Using Government Information Sources

Electronic and Print
Third Edition

Using Government Information Sources

Electronic and Print
Third Edition

Jean L. Sears and Marilyn K. Moody

Oryx Press
2001

The rare Arabian Oryx is believed to have inspired the myth of the unicorn. This desert antelope became virtually extinct in the early 1960s. At that time, several groups of international conservationists arranged to have nine animals sent to the Phoenix Zoo to be the nucleus of a captive breeding herd. Today, the Oryx population is over 1,000, and over 500 have been returned to the Middle East.

© 2001 by Marilyn K. Moody and Jean L. Sears
Published by The Oryx Press
4041 North Central at Indian School Road
Phoenix, Arizona 85012-3397
http://www.oryxpress.com

Published simultaneously in Canada
Printed and bound in the United States of America

∞ The paper used in this publication meets the minimum requirements of
American National Standard for Information Science—Permanence
of Paper for Printed Library Materials, ANSI Z39.48, 1984.

Library of Congress Cataloging-in-Publication Data

Sears, Jean L.
  Using government information sources : electronic and print / Jean L.
Sears and Marilyn K. Moody.— 3rd ed.
      p. cm.
  Includes bibliographical references and index.
  ISBN 1-57356-288-2 (alk. paper)
   1. Government publications—United States—Handbooks, manuals, etc.
  2. Government publications—United States—Bibliography. 3. Elec-
tronic information resources—United States—Handbooks, manuals, etc.
  4. Electronic information resources—United States—Catalogs.
  I. Moody, Marilyn K. II. Title.
  Z1223.Z7 S4 2000
  [J83]
  015.73'053—dc21
                                                        00-009773
                                                        CIP

To Katie, Daniel, Emily, Tera, and Ryan

Contents

List of Illustrations

Preface to the Third Edition

Using Government Information Sources is a reference guide to U.S. government publications and information designed for both beginning and experienced researchers. Its purpose is to provide a guide to the most commonly used government information sources and an introduction to related research strategies.

When the second edition of this book was published in 1994 electronic information resources were beginning to play an important role in access to government information. The second edition cited several online bulletin boards, gopher sites, and CD-ROMs. Since then the World Wide Web has developed into the premiere method for the dissemination of government information. The most notable change in the third edition is the inclusion of selected federal agency Web sites, Web titles, and URLs for publications now also available on the Web.

All of the resources included in the second edition have been reviewed and reevaluated for the third edition. Discontinued titles have been eliminated and new resources added. Bibliographic information has been updated to reflect title and classification number changes and Web availability.

The chapter topics and organization are very similar to the last edition. Chapters are grouped into four search strategy categories: the subject search, the agency search, the statistical search, and special techniques. This edition includes one new chapter on "Housing and Construction Statistics." Many of these sources were formerly included in the "Business and Industry Statistics" chapter. A small number of previous chapters have been consolidated. Former chapters on "Occupations" and "Federal Government Jobs" have been merged into the "Occupations and Jobs" chapter. The "Foreign Broadcast Information Service Reports (JPRS/FBIS)" chapter has been incorporated into the chapter on "Foreign Countries."

Acknowledgments

The authors acknowledge the support of the Miami University Libraries and the University at Buffalo Libraries. Support was also received through the Professional Development & Quality of Work Life (PDQWL) program of the State of New York and United University Professions.

CHAPTER 1
Introduction

Using Government Information Sources is a basic reference guide to U.S. government publications and information. This book not only lists sources for information on specific topics but also suggests general and specific strategies for finding additional information or for finding information on topics not covered. These source listings and search strategies make it easier for users to organize research and identify information sources.

USING THE BOOK

This book is designed to deal with specific search situations. An important tool in locating government information sources is the search strategy, which provides an overall plan for approaching research and finding information. The chapters in this book are arranged into four main sections, which correspond to four of the five main types of search strategies: subject, agency, statistical, and special techniques. More information on these search strategies, as well as a discussion of the fifth type of search strategy, known item, may be found in Chapter 2, "Search Strategy and Government Information Sources."

Beginning with Chapter 4, "Foreign Policy," each chapter is self-contained, focuses on a specific topic, and follows or illustrates one type of search strategy. Each of these chapters begins with a specific search strategy, followed by checklists of sources, narrative descriptions of sources covered, and indexes and other related materials to consult for more detailed and specialized materials.

The specific search strategy is a step-by-step plan for research that relates individual topics to one of the five general search strategies, and it is a suggested framework for organizing research on a particular topic. To identify specific materials on a topic, researchers can use the lists of sources given in each chapter. Sources of information are grouped into small subcategories of similar or related material, each with a checklist of sources and a narrative discussion. The checklist provides full bibliographic information for each title in the subcategory. Titles are listed in order of importance or in order of logical progression. Individual sources are repeated wherever relevant; one source may answer many different types of questions and will be included in every chapter to which it is applicable.

The combination of checklists with coverage and content notes, search strategies, and analyses provides a flexible approach for all users, ranging from experienced researchers or government information librarians to librarians and researchers unfamiliar with the field of government information to students and novice government information users. This book serves both as a "point of use" guide to answer specific questions and as a more general guide to search strategies that may prove effective in a variety of situations.

Experienced or hurried users may only want to scan the checklists of titles in each chapter to quickly identify or remind themselves of sources. If more information is needed than that provided by the checklists, read and follow the suggested search strategy at the beginning of the chapter. For a better understanding of differences between sources, scan the coverage and content notes in the checklists for each unit of the chapter. Finally, to obtain the most information and detail about sources, consult the narrative descriptions that follow the checklists.

INCLUSION OF MATERIALS

Only those subjects, types of materials, and search techniques most often associated with government publications and information are included. Similarly, only the most basic and important sources are listed. Individual series and titles have been selected on the basis of reference value, general interest value, currency, and availability. This book can also be useful to librarians as a selection tool to help decide which government publications to acquire. However, no attempt is made to list government sources comprehensively or to identify the many nongovernment sources that apply to a particular topic.

Depository and Nondepository Libraries

Depository libraries are those libraries specifically designated by the Government Printing Office to receive U.S. government publications. In depository collections arranged by Superintendent of Documents (SuDocs) number, readers will be able to retrieve materials directly, using the information provided in each entry. In other government publication collection arrangements, additional searching may be required in the individual library's records for an alternate classification number. Depository libraries also provide free Internet access for government information available on the Web. In designing this book for use with depository libraries, we have followed two guidelines for the inclusion of material. First, most publications included are available through the depository library system or the Internet. Selected nondepository documents have been included, however, when they are important to the topic under discussion. Second, inclusion of commercially published items relating to government publications is kept to a minimum. We include basic items that most libraries with a government publications collection would purchase or unique items that are essential to a particular search strategy.

While this book is directed toward depository libraries, nondepository libraries will also find it useful. Libraries and individuals with Internet access will be able to locate many of the sources online. Nondepository libraries may also acquire a limited number of government publications, so this book can serve as a guide to publications that the library may have in its collection. The book also identifies and describes publications that nearby depository libraries own and that nondepository library users may be able to obtain through interlibrary loan or through a visit to a local depository library. Additionally, this book identifies key government information resources that nondepository libraries may want to acquire; the following availability section gives information on how these publications may be obtained.

AVAILABILITY OF MATERIALS

Many of the publications listed in this book are available on the Internet. Bibliographic entries include URLs.

Publications available from the Government Printing Office are indicated in the bibliographic entry by the designation "GPO." Full ordering information for these publications is available from the Government Printing Office Online Bookstore <http://bookstore.gpo.gov>. *Subject Bibliographies* also contain ordering information and are available free of charge from the Government Printing Office. They list publications on individual topics that are for sale by the GPO. They are also available on the GPO Web site <http://bookstore.gpo.gov/sb/about.html>. (Chapter 3, "The Basics of Searching," provides more information on using the Online Bookstore's *Sales Product Catalog* and *Subject Bibliographies*.)

Publications not for sale by the Government Printing Office are occasionally available by contacting the issuing agency directly. The *United States Government Manual* and other similar directories can be used to locate agency addresses. Chapter 9, "Directories," gives a comprehensive listing of government directories.

Congressional documents are available from a variety of sources. Selected congressional publications are available for sale through the GPO. The Senate Document Room and House Legislative Resource Center distribute copies of reports, documents, bills, and laws. Individual congressional committees may also be able to provide copies of their publications.

Some publications are also available through commercial publishers. Statistical publications indexed in *American Statistics Index (ASI)* or congressional publications indexed in *CIS/Index*, for example, are available in microfiche from the publisher, Congressional Information Service, Inc., either by subscription or individually. The CIS Web products, *Congressional Universe* and *Statistical Universe* also include some full-text materials. The addresses of commercial vendors cited in this book are listed in the appendix.

ELECTRONIC INFORMATION SOURCES

The Internet, particularly the World Wide Web (WWW), has become one of the primary vehicles for the dissemination of government information. The World Wide Web is a network of interconnected, linked documents (hypertext) that can also incorporate other media such as images and sound. Virtually every government agency has a Web site and many provide full-text publications and databases. While many government publications continue to be available in print or microfiche format, other government agencies have discontinued some of their print publications, relying on the Web to make information available. In some instances, information that was not previously available in print may now be available via the Web, such as agency databases. Even so, many government publications are not on the Internet. Publications and information available on the Internet are selective and tend to be recent materials of a popular or reference nature. This book emphasizes reference and serial titles and a large number of these titles are available on the Internet, at least for current editions or recent years. Bibliographic entries incorporate URLs (Uniform Resource Locators) for sources covered when available. Entries for Web sites are also included. Criteria for inclusion of Web resources is the same as for print or microfiche and is limited to those titles judged to be the most useful for the topics covered. For more comprehensive guides and directories to government Web sites see federal agency directories (such as those listed in Chapter 9, "Directories") and sources such as the following:

Government Information on the Internet. 3rd ed. 2000. Greg R. Notess. Lanham, MD: Bernan Press.

How to Access the Federal Government on the Internet. 4th ed. 1999. Bruce Maxwell. Washington, D.C.: CQ Press.

Government information is available on the Internet in many formats. These include HTML, PDF, ASCII text, word processing documents (Word, WordPerfect), and spreadsheet files (Excel, Lotus). This book emphasizes sources that can be viewed directly online, although occasional references to files available for downloading are included. Hypertext documents on the World Wide Web are written in HTML (Hypertext Markup Language) and are viewable with an Internet browser. PDF (Portable Document Format) documents incorporate the original fonts, formatting, and graphics to provide an exact replica of the original publication. These files require Adobe Acrobat Reader software that can be downloaded free from the Adobe Web site <http://www.adobe.com/products/acrobat/readstep.html>.

Web resources are much less stable than print and microfiche. Agencies may drop particular titles from their Web sites and add others. Web sites are often redesigned and URLs frequently change. The URL specifies the location or address of a particular resource on the Internet. While every attempt was made to ensure that the URLs cited in this book were current at press time, it is inevitable that changes will occur. The Government Printing Office selectively assigns PURLs (Persistent Uniform Resource Locators) to some government Internet titles, and these have been included in bibliographic citations when available. A PURL is a URL that points to an intermediate resolution service that can redirect the request to a new URL when a new URL has been identified by GPO. Another method of dealing with changed URLs is to go to the agency home page, which may be represented by the first part of the URL up to the initial slash (/) or may be identified using federal agency Internet directories (see Chapter 9, "Directories"), and browse or search the Web site for the desired resource. (Chapter 3, "The Basics of Searching," also discusses government information on the Web.)

Government agencies also continue to provide publications and data on CD-ROMs. Some of the same information that is on a CD-ROM may also be available on the agency's Web site. As with Web resources, CD-ROM titles are included in chapter listings when relevant. Emphasis is on titles available to depository libraries. Nondepository and commercial products are included on a selective basis.

Other types of electronic information resources are occasionally included, such as commercial online databases.

BIBLIOGRAPHIC ENTRIES

A sample bibliographic entry is reproduced in Figure 1.1. Each element in the entry is identified by number and described below.

1. **Title.** Current title of publication.

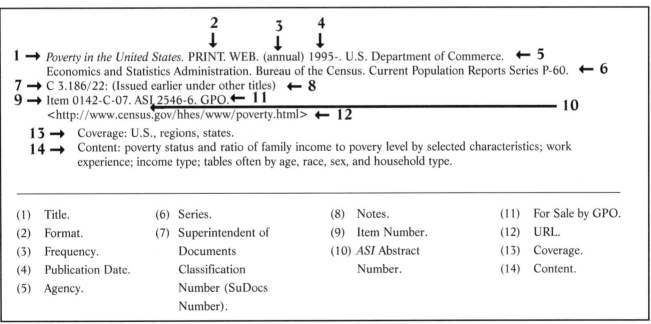

(1) Title.	(6) Series.	(8) Notes.	(11) For Sale by GPO.
(2) Format.	(7) Superintendent of	(9) Item Number.	(12) URL.
(3) Frequency.	Documents	(10) *ASI* Abstract	(13) Coverage.
(4) Publication Date.	Classification	Number.	(14) Content.
(5) Agency.	Number (SuDocs		
	Number).		

Figure 1.1: Sample Bibliographic Entry.

2. **Format.**   Current format(s) available to depository libraries. Commonly used formats include PRINT, MF (microfiche), WEB (World Wide Web/Internet), and CD-ROM. Use of the MF and WEB formats do not necessarily mean that the title does not exist in print, but that print copies are not currently distributed to depository libraries. Libraries may own earlier issues in print, in some of these cases. Some series may contain a current mixture of paper and microfiche material. Other series are offered to depositories in either format with the choice left up to the individual library.

3. **Frequency.**   Present publishing frequency, such as monthly, annual, biennial, etc.

4. **Publication Date.**   Dates enclosed in parentheses are publication dates for monographs. Beginning dates, given for serials, are usually dates of coverage, although occasionally a publication date may be used. Dates not positively determined are omitted.

5. **Agency.**   The government agency that presently issues the publication. Complete agency hierarchy is given, taken whenever possible from the title page or cover of the publication.

6. **Series.**   Series information is included when applicable.

7. **Superintendent of Documents Classification Number (SuDocs Number).**   The present SuDocs number is given. If the number has been recently changed, an earlier classification number may be shown, but no attempt is made to provide a complete SuDocs number history. In cases where a title recurs in a series along with other titles, the exact SuDocs number of the most recent issue or edition as of this writing is included in a parenthetical statement following the SuDocs number. SuDocs numbers are also assigned to Web-only resources—the presence of a SuDocs number does not always mean that depository libraries using this classification system will have physical materials shelved under this number.

8. **Notes.**   Additional notes of various kinds are added as needed. These notes may relate to the history of the source or to variations or special features of the publication.

9. **Item Number.**   Item numbers are used for selection by depository libraries. Some series are offered to depository libraries in either print or microfiche. In such cases, two item numbers are indicated, one of which is followed by the "MF" designation.

10. *ASI* **Abstract Number.**   For titles appearing in the *American Statistics Index (ASI)*, the abstract number is given, for two reasons: (1) some libraries have access to the full-text publications through the *ASI* microfiche collection arranged by the *ASI* number or through the Web service, *Statistical Universe*, and (2) additional information about the publication that a user may find helpful may be found in the *ASI* abstract. Only sources that are primarily statistical in nature will appear in *ASI* and thus have an *ASI* abstract number.

For monograph publications, the year of *ASI* is given, followed by the abstract number, for example, ASI (98) 5606-2. For recurring publications, no year is given. Recurring publications may retain the same *ASI* number over a period of time, so abstract numbers may be checked in any *ASI* annual, depending on time period desired. There are exceptions, but because of the complexity of listing the complete *ASI* number history, usually only the current abstract number is given.

11. **For Sale by GPO.**   Items for sale by the Government Printing Office are indicated by the designation "GPO." In the case of a series, the GPO designation indicates that at least some of the latest items in the series are available for sale. Availability from GPO may vary, as items go in and out of stock. Occasionally the designation NTIS is given instead of GPO. This indicates that the publication is available for sale from the National Technical Information Service.

12. **URL.**   Uniform Resource Locator for resources available on the Web. Multiple URLs may be listed in cases where the resource is available in more than one location or from more than one approach. PURLs (Persistent Uniform Resource Locator) created by GPO are also listed when available. A PURL can locate a resource even when the URL has changed.

13. **Coverage.**   "Coverage" indicates geographic coverage and is used primarily with statistical sources. Terms used are usually those found within the source itself. If no coverage note appears, geographic breakdowns are not particularly relevant to the source. Coverage refers to the geographic coverage as it relates to the topic under discussion, not necessarily to the geographic coverage of the source as a whole.

14. **Content.**   Content notes briefly summarize a title's contents as they relate to the topic under consideration. Content notes for the same source will vary from chapter to chapter, depending on the topic being discussed. Notes reflect current content and may not accurately describe content of older issues; format and content may change substantially over the years.

CHAPTER 2
Search Strategy and Government Information Sources

This chapter discusses the search strategy or research process required to locate government information. The phrase "search strategy" is used here to mean a series of specific steps, usually based on categories of information sources that can be followed to locate relevant materials to answer a specific question. In previous editions of this book, we considered the question of whether there was a search strategy for using government publications and information, and whether it differed from a general reference search strategy. Arguing that the answer was yes, there are specific search strategies for government information and they do differ from general reference strategies, we then described the five types of search strategies that we found useful in working with government information: known item, subject, agency, statistical, and special techniques. These proposed strategies then formed the basis of the chapters in the earlier editions of this work, as they do in the chapters of this current work as well.

Subsequent experience with these strategies, the search process steps detailed within the strategies, and the types of resources used in carrying out the strategies have proven their worth as a framework for successfully planning and completing government information searches. Since the last edition of this book, however, the proliferation of Web-based and electronic government information resources has also changed the use of these search strategies somewhat as well as affected the types of resources that are consulted at each step in the search process. The search strategies included in each chapter of this work reflect those changes, and in many cases also reflect the increased availability and accessibility of the Web-based resources.

This chapter considers, then, these basic questions: (1) What search strategies can be used to locate government information sources? (2) How are these search strategies categorized, what types of sources can be identified for use within the search strategies, and what major individual sources can be identified for use with these strate-

gies? (3) What aspects of these governmental search strategies are unique and differ from general reference search strategies? (4) How has the addition of Web-based and other electronic governmental information resources affected these strategies?

GOVERNMENT INFORMATION SEARCH STRATEGIES

The first step in developing government information search strategies is to categorize government information queries by type. In this book, we have categorized searches as falling into one of five categories: (1) Known Item, (2) Subject, (3) Agency, (4) Statistical, and (5) Special Technique. A general model for each of these types of searches can then be developed by identifying the types of sources to be consulted and eventually identifying individual titles. Each of these search strategies will be discussed individually in this chapter, with other chapters in this volume providing more detailed search strategies for each of the five types, including specific titles and a "Search Strategy" section relating to the topic being discussed.

In addition to questions concerning these search strategies, another type of question that is often asked is the ready-reference question. Ready-reference questions can be answered by using basic sources (print or electronic formats) such as the *Statistical Abstract of the United States*, the *U.S. Government Manual*, or a statistical compilation such as *Agricultural Statistics*. Ready-reference questions are usually simple questions that require one step to answer the question and do not involve the formation of a search strategy. Ready-reference sources are often used in the subsearch of a more complicated strategy or are sometimes used as the first step of a search strategy. Ready reference sources are included in the individual topic chapters when appropriate.

ANALYSIS OF SEARCH STRATEGY

Known Item Searches

The known item search involves the user looking for a distinct bibliographic item. (See Figure 2.1.)

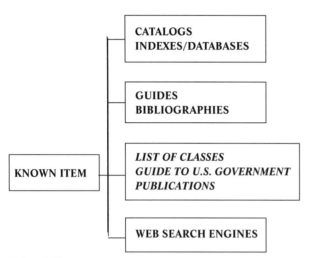

Related Chapter:

3. The Basics of Searching

Figure 2.1: Known Item Search Strategy.

A typical question in such a search might be "Can you locate the title *Country Reports on Human Rights Practices*?" or "How do I locate the citation to the technical report footnoted in this article?" Known item searches may be more or less specific in the information that a user has in hand, but the user IS looking for a specific item as he or she searches.

While the manner of approaching this may be somewhat similar to approaching the searching of other nongovernmental known items, there are some significant differences. First, a specific known item governmental "title" may be in a variety of formats—print, microform, and electronic. Preprints and preliminary versions of an item may also be available. Although this may also occur with nongovernment information, it is more common with government information. The bibliographic control of the known item may also be weaker—it may be somewhat harder to actually identify the item or find bibliographic records describing it. The addition of Web-based or other electronic versions of the item, which may not exactly mimic earlier print or microfiche versions, adds to this confusion.

The methods of citing a particular item may also vary. It is not uncommon to see widely varying citations for the same government item. Whether agency or personal authors, identifying numbers such as SuDocs and technical report numbers, series information, format information, or version or edition information are included in a citation can make a large difference in how easy it is to identify the item. While this problem is also found in non-

government citations, it tends to be a more difficult one with government sources.

Just the step of identifying a government source clearly and completely may require the use of multiple catalogs and databases of one sort or another. As the suggested search strategy for known items shows, this tends to be more multifaceted and complex than nongovernment sources. Search steps for a known item search might include searching such resources as catalogs; indexes, abstracts, and databases; guides and bibliographies; the *List of Classes* and the *Guide to U.S. Government Publications*; and Web search engines.

The exact tools and steps used may vary, depending on the resources available to the searcher. In some library settings, for example, searching an enhanced online library catalog that includes access to governmental information sources in many different formats, including electronic only resources, might be an excellent first step. In other situations, searching indexes or databases such as the *Monthly Catalog, ASI,* or *CIS/Index* might be the most useful first step. If the exact title is unknown, searching by keywords, series name, series number, agency name, subjects, or combinations of these might be needed. Searching by governmental series or browsing listings of series of a particular agency can also be a successful strategy when the series name and/or agency author is known. Bibliographies and guides may also prove useful, particularly Web-based guides and directories that allow for searching and browsing functions. The use of Web search engines, particularly those searching only governmental sites, can also be used as a step in the known item process. Because of some of the complexities of bibliographically identifying a specific governmental source, even when a complete title of a source is known, it may be difficult to narrow Web search results to identify the known item desired.

Subject Searches

Subject searches (see Figure 2.2) are those queries involving more than a ready-reference question, going beyond consulting one source for an answer, and involving the formulation of a search strategy. In such a search, the user is requesting information in a more general way. The request may be satisfied by consulting two items or hundreds, depending on the complexity and comprehensiveness of the user's needs. Indexes, databases, catalogs, and Web search engines are probably the most commonly used tools to answer these types of questions, but bibliographies and guides (especially Web-based ones) are also an important type of tool in subject searches.

Subject searches may also include the use of other types of searches as subsearches or tangential searches to the main query. It is often not enough to consult only the *Monthly Catalog* or a database such as *CIS/Index* or a Subject Bibliography on the topic. To find *all* relevant material, some of the other search strategies discussed in this chapter may be needed. The regulations and activities of a government agency may be applicable to a particular search, for example, and could be found through the agency search strategy. A bibliography or guide may produce a reference to a key item that will require a known item search. The need for statistics on a subject will require the use of a statistical search strategy. Ready-reference sources may also be consulted at various points in the search strategy.

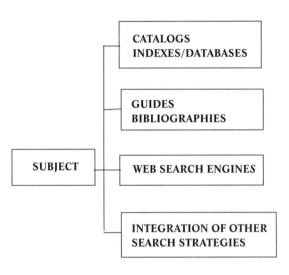

Related Chapters:
 3. The Basics of Searching
 4. Foreign Policy
 5. Foreign Countries
 6. Occupations and Jobs
 7. Selling to the Government
 8. Business Aids
 9. Directories
10. Tax Information
11. Travel Information
12. Audiovisual Information
13. Copyright
14. Climate
15. Elections
16. Maps
17. Genealogy
18. Agriculture
19. Health
20. Education
21. Geology
22. Environment
23. Astronomy and Space

Figure 2.2: Subject Search Strategy.

Subject searching for government information often follows the type of search strategy for more general reference materials, but there are some important differences. There is often a greater need to incorporate various strategies within the subject search, such as statistical subsearches or agency searches. The sheer enormity of subjects involved and the amount of information available can add to the complexity. It may not be obvious where to best start the search, and it may be more difficult to choose relevant sources as the search progresses. There is often a lack of good filtering mechanisms to help narrow the subject search, and users may find themselves combing through a wide variety of sources, of which only some will be relevant.

Subject searches may include such categories of resources as online catalogs; indexes, abstracts, and data-bases; bibliographies; guides and listings; Web search engines; and sources used in other types of search strategies such as agency or statistical searches. Many of the chapters of this book involve subject searches. The subjects chosen for inclusion are popular topics, recurring topics, topics that have proven difficult to search, or subject areas that are well represented by government information resources. The individual chapters are the result of applying the subject search strategy and selecting major series and reference sources that have general application. Each chapter groups the most relevant sources into smaller subgroups of related materials and identifies the most fruitful search strategies for that subject.

Agency Searches

The agency search is perhaps the most distinctive of the governmental search strategies. It is a search by agency, subagency, or issuing group. It may include the use of agency bibliographies, listings, and agency Web sites as the focus of a search. While a search by agency or issuing group is sometimes used in the general reference search strategy, its use with government information is quite extensive. While there is a parallel with the corporate search for general reference, this type of search is rarely emphasized in general reference searches. It requires the searcher to approach the information gathering from a new perspective in order to use fully the agency approach. A familiarity with governmental structure and agency missions and purposes is also necessary. The advent of the Web and agency Web sites has made this approach extremely useful, yet it remains difficult for those not familiar with government information to grasp the power of this approach. (See Figure 2.3.)

For some types of queries, an agency search is the fastest and most productive search strategy to follow. This is especially true for more experienced government information searchers. The agency chapters within this book try to duplicate the resources and strategy that an experienced searcher might follow to obtain information about or by a specific agency. Types of sources consulted in an agency search strategy might include the *List of Classes*; ready reference sources such as the *Government Manual*; agency Web sites and directories of agency Web sites; agency annual reports and other agency sources; regulations; catalogs, indexes, and databases; and Web search engines.

Ready-reference sources are often a first step to follow in obtaining agency information. The *U.S. Government Manual* is one heavily used source. Another commonly used source is the *List of Classes*. Many known item and subject subsearches can also be answered by using the *List of Classes*, such as whether an agency produces a particular source or title. The *Guide to U.S. Government Publications* (formerly known as *Andriot* for its original author), can also be used in a similar way. The *Guide to U.S. Government Publications* provides an expanded and often annotated listing of both current and discontinued SuDocs classes.

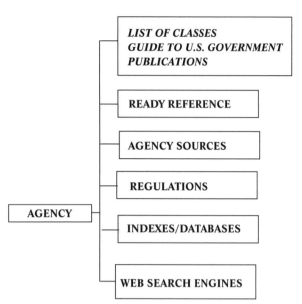

Related Chapters:
 3. The Basics of Searching
24. Government Programs and Grants
25. Regulations and Administrative Actions
26. Administrative Decisions
27. The President

Figure 2.3: Agency Search Strategy.

Agency Web sites have become an integral part of the agency search. Directories of the agency sites are useful for identifying URLs for the sites and often help in identifying the appropriate individual office, bureau, and sub-agency within a larger agency. The agency's annual reports and other recurring reports describing agency activities can also be useful tools in the agency search process.

Consulting regulations and other regulatory materials is often required as a part of an agency search. This usually requires searching the *Federal Register* or the *Code of Federal Regulations*, although increasingly agency Web sites include information about an agency's regulatory activities. For example, gaining information about the workings of the Consumer Product Safety Commission (CPSC) may require reading its regulations to find the commission's purpose and powers; the CPSC Web site also provides links to much of this regulatory information.

Statistical Searches

Many governmental information queries can be categorized as statistical in nature. (See Figure 2.4.) The use of governmental sources for statistical queries is one of the most well known and recognized uses. The statistical search encompasses all searches for statistics, including the use of census information as a distinct subsearch. The types of information to be searched include ready reference sources; statistical compilations; census sources; and indexes, abstracts, and databases. Many of the sources used in a subject search may also be used in statistical searches, especially bibliographies and subject oriented guides and listings. Using statistical sources requires the use of specialized sources and the ability to understand clearly the level of detail and the type of statistic needed. While statistical searches are also carried out using non-government sources, the use of government statistics requires an additional understanding of a multitude of governmental statistics-gathering programs. The use of census data is often required and adds further complexity to the search.

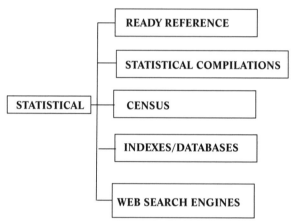

Related Chapters:

 3. The Basics of Searching
28. Population Statistics
29. Vital Statistics
30. Economic Indicators
31. Business and Industry Statistics
32. Housing and Construction Statistics
33. Income
34. Earnings
35. Employment
36. Prices
37. Consumer Expenditures
38. Foreign Trade Statistics
39. Crime and Criminal Justice Statistics
40. Defense and Military Statistics
41. Energy Statistics
42. Projections
43. State and Local Government Statistics
44. Transportation Statistics

Figure 2.4 Statistical Search Strategy.

A given statistic may be identified in multiple sources, and the searcher must learn which search source is most appropriate for the search in process. The Web has made governmental statistical information much more accessible, but Web sources are not always as well documented in terms of describing the origination of the statistics and the statistical methods used in collecting the data. Providing this sort of context is important in ensuring that the results of a statistical search are truly meaningful and accurately applied.

A statistical question may very well be answered by a ready-reference source, and some statistical search strategies may end at that point. The ready-reference checking of the *Statistical Abstract* is a standard step that, by itself, can solve a large percentage of statistical questions. The citations to the sources from which the statistical tables in the *Statistical Abstract* are derived often lead the user to more detailed statistical sources to use with the search strategy.

As another step of the search strategy, other types of statistical compilations may be consulted. These often emphasize a particular subject area and can be an extension of the ready-reference step. Statistical compilations such as *Agricultural Statistics*, *County and City Data Book*, and the *World Factbook* are issued by a number of agencies and encompass a wide range of subject areas. While some of these statistical compilations are easily identifiable as ready-reference tools, others are more difficult to identify. Within each statistical chapter, these types of compilations are included as part of the search strategy.

Census publications make up a special category and should be consulted for many statistical searches. This is even more important as the number of electronic products providing more detailed data from the censuses is steadily increasing. The use of census information is not always obvious. Because of the sheer number and complexity of sources, this category requires its own techniques for locating information. Within many of the statistical chapters, census sources are included as a separate search strategy step.

Consulting indexes and databases is an important part of the statistical search strategy and is usually carried out when searches in the known sources previously mentioned have been exhausted. *American Statistics Index (ASI)*, available in both print and electronic formats, is an extremely valuable source for the statistical search strategy. Within the statistical chapters, the results of using *ASI* as part of the search strategy are often given and selected sources obtained from using *ASI* are shown. *ASI* is also one of the last steps in the search strategy if the search steps within the chapter are exhausted and a query still has not been answered. While the *Monthly Catalog* can also be used as an index for statistical searching, its lack of specificity for statistical searches as compared to *ASI* makes it much less useful.

The use of Web search engines and the searching of agency Web sites and subject guides and directories to statistical information available on the Web are also a part of the statistical search strategy. These sources are generally used when other steps have failed, or if *ASI* is not available. There are exceptions, however—in the case of the Census Bureau site, for example, the excellent search directories and search engines available on the site make it easy to locate specific sources on a wide range of topics, and make searching the Census Bureau site an effective and efficient strategy.

Special Techniques

Special technique search strategies are those involving a specialized technique unique to a specific situation or type of material. (See Figure 2.5.) The searches often involve complex multistep, multifaceted search techniques. Some searches require steps that are not logical or intuitive. They also often include the use of specialized indexes, databases, or other tools. A special technique may be impossible to carry out without a guide, specific directions, or past experience in using the technique. Special technique searches may use every type of source previously mentioned in the other searches. While the Web has made access to the resources needed for special technique searching more accessible, some Web-based sources provide even less help and documentation than their print counterparts.

Some steps of a special techniques strategy might include the use of specialized guides, specialized databases, agency Web sites, and specialized search engines. The individual chapters go step by step through the sources and strategy needed for such activities as locating a patent, finding a treaty, or following a legislative history.

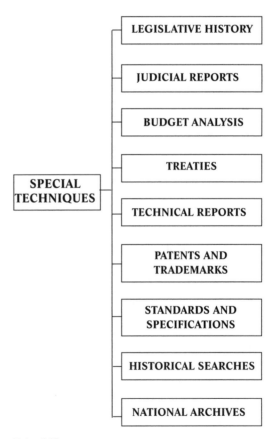

Related Chapters:
45. Legislative History   50. Patents and Trademarks
46. Judicial Reports   51. Standards and Specifications
47. Budget Analysis   52. Historical Searches
48. Treaties   53. National Archives
49. Technical Reports

Figure 2.5: Special Techniques Search Strategy.

CHAPTER 3
The Basics of Searching

This chapter discusses the depository library system; the use of the World Wide Web for accessing and using government information; the Superintendent of Documents classifications system used throughout this book; and the basic government publications indexes, abstracts, databases, search engines, and Web sites that are most often used to locate government publications. (For information on searching historical indexes, see Chapter 53, "Historical Searches.")

THE DEPOSITORY LIBRARY SYSTEM

Locate Federal Depository Libraries by State or Area Code. WEB. U.S. Government Printing Office. Superintendent of Documents. <http://www.gpo.gov/su_docs/dpos/adpos003.html>.
> Content: searchable directory of federal depository libraries.

Government publications in both print and electronic formats are distributed free of charge to nearly 1,400 specially designated depository libraries throughout the country. These libraries automatically receive publications from the U.S. Government Printing Office that are designated for general distribution. Some depository libraries are regional depositories and must receive all publications distributed. Other libraries are selective depositories and can control the selection of their documents by choosing which item numbers they wish to receive. Item numbers correspond to individual titles or groups of titles. For example, item number 0431-I-04(MF), is the item number for the class "Annual Report," of the Environmental Protection Agency. All libraries selecting Item 0431-I-04(MF) will receive this title, which is distributed in a microfiche format. A depository library, then, can determine whether it has received or will receive a publication through the depository program by its item number. The item number is found in the bibliographic entries throughout this book.

Depository libraries will have the most complete and accessible collections of government publications, particu-larly for items distributed in print, microfiche, and CD-ROM formats. Most depositories will also provide access to electronic databases and reference tools and specialized indexes, abstracts, and reference tools needed to access and use government publications and information. Depository libraries are also required to provide Internet access to make government information available to the general public. Depository libraries are required by law to make their documents available to all citizens and to furnish the hardware and software necessary to provide Internet access to government information available on the Web.

ACCESS TO GOVERNMENT INFORMATION THROUGH THE WORLD WIDE WEB

A huge number of government publications as well as a vast amount of government information is now also being distributed via the World Wide Web. Most agencies provide agency Web sites that include information in a variety of formats. Versions of some publications are found in HTML formats. The PDF (Portable Document Format) is also used for many publications, particularly those originally published in a print format. Versions of databases or information distributed in CD-ROM formats may also sometimes be accessible via the Web. Some publications and information are only available in a Web-accessible format. Throughout this book, the designation "WEB" is used to indicate that a publication, site, or Web page is accessible via the Web. For simplicity, this designation indicates only that the material is accessible via the Web; it does not indicate the format the information is in, such as HTML or PDF.

The Uniform Resource Locator (URL) is included whenever a source is designated "WEB." In some cases, more than one URL may lead to a particular source, and the entries in this book include multiple URLs where appropriate. Governmental URLs will end with the .gov or .mil extension in their URLs. For example, the URL for the Census Bureau Web site is http://www.census.gov. Some governmental Web sources have also been assigned a Persistent Uniform Resource Locator (PURL). Instead of pointing directly to a URL, a PURL points to an intermediate URL resolver. The hoped-for result is that a PURL will remain a constant unchanging address to a resource, even if its URL changes multiple times. PURLs are included wherever possible in the entries in this book.

SUDOCS CLASSIFICATION SYSTEM

The Superintendent of Documents (SuDocs) classification system is an alphanumeric system used to classify federal government publications. Many libraries also use the SuDocs system to physically arrange their collections of government publications. SuDocs numbers are assigned by the Government Printing Office. Figure 3.1 shows the basic elements of a SuDocs number. Each publication is assigned a letter based on the issuing department (A=Agriculture Department, C=Commerce Department, EP=Environmental Protection Agency, and so on). Subagencies within each department may also be assigned a number. The Census Bureau, for example, is given the number 3 under the Commerce Department. All Census Bureau publications, therefore, have call numbers beginning with C 3. Within an agency or subagency, each series is also assigned a number. For example, the Census Bureau's annual *Statistical Abstract of the United States* is given the SuDocs number C 3.134:. Each individual issue of a periodical or individual title in a series is then assigned a unique number or alphabetical symbol based on year, volume, series number, or title. This unique publication number follows the colon. Thus, C 3.134:999 is the SuDocs number for the 1999 edition of the *Statistical Abstract of the United States*. (See Figure 3.1.)

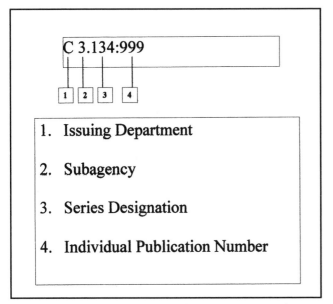

Figure 3.1: Basic Elements of a SuDocs Number.

In summary, the first half of the number (up to the colon) identifies the agency and series, and the last half identifies the specific publication. Publications are filed alphabetically by letter and then numerically, first grouped by subagency, then by series, and finally, arranged alphabetically or numerically within each series.

GPO ACCESS

GPO Access. WEB. U.S. Government Printing Office. Superintendent of Documents <http://www.access.gpo.gov/su_docs/index.html>.

The *GPO Access* initiative provides free online access to many governmental databases and other information resources. The site also provides access to many full-text materials, such as the full text of congressional bills and of the *Code of Federal Regulations*. Congressional materials and regulatory materials are particularly well represented in the materials available through *GPO Access*. Typically, *GPO Access* also provides a search interface for these databases of materials.

GPO Access also includes many search tools to help the user more readily locate government information resources. The databases in this category include such items as the *Catalog of Government Publications (Monthly Catalog)* and the *Sales Product Catalog* (described individually later in this chapter). Additional noteworthy resources include *Browse Topics, New Electronic Titles,* and the *U.S. Federal Government Agencies Directory* (also titled *Federal Agency Internet Sites.)* The *Browse Topics* tool gives links to agency sites and governmental resources dealing with some of the most popular or often-requested topics, such as "Native Americans," "Conservation," "Weather," and "Health Care." The *New Electronic Titles* gives listings and links to new items added to the Federal Depository Library Program Electronic Collection during the previous four weeks. In partnership with Louisiana State University, the *U.S. Federal Government Agenicies Directory* is a constantly updated set of links to agency and subagency Web sites.

The *GPO Access* site is continually expanding, and the fact that it is free-of-charge to users makes it one of the basic resources for finding and using government resources in electronic formats.

SOURCES AND GUIDES

GPO-Produced *Monthly Catalog/Catalog of United States Government Publications*

Catalog of United States Government Publications (MOCAT). WEB. 1994–. U.S. Government Printing Office. Superintendent of Documents. <http://www.gpo.gov/catalog>; <http://www.access.gpo.gov/su_docs/locafocs/cgp/index.html>; <http://purl.access.gpo.gov/GPO/LPS844>.

Monthly Catalog of United States Government Publications. CD-ROM. 1996–. U.S. Government Printing Office. Superintendent of Documents. GP 3.8/7: Item 0557-C. GPO.

Monthly Catalog of United States Government Publications (Condensed version). PRINT. (monthly) 1996–. U.S. Government Printing Office. Superintendent of Documents. GP 3.8/8: (Earlier full version, GP 3.8:, 1895–1995). Item 0557-D. GPO.

Commercial Versions of the *Monthly Catalog*

GPO Monthly Catalog. WEB. July 1976–. Dublin, OH: OCLC Computer Library Center, Inc. (FirstSearch).

GPO on SilverPlatter. WEB. CD-ROM. July 1976–. Norwood, MA: SilverPlatter Information, Inc.

GPO Monthly Catalog. WEB. July 1976–. Palo Alto, CA: Dialog Information Services, Inc. <www.dialog.com>.

Impact/ACCESS Government Documents Catalog Service (GDCS). WEB. July 1976–. Pomona, CA: Auto-Graphics, Inc.

Impact/CD Government Documents Catalog Services (GDCS). CD-ROM. July 1976–. Pomona, CA: Auto-Graphics, Inc.

Government Publications Index. WEB. CD-ROM. July 1976–. Farmington Hills, MI: Gale Group.

MarciveWeb DOCS. WEB. July 1976–. San Antonio, TX: MARCIVE, Inc.

GPO CAT/PAC and GPO CAT/PAC Plus. CD-ROM. July 1976–. San Antonio, TX: MARCIVE, Inc.

The *Monthly Catalog* is the basic index/database to government publications, including both depository and nondepository publications, and publications produced in all types of formats from all agencies. The *Monthly Catalog* is currently produced in a number of formats, all of which are derived from the database produced by GPO. Historically, the print version of the *Monthly Catalog* began production in 1895. A full print version is no longer being produced, and most users access one of the electronic versions of the database.

About the *Monthly Catalog* Bibliographic Database

The *Monthly Catalog* bibliographic database is the electronic bibliographic product from which all current versions of the *Monthly Catalog* are produced. The Government Printing Office (GPO) is responsible for creating and disseminating the database. Besides the versions of the *Monthly Catalog* listed above that are used as searching tools, electronic bibliographic records produced during the production of the *Monthly Catalog* are also available for use in locally produced databases and catalogs. GPO has been producing this database since 1976, and it follows standard cataloging practices, including the use of the MARC format.

The *Monthly Catalog* includes both depository and nondepository items in all formats, and is the most complete of the general bibliographic databases for federal publications. The database includes over 500,000 records. Increasingly, the *Monthly Catalog* database includes Web-based electronic resources from agency Internet sites. There are federal sources, however, that are not included in the *Monthly Catalog*, and it is not totally comprehensive. In particular, much of the technical report literature produced by government agencies is not included in the *Monthly Catalog* database.

Using the *Catalog of United States Government Publications* (GPO Access Version)

The *Catalog of United States Government Publications* is a publicly accessible Web version of the *Monthly Catalog* that provides coverage of sources from 1994–. Search fields include keywords, title, SuDocs number, item number, GPO stock number, and publication date. Boolean searching and phrase searching are possible and search terms may be truncated. Records returned as a result of a search are ranked according to relevance and are displayed as short summary records. A "Locate Libraries" link connects to the "GPO Access Federal Locator Services" search box that allows the user to locate depository libraries that select the item number associated with the document (if the publication was a depository item). (See Figure 3.2.) Once the results are displayed, the user has the option of retrieving either a short record, or a longer full record in the MARC format. (See Figures 3.3 and 3.4.) Short records include the following labeled display fields: "SuDocs Call No.," "Title," "Author," "Published," "Internet Access," "Description," "Item No.," "Subject," and "Entry No." The "Internet Access" field provides a direct URL or PURL link to any publications available on the Web. This is a very convenient feature that makes it easy to locate the electronic versions of sources. The "Entry No." is an accession number for the *Monthly Catalog* database. The full record gives a tagged MARC record display of all the fields and information in the full bibliographic record. It also provides the linking URL or PURL to the electronic version of the source, if available.

Catalog of U.S. Government Publications Search Results

The search was:

> ("BOSNIA")
> Records returned: 40

To locate Federal depository libraries that are likely to have a publication, select [Locate Libraries]

For the cataloging information for a publication, select either SHORT RECORD (for the user-friendly display) or FULL RECORD (for the full cataloging record).

When electronic access is available, click on the highlighted URL or PURL to go directly to the electronic document.

Publications with a GPO Stock Number may be available for purchase. Contact the nearest GPO Bookstore to determine if a publication is currently for sale from GPO. (Note the Title and Stock Number)

---

[1]
Bombs over **Bosnia** : the role of airpower in **Bosnia**-Herzegovina. Microfiche. [1997] Air University (U.S.). D 301.26/6-9:B 63. [[0422-K-02 (MF)]].
   Rank: 1000 Locate Libraries , [Short Record] , [Full Record]

---

[2]
Efforts to achieve peace and security in **Bosnia**-Herzegovina : communication from the President of the United States transmitting developments since his last report on August 22, 1994, on our support for the United Nations and North Atlantic Treaty Organization's (NATO) efforts to achieve peace and security in **Bosnia**-Herzegovina. 1994. United States. Y 1.1/7:103-336. [[0996-A]].
   Rank: 983 Locate Libraries , [Short Record] , [Full Record]

---

[3]
Employment : agreement between the United States of America and **Bosnia**-Herzegovina effected by exchange of notes, dated

Source: *Catalog of United States Government Publications*, <http://www.access.gpo.gov/su_docs/dpos/adpos400.html>

Figure 3.2: *Catalog of United States Government Publications* **Summary Display.**

SuDocs Call No.:	Y 4.SE 2:104-1-7
Title:	The latest crisis in Bosnia-Herzegovina : hearing before the Commission on Security and Cooperation in Europe, One Hundred Fourth Congress, first session, June 8, 1995.
Author:	United States. Congress. Commission on Security and Cooperation in Europe.
Published:	Washington : U.S. G.P.O. : For sale by the U.S. G.P.O., Supt. of Docs., Congressional Sales Office,
Date:	1996.
Internet Access:	http://purl.access.gpo.gov/GPO/LPS1572
Description:	iii, 12 p. ; 23 cm.
Item No.:	1089-C 1089-C (online) 1089-D (MF) 1089-D (online)
	Yugoslav War, 1991- -- Bosnia and Hercegovina. Embargo.
Subject:	Arms transfers -- Bosnia and Hercegovina. Arms transfers -- Government policy -- United States. United States
Entry No.:	98-19449

Source: *Catalog of United States Government Publications*, <http://www.access.gpo.gov/su_docs/dpos/adpos400.html>

Figure 3.3: *Catalog of United States Government Publications Short Record Example.*

```
Genocide in Bosnia-Herzegovina : hearing before the
Commission on Security and Cooperation in Europe, One
Hundred Fourth Congress, first session, April 4, 1995. 1995.
United States. Y 4.SE 2:104-1-4.
[[1089-C]].
 http://purl.access.gpo.gov/GPO/LPS1571


<001>  ocm33051464
<005>  19980917095854.0
<010a>  95220519
<040a>  DGPO
<040c>  DLC
<040d>  GPO
<020a>  0160474442
<035a>  (GPO)apn95-040913
<042a>  lccopycat
<043a>  e-bn---
<043a>  e-yu---
<050a>  DR1313.7.A85
<050b>  U54 1995
<074a>  1089-C
<074a>  1089-C (online)
<074a>  1089-D (MF)
<074a>  1089-D (online)
<082a>  949.702/4
<0822>   20
<086a>  Y 4.SE 2:104-1-4
<088a>  CSCE 104-1-4
<099a>  Y 4.SE 2:104-1-4
<049a>  GPOO
<110a>  United States.
<110b>  Congress.
```

Source: *Catalog of United States Government Publications,* <http://www.access.gpo.gov/su_docs/dpos/adpos400.html>

Figure 3.4: *Catalog of United States Government Publications* **Full Record Example.**

GPO CD-ROM and Print Versions of the Monthly Catalog

The Government Printing Office also produces a CD-ROM version of the *Monthly Catalog* with records available from 1996 to the present. A condensed version of the print *Monthly Catalog* that includes brief bibliographic entries along with a title keyword index has also been published by GPO since 1996. From 1895–1995, GPO published the *Monthly Catalog* in a full print version. Searching for items before 1976 will require the use of the print *Monthly Catalog* version, as all of the electronic versions available start with 1976. The format and information included in the print *Monthly Catalog* varied over its 100 year life span. Various cumulative subject, author, and title indexes provide for annual and multiyear searching.

Commercial Versions of the *Monthly Catalog*

A number of commercial versions of the *Monthly Catalog* are produced by various vendors. All of them are based on the *Monthly Catalog* database, and start their coverage with July 1976. Since the *Catalog of United States Government Publications* does not start its coverage until 1994,

using one of these versions with the longer coverage can be a distinct advantage. Boolean searching is a standard feature, and many of the databases provide the ability to search and combine additional fields beyond those provided by the *Catalog of United States Government Publications*. For example, the OCLC FirstSearch version of the *Monthly Catalog* provides fielded searching for the following fields: "Subject," "Author," "Title," "Edition," "Gov doc number," "Item number," "Map data," "Monthly catalog number," "Notes," "Publication place," "Publisher," "Report number," "Series Standard number," "Stock number," and "Subject headings."

Sales Product Catalog

Sales Product Catalog. WEB. U.S. Government Printing Office. Superintendent of Documents. Earlier title *Publications Reference File (PRF)* <https://orders.access.gpo.gov/su_docs/sale/index.html>; <http://purl.access.gpo.gov/GPO/LPS3766>.

The *Sales Product Catalog (SPC)* is an online database of all items for sale by the Government Printing Office. Included are such items as books, reports, maps, posters, periodicals, and other resources published in paper, microfiche, and electronic formats. Only a small proportion of the sources produced by the government are made available for sale. The *Sales Product Catalog* allows fielded searching by stock number, title, author, document source, key phrase, and description. Keyword searching of the entries is also provided. Entries provide information on the current status of the item—whether in stock, out-of-print, superseded, being reprinted, etc. (See Figure 3.5.)

Sales Product Catalog, <https://orders.access.gpo.gov/su_docs/sale/prf/prf.html>. While the *SPC* is primarily a database of items currently available, it does include items that have recently gone out-of-print and new requisition items that will be available for purchase in the near future.

```
PRF Online Via GPO Access

Title:                  Congressional Budget Request, FY 1998, United
                        States Department of Energy, V. 2, Energy Supply
                        Research and Development, Energy Assets Acquisition


Stock Number:           061-000-00882-9
Availability:           0. out of print GPO
Price:                  $57.00
Price (non-U.S.):       $71.25
Description:            DOE/CR-0042, V. 2. FY 1998 Congressional Budget
                        Request: Energy Supply Research and Development,
                        Energy Assets Acquisition. Includes detailed
                        information on Energy Supply Research and Development;
                        and Energy Assets Acquisition. Item 0429-T-46.


Publisher:              Energy Dept., Office of the Chief Financial Officer
Year/pages:             1997: 467 p.; ill.
Note:                   NB1258
Key Phrases:            DOE CR 0042, V. 2, Energy Supply Research and
                        Development, Energy Assets Acquisition, Research
                        and Development, Budgets, Energy Department,
                        Energy Supplies
SuDocs Class:           E 1.34:998/V.3
ISBN:                   0-16-063428-8
Extra Description:      individual mailing box
Weight:                 3 lbs 11 oz
Quantity Price:         discount
Binding:                perfect binding
Cover:                  paper
Available date:         02-11-97
Subject Bibliography:   900
Status date:            02-16-00
Unit:                   each
```

Figure 3.5: Sample Entry from *Sales Product Catalog*.

CIS/Index/Congressional Universe

CIS/Index. PRINT. (monthly) 1970–. Bethesda, MD: Congressional Information Service.

Congressional Universe. WEB. Bethesda, MD: Congressional Information Service.

CIS/Index is a comprehensive index to the publications of the U.S. Congress. Publications indexed include hearings, committee prints, House and Senate reports and documents, Senate executive reports, Senate treaty documents, and special publications of the House and Senate. Publications of joint committees and subcommittees, special commissions, special committees, and other congressionally affiliated agencies are also indexed. Coverage extends back to 1970. *CIS/Index* is available as a print version, and as a Web version within *Congressional Universe.*

The Print Version of *CIS/Index*

The print *CIS/Index* consists of three parts: an index volume, an abstract volume, and a legislative histories volume. The index and abstract volumes are published as separate monthly issues, with cumulated annual volumes. The legislative histories volume is published only as an annual volume. Index volumes are also cumulated quarterly, and multiyear cumulative index volumes are also issued: the last cumulative index was a four-year volume covering the time period 1995–98.

Using *CIS/Index*

The index volume of *CIS/Index* consists of several separate indexes. The "Index of Subjects and Names" covers subjects, corporate and individual names of authors and witnesses, affiliations of witnesses, names of subcommittees, and official and popular names of laws, bills, etc. The "Index of Titles" alphabetically lists the names of all publications abstracted. The "Index of Bill Numbers" provides an index by bill number, arranged by house, and within house, by Congress and type of bill. The "Index of Report Numbers" indexes House, Senate, and Executive Reports, arranged by report number. The "Index of Document Numbers" does the same for House, Senate, and Treaty Documents. The "Index of Senate Hearing Numbers" and "Index of Senate Print Numbers" are similarly arranged. The "Index of Superintendent of Documents Numbers" allows the user to go from a SuDocs number obtained elsewhere to the CIS accession number. The "Index of Committee and Subcommittee Chairmen" provides a listing of chairs, followed by the CIS committee codes.

The abstract volume of *CIS/Index* includes a "Table of Contents" broken down by committee, which is useful for browsing the publications of a committee. Each abstract entry includes complete bibliographic data. A *CIS/Index* assigned accession number (e.g., S361-27) is used to indicate the committee and specific document being described. Elements such as the SuDocs number, item number, *Monthly Catalog* entry number, and GPO stock

number are included in the bibliographic data. (See Figure 3.6.)

An abstract describing the entire document is included. Abstracts describe the subject covered by the document and cite texts of legislation appearing in the publication and many of the papers printed or reprinted in the document. Other items of possible interest to researchers, such as tables or lists are also often included in the abstract. Hearings will have additional "testimony abstracts" iden-

H271   **Hearings**
COMMERCE
Committee, House

H271–81   IMPACT OF MARKET VOLATILITY ON SECURITIES TRANSACTION FEES.
July 27, 1999. 106-1.
iii+43 p. GPO $2.50
S/N 552-070-24309-7.
CIS/MF/3
•Item 1019-A-01; 1019-B-01.
▼Y4.C73/8:106-41.

Committee Serial No. 106-41. Hearing before the *Subcom on Finance and Hazardous Materials* to examine a proposal to reduce fees imposed by SEC on securities transactions under section 31 of the Securities Exchange Act of 1934.

Supplementary material (p. 40-43) includes a submitted statement.

H271–81.1: July 27, 1999. p. 5-40.

Witnesses: **BRODSKY, William J.,** Chairman and CEO, Chicago Board Options Exchange.
CADER, Andrew, Vice President and Board Member, Specialist Association, New York Stock Exchange.
NELSON, Stephen J., Vice President, Herzog Heine Geduld; representing Securities Industry Association.
KEARNEY, Arthur J., Board Member and Director, Capital Markets, John G. Kinnard & Co.; representing Security Traders Association.

Statements and Discussion: Support for reduction of section 31 fees imposed on exchange-traded securities to promote competition among financial markets; need to reduce section 31 fees to bring fees collected into line with SEC operating costs and reduce burdens on stock exchanges; negative impact of excessive section 31 fees on private investment decisions.

Figure 3.6: Sample *CIS/Index* Abstract.

tifying and abstracting witnesses' statements and materials submitted by witnesses.

Using the index and abstract volumes of *CIS/Index* is a two-step process: (1) find the subject, name, title, bill number, etc., in the index volume and select a document entry (each entry is followed by an accession number such as S521-62) and (2) find the accession number in the abstract volume to find out more about the publication and to obtain retrieval information, such as the SuDocs number.

The annual legislative histories volume abstracts each public law except those of a ceremonial or housekeeping nature. Citations for documents relating to each public law are also included. Publications cited include slip laws; committee reports, prints, and hearings; House and Senate Documents; citations to the *Congressional Record*; and citations to the presidential signing statements included in the *Weekly Compilation of Presidential Documents*.

Approximately 10 percent of the laws are deemed by CIS to be "major enactments," and these histories include additional information. Included for these laws are the *CIS/Index* abstracts for the reports, hearings, prints, and documents cited; citations to relevant bills; more extensive *Congressional Record* citations; and citations for "Related" reports, hearings, prints, and documents.

Congressional Universe

The *Congressional Universe* is a comprehensive information system covering all aspects of congressional activity. One major component of *Congressional Universe* is an electronic version of the *CIS/Index*, providing coverage back to 1970. In addition, *Congressional Universe* includes the full text of many congressional publications, and such legal and regulatory materials as the *United States Code*, the *Federal Register*, and the *Code of Federal Regulations*. It also includes sources of information about congressional members and analysis of congressional activities, such as the full-text of the periodicals *National Journal* and *Congress Daily*.

Using *Congressional Universe*

The electronic version of the *CIS/Index* included in *Congressional Universe* provides a wide range of searching capabilities. Search screen options include searching by subject (including CIS subject descriptors); by title; by document number, such as House Report number or Senate Document number; by bibliographic numbers, such as SuDocs, LC "Card" (control number), *Monthly Catalog* entry number, or CIS accession number; by committee (House, Senate, or Joint committee issuing the publication); by witness (for searching for testimony in hearings); and by bill number (to locate all publications associated with a particular bill). (See Figure 3.7.)

As in the print version, abstracts are included for the items retrieved. Increasingly, *Congressional Universe* makes the full text of indexed and abstracted publications available as part of its subscription service.

The *Congressional Universe CIS/Index* also provides special searching for the Legislative Histories section. Legislative Histories may be searched by keyword or CIS subject descriptor, by public law or bill number, or by the *Statutes at Large* citation. As in the print index, the Legislative Histories provide a comprehensive record of the history of the bill. The *Congressional Universe* version also provides many links to the abstracts or full text of the items being cited.

Congressional Universe also includes many other features that go beyond bibliographic searching. It includes the full text of bills and a bill tracking feature, a "Hot Bills and Topics" feature, information about members of Congress and their voting records, Congressional committee information, and the full text of *Public Laws*, the *U.S. Code*, the *Congressional Record*, the *Federal Register*, and the *Code of Federal Regulations*.

ASI

American Statistics Index (ASI). PRINT. (monthly) 1973–. Bethesda, MD: Congressional Information Service.

Statistical Universe. WEB. 1973–. Bethesda, MD: Congressional Information Service.

The *American Statistics Index* (*ASI*) is a comprehensive index to government statistics that is invaluable—even indispensable—for locating any statistics published by a government agency. *ASI* is constantly updated and is available in a print- and a Web-based version. Indexing starts with 1973, with some selected retrospective coverage of sources from the 1960s included.

The Print Version of *ASI*

The print version of *ASI* consists of a base retrospective edition covering the years 1960–73, with annual supplements for each year thereafter. Five multiple-year cumulative indexes for the years 1974–79, 1980–94, 1985–88, 1989–92, and 1993–96 have been published. Each annual supplement (and the retrospective edition) consists of two parts: an index and an abstract volume. Monthly issues are published for the current year, with the indexes cumulated quarterly.

Using *ASI*

The index volume contains a subject and names index, an index by categories, a title index, an agency report number index, and an index by Superintendent of Documents numbers (annual volume only). The subject and names index includes subjects, place names, government agency names, major related government program or proposal names, special classes of publications or data (for example, "Directories"), individual personal names, companies and institutions, and major data surveys names. The category index allows a researcher to look up material according to how the statistics are arranged, rather than just by sub-

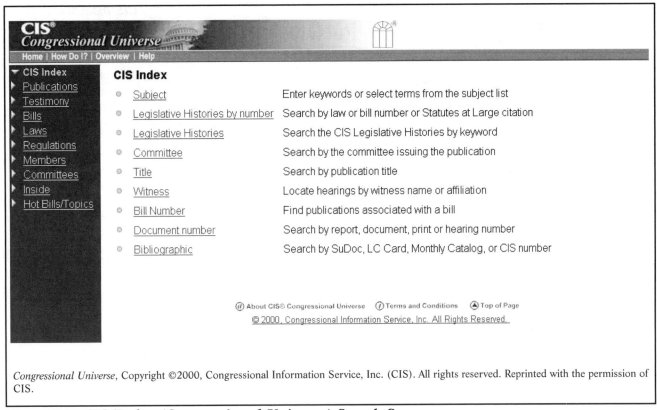

Congressional Universe, Copyright ©2000, Congressional Information Service, Inc. (CIS). All rights reserved. Reprinted with the permission of CIS.

Figure 3.7: *CIS/Index (Congressional Universe)* **Search Screen.**

ject. This can be a useful shortcut. Categories in the index include geographic (for statistics arranged "By city," By state," etc.); economic ("By commodity," "By industry"); and demographic ("By age," "By race").

Abstracts are arranged in accession number order and grouped by agency. (See Figure 3.8.) Each publication or series has a unique number and recurring publications generally have the same number each year. Thorough descriptions of the contents of the publications are given, often down to a listing of each statistical table. A given publication may be broken down into several abstract numbers by the use of decimals in the accession number. The publication assigned the accession number 2024-2, for example, may be subdivided into 2024-2.1, 2024-2.2, etc. Using *ASI* is a two-step process: (1) Find the subject, category, or title in the index volume and select a publication entry (each entry is followed by an accession number), and (2) find the accession number in the abstract volume to read more about the publication and to get retrieval information. The entry may include SuDocs numbers and indicate when a publication is also available on the Internet.

Statistical Universe

Statistical Universe is an online statistical information system produced by Congressional Information Service. Included in *Statistical Universe* is a Web-based version of

ASI. The other products included within *Statistical Universe* are the *Index to International Statistics (IIS)* (covering international intergovernmental organizations) and *Statistical Reference Index (SRI)* (covering state government agencies and a variety of private organization sources).

Within *Statistical Universe*, *ASI* can be searched by subject, including keyword and subject descriptors assigned by CIS. As in the print *ASI*, category searching is available, and is especially useful when combined with subject descriptor or subject keyword searching. Title searching and a "publisher" search that searches by the issuing agency are also available. An author search allows searching by personal names, and a number search provides searching by SuDocs number, *Monthly Catalog* entry number, *ASI* accession number, and LC "Card" (control) number.

A "Power Tables" section also allows the user to search the content of specific statistical tables, taken from sources indexed by Statistical Universe. Subject descriptors and bibliographic information pertaining to the tables are also searchable. Keyword and phrase searching are included, and results may be limited by geographic coverage or dates. Category searching is also available. Results display a gif file of the actual table, with links to the abstract and bibliographic data for the source from which the table is taken.

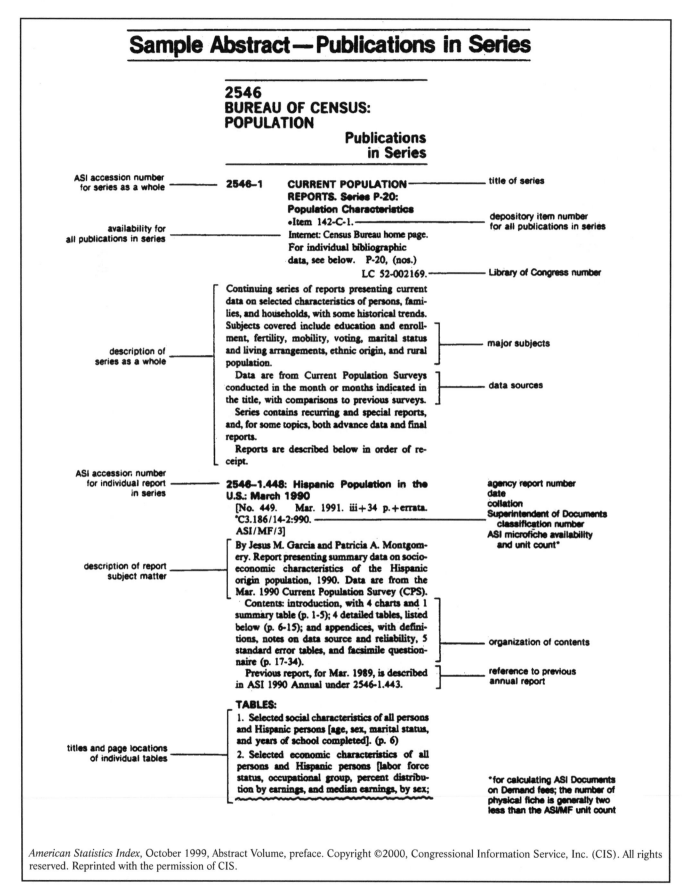

Sample Abstract—Publications in Series

**2546
BUREAU OF CENSUS:
POPULATION**

Publications
in Series

ASI accession number
for series as a whole — **2546–1** — **CURRENT POPULATION** — title of series
**REPORTS. Series P-20:
Population Characteristics**
availability for — •Item 142-C-1. — depository item number
all publications in series — Internet: Census Bureau home page. — for all publications in series
For individual bibliographic
data, see below. P-20, (nos.)
LC 52-002169. — Library of Congress number

description of
series as a whole —
Continuing series of reports presenting current
data on selected characteristics of persons, families, and households, with some historical trends.
Subjects covered include education and enrollment, fertility, mobility, voting, marital status
and living arrangements, ethnic origin, and rural
population. — major subjects

Data are from Current Population Surveys
conducted in the month or months indicated in
the title, with comparisons to previous surveys. — data sources

Series contains recurring and special reports,
and, for some topics, both advance data and final
reports.

Reports are described below in order of receipt.

ASI accession number
for individual report — **2546–1.448: Hispanic Population in the** — agency report number
in series — **U.S.: March 1990** — date
[No. 449. Mar. 1991. iii+34 p.+errata. — collation
°C3.186/14-2:990. — Superintendent of Documents
ASI/MF/3] — classification number
— ASI microfiche availability
and unit count*

description of report
subject matter —
By Jesus M. Garcia and Patricia A. Montgomery. Report presenting summary data on socioeconomic characteristics of the Hispanic
origin population, 1990. Data are from the
Mar. 1990 Current Population Survey (CPS).

Contents: introduction, with 4 charts and 1
summary table (p. 1-5); 4 detailed tables, listed
below (p. 6-15); and appendices, with definitions, notes on data source and reliability, 5
standard error tables, and facsimile questionnaire (p. 17-34). — organization of contents

Previous report, for Mar. 1989, is described
in ASI 1990 Annual under 2546-1.443. — reference to previous
annual report

titles and page locations
of individual tables —
TABLES:
1. Selected social characteristics of all persons
and Hispanic persons [age, sex, marital status,
and years of school completed]. (p. 6)
2. Selected economic characteristics of all
persons and Hispanic persons [labor force
status, occupational group, percent distribu-
tion by earnings, and median earnings, by sex; — *for calculating ASI Documents
on Demand fees; the number of
physical fiche is generally two
less than the ASI/MF unit count

Figure 3.8: *ASI* **Sample Abstract.**

Availability

Many of the publications in *ASI* are made available to depository libraries. Some are available electronically from agency Web sites. *Statistical Universe* itself includes the full text of some publications, depending on the subscription options selected by the subscribing library. Microfiche copies of all publications indexed by *ASI* can also be purchased from Congressional Information Service, Inc.

Web Search Engines and Directories

GovBot. WEB. University of Massachusetts. Center for Intelligent Information Retrieval. <http://ciir2.cs.umass.edu/Govbot/>.

Google Search UncleSam. WEB. Google Inc. <http://www.google.com/unclesam>.

UsGovSearch Free Edition. WEB. Northern Light. <http://usgovsearch.northernlight.com/publibaccess/>.

Government Information Exchange. WEB. General Services Administration. Federal Technology Service. Center for Emerging Technologies. <http://www.info.gov/>.

Providing access to electronic publications and information through the World Wide Web is now one of the primary ways that government agencies distribute information. The use of Web search engines has become essential in accessing governmental information. This section lists a selection of Web search engines that are particularly useful for searching for federal government information. Most of them search only Internet sites with .gov and/or .mil extensions. *GovBot* is one of the most extensive of these search engines and provides sophisticated search options. One of *Google Search UncleSam's* unique features is that it caches pages to provide a backup version of the pages it indexes. The *UsGovSearch Free Edition* is available to libraries free of charge and features Northern Light's "Custom Search Folders," which organizes search results into specialized categories. It also includes power and agency searches that allow searches to be limited to specific agencies, subjects, or dates.

The *Government Information Exchange* site provides directories and links to a variety of government information sources, but it also includes a search engine within its site. It allows searches to be limited by "All Federal Government," "Federal Civilian Agencies Only," Dept. of Defense Agencies Only," and "Federal Kids-Related Sites."

CIS Government Periodicals Universe/ U.S. Government Periodicals Index

CIS Government Periodicals Universe. WEB. (quarterly) 1988–. Bethesda, MD: Congressional Information Service, Inc.

U.S. Government Periodicals Index. PRINT. (quarterly) 1988–. Bethesda, MD: Congressional Information Service, Inc.

The *CIS Government Periodicals Universe* is the Web version of the *U.S. Government Periodicals Index*, the only major index indexing government periodical articles. Coverage goes back to 1988, and approximately 170 current periodicals are covered. Titles covered range from the popular to the research journal. Sample titles include *Naval War College Review*, *Agricultural Outlook*, *Monthly Labor Review*, and *Environmental Health Perspectives*. Both versions are updated quarterly. A previous CD-ROM version titled *US Government Periodicals Index on CD-ROM* has been discontinued.

List of Classes

List of Classes of United States Government Publications Available for Selection by Depository Libraries. PRINT. WEB. (semiannual). U.S. Government Printing Office. Superintendent of Documents. Library Programs Service. Library Division. Depository Administration Branch. GP 3.24: Item 0556-C. <http://www.du.edu/~ttyler/locintro.htm#gtr00>; <http://www.access.gpo.gov/su_docs/fdlp/pubs/loc/index.html>; <http://fedbbs.access.gpo.gov/libs/CLASS.htm>; <http://purl.access.gpo.gov/GPO/LPS1480>.
> Content: depending on version, listing or database of depository series available for distribution.

The *List of Classes* provides information about the sources currently available for selection by selective depository libraries and received in entirety by regional depository libraries. Increasingly, the *List of Classes* also lists electronic versions of items accessible through the Web that are only available that way—and are not otherwise distributed to depository libraries or are not produced in any other format.

The print version of the *List of Classes* is arranged by agency in SuDocs number order. For each class under an agency, the title, SuDocs number, item number, and often the frequency of the title is given. The format designations Print (P), Microfiche (MF), CD-ROM (CD-ROM), Electronic (E), and Electronic Library (EL) are also included. The print version includes an alphabetical list of government authors and a list of item numbers, giving SuDocs. The HTML version of the *List of Classes* at the *Basic Depository Library Documents* (*BDLD*) site provides a similarly formatted version, and also includes a list of government authors arranged by government author name, and a list of classes arranged by item number. (See Figure 3.9.)

A searchable version of the *List of Classes* is also available at the *Documents Data Miner©* Web site. This site allows Boolean searching of the agency, item number, SuDocs stem, title, formats, and status fields. Truncated and wild card searching is also included. This version also allows you to easily display the libraries selecting the item for a particular class, according to user-defined filters for the geographic areas of the depository libraries that should be included.

A GPO version of the *List of Classes* is made available through the *Federal Bulletin Board File Libraries* as ASCII comma-delimited files. Although somewhat unwieldy to search and use, these files can be downloaded and manipulated. They also provide the data for the two versions of the *List of Classes* previously described.

Guide to U.S. Government Publications

Guide to U.S. Government Publications. PRINT. (annual) 1959–. Donna Batten, Editor. Farmington Hills, MI: Gale Group, Inc. (Earlier published by Documents Index.)

The *Guide to U.S. Government Publications*, previously known as *Andriot* (for its original author), also provides a listing of classes in a SuDocs number arrangement. Entries include the SuDocs number, title, and item number if depository; other elements that are sometimes included are dates, frequency of publication, ISSN number; notes about title and SuDocs number changes, and descriptions of the title. Information about the creation, authority, and establishment dates of each individual agency is included at the beginning of an agency's listing. Entries are often annotated, and individual documents within a series are sometimes noted and annotated. An "Agency Class Chronology" section gives a historical SuDocs numbers listing for each agency, and an agency, title, and keyword-in-title index are included within the volume. In many ways, The *Guide to U.S. Government Publications* can be used as an expanded *List of Classes*. The *Guide*, however, includes nondepository titles and discontinued classes, whereas the *List of Classes* includes current depository classes only.

Subject Bibliographies

GPO *Subject Bibliographies*. PRINT. WEB. GP 3.22/2: <http://bookstore.gpo.gov/sb/about.html>.

The Government Printing Office issues over 150 bibliographies of current, in-print titles available for sale on different topics. These *Subject Bibliographies* are available in both Web and print formats. An index to the topics covered is issued in a print format and is also available on the Web with links to the individual bibliographies indexed. Sample titles of Subject Bibliographies include *Wildlife Management* (GP 3.22/2:116); *Childhood and Adolescence* (GP 3.22/2:35); and *Federal Trade Commission* (GP 3.22/2:100).

LIST OF CLASSES - June 2, 2000
ARRANGED BY ITEM NUMBER
(continued)

Item No.	Class Stem	Series Title	Frequency	Format
0001	A 1.47:	Agricultural Statistics		EL, P
0001-A	A 1.47/2:	Agricultural Statistics)	Annual	CD
0002	A 1.116:	Rural Telephone Bank		MF
0002	A 1.58/A:	Agriculture Decisions	Semiannual	P
0003	A 1.76:	Agriculture Handbooks		EL, P
0004	A 1.75/2:	Structural and Financial Characteristics of U.S. Farms)	Annual	MF
0004	A 1.75:	Agriculture Information Bulletin (AIB series)		EL, MF
0006	A 1.1:	Annual Report	Annual	MF
0006-C	A 93.43:	Outlook for U.S. Agricultural Trade		EL
0006-G	A 1.1/3:	Semiannual Report, Office of Inspector General	Semiannual	MF
0006-H	A 1.93:	Budget Estimates for the United States Department of Agriculture for Fiscal Year ...	Annual	MF
0006-J	A 1.1/4-2:	Annual Report on the Food and Agricultural Sciences	Annual	MF
0006-J	A 1.1/5:	Report on USDA Human Nutrition Research and Education Activities, A Report to Congress)	Annual	MF
0006-J	A 1.1/6:	Office of Inspector General FY, Annual Plan	Annual	MF
0006-K	A 1.2/12:	Accomplishments for Research, Extension, and Higher Education)	Annual	MF
0006-L	A 1.2/11:	Five-Year Plan for the Food and Agricultural Sciences	Biennial	MF

List of Classes, June 2, 2000, Agriculture Department. <http://www.du.edu/~ttyler/loci100.htm#gtr00>

Figure 3.9: Sample Listing from the *List of Classes* (Basic Depository Library Documents Version).

The Subject Search

The subject search is used to answer questions such as "Do you have any publications on child abuse?" or "Do you have any information on U.S. involvement in economic boycotts?" or "Has the government completed any studies on dioxin?" The usual strategy is to consult basic government publication indexes (or local and electronic catalog equivalents). These indexes form the basic component of the subject search strategy.

This section contains chapters on topics for which government publications are an important source and for which questions frequently arise. The object of these chapters is to list major sources in each area and thus make it possible to answer some basic questions without engaging in the more time-consuming index search. Searching indexes is, however, necessary for locating more specialized information and for locating materials in subject areas not covered here.

Subject searches may be expanded by including other search strategies as part of the search. If a government agency that has a particular interest in the subject can be identified (for example, the Environmental Protection Agency for environmental topics), that agency's publications can be scanned in the *List of Classes* or the *Guide to U.S. Government Publications*. In many cases, statistical searches also provide useful information.

CHAPTER 4
Foreign Policy

U.S. foreign policy is a very broad topic covering many different areas. This chapter concentrates on describing overview publications from Congress and the Department of State, including both current and historical sources. Two specific topics also included in this chapter are foreign aid and foreign economic relations. For information on other related areas not covered in this chapter, use the "Related Material" section at the end of the chapter and the search strategy provided below.

SEARCH STRATEGY

1. Try the major sources and series of publications and Web sites listed within this chapter, such as the *U.S. Department of State Dispatch* or the *Foreign Relations of the United States* series;
2. Search the Department of State Web site;
3. Check the "Related Material" section, especially for other chapters that relate to this subject;
4. Use the print or electronic forms of the indexes and databases listed to locate further information; and
5. If searching for other subtopics that are statistical in nature, such as the foreign aid section, use *American Statistics Index (ASI)*, either in print or on the Web in *Statistical Universe*.

CONGRESSIONAL ACTIVITIES SOURCES
Checklist

House Committee on International Relations Web Site. WEB. U.S. Congress. House. Committee on International Relations. <http://www.house.gov/international_relations/>.
  Content: background information on the committee; information about hearings, meetings, and reports; overview of activities; committee schedules; information on subcommittees.

Senate Foreign Relations Committee Web Site. WEB. U.S. Congress. Senate. Committee on Foreign Relations. <http://www.senate.gov/~foreign/>.
  Content: background information on the committee; hearing schedule; prepared witness statements.

Hearings, Prints, and Miscellaneous Publications. PRINT. MF. U.S. Congress. House. Committee on International Relations. Y 4.IN 8/16: Items 1017-A-01 or -B(MF).
  Content: hearings, committee prints, and other publications from the House Committee on International Relations.

Hearings, Prints, and Miscellaneous Publications. PRINT. MF. U.S. Congress. Senate. Committee on Foreign Relations. Y 4.F 76/2: Items 1039-A or -B(MF).
  Content: hearings, committee prints, and other publications from the Senate Committee on Foreign Relations.

Senate Reports. PRINT. MF. (irregular) U.S. Congress. Senate. Y 1.1/5: Items 1008-C or -D(MF).
  Content: Senate Reports, including those from the Senate Committee on Foreign Relations.

Senate Executive Reports. PRINT. MF. (irregular) U.S. Congress. Senate. Y 1.1/6: Items 1008-C or -D(MF).
  Content: Senate Executive Reports, issued by the Senate Committee on Foreign Relations.

Senate Documents. PRINT. MF. (irregular) U.S. Congress. Senate. Y1.1/3: Items 0996-A or -B(MF).
  Content: Senate Documents, including those issued by the Senate Committee on Foreign Relations.

Senate Treaty Documents. PRINT. MF. U.S. Congress. Senate. Y 1.1/4: Items 0996-A or -B(MF).
  Content: Senate Treaty Documents issued by the Senate Committee on Foreign Relations.

House Reports. PRINT. MF. U.S. Congress. House. Y 1.1/8: Items 1008-C or -D(MF).
  Content: House Reports, including those issued by the House Committee on International Relations.

House Documents. PRINT. MF. U.S. Congress. House. Y 1.1/7: Items 0996-A or -B(MF).

> Content: House Documents, including those issued by the House Committee on International Relations.

Committee Reports. WEB. 1995–. U.S. Congress. (*THOMAS*) <http://thomas.loc.gov/>.

> Content: full text of House and Senate Committee Reports, including the Senate Committee on Foreign Relations and the House Committee on International Relations.

Senate, House, and Executive Reports. WEB. 1995–. U.S. Congress. (*GPO Access*) <http://www.access.gpo.gov/congress/cong005.html>.

> Content: full text of House and Senate Committee Reports, including the Senate Committee on Foreign Relations and the House Committee on International Relations.

Senate, House, and Treaty Documents. WEB. 1994–. U.S. Congress (*GPO Access*) <http://www.access.gpo.gov/congress/cong006.html>.

> Content: full text of House and Senate Committee Documents, including the Senate Committee on Foreign Relations and the House Committee on International Relations.

Country Reports on Human Rights Practices for [year]. PRINT. MF. WEB. (annual) 1977–. U.S. Congress. House. Committee on International Relations. Senate. Committee on Foreign Relations. Y 4.IN 8/16-15: (Prepared by the Department of State; issued as a Joint Committee Print) Items 1017-A-03 ; 1017-B-03(MF). ASI 21464-3. GPO. <http://www.state.gov/www/global/human_rights/hrp_reports_mainhp.html>; <http://purl.access.gpo.gov/GPO/LPS1236>.

> Content: country-by-country review and analysis of human rights practices.

Annual Report to Congress on International Religious Freedom. PRINT. MF. WEB. (annual) 1999–. U.S. Congress. Senate. Committee on Foreign Relations. Y 4.IN8/16: (1999 is Y 4.IN8/16:R27/3) Items 1017-A-01; 1017-B-01(MF). <http://www.state.gov/www/global/human_rights/irf/irf_rpt/index.html>; <http://purl.access.gpo.gov/GPO/LPS3421>.

> Content: country-by-country analysis of religious freedom and any human rights violations of religious freedom.

Legislation on Foreign Relations through [year]. PRINT. MF. (irregular) 1977–. U.S. Congress. Senate. Committee on Foreign Relations. U.S. Congress. House. Committee on International Relations. (Issued as a joint committee print) Y 4.F 76/2-10: year. Items 1039-A or -B(MF). GPO.

> Content: annotated copies of legislation, executive orders, and treaties pertaining to foreign policy.

Legislative Review Activities of the Committee on International Relations. PRINT. MF. WEB. (biennial) U.S. Congress. House. Committee on International Relations. House Report. Y 1.1/8: (105th Congress is Y 1.1/8:105-838) Items 1008-C or -D(MF). <http://www.access.gpo.gov/congress/cong005.html>.

Discussion

The two congressional committees most involved with foreign policy are the House Committee on International

Relations and the Senate Committee on Foreign Policy. Each of these committees issues numerous hearings, committee prints, and miscellaneous publications dealing with foreign policy. *CIS/Index,* cited in the "Indexes" section of this chapter, can be used to further identify the individual titles of publications issued by these two committees. The full-text of some of these publications are also available through *THOMAS* and the *GPO Access* Web sites.

Both the House Committee on International Relations and the Senate Committee on Foreign Policy maintain committee Web sites that provide some general background information about the committee's members and work of the committees. The *House Committee on International Relations Web Site* also provides links to its committee reports via *THOMAS* and includes transcripts of hearings. A weekly updated "Survey of Activities" section lists all hearings and meetings scheduled that week, as well as listing any reports received by the committee. The *Senate Committee on Foreign Policy Web Site* is less complete, but does provide some information on its members and its work.

Hearings, prints, and other miscellaneous publications from these two committees are distributed to depository libraries in print or microfiche formats. *Senate and House Reports, Senate and House Documents, Senate Executive Reports,* and *Senate Treaty Documents* are also made available to depository libraries. Increasingly, the full text of these documents are also available online from either *THOMAS* or the *GPO Access* Web sites, and links to the relevant sections of these sites are cited here.

Two important recurring reports relating to foreign policy and human rights are issued by these two committees. The first, *Country Reports on Human Rights Practices for [year]* is issued as a joint committee print by both the House Committee on International Relations and the Senate Committee on Foreign Affairs. *Country Reports on Human Rights Practices* is a lengthy annual report that contains individual country reports on human rights conditions. Information included within the report is obtained from many sources, including U.S. officials (particularly State Department officials), officials of foreign governments, private citizens, intelligence information, journalists, international organizations, and nongovernmental human rights organizations. Sections of the report for each country include the following: (1) "Respect for the Integrity of the Person"; (2) "Respect for Civil Liberties"; (3) "Respect for Political Rights: The Right of Citizens to Change Their Government"; (4) "Government Attitude Regarding International and Nongovernmental Investigation of Alleged Violations of Human Rights"; (5) "Discrimination Based on Race, Sex, Religion, Language, or Social Status"; and (6) "Worker Rights."

The second report, the *Annual Report to Congress on International Religious Freedom* is a similarly compiled report on religious freedom and human rights violations regarding religious freedom issued by the Senate Committee on Foreign Relations. Each country-by-country listing includes the following sections: "Freedom of Religion," "Societal Attitudes," and "U.S. Government Policies." Background information, information on the current status of religious activity and religious freedom of the country, and examples of any religious freedom violations are included in the narrative.

Legislation on Foreign Relations is a five-volume set that reprints the text of legislation, executive orders, and treaties pertaining to foreign policy. Annotations are included with the text, along with subject indexes.

Legislative Review Activities of the Committee on International Relations summarizes the Committee's and its Subcommittees' work of the last Congress. The report includes lists of meetings and hearings, lists of witnesses who testified at meetings, lists of foreign dignitaries and U.S. officials received by the Committee, and a listing of members of the committee. The report serves as a good summary and record of the Committee's work in each congressional session.

DEPARTMENT OF STATE PUBLICATIONS

Checklist

Department of State Web Site. WEB. U.S. Department of State. <http://www.state.gov>.

> Content: information about the State Department; foreign policy information; press briefings and publications; information about State Department services.

Patterns of Global Terrorism. WEB. (annual) 1976–. U.S. Department of State. Office of the Secretary of State. Office of the Coordinator for Counterterrorism. S 1.138: (Earlier, PREX 3.10/7:) (Title varies) Item 0876-A-06. ASI 7004-13. <http://www.state.gov/www/global/terrorism/annual_reports.html#patterns>; <http://www.usis.usemb.se/terror/index.html>; <http://purl.access.gpo.gov/GPO/LPS1488>.

> Content: country-by-country review and analysis of terrorist attacks; statistics on terrorism attacks and casualties; description of and background information on organizations engaging in terrorism.

Significant Incidents of Political Violence Against Americans. PRINT. WEB. (annual) 1988–. U.S. Department of State. Bureau of Diplomatic Security. Office of Intelligence and Threat Analysis. S 1.138/2: Item 0876-A-07. ASI 7004-22. <http://www.state.gov/www/global/terrorism/annual_reports.html>.

> Content: descriptions of and statistics relating to terrorist attacks directed against U.S. citizens; data given by country and world region.

International Narcotics Control Strategy Report. PRINT. WEB. (annual) 1984–. U.S. Department of State. Bureau for International Narcotics and Law Enforcement Affairs. S 1.146: (Earlier, S 1.2:N 16/3/year) Item 0876-A-06. ASI 7004-17. GPO. <http://www.state.gov/www/global/narcotics_law/narc_reports_mainhp.html>; <http://purl.access.gpo.gov/GPO/LPS3635>.

> Content: overview of U.S. involvement in drug control throughout the world; country-by-country descriptions of drug industries and drug control activities.

Voting Practices in the United Nations: Report to Congress Submitted Pursuant to Public Law 101-167. MF. WEB. (annual) 1983–. U.S. Department of State. Bureau of International Organization Affairs. S 1.1/8: (Title varies) Item 0876-A-05(MF). ASI 7004-18. <http://www.state.gov/www/issues/io_ann_reports.html>.

> Content: analysis of the voting practices of U.N. member states as it relates to United States policy.

United States Participation in the U.N.: Report by the President to the Congress for the Year [year]. MF. WEB. U.S. Department of State. Bureau of International Organization Affairs. S 1.70/8: (Earlier S 1.70:) Item 0882-B(MF). ASI 7004-5. GPO. <http://www.state.gov/www/issues/ioparticipation.html>.

> Content: comprehensive review of the United States' involvement with U.N. activities.

Background Notes. PRINT. WEB. (irregular) 1964–. U.S. Department of State. S 1.123: (Indexes, S 1.123/2:) Item 0862-B. ASI 7006-2. GPO. <http://www.state.gov/www/background_notes/index.html>; <http://purl.access.gpo.gov/GPO/LPS2003>.

> Content: basic information on a country's geography, government, economy, history, people, political conditions, foreign relations, and travel and business information.

Diplomatic List. PRINT. WEB. (quarterly) U.S. Department of State. S 1.8: Item 0865. GPO. <http://www.state.gov/www/about_state/contacts/diplist/index.html>; <http://purl.access.gpo.gov/GPO/LPS2407>.

> Content: listing of foreign missions in the United States; diplomatic staff and spouses of those missions.

Foreign Consular Offices in the United States. WEB. (annual) U.S. Department of State. S 1.69/2: Item 0963. GPO. <http://www.state.gov/www/travel/consular_offices/fco_index.html>; <http://purl.access.gpo.gov/GPO/LPS1388>.

> Content: listing of Washington DC chanceries; listing by country of foreign consular offices and officers in the United States.

Key Officers of Foreign Service Posts: Guide for Business Representatives. WEB. (irregular) U.S. Department of State. S 1.40/5: Item 0876-B. <http://www.state.gov/www/about_state/contacts/keyofficer_index.html>; <http://purl.access.gpo.gov/GPO/LPS2408>.

> Content: key officers (chiefs, assistant chiefs of missions, economic offices, consular offices, etc.) of missions and consulates.

Discussion

The Department of State is the executive branch agency most closely involved with foreign policy. Its agency Web site is a good starting point for accessing many of its publications and for locating information on its activities and on the activities of its many offices and bureaus. Many of the bureaus and offices have their own Web pages, and often include press releases and information about current foreign policy–related events.

Patterns of Global Terrorism is a detailed analysis of worldwide terrorism, particularly noting those acts against

U.S. targets. It provides a country-by-country overview (organized by regions) of terrorist attacks and incidents. The report also includes detailed statistics on incidents, casualties, and facilities attacked. Background information on terrorist groups and a chronology of incidents for the year are also included. This source is one of the best and most complete for looking at terrorism from a U.S. foreign policy perspective. *Significant Incidents of Political Violence Against Americans* is a related report that concentrates on describing through descriptions, statistical tables, charts, and photos, the extent of terrorist attacks directed against U.S. citizens.

The *International Narcotics Control Strategy Report* describes the U.S. Government's policies and programs for combating the drug trade worldwide. The report includes statistics on drug production and on the U.S.'s assistance to other countries in eradication and drug enforcement programs. It also includes country-by-country descriptions of drug production, drug trade, eradication efforts, and drug supply and demand in the country, along with other information such as the U.S.'s policies and programs in the country, relevant agreements and treaties, and money laundering activities taking place.

Section I of the *Voting Practices in the United Nations: Report to Congress Submitted Pursuant to Public Law 101-167* contains a short introduction summarizing the U.N.'s activities during the year, written from a U.S. point of view. It also includes a series of graphs summarizing the voting coincidence percentage (as compared to the United States), for selected geographic and political groups. Section II summarizes the U.S. vote in the General Assembly, and also includes a table arranged by country, listing the number of General Assembly identical votes, opposite votes, abstention, and absences, along with the voting coincidence percentage. Section III compares selected U.S. votes on key issues in a similar fashion. Section IV analyzes Security Council votes. Section V compiles voting information for each country. (See Figure 4.1.)

United States Participation in the U.N.: Report by the President to the Congress for the Year [year] provides a comprehensive and analytical overview of the United States activities in the United Nations. Sections of the report cover broad topics such as "Economic and Social Affairs," "Science, Technology, and Research," and "Reform of the United Nations." The United States' role in United Nations' activities in these areas is then discussed in detail.

Each issue of *Background Notes* provides basic information on an individual country. A profile of the country starts each *Note*, and provides brief statistical and factual information. The *Background Notes* include a broad overview of a country and its people, history, economy, geography, and government. *Notes* also includes a discussion of U.S. relations with the country and the country's relationships with other countries.

Several directories published by the Department of State list U.S. diplomatic staff and consular offices and

HISTORICAL SOURCES
Checklist

Foreign Relations of the United States. PRINT. MF. WEB. (annual) 1818–. U.S. Department of State. Bureau of Public Affairs. Office of the Historian. S 1.1: (Earliest volumes issued in the *Serial Set*) Items 0872-B or -C(MF), 0872-D(MF). GPO. Selected volumes: <http://www.state.gov/www/about_state/history/frusonline.html>.

Content: official record of U.S. foreign policy with correspondence and papers on major policies and decisions.

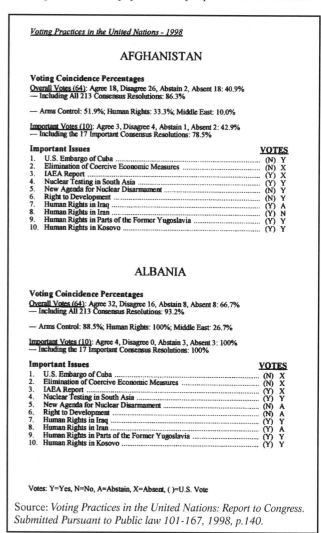

Figure 4.1: Sample Page from *Voting Practices in the United Nations.*

officers of other countries. The *Diplomatic List* is a directory of the diplomatic staff and their spouses of all missions located in the United States. The *Foreign Consular Offices in the United States* lists offices and their staff located in both Washington, D.C., and in states. *Key Officers of Foreign Service Posts* lists the U.S. officers in other countries who can be of help in developing international trade and business opportunities.

Foreign Relations of the United States. Diplomatic Papers. Conferences. PRINT. U.S. Department of State. Bureau of Public Affairs. Office of the Historian. S 1.1/3: Item 0872.

> Content: official record of United States involvement with foreign policy conferences.

A Decade of American Foreign Policy: Basic Documents, 1941–1949. PRINT. (1985) U.S. Department of State. Bureau of Public Affairs. Office of the Historian. Foreign Service Series No. 415. S 1.69:415. Item 0863.

> Content: basic collection of public documents on U.S. foreign policy.

American Foreign Policy 1950–55: Basic Documents. PRINT. (1957) U.S. Department of State. Historical Division. S 1.71:117. Item 0875.

> Content: basic collection of public documents on foreign policy.

American Foreign Policy: Current Documents. PRINT. (annual) (1955–67) (1981–1990) U.S. Department of State. Bureau of Public Affairs. Office of the Historian. S 1.71/2: Item 0875.

> Content: annual compilations of texts of major official messages; addresses, statements, reports, and communications relating to foreign policy.

American Foreign Policy: Basic Documents, 1977–1980. PRINT. (1983) U.S. Department of State. Bureau of Public Affairs. Office of the Historian. Department and Foreign Service Series 346. S 1.69:346. Item 0863.

> Content: text of major official messages, addresses, statements, reports, and communications relating to foreign policy.

U.S. Department of State Dispatch. PRINT. WEB. (10 times per year) (1990-1999) U.S. Department of State. Office of Public Communication. Bureau of Public Affairs. S 1.3/5: Item 0864. GPO. <http://www.state.gov/www/publications/dispatch/index.html>; <http://dosfan.lib.uic.edu/ERC/briefing/dispatch/index.html>; <http://purl.access.gpo.gov/GPO/LPS1701>.

> Content: record of official activities dealing with U.S. foreign affairs activities.

Department of State Bulletin. (monthly) (1939–89) U.S. Department of State. Bureau of Public Affairs. S 1.3: Item 0864.

> Content: articles, addresses, messages, statements, and press releases dealing with foreign policy and the work of the Department of State.

Executive Sessions of the Senate Foreign Relations Committee (Historical Series). PRINT. MF. (irregular) (1976–93) U.S. Congress. Senate. Committee on Foreign Relations. Y 4.F76/2:Ex3/2/v.1-18. Items 1039-A or -B(MF).

> Content: compilation of historical transcripts of the Senate Foreign Relations Committee, 1947–1966.

Historical Series. PRINT. (irregular) (1976–80) U.S. Congress. House. Committee on International Relations; Committee on Foreign Affairs. Y 4.IN 8/16:H 62/v.1-8; Y 4.F76/1:H 62/v.9-18. Item 1017.

> Content: compilation of historical transcripts of the House Committee on Foreign Affairs, 1943-60.

Principal Officers of the Department of State and United States Chiefs of Mission 1778–1990. PRINT. (1991) U.S. Department of State. Office of the Historian. Bureau of Public Affairs. Department of State Publication 9825. S 1.2:OF 2/1778–1990.

(Various earlier editions have also been issued by the Department of State) Item 0876. ASI (91) 7008-1.

> Content: historical directory of Department of State secretaries; deputy, under, and assistant secretaries; counselors; ambassadors at large; heads of foreign assistance agencies; and chiefs of mission.

Electronic Research Collection. WEB. U.S. Department of State; University of Illinois at Chicago Library; U.S. Government Printing Office. Superintendent of Documents. Federal Depository Library Program. <http://dosfan.lib.uic.edu/ERC/index.html>.

> Content: archives of older material taken from the Department of State Web site and the discontinued U.S. Arms Control and Disarmament Agency Web site.

The National Security Archive. WEB. George Washington University. Gelman Library. National Security Archive <http://www.gwu.edu/~nsarchiv/>.

> Content: collections of declassified documents obtained as a result of Freedom of Information Act requests; other documents in selected areas of international relations and foreign policy.

Discussion

The *Foreign Relations of the United States* series is a basic tool for historical research on U.S. foreign policy and U.S. history in general. The editors of the series endeavor to include all documents needed to objectively record the foreign relations of the United States during the time period covered. Documents from all agencies concerned with foreign policy are included.

Volumes in the set are usually published about 30 years after the time period covered. For example, volumes published in 1999 generally covered the time period of 1964–68. Each time period is issued in several volumes, arranged by geographic area or topic. Editorial notes and references are added to the documents as deemed necessary for clarification. Selected volumes of the set are being made available electronically at the *Department of State Web Site.* The volumes covering the conferences are similar in format and content but were issued as a separate series. They cover conferences, such as the Malta Conference, held during the World War II period.

The next series of sources provides convenient compilations of foreign policy documents. They include *A Decade of American Foreign Policy: Basic Documents, 1941–1949; American Foreign Policy 1950–55: Basic Documents; American Foreign Policy: Current Documents;* and *American Foreign Policy: Basic Documents, 1977–1980.* The *American Foreign Policy: Current Documents,* was issued as an annual title, with volumes issued for the years 1955–67 and 1981–90.

The *U.S. Department of State Dispatch* provided compilations of major speeches and congressional testimony given by Department of State staff. It also included information on treaty actions.

The *Department of State Bulletin* is the predecessor to the *Department of State Dispatch* and a valuable source of historical foreign policy information. The *Bulletin* reprinted major addresses and news conferences of the President and secretary of state, testimony of Department of State officials before Congress, and selected press releases, treaties, and agreements.

The next two historical sources are compilations of historical transcripts of meetings not previously published. The *Executive Sessions of the Senate Foreign Relations Committee (Historical Series)* include transcripts selected to provide the most useful and interesting record of the meetings. Editorial notes and references have sometimes been added, and any deleted material is noted. The *Historical Series* is a similar series covering the executive session hearings of the House Committee on Foreign Affairs.

Principal Officers of the Department of State and United States Chiefs of Mission 1778–1990 provides a historical listing of people holding the most important U.S. diplomatic posts. This is a convenient compilation of this information that is otherwise scattered.

The *Electronic Research Collection* is a cooperative project of the Department of State, the Federal Depository Library Program, and the University of Illinois at Chicago Library to electronically archive material from the Department of State Web site. As material is superceded or new editions of materials are compiled, the older electronic versions are moved to this Web site. The *National Security Archive* is a nongovernmental, nonprofit organization, which has among its goals the creation of an archive of declassified government publications and information. Most of the documents have been obtained as a result of Freedom of Information Act requests. Their Web site provides access to the full text of many publications relating to foreign policy and international relations. Of particular interest are their "Electronic Briefing Books," which bring together selected documents on specific topics, such as " Kennedy and Castro: The Secret Quest for Accommodation," "Record of Richard Nixon-Zhou Enlai Talks, February 1972," and " 20 Years after the Hostages: Declassified Documents on Iran and the United States."

FOREIGN AID STATISTICAL SOURCES
Checklist

Statistical Abstract of the United States. PRINT. WEB. (annual) 1878–. U.S. Department of Commerce. Economics and Statistics Administration. Bureau of the Census. C 3.134: Item 0150. ASI 2324-1. GPO. <http://www.census.gov/statab/www/>; <http://purl.access.gpo.gov/GPO/LPS2878>.
> Coverage: world, world regions, countries.
> Content: U.S. foreign and military assistance.

Statistical Abstract of the United States. CD-ROM. (annual) 1993–. U.S. Department of Commerce. Bureau of the Census. C 3.134/7: Item 0150-B. ASI 2324-14.
> Content: CD-ROM version of the *Statistical Abstract*.

Historical Statistics of the United States: Colonial Times to 1970. Parts 1-2. PRINT. (1975) U.S. Department of Commerce. Bureau of the Census. C 3.134/2:H 62/789-970/pt.1-2. Item 0151. ASI (76) 2328-2. GPO.
> Coverage: world, world regions, countries.
> Content: U.S. foreign assistance.

Historical Statistics of the United States on CD-ROM: Colonial Times to 1970. CD-ROM. (1997) New York, NY: Cambridge University Press.
> Content: CD-ROM version of *Historical Statistics of the United States*.

Foreign Military Sales: Foreign Military Construction Sales and Military Assistance Facts. MF. WEB. (annual) U.S. Department of Defense. Defense Security Cooperation Agency. D 1.66: (Earlier, D 1.2:F 76/year) Item 0310-E-11(MF). ASI 3904-3. <http://www.dsca.osd.mil/publications.htm>.
> Coverage: world, world regions, countries.
> Content: U.S. military assistance.

"U.S. International Transactions." *Survey of Current Business.* PRINT. WEB. (quarterly) 1921–. U.S. Department of Commerce. Bureau of Economic Analysis. C 59.11: Item 0228. ASI 2702-1. GPO. <http://www.bea.doc.gov/bea/pubs.htm>; <http://purl.access.gpo.gov/GPO/LPS1730>.
> Coverage: world, world regions, selected countries.
> Content: U.S. foreign and military assistance.

Survey of Current Business. CD-ROM. (annual) 1994–. U.S. Department of Commerce. Economics and Statistics Administration. Bureau of Economic Analysis. C 59.11/1: Item 0228-A. GPO.
> Content: CD-ROM version of *Survey of Current Business*.

U.S. Agency for International Development Web Site. WEB. U.S. Agency for International Development. <http://www.info.usaid.gov/>.
> Content: information on the work of the USAID; statistics and information on foreign economic and humanitarian aid.

USAID Congressional Presentation. WEB. U.S. Agency for International Development. ASI 9914-3. NTIS. <http://www.info.usaid.gov/pubs/>.
> Coverage: world regions, countries.
> Content: USAID program descriptions; budget requests; statistics and narrative on USAID programs in individual countries.

U.S. Overseas Loans and Grants and Assistance from International Organizations. PRINT. (annual) U.S. Agency for International Development. S 18.2: OV 2/years. Item 0900-C-02. ASI 9914-5.
> Coverage: world, world regions, countries.
> Content: U.S. foreign economic and military assistance.

Discussion

The *Statistical Abstract of the United States* has an entire section on "Foreign Commerce and Aid." Included are tables on foreign grants and credits and military assistance. One important series included is the "U.S. Government Foreign Grants and Credits by Type and Country." It gives a country-by-country listing of total U.S. grants. This series is also published with year-by-year statistics in *Historical Statistics of the United States*. Summary tables on foreign economic and military aid are also included in the *Statistical Abstract*.

The *Foreign Military Sales: Foreign Military Construction Sales and Military Assistance Facts* includes a series of statistical tables and charts that include expenditures for military assistance programs to other countries. The Web version of the report also provides statistical information in Excel spreadsheet format that can be downloaded.

The *Survey of Current Business*, available in print, Web, and CD-ROM versions, also includes a quarterly report titled "U.S. International Transactions," that provides recurring statistics on foreign and military aid.

The United States Agency for International Development (USAID) is charged with implementing foreign assistance economic and humanitarian programs. The agency's Web site provides a good starting point for information about the programs administered by the agency and U.S. foreign assistance in general. The full text of many publications are included, as well as numerous reports, press releases, news reports, and other information about the USAID's work, including some statistical information.

Each year the USAID compiles a vast amount of information as part of its *Congressional Presentation*. The information in this report describes and justifies USAID's programs and activities. The report provides summary statistics and information, as well as information on a country-by-country basis. This report is one of the best sources for obtaining both an overview and specific data on foreign aid programs administered by the USAID.

The *U.S. Overseas Loans and Grants and Assistance from International Organizations* report includes detailed statistics on U.S. foreign economic and military assistance from 1945 to the present. A.I.D. (Agency for International Development), P.L. 480 (Food for Peace), and the Peace Corps programs are included, along with international narcotics control, Eximbank and Overseas Private Investment Corporation loans, and other economic and military grants and loans. Statistics for each program are given by region and individual country. The U.S. contributions to international organizations and the assistance provided by those organizations is also included. This report is also sometimes known as the "Green Book."

FOREIGN ECONOMIC RELATIONS
Checklist

Trade Policy Agenda and Annual Report of the President of the United States on the Trade Agreements Program. PRINT. WEB. (annual) 1960–. U.S. Executive Office of the United States Trade Representative. PREX 9.11: (Earlier, PR 40.11: and PR 39.13:) Item 0857-G-01. ASI 444-1. GPO. <http://www.ustr.gov/reports/index.html>.
    Content: overview of trade policy.

[Year] National Trade Estimate Report on Foreign Trade Barriers. PRINT. WEB. (annual) 1984–. U.S. Office of the United States Trade Representative. PREX 9.10: Item 0766-C-09. ASI 444-2. GPO. <http://www.ustr.gov/reports/index.html>.
    Content: country-by-country review of foreign policies that are barriers to U.S. exports.

Bureau of Economic Analysis: International Accounts Data. WEB. U.S. Department of Commerce. Economics and Statistics Administration. Bureau of Economic Analysis. <http://www.bea.doc.gov/bea/di1.htm>.
    Content: data relating to direct investment abroad and foreign direct investment in the U.S. in a variety of file formats.

Foreign Direct Investment in the United States: Operations of U.S. Affiliates of Foreign Companies. PRINT. WEB. (annual) 1981–. U.S. Department of Commerce. Economics and Statistics Administration. Bureau of Economic Analysis. C 59.20: (Includes both preliminary and revised estimates) Item 0130-D-07. ASI 2704-4. GPO. <http://www.bea.doc.gov/bea/ai/12-99.htm#FDIUS>.
    Coverage: world, world regions, countries, U.S., regions, states.
    Content: financial and operating data; balance sheets; property, plant, and equipment; income and taxes; employment and employee compensation; foreign trade.

U.S. Direct Investment Abroad: Operations of U.S. Parent Companies and Their Foreign Affiliates. PRINT. WEB. (annual) 1983–. U.S. Department of Commerce. Economics and Statistics Administration. Bureau of Economic Analysis. C 59.20/2: (Includes both preliminary and revised estimates) Item 0130-D-06. ASI 2704-5. GPO. <http://www.bea.doc.gov/bea/ai/12-99.htm#USDIA>.
    Coverage: world, world regions, U.S., countries.
    Content: assets; income statements; sales; employment and employee compensation; exports and imports of goods balance sheet; research and development.

Foreign Direct Investment in the United States: Establishment Data for 1992. PRINT. (1997). U.S. Department of Commerce. Economics and Statistics Administration. Bureau of Economic Analysis.; U.S. Bureau of the Census. C 59.20/3: Item 0130-D-11. ASI (97) 2708-48. GPO.
    Coverage: U.S., states.
    Content: number, employment, payroll, shipments, sales of foreign-owned establishments; for manufacturing foreign-owned establishments includes value added, total compensation of employees; hourly wage rates of production workers, and expenditures for new plant and equipment.

Foreign Direct Investment in the United States: 1992 Benchmark Survey, Final Results. PRINT. WEB. (1995). U.S. Department of Commerce. Economics and Statistics Administration. Bureau of Economic Analysis. C 59.2:F 76/4/992/final. Item 0130-D-01. ASI (95) 2704-4. GPO. <http://www.bea.doc.gov/bea/ai/12-99.htm#FDIUS>.
    Coverage: world, world regions, U.S., regions, states.
    Content: detailed statistics on financial and operating data; direct investment position and balance of payments data; balance sheets; income statements; assets; employment and employees' compensation; foreign trade; research and development.

U.S. Direct Investment Abroad: 1994 Benchmark Survey, Final Results. PRINT. WEB. (1998). U.S. Department of Commerce. Economics and Statistics Administration. Bureau of Economic Analysis. C 59.2: IN8/4/994/final. Item 0130-D-01. ASI (98) 2704-5. GPO. <http://www.bea.doc.gov/bea/ai/12-99.htm #USDIA>.

> Coverage: world, world regions, U.S., countries.
> Content: balance sheets; income, employment and employee compensation; sales; research and development; imports and exports; direct investment position; financial and operating data.

Survey of Current Business. PRINT. WEB. (monthly) 1921–. U.S. Department of Commerce. Bureau of Economic Analysis. C 59.11: Item 0228. ASI 2702-1. GPO. <http://www.bea.doc.gov/bea/pubs.htm>; <http://purl.access.gpo.gov/GPO/LPS1730>.

> Content: articles on foreign direct investment; U.S. direct investment abroad; and U.S. affiliates of foreign companies operations.

Survey of Current Business. CD-ROM. (annual) 1994–. U.S. Department of Commerce. Economics and Statistics Administration. Bureau of Economic Analysis. C 59.11/1: Item 0228-A. GPO.

> Content: CD-ROM version of *Survey of Current Business.*

Foreign Direct Investment in the United States: An Update, Review and Analysis of Current Developments. (biennial) U.S. Department of Commerce. Economics and Statistics Administration. Office of the Chief Economist. C 59.2:F76/6/update/year. Item 0130-D-01. ASI 2004-9. GPO.

> Coverage: world, world regions, selected countries, country groupings, states.
> Content: articles and statistical tables about foreign direct investment.

International Direct Investment: Studies by the Bureau of Economic Analysis. PRINT. (1999). U.S. Department of Commerce. Bureau of Economic Analysis. C 59.2:IN 8/6. Item 0130-D-01. GPO.

> Content: compilation of articles from the *Survey of Current Business* dealing with direct investment abroad and foreign direct investment in the United States.

National Trade Data Bank: The Export Connection. WEB. CD-ROM. (monthly) Oct. 1990–. U.S. Department of Commerce. STAT-USA. C 1.88: (Depository distribution of CD-ROM discontinued with Oct. 2000 disk) Item 0128-L. ASI 2002-6. <http://www.stat-usa.gov/tradtest.nsf>; <http://purl.access.gpo.gov/GPO/LPS1777>.

Country Reports on Economic Policy and Trade Practices. PRINT. MF. WEB. (annual) 1989–. U.S. Congress. House. Committee on International Relations. Or U.S. Congress. Senate. Committee on Foreign Relations. (Report is published in alternate years by the two committees) Y 4.IN 8/16:C 83/year or Y 4.F 76/2:S.PRT.(no.) (1999 report is Y 4.IN8/16: C83/999; 2000 report is Y 4.F76/2: S.PRT. 106–45). Items 1017-A-01 or -B-01(MF); 1039-A or -B(MF). ASI 21464-2; ASI 25384-2. GPO. <http://www.state.gov/www/issues/economic/trade_reports/index.html>; <http://purl.access.gpo.gov/GPO/LPS2637>.

> Content: general overview of the country's situation; exchange rate policies; structural policies; debt management policies; barriers to U.S. exports and investments; export subsidies policies; intellectual property policies; worker rights.

Discussion

The title *Trade Policy Agenda and Annual Report of the President of the United States on the Trade Agreements Program* includes two distinct reports. The first, the *Trade Policy Agenda*, discusses foreign policy regarding trade. It looks at initiatives for the coming year and reviews the previous year's accomplishments. The *Annual Report* looks at U.S. trade in general, multilateral and bilateral negotiations, and the implementation of U.S. trade law. It also reviews trade policy enforcement and development. This source is an excellent tool for providing a broad overview of foreign policy in the trade policy arena. Another section reviews World Trade Organization actions.

The *National Trade Estimate Report on Foreign Trade Barriers* provides a country-by-country review of trade barriers. For each country, the report reviews the following categories: (1) import policies, other import charges, quantitative restrictions, import licensing, and customs barriers; (2) standards, testing, labeling, and certification; (3) government procurement; (4) export subsidies; (5) lack of intellectual property protection; (6) services barriers; (7) investment barriers; (8) anticompetitive practices; (9) trade restrictions affecting electronic commerce; and (10) other barriers (such as bribery and corruption). This report is an excellent source for obtaining a concise summary and overview of the U.S.'s trade relations with each country.

The Bureau of Economic Analysis (BEA) collects a series of data on U.S. direct investment in other countries and foreign direct investment in the United States. The data are reported in several recurring reports, with data also often available from the BEA Web site in various formats. The BEA also makes much of this data available for purchase on diskettes, but in almost all cases, the data are also available free-of-charge for downloading from their Web site. The *Bureau of Economic Analysis: International Accounts Data* Web page from the BEA Web site is a good starting point for accessing much of the direct investment and foreign direct investment data.

The *Foreign Direct Investment in the United States: Operations of U.S. Affiliates of Foreign Companies* and the *U.S. Direct Investment Abroad: Operations of U.S. Parent Companies and Their Foreign Affiliates* titles collect similar sorts of data. One report looks at foreign companies in the United States, while the other looks at U.S. companies in other countries. Detailed statistical tables analyzed by geographic region and industry are included in both reports. The *Bureau of Economic Analysis: International Accounts Data* Web page also includes numerous tables and spreadsheets and other downloadable files from the data collection used to compile these two reports. The text and tables of this report are also downloadable from the BEA Web site and the URL for that page is also cited in the entries for these two sources.

Foreign Direct Investment in the United States: Establishment Data for 1992 reports on a series of data concerning the operation of establishments of U.S. affiliates of foreign companies (foreign-owned establishments). The collection of this data is a joint project between the Bureau of Economic Analysis and the Census Bureau. There is a long lag in the reporting of data—the 1992 report was published in 1997. The volume is compiled in two parts, with the first reporting on all establishments, and the second providing more detailed reporting by industry for manufacturing establishments. This report updates the report of 1987 establishment data published under the title *Foreign Direct Investment in the United States: Establishment Data for 1987*, and individual year reports on manufacturing data for the years 1988–1991, titled *Foreign Direct Investment in the United States: Establishment Data for Manufacturing*.

The BEA also compiles benchmark surveys of detailed data on U.S. direct investment abroad and foreign direct investment. Data from these reports, including updates and preliminary data, appear regularly in the *Survey of Current Business*. The final reports of two of the most recent benchmark data are included here, *Foreign Direct Investment in the United States: 1992 Benchmark Survey, Final Results*, and *U.S. Direct Investment Abroad: 1994 Benchmark Survey, Final Results*. The BEA Web site includes the full text and statistical tables from these two reports available for download.

The biennial *Foreign Direct Investment in the United States: An Update, Review and Analysis of Current Developments* includes articles (most reprinted from *Survey of Current Business*) along with numerous statistical charts. Some data are given for individual countries. *International Direct Investment: Studies by the Bureau of Economic Analysis* is a similar compilation of articles. In addition to the articles reprinted from the *Survey of Current Business*, it also includes a user's guide to BEA direct investment statistics and information on the methodologies that BEA uses for direct investment data collection.

The *National Trade Data Bank* is available both on CD-ROM and as part of the *STAT-USA Internet* site. It contains publications and statistics related to international trade, including statistics on foreign direct investment.

Each *Country Report on Economic Policy and Trade Practices* includes an extensive review of the economic and trade factors and policies of the country covered. The individual country reports are in a standardized format, which allows for easy comparison of one country to another. *Country Reports on Economic Policy and Trade Practices* is prepared by the Department of State for the guidance of Congress. The report has been issued alternately by the House and the Senate and the SuDocs number has

varied accordingly. It is a good source for understanding better the foreign policy implications of trade with other countries.

INDEXES
Checklist

American Foreign Policy and Treaty Index. PRINT. (quarterly) 1993–. Bethesda, MD: Congressional Information Service.

CIS/Index. PRINT. (monthly) 1970–. Bethesda, MD: Congressional Information Service.

Congressional Universe. WEB. Bethesda, MD: Congressional Information Service.

American Statistics Index (ASI). PRINT. (monthly) 1973–. Bethesda, MD: Congressional Information Service.

Statistical Universe. WEB. Bethesda, MD: Congressional Information Service.

Catalog of United States Government Publications (MOCAT). WEB. 1994–. U.S. Government Printing Office. Superintendent of Documents. <http://www.gpo.gov/catalog>; <http://www.access.gpo.gov/su_docs/locators/cgp/index.html>; <http://purl.access.gpo.gov/GPO/LPS844>.

Monthly Catalog of United States Government Publications. CD-ROM. 1996–. U.S. Government Printing Office. Superintendent of Documents. GP 3.8/7: Item 0557-C. GPO.

Monthly Catalog of United States Government Publications (Condensed version). PRINT. (monthly) 1996–. U.S. Government Printing Office. Superintendent of Documents. GP 3.8/8: (Earlier full version, GP 3.8:, 1895-1995). Item 0557-D. GPO.

Discussion

Congressional Information Service (CIS) publishes the *American Foreign Policy and Treaty Index*, a comprehensive index to key foreign policy documents produced by the executive branch, Congress, and independent agencies. A wide range of both depository and nondepository documents are included. Defining foreign policy broadly, the index covers such topics as human rights, arms control, economic and military assistance, and international finance. It also comprehensively covers sources related to the treaty process. In format, the index is similar to CIS's other products, and it includes extensive abstracts. CIS also produces an accompanying microfiche set of the full text of the publications described in the index.

CIS/Index is a comprehensive index to congressional publications found in both a print and electronic format, and is discussed in greater detail in Chapter 3, "The Basics of Searching." To locate additional congressional publications on foreign policy, search subject terms such as "Foreign Assistance," "Foreign Relations," "Military Assistance," and the names of specific acts and programs dealing with foreign policy.

American Statistics Index (ASI) is a comprehensive index to government statistics. (For more information, see Chapter 3.) To find statistics on foreign policy, search under such headings as "Foreign assistance," "Military assistance," and "Foreign relations."

The *Monthly Catalog* is a comprehensive index to government publications and is also discussed in greater detail in Chapter 3. To locate more publications on foreign policy through the *Monthly Catalog*, search subject indexes with headings beginning with "Economic assistance, American"; "Military assistance, American"; "Technical Assistance, American"; "United States-Foreign economic relations"; "United States-Foreign relations"; and "International Relations." Keyword searching on similar terms and names of individual countries and foreign policy topics can also be used. The complete version of the *Monthly Catalog* is available on the Web and CD-ROM. Commercial online and CD-ROM versions of the *Monthly Catalog* are also available.

RELATED MATERIAL
Within this Work

Chapter 5   Foreign Countries

Chapter 38   Foreign Trade Statistics

Chapter 45   Legislative History

Chapter 48   Treaties

GPO Subject Bibliographies. PRINT. WEB. GP 3.22/2:

<http://bookstore.gpo.gov/sb/about.html>

No. 75   "Foreign Affairs of the United States"

No. 123   "International Trade"

No. 210   "Foreign Relations of the United States"

CHAPTER 5
Foreign Countries

The U.S. government publishes a great deal of information about other countries, ranging from general descriptions to detailed statistical compilations on an individual country or subject, such as foreign agricultural trade. Information compiled by the United States, especially statistical information, is often more current and detailed than information from an individual country or international organization. Within this chapter, general background and statistical sources are discussed first, followed by major sources in a sampling of subject areas. This chapter is not comprehensive, but it does give an idea of the coverage and types of materials available that deal with foreign countries.

SEARCH STRATEGY

Information about foreign countries generally follows the subject search strategy. Statistical subsearches and sources are included where appropriate. The following strategy can usually be applied:
1. Try the general background and general statistical sources given in this chapter;
2. Consult the topical sources sections; and
3. Use the indexes and databases listed for further, more comprehensive searching.

GENERAL BACKGROUND SOURCES
Checklist

Background Notes. PRINT. WEB. (irregular) 1964–. U.S. Department of State. S 1.123: (Indexes, S 1.123/2:) Item 0862-B. ASI 7006-2. GPO. <http://www.state.gov/www/background_notes/index.html>; <http://purl.access.gpo.gov/GPO/LPS2003>.
> Coverage: selected countries and international organizations.
> Content: basic information on a country's geography, government, economy, history, people, political conditions

and foreign relations, and travel and business information.

Post Reports. PRINT. (irregular) U.S. Department of State. S 1.127: Item 0869-C.
> Coverage: selected countries.
> Content: basic information on the host country, the U.S. Embassy, travel within the country, and everyday life.

Tips for Travelers to [country]. PRINT. WEB. (irregular) U.S. Department of State. S 1.2: (Included in the *General Publications* series of the Department of State) Item 0876. GPO. <http://travel.state.gov/travel_pubs.html>.
> Coverage: selected countries.
> Content: brief pamphlets giving basic country information for travelers.

Country Studies. PRINT. WEB. (irregular) U.S. Department of Defense. Army Department. U.S. Library of Congress. Federal Research Division. D 101.22:550-# (Earlier title: *U.S. Area Handbooks for [country]*) Item 0327-J. GPO. <http://lcweb2.loc.gov/frd/cs/cshome.html>.
> Coverage: approximately 100 countries.
> Content: comprehensive coverage of a country's history, social conditions, economy, politics, and military organization.

USAID Regions and Countries. WEB. U.S. Agency for International Development. <http://www.info.usaid.gov/regions/>.
> Content: background information on individual countries; USAID programs and activities; U.S. assistance to the country; links to information about the country.

Discussion

Each issue of *Background Notes* provides basic information on an individual country. A profile of the country starts each *Note*, and provides brief statistical and factual information. The *Background Notes* include a broad overview of a country and its people, history, economy, geography, and government. *Notes* also include a discussion of U.S. relations with the country and the country's relationships with other countries. Frequently updated, the *Background*

Notes provide an excellent concise overview of a country, and serve as ready-reference sources for basic factual information.

Post Reports provide a unique insight into daily life in other countries as seen from a U.S. perspective. The reports are written for use as guides for Department of State employees living abroad and provide general information about the U.S. Embassy in the country, including maps and photographs of the embassy and U.S. diplomatic facilities. *Post Reports* are especially useful for travelers planning to visit a country. The reports provide specific, practical information on what types of food, clothing, supplies, and services are available locally and what items should be brought to the country. Entertainment, educational, recreational, and social activities are also discussed.

Tips for Travelers to [country] is a series of small pamphlets giving information on such topics as entry and exit requirements, safety tips and information on crime, travel advisories, advice for those with dual nationality, avoiding legal problems, and health and medical care information. They provide basic information about a country from a traveler's point of view.

Country Studies are prepared by a multidisciplinary team of experts under the auspices of the Federal Research Division of the Library of Congress and sponsored by the Department of the Army. Each *Country Study* attempts to provide a comprehensive analysis of a country's economic conditions, national security situation, political structure, and social systems and institutions. A brief country profile gives basic information about the country and is followed by more lengthy chapters addressing individual topics. An appendix of statistical tables is included, along with another appendix containing an extensive bibliography. The electronic version of the *Country Studies* provides searching capabilities for the text in each *Study*, and also allows for searching across the full text of either all *Country Studies* or selected titles within the series. Reports in the *Country Studies* series rate as some of the best reference sources—governmental or nongovernmental—for providing a careful, detailed overview of a country. This series was formerly titled and widely known as *Area Handbooks*.

The U.S. Agency for International Development (USAID) oversees the delivery of humanitarian and economic aid to other countries. One section of the USAID Web site, titled *USAID Regions and Countries*, gives country-by-country profiles of the work of the USAID in the country and the assistance provided by the U.S, along with background information about the country. The content of the profiles varies, but many include maps, links to the appropriate *World Factbook* entries and other relevant U.S. governmental publications about the country, and links to news reports and newspapers.

GENERAL STATISTICAL SOURCES
Checklist

Statistical Abstract of the United States. PRINT. WEB. (annual) 1878–. U.S. Department of Commerce. Economics and Statistics Administration. Bureau of the Census. C 3.134: Item 0150. ASI 2324-1. GPO. <http://www.census.gov/statab/www/>; <http://purl.access.gpo.gov/GPO/LPS2878>.

> Coverage: world, selected countries.
> Content: area; population; demographics; vital statistics; environmental data; social and industrial indicators; finances; economic indicators; agriculture; transportation; communication; military.

Statistical Abstract of the United States. CD-ROM. (annual) 1993–. U.S. Department of Commerce. Bureau of the Census. C 3.134/7: Item 0150-B. ASI 2324-14.

> Content: CD-ROM version of the *Statistical Abstract*.

The World Factbook. PRINT. WEB. (annual) 1981–. U.S. Central Intelligence Agency. Directorate of Intelligence. PREX 3.15: (Earlier title: *National Basic Intelligence Factbook*, PREX 3.10:N31) Item 0856-A-07. ASI 244-11. GPO. <http://www.odci.gov/cia/publications/factbook/index.html>; <http://purl.access.gpo.gov/GPO/LPS5527>.

> Coverage: countries, dependent areas.
> Content: geography; people; government; economy; communications; defense forces.

The World Factbook. CD-ROM. (annual) U.S. Central Intelligence Agency. Directorate of Intelligence. PREX 3.15/2: Item O856-A-10. ASI 9114-11.GPO.

> Content: CD-ROM version of *The World Factbook*.

Discussion

The *Statistical Abstract of the United States* includes a 35–40 page section on comparative international statistics. The statistics cover a wide range of subjects and are drawn from a variety of sources, including international organizations. Typical tables include "Energy Consumption and Production by Country," "Newspapers, Radio, Television, Telephones, and Computers by Country," and "Death Rates, by Cause and Country." The major strength of the *Statistical Abstract* is in its side-by-side country comparisons that make it easy to quickly grasp a wide range of information about individual countries. It is also a first ready-reference source to check when searching for any statistical information on other countries. A PDF version of the *Statistical Abstract* is available at the Census Bureau Web site, and a CD-ROM version is also produced.

The World Factbook provides a country-by-country listing of basic statistical and factual information. Dependencies and areas of special sovereignty such as Guam and Hong Kong and miscellaneous areas such as the Antarctica and the West Bank are included as well as independent states. Each individual entry averages two print pages in length. Major sections of each entry include "Introduction," "Geography," "People," "Government," "Economy," "Communications," "Transportation," "Military," and "Transnational Issues." Information such as

The Library of Congress Country Studies

Search the Country Studies

Type as many words as you wish in the box below.
Press the SEARCH button to start your search.

[   ]   SEARCH   Clear Search

⊙ Search for variants of search words, e.g. plurals.
○ Search for words exactly as entered

Limit your search to one or more countries:
Use the CTRL key to make more than one selection.

Albania	Ecuador	Laos	Romania
Algeria	Egypt	Lebanon	Russia
Angola	El Salvador	Libya	Saudi Arabia
Armenia	Estonia	Lithuania	Seychelles
Austria	Ethiopia	Macau	Singapore
Azerbaijan	Finland	Madagascar	Somalia
Bahrain	Georgia	Maldives	South Africa
Bangladesh	Germany	Mauritania	South Korea
Belarus	Ghana	Mauritius	Soviet Union
Belize	Guyana	Mexico	Spain
Bhutan	Haiti	Moldova	Sri Lanka
Bolivia	Honduras	Mongolia	Sudan
Brazil	Hungary	Nepal	Syria
Bulgaria	India	Nicaragua	Tajikistan
Cambodia	Indonesia	Nigeria	Thailand

The Library of Congress Country Studies: Search the Country Studies. <http://lcweb2.loc.gov/frd/csquery.html>

Figure 5.1: *Country Studies* Search Page.

population, type of legal system, national holidays, number of railroads, and military strength is included. *The World Factbook* also includes an appendix listing membership in selected U.N. and international organizations and a series of reference maps of the world. *The World Factbook* is an excellent source for obtaining a quick up-to-date overview of a country. The Web-based version of *The World Factbook* is made available in an easy-to-use nicely formatted and organized HTML version.

AGRICULTURAL SOURCES
Checklist

Agricultural Statistics. PRINT. WEB. (annual) 1936–. U.S. Department of Agriculture. National Agricultural Statistics Service. A 1.47: Item 0001. ASI 1004-1. GPO. <http://www.usda.gov/nass/pubs/agstats.htm>; <http://purl.access.gpo.gov/GPO/LPS1063>.
> Coverage: selected countries.
> Content: commodities; production and trade; foreign imports and exports.

Agricultural Statistics. CD-ROM. (annual) 1994–. U.S. Department of Agriculture. A 1.47/2: Item 0001-A. GPO.
> Content: CD-ROM version of Agricultural Statistics.

Attache Reports. WEB. (irregular) U.S. Department of Agriculture. Foreign Agricultural Service. <http://www.fas.usda.gov/scriptsw/attacherep/default.htm>.
> Coverage: selected countries.
> Content: reports on commodity production in individual countries; marketing and trade in individual countries.

Discussion

While *Agricultural Statistics* lists primarily U.S. agricultural statistics, it also includes some statistics on foreign agriculture. It is especially useful for foreign trade and import and export statistics. A good portion of *Agricultural Statistics* consists of a commodity-by-commodity statistical listing that includes statistics from other countries. A PDF version of *Agricultural Statistics* is available on the Web, and a CD-ROM version is also available.

Attache Reports are reports on agricultural production, marketing, and trade in other countries. A typical report might deal with the retail food sector in Argentina or strawberry production in Chile. Reports mix narrative and statistical tables to provide an analysis of their topic. New reports are constantly being issued. The *Attache Reports* Web site allows you to search for reports from a specific time frame, by topic, and by country. Reports are available in PDF and in WordPerfect format files.

There are many more sources dealing with foreign agriculture—see Chapter 18, "Agriculture," for additional detailed sources.

BUSINESS SOURCES

Checklist

Country Commercial Guides. WEB. (annual) U.S. Department of State. Bureau of Economic and Business Affairs. S 1.40/7: Item 0863-B. ASI 2046-17. NTIS. <http://www.state.gov/www/about_state/business/com_guides/>; <http://www.usatrade.gov/website/ccg.nsf>; <http://purl.access.gpo.gov/GPO/LPS303>.
>   Coverage: selected countries.
>   Content: guides for U.S. businesspersons; analysis of political, economic, and market environment of individual countries.

STAT-USA Internet. WEB. U.S. Department of Commerce. C 1.91: Item 0128-P. <http://www.stat-usa.gov/>.
>   Coverage: selected countries.
>   Content: *National Trade Data Bank*; *Country Commercial Guides*; country and industry market research reports, *Attache Reports*.

National Trade Data Bank: The Export Connection. WEB. CD-ROM. (monthly) Oct. 1990–. U.S. Department of Commerce. STAT-USA. C 1.88: (Depository distribution of CD-ROM discontinued with Oct. 2000 disc.) Item 0128-L. ASI 2002-6. <http://www.stat-usa.gov/tradtest.nsf>; <http://purl.access.gpo.gov/GPO/LPS1777>.
>   Coverage: selected countries.
>   Content: exports and imports by country and commodity; *Country Commercial Guides*; country and industry market research reports, *Attache Reports*.

Foreign Labor Trends. PRINT. (annual) 1982–. U.S. Department of Labor. Bureau of International Labor Affairs. L 29.16: Item 0749-E. ASI 6366-4. GPO.
>   Coverage: selected countries.
>   Content: key labor indicators; descriptions of major labor issues in each country.

Discussion

Country Commercial Guides are geared toward providing U.S. businesses with the information needed to increase trade in a country. The guides are prepared in conjunction with the U.S. embassies in each country. Guides provide a comprehensive look and analysis of a country's economic, political, and market environment. Each guide provides chapters on the following major topics: "Economic Trends and Outlook," "Political Environment," "Marketing U.S. Products and Services," "Leading Sectors for U.S. Exports and Investments," "Trade Regulations and Standards," "Investment Climate," "Trade and Project Financing," and "Business Travel." Most reports also include appendices with information on the topics of "Economic and Trade Statistics," "U.S. and Country Contacts," and "Market Research and Trade Events."

The *National Trade Data Bank*, included in the subscription for the *STAT-USA* service and distributed on CD-ROM, includes the full text of the *Country Commercial Guides*. The *National Trade Data Bank* is available as part of the *STAT-USA Internet* site. *STAT-USA Internet* is a fee-based service, but federal depository libraries may register for free access for two workstations. A CD-ROM version of the *National Trade Data Bank* is also produced, but not distributed to depository libraries after Oct. 2000. It also includes the *Attache Reports*, described in the Agricultural Sources section, as well as other reports on trade and marketing that include some information on foreign trade and other countries.

Foreign Labor Trends are published as individual reports for each country. In an average 20 to 30 print pages, the major issues and political, economic, and social structures having an effect on labor are described. Although the individual issues vary in the depth of their coverage, each issue begins with a standard statistical table of key labor indicators. This table, which includes such items as population, the unemployment rate, minimum wage rates, average hourly earnings, and average hours worked per week, allows for an easy comparison of countries. Most reports are prepared by the U.S. Embassy in each country.

ECONOMIC SOURCES

Checklist

Handbook of International Economic Statistics. PRINT. WEB. (annual) 1992–. U.S. Central Intelligence Agency. Directorate of Intelligence. PREX 3.16: (Issued earlier as *Handbook of Economic Statistics*, PREX 3.10/7-5:) Item 0856-A-09. ASI 9114-4. GPO. <http://www.cia.gov/cia/di/products/hies/index.html>; <http://purl.access.gpo.gov/GPO/LPS2917>.
>   Coverage: world, world regions, country groupings, selected countries, U.S.
>   Content: basic general country statistics; economic indicators; energy; agriculture; minerals and metals; chemicals and manufactured goods; foreign trade and aid; environment.

The World Factbook. CD-ROM. (annual) U.S. Central Intelligence Agency. Directorate of Intelligence. PREX 3.15/2: Item 0856-A-10. ASI 9114-11.GPO.

> Content: CD-ROM version of the *Handbook of International Economic Statistics.*

Country Reports on Economic Policy and Trade Practices. PRINT. MF. WEB. (annual) 1989–. U.S. Congress. House. Committee on International Relations. Or U.S. Congress. Senate. Committee on Foreign Relations. (Report is published in alternate years by the two committees) Y 4. IN 8/16:C 83/year or Y 4.F 76/2:S.prt.(no.). (1999 is Y 4.IN 8/16:C 83/999.) (2000 is Y 4.F 76/2: S.PRT 106-45.) Items 1017-A-01 or -B-01(MF); 1039-A or -B(MF). ASI 21464-2; ASI 25384-2. GPO. <http://www.state.gov/www/issues/economic/trade_reports/index.html>; <http://purl.access.gpo.gov/GPO/LPS2637>.

> Coverage: approximately 77 countries, customs territories, and customs unions.
> Content: general overview of the country's situation; exchange rate policies; structural policies; debt management policies; barriers to U.S. exports and investments; export subsidies policies; intellectual property policies; worker rights.

Discussion

The *Handbook of International Economic Statistics* consists of a series of tables and charts comparing economic data for everything from gross national product to natural gas production. Historical data are included on many of the charts. The *Handbook* often compares groups of countries such as the OECD (Organization of Economic Cooperation and Development) or the Big Six (Canada, France, Germany, Italy, Japan, United Kingdom) countries. With more than 85 economic tables, the *Handbook* provides extensive analysis and economic comparisons. A CD-ROM version of the *Handbook* is included on the *World Factbook* CD-ROM.

Each *Country Report on Economic Policy and Trade Practices* includes an extensive review of the economic and trade factors and policies of the country covered. The individual country reports are in a standardized format, which allows for easy comparison of one country to another. A chart titled "Key Economic Indicators" is given for each country, and provides around 30 key indicators, such as consumer price inflation and external public debt, for the last three years. *Country Reports on Economic Policy and Trade Practices* is prepared by the Department of State for the guidance of Congress. The report has been issued alternately by the House and the Senate and the SuDocs number has varied accordingly.

DEMOGRAPHIC SOURCES

Checklist

World Population Profile: [year]. PRINT. WEB. (biennial) 1985–. U.S. Department of Commerce. Economics and Statistics Administration. Bureau of the Census. C 3.205/3: WP/(year). (Issued earlier under other titles.) Item 0146-F. ASI 2324-9. GPO.

<http://www.census.gov/ipc/www/world.html>; <http://www.census.gov/ipc/www/publist.html>; <http://purl.access.gpo.gov/GPO/LPS2698>.

> Coverage: over 225 countries and territories with a population of 5,000 or more.
> Content: population; population by sex and age group; growth rates; women of reproductive age; fertility; contraceptive use; life expectancy.

World Population Information Web Page. WEB. U.S. Department of Commerce. Bureau of the Census. <http://www.census.gov/ipc/www/world.html>.

> Content: tables, charts, publications, and databases on world population.

International Data Base (IDB). WEB. U.S. Department of Commerce. Bureau of the Census.<http://www.census.gov/ipc/www/idbnew.html>.

> Coverage: 227 countries and areas of the world.
> Content: database of demographic and socioeconomic statistics.

Discussion

World Population Profile consists of a narrative analysis of world population trends followed by an appendix of more detailed tables on population and factors affecting population growth. Covering most countries and territories of the world, it provides a good overview of population statistics and trends for individual countries or areas.

The U.S. Census Bureau collects and disseminates a large amount of information on world population and demographics. Its *World Population Information* Web page includes graphs and charts, links to publications, and a "World POPClock" that provides up-to-the second projections of world population figures. A link to this page also goes to the *International Data Base (IDB)*, a database of demographic information for selected years from 1950 to the present, along with projections to 2050. Information categories in the database include population by age and sex; vital rates, infant mortality, and life tables; fertility and child survivorship; migration; marital status; family planning; ethnicity, religion, and language; literacy; and labor force, employment, and income. Data may be displayed to the screen, downloaded, or downloaded in a spreadsheet format.

FOREIGN BROADCAST INFORMATION SERVICE (FBIS)
Checklist

World News Connection. WEB. U.S. Department of Commerce. National Technical Information Service. NTIS. <http://wnc.fedworld.gov/>.

> Content: subscription online news service that includes translated and English-language information from other countries.

FBIS Publications. CD-ROM. (quarterly) PrEx 7.10/3: Item 0856-A-11. U.S. Foreign Broadcast Information Service.
    Content: individual FBIS reports.

FBIS Index, 1975–1996. CD-ROM. New Canaan, CT: NewsBank, Inc.
    Content: cumulated index to *FBIS Daily Reports*, 1975-1996.

Discussion

The Foreign Broadcast Information Service (FBIS) collects and distributes English-language material and translations of information gathered from other countries. Information is obtained from the full text and summaries of newspaper articles, conference proceedings, television and radio broadcasts, periodicals, and nonclassified technical reports. In organizing the information, FBIS divides the information into regional categories, which presently include: "Central Eurasia"; "China"; "East Asia"; "Near East & South Asia"; "East Europe"; "West Europe"; "Latin America"; and "Sub-Saharan Africa." This FBIS information is an excellent source of information on other countries on both a current and historical basis.

While the individual reports from the FBIS were earlier distributed to depository libraries in a microfiche format, since 1996 they have only been distributed on a quarterly basis through the CD-ROM title, *FBIS Publications*. Indexing to the individual reports was never provided through the depository system. The *FBIS Index CD-ROM* from NewsBank is a cumulated index on CD-ROM to these older reports. NewsBank also sells microfiche copies of the older FBIS reports.

The *World News Connection (WNC)* service through the National Technical Information Service (NTIS) provides current access to the full text of the reports as they are published. The "WNC Latest Headlines" section shows the reports of the last few days in each regional category. Reports are typically submitted to *WNC* within 48-72 hours of the original broadcast or publication. *WNC* also provides free-text searching, Boolean searching, and searching by region and topic.

MISCELLANEOUS SOURCES

Checklist

Chiefs of State and Cabinet Members of Foreign Governments. PRINT. WEB. (monthly) U.S. Central Intelligence Agency. Directorate of Intelligence. PREX 3.11/2: Item 0856-A-05.ASI 9112-4. <http://www.odci.gov/cia/publications/chiefs/>; <http://purl.access.gpo.gov/GPO/LPS1653>.
    Coverage: countries.
    Content: chiefs of state; cabinet members.

Key Officers of Foreign Service Posts: Guide for Business Representatives. WEB. (irregular) U.S. Department of State. S 1.40/5: Item 0876-B. <http://www.state.gov/www/about_state/contacts/keyofficer_index.html>; <http://purl.access.gpo.gov/GPO/LPS2408>.

    Content: key officers (chiefs, assistant chiefs of missions, economic offices, consular offices, etc.) of missions and consulates.

Country Reports on Human Rights Practices for [year]. PRINT. MF. WEB. (annual) 1977–. U.S. Congress. House. Committee on International Relations. Senate. Committee on Foreign Relations. Y 4.In8/16-15: (Prepared by the Department of State; issued as a Joint Committee Print) Item 1017-A-03; 1017-B-03(MF). ASI 21464-3. GPO. <http://www.state.gov/www/global/human_rights/hrp_reports_mainhp.html>; <http://purl.access.gpo.gov/GPO/LPS1236>.
    Coverage: countries that are U.N. members; countries that are the recipients of U.S. assistance; selected other countries.
    Content: country-by-country review and analysis of human rights practices.

Annual Report to Congress on International Religious Freedom. PRINT. MF. WEB. (annual) 1999–. U.S. Congress. Senate. Committee on Foreign Relations. Y 4.F 76/2: (1998 is Y 4.F76/2: S.Hrg.105-591) Item 1039-A or-B(MF). <http://www.state.gov/www/global/human_rights/irf/irf_rpt/index.html>; <http://purl.access.gpo.gov/GPO/LPS3421>.
    Coverage: 194 countries.
    Content: country-by-country analysis of religious freedom and any human rights violations of religious freedom.

CIA Maps and Atlases. PRINT. (irregular) U.S. Central Intelligence Agency. PREX 3.10/4: Item 0856-A-01. GPO. NTIS.
    Content: assorted political, geographical, and thematic maps.

CIA Maps and Publications Released to the Public. WEB. U.S. Central Intelligence Agency. <http://www.odci.gov/cia/publications/mapspub/index.html>.
    Content: catalog of CIA maps and other publications released for public use since 1971.

Perry-Castañeda Library Map Collection. WEB. University of Texas at Austin. <http://www.lib.utexas.edu/Libs/PCL/Map_collection/Map_collection.html>.
    Content: digitized CIA maps.

Discussion

Chiefs of State and Cabinet Members of Foreign Governments provides an up-to-date listing by country of each nation's leaders. The listing is as complete as possible, including countries not yet fully independent and countries not officially recognized by the United States. This directory is one of the most current reference sources that compiles this information in one place, with the print version issued monthly and the Web version constantly updated.

Key Officers of Foreign Service Posts lists the major U.S. officers in other countries who can be of assistance to U.S. citizens in other countries. This guide is of particular help to business people.

Country Reports on Human Rights Practice is a lengthy annual report containing individual country reports on human rights conditions. Information included within the report is obtained from many sources, including U.S. officials (particularly State Department officials), officials of foreign governments, private citizens, intelligence information, journalists, international organizations, and nongovernmental human rights organizations. Sections of the report for each country include the following: (1) "Respect for the Integrity of the Person"; (2) "Respect for Civil Liberties"; (3) "Respect for Political Rights: The Right of Citizens to Change Their Government"; (4) "Government Attitude Regarding International and Nongovernmental Investigation of Alleged Violations of Human Rights"; (5) "Discrimination Based on Race, Sex, Religion, Language, or Social Status"; and (6) "Worker Rights."

The *Annual Report to Congress on International Religious Freedom* is a similarly compiled report on religious freedom and human rights violations regarding religious freedom. Each country-by-country listing includes the following sections: "Freedom of Religion," "Societal Attitudes," and "U.S. Government Policies." Background information, information on the current status of religious activity and religious freedom of the country, and examples of any religious freedom violations are included in the narrative.

The Central Intelligence Agency (CIA) produces a number of excellent maps of individual countries and the world. The maps are primarily for individual countries, although some maps are for smaller geographic areas, and some world maps are also produced. While most maps are political or geographical, the CIA also produces thematic maps on varying topics. A Web-based catalog listing these publications, along with ordering information (including price) for print copies of the maps, is listed here. The *Perry-Castañeda Library Map Collection* has made many of these maps available to the public in digitized format, and their online collection is an excellent source for obtaining copies of these maps. Maps are made available primarily in JPEG format, with some maps in a PDF format. Since the maps are in the public domain they may be freely downloaded or printed.

INDEXES
Checklist

Catalog of United States Government Publications (MOCAT). WEB. 1994–. U.S. Government Printing Office. Superintendent of Documents. <http://www.gpo.gov/catalog>; <http://www.access.gpo.gov/su_docs/locators/cgp/index.html>; <http://purl.access.gpo.gov/GPO/LPS844>.

Monthly Catalog of United States Government Publications. CD-ROM. 1996–. U.S. Government Printing Office. Superintendent of Documents. GP 3.8/7: Item 0557-C. GPO.

Monthly Catalog of United States Government Publications (Condensed version). PRINT. (monthly) 1996–. U.S. Government Printing Office. Superintendent of Documents. GP 3.8/8: (Earlier full version, GP 3.8:, 1895-1995). Item 0557-D. GPO.

American Statistics Index (ASI). PRINT. (monthly) 1973–. Bethesda, MD: Congressional Information Service.

Statistical Universe. WEB. Bethesda, MD: Congressional Information Service.

Discussion

A comprehensive indexing of government publications can be found in the *Monthly Catalog*. To locate additional publications on foreign countries, search the *Monthly Catalog* subject headings under the names of individual countries or subjects subdivided by the names of countries (e.g., Education—Norway). The complete version of the *Monthly Catalog* is available on the Web and CD-ROM. Commercial online and CD-ROM versions of the *Monthly Catalog* are also available.

American Statistics Index (ASI) is a comprehensive listing of statistical information. To find additional statistical information on foreign countries, search subject headings starting with "Foreign" or "Foreign countries" or names of individual countries, regions, or groups of regions. The category index can be searched under the term "By Foreign Country."

For more information on these indexes, see Chapter 3, "The Basics of Searching."

RELATED MATERIAL
Within this Work

Chapter 4   Foreign Policy

Chapter 11 Travel Information

Chapter 18 Agriculture

Chapter 38 Foreign Trade Statistics

GPO Subject Bibliographies. PRINT. WEB. GP 3.22/2:

<http://bookstore.gpo.gov/sb/about.html>

No. 93   "Background Notes"

No. 123 "International Trade"

No. 166 "Foreign Country Studies"

No. 278 "Canada"

No. 279 "Soviet Union"

No. 284 "Africa"

No. 286 "Middle East"

No. 287 "The Americas"

No. 288 "Asia"

No. 289 "Europe"

No. 299 "China"

No. 318 "Pacific Rim"

CHAPTER 6
Occupations and Jobs

The government publishes some important general reference sources on occupations and information on the federal government civil service system. The government has not published any recent, comprehensive guides to working for the government, although several such guides are available from commercial publishers. Government agency Web sites often provide information on employment with specific agencies and information on specific job vacancies.

SEARCH STRATEGY

This chapter shows a subject search strategy. The steps to follow are
1. For general information on occupations, begin with the *Occupational Outlook Handbook*, a key ready-reference tool listed under "Reference Sources" in this chapter;
2. Consult the other titles under "Reference Sources" and the "Additional Occupation Sources" section for other basic guides;
3. For information on specific job openings, consult "Job Vacancy Sources: General" and "Job Vacancy Sources: Federal Government";
4. For more specific information on federal government jobs and vacancies, consult the "Individual Agency Information" sources;
5. For more background information on federal government jobs, consider the sections on "Federal Position Descriptions," Civil Service Exam Sources," and "Federal Salary and Wage Information Sources;"
6. Consider the "Related Material"; and
7. Use the appropriate indexes for more comprehensive coverage of the topic.

REFERENCE SOURCES
Checklist

Occupational Outlook Handbook. PRINT. WEB. (biennial) 1949–. U.S. Department of Labor. Bureau of Labor Statistics. Bulletin series. L 2.3/4: (Earlier, L 2.3:) Item 0768-C-02. ASI 6744-1. GPO. <http://stats.bls.gov/ocohome.htm>.
> Content: occupational descriptions with information on nature of the work, working conditions, employment, qualifications, job outlook, earnings, and sources for additional information.

Occupational Outlook Handbook. CD-ROM. (biennial) 1992/93–. U.S. Department of Labor. Bureau of Labor Statistics. L 2.3/4-4: Item 0744-G-02. GPO.
> Content: CD-ROM version of the *Occupational Outlook Handbook*.

Career Guide to Industries. PRINT. WEB 1992– . U.S. Department of Labor. Bureau of Labor Statistics. Bulletin. L 2.3/4-3: Item 0768-A-01. ASI 6748-87. GPO. <http://stats.bls.gov/cghome.htm>; <http://purl.access.gpo.gov/GPO/LPS4409>.
> Content: industry descriptions with information on nature of the industry, employment, working conditions, occupations, training, earnings, outlook, and sources for additional information.

O*NET Online. WEB. U.S. Department of Labor. Employment and Training Administration. <http://online.onetcenter.org/>;<http://www.doleta.gov/programs/onet/>.
> Content: database of over 950 occupational titles, descriptions, and related classification codes.

*O*NET 98: Keeping Pace With Today's Changing Workplace.* CD-ROM. WEB. (1998) U.S. Department of Labor. Employment and Training Administration. L 37.25:OC 1/CD. Item 0744-G-04. GPO. <http://www.doleta.gov/programs/onet/>; <http://www.access.gpo.gov/o_net/download_onet.html>; <http://purl.access.gpo.gov/GPO/LPS4232>.
> Content: database of 1,100 occupational titles, descriptions, and related classification codes.

Dictionary of Occupational Titles. PRINT. 2 vols. 4th ed. revised. (1991) U.S. Department of Labor. Employment and Training Administration. Employment Service. L 37.2:OC 1/2/991/ v.1-2. Item 0780-A-01. ASI (91) 6406-1. GPO. <http://www.oalj.dol.gov/libdot.htm>.

> Content: standardized job descriptions and classification numbers for more than 20,000 occupations.

Selected Characteristics of Occupations Defined in the Revised Dictionary of Occupational Titles. PRINT. (1993) U.S. Department of Labor. Employment and Training Administration. L 37.2:OC 1/4. Item 0780-A-01. GPO.

> Content: physical demands, environmental conditions, and training time for jobs listed in the *Dictionary of Occupational Titles.*

Discussion

The *Occupational Outlook Handbook* is a major reference source for information on occupations. It provides detailed descriptions of about 250 occupations and summary information on about 70 additional occupations. Occupations are grouped by broad categories, such as "Executive, Administrative, and Managerial Occupations" or "Service Occupations." Each description contains information on the nature of the job, qualifications and training, earnings, and hiring trends. The narrative analysis includes basic statistics on the number of people employed in the occupation and on earnings. Introductory chapters discuss economic and demographic trends and methods for obtaining additional information on occupations, including addresses of state employment information offices. There is an alphabetical index and an index by *Dictionary of Occupational Titles* classification numbers. The *Occupational Outlook Handbook* is also available on the Internet and on CD-ROM.

The *Career Guide to Industries* is a companion to the *Occupational Outlook Handbook.* Rather than describing individual occupations, it describes 40 major industries and the types of occupations within each industry. Industries are grouped by broad sector such as agriculture, mining, and construction; manufacturing; and transportation, communications and public utilities. Examples of specific industries discussed include electronic equipment manufacturing, food processing, air transportation, telephone communications, motor vehicle dealers, banking, childcare services, and health services. Each industry profile includes SIC numbers, a "significant points" summary, a narrative analysis, and selected statistics. (See Chapter 31, "Business and Industry Statistics," for an explanation of SIC numbers.) Each profile contains sections on the nature of the industry, employment, working conditions, occupations in the industry, training and advancement, earnings, outlook, and sources of additional information. Statistical tables generally give the percentage of establishments by employment size, employment by occupation, and sometimes average earnings.

*O*NET (Occupational Information Network*) is a developing database that will eventually replace the *Dictionary of Occupational Titles* discussed below. The database provides detailed information on each occupation in the areas of worker characteristics, worker requirements, experience requirements, occupation characteristics, occupation requirements, occupation-specific information, related occupations, and associated classification codes. Information available in the worker characteristics and worker requirements areas covers abilities, interests, work values, skills, knowledge, and instructional programs. The experience category gives a job zone rating based on amount of experience and education required. Occupation characteristics covers outlook and earnings. Occupation requirements covers generalized work activities, while occupation-specific information covers important job tasks. More detailed levels of information include ratings for the ability level and importance of each skill or task. Plans for the database call for additional information to be added with a more comprehensive database available in 2001.

Many occupational guides make references to the *Dictionary of Occupational Titles (DOT).* The *DOT* is both a numerical classification system for jobs and a set of job definitions. The job definitions provide a comprehensive guide to job titles, types of jobs, and job duties. The *DOT* classification numbers are often used by employment services, job information centers, and personnel professionals to classify job information, applicants, and openings. The classification system groups related occupations together. The 020 classification, for example, is for occupations in mathematics and gives paragraph descriptions of the duties of such jobs as mathematical technician (020.162-010) and statistician, applied (020.167-026). The definitions are arranged by classification number. Indexes include an industry index, an alphabetical index of occupational titles, and occupational titles arranged by industry designation.

Additional factors to consider in a job are found in *Selected Characteristics of Occupations Defined in the Revised Dictionary of Occupational Titles.* This book is arranged by interest area such as artistic occupations or mechanical occupations. An index by *DOT* classification number is also provided. Each job is given a rating for specific vocational preparation (SVP) that represents the amount of time required to attain the knowledge and necessary skills to perform the job. Ratings are also provided for strength level and various physical demand components of the job and for environmental condition factors.

ADDITIONAL OCCUPATION SOURCES
Checklist

Occupational Outlook Quarterly. PRINT. WEB. (quarterly) 1957–. U.S. Department of Labor. Bureau of Labor Statistics. L 2.70/4: (Title varies) Item 0770-A. ASI 6742-1. GPO. <http://www.bls.gov/opub/ooq/ooqhome.htm>; <purl.access.gpo.gov/GPO/LPS3410>.

> Content: articles on occupations, job outlook and trends, earnings trends, education and training, and career planning.

Occupational Projections and Training Data. MF. (biennial) 1971–. U.S. Department of Labor. Bureau of Labor Statistics. Bulletin series. L 2.3/4-2: (Earlier, L 2.3:) Item 0768-A-10. ASI 6744-3.

> Content: occupational rankings by selected characteristics; projected annual average openings by occupation; projected changes in employment by occupation; degrees by field of study; replacement rates by occupation.

Employment Outlook. PRINT. (biennial) 1957–. U.S. Department of Labor. Bureau of Labor Statistics. Bulletin series. L 2.3: (1998 edition is L 2.3:2502) (Title varies) Item 0768-A-01. ASI 6744-19. (Earlier, 6748-91, 6728-29). GPO.

> Coverage: U.S.
> Content: economic and employment projections for the labor force, employment by industry and occupation, employment change, and fastest growing and declining occupations.

Employment Projections Web Page. WEB. U.S. Department of Labor. Bureau of Labor Statistics. <http://stats.bls.gov/emphome.htm>.

> Content: selected data tables on employment projections by occupation, industry, education, and earnings; publication information.

Discussion

The *Occupational Outlook Quarterly* supplements and updates the *Occupational Outlook Handbook*. It covers employment and occupational trends and forecasts. The articles are written for a general audience and are attractively presented and illustrated with graphs and charts. Articles often summarize the contents of recently released government publications or profile specific occupations. The winter issue includes an index for the most recent five years. Recent articles include "Work More, Earn More? How Hours of Work Affect Occupational Earnings" (Vol. 43, No. 1), "You're a What? Telemarketer" (Vol. 43, No. 1), "Charting the Projections: 1996–2006" (Vol. 41, No. 4), and "A Portrait of the M.B.A." (Vol. 41, No. 3).

Occupational Projections and Training Data is a statistical supplement to the *Occupational Outlook Handbook*. It provides the statistical basis for the general outlook information provided in the *Handbook*. Data are given on current and projected employment by detailed occupation. Occupations are also ranked by selected characteristics, such as change in employment, projected annual average openings, median hourly earnings, unemployment rate, and percent of part-time workers. The most significant source of training is also given for each occupation, such as bachelor's degree or short-term-on-the-job-training. This source can answer such questions as "What is the current employment and projected change in employment for child care workers?" and "What occupations in the food preparation area will have a lot of job openings?" and "What level of training do secretaries require?"

Employment Outlook 1996–2006 contains economic projections and projections of employment by occupation and industry. It summarizes more detailed articles that appeared in the agency's periodical, *Monthly Labor Review* (L 2.6:). The subtitle of this report, and sometimes the title, change with each edition. Narrative analysis summarizes trends and issues in employment. Detailed tables on employment by industry and by occupation give statistics on current and projected employment and on projected employment change. Charts show the industries and occupations with the fastest growing employment. Additional industry and occupation tables list factors affecting demand or growth.

The *Employment Projections Web Page* provides access to the Bureau of Labor Statistics' most popular tables on employment and occupation projections. A menu of data items covers "Most Requested Tables" and specific topics such as "Occupational," "Industry," "Labor force (demographic)," and "State occupational employment projections." Each topic choice offers statistical tables, recent articles, datafiles, and related information sources. An "Education and training" option includes a "Compare occupations" feature that allows searching by occupation or level of education to retrieve specified tables on employment and projected change or growth.

JOB VACANCY SOURCES: GENERAL

Checklist

America's Job Bank. WEB. U.S. Department of Labor. Employment and Training Administration. <http://www.ajb.dni.us/>.

> Content: nationwide job postings for all types of jobs.

Discussion

America's Job Bank is a nationwide network of job openings sponsored by the U.S. Department of Labor and maintained by a network of state employment offices. The majority of jobs are in the private sector and represent all areas of work including professional, technical, managerial, blue-collar, sales, and clerical. Job seekers may search for jobs by occupation, keyword, zip code, or state. Registered users may also create and post resumes. Employers may post jobs and search electronic resumes. Users can also link to *America's Career InfoNet* from the home page. *America's Career InfoNet* provides general outlook information on the U.S. job market, wage and trend information by occupation, state profiles, links to state employment resources and job banks, and career information guides.

JOB VACANCY SOURCES: FEDERAL GOVERNMENT

Checklist

USAJobs. WEB. U.S. Office of Personnel Management. <http://www.usajobs.opm.gov/>.

> Content: current job openings; general information on federal employment.

FedWorld Federal Jobs. WEB. U.S. Department of Commerce. National Technical Information Service. <http://www.fedworld.gov/jobs/jobsearch.html>.

> Content: current job openings; shareware software for application forms OF-612 and SF-171.

Federal Jobs Digest. WEB. Breakthrough Publications, Inc. <http://www.jobsfed.com/>.

> Content: current job openings.

Discussion

The *USAJobs* Web site is the official federal government source for information on federal jobs. It provides current worldwide job vacancy information and is updated each business day. The "General Information" main menu selection provides information on applying for federal jobs, salaries, and other topics. The current job openings can be searched by category, agency, alphabetically, or by series code. Searches can also specify all geographic areas or a specific state. The site also offers online resume creation and copies of the "Optional Application for Federal Employment" form OF-612. For some positions, resumes can be submitted electronically. The job vacancy database is also accessible by telephone at 912-757-3000 or TDD 912-744-2299 or by calling one of the 17 OPM service centers around the country. *USAJobs* is a Web version of the *Federal Job Opportunity Board* (*FJOB*) also available at 912-757-3100 or via telnet at fjob.opm.gov.

The *FedWorld Federal Jobs* Web site provides another option for searching current federal vacancy announcements. *FedWorld* downloads the data from the Office of Personnel Management and links to the fuller vacancy announcements on the *USAJobs* Web site. *FedWorld* offers word searches with Boolean search options. Searches may be done for all states or for a specific state.

The *Federal Jobs Digest* Web site is a nongovernment source of federal job listings. Although there is no fee to view current job vacancies, registration is required. Jobs are listed by broad subject categories. Additional fee-based sources include an email hotline notification service and hardcopy subscriptions to *Federal Jobs Digest*.

INDIVIDUAL AGENCY INFORMATION

Checklist

United States Government Manual. PRINT. WEB. (annual) 1935–. U.S. National Archives and Records Administration. Office of the Federal Register. AE 2.108/2: (Earlier, GS 4.109:) Item 0577. GPO. <http://www.access.gpo.gov/nara/nara001.html>; <http://purl.access.gpo.gov/GPO/LPS2410>.

> Content: descriptions, addresses, and telephone numbers of federal government agencies.

Federal Jobs.Net. WEB. Bookhaven Press. <http://federaljobs.net/>.

> Content: information and resources on federal employment; links to federal agency vacancy listings and employment Web pages.

The Federal Web Locator. WEB. The Center for Information Law and Policy. Illinois Institute of Technology's Chicago-Kent College of Law. <http://www.infoctr.edu/fwl/>.

> Content: list of federal government agency Web sites.

U.S. Federal Government Agencies Directory. WEB. (Also titled: *Federal Agency Internet Sites.*) U.S. Government Printing Office. Superintendent of Documents and Louisiana State University Libraries. <http://www.access.gpo.gov/su_docs/locators/agency/index.html>; <http://purl.access.gpo.gov/GPO/LPS849>.

> Content: list of federal government agency Web sites.

Discussion

The *United States Government Manual* provides general information about each federal government agency, as well as addresses and telephone numbers. Many descriptions include a "Sources of Information" section at the end that often contains an "Employment" subheading with addresses and telephone numbers for employment information.

Federal Jobs.Net provides general information on government employment, including types of jobs, identifying jobs, the application process, civil service exams, telephone numbers of agency personnel offices, and job hotlines. This site also provides links to federal government agency Web site job lists and employment information sites.

Many individual government agency Web sites include information about employment at the agency. Two Web sites that can be used to identify agency Web sites are *The Federal Web Locator* and the *U.S. Federal Government Agencies Directory*. Both offer searchable and browsable lists of federal government agency Web sites. Agency Web sites may include specific vacancy announcements as well as general employment information.

Some agencies may publish brochures on their employment opportunities. The number of such publications distributed to depository libraries has decreased in recent years. To identify such publications, consult the indexes listed in the "Index" section at the end of this chapter.

FEDERAL POSITION DESCRIPTIONS

Handbook of Occupational Groups and Families. PRINT. WEB. 1989–. U.S. Office of Personnel Management. Workforce Compensation and Performance Service. Classification Programs Division. PM 1.8/2: Item 0296. (Title varies) GPO. <http://www.opm.gov/fedclass/>.

> Content: outline and series definitions for classification of federal positions under the General Schedule (GS) and the Federal Wage System (FWS).

HRCD. CD-ROM. (semiannual) 1996–. U.S. Office of Personnel Management. PM 1.59/2: Item 0295-D-01. GPO.

> Content: GS classification standards; FWS job grading standards; GS qualification standards; *Handbook of Occupational Groups and Families*; significant classification appeal decisions; *United States Code* Title 5; salary tables; other related titles.

Operating Manual Qualification Standards for General Schedule Positions. PRINT. WEB. (loose-leaf) PM 1.8/14: Item 0290-A-01. U.S. Office of Personnel Management. GPO. <http://www.opm.gov/qualifications/index.htm>.

> Content: minimum education, training, experience, and other requirements for General Schedule position series.

Federal Classification Systems. WEB. U.S. Office of Personnel Management. <http://www.opm.gov/fedclass/>.

> Content: news and publications relating to the General Schedule and Federal Wage System classification systems; text of selected position standards.

United States Government Policy and Supporting Positions. PRINT. MF. WEB. (quadrennial) 1960–. U.S. Congress. House. Committee on Government Reform and Oversight. Y 4.G 74/7: P 75/6/. (Earlier, Y 4.G 74/9:, Y 4. P 84/10:) (Title and issuing committee vary) (Also known as the "Plum Book") Items 1016-A or -B(MF). GPO. <http://www.access.gpo.gov/plumbook/toc.html>.

> Content: list by agency of positions filled by Presidential appointment, positions excepted from competitive civil service, Senior Executive Service positions, and noncareer executive positions; information for each position includes location, position title, incumbent, pay plan, type of appointment, level or grade, tenure, and expiration date.

Discussion

This section lists sources from the U.S. Office of Personnel Management that provide guidance to the position classifications and requirements for the federal government personnel system. These publications are useful for determining the types of positions in the federal government, the nature of the work, and the qualification requirements. Classification series numbers identified from these sources may also be used in searching job vacancy listings.

The *Handbook of Occupational Groups and Families* contains outlines and series definitions for the two basic federal position classification systems. The General Schedule (GS) covers most white-collar positions, including professional, administrative, technical, and clerical positions. Positions are numerically organized into related occupational groups. The GS-0300 group, for example, is the "General Administration, Clerical, and Office Services Group." Each group contains individual series, such as GS-0334, the "Computer Specialist" series. The Federal Wage System (FWS) covers trades and labor jobs. Positions are also organized numerically into job families, with specific occupations listed under each family. The section for each classification system begins with a numerical outline and is followed by brief definitions of each group or family and each series or occupation. There is a separate alphabetical index for each classification system.

The *HRCD* CD-ROM contains several publications that provide detailed position descriptions and qualification standards for General Schedule and Federal Wage System positions. Some of these publications have been discontinued in paper format. The CD-ROM can be used with Adobe Acrobat software. The "General Schedule

(GS) Classification Standards" section describes each GS series group in detail, including a series definition, detailed occupational description, glossary, job titles, instructions on evaluating positions, a grade conversion table, and detailed evaluation factor level descriptions. Factors include such categories as knowledge required, supervisory controls, complexity, personal contacts, physical demands, and work environment. A former print publication, *Position Classification Standards for Positions under the General Schedule Classification System* (PM 1.30:), has been discontinued. The "General Schedule Qualification Standards" section provides information on the minimum education, experience, and other requirements needed to qualify for a particular GS series. Group standards cover several series. Figure 6.1 illustrates a page from the "Administrative and Management Positions" group standard. Each group standard discusses the education and experience requirements that are common to all the series in the group and lists the specific GS series numbers to which it applies. There is also a separate section of individual series standards for those series that have more specific requirements. Additional sections list series with test and medical requirements. This title is also available in print and on the agency's Web site as *Operating Manual Qualification Standards for General Schedule Positions.* The "Federal Wage System (FWS) Classification Standards" section contains detailed job descriptions for each occupation. These descriptions, or standards, describe the work covered, job titles, and specific grade levels. The grade level sections discuss skill and knowledge required, level of responsibility, physical effort, and working conditions. A former print publication, *Job Grading System for Trades and Labor Occupations* (PM 1.14/3:512-1), has been discontinued.

The *Federal Classification Systems* Web page contains menu choices for both General Schedule classification documents and Federal Wage System classification documents, as well as current news items. Both of the classification system areas include selected publications, an introduction to that particular classification system, and the full text of position classification standards.

United States Government Policy and Supporting Positions ("Plum Book") lists positions that may be filled by appointment, including Executive Schedule positions, Senior Executive Service general positions, Senior Foreign Service positions, and other positions excepted from competitive service due to their confidential or policy-determining nature. Appendices summarize number of positions of each type by agency and provide additional information on types of positions and pay schedules. The publication is presently issued alternately by the House Committee on Government Reform and Oversight and the Senate Committee on Governmental Affairs.

QUALIFICATION STANDARDS OPERATING MANUAL

**Group Coverage Qualification Standard for
Administrative and Management Positions**

This qualification standard covers positions in the General Schedule that involve the performance of two-grade interval administrative and management work. It contains common patterns of creditable education and experience to be used in making qualifications determinations. Section IV-B of this Manual contains individual occupational requirements for some occupations that are to be used in conjunction with this standard. Section V identifies the occupations that have test requirements.

A list of the occupational series covered by this standard is provided on pages IV-A-13 and IV-A-14. This standard may also be used for two-grade interval positions other than those listed if the education and experience pattern is determined to be appropriate.

EDUCATION AND EXPERIENCE REQUIREMENTS

The following table shows the amounts of education and/or experience required to qualify for positions covered by this standard.

| GRADE | EDUCATION | OR EXPERIENCE | |
		GENERAL	SPECIALIZED
GS-5	4-year course of study leading to a bachelor's degree	3 years, 1 year of which was equivalent to at least GS-4	None
GS-7	1 full year of graduate level education *or* superior academic achievement	None	1 year equivalent to at least GS-5
GS-9	master's or equivalent graduate degree *or* 2 full years of progressively higher level graduate education leading to such a degree *or* LL.B. or J.D., if related	None	1 year equivalent to at least GS-7
GS-11	Ph.D. or equivalent doctoral degree *or* 3 full years of progressively higher level graduate education leading to such a degree *or* LL.M., if related	None	1 year equivalent to at least GS-9
GS-12 and above	None	None	1 year equivalent to at least next lower grade level

Equivalent combinations of education and experience are qualifying for all grade levels for which both education and experience are acceptable.

Some of the occupational series covered by this standard include both one- and two-grade interval work. The qualification requirements described in this standard apply only to those positions that typically follow a two-grade interval pattern. While the levels of experience shown for most positions covered by this standard follow the grade level progression pattern outlined in the table, users of the standard should refer to E.3.(p) in the "General Policies and Instructions" (Section II of this Manual) for guidance on crediting experience for positions with different lines of progression.

Undergraduate Education: Successful completion of a full 4-year course of study in *any field* leading to a bachelor's degree, in an accredited college or university, meets the GS-5 level requirements for many positions covered by this standard. Others have individual occupational requirements in Section IV-B that specify that applicants must, in general, (1) have specific course work that meets the requirements for a major in a *particular field(s)*, or (2) have at least 24 semester hours of course work in the field(s) identified. Course work in fields closely related to those specified may be accepted if it clearly provides applicants with the background of knowledge and skills necessary for successful job performance. One year of full-time undergraduate study is defined as 30 semester hours or 45 quarter hours.

Superior Academic Achievement: The superior academic achievement provision is applicable to all occupations covered by this standard. See the "General Policies and Instructions" for specific guidance on applying the superior academic achievement provision.

Graduate Education: Education at the graduate level in an accredited college or university in the amounts shown in the table meets the requirements for positions at GS-7 through GS-11. Such education must demonstrate the knowledge, skills, and abilities necessary to do the work.

One year of full-time graduate education is considered to be the number of credit hours that the school attended has determined to represent 1 year of full-time

Figure 6.1: Sample Page from *Operating Manual Qualification Standards for General Schedule Positions*.

CIVIL SERVICE EXAM SOURCES

Discussion

Study guides or sample test questions for civil service exams are often in demand. Only limited information has been available through the federal depository library system and none of it is recent. Guides to civil service exams have traditionally been published only by the private sector. Sample questions can sometimes be found in general books on federal government jobs. Two publishers that publish a large number of test guides are Arco (Peterson's) and National Learning Corporation.

FEDERAL SALARY AND WAGE INFORMATION SOURCES

Checklist

United States Code. Title 5, Section 5332. PRINT. WEB. CD-ROM. (annual supplements; revised every 6 years) 1926–. U.S. Congress. House. Y 1.2/5:, Y 1.2/5-2: (CD) (Annotated commercial editions also available) Items 0991-A or -B(CD). GPO. <http://www.access.gpo.gov/congress/cong013.html>; <http://purl.access.gpo.gov/GPO/LPS2873>; <http://uscode.house.gov/uscode.htm>; <http://www4.law.cornell.edu/uscode/>.
    Content: government employee salary schedules.

Federal Register. PRINT. MF. WEB. (daily, Mon.-Fri.) 1936–. National Archives and Records Administration. Office of the Federal Register. AE 2.106: (Earlier, GS 4.107:) Items 0573-C, -D(MF), -F(EL). GPO. <http://www.access.gpo.gov/su_docs/aces/aces140.html>; <http://purl.access.gpo.gov/GPO/LPS1756>.
    Content: annual December executive order adjusting government employee pay rates.

Salary Tables for [year]: Executive Branch of the Government. PRINT. (annual) U.S. Office of Personnel Management. Workforce Performance and Compensation Service. PM 1.9: (Earlier, CS 1.73:) (Title varies) Item 0290-F. GPO.
    Content: General Schedule salary tables showing annual and hourly basic and overtime rates and deductions for each grade and step; tables for locality pay rates, law enforcement officers, and senior-level positions; fact sheets and miscellaneous information on pay computation and deductions; biweekly income tax withholding tables.

Salaries and Wages. WEB. U.S. Office of Personnel Management. <http://www.opm.gov/oca/payrates/index.htm>; <http://purl.access.gpo.gov/GPO/LPS2858>.
    Content: recent salary tables and Federal Wage System information.

Discussion

At the end of each year, the President issues an executive order setting the rates of pay for several government employee salary schedules. These include the General Schedule, the Foreign Service Schedule, Veterans Health Administration Schedules, the Senior Executive Service, Executives, the Vice President and Members of Congress, judicial salaries, pay and allowances of the uniformed services, and geographic adjustments for certain employees. This executive order appears in the *Federal Register*. Eventually it is also incorporated into the *United States Code* at Title 5, section 5332 (5 *USC* 5332).

The *Salary Tables for [year]* contains detailed pay rate schedules for the General Schedule and law enforcement officers by grade and step. Tables for specific localities are included. Each table gives annual rates and hourly basic and overtime rates. Tables are also given for the Senior Executive Service, employees in senior-level and scientific and professional positions, administrative law judges, members of boards of contract appeals, and the executive schedule. Some additional general information related to pay computation and deductions is also included.

The *Salaries and Wages* Web page from the Office of Personnel Management provides current salary tables for the General Schedule, including locality pay tables, law enforcement officers, executives, senior executive service and other senior-level positions, and information on pay adjustments and special rates. Information is also given on how to obtain Federal Wage System schedules.

INDEXES

Checklist

Catalog of United States Government Publications (MOCAT). WEB. 1994–. U.S. Government Printing Office. Superintendent of Documents. <http://www.gpo.gov/catalog>; <http://www.access.gpo.gov/su_docs/locators/cgp/index.html>; <http://purl.access.gpo.gov/GPO/LPS844>.

Monthly Catalog of United States Government Publications. CD-ROM. 1996–. U.S. Government Printing Office. Superintenent of Documents. GP 3.8/7: Item 0557-C. GPO.

Monthly Catalog of United States Government Publications (Condensed version). PRINT. (monthly) 1996–. U.S. Government Printing Office. Superintendent of Documents. GP 3.8/8: (Earlier full version, GP 3.8:, 1895-1995). Item 0557-D. GPO.

CIS/Index. PRINT. (monthly) 1970–. Bethesda, MD: Congressional Information Service.

Congressional Universe. WEB. Bethesda, MD: Congressional Information Service.

Discussion

The *Monthly Catalog* is the most comprehensive index for government publications and is discussed in greater detail in Chapter 3, "The Basics of Searching." To locate more publications on occupations look under subject headings beginning with "Occupations," "Vocational Guidance," "Military Occupations," and the subheading "Vocational Guidance" under specific subjects. See also names of specific occupations. For information on federal jobs look under headings beginning with "Civil Service" or "United States — Officials and Employees." See also the names of specific government agencies (e.g., "United States. Dept. of Agriculture — Officials and Employees"). The complete version of the *Monthly Catalog* is available on the Web and on CD-ROM. Commercial online and CD-ROM versions of the *Monthly Catalog* are also available.

CIS indexes congressional publications on agency personnel programs and policies. Look under such subject headings as "Federal employees," "Congressional employees," "Diplomatic and consular service," "Military personnel," and "Civil service system." *CIS* is also available online through *Congressional Universe*.

RELATED MATERIAL
Within this Work

Chapter 33 Income

Chapter 34 Earnings

Chapter 35 Employment

GPO Subject Bibliographies. PRINT. WEB. GP 3.22/2:

<http://bookstore.gpo.gov/sb/about.html>.

No. 44   "Employment and Occupations"

No. 110 "Career Education"

No. 202 "Personnel Management"

No. 270 "Occupational Outlook Handbook"

No. 300 "Office of Personnel Management"

Other

Federal Jobs Digest. (biweekly) Ossining, NY: Breakthrough Publications, Inc. <http://jobsfed.com>.
> Content: federal job vacancy listings; hardcopy subscription for a fee; Web access free with registration.

Federal Career Opportunities. (biweekly) 1974–. Vienna, VA: Federal Research Service, Inc. <http://www.fedjobs.com/>.
> Content: fee-based access to federal job vacancy listings through hardcopy subscription or online and Web databases.

CHAPTER 7
Selling to the Government

The U.S. government purchases many different types of products and services. Several different sources provide information about this process. Major sources listing procurement contracts and selling opportunities are included in this chapter. Regulations pertaining to the procurement process are also discussed, along with guides to the government procurement and contracting process. The majority of this information is available on the Web, with the advantage of information being more easily accessible and often more easily kept up-to-date and current.

SEARCH STRATEGY

This chapter shows a subject search strategy. Search steps are

1. If searching for a specific procurement opportunity, use the *Commerce Business Daily*, available in print and a publicly accessible electronic format that is especially useful;
2. Check other sources described in this chapter as including specific procurement opportunities;
3. Consult the "Regulations" section of this chapter if specific regulations are needed;
4. Use the sources listed in the "General Guides and Information" section;
5. If agency-specific information is needed, consult the guides and agency Web sites relating to procurement listed in the "Agency Guides and Agency Specific Information" section; and
6. Search the indexes and databases listed for additional information.

COMMERCE BUSINESS DAILY AND CONTRACT AWARDS SOURCES
Checklist

Commerce Business Daily. PRINT. (daily, Mon.-Fri.) U.S. Department of Commerce. C 1.76: Item 0231-G-03. GPO.
> Content: listing of all proposed federal procurements and contract awards of $25,000 or more.

CBD Net. WEB. December 2, 1996–. U.S. Department of Commerce. C 1.76/2: Item 0231-G-04.
> Content: searchable database version of *Commerce Business Daily*. <http://cbdnet.access.gpo.gov/index.html>; <http://purl.access.gpo.gov/GPO/LPS2835>.

STAT-USA Internet. WEB. U.S. Department of Commerce. C 1.91: Item 0128-P. <http://www.stat-usa.gov/>.
> Content: current *Commerce Business Daily* notices.

DMS/FI Contract Awards. WEB. Dialog. <www.dialog.com>.
> Content: data on awarded individual prime contract awards of $25,000 or more.

Federal Prime Contracts Data Base. CD-ROM. (formerly titled *ICAR CD-ROM*) Fairfax City, VA: Eagle Eye Publishers.
> Content: data on awarded individual prime contract awards of $25,000 or more.

Discussion

The *Commerce Business Daily (CBD)* lists all proposed federal procurements greater than $25,000. Summaries of recent contract awards greater than $25,000 are also listed along with their recipients. Brief news and announcements of interest to government contractors are also included. Each *Commerce Business Daily* includes 500–1000 notices. The individual listings are placed under classification codes (category headings) such as "Salvage Services," "Utilities and Housekeeping Services," "Information Technology Services, including Telecommunication Services," and "Instruments and Laboratory Equipment." Listings range from contracts to provide paint products to contracts to provide specialized research and development activities. Some procurement opportunities are specifically for special programs, such as the Small Business Set Aside program, and these are noted in the entries.

The *Commerce Business Daily* is available in a searchable database format, titled *CBD Net. CBD Net* is available free-of-charge and provides sophisticated fielded searching of the entries in the *Commerce Business Daily*. Fifteen days worth of the most current *Commerce Business Daily* issues are available in the "Active Notices" database. Older issues are searchable in the "Archive of Notices" database. Fielded searching allows for keyword and phrase searching of the full text of the *Commerce Business Daily*. Other fields include the "Posted Date," "Printed Date," "Part" (sections of the *CBD*, including U.S. Government Procurements, Sources Sought, Contract Awards, Sale of Surplus Property, Special Notices, and Foreign Government Standards), "SubPart" (including Services, or Supplies and Equipment), "Classification Code," "Contracting Officers Address," "Subject," "Solicitation Number," "Response Date," "Point of Contact," "Description," "Awardee," "Award Number," "Award Amount," "Award Line Number," "Award Date," "E-Mail Description," "E-Mail Address," "Internet Link Description," "Internet Link URL," and "Cite."

For the current isssues, *CBD Net* also includes a browsing feature for each section of the *CBD*. Browsing by classification code is also available. In addition to the fielded search described above, a "Simple Search" screen is also available. A "Reader's Guide," "Search Help," and "Search FAQ's" provide information about the *CBD* and searching assistance. *CBD Net* is a powerful search tool and one of the first sources to consult if searching for procurement opportunities.

Current notices from the *Commerce Business Daily* are also available from *STAT-USA*. Several commercial vendors also provide access to *Commerce Business Daily*, including Dialog (CD-ROM and Files 194 and 195), CompuServe, and LEXIS-NEXIS (current and historical files included in several different libraries.)

Two commercial databases of prime contract awards data are also included here. Both databases provide information on specific individual contracts awarded. The *DMS/FI Contract Awards* is available through Dialog as File 588. It includes awarded nonclassified prime contract awards of $25,000 or more. Each individual entry includes the name of the company receiving the money, the dollar amount awarded, contract type and number, date of award, place of performance, awarding agency, defense program involved, and the digital Federal Supply Classification (FSC) code. *Federal Prime Contracts Data Base* covers similar contract awards, providing over 140 fields of information for individual contracts in a CD-ROM format.

REGULATIONS
Checklist

Federal Acquisition Regulation System. Code of Federal Regulations, Title 48. PRINT. MF. WEB. (annual) 1938–. U.S. National Archives and Records Administration. Office of the Federal Register. AE 2.106/3: (*CFR Index and Finding Aids*, AE 2.106/3-2:). (Earlier, GS 4.108:, GS 4.108/4:) Items 0572, 0572-B or -C(MF). GPO. <http://www.access.gpo.gov/nara/cfr/index.html>; <http://purl.access.gpo.gov/GPO/LPS3384>.

    Content: policies and procedures for the acquisition of supplies and services.

Title 48, Federal Acquisition Regulation System: Chapter 1: Federal Acquisition Regulation. PRINT. WEB. (loose-leaf) U.S. General Services Administration; Department of Defense; National Aeronautics and Space Administration. GS 1.6/10: Item 0559-K. GPO. <http://www.arnet.gov/far/>.

    Content: full text of *Federal Acquisition Regulation (FAR)*.

Federal Acquisition Regulation System (Title 48, CFR). CD-ROM. (quarterly) U.S. Government Printing Office. GP 3.38/2: Item 552-D-01. GPO.

    Content: Title 48 of the *Code of Federal Regulations, Federal Register* updates, related circulars, forms, pricing guides, and other material.

FARSite. WEB. U.S. Department of Defense. Department of the Air Force. Air Force Contracting Laboratory. <http://farsite.hill.af.mil/>.

    Content: full text of *FAR* and supplements; links to other related materials.

Federal Acquisition Regulation (FAR). WEB. Dialog. <http://www.dialog.com>.

    Content: *FAR* and supplements; other related sources.

Agency for International Development Acquisition Regulation (AIDAR). WEB. U.S. Agency for International Development. <http://www.info.usaid.gov/pubs/ads/aidar9-1.pdf>.

    Content: text of *Agency for International Development Acquisition Regulation (AIDAR)*.

Agriculture Acquisition Regulation (AGAR). WEB. U.S. Department of Agriculture. <http://www.usda.gov/da/procure/agar.htm>.

    Content: HTML, PDF, and WordPerfect format files of the *Agriculture Acquisition Regulation (AGAR)*.

Air Force FAR Supplement. WEB. U.S. Department of Defense. Department of the Air Force. Air Force Contracting Laboratory. <http://FARSITE.HILL.AF.MIL/vfaffar1.htm>.

    Content: text of *Air Force Federal Acquisition Regulation Supplement (AFFARS)*.

Army Federal Acquisition Regulation Supplement. WEB. U.S. Department of Defense. Department of the Army. Deputy Assistant Secretary of the Army (Procurement). <http://acqnet.sarda.army.mil/library/zpafar.htm>.

    Content: *Army Federal Acquisition Regulation Supplement (AFARS)* in HTML and Word formats and in a downloadable "Electronic AFARS Desk Reference" program.

Structure of the EFARS to the Subpart Level. WEB. U.S. Department of Defense. Department of the Army. Army Corps of Engineers. <http://www.hq.usace.army.mil/cepr/efars.html>.

   Content: PDF format files for each part of the *Engineer Federal Acquisition Regulation Supplement (EFARS)*.

U.S. Department of Commerce Acquisition Community: Policy and Guidance. WEB. U.S. Department of Commerce. <http://oamweb.osec.doc.gov/policy/>.

   Content: *Federal Acquisition Regulation (FAR), Commerce Acquisition Regulation (CAR), Commerce Acquisition Manual (CAM)*.

Defense Federal Acquisition Regulation Supplement. PRINT. WEB. (looseleaf) U.S. Department of Defense. D 1.6:AC 7/year. Item 0309. GPO. <http://www.acq.osd.mil/dp/dars/dfars.html>; <http://purl.access.gpo.gov/GPO/LPS2140>.

   Content: Department of Defense *Federal Acquisition Regulation Supplement (DFAS)*.

Defense Logistics Agency Regulations. WEB. U.S. Department of Defense. Defense Logistics Agency. Defense Logistics Support Command. <http://www.procregs.hq.dla.mil/>.

   Content: PDF version of *Defense Logistics Acquisition Directive (DLAD)*.

Department of Education Acquisition Regulation. WEB. U.S. Department of Education. Office of the Chief Financial Officer. <http://ocfo.ed.gov/coninfo/clibrary/edar.htm>.

   Content: text of *Department of Education Acquisition Regulation (EDAR)*.

EPA Acquisition Policy Information. WEB. U.S. Environmental Protection Agency. Office of Acquisition Management. <http://www.epa.gov/oamrfp12/ptod/>.

   Content: PDF version of *EPA Acquisition Regulation (EPAAR)*.

Department of Energy Acquisition Regulation. WEB. U.S. Department of Energy. Office of Procurement and Assistance Management. <http://www.pr.doe.gov/dear.html>.

   Content: *Department of Energy Acquisition Regulation (DEAR)*.

Department of the Interior Acquisition Regulation (DIAR). WEB. U.S. Department of the Interior. <http://www.ios.doi.gov/pam/aindex.html>.

   Content: *Department of the Interior Acquisition Regulation (DIAR)*.

Justice Acquisition Regulations. WEB. U.S. Department of Justice. <http://www.usdoj.gov/jmd/pss/jarinet.htm>.

   Content: text of *Justice Acquisition Regulation (JAR)*.

Department of Labor Acquisition Regulation (DOLAR). WEB. U.S. Department of Labor. Office of the Assistant Secretary for Administration and Management. <http://www.dol.gov/dol/oasam/public/regs/cfr/48cfr/toc_Part2900-2999/Part2900-2999_toc.htm>.

   Content: *Department of Labor Acquisition Regulation (DOLAR)*.

NASA FAR Supplement. WEB. U.S. National Aeronautics and Space Administration. <http://www.hq.nasa.gov/office/procurement/regs/nfstoc.htm>.

   Content: text of *NASA Acquisition Regulation (NASA FAR)* in Word and HTML format.

Navy Acquisitions Procedures Supplement. WEB. U.S. Department of Defense. Department of the Navy. Acquisition and Business Management. <http://www.abm.rda.hq.navy.mil/naps/index.html>.

   Content: text of *Navy Acquisitions Procedures Supplement (NAPS)*; searchable full text.

NRC Acquisition Regulations. WEB. U.S. Nuclear Regulatory Commission. <http://www.nrc.gov/ADM/CONTRACT/NRCAR.html>.

   Content: text of *Nuclear Regulatory Commission Acquisition Regulation (NRCAR)*.

Department of State Acquisition Regulations—DOSAR. WEB. U.S. Department of State. <http://www.statebuy.gov/dosar/dosartoc.htm>.

   Content: text of *Department of State Acquisition Regulation (DOSAR)*; searchable *DOSAR* database.

Transportation Acquisition Regulation and Transportation Acquisition Manual. WEB. U.S. Department of Transportation. Office of the Secretary. <http://www.dot.gov/ost/m60/tamtar/>.

   Content: text of *Transportation Acquisition Regulation (TAR)* and *Transportation Acquisition Manual (TAM)*.

Treasury DTAR. WEB. U.S. Department of the Treasury. Office of Procurement. <http://www.ustreas.gov/procurement/dtar.html/>.

   Content: text of *Department of Treasury Acquisition Regulation (DTAR)*.

Selling to the USPS. WEB. U.S. Postal Service. <http://www.usps.gov/business/pub41.htm>.

   Content: text of the *U.S. Postal Service Procurement Manual (PM)* in PDF format.

VAAR On-Line. WEB. U.S. Department of Veterans Affairs. Office of Acquisition and Materiél Management. <http://www.va.gov/oa&mm/vaar/>.

   Content: text of *Veterans Affairs Acquisition Regulation (VAAR)*.

Discussion

The Federal Acquisition Regulation System governs acquisition procedures for all executive agencies. It is published in Title 48 of the *Code of Federal Regulations*. Chapter 1 of Title 48 is the *Federal Acquisition Regulation (FAR)*, which contains general regulations pertaining to all agencies. Chapters 2 through 59 of Title 48 are supplements to the *FAR* covering specific acquisition regulations for individual agencies. The *Code of Federal Regulations* is also available in many electronic editions, and the *FAR* is included in those versions. The *Code of Federal Regulations* is available on the Web from the Government Printing Office's *GPO Access* Web site (July 1996–). Online commercial services also include the *CFR*, including *CIS Congressional Universe* (current), *LEXIS-NEXIS* (1981–), *LEXIS-NEXIS Academic Universe* (current), *Westlaw* (1984–), and *CQ.com On Congress*. The *LEXIS* file is called CFR and is available in several libraries, including GENFED, CODES, and EXEC. The GENFED library offers the most options, including different editions of the

CFR. Relevant titles of the *CFR* also appear in appropriate subject libraries. A CD-ROM version is available from West.

The *FAR* is also published jointly by three agencies as a separate print looseleaf edition and as a Web version. The Government Printing Office publishes a CD-ROM version. The Department of Defense's *FARSite* also provides the text of *FAR* and *FAR* supplements. *FAR* is also available from Dialog, as File 665.

Many of the agencies issuing *FAR* supplements now make them available from their agency Web sites. A selection of the major departments and agencies making their agency *FAR* supplements available is listed here. The agency versions of the *FAR* supplements often include other related information on their sites, which can be an advantage in using these versions.

GENERAL GUIDES AND INFORMATION
Checklist

Acquisition Reform Network. WEB. U.S. Office of Federal Procurement Policy. <http://www.arnet.gov>.
> Content: comprehensive guide to the procurement process; searchable database of business opportunities; other resource information.

Federal Acquisition Jumpstation. WEB. U.S. National Aeronautics and Space Administration. Marshall Space Flight Center. Procurement Office. <http://nais.nasa.gov/fedproc/home. html>.
> Content: links to agencies with procurement Web sites; links to other acquisition information.

Electronic Posting System (EPS) Home Page. WEB. U.S. General Services Administration. <http://www.eps.gov/>.
> Content: electronic posting system for procurement opportunities; searchable database of business opportunities.

SBA PRO-Net. WEB. U.S. Small Business Administration. <http://pro-net.sba.gov/>.
> Content: procurement gateway for small businesses; includes procurement and subcontracting opportunities; searchable database of small, disadvantaged, 8(a) and women-owned businesses.

Women Business Owners: Selling to the Federal Government. WEB. U.S. Small Business Administration. Office of Women's Business Ownership. <http://www.onlinewbc.org/docs/procure/table_of_contents.html>.
> Content: overview of the government procurement process; steps for selling to the government; descriptions of other resources of interest.

Library and Resources. WEB. U.S. Small Business Administration. Office of Technology. <http://www.sba.gov/SBIR/library.html>.
> Content: links to information about the Small Business Innovation Research (SBIR) program and Small Business Technology Transfer (STTR) program, which provide special contracting opportunities for small businesses; pre-solicitation announcements; guides and general information about SBIR and STTR programs.

Discussion

This section lists selected resources that provide information about the procurement process in general, or provide information about a number of agencies, not just a single individual agency.

The *Acquisition Reform Network (ARN)* serves as a comprehensive gateway to federal procurement information. Included is a "Virtual Library" of links to procurement resources, covering resources such as presolicitations, solicitations, awards, contract administration, laws, policies, regulations, and forms. The "Federal Business Opportunities" section provides a multiagency database of information. The search interface allows the user to easily locate an agency's home page, and its small business information, business opportunities, and procurement forecasts. Other sections of the *ARN* link to procurement regulations and federal committees and councils dealing with procurement.

The *Federal Acquisition Jumpstation* is another good starting point for locating procurement information for a number of agencies. It provides links to procurement and acquisition related agency Web sites as well as links to general resources, such as the *Commerce Business Daily.*

The General Services Administration's *Electronic Posting System (EPS)* has been designed as a government-wide tool to provide online business opportunities postings. Postings can be searched by agency, solicitation/award number, procurement/classification code, and date. The last thirty days of postings can also be browsed by agency.

SBA PRO-Net (Procurement Marketing and Access Network) is a procurement gateway specifically for small businesses. One of its most useful features is a database of information on more than 171,000 small, disadvantaged, 8(a) and women-owned businesses. *SBA PRO-Net* also includes links to business opportunities at selected agencies and a database of subcontracting opportunities.

Women Business Owners: Selling to the Federal Government is a general guide to the procurement process, aimed at women-owned businesses. The guide explains the steps in the procurement process and describes resources for use in the procurement process. It also describes the subcontracting process and details responsibilities of governmental contractors.

Two procurement programs of interest to small businesses are the Small Business Innovation Research (SBIR) program and Small Business Technology Transfer (STTR) program, which provide special contracting opportunities for small businesses. The Small Business Administration Office provides a *Library and Resources* Web site of links to resources for those interested in this program. Included are SBIR and STTR presolicitations and solicitations, and statistics on awards

AGENCY GUIDES AND AGENCY SPECIFIC INFORMATION

Checklist

United States Agency for International Development

USAID Office of Procurement Announcements, Solicitations and Resources. WEB. U.S. Agency for International Development. Office of Procurement. <http://www.info.usaid.gov/procurement_bus_opp/procurement/>.

> Content: solicitations, regulations, recent award notices, links to other related procurement information.

Department of Agriculture

USDA Procurement. WEB. U.S. Department of Agriculture. Office of Procurement, Property & Emergency Preparedness. <http://www.usda.gov/da/procure.html>.

> Content: general information about USDA procurement and acquisition activities; links to numerous other related sites; links to points of contact and solicitations at USDA Web sites.

Doing Business with USDA. WEB. (1998). U.S. Department of Agriculture. USDA Office of Procurement & Property Management and Office of Small & Disadvantaged Business Utilization.<http://www.usda.gov/da/procure/dobiz.htm>.

> Content: procurement policies and procedures; programs for small, disadvantaged and women-owned businesses; types of products and services purchased; Web site addresses; directory of purchasing offices.

Department of Commerce

U.S. Department of Commerce Acquisition Community. WEB. U.S. Department of Commerce. <http://oamweb.osec.doc.gov/>.

> Content: general Department of Commerce acquisitions information; links to other agency Web sites and resources.

Office of Small and Disadvantaged Business Utilization Web Site. WEB. U.S. Department of Commerce. Office of Small and Disadvantaged Business Utilization. <http://www.doc.gov/osdbu/>.

> Content: information about programs to increase contract and subcontract awards to small, minority, women-owned and minority small businesses; contracting and subcontracting information; procurement process information; directories of relevant offices and contact information.

Department of Defense

Selling to the Military, Army, Navy, Air Force, Defense Logistics Agency, Other Defense Agencies: General Information, Items Purchased, Location of Military Purchasing Offices. PRINT. WEB. (1998) U.S. Department of Defense. Office of the Secretary of Defense. D 1.2:SE 4/998. Item 0306. <http://www.acq.osd.mil/sadbu/publications/selling/index.html>.

> Content: comprehensive directory and guide to military procurement.

Doing Business with the Department of Defense. WEB. U.S. Department of Defense. <http://www.defense/ink.mil/other_info/business.html>.

> Content: links to relevant Web sites, including business opportunities, guides, and other Department of Defense Web Sites.

Defense Acquisition Deskbook. WEB. U.S. Department of Defense. Deputy Under Secretary of Defense (Acquisition Reform) ODUSD(AR) and Office of the Under Secretary of Defense (Acquisition, Technology, and Logistics) Systems Acquisition. <http://www.deskbook.osd.mil/>.

> Content: *FAR*; *DFARS*, and other *FAR* supplements; text of related laws and regulations; library of acquisition documents and forms; other general information.

Defense Acquisition Deskbook. CD-ROM. (quarterly) U.S. Department of Defense. Aeronautical Systems Center. Defense Acquisition Deskbook Joint Program Office. D 1.95/2: Item 0307-A-11. GPO. <http://www.deskbook.osd.mil/>; <http://purl.access.gpo.gov/GPO/LPS1506>.

> Content: *FAR*; *DFARS*, and other *FAR* supplements; text of related laws and regulations; library of acquisition documents and forms; other general information; URL listed provides a downloadable version of the CD-ROM.

Defense Procurement Home Page. WEB. U.S. Department of Defense. Director of Defense Procurement. <http://www.acq.osd.mil/dp/>.

> Content: general information about defense procurement; links to related sources and agencies.

Department of Defense Procurement Gateway. WEB. U.S. Department of Defense. Defense Automated Printing Service. <http://progate.daps.mil/home/>.

> Content: searchable database of Department of Defense request for quotations and contract awards.

Department of Defense Business Opportunities (DoDBusOpps). WEB. U.S. Department of Defense. Joint Electronic Commerce Program Office. <http://dodbusopps.com/>.

> Content: general information about contracting opportunities; searchable database of solicitations; links to other agency sites.

Defense Logistics Agency Logistics Operations (J-3) Home Page. WEB. U.S. Department of Defense Logistics Agency. Defense Logistics Operations <http://www.supply.dla.mil/mmhome.htm>.

> Content: guide to procurement procedures; regulations; links to other related information.

Air Force Contracting. WEB. U.S. Department of Defense. Air Force Department. Deputy Assistant Secretary (DAS) for Contracting. <http://www.safaq.hq.af.mil/contracting/>.

> Content: general information about Air Force contracts and procurements; business opportunities; contracting tool kit; contact information.

Army Acquisition Website. WEB. U.S. Department of Defense. Department of the Army. Deputy Assistant Secretary of the Army (Procurement). <http://acqnet.sarda.army.mil/>.

> Content: general information about Army acquisition programs; business opportunities.

Army Single Face to Industry (ASFI) Acquisition Business Web Site. WEB. U.S. Department of Defense. Department of the Army. Assistant Secretary of the Army for Acquisition, Logistics, and Technology. <http://acquisition.army.mil/default.htm>.

> Content: searchable database of Army contracting opportunities.

abm online. WEB. U.S. Department of Defense. Department of the Navy. Acquisition and Business Management. <http://www.abm.rda.hq.navy.mil/>; <http://purl.access.gpo.gov/GPO/LPS940>.

> Content: comprehensive gateway to Navy procurement process and resources relating to procurement.

Navy Electronic Commerce Online. WEB. U.S. Department of Defense. Department of the Navy. <http://www.neco.navy.mil/>.

> Content: general information about Navy procurement and contracting; searchable database of presolicitation notices; searchable database of current procurement transactions.

Department of Education

Contracts Information. WEB. U.S. Department of Education. <http://gcs.ed.gov/Coninfo.htm>.

> Content: contract award database; U.S. Department of Education currently available solicitations; contract solicitations and work statements online; forecast of upcoming contract activity; other general information about the contract process.

Doing Business with the Department of Education. WEB. U.S. Department of Education. Office of the Chief Financial Officer/Contracts and Purchasing Operations; Office of Small and Disadvantaged Business Utilization. <http://gcs.ed.gov/coninfo/booklet1.htm>.

> Content: overview of the Department of Education and its programs; general contracting information; description of preferential acquisitions programs.

Department of Energy

U.S. Department of Energy (DOE), Office of Procurement and Assistance Management Web Page. WEB. U.S. Department of Energy. Office of Procurement and Assistance Management. <http://www.pr.doe.gov/>.

> Content: general information about procurement; DOE regulations and procedures; links to other Web sites of interest.

Doing Business with the Department of Energy Business Communications Center. WEB. U.S. Department of Energy. Office of Procurement and Assistance Management. <http://www.pr.doe.gov/prbus.html>.

> Content: business opportunities; procurement information and resources; contact information; regulations, directives and guides; other information related to Department of Energy procurement activities.

How to Do Business with DOE. WEB. U.S. Department of Energy. <http://www.pr.doe.gov/prhow.html>.

> Content: general guide and description of Department of Energy procurement methods.

Environmental Protection Agency

Doing Business With EPA. WEB. U.S. Environmental Protection Agency. Office of Acquisition Management. <http://www.epa.gov/oam/>.

> Content: business opportunities; EPA procurement policies and regulations; small business opportunities; other related links.

Federal Emergency Management Administration

Doing Business With FEMA. WEB. U.S. Federal Emergency Management Administration. <http://www.fema.gov/ofm/toc.htm>.

> Content: general guide and description of FEMA procurement and contracting procedures.

General Services Administration

Contracting Opportunities with GSA. WEB. (1997) U.S. General Services Administration. <http://www.gsa.gov/pubs/ctropgsa/ctropgsa.htm>.

> Content: brief description of GSA contracts and bidding process; directory of GSA small business centers.

Department of Health and Human Services

Office of Acquisition Management Web Page. WEB. U.S. Department of Health and Human Services. Office of the Assistant Secretary for Management and Budget. Office of Acquisition. <http://www.dhhs.gov/progorg/oam/>.

> Content: general procurement information; links to other relevant Web sites.

Doing Business with the Department of Health and Human Services. WEB. U.S. Department of Health and Human Services. Office of Small and Disadvantaged Business Utilization. <http://www.hhs.gov/progorg/osdbu/howto97.html>.

> Content: products and services purchased; directory of contacts; information geared specifically to small businesses.

Department of Housing & Urban Development.

HUD Contracting. WEB. U.S. Department of Housing & Urban Development. <http://www.hud.gov/cts/ctshome.html>.

> Content: general information; contracting opportunities; contact information; recent contract awards; grantee technical assistance.

Contracting with HUD. WEB. (2000) U.S. Department of Housing & Urban Development. Office of the Chief Procurement Officer. <http://www.hud.gov:80/cts/guide/guide.pdf>.

> Content: general information; what HUD buys; what HUD spends; procurement opportunity programs; contact information.

Department of the Interior

Office of Acquisition and Property Management Home Page. WEB. U.S. Department of the Interior. Office of Acquisition and Property Management. <http://www.ios.doi.gov/pam/pamhome.html>.

> Content: general information on doing business with the Department of the Interior; acquisition policy and regulations; links to other relevant home pages.

Bureau of Land Management Acquisitions. WEB. U.S. Department of the Interior. Bureau of Land Management. Acquisition Office. <http://www.blm.gov/natacq/>.

> Content: general information about the BLM procurement process; contact information; BLM procurement initiatives; links to other resources.

Department of Justice

Business with DOJ. WEB. U.S. Department of Justice. <http://www.usdoj.gov/07business/index.html>.

>Content: general information; directory of procurement offices; procurements and solicitations; links to other departmental Web sites and resources relating to procurement.

Department of Labor

Contract Information and Resources. WEB. U.S. Department of Labor. Office of the Assistant Secretary for Administration and Management. <http://www.dol.gov/dol/oasam/public/grants/contract.htm>.

>Content: Department of Labor related procurement information; manuals and procedures; links to related contract information.

National Aeronautics and Space Administration

NAIS Home Page. WEB. U.S. National Aeronautics and Space Administration. <http://procurement.nasa.gov/>.

>Content: Web site of the NASA Acquisition Internet Service (NAIS); business opportunities; procurement reference library; center procurement sites; NASA regulations, handbooks, and other procurement information.

NASA Office of Procurement. WEB. U.S. National Aeronautics and Space Administration. Office of Procurement. <http://www.hq.nasa.gov/office/procurement/>.

>Content: business opportunities; small business programs; general information about NASA procurement.

Nuclear Regulatory Commission

Doing Business with NRC. WEB. U.S. Nuclear Regulatory Commission. <http://www.nrc.gov/ADM/CONTRACT/contract.html>.

>Content: contract opportunities; small business opportunities; how the NRC buys; other general information and links to related resources.

Small Business Administration

The Facts About—Doing Business with the Federal Government. PRINT. WEB. (1999) U.S. Small Business Administration. SBA 1.2:F 11/GOVERN./999. Item 0901-B. <http://www.sba.gov/library/pubs.html>.

>Content: short pamphlet of general information about SBA procurement assistance programs; directory of SBA government contracting offices.

Department of State

Office of the Procurement Executive (A/OPE) Acquisition Web Site. WEB. U.S. Department of State. Office of the Procurement Executive. <http://www.statebuy.gov/home.htm>.

>Content: procurement programs; acquisition policy information; links to other acquisition sources.

A Guide to Doing Business with the Department of State. PRINT. WEB. (semiannual) U.S. Department of State. Office of Small and Disadvantaged Business Utilization. S 1.40/2:B 96/year. GPO. <http://www.mindspring.com/~l.taylor/osguide.htm>; <http://purl.access.gpo.gov/GPO/LPS2916>.

>Content: summary of Department of State procurement programs; information about the department's Small, Disadvantaged, and Female Business Program; subcontracting opportunities.

Department of Transportation

U.S. Department of Transportation Acquisition and Grants Home Page. WEB. U.S. Department of Transportation. Office of the Senior Procurement Executive. <http://www.dot.gov/ost/m60/>.

>Content: business opportunities and vendor information; tools for procurement professionals; reference materials.

Contracting with the United States Department of Transportation. WEB. U.S. Department of Transportation. <http://osdbuweb.dot.gov/business/mp/contract.html>.

>Content: general information; procurement programs; information on the procurement activities of individual departments and offices; contact information.

Doing Business with FHWA. WEB. U.S. Department of Transportation. Federal Highway Administration. <http://www.fhwa.dot.gov/doingbiz.htm>.

>Content: general information; links to relevant Federal Highway Administration Web sites.

Department of the Treasury

Treasury Procurement Information Web Site. WEB. U.S. Department of the Treasury. Office of Procurement. <http://www.ustreas.gov/procurement/>.

>Content: business opportunities; procurement regulations; policies and procedures; small business information; references and resources.

How to Do Business with Treasury. WEB. U.S. Department of the Treasury. Office of Small and Disadvantaged Business Utilization. <http://www.treas.gov/sba/htdbwt1.html>.

>Content: basic guide to the procurement process; information for small businesses; information about treasury offices; contact information.

USSS Procurement. WEB. U.S. Department of the Treasury. Secret Service. Procurement Division. <http://www.ustreas.gov/usss/proc/index.htm>.

>Content: procurement opportunities; procurement virtual library; small business information.

Department of Veterans Affairs

VA Business Opportunities. WEB. U.S. Department of Veterans Affairs. Office of Acquisition and Matériel Management. <http://www.va.gov/oa&mm/busopp/index.htm>.

>Content: Veterans Affairs solicitations; policies and regulations; forms; general information.

Doing Business with the Department of Veterans Affairs. WEB. U.S. Department of Veterans Affairs. Office of Acquisition and Matériel Management. <http://www.va.gov/oa&mm/busopp/doingbusiness.htm>.

>Content: general information; information on opportunities with specific VA centers; information for small businesses; contact information.

Discussion

There are numerous agency Web sites from procurement offices and other offices dealing with the procurement process that provide current information on specific agency procurement opportunities and processes. Some agencies also issue individual guides to the procurement and contracting processes. This section lists these guides, along with any current print versions of the guides. Because of the timeliness of the information, most agencies are now using the Web to distribute this type of information. This listing of resources is not a comprehensive list, but does include resources from the departments and agencies most heavily involved with governmental procurement. The sources listed here also serve as examples of the kinds of information available.

INDEXES
Checklist

Catalog of United States Government Publications (MOCAT). WEB. 1994–. U.S. Government Printing Office. Superintendent of Documents. <http://www.gpo.gov/catalog>; <http://www.access.gpo.gov/su_docs/locators/cgp/index.html>; <http://purl.access.gpo.gov/GPO/LPS844>.

Monthly Catalog of United States Government Publications. CD-ROM. 1996–. U.S. Government Printing Office. Superintendent of Documents. GP 3.8/7: Item 0557-C. GPO.

Monthly Catalog of United States Government Publications (Condensed version). PRINT. (monthly) 1996–. U.S. Government Printing Office. Superintendent of Documents. GP 3.8/8: (Earlier full version, GP 3.8:, 1895–1995). Item 0557-D. GPO.

CIS/Index. PRINT. (monthly) 1970–. Bethesda, MD: Congressional Information Service.

Congressional Universe. WEB. Bethesda, MD: Congressional Information Service.

Discussion

The *Monthly Catalog* is the most comprehensive index for government publications and is discussed in greater detail in Chapter 3, "The Basics of Searching." To locate more publications on selling to the government, look under subject headings and keywords beginning with "Government Purchasing," "Contracts," "Contractors," and "Employees." The complete version of the *Monthly Catalog* is available on the Web and CD-ROM. Commercial online and CD-ROM versions of the *Monthly Catalog* are also available.

RELATED MATERIAL
Within this Work

Chapter 8   Business Aids

Chapter 40   Defense and Military Statistics

Chapter 51   Standards and Specifications

GPO Subject Bibliographies. PRINT. WEB. GP 3.22/2:

<http://bookstore.gpo.gov/sb/about.html>

No. 129   "Procurement"

No. 231   "Specifications and Standards"

CHAPTER 8
Business Aids

The U.S. government publishes many resources that provide information and assistance to businesses. While much of this information is geared toward use by small businesses, some sources are more generally applicable to all businesses. The Small Business Administration is one of the most prolific producers of this information. Many of its publications are now available on the Web. Another publisher of business guides is the International Trade Administration, which publishes aids for businesses exporting to and operating in other countries. Some of its more general guides and sites of interest to businesses are included here. Agency Web sites, major series, and examples of the types of materials available as aids to businesses from other agencies are also included.

SEARCH STRATEGY

This chapter shows a subject search strategy. The steps to follow are
1. Check the major series and publications listed in this chapter;
2. Search the Web sites of the Small Business Administration and the International Trade Administration; and
3. Search the *Monthly Catalog* for additional publications.

SMALL BUSINESS ADMINISTRATION SOURCES
Checklist

SBA: Small Business Administration Home Page. WEB. U.S. Small Business Administration. <http://www.sba.gov/>.
> Content: general information about the SBA; starting, financing, and expanding small businesses; SBA services and programs; topics of interest to small businesses.

SBA: Starting Your Business. WEB. U.S. Small Business Administration. <http://www.sba.gov/starting/>.
> Content: SBA resources and information about starting a small business.

SBA: Financing Your Business. WEB. U.S. Small Business Administration. <http://www.sba.gov/financing/>.
> Content: SBA resources and information about financing your business.

SBA: Expanding and Growing Your Business. WEB. U.S. Small Business Administration. <http://www.sba.gov/expanding/>.
> Content: SBA resources and information on business development.

Online Library Reading Rooms. WEB. U.S. Small Business Administration. <http://www.sba.gov/library/>.
> Content: collection of publications, regulations, forms, directories, records, shareware, and other resources pertaining to small businesses.

Publications Room. WEB. U.S. Small Business Administration. <http://www.sba.gov/library/pubs.html>.
> Content: online versions of SBA publications, including many business guides.

General Publications. PRINT. (irregular) U.S. Small Business Administration. SBA 1.2: Item 0901-B.
> Content: guides and publications on small business topics.

Handbooks, Manuals, Guides. PRINT. (irregular) U.S. Small Business Administration. SBA 1.19: Item 0901-P.
> Content: guides to SBA programs and basic business topics.

Facts About ... (series). PRINT. WEB. U.S. Small Business Administration. SBA 1.49/2: Item 0901-B-13. <http://www.sba.gov/library/pubs.html>.
> Content: fact sheets on SBA and other governmental programs and small business topics.

U.S. Business Advisor. WEB. U.S. Small Business Administration. <http://www.business.gov/busadv/index.cfm>.
> Content: gateway to business information from a variety of government agencies.

The Small Business Advocate. WEB. PRINT. U.S. Small Business Administration. Office of Advocacy. SBA 1.51: Item 0901-

B-12. <http://www.sba.gov/ADVO/news/>; <http://purl.access.gpo.gov/GPO/LPS2001>.

Content: newsletter with information geared towards small businesses; includes articles on regulatory activities, economic issues, and programs of the SBA.

The State of Small Business: A Report of the President Transmitted to the Congress [year]. WEB. PRINT. (annual) 1981–. SBA 1.1/2: Item 0901-A. ASI 9764-6. GPO. U.S. Small Business Administration. <http://www.sba.gov/ADVO/stats/ec_state.html>; <http://purl.access.gpo.gov/GPO/LPS1196>.

Coverage: U.S., states.

Content: comprehensive narrative and statistical report on small businesses.

Discussion

The *Small Business Administration* Web site includes a vast amount of information on all aspects of small businesses. The home page of the site gives the user the option of selecting different sections of the Web site. Options available from this page include "Starting," "Financing," "Expanding," "Offices & Services," "Local SBA Resources," "PRO-Net" (procurement information), "Freedom of Information," "Disaster Assistance," "Regulatory Fairness," "SBA Classroom," "Business Cards," "Your Government," and "Outside Resources." The site also includes a site map, search engine, and listing of popular topics.

Within the SBA site is the *Starting Your Business* page. This page describes the many SBA programs that help small businesses get started, such as Business Information Centers and Small Business Development Centers. An "FAQ" page provides answers to the most commonly asked questions about starting a business. A "Start-up Kit Page" provides a comprehensive look at topics like "Finding the Money You Need," "Regulations," "SBA Assistance," and "Local Sources of Assistance." Other areas cover such topics as research aids, business plans, counseling help, patents and trademarks, and workshops.

The *Financing Your Business* page comprehensively and individually describes the myriad of loan programs available from the SBA. Forms needed for the program and other detailed information is available from this part of the SBA site. Sample programs covered include the 7(A) Loan Guaranty Program, the SBALowDoc Loan Program, International Trade Loans, and the Certified Development Company (504) Loan Program. Information on lender programs is also included. Additional links from this page provide information on other sources of financing, such as investment firms.

The *SBA: Expanding and Growing Your Business* page describes SBA programs to help small businesses in their expansion efforts. One of the resources described is Pro-Net, an electronic gateway of information about procurement, including procurement opportunities. Help in finding investors is provided through the SBA sponsored *Angel Capital Electronic Network, ACE-Net.* Other programs

described include the Small Business Innovation Research (SBIR) Program, the Small Business Technology Transfer (STTR) Program, and export assistance programs.

The *Online Library Reading Rooms* contain an immense amount of information of use to small businesses. "FAQ's" cover all aspects of SBA programs and small business topics. "Laws and Regulations" provide the complete text of relevant sections of the *Code of Federal Regulations*, individual laws, and reports about regulations and laws. Examples of items in the listings and directories section include directories of the Offices of Small & Disadvantaged Business Utilization (OSDBU), listings of SBA job announcements, and a directory of Small Business Development Centers (SBDCs). Other sections include "Loan Information," "Programs," "Reports, Statistics, Studies," and "Shareware & Files."

Also included in the *Online Library Reading Rooms* is the *Publications Room* page. This page includes the text of many small business guides, often issued in series of publications. Among the series are the *Small Business Management Series.* Subseries within this include the *Emerging Business Series*, the *Financial Management Series*, the *Managing and Planning Series*, the *Marketing Series*, the *Products/Ideas/Inventions Series*, the *Personnel Management Series*, and the *Crime Prevention Series.* Some of these are older publications that were originally issued to depository libraries in print formats, but they still provide valuable information. Also included at this site is the *Facts About ... (series)*, described separately later in this section. *A Business Plan Workbook, Marketing Plan Workbook, Financing Workbook*, and *Franchising Workbook* are also included. An additional series at the site is the *Small Business Success Series.* Publications from the site are available in text, PDF, and Word97 formats.

The *General Publications* series and *Handbooks, Manuals, Guides* series include guides on various topics relating to SBA programs and areas of interest. Titles within the *General Publications* series include: *Business Coaches: Mentors for Small Business Success* (SBA 1.2:M 52), *The Facts About—The New SBA Franchise Registry* (SBA 1.2:F 11/FRANCHISE), and *The Small Business Loan Prequalification Program*, (SBA 1.2:L 78/999). The *Handbooks, Manuals, Guides* series includes a limited number of similar titles, such as *Loan Servicing Requests Guidelines* (SBA 1.19:L 78) and *Guidelines for Small Business Award Nominations: Small Business Week 1998* (SBA 1.19:AW 1/998). *The Facts About...* (series) consists of a series of short fact sheets. Sample titles include *The Facts About—: Small Business Development Centers* (SBA 1.49/2:43), *The Facts About—: SBA On the Information Superhighway* (SBA 1.49/2:65), and *The Facts About—: Starting a Small Business* (SBA 1.49/2:28).

The *U.S. Business Advisor* Web site strives to be a one-stop gateway to federal information about small businesses. It includes links to agency information from many different agencies throughout the government. Major sections of the site include: "Business Development," "Financial Assistance," "Taxes," "Laws and Regulations," "International Trade," "Workplace Issues," "Buying and Selling," and "Agencies and Gateways." The "InfoDesk" area provides links to many agency publications of interest.

Each area tries to bring together all the resources scattered among agencies, describe them, and provide an organized approach to using them

The Small Business Advocate is a newsletter issued by the Small Business Administration's Office of Advocacy. Articles often explain the impact of regulatory actions or proposed regulatory actions on small businesses, such as a recent article titled, "Small Businesses Will Feel the Effect of New USPS Regs" (Vol. 18, No. 6, 1999). Other articles report on economic news impacting small businesses, such as "New Edition of Report on 'Micro-Business-Friendly Banks' Issued" (Vol. 18, No. 5, 1999), or describe SBA programs "After 20 Years, Advocacy Still Has a Vital Role to Play" (Vol. 18, No. 4, 1999).

The State of Small Business is an annual analysis of small business activity that can be used as a guide to the current business climate. The report includes numerous statistical tables and covers such topics as business start-ups and closings, business earnings, employment creation, small business financing, federal procurement, women-owned businesses, and minority-owned businesses.

INTERNATIONAL TRADE ADMINISTRATION SOURCES

Checklist

United States International Trade Administration Web Site. WEB. U.S. International Trade Administration. <http://www.ita.doc.gov/ita_home/>.
>   Content: information about ITA programs and services; countries; industries and sectors; announcements and press releases; trade missions and events; trade rights and agreements; trade statistics.

Countries and Regions. WEB. U.S. International Trade Administration. <http://www.ita.doc.gov/ita_home/itacnreg.htm>.
>   Content: links to information about specific countries and regions.

Trade Development Home Page. WEB. U.S. International Trade Administration. <http://www.ita.doc.gov/td/td_home/tdhome.html>.
>   Content: information on increasing exports in specific industries; information about the Trade Development Division's programs and services.

Trade Information Center. WEB. U.S. International Trade Administration. Trade Development. <http://tradeinfo.doc.gov>.
>   Content: country information; trade offices; tariff and tax information; publications; trade events; other export and trade information.

USATRADE.gov. WEB. U.S. Department of Commerce. International Trade Administration. U.S. Commercial Service. <http://www.usatrade.gov/website/>.
>   Content: ITA services; market research; trade events; exporting resources.

A Basic Guide to Exporting. PRINT. WEB. (1998) U.S. Department of Commerce. International Trade Administration. C 61.8:EX 7/3/998. Item 0231-B-05. GPO. <http://www.unzco.com/basicguide/index.html>.
>   Content: comprehensive guide to all aspects of exporting, such as contact information; conducting business abroad; shipping information; financing information; export advice; preparing products for exports.

Export Programs: A Business Guide to Federal Export Assistance Programs. PRINT. WEB. (1998?) Web version: (2000) U.S. Department of Commerce. International Trade Administration. C 61.8:EX 7/8/997. Item 0231-B-05. <http://infoserv2.ita.doc.gov/tic.nsf/037197a7338428ca852566330051710b/dcdd173db9e6cb04852566330052983e?OpenDocument>; <http://purl.access.gpo.gov/GPO/LPS174>.
>   Content: counseling and assistance information; trade contacts and market information programs; financing, grants, and tax incentives; agriculture export and financing programs; export licenses and controls.

Export America. PRINT. WEB. 1999–. U.S. Department of Commerce. International Trade Administration. C 61.18/2: Item 0127-A. <http://exportamerica.doc.gov/>.
>   Content: articles on exporting and international trade; news; trade events; market opportunities.

Discussion

The International Trade Administration (ITA) carries out programs and services to help U.S. businesses succeed in the global marketplace. Its home page provides a gateway to accessing ITA information and provides links to other areas of the ITA Web site. It is a good starting point for understanding the role of the ITA, the extent of its services, and for accessing ITA publications and resources.

Two pages within the ITA site are especially useful as business aids. The *Countries and Regions* page provides links to information on specific countries and regions. Especially covered are the Big Emerging Markets, or BEMs, which include such countries as Brazil, China, Turkey, and Malaysia. The page is arranged by geographic regions, then provides links to specific country pages or other resources for the region as a whole. The *Trade Development Home Page* provides links to areas within the Trade Development Division and describes its programs and services to increase exports. Information is available by specific industry, such as "Environmental Technologies," "Consumer Goods," or "Microelectronics."

USATRADE.gov is a Web site of the U.S. Commercial Service. The U.S. Commercial Service maintains a presence in 78 countries and operates 92 Export Assistance Centers in the United States. It promotes and protects business in other countries and strives to increase export opportunities through a series of programs and services. *USATRADE.gov* includes sections on "Services," "Market Research," "Trade Events," "Exporting Resources," and "Other Site Features." Of particular interest are the "Market Research," and the "Exporting Resources" sections. The "Market Research" section includes detailed information accessible by industry or country. The "Exporting Resources" section includes links to export guides and information about export regulations, tariffs, and rates.

Two guidebooks from the ITA provide additional assistance for businesses wishing to start or expand their export trade. *A Basic Guide to Exporting* is a comprehensive manual on export trade. It offers a step-by-step approach to developing a company export strategy. Sections of the guide cover such topics as "Preparing Your Product for Export," "International Legal Considerations," "Financing Export Transactions," and "Selling Overseas." The *Export Programs: A Business Guide to Federal Export Assistance Programs* provides extensive contact information for export assistance, including general assistance, industry-specific, and country-specific directories. Various export programs and assistance programs are also described.

Export America is a glossy, highly readable magazine that provides practical and technical advice to businesses concerning export trade and opportunities. Included are news announcements and articles about new export opportunities. Other articles deal with specific regions and markets, or describe "success stories" in export trade. Information on trade events, marketing tips, Internet marketing, and federal government programs are also included.

ADDITIONAL SOURCES
Checklist

Minority Business Development Agency Web Site. WEB. U.S. Department of Commerce. Minority Business Development Agency. <http://www.mbda.gov/>.
> Content: general information; database of minority businesses; local MBDA centers; online resources; events; FAQ.

Country Commercial Guides. WEB. (annual) U.S. Department of State. Bureau of Economic and Business Affairs. S 1.40/7: Item 0863-B. ASI 2046-17. NTIS. <http://www.state.gov/www/about_state/business/com_guides/>; <http://www.usatrade.gov/website/ccg.nsf>; <http://purl.access.gpo.gov/GPO/LPS303>.
> Content: guides for U.S. businesspersons; analyses of political, economic, and market environment of individual countries.

Small Business Handbook. WEB. U.S. Department of Labor. Office of the Assistant Secretary for Policy. <http://www.dol.gov/dol/asp/public/programs/handbook/main.htm>.
> Content: handbook on statutes and regulations administered by the Department of Labor.

Small Business Information. WEB. U.S. Securities and Exchange Commission (SEC). <http://www.sec.gov/smbus1.htm>.

> Content: Q&A about small business and the SEC; small business forms and regulations; how to reach the SEC; links to other information.

Q&A: Small Business and the SEC. PRINT. WEB. (1999) U.S. Securities and Exchange Commission. Division of Corporation Finance. Office of Small Business. <http://www.sec.gov/smbus/qasbsec.htm>.
> Content: guide to raising capital and complying with federal securities laws.

Small Business Corner. WEB. U.S. Department of the Treasury. Internal Revenue Service. <http://www.irs.ustreas.gov/prod/bus_info/sm_bus/index.html>.
> Content: variety of links to information of use to small businesses; tax information and tax issues.

Tax Guide for Small Business. PRINT. WEB. (annual) 1956–. U.S. Department of the Treasury. Internal Revenue Service. Publication 334. T 22.19/2-3: (Earlier, T 22.19/2:SM 1/) Item 0956-A. GPO. <http://www.irs.ustreas.gov/forms_pubs/pubs/p334toc.htm>; <http://purl.access.gpo.gov/GPO/LPS814>; <http://www.irs.ustreas.gov/forms_pubs/pubs.html>; <http://purl.access.gpo.gov/GPO/LPS533>.
> Content: basic information on business taxes, including how to file, dispositions of business property, business income, cost of goods sold, gross profit, business expenses, net profit or loss, and sample forms.

Starting a Business and Keeping Records. PRINT. WEB. (annual) U.S. Department of the Treasury. Internal Revenue Service. Publication 583. T 22.44/2:583/year. Item 0964-B. <http://www.irs.ustreas.gov/prod/forms_pubs/pubs/p583toc.htm>; <http://www.irs.gov/prod/forms_pubs/pubs.html>; <http://purl.access.gpo.gov/GPO/LPS5337>.
> Content: kinds of federal business taxes; identification numbers; record keeping.

Key Officers of Foreign Service Posts: Guide for Business Representatives. WEB. (irregular) U.S. Department of State. S 1.40/5: Item 0876-B. <http://www.state.gov/www/about_state/contacts/keyofficer_index.html>; <http://purl.access.gpo.gov/GPO/LPS2408>.
> Content: key officers (chiefs, assistant chiefs of missions, economic offices, consular offices, etc.) of missions and consulates.

Small Business Guide. PRINT. WEB. (1998) U.S. Pension Benefit Guaranty Corporation. <http://www.pbgc.gov/publications/SMBUS.htm>; <http://purl.access.gpo.gov/GPO/LPS2710>.
> Content: guide to understanding the requirements of the federal pension insurance program.

Small Business. WEB. U.S. Department of Labor. Occupational Safety and Health Administration. <http://www.osha-slc.gov/SmallBusiness/index.html>.
> Content: information about OSHA programs and services; publications; safety and health; workplace hazards.

OSHA Handbook for Small Businesses. PRINT. WEB. (1996) U.S. Department of Labor. Occupational Safety and Health Administration. L 35.19:B 96/996. Item 0766-K. GPO. <http://www.osha-slc.gov/Publications/Osha2209.pdf>.

Content: small business guide for establishing safety and health programs.

Welcome to the U.S. Trade Center. WEB. U.S. Department of Commerce. <http://usatc.doc.gov/>.

Content: information on Trade Center programs and services; links to centers and other sources of information.

National Trade Data Bank: The Export Connection. WEB. CD-ROM. (monthly) Oct. 1990–. U.S. Department of Commerce. STAT-USA. C 1.88: (Depository distribution of CD-ROM discontinued with Oct. 2000 disc.) Item 0128-L. ASI 2002-6. <http://www.stat-usa.gov/tradtest.nsf>; <http://purl.access.gpo.gov/GPO/LPS1777>.

Content: full text of *Country Commercial Guides*; *A Basic Guide to Exporting*, and *Key Officers of Foreign Service Posts*; market research reports; exporting guides; trade-related publications.

Discussion

The Minority Business Development Agency's (MBDA) mission is to "encourage the creation, growth, and expansion of minority-owned businesses in the United States." The MBDA's programs include Minority Business Development Centers and Native American Development Centers. The MBDA also sponsors programs to encourage minority entrepeneurship. The MBDA Web site provides access to information about MBDA programs and services, along with other resources. A database of minority businesses and business opportunities available to minority businesses is available at the site. Virtual business centers provide extensive information on the topics of "Aquaculture," "International Trade," "Franchising," "Manufacturing Technology," and "Capital Access."

Country Commercial Guides are geared towards providing U.S. businesses with the information needed to increase trade in a country. The guides are prepared in conjunction with the U.S. Embassies in each country. Guides provide a comprehensive look and analysis of a country's economic, political, and market environment. Each guide provides chapters on the following major topics: "Economic Trends and Outlook," "Political Environment," "Marketing U.S. Products and Services," "Leading Sectors for U.S. Exports and Investments," "Trade Regulations and Standards," "Investment Climate," "Trade and Project Financing," and "Business Travel." Most reports also include appendices with information on the topics of "Economic and Trade Statistics," "U.S. and Country Contacts," and "Market Research and Trade Events."

The Department of Labor's *Small Business Handbook* is designed to give small businesses an overview and familiarity with the laws and regulations affecting them. Laws and regulations in the broad categories of "Retirement and Health Benefit Standards," "Safety and Health Standards," "Wage, Hour, and Other Workplace Standards," and "Workplace Standards for Federally Assisted or Funded Contracts" are described. Typical descriptions give information on who is covered, basic provisions and re-

quirements, assistance available to help businesses comply, and a description of what authority is available to investigate noncompliance and any applicable fines and penalties.

The SEC's *Small Business Information* Web site provides information of use to small businesses in complying with federal securities laws. Available at this site is the publication *Q&A, Small Business and the SEC*, which is also issued in a print format. This guide gives basic information that small businesses need to know about securities laws and how they affect a company wishing to go public. Lists of resources for more information are also included. Other sections of the Web site cover the work of the SEC, how to contact the SEC, and give information on forms and regulations of the SEC.

The *Small Business Corner* Web site of the Internal Revenue Service provides extensive information and links to other resources about taxes and tax questions for small businesses. The site covers employment taxes, self-employment taxes, business taxes, and other taxes of concern to businesses. News and reports concerning small businesses are also included at the site, as well as links to general small business resources. The IRS also publishes many tax guides—two of particular interest to small businesses are the *Tax Guide for Small Business* and *Starting a Business and Keeping Records*.

The *Tax Guide for Small Business* describes the taxes affecting small businesses. Topics covered include capital expenses, employees' pay, gains and losses, travel and entertainment, insurance, and depreciation. It includes sample returns and an index. *Starting a Business and Keeping Records* covers what kinds of taxes businesses pay, the records a business should keep, and the tax identification numbers used by businesses.

Key Officers of Foreign Service Posts lists the U.S. officers in other countries who can be of help in developing international trade and business opportunities. It is frequently updated and gives the names of officers, addresses, and telephone and fax numbers. It also includes e-mail addresses and URLs for the offices involved.

The *Small Business Guide* from the Pension Benefit Guaranty Corporation (PBGC) is designed to help businesses understand the requirements of the federal pension insurance program that covers most defined benefit insurance programs. The plan ensures workers of retirement payments if their company goes bankrupt. This guide comprehensively covers the many requirements that exist for carrying out these plans, including descriptions of the premiums to be paid to PBGC and the disclosures required to be given to employees.

The *OSHA Small Business* Web site brings together OSHA resources of interest to small businesses. It includes contact information, information on training resources, safety and health data tools, and workplace hazards. A publications section includes an extensive collection of the full text of OSHA publications, including the *OSHA Hand-*

book for Small Businesses. This source is a detailed guide designed to help small businesses achieve compliance with the Occupational and Safety Health Act. It explains the importance of the "Four-Point Workplace Program," which includes voluntary guidelines that OSHA has designed to help worksites protect workers. Self-inspection safety checklists, a directory of sources for further assistance, and a directory of OSHA offices are also included.

The *USA Trade Center* is a Department of Commerce initiative to provide a centralized source for export products and information. The Web site provides links to the Trade Information Center, the Business Information Service of the Newly Independent States (BISNIS), the Central and Eastern Europe Business Information Center (CEEBIC), the Multilateral Development Bank Operations (MDBO), the Trade Reference and Assistance Center (TRAC), the Bureau of Export Administration (BXA), and the Export Research and Assistance Center (ERAC). All of these centers and bureaus provide specialized assistance and information for exporters. The site also provides general information about the USA Trade Center's programs and services.

The *National Trade Data Bank: The Export Connection* includes online versions of some of the guides previously cited in this chapter, including the *Country Commercial Guides*, *A Basic Guide to Exporting*, and *Key Officers of Foreign Service Posts*. The site also includes various market research and analysis reports. The "International Trade Library" portion of the site includes several other exporting and trade guides.

INDEXES
Checklist

Catalog of United States Government Publications (MOCAT). WEB. 1994–. U.S. Government Printing Office. Superintendent of Documents. <http://www.gpo.gov/catalog>; <http://www.access.gpo.gov/su_docs/locators/cgp/index.html>; <http://purl.access.gpo.gov/GPO/LPS844>.

Monthly Catalog of United States Government Publications. CD-ROM. 1996–. U.S. Government Printing Office. Superintendent of Documents. GP 3.8/7: Item 0557-C. GPO.

Monthly Catalog of United States Government Publications (Condensed version). PRINT. (monthly) 1996–. U.S. Government Printing Office. Superintendent of Documents. GP 3.8/8: (Earlier full version, GP 3.8:, 1895-1995). Item 0557-D. GPO.

Discussion

A comprehensive index of government publications can be found in the *Monthly Catalog*. To locate additional publications on business aids, search the *Monthly Catalog* under subject headings and key words beginning with "Business" and "Small Business." The complete version of the *Monthly Catalog* is available on the Web and CD-ROM. Commercial online and CD-ROM versions of the *Monthly Catalog* are also available. For more information on the *Monthly Catalog*, see Chapter 3, "The Basics of Searching."

RELATED MATERIAL
Within this Work

Chapter 7   Selling to the Government

Chapter 31 Business and Industry Statistics

Chapter 38 Foreign Trade Statistics

GPO Subject Bibliographies. PRINT. WEB. GP 3.22/2:

<http://bookstore.gpo.gov/sb/about.html>

No. 4   "Business"

No. 307 "Small Business"

CHAPTER 9
Directories

There are a number of sources available for obtaining the name, address, telephone number, fax, e-mail address, or URL of a government agency or an individual government employee. Agency Web sites often provide directories of the agency's offices and key contact persons, and sometimes also include directories of individual employees of the agency. Several comprehensive listings of U.S. governmental agency sites have been compiled and are included in this chapter.

Some departments publish print versions of organizational or telephone directories and some of these directories are distributed to depository libraries. However, these print directories have the disadvantage of being sporadically distributed to depository libraries and are often out-of-date by the time they are distributed. In general, if available, information from agency Web sites is a more accessible and up-to-date option.

There are also a number of commercially published government directories in both print and electronic formats. These directories are sometimes more complete and current than the directories compiled by the government agencies, especially when they are directories of individuals or offices within a department. Electronic versions of directories often include the capability to create subsets of the information in the directories and/or to create mailing lists. Commercially published directories are often duplicative in nature, and a great number of them are published. Examples of some of the most common commercially published directories are listed in the commercial directory section of this chapter. The specific directories accessible in an individual library will depend on the institution's needs, budget, and unique situation.

Government agencies also publish an extensive array of directories on a variety of other subjects in addition to the agency directories discussed here. These subject directories, covering topics ranging from adult care facilities to unions, may be located by searching for the individual subject in the *Monthly Catalog* or in some cases through searching agency Web sites or using government Web search engines. (See Chapter 3, "The Basics of Searching.")

SEARCH STRATEGY

This chapter illustrates a subject search strategy. The steps to follow are

1. Consult an appropriate basic directory or one of the Web-based agency directories listed here;
2. Check available commercial directories in print or electronic format for more comprehensive listings, particularly of individuals;
3. Use the *U.S. Federal Government Agencies Directory* or *Federal Web Locator* to locate additional agency Web sites that may include directory information; and
4. Search the *Monthly Catalog* by agency or subject to locate additional directories, particularly subject-oriented directories.

BASIC DIRECTORIES
Checklist

United States Government Manual. PRINT. WEB. (annual) 1935–. U.S. National Archives and Records Administration. Office of the Federal Register. AE 2.108/2: (Earlier, GS 4.109:) Item 0577. GPO. <http://www.access.gpo.gov/nara/nara001.html>; <http://purl.access.gpo.gov/GPO/LPS2410>.
> Content: agencies of the legislative, judicial, and executive branches; independent establishments and government corporations; quasi-official agencies; selected international organizations.

Internet Blue Pages: The Guide to Federal Government Web Sites. PRINT. WEB. (1998). Laurie Andriot. Medford, NJ: Information Today, Inc. <http://www.fedweb.com/>.
> Content: directory of federal agency URLs; brief description of agencies.

U.S. Federal Government Agencies Directory. WEB. (Also titled: *Pathway Services: Federal Agency Internet Sites.*) U.S. Government Printing Office. Superintendent of Documents and Louisiana State University Libraries. <http://www.access.gpo.gov/su_docs/locators/agency/index.html>; <http://purl.access.gpo.gov/GPO/LPS849>.

> Content: listing of links to federal government agency Web sites; keyword searchable index.

The Federal Web Locator. WEB. The Center for Information Law and Policy and the Illinois Institute of Technology's Chicago-Kent College of Law. <http://www.infoctr.edu/fwl/>.

> Content: links to federal government agency Web sites.

Official Congressional Directory. PRINT. WEB. (annual) 1809–. U.S. Congress. Joint Committee on Printing. Y4.P 93/1:1/year. Item 0992. GPO. <http://www.access.gpo.gov/congress/cong016.html>; <http://purl.access.gpo.gov/GPO/LPS194>.

> Content: members of Congress; committees of Congress; Capitol officers and officials; officials in executive and independent agencies; directory of the judiciary; international organizations; foreign diplomatic representatives and consular offices; press, radio, television, and periodical press galleries.

Members and Committees. WEB. U.S. Congress. House. Office of the Clerk. <http://clerkweb.house.gov/mbrcmtee/mbrcmtee.htm>.

> Content: member lists; telephone directory; committee lists; member Web pages.

U.S. Senators. WEB. U.S. Congress. Senate. http://www.senate.gov/senators/index.cfm>.

> Content: directories of Senators by name, state, and class; directory of Senators' contact information; Senate leadership; committee assignments.

Government Information Exchange. WEB. General Services Administration. Federal Technology Service. Center for Emerging Technologies. <http://www.info.gov/>.

> Content: federal agency listings; federal telephone directories; federal yellow pages.

U.S. Blue Pages, WEB. General Services Administration. Federal Technology Service. <http://www.usbluepages.gov>.

> Content: searchable telephone blue page directories.

Federal Telephone Directories. WEB. General Services Administration. Federal Technology Service. Center for Emerging Technologies. <http://www.info.gov/fed_directory/phone.shtml>.

> Content: links to telephone directories for House and Senate and other agencies.

Discussion

The *United States Government Manual* is a directory of agencies and major officials within agencies. Each listing also includes information on the agency's responsibilities and duties. Entries may include information about programs, personnel contacts for further information about programs, and information on obtaining agency publications. Agency regional and field offices are also often listed. The Web version of the *Government Manual* provides keyword and phrase searching capabilities. (See Figure 9.1.)

Following the general arrangement of the *United States Government Manual*, the print *Internet Blue Pages* gives a short description of the agency or subagency, followed by its URL. An accompanying Web site provides an updated listing of agencies and links to the URLs provided in the book.

Two comprehensive directories of federal agency Web sites are listed here. Both are similar in approach and follow the federal government organizational structure to organize their listings of links. The *U.S. Federal Government Agencies Directory* is a partnership between the Federal Depository Library Program (FDLP) and Louisiana State University Libraries. Agency Web sites are organized into executive; judicial; legislative; independent boards, commissions, and committees; and quasi-official categories. The *Federal Web Locator* takes a similar approach in organizing its links. Both of these Web sites are updated frequently and provide one of the easiest ways to locate an agency or subagency Web site.

In addition to listing addresses, telephone numbers, e-mail addresses, and URLs, the *Official Congressional Directory* also includes biographical sketches of the members of Congress. House and Senate committee members and congressional staff members are also listed. Directory information for agencies outside of Congress is also included in an extensive listing. One special feature of the *Directory* is a section containing current maps of congressional districts. The Web version of the *Congressional Directory* allows keyword and phrase searching through a GPO Access search interface. A browsing version of the *Directory*, consisting of PDF and ASCII text files of each section of the *Directory*, is also available at the site.

Web-based directories of the House and Senate are also available and are listed here. They have the advantage of being easily updated and include a variety of information about the members of Congress.

The *Government Information Exchange* serves as a gateway to governmental information with a number of access points. Included at the site are links to federal agencies, links to federal telephone and employee directories, and a "yellow pages" of links to federal information and agencies by topic.

The U.S. Government Blue Pages Project is an initiative to improve the governmental listings in commercial telephone directories. Its Web site, *U.S. Blue Pages,* includes links to the most requested Federal agency Web sites, along with frequently requested toll-free and customer service numbers. The *Federal Telephone Directories* page, part of the *Government Information Exchange* site, provides links to Web-based congressional and agency telephone directories.

NATIONAL ARCHIVES AND RECORDS ADMINISTRATION

8601 Adelphi Road, College Park, Maryland 20740–6001
Phone, 301–713–6800. Internet, http://www.nara.gov/.

Archivist of the United States	JOHN W. CARLIN
Deputy Archivist of the United States	LEWIS J. BELLARDO
Executive Director, National Historical Publications and Records Commission	ANN CLIFFORD NEWHALL
Director of the Federal Register	RAYMOND A. MOSLEY
Assistant Archivist for Regional Records Services	RICHARD L. CLAYPOOLE
Assistant Archivist for Presidential Libraries	DAVID F. PETERSON
Assistant Archivist for Records Services— Washington, DC	MICHAEL J. KURTZ
Assistant Archivist for Human Resources and Information Services	L. REYNOLDS CAHOON
Assistant Archivist for Administrative Services	ADRIENNE C. THOMAS
General Counsel	GARY M. STERN
Inspector General	KELLY A. SISARIO
Director, Information Security Oversight Office	STEVEN GARFINKEL

[For the National Archives and Records Administration statement of organization, see the *Federal Register* of June 25, 1985, 50 FR 26278]

The National Archives and Records Administration (NARA) ensures, for citizens and Federal officials, ready access to essential evidence that documents the rights of American citizens, the actions of Federal officials, and the national experience. It establishes policies and procedures for managing U.S. Government records and assists Federal agencies in documenting their activities, administering records management programs, scheduling records, and retiring noncurrent records. NARA accessions, arranges, describes, preserves, and provides access to the essential documentation of the three branches of Government; manages the Presidential Libraries system; and publishes the laws, regulations, and Presidential and other public documents. It also assists the Information Security Oversight Office, which manages Federal classification and declassification policies, and the National Historical Publications and Records Commission, which makes grants nationwide to help nonprofit organizations identify, preserve, and provide access to materials that document American history.

The National Archives and Records Administration is the successor agency to the National Archives Establishment, which was created in 1934 and subsequently incorporated into the General Services Administration as the National Archives and Records Service in 1949. NARA was established as an independent agency in the executive branch of the Government by act of October 19, 1984 (44 U.S.C. 2101 *et seq.*), effective April 1, 1985.

Activities

Archival Program   The National Archives and Records Administration maintains the historically valuable records of the U.S. Government dating from the Revolutionary War era to the recent past; arranges and preserves records and prepares finding aids to facilitate their use; makes records available for use in research rooms in its facilities; answers written and oral

Figure 9.1: Sample Page from the *United States Government Manual*.

COMMERCIAL DIRECTORIES

Checklist

Washington Information Directory. PRINT. (annual) 1975/76–. Washington, DC: CQ Press.

Content: directory of Congress; agencies; nongovernmental organizations in the Washington, DC, area; and foreign embassies.

Federal Regulatory Directory. PRINT. (irregular) 1979/80–. Washington, DC: CQ Press.

Content: directory of regulatory agencies.

Congressional Staff Directory. PRINT. WEB. (3 times per year) (weekly Web updates) 1959–. Washington, DC: CQ Press. (previously published by Staff Directories, Ltd.) <http://store.yahoo.com/cq-press/cqdirectories.html>.

Content: directory of members of Congress and their staffs.

Federal Staff Directory. PRINT. WEB. (3 times per year) (weekly Web updates) 1982–. Washington, DC: CQ Press. (previously published by Staff Directories, Ltd.) <http://store.yahoo.com/cq-press/cqdirectories.html>.

Content: directory of federal agency staff.

Judicial Staff Directory. PRINT. WEB. (3 times per year) (weekly Web updates) 1987–. Washington, DC: CQ Press. (previously published by Staff Directories, Ltd.) <http://store.yahoo.com/cq-press/cqdirectories.html>.

Content: directory of federal judges and their staff; other judicial branch staff.

Staff Directories on CD-ROM. CD-ROM. (3 times per year). Washington, DC: CQ Press.

Content: CD-ROM version of the *Congressional Staff Directory*, *Federal Staff Directory*, and *Judicial Staff Directory*.

Federal Yellow Book. PRINT. (quarterly) New York, NY: Leadership Directories, Inc.

Content: directory of the executive office of the President; office of the Vice-President; departments, and independent agencies.

Federal Regional Yellow Book. PRINT. (semiannual) New York, NY: Leadership Directories, Inc.

Content: directory of federal regional offices and staff members; administrators and professional staff at federal laboratories, research centers, military installations, and service academies; regional offices of congressional support agencies; U.S. ambassadors and staff of federal departments and agencies with offices abroad.

Congressional Yellow Book. PRINT. (quarterly) New York, NY: Leadership Directories, Inc.

Content: directory of members of Congress, congressional committees, and staff members.

Judicial Yellow Book. PRINT. New York, NY: Leadership Directories, Inc.

Content: includes listings of judges in the federal court system; staff in judges' chambers; administrative court staff.

The Leadership Library. WEB. New York, NY: Leadership Directories, Inc. <http://www.leadershipdirectories.com/lloi.htm>.

Content: database of directories published by Leadership Directories, Inc., including *Federal Yellow Book*, *Federal Regional Yellow Book*, *Congressional Yellow Book*, and *Judicial Yellow Book*.

The Leadership Library. CD-ROM. (quarterly) New York, NY: Leadership Directories, Inc.

Contents: database of directories published by Leadership Directories, Inc., including *Federal Yellow Book*, *Federal Regional Yellow Book*, *Congressional Yellow Book*, and *Judicial Yellow Book*.

Federal Directory. PRINT. WEB. (semiannual) Carroll Publishing. <http://www.carrollpub.com/>.

Content: directory of executive office of the President; departments; administrative agencies; Congress; federal court system.

Federal Directory. CD-ROM. (bimonthly) Carroll Publishing.

Content: CD-ROM version of *Federal Directory*.

Federal Regional Directory. PRINT. WEB. (semiannual) Carroll Publishing. <http://www.carrollpub.com/>.

Content: directory of major agency offices outside Washington, DC; non-Washington, DC– based executives in departments, agencies, the courts, and military bases.

Federal Regional Directory. CD-ROM. (bimonthly) Carroll Publishing.

Content: CD-ROM version of *Federal Regional Directory*.

Encyclopedia of Governmental Advisory Organizations. PRINT. (annual) 1973–. Farmington Hills, MI: Gale Group.

Content: government advisory committees; task forces; and commissions.

Discussion

Several commercial publishers produce various detailed and comprehensive congressional and agency directories. This section cites print, CD-ROM, and Web directories compiled by three major publishers, CQ Press, Leadership Directories, Inc., and Carroll Publishing, as examples of commercial directories. If available, these directories serve as convenient compilations and often provide much greater coverage in terms of detailed personnel listings. The Web and CD-ROM versions of these directories provide sophisticated searching techniques and frequently updated information.

The *Encyclopedia of Governmental Advisory Organizations,* compiled by Gale Group, is one of the few comprehensive sources for information on government advisory committees, task forces, and commissions. Coverage is both current and historical. Organizations are arranged by broad subject categories such as agriculture; business, economics, industry, and labor; and defense and military science. Indexes provide access by names of individuals, titles of publications and reports, the Presidential administration involved, and names of federal departments or agencies. An alphabetical keyword index is also included.

AGENCY DEPARTMENTAL DIRECTORIES
Checklist
Department of Agriculture

About USDA. WEB. U.S. Department of Agriculture. <http://www.usda.gov/about.htm>.
> Content: directory of agencies and staff offices; headquarters organizational charts; photos and biographical information; county office locator.

USDA Telephone Directory. WEB. U.S. Department of Agriculture. <http://www.usda.gov/phonebook/>.
> Content: searchable phone directory of USDA Metropolitan Washington, DC area.

Department of Commerce

U.S. Department of Commerce Person Finder. WEB. U.S. Department of Commerce. <http://204.193.246.62/public.nsf/docs/person-finder>.
> Content: searchable databases of phone numbers and e-mail addresses; listing of organizational phone numbers.

Department of Defense

DefenseLink. WEB. U.S. Department of Defense. <http://www.defenselink.mil/index.html>.
> Content: gateway site for information about the Department of Defense.

Department of Defense Telephone Directory. CD-ROM. (3 times per year) U.S. Department of Defense. D 1.7/1: Item 0304-H-02. GPO.
> Content: searchable database of Department of Defense (including Department of Army, Department of Navy, and Department of Air Force) personnel.

Department of Education

U.S. Department of Education Directories. WEB. U.S. Department of Education. <http://www.ed.gov/dirs.html>.
> Content: electronic phone book; organizational directory.

United States Department of Education Directory. MF. U.S. Department of Education. ED 1.24: Item 0455-K.
> Content: Department of Education telephone directory.

Department of Energy

U.S. Department of Energy People and Pages. WEB. U.S. Department of Energy (DOE). <http://www.doe.gov/people.htm>.
> Content: directory assistance; headquarters programs offices; field, regional and operations offices; DOE laboratories; power administrations.

Health and Human Services Department

Employee Information. WEB. U.S. Health and Human Services Department. <http://www.hhs.gov/progorg/ohr/eis_hom1.html>.
> Content: organizational directory; employee directory.

Department of Housing and Urban Development

About HUD. WEB. U.S. Department of Housing and Urban Development. <http://www.hud.gov/abouthud.html>.
> Content: HUD staff; HUD offices; employee directory.

Telephone Directory. MF. (irregular) U.S. Department of Housing and Urban Development. HH 1.92. Item 0581-E-33.
> Content: HUD telephone directory.

Department of the Interior

Obtaining Information. WEB. U.S. Department of the Interior. Office of the Solicitor. <http://www.doi.gov/sol/solfreq.html>.
> Content: office mailing addresses directory; telephone directory.

Telephone Directory. MF. U.S. Department of the Interior. I 1.86: Item 0601-C.
> Content: Department of the Interior telephone directory.

Department of Justice

U.S. Department of Justice Organizations & Information. WEB. U.S. Department of Justice. <http://www.usdoj.gov/02organizations/index.html>.
> Content: alphabetical listing of Department of Justice Offices; organization chart.

Department of Labor

About DOL. WEB. U.S. Department of Labor. <http://www.dol.gov/dol/public/aboutdol/main.htm>.
> Content: organizational chart; key personnel and phone numbers.

DOL Telephone Directory. MF. U.S. Department of Labor. L 1.67: Item 0754-E.
> Content: Department of Labor telephone directory.

Department of State

U.S. Department of State Telephone Numbers. WEB. U.S. Department of State. <http://www.state.gov/www/about_state/contacts/phbook/phbook.html>.
> Content: employee telephone directory.

Telephone Directory. MF. U.S. Department of State. S 1.21: Item 0876-C.
> Content: Department of State telephone directory; includes related agencies of Agency for International Development; Overseas Private Investment Corporation; Trade and Development Agency; and Broadcasting Board of Governors.

Department of Transportation

U.S. Department of Transportation Organizations. WEB. U.S. Department of Transportation. <http://www.dot.gov/organizations.htm>.
> Content: listing and links to DOT organizations.

Department of the Treasury

About Treasury. WEB. U.S. Department of the Treasury. <http://www.ustreas.gov/about.html>.
> Content: contact information; organizational information.

Department of Veterans Affairs

About VA. WEB. U.S. Department of Veterans Affairs. <http://www.va.gov/About_VA/index.htm>.
    Content: VA organizations; VA facilities locator.

Discussion

Agency Web sites are now one of the best sources of current agency directory and organizational information. Many agency Web sites include telephone and employee directories. Agency sites also usually include contact information for the agency. This listing provides some examples of agency directory information included at the departmental level. Many agencies and subagencies within a department include this type of information for their own agency on their individual Web sites. The Web site directories included in the "Basic Directories" section of this chapter can be used to identify the URLs of additional agency sites, and from there, locate agency directory information. Examples of telephone directories currently being distributed to depository libraries are also included in this listing.

INDEXES

Checklist

Catalog of United States Government Publications (MOCAT). WEB. 1994–. U.S. Government Printing Office. Superintendent of Documents. <http://www.gpo.gov/catalog>; <http://www.access.gpo.gov/su_docs/locators/cgp/index.html>; <http://purl.access.gpo.gov/GPO/LPS844>.

Monthly Catalog of United States Government Publications. CD-ROM. 1996–. U.S. Government Printing Office. Superintendent of Documents. GP 3.8/7: Item 0557-C. GPO.

Monthly Catalog of United States Government Publications (Condensed version). PRINT. (monthly) 1996–. U.S. Government Printing Office. Superintendent of Documents. GP 3.8/8: (Earlier full version, GP 3.8:, 1895-1995). Item 0557-D. GPO.

Discussion

The *Monthly Catalog* is a comprehensive index to government publications. The complete version of the *Monthly Catalog* is available on the Web and CD-ROM. Commercial online and CD-ROM versions of the *Monthly Catalog* are also available. (For more information on the *Monthly Catalog*, see Chapter 3, "The Basics of Searching.") To locate additional directories in the *Monthly Catalog*, search by subject or keyword under the names of subjects or agencies with the term "Directories."

GPO Subject Bibliographies. PRINT. WEB. GP 3.22/2:

<http://bookstore.gpo.gov/sb/about.html>

No. 114 "Directories"

CHAPTER 10
Tax Information

There are three main kinds of tax information available from the government: (1) guides on preparing and filing income tax returns; (2) statistics derived from tax returns; and (3) tax laws, regulations, and decisions.

SEARCH STRATEGY

This chapter shows a subject search strategy. The steps for locating materials are

1. Begin with the "General Guides" section to identify comprehensive tax information sources;
2. See the "Tax Information Publications" section for more specific publications on various tax topics;
3. Check the "Tax Form Sources" section to locate copies of tax return forms;
4. Consult "Tax Statistics" to find sources giving statistical data;
5. Examine the "Legal and Judicial Sources" for laws, regulations, and court decisions;
6. Use "Congressional Sources" for publications on legislative and policy issues; and
7. Search the indexes and consider the "Related Material."

GENERAL GUIDES
Checklist

Your Federal Income Tax for Individuals. PRINT. WEB. (annual) U.S. Department of the Treasury. Internal Revenue Service. Publication 17. T 22.44: Item 0964-B. GPO. <http://www.irs.ustreas.gov/forms_pubs/pubs/p17toc.htm >; <http://www.irs.ustreas.gov/forms_pubs/pubs.html>; <http://purl.access.gpo.gov/GPO/LPS533>.

> Content: basic information on how to file an income tax return, which forms to use, determining filing status, exemptions, income, gains and losses, itemized deductions, credits, adjustments, and tax tables.

Tax Guide for Small Business. PRINT. WEB. (annual) 1956–. U.S. Department of the Treasury. Internal Revenue Service. Publication 334. T 22.19/2-3: (Earlier, T 22.19/2:SM 1/) Item 0956-A. GPO. <http://www.irs.ustreas.gov/forms_pubs/pubs/p334toc.htm>; <http://purl.access.gpo.gov/GPO/LPS814>; <http://www.irs.ustreas.gov/forms_pubs/pubs.html>; <http://purl.access.gpo.gov/GPO/LPS533>.

> Content: basic information on business taxes, including how to file, dispositions of business property, business income, cost of goods sold, gross profit, business expenses, net profit or loss, and sample forms.

Farmer's Tax Guide. PRINT. WEB. (annual) 1955–. U.S. Department of the Treasury. Internal Revenue Service. Publication 225. T 22.44/2:225/[year]. (Earlier, T 22.19/2:F 22/) Item 0964-B. <http://www.irs.ustreas.gov/forms_pubs/pubs/p225toc.htm>; <http://purl.access.gpo.gov/GPO/LPS798>; <http://www.irs.ustreas.gov/forms_pubs/pubs.html>; <http://purl.access.gpo.gov/GPO/LPS533>.

> Content: basic information on filing requirements, farm income, farm business expenses, soil and water conservation expenses, depreciation, gains and losses, and a sample return.

Discussion

Your Federal Income Tax for Individuals is the basic tax guide for individuals. It covers basic information on filing a return and on personal exemptions and deductions. More detailed information covers such things as selling a home, moving expenses, individual retirement arrangements, alimony, medical expenses, child care, and other topics. Explanations often include examples, worksheets, and charts. There is an order form for obtaining additional publications and forms. An index is also included.

The *Tax Guide for Small Business* describes the taxes affecting small businesses. Topics covered include capital expenses, employees' pay, gains and losses, travel and entertainment, insurance, and depreciation. There are sample returns and an index. The *Farmer's Tax Guide* provides similar information for farmers. Both of these guides are also available in *Business Taxpayer Information Publications* discussed in the "Tax Information Publications" section.

TAX INFORMATION PUBLICATIONS
Checklist

Taxpayer Information Publications. PRINT. (annual) U.S. Department of the Treasury. Internal Revenue Service. Publication 1194. T 22.44/2:1194/[year]/[v.] Item 0964-B. GPO.

> Content: multivolume collection of IRS informational publications.

Business Taxpayer Information Publications. PRINT. (annual) U.S. Department of the Treasury. Internal Revenue Service. Publication 1194-B. T 22.44/2:1194-B/[year]. Item 0964-B. GPO.

> Content: collection of IRS informational publications related to business.

Tax Information: IRS Publications. PRINT. WEB. 1968–. U.S. Department of the Treasury. Internal Revenue Service. T 22.44/2: Item 0964-B. <http://www.irs.ustreas.gov/prod/forms_pubs/pubs/index.htm>; <http://www.irs.ustreas.gov/forms_pubs/pubs.html>; <http://purl.access.gpo.gov/GPO/LPS533>.

> Content: series of individual IRS information publications.

Forms and Publications Web Page. WEB. U.S. Department of the Treasury. Internal Revenue Service. <http://www.irs.ustreas.gov/forms_pubs/index.html>.

> Content: current and prior years tax forms, instructions, and informational publications.

Federal Tax Products. CD-ROM. U.S. Department of the Treasury. Internal Revenue Service. T 22.51/4: Item 0923-B-01. GPO. NTIS.

> Content: current and prior years tax forms, instructions, and informational publications.

Guide to Free Tax Services. PRINT. WEB. U.S. Department of the Treasury. Internal Revenue Service. Publication 910. T 22.44/2:910/[year]. (Title varies) Item 0964-B. <http://www.irs.ustreas.gov/forms_pubs/pubs.html>; <http://purl.access.gpo.gov/GPO/LPS533>.

> Content: IRS tax information services; Tele-Tax phone numbers; filing addresses; list and description of tax information publications with subject index; electronic services; and electronic filing.

Discussion

The Internal Revenue Service issues numerous informational publications on specific tax topics in the *Tax Information: IRS Publications* series. Most of the publications are revised annually. Sample titles include *Tax Withholding and Estimated Tax* (No. 505), *Educational Expenses* (No. 508), *Credit for the Elderly or the Disabled* (No. 524), and *Tax Information for First-Time Homeowners* (No. 530). The most frequently requested of these publications

have been compiled in a multivolume set called *Taxpayer Information Publications*. Publications are arranged in publication number order within each volume. *Business Taxpayer Information Publications* is a similar collection for business publications. It includes the *Tax Guide for Small Business* and the *Farmer's Tax Guide* listed in the "General Guides" section.

The *Forms and Publications Web Page* provides several options for electronic access to tax information publications. The "Publications and Notices" option lists all current year information publications by number. Full text for each publication is available in PDF, PCL, PostScript, and SGML formats. The "Publications Online" option lists selected information publications that can be browsed online. A search option offers a keyword search of both information publications and forms. Other options include an expert FTP option, a numerical list of publications and forms arranged by date, and publications for previous years by year.

The *Federal Tax Products* CD-ROM also contains the full text of current and prior years' tax information publications. The CD is issued in two releases each year—an early release with forms approved at that time and a later final release. The NTIS and GPO CDs are slightly different. Depository libraries receive the NTIS edition. The GPO edition is titled *Federal Tax Forms and Publications on CD-ROM* and does not contain a set of forms in SGML format.

Guide to Free Tax Services lists all of the tax information publications available. Publications are listed numerically with brief contents descriptions. A subject index indicates which publications cover specific topics. The *Guide* also provides information on basic tax filing procedures and on other assistance and information available from the IRS.

TAX FORM SOURCES
Checklist

Reproducible Copies of Federal Tax Forms and Instructions. PRINT. (annual) 1981–. U.S. Department of the Treasury. Internal Revenue Service. Publication 1132. T 22.57: (Earlier, T 22.2:T 19/20/) (Title varies) Item 0956-F. GPO.

> Content: selected tax forms and instructions that can be photocopied for taxpayers' use.

Package X: Reference Copies of Federal Tax Forms and Instructions. PRINT. (annual) U.S. Department of the Treasury. Internal Revenue Service. T 22.2/12: (Earlier, T 22.2:P 12/) (Title varies) Item 0956. GPO.

> Content: selected tax forms and instructions.

Forms and Publications Web Page. WEB. U.S. Department of the Treasury. Internal Revenue Service. <http://www.irs.ustreas.gov/forms_pubs/index.html>.

> Content: current and prior years tax forms, instructions, and informational publications.

Federal Tax Products. CD-ROM. U.S. Department of the Treasury. Internal Revenue Service. T 22.51/4: Item 0923-B-01. GPO. NTIS.

> Content: current and prior years tax forms, instructions, and informational publications.

IRS Publications and Forms. Toll-Free Telephone Number: (800) 829-3676.

Discussion

Photocopies of official IRS tax forms may be submitted by taxpayers in place of original copies. *Reproducible Copies of Federal Tax Forms and Instructions* is specifically designed for this purpose and is in loose-leaf format to allow for easy photocopying. *Package X* is a collection of perforated tear sheets designed primarily as reference copies. The content of the two titles is very similar. Instructions for each form are also included.

In addition to the GPO depository system, the Internal Revenue Service has a Banks, Post Office, and Library Program (BPOL) to distribute *Reproducible Copies of Federal Tax Forms and Instructions*, informational publications, and multiple copies of tax forms and instructions free to any library, bank, or post office that wishes to participate.

The *Forms and Publications Web Page* provides several options for electronic access to tax forms. The "Forms and Instructions" option lists all current year forms by number. Copies of each form and instructions are available in PDF, PCL, PostScript, and SGML formats. A search option offers a keyword search of both information publications and forms. A fill-in forms option is also available. Data may be entered into a form online using Adobe Acrobat software and then printed. Forms cannot be transmitted to the IRS electronically using this method. Other options include requesting forms to be sent by mail, an expert FTP option, a numerical list of publications and forms arranged by date, and forms for previous years by year.

The *Federal Tax Products* CD-ROM also contains the full text of current and prior years' tax forms. The CD offers the ability to fill in forms on screen for printing, but does not provide electronic submission of forms. The CD is issued in two releases each year—an early release with forms approved at that time and a later final release. The NTIS and GPO CDs are slightly different. Depository libraries receive the NTIS edition. The GPO edition is titled *Federal Tax Forms and Publications on CD-ROM* and does not contain a set of forms in SGML format.

Free copies of forms and IRS publications can also be requested by calling the IRS toll-free telephone number listed above or by writing to the appropriate IRS distribution center listed in *Guide to Free Tax Services* discussed in the previous section.

TAX STATISTICS
Checklist

Statistics of Income: Individual Income Tax Returns. PRINT. WEB. (annual) 1916–. U.S. Department of the Treasury. Internal Revenue Service. Statistics of Income Division. T 22.35/8: (Earlier, T 22.35/2:IN 2/, T 22.35:) (Title varies) Item 0964. ASI 8304-2. GPO. Selected tables: <http://www.irs.ustreas.gov/tax_stats/soi/ind_gss.html>.

> Coverage: U.S.
> Content: number and characteristics of returns by size of adjusted gross income; sources of income; exemptions and deductions by size of adjusted gross income; some data by marital status.

Statistics of Income: Corporation Income Tax Returns. PRINT. WEB. (annual) 1916–. U.S. Department of the Treasury. Internal Revenue Service. T 22.35/5: (Earlier, T 22.35/2:C 81/year. Earlier title, *Statistics of Income*, T 22.35:). Item 0964. ASI 8304-4. GPO. <http://www.irs.ustreas.gov/prod/tax_stats/soi/corp_id.html>.

> Coverage: U.S.
> Content: data by industry on number of returns, assets, liabilities, receipts, deductions, net income, taxable income, credits.

Statistics of Income SOI Bulletin. PRINT. WEB. (quarterly) 1981–. U.S. Department of the Treasury. Internal Revenue Service. T 22.35/4: Item 0964-C. ASI 8302-2. GPO. <http://www.irs.ustreas.gov/prod/tax_stats/soi/soi_bul.html>; <http://purl.access.gpo.gov/GPO/LPS3363>.

> Coverage: U.S., states; occasionally world, world regions, country groupings, selected countries.
> Content: earliest published statistics on income tax returns of corporations, partnerships, and sole proprietorships; number of returns, assets, receipts, deductions, net income, tax by broad industry sector; articles on tax return statistics.

Discussion

The Internal Revenue Service publishes statistical reports based on income tax returns. *Statistics of Income: Individual Income Tax Returns* gives statistics on the number of tax returns in each adjusted gross income category as well as various characteristics of these returns. Income groups are analyzed by source of income and by other tax return items, such as deductions and exemptions. Examples of data available include the number of returns taking advantage of the child care credit or the number of returns with adjusted gross income of a million dollars or more that reported receiving alimony. Selected tables can be downloaded from the Internet in Excel format.

Statistics of Income: Corporation Income Tax Returns contains data on returns, balance sheet items, income, and tax items by industry. Examples of statistics available include the total assets of grocery stores or the type of deductions taken by the paper industry. Recent years of this title can be downloaded from the IRS Web site in Excel format, but cannot be viewed directly on the site.

The *Statistics of Income: SOI Bulletin* contains preliminary statistics from the above reports and statistics on areas that are not covered in separate reports. Each issue also contains a "Selected Historical and Other Data" section with tables on income tax returns and related statistics such as income, amount of tax, reported deductions, refunds, and corporation balance sheet data. Sample articles include "Individual Income Tax Rates and Tax Shares, 1996" (Spring 1999), "Federal Estate Tax Returns, 1995–1997" (Summer 1999), and "Private Foundations and Charitable Trusts, 1995" (Winter 1998–1999). Articles from recent issues are available for downloading in Excel format.

LEGAL AND JUDICIAL SOURCES

Checklist

United States Code. Title 26, Internal Revenue Code. PRINT. CD-ROM. WEB. (annual supplements; revised every 6 years) 1926–. U.S. Congress. House. Y 1.2/5:, Y 1.2/5-2: (CD) (Sample citation: 26 *U.S.C.* 2044) (Annotated commercial editions also available) Items 0991-A or -B(CD). GPO. <http://www.access.gpo.gov/congress/cong013.html>; <http://purl.access.gpo.gov/GPO/LPS2873>; <http://uscode.house.gov/uscode.htm>; <http://www4.law.cornell.edu/uscode/>.

    Content: current tax laws, as amended.

Code of Federal Regulations. Title 26, Internal Revenue. PRINT. MF. WEB. (annual) 1938–. U.S. National Archives and Records Administration. Office of the Federal Register. AE 2.106/3: (Sample citation: 26 *CFR* 1.69-9) (*CFR Index and Finding Aids*, AE 2.106/3-2:). (Earlier, GS 4.108:, GS 4.108/4:) Items 0572, 0572-B or -C(MF). GPO. <http://www.access.gpo.gov/nara/cfr/index.html>; <http://purl.access.gpo.gov/GPO/LPS3384>.

    Content: current tax regulations, as amended.

Internal Revenue Bulletin. PRINT. WEB. (weekly) 1922–. U.S. Department of the Treasury. Internal Revenue Service. T 22.23: (Sample citation: 1999-34 I.R.B. 278) Item 0957. GPO. <http://www.irs.ustreas.gov/prod/bus_info/bullet.html>; <http://purl.access.gpo.gov/GPO/LPS1636>.

    Content: official rulings and procedures (revenue rulings and revenue proceedings), treasury decisions, executive orders, tax conventions, legislation, court decisions, and other tax-related items.

Internal Revenue Cumulative Bulletin. PRINT. (semiannual) 1922–. U.S. Department of the Treasury. Internal Revenue Service. T 22.25: (Sample citation: 1991-1 C.B. 286). Item 0960. GPO.

    Content: consolidation of items of a permanent nature from the weekly *Internal Revenue Bulletin*.

Tax Regs in Plain English Web Page. WEB. U.S. Department of the Treasury. Internal Revenue Service. <http://www.irs.ustreas.gov/prod/tax_regs/index.html>.

    Content: tax regulations listing with summaries and full text; laws; link to Title 26 of the *Code of Federal Regulations* on *GPO Access;* link to the *Internal Revenue Bulletin*.

Federal Tax Products. CD-ROM. U.S. Department of the Treasury. Internal Revenue Service. T 22.51/4: Item 0923-B-01. GPO. NTIS.

    Content: most recent year of the *Internal Revenue Bulletin*.

Reports of the United States Tax Court. PRINT. WEB. (semiannual) 1942–. U.S. Tax Court. JU 11.7: (Title varies) (Monthly advance sheets titled *Reports*, JU 11.7/A 2:) (Sample citation: 95 T.C. 1) Item 0742. GPO. <http://www.ustaxcourt.gov/UstcInOp/asp/HistoricOptions.asp>.

    Content: U.S. Tax Court decisions.

T.C. Memo. MF. WEB. (irregular) U.S. Tax Court. JU 11.7/2: Item 0742-B. <http://www.ustaxcourt.gov/UstcInOp/asp/HistoricOptions.asp>.

    Content: individual U.S. Tax Court memorandum decisions.

LEXIS-NEXIS. <http://www.lexis-nexis.com/lncc/>.

    Content: tax laws, regulations, court cases, IRS rulings, and related materials.

LEXIS-NEXIS Academic Universe. <http://www.lexis-nexis.com/cispubs/Catalog/Universe/Academic%20Universe/index.htm>.

    Content: tax laws, regulations, court cases, IRS rulings, and related materials

Westlaw. <http://www.westlaw.com/>.

    Content: tax laws, regulations, court cases, IRS rulings, and related materials.

West's Federal Taxation Library. CD-ROM. St. Paul, MN: West Group.

    Content: tax laws, regulations, court cases, IRS rulings, and related materials.

Discussion

The major elements of the legal and judicial process include tax laws passed by the U.S. Congress, regulations developed by the Internal Revenue Service (IRS) to implement these laws, IRS revenue rulings on specific problems, and court decisions involving disputes between taxpayers and the IRS.

The *United States Code* is a subject arrangement of current laws. It is divided into subject categories called "titles." Title 26 contains the laws relating to taxes and is known as the *Internal Revenue Code*. The IRS regulations interpreting the code are found in the *Code of Federal Regulations*, also in Title 26. Section numbers in the two codes generally correspond. The regulations affecting section 172 in the *United States Code* (26 *USC* 172), for example, can be found in section 1.172 of Title 26 in the *Code of Federal Regulations* (26 *CFR* 1.172).

The *Internal Revenue Bulletin* announces changes in tax laws and regulations (the latter are referred to as Treasury Decisions [T.D.]). It is also the source for revenue rulings and revenue proceedings concerning specific tax matters and procedures not clearly covered in laws and regulations. (See Figure 10.1.) Each issue contains a nu-

Internal Revenue bulletin

Bulletin No. 1999–34
August 23, 1999

HIGHLIGHTS
OF THIS ISSUE
These synopses are intended only as aids to the reader in identifying the subject matter covered. They may not be relied upon as authoritative interpretations.

INCOME TAX

Rev. Rul. 99–33, page 251.
Fringe benefits aircraft valuation formula. For purposes of section 1.61–21(g) of the Income Tax Regulations, relating to the rule for valuing noncommercial flights on employer-provided aircraft, the Standard Industry Fare Level (SIFL), cents-per-mile rates, and terminal charges in effect for the second half of 1999 are set forth.

Rev. Rul. 99–35, page 278.
Mutual life insurance companies; differential earnings rate. The differential earnings rate for 1998 and the recomputed differential earnings rate for 1997 are set forth for use by mutual life insurance companies to compute their income tax liabilities for 1998.

T.D. 8831, page 264.
REG–252487–96, page 303.
Final, temporary, and proposed regulations implementing sections 672(f) and 643(f) of the Code relate to the application of the grantor trust rules to certain trusts established by foreign persons. A public hearing is scheduled for November 2, 1999.

T.D. 8834, page 251.
Temporary regulations are removed and final regulations are added under section 367(e) of the Code relating to the treatment of distributions to foreign persons.

Rev. Proc. 99–32, page 296.
Procedures are provided for the repatriation of cash by a United States taxpayer via an interest-bearing account receivable or payable in an amount corresponding to the amount allocated under section 482 of the Code from, or to, a related person with respect to a controlled transaction. Rev. Procs. 65–17, 65–31, 70–23, 71–35, 72–22, 72–46, 72–48, 72–53, superseded. Rev. Rul. 82–80, superseded.

EMPLOYEE PLANS

Rev. Proc. 99–31, page 280.
This procedure sets forth acceptable correction methods and examples under the Employee Plans Compliance Resolution System that can be used to correct common problems in complying with the rules governing qualified plans. Rev. Proc. 98–22, clarified and supplemented.

Notice 99–39, page 313.
Weighted average interest rate update. The weighted average interest rate for August 1999 and the resulting permissible range of interest rates used to calculate current liability for purposes of the full funding limitation of section 412(c)(7) of the Code are set forth.

EXEMPT ORGANIZATIONS

Announcement 99–80, page 310.
A list is given of organizations now classified as private foundations.

ADMINISTRATIVE

Rev. Proc. 99–33, page 301.
Low-income housing tax credit. This procedure publishes the amounts of unused housing credit carryovers allocated to qualified states under section 42(h)(3)(D) of the Code for calender year 1999.

REG–106527–98, page 304.
Proposed regulations under section 1223 of the Code relate to the sales or exchanges of interests in partnerships, S corporations, and trusts. A public hearing is scheduled for November 18, 1999.

Finding Lists begin on page ii.

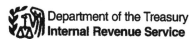 Department of the Treasury
Internal Revenue Service

Figure 10.1: Sample Page from the *Internal Revenue Bulletin*.

merical finding list and a finding list of current action on previously published items that cumulate over six months. The first issue of each month contains a subject index that cumulates over six months. A cumulative subject index covering January through June appears in the first issue of July. An annual subject index and finding lists for January through December appear in the first issue of the following year. The annual listings include some additional materials not found in other issues, including a cumulative list of actions relating to decisions of the Tax Court. The materials published in the *Internal Revenue Bulletin* are eventually collected in the *Cumulative Bulletin* where they are presented primarily in *Internal Revenue Code* section order with indexes and finding lists.

The *Tax Regs in Plain English Web Page* provides a list of tax regulations issued since Aug. 1, 1995, with summaries and links to the full text. Current proposed regulations are also available for comment. This page also provides links to Title 26 (Internal Revenue) of the *Code of Federal Regulations* from the *GPO Access* Web site and to the *Internal Revenue Bulletin*.

The *Federal Tax Products* CD-ROM contains the *Internal Revenue Bulletin* for the most recent year, as well as tax forms and information publications. The CD is issued in two releases each year—an early release with forms approved at that time and a later final release.

There are several federal courts that may handle tax-related matters. Court decisions involve disputes over laws. The only court that deals entirely with tax law is the U.S. Tax Court. This court handles cases involving tax deficiencies assessed by the IRS. Full decisions are published in *Reports of the United States Tax Court*. Memorandum decisions are also published and became available to depositories in 1981 on microfiche. Memorandum cases do not establish new legal principles, but are primarily factual determinations. U.S. district courts and the U.S. Court of Federal Claims handle cases involving claims for refunds. The decisions of these courts are not available through the depository library program. They can be purchased from the West Group. Some recent decisions from these courts are also available on the Internet. See Chapter 46, Judicial Reports, for more information on these courts.

LEXIS-NEXIS and *Westlaw* provide fee-based online access to the full texts of laws and court cases as well as extensive collections of analytical material from such sources as the Bureau of National Affairs, CCH, Research Institute of America, and Tax Analysts. Both have libraries specifically for tax law. On *LEXIS* the tax materials are in the FEDTAX library. This library contains the *Internal Revenue Code*, tax regulations, congressional reports, the *Internal Revenue Bulletin* and *Cumulative Bulletin*, Tax Court decisions, other federal court decisions, and other IRS materials. The *Westlaw* "Taxation Library" contains similar materials. West also offers a CD-ROM. *LEXIS-NEXIS Academic Universe* also contains a Tax Law area

with a smaller selection of materials. It includes federal court cases, regulations, the *Internal Revenue Bulletin*, other IRS rulings and materials, law journals, and a selection of materials from the Research Institute of America and Tax Analysts.

Some libraries may purchase loose-leaf tax services or electronic tax products from individual publishers that include tax laws, regulations, and information on tax-related court decisions all in one place. These may be more convenient to use and are sometimes more current than some of the government publications discussed above. Examples of companies providing such services are CCH and Research Institute of America (RIA).

CONGRESSIONAL SOURCES
Checklist

Hearings, Prints, and Miscellaneous Publications. PRINT. MF. (irregular) U.S. Congress. Senate. Committee on Finance. Y 4.F 49: Items 1038-A or -B(MF). GPO. Limited publications: <http://www.senate.gov/~finance/>; <http://www.access.gpo.gov/congress/senate/senate10.html>.

> Content: hearings and research reports on tax legislation and issues.

Hearings, Prints, and Miscellaneous Publications. PRINT. MF. (irregular) U.S. Congress. Joint Committee on Taxation. Y 4.T 19/4: Items 1002-A or -B(MF). GPO. Limited publications: <http://www.house.gov/jct/>; <http://www.access.gpo.gov/congress/joint/hjoint01cp.html>.

> Content: hearings and research reports on tax legislation and issues.

Hearings, Prints, and Miscellaneous Publications. PRINT. MF. (irregular) U.S. Congress. House. Committee on Ways and Means. Y 4.W 36: Items 1028-A or -B(MF). GPO. Limited publications: <http://www.house.gov/ways_means/>; <http://www.access.gpo.gov/congress/house/house19.html>.

> Content: hearings and research reports on tax legislation and issues.

Discussion

These congressional committees publish hearings and analyses on tax legislation and issues. Examples of recent titles from these committees include *Complexity of the Individual Income Tax* (Y 4.F 49:S.HRG.106-165), *The Impact on Individuals and Families of Replacing the Federal Income Tax* (Y 4.W 36:105-15), *Oversight of Tax Law Related to Health Insurance* (Y 4.W 36:105-54), and *General Explanation of Tax Legislation Enacted in 1998* (Y 4.T 19/4:L 52/2/998). For complete listings of congressional publications on specific topics, consult the *Monthly Catalog* and *CIS/Index* listed in the "Indexes" section below. A limited number of congressional committee publications are available on the Internet. Commercial online services such as *Congressional Universe* and LEXIS-NEXIS provide testimony transcripts.

INDEXES
Checklist

Catalog of United States Government Publications (MOCAT). WEB. 1994–. U.S. Government Printing Office. Superintendent of Documents. <http://www.gpo.gov/catalog>; <http://www.access.gpo.gov/su_docs/locators/cgp/index.html>; <http://purl.access.gpo.gov/GPO/LPS844>.

Monthly Catalog of United States Government Publications. CD-ROM. 1996–. U.S. Government Printing Office. Superintendent of Documents. GP 3.8/7: Item 0557-C. GPO.

Monthly Catalog of United States Government Publications (Condensed version). PRINT. (monthly) 1996–. U.S. Government Printing Office. Superintendent of Documents. GP 3.8/8: (Earlier full version, GP 3.8:, 1895–1995). Item 0557-D. GPO.

CIS/Index. PRINT. (monthly) 1970–. Bethesda, MD: Congressional Information Service.

Congressional Universe. WEB. Bethesda, MD: Congressional Information Service.

American Statistics Index (ASI). PRINT. (monthly) 1973–. Bethesda, MD: Congressional Information Service.

Statistical Universe. WEB. Bethesda, MD: Congressional Information Service.

Discussion

The *Monthly Catalog* provides comprehensive access to government publications. For tax information, look in the subject index under headings beginning with "Tax" or "Taxation" and under "Income Tax." The complete version of the *Monthly Catalog* is available on the Web and CD-ROM. Commercial online and CD-ROM versions of the *Monthly Catalog* are also available.

CIS indexes congressional hearings and research reports relating to taxes under headings beginning with "Tax," "Taxation," "Income taxes," and specific types of taxes.

Statistical materials can be located through *American Statistics Index (ASI)*. Look under "Income taxes," headings beginning with "Tax," and specific types of taxes. *Statistical Universe* includes a Web version of *ASI*.

For more information on these indexes, see Chapter 3, "The Basics of Searching."

RELATED MATERIAL
Within this Work

Chapter 46 Judicial Reports

GPO Subject Bibliographies. PRINT. WEB. GP 3.22/2:

<http://bookstore.gpo.gov/sb/about.html>

No. 66   "Internal Revenue Cumulative Bulletins"

No. 67   "Tax Court Reports"

No. 195 "Taxes"

CHAPTER 11
Travel Information

The majority of government travel information is produced by the Interior Department, as National Park System guides, both in electronic and print format. The National Park System includes national parks, monuments, preserves, lakeshores, seashores, rivers, wild and scenic riverways, scenic trails, historic sites, historical parks, memorials, recreation areas, and parkways. Several other agencies publish travel-related guides, and a sampling of these is included. General information for international travelers, particularly from the Department of State, is also included within this chapter. Additional information about specific countries may also be found in Chapter 5, "Foreign Countries."

SEARCH STRATEGY

This chapter shows a subject search strategy. The steps to follow are
1. Check major guides, series, and Web sites listed in this chapter;
2. Scan the "Related Material" section, especially the *GPO Subject Bibliographies*; and
3. Search the *Monthly Catalog* by subject for additional materials.

NATIONAL PARK SYSTEM
Checklist

Visit Your Parks. WEB. U.S. Department of the Interior. National Park Service. <http://www.nps.gov/parks.html>.
　　Content: general information about parks and park fees; links to park maps; search features to locate parks.

National Park Service Cartographic Resources Home Page. WEB. U.S. Department of the Interior. National Park Service. <http://www.nps.gov/carto/>.
　　Content: digital versions of the maps used in the national park system brochures.

Maps of United States National Parks and Monuments. WEB. University of Texas at Austin. Perry-Castañeda Library Map Collection. <http://www.lib.utexas.edu/Libs/PCL/Map_collection/National_parks/National_parks.html>.
　　Content: digital versions of maps of national parks and monuments.

National Park Reservation Service. WEB. Biospherics Inc. <http://reservations.nps.gov/>.
　　Content: online reservation system for National Park Service campgrounds and tours.

Wild & Scenic Rivers. WEB. U.S. Department of the Interior. National Park Service. <http://www.nps.gov/rivers/>.
　　Content: listing of wild and scenic rivers; background information and description of wild and scenic rivers.

National Park System: Map and Guide. PRINT. WEB. (1999) U.S. Department of the Interior. National Park Service. I 29.9/2:P 21/2/999. Item 0648-A. GPO. <http://www.nps.gov/carto/NPSMAP.html>.
　　Content: map of the U.S. showing the location of areas in the National Park System, with the reverse side providing a state-by-state listing of areas, addresses, and activities.

The National Parks: Index [year]. PRINT. (biennial) U.S. Department of the Interior. National Park Service. Office of Public Affairs and the Division of Publications. I 29.103: Item 0648-G. GPO.
　　Content: state-by-state listing and description of park service areas.

National Parks, Information Circulars. PRINT. (irregular) U.S. Department of the Interior. National Park Service. I 29.6: Item 0651.
　　Content: pamphlets describing individual national parks.

National Seashores, Information Circulars. PRINT. (irregular) U.S. Department of the Interior. National Park Service. I 29.6/2: Item 0651-B.
　　Content: pamphlets describing individual national seashores.

National Lakeshores, Information Circulars. PRINT. (irregular) U.S. Department of the Interior. National Park Service. I 29.6/3: Item 0651-B-01.
　　Content: pamphlets describing individual national lakeshores.

National Rivers, Information Circulars. PRINT. (irregular) U.S. Department of the Interior. National Park Service. I 29.6/4: Item 0651-B-02.

Content: pamphlets describing individual national rivers.

National Scenic Trails, Information Circulars. PRINT. (irregular) U.S. Department of the Interior. National Park Service. I 29.6/5: Item 0651-B-03.

Content: pamphlets describing individual national scenic trails.

National Historic Site, Information Circulars. PRINT. (irregular) U.S. Department of the Interior. National Park Service. I 29.6/6: Item 0651-B-04.

Content: pamphlets describing individual national historic sites.

National Monuments and Military Parks, Information Circulars. PRINT. (irregular) U.S. Department of the Interior. National Park Service. I 29.21: Item 0650.

Content: pamphlets describing individual national monuments and military parks.

National Recreational Areas, Information Circulars. PRINT. (irregular) U.S. Department of the Interior. National Park Service. I 29.39: Item 0654.

Content: pamphlets describing individual national recreational areas.

National Historical Parks, Information Circulars. PRINT. (irregular) U.S. Department of the Interior. National Park Service. I 29.88/6: Item 0651.

Content: pamphlets describing individual national historical parks.

National Park Service Handbooks. PRINT. (irregular) U.S. Department of the Interior. National Park Service. I 29.9/5: Item 0649. GPO.

Content: detailed, highly illustrated guides to areas within the National Park system.

Discussion

Information about the National Park system in general, and individual areas of the system in particular, is now available on the Web. *Visit Your Parks* is the National Park Service gateway to much of this information. The site includes information about park fees in general, including lists of park entrance and recreational use fees and infor-

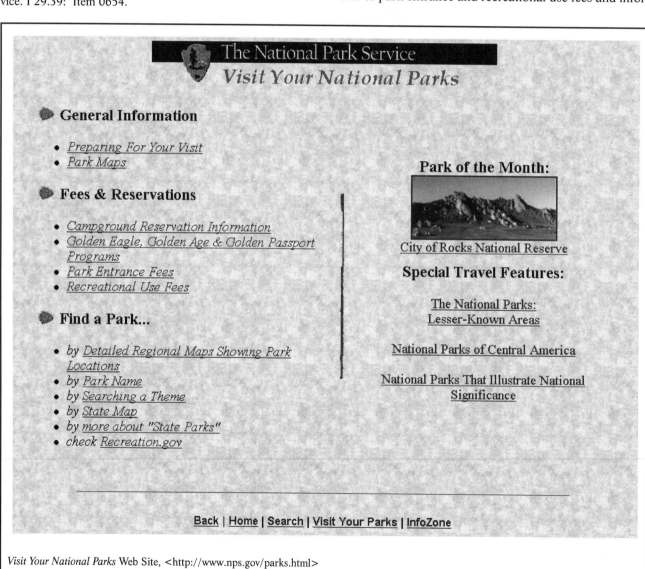

Visit Your National Parks Web Site, <http://www.nps.gov/parks.html>

Figure 11.1: *Visit Your Parks* Web Site.

mation about special fee programs such as the Golden Eagle, Golden Age, and Golden Access Passport programs. The site also includes a link to the National Park Service campground online reservation system described later in this section.

The "Find A Park" section of the site allows the user to search by name, by theme, and by clicking on state maps. Once an entry for a park is found, it includes basic information about the National Park area, links to any individual home pages for the area, and other related links of interest.

The *National Park Service Cartographic Resources Home Page* includes digital versions of maps of areas of the National Park System used in the brochures describing the areas. These maps are made available in a variety of formats, and are in the public domain. Between *Visit Your Parks* and the *National Park Service Cartographic Home Page,* very complete information about the National Park System can be obtained. The Perry-Castañeda Library Map Collection has also made many national park and monument maps available to the public in digital formats.

The *National Park Reservation Service* provides an online service for making reservations for National Park Service campgrounds and tours. A commercial firm, Biospherics, Inc., runs the service itself. The site also includes descriptive information about the campgrounds and tours.

The *Wild & Scenic Rivers* Web site gives background information and describes the legislation that led to the creation of the wild and scenic rivers system. A state-by-state listing gives brief information about each wild and scenic river.

The *National Park System: Map and Guide* is an attractive folder showing the location of the different areas of the National Park System. One side shows a large map of the United States with areas of the National Park System pinpointed. The reverse side has a state-by-state listing of the areas, their addresses, and the services available in each area. A digital version of the *Map and Guide* is also available. New versions are periodically issued, and the *Map and Guide* is kept up-to-date. *The National Park System: Map and Guide* is particularly helpful for planning trips and locating National Park System areas on travel routes.

National Parks: Index [year] includes some general information, along with a brief description and the address of each area. Included in each annotation is the date of establishment and total acreage of the area.

The *Information Circulars* series listed in this section consist of print pamphlets describing individual areas of the National Park System. The format of these colorful guides varies, but they often include maps and illustrations. They serve as basic introductions to the area that they describe. In most cases, these are the pamphlets you would receive if you visited one of these areas in person.

Although they are available for only a limited number of areas, the *National Park Service Handbooks* contain well-researched, in-depth guides, suitable for the traveler wanting to know more about an area.

ADDITIONAL TRAVEL GUIDES
Checklist

Recreation.Gov. WEB. U.S. Department of the Interior. National Park Service; U.S. Department of the Army. Army Corps of Engineers; U.S. Department of the Interior. Bureau of Land Management; U.S. Tennessee Valley Authority; U.S. Department of Agriculture. Fish and Wildlife Service; U.S. Department of the Interior. Bureau of Reclamation.; U.S. Department of Transportation. Federal Highway Administration. <http://www.recreation.gov/>.
> Content: information about federal recreation areas.

National Forests. WEB. U.S. Department of Agriculture. Forest Service. <http://www.fs.fed.us/links/forests.shtml>.
> Content: directory of National forests and their Web sites; information about National Forests.

Guide to Your National Forests and Other Lands Administered by the Forest Service. PRINT. (1996) U.S. Department of Agriculture. Forest Service. A 13.36/2:N 21/21/996. Item 0086-C.
> Content: map of the United States giving the location of National Forests; listing of National Forests by state.

Information Pamphlets Relating to National Forests. PRINT. (irregular) U.S. Department of Agriculture. Forest Service. A 13.13: Item 0085.
> Content: pamphlets describing individual national forests.

Welcome to Your National Grasslands. WEB. U.S. Department of Agriculture. Forest Service. <http://www.fs.fed.us/grasslands/>.
> Content: descriptions and information about National Grasslands.

National Wildlife Refuge System. WEB. U.S. Department of the Interior. Fish and Wildlife Service. <http://bluegoose.arw.r9.fws.gov/>.
> Content: information about Wildlife Refuges; access to searchable databases on Wildlife Refuges and Endangered Species.

National Wildlife Refuges. PRINT. (1996) U.S. Department of the Interior. Fish and Wildlife Service. I 49.44/2:V 82/996. Item 0612-C.
> Content: map and guide to National Wildlife Refuges.

National Wildlife Refuges. PRINT. (irregular) U.S. Department of the Interior. Fish and Wildlife Service. I 49.44/2: Item 0612-C.
> Content: pamphlets describing wildlife refuges.

National Fish Hatchery. PRINT. (irregular) U.S. Department of the Interior. Fish and Wildlife Service. I 49.86: Item 0610-C.
> Content: pamphlets describing individual hatcheries.

U.S. Army Corps of Engineers Recreation Services. WEB. U.S. Department of Defense. Army Corps of Engineers. <http://www.usace.army.mil/recreation/>.
> Content: brochures on recreation sites; online campsite reservations.

National Recreation Reservation Service. WEB. National Recreation Reservation Service. <http://www.reserveusa.com/>.
> Content: reservation service for U.S. Army Corps of Engineers and U.S. Forest Service administered campgrounds, cabins, and wilderness camping.

General Publications. PRINT. (irregular) U.S. Department of Defense. Army Corps of Engineers. D 103.2: Item 0337.
> Content: Corps of Engineers projects.

Beyond the National Parks: A Recreation Guide to Public Lands in the West. PRINT. (1998) Mary E. Tisdale. Washington, DC: Smithsonian Press.
> Content: highly illustrated travel guide to BLM Public Lands.

Discussion

The *Recreation.Gov* site is a cooperative effort among several different governmental agencies to provide information on recreational activities in public lands. A highly flexible search interface allows the user to limit the search by state or groups of states. The user can further limit the search by over 20 activities or uses, such as "AutoTouring," "Hiking," or "Picnic Areas." The entries retrieved give a short description of the area, list the recreational features of the area, give addresses and contact information, and provide links to any related Web sites.

The *National Forests* Web site allows you to search for National Forests by an interactive map, by name, and by state. Information about each National Forest is either provided, or the link may go to an individual Web site for the National Forest. A listing of National Forest Web sites by region is also included.

The *Guide to Your National Forests and Other Lands Administered by the Forest Service* is a folder with a map of the United States that identifies National Forests. The brochure also provides the addresses and telephone numbers of national and regional Forest Service offices. The *Information Pamphlets Relating to National Forests* are small brochures describing individual national forests, similar to the National Park System *Information Circulars* folders described earlier.

The *Welcome to Your National Grasslands* Web site provides a directory of the 20 grasslands administered by the Forest Service. Contact information and links to individual Web sites for the national grasslands are included at the site.

The *National Wildlife Refuge System Web* site provides general information about National Wildlife Refuges, as well as linking to searchable databases of information about national wildlife refuges. The "National Wildlife Refuge System Profiles Database" allows the user to search by a variety of criteria, including specific recreational opportunities. The profiles in the database include extensive information on each refuge, and include links for further information. The "National Wildlife Refuge System Endangered Species Database" allows searching by species or by unit. Other searchable databases include a database

to locate addresses of National Wildlife Refuges and a "Lands Database" that provides information on the acreage of national wildlife refuges.

National Wildlife Refuges is published as a folder with a map of the United States. The map designates wildlife refuges that provide visitor opportunities. A chart on the reverse indicates the location of the refuges and their facilities and programs.

Individual print information brochures are also published for wildlife refuges. Similar brochures are published for national fish hatcheries.

The *U.S. Army Corps of Engineers Recreation Services* Web site provides access to descriptions of the recreational areas at lakes and reservoirs administered by the Corps of Engineers. A link to the online reservation system, the *National Recreation Reservation Service,* for these sites is included. *The National Recreation Reservation Service* also provides reservations for the U.S. Forest Service. The *General Publications* series of the Army Corps of Engineers includes small pamphlets describing the Corps' recreational areas.

Beyond the National Parks: A Recreation Guide to Public Lands in the West, was produced under the direction of the Bureau of Land Management and published by Smithsonian Institution Press. It is a highly illustrated travel guide to the Public Lands and the unique features of those lands.

TRAVEL TO OTHER COUNTRIES
Checklist

Travel Publications. WEB. U.S. Department of State. Bureau of Consular Affairs. <http://travel.state.gov/travel_pubs.html>.
> Content: listing of publications available in full text on the Web.

Tips for Travelers to [country]. PRINT. WEB. (irregular) U.S. Department of State. Bureau of Consular Affairs. S 1.2: (Included in the *General Publications* series of the Department of State.) Item 0876. GPO.
> Content: series of individual country travel guides.
> *Tips for Travelers to Canada.* S 1.2:C 16/2. <http://travel.state.gov/tips_canada.html>.
> *Tips for Travelers to the Caribbean.* S 1.2:C 19/2/993. <http://travel.state.gov/tips_caribbean.html>.
> *Tips for Travelers to Central and South America.* S 1.2:SO 8/14. <http://travel.state.gov/tips_samerica.html>.
> *Tips for Travelers to Mexico.* S 1.2:M 57/7/995. <http://travel.state.gov/tips_mexico.html>.
> *Tips for Travelers to the Middle East and North Africa.* S 1.2:M 58/4/994. <http://travel.state.gov/tips_mideast&nafrica.html>.
> *Tips for Travelers to the People's Republic of China.* S 1.2:T 69/4/995. <http://travel.state.gov/tips_china.html>.
> *Tips for Travelers to Russia and the Newly Independent States.* S 1.2:T 69/7/995. <http://travel.state.gov/tips_russia.html>.
> *Tips for Travelers to South Asia.* S 1.2:SO 8/13/995. <http://travel.state.gov/tips_sasia.html>.

Tips for Travelers to Sub-Saharan Africa. S 1.2:AF 8/6/994. <http://travel.state.gov/tips_sub-saharanafica.html>.

Your Trip Abroad. PRINT. WEB. (1998) U.S. Department of State. Bureau of Consular Affairs. S 1.2:T 73/2/998. Item 0876. GPO. <http://travel.state.gov/yourtripabroad.html>.
Content: basic State Department travel requirements; information for international travelers.

Travel Tips for Older Americans. PRINT. WEB. (1996) U.S. Department of State. Bureau of Consular Affairs. S 1.2:T 9/3/996. Item 0876. <http://travel.state.gov/olderamericans.html>.
Content: basic international travel information for older U.S. citizens.

A Safe Trip Abroad. PRINT. WEB. (1996) U.S. Department of State. Bureau of Consular Affairs. S 1.2:T 73/996. Item 0876.
Content: discussion of safety problems when traveling in other countries.

Travel Warning on Drugs Abroad—Things You Should Know Before You Go Abroad. WEB. (2000) U.S. Department of State. Bureau of Consular Affairs. <http://travel.state.gov/drug_warning.html>; <http://purl.access.gpo.gov/GPO/LPS689>.
Content: information on penalties for drug use and possession in other countries; consular officer's role in helping U.S. citizens.

Medical Information for Americans Traveling Abroad. WEB. U.S. Department of State. Bureau of Consular Affairs. S 1.2:96038595. Item 0876. <http://travel.state.gov/medical.html>.
Content: information about medical coverage abroad; listing of private organizations providing medical insurance, medical information, or medical evacuation abroad.

Foreign Entry Requirements. PRINT. WEB. (1999) U.S. Department of State. Bureau of Consular Affairs. S 1.2:F 76E/999. Item 0876. <http://travel.state.gov/foreignentryreqs.html>.
Content: country-by-country listing of entry requirements.

Passport Services and Information. WEB. U.S. Department of State. <http://travel.state.gov/passport_services.html>.
Content: information about passports; passport application forms.

Applying for Your U.S. Passport the Easy Way. WEB. (1998?) U.S. Department of State. Bureau of Consular Affairs. S 1.2:98020909. Item 0876. <http://travel.state.gov/passport_easy.html>; <http://purl.access.gpo.gov/GPO/LPS991>.
Content: basic passport application information.

Travel Warnings. WEB. U.S. Department of State. Bureau of Consular Affairs. <http://travel.state.gov/travel_warnings.html>.
Content: warnings issued when for safety reasons U.S. citizens are advised to avoid visiting a country.

Consular Information Sheets. WEB. U.S. Department of State. Bureau of Consular Affairs. <http://travel.state.gov/travel_warnings.html>.
Content: individual country information sheets issued by the U.S. Embassy or Consulate in each country.

Traveler Information. WEB. U.S. Department of the Treasury. U.S. Customs Service. <http://www.customs.gov/travel/travel.htm>.

Content: publications and information about Customs and traveling in other countries.

Know Before You Go: Customs Regulations for U.S. Residents. PRINT. WEB. (2000) U.S. Department of the Treasury. U.S. Customs Service. T 17.2:C 96/3/2000. Item 0950. <http://www.customs.gov/travel/travel.htm>.
Content: basic information on customs for U.S. residents.

CDC Traveler's Health. WEB. U.S. Department of Health and Human Services. Centers for Disease Control and Prevention. National Center for Infectious Disease. Division of Quarantine. <http://www.cdc.gov/travel/>.
Content: health information and information about vaccinations of interest to travelers.

Health Information for International Travel. PRINT. WEB. (biennial) U.S. Department of Health and Human Services. Public Health Service. Centers for Disease Control and Prevention. National Center for Infectious Diseases. Division of Quarantine. HE 20.7818: Item 0504-K-03. GPO. <http://www.cdc.gov/travel/reference.htm>.
Content: vaccination information; general health-related information for international travelers.

Summary of Health Information for International Travel. PRINT. WEB. (biweekly) U.S. Department of Health and Human Services. Public Health Service. Centers for Disease Control and Prevention. National Center for Infectious Diseases. Division of Quarantine. HE 20.7818/2: Item 0504-K-04. <http://www.cdc.gov/travel/blusheet.htm>; <http://purl.access.gpo.gov/GPO/LPS1611>.
Content: updated listing of countries with cholera, yellow fever, and plague outbreaks.

Health Information for Travelers to [region]. WEB. U.S. Department of Health and Human Services. Centers for Disease Control and Prevention. National Center for Infectious Diseases. Division of Quarantine. <http://www.cdc.gov/travel/>.
Content: individual guides to health risks associated with a world region.

Discussion

The Department of State publishes a number of publications of interest to international travelers. Its *Travel Publications* Web page provides links to a number of publications in full-text electronic formats (primarily HTML), and it is a first place to check for information. Many of the publications discussed in this section are linked from this Web page.

Tips for Travelers to [country] is a series of small pamphlets giving information on such topics as entry and exit requirements; safety tips and information on crime; travel advisories; advice for those with dual nationality; avoiding legal problems; and health and medical care information. The titles in this series give a good review of basic information written from a State Department viewpoint.

The State Department also issues several other small pamphlets dealing with travel to other countries that are periodically revised and updated. The latest editions of some of these publications are listed here. *Your Trip Abroad* includes information on items (such as passports, visa, immunizations, and health insurance) to check before leaving the country. It also gives tips on how to deal with different situations encountered in other countries. *Travel Tips for Older Americans* covers some of this same type of information, geared towards the older traveler. *A Safe Trip Abroad* concentrates on ways to avoid dangerous situations and safety tips for dealing with various situations, such as using public transportation, travel to high-risk areas, and hijacking/hostage situations. *Travel Warning on Drugs Abroad—Things You Should Know Before You Go Abroad* is a blunt document that details the sometimes harsh penalties that other countries impose on drug use and trafficking. *Medical Information for Americans Traveling Abroad* provides a summary of basic information, along with a directory of air ambulance/medical evacuation companies, travel insurance companies, and executive medical services. *Foreign Entry Requirements* is an annual summary of the items required by each country for entrance by U.S. citizens (passports; visas; immunizations; proof of sufficient funds; onward/return tickets; AIDS/HIV testing; etc.).

Comprehensive information about passports is included on the Department of State's *Passport Services and Information* page. It details how to apply for passports and passport renewals, how to replace lost or stolen passports, and how to get a passport in a hurry. It also provides information on passport fees and passport processing times, and directions on where to apply for passports. Downloadable copies of passport application fees are also included at the site. A publication summarizing passport application information titled *Applying for Your U.S. Passport the Easy Way*, is available from this site.

The Department of State also issues *Travel Warnings*, which inform U.S. citizens when the Department of State has deemed a country unsafe to visit, and these are now available on the Web. At the same Web site are the *Consular Information Sheets*, which are produced by the consular offices in each country. They provide information on immigration practices, health conditions, minor political disturbances, unusual currency and entry regulations, crime and security information, and drug penalties in each country. They provide a concise overview of some of the most important information about entering and traveling in another country.

The U.S. Customs Bureau also provides information for travelers on customs information and the procedures for reporting to customs. Their *Traveler Information* Web site links to publications and Web pages discussing all aspects of custom procedures, rules, and regulations. *Know Before You Go: Customs Hints for Returning Residents* is a helpful brochure available from the *Traveler Information* Web site and in a print format. It provides the instructions U.S. citizens need to follow concerning customs rules and regulations when returning to the U.S. It also discusses exemptions, gifts, rates of duty, and prohibited and restricted articles.

The Centers for Disease Control and Prevention provide links to their publications and other information of interest to international travelers through their *CDC Traveler's Health* site. *Health Information for International Travel* is a comprehensive guide to the vaccination requirements of different countries. A country-by-country listing gives information on the vaccinations required. Information on yellow fever vaccination requirements and malaria risk is also given. U.S. Public Health Service recommendations for vaccinations and disease prevention are also discussed. Another section of the report discusses the health risks present in different regions of the world. The biweekly *Summary of Health Information for International Travel* lists cholera-infected, yellow fever–infected, and plague-infected countries. The *Health Information for Travelers to [region]* series includes individual guides for seventeen regions of the world. Each guide discusses diseases prominent in the region and vaccinations needed, along with tips for remaining healthy.

INDEXES
Checklist

Catalog of United States Government Publications (MOCAT). WEB. 1994–. U.S. Government Printing Office. Superintendent of Documents. <http://www.gpo.gov/catalog>; <http://www.access.gpo.gov/su_docs/locators/cgp/index.html>; <http://purl.access.gpo.gov/GPO/LPS844>.

Monthly Catalog of United States Government Publications. CD-ROM. 1996–. U.S. Government Printing Office. Superintendent of Documents. GP 3.8/7: Item 0557-C. GPO.

Monthly Catalog of United States Government Publications (Condensed version). PRINT. (monthly) 1996–. U.S. Government Printing Office. Superintendent of Documents. GP 3.8/8: (Earlier full version, GP 3.8:, 1895–1995). Item 0557-D. GPO.

Discussion

The *Monthly Catalog* is the most comprehensive index for government publications. For publications with travel information, search under the following subjects: "Travel" or "Travelers," "National Parks and Reserves," "Forest Reserves," and the names of individual areas, places, or locations. The complete version of the *Monthly Catalog* is available on the Web and CD-ROM. Commercial online and CD-ROM versions of the *Monthly Catalog* are also available. For more information on the *Monthly Catalog*, see Chapter 3, "The Basics of Searching."

RELATED MATERIAL
Within this Work

Chapter 5   Foreign Countries

GPO Subject Bibliographies. **PRINT. WEB. GP 3.22/2:**

<http://bookstore.gpo.gov/sb/about.html>

No. 16   "National Park Service Handbooks"

No. 17   "Recreation"

No. 140   "Buildings, Landmarks, and Historical Sites"

No. 302   "Travel and Tourism"

CHAPTER 12
Audiovisual Information

Audiovisual materials have generally been excluded from the depository library program. Depository libraries do receive many CD-ROMs, posters, and a small number of kits and videotapes. Some attempt has been made to centralize government-produced audiovisual materials through the National Audiovisual Center, but agencies still handle some of their own materials. Materials must be obtained directly from the National Audiovisual Center or the individual agencies in accordance with each agency's procedures.

SEARCH STRATEGY

This chapter shows a subject search strategy. The steps to follow are
1. Consult the National Audiovisual Center Web site;
2. Look for individual agency information using the sources in the sections on "Agency Information Sources," "National Library Service for the Blind and Physically Handicapped Sources," and "National Archives and Records Administration Sources";
3. Consider the "Related Material" section; and
4. Search the indexes for additional catalogs, posters, and related materials.

NATIONAL AUDIOVISUAL CENTER SOURCES
Checklist

National Audiovisual Center Web Page. WEB. U.S. Department of Commerce. National Technical Information Service. National Audiovisual Center. <http://www.ntis.gov/nac/index.html>.
> Coverage: database of federally produced audiovisual materials; selected subject catalogs; ordering information.

Discussion
The National Audiovisual Center is a central distribution source for government-produced audiovisual materials. Its Web site provides keyword searching of a database of over 9,000 audiovisual and media productions. Types of media represented include films, videocassettes, filmstrips, slide sets, and multimedia kits. Users may also browse by broad subject categories such as business, environment, and health. PDF versions of popular catalogs on occupational safety and health training, foreign language training, and law enforcement training are also available. The center is the official distributor for foreign language training programs developed by the Foreign Service Institute and the Defense Language Institute. These courses are the same ones used to train diplomatic and military personnel.

AGENCY INFORMATION SOURCES
Checklist

United States Government Manual. PRINT. WEB. (annual) 1935–. U.S. National Archives and Records Administration. Office of the Federal Register. AE 2.108/2: (Earlier, GS 4.109:) Item 0577. GPO. <http://www.access.gpo.gov/nara/nara001.html>; <http://purl.access.gpo.gov/GPO/LPS2410>.
> Content: sources of information on federal government agencies, including availability of films.

The Federal Web Locator. WEB. The Center for Information Law and Policy. Illinois Institute of Technology's Chicago-Kent College of Law. <http://www.infoctr.edu/fwl/>.
> Content: list of federal government agency Web sites.

U.S. Federal Government Agencies Directory. WEB. (Also titled: *Federal Agency Internet Sites.*) U.S. Government Printing Office. Superintendent of Documents and Louisiana State University Libraries. <http://www.access.gpo.gov/su_docs/locators/agency/index.html>; <http://purl.access.gpo.gov/GPO/LPS849>.
> Content: list of federal government agency Web sites.

List of Classes of United States Government Publications Available for Selection by Depository Libraries. PRINT. WEB. (semi-annual) U.S. Government Printing Office. Superintendent of Documents. Library Programs Service. Library Division. Depository Administration Branch. GP 3.24: Item 0556-C. <http://www.du.edu/~ttyler/locintro.htm#gtr00>; <http://www.access.gpo.gov/su_docs/fdlp/pubs/loc/index.html>; <http://fedbbs.access.gpo.gov/libs/CLASS.htm>; <http://purl.access.gpo.gov/GPO/LPS1480>.

> Content: list by agency of series available to depository libraries, such as poster series.

Documents Data Miner. WEB. Wichita State University. <http://govdoc.wichita.edu/ddm/GdocFrames.asp>.

> Content: collection management tool for depository libraries; includes a searchable version of the *List of Classes*.

Discussion

Although many agency films are available through the National Audiovisual Center, additional materials may be available from some individual agencies. The *United States Government Manual* contains a basic description of each federal government agency. At the end of each major agency chapter is a section on "Sources of Information." This section sometimes contains a category for films or audiovisuals. A short paragraph describes the types of films available from the agency. A general information address, usually a public affairs office, is always listed at the end of the section. In some cases, a specific address for films may be provided.

Many individual government agency Web sites include images, graphics, sound clips, and videos. Two Web sites that can be used to identify agency Web sites are *The Federal Web Locator* and the *U.S. Federal Government Agencies Directory*. Both offer searchable and browsable lists of federal government agency Web sites.

Occasionally, catalogs of audiovisual materials are issued by individual agencies. Some of these catalogs list government-produced programs, while others list programs available from many different sources. The number of such publications distributed to depository libraries has decreased in recent years. To identify such publications consult the indexes listed in the "Index" section at the end of this chapter.

Agencies also occasionally issue posters, which may be distributed to depository libraries. Some posters are also available on agency Web sites. The *List of Classes of United States Government Publications Available for Selection by Depository Libraries* can be used to determine whether a poster series is available from a particular agency. Some poster series may contain only one or two items. Depository libraries may receive several posters from an agency during a particular time period, then none for many years. Posters can also be identified by searching the indexes listed in the "Index" section at the end of this chapter.

Poster series may contain a variety of materials in different sizes. These include signs and posters directed toward agency employees relating to internal procedures or promoting desirable employee behavior. Other posters are designed for the public and reflect the agency's mission. Such posters encourage participation in agency programs or promote health and environmental responsibility. Posters also commemorate significant events and special occasions. Some posters and signs are strictly utilitarian; others are art posters. Many of the posters available relate to the environment, health and safety, natural resources, space, and the armed forces.

NATIONAL LIBRARY SERVICE FOR THE BLIND AND PHYSICALLY HANDICAPPED SOURCES

Checklist

National Library Service for the Blind and Physically Handicapped Web Site. WEB. Library of Congress. National Library Service for the Blind and Physically Handicapped. <http://lcweb.loc.gov/nls/>.

> Content: eligibility and program information; Web-BLND online catalog of recorded and braille books; other catalogs.

CD BLND. CD-ROM. (quarterly) Library of Congress. National Library Service for the Blind and Physically Handicapped. LC 19.24: Item 0806-A-21.

> Content: catalog of recorded and braille books.

Cassette Books. PRINT. WEB. (annual) Library of Congress. National Library Service for the Blind and Physically Handicapped. LC 19.10/3: Item 0806-A-09. <http://www.loc.gov/nls/catalogs/catalogs.html>.

> Content: cassette books produced during the year for loan to individuals with reading problems due to visual or physical limitations.

For Younger Readers: Braille and Talking Books. PRINT. WEB. (biennial) Library of Congress. National Library Service for the Blind and Physically Handicapped. LC 19.11/2: Item 0806-A-13. <http://www.loc.gov/nls/catalogs/catalogs.html>.

> Content: cassette and braille books produced during the two year period; available on loan to people with visual or physical limitations.

Magazines in Special Media. PRINT. (biennial) Library of Congress. National Library Service for the Blind and Physically Handicapped. LC 19.11/2-2: Item 0806-A-17.

> Content: magazine subscriptions available in braille, cassette, large type, and other formats; available to people with visual or physical limitations either through the National Library Service program or through other sources.

Talking Book Topics. PRINT. WEB. (bimonthly) 1935–. Library of Congress. National Library Service for the Blind and Physically Handicapped. LC 19.10: (Title varies). Item 0806-A-02. <http://www.loc.gov/nls/tbt/tbt.html>; <http://purl.access.gpo.gov/GPO/LPS1694>.

> Content: recent books and magazines made available on cassette or disc; related news items.

Discussion

The National Library Service for the Blind and Physically Handicapped provides materials for loan to qualified persons through a network of cooperating libraries. Books and magazines are provided in various formats, including cassettes and braille. The *National Library Service for the Blind and Physically Handicapped Web Site* describes the program and how to participate. The Web-BLND online catalog lists the resources available. Searching can be done by author, title, subject, book number, Dewey number, and keyword. Searches may be limited by various characteristics including format, holding code, and intellectual level. A CD-ROM version, *CD BLND*, is also available. The National Library Service also produces book catalogs. Some of the more general catalogs are listed above. These list recent materials available through the network.

Cassette Books is arranged by subject category and contains fiction and nonfiction books that have been produced during the year. A description is given for each title. Title and author indexes are included. *For Younger Readers: Braille and Talking Books* is a similar catalog for children and young adults. *Magazines in Special Media* lists magazines available in braille, cassette, computer diskette, large type, electronic access, and other special formats. The first part of the catalog lists magazines produced by the National Library Service. These are available as free subscriptions to qualified persons through participating libraries. A second section lists magazines available through other sources. Some of these are free; others are available for purchase. Indexes provide access by title, subject, and media.

Talking Book Topics updates the various catalogs of the National Library Service. It lists recent recorded books by category, including books for adults, books for children, foreign language books, and talking book magazines. As with the catalogs, a description is given for each title. A combined author and title index is provided. Order forms are also included. A short news section highlights books on selected topics and announces new catalogs and selected titles from other sources.

NATIONAL ARCHIVES AND RECORDS ADMINISTRATION SOURCES

Checklist

National Archives and Records Administration: The Research Room Web Page. WEB. U.S. National Archives and Records Administration. <http://www.nara.gov/research/>.
> Content: information on holdings by media, including film-video-sound, photographs, and cartographic and architectural records.

Select List of Publications of the National Archives and Records Administration. PRINT. WEB. (1994) U.S. National Archives and Records Administration. General Information Leaflet No. 3. AE 1.113:3/994. Item 0569. <http://www.nara.gov/publications/gil3home.html>.

> Content: list of National Archives publications currently in print by series; includes *Select Audiovisual Records* series and *General Information Leaflets* series.

General Information Leaflets. PRINT. U.S. National Archives and Records Administration. AE 1.113: Item 0569.
> Content: small pamphlets on the National Archives, its resources, facilities, and services.

Discussion

The National Archives contains a large collection of pictures, motion pictures, videotapes, and sound recordings. The *National Archives and Records Administration: The Research Room Web Page* lists types of media available, including "Film-Video-Sound," "Photographs," and "Cartographic & Architectural Records." Selecting any of these media types leads to additional information on holdings, online resources, and information on obtaining reproductions. Online resources include the full text of selected descriptive leaflets in the agency's *Select Audiovisual Records* and *General Information Leaflet* series.

The *Select List of Publications of the National Archives and Records Administration* contains a list of the *Select Audiovisual Records* and *General Information Leaflets* titles available. Many of the brochures mentioned are available on request from the National Archives. Some are also available on their Web site.

The *General Information Leaflets* series includes small brochures on the National Archives and its services. Brochures relating to audiovisual materials include *Ordering Reproductions From the National Archives* (AE 1.113:13/987), *Motion Pictures & Sound and Video Recordings in the National Archives* (AE 1.113:33/994), and *Information for Prospective Researchers about the Still Picture Branch of the National Archives* (AE 1.113:38).

INDEXES

Checklist

Catalog of United States Government Publications (MOCAT). WEB. 1994–. U.S. Government Printing Office. Superintendent of Documents. <http://www.gpo.gov/catalog>; <http://www.access.gpo.gov/su_docs/locators/cgp/index.html>; <http://purl.access.gpo.gov/GPO/LPS844>.

Monthly Catalog of United States Government Publications. CD-ROM. 1996–. U.S. Government Printing Office. Superintendent of Documents. GP 3.8/7: Item 0557-C. GPO.

Monthly Catalog of United States Government Publications (Condensed version). PRINT. (monthly) 1996–. U.S. Government Printing Office. Superintendent of Documents. GP 3.8/8: (Earlier full version, GP 3.8:, 1895–1995). Item 0557-D. GPO.

Discussion

The *Monthly Catalog* is the most comprehensive index to government publications. Information can be found under the heading "Audio-Visual Materials" and under specific kinds of media such as "Filmstrips," "Motion Pictures," and "Video Tapes." Look also under specific topics with the subheadings "Audio-visual Aids," "Film Catalogs," or "Posters." The complete version of the *Monthly Catalog* is available on the Web and CD-ROM. Commercial online and CD-ROM versions of the *Monthly Catalog* are also available. For more information, see Chapter 3, "The Basics of Searching."

RELATED MATERIAL
Within this Work

Chapter 16　Maps

GPO Subject Bibliographies. **PRINT. WEB. GP 3.22/2:**

<http://bookstore.gpo.gov/sb/about.html>.

No. 57　"Posters and Prints"

No. 107　"Art and Artists"

No. 72　"Photography"

No. 73　"Films and Audiovisual Information"

CHAPTER 13
Copyright Information

The United States copyright law has its origins in the U.S. Constitution, which authorizes the government to grant authors the exclusive right to their writings for a limited period of time (Article I, Section 8, Clause 8). The purpose of copyright is to promote creativity by rewarding authors and to provide eventual public access to creative works after the copyright expires. Copyrights protect literary, dramatic, musical, artistic, and other intellectual works and reserve to the author the right to reproduce, distribute, perform, or display the work. Although copyrights are often associated with patents and trademarks, they are different and are handled by a different office, the Copyright Office of the Library of Congress. Patents and trademarks are issued by the Patent and Trademark Office of the Department of Commerce. See Chapter 50, "Patents and Trademarks," for more information.

SEARCH STRATEGY

This chapter shows a subject search strategy. There are three basic steps for locating copyright information:
1. See the "General Sources" section of this chapter for basic, descriptive information sources on copyrights;
2. See the "Copyright Status Sources" section to locate material on determining copyright status; and
3. Consult the "Indexes" and "Related Material" sections for additional sources.

GENERAL SOURCES
Checklist

U.S. Copyright Office Web Site. WEB. Library of Congress. Copyright Office. <http://lcweb.loc.gov/copyright/>.
> Content: basic information on copyright; copyright records; publications and forms; legislation; agency information and news; related resources.

Copyright Basics. PRINT. WEB. (irregular) Library of Congress. Copyright Office. Circular 1. LC 3.4/2:1/year. Item 0802-A.

<http://www.loc.gov/copyright/circs/circ1.html>; <http://lcweb.loc.gov/copyright/circs/circ01.pdf>; <purl.access.gpo.gov/GPO/LPS471>; <http://www.loc.gov/copyright/circs/>.
> Content: what a copyright is; what can be copyrighted; notice of copyright; duration; registration procedures; application; fees.

Publications on Copyright. PRINT. WEB. (irregular) Library of Congress. Copyright Office. Circular 2. LC 3.4/2:2/year. Item 0802-A. <http://lcweb.loc.gov/copyright/circs/circ02.pdf>; <http://www.loc.gov/copyright/circs/>.
> Content: list of forms and publications currently available with ordering information.

Circulars. PRINT. WEB. (irregular) Library of Congress. Copyright Office. LC 3.4/2: Item 0802-A. <http://www.loc.gov/copyright/circs/>.
> Content: numerous informational brochures on copyright topics.

Discussion

The *U.S. Copyright Office Web Site* provides comprehensive information on copyright, including copies of all copyright forms, full-text publications, and an online database. The "General Information" menu category includes the *Copyright Basics*, information on registration procedures, and frequently asked questions. The "Publications" category includes application forms, information circulars, factsheets, regulations, and other reports. The Copyright Office online registration files are accessible from the "Copyright Office Records" category. A "Legislation" category provides the text of the copyright law and information on new and pending legislation. Other categories cover international copyright information, announcements, and links to related resources.

Copyright Basics explains what copyright is, who can claim it, and what materials can be copyrighted. Information is given on how to secure copyright and on registration and application procedures. Other basic information on the characteristics of copyrights is included.

Publications on Copyright lists forms and publications available from the Copyright Office, other Library of Congress offices, the Government Printing Office, and the National Technical Information Service. Ordering information is given for each source. Instructions about obtaining information on the Internet or by fax are also given.

The *Circulars* series contains additional brochures on more specific aspects of copyright, including particular types of materials and specific procedures. Examples of titles include *Renewal of Copyright* (No. 15), *Reproduction of Copyrighted Works by Educators and Librarians* (No. 21), and *Copyright Registration for Works of the Visual Arts* (No. 40). A complete list of circulars can be found in *Publications on Copyright* discussed above. In addition to being available to depository libraries, frequently requested titles are available on the agency's Web site, by fax, or free from the Copyright Office, Library of Congress, Publications Section, LM-455, 101 Independence Avenue, S.E., Washington, D.C. 20559-6000.

COPYRIGHT STATUS SOURCES
Checklist

How to Investigate the Copyright Status of a Work. PRINT. WEB. (irregular) Library of Congress. Copyright Office. Circular 22. LC 3.4/2:22/year. Item 0802-A. <http://lcweb.loc.gov/copyright/circs/circ22.pdf>; <http://www.loc.gov/copyright/circs/>.

    Content: methods of copyright investigation; Copyright Office records and searches; copyright notice.

Searching Online U.S. Copyright Office Records Web Page. WEB. 1978–. Library of Congress. Copyright Office. <http://www.loc.gov/copyright/rb.html>; <telnet://locis.loc.gov>.

    Content: overview and instructions for using the *LOCIS* telnet catalog containing copyright registration information; telnet link to *LOCIS*.

Catalog of Copyright Entries. 4th series. MF. 1978–1982. Library of Congress. Copyright Office. LC 3.6/6: (Issued in previous series since 1891) Items 0791, 0793, 0794, 0795, 0797, 0798, 0800.

    Content: list of registered copyrighted materials by type.

Dialog. <http://www.dialog.com/>.

    Content: comprehensive online data provider; files include *U.S. Copyrights*, the Copyright Office online catalog.

Discussion

How to Investigate the Copyright Status of a Work briefly explains the many factors that affect copyright status and the methods for determining status. These methods include locating and analyzing copyright notices, searching the Copyright Office catalogs and files, or requesting a search from the Copyright Office. Information is given on each method and its limitations. Changes in copyright law and their implications for copyright status are discussed. The changing requirements for copyright notice and the significance of the copyright date are covered. Due to the complexity of determining status, the brochure recommends consulting a copyright attorney. Figure 13.1 summarizes some general principles of copyright status based on the date in a copyright notice.

WORKS PUBLISHED AND COPYRIGHTED:

1. Before Jan. 1, 1978, but within past 75 years—   May be protected for 95 years from date if copyright was renewed.

2. Before Jan. 1, 1978, but more than 75 years ago—   Copyright has expired.

3. Between Jan. 1, 1923 and Dec. 31, 1949—   Expired if not renewed in 28th year after copyright; if in renewal term on Dec. 31, 1977, copyright will last 95 years from original date.

4. Between Jan. 1, 1950, and Dec. 31, 1963—   If in its first term, it must be renewed in the 28th year—then copyright lasts 95 years from original date. Otherwise copyright expires after 28th year.

5. Between Jan. 1, 1964 and Dec. 31, 1977—   Automatic renewal—copyright lasts 95 years from original date.

6. Unpublished, unregistered works prior to 1978—   Now protected, but length of time varies. None will expire before Dec. 31, 2002.

7. Works created on or after Jan. 1, 1978—   Automatic protection from time of creation for the author's lifetime plus 70 years.

Based on information in *How to Investigate the Copyright Status of a Work*, 1999.

Figure 13.1: Outline of Status Based on Copyright Date.

One way to determine copyright status is to search the Copyright Office's catalogs and records. An online catalog of registrations is available from 1978 on through *LOCIS (Library of Congress Information System). LOCIS* requires the use of a telnet application. The *Searching Online U.S. Copyright Office Records Web Page* provides information on the system and how to use it, as well as a telnet link to the catalog. Once connected to *LOCIS,* select "Copyright Information" from the main menu. Three files are available. "Works registered for copyright since 1978" (COHM) contains records for monographs, including books, film, music maps, sound recordings, software, and other materials. A "Serials" file (COHS) covers periodicals and newspapers. A "Documents" file (COHD) contains records relating to copyright ownership, including name changes and transfers.

The catalog was published as the *Catalog of Copyright Entries* through 1982. The 4th (and last) series was published in microfiche from 1979–82. This catalog lists registered materials alphabetically by title, author, and claimant. Each entry includes bibliographic information, name of copyright claimant, date of creation, date of registration, registration number, and other copyright information. The catalog was issued in eight parts, with each part covering a specific type of material such as nondramatic literary works, serials and periodicals, performing arts, or motion pictures and filmstrips. Part 8 was devoted to renewals of all types. Previous series of catalogs were published in print format since 1891. A cumulation for motion picture registrations beginning with 1894 and ending with 1969 has been done (LC 3.8:, Item 0803-A). The Copyright Office card catalog, covering 1870–1977 may be searched in person at the Copyright Office. The Copyright Office will also do a search of their records for an hourly fee.

The online catalog of the Copyright Office is also available through Dialog as the *U.S. Copyrights* file. The database contains registration, renewal, and ownership information since 1978.

INDEXES
Checklist

Catalog of United States Government Publications (MOCAT). WEB. 1994–. U.S. Government Printing Office. Superintendent of Documents. <http://www.gpo.gov/catalog>; <http://www.access.gpo.gov/su_docs/locators/cgp/index.html>; <http://purl.access.gpo.gov/GPO/LPS844>.

Monthly Catalog of United States Government Publications. CD-ROM. 1996–. U.S. Government Printing Office. Superintendent of Documents. GP 3.8/7: Item 0557-C. GPO.

Monthly Catalog of United States Government Publications (Condensed version). PRINT. (monthly) 1996–. U.S. Government Printing Office. Superintendent of Documents. GP 3.8/8: (Earlier full version, GP 3.8:, 1895–1995). Item 0557-D. GPO.

CIS/Index. PRINT. (monthly) 1970–. Bethesda, MD: Congressional Information Service.

Congressional Universe. WEB. Bethesda, MD: Congressional Information Service.

Discussion

These basic indexes provide access to general publications on copyright issues. The *Monthly Catalog* covers the full range of government publications that might be available. The complete version of the *Monthly Catalog* is available on the Web and CD-ROM. Commercial online and CD-ROM versions of the *Monthly Catalog* are also available. *CIS/Index* covers congressional publications. *Congressional Universe* includes a Web version of *CIS.* The subject heading to look under is the same for all of these indexes: "Copyright." (For more information on these indexes, see Chapter 3, "The Basics of Searching.")

RELATED MATERIAL
Within this Work
Chapter 50 Patents and Trademarks

GPO Subject Bibliographies. PRINT. WEB. GP 3.22/2:
<http://bookstore.gpo.gov/sb/about.html>.

No. 126 "Copyright"

CHAPTER 14
Climate

This chapter covers materials that deal with both general climate averages and daily weather information. Many of the sources in this chapter originate from the National Climatic Data Center.

SEARCH STRATEGY

This chapter shows a subject search strategy. The steps to follow are

1. Look at the titles under the "General Statistical Sources" section of this chapter to find basic temperature and precipitation data;
2. Consult the "National Climatic Data Center" section for online climate data and information on the resources available;
3. Consult the titles listed under the "Detailed Climatological Data" and "Other Climate Sources" sections for a greater variety of data and greater levels of detail;
4. If interested in international data, see the "World Climate Sources" section;
5. For specialized information, consider the "Climate CD-ROM Datasets" section. Use of some of these titles may require programming skills;
6. Search the indexes for more publications on other aspects of climate; and
7. Check the "Related Material" section of this chapter.

GENERAL STATISTICAL SOURCES
Checklist

Statistical Abstract of the United States. PRINT. WEB. (annual) 1878–. U.S. Department of Commerce. Economics and Statistics Administration. Bureau of the Census. C 3.134: Item 0150. ASI 2324-1. GPO. <http://www.census.gov/statab/www/>; <http://purl.access.gpo.gov/GPO/LPS2878>.
    Coverage: selected cities.

Content: normal daily mean, maximum, and minimum temperature for January and July, and annual average; highest and lowest recorded temperatures; normal monthly and annual precipitation; average number of days with precipitation of .01 inch or more; snow and ice pellets; sunshine; average wind speed; average relative humidity; heating and cooling degree days; major weather disasters; number and types of storms with number of lives lost and property loss.

Statistical Abstract of the United States. CD-ROM. (annual) 1993–. U.S. Department of Commerce. Bureau of the Census. C 3.134/7: Item 0150-B. ASI 2324-14.
    Content: CD-ROM version of the *Statistical Abstract.*

Historical Statistics of the United States: Colonial Times to 1970. Parts 1-2. PRINT. (1975) U.S. Department of Commerce. Bureau of the Census. C 3.134/2:H 62/789-970/pt.1-2. Item 0151. ASI (76) 2328-2. GPO.
    Coverage: selected cities.
    Content: monthly, seasonal, and annual temperature and precipitation; tornadoes, floods, and cyclones.

Historical Statistics of the United States on CD-ROM: Colonial Times to 1970. CD-ROM. (1997) New York, NY: Cambridge University Press.
    Content: CD-ROM version of *Historical Statistics of the United States.*

County and City Data Book. PRINT. WEB. (quinquennial) 1947–. U.S. Department of Commerce. Economics and Statistics Administration. Bureau of the Census. C 3.134/2:C 83/2/year. Item 0151. ASI 2328-1. GPO. <http://fisher.lib.Virginia.EDU/ccdb/>.
    Coverage: cities of 25,000 people or more.
    Content: average daily mean temperature and limits for January and July; annual precipitation; heating and cooling degree days.

County and City Data Book. CD-ROM. (quinquennial) 1988–. U.S. Department of Commerce. Bureau of the Census. C 3.134/2-1: (Earlier, C 3.134/2:C 83/2/) Item 0151-D-01. ASI 2328-103.
    Content: CD-ROM version of the *County and City Data Book.*

County and City Extra: Annual Metro, City, and County Data Book. PRINT. (annual) 1992–. Lanham, MD: Bernan Press.
> Coverage: cities of 25,000 people or more.
> Content: updated version of the *County and City Data Book.*

Discussion

These sources can be used to quickly locate basic climatic data. The *Statistical Abstract of the United States* contains a chapter on "Geography and Environment," which gives temperature and precipitation data for selected U.S. cities as well as some other miscellaneous climate information. The full text of recent editions of the *Statistical Abstract* is available on the Census Bureau Web site as PDF files. The *Statistical Abstract* is also available on CD-ROM. The CD uses Adobe Acrobat software and contains some additional geographic areas and time series in the form of spreadsheet files that are not in the printed version. *Historical Statistics of the United States* contains similar information for earlier years. A CD-ROM version of *Historical Statistics* is available from Cambridge University Press. *The County and City Data Book* gives basic temperature and precipitation data for all cities with a population over 25,000. The *County and City Data Book* is also available in CD-ROM from the Census Bureau. The University of Virginia Library Geospatial and Statistical Data Center offers recent editions of the *County and City Data Book* on the Internet in their interactive data area. Users select the desired edition, geography, and variables to create a customized data display. *County and City Extra* is a commercially produced annual version of the *County and City Data Book* with identical climate data.

NATIONAL CLIMATIC DATA CENTER

Checklist

National Climatic Data Center Web Site. WEB. U.S. Department of Commerce. National Oceanic and Atmospheric Administration. National Climatic Data Center. <http://www.ncdc.noaa.gov/>.
> Content: full text climate data, product listings, agency information.

CLIMVIS. WEB. U.S. Department of Commerce. National Oceanic and Atmospheric Administration. National Climatic Data Center. <http://www.ncdc.noaa.gov/onlineprod/drought/xmgr.html>.
> Content: interactive time series graphs and contour map analyses of climate data.

Discussion

The National Climatic Data Center (NCDC) is the central source for current and historical U.S. climate and weather records. The *National Climatic Data Center Web Site* serves as a guide to climatological information products in a variety of formats. A "Locate NCDC Products by" menu option is subdivided into "Most Popular Products," "Weather Station, City, County, and more," and "Category/Type." The "Most Popular Products" option lists the most popular climate data resources by such categories as "Most Requested," "CD-ROMs," Publications," and "Digital ASCII Files." The "Weather Station" choice provides various options for searching for a particular weather station such as lists by state/division/county/city or searches by station name/city, zip code, county, or various identification numbers. Data available for a station include station history, downloadable ASCII data files, information on related products, and related Web links. The "Category/Type" menu option is a database of NCDC products with descriptions, information on formats, and price information. Links are available to any data that are available online. Users can search all products or select a general subject category such as "Climate" or "Oceanographic." Searches can be further defined by selecting product types, such as CD-ROM, online, or publication. Other options include a keyword search that allows users to specify a time range, geographical coverage, and specific databases. The same database is also available from the "Online Store" main menu choice. The main menu also includes a "Browse by Data Type" selection. Users may choose satellite, climate, or radar data. The climate data choice leads to a "Climate Resources" page with categories covering online climate data, products and publications listings, research and applications, and an online document library. Some resources may be viewed online and some may be downloaded. Some resources are free, but many must be purchased. Federal depository libraries have been provided free access to selected publications and, at present, free access is also available to .edu domain Internet addresses.

The "Climate Resources" page includes a "Get/View Online Climate Data" option that is arranged by categories such as "Climatology & Extreme Events," "Surface Data," or "Upper Air Data." "Surface Data" is the largest category and is further subdivided into graphs, hourly, daily, monthly, and modeled data. Examples of specific types of data available include U.S. climatological averages and normals, U.S. storm events database, and graphs of selected temperature and precipitation data by station.

The "Products & Publications" option under "Climate Resources" lists products by category such as CD-ROM, climatic reports, or online store. A *Products & Services Guide* is available in PDF format and WordPerfect format and may also be ordered online in print format for a service charge.

The "Research & Applications" category under "Climate Resources" contains annual climate reviews for recent years. Data for each year include monthly and annual reports and special reports on climatic extremes and weather events. Each monthly report includes global, national, and regional analyses and coverage of extreme events. The research area also includes a climatic extremes and weather events section with information on specific events and issues such as El Nino/La Nina, global climate change, and billion dollar weather disasters. Other choices in the research area include a global warming section and information on research programs.

The "Online Document Library" includes a publications category that lists the major climatological data serials available from the NCDC. Each title includes a description, sample issue, ordering information, and limited free full-text access for recent years for those who qualify, including federal depository libraries and .edu domain Internet addresses. These titles include *Monthly Climatic Data for the World, Storm Data, Local Climatological Data, Climatological Data, Hourly Precipitation Data*, and *Heating and Cooling Degree Day Data*. Some of these titles are discussed in the "Detailed Climatological Data" section of this chapter. The *National Climatic Data Center Web Site* main page also includes an "About NCDC" section and links to Regional Climate Centers and State Climatologists. These sources can provide additional regional and state climate resources.

CLIMVIS is an interactive climate visualization tool available through the NCDC Web site. It can also be found through the "Get/View Online Climate Data" menu option discussed above. Users select data sets and variables to create graphs or contour maps. Four datasets are currently available: "National Weather Service Summary of the Day," "Global Summary of the Day," "Climate Division Precipitation, Temperature, and Drought Data," and "Global Historical Climatological Network Data." The "National Weather Service Summary of the Day" covers approximately 300 U.S. stations with data as far back as 1869 for some stations. Data include daily maximum and minimum temperatures, departures from normal temperature, daily precipitation and snowfall, snow depth, heating and cooling degree days, sunshine, wind, pressure, and humidity. Users can select parameters for time series graphs or for contour plots by region or state. The other three data sets offer time series graphs only. "Global Summary of the Day" covers approximately 8000 global stations from 1994 on and includes daily mean, maximum, and minimum temperature, precipitation, snow depth, wind, visibility, and selected weather events such as fog or thunder. "Climate Division Precipitation, Temperature, and Drought Data" contains monthly data for U.S. divisions for temperature, precipitation, and drought indexes since 1895. "Global Historical Climatological Network" covers global station data on precipitation as far back as 1697 for some stations and minimum and maximum temperature data as far back as the early 1700s.

DETAILED CLIMATOLOGICAL DATA
Checklist

Climatological Data [state]. WEB. (monthly) 1914–. U.S. Department of Commerce. National Oceanic and Atmospheric Administration. National Environmental Satellite, Data and Information Service. National Climatic Data Center. C 55.214/48: (Earlier MF, C 55.214/2: to C 55.214/47:) (Published before 1914 under other titles) Item 0277-B. <http://www5.ncdc.noaa.gov/pubs/publications.html#CD>; <http://purl.access.gpo.gov/GPO/LPS1895>.

> Coverage: individual U.S. weather stations.
> Content: daily precipitation; daily maximum and minimum temperatures; monthly and annual temperature averages, departures from normal, highest and lowest; heating and cooling degree days; monthly and annual precipitation totals, departures from normal, greatest day; some stations provide daily snowfall and snow on ground, evaporation and wind, and soil temperature.

Local Climatological Data [station]. WEB. (monthly) 1897–. U.S. Department of Commerce. National Oceanic and Atmospheric Administration. National Environmental Satellite, Data and Information Service. National Climatic Data Center. C 55.286/6-54: (Earlier MF, C55.286/6: to C55.286/6-53:) (Title varies) Item 0274-G. <http://www5.ncdc.noaa.gov/pubs/publications.html#LCD>; <http://purl.access.gpo.gov/GPO/LPS1384>.

> Coverage: selected U.S. weather stations.
> Content: daily temperature averages, maximums, and minimums; departure from normal; heating and cooling degree days; snow and ice on the ground; daily precipitation; pressure; wind direction and speed; sunshine; cloudiness; visibility; hourly precipitation; three-hour–interval observations for temperature and other variables; annual issue contains narrative climate description; monthly and annual totals and averages; and historical normals, means, and extremes.

Hourly Precipitation Data [state]. WEB. (monthly) 1951–. U.S. Department of Commerce. National Oceanic and Atmospheric Administration. National Environmental Satellite, Data and Information Service. National Climatic Data Center. C 55.216/45: (Earlier MF, C 55.216: to C 55.216/44:) (Published before 1951 in other titles) Item 0274-A-57. <http://www5.ncdc.noaa.gov/pubs/publications.html#HPD>; <http://purl.access.gpo.gov/GPO/LPS1970>.

> Coverage: individual U.S. weather stations.
> Content: daily and hourly precipitation; maximum precipitation for selected intervals; monthly and annual totals.

Storm Data. WEB. (monthly) 1959–. U.S. Department of Commerce. National Oceanic and Atmospheric Administration. National Environmental Satellite, Data and Information Service. National Climatic Data Center. C 55.212: Item 0274-B. (Earlier MF) ASI 2152-3. <http://www5.ncdc.noaa.gov/pubs/publications.html#SD>; <http://purl.access.gpo.gov/GPO/LPS1383>.

> Coverage: U.S., states, selected places.
> Content: storm listings; type of storm; location; date; time; length and width of path; number killed or injured; property and crop damage; descriptions and photographs of major storms; annual and historical summary data on floods, lightning, tornadoes, and hurricanes.

National Climatic Data Center Periodical Publications. CD-ROM. (quarterly) 1998–. U.S. Department of Commerce. National Oceanic and Atmospheric Administration. National Climatic Data Center. C 55.287/63: Item 0274-G-01.

Content: full-text issues of periodicals issued each quarter; includes *Climatological Data, Local Climatological Data, Hourly Precipitation Data, Storm Data,* and *Monthly Climatic Data for the World.*

Climatedata NCDC Summary of the Day. CD-ROM. (annual) 1867–. Boulder, CO: Hydrosphere Data Products, Inc.

Coverage: individual weather stations.

Content: daily maximum, minimum, and average temperature; precipitation; snowfall; evaporation.

Climatedata NCDC Hourly Precipitation. CD-ROM. (annual) 1902–. Boulder, CO: Hydrosphere Data Products, Inc.

Coverage: individual weather stations.

Content: hourly precipitation data.

Climatedata NCDC Quarter-Hourly Precipitation. CD-ROM. (annual) 1970–. Boulder, CO: Hydrosphere Data Products, Inc.

Coverage: individual weather stations.

Content: 15-minute precipitation data.

Discussion

Climatological Data is the major source for daily weather data. It is issued monthly for each state (in some cases, groups of states) with an annual cumulation. Each issue contains monthly totals and averages (see Figure 14.1) and daily temperature and precipitation data for most of the weather stations in the state. A smaller number of stations also report data on daily soil temperatures, evaporation, wind, and snowfall. The July issue contains additional tables on heating degree days for the year and annual snowfall data. Within each table, stations are listed by divisions. There is a station index that identifies division number, county, latitude and longitude, elevation, observation times, and type of information gathered for each station. The annual summary gives monthly and annual data for total precipitation, average temperatures, departures from normal, temperature extremes and freeze data, cooling degree days, soil temperatures, evaporation, and wind movement. *Climatological Data* is available on the agency's Web site, with limited free access to those who qualify, including federal depository libraries and .edu domain Internet addresses.

Local Climatological Data is issued for each of nearly 300 weather stations, located mainly in large cities. For these stations, more information is provided here than in *Climatological Data.* The monthly summary table gives daily and monthly temperature data, degree days, precipitation, average pressure, wind data, sunshine, and occurrence of other phenomena, such as fog or hail. Additional tables give hourly precipitation for each day and observations at three-hour intervals for temperature, wind, vis-

ibility, sky cover, pressure, and relative humidity. The annual contains a narrative climate summary and tables showing monthly and annual data similar to that in the monthly report. A "Normals, Means, and Extremes" table gives a good overview of a city's weather based on historical averages. This table gives monthly and annual historical norms for such items as mean maximum and minimum temperature, heating and cooling degree days, pressure, winds, maximum and minimum precipitation and snowfall, sunshine, and cloudiness. *Local Climatological Data* is available on the agency's Web site, with limited free access to those who qualify, including federal depository libraries and .edu domain Internet addresses.

Hourly Precipitation Data provides more detail than *Climatological Data* on the subject of precipitation. In addition to showing daily totals, this title shows totals by hour for each station. Another table gives maximum precipitation for selected time intervals ranging from 15 minutes to 24 hours. The December issue contains monthly and annual precipitation totals. *Hourly Precipitation Data* is available on the agency's Web site, with limited free access to those who qualify, including federal depository libraries and .edu domain Internet addresses.

Storm Data lists major storms by state and place of occurrence. These include a wide range of events such as tornadoes, hurricanes, high winds, heavy rain and snow, thunderstorms, hail, floods, lightning, blizzards, winter storms, drought, and wild/forest fires. A brief description of the event is often included along with data on injuries and estimated damage. An "Outstanding Storms of the Month" section describes major storms with photographs. An annual summary is published separately or included in the December issue. The annual summary covers floods, lightning, tornadoes, and hurricanes and includes historical statistics. For most of these events, data include number of events, location, and number of deaths. The most detailed data are available for tornadoes, including injuries and property damage. The least detailed data are available for hurricanes, covering the current year only. *Storm Data* is available on the agency's Web site, with limited free access to those who qualify, including federal depository libraries and .edu domain Internet addresses. A storm events database is also available from the NCDC Home Page under "Climate Resources." It covers most storms since 1993 and tornadoes, wind, and hail since 1950. Storms can be searched by state, county, type of event, and event characteristics.

The National Climatic Data Center Periodical Publications CD-ROM contains issues of the agency's periodicals for each quarter. Publications are in PDF format.

OHIO
MAY 1999

MONTHLY STATION AND DIVISION SUMMARY

STATION	TEMPERATURE (°F)										NO. OF DAYS			
	AVERAGE MAXIMUM	AVERAGE MINIMUM	AVERAGE	DEPARTURE FROM NORMAL	HIGHEST	DATE	LOWEST	DATE	HEATING DEGREE DAYS	COOLING DEGREE DAYS	MAX		MIN	
											90 OR ABOVE	32 OR BELOW	32 OR BELOW	0 OR BELOW
OHIO														
NORTHWEST 01														
BOWLING GREEN WWTP	74.5	49.7	62.1	2.5	91	18	38	1	131	48	1	0	0	0
DEFIANCE	74.3	50.4	62.4	3.6	89	18	41	27	125	52	0	0	0	0
FINDLAY FAA AIRPORT	73.9	51.1	62.5	2.8	90	17	43	27+	118	49	1	0	0	0
FINDLAY WPCC	75.2	51.9	63.6	3.7	89	17	43	27+	92	56	0	0	0	0
HOYTVILLE 2 NE	74.6	47.6	61.1	1.9	90	18	36	2+	160	47	1	0	0	0
LIMA WWTP	74.8	52.8	63.8	3.3	86	30+	40	27	93	64	0	0	0	0
MONTPELIER	75.6	47.2	61.4	3.5	90	30	37	1	145	42	1	0	0	0
PANDORA	75.0	50.7	62.9	2.8	89	17	39	1	111	54	0	0	0	0
PAULDING	74.3	49.8	62.1	3.2	90	18	38	9	136	52	1	0	0	0
TOLEDO EXPRESS WSO AP R	74.3	50.8	62.6	4.0	90	17	42	2	113	46	1	0	0	0
TOLEDO BLADE	M	M	M		91	18	40	3			1	0	0	0
VAN WERT 1 S	75.3	52.5	63.9	3.1	89	30+	42	27	103	74	0	0	0	0
WAUSEON WATER PLANT	74.2	49.5	61.9	1.8	88	18	43	28+	137	49	0	0	0	0
--DIVISIONAL DATA------>			62.5	2.7										
NORTH CENTRAL 02														
BUCYRUS	75.5	48.3	61.9	3.6	88	31+	40	27	130	41	0	0	0	0
ELYRIA 3 E	75.7	49.8	62.8	2.6	90	30	37	1	116	52	1	0	0	0
FREMONT	74.4	50.2	62.3	3.3	90	18	38	1	136	62	1	0	0	0
FREMONT AG STA	74.3	46.2	60.3		90	18	34	2+	189	49	1	0	0	0
NORWALK WWTP	72.3	50.1	61.2	2.9	88	31	36	1	165	56	0	0	0	0
OBERLIN	74.7	49.4	62.1	4.3	87	30+	38	1	130	48	0	0	0	0
SANDUSKY	69.8	52.3	61.1	1.8	88	18	43	2	164	50	0	0	0	0
TIFFIN	74.8	50.8	62.8	3.1	89	30+	39	1	121	58	0	0	0	0
UPPER SANDUSKY	74.8	50.0	62.4	2.7	87	31+	39	1	128	54	0	0	0	0
--DIVISIONAL DATA------>			61.9	2.6										
NORTHEAST 03														
AKRON CANTON WSO AP R	72.7	50.0	61.4	2.4	83	30+	42	27+	134	29	0	0	0	0
AKRON R	74.8	54.2	64.5		88	30+	46	27	81	73	0	0	0	0
CHARDON	71.2	46.4	58.8	2.9	84	31+	36	27	197	15	0	0	0	0
CHIPPEWA LAKE	72.6	49.3	61.0	3.4	85	31	40	28+	144	24	0	0	0	0
CLEVELAND WSFO AP R	71.9	50.0	61.0	3.0	85	30+	40	27	155	39	0	0	0	0
DORSET	72.1	45.5	58.8	3.0	86	31	33	11+	206	20	0	0	0	0
HIRAM	71.5	47.6	59.6	1.4	84	31	37	27	177	16	0	0	0	0
KIRTLAND-HOLDEN 2	70.1	48.3	59.2		86	31	36	10	200	27	0	0	0	0
MINERAL RIDGE WTR WKS	76.8	49.4	63.1	3.2	88	31+	38	13	104	53	0	0	0	0
PAINESVILLE 4 NW	70.1	51.7	60.9	2.6	88	17	42	27+	174	52	0	0	0	0
WARREN 3 S	74.2	44.1	59.2	1.4	86	31+	34	1	192	17	0	0	0	0
YOUNGSTOWN WSO AP R	72.9	47.0	60.0	2.5	84	30	35	10	170	21	0	0	0	0
--DIVISIONAL DATA------>			60.6	2.5										
WEST CENTRAL 04														
BELLEFONTAINE	74.3	51.7	63.0	3.4	86	31+	37	27	120	66	0	0	0	0
CELINA 3 NE	75.8	52.0	63.9	2.3	87	17	41	2+	96	71	0	0	0	0
GREENVILLE WATER PLANT	74.5	49.4	62.0	2.5	86	30+	39	1	136	49	0	0	0	0
KENTON	75.7	51.2	63.5	3.7	90	30	42	27	102	58	1	0	0	0
SIDNEY 1 S	74.8	46.6	60.7		87	31+	38	28+	160	33	0	0	0	0
SPRINGFIELD NEW WTR WK	75.4	47.7	61.6	2.2	88	31	39	27	144	43	0	0	0	0
URBANA WWTP	75.0	52.3	63.7	4.2	89	31	41	27+	109	74	0	0	0	0
--DIVISIONAL DATA------>			62.6	2.3										
CENTRAL 05														
CIRCLEVILLE	76.4	50.5	63.5	1.9	89	31	40	1	90	50	0	0	0	0
COLUMBUS VLY CROSSING	77.7	51.0	64.4	2.2	88	30	41	27	72	59	0	0	0	0
COLUMBUS WSO AIRPORT R	76.7	52.9	64.8	3.6	87	30+	43	27	68	69	0	0	0	0
DELAWARE	77.3	48.7M	63.0M	3.8	88	31+	42	27	106	49	0	0	0	0
LANCASTER	77.2	50.7	64.0		89	13	42	4+	85	61	0	0	0	0
LONDON	75.1	48.3	61.7	1.5	88	31	38	1	141	44	0	0	0	0
MARION 2 N	74.8	49.4	62.1	2.6	88	18	41	3+	127	46	0	0	0	0
MARYSVILLE	76.9	50.5	63.7	3.4	89	30	41	1	89	56	0	0	0	0
NEWARK WATER WORKS	74.9	45.6	60.3	-1.0	85	31+	39	2+	160	18	0	0	0	0
WASHINGTON COURT HOUSE	75.7	51.5	63.6	1.5	85	12	43	27	89	53	0	0	0	0
WESTERVILLE	78.1	50.0M	64.1M	2.8	87	31+	39	27+	90	72	0	0	0	0
--DIVISIONAL DATA------>			63.2	2.1										
CENTRAL HILLS 06														
ASHLAND 2 SW	74.0	48.8	61.4	3.6	87	30+	40	2	141	35	0	0	0	0
CENTERBURG 2 SE	74.4	49.8M	62.1M	3.3	86	31+	43	27	130	44	0	0	0	0
COSHOCTON WPC PLANT	75.1	47.8	61.5	1.5	85	29+	40	27	129	25	0	0	0	0
COSHOCTON AGR RES STN R	73.8	51.8	62.8	3.2	86	30	43	25	105	46	0	0	0	0
DANVILLE 2 W	73.5	44.4	59.0	1.5	86	13	36	5+	198	15	0	0	0	0
FREDERICKTOWN 4 S	74.6	43.5	59.1	1.0	85	30+	33	1	194	17	0	0	0	0

Source: *Climatological Data. Ohio*, v. 104, no. 5 (May, 1999), p. 2.

Figure 14.1: Sample Page from *Climatological Data*.

The CD is issued several months after the end of the quarter covered.

Hydrosphere Data Products provides CD-ROM titles based on National Climatic Data Center files. *Climatedata NCDC Summary of the Day* contains daily precipitation and temperature data for more than 18,000 stations. *Climatedata NCDC Hourly Precipitation* contains hourly precipitation data for more than 6,000 stations. *Climatedata NCDC 15-Minute Precipitation* contains 15-minute precipitation data for more than 3,000 stations.

OTHER CLIMATE SOURCES

Checklist

Comparative Climatic Data for the United States through [year]. WEB. (annual) U.S. Department of Commerce. National Oceanic and Atmospheric Administration. National Environmental Satellite, Data and Information Service. National Climatic Data Center. (Earlier, C 55.202:C 61/2/(year), Item 0273-D-01) ASI 2154-8. <http://nndc.noaa.gov/?http://ols.nndc.noaa.gov:7777/plolstore/plsql/olstore.prodspecific?prodnum=C00095-PUB-A0001>.

Coverage: selected U.S. weather stations.

Content: highest and lowest recorded temperatures; mean number of days with minimum temperature freezing or below or maximum temperature 90 degrees or above; mean number of days with more than .01 inch of precipitation; snowfall; wind speed; sunshine; cloudiness; average relative humidity; normal daily maximum, minimum, and mean temperature; normal heating and cooling degree days; normal precipitation.

Climate Prediction Center Web Site. WEB. U.S. Department of Commerce. National Oceanic and Atmospheric Administration. National Centers for Environmental Prediction. Climate Prediction Center. <http://www.cpc.ncep.noaa.gov/>.

Content: climate forecasts, highlights, trends, and analyses.

Weekly Weather and Crop Bulletin. PRINT. WEB. (weekly) 1924–. U.S. Department of Commerce. National Oceanic and Atmospheric Administration. National Weather Service/U.S. Department of Agriculture. National Agricultural Statistics Service and World Agricultural Outlook Board. C 55.209: (Issued since 1872 under other titles) Item 0273-D-12. ASI 2182-7. (Earlier, 2152-2). <http://www.usda.gov/oce/waob/jawf/wwcb.html>; <http://purl.access.gpo.gov/GPO/LPS1468>.

Coverage: world regions, U.S. regions, states, selected U.S. and world cities.

Content: national, state, and world weather and agriculture highlights; precipitation data; temperature data with departures from the norm; seasonal data on crop progress and conditions; snow; freeze dates; soil temperature; crop moisture; drought; and growing degree days.

Daily Weather Maps, Weekly Series. PRINT. (weekly) 1968–. U.S. Department of Commerce. National Oceanic and Atmospheric Administration. National Weather Service. National Centers for Environmental Prediction. Hydrometeorological Prediction Center and Climate Prediction Center. C 55.195: (Earlier, C 55.213:) Item 0273-D-04.

Coverage: North America, U.S.

Content: surface weather map, 500-millibar height contours chart, highest and lowest temperatures chart, precipitation areas and amounts chart.

Monthly State, Regional, and National (Heating/Cooling) Degree Days Weighted by Population (Includes Aerially Weighted Temperature and Precipitation). WEB. (monthly) U.S. Department of Commerce. National Oceanic and Atmospheric Administration. National Environmental Satellite, Data and Information Service. National Climatic Data Center. Historical Climatology Series 5-1, 5-2. C 55.287/60-2:; C 55.287/60-3: Items 0274-D-01; 0274-D-02. (Earlier MF) ASI 2152-13. <http://www.ncdc.noaa.gov/ol/documentlibrary/hcs/hcs.html>; <http://purl.access.gpo.gov/GPO/LPS3575>; <http://purl.access.gpo.gov/GPO/LPS3576>.

Coverage: U.S., divisions, states.

Content: heating or cooling degree days; accumulated degree days; ratio of accumulated days to the norm; state, regional, and national average temperatures and precipitation by month.

National Weather Service Web Site. WEB. U.S. Department of Commerce. National Oceanic and Atmospheric Administration. National Weather Service. <http://www.nws.noaa.gov/>.

Content: current weather conditions, forecasts, and warnings; agency information.

Discussion

Comparative Climatic Data for the United States is based on data from the "Normals, Means, and Extremes" table in annual issues of *Local Climatological Data*, although it is less detailed. Tables give monthly and annual averages for about 290 weather stations, usually located within large cities. There is a separate table for each topic that lists all the areas alphabetically by state, making it easy to compare different cities. The normal tables are based on 30-year averages that are updated every decade. *Comparative Climatic Data* tables are available at no charge on the agency's Web site.

The *Climate Prediction Center Web Site* contains climate forecasts and analyses. A climate highlights box lists current assessments such as U.S. threats, drought, hurricane outlook, or La Nina advisory. Other main menu items include "Expert Assessments," "Outlooks (Forecasts)," "Monitoring and Data," and "Most Popular Products." The "Expert Assessments" category is a more complete list of current weather and climate assessments, advisories, and special outlook discussions of seasonal events. The "Outlooks (Forecasts)" category lists outlook maps and graphs for various timeframes ranging from "0-48 Hours" to "Seasonal." Brief narrative discussion accompanies some of the outlook maps. The "0-48 Hours" forecast provides information on current conditions. The "Monitoring and Data" menu selection provides U.S. and global maps and time series data for selected climate indicators such as temperature and precipitation. The "Most Popular Products" menu option provides a selection of the most popular assessments and outlooks.

Weekly Weather and Crop Bulletin summarizes the week's weather with emphasis on its effects on crops. Standard narrative sections include a highlights section, national agricultural summary, state agricultural summaries, and international weather and crop summary. Regular tables contain temperature and precipitation data for selected cities. The temperature and precipitation tables for U.S. cities appear in every issue; tables for selected world cities appear monthly. The U.S. city table contains data on average temperature, average maximum and minimum temperature, extreme low and high temperature, and departure from normal. Precipitation data include weekly total, departure from normal, greatest amount in 24 hours, and totals and percentage of normal since January 1 and June 1. Other data include average maximum and minimum relative humidity, number of days with temperature 90° F and above or 32° F and below, and number of days with precipitation of .01 inch or more or .50 inch or more. The tables for world cities are much more limited. These include average temperature, average maximum and minimum temperature, high and low temperatures, total precipitation, and departures from normal. Temperature and precipitation maps for the U.S. appear in each issue. Precipitation maps for world regions appear in each issue, with temperature maps appearing monthly. Monthly summary data are published soon after the close of each month. The last issue of the year contains an index to special articles and regular features. (See Figure 14.2.) Some data appear only at certain times of the year or in certain issues.

Each *Daily Weather Map* weekly issue contains a page of charts for each day of the week. These charts show the positions, development, and movements of weather systems. The surface weather map shows selected station data, precipitation, and pressure areas for 7:00 a.m. EST. The 500-millibar chart indicates winds, temperatures, and humidities above the earth. The highest and lowest temperatures chart shows temperatures for selected stations. The precipitation areas and amounts chart shows areas of precipitation with selected station amounts. All charts cover the United States and some include portions of Canada and Mexico.

Degree day data are found in many of the sources in this chapter, but *Monthly State, Regional and National (Heating/Cooling) Degree Days* is the only source that gives state data. Degree days provide a relative measure of the energy required to heat and cool buildings. One degree day is accumulated for each degree the mean daily temperature is above (cooling degree day) or below (heating degree day) 65° F. A mean daily temperature of 67° F, for example, generates two cooling degree days. These two sources are designed to provide information on heating fuel and cooling energy demand on a statewide basis. Degree days, accumulated degree days, and a ratio of accumulated to normal days are given for the current and previous season. There are also tables on average temperature and precipitation for each month for states, divisions, and the United States. These titles are available on the agency's Web site, with limited free access to those who qualify, including federal depository libraries and .edu domain Internet addresses.

The *National Weather Service Web Site* contains information on recent and current weather conditions and forecasts rather than on specific past observations. The "National" menu options include a choice for current conditions. Users select a state and then a weather station for information on current conditions and a 24-hour summary. A forecasts option is also available by county or city. The main page also contains the Interactive Weather Information Network that displays a national map showing states with current weather warnings. Clicking on a state displays a more detailed state map with the option to display a variety of current weather data, including any active warnings or to click on a specific station for local conditions. The main page also contains links to regional National Weather Service offices that offer additional local information and resources.

WORLD CLIMATE SOURCES
Checklist

Climates of the World. WEB. 1969, revised 1991. U.S. Department of Commerce. National Oceanic and Atmospheric Administration. National Environmental Satellite, Data and Information Service. National Climatic Data Center. Nondepository. (Original 1969 edition was C 52.2:C 61/3) <http://www.ncdc.noaa.gov/ol/climate/climateproducts.html#PUBS>.

> Coverage: approximately 800 weather stations.
> Content: world temperature and precipitation maps; average daily maximum and minimum temperatures for selected months; maximum and minimum extreme temperatures; monthly and annual average precipitation.

Monthly Climatic Data for the World. WEB. (monthly) 1948–. U.S. Department of Commerce. National Oceanic and Atmospheric Administration. National Environmental Satellite, Data and Information Service. National Climatic Data Center. C55.211: (Title varies) Item 0273-D-22. (Earlier MF) ASI 2152-4. <http://www5.ncdc.noaa.gov/pubs/publications.html#MCDW>; <http://purl.access.gpo.gov/GPO/LPS1382>.

> Coverage: individual world and U.S. weather stations.
> Content: mean station and sea level pressure; mean vapor pressure and departure from the norm; mean temperature and departure from the norm; total precipitation and departure from the norm; days with precipitation of 1 mm or more; sunshine; upper air mean temperature, pressure, and wind data.

World Weather Records. PRINT. (decennial) 1921–. U.S. Department of Commerce. National Oceanic and Atmospheric Administration. National Environmental Satellite, Data and Information Service. National Climatic Data Center. C 55.281:W 89/(years) (Earlier, C 30.2:W 89/; SI 1.7:) Item 0274-A. ASI 2156-4.

10 **Weekly Weather and Crop Bulletin** December 29, 1998

1998 Bulletin Index
Volume 85

*Regular Features**

Text:

U.S. Weather Highlights	w/s
U.S. Weather and Crop Summary	m
National Agricultural Summary	w
Spring Wheat (April - September)	w
Rice (April - November)	w
Sorghum (April - November)	w
Corn (April - November)	w
Cotton (April - November)	w
Oats (April - September)	w
Barley (April - September	w
Peanuts (April - November)	w
Soybeans (May - November)	w
Winter Wheat (September - August)	w
U.S. Crop Production Highlights	m
State Summaries of Weather and Agriculture (April - November)	w
State Summaries of Weather and Agriculture (December - March)	m
International Weather and Crop Summary	w/m

National Charts:

Precipitation	w/m/s
Percent of Normal Precipitation	m/s
Average Temperature	m/s
Departure of Average Temperature from Normal	w/m/s
Extreme Minimum Temperature (September - April)	w
Extreme Maximum Temperature (April - September)	w
Snow Depth (December - March)	w
Average Soil Temperature, 4-Inch Depth, Bare Soil (March - May)	w
Pan Evaporation Map (May - September)	w
Growing Degree Days (May - October)	w
Crop Moisture Index (April - October)	w
Palmer Drought Severity Index (April - October)	w
Additional Precipitation Needed to End Drought (April - October)	w

International Charts (major crop areas):

Precipitation	w/m
Percent of Normal Precipitation	m
Average Temperature	m
Departure of Average Temperature from Normal	m

National Tabulations:

Weather Data for Selected Cities	w
Precipitation and Temperature	m
Crop Progress: Planting, Development, Harvesting (April - November)	w
Crop Condition (April - November)	w

International Tabulation:

Precipitation and Temperature	m

* w = weekly, m = monthly, s = seasonal (published every March, June, September, and December for the preceding 3 months)

Source: *Weekly Weather and Crop Bulletin*, v. 85, no. 52 (Dec. 29, 1998), p. 10.

Figure 14.2: Index to *Weekly Weather and Crop Bulletin*.

Coverage: individual world and U.S. weather stations.
Content: mean station and sea-level pressure; mean temperature; total precipitation.

International Station Meteorological Climate Summary. CD-ROM. (1996) U.S. Department of the Navy/U.S. Department of Commerce/U.S. Department of the Air Force. Jointly produced by Fleet Numerical Meteorology and Oceanography Detachment, National Climatic Data Center, and USA FETAC OL-A. D 201.40:M 56/996/CD. Item 0307-A-02.
Coverage: individual world weather stations.
Content: station climate summaries; temperature; humidity; winds; precipitation.

World WeatherDisc. CD-ROM. Seattle: WeatherDisc Associates, Inc.
Coverage: individual weather stations.
Content: temperature; precipitation; heating and cooling degree days.

Discussion

These sources cover world climatological data. *Climates of the World* contains a brief discussion of the climate of each continent with maps that illustrate average January and July temperatures and annual precipitation. Tables cover approximately 800 stations representing every country for which data could be obtained. Data given for each city include average maximum and minimum temperatures for selected months, extreme temperatures, and average monthly and annual precipitation. A map also illustrates temperature and precipitation extremes.

Monthly Climatic Data for the World contains two tables: one for surface data and one for upper-air data. Surface data cover temperature, pressure, precipitation, and sunshine. Upper-air data give temperature and wind data for different levels. Wind data includes steadiness, direction, and speed. Within each table, stations are arranged first by continent and then by country. Data are gathered from countries that are members of the World Meteorological Organization. A complete list of stations appears in the January and July issues. A shorter list of stations for which current data have been received appears in other issues. There is no annual summary. *Monthly Climatic Data for the World* is available on the agency's Web site, with limited free access to those who qualify, including federal depository libraries and .edu domain Internet addresses. This title is also included on the *National Climatic Data Center Periodical Publications* CD-ROM discussed in the "Detailed Climatological Data" section of this chapter.

World Weather Records is issued every 10 years. The last complete set covers 1971–80. Two volumes have been issued for 1981–90, but these have not been distributed to depository libraries. Recent sets have consisted of six volumes with each volume covering one world region, such as North America or Europe. Tables are arranged alphabetically by country, then by station. There is a page of data for each weather station. Some countries have only

one station, others several. Monthly and annual data for the decade are given on station pressure, sea-level pressure, mean temperature, and precipitation. The climatological normal for each month is also given. Two indexes list all the stations in each volume alphabetically and by country.

The *International Station Meteorological Climate Summary* CD-ROM contains climate summaries from several agency sources. The data available vary depending on the source. Detailed summaries are available for 2,600 stations, with more limited data available for an additional 4,000 stations. Detailed summaries include daily maximum, minimum, and mean temperature; daily precipitation; daily snowfall and snow depth; extreme precipitation and temperatures; wind data; pressure; humidity; visibility; specific weather phenomena; a summary table; and a narrative overview.

World WeatherDisc contains extensive climatological data from the records of the National Climatic Data Center and the National Center for Atmospheric Research. Data are provided for thousands of weather stations in the U.S. and throughout the world. Global information includes monthly mean temperature, precipitation, pressure, and wind data. U.S. weather station data include monthly temperature means and extremes, precipitation, heating and cooling degree days, daily maximum and minimum temperature, and daily precipitation.

Weekly Weather and Crop Bulletin discussed in the "Other Climate Sources" section of this chapter, the *CLIMVIS* Web site discussed in the "National Climatic Data Center" section, and some of the CD-ROMs in the "Climate CD-ROM Datasets" section also contain world weather information.

CLIMATE CD-ROM DATASETS
Checklist

1961–1990 Global Climate Normals. CD-ROM. (1998) U.S. Department of Commerce. National Oceanic and Atmospheric Administration. National Environmental Satellite, Data and Information Service. National Climatic Data Center. C 55.281/2-2:G 51/2/CD. Item 0274-F.
Coverage: individual world weather stations.
Content: maximum, minimum, and mean temperature; precipitation and snowfall; snow depth; humidity; pressure; wind; cloud cover; sunshine; and number of days with various weather phenomena.

U.S. Divisional and Station Climatic Data and Normals, Vol. 1. CD-ROM. (1994) U.S. Department of Commerce. National Oceanic and Atmospheric Administration. National Environmental Satellite, Data and Information Service. National Climatic Data Center. C 55.281/2-3: Item 0274-F-01.
Coverage: divisions, individual weather stations.
Content: temperature, precipitation, degree days, and Palmer Drought Index.

Cooperative Summary of the Day: TD 3200. CD-ROM. (annual) 1993–. U.S. Department of Commerce. National Oceanic and Atmospheric Administration. National Environmental Satellite, Data and Information Service. National Climatic Data Center. C 55.281/2-4: Item 0274-F-02.

> Coverage: individual U.S. weather stations.
>
> Content: daily maximum and minimum temperatures; daily rainfall; daily snowfall and snow depth; evaporation; wind; weather phenomena.

International Surface Weather Observations, 1982–1997. CD-ROM. (1998) U.S. Department of Commerce. National Oceanic and Atmospheric Administration. National Climatic Data Center. U.S. Department of the Air Force. C 55.54:W 37/v.1-5/CD. Item 0128-M-02.

> Coverage: individual weather stations.
>
> Content: hourly and three-hourly data on temperature, clouds, visibility, pressure, wind, and present and past weather.

Hourly United States Weather Observations, 1990–1995. CD-ROM. (1997) U.S. Department of Commerce. National Oceanic and Atmospheric Administration. National Climatic Data Center. U.S. Environmental Protection Agency. C 55.54:H 81/CD. Item 0128-M-02.

> Coverage: individual U.S. weather stations.
>
> Content: sky cover; temperature; humidity; pressure; wind; visibility; present weather; cloud layers; precipitation; and snow depth.

Probabilities of Temperature Extremes in the U.S.A. CD-ROM. (1999) U.S. Department of Commerce. National Oceanic and Atmospheric Administration. National Climatic Data Center. C 55.54:T 24/CD. Item 0128-M-02.

> Coverage: 332 locations in 50 states.
>
> Content: software and data to estimate extreme temperature probabilities and examine climate change scenarios.

National Virtual Data System (Online Store). WEB. U.S. Department of Commerce. National Oceanic and Atmospheric Administration. National Climatic Data Center. <http://www.nndc.noaa.gov/onlinestore.html>.

> Content: list of CD-ROM titles with descriptions of content and specifications.

CD-ROM Hints. WEB. U.S. Department of Commerce. National Oceanic and Atmospheric Administration. National Climatic Data Center. <http://www.ncdc.noaa.gov/ol/about/cdhints.html>.

> Content: troubleshooting information and hints for specific NCDC CD-ROM titles.

Discussion

The National Climatic Data Center issues many CD-ROMs containing extensive collections of climate data. Many contain raw data with no software. Most CD-ROMs produced before the late 1990s were produced for the DOS environment rather than Windows or Macintosh. Many of the CDs are one-time publications or infrequently updated, so they are not useful for current information. A selection of the more comprehensive titles is listed here.

1961–1990 Global Climate Normals contains normals (averages) data for over 4,000 weather stations world-wide. The CD contains eye-readable ASCII table files. It also contains large ASCII data files that can be read by user-written software or opened in an ASCII-compatible application that can handle large files. Also available are graphics files showing which countries submitted data (.pcx format) and limited DOS data extraction software.

U.S. Divisional and Station Climatic Data and Normals covers approximately 6,600 precipitation stations and 4,700 temperature stations. Data cover the current normals period 1961–90 with earlier data provided for comparison. Some monthly data are available back to 1931 and drought data are available back to 1895. Monthly divisional files include cooling and heating degree days, precipitation normals, and temperature normals. Daily and monthly station files cover cooling and heating degree days; precipitation normals; and average, maximum, and minimum temperature normals. Files also cover divisional monthly drought index and state, regional, and national heating and cooling degree days. Files are in the form of ASCII text data with no software or extraction programs provided.

Cooperative Summary of the Day consists of a 21-volume base set covering the earliest data available through 1993 with annual updates. Data in the base set are generally available for the time period 1948–93, but can go back as far as the 1850s for selected stations. Approximately 8,000 active stations are covered with many more historical stations included for selected years. Data are in the form of ASCII files with no software provided. Files in the base set are extremely large. Extraction programs may be downloaded from the agency Web site. See Appendix E of the *CD-ROM Hints* Web site. Extracted files are in the same format as the original and are not directly importable into spreadsheets. Extracted data files can be read using sequential access reads using BASIC, FORTRAN, or DATA BASE software. More recent annual updates include an extraction program for the update. Data from this set form the basis for the publication *Climatological Data* and for the commercial CD-ROM product *Climatedata NCDC Climate Summary of the Day*, discussed in the "Detailed Climatological Data" section of this chapter.

International Surface Weather Observations covers hourly and three-hourly weather observations for 1500 worldwide weather stations. Data cover wind direction and speed, ceiling, sky cover, types of clouds, visibility, and numerous indicators of specific current or recent weather conditions. Each data file contains data for one station year in compressed form. Software for uncompressing files is included on the CD.

Hourly United States Weather Observations contains hourly weather observations for 262 U.S. weather stations. A map interface and station list can be used to access data or data files can be copied directly from the CD. The CD includes instructions for operating in Windows 95, but may work best in DOS mode.

Probabilities of Temperature Extremes in the U.S.A. can estimate the probability for a specific location that an extreme temperature will occur for one or more consecutive days or for any number of days in a specified month or season. Users may also adjust the normal temperatures or use climate model projections to view probabilities under different scenarios. Results are shown as graphs.

The *National Virtual Data System* Web site is a database of National Climatic Data Center products, including CD-ROM titles. Users may select the "All" category or a general subject area, such as "Climate," and select CD-ROM as the product type to produce a list of CD-ROM titles available. Click on a title for a description and availability information. The *CD-ROM Hints* Web site provides some additional information on using selected CD titles.

INDEXES
Checklist

Catalog of United States Government Publications (MOCAT). WEB. 1994–. U.S. Government Printing Office. Superintendent of Documents. <http://www.gpo.gov/catalog>; <http://www.access.gpo.gov/su_docs/locators/cgp/index.html>; <http://purl.access.gpo.gov/GPO/LPS844>.

Monthly Catalog of United States Government Publications. CD-ROM. 1996–. U.S. Government Printing Office. Superintendent of Documents. GP 3.8/7: Item 0557-C. GPO.

Monthly Catalog of United States Government Publications (Condensed version). PRINT. (monthly) 1996–. U.S. Government Printing Office. Superintendent of Documents. GP 3.8/8: (Earlier full version, GP 3.8:, 1895-1995). Item 0557-D. GPO.

American Statistics Index (ASI). PRINT. (monthly) 1973–. Bethesda, MD: Congressional Information Service.

Statistical Universe. WEB. Bethesda, MD: Congressional Information Service.

Discussion

The *Monthly Catalog* is the most comprehensive index to government publications. Additional materials can be found under such subject headings as "Climatology," "Temperature," "Precipitation (Meteorology)," "Weather," "Storms," "Winds," "Rain and Rainfall," "Meteorology," and "Tornadoes." The complete version of the *Monthly Catalog* is available on the Web and CD-ROM. Commercial online and CD-ROM versions of the *Monthly Catalog* are also available.

ASI indexes statistical data on weather under such headings as "Weather," "Meteorology," and "Storms." *Statistical Universe* includes a Web version of *ASI*.

For more information on these indexes, see Chapter 3, "The Basics of Searching."

GPO *Subject Bibliographies*. PRINT. WEB. GP 3.22/2:

<http://bookstore.gpo.gov/sb/about.html>

No. 234 "Weather"

Other

The Weather Almanac: A Reference Guide to Weather, Climate, and Related Issues in the United States and its Key Cities. PRINT. 8th ed. (1998) Detroit, MI: Gale Research Co.

Weather of U.S. Cities: A Guide to the Weather Histories of 268 Key Cities and Weather Observation Stations in the United States and its Island Territories. PRINT. 5th ed. (1996) Detroit, MI: Gale Research, Inc.

The *Weather Almanac* contains maps, several narrative chapters on weather topics, and climatological data for more than 100 U.S. cities. Each city report includes a normals, means, and extremes table; precipitation; average temperature; heating and cooling degree days; snowfall; and a brief description of the city location and weather. Data are given for several years. The information is similar to that found in the annual issue of *Local Climatological Data*.

Weather of U.S. Cities is similar to the city section of *The Weather Almanac*, but covers more cities.

CHAPTER 15
Elections

The government publishes basic election results and statistics on the voting age population and voter participation. There is also information available from the government on campaign procedures and financing. More detailed election result data can be obtained from nongovernmental sources, such as Congressional Quarterly publications, some of which are listed in this chapter.

SEARCH STRATEGY

This chapter shows a subject search. The steps to follow are

1. Consult the "General Statistical Sources" section of this chapter to identify resources giving basic election and voting statistics;
2. Try the "Sources for Election Results" listings for titles giving election results;
3. Examine any of the special topic sections that seem relevant — "Sources for Voting Population and Participation," "Congressional District Data," or "Campaign Finance Sources";
4. Locate miscellaneous materials, including campaign procedures and laws, in the "Other Election Information Sources" category; and
5. Consider the "Indexes" and "Related Material" sections.

GENERAL STATISTICAL SOURCES
Checklist

Statistical Abstract of the United States. PRINT. WEB. (annual) 1878–. U.S. Department of Commerce. Economics and Statistics Administration. Bureau of the Census. C 3.134: Item 0150. ASI 2324-1. GPO. <http://www.census.gov/statab/www/>; <http://purl.access.gpo.gov/GPO/LPS2878>.
> Coverage: U.S., regions, states, congressional districts.
> Content: electoral and popular vote cast for President by state and party; vote cast for senators and representatives

by party; composition and characteristics of Congress; vote cast for governors; composition of state legislatures; office holders by race and sex; voting age population; voting registration and participation; characteristics of voters; campaign finance.

Statistical Abstract of the United States. CD-ROM. (annual) 1993–. U.S. Department of Commerce. Bureau of the Census. C 3.134/7: Item 0150-B. ASI 2324-14.
> Content: CD-ROM version of the *Statistical Abstract.*

Historical Statistics of the United States: Colonial Times to 1970. Parts 1-2. PRINT. (1975) U.S. Department of Commerce. Bureau of the Census. C 3.134/2:H 62/789-970/pt.1-2. Item 0151. ASI (76) 2328-2. GPO.
> Coverage: U.S., states.
> Content: electoral and popular vote cast for President by state and party; voter participation in Presidential elections; cost of Presidential elections; party affiliations in Congress and the Presidency; votes cast for representatives by party.

Historical Statistics of the United States on CD-ROM: Colonial Times to 1970. CD-ROM. (1997) New York, NY: Cambridge University Press.
> Content: CD-ROM version of *Historical Statistics of the United States.*

State and Metropolitan Area Data Book. PRINT. WEB. (irregular) 1979–. U.S. Department of Commerce. Economics and Statistics Administration. Bureau of the Census. C 3.134/5: Item 0150. ASI 2328-54. GPO. <http://www.census.gov/statab/www/smadb.html>.
> Coverage: U.S., states.
> Content: vote cast for President and senators in recent elections by party; party composition of Congress and state legislatures; vote cast for governor; voting age population; minority office holders.

State and Metropolitan Area Data Book. CD-ROM. (irregular) 1997/98–. U.S. Department of Commerce. Economics and Statistics Administration. Bureau of the Census. (Not distributed to depository libraries).

Content: CD-ROM version of the *State and Metropolitan Area Data Book*.

County and City Data Book. PRINT. WEB. (quinquennial) 1947–. U.S. Department of Commerce. Economics and Statistics Administration. Bureau of the Census. C 3.134/2:C 83/2/year. Item 0151. ASI 2328-1. GPO. <http://fisher.lib.Virginia.EDU/ccdb/>.

Coverage: states, counties.
Content: total vote cast for President and percentage of vote for leading candidates.

County and City Data Book. CD-ROM. (quinquennial) 1988–. U.S. Department of Commerce. Bureau of the Census. C 3.134/2-1: (Earlier, C 3.134/2:C 83/2/) Item 0151-D-01. ASI 2328-103.

Content: CD-ROM version of the *County and City Data Book*.

County and City Extra: Annual Metro, City, and County Data Book. PRINT. (annual) 1992–. Lanham, MD: Bernan Press.

Coverage: U.S., states, counties, metropolitan areas.
Content: percentage of vote cast for president by party for most recent presidential election.

USA Counties. CD-ROM. WEB. (irregular) 1992–. U.S. Department of Commerce. Economics and Statistics Administration. Bureau of the Census. C 3.134/6: Item 0150-B-01. ASI 2324-17. <http://govinfo.kerr.orst.edu/usaco-stateis.html>; <http://tier2.census.gov/usac/index.html-ssi>.

Coverage: U.S., states, counties.
Content: number and percentage of vote cast for president by party for recent elections.

Discussion

The *Statistical Abstract of the United States* contains a chapter on "Elections" that gives election results for Presidential and congressional elections. The Presidential election tables cover several years. Congressional election data are for recent elections only. There are also statistics on the characteristics of voters, political party identification of voters, the composition of Congress, and campaign finance. The full text of recent editions of the *Statistical Abstract* is available on the Census Bureau Web site as PDF files. The *Statistical Abstract* is also available on CD-ROM. The CD uses Adobe Acrobat software and contains some additional geographic areas and time series in the form of spreadsheet files that are not in the printed version. Additional, but more limited, historical statistics can be found in *Historical Statistics of the United States: Colonial Times to 1970*, which emphasizes presidential election data. A CD-ROM version of *Historical Statistics* is available from Cambridge University Press.

The *State and Metropolitan Area Data Book* gives state data on presidential and senatorial elections by party, but not by individual candidate. The book includes additional statistics on the party composition of Congress and the voting age population. There are no election statistics at the metropolitan area level.

The *County and City Data Book* contains only two items related to elections: total vote cast for President and percentage of vote for leading candidates. This book covers the most recently available presidential election. This title is also available on CD-ROM. *County and City Extra* is a commercially produced annual version of the *County and City Data Book*.

The *USA Counties* CD-ROM contains county and state data from the last two or three issues of the *County and City Data Book* and the *State and Metropolitan Area Data Book* to provide several years of data in one source. The data are similar to that found in the two data books and include vote cast for president, total and by party, for recent elections. The Oregon State University Government Information Sharing Project provides access to the current issue on the Internet. Users select a geographic area profile or an area comparison and then the desired geography. A subject area can then be selected or a keyword search conducted to display data. The Census Bureau Web site contains a similar version.

SOURCES FOR ELECTION RESULTS
Checklist

Federal Elections [year]: Election Results for U.S. President, the U.S. Senate and the U.S. House of Representatives. MF. WEB. (biennial) 1982–. U.S. Federal Election Commission. Y 3.EL 2/3:16/ (Earlier, Y 3.EL 2/3:2 F 31/4/) (Subtitle varies in nonpresidential years: *Federal Elections [year]: Election Results for the U.S. Senate and the U.S. House of Representatives*) Item 1091-A. ASI 9274-5. <http://www.fec.gov/elections.html>.

Content: official election results by state giving candidates, party, total votes, and percentage of votes for President, Senate, and House; House results by congressional district.

Statistics of the Presidential and Congressional Election. PRINT. WEB. (biennial) 1920–. U.S. Congress. House of Representatives. Y 1.2:EL 2/. (Title varies in nonpresidential years: *Statistics of the Congressional Election*; generally nondepository) Item 998. ASI 21944-3. <http://clerkweb.house.gov/elections/elections.htm>.

Content: listing by state of votes cast for presidential electors by party, for senators by candidate and party, and for representatives by district, candidate, and party; summary totals of votes cast for each office by party.

Official Congressional Directory. PRINT. WEB. (annual) 1809–. U.S. Congress. Joint Committee on Printing. Y 4.P 93/1:1/ Item 0992. ASI 23874-1. GPO. <http://www.access.gpo.gov/congress/cong016.html>.

Content: number of votes cast for senators and representatives in last three elections by state and party; House data by congressional district; number of representatives under each apportionment; congressional district maps.

CQ Weekly. PRINT. WEB. (weekly) 1946–. (Title varies. Earlier, *Congressional Quarterly Weekly Report*) Washington, D.C.: Congressional Quarterly, Inc. CQ Library: <http://libraryip.cq.com/>.

Content: votes for each candidate and governors by state; percentage of total votes; analytical articles on election results.

America Votes: A Handbook of Contemporary American Election Statistics. (biennial) 1956–. Richard M. Scammon, Alice V. McGillivray, and Rhodes Cook, comps. Washington, D.C.: CQ Press.

Content: election results by state, county, and selected large cities; total vote and percentage by candidate and party; historical tables.

Congressional Quarterly Almanac. PRINT. (annual) 1945–. Washington, D.C.: Congressional Quarterly, Inc.

Content: votes and percentage of total votes for presidential candidates; summary data on congressional and gubernatorial elections; analytical articles on election results.

Discussion

Federal Elections reports the official election results for each biennial election. It contains the most complete information on individual candidates, with all parties represented. There are separate sections for the President (when appropriate), Senate, and House. Each section is arranged alphabetically by state. The House section is further subdivided by congressional district. The full name of each candidate is given, along with party affiliation, number of votes, and percentage of votes. Votes are given for primaries, runoffs, and general elections. For the Senate, there is also a list of incumbents arranged by the year their term expires. Summary tables give total votes cast by state and party. Maps illustrate Senate victors by party, Senate incumbents re-elected or defeated, House delegations by majority party, and party gains in the House. In presidential election years, tables and maps show the popular and electoral votes for president. Recent editions are available on the Web.

Statistics of the Presidential and Congressional Election has not generally been distributed to depository libraries, but all issues since 1920 are available on the Web. Data for the President (when appropriate), Senate, and House are given for each state, along with a statistical summary table. Votes cast for the President are given by party, not by candidate names. Individual candidates are named for the Senate and House, along with the candidate's party affiliation. House candidates are listed by congressional district. Minor party candidates are included. A summary table shows votes cast for each office by party and total vote cast.

The *Official Congressional Directory* gives congressional election results, but not results for presidential elections. The data are limited to vote cast by major party for recent elections. Total vote cast is given only for the most recent election. House data are given by congressional district. Individual candidates, however, are not named.

CQ Weekly produces an election issue shortly after each biennial November election with complete election results by individual candidate. Information includes the number and percentage of votes for each candidate. *CQ Weekly* also contains many analytical articles on election results, the campaign, and campaign funding.

America Votes contains voting results for the U.S., states, counties, and a small number of large cities. A volume is issued for each election year. Volumes contain historical statistics, as well as detailed statistics on the current election. The introduction contains summary tables on voter turnout and the total vote for governors, senators, and representatives by state. A brief United States overview gives historical statistics on the popular and electoral vote for president. Sections for each state include district maps and historical state tables on elections for presidents, governors, and senators. Data on elections for representatives are given by congressional district for recent elections. County data for the most recent election are given for governors and senators. Information provided includes total vote, Republican and Democratic vote by candidate, other vote, plurality, and percentage of total and major vote for Republican and Democratic parties. Primary elections are also covered.

Congressional Quarterly Almanac often contains a "Political Report" chapter or appendix in election years, giving election results and analytical articles. In recent years, the results for congressional elections have been reduced to summary data and lists of new members, without the full candidate lists and vote totals of previous years.

SOURCES FOR VOTING POPULATION AND PARTICIPATION

Checklist

Voting and Registration in the Election of [date]. PRINT. WEB. (biennial) 1964–. U.S. Department of Commerce. Economics and Statistics Administration. Bureau of the Census. Current Population Reports: Population Characteristics, Series P-20. C 3.186/3-2: (Earlier, C 3.186:P-20/). Item 0142-C-01. ASI 2546-1. GPO. <http://www.census.gov/population/www/socdemo/voting.html>; <http://www.census.gov/prod/www/abs/popula.html#pop>; <http://www.census.gov/mp/www/pub/pop/mspop01.html>.

Coverage: U.S., regions, divisions (Web), states (Web). Content: percentage of persons voting and registered by age, race, sex, education, marital status, income, housing characteristics, employment status, and occupation characteristics; percentage registered but not voting by age, race, sex, education; reason for not voting.

Projections of the Voting-Age Population for States: November [year]. PRINT. WEB. (biennial) U.S. Department of Commerce. Economics and Statistics Administration. Bureau of the Census. Current Population Reports: Population Characteristics, Series P-25. C 3.186/26: (Title varies: *Projections of the Population of Voting Age for States: November [year]*) Item 0142-C-03. ASI 2546-3.[no]. <http://www.census.gov/population/www/socdemo/voting.html>; <http://www.census.gov/prod/www/abs/popula.html#popest>; <http://www.census.gov/mp/www/pub/pop/mspop05.html>.

Coverage: U.S., regions, divisions, states.

Content: projections of the voting-age population by age group, sex, and race; population of voting age and percent voting in previous elections; participation in elections.

Voting and Registration Web Page. WEB. U.S. Department of Commerce. Bureau of the Census. <http://www.census.gov/population/www/socdemo/voting.html>.

Content: tables and links to full-text publications on voting participation and registration and on the voting-age population.

About Elections and Voting Web Page. WEB. U.S. Federal Election Commission. <http://www.fec.gov/elections.html>.

Coverage: countries, U.S., states.

Content: current and historical statistics on voter registration and turnout.

Discussion

Voting and Registration in the Election of [date] is the most detailed statistical report on voter participation. A print summary is published every other election year with more detailed tables available on the Census Bureau Web site. Similar detailed tables were included in the print version through 1992. In alternate election years tables are published only on the Web site. The print version gives summary statistics with some historic trends. Examples of data items include the percentage of people in the 18-to-24 years age group that voted in 1964 compared to 1996 or how many registered voters did not vote due to illness. The detailed Web tables cover persons registered, persons voting, persons registered but not voting, and persons not registered by a variety of demographic, social, and economic variables. (See Figure 15.1.) A set of state tables is also available on the Web.

Projections of the Voting-Age Population for States: November [year] is issued during election years and projects the number of voting-age persons for the coming election. Print versions are published every other election year. Alternate year tables are available only on the Web. Projections are given by state, sex, race, and age group. The print version also contains tables on the voting-age population in previous election years and the percent casting votes in previous elections. This source answers such questions as "What is the population of black women between 25 and 44 years of age expected to be at election time?" or "What percentage of the voting-age population voted for President in the 1988 election?" (print edition).

The *Voting and Registration Web Page* includes the full text of recent editions of *Voting and Registration in the Election of [date]* and *Projections of the Voting-Age Population for States: November [year]* plus additional detailed tables not included in the printed reports. Tables are also available for alternating election years when these two reports are not published in print. The Web page also includes other related publications and a set of historical time series tables.

The *About Elections and Voting Web Page* contains several statistical tables on voter registration and turnout that cover several years. Data are given by state, type of election (presidential or congressional), age, race, and sex. Total turnout is also given for recent elections in other countries.

CONGRESSIONAL DISTRICT DATA
Checklist

Population and Housing Characteristics for Congressional Districts of the 103rd Congress. PRINT. (decennial) 1980–. U.S. Department of Commerce. Bureau of the Census. C 3.223/20: (Title varies; before 1980 data were published in *Congressional District Data Book*) Item 0159-C-01 to 53. ASI 2551-4.

Coverage: congressional districts, counties, places of 10,000 or more, minor civil divisions of 10,000 or more.

Content: population and housing characteristics; age, sex, race, marital status, family and household characteristics, education, ancestry, language, employment and occupation, income, housing occupancy, housing structure, plumbing, equipment, and financial characteristics.

Congressional Districts of the United States Summary Tape File 1D; Summary Tape File 3D. CD-ROM. WEB. U.S. Department of Commerce. Bureau of the Census. C 3.282/4: Item 0154-F-05. ASI 2551-18. <http://www.census.gov/prod/www/abs/congprof.html>.

Coverage: states, congressional districts, counties, places, American Indian areas.

Content: population and housing characteristics; age, sex, race, marital status, family and household characteristics, education, ancestry, language, employment and occupation, income, housing occupancy, housing structure, plumbing, equipment, and financial characteristics.

Congressional District Atlas. PRINT. (irregular) 1960–. U.S. Department of Commerce. Economics and Statistics Administration. Bureau of the Census. C 3.62/5: Item 0140-B. ASI 2448-3. GPO.

Content: maps for each state showing county and district boundaries; lists correlating cities and counties to congressional district number.

Congressional District Atlas. CD-ROM. (biennial) U.S. Department of Commerce. Economics and Statistics Administration. Bureau of the Census. Geography Division. C 3.282/5: Item 0154-F-06.

Content: CD-ROM version of the *Congressional District Atlas.*

Official Congressional Directory. PRINT. WEB. (annual) 1809–. U.S. Congress. Joint Committee on Printing. Y 4.P 93/1:1/ Item 0992. ASI 23874-1. GPO. <http://www.access.gpo.gov/congress/cong016.html>.

Content: maps for each state showing county and congressional district boundaries.

5

Table 2. Reported Voting and Registration, by Race, Hispanic Origin, Sex, and Age, for the United States and Regions—Continued

(November 1996. Numbers in thousands. For meaning of symbols, see text)

Region, race, Hispanic origin, sex, and age	All persons	Reported registered		Reported voted		Reported that they did not vote[1]				
								Not registered		
		Number	Percent	Number	Percent	Total	Registered	Total[2]	Not a U.S. citizen	Do not know and not reported on registration
UNITED STATES—CONTINUED										
Black										
Both Sexes										
Total, 18 years and over	22,483	14,267	63.5	11,386	50.6	11,098	2,881	8,216	997	2,379
18 to 20 years	1,621	689	42.5	461	28.4	1,161	228	933	71	193
21 to 24 years	1,992	1,094	54.9	709	35.6	1,283	385	898	82	222
25 to 34 years	5,315	3,106	58.4	2,338	44.0	2,976	768	2,209	273	595
35 to 44 years	5,338	3,432	64.3	2,757	51.7	2,581	674	1,906	310	616
45 to 54 years	3,472	2,408	69.4	2,098	60.4	1,374	310	1,064	152	342
55 to 64 years	2,122	1,567	73.8	1,351	63.7	771	216	555	70	190
65 to 74 years	1,568	1,220	77.8	1,062	67.7	506	158	348	20	119
75 years and over	1,055	752	71.3	610	57.8	445	142	303	21	102
Male										
Total, 18 years and over	9,993	6,001	60.0	4,658	46.6	5,335	1,343	3,992	506	1,142
18 to 20 years	772	297	38.4	171	22.1	602	126	475	39	94
21 to 24 years	890	457	51.3	252	28.4	638	204	433	34	116
25 to 34 years	2,380	1,290	54.2	960	40.3	1,420	330	1,090	136	292
35 to 44 years	2,437	1,499	61.5	1,187	48.7	1,250	312	938	150	314
45 to 54 years	1,563	1,013	64.8	870	55.7	693	143	550	102	144
55 to 64 years	919	665	72.3	581	63.2	338	84	254	30	86
65 to 74 years	663	502	75.7	412	62.1	252	90	161	9	62
75 years and over	368	278	75.4	225	61.2	143	52	91	6	33
Female										
Total, 18 years and over	12,490	8,266	66.2	6,728	53.9	5,762	1,538	4,224	491	1,237
18 to 20 years	849	392	46.1	290	34.2	559	102	457	31	99
21 to 24 years	1,102	637	57.8	456	41.4	645	181	465	48	106
25 to 34 years	2,934	1,815	61.9	1,378	47.0	1,556	437	1,119	137	304
35 to 44 years	2,901	1,932	66.6	1,571	54.1	1,331	362	969	160	301
45 to 54 years	1,909	1,395	73.1	1,228	64.3	681	167	514	50	198
55 to 64 years	1,203	902	75.0	770	64.0	433	132	301	40	104
65 to 74 years	905	718	79.4	650	71.8	255	68	187	10	57
75 years and over	687	474	69.0	385	56.0	302	89	213	14	69
Hispanic origin[3]										
Both Sexes										
Total, 18 years and over	18,426	6,573	35.7	4,928	26.7	13,497	1,645	11,853	7,217	1,184
18 to 20 years	1,421	386	27.1	228	16.1	1,193	158	1,036	454	95
21 to 24 years	2,031	567	27.9	294	14.5	1,736	273	1,464	824	139
25 to 34 years	5,228	1,454	27.8	1,026	19.6	4,202	428	3,774	2,493	304
35 to 44 years	4,322	1,580	36.6	1,163	26.9	3,158	416	2,742	1,741	289
45 to 54 years	2,310	999	43.2	830	36.0	1,479	168	1,311	844	145
55 to 64 years	1,626	781	48.0	677	41.6	950	104	845	492	104
65 to 74 years	1,003	532	53.1	489	48.7	514	43	471	248	81
75 years and over	485	275	56.6	220	45.4	265	54	211	122	27
Male										
Total, 18 years and over	9,213	3,028	32.9	2,233	24.2	6,980	795	6,185	3,805	651
18 to 20 years	746	179	24.0	93	12.4	653	86	567	242	63
21 to 24 years	1,062	270	25.4	125	11.7	938	146	792	470	92
25 to 34 years	2,748	685	24.9	472	17.2	2,275	213	2,063	1,374	155
35 to 44 years	2,195	760	34.6	561	25.6	1,634	199	1,435	933	160
45 to 54 years	1,109	422	38.1	345	31.1	764	78	687	431	76
55 to 64 years	730	326	44.7	284	38.8	447	43	404	224	54
65 to 74 years	426	248	58.3	233	54.7	193	15	177	94	38
75 years and over	197	137	69.8	121	61.5	76	16	59	38	13
Female										
Total, 18 years and over	9,213	3,545	38.5	2,695	29.3	6,517	850	5,668	3,411	533
18 to 20 years	675	207	30.6	135	20.0	540	71	468	212	31
21 to 24 years	968	297	30.6	170	17.5	798	127	672	354	47
25 to 34 years	2,480	769	31.0	553	22.3	1,927	215	1,711	1,119	149
35 to 44 years	2,127	820	38.6	602	28.3	1,524	218	1,306	808	129
45 to 54 years	1,201	577	48.0	486	40.5	715	91	624	413	69
55 to 64 years	896	455	50.8	393	43.9	503	62	441	268	50
65 to 74 years	577	284	49.2	256	44.3	321	28	293	154	42
75 years and over	289	137	47.6	99	34.4	189	38	151	83	14

See footnotes at end of table.

Source: *Voting and Registration in the Election of November 1996, Detailed Tables*, Table 2. U.S. Census Bureau Web Site <http://www.census.gov/prod/3/98pubs/p20-504u.pdf>

Figure 15.1: Sample Page from *Voting and Registration in the Election of November 1996, Detailed Tables*.

Discussion

Congressional district data are useful in analyzing elections for the House of Representatives. The *Census of Population and Housing* contains a series of reports titled *Population and Housing Characteristics for Congressional Districts*. A report is issued for each state and provides a demographic and economic portrait of each individual district. The only statistic directly related to elections is the number of voting-age persons by sex and race. *Congressional Districts of the United States Summary Tape File 1D; Summary Tape File 3D* provides detailed demographic and economic data for congressional districts on CD-ROM. The CD-ROM is updated periodically to reflect changes in congressional district boundaries since the census. Similar data are also available on the Census Bureau *Congressional District Profiles* Web page. The 1980 census *Supplementary Report* series also contained a report on congressional districts titled *Congressional District Profiles, 98th Congress* (C 3.223/12:80-S1-11). This was a single report with somewhat different, but more limited, data on all states and congressional districts.

The *Congressional District Atlas* shows district boundaries and indicates in which district each county and city is located. More current, but smaller maps can be found in the *Official Congressional Directory*.

OTHER ELECTION INFORMATION SOURCES
Checklist

Federal Election Commission Home Page. WEB. U.S. Federal Election Commission. <http://www.fec.gov/>.
> Content: election and campaign finance information and law; campaign finance database; election results; agency information and services.

Record. PRINT. WEB. (monthly) 1975–. U.S. Federal Election Commission. Y 3.EL 2/3:11. Item 1091-A. <http://www.fec.gov/pages/infosub1.htm>; <http://purl.access.gpo.gov/GPO/LPS3392>; <http://www.fec.gov/finance_law.html>.
> Content: public funding news and statistics; legal and regulatory activities; summaries of court cases and advisory opinions; schedules for filing reports; matching funds eligibility, payments, statistics; PACs and party committee statistics; publication announcements.

Senate Election Law Guidebook 1998: A Compilation of Senate Campaign Information, Including Federal and State Laws Governing Election to the United States Senate. PRINT. MF. WEB. (1998) U.S. Congress. Senate. Committee on Rules and Administration. Senate Document No. 105-12. Y 1.1/3:105-12. Items 0996-A or -B(MF). <http://www.access.gpo.gov/congress/cong006.html>.
> Content: federal laws relating to the nomination and election of senators; senate election rules; state election laws; information on campaign activities, ethics laws, and member qualifications.

Discussion

The *Federal Election Commission Home Page* provides information on election law, administration, and campaign finance. Main menu categories include "About the FEC," "FEC Services," "Campaign Finance Reports and Data," "Campaign Finance Law Resources," and "Elections and Voting." Also available are news releases and a site index. "Campaign Finance Reports and Data" provides access to campaign finance reports filed by candidates, political parties, and political action committees (PACs). This category is discussed further in the "Campaign Finance Sources" section of this chapter. The "Campaign Finance Law Resources" area includes agency regulations, a database of advisory opinions, recent *Federal Register* notices, campaign guides and other agency publications, and selected court case abstracts. The "Elections and Voting" category provides recent election results, information and statistics on voter registration, a directory of election officials, and information on the electoral college and voting systems.

The *Record* reports on new legislation, regulations, advisory opinions, and court cases related to elections. It also covers news on report filing and campaign financing. News items are arranged by such categories as "Public Funding," "Statistics," and "Reports." Examples of statistics reported include number of PACs by type, PAC contributions, and candidate and party receipts and expenditures. Each issue contains an index that cumulates throughout the year. A separate annual index is published at the end of the year.

The *Senate Election Law Guidebook* covers laws and rules relating to the election and nomination of senators, including material on campaign financing and financial disclosure. The guidebook is updated periodically. It is available on the Internet by searching the congressional documents database on *GPO Access*.

CAMPAIGN FINANCE SOURCES
Checklist

Combined Federal/State Disclosure and Election Directory. MF. WEB. 1992–. U.S. Federal Election Commission. Public Disclosure Division. Y 3.EL 2/3:14-2/year. (Title varies) Item 1091-A. <http://www.fec.gov/pubrec/cfsdd.htm>.
> Content: directory of national and state offices that provide information on campaign financing, lobbies, candidate financial statements, other public finance data, and voting and election information.

Campaign Finance Reports and Data Web Page. WEB. U.S. Federal Election Commission. <http://www.fec.gov/finance_reports.html>.
> Content: database on campaign contributions to candidates, parties, and political action committees (PACs); images of campaign finance reports filed; summary reports on current and previous campaigns.

FECInfo Web Site. WEB. Netivation.com, Inc. <http://www.tray.com/>.

>   Content: database on campaign contributions to candidates, parties, and political action committees (PACs); House and Senate financial disclosure reports; candidate and PAC money leaders.

Your Guide to Researching Public Records. PRINT. WEB. U.S. Federal Election Commission. Y 3.EL 2/3:8 R 31/998. Item 1091-A. <http://www.fec.gov/publicrecords.html>.

>   Content: information on the campaign finance records, indexes, and databases maintained by the Federal Election Commission.

Availability of FEC Information. PRINT. (1999) U.S. Federal Election Commission. Y 3.EL 2/3:2 IN 3. Item 1091-A.

>   Content: types of information available and how to obtain it.

FEC Reports on Financial Activity. MF. (biennial) 1976–. U.S. Federal Election Commission. Y3.EL 2/3:15/ (Earlier title: *FEC Disclosure*) Item 1091-A. ASI 9276-2.

>   Coverage: U.S., states, individual candidates, individual political committees.
>   Content: financial statistics for campaigns and political committees; receipts and disbursements; contributions received by source; expenditures for and against candidates; data by office, party, and type of campaign.

Financial Disclosure Reports of Members of the U.S. House of Representatives for the Period between Jan. 1, [year] and Dec. 31, [year]. PRINT. MF. (annual) 1977–. U.S. Congress. House. House Document. Y 1.1/7: (1998 edition is Y 1.1/7:106-103/v.1-3) Items 0996-A or -B(MF).

>   Content: personal financial statements for each member of the House of Representatives; income, assets, transactions, liabilities, travel payments, and gifts.

Public Document Service for Public Financial Disclosure Reports Web Page. WEB. U.S. Office of Government Ethics. <http://www.usoge.gov/usoge004.html#document>.

>   Content: how to obtain executive branch financial disclosure reports; copy of standardized request form.

Congressional Universe. WEB. Bethesda, MD: Congressional Information Service. <http://www.lexis-nexis.com/cispubs/Catalog/Universe/Congressional%20Universe/index.htm>.

>   Content: campaign finance reports, financial disclosure reports, and campaign contributions for members of Congress.

LEXIS-NEXIS. <http://www.lexis-nexis.com/lncc/>.

>   Content: campaign finance reports, financial disclosure reports, campaign contributions, and Federal Election Commission releases.

Discussion

The *Combined Federal/State Disclosure and Election Directory* lists sources of information on political funding and elections. The directory lists offices, individual contacts, addresses, telephone numbers, URLs, and types of information available from each source. Federal Election Commission contacts are listed first, followed by other national offices, then state offices arranged alphabetically by state. The offices included are responsible for providing campaign and candidate financial information to the public

Presidential and House candidates, political parties, and political action committees (PACs) must file campaign finance reports with the Federal Election Commission (FEC). The FEC's *Campaign Finance Reports and Data Web Page* provides access to these reports and to summary statistics based on the reports. Images of the original financial reports are available for Presidential campaign committees, party committees, and PACs since 1993 and for House campaign committees since 1996. An option to view electronically filed reports allows access to reports shortly after they are submitted—sooner than they are available in the image database. A database search option is also available, covering selected contributions to House, Senate, and Presidential campaigns, parties, and PACs. It presently covers only the current and one previous election cycle. Users can search by individual contributor, committee name, or candidate name. Other search options include city, zip code, or party for committees and candidates. Summary statistical reports are available for Presidential, Senate, and House campaigns and political parties and PACs since 1996. Data files are also available for downloading beginning with the 1993–1994 election cycle.

The *FECInfo Web Site* is a nongovernment site based on Federal Election Commission data. Its exceptional presentation and coverage makes this a premiere site for campaign finance information. *FECInfo* provides more historical data than the FEC's own site with some data going back to 1980. Database choices include House/Senate campaign money, U.S. Presidential candidate money, PAC and party committees, and options to look up contributors by name, occupation/employer, donations outside of home state, and zip code. House and Senate candidates can be located by name, state, and election cycle. Presidential candidates are listed by election cycle, then by name. PACs and party committees can be searched by name, election cycle, or Standard Industrial Classification (SIC) category. Other features include candidate and PAC money leaders and financial news relating to the current President and Vice-President. One area of the Web site, *FECInfoPro,* is only available by subscription. It includes a soft money database and lobby reports and registrations.

Your Guide to Researching Public Records describes the records maintained by the Federal Election Commission. Categories covered include candidates; PACs, party and other committees; individual contributors; and commission activity. Each category generally includes a list of indexes or search options and a research checklist. Information is provided on how to obtain data. Some data, especially for earlier election years, are only available from the FEC's own files and databases.

Availability of FEC Information summarizes the types of information available from the FEC for campaign finance and other areas. Methods of obtaining information include visiting the FEC, telephone, fax, computer access, and visiting state offices. A chart lists each type of information and related access methods.

The *FEC Reports on Financial Activity* series contains summary statistics produced from the reports filed with the FEC by candidates and political committees. There are generally two titles for each two-year period. These consist of a one-volume *Final Report: U.S. Senate and House Campaigns* and a four-volume *Final Report: Party and Non-Party Political Committees*.

The *Final Report: U.S. Senate and House Campaigns* contains national and state summary tables and a table listing individual candidates. The individual candidate and state tables provide data on total receipts, sources of receipts, cash on hand, and support or opposition by types of political committee. The national tables give similar data by campaign type and office. An appendix gives a six-year summary of Senate campaign receipts and disbursements by candidate.

The *Final Report: Party and Non-Party Political Committees* gives information on contributions made by individual political committees by office and party, but not by individual candidate. Volume 1 covers national Democratic and Republican committees and contains summary data on other types of committees. Volume 2 covers state and local Democratic and Republican committees. Volumes 3 and 4 cover nonparty committees by type, such as corporation, labor organizations, and trade organizations.

Although these reports give individual candidate and committee data, they do not correlate specific committees to specific candidates. It is possible to determine, for example, how much money a candidate received from corporate political committees, but not which committees were involved. Similarly, information is available on how much money a specific corporate committee gave to Democratic candidates, but not how much was given to a specific candidate. More detailed and more current information is available from the FEC's *Campaign Finance Reports and Data Web Page* and the *FECInfo Web Site*.

The Federal Election Commission began collecting campaign data with the 1976 campaign. Detailed reports on the 1972 campaign were published by the General Accounting Office and the Congress. No data on the 1974 campaign were published. The 1972 titles are *Federal Election Campaign Act of 1971: Alphabetical Listing of 1972 Presidential Campaign Receipts* (GA 1.20:972/v.1-2); *Annual Statistical Report of Contributions and Expenditures Made During the 1972 Election Campaigns for the U.S. House of Representatives* (House Document No. 93-284, Serial Set 13077-2, -3); *Annual Statistical Report of Receipts and Expenditures Made in Connection with Elections for the U.S. Senate in 1972* (Y 1.3/6:972); and *1972 Annual Reports of Political Committees Supporting Candidates for the U.S. House of Representatives* (Y 1.2/4:).

The Ethics in Government Act of 1978, as amended, requires the President, Vice President, and members of Congress, as well as certain other federal officials, to file personal financial reports. *Financial Disclosure Reports of Members of the U.S. House of Representatives* contains individual reports from each representative on income sources, assets, and financial transactions. The reports of the President, Vice-President, and Senate are not published. The *FECInfo Web Site* includes personal financial reports for House and Senate members in their House and Senate campaign data category. Reports for senators can also be obtained from the Secretary of the Senate. (See the *Combined Federal/State Disclosure and Election Directory* above for information on addresses and the types of information available.) Copies of financial reports for the President and Vice-President may be obtained from the Office of Government Ethics. Instructions and a copy of the request form are available from the *Public Document Service for Public Financial Disclosure Reports Web Page*.

Campaign finance information and financial disclosure reports are also available from commercial sources, including *Congressional Universe* and LEXIS-NEXIS. *Congressional Universe* campaign finance information can be found under the "Members" main menu category. Data available include candidates' campaign finance reports filed with the FEC since 1989, financial disclosure reports since 1991, and individual and PAC contributions since 1987.

On LEXIS-NEXIS, campaign finance information can be found in the LEGIS or CMPGN libraries. Files include "Campaign Summary Reports" (CMPSUM), "Political Action Committee Contributions Reports" (PAC), "Political Action Committee Summary Reports" (PACSUM), "Congressional/Presidential Candidate Receipts Report" (MEMFIN), and "Congressional Member Financial Disclosures" (MEMFD). Files begin with the 1989/1990 election cycle, except for the "Congressional Member Financial Disclosures" which begin with 1991. The "Campaign Summary Reports" file contains campaign finance reports for each candidate with information on the amount and types of receipts, disbursements, and cash on hand. The "Political Action Committee Contributions Reports" provide data on contributions to individual candidates by each committee. The "Political Action Committee Summary Reports" consist of financial reports for each political action committee with information on amount and types of contributions, expenditures, and cash on hand. The "Congressional/Presidential Candidate Receipts Report" file contains data on contributions to candidates by individuals and political committees. Also available are Federal Election Commission news releases, which contain summary statistics on campaign financing.

INDEXES

Checklist

Catalog of United States Government Publications (MOCAT). WEB. 1994–. U.S. Government Printing Office. Superintendent of Documents. <http://www.gpo.gov/catalog>; <http://www.access.gpo.gov/su_docs/locators/cgp/index.html>; <http://purl.access.gpo.gov/GPO/LPS844>.

Monthly Catalog of United States Government Publications. CD-ROM. 1996–. U.S. Government Printing Office. Superintendent of Documents. GP 3.8/7: Item 0557-C. GPO.

Monthly Catalog of United States Government Publications (Condensed version). PRINT. (monthly) 1996–. U.S. Government Printing Office. Superintendent of Documents. GP 3.8/8: (Earlier full version, GP 3.8:, 1895-1995) Item 0557-D. GPO.

CIS/Index. PRINT. (monthly) 1970–. Bethesda, MD: Congressional Information Service.

Congressional Universe. WEB. Bethesda, MD: Congressional Information Service.

American Statistics Index (ASI). PRINT. (monthly) 1973-. Bethesda, MD: Congressional Information Service.

Statistical Universe. WEB. Bethesda, MD: Congressional Information Service.

Discussion

The *Monthly Catalog* is the most comprehensive index to government publications. To find materials relating to elections, look under the subject heading "Elections—United States" and headings beginning with "Election," such as "Election Law." Other relevant headings include "Campaign Funds," "Presidents—United States—Election," "Voting," and "Voter Registration." The complete version of the *Monthly Catalog* is available on the Web and CD-ROM. Commercial online and CD-ROM versions of the *Monthly Catalog* are also available.

CIS/Index indexes congressional publications under such headings as "Elections," "Campaign funds," "Presidential elections," and "Congressional elections." *Congressional Universe* includes a Web version of *CIS*.

American Statistics Index (ASI) indexes statistical data. Information can be found under the subject headings "Elections" and "Campaign funds." *Statistical Universe* includes a Web version of *ASI*.

For more information on these indexes, see Chapter 3, "The Basics of Searching."

GPO Subject Bibliographies. PRINT. WEB. GP 3.22/2:

<http://bookstore.gpo/gov/sb/about.html>

No. 245 "Voting and Elections"

CHAPTER 16
Maps

The U.S. government produces a great deal of cartographic material. The majority of it is produced by the U.S. Geological Survey (USGS) and the National Imagery and Mapping Agency (NIMA), although other agencies also publish and produce maps. Increasingly, maps are being produced and made available in various digital formats. This chapter describes only the most basic series of maps, and concentrates on describing the most common maps presently or recently distributed to depository libraries or publicly accessible on agency Web sites. It does not attempt to describe the use of maps, digital data, or specialized cartographic materials in detail, but includes several sources to consult for this information.

SEARCH STRATEGY

This chapter shows a map search strategy, which generally follows the steps of a subject search strategy. Maps are selected for use by the type of map, geographic coverage, and date, as well as the subject matter. Steps to follow include

1. Locate needed maps through the citations presented in this chapter;
2. Check appropriate agency Web sites;
3. Check the *Monthly Catalog* to identify additional maps; and
4. Use the sources in the "Related Material" section, especially the book *Map Librarianship,* for additional assistance in using maps.

USGS GENERAL SOURCES
Checklist

USGS National Mapping Information. WEB. U.S. Department of the Interior. Geological Survey. <http://mapping.usgs.gov/>.
Content: general information about USGS mapping activities; national mapping program information; mapping products and information; mapping news; regional mapping centers.

USGS Maps. PRINT. WEB. (1995) U.S. Department of the Interior. Geological Survey. I 19.14/2:M 32/11/995. Item 0619-B. <http://mapping.usgs.gov/mac/isb/pubs/booklets/usgsmaps/usgsmaps.html>.
Content: descriptions and examples of the types of maps produced by the USGS.

Maps for America: Cartographic Products of the United States Geological Survey and Others. (1988) U.S. Department of the Interior. Geological Survey. I 19.2:M 32/987. Item 0621.
Content: guide to U.S. maps, especially U.S. Geological Survey Maps.

National Mapping Program. PRINT. (irregular) U.S. Department of the Interior. Geological Survey. I 19.80: Item 0619-G-02.
Content: series of leaflets describing different aspects of the National Mapping Program.

Search Publications of the U.S. Geological Survey. WEB. 1880–. U.S. Department of the Interior. Geological Survey. <http://usgs-georef.cos.com/>.
Content: bibliographic database of all U.S. Geological Survey reports.

Guide to USGS Publications. PRINT. 1996–. (irregular) (Earlier titled: *Guide to USGS Geologic and Hydrologic Maps*) McLean, VA: Documents Index. (Future editions to be published by Gale Group, Inc.).
Content: guide to USGS thematic maps series.

Discussion

The *USGS National Mapping Information* does an excellent job of providing information on USGS's many mapping and mapping-related programs. Included at this page are links to online maps and services and information about USGS mapping products in general. Its many links and referral points serve as a comprehensive guide to navigating the USGS mapping services and Web sites.

The *USGS Maps* title describes and provides examples of the most used series of primarily print USGS products, many of which are included in this chapter. This source, especially in its revised Web version, is an excellent introduction to the sources most often used in libraries and by the general public. Included are descriptions of USGS topographic maps, geologic maps, hydrologic maps, photoimage maps, and *National Atlas* maps.

Although an older publication, *Maps for America: Cartographic Products of the United States Geological Survey and Others*, is still a valuable guide to U.S. maps and mapping. While concentrating on USGS cartographic products and services, it describes specific types of maps and chronicles the development of American mapping. It is also an excellent source for general map information, as well as a reference guide to specific types of government maps.

Each individual brochure of the *National Mapping Program* series describes a product or product area of the National Mapping Program or provides information about some aspect of mapping. Titles include *Maps of the United States* (I 19.80:UN 8/998), *Finding Your Way with Map and Compass* (I 19.80:M 32/3/997), and *The National Aerial Photography Program* (I 19.80:AE 8/4/996).

The *Search Publications of the U.S. Geological Survey* Web database covers all USGS publications and non-USGS publications by USGS authors since 1983. The database is a subset of the American Geological Institute's *GeoRef* database. Some entries contain abstracts. The database can be searched by numerous fields, including subject, title, author, keyword, journal or proceedings title, date, and type of map or document. The database can be used to locate USGS publications that include maps.

The *Guide to USGS Publications* is an index to the thematic maps of the USGS. It indexes the thematic series listed in the "USGS Geologic and Hydrologic Maps" section of this chapter, as well as some other USGS series, most notably the *USGS Professional Papers* series. It does not include information about the USGS topographic series. The first part of the guide describes individual publications in each series, listed by series. This is followed by area, subject, coordinate, and author indexes.

USGS TOPOGRAPHIC MAPS

Checklist

7.5' Series. (1:24,000) PRINT. I 19.81: Item 0619-M-01 to 53.

15' Series. (1:62,500) PRINT. I 19.81/2: Item 619-M-01 to 53.

1:50,000 Series (Alaska) (1:50,000) PRINT. I 19.81/2: Item 0619-M-02.

United States 1:100,000 Scale Series. (1:100,000) PRINT. I 19.110: Item 0619-G-25.

U.S. Series of Topographic Maps. (1:250,000) PRINT. I 19.98: Item 0619-G-17.

Alaska 1:250,000 Series. (1:250,000) PRINT. I 19.99: Item 0619-G-18.

Antarctica Topographic Series. (1:50,000) PRINT. I 19.100: Item 0619-G-19.

Antarctica Topographic Series. (1:250,000) PRINT. I 19.100/2. Item 0619-G-19.

Antarctica Topographic Series. (1:500,000) (with contours) PRINT. I 19.100/3: Item 0619-G-19.

Antarctica Topographic Series. (1:500,000) (without contours) PRINT. I 19.100/4: Item 0619-G-19.

Antarctica Topographic Series. (1:1,000,000) PRINT. I 19.100/5: Item 0619-G-19.

State Map Series: Planimetric, Topographic and Shaded Relief. (scale varies) PRINT. I 19.102/1:-I 19.102/53: Item 619-H-01 to 53.

National Park Series. (scale varies) PRINT. I 19.106: Item 0619-G-21.

County Map Series. (scale varies, usually 1:50,000 or 1:100,000) PRINT. I 19.108: Item 619-P-01 to 50.

Finding and Ordering USGS Topographic Maps. WEB. U.S. Department of the Interior. Geological Survey. <http://mapping.usgs.gov/mac/findmaps.html>.
  Content: series of searchable databases and finding aids to identify and order appropriate maps.

[Name of State]: Index to Topographic and Other Map Coverage. PRINT. U.S. Department of the Interior. U.S. Geological Survey. I 19.41/6-3: Item 0619-M-01 to 53.
  Content: provides index maps for the 7.5' series and other topographic USGS series.

TopoZone. WEB. Maps a la carte, Inc. <www.topozone.com>.
  Content: Web-accessible digital topographic maps of the United States.

Discussion

Topographic maps portray the position of selected features and the shape and elevation of the terrain. They are used extensively for all types of planning and land management purposes, as well as for recreational purposes. Topographic maps are usually issued in series, covering different geographic areas and different scales.

Scales of maps can be roughly divided into three groups—large, intermediate, and small. Large-scale maps are those of a scale less than 1:50,000. These maps cover the smallest geographic area on one sheet. Intermediate-scale maps are those from 1:50,000 to 1:100,000. Small-scale maps cover the scales greater than 1:100,000 and have the largest areas on a single sheet.

The maps listed here are for the most part series currently being distributed or recently distributed to depository libraries. The most widely used of these series are the 7.5' series of maps, which cover the entire United States. The 15' series is not a current series, and maps were primarily done before 1950, but it is listed here because it is still a heavily used series.

The *Finding and Ordering USGS Topographic Maps* Web page provides various methods for identifying USGS maps and then ordering them. The "Map Finder" provides an easy interface for locating the popular 7.5' topographic series. Name or zip codes can be entered into the search interface, or the user may click on maps that will locate the appropriate quadrangle. The "USGS Map Lists" can be used to generate listings of maps for each state at different scales. Two additional search databases allow for more sophisticated searching for large-scale and small-scale maps. The *Finding and Ordering USGS Topographic Maps* Web page is the most current and efficient way of locating the individual topographic maps needed. A print index to topographic maps is also published, titled *[Name of State]: Index to Topographic and Other Map Coverage*.

The USGS partners with businesses to make the digital raster data that are the basis for the topographic maps available. One of these partners, Maps a la carte, Inc., has created the publicly accessible Web site, *TopoZone*. *TopoZone* provides digital online topographic maps of the entire United States. Access to the site is free of charge, and interactively created map images can be downloaded or printed out. Maps can be searched by place name or latitude and longitude. USGS quad names are indicated in the search results.

USGS GEOLOGIC AND HYDROLOGIC MAPS
Checklist

National Geologic Map Database. WEB. U.S. Department of the Interior. United States Geological Survey. <http://ngmdb.usgs.gov/>.
> Content: database of information about geologic paper and digital maps.

Coal Investigations. (scale varies) PRINT. I 19.85: Item 0619-G-03.

Geologic Quadrangle Maps. (1:24,000 or 1:62,500) PRINT. I 19.88: Item 0619-G-05.

Geophysical Investigations. (scale varies) PRINT. I 19.87: Item 0619-G-04.

Hydrologic Investigations Atlases. (scale varies; usually 1:24,000 or 1:250,000) PRINT. I 19.89: Item 0619-G-06.

Geologic Investigations. (scale varies) PRINT. WEB. I 19.91: (Earlier title: *Miscellaneous Geologic Investigations*) Item 0619-G-08. Selected publications: <http://geology.usgs.gov/i-maps.html>.

Miscellaneous Field Studies Maps. (scale varies: usually 1:24,000 or 1:250,000) MF. WEB. I 19.113: Item 0619-G-11. Selected publications: <http://geology.usgs.gov/mf-maps.html>; <http://purl.access.gpo.gov/GPO/LPS3397>.

Oil and Gas Investigations Maps. (scale varies) PRINT. I 19.93: Item 0619-G-10.

Oil and Gas Investigations Charts. (scale varies) PRINT. I 19.92: Item 0619-G-09.

Hydrologic Unit Map. (1:500,000) PRINT. I 19.89/2: Item 0619-G-06.

Circum-Pacific (CP) Map Series. (1:10,000,000 or 1:17,000,000) PRINT. I 19.91/2: Item 0619-G-08.

Maps. WEB. U.S. Department of the Interior. Geological Survey. <http://geology.usgs.gov/maps.html>.
> Content: digital maps from USGS formal series of publications and informal series, such as the *Open-File Reports* available on the Web.

Daily Streamflow Conditions Map of the United States. WEB. (Daily) U.S. Department of the Interior. United States Geological Survey. Office of Surface Water. <http://water.usgs.gov/dwc/>.
> Content: daily updated online map of streamflow conditions.

National Water Conditions. WEB. (monthly) U.S. Department of the Interior. United States Geological Survey. I 19.42: Item 0624-B. <http://water.usgs.gov/nwc/>.
> Content: monthly U.S. map and report of water conditions.

Discussion

Several thematic series of maps pertaining to geology and hydrology are published by the USGS. Series currently or recently distributed to depository libraries are included in this listing. Individual maps in most of these series are described and indexed in the *Guide to USGS Publications* and also indexed by the *Search Publications of the U.S. Geological Survey*, cited in the "USGS General Sources" section of this chapter. Many of the publications in these series consist of maps and accompanying reports.

Geologic maps in these series and additional maps are also indexed by the online *National Geologic Map Database*. This database provides indexing for state, federal, and other map, producing organizations. While the database is still under construction, the indexing for USGS maps is almost complete. Very detailed searching criteria allow searching by geologic themes, such as magnetics, geophysics, or volcanoes. Maps can also be searched by geographic area, coordinates, scale, author, title map number, publisher, date, and map format. This is one of the best resources for easily identifying USGS geologic maps.

The *Coal Investigations* series provides geologic maps of areas with significant coal resources. The *Geologic Quadrangle Maps* are geological maps on topographic bases. *Geophysical Investigations* are maps on topographic or planimetric bases that provide the results of surveys using geophysical techniques. The *Hydrologic Investigations Atlases* series cover a wide range of hydrologic and hydrogeologic subjects. *Geologic Investigations* include maps of varying scales, formats, and subjects. This series includes everything from earthquake epicenter maps to geologic maps of the moon. The *Miscellaneous Field Stud-*

ies Maps series includes similar types of maps with the addition of metallic mineral resources and mining maps. Environmental topics are also often covered in this series.

The *Oil and Gas Investigations* maps and charts series consist of geologic maps and charts covering areas with oil and gas fields. The *Hydrologic Unit Maps* portray the hydrographic boundaries of major U.S. river basins for each state. The *Circum-Pacific (CP) Map Series* includes base, geographic, geodynamic, plate-tectonic, geologic, tectonic, mineral-resources, energy-resources maps, and other maps for the Pacific Basin and Arctic and Antarctic regions.

Digital maps available from these "formal" series of publications are accessible from the *Maps* Web site. Entries are arranged by these publication series, so that you can easily see all the digital maps available from the *Miscellaneous Field Studies Maps* series, for example. Maps from "informal" series of USGS publications, most notably *Open-File Reports*, are also included.

Two online maps relating to streamflow are made available from the USGS site. The first, *Daily Streamflow Conditions Map of The United States*, plots streamflow conditions from USGS gaging stations. Streamflow conditions are represented as a percentile, computed from the average streamflow for that day and station over a number of years. Individual state maps can also be created from this site. The *National Water Conditions* uses water resources data to create a monthly map and report of above normal, normal, and below normal streamflow conditions.

NATIONAL IMAGERY AND MAPPING AGENCY MAPS (NIMA)
Checklist

National Imagery and Mapping Agency Home Page. WEB. U.S. Department of Defense. <http://164.214.2.59/publications/pub.html>.
> Content: general information about NIMA; imagery; maps and geodata; publications.

Catalog of Public Sale Topographic Maps, Publications, and Digital Products. WEB. U.S. Department of Defense. National Imagery and Mapping Agency. <http://mapping.usgs.gov/mac/nimamaps/index.html>.

Series 1105 - Area Outline Maps. (1:20,000,000) PRINT. D 5.355: Item 0378-E-04.

Series 1308 - Middle East Briefing Map. (1:1,500,000) PRINT. D 5.355: Item 0378-E-09.

Series 5211 - Arabian Peninsula. (1:2,000,000) PRINT. D 5.355: Item 0378-E-10.

Series 2201 - Africa. (1:2,000,000) PRINT. D 5.355: Item 0379-F-04.

Series 5213 - Southeast Asia Briefing Map. (1:2,000,000) PRINT. D 5.355: Item 0379-F-07.

Discussion
The National Imagery and Mapping Agency (NIMA) is the primary mapping agency for the Department of Defense. Its Web site provides an introduction to the products and services of NIMA. The USGS handles the sale of many NIMA products. The *Catalog of Public Sale Topographic Maps, Publications, and Digital Products* not only provides the ordering information for these products, but it also gives a good description of the most popular NIMA products. Of particular interest are the descriptions of topographic maps and digital products. NIMA is particularly known for its series of topographic maps. Many of these maps have been distributed to depository libraries, and the currently or recently received series are listed here.

OTHER SELECTED SOURCES
Checklist

CIA Maps and Atlases. PRINT. (irregular) U.S. Central Intelligence Agency. PREX 3.10/4: Item 0856-A-01. GPO. NTIS.
> Content: assorted political, geographical, and thematic maps.

CIA Maps and Publications Released to the Public. WEB. U.S. Central Intelligence Agency. <http://www.odci.gov/cia/publications/mapspub/index.html>.
> Content: catalog of CIA maps and other publications released for public use since 1971.

Perry-Castañeda Library Map Collection. WEB. University of Texas at Austin. <http://www.lib.utexas.edu/Libs/PCL/Map_collection/Map_collection.html>.
> Content: digitized CIA maps.

National Park Service Cartographic Resources Home Page. WEB. U.S. Department of the Interior. National Park Service. <http://www.nps.gov/carto/>.
> Content: digital versions of the maps used in the national park system brochures.

EnviroMapper. WEB. U.S. Environmental Protection Agency. <http://www.epa.gov/enviro/html/em/index.html>.
> Content: maps of environmental information, including drinking water, toxic and air releases, hazardous waste, water discharge permits, and Superfund sites.

Environmental Atlas. WEB. U.S. Environmental Protection Agency. Center for Environmental Information and Statistics. <http://www.epa.gov/ceisweb1/ceishome/atlas/>.
> Content: online environmental map collection.

National Wetlands Inventory Maps. (1:24,000) MF. (irregular) U.S. Department of the Interior. Fish and Wildlife Service. I 49.6/7-: to I 49.6/7-53. Item 0611-W-01 to 53.
> Content: maps of wetlands regions.

Wetlands Interactive Mapper. WEB. U.S. Department of the Interior. Fish and Wildlfe Service. <http://www.nwi.fws.gov/wetlands_interactive_mapper_tool.htm>.
> Content: interactive mapping program using Wetlands Inventory data.

Daily Weather Maps, Weekly Series. PRINT. (weekly) 1968–. U.S. Department of Commerce. National Oceanic and Atmospheric Administration. National Weather Service. National Centers for Environmental Prediction. Hydrometeorological Prediction Center and Climate Prediction Center. C 55.195: (Earlier, C 55.213:) Item 0273-D-04.

> Content: surface weather map, 500-millibar height contours chart, highest and lowest temperatures chart, precipitation areas and amounts chart.

NWS Fax Charts. WEB. U.S. Department of Commerce. National Oceanic and Atmospheric Administration. National Weather Service. <http://weather.noaa.gov/fax/nwsfax.shtml>.

> Content: U.S. weather charts

Miscellaneous NWS Facsimile Charts. WEB. U.S. Department of Commerce. National Oceanic and Atmospheric Administration. National Weather Service. <http://weather.noaa.gov/fax/otherfax.shtml>.

> Content: international weather charts.

Maps and Charts. PRINT. U.S. Department of the Interior. Forest Service. A 13.28: Item 0080-G.

> Content: maps of National Forests.

BLM 1:100,000 Scale Maps, Surface Management Status. PRINT. U.S. Department of the Interior. Bureau of Land Management. I 53.11/4: Item 0619-G-16.

> Content: topographic maps showing land use.

BLM 1:100,000 Scale Maps, Surface and Minerals Management Status. PRINT. U.S. Department of the Interior. Bureau of Land Management. I 53.11/4-2: Item 0619-G-16.

> Content: topographic maps showing land use and minerals.

National Atlas of the United States. (separate maps) (scale varies) PRINT. (irregular) U.S. Department of the Interior. Geological Survey. I 19.111/A Item 0619-G-26.

> Content: individual sheet maps produced as part of the *National Atlas.*

National Atlas of the United States. WEB. U.S. Department of the Interior. <http://nationalatlas.gov>.

> Content: information about ongoing work on the *National Atlas*; *Atlas* maps; interactive map browser.

Map Collections 1544–1999. WEB. U.S. Library of Congress. Geography and Map Division. (American Memory Project) <http://lcweb2.loc.gov/ammem/gmdhtml/gmdhome.html>.

> Content: selected maps from the Library of Congress collection; primarily historical maps.

Discussion

The Central Intelligence Agency (CIA) produces a number of excellent maps. The maps are primarily for individual countries, although some maps are for smaller geographic areas, and some world maps are also produced. While most maps are political or geographical, the CIA also produces thematic maps on varying topics. A Web-based catalog listing these publications, along with ordering information (including price) for print copies of the maps, is given here. The *Perry-Castañeda Library Map Collection* has made many of these maps available to the public in digitized format, and their online collection is an excellent source for obtaining copies of these maps. Maps are made available primarily in JPEG format, with some maps in a PDF format. Since the maps are in the public domain, they may be freely downloaded or printed.

The *National Park Service Cartographic Resources Home Page* includes digital versions of maps of areas in the National Park System used in the brochures describing the areas. These maps are made available in a variety of format and are in the public domain.

EnviroMapper provides local maps showing environmental features, such as EPA-regulated facilities, Superfund sites, watershed characteristics, and toxic releases. It displays maps from the national level to the local level with feature identification and zoom and pan capabilities.

The *Environmental Atlas* offers online maps with environmental information. Main menu choices include USA maps and state and regional maps. USA maps are subdivided into air, land, or water. Individual maps are listed under each category. Maps come from various federal agencies and other sources. Examples of some of the specific maps available include total wetlands acres, pollutant loads discharged above permitted limits, and density map of carbon monoxide emissions by county. The state and regional map option allows the user to select a specific region or state and view a list of maps, including general base maps as well as those with environmental information. The main page also contains an interactive mapper option that links to the *EnviroMapper* Web site.

The National Wetlands Inventory project is a major initiative of the U.S. Fish and Wildlife Service to describe the characteristics, extent, and status of U.S. wetlands and deepwater habitats. As part of that project, *National Wetlands Inventory Maps* at a 1:24,000 scale have been produced that show the location and characteristics of wetlands. These maps have been distributed to depository libraries in a microfiche format. The *Wetlands Interactive Mapper* uses data collected from the National Wetlands Inventory program to provide a Web-accessible mapping program. Users can first select the geographic area to be covered by latitude and longitude or county, zip code, or name of place or name of U.S. Fish and Wildlife Service Refuge. Users are then presented with a variety of options for manipulating data and creating maps.

Each *Daily Weather Map* weekly issue contains a page of charts for each day of the week. These charts show the positions, development, and movements of weather systems. The surface weather map shows selected station data, precipitation, and pressure areas for 7:00 a.m. EST. The 500-millibar chart indicates winds, temperatures, and humidities above the earth. The highest and lowest temperatures chart shows temperatures for selected stations. The precipitation areas and amounts chart shows areas of precipitation with selected station amounts. All charts cover the United States and some include portions of Canada and Mexico.

Additional U.S. and International weather charts are also available from National Weather Service Web pages listed here. Many of the charts are updated frequently. Sample U.S. charts include charts of standard barotropic levels, winds/streamlines, surface analysis, weather depiction/significant weather, radar summary, thickness, forecast series, and hemispheric products. Images are available as TIFF files. Selected international charts are also available.

A series of 1:24,000 scale maps of National Forests have been distributed to depository libraries through the *Maps and Charts* series. Trail maps and other miscellaneous maps of forests are also distributed through this series. The Bureau of Land Management also distributes two series of topographic maps at the 1:100,000 scale. These use the USGS topographic bases, and then add information on land use and minerals.

The *National Atlas of the United States* is a comprehensive atlas that was published in 1970 and is now out of print. A new version of the *National Atlas* is being developed by the U.S. Geological Survey, which includes a variety of products. Some separate print sheet maps are being produced for the series and distributed to depository libraries. Titles of recent individual sheet maps include *Federal and Indian Lands* (I 19.111/A:998/L 23), *Hydrologic Units* (I 19.111/A:998/H 99), and Principal Aquifers (a I 19.111/A:998/AQ 5). The *National Atlas of the United States* Web site describes the products available from the National Atlas. A Web-based map browser allows the user to view maps digitally and to combine layers and data to create customized maps. Some of the many map layers available include "Land Cover Diversity," "Metropolitan Areas," "Superfund Sites," "Toxic Releases," "Agricultural Minerals Operations," "Ethnic Population," "Per Capita Income," "Railroads," and "Streams and Waterbodies."

Map Collections 1544–1999 is a collection of digitized maps produced by the Library of Congress as part of the American Memory Project. Most maps included are historical American maps. Maps are available in the categories of "Cities and Towns," "Conservation and Environment," "Discovery and Exploration," "Immigration and Settlement," "Military Battles and Campaigns," "Transportation and Communication," and "General." Maps may be searched by subject, creator, geographic location, and title indexes.

DIGITAL DATA PRODUCTS
Checklist

USGS Geospatial Data Clearinghouse. WEB. U.S. Department of the Interior. United States Geological Survey. National Geospatial Data Clearinghouse. <http://nsdi.usgs.gov/>.

Digital Products. WEB. U.S. Department of the Interior United States Geological Survey. National Geospatial Data Clearinghouse. <http://nsdi.usgs.gov/pages/nsdi005.html>.
  Content: description of USGS digital data set product categories.

USGS Geographic Data Download. WEB. U.S. Department of the Interior. Geological Survey. <http://edc.usgs.gov/doc/edchome/ndcdb/ndcdb.html>.
  Content: downloadable files of geographic data sets.

Digital Data Series. CD-ROM. U.S. Department of the Interior. Geological Survey. I 19.121: Item 0621-K.
  Content: USGS digital data files and products.

Digital Data Series [Online]. WEB. U.S. Department of the Interior. Geological Survey. <http://geology.usgs.gov/digital.html>.
  Content: selected reports, data, and excerpts of reports from the *Digital Data Series*.

DoD and NIMA Publications and Digital Products. WEB. U.S. Department of the Interior. Geological Survey. <http://mapping.usgs.gov/mac/nimamaps/dodnima.html>.
  Content: information on NIMA digital products available for sale.

Vector Map Level O (VMAPO). (Previously titled *Digital Chart of the World (DCW)*. D 5.358: Item 0378-E-36.
  Content: vector-based geospatial data for the world viewable at 1:1,000,000 scale.

LandView III: Environmental Mapping Software. CD-ROM. U.S. Environmental Protection Agency and U.S. Department of Commerce. National Oceanic and Atmospheric Administration and U.S. Department of Commerce. Bureau of the Census. EP 1.104/4: Item 0431-R-03.
  Content: electronic mapping system that combines census data, TIGER/Line data, and information on hazardous waste sites.

TIGER: Topologically Integrated Geographic Encoding and Referencing System Web Site. WEB. U.S. Department of Commerce. Bureau of the Census. <http://www.census.gov/geo/www/tiger/index.html>.
  Content: descriptions of TIGER/LINE files; information on TIGER releases; links to TIGER related products and documentation; links to other related on-line mapping, cartographic and geographic resources

TIGER/Line Census Files. CD-ROM. U.S. Department of Commerce. Bureau of the Census. C 3.279: Item 0154-E.
  Content: TIGER/Line files of coordinate-based geographic information.

Discussion

This section describes some of the major sources of information about digital mapping products and describes selected products that have been distributed to depository libraries. This section does not attempt to comprehensively describe the many products available.

The *USGS Geospatial Data Clearinghouse Web Site* is a major source for locating information about geospatial or spatially referenced data available from USGS. Finding aids for locating the information and products included are available from the site. Many of the data sets are available for sale and some can be downloaded from the site. Many of the data sets are also used in conjunction with the production of other products, such as paper. Most products described at this site are designed to be used with geographic information systems (GIS), image processing systems, or similar computer applications. *The Digital Products Page* from this site that describes USGS data sets in more detail is also included here.

The *USGS Geographic Data Download* Web site provides an easy way to obtain USGS geographic data sets. Data sets at this site are not viewable from a browser and require the use of geographical information systems (GIS) software. Included at this site are *1:250,000 Scale Digital Elevation Models (DEM)*, *1:24,000 Scale Digital Elevation Models (DEM) SDTS Format*, *1:2,000,000 Digital Line Graphs (DLG) SDTS Format*, *1:100,000 Scale Digital Line Graphs (DLG)*, and *1:24,000 Scale Digital Line Graphs (DLG) SDTS Format* data sets.

Depository libraries have received the *Digital Data Series* on CD-ROM from the USGS. This series has included a broad range of digital products, in various data formats, and with varying abilities to manipulate the data included with the CD-ROM. Sample titles from this series have included *Sea-Floor Images and Data from Multibeam Surveys in San Francisco Bay, Southern California, Hawaii, the Gulf of Mexico, and Lake Tahoe, California-Nevada* (I 19.121:55); *Gravity Data of Nevada* (I 19.121:42); and *The Mineral Economy of Brazil* (I 19.121:53). Some of the data and report material from this series are available online, from the *Digital Data Series [Online]* Web site. The information available varies—for some reports full data sets may be downloaded or FTP'ed. Other reports may only include partial data or may only include textual report material, often available in a PDF format.

USGS also distributes products for the Department of Defense National Imagery and Mapping Agency (NIMA), and the site listed here describes the public products available for sale. It is a part of the larger *Catalog of Public Sale Topographic Maps, Publications, and Digital Products* described earlier in the "National Imagery and Mapping Agency (NIMA)" section of this chapter. It includes the *Vector map level O (VMAPO)*, which has been distributed to depository libraries in a CD-ROM format. This data set consists of vector-based data that provides worldwide coverage and can be viewed at the 1:1,000,000 scale.

LandView III: Environmental Mapping Software provides the user the direct capability of manipulating data and producing maps. Included are TIGER/Line files, economic and demographic data from the 1990 census, and data from the Environmental Protection Agency on Superfund and hazardous waste sites. This EPA information includes air facilities, air quality monitoring sites,

brownfields pilots, (U.S. Summary disc only) hazardous waste facility information, hydrologic area boundaries, Superfund sites, toxic release inventory sites, and waste water discharger sites. In combination with the TIGER/Line data and the census data, various detailed maps can be created. Census data down to the block level are included and the user has the capability of easily manipulating data and deciding what map features will be included.

The *TIGER/LINE Census Files* are files that contain extracts of geographic and cartographic information. TIGER stands for "Topologically Integrated Geographic Encoding and Referencing System." TIGER files contain information such as geographic area codes, latitude/longitude coordinates of features and boundaries, and the name and type of feature for each individual feature (for example, an individual segment of a road). Used with Geographic Information System (GIS) software, these files can be used to create maps. The geographic and cartographic information from the TIGER files can also be combined with statistical data, such as STF data. TIGER/Line files are distributed to depository libraries in a CD-ROM format, but GIS software is not provided to depository libraries by the Census Bureau and must be obtained from commercial vendors or other sources. The TIGER/Line files are periodically revised, and new versions are produced.

The *TIGER: Topologically Integrated Geographic Encoding and Referencing System Web Site* includes extensive information about and documentation for the TIGER/Line files. The site provides links to a wide variety of other related resources, including a searchable directory of companies that provide services related to the TIGER/Line data or use TIGER extract products.

INDEXES
Checklist

Catalog of United States Government Publications (MOCAT). WEB. 1994–. U.S. Government Printing Office. Superintendent of Documents. <http://www.gpo.gov/catalog>; <http://www.access.gpo.gov/su_docs/locators/cgp/index.html>; <http://purl.access.gpo.gov/GPO/LPS844>.

Monthly Catalog of United States Government Publications. CD-ROM. 1996–. U.S. Government Printing Office. Superintendent of Documents. GP 3.8/7: Item 0557-C. GPO.

Monthly Catalog of United States Government Publications (Condensed version). PRINT. (monthly) 1996–. U.S. Government Printing Office. Superintendent of Documents. GP 3.8/8: (Earlier full version, GP 3.8:, 1895–1995). Item 0557-D. GPO.

Discussion

The Monthly Catalog is a comprehensive index to government publications. The complete version is available on the Web and on CD-ROM. (See Chapter 3, "The Basics of Searching," for more information.) To find additional maps and cartographic materials, search the subject headings and keywords beginning with the terms "Maps," and "Cartography" and headings such as "Bathymetric Maps," "Nautical Charts," "Outline Maps," and "World Maps." Subject headings combined with the term "Maps" may also be used.

RELATED MATERIAL
Within this Work

Chapter 21   Geology

GPO Subject Bibliographies. PRINT. WEB. GP 3.22/2:

<http://bookstore.gpo.gov/sb/about.html>

No. 102 "Maps and Atlases"

No. 183 "Surveying and Mapping"

Other Sources

Map Librarianship: An Introduction. PRINT. 3rd edition. (1998) Mary Lynette Larsgaard. Englewood, CO: Libraries Unlimited, 1998.

Map Librarianship is the classic guide to the organization and use of maps. While geared to librarians, it is a helpful source for anyone needing guidance in the use of maps.

CHAPTER 17
Genealogy

There are many governmental publications, Web sites, and other resources of value to genealogical researchers. The federal population census name schedules are some of the most popular genealogical tools. This chapter describes resources of general interest to genealogists and gives examples of the types of governmental resources available for genealogical research. Many of these sources are produced by the National Archives and Records Administration (NARA) or are guides to materials in the National Archives.

SEARCH STRATEGY

This chapter shows a subject search strategy. Steps to follow are
1. Check major materials listed in this chapter;
2. Use guides and Web sites cited in this chapter to locate additional resources; and
3. Check Chapter 53, "National Archives," for more information.

NATIONAL ARCHIVES GUIDES AND SOURCES
Checklist

Guide to Federal Records in the National Archives of the United States. PRINT. WEB. (1995) U.S. National Archives and Records Administration. AE 1.108:G 94/v. Item 0569-B. <http://www.nara.gov/guide/>.
  Content: description of records in the National Archives, arranged by record group number, with subject index.

NARA Archival Information Locator (NAIL). WEB. U.S. National Archives and Records Administration. <http://www.nara.gov/nara/nail.html>.
  Content: prototype online information system of NARA archival and microfilm holdings, including selected digital images.

Information about the National Archives for Researchers. PRINT. (1994) U.S. National Archives and Records Administration. General Information Leaflet No. 30. AE 1.113:30/994. Item 0569.
  Content: basic information on the facilities of the National Archives and how to use them; addresses of regional archives and presidential libraries.

National Archives and Records Administration Web Site. WEB. U.S. National Archives and Records Administration. <http://www.nara.gov/>.
  Content: guides to material in the National Archives; how to do research; locations and hours of research facilities; publication catalogs; classroom activities; general agency information.

The Genealogy Page. WEB. U.S. National Archives and Records Administration. <http://www.nara.gov/genealogy/genindex.html>.
  Content: guide to National Archives facilities and resources for doing genealogical research.

Aids for Genealogical Research Catalog. WEB. U.S. National Archives and Records Administration. <http://www.nara.gov/publications/genihome.html>.
  Content: links to NARA publications and other information of interest to genealogists.

Guide to Genealogical Research in the National Archives. PRINT. (1985) U.S. National Archives and Records Administration. (Nondepository; for sale by the National Archives Trust Fund Board).
  Content: genealogical materials available and how to use them, with chapters on population and immigration records, military records, women, Blacks, Native Americans, land, and other areas; includes references to additional published materials.

Using Records in the National Archives for Genealogical Research. PRINT. (1990) U.S. National Archives and Records Administration. AE 1.113:5/990. Item 0569.
  Content: brief guide to the types of records of interest to genealogists, such as census schedules, land records, naturalization records, service records, and others.

Genealogical and Biographical Research: A Select Catalog of National Archives Microfilm Publications. PRINT. WEB. (1983) U.S. General Services Administration. National Archives Trust Fund Board. (Nondepository; available from National Archives Trust Fund Board or Scholarly Resources, Inc.) <http://www.nara.gov/publications/microfilm/biographical/genbio.html>.

> Content: description of microfilmed records useful for genealogical and biographical research; arranged by broad area and record group with microfilm reel listings.

Immigrant and Passenger Arrivals: A Select Catalog of National Archives Microfilm Publications. PRINT. WEB. 2d ed. (1991) U.S. General Services Administration. National Archives Trust Fund Board. (Nondepository; available from National Archives Trust Fund Board or Scholarly Resources, Inc.) <http://www.nara.gov/publications/microfilm/immigrant/immpass.html>.

> Content: description of microfilmed records of the U.S. Customs Service and the Immigration and Naturalization Service; arranged by port with microfilm reel listings.

Military Service Records: A Select Catalog of National Archives Microfilm Publications. PRINT. WEB. (1985) U.S. National Archives and Records Administration. National Archives Trust Fund Board. (Nondepository; available from National Archives Trust Fund Board or Scholarly Resources, Inc.) <http://www.nara.gov/publications/microfilm/military/service.html>.

> Content: description of microfilmed military records; arranged by broad area and record group with microfilm reel listings.

Black Studies: A Select Catalog of National Archives Microfilm Publications. PRINT. WEB. (1984) U.S. General Services Administration. National Archives Trust Fund Board. (Nondepository; available from National Archives Trust Fund Board or Scholarly Resources, Inc.) <http://www.nara.gov/publications/microfilm/blackstudies/blackstd.html>.

> Content: description of microfilmed records relating to African Americans; arranged by record group with microfilm reel listings.

American Indians: A Select Catalog of National Archives Microfilm Publications. PRINT. WEB. (1995) U.S. National Archives and Records Administration. National Archives Trust Fund Board. (Nondepository; available from National Archives Trust Fund Board or Scholarly Resources, Inc.) <http://www.nara.gov/publications/microfilm/amerindians/indians.html>.

> Content: description of microfilmed records relating to Native Americans; arranged by broad area and record group with microfilm reel listings.

General Information Leaflets. PRINT. U.S. National Archives and Records Administration. AE 1.113: Item 0569.

> Content: small pamphlets on the National Archives, its resources, facilities, and services.

Special Lists. MF. 1942–. U.S. National Archives and Records Administration. AE 1.115: (Earlier, GS 4.7:). Item 0570-A.

> Content: listings of individual records or data items in a specific area, such as a list of black servicemen in the Revolutionary War or a list of population and mortality schedules.

Discussion

The National Archives is a prime source for information and records of interest to genealogists. The first four sources in this chapter give general information about using the National Archives. Chapter 53, "National Archives," should also be consulted for more complete information about using the National Archives.

The *Guide to Federal Records in the National Archives of the United States* describes the holdings of the National Archives. The chapters, arranged by record group, give brief descriptions of the content and amount of material in each group, agency organizational history, information on printed guides, microform availability, and any use restrictions. An alphabetical list of agencies are included at the beginning of Vol. 1. Vol. 3 is an index by subject and name. A Web version of the guide offers keyword and record-group-number searching. The Web version is updated regularly.

The *Guide* may indicate that some material is available for purchase in microfilm. Some microfilm records may be available in large libraries. Otherwise the researcher may need to visit the National Archives to use the materials. Some microfilm records and regional records may also be consulted at regional archives branches.

The *NARA Archival Information Locator (NAIL)* is a prototype online database of holdings in Washington, DC regional archives, and presidential libraries. *NAIL* contains a selection of archival, microfilm, and audiovisual materials, including more than 100,000 full-text documents and images. Although it contains thousands of entries, these represent only a small portion of NARA holdings at this time. Separate searches for archival or microfilm materials are available. The archival search includes a standard and expert search option and an option to search the digital collection only.

Information on using the National Archives in person can be found in *Information about the National Archives for Researchers*, which contains information on hours, application and use procedures, and addresses of branches and presidential libraries.

The *National Archives and Records Administration Web Site* provides information on doing research at the National Archives, digital classroom materials, online exhibits, and information on records management, grants, and archival preservation. A "Quick Links" menu includes links to "Nationwide Facilities: Locations, Hours & Accessibility" and "NARA Publications." The main menu includes "The Research Room" which provides information for researchers on facilities, how to do research, and guides to holdings.

The *Genealogy Page* provides essential information for any genealogist using the National Archives. Part 1 of the site is a directory of the National Archives research facilities, including regional facilities. Information given for the facilities includes hours, locations, directions, and accessibility information. Part 2 is titled "Online Information" and includes genealogical research guides to such items as census records, immigration and naturalization records, and military records. It also includes links to a limited number of sets of digitized genealogical data available online. In addition, links to Web versions of microfilm catalogs and finding aids are included. Part 3 describes National Archives and Records policies affecting genealogists. Part 4 gives information on NARA publications, with links to pages describing the publications in more detail and ordering information for sales publications. Included here is information on the sale of NARA microfilm publications. Part 5 describes genealogical workshops and courses held by NARA in both the Washington, DC area and its regional facilities. Part 6 provides a limited number of links to other genealogical sites on the Web.

The *Aids for Genealogical Research Catalog* also provides genealogical information, particularly concentrating on describing NARA's publications of interest. It includes links to pages that describe guides and finding aids, microfilm catalogs, and other sources for research. It also includes information on electronic access to NARA publications, genealogy workshops, and information on how to obtain reproductions of NARA materials.

The *Guide to Genealogical Research in the National Archives* is an excellent guide to using the National Archives and also serves as a guide to many general aspects of genealogical research. Topics covered within the guide include census records, passenger arrival lists, naturalization records, military records, records of American Indians, Black Americans, merchant seamen, court records, land records, and claim records. This is a good starting point for beginning any genealogical research in the National Archives.

Using Records in the National Archives for Genealogical Research is a short leaflet describing the major records in the Archives. This leaflet provides a good introduction to the types of records available.

Many National Archives records are available in microfilm from the National Archives or from Scholarly Resources, Inc., an authorized vendor for National Archives microfilm. This microfilm provides facsimile reproductions of original (often handwritten) records judged to have high research value. The microfilm is not available through the depository library program, but must be purchased separately. A series of select catalogs on popular subject areas provides more detailed descriptions and reel listings for microfilm in these areas. All microfilmed records have been surveyed for material that relates to the selected subject. Background information and descriptions of the records in the subject area are provided, as well as detailed microfilm reel listings. Five of these catalogs of particular interest to genealogists are listed here: *Genealogical and Biographical Research: A Select Catalog of National Archives Microfilm Publications*; *Immigrant and Passenger Arrivals: A Select Catalog of National Archives Microfilm Publications*; *Military Service Records: A Select Catalog of National Archives Microfilm Publications*; *Black Studies: A Select Catalog of National Archives Microfilm Publications*; and *American Indians: A Select Catalog of National Archives Microfilm Publications*. Census record catalogs are listed in the next section, "Census Sources."

The *General Information Leaflets* series includes small brochures that provide a good introduction to the National Archives and its services. Leaflets of interest to genealogists include *Using Records in the National Archives for Genealogical Research* (AE 1.113:5), *Military Service Records in the National Archives* (AE 1.113:7), *Using the Census Soundex* (AE 1.113:55), and *Fast Facts about the 1920 Census* (AE 1.113:43).

The *Special Lists* series consists of guides and descriptions of records series. Information held in other record depositories besides the National Archives may also be included. *Special Lists* cover a wide range of topics, including several pertaining to genealogical research. Examples of interest to genealogists include *List of Free Black Heads of Families in the First Census of the United States, 1790* (GS 4.7:34); *Federal Population and Mortality Census Schedules, 1780–1910, in the National Archives and the States: Outline of a Lecture on Their Availability, Content and Use* (GS 4.7:24); and *List of Black Servicemen Compiled from the War Department Collection of Revolutionary War Records* (GS 4.7:36).

CENSUS SOURCES
Checklist

The 1790–1890 Federal Population Censuses: Catalog of National Archives Microfilm. PRINT. WEB. (1997) U.S. National Archives and Records Administration. National Archives Trust Fund Board. (Nondepository; available from National Archives Trust Fund Board or Scholarly Resources, Inc.) <http://www.nara.gov/publications/microfilm/census/1790–1890/17901890.html>.

> Content: microfilmed census schedules by year, state, and county.

1900 Federal Population Census: Catalog of National Archives Microfilm. PRINT. WEB. (1996) U.S. National Archives and Records Administration. National Archives Trust Fund Board. (Nondepository; available from National Archives Trust Fund Board or Scholarly Resources, Inc.) <http://www.nara.gov/publications/microfilm/census/1900/1900.html>.

> Content: microfilmed census schedules by state and county.

The 1910 Federal Population Census: A Catalog of Microfilm Copies of the Schedules. PRINT. WEB. (1982) National Archives Trust Fund Board. (Nondepository; available from National Archives Trust Fund Board or Scholarly Resources, Inc.) <http://www.nara.gov/publications/microfilm/census/1910/1910.html>.

> Content: microfilmed census schedules by state and county.

The 1920 Federal Population Census: Catalog of National Archives Microfilm. PRINT. WEB. 2d ed. (1992) U.S. National

Archives and Records Administration. National Archives Trust Fund Board. (Nondepository; available from National Archives Trust Fund Board or Scholarly Resources, Inc.) <http://www.nara.gov/publications/microfilm/census/1920/1920.html>.

> Content: microfilmed census schedules by state and county.

How to Use NARA's Census Microfilm Catalogs Web Page. WEB. U.S. National Archives and Records Administration. <http://www.nara.gov/genealogy/microcen.html>.

> Content: information on how to use the census microfilm catalogs and microfilm soundex indexes; link to information on the microfilm rental program.

The USGenWeb Archives: Census Project: Census Images. WEB. USGenWeb. <http://www.rootsweb.com/~usgenweb/cen_img.htm>.

> Content: state by state listing and linking of federal census record images available through the *USGenWeb Archives.*

Family Quest Archives™ Digital Microfilm. CD-ROM. Listing of CDs available: <http://www.heritagequest.com/ProdFind2/digital.htm>.

> digitized versions of federal census record images.

Family Archive CDs: United States Census CDs. CD-ROM. FamilyTreeMaker.com. Listing of available CDs: <http://www.familytreemaker.com/cenmicro.html>.

> Content: digitized versions of federal census record images.

SK Publications Census CDs. CD-ROM. WEB. SK Publications. <http://www.skpub.com/genie/>.

> Content: digitized versions of federal census record images; Web includes links to images from *USGenWeb Archives.*

CensusView Census on CD-ROM. CD-ROM. Ripley, OK: CensusView. Listing of CDs available: <http://www.galstar.com/~censusvu/>.

> Content: digitized versions of federal census records images.

U.S. Federal Census Records. CD-ROM. ALLCENSUS. Listing of CDs available:

> Content: digitized versions of federal census record images.

Heads of Families of the First Census of the States Taken in the Year 1790. PRINT. 12 vols. (1907–08) U.S. Department of Commerce and Labor. Bureau of the Census. C 3.11: (Reprint edition: Baltimore, MD: Genealogical Publishing Co., Inc., 1992)

> Coverage: Vermont, New Hampshire, Connecticut, Virginia, North Carolina, South Carolina, New York, Pennsylvania, Rhode Island, Massachusetts, Maine, Maryland. Content: name of head of family and number of people in household, taken from the 1790 census.

The USGenWeb Census Project. WEB. USGenWeb. <http://www.rootsweb.com/~usgenweb/census/>.

> Content: transcriptions of federal censuses.

Census Online: Census Sites on the Web. WEB. Mark E. Reed. <http://www.census-online.com/>.

> Content: links to sites with census information of interest to genealogists; state-by-state links to Web accessible census indexes and schedules.

African-American Census Schedules Online. WEB. B.J. Smothers. <http://www.afrigeneas.com/aacensus/>.

> Content: state-by-state listing and link to federal census schedule indexes and transcriptions pertaining to African Americans.

AIS Census Indexes. WEB. Ancestry.com <http://www.ancestry.com/search/rectype/census/ais/main.htm>.

> Content: fee based search service for census indexes.

Cyndi's List: U.S. Census. WEB. Cyndi Howells. <http://www.CyndisList.com/census.htm>.

> Content: comprehensive list of links to Web sites with U.S. Census information and sources.

200 Years of U.S. Census Taking: Population and Housing Questions, 1790–1990. PRINT. (1989) U.S. Department of Commerce. Bureau of the Census. C 3.2:T 93. Item 0146.

> Content: instructions to enumerators for censuses; questions asked on each census.

Age Search Service. WEB. U.S. Department of Commerce. Bureau of the Census. <http://www.census.gov/genealogy/www/agesearch.html>.

> Content: information on age search service and the fees involved; application form.

Availability of Census Records about Individuals. PRINT. WEB. (1997) U.S. Department of Commerce. Bureau of the Census. Factfinder for the Nation No. 2. C 2.252:2/ <http://www.census.gov/prod/2/gen/cff/cff-9702.pdf>.

> Content: short pamphlet describing what census information has been collected about individuals and how to obtain that information.

Discussion

Information about specific individuals collected during the federal census is not released until 72 years after the census is taken. Thus, the latest census data released are from 1920 (which were released in 1992). Data available from the census vary from year to year. Depending on the year, data may include a person's name and age, number of years in the United States, marital status, birthplace of father and mother, and number of children born. The *Guide to Genealogical Research in the National Archives,* cited in the "National Archives Guides" section of this chapter, provides a description of the types of information available from each census.

The census catalogs cited here provide detailed reel listings for the more than 35,000 rolls of film that reproduce original census forms and related indexes. This microfilm allows users to find information on specific individuals, such as occupation, birthplace, and names of children. It is an important source of information for genealogists and historians. Catalogs list the reels for each census by state and then by county. They give ordering information and may also serve as guides to locating specific rolls in a census microfilm collection.

Individual National Archives microfilm rolls are available for purchase from the National Archives or from Scholarly Resources, Inc. A microfilm rental program is conducted by the National Archives. Microfilm may often be rented from genealogical research firms. Many large libraries and genealogical societies have purchased the microfilm and make it available for use. The four census guides cited here, *The 1790–1890 Federal Population Censuses: Catalog of National Archives Microfilm*; *1900 Federal Population Census: Catalog of National Archives Microfilm*; *The 1910 Federal Population Census: A Catalog of Microfilm Copies of the Schedules*; and *The 1920 Federal Population Census: Catalog of National Archives Microfilm*, provide the roll numbers and geographic area covered on each roll. (See Figure 17.1.)

How to Use NARA's Census Microfilm Catalogs Web Page provides information on using the census microfilm catalogs, using the microfilm soundex indexes, and using the microfilm rental program.

Increasingly, commercial genealogical research firms or other genealogical organizations are digitizing the census microfilm records and creating records accessible through the Web or more typically available for a fee on CD-ROM. In most cases, the images themselves are being digitized—not the information included in the images. It is still necessary to use other indexes or guides to identify the image needed. This section cites some of the major companies or organizations providing digital census records. The coverage of records is not comprehensive, varies from vendor to vendor, and is constantly changing as new census microfilm rolls are digitized. Consult the URLs given in the entries for listings of products currently available from each source.

The *USGenWeb Archives: Census Project: Census Images* page provides links to freely available census images made available through a cooperative project. The *Family Quest Archives Digital Microfilm* CD-ROMs are some of the more comprehensive in terms of the number of CDs available for purchase. *Family Archive CDs: United States Census CDs* is another series of CD-ROM products available from FamilyTreeMaker. SK Publications provides CD-ROMs available for purchase, but also provides links to lower-resolution images of the census records from their Web site. CensusView and ALLCENSUS are two additional vendors making CD-ROMs of the federal census images available.

In order to locate the appropriate pages of the census records—whether on microfilm or a digitized microfilm version—it is necessary to use an index to locate the appropriate page. Commercial sources and genealogical and historical societies have published many individual indexes to census materials for particular states and counties. Overall indexes available are the Soundex indexes included within the federal census and available on National Archives microfilm for 1880, 1900, 1910, and 1920. The Soundex system allows users to locate specific names (for

an exact geographic location) when they do not know the exact spelling of the name. (See Figure 17.2) An alphabetical name index for the existing records of the 1890 census is also available, although most of the 1890 census was destroyed by fire. The 1790 schedule was reprinted by the Census Bureau in 1907 and 1908 and includes its own index. Many research libraries own this 12-volume set. The 1790 census is also available on National Archives microfilm rolls and was recently reprinted by a commercial publisher.

The *USGenWeb Census Project* is a volunteer project to provide transcriptions of the Census Records. Volunteers transcribe the names and information on individual rolls of the federal census microfilm. The information is then made available in text files, accessible by state, county, and census year. *Census Online: Census Sites on the Web* is a guide to federal census information available on the Web of interest to genealogists. It includes links to some of the census resources already described, and through its "Links to Online Data" section, census indexes available on the Web can be found, arranged by state and county. For example, if a local historical society has indexed the schedules for its county and placed them on the Web, this site will link to that index.

African-American Census Schedules Online provides a similar type of listing for census schedule indexes and transcriptions pertaining to African Americans. Information from federal censuses is listed, including slave schedules and mortality schedules. *AIS Census Indexes* is a fee-based comprehensive Web-based searchable census records index of over 35 million people that includes the *Federal Census Indexes*. It is available through the popular genealogical Web site, *Ancestry.com*.

Cyndi's List: U.S. Census is a comprehensive list of links about the U.S. Census of interest to genealogists. Many of the Web sources discussed in this chapter are included in this list. The list also links to items of more specialized interest, such as individual county census indexes. Additional guides to using the federal census records are also included in the listing.

200 Years of U.S. Census Taking: Population and Housing Questions 1790–1990 reprints the instructions to enumerators and the questions asked for each census. The detailed instructions and explanation of the questions asked are helpful sources for interpreting the federal population schedules. An essay covering the historical background of the census and a section titled "Availability of Population Schedules" are also included.

For a fee, the Census Bureau will perform searches of the census records not yet released for public use. To release information, the permission of the person involved must be obtained, or in the case of deceased persons, will only be released to blood relatives, surviving spouses, administrators or executors of estates, or beneficiaries by will or insurance. The *Age Search Service Web Site* describes this service. *Availability of Census Records about*

ALABAMA

1. Autauga, Baldwin, and Barbour (ED's 1–12) Counties.
2. Barbour (ED's 13–26), Bibb, and Blount Counties.
3. Bullock and Butler (ED's 16–25, 29) Counties.
4. Butler (ED's 26–28, 30–33) and Calhoun Counties.
5. Chambers and Cherokee Counties.
6. Chilton, Choctaw, and Clarke Counties.
7. Clay, Cleburne, and Coffee Counties.
8. Colbert, Conecuh, and Coosa Counties.
9. Covington and Crenshaw Counties.
10. Cullman, De Kalb (ED's 35–43, *see also* roll 12), and Dale Counties.
11. Dallas County.
12. De Kalb (ED's 44–55, *see also* roll 10), Elmore, and Geneva (ED's 95–99, *see also* roll 14) Counties.
13. Escambia, Etowah, and Fayette Counties.
14. Franklin, Geneva (ED's 100–114, *see also* roll 12), and Greene (ED's 19–35) Counties.
15. Greene (ED's 36–48, 194), Hale, Limestone (ED's 94–98, see also roll 22), and Henry Counties.
16. Houston and Jackson Counties.
17. Jefferson (ED's 30–41, 93, 105–128) County.
18. Jefferson (ED's 42–60, 129–136) County.
19. Jefferson (ED's 61–87, 154) County.
20. Jefferson (ED's 88–92, 94–104), Lamar, and Lauderdale (ED's 49–57, 71–73) Counties.
21. Lauderdale (ED's 58–70), Lawrence, and Lee (ED's 157–168) Counties.
22. Lee (ED's 169–173, 175–180), Limestone (ED's 99–110, 173, *see also* roll 15), and Lowndes Counties.
23. Macon and Madison (ED's 111–129) Counties.
24. Madison (ED's 130–145) and Marengo Counties.
25. Marion, Marshall, and Monroe Counties.
26. Mobile (ED's 61–77) County.
27. Mobile (ED's 78–117) County.
28. Montgomery (ED's 83–90, 102–124) County.
29. Montgomery (ED's 91–101) and Morgan Counties.
30. Perry and Pickens Counties.
31. Pike and Randolph Counties.
32. Russell, St. Clair, and Shelby (ED's 102–113) Counties.
33. Shelby (ED's 114–119), Sumter, and Talladega (ED's 120–130, 143) Counties.
34. Talladega (ED's 131–142) and Tallapoosa Counties.
35. Tuscaloosa and Walker (ED's 170–180, 192, 193, 196, 197) Counties.
36. Walker (ED's 181–191, 195), Washington, and Wilcox (ED's 144–154) Counties.
37. Wilcox (ED's 155–168) and Winston Counties.

ARIZONA

38. Apache and Cochise Counties.
39. Coconino, Gila, and Graham Counties.
40. Maricopa County.
41. Mohave, Yuma, Navajo, and Pima Counties.
42. Pinal, Santa Cruz, and Yavapai Counties.

ARKANSAS

43. Arkansas, Ashley, Baxter, and Boone Counties.
44. Benton, Bradley, and Calhoun Counties.
45. Carroll, Chicot, and Clark Counties.
46. Clay, Cleburne, Cleveland, and Columbia Counties.
47. Conway and Craighead Counties.
48. Crawford, Crittenden, Cross, and Dallas Counties.
49. Desha, Drew, and Faulkner Counties.
50. Franklin, Fulton, and Garland Counties.
51. Grant, Hot Springs, and Greene Counties.
52. Hempstead, Howard, and Independence Counties.
53. Izard, Lafayette, and Jackson Counties.
54. Jefferson and Johnson Counties.
55. Lawrence, Lee, Little River, and Lincoln Counties.
56. Logan and Lonoke Counties.
57. Madison, Marion, and Miller Counties.
58. Mississippi and Monroe Counties.
59. Newton, Montgomery, Nevada, and Ouachita Counties.
60. Perry, Phillips, and Pike Counties.
61. Poinsett, Prairie, Polk, and Pope Counties.
62. Pulaski (ED's 98–144) County.
63. Pulaski (ED's 145–157), Randolph, and St. Francis Counties.
64. Saline, Scott, Sharp, Searcy, and Stone Counties.
65. Sebastian County.
66. Sevier, Union, and Van Buren Counties.
67. Washington and White Counties.
68. Woodruff and Yell Counties.

CALIFORNIA

69. Alameda (ED's 1–17, 30–37, 39, 74–86, 215, 216) County.
70. Alameda (ED's 87–126, 214) County.
71. Alameda (ED's 18–29, 127–150, 207–213) County.
72. Alameda (ED's 38, 40–73, 151–160, 218) County.
73. Alpine, Amador, Calaveras, and Butte (ED's 1–13, 197–201) Counties.
74. Butte (ED's 14–18), Colusa, Del Norte, and El Dorado Counties.
75. Contra Costa and Fresno (ED's 26–28, 42, 45–50, 179) Counties.
76. Fresno (ED's 29–41, 43, 44, 51–73, 176–178, 183) County.
77. Glenn, Imperial, and Humboldt Counties.
78. Inyo, Lake, Lassen, and Kern Counties.
79. Kings and Los Angeles (ED's 1–16, 71, 113–116, 278, 348, 360, 369) Counties.
80. Los Angeles (ED's 117–127, 207, 213–242, 275, 359, 364) County.
81. Los Angeles (ED's 128–133, 138–144, 153, 154, 243–274, 365) County.
82. Los Angeles (ED's 104, 105, 134–137, 145–152, 155–164, 168–173, 176–181, 185, 189, 193–206, 208–212, 361) County.
83. Los Angeles (ED's 46–70, 72, 73, 165–167, 174, 175, 182–184, 186–188, 190–192, 355) County.
84. Los Angeles (ED's 74–103, 106–112, 276, 277, 279, 362, 363) County.
85. Los Angeles (ED's 17–45, 280–291, 320, 349, 354) County.
86. Los Angeles (ED's 292–319, 321–323, 336–339, 341, 350, 356–358, 366, 368) County.
87. Los Angeles (ED's 324–335, 340, 342–347, 351–353, 367), Madera, Mariposa, and Modoc Counties.
88. Marin and Mendocino Counties.
89. Merced, Mono, and Monterey Counties.
90. Napa, Nevada, and Orange Counties.
91. Placer, Plumas, and Riverside Counties.
92. Sacramento (ED's 87–115, 131–135) County.
93. Sacramento (ED's 116–130, 196), San Benito, and San Bernardino (ED's 91, 93–96, 104) Counties.
94. San Bernardino (ED's 92, 97–103, 105–124, 224, 226, 228) and San Diego (ED's 140–152) Counties.
95. San Diego (ED's 125–139, 153–165, 239) and San Francisco (ED's 1–6, 13–19) Counties.
96. San Francisco (ED's 7–12, 20–58, 139–150) County.
97. San Francisco (ED's 59–101) County.
98. San Francisco (ED's 102–166) County.
99. San Francisco (ED's 167–205) County.
100. San Francisco (ED's 206–242) County.
101. San Francisco (ED's 243–294) County.

The 1910 Federal Population Census: A Catalog of Microfilm Copies of the Schedules, p. 1.

Figure 17.1: Sample Page from *The 1910 Federal Population Census*.

The Soundex Coding System

Every Soundex code consists of a letter and three numbers, such as S-650. The letter is always the first letter of the surname, whether it is a vowel or a consonant. Disregard the remaining vowels and W, Y, and H and assign numbers to the next three consonants of the surname according to the Soundex coding guide. If there are not three consonants following the initial letter, use zeros to fill out the three-digit code.

Most surnames can be coded using the Soundex coding guide. Names with prefixes, double letters, or letters side by side that have the same number of the Soundex coding system are described below.

NAMES WITH PREFIXES

If the surname has a prefix, such as van, Von, De, Di, or Le, code it both with and without the prefix because it might be listed under either code. The surname vanDevanter, for example, could be V-531 or D-153.

Mc and Mac are not considered prefixes.

NAMES WITH DOUBLE LETTERS

If the surname has any double letters, they should be treated as one letter. Thus, in the surname Lloyd, the second L should be crossed out, in the surname Gutierrez, the second R should be crossed out.

NAMES WITH LETTERS SIDE BY SIDE THAT HAVE THE SAME NUMBER ON THE SOUNDEX CODING GUIDE

A surname may have different letters that are side by side and have the same number on the Soundex coding guide; for example, PF in Pfister (1 is the number for both P and F); CKS in Jackson (2 is the number for C, K, and S). These letters should be treated as one letter. Thus in the name Pfister, F should be crossed out; in the name Jackson, K and S should be crossed out.

Source: The 1920 Federal Population Census: *Catalog of National Archives Microfilm*, p.3.

Figure 17.2: Soundex Guide.

Individuals also gives information about the census data available for an individual. It describes the circumstances under which this information can be released and lists the census questions asked in each census.

CONGRESSIONAL SERIAL SET

Checklist

U.S. Congressional Serial Set. PRINT. MF. WEB. 1817–. U.S. Congress. Y 1.1/2: (Before 1817, see the *American State Papers*). Items 0996-B(MF) or -C; 1008-D(MF) or –E; 1008-F (105th Congress –, regional depository libraries only) Early volumes: <http://lcweb2.loc.gov/ammem/amlaw/lwss.html>; Individual documents and reports since 1995: <http://www.access.gpo.gov/su_docs/legislative.html>.

> Content: bound collection of congressional publications consisting of the numbered series of House and Senate reports and House and Senate documents.

CIS U.S. Serial Set Index, 1789–1969. PRINT. (1975–79) Washington, DC: Congressional Information Service, Inc.

> Content: index to *U.S. Congressional Serial Set.*

Congressional Masterfile 1. CD-ROM. Bethesda, MD: Congressional Information Service.

> Content: includes CD-ROM version of the *CIS U.S. Serial Set Index.*

Grassroots of America. PRINT. (1972) Philip W. McMullin. Salt Lake City, UT: Gendex Corporation.

> Content: index to names appearing in *Serial Set* volumes 28–36.

Discussion

The *U.S. Congressional Serial Set* is a bound compilation of congressional reports and documents and serves as a detailed record of congressional activities. Various executive agency reports and documents were also issued as part of the *Serial Set*, especially in earlier years. Each volume within the *Serial Set* is individually numbered, and may contain one report or a series of individual reports. Examples useful to genealogical research include *Historical Register and Dictionary of the United States Army from Its Organization September 29, 1789 to March 2, 1903* (Serial Set 4535, 4536); *Letter from the Secretary of State with a Transcript of the List of Passengers Who Arrived in the United States from the 1st October, 1819, to the 30th September, 1820* (Serial Set 45); and *List of Private Land Claims, Senate, 14th–46th Congress* (Serial Set 1945, 1946).

The *CIS U.S. Serial Set Index, 1789–1969* provides a comprehensive index to the *Serial Set* volumes. It is also available in a CD-ROM format as part of the Congressional Masterfile I. (See Chapter 52, Historical Searches," for more information on using the *Serial Set* and *Serial Set Index.*)

The *Grassroots of America* volume provides a listing of names included in volumes 28–36 of the *Serial Set.* These volumes are part of the *American State Papers* and deal with land grants and claims during the period 1789–1837.

MISCELLANEOUS SOURCES
Checklist

War of the Rebellion. Official Records of the Union and Confederate Armies. PRINT. WEB. 130 vols. (1880–1901) U.S. War Department. W 45.5: or Serial Set. <http://moa.cit.cornell.edu/MOA/MOA-JOURNALS/WARO.html>.; Guide to volumes in the *Serial Set:* <http://www.access.gpo.gov/su_docs/fdlp/pubs/techsup/ts120197.html>.

> Content: army records of the Civil War, including an index to individual's names.

Army Official Records. Official Records of the Union and Confederate Armies. CD-ROM. (1995) Wilmington, NC: Broadfoot Publishing Co.

> Content: CD-ROM version of the *War of the Rebellion.*

Official Records of the Union and Confederate Navies in the War of the Rebellion. PRINT. WEB. 22 vols. (1894–1927) U.S. Department of the Navy. Library and Naval War Records Office. N 16.6: or Serial Set. <http://moa.cit.cornell.edu/MOA/MOA-JOURNALS/OFRE.html>; Guide to volumes in the *Serial Set:* <http://www.access.gpo.gov/su_docs/fdlp/pubs/techsup/ts120197.html>.

> Content: naval records of the Civil War, including an index to individual's names.

The Official Federal Land Patent Records Site. WEB. U.S. Department of the Interior. Bureau of Land Management. <http://www.glorecords.blm.gov/>.

> Content: database of images of federal land title records issued between 1820 and 1908.

General Land Office Automated Records Project. CD-ROM. U.S. Department of the Interior. Bureau of Land Management. I 53.57: Item 0600-D-01. GPO.

> Content: database of federal land title records issued prior to 1908.

Social Security Death Index. WEB. Ancestry.com <http://www.ancestry.com/search/rectype/vital/ssdi/main.htm>.

> Content: Social Security Administration database of death records.

Local History & Genealogy Reading Room. WEB. U.S. Library of Congress. Humanities and Social Sciences Division. <http://lcweb.loc.gov/rr/genealogy/>.

> Content: general information about the reading room; information about the collections; bibliographies and guides; links to Internet sources on genealogy and local history.

Genealogical Research at the Library of Congress. WEB. PRINT. (1999) U.S. Library of Congress. LC 1.2:G 28/999. Item 0786. <http://lcweb.loc.gov/rr/genealogy/bib_guid/guide0.html>.

> Content: brief genealogical research guide.

Using Maps in Genealogy. WEB. (1999) U.S. Department of the Interior. U.S. Geological Survey. <http://mapping.usgs.gov/mac/isb/pubs/factsheets/fs14099.html>.

> Content: brief guide to the use of maps in genealogy.

Where to Write for Vital Records, Births, Deaths, Marriages, and Divorces. PRINT. WEB. (irregular). U.S. Department of Health and Human Services. Public Health Service. Centers for Disease Control and Prevention. National Center for Health Statistics. HE 20.6210/2: Item 0510-A-01. ASI 4128-11. GPO. <http://www.cdc.gov/nchswww/howto/w2w/w2welcom.htm>; <http://purl.access.gpo.gov/GPO/LPS2642>.

> Coverage: states.
>
> Content: addresses, telephone numbers, URLs for state Web sites, and other information needed to obtain individual birth, death, marriage, and divorce records.

Discussion

Two sets of Civil War military records, *War of the Rebellion. Official Records of the Union and Confederate Armies*, and *Official Records of the Union and Confederate Navies in the War of the Rebellion* are often used to identify persons serving during the war. Both of these sets include indexes to the names found within. Actual information given on any individual will vary depending on what type of military record the person's name is found in. Some records are merely lists of names, while others give more detailed information. Web versions of both sets are available, and a CD-ROM version of the *War of the Rebellion. Official Records of the Union and Confederate Armies* has also been published.

The Bureau of Land Management is providing a database of their land patent records from 1820 to 1908 on their *The Official Federal Land Patent Records Site.* Records in the database include two million Federal land title records for Eastern Public Land States. Plans are to add additional records from 1908 to the 1960s. Land patents document the transfer of land ownership from the federal government to individuals. The search interface for the database allows searching by the patentee's (individual receiving the transfer of land) first, middle, and last names, along with a number of search fields, including geographic location fields. A CD-ROM version of this database was also distributed to depository libraries.

The Social Security Administration compiles a database of death records of those persons with social security numbers who have been reported as deceased to the Social Security Administration. While the Social Security Administration does not provide a publicly searchable version of this database, it does sell a version on magnetic tape. This version has been distributed commercially in CD-ROM and other electronic formats by various vendors. The free-of-charge *Social Security Death Index* available at the *Ancestry.com* Web site is one of the most popular versions of this database, and provides various searching capabilities, including name and geographic location searches.

The Library of Congress maintains extensive genealogical holdings in its collections. The Web page of the *Library of Congress Local History & Genealogy Reading Room* is an excellent guide to the resources available. The site also includes numerous guides to genealogical research and links to additional Internet resources. *Genealogical Research at the Library of Congress* is a small guide that describes some of the basic procedures and resources for conducting research in the Library of Congress. The Library of Congress periodically publishes some print book and guides to various aspects of genealogical research or to specific genealogical collections in the Library of Congress. Use the *Monthly Catalog* to locate additional genealogical guides published by the Library of Congress.

Using Maps in Genealogy is a basic guide to using maps in genealogical research that gives examples and suggests strategies. It also cites numerous related map and place-name sources. Relevant resources of the Geological Survey, such as the *Geographic Names Information System*, are also discussed.

Where to Write for Vital Records: Births, Deaths, Marriages, and Divorces provides a state-by-state directory of where and how to obtain these records. It is available in print, PDF, and HTML formats. Complete information for obtaining records from state offices is given in a state-by-state listing. These listings also indicate when records are available from county offices, but do not give individual county contact information.

INDEXES
Checklist

Catalog of United States Government Publications (MOCAT). WEB. 1994–. U.S. Government Printing Office. Superintendent of Documents. <http://www.gpo.gov/catalog>; <http://www.access.gpo.gov/su_docs/locators/cgp/index.html>; <http://purl.access.gpo.gov/GPO/LPS844>.

Monthly Catalog of United States Government Publications. CD-ROM. 1996–. U.S. Government Printing Office. Superintendent of Documents. GP 3.8/7: Item 0557-C. GPO.

Monthly Catalog of United States Government Publications (Condensed version). PRINT. (monthly) 1996–. U.S. Government Printing Office. Superintendent of Documents. GP 3.8/8: (Earlier full version, GP 3.8:, 1895-1995). Item 0557-D. GPO.

Discussion

The Monthly Catalog is a comprehensive index to government publications. The complete version is available on the Web and on CD-ROM. (See Chapter 3, "The Basics of Searching," for more information.) To find additional genealogical materials, search the *Monthly Catalog* under headings and keywords such as "Genealogy," and "United States. National Archives and Records Administration."

RELATED MATERIAL
Within this Work

CHAPTER 18
Agriculture

The U.S. government produces an immense amount of material on agriculture and agriculture-related topics. This chapter includes only the most important or basic sources. Some of the annuals and series included have been published for many years and are good sources of historical information. The Department of Agriculture has also begun publishing many of its sources, particularly statistical sources, on the Web. Some areas of agriculture are covered extensively in other chapters of this book. (See the "Related Material" section at the end of this chapter.)

SEARCH STRATEGY

This chapter shows a subject search strategy. One major subsearch also included is the statistical search strategy, as the Department of Agriculture collects, compiles, and makes available a great deal of statistical information. Search steps for this chapter are

1. Check major sources in the categories given here;
2. Use the *Monthly Catalog* for further searching;
3. Use *American Statistics Index (ASI)* to locate additional statistical materials not included in this chapter; and
4. Consult "Related Material," particularly other related chapters within this book.

GENERAL SOURCES
Checklist

United States Department of Agriculture Web Site. WEB. U.S. Department of Agriculture. <http://www.usda.gov/>.
> Content: General information about the USDA; links to agencies within the USDA; links to information on a variety of USDA-related topics.

General Publications. PRINT. MF. (irregular) U.S. Department of Agriculture. A 1.2: Item 0010.

> Content: miscellaneous publications in agriculture-related areas.

Report of the Secretary of Agriculture. MF. WEB. (annual) 1862–. U.S. Department of Agriculture. A 1.1: (title varies) Item 0006. ASI 1004-3. <http://www.usda.gov/news/pubs/>; <http://purl.access.gpo.gov/GPO/LPS2976>.
> Content: activities and accomplishments of the various Agriculture Department agencies.

Miscellaneous Publications. MF. (irregular) 1927–. U.S. Department of Agriculture. A 1.38: Item 0013-A.
> Content: variety of publications on agricultural topics.

Agriculture Fact Book. PRINT. WEB. (annual) 1979–. U.S. Department of Agriculture. Office of Communications. A 1.38/2: (Earlier title: *Fact Book of Agriculture*) Item 0013-A-01. ASI 1004-14. GPO. <http://www.usda.gov/news/pubs/index.htm>; <http://purl.access.gpo.gov/GPO/LPS2942>.
> Content: information and trends concerning topics such as U.S. agriculture, rural America, food safety, nutrition, natural resources, trade, and consumer issues.

Program Aids. PRINT. 1946–. U.S. Department of Agriculture. A 1.68: Item 0014-A.
> Content: small brochures on USDA programs and services.

Agriculture Information Bulletin. MF. WEB. (irregular) U.S. Department of Agriculture. A 1.75: Item 0004. URLs for individual publications vary.
> Content: pamphlets on farming, land ownership, pesticides, and other agricultural topics.

Agriculture Handbooks. PRINT. Some MF. (irregular) 1950–. U.S. Department of Agriculture. A 1.76: Item 0003.
> Content: monographs on scientific and agricultural topics.

Home and Garden Bulletins. PRINT. WEB. (irregular) U.S. Department of Agriculture. A 1.77: Item 0011. URLs for individual publications vary; some titles at: <http://www.ams.usda.gov/howtobuy/>.
> Content: pamphlets on gardening, care and maintenance of homes, food and nutrition, and budgeting.

Discussion

The *United States Department of Agriculture Web Site* is a good source of general information about the activities and programs of the Department of Agriculture. It provides numerous links to agencies within the Department and to topics of general interest. It also includes links to a few full-text publications of broad interest. The site is a good first resource to consult when researching information about agriculture and agriculture-related topics. It is also a useful site for understanding the organization of the Department of Agriculture and the responsibilities of the many subagencies and offices within the Department of Agriculture.

The *General Publications* series of the Agriculture Department contains a small number of miscellaneous publications. Recent publications in this series include *Sustaining the People's Lands: Recommendations for Stewardship of The National Forests and Grasslands into the Next Century* (A 1.2:P 39/2); *Building a Risk Management Plan: Risk-Reducing Ideas that Work* (A 1.2:B 86/2), and *Water Quality: A Report of Progress* (A 1.2: W 29/9/997).

In short summary sections arranged by topics, the *Report of the Secretary of Agriculture* looks at the year's activities and accomplishments for the Department of Agriculture. Information on the mission and accomplishments of individual subagencies such as the Forest Service, Agricultural Marketing Service, Food and Nutrition Service, and the Natural Resources Conservation Service are included. This report provides an excellent overview of the Department's programs.

The *Miscellaneous Publications* series is a long-standing one that includes research and technical sorts of publications as well as more general ones. Titles in this series include *A Time to Act: A Report of the USDA National Commission on Small Farms* (A 1.38:1545); *Managing Wildlife Damage: The Mission of Aphis' Wildlife Services Program* (A 1.38:1543/999); and *Food Cost Indexes for Low-Income Households and the General Population* (A 1.38:1872).

The annual *Agriculture Fact Book* provides narrative and statistics that describe the state of U.S. agriculture and rural America. As its name implies, it is full of facts about all areas that the Department of Agriculture covers, including foreign agriculture and trade, food and nutritional services, natural resources and the environment, and agricultural research and education.

Program Aids are primarily small brochures on agriculture programs and services. Brochures may describe a particular agency or program, give guidance on using services, or offer practical advice in an area related to agriculture or one of the other areas covered by Department of Agriculture agencies. Titles include *Facts about the Food Stamp Program* (A 1.68:1340/999), *Pink Hibiscus Mealybug* (A 1.68:1605), *Rural Youth Loans* (A 1.68:1630), and *Cooperative Stock Purchase Program* (A 1.68:1640).

The *Agriculture Information Bulletin* series contains small pamphlets on miscellaneous agricultural topics. Many of the recently published titles in this series are also being made available on the Web, but the individual URLs vary. Recent titles include *Agricultural Productivity in the United States* (A 1.75:740), *Injuries and Fatalities on U.S. Farms* (A 1.75:739), *The Food and Fiber System: Contributing to the U.S. and World Economies* (A 1.75:742), and *Broiler Farms' Organization, Management, and Performance* (A 1.75:748).

The *Agriculture Handbooks* series consists of monographs, often substantial in size, that are often more scientific and specialized than the other series in this section. Titles include *The Classification of Cotton* (A 1.76:566/999), *Forest Production for Tropical America* (A 1.76:710), *Soil Taxonomy: A Basic System of Soil Classification for Making and Interpreting Soil Surveys* (A 1.76:436/999), and *Consumer Use of Information: Implications for Food Policy* (A 1.76:715).

The *Home and Garden Bulletins* series provides practical information on a wide range of everyday subjects, including the purchase and preparation of food, nutrition, budgeting, home care, growing flowers and plants, and dealing with insects. Examples of titles include: *The Food Guide Pyramid* (A 1.77:252/996), *How to Buy Fresh Fruits* (A 1.77:260), and *Making Healthy Food Choices* (A 1.77:250/998).

AGRICULTURAL STATISTICAL SOURCES
Checklist

National Agricultural Statistical Services Web Site. WEB. U.S. Department of Agriculture. National Agricultural Statistical Services. <http://www.usda.gov/nass/>.

> Content: access to and information about a wide variety of statistical sources and services pertaining to agriculture.

Agricultural Statistics. PRINT. WEB. (annual) 1936–. U.S. Department of Agriculture. National Agricultural Statistics Service. A 1.47: Item 0001. ASI 1004-1. GPO. <http://www.usda.gov/nass/pubs/agstats.htm>; <http://purl.access.gpo.gov/GPO/LPS1063>.

> Coverage: world, world regions, countries, U.S., states.
> Content: specific commodity data such as area harvested, yield, production, disposition, value, supply, price or trade; farm income and expenses; price-support program data; conservation and forestry; food prices and consumption.

Agricultural Statistics. CD-ROM. (annual) 1994–. U.S. Department of Agriculture. A 1.47/2: Item 0001-A.

> Content: CD-ROM version of *Agricultural Statistics.*

Census of Agriculture. PRINT. WEB. CD-ROM. (quinquennial) 1840–. U.S. Department of Agriculture. National Agricultural Statistics Service. A 92.53/1:-A 92.53/56:; A 92.54: (Earlier, U.S. Department of Commerce, Bureau of the Census, C3.31/.) Items 0015-B-01-57. ASI 1661-1; 1663-2. <http://www.nass.usda.gov/census/>; <http://govinfo.kerr.orst.edu/ag-stateis.html>.

Coverage: U.S., regions, divisions, states, counties.
Content: statistics relating to all aspects of agriculture, including farms; acreage; crops; fruit and nut production; vegetables; nursery and greenhouse products; value of sales; land use; irrigation; livestock and poultry; specialty products; operator characteristics; finances and operations; production expenses; federal programs; machinery and equipment; market value of land; use of agricultural chemicals; farm finance.

Agricultural Outlook. PRINT. WEB. (10 issues a year) 1975–. U.S. Department of Agriculture. Economic Research Service. A 93.10/2: Item 0042-M. ASI 1502-4. GPO. <http://www.ers.usda.gov/epubs/pdf/agout/ao.htm>; <http://purl.access.gpo.gov/GPO/LPS4107>; <http://usda.mannlib.cornell.edu/reports/erssor/economics/ao-bb/>; <http://purl.access.gpo.gov/GPO/LPS1093>.
Coverage: world, world regions, selected countries, U.S., states.
Content: commodity prices; production and supplies; trade indicators; farm income; food prices and consumption; trends and outlook; agricultural policy.

Agricultural Income and Finance Situation and Outlook Report. WEB. (three times per year) 1961–. U.S. Department of Agriculture. Economic Research Service. A 93.9/8: (Title varies) Item 0042-D. ASI 1541-1. <http://usda.mannlib.cornell.edu/reports/erssor/economics/ais-bb/>; <http://purl.access.gpo.gov/GPO/LPS1092>.
Coverage: U.S.
Content: statistics on agricultural income and finance.

Statistical Bulletins. MF. (irregular) 1923–. U.S. Department of Agriculture. A 1.34: Item 0015.
Coverage: varies; world, world regions, countries, U.S., states.
Content: detailed statistical reports on commodity production, prices, sales, supply, consumption, trade, or marketing.

USDA Economics and Statistics System. WEB. Cornell University. Albert R. Mann Library. <http://usda.mannlib.cornell.edu/>.
Content: searchable database with links to full-text reports and data sets from economics agencies of the USDA; includes many statistical reports.

Discussion

The National Agricultural Statistics Service (NASS) is the agency of the Department of Agriculture responsible for compiling and distributing agricultural statistical information. Its Web site provides a wide range of information about the activities of the NASS, including the full-text of many of its publications.

Agricultural Statistics is the most valuable ready reference source for information on U.S. agriculture. It also includes data on U.S. agricultural trade and some statistics on agricultural production in other countries. *Agricultural Statistics* brings together statistical tables from many different sources. Topics covered include farm resources, income, and expenses; taxes, insurance, cooperative, and credit; and stabilization and price-support programs. Also included are detailed statistics on such commodities as grains, vegetables, and melons; cattle, hogs, and sheep; and oilseeds, fats, and oils. Most commodity statistics include statistics for each state involved in production of the commodity. A PDF format version of *Agricultural Statistics* is made available on the Web. A CD-ROM version, which allows for more sophisticated searching functions, is also produced.

Data for the *Census of Agriculture* are collected every five years. In the past, the Census Bureau produced the *Census of Agriculture*, but starting with the 1992 Census, the Department of Agriculture, National Agricultural Statistics Service, has conducted the survey. The format of the *Census of Agriculture* has varied over the years, but the current format includes a series of three volumes. Volume 1 is the *Geographic Area Series* volume and includes a U.S. summary report, statistical summaries for states, and reports at the county level. (See Figure 18.1.)

Volume 2 of the *Census of Agriculture* includes subject reports. For the 1997 Census, three titles were produced: *Agricultural Atlas of the United States, Rankings of States and Counties,* and *Zip Code Tabulations of Selected Items.* Volume 3 includes special studies. Titles included are: *Farm and Ranch Irrigation Survey, Census of Horticultural Specialties, Census of Aquaculture,* and *Agricultural Economics and Land Ownership Survey.*

Data from the *Census of Agriculture* are also issued on CD-ROM and in PDF formats on the Web. The CD-ROM includes additional searching capabilities. Through the Government Information Sharing Project, data from the *Census of Agriculture Geographic Area* series are made available through the Web in a searchable format. The easy-to-use interface allows reports to be quickly obtained by state, county, or zip code.

Agricultural Outlook contains regular sections on such topics as agricultural economy, commodities, farm finance, world agriculture and trade, resources and environment, risk management, research and technology, farm and rural communities, and food and marketing, The statistical section contains tables on key statistical indicators, foreign and economic data, producer and consumer prices, farm-retail price spreads, livestock, crops, world agriculture, U.S. agricultural trade, farm income, food expenditures, transportation, farm productivity, and food supply and use. *Agricultural Outlook* is a good source for information on current statistics and trends.

Agricultural Income and Finance Situation and Outlook Report includes both narrative and statistical tables and charts. Topics covered include such items as farm debt, real estate debt, loans, farm business balance sheets, farm income, and production costs. An appendix of statistical tables includes current forecast data as well as historical data for the past five years. Articles on special topics are also included within each issue.

The *Statistical Bulletin* series contains detailed statistical reports. Most of these reports cover several years

Table 29. **Vegetables, Sweet Corn, and Melons Harvested for Sale: 1997 and 1992**–Con.

[For meaning of abbreviations and symbols, see introductory text]

Geographic area	1997 Harvested Farms	Harvested Acres	Irrigated Farms	Irrigated Acres	1992 Harvested Farms	Harvested Acres	Irrigated Farms	Irrigated Acres
LETTUCE AND ROMAINE								
State Total								
New York	156	1 384	80	792	172	1 537	73	1 102
Counties								
Cattaraugus	3	1	–	–	3	1	–	–
Columbia	6	39	3	35	4	17	3	11
Dutchess	4	17	2	(D)	7	10	3	(D)
Erie	6	51	3	48	8	18	5	17
Greene	3	(D)	–	–	(NA)	(NA)	(NA)	(NA)
Nassau	4	7	4	7	3	8	3	8
Niagara	5	1	1	(D)	5	7	1	(D)
Orange	13	489	8	296	13	484	6	341
Oswego	6	(D)	2	(D)	7	600	4	522
St. Lawrence	4	1	2	(D)	7	1	–	–
Saratoga	4	2	2	(D)	8	2	3	(Z)
Schoharie	4	13	1	(D)	–	–	–	–
Suffolk	27	167	23	148	31	130	23	121
Sullivan	5	5	2	(D)	(NA)	(NA)	(NA)	(NA)
Tioga	4	3	3	3	(NA)	(NA)	(NA)	(NA)
Tompkins	4	2	1	(D)	6	3	1	(D)
Ulster	7	(D)	2	(D)	9	84	3	(D)
Washington	6	3	4	3	7	4	6	3
All other counties	41	252	19	39	(NA)	(NA)	(NA)	(NA)
MUSTARD GREENS								
State Total								
New York	27	86	12	72	32	131	13	63
Counties								
Monroe	4	2	–	–	(NA)	(NA)	(NA)	(NA)
Niagara	3	1	–	–	(NA)	(NA)	(NA)	(NA)
Suffolk	4	57	4	57	5	54	5	54
All other counties	16	26	8	15	(NA)	(NA)	(NA)	(NA)
DRY ONIONS								
State Total								
New York	265	11 792	96	2 951	292	12 066	43	1 080
Counties								
Cattaraugus	3	1	–	–	3	2	–	–
Cayuga	6	34	–	–	5	(D)	–	–
Dutchess	3	(D)	2	(D)	4	(D)	–	–
Genesee	11	1 045	7	199	7	232	1	(D)
Madison	6	284	3	129	10	736	–	–
Monroe	3	3	1	(D)	3	2	1	(D)
Niagara	10	1	4	1	5	3	2	(D)
Orange	89	5 248	17	1 116	99	5 274	2	(D)
Orleans	17	2 137	9	481	18	2 273	2	(D)
Oswego	20	1 671	3	(D)	24	1 823	6	309
Otsego	3	1	–	–	(NA)	(NA)	(NA)	(NA)
St. Lawrence	4	1	1	(D)	6	1	1	(D)
Schuyler	3	1	1	(D)	(NA)	(NA)	(NA)	(NA)
Steuben	4	(D)	1	(D)	4	427	1	(D)
Suffolk	10	40	8	34	14	57	11	46
Tompkins	5	2	2	(D)	5	1	1	(D)
Ulster	3	(D)	1	(D)	4	1	–	–
Washington	4	2	2	(D)	8	3	4	2
Wayne	20	527	15	418	20	538	1	(D)
Yates	7	359	5	207	5	(D)	–	–
All other counties	34	138	14	7	(NA)	(NA)	(NA)	(NA)
GREEN ONIONS								
State Total								
New York	53	287	18	23	86	885	25	25
Counties								
Niagara	5	1	2	(D)	7	4	2	(D)
Orange	5	35	1	(D)	7	329	1	(D)
Oswego	5	206	–	–	–	–	–	–
Rensselaer	4	1	–	–	(NA)	(NA)	(NA)	(NA)
St. Lawrence	4	1	2	(D)	7	2	2	(D)
Suffolk	6	10	6	10	10	17	7	10
All other counties	24	32	7	11	(NA)	(NA)	(NA)	(NA)
OKRA								
State Total								
New York	9	5	2	(D)	9	(D)	4	(Z)

1997 CENSUS OF AGRICULTURE—COUNTY DATA **NEW YORK 397**

USDA, National Agricultural Statistics Service

Source: 1997 *Census of Agriculture*, Volume 1, *Geographic Area Series, New York*, Table 29.

Figure 18.1: Sample Table from 1997 *Census of Agriculture*.

of statistical data. Sample titles in this series include: *European Agricultural Statistics* (A 1.34:937), *Overview of U.S. Horticultural Exports to Asia* (A 1.34:934), and *Forecasting Seven Components of the Food CPI: An Initial Assessment* (A 1.34:1851).

The Mann Library at Cornell University maintains the *USDA Economics and Statistics System.* The system includes reports and data sets from the Economic Research Service, National Agricultural Statistics Service, and World Agricultural Outlook Board. Over 100 reports and 200 data sets are available for use. A searchable database provides an easy-to-use interface for locating the reports and data sets. Many of the reports listed in this chapter are available from this site.

COMMODITY STATISTICAL SOURCES
Checklist

Reports by Commodity: Index of Estimates. WEB. U.S. Department of Agriculture. National Agricultural Statistics Service. <http://www.usda.gov/nass/pubs/estindx.htm>.
> Content: report locator interface that indexes commodity reports of the Agricultural Statistics Board.

Crop and Livestock Reports. WEB. (frequencies and dates vary) U.S. Department of Agriculture. National Agricultural Statistics Service. Agricultural Statistics Board. A92.9-A92.50: (with exceptions). <http://usda.mannlib.cornell.edu/reports/nassr/>.
> Coverage: U.S., states.
> Content: numerous commodity reports with data on production, stocks, acreage, yield, use, value, and prices.

Acreage. MF. WEB. (annual) A 92.39: Item 0020-B-04. ASI 1621-23. <http://jan.mannlib.cornell.edu/reports/nassr/field/pcp-bba/>.

Agricultural Chemical Usage. WEB. (annual or biennial) A 92.50: (includes various individual titles) Item 0122-A-10. ASI 1616-1. <http://usda.mannlib.cornell.edu/reports/nassr/other/pcu-bb/>; <http://purl.access. gpo.gov/GPO/LPS1116>.

Agricultural Prices. WEB. (monthly) A 92.16: Item 0018-C. ASI 1629-1. <http://jan.mannlib.cornell.edu/reports/nassr/price/pap-bb/>.

Agricultural Prices [fiscal year] Summary. WEB. (annual) A 92.16/2: Item 0018-C. ASI 1629-5. <http://jan.mannlib.cornell.edu/reports/nassr/price/pap-bb/>; <http://purl.access.gpo.gov/GPO/LPS3074>.

Broiler Hatchery. WEB. (weekly) A 92.46: Item 0021-F-01. ASI 1625-11. <http://jan.mannlib.cornell.edu/reports/nassr/poultry/pbh-bb/>; <http://purl.access. gpo.gov/GPO/LPS1121>.

Capacity of Refrigerated Warehouses [year] Summary. WEB. (biennial) A 92.21/3: Item 0024-G. ASI 1614-2. <http://jan.mannlib.cornell.edu/reports/nassr/other/pcs-bbc/>; <http://purl.access.gpo.gov/GPO/LPS1122>.

Catfish Processing. WEB. (monthly) A 92.44: Item 0021-F-04. ASI 1631-14. <http://jan.mannlib.cornell.edu/reports/nassr/other/pcf-bb/>; <http://purl.access. gpo.gov/GPO/LPS1123>.

Catfish Production. WEB. (quarterly) A 92.44/2-2: Item. 0021-F-04. ASI 1631-18. <http://jan.mannlib. cornell.edu/reports/nassr/other/pcf-bbc/>; <http://purl.access.gpo.gov/GPO/LPS1124>.

Cattle. WEB. (semiannual) A 92.18/6-2: Item 0021-N. ASI 1623-1. <http://jan.mannlib.cornell.edu/reports/nassr/livestock/pct-bb/>; <http://purl.access.gpo.gov/GPO/LPS1125>.

Cattle on Feed. WEB. (monthly) A 92.18/6: Item 0021-N-01. ASI 1623-2. <http://jan.mannlib.cornell.edu/reports/nassr/livestock/pct-bbc/>; <http://purl.access. gpo.gov/GPO/LPS1126>.

Cherry Production. WEB. (annual) A 92.11/3: Item 0122-A-13. ASI 1621-18.2. <http://jan.mannlib.cornell.edu/reports/nassr/fruit/zcp-bb/>; <http://purl.access. gpo.gov/GPO/LPS1128>.

Chickens and Eggs. WEB. (monthly) A 92.9/16: Item 0021-F-01. ASI 1625-1. <http://usda. mannlib.cornell.edu/reports/nassr/poultry/pec-bb/>; <http://purl.access.gpo.gov/GPO/LPS1129>.

Chickens and Eggs [year] Summary. WEB. (annual) A 92.9/13: Item 0021-F-02. ASI 1625-7. <http://usda.mannlib.cornell.edu/reports/nassr/poultry/pec-bbl/>; <http://purl.access.gpo.gov/GPO/LPS1151>.

Citrus Fruits [year] Summary. WEB. (annual) A 92.11/8: Item 0024-E-01. ASI 1621-18.5. <http://jan.mannlib.cornell.edu/reports/nassr/fruit/zcf-bb/>; <http://purl.access.gpo.gov/GPO/LPS1130>.

Cold Storage. WEB. (monthly) A 92.21: Item 0024-G-01. ASI 1631-5. <http://jan.mannlib.cornell.edu/reports/nassr/other/pcs-bb/>; <http://purl.access.gpo.gov/GPO/LPS1131>.

Cold Storage [year] Summary. WEB. (annual) A 92.21/2: Item 0024-G-04. ASI 1631-11. <http://jan.mannlib.cornell.edu/reports/nassr/other/pcs-bban/>; <http://purl.access.gpo.gov/GPO/LPS1132>.

Cotton Ginnings. WEB. (semimonthly) A 92.47: Item 0141. ASI 1631-19. <http://jan.mannlib.cornell.edu/reports/nassr/field/pcg-bb/>; <http://purl.access. gpo.gov/GPO/LPS1134>.

Cranberries. WEB. (annual) A 92.11/6: Item 0122-A-04. ASI 1621-18.4. <http://jan.mannlib.cornell.edu/reports/nassr/fruit/zcr-bb/>; <http://purl.access.gpo.gov/GPO/LPS1135>.

Crop Production. WEB. (monthly) A 92.24: Item 0020-B. ASI 1621-1. <http://jan.mannlib.cornell.edu/reports/nassr/field/pcp-bb/>; <http://purl.access.gpo.gov/GPO/LPS1136>.

Crop Production [year] Summary. WEB. (annual) A 92.24/4: Item 0020-B-02. ASI 1621-1. <http://jan. mannlib.cornell.edu/reports/ nassr/field/pcp-bban/>; <http://purl.access.gpo.gov/GPO/LPS1137>.

Crop Progress. WEB. (Weekly) <http://jan.mannlib.cornell.edu/reports/nassr/field/pcr-bb/>.

Crop Values [year] Summary. WEB. (annual) A 92.24/3: Item 0020-B-05. ASI 1621-2. <http://jan.mannlib.cornell.edu/reports/nassr/price/zcv-bb/>; <http://purl.access.gpo.gov/GPO/LPS3076>.

Dairy Products. WEB. (monthly) A 92.10/7: Item 0024-F. ASI 1627-3. <http://usda.mannlib.cornell.edu/reports/nassr/

dairy/pdp-bb/>; <http://purl.access. gpo.gov/GPO/LPS1139>.

Dairy Products [year] Summary. WEB. (annual) A 92.10/5: Item 0024-F. ASI 1627-5. <http://usda. mannlib.cornell.edu/reports/nassr/dairy/pdp-bban/>; <http://purl.access. gpo.gov/GPO/LPS1140>.

Dairy Products Prices. WEB. (weekly) A 92.10/8: (Earlier title *Cheddar Cheese Prices*) Item 0015-A-03. ASI 1629-12. <http://usda.mannlib.cornell.edu/reports/nassr/price/dairy/>.

Egg Products. WEB. (monthly) A 92.9/4: Item 0021-F-02. ASI 1625-2. <http://jan.mannlib.cornell.edu/reports/nassr/poultry/pep-bb/>; <http://purl.access.gpo.gov/GPO/LPS1141>.

Farms and Land in Farms. WEB. (annual) A92.24/5: Item 0018-A. Item ASI 1614-4. <http://usda.mannlib.cornell.edu/reports/nassr/other/zfl-bb/>; <http://purl.access.gpo.gov/GPO/LPS1143>.

Farm Labor. WEB. (quarterly) A 92.12: Item 0021-F-05. ASI 1631-1. <http://jan.mannlib.cornell.edu/reports/nassr/other/pfl-bb/>; <http://purl.access.gpo.gov/GPO/LPS1142>.

Farm Production Expenditures Summary. WEB. (annual) A 92.40: Item 0018-A. ASI 1614-3. <http://jan. mannlib.cornell.edu/reports/nassr/price/zpe-bb/>; <http://purl.access.gpo.gov/GPO/LPS4599>.

Floriculture Crops Summary. WEB. (annual) A 92.32: Item 0024-L. ASI 1631-8. <http://jan.mannlib.cornell.edu/reports/nassr/other/zfc-bb/>; <http://purl.access. gpo.gov/GPO/LPS1144>.

Grain Stocks. WEB. (quarterly) A 92.15: Item 0122-A-03. ASI 1621-4. <http://jan.mannlib.cornell.edu/reports/nassr/field/pgs-bb/>; <http://purl.access.gpo.gov/GPO/LPS1145>.

Hatchery Production [year] Summary. WEB. (annual) A 92.9/6: Item 0021-F. ASI 1625-8. <http://usda. mannlib.cornell.edu/reports/nassr/poultry/pbh-bbh/>; <http://purl.access.gpo.gov/GPO/LPS1146>.

Hogs and Pigs. WEB. (quarterly) A 92.18/7: Item 0024-H. ASI 1623-3. <http://jan.mannlib.cornell.edu/reports/nassr/livestock/php-bb/>; <http://purl.access.gpo.gov/GPO/LPS1148>.

Honey. WEB. (annual) A 92.28/2: Item 0018-E. ASI 1631-6. <http://jan.mannlib.cornell.edu/reports/nassr/other/zho-bb/>; <http://purl.access.gpo.gov/GPO/LPS1149>.

Hop Stocks. WEB. (semiannual) A 92.30: Item 0122-A-03. ASI 1621-8. <http://jan.mannlib.cornell.edu/reports/nassr/field/phs-bb/>; <http://purl.access.gpo.gov/GPO/LPS1150>.

Livestock Slaughter Summary. WEB. (annual) A 92.18: Item 0024-J. ASI 1623-10. <http://jan.mannlib.cornell.edu/reports/nassr/livestock/pls-bban/>; <http://purl.access. gpo.gov/GPO/LPS1153>.

Livestock Slaughter. WEB. (monthly) A 92.18/3: Item 0024-J. ASI 1623-9. <http://usda.mannlib.cornell.edu/reports/nassr/livestock/pls-bb/>; <http://purl. access.gpo.gov/GPO/LPS1152>.

Meat Animals Production, Disposition, and Income Summary. WEB. (annual) A 92.17: Item 0024-H. ASI 1623-8. <http://jan.mannlib.cornell.edu/reports/nassr/livestock/zma-bb/>; <http://purl.access.gpo.gov/GPO/LPS1154>.

Milk Production. WEB. (monthly) A 92.10: Item 0024-F. ASI 1627-1. <http://jan.mannlib.cornell.edu/reports/nassr/dairy/pmp-bb/>; <http://purl.access.gpo.gov/GPO/LPS1156>.

Milk Production, Disposition and Income Summary. WEB. (annual) A 92.10/2: Item 0024-F. ASI 1627-4. <http://jan.mannlib.cornell.edu/reports/nassr/dairy/pmp-bbm/>; <http://purl.access.gpo.gov/GPO/LPS1157>.

Mink. WEB. (annual) A 92.18/11: Item 0024-J. ASI 1631-7. <http://jan.mannlib.cornell.edu/reports/nassr/other/zmi-bb/>; <http://purl.access.gpo.gov/GPO/LPS1158>.

Mushrooms. WEB. (annual) A 92.11/10-5: Item 0024-E. ASI 1631-9. <http://jan.mannlib.cornell.edu/reports/nassr/other/zmu-bb/>; <http://purl.access.gpo.gov/GPO/LPS1159>.

Noncitrus Fruits and Nuts. WEB. (annual) (includes both preliminary summary and summary report) A 92.11/2-2: Item 0122-A-04. ASI 1621-18. [no.] <http://jan.mannlib. cornell.edu/reports/nassr/fruit/pnf-bb/>; <http://purl. access.gpo.gov/GPO/LPS1160>.

Peanut Stocks and Processing. WEB. (monthly) A 92.14: Item 0122-A-03. ASI 1621-6. <http://jan. mannlib.cornell.edu/reports/nassr/field/pps-bb/>; <http://purl.access.gpo.gov/GPO/LPS1161>.

Potatoes. WEB. (annual) A 92.11/4: Item 0020-B-01. ASI 1621-11. <http://jan.mannlib.cornell.edu/reports/nassr/field/ppo-bbp/>; <http://purl.access.gpo.gov/GPO/LPS2402>.

Potato Stocks. WEB. (monthly, December-May) A 92.11/11: Item 0020-B-01. ASI 1621-10. <http://jan. mannlib. cornell.edu/reports/nassr/field/ppo-bb/>; <http://purl.access.gpo.gov/GPO/LPS1163>.

Poultry Slaughter. WEB. (monthly) A 92.9/5: Item 0021-F. ASI 1625-3. <http://jan.mannlib.cornell.edu/reports/nassr/poultry/ppy-bb/>; <http://purl.access.gpo.gov/GPO/LPS1162>.

Poultry—Production and Value, Summary. WEB. A 92.9/3: Item 0021-F; ASI 1625-5. <http://usda.mannlib.cornell.edu/reports/nassr/poultry/pbh-bbp/>; <http://purl.access.gpo.gov/GPO/LPS1164>.

Prospective Plantings. WEB. (annual) A 92.24/2: Item 0020-B-03. ASI 1621-22. <http://usda. mannlib.cornell.edu/reports/nassr/field/pcp-bbp/>; <http://purl.access.gpo.gov/GPO/LPS1136>.

Rice Stocks. WEB. (quarterly) A 92.43: Item 0122-A-03. ASI 1621-7. <http://usda.mannlib.cornell.edu/reports/nassr/field/prs-bb/>; <http://purl.access.gpo.gov/GPO/LPS1165>.

Sheep. WEB. (3 times per year) A 92.18/9: Item 0021-N-10. ASI 1623-5. <http://usda.mannlib.cornell.edu/reports/nassr/livestock/pgg-bbs/>; <http://purl. access.gpo.gov/GPO/LPS1166>.

Sheep and Goats. WEB. (annual) A92.18/8: Item 0021-N. ASI 1623-4. <http://jan.mannlib.cornell.edu/reports/nassr/livestock/pgg-bb/>; <http://purl.access.gpo.gov/GPO/LPS4781>.

Small Grains Summary. WEB. (annual) A 92.42: Item 0122-A-06. ASI 1621-24. <http://jan.mannlib.cornell.edu/reports/nassr/field/pcp-bbs/>; http://purl.access.gpo.gov/GPO/LPS4614>.

Trout Production. WEB. (annual) A 92.44/3: Item 0021-F-07. ASI 1631-16. <http://jan.mannlib.cornell.edu/reports/nassr/other/ztp-bb/>; <http://purl.access. gpo.gov/GPO/LPS1168>.

Turkey Hatchery. WEB. (annual) A 92.9/17-2: Item 0021-F-01. ASI 1625-10. <http://jan.mannlib.cornell.edu/reports/nassr/poultry/pth-bb/>; <http://purl.access. gpo.gov/GPO/LPS1169>.

Turkeys. WEB. (semiannual) A 92.9/17: Item 0021-F-01. ASI 1625-6. <http://jan.mannlib.cornell.edu/reports/nassr/poultry/pth-bbt/>; <http://purl.access.gpo.gov/GPO/LPS2534>.

Vegetables. WEB. (5 times per year) A 92.11: Item 0024-E. ASI 1621-12. <http://jan.mannlib.cornell.edu/reports/nassr/fruit/pvg-bb/>; <http://purl.access. gpo.gov/GPO/LPS1170>.

Vegetables Summary. WEB. (annual) A 92.11/10-2: Item 0024-E. ASI 1621-25. <http://jan.mannlib.cornell.edu/reports/nassr/fruit/pvg-bban/>; <http://purl.access. gpo.gov/GPO/LPS1171>.

Weekly Weather and Crop Bulletin. WEB. (weekly) <http://jan.mannlib.cornell.edu/reports/nassr/field/weather/>.

Winter Wheat and Rye Seedings. WEB. (annual) A 92.42: Item 0122-A-06. ASI 1621-30. <http://jan.mannlib.cornell.edu/reports/nassr/field/pcp-bbw/>.

Wool and Mohair. WEB. (annual) A 92.29/5: Item 0021-N-09. ASI 1623-6. <http://jan.mannlib.cornell.edu/reports/nassr/livestock/pgg-bbw/>; <http://purl. access.gpo.gov/GPO/LPS1173>.

Commodity Situation and Outlook Reports. MF. WEB. (frequency varies) (Dates and titles vary) U.S. Department of Agriculture. Economic Research Service. <http://www.ers.usda.gov/prodsrvs/periodic.htm#SandO>.

> Coverage: varies; world, U.S., regions, states, selected market cities.
>
> Content: commodity reports that provide statistics on production, prices, trade, forecasts, and current situation.

Cotton and Wool Outlook. WEB. (monthly) A 93.24/2: Item 0021-M. ASI 1561-1. <http://usda.mannlib.cornell.edu/reports/erssor/field/cws-bb/>.

Feed Outlook. WEB. (monthly) A 93.11/2: Item 0021-E. ASI 1561-4. <http://usda.mannlib.cornell.edu/reports/erssor/field/fds-bb/>; <http://purl.access.gpo.gov/GPO/LPS1100>.

Fruit and Tree Nuts Situation and Outlook. MF. WEB. (three issues a year) A 93.12/3: Item 0021-K. ASI 1561-6. GPO. <http://usda.mannlib.cornell.edu/reports/erssor/specialty/fts-bb/>; <http://purl.access.gpo.gov/GPO/LPS3327>.

Livestock, Dairy, and Poultry Situation and Outlook. WEB. (monthly) A 93.46/3: Item 0024-C. ASI 1561-19. <http://usda.mannlib.cornell.edu/reports/erssor/livestock/ldp-mbb/>; <http://purl.access.gpo.gov/GPO/LPS2552>.

Oil Crops Outlook. WEB. (monthly) A 93.23/2: Item 0021-D. ASI 1561-3. <http://usda.mannlib.cornell.edu/reports/erssor/field/ocs-bb/>; <http://purl.access.gpo.gov/GPO/LPS1105>.

Rice Outlook. WEB. (monthly) A 93.11/3: Item 0021-P. ASI 1561-8. <http://usda.mannlib.cornell.edu/reports/erssor/field/rcs-bb/>.

Sugar and Sweetener. MF. WEB. (two issues a year) A 93.31/3: Item 0024-R. ASI 1561-14. GPO. <http://usda.mannlib.cornell.edu/reports/erssor/specialty/sss-bb/>; <http://purl.access.gpo.gov/GPO/LPS1109>.

Tobacco Situation and Outlook. MF. WEB. (three issues a year) A 93.25: Item 0024-D-01. ASI 1561-10. GPO. <http://usda.mannlib.cornell.edu/reports/erssor/specialty/tbs-bb/>; <http://purl.access.gpo.gov/GPO/LPS1110>; <http://www.ers.usda.gov/briefing/tobacco/index.htm>.

Vegetables and Specialties Situation and Outlook. MF. WEB. (three issues a year) A 93.12/2: Item 0021-L. ASI 1561-11. GPO. <http://usda.mannlib.cornell.edu/reports/erssor/specialty/vgs-bb/>; <http://purl.access.gpo.gov/GPO/LPS3325>.

Wheat Outlook. WEB. (monthly) A 93.11: Item 0021-I. ASI 1561-12. <http://usda.mannlib.cornell.edu/reports/erssor/field/whs-bb/>; <http://purl.access.gpo.gov/GPO/LPS1112>.

Guide to Products and Services: National Agricultural Statistics Service, USDA. PRINT. (irregular) U.S. Department of Agriculture. National Agricultural Statistics Service. Agricultural Statistics Board. A 92.35/2: (Earlier titled *Agricultural Statistics Board Catalog.*) Item 0122-A-08. (Some issues not sent to depository libraries) ASI 1614-1.

> Content: descriptions of Agricultural Statistics Board and other National Agricultural Statistics publications; release dates.

Discussion

The *Crop and Livestock Reports* of the Agricultural Statistics Board consist of numerous detailed statistical reports on various commodities. Individual titles of the reports are listed above. Distribution of these reports is now primarily on the Web. Reports may give data on production or data related to production. The frequency of the reports vary. The *Reports by Commodity: Index of Estimates* provides an easy-to-use interface for locating the appropriate report by the name of the commodity. For example, using this locator and selecting "carrots," provides the titles and links to three reports including data on carrots.

The *Commodity Situation and Outlook Reports* are a group of periodic reports, each on an individual commodity or commodity group. Each report begins with a summary consisting of a narrative description of the current situation with numerous charts and tables covering a variety of basic data on the commodity. Occasionally there is a special article on some aspect of the commodity. Reports are primarily distributed on the Web, with text and PDF versions of the reports available. Several years worth of the reports are usually available.

A print catalog of Agricultural Statistics Board publications and other selected NASS publications titled, *Guide to Products and Services: National Agricultural Statistics Service, USDA* is also produced.

FOREIGN AGRICULTURE SOURCES
Checklist

Foreign Agricultural Service Web Site. WEB. <http://www.fas.usda.gov>.

>Content: links to foreign agricultural resources, including news items, countries, commodities, exporter assistance, FAS programs, and other information about FAS.

AgExporter. PRINT. WEB. (monthly) 1989–. U.S. Department of Agriculture. Foreign Agricultural Service. A 67.7/3: Item 0076. ASI 1922-2. GPO.

>Coverage: U.S., selected countries. <http://www.fas.usda.gov/info/agexporter/agexport.html>; <http://purl.access.gpo.gov/GPO/LPS1647>.

>Content: popular articles about exporting of agricultural products; descriptions of markets, and Foreign Agricultural Service programs.

World Agricultural Supply and Demand Estimates. WEB. (monthly) U.S. Department of Agriculture. Economic Research Service. A 93.29/3: Item 0011-F. ASI 1522-5. <http://jan.mannlib.cornell.edu/reports/waobr/wasde-bb/>; <http://purl.access.gpo.gov/GPO/LPS1847>.

>Coverage: world, country groupings, selected countries, U.S.

>Content: quantity of agricultural exports and imports by commodity and geographic area.

World Markets and Trade, Circular Series. MF. WEB. (1994-) U.S. Department of Agriculture. Foreign Agricultural Service. A 67.18: Item 0076-J. ASI 1925–. <http://ffas.usda.gov/currwmt.html>; <http://ffas.usda.gov/archive.html>.

>Coverage: countries.

>Content: statistics on U.S. and foreign production, trade, use, prices, and other related information for agricultural products covered.

Cotton: World Markets and Trade. MF. WEB. (monthly) A 67.18:FC. Item 0076-J. ASI 1925-4.<http://ffas.usda.gov/currwmt.html>; <http://ffas.usda.gov/archive.html>; <http://ffas.usda.gov/cotton_arc.html>; <http://purl.access.gpo.gov/GPO/LPS1868>.

Dairy, Livestock and Poultry: U.S. Trade and Prospects. MF. WEB. (monthly) A 67.18:FDLP. Item 0076-J. ASI 1925-32. <http://ffas.usda.gov/currwmt.html>; <http://ffas.usda.gov/archive.html>; <http://ffas.usda.gov/ust&p_arc.html>; <http://purl.access.gpo.gov/GPO/LPS2550>.

Dairy Monthly Imports. MF. WEB. (monthly) A 67.18:FDMI. Item 0076-J. ASI 1925-31. <http://ffas.usda.gov/currwmt.html>; <http://ffas.usda.gov/archive.html>; <http://ffas.usda.gov/dmi_arc.html>; <http://purl.access.gpo.gov/GPO/LPS1800>.

Dairy: World Markets and Trade. MF. WEB. (semiannual) A 67.18:FD. Item 0076-J. ASI 1925-10. <http://ffas.usda.gov/currwmt.html>; <http://ffas.usda.gov/archive.html>; <http://ffas.usda.gov/dairy_arc.html>; <http://purl.access.gpo.gov/GPO/LPS1770>.

Fishery Products Circular. WEB. (quarterly) <http://ffas.usda.gov/currwmt.html>; <http://ffas.usda.gov/ffpd/Fish-Circular/fish.html>.

Grain: World Markets and Trade. MF. WEB. (monthly) A 67.18:FG Item 0076-J. ASI 1925-2. <http://ffas.usda.gov/currwmt.html>; <http://ffas.usda.gov/archive.html>; <http://ffas.usda.gov/grain_arc.htm>; <http://purl.access.gpo.gov/GPO/LPS1868>.

Livestock and Poultry: World Markets and Trade. MF. WEB. A 67.18:FL&P. Item 0076-J. ASI 1925-33. <http://ffas.usda.gov/currwmt.html>; <http://ffas.usda.gov/archive.html>; <http://ffas.usda.gov/livestock_arc.html>; <http://purl.access.gpo.gov/GPO/LPS1796>.

Oilseeds: World Markets and Trade. MF. WEB. A 67.18:FOP. Item 0076-J. ASI 1925-1. <http://ffas.usda.gov/currwmt.html>; <http://ffas.usda.gov/archive.html>; <http://ffas.usda.gov/oilseeds_arc.htm>; <http://purl.access.gpo.gov/GPO/LPS3505>.

Organic Perspectives. WEB. <http://ffas.usda.gov/currwmt.html>; <http://ffas.usda.gov/archive.html>; <http://ffas.usda.gov/organics_arc.html>.

Sugar: World Markets and Trade. MF. WEB. A 67.18:FS. Item 0076-J. ASI 1925-14. <http://ffas.usda.gov/currwmt.html>; <http://ffas.usda.gov/archive.html>; <http://ffas.usda.gov/sugar_arc.html>; <http://purl.access.gpo.gov/GPO/LPS1868>.

Tobacco: World Markets and Trade. MF. WEB. A 67.18:FT. Item 0076-J. ASI 1925-16. <http://ffas.usda.gov/currwmt.html>; <http://ffas.usda.gov/archive.html>; <http://ffas.usda.gov/tobacco_arc.htm>; <http://purl.access.gpo.gov/GPO/LPS3506>.

Tropical Products: World Markets and Trade. MF. WEB. A 67.18:FTROP. Item 0076-J. ASI 1925-37. <http://ffas.usda.gov/currwmt.html>; <http://ffas.usda.gov/archive.html>; <http://ffas.usda.gov/tropical_arc.html>; <http://purl.access.gpo.gov/GPO/LPS3507>.

U.S. Planting Seed Trade. MF. WEB. (monthly) A 67.18:FFVS-. Item 0076-J. ASI 1925-13. <http://ffas.usda.gov/currwmt.html>; <http://ffas.usda.gov/archive.html>; <http://ffas.usda.gov/seed_arc.html>; <http://purl.access.gpo.gov/GPO/LPS1768>.

Wood Products: International Trade and Foreign Markets. WEB. MF. (quarterly) A 67.18:WP. Item 0076-J. ASI 1925-36. <http://ffas.usda.gov/currwmt.html>; <http://ffas.usda.gov/ffpd/forestcirculars.htm>.

World Agricultural Production. MF. WEB. A 67.18:WAP. Item 0076-J. ASI 1925-28. <http://ffas.usda.gov/currwmt.html>; <http://ffas.usda.gov/archive.html>; <http://ffas.usda.gov/wap_arc.htm>; <http://purl.access.gpo.gov/GPO/LPS3508>.

World Horticultural Trade and U.S. Export Opportunities. MF. WEB. (monthly) ASI 1925-34. A 67.18:FHORT. Item 0076-J. ASI 1925-34. <http://ffas.usda.gov/currwmt.html>; <http://ffas.usda.gov/archive.html>; <http://ffas.usda.gov/htp_arc.htm>; <http://purl.access.gpo.gov/GPO/PS3504>.

Foreign Agricultural Trade of the United States (FATUS) Calendar Year Supplement. MF. (annual) U.S. Department of Agriculture. Economic Research Service. A 93.17/7-3: Item 0042-E. ASI 1522-4. GPO. Selected tables <http://www.ers.usda.gov/briefing/AgTrade/htm/Data.htm>.

>Coverage: world, world regions, country groupings, countries, U.S.

Content: value and quantity of agricultural exports and imports for commodities, countries, and commodities by country; balance of trade.

Foreign Agricultural Trade of the United States — Briefing Room. WEB. U.S. Department of Agriculture. Economic Research Service. <http://www.ers.usda.gov/briefing/AgTrade/>.

Coverage: world, world regions, country groupings, countries, U.S.

Content: Foreign Agricultural Trade of the United States (FATUS) database; quantity and value of agricultural exports and imports by commodity and country.

Attache Reports. WEB. (irregular) U.S. Department of Agriculture. Foreign Agricultural Service. <http://www.fas.usda.gov/scriptsw/attacherep/default.htm>.

Coverage: selected countries.

Content: reports on commodity production in individual countries; marketing and trade in individual countries.

Discussion

Agricultural Statistics, cited in the "Agricultural Statistical Sources" section of this chapter, includes some statistics on foreign agriculture and should be consulted first if searching for statistical information.

The Foreign Agricultural Service (FAS) is the major Department of Agriculture agency involved with foreign agriculture. It is particularly concerned with foreign agricultural trade and exporting issues. FAS also collects and compiles numerous statistics on the worldwide supply and trade of agricultural commodities. The *Foreign Agricultural Service Web Site* is a good source to begin searching for information on foreign agriculture.

AgExporter is a popular-oriented magazine that includes short articles and numerous photographs. The magazine is directed towards an audience of U.S. agricultural producers, exporters, trade organizations, state departments of agriculture and other export-oriented organizations. Typical articles include "Guatemala's Cool Dessert Craze: A Growing U.S. Opportunity" (Vol. XI, No. 12), "Sweetening the Deal for U.S. Snack Food Producers" (Volume XI, No. 1), and "Mexico: Making the Connection" (Volume XI, No. 11).

Each issue of the *World Agricultural Supply and Demand Estimates* includes a short summary section that reviews world agricultural production and trade. The majority of the report consists of a series of statistical tables charting world, U.S., and selected countries' use of individual commodities, such as rice, soybeans, animal products, and cotton.

Each *World Markets and Trade, Circular Series* offers detailed reports on an individual commodity. The information included varies from report to report, but combines text and statistics to provide a comprehensive report on a commodity's worldwide production and trade. Many of the reports contain production estimates, forecasts, and outlooks. These reports are one of the first sources to

search if looking for information on a specific commodity.

Foreign Agricultural Trade of the United States (FATUS) contains detailed statistical tables on agricultural trade. There are some summary tables on total trade, some historical tables, and a set of detailed tables for both exports and imports. The detailed tables include commodity by country data for the last two years.

The *Foreign Agricultural Trade of the United States — Briefing Room* Web site provides access to the Foreign Agricultural Trade of the United States (FATUS) database. Users may select exports and imports, then either a commodity or a country/region. The individual commodity reports list exports or imports for all geographic areas. The country/region reports list all commodities for that area. An option to produce more customized reports is also available. This site also offers several tables from FATUS in downloadable spreadsheet format. Links are provided to publications and other Web sites.

Attache Reports are reports on agricultural production, marketing, and trade in other countries. A typical report might deal with the retail food sector in Argentina or strawberry production in Chile. Reports mix narrative and statistical tables to provide an analysis of their topic. New reports are constantly being issued. The *Attache Reports* Web site allows you to search for reports from a specific time frame, by topic, and by country. Reports are available in PDF and in WordPerfect format files.

See Chapter 38, "Foreign Trade Statistics," for more information on agricultural trade.

AGRICULTURAL AND SOIL CONSERVATION SOURCES
Checklist

Natural Resources Conservation Service Web Site. WEB. U.S. Department of Agriculture. Natural Resources Conservation Service. <http://www.nrcs.usda.gov/>.

Content: general information about the National Resources Conservation Service (NRCS) and its programs; links to specific offices and areas of NRCS.

General Publications. PRINT. (irregular) U.S. Department of Agriculture. Natural Resources Conservation Service. A 57.2: Item 0120.

Content: general publications on a wide variety of topics relating to the programs and activities of the NRCS.

Handbooks, Manuals, Guide. PRINT. (irregular) U.S. Department of Agriculture. Natural Resources Conservation Service. A 57.6/2: Item 0120-A.

Content: guides and manuals to a wide range of conservation topics covered by the NRCS.

Soil Survey Division Web Site. WEB. U.S. Department of Agriculture. Natural Resources Conservation Center. Soil Survey Division. <http://www.statlab.iastate.edu/soils/soildiv/index.html>.

Content: information about programs of the Soil Survey Division; links to other offices and centers relating to soil programs; information about soils, soil surveys, and soils data.

National Soil Survey Center. WEB. U.S. Department of Agriculture. Natural Resources Conservation Service. National Soil Survey Center. <http://www.statlab.iastate.edu/soils/nssc/>.

Content: information about soil survey programs; directory of services and personnel; lists of published soil surveys; links to publications of the National Soil Survey Center.

Soil Survey Reports. PRINT. (irregular) U.S. Department of Agriculture. Natural Resources Conservation Center. A 57.38: to A 57.38/51: Item 0102-B-01 to 53; Item 102-A.

Content: soil surveys of individual counties; includes both report and maps.

On-Line Soil Survey Manuscripts. WEB. (irregular) U.S. Department of Agriculture. Natural Resources Conservation Service. Soil Survey Division. <http://www.statlab.iastate.edu/soils/soildiv/surveys/onlineman.html>.

Content: prototype system for delivering soil surveys electronically.

Discussion

The Natural Resources Conservation Service (NRCS) is the agency most involved with agricultural conservation issues. It carries out a number of initiatives and programs in this area, particularly in the area of soil conservation. Its agency Web site is a good source to consult for an overview of these programs and links to more specific information on the programs.

The *General Publications* and *Handbooks, Manuals, Guides* series include a wide range of publications from the NRCS. Some reports are geared to a specific geographic area, while others have more general applications. Titles in the *General Publications* series include *Environmental Quality Incentives Program in the Shawano Lake Watershed, Shawano County, Wisconsin* (A 57.2:EN 8/2/SHAWANO); *Prairie Plants: Warm Season Grasses, Glowers and Legumes* (A 57.2:P 88/2); and *Grazing Lands Conservation Initiative in Oklahoma* (A 57.2:G 79/14). Titles in the *Handbooks, Manuals, Guides* series include *The Northeast Missouri Soil Health Guide* (A 57.6/2:M 69 O), *National Forestry Manual,* (A 57.6/2:F 76), and *Landowner Responsibility for Constructed Conservation Systems: A Guide* (A 57.6/2:L 23/2).

One major and important program of the NRCS is its work with soil surveying programs. The Soil Survey Division is particularly charged with carrying out soil surveying, soils classification, and other soils research for both U.S. soils and soils worldwide. Their Web site is a good source of current information about these programs and includes much information on soils in general. The *National Soil Survey Center* is particularly charged with carrying out and publishing the U.S. soil survey program.

Detailed information about the soil survey program is included at its site.

The U.S. soil surveys produced as a result of the NRCS programs are extremely detailed reports describing and analyzing the types of soils found in a particular area, usually a county. The text of each report describes the properties of each type of soil found in the area. Tables describe soil characteristics even more extensively when used for such activities as woodland management and productivity, building site development, sanitary facilities, or recreational development. Tables on engineering index properties, physical and chemical properties, water features, soil features, and classification of the soils are included. Each *Soil Survey* also includes a series of soil maps keyed to the written report.

Soil Survey Reports are distributed to depository libraries in a print format. *The National Soil Survey Center* Web site includes information about the availability of soil surveys, as well as a listing of published soil surveys by state that indicates whether a report is still in-print and available. In general, individual copies of soil surveys are available from state or local offices of the Natural Resources Conservation Service, from county agents, and from congressional representatives. A prototype system for distributing soil surveys electronically, called the *On-Line Soil Survey Manuscripts*, is being developed, but only includes selected reports at this point. It also does not generally include the soil survey maps accompanying the reports. Reports at this site are in HTML and PDF formats, or combinations of the two formats.

AGRICULTURAL RESEARCH
Checklist

Agricultural Research Service Web Site. WEB. U.S. Department of Agriculture. Agricultural Research Service. <http://www.ars.usda.gov/>.

Content: ARS programs; news and information; find the expert at ARS; research opportunities; general information about ARS.

General Publications. PRINT. (irregular) U.S. Department of Agriculture. Agricultural Research Service. A 77.2: Item 0026-A-01.

Content: general publications reporting on the work and programs of the Agricultural Research Service.

Agricultural Research. PRINT. WEB. (monthly) 1953–. U.S. Department of Agriculture. Agricultural Research Service. A 77.12: Item 0025-A. <http://www.ars.usda.gov/is/AR/>.

Content: articles on agricultural research.

Technical Bulletins. MF. WEB. (irregular) 1927–. U.S. Department of Agriculture. A 1.36: Item 0016. Selected *Technical Bulletins* authored by the Economic Research Service: <http://www.ers.usda.gov/Prodsrvs/reports.htm>.

Content: technical research reports on a variety of agricultural subjects.

Inventory of Agricultural Research Fiscal Year [year]. MF. (annual) 1969/70–. U.S. Department of Agriculture. Cooperative State Research, Education, and Extension Service. A 94.14: Item 0040-A-05. ASI 1744-2.

> Coverage: U.S., regions, states.
>
> Content: statistics on agricultural research funding.

The National Agricultural Library Home Page. WEB. U.S. Department of Agriculture. Agricultural Research Service. National Agricultural Library. <http://www.nal.usda.gov/>.

> Content: general information about the National Agricultural Library (NAL) and its services and programs; search engine for site; links to AGRICOLA, publications and other databases; site map.

*AGRICOLA.*WEB. 1970–. U.S. Department of Agriculture. Agricultural Research Service. National Agricultural Library. <http://www.nal.usda.gov/ag98/>; <http://purl.access. gpo.gov/GPO/LPS1292>.

> Content: index to publications and resources concerning all aspects of agriculture and allied disciplines; includes bibliographic records for books, journal articles, theses, patents, technical reports, software, multimedia, and other resources.

Discussion

The Agricultural Research Service (ARS) is the primary division of the Department of Agriculture involved in agricultural research. Its Web site is a good starting point for locating information about the programs of the ARS. The *General Publications* series of the ARS includes publications describing ARS polices and procedures as well as some documents on more specific research programs and topics. Typical titles include *Gleaning at ARS: Harvesting all the Benefits of Agricultural Research* (A 77.2:G 47); *Silverleaf Whitefly: National Research, Action, and Technology Transfer Plan* (A 77.2:SI 3); and *Technology Transfer Agreements with the Agricultural Research Service* (A 77.2:T 22/2/997).

Agricultural Research contains short articles on agricultural research topics. Articles are technical in content but are written in a very readable, highly illustrated style. Topics covered vary, including crop production and crop sciences; forage and range sciences; livestock and veterinary sciences; soil, water, and air sciences; insect research; and postharvest science and technology.

Technical Bulletins are technical reports on research projects. Reports cover scientific and technological areas related to agriculture and are produced by different subagencies within the Department of Agriculture. Reports vary from a few pages in length to book-length reports. Titles include *Price Determination for Corn and Wheat: The Role of Market Factors and Government Programs* (A 1.36:1878), *Validation of a Self-Reported Measure of Household Food Insufficiency With Nutrient Intake Data* (A 1.36:1863), and *Composite Breeds to Use Heterosis and Breed Differences to Improve Efficiency of Beef Production* (A1.36:1875).

Inventory of Agricultural Research provides funding and scientist years data for Department of Agriculture research agencies, state agricultural experiment stations, forestry and veterinary schools, Colleges of 1890 and Tuskegee University, and other cooperating institutions. Tables report scientist year (similar to full-time equivalent figures) and amount of funds allocated for research for the USDA as a whole, for USDA agencies, and for other institutions as a group by designated Research Problem Areas and commodity subdivision. Also included are tables giving scientist years and funds for state agricultural experiment stations, forestry schools, other cooperating institutions, and USDA agencies. Tables showing funding by sources of funds and statistics on funding for state stations and other nonfederal institutions by source of funds are included.

The National Agricultural Library is the largest agricultural library in the world. It contains vast collections and provides numerous services to researchers and users. The home page of the National Agricultural Library provides a gateway to accessing these resources and services.

AGRICOLA is an online database produced by the National Agricultural Library. It is available from the National Agricultural Library Web site free-of-charge. It includes bibliographic records for materials covering "all aspects of agriculture and allied disciplines, including plant and animal sciences, forestry, entomology, soil and water resources, agricultural economics, agricultural engineering, agricultural products, alternative farming practices, and food and nutrition." Resources on agricultural trade and marketing, rural information, and animal welfare, are also represented. One section of the database includes information on books, serials, and audiovisual materials, theses, patents, software, and technical reports related to agriculture held by the National Agricultural Library. The other part of the database covers journals, book chapters, reports, and reprints. Bibliographic records began production with 1970, but material from the 16th century to the present is represented in the database. Many commercial versions of AGRICOLA are also being produced.

Vendors of the AGRICOLA database include Dialog (File 10), CompuServe Information Service, OCLC FirstSearch, STN International, Ovid Technologies, and the National Information Services Corporation (NISC). Web and CD-ROM versions are available from SilverPlatter Inc. A large subset of the AGRICOLA database is also available in print from The Oryx Press in the *Bibliography of Agriculture.*

DEPARTMENT OF AGRICULTURE SOURCES ON FOODS

Checklist

FNS Online. WEB. U.S. Department of Agriculture. Food and Nutrition Service. <http://www.fns.usda.gov/fns/>.

Content: general information about the Food and Nutrition Services' food assistance programs; agency activities and organization.

Food Review: The Magazine of Food Economics. PRINT. WEB. (quarterly) 1978–. U.S. Department of Agriculture. Economic Research Service. A 93.16/3: (Earlier, A 105.15:) (Before 1991 titled *National Food Review*) Item 0021-H. ASI 1541-7. GPO. <http://www.ers.usda.gov/epubs/pdf/foodrevw/foodrevw.htm>.
> Content: articles on various food topics of interest to USDA researchers.

Food Consumption, Prices, and Expenditures. MF. WEB. (annual) U.S. Department of Agriculture. Economic Research Service. Statistical Bulletin series. A 1.34/4: (Earlier, A 1.34:) Item 0015. ASI 1544-4. <http://www.ers.usda.gov/prodsrvs/rept-fd.htm#consumption>; <http://purl.access.gpo.gov/GPO/LPS3832>; 1970–97 edition: <http://www.ers.usda.gov/epubs/pdf/sb965/>.
> Coverage: selected countries, U.S.
> Content: food expenditures as share of all disposable personal income; percentage of food expenditures by income range; percentage of personal consumption expenditures for food and alcoholic beverages; total expenditures for food and alcoholic beverages at home and away from home; food expenditures by source of funds; average retail food prices for individual items; consumer price index for food items; per capita annual consumption of individual food items.

Food Cost Review. MF. WEB. (annual) U.S. Department of Agriculture. Economic Research Service. Agricultural Economic Report series. A 1.107/2: (Earlier, A 1.107:) (Earlier title: *Developments in Farm to Retail Price Spreads for Food Products*) Item 0042-C. ASI 1544-9. Tables: <http://www.ers.usda.gov/briefing/foodmark/cost/cost.htm>.
> Coverage: U.S.
> Content: food price developments; consumer price index; retail food prices for individual items; farm-retail price spreads; food expenditures as share of disposable food income; annual food expenditures by income range and food product.

Family Economics and Nutrition Review. MF. WEB. (quarterly) 1995–. U.S. Department of Agriculture. Food and Consumer Service. A 98.20: (Earlier, A 77.245:) (Issued since 1957 as *Family Economics Review*) Item 0074-A-09. ASI 1362-17. GPO. <http://www.usda.gov/cnpp/FENR.htm>; <http://purl.access.gpo.gov/GPO/LPS5323>.
> Content: research articles on food and nutrition.

Official USDA Food Plans: Cost of Food at Home at Four Levels. WEB. (monthly) U.S. Department of Agriculture. Food and Consumer Service. A 98.19/2: Item 0074-A-08. <http://www.usda.gov/cnpp/using3.htm>; <http://purl.access.gpo.gov/GPO/LPS1848>.
> Content: average cost per week for food at four cost levels by family size and age group.

Food and Nutrition Information Center Web Site. WEB. U.S. Department of Agriculture. Agricultural Research Service. National Agricultural Library. Food and Nutrition Information Center. <http://www.nal.usda.gov/fnic/>.

Content: general information about the work of the Food and Nutrition Information Center (FNIC); links to reports and studies; FNIC databases; links to individual topic pages such as "food composition," "dietary supplements," and "dietary guidelines."

USDA Food Composition Data. WEB. U.S. Department of Agriculture. Agricultural Research Service. National Agricultural Library. Food and Nutrition Information Center. Nutrient Data Laboratory. <http://www.nal.usda.gov/fnic/foodcomp/Data/index.html>.
> Content: databases and publications providing food composition data.

Discussion

Within the Department of Agriculture is the Food and Nutrition Service, which administers the 15 food assistance programs carried out by the Department of Agriculture. Included are such programs as the Food Stamp Program; the Special Supplemental Nutrition Program for Women, Infants, and Children (WIC); the National School Lunch Program; and the School Breakfast Program. The agency Web site describes these programs and provides links to more specific information about each program. It is a good source for beginning research on the Department of Agriculture's major role in carrying out these food assistance programs.

Food Review: The Magazine of Food Economics publishes short research-oriented articles written by USDA specialists. Most articles include a list of references, and many include statistical tables, charts, and graphs. Reports on the impact of federal legislation and regulations are also included. Sample articles include "Minimum Wage Increases Have Little Effect on Prices of Food away from Home;" "Characteristics of Mid-Atlantic Food Banks and Food Rescue Organizations" (both in Volume 22, Issue 1, September 1999); "Food Companies Spread Nutrition Information through Advertising and Labels;" and "Prices and Incomes Affect Nutrients Consumed" (both in Volume 21, Issue 2, May 1999).

Food Consumption, Prices, and Expenditures is a detailed statistical annual report. Over 100 tables cover the consumption, supply, and prices of individual food items. The per capita annual food consumption for such items as apples, potatoes, candy, and eggs is provided. Average retail prices are given for specific items, such as white bread, frankfurters, or coffee. The price index tables give the consumer price index for food items. Data are given for several years.

Food Cost Review is a narrative report with numerous statistical tables. There is an overview section and sections on "Market Basket Prices," and "Price Spreads for Selected Foods." The market basket price tables give retail prices, farm value, and farm value share of retail prices for specific food items. Related price indexes are given for broad food groups. The price spread tables give retail price, wholesale value, price spreads, and farm value share for selected food items.

Family Economics and Nutrition Review includes a variety of research oriented articles about food and nutrition. Typical articles include "Nutrition and Dairy Industry Benefits Associated with Promoting Lowfat Milk: Evidence from the 1989 CSFII," and "The Diet Quality of Americans: Strong Link with Nutrition Knowledge" (both from Vol. 12, No. 1, 1999). The journal also regularly contains a widely cited and used table on cost of food at home. It gives the weekly and monthly cost of food at four different levels ranging from a thrifty plan to a liberal plan. Information is given for families of two, families of four, and for individuals by age group and sex. This table, *Official USDA Food Plans: Cost of Food at Home at Four Levels*, also appears monthly on the USDA Web site.

The Food and Nutrition Information Center (FNIC) is concerned with and disseminates information on many aspects of human nutrition. In particular, information on food safety, dietary guidelines, and the composition of foods is available from the FNIC site. One individual page from the FNIC site, titled *USDA Food Composition Data* is also cited here. This page provides links to a wide range of food composition databases and publications. Included among these are the *USDA Nutrient Database for Standard Reference*, which gives data for over 6,200 foods for up to 82 nutrients, and *Nutritive Value of Foods*, which includes data on over 900 foods expressed in terms of common household units.

INDEXES
Checklist

Catalog of United States Government Publications (MOCAT). WEB. 1994 0150. U.S. Government Printing Office. Superintendent of Documents. <http://www.gpo.gov/catalog>; <http://www.access.gpo.gov/su_docs/locators/cgp/index.html>; <http://purl.access.gpo.gov/GPO/LPS844>.

Monthly Catalog of United States Government Publications. CD-ROM. 1996–. U.S. Government Printing Office. Superintendent of Documents. GP 3.8/7: Item 0557-C. GPO.

Monthly Catalog of United States Government Publications (Condensed version). PRINT. (monthly) 1996–. U.S. Government Printing Office. Superintendent of Documents. GP 3.8/8: (Earlier full version, GP 3.8:, 1895–1995). Item 0557-D. GPO.

American Statistics Index (ASI). PRINT. (monthly) 1973–. Bethesda, MD: Congressional Information Service.

Statistical Universe. WEB. Bethesda, MD: Congressional Information Service.

DISCUSSION

The *Monthly Catalog* is the most comprehensive index for government publications. The complete version is available on the Web and on CD-ROM. For publications on agriculture and related topics, search headings and keywords such as those beginning with "Agriculture," "Agricultural," "Farm," "Farms," "Crop," "Crops," "Plant," "Plants" "Seeds," "Soil," and "Soils," and the names of individual agricultural products.

To locate additional statistical materials relating to agriculture in *American Statistics Index (ASI),* search headings such as those beginning with "Agricultural," "Botany," "Census of Agriculture," "Farm income," "Farms and farmland," "Fertilizers," "Food and food industry," "Foreign agriculture," "Irrigation," "Pesticides," "Pests and pest control," "Rural areas," "Soils and soil conservation," "Wildlife and wildlife conservation," and the names of individual commodities. *Statistical Universe* includes a Web version of *ASI*.

See Chapter 3, "The Basics of Searching," for more information.

RELATED MATERIAL
Within this Work

Chapter 5   Foreign Countries

Chapter 22   Environment

Chapter 36   Prices

Chapter 37   Consumer Expenditures

Chapter 42   Projections

Chapter 38   Foreign Trade Statistics

GPO Subject Bibliographies. PRINT. WEB. GP 3.22/2:

<http://bookstore.gpo.gov/sb/about.html>

No. 162 "Agriculture"

No. 238 "Conservation"

No. 277 "Census of Agriculture"

CHAPTER 19
Health

Health is a general subject area that is heavily represented in government publications, particularly in the publications of the Department of Health and Human Services and the U.S. Congress. This chapter lists selected basic titles and series that might be useful to consult for a search involving a health topic.

SEARCH STRATEGY

This chapter is an example of a subject search. The suggested strategy is as follows:
1. Begin with the sources in the general categories such as "General Health Sources" or "General Health Statistics Sources" (for statistics begin with the title *Health United States*);
2. Examine sources in the sections on more specific topics that may be relevant;
3. Consider the "Related Material" listed at the end of this chapter; and
4. Search the indexes for comprehensive coverage of specific topics.

GENERAL HEALTH SOURCES

Checklist

Health Hotlines: Toll-Free Numbers from the National Library of Medicine's DIRLINE Database. PRINT. WEB. (irregular) National Institutes of Health. National Library of Medicine. HE 20.3602:H 34/6/(year). Item 0508-D. <http://newsis. nlm.nih.gov/hotlines/>.
> Content: directory of health organizations with toll-free telephone numbers.

DIRLINE. WEB. TELNET. U.S. Department of Health and Human Services. National Library of Medicine. <http:// igm.nlm.nih.gov/>; <http://purl.access.gpo.gov/GPO/ LPS1783>; <telnet://locator.nlm.nih.gov>. (Select Directory of Information Resources).
> Content: directory of health information organizations.

Health Information Resource Database. WEB. National Health Information Center. <http://nhic-nt.health.org/>.
> Content: directory of health information organizations.

Healthfinder. WEB. U.S. Department of Health and Human Services. Office of Disease Prevention and Health Promotion. <http://www.healthfinder.org/default.htm>.
> Content: gateway for consumer health information on the Internet.

FDA Consumer. PRINT. WEB. (bimonthly) 1972–. U.S. Department of Health and Human Services. Public Health Service. Food and Drug Administration. HE 20.4010: (Earlier title: *FDA Papers*). Item 0475-H. GPO. <http://www.fda.gov/fdac/>; <http://purl.access.gpo.gov/GPO/LPS1609>.
> Content: articles on health, nutrition, and medicines.

Food and Drug Administration Web Site. WEB. U.S. Food and Drug Administration. <http://www.fda.gov/>.
> Content: FDA news and publications.

Public Health Reports. PRINT. (bimonthly) 1878–. U.S. Department of Health and Human Services. Public Health Service. HE 20.30: (Earlier, HE 20.6011:; HE 20.5009:; HE 20.2010/2:). (Title varies). Item 0497. ASI 4042-3.

Discussion

Health Hotlines: Toll-Free Numbers from the National Library of Medicine's DIRLINE Database is available in print and on the Internet. It lists the names and addresses of health organizations with toll-free telephone numbers. The directory is arranged alphabetically by organization name with a subject index. The listing is extracted from the National Library of Medicine's *DIRLINE* database. *DIRLINE* contains a more comprehensive directory of organizations that provide health information services. It includes government agencies, information centers, professional societies, support groups, academic and research institutions, and research facilities. Information available includes organization names, addresses, telephone numbers, descriptions of services, and publications. The *Health Informa-*

tion Resource Database is another Internet version of the *DIRLINE* database.

Healthfinder provides links to basic Internet health care resources and to agencies and organizations that can provide health information. The information selected comes primarily from government agencies, professional and nonprofit organizations, and educational institutions. Main menu categories include Hot Topics (AIDS, Cancer), News, Smart Choices (prevention and self-care, choosing quality care), More Tools (libraries, online journals, databases), and Just for You (infants, seniors, women). Hot Topics listings are often divided into two groups: Web resources and organizations.

FDA Consumer is an attractive general-interest periodical on health and related consumer issues. Articles are often based on research and investigative findings of FDA staff. The periodical also contains agency news, notes on publications and information resources, information on investigations, and summaries of court actions. A cumulative index is issued periodically. The most recent index covers 1980–93. Articles cover diet, specific illnesses, medicines, health care issues, and health technology. Examples of recent articles include "Miracle Drugs vs. Superbugs" (Vol. 32, No. 6); "Epilepsy: Taming the Seizures, Dispelling the Myths" (Vol. 33, No. 1); "An FDA Guide to Dietary Supplements" (Vol. 32, No. 5); and "Critical Controls for Juice Safety" (Vol. 32, No. 5). Issues of *FDA Consumer* are also available on the FDA's Web site since July/August 1995 with selected articles back to April 1989. The Web site includes an index from 1985 to the present.

The *Food and Drug Administration Web Site* contains links to FDA news and publications. Information is grouped by the agency's areas of responsibility, including Foods, Human Drugs, Biologics, Cosmetics, and Medical Devices/Radiological Health. An index to the site provides access by topics, categories of material, and selected titles. A search option is also available. Types of materials available include press releases, standards, product approvals, *Federal Register* announcements, speeches, publications, and congressional testimony.

Public Health Reports contains articles on public health research, issues, policy, and programs. Articles include scientific investigation reports, analyses of health data collection, program planning and evaluation studies, commentaries, and viewpoints on issues. Regular departments include News and Notes, Overseas Observer, Information Technology, and Data Line from the National Center for Health Statistics. Articles begin with a synopsis, often contain tables and charts, and conclude with a list of references. Some of the subject areas covered are prenatal care, alcohol use, drug use, AIDS, violence, smoking, availability of health care services, mortality, injuries, and diseases. Articles have reported on such diverse topics as dog and cat bites (Vol. 113, No. 3) to smoke alarms (Vol. 113, No. 5). Examples of recent articles include "Drug Prohi-

bition and Public Health: 25 Years of Evidence" (Vol. 114, No. 1), "Poisoning Mortality, 1985–95" (Vol. 113, No. 3), "State Estimates of Total Medical Expenditures Attributable to Cigarette Smoking, 1993" (Vol. 113, No. 5), and "Farm Tractor Safety in Kentucky, 1995" (Vol.114, No. 1). Occasional supplements cover special topics, such as HIV prevention (Vol. 113, Supp.1).

GENERAL HEALTH STATISTICS SOURCES
Checklist

Health United States. PRINT. WEB. (annual) 1976–. U.S. Department of Health and Human Services. Centers for Disease Control and Prevention. National Center for Health Statistics. HE 20.7042/6: (Earlier, HE 20.6223:; HE 20.21:). Item 0483-A-19. ASI 4144-11. GPO. <http://www.cdc.gov/nchswww/ products/pubs/pubd/hus/2010/2010.htm>.
>   Coverage: selected countries, U.S., regions, divisions, states, limited urban areas.
>   Content: fertility; births; deaths; smoking; alcohol; drugs; air pollution; disease; physician and dentist visits; hospital admissions and discharges; nursing homes; health personnel; health facilities; health care expenditures; data often by age, race, and sex.

Healthy People 2000 Review. PRINT. WEB. 1992–. U.S. Department of Health and Human Services. Centers for Disease Control and Prevention. National Center for Health Statistics. HE 20.7042/5: Item 0483-A-18. ASI 4144-17. <http:// www.cdc.gov/nchswww/products/pubs/pubd/hp2k/review/ review.htm>; <http://www.cdc.gov/nchs/hphome.htm>.
>   Coverage: U.S.
>   Content: statistics on progress toward national health goals for specific diseases and health-related behaviors; some data by age, race and sex.

[State] Health Profile. MF. (annual) 1987–. U.S. Department of Health and Human Services. Public Health Service. Centers for Disease Control and Prevention. HE 20.7043/(1-51): Item 0504-X-01 to 51.
>   Coverage: U.S., states.
>   Content: causes of death, childhood health, environmental health, occupational health, infectious diseases, chronic diseases, and health promotion.

HRSA Web Site. WEB. U.S. Department of Health and Human Services. Public Health Service. Health Resources and Services Administration. <http://www.hrsa.gov/>.
>   Coverage: U.S., states, counties.
>   Content: state health profiles, community health status indicators by county, agency programs, and news.

Health and Healthcare in the United States County and Metro Area Data. PRINT. CD-ROM. (annual) 1999–. Lanham, MD: Bernan Press.
>   Coverage: U.S., states, counties, metropolitan areas.
>   Content: population, births, fertility, deaths, physicians, hospitals, nursing homes, medical offices, medicare enrollees.

Publications from the National Center for Health Statistics. CD-ROM. (annual) 1995–. Centers for Disease Control and Prevention. National Center for Health Statistics. HE 20.7042/7: Item 0483-A-20. GPO.

> Content: full text of selected publications, including *Health, United States*; *Vital and Health Statistics* series reports; and *National Vital Statistics Reports*.

National Center for Health Statistics Web Site. WEB. U.S. Department of Health and Human Services. Centers for Disease Control and Prevention. National Center for Health Statistics. <http://www.cdc.gov/nchs/default.htm>.

> Content: full text of selected publications including *Health, United States*; *Vital and Health Statistics* series reports; and *National Vital Statistics Reports*.

Vital and Health Statistics. PRINT. MF. WEB. (irregular) 1962–. U.S. Department of Health and Human Services. Centers for Disease Control and Prevention. National Center for Health Statistics. HE 20.6209:; HE 20.6209/. Item 0500-E. ASI 4147-. GPO. <http://www.cdc.gov/nchs/products/pubs/pubd/series/ser.htm>.

> Coverage: varies; selected countries, U.S., regions, divisions, states.
>
> Content: statistics from health surveys; incidence of disease and injury; disability; use of health care services; physical characteristics; nutrition; health personnel and facilities; mortality; natality; marriage and divorce; family planning; fertility.

Vital and Health Statistics Series: An Annotated Checklist and Index to the Publications of the "Rainbow Series." PRINT. (1991) Jim Walsh and A. James Bothmer. Westport, CT: Greenwood Press.

> Content: index and annotations of individual reports in the *Vital and Health Statistics* series.

Advance Data from Vital and Health Statistics of the Centers for Disease Control and Prevention, National Center for Health Statistics. PRINT. WEB. (irregular) 1976–. U.S. Department of Health and Human Services. Centers for Disease Control and Prevention. National Center for Health Statistics. HE 20.6209/3: (Compiled in HE 20.6209:16/). Item 0500-E. ASI 4146-8. <http://www.cdc.gov/nchs/products/pubs/pubd/ad/ad.htm>; <http://purl.access.gpo.gov/GPO/LPS3741>.

> Coverage: varies; selected countries, U.S.
>
> Content: summary data from health surveys on health condition and use of health care services.

Discussion

Health United States is a key reference source for health statistics. Tables are grouped into six major subject areas: health status and determinants, utilization of health resources, health care resources, health care expenditures, health care coverage, and major federal programs and state health expenditures. Statistics cover causes of death, specific diseases, health-related behaviors, and health conditions. A subject index to the statistical tables is provided. A "Chartbook" section analyzes a special topic each year. Recent "Chartbooks" have covered socioeconomic status and health (1998), injury (1996–97), and women's health (1995).

Healthy People 2000 Review reports on progress toward an established set of health promotion and disease prevention goals and objectives. Sections on each of 22 priority areas give narrative highlights, data sources, a chart representing progress for a selected data item, and a more detailed table listing each objective with related statistics for recent years. Some of the priority areas covered include physical activity and fitness; nutrition; substance abuse; violence and abusive behavior; environmental health; heart disease and stroke; and cancer. Statistics for several data items are given for each area to illustrate related trends. A small sampling of topics covered includes adolescent pregnancies, cancer deaths, cigarette smoking, dietary fat intake, and work-related injuries. Beginning with the 1995–96 report, a special chart section on a selected population group has been included. The 1995–96 topic was racial and ethnic minority groups. The 1997 report topic was disability. Recent issues of this report have not been distributed to depository libraries, but are available on the Internet at the address given in the citation above. A related site, also cited above, provides more current progress reviews for selected topics and reports on the development of new goals and objectives for 2010.

The *[State] Health Profile* series consists of individual state reports on health status. Bar charts, maps, and graphs illustrate selected health status indicators and compare state data to national data. Health status indicators include leading causes of death, births to adolescents, childhood poverty, homicide, air quality, and data on selected diseases. This series was first distributed to depository libraries beginning with 1998.

The *HRSA Web Site* offers two statistical databases, HRSA State Profiles and Community Health Status Indicators. HRSA State Profiles provides six page profiles for each state covering grant funds awarded, access to health care, health care providers, and selected health status indicators such as leading causes of death, maternal and child health indicators, and infectious diseases. A query option allows the user to search by specific element. The Community Health Status Indicators database provides 16-page county profiles. Profiles cover basic demographic data, health measures, birth and death measures, environmental health, risk factors, and access to care. Specific elements include life expectancy, death rate, death from selected causes, infectious disease cases, and attainment of national air quality standards. Data are often shown in comparison to a selection of peer counties with similar demographics.

Health and Healthcare in the United States County and Metro Area Data compiles basic statistics on population, vital statistics, and healthcare resources for counties and metropolitan areas. Data on medicare eligibles and enrollees are given for counties. Statistics include births, deaths by cause, fertility rate, number of physicians, number of hospitals, and number and type of other medical facilities. Data come from such government agencies as the National Center for Health Statistics and from private sources.

Publications from the National Center for Health Statistics CD-ROM contains the full text of many reports from the agency's major publication series. The CD contains recent editions of *Health, United States* and reports from the *Vital and Health Statistics* series, *Advance Data* series, *National Vital Statistics Reports* (formerly *Monthly Vital Statistics Reports*), and *Healthy People 2000* reviews and newsletters. Selected other titles available include *America's Children: Key National Indicators of Well-Being*, *Atlas of United States Mortality*, and the agency's catalog of publications.

The *National Center for Health Statistics Web Site* also includes the full text of many of the agency's publications under the "Publications and Information Products" menu selection. Publications available in full text are similar to those included on the CD-ROM described above, but the Web site is more current. The Web site also provides more complete listings of all publications issued in each series with links to abstracts and full text when available. Another feature of the Web site is the "Surveys and Data Collection Systems" menu choice that pulls information together for each individual survey the agency conducts. Selecting the National Health Interview Survey, for example, leads to sources of descriptive data, related news releases, data highlights, methods, publications, and micro-data. Another main menu selection is "FASTATS A-Z." Users can pick topics from an alphabetical list that includes specific diseases, states, and health topics. Summary statistics are presented on each topic with links to more detailed publications. Examples of topics include births, chicken pox, elderly health, and suicide.

The *Vital and Health Statistics* series presently contains 14 active subseries, each on a different subject area. Reports are usually a few years behind in coverage. Some of the series of more general interest are mentioned here. A complete listing of the publications in each series, as well as abstracts or full text for many recent publications, is available on the *National Center for Health Statistics* Web site at the address listed in the citation above. The original survey data used to produce these reports is also available on several CD-ROM series containing tabulation software for users who wish to do their own analyses of the survey data (HE 20.6209/; Items 0500-E-, 0508-W).

Series 3, *Analytical and Epidemiological Studies*, analyzes trends in some depth (HE 20.6209: 3/). Recent titles include *Trends in the Health of Older Americans: United States, 1994* (HE 20.6209:3/30) and *Women: Work and Health* (HE 20.6209:3/31). This series does not contain a large number of publications.

Series 5, *International Vital and Health Statistics Reports*, contains a small number of reports comparing United States data to other countries. Examples include *Disability Among Older People: United States and Canada* (HE 20.6209:5/8) and *Maternal and Child Health Statistics: Russian Federation and United States, Selected Years 1985-95* (HE 20.6209:5/10).

Series 10 is a large series of reports from the National Health Interview Survey, a continuing household

survey (HE 20.6209:10/). This survey covers illness, injury, disability, and use of health care services. Examples of recent titles include *Health and Selected Socioeconomic Characteristics of the Family: United States, 1988–90* (HE 20.6209:10/195); *Access to Health Care, Part 1 Children* (HE 20.620910/196); and *Prevalence of Selected Chronic Conditions: United States, 1990–92* (HE 20.6209:10/194). One recurring title in this series has been given a separate classification number. *Current Estimates from the National Health Interview Survey* (HE 20.6209/4:) is a detailed annual report on survey results. Statistics cover the incidence of acute conditions, injuries, prevalence of chronic conditions, related activity restrictions and limitations, self-assessment of health status, physician contacts, and hospitalization.

Series 11 contains data from the National Health Examination Survey and the National Health and Nutrition Examination Survey (HE 20.6209:11/). These reports are based on examinations and measurements and cover disease and physical characteristics. Recent titles include *Clinical Chemistry Profile Data for Hispanics, 1982–84* (HE 20.6209:11/241) and *Serum Lipids of Adults 20–74 Years: United States, 1976–80* (HE 20.6209:11/242).

Series 13 deals with health resources and contains reports on the use of health personnel and facilities (HE 20.6209:13/). It includes reports on hospital and nursing home use with detailed data on the characteristics and diagnoses of persons using these facilities. Recent reports include *Injury Visits to Hospital Emergency Departments: United States, 1992–95* (HE 20.6209:13/131) and *Ambulatory Health Care Visits by Children: Principal Diagnosis and Place of Visit* (HE 20.6209:13/137). Some recurring titles in this series have been given separate classification numbers. These include *National Hospital Discharge Survey: Annual Summary* (HE 20.6209/7:) and *Detailed Diagnoses and Procedures, National Hospital Discharge Survey* (HE 20.6209/9:).

Series 23, Data from the National Survey of Family Growth, contains a small number of reports on fertility and family planning. Examples include *Fertility, Family Planning, and Women's Health: New Data from the 1995 National Survey of Family Growth* (HE 20.6209:23/19) and *Surgical Sterilization in the United States: Prevalence and Characteristics, 1965–95* (HE 20.6209:23/20).

The *Vital and Health Statistics Series: An Annotated Checklist and Index to the Publications of the "Rainbow Series"* is a comprehensive index to the *Vital and Health Statistics* series, with author, title, and subject indexes; annotations, and a listing of individual reports by series.

The *Advance Data from Vital and Health Statistics* series consists of brief reports from the same health surveys on which the *Vital and Health Statistics* reports are based. These reports contain early summary results that are often followed up by more detailed reports in the *Vital and Health Statistics* series at a later date. Reports contain a brief narrative analysis with numerous charts and statistical tables. Recent reports include *Characteristics of Hospice Care Users: Data from the 1996 National Home and Hospice Care Survey* (HE 20.6209/3:299) and *Office Visits to Orthopedic Surgeons: United States, 1995–96* (HE 20.6209/3:302).

SOURCES ON DISEASES
Checklist

Morbidity and Mortality Weekly Report: MMWR. PRINT. WEB. (weekly) 1952–. U.S. Department of Health and Human Services. Centers for Disease Control and Prevention. HE 20.7009: (Title varies). Item 0508-A. ASI 4202-1. (Annual summary titled *Summary of Notifiable Diseases, U.S.,* ASI 4204-1). GPO. <http://www2.cdc.gov/mmwr/mmwr_wk.html>; <http://purl.access.gpo.gov/GPO/LPS2051>; *Summary of Notifiable Diseases, U.S.:* <http://www2.cdc.gov/mmwr/summary.html>.

    Coverage: U.S., divisions, states, 122 cities.

    Content: number of cases of selected diseases; deaths from all causes by age group for selected cities; articles on diseases and related topics; annual summary contains age, sex and race data for each disease, graphs and maps, and historical data.

Morbidity and Mortality Weekly Report. CDC Surveillance Summaries: MMWR. PRINT. WEB. (5 or 6 a year) U.S. Department of Health and Human Services. Centers for Disease Control and Prevention. HE 20.7009/2: Item 0508-A. ASI 4202-7. GPO. <http://www2.cdc.gov/mmwr/mmwr_ss.html>.

    Coverage: varies; countries, U.S., states, selected metropolitan areas.

    Content: summary analyses with statistics on diseases and injuries monitored by the Centers for Disease Control and Prevention.

Morbidity and Mortality Weekly Report. Recommendations and Reports: MMWR. PRINT. WEB. (irregular) 1990–. U.S. Department of Health and Human Services. Centers for Disease Control and Prevention. HE 20.7009/2-2: Item 0508-A. ASI 4206-2. GPO. <http://www2.cdc.gov/mmwr/mmwr_rr.html>; <http://purl.access.gpo.gov/GPO/LPS2058>.

    Content: guidelines on prevention and treatment of infectious diseases.

Morbidity and Mortality Weekly Report: MMWR. CD-ROM. 1993-. Centers for Disease Control and Prevention. HE 20.7039/3: Item 0504-W-01. GPO.

    Content: full text of MMWR publications and selected other CDC publications.

National Institutes of Health Web Site. WEB. U.S. Department of Health and Human Services. National Institutes of Health. <http://www.nih.gov/>.

    Content: health publications and information resources; gateway to individual institutes that provide publications and resources on various diseases.

Centers for Disease Control and Prevention Home Page. WEB. Centers for Disease Control and Prevention. <http://www.cdc.gov/default.htm>.

    Content: health and disease databases, publications, and statistics.

CHID Online: The Combined Health Information Database. WEB. U.S. Department of Health and Human Services. <http://chid.nih.gov/>; <http://purl.access.gpo.gov/GPO/LPS1642>.

    Content: bibliographic databases produced by health-related agencies covering health education and promotion resources.

CDP File. CD-ROM. 1991–. U.S. Department of Health and Human Services. Centers for Disease Control and Prevention. National Center for Chronic Disease Prevention and Health Promotion. HE 20.7616: Item 0444-P-01. GPO.

    Content: bibliographic health databases on health promotion, cancer, smoking, epilepsy; directories of health promotion organizations and state officials.

Cancer

General Publications. PRINT. (irregular) U.S. Department of Health and Human Services. Public Health Service. National Institutes of Health. National Cancer Institute. HE 20.3152: Item 0507-G-02.

    Content: informational brochures on cancer in general and on specific types of cancer; cancer research results; cancer mortality statistics.

CancerNet. WEB. National Cancer Institute. <http://cancernet.nci.nih.gov/>.

    Content: selected information from the *PDQ* database on cancer treatment, screening, prevention and supportive care; clinical trials; *CANCERLIT* bibliographic database; general cancer information and resources.

SEER Cancer Statistics Review. MF. WEB. (annual) U.S. Department of Health and Human Services. Public Health Service. National Institutes of Health. National Cancer Institute. HE 20.3186: Item 0507-G-42. ASI 4474-35. <http://www-seer.ims.nci.nih.gov/Publications/>; <http://purl.access.gpo.gov/GPO/LPS3349>.

    Coverage: U.S., states, registry areas.

    Content: cancer incidence, mortality, survival and trends; data often given by age, race, and sex.

Journal of the National Cancer Institute. PRINT. (semimonthly) 1940–. Oxford University Press. HE 20.3161: Item 0488. <http://jnci.oupjournals.org/>; <http://purl.access.gpo.gov/GPO/LPS1716> (subscribers may register for full-text access).

    Content: scientific articles on the latest developments in cancer research, treatment, prevention, and control.

AIDS

HIV/AIDS Surveillance Report. PRINT. WEB. (semiannual) Sept. 1982–. U.S. Department of Health and Human Services. Public Health Service. Centers for Disease Control and Prevention. National Center for HIV, STD, and TB Prevention. Division of HIV/AIDS. HE 20.7320: (Earlier, HE 20.7011/38:) (Title and frequency vary). Item 0494-K-11. ASI 4202-9. <http://www.cdc.gov/hiv/stats/hasrlink.htm>; <http://purl.access.gpo.gov/GPO/LPS1040>.

    Coverage: U.S., regions, states, selected metropolitan areas.

    Content: number of cases and rates; cases by age, cause of transmission, race and sex; deaths.

National Center for HIV, STD, & TB Prevention Divisions of HIV/AIDS Prevention Web Site. WEB. Centers for Disease Control.

National Center for HIV, STD, and TB. Divisions of HIV/AIDS Prevention. <http://www.cdc.gov/hiv/dhap.htm>.

Content: information on AIDS/HIV treatment and prevention; publications; and statistics.

HIV/AIDS Information Web Page. WEB. National Library of Medicine. Specialized Information Services. <http://sis.nlm.nih.gov/hiv.cfm>.

Content: databases relating to AIDS, including *AIDSLINE, AIDSTRIALS,* and *AIDSDRUGS.*

MMWRs on HIV/AIDS Web Page. WEB. Centers for Disease Control and Prevention. National Center for HIV, STD, & TB Prevention. Divisions of HIV/AIDS Prevention. (Earlier print title: *Reports on HIV/AIDS,* HE 20.7009/5:, HE 20.7009/A:AC 7/. Item 0508-A-06). <http://www.cdc.gov/hiv/pubs/mmwr.htm>.

Content: compilation of AIDS articles from *Morbidity and Mortality Weekly Report.*

Other

National Institute of Allergy and Infectious Diseases Web Site. WEB. National Institutes of Health. National Institute of Allergy and Infectious Diseases. <http://www.niaid.nih.gov/>.

Content: publications on allergies, asthma, autoimmune diseases, influenza and colds, and other diseases.

Handout on Health. PRINT. (irregular) U.S. Department of Health and Human Services. Public Health Service. National Institutes of Health. National Institute of Arthritis and Musculoskeletal and Skin Diseases. HE 20.3916: (Earlier, HE 20.3902:) Item 0508-T-02.

Content: pamphlets on arthritis, musculoskeletal, and skin diseases.

NIAMS National Institute of Arthritis and Musculoskeletal and Skin Diseases Web Site. WEB. National Institutes of Health. National Institute of Arthritis and Musculoskeletal and Skin Diseases. <http://www.nih.gov/niams/>.

Content: publications on arthritis, fibromyalgia, lupus, osteoporosis, skin diseases, and other related diseases.

National Institute of Diabetes and Digestive and Kidney Diseases Web Site. WEB. National Institutes of Health. National Institute of Diabetes and Digestive and Kidney Diseases. <http://www.niddk.nih.gov/>.

Content: publications, fact sheets, educational materials, and other resources for diabetes, digestive diseases, and kidney diseases.

General Publications. PRINT. (irregular) U.S. Department of Health and Human Services. National Institutes of Health. National Eye Institute. HE 20.3752: Item 0507-Y-01.

Content: miscellaneous publications on eye diseases.

National Eye Institute Web Site. WEB. National Institutes of Health. National Eye Institute. <http://www.nei.nih.gov/>.

Content: publications on eye diseases.

Fact Sheets. PRINT. (irregular) U.S. Department of Health and Human Services. Public Health Service. National Institutes of Health. National Heart, Lung, and Blood Institute. HE 20.3218: Item 507-E-01.

Content: fact sheets on heart, lung, and blood diseases and related health factors.

National Heart, Lung, and Blood Institute Web Site. WEB. National Institutes of Health. National Heart, Lung, and Blood Institute. <http://www.nhlbi.nih.gov/index.htm>.

Content: publications on heart, lung, and blood diseases and related health factors; agency news and press releases; research funding.

General Publications. PRINT. (irregular) U.S. Department of Health and Human Services. National Institutes of Health. National Institute of Neurological Disorders and Stroke. HE 20.3502: Item 0507-L-02. GPO.

Content: miscellaneous publications on neurological disorders and stroke.

Fact Sheets. PRINT. (irregular) U.S. Department of Health and Human Services. Public Health Service. National Institutes of Health. National Institute of Neurological Disorders and Stroke. HE 20.3520: Item 0507-L-13.

Content: fact sheets on specific neurological disorders.

National Institute of Neurological Disorders and Stroke Web Site. WEB. U.S. Department of Health and Human Services. National Institutes of Health. National Institute of Neurological Disorders and Stroke. <http://www.ninds.nih.gov/>.

Content: guides to strokes, epilepsy, and Parkinson's disease; health information and publications on neurological conditions.

Discussion

Morbidity and Mortality Weekly Report (MMWR) contains statistics on selected infectious diseases reported to the Centers for Disease Control and Prevention by state health departments. Regular tables near the end of each issue give number of cases for such diseases as AIDS, gonorrhea, hepatitis, legionellosis, Lyme disease, malaria, measles, mumps, rubella, toxic shock syndrome, tuberculosis, typhoid fever, and others. One table gives number of total deaths in selected cities by age group. The city data do not include information on specific diseases. Each weekly issue also contains brief articles on infectious diseases, chronic conditions, injuries, and related topics. Examples of recent articles include "Update: Influenza Activity—United States, 1998–99 Season," (Vol. 48, No. 2), "All-Terrain Vehicle-Related Deaths—West Virginia, 1985–1997," (Vol. 48, No. 1), and "Self-Reported Prevalence of Diabetes Among Hispanics—United States, 1994–1997" (Vol. 48, No. 1). An annual report at the end of the year is titled *Summary of Notifiable Diseases, United States.* It covers a larger number of diseases and provides more detailed data by age, race, and sex. A section of graphs and maps illustrates rates and trends for selected diseases. There is also a section of historical tables.

Morbidity and Mortality Weekly Report. CDC Surveillance Summaries: MMWR contains reports on a variety of public health matters kept under surveillance by the Centers for Disease Control and Prevention. Topics cover infectious diseases, human reproduction, injuries, chronic diseases, and behaviors affecting health. Reports contain narrative analysis and statistical tables. Examples of these surveillance reports include "Abortion Surveillance—United States, 1995" (Vol. 47, SS-2); "Youth Risk Behavior Surveillance—United States, 1997" (Vol. 47, SS-3), and "Surveillance for Asthma—United States, 1960–1995" (Vol. 47, SS-1).

Morbidity and Mortality Weekly Report. Recommendations and Reports: MMWR contains CDC guidelines on disease prevention, control, and treatment. Before 1990, these reports appeared as supplements to the *Morbidity and Mortality Weekly Report*. Examples of recent titles include "Prevention and Treatment of Tuberculosis Among Patients Infected with Human Immunodeficiency Virus: Principles of Therapy and Revised Recommendations" (Vol. 47, RR-20) and " Preventing Emerging Infectious Diseases: A Strategy for the 21st Century Overview of the Updated CDC Plan" (Vol. 47, RR-15).

The *Morbidity and Mortality Weekly Report: MMWR* CD-ROM contains the full text of the *MMWR* titles described above. A small number of other titles from the National Center for Infectious Diseases are also included on the CD-ROM. Titles include *Emerging Infectious Diseases Journal, The ABC's of Safe and Healthy Child Care*, and *Isolation Precautions in Hospitals*.

The *MMWR* publications are also available on the Internet on the Centers for Disease Control and Prevention Web site. Coverage on the Internet is more extensive than on the CD-ROM with some issues dating from the 1980's. Issues on the Internet are also more current. A search feature allows keyword or phrase searching beginning with 1993 issues.

The *National Institutes of Health Web Site* offers a Health Information section, which includes a health information index that lists diseases and health issues in alphabetical order with links to the appropriate institute's Web site. Individual institutes, such as the National Institute of Allergy and Infectious Diseases or the National Institute of Diabetes and Digestive and Kidney Diseases, provide information resources and full-text publications on diseases in their research areas. The NIH Health Information section also has a publications category for full-text consumer health publications that lists the NIH's most frequently requested publications by institute and provides full text. A clinical trials menu choice provides links to all of the NIH's clinical trial databases. Other sections list NIH toll-free information lines and other popular NIH resources, including the *MEDLINE* bibliographic database, which is discussed later in this chapter.

The *Centers for Disease Control and Prevention Home Page* provides access to data and information on infectious diseases and public health. A main menu choice on "Health Topics A-Z" lists many specific diseases and health topics with links to summary information and publications. Examples of topics include bacterial diseases, behavioral risk factors, chronic fatigue syndrome, ebola, flu, suicide, and vaccine safety. Another main menu option on "Data & Statistics" lists scientific data resources, sur-

veillance program data, and laboratory information. Scientific data include the CDC Wonder database that provides a single point of access to CDC reports and numeric data sets. Structured query forms provide easy access to data sets and reports, such as AIDS—Public Use, Injury Mortality Data, Linked Birth/Infant Death, MMWR—Morbidity and Mortality Weekly Report, Mortality, and Natality. Also available under the "Data & Statistics" area are surveillance data in such areas as behavioral risk, sexually transmitted diseases, and tuberculosis. The CDC home page has a "Publications, Software & Products" category, which lists online publications and software by CDC agency.

CHID Online is a bibliographic database that combines files from several health agencies. The database provides titles, abstracts, and availability information for educational and promotional materials related to health. References include journal articles, books, reports, curricular materials, audiovisuals, and other types of resources. The database is updated quarterly. Sixteen topics are currently covered, including "AIDS, STD and TB Education," "Alzheimer's Disease," "Cancer Prevention and Control," "Complementary and Alternative Medicine," "Diabetes," "Health Promotion and Education," "Medical Genetics and Rare Disorders," and "Weight Control." Searches can be done on the entire database or on individual topics. The materials themselves must be obtained through libraries or by contacting the issuing organization. Four of the individual databases are also available on the *CDP File* CD-ROM discussed below.

The *CDP File* CD-ROM contains eight databases. The "Health Promotion and Education (HE)" database contains bibliographic references to health education materials from journal articles, books, proceedings, and other types of publications. The "Cancer Prevention and Control (CP)" database contains references to similar types of material on breast, cervical, and skin cancer detection and control. Additional databases available are the "Prenatal Smoking Cessation (PS)" database, "Epilepsy Education and Prevention Activities (EP)" database, "NCCDPHP Publications" database, and "Smoking and Health (SH)" database. A "Chronic Disease Prevention Directory" gives names and addresses of key persons and organizations in health promotion and disease prevention. The "State Profile Database" gives information on state contacts and programs.

Government resources provide particularly strong coverage of cancer and AIDS. Many publications on cancer can be found in the *General Publications* series of the National Cancer Institute. This series contains a mixture of materials ranging from small brochures to multivolume statistical reports. One series of brochures is titled *What You Need to Know about...* and provides background information on more than 20 specific types of cancer. Examples of these titles include *What You Need to Know about Lung Cancer* (HE 20.3152:L 97/998) and *What You Need to Know about Breast Cancer* (HE 20.3152:B

74/6/998). Each brochure describes the disease, its symptoms, diagnosis, treatment, and additional information sources. Also in the *General Publications* series are historical cancer mortality statistics. *U.S. Cancer Mortality Rates and Trends 1950–1979* (HE 20.3152:M 84/950-79/v.1-3), for example, gives detailed statistics to the county level on deaths from every type of cancer. Examples of other titles include *Closing in on Cancer: Solving a 5000-Year-Old Mystery* (HE 20.3152:C 62/998), *When Cancer Recurs: Meeting the Challenge* (HE 20.3152:M 47/997), and *Cancer in Populations Living Near Nuclear Facilities* (HE 20.3152:N 88/v.1-3).

CancerNet provides a wide range of cancer information from National Cancer Institute databases and publications. Selected information from the *PDQ (Physician Data Query)* database provides treatment information summaries, screening and prevention information summaries and supportive care information summaries for specific types of cancer. Summaries are available in two versions—a technical version for health professionals and a less technical version for patients and the public. Information is regularly reviewed by cancer experts and updated to incorporate the latest research available. An extensive *PDQ* database of ongoing clinical trials is also available. The full *PDQ* database, which also includes a directory of physicians and cancer programs, is available online from Ovid Technologies and Lexis-Nexis. A CD-ROM version is available from SilverPlatter.

Another database offered through *CancerNet* is the bibliographic database, *CANCERLIT*. It contains more than a million bibliographic citations and abstracts on cancer since 1963. More than 4000 sources are indexed, including journal articles, government reports, meeting papers, and monographs. The database is updated monthly. The articles themselves are not provided, but must be obtained from libraries or other sources. *CANCERLIT* is derived primarily from the National Library of Medicine's online database, *MEDLINE*, but additional foreign journals and other literature are included. (For more information on *MEDLINE* see the "Medical Indexes and Bibliographies" section later in this chapter). *CANCERLIT* is also available online from Ovid Technologies, Knight-Ridder Information (DataStar, DIALOG), CompuServe Information Service Knowledge Index, and STN International. CD-ROM versions are available from Ovid Technologies and SilverPlatter.

CancerNet also contains general cancer information fact sheets and brochures on such topics as living with cancer, nutrition, and managing side effects. The *What You Need to Know About* publications mentioned under the *General Publications* series discussion above are also available in full text on this site. The public can also obtain information from *CancerNet* resources by calling the National Cancer Institute's Cancer Information Service at 1-800-4-CANCER and requesting cancer information.

SEER Cancer Statistics Review contains detailed statistics on cancer. An overview chapter summarizes major

trends. Tables in this chapter give number of cases by specific body sites and show trends for several years. Changes in incidence and survival rates over the years are also shown. Additional statistics give median age of cancer patients for each cancer site. Additional chapters give detailed data on incidence, mortality, and survival rates for all cancer sites and for each individual site. Data are given for year groups and individual years and by race, sex, and age group.

The *Journal of the National Cancer Institute* contains scientific articles on the latest cancer research findings and news items. Regular features include "In This Issue," a one-page summary of selected articles and a news section on cancer programs, funding, and other related activities. Articles are categorized by type and length and include reviews, articles, reports, brief communications, and commentaries. Reviews are comprehensive overviews of an area or issue. Articles present major new findings. Reports present new findings in less extensive format. Brief communications are concise descriptions of new findings. Commentaries are informal summaries of current activities and events. There are also editorials, book reviews, and a correspondence section. Articles contain abstracts, tables and charts, and a list of references. Examples of recent articles and reports include "Estrogen Replacement Therapy and Breast Cancer Survival in a Large Screening Study" (Vol. 91, No. 3); "Plasma Levels of Insulin-Like Growth Factor-I and Lung Cancer Risk: a Case-Control Analysis" (Vol. 91, No. 2); "Sunscreen Use, Wearing Clothes, and Number of Nevi in 6- to 7-Year-Old European Children" (Vol. 90, No. 24). The Web site contains abstracts of articles from 1989–1996 and full text from 1997. The online version is available to individuals and institutions with a print subscription.

HIV/AIDS Surveillance Report contains detailed statistics on AIDS and HIV. Tables show the number and rate of AIDS cases by state and selected large metropolitan areas. Maps illustrate the state data. National statistics are given on the method of exposure by various demographic variables. Data are also given on age at diagnosis and on deaths. Separate tables cover HIV infection. Examples of data available include number of women exposed via heterosexual contact with injecting drug users and number of Black males diagnosed with AIDS at the age of 20–24. The "Mid-Year Edition" covers the first six months of the year. The "Year-End Edition" contains annual data and additional tables. The additional information includes AIDS deaths by race, age group, and sex; cases and annual rates by race, age group, and sex; and AIDS-indicator conditions by age group. This publication was initially intended for internal use only. It was first supplied to depository libraries in 1989.

The *National Center for HIV, STD, & TB Prevention Divisions of HIV/AIDS Prevention Web Site* offers AIDS/HIV information by topic or category. Some of the topics available include basic science, surveillance, prevention research, prevention tools, and treatment. General information categories that can be selected include basic statistics, brochures, fact sheets, FAQs, and publications. One useful feature available from the home page is an index of HIV/AIDS-related articles in *Morbidity and Mortality Weekly Report (MMWR)* since 1981. Links to other AIDS-related sites are also provided.

The *HIV/AIDS Information Web Page* provides convenient access to National Library of Medicine databases related to AIDS through the HIV/AIDS search button. Databases available include *AIDSLINE, AIDSDRUGS, AIDSTRIALS, HSTAT* (clinical guidelines), *DIRLINE* (directory of organizations), and *Health Hotlines*. Tutorials on some of the databases are also available. *AIDSLINE* contains bibliographic references to journal articles, government reports, technical reports, meeting papers, and monographs since 1980 on all aspects of AIDS. It is derived in part from the National Library of Medicine's online database, *MEDLINE*, with additions from other NLM databases and AIDS-related journals and newsletters. (For more information on *MEDLINE*, see the "Medical Indexes and Bibliographies" section later in this chapter). A print version of *AIDSLINE*, *AIDS Bibliography*, was published from 1988 to 1995 (HE 20.3615/3:, Item 0508-F-02). The *AIDSTRIALS* database provides information on clinical trials to evaluate experimental drugs. The *AIDSDRUGS* database contains descriptive information on experimental drugs. *AIDSLINE* is also available online from Ovid Technologies, Knight-Ridder Information (DIALOG, DataStar), CompuServe Information Service Knowledge Index, and STN International. CD-ROM versions are available from Aries Systems (Knowledge Finder), Ovid Technologies, and SilverPlatter.

The *MMWRs on HIV/AIDS Web Page* provides access to all of the articles on AIDS published in *Morbidity and Mortality Weekly Report* from 1981 on, arranged by year. It is comparable to the print title *Reports on HIV/AIDS*, which covers 1981–95 (HE 20.7009/5:, HE 20.7009/A:AC 7; Item 0508-A-06).

Many of the individual institutes in the National Institutes of Health publish informational publications on diseases in their area of research. Most of the institutes' Web sites also provide the full text of recent informational publications. In many cases, there are more extensive and more recent publications on the Web site than are distributed to depository libraries. The *National Institutes of Health Web Site* listed earlier in this section can serve as a gateway to the Web sites of individual institutes. Selected publication series that contain several recent informational publications on specific diseases are listed in the "Other" section in the checklist above, along with selected institute Web sites.

SOURCES ON ALCOHOL
Checklist

Special Report to the U.S. Congress on Alcohol and Health. PRINT. (triennial) 1971–. U.S. Department of Health and Hu-

man Services. Public Health Service. National Institutes of Health. National Institute on Alcohol Abuse and Alcoholism. HE 20.8313: Item 0498-C-06. ASI 4488-4. GPO.
Coverage: varies; selected countries, U.S., states, regions. Content: overview of alcohol research; consumption; related illness and death; medical and social consequences; prevention and treatment.

Alcohol Research & Health. PRINT. WEB. (quarterly) 1973/74–. U.S. Department of Health and Human Services. Public Health Service. National Institutes of Health. National Institute on Alcohol Abuse and Alcoholism. HE 20.8309: (Earlier title, *Alcohol Health and Research World)* Item 0507-B-19. ASI 4482-1. GPO. <http://silk.nih.gov/silk/niaaa1/publication/aharw.htm>; <http://purl.access.gpo.gov/GPO/LPS1441>.
Content: articles on alcohol problems, effects and research findings.

General Publications. PRINT. (irregular) U.S. Department of Health and Human Services. Public Health Service. National Institutes of Health. National Institute on Alcohol Abuse and Alcoholism. HE 20.8302: Item 0498-C-01.
Content: miscellaneous publications on alcohol abuse.

Alcohol Alert series. PRINT. WEB. (irregular) U.S. Department of Health and Human Services. Public Health Service. National Institutes of Health. National Institute on Alcohol Abuse and Alcoholism. HE 20.8322: Item 0483-G-02. <http://silk.nih.gov/silk/niaaa1/publication/alalerts.htm>; <http://purl.access.gpo.gov/GPO/LPS1579>.
Content: brief overviews of specific alcohol problems.

Research Monographs. MF. (irregular) 1979–. U.S. Department of Health and Human Services. Public Health Service. National Institutes of Health. National Institute on Alcohol Abuse and Alcoholism. HE 20.8315: Item 0498-C-10. ASI 4488-. <http://silk.nih.gov/silk/niaaa1/publication/monograp.htm> (list of recent titles with abstracts).
Content: research reviews on alcohol-related issues.

National Institute on Alcohol Abuse and Alcoholism Web Site. WEB. U.S. Department of Health and Human Services. National Institutes of Health. National Institute on Alcohol and Alcoholism. <http://www.niaaa.nih.gov/>.
Content: agency news and information; publications; databases; general information and resources on alcohol abuse.

Alcohol and Alcohol Problems Science Database (ETOH). WEB. 1972–. National Institute on Alcohol Abuse and Alcoholism. <http://etoh.niaaa.nih.gov/>.
Content: citations and abstracts for journal articles and reports on alcohol research.

Quick Facts Web Page. WEB. U.S. Department of Health and Human Services. National Institutes of Health. National Institute on Alcohol Abuse and Alcoholism. <http://silk.nih.gov/silk/niaaa1/database/qf.htm>.
Coverage: countries, U.S., states. Content: statistics on alcohol abuse, consumption, economic costs, morbidity, mortality, patterns of use.

PREVLINE Prevention Online. WEB. National Clearinghouse for Alcohol and Drug Information. Substance Abuse and Mental Health Services Administration. <http://www.health.org>.

Content: alcohol abuse information, databases, and publications.

See also Sources on Drugs below.

Discussion

The *Special Report to the U.S. Congress on Alcohol and Health* is a survey of knowledge and recent research advances on the health and social consequences of alcohol use and abuse. The content of each report reflects current research trends. Chapters in the ninth report cover epidemiology (consumption, alcohol-related diseases, mortality); genetic, psychological and sociocultural influences; actions of alcohol on the brain; neurobehavioral effects; effects of alcohol on the body; effects on fetal and postnatal development; effects on behavior and safety; economic aspects; prevention; treatment; and alcohol health services. An overview gives highlights of each chapter. Each individual chapter begins with an introduction and concludes with a summary and list of references. A limited number of statistical tables throughout the text cover data on such topics as consumption, characteristics of drinkers, alcohol involvement among emergency room patients, and college students' risk of alcohol problems. This is an excellent source for information on all aspects of alcoholism.

Alcohol Research & Health is a glossy periodical with articles on current alcohol research. Issues are usually devoted to a particular theme such as children of alcoholics, alcohol withdrawal, and alcohol and youth. Recent articles include "Alcohol Use Among Adolescents" (Vol. 22, No. 2), "Alcohol Hangover: Mechanisms and Mediators" (Vol. 22, No.1), and "New Genetic Technologies in Alcohol Research" (Vol. 21, No. 4). The agency's Web site provides full-text for the most recent issues and article lists, issue overviews, and selected article abstracts for ealier issues.

The *General Publications* series of the National Institute on Alcohol Abuse and Alcoholism contains brochures and monographs on topics of interest to the Institute. Examples of recent titles include *Drinking and Your Pregnancy* (HE 20.8302:D 83/10); *The Economic Costs of Alcohol and Drug Abuse in the United States, 1992* (HE 20.8302:EC 7); and *Alcoholism: Getting the Facts* (HE 20.8302:F 11/2).

The *Alcohol Alert* series consists of four page overviews on specific alcohol-related problems, such as *Alcohol and the Liver* (No. 42), *Alcohol and Sleep* (No. 41), and *Alcohol and Aging* (No. 40). Each *Alcohol Alert* summarizes current research on the nature of the problem and concludes with a paragraph commentary from the Institute's director. A list of bibliographic references is also included. The full text of each issue is on the agency's Web site.

The *Research Monograph* series is based on papers presented at conferences sponsored by the National Institute on Alcohol Abuse and Alcoholism. Each report is a collection of research reviews on a specific theme with bibliographic references. Recent reports include *Alcohol Problems and Aging* (HE 20.8315:33), *Alcohol and the Cardiovascular System* (HE 20.8315:31), and *Alcohol and Tobacco: From Basic Science to Clinical Practice* (HE 20.8315:30).

The *National Institute on Alcohol Abuse and Alcoholism Web Site* contains information on alcohol abuse, agency publications, and databases. The "Publications" and "Databases" menu choices provide access to some of the resources mentioned in this section, as well as additional miscellaneous publications. A "Frequently Asked Questions" menu choice provides basic information on alcohol abuse with brief answers to such questions as "Is alcoholism a disease?" and "Can alcoholism be cured?" Links to relevant publications are also included with the answers. The Web site provides agency press releases and information on the agency's research programs.

The *Alcohol and Alcohol Problems Science Database* or *ETOH* is a comprehensive bibliographic database on alcohol-related research. *ETOH* contains references and abstracts for journal articles, books, reports, and other research sources. The database covers medical, psychological, social, and public policy aspects of alcohol use and is updated monthly. *ETOH* is also available online from Ovid Technologies.

The *Quick Facts Web Page* contains extensive statistics on alcohol abuse. Data include estimated number of alcohol abusers; per capita consumption by type of beverage; costs to society; hospital discharges; deaths from cirrhosis; traffic fatalities; and frequency of use by demographic characteristics.

PREVLINE contains a variety of information resources on alcohol abuse. An "Alcohol & Drug Facts" menu choice leads to a list of topics, including alcohol. Under alcohol is a list of fact sheets, articles, publications, and other resources with links to the full text or resource. Alcohol-related material can also be found under other topics, such as "College Students." More substantial research publications and statistics are available under the main menu choice "Research Briefs." A "Databases" category provides access to such databases as *ETOH, Information about Drugs and Alcohol, SAMHSA's Substance Abuse Treatment Facility Locator* and *SAID* (Department of Labor's *Substance Abuse Information Database*). The database section includes a search feature for authoritative substance abuse Web sites, *NSAWI (National Substance Abuse Web Index)*. An online catalog main menu option is available, which includes a list of online publications and the NCADI (National Clearinghouse for Alcohol and Drug Information) catalog. Many of these publications can be requested at no charge.

The first three titles under "Sources on Drugs" below include data on the prevalence and frequency of alcohol use. The data on alcohol are comparable to the data on drugs as described below.

SOURCES ON DRUGS

Checklist

National Household Survey on Drug Abuse. PRINT. WEB. (annual) 1971–. U.S. Department of Health and Human Services. Substance Abuse and Mental Health Services Administration. Office of Applied Studies. (Title and frequency vary). ASI 4096-3 (Earlier, 4094-3, 4494-5, 4498-4). GPO. <http://www.samhsa.gov/OAS/p0000016.htm>.

> *Main Findings.* PRINT. WEB. HE 20.417/3: (Earlier, HE 20.402:D 84/, HE 20.8202:H 81/, HE 20.8202: SU 7/). Item 0497-D-26.
>
> > Coverage: U.S., regions.
> > Content: prevalence, trends, and frequency of drug use for marijuana, cocaine, inhalants, hallucinogens, heroin, psychotherapeutic drugs, alcohol, cigarettes, and smokeless tobacco; by age group, sex, race, education, employment status; problems associated with drug use; use patterns; perceptions of risk; availability.
>
> *Population Estimates.* PRINT. WEB. HE 20.417/2: (Earlier, HE 20.402:D 84/, HE 20.2:H 81/, HE 20.8202:H 81/2/). Item 0497-D-24.
>
> > Coverage: U.S., regions.
> > Content: prevalence and frequency of drug use by sex, race, age group.
>
> *Summary of Findings from the [year] National Household Survey on Drug Abuse.* PRINT. WEB. 1992–. HE 20.417/5: (Title varies. Earlier, HE 20.417/4:, HE 20.417/2:, HE 20.421:). Item 0497-D-39.
>
> > Coverage: U.S., regions, divisions.
> > Content: prevalence and frequency of drug use by sex, race, age group and other characteristics.

National Survey Results on Drug Use from the Monitoring the Future Study. PRINT. (annual) 1975–. U.S. Department of Health and Human Services. Public Health Service. National Institutes of Health. National Institute on Drug Abuse. HE 20.3968: (Earlier, HE 20.3952:D 84/). Item 0467-A-32. ASI 4494-4. GPO. <http://monitoringthefuture.org/data/data.html> (selected data).

> Coverage: U.S., regions.
> Content: prevalence and frequency of drug use for various drugs, alcohol, and tobacco; differences in use by sex, race and selected socioeconomic factors; grade of first use; degree and duration of highs; attitudes and beliefs; social milieu.

Substance Abuse and Mental Health Statistics Source Book. PRINT. 1998. 2nd ed. U.S. Department of Health and Human Services. Substance Abuse and Mental Health Services Administration. Office of Applied Studies. HE 20.424:4. Item 0497-D-34. ASI 4096-6.

> Coverage: U.S., selected states, selected metropolitan areas.
> Content: statistics on nature, extent, and trends of substance abuse; social costs; prevention and treatment.

General Publications. PRINT. (irregular) U.S. Department of Health and Human Services. National Institutes of Health. National Institute on Drug Abuse. HE 20.3952: (Earlier, HE 20.8202:) Item 0467-A-01. GPO.

> Content: miscellaneous publications on drug topics.

Research Monographs. PRINT. WEB. (irregular) 1975–. U.S. Department of Health and Human Services. National Institutes of Health. National Institute on Drug Abuse. HE 20.3965: (Earlier, HE 20.8216:) Item 0831-C-12. ASI 4498-. GPO. <http://www.nida.nih.gov/PublicationsIndex.html>; http://165.112.78.65/pubs/rmpubs2.taf?function=form>.

> Content: surveys of research and issues in drug abuse.

NIDA National Institute on Drug Abuse Web Site. WEB. U.S. Department of Health and Human Services. National Institutes of Health. National Institute on Drug Abuse. <http://www.nida.nih.gov/NIDAHome2.html>.

> Content: agency news and information; publications on drug abuse.

PREVLINE Prevention Online. WEB. National Clearinghouse for Alcohol and Drug Information. Substance Abuse and Mental Health Services Administration. <http://www.health.org>.

> Content: drug, alcohol, and tobacco information, databases, and publications.

Discussion

The *National Household Survey on Drug Abuse Main Findings* covers the U.S. household population aged 12 and up and is a comprehensive report on the prevalence and frequency of drug use. The report contains a trends chapter and chapters for each type of drug. Each chapter contains a narrative overview and statistical tables. Statistics show percentage of persons who have ever used drugs, used drugs during the past year, or used drugs during the past month by demographic characteristics for each drug. Additional chapters cover problems associated with use, use patterns, and special topics. These provide data in such areas as age at first use, multiple drug use, dependence, and binge alcohol use. The *Population Estimates* report is entirely statistical. It contains a set of prevalence tables for each drug, giving the percent and number of persons who have ever used the drug, used it in the past year, or in the past month. Tables are broken down by sex and age group with separate tables for each race category and region. A similar set of tables shows frequency of use during the past year. The *Summary of Findings* report provides early estimates from the survey and covers the same type of data as the other two reports. The first part of the report gives narrative highlights illustrated with graphs and charts. An appendix contains detailed tables of preliminary data on percentages of people reporting lifetime, past year, or past month use; number reporting first use each year and age at first use; availability; and perceptions of risk.

Another drug use survey of secondary school students, college students, and young adults is also conducted annually. *National Survey Results on Drug Use from the Monitoring the Future Study* also covers prevalence and frequency of use, but contains slightly different variables than the household survey above. Drug use data are analyzed in relation to college attendance plans and the level of parental education. Information is also collected on the grade in which drugs were first used, the degree and duration of the high, and attitudes and social factors involved. The latter two areas involve beliefs regarding the harmfulness of drugs, extent of disapproval of drugs, attitudes toward legality, and perceived attitudes of friends. Volume 1 covers secondary school students, and volume 2 covers college students and young adults. Selected data from recent surveys are available on the Internet.

The *Substance Abuse and Mental Health Statistics Source Book* contains a series of fact sheets on individual data items. Each fact sheet is two pages and includes brief narrative highlights, one statistical table, one graphic, and source notes. Fact sheets are organized by broad categories: prevalence of substance abuse; substance abuse by substance and various demographic variables; risk factors; social costs and consequences; and prevention and treatment. The substance abuse section covers trends in use for specific substances and by race, age, region, academic standing, employment status, and occupation. Risk factors cover family structure and violence. Costs to society topics include health care costs, loss of productivity, AIDS, emergency department episodes, deaths, and crime. Prevention and treatment topics include impact of drug prevention programs, funding for treatment, types of treatment, treatment admissions by demographic variables, and health insurance.

The *General Publications* series of the National Institute on Drug Abuse contains brochures and monographs on drug abuse topics. Examples of recent titles include *Marijuana: Facts Parents Need to Know* (HE 20.3952:M 33/3/998), *Drug Addiction Research and the Health of Women* (HE 20.3952:W 84/2), and *Assessing Drug Abuse within and across Communities* (HE 20.3952:C 73).

The *Research Monograph* series is based on papers and discussions from technical review meetings sponsored by the National Institute on Drug Abuse. Each monograph contains contributions from various researchers on a selected drug topic. Recent monograph titles include *Cost-Benefit/Cost-Effectiveness Research of Drug Abuse Prevention: Implications for Programming and Policy* (HE 20.3965:176), *Medication Development for the Treatment of Cocaine Dependence: Issues in Clinical Efficacy Trials* (HE 20.3965:175), and *Laboratory Behavioral Studies of Vulnerability to Drug Abuse* (HE 20.3965:169). The text of recent reports is available on the agency's Web site.

The *NIDA National Institute on Drug Abuse Web Site* contains announcements and summaries of current reports with links to full text. An "Information on Drugs of Abuse" menu choice leads to an alphabetical list of drugs with links to related publications and articles. A "Publications" menu choice gives a list of publications arranged by category or series including an option to view popular online publications. A "Popular Publications Online" menu choice is also available from the home page. Additional information available includes agency news releases, scientific meeting dates and summaries, funding opportunities, and agency organizational information.

PREVLINE contains a variety of information resources on drug abuse. An "Alcohol & Drug Facts" menu choice leads to a list of topics, including specific drugs such as cocaine/crack and marijuana. Under each drug is a list of fact sheets, articles, publications and other resources with links to the full text or resource. Drug-related material can also be found under other topics such as "Family & Friends." More substantial research publications and statistics are available under the main menu choice "Research Briefs." A "Databases" category provides access to such databases as *Information about Drugs and Alcohol*, *SAMHSA's Substance Abuse Treatment Facility Locator* and *SAID* (Department of Labor's *Substance Abuse Information Database*). The database section includes a search feature for authoritative substance abuse Web sites, *NSAWI (National Substance Abuse Web Index)*. An online catalog main menu option is available, which includes a list of online publications and the NCADI (National Clearinghouse for Alcohol and Drug Information) catalog. Many of these publications can be requested at no charge.

SOURCES ON SMOKING
Checklist

Reports of the Surgeon General on the Health Consequences of Smoking. PRINT. 1964–. U.S. Department of Health and Human Services. Centers for Disease Control and Prevention. National Center for Chronic Disease Prevention and Health Promotion. Office on Smoking and Health. HE 20.7615: (Earlier, HE 20.7614:, HE 20.25/2:; HE 20.7016:; HE 20.2:SM 7/5. Title varies). Item 0483-L-06. ASI 4204-18. (Earlier, ASI 4044-6). GPO.

> Content: review of the literature on various aspects of smoking and health with extensive bibliographic references.

The Virtual Office of the Surgeon General. WEB. U.S. Department of Health and Human Services. Public Health Service. Office of the U.S. Surgeon General. <http://www.surgeongeneral.gov/library/publications.htm>.

> Content: complete list of Surgeon General reports with full text for recent reports.

Smoking and Tobacco Control Monographs. PRINT. WEB. (irregular) 1991–. U.S. Department of Health and Human Services. Public Health Service. National Institutes of Health. National Cancer Institute. HE 20.3184/2: Item 0507-G-40. ASI 4476-7. <http://rex.nci.nih.gov/NCI_MONOGRAPHS/LIST.HTM>.

> Content: research reviews on smoking and tobacco control issues.

CDC's TIPS Tobacco Information and Prevention Source Web Site. WEB. Centers for Disease Control and Prevention. <http://www.cdc.gov/tobacco>.

> Content: information, publications, and databases on tobacco.

Smoking and Health Database. WEB. 1960-. Centers for Disease Control and Prevention. Office of Smoking and Health. <http://www.cdc.tobacco/search/index.htm>.

Content: bibliographic references to journal articles, books, and other materials on tobacco and tobacco use.

CDP File. CD-ROM. 1991–. U.S. Department of Health and Human Services. Centers for Disease Control and Prevention. National Center for Chronic Disease Prevention and Health Promotion. HE 20.7616: Item 0444-P-01. GPO.

Content: bibliographic health databases, including *Smoking and Health Database*.

See also Sources on Drugs above.

Discussion

The *Reports of the Surgeon General on the Health Consequences of Smoking* series contains comprehensive periodic reports on smoking and health research from the Surgeon General. Each report has a different theme and a distinctive title. Recent reports include *Tobacco Use Among U.S. Racial/Ethnic Minority Groups* (HE 20.7615:R 11) and *Preventing Tobacco Use Among Young People* (HE 20.7615:T 55). Other topics covered over the years include benefits of smoking cessation, nicotine addiction, and involuntary smoking. Chapters summarize research on various aspects of the topic and frequently contain statistics. Bibliographic references are included.

The Virtual Office of the Surgeon General contains a complete list of the Surgeon General reports since 1964, many of which deal with smoking. Full text is available for a small number of recent reports.

The *Smoking and Tobacco Control Monographs* series consists of research reports on tobacco and health issues. The reports analyze topics affecting public health and control of tobacco use. Statistical tables, graphs, and bibliographical references are included. Recent titles include *Cigars Health Effects and Trends* (HE 20.3184/2:9) and *Changes in Cigarette-Related Disease Risks and Their Implication for Prevention and Control* (HE 20.3184/2:8).

CDC's TIPS Tobacco Information and Prevention Source Web Site provides extensive data on tobacco and health issues. The "Overview" menu selection gives a brief summary of deaths related to smoking and provides links to additional overview data on such topics as "Tobacco Use in the United States—Overview" and "Significant Developments Related to Smoking and Health 1964–1996." The "Surgeon General's Reports" menu selection offers the full text of the most recent tobacco-related report, a complete list of reports, and a history of the 1964 Surgeon General's report. A "Research, Data, & Reports" menu choice leads to a list of topics such as "Addiction/Nicotine Dependence," "Cessation," "Economics," "Legal and Policy Issues," and "Secondhand Smoke." Under each topic is a list of articles, fact sheets, tables, and reports with links to full text. Also available from the home page is "Tobacco Control Highlights." This selection provides U.S. summary data and individual state data on tobacco issues, including adult and youth cigarette and smokeless tobacco use, deaths, health care costs, and tobacco control legislation. Other features of the Web site

include recent news items, guides on how to quit smoking, bibliographic citations to recently published articles and reports, educational materials, and a catalog of publications.

The *Smoking and Health Database* is also available via *CDC's TIPS* Web site. It contains bibliographic citations and abstracts to scientific reports and journal articles on smoking. Materials cover health and medical aspects, psychological aspects, policy and legal aspects, smoking prevention and cessation, and the tobacco industry. This database is also available on the *CDP File* CD-ROM.

The first two titles under "Sources on Drugs" above include data on the prevalence and frequency of tobacco use. The data on tobacco are comparable to the data on drugs as described above.

SOURCES ON MENTAL HEALTH
Checklist

Mental Health, United States. PRINT. (biennial) 1983–. U.S. Department of Health and Human Services. Public Health Service. Substance Abuse and Mental Health Services Administration. Center for Mental Health Services. HE 20.8137: Item 0506-C. ASI 4094-1. GPO.

Coverage: U.S., divisions, states.

Content: mental health care issues; number, types, and characteristics of mental health organizations; number and categories of patients; mental health personnel; funding and expenditures.

Substance Abuse and Mental Health Statistics Source Book. PRINT. 1998. 2nd ed. U.S. Department of Health and Human Services. Substance Abuse and Mental Health Services Administration. Office of Applied Studies. HE 20.424:4. Item 0497-D-34. ASI 4096-6.

Coverage: U.S., selected states, selected metropolitan areas.

Content: statistics on nature, extent, and trends of mental disorders; social costs; prevention and treatment.

General Publications. PRINT. (irregular) U.S. Department of Health and Human Services. National Institutes of Health. National Institute of Mental Health. HE 20.8102: Item 0507-B-05. GPO.

Content: miscellaneous publications on mental health.

National Institute of Mental Health Web Site. WEB. U.S. Department of Health and Human Services. National Institutes of Health. National Institute of Mental Health. < http://www.nimh.nih.gov/ >.

Content: general information and resources on mental disorders; agency information and news.

Schizophrenia Bulletin. PRINT. (quarterly) Dec. 1969–. U.S. Department of Health and Human Services. Public Health Service. National Institutes of Health. National Institute of Mental Health. HE 20.8115: (Earlier, HE 20.2414:). Item 0507-B-07. GPO.

Content: articles on schizophrenia research.

Discussion

Mental Health, United States is a combination of analysis and statistics on the mental health care system. Chapters highlight major policy concerns and vary from edition to edition. There is generally a chapter on highlights and trends in mental health services with statistics on the availability of services, volume of services, staffing, and financing for different types of mental health organizations, such as state and county mental hospitals or private psychiatric hospitals. Other topics that have been discussed in recent issues include the growth and direction of managed care; prevalence of serious emotional disturbances; and national prevalence and treatment of mental and addictive disorders. Each chapter includes bibliographical references. Examples of information available include number of residential treatment beds by type of facility, number of psychiatrists in residential treatment centers for emotionally disturbed children, and number of active mental health personnel in marriage and family therapy in New Jersey.

The *Substance Abuse and Mental Health Statistics Source Book* contains a series of fact sheets on individual data items. Each fact sheet is two pages and includes brief narrative highlights, one statistical table, one graphic, and source notes. Fact sheets are organized by broad categories: prevalence of mental disorders; mental disorders by various demographic variables; risk factors; social costs and consequences; and prevention and treatment. The mental disorders section covers prevalence of specific disorders by race, age, sex, and employment status. Risk factors cover the impact of violence. Costs to society topics include health care costs and suicide. Prevention and treatment topics include funding for treatment and facilities; types of treatment; facilities and staffing; facility admissions; treatment by sex, age, race, diagnosis; and health insurance.

The *General Publications* series of the National Institute of Mental Health contains brochures and monographs on mental health topics. Examples of recent titles include *Anxiety Disorders: Decade of the Brain* (HE 20.8102:AN 9/997); *Let's Talk About Depression: the Good News Is That You Can Get Treatment and Feel Better Soon* (HE 20.8102:D 44/21/997); and *Parity in Financing Mental Health Services: Managed Care Effects on Cost, Access, and Quality: An Interim Report to Congress* (HE 20.8102:F 49/3).

The *National Institute of Mental Health Web Site* contains general agency information, news and press releases, and information on mental disorders. The "For the Public" section contains brochures, fact sheets, and educational materials on specific disorders. Some of the disorders covered include anxiety disorders, depression, attention deficit hyperactivity disorder, autism, and learning disabilities. Resources available on each disorder include general summary information or full-text publications. The Web site also offers sections for practitioners and researchers and information on funding opportunities.

Schizophrenia Bulletin is devoted to disseminating information and research on schizophrenia. Each issue is approximately 180 pages and contains several articles. An "At Issue" section contains viewpoints and arguments on controversial issues. Articles include critical literature reviews, reports of original laboratory and clinical research, and first person accounts. Each issue has a theme or featured topics, such as treatment recommendations and outcomes (Vol.24, No. 1) or new models of the pathophysiology of schizophrenia (Vol. 24, No.2). Issues regularly contain first person accounts by persons with schizophrenia or by members of their family. Examples of recent articles include "Family Caregiving in Schizophrenia" (Vol. 24, No. 4); "Facial Expressions of Emotions and Schizophrenia" (Vol. 24, No. 3); and "Schizophrenia, Alcohol Abuse, and Violent Behavior" (Vol. 24, No. 3).

SOURCES ON CHILDREN

Checklist

Trends in the Well-Being of America's Children and Youth. PRINT. WEB. (annual) 1996–. U.S. Department of Health and Human Services. Office of the Assistant Secretary for Planning and Evaluation. HE 1.63: Item 0455-M-01. ASI 4004-37. GPO. <http://aspe.os.dhhs.gov/hsp/hspyoung.htm#indicators>.

> Coverage: U.S.
>
> Content: statistical indicators on the condition of children; population; economic security; health; social development; education.

America's Children: Key National Indicators of Well-Being. PRINT. WEB. (annual) 1997–. Federal Interagency Forum on Child and Family Statistics. PR 42.8:C 43/C 43/. Item 0851-J. ASI 14434-1. GPO. <http://childstats.gov/>.

> Coverage: U.S.
>
> Content: statistical indicators on well-being of children; economic security; health; behavior and social environment; education.

Child Health USA. PRINT. (annual) 1989–. U.S. Department of Health and Human Services. Health Resources and Services Administration. Maternal and Child Health Bureau. HE 20.9213: (Earlier, HE 20.9202:C 43/2/). Item 0486-A-13. ASI 4104-19. GPO.

> Coverage: U.S., states.
>
> Content: statistical indicators on the health status and service needs of children.

Administration for Children and Families Web Site. WEB. U.S. Department of Health and Human Services. Administration for Children and Families. <http://www.acf.dhhs.gov/>.

> Content: fact sheets, statistics, press releases on agency program areas and subagencies; information relating to child care, child support, child welfare, welfare programs.

Discussion

All three of the publications listed above present statistical data on the well-being of children. *Trends in the Well-Being of America's Children and Youth* is the most extensive. It covers more than 90 indicators of well-being in such areas as child population characteristics, family structure, neighborhoods, poverty and income, mortality, health conditions, substance abuse, sexual activity, educational enrollment, and educational achievement. The health conditions section covers such topics as mortality, healthy births, chronic health conditions, overweight, abuse and neglect, violent victimization, and immunization. A brief narrative section for each indicator summarizes its significance and highlights key data. Tables provide more detailed information. Graphs or charts illustrate key trends. Data are often given by sex, age group, and race. A special section analyzes a different topic each year. The 1998 edition special section is on the well-being of immigrant children.

America's Children: Key National Indicators of Well-Being covers 23 key indicators that are reliable and measured regularly. A section on population and family characteristics presents important demographic trends in the child population. A section on indicators of well-being contains data on economic security, educational opportunity, and a healthy environment. A brief narrative section discusses each indicator and is illustrated with graphs and charts. More detailed tables keyed to each chart are available in an appendix. The health indicators section covers general health status, activity limitation, low birthweight, mortality, immunization, and adolescent births.

Child Health USA covers 55 health status indicators at a more succinct level than the other two publications. A brief statement is given on each indicator along with one or two graphs or charts. Sections cover population characteristics, health status, and health services utilization. A state data section provides state data for a small number of data items. Examples of topics discussed include child care, infant mortality, hospitalization, vaccine-preventable diseases, child abuse and neglect, and substance abuse.

The *Administration for Children and Families Web Site* contains information on agency programs to promote the well-being of children. Fact sheets give overview information on the agency and its subagencies and on such topics as the child support enforcement program, child welfare, domestic violence, and Head Start. The ACF press room area contains agency press releases. The press room area includes a statistical area with data on child care, child support, child welfare, Head Start, refugees, and welfare. From the home page a user can also select from a list of programs or topics. Some of the topics include adoption and foster care, child abuse and neglect, child care, runaway and homeless youth, and welfare reform. Program listings include subagencies such as the Children's Bureau and Child Care Bureau. Each subagency has additional information resources including publications, databases, and additional Web links.

SOURCES ON AGING

Checklist

Developments in Aging. PRINT. WEB. (annual) 1959–. U.S. Congress. Senate. Special Committee on Aging. Senate Report. Y 1.1/5: (1997–98 is Y1.1/5:106-229/v.). Items 1008-C or 1008-D(MF). <http://www.access.gpo.gov/congress/cong005.html>; <http://purl.access.gpo.gov.GPO/LPS702>.

Content: review of congressional and agency activities, federal programs, and policies affecting the aged.

General Publications. PRINT. (irregular) U.S. Department of Health and Human Services. Public Health Service. National Institutes of Health. National Institute of Aging. HE 20.3852: Item 0447-A-26. GPO.

Content: miscellaneous publications on aging.

National Institute on Aging Web Site. WEB. National Institutes of Health. National Institute on Aging. <http://www.nih.gov/nia/>.

Content: publications on health and aging; agency news; research programs; and funding.

General Publications. PRINT. MF. (irregular) U.S. Department of Health and Human Services. Administration on Aging. HE 1.1002: Item 0447-A-01.

Content: project reports and miscellaneous publications of the Administration on Aging.

Administration on Aging Web Site. WEB. U.S. Department of Health and Human Services. Administration on Aging. <http://www.aoa.dhhs.gov/>.

Content: resources for the elderly, directories, fact sheets, publications, press releases, and Web sites.

Access America for Seniors Web Site. WEB. <http://www.seniors.gov/>.

Contents: federal government services and resources for seniors.

Progress Report on Alzheimer's Disease. PRINT. WEB. (annual) U.S. Department of Health and Human Services. National Institutes of Health. National Institute on Aging. HE 20.3869: (Earlier, HE 20.3852:AL 9/. Frequency varies). Item 0447-A-25. <http://www.alzheimers.org/pubs/pubs.html>.

Content: recent research findings on Alzheimer's disease.

Hearings, Prints, and Miscellaneous Publications. PRINT. MF. U.S. Congress. Senate. Special Committee on Aging. Y 4.AG 4: Items 1009-B-01 or -C-01(MF). GPO.

Content: committee hearings and research reports on issues related to aging.

Discussion

Developments in Aging is a comprehensive annual review of federal agency activities and programs affecting the aged. The report is issued in two or three volumes. Volume 1 summarizes congressional activity and provides background information on many issues and programs. These include Social Security, pensions, taxes, employment, food stamps, Medicare, Medicaid, other health issues, housing, the Older Americans Act, social services, and crime. Volumes 2 and 3 contain reports from many federal agencies regarding activities related to the aged. These include reports from agencies with a direct mission to the aged, such as the Administration on Aging, the National Institutes on Health (National Institute on Aging), and the Social Security Administration. Many less obvious agencies are included also, however. Some agencies report on specific research projects and findings, such as an Agricultural Research Service nutrition study on the role of vitamin E in enhancing immune response or a study being conducted by the National Institute of Mental Health on recurring depression in the elderly. Other reports cover projects, grants, investigations, publications, databases, educational activities, or regular program activities.

The *General Publications* series of the National Institute on Aging contains a small number of brochures, pamphlets, and books on aging. Examples of titles include *In Search of the Secrets of Aging* (HE 20.3852:AG 4/13/996), *Alzheimer's Disease Genetics* (HE 20.3852:D 63/2), and *Menopause* (HE 20.3852:M 52/3/994).

The *National Institute on Aging Web Site* contains a health information area with subcategories for publications, a resource directory, public service ads, Alzheimer's disease, and other Internet links. The publications section consists of a searchable database. Publications can be searched by keyword, title, subject, or publication type. All subjects or publication types can be selected to produce a complete list. Links to full-text are available. The Alzheimer's disease section contains several types of resources, including publications, agency press releases, sources of additional information, and clinical trials. Alzheimer's publications include several full-text publications that can be selected by category or listed alphabetically. Publications include fact sheets, *Age Pages,* and recent years of the *Progress Report on Alzheimer's Disease. Age Pages* are fact sheets on health topics affecting older persons. They are based on current scientific information, emphasize practical advice, and include suggestions for additional resources and information sources. A complete list of *Age Pages* can be found in the publications database by choosing the publication type "Age Page."

The *General Publications* series of the Administration on Aging contains miscellaneous publications on aging. Many of these reports are the result of projects funded by the agency and are issued almost entirely in microfiche. Recent titles include *Informal Caregiving: Compassion in Action* (HE 1.1002:IN 3); *Living Longer, Growing Stronger in America* (HE 1.1002:OL 1/13/KIT); and *Final Report to the Administration on Aging for Restructuring Aging and Domestic Violence Services for Elderly Battered Women* (HE 1.1002:B 32/2 (MF)).

The *Administration on Aging Web Site* provides extensive listings of resources for the elderly. Information pages are available for older persons and their families; practitioners and other professionals; and researchers and students. Examples of some of the resources listed under older persons and their families include "Eldercare Locator"; state and area aging agencies; AoA fact sheets on such topics as age discrimination, elder abuse, and nutrition; retirement and financial planning resources; information on housing concerns; and links to a variety of organizations and agencies.

The *Access America for Seniors Web Site* provides a centralized source for federal government resources, services, and information of interest to seniors. Resources are grouped by subject areas such as health, consumer protection, services, employment and volunteer activities, tax assistance, and education and training. Links to federal agencies and state Web sites are also available.

The *Progress Report on Alzheimer's Disease* is a survey of the latest findings on the disease. The report gives basic information on the prevalence and costs of the disease, research directions, and advances in various areas. Examples of areas covered include structure and function of the brain, changes in the brain in Alzheimer's, genetic factors, risk factors, diagnosis, and treatment and prevention.

The Senate has a committee devoted exclusively to aging. Publications include transcripts of committee hearings on bills, programs, and issues, as well as occasional studies and guides. Examples of recent Senate hearings include *Transforming Health Care Systems for the 21st Century: Issues and Opportunities for Improving Health Care* (Y 4.AG 4:S.HRG.105-631), *The Graying of Nations: Productive Aging Around the World* (Y 4.AG 4:S.HRG.105-635), and *Betrayal: The Quality of Care in California Nursing Homes* (Y 4.AG 4:S.HRG.105-735). Other congressional committees also occasionally publish materials on aging.

SOURCES ON DISABILITY
Checklist

American Rehabilitation. PRINT. (quarterly) Sept./Oct. 1975–. U.S. Department of Education. Office of Special Education and Rehabilitative Services. Rehabilitation Services Administration. ED 1.211: (Earlier, HE 1.612:). Item 0506-C-04. GPO.
> Content: articles on rehabilitation; publication announcements.

NARIC Web Site. WEB. National Rehabilitation Information Center. <http://www.naric.com/>.
> Content: disability and rehabilitation publications and databases.

ABLEDATA. WEB. U.S. Department of Education. National Institute on Disability and Rehabilitation Research. High graphics: <http://www.abledata.com/Site_2/search.htm>; Low graphics: <http://www.abledata.com/text2/search.htm>.
> Content: database of products that assist the disabled.

Access to Disability Data Web Site. WEB. National Institute on Disability and Rehabilitation Research. InfoUse. <http://www.infouse.com/disabilitydata/>.
> Content: disability chartbooks; number and characteristics of people with disabilities.

Disability Web Page. WEB. U.S. Bureau of the Census. <http://www.census.gov/hhes/www/disability.html>.
> Coverage: U.S., states, counties, metropolitan areas.
> Content: disability data from Census surveys and reports; disability and employment status; earnings; receipt of benefits and personal assistance; degree and type of disability; data often by age, race, and sex.

disAbility.gov Access America Web Site. WEB. <http://disability.gov/>

Content: federal government resources on disability.

Library Resources for the Blind and Physically Handicapped: A Directory with FY Statistics on Readership, Circulation, Budget, Staff, and Collections. PRINT. WEB. (annual) 1976–. Library of Congress. National Library Service for the Blind and Physically Handicapped. LC 19.16: Item 0806-A-14. ASI 26404-3. HTML version: <http://www.loc.gov/nls/reference/address.html>.

Content: directory of libraries providing recorded and braille materials and related services to the blind and physically handicapped.

Discussion

American Rehabilitation contains articles on rehabilitation programs, services, and issues. Topics cover education, employment, technology, specific disabilities, and other aspects of rehabilitation. Individual issues often have a central theme, such as personal assistance services or community rehabilitation programs. Examples of recent articles include "Home Care Benefits for Persons with Disabilities" (Vol. 24, No. 3), "Moving Beyond the Traditional Job Placement Role" (Vol. 24, No. 1) and "Making Mass Transit User-Friendly for Blind Commuters" (Vol. 23, No. 3). A "New Publications and Films" section is a regular feature. An index for each volume is included in the last issue of the year or shortly thereafter.

The *NARIC Web Site* contains publications, databases, and other disability resources. The publications main menu option provides a list of publications including the *Disability Statistics Abstracts* and *Disability Statistics Reports* series. Brief abstracts are provided as well as links to online data. The *Disability Statistics Abstracts* series contains short reports summarizing data on disability from more extensive surveys and sources. Examples of topics covered include education of children with disabilities, trends in disability rates, and health conditions and impairments causing disabilities. The *Disability Statistics Reports* series are more detailed research reports. The main menu also offers a database option. Databases available include the *NARIC Knowledgebase, REHABDATA, NIDRR Program Directory* of current research, and the *NIDRR Compendium* of literature from NIDRR-funded projects. The database search screen includes a list of frequently requested topics offering predefined search options.

The *NARIC Knowledgebase* of disability resources contains information on organizations, journals, Internet sites, databases, and directories. The database can be searched by keyword, by type of resource (database, Internet), and by state, city or zip code. Information available includes address or URL, telephone number, types of disabilities served, types of users served, and a description. For organizations, information is given on publications available and organization type. A print publication based on the database, *Directory of National Information Sources on Disabilities* (ED 1.30/2:D 63/, Item 0461-B-10), has not been issued in recent years.

REHABDATA contains bibliographic references on the rehabilitation of physically or mentally disabled persons. Information includes research reports funded by the National Institute on Disability and Rehabilitation Research (NIDRR) and the Rehabilitation Services Administration, as well as journal articles, books, and audiovisual materials.

ABLEDATA contains data on more than 17,000 commercially available products that assist the disabled. Information includes product name, brand name, manufacturer, cost, and description. Searches can be conducted by key word, company name, or brand name.

The *Access to Disability Data Web Site* provides chartbooks on disability statistics in the "Data Resources" area. Titles include *Chartbook on Women and Disability in the United States, Chartbook on Work and Disability in the United States,* and *Chartbook on Disability in the United States.* All of the chartbooks present basic statistical data in a nontechnical, easy-to-use format. Each page is centered around a single topic question, such as "How does activity limitation differ by gender?," "Which chronic health conditions cause activity limitations most often?," and "What are the median earnings of working people by disability status?" A brief explanatory paragraph answers the question and summarizes key statistics. Data are also illustrated by a chart or graph. The source for each statistic is given. There is a bibliography, a glossary, and an appendix on sources and their limitations.

The *Disability Web Page* contains full-text publications and data tables from surveys and from the *Census of Population.* Statistics are given for the number of persons with disabilities by age, race, employment status, and other variables.

The *disAbility.gov Access America Web Site* provides a centralized source for federal government resources, services, and information on disability. Resources are grouped by subject areas such as children and youth, choice and self-determination, civil rights and protections, employment, and health.

The National Library Service for the Blind and Physically Handicapped (NLS) of the Library of Congress selects, produces, and distributes reading materials in braille and on recorded discs and cassettes. A network of libraries circulates these materials to eligible borrowers by postage-free mail. The NLS publishes several catalogs and other materials related to this service. *Library Resources for the Blind and Physically Handicapped* is a directory of the libraries participating in this program. The directory is arranged by state. Regional libraries are listed first, followed by subregional libraries, if any. Subregional libraries are listed by city. Information includes the library name, address, telephone numbers, librarian name, hours, services, and publications.

CONGRESSIONAL SOURCES

Many congressional committees publish materials on health programs and issues. Some of these include the

House Committee on Commerce (Y 4.C 73/8:), the Senate Committee on Labor and Human Resources (Y 4.L 11/4:), the Senate Committee on Finance (Y 4.F 49:), and the House Committee on Ways and Means (Y 4.W 36:). Recent examples of publications from some of these committees include *Federal Legislation Relating to Health Care Quality* (Y 4.L 11/4: S.HRG.105-510); *State and Local Views of Proposed National Tobacco Policy* (Y 4.L 11/4:S.HRG.105-466); *Substance Abuse, the Science of Addiction and Options for Treatment* (Y 4.L 11/4: S.HRG.105-645); *The State of Cancer Research* (Y 4.C 73/8:105-128); and *Increasing Children's Access to Health Care* (Y 4.F 49:S.HRG.105-459). For complete listings of congressional publications, consult the *Monthly Catalog* and *CIS/Index* listed in the "Indexes" section below.

MEDICAL INDEXES AND BIBLIOGRAPHIES
Checklist

Index Medicus. PRINT. (monthly, annual cumulation) 1960–. U.S. Department of Health and Human Services. Public Health Service. National Institutes of Health. National Library of Medicine. HE 20.3612:, HE 20.3612/3: (Issued earlier as *Current List of Medical Literature*). Item 0508-E. GPO.

> Content: index to articles from more than 4300 biomedical journals from around the world.

MEDLINE: PubMed and Internet Grateful Med. WEB. 1966–. National Library of Medicine. <http://www.nlm.nih.gov/databases/freemedl.html>.

> Content: Web versions of *Index Medicus*; additional medical databases are available on *Internet Grateful Med*, including *AIDSLINE, AIDSDRUGS, AIDSTRIALS, HealthSTAR,* and *TOXLINE.*

MEDLINEplus. WEB. 1966-. National Library of Medicine. <http://www.nlm.nih.gov/medlineplus/>.

> Content: collection of health resource information sources, including *MEDLINE.*

Current Bibliographies in Medicine. WEB. (irregular) 1988–. U.S. Department of Health and Human Services. Public Health Service. National Institutes of Health. National Library of Medicine. HE 20.3615/2: Item 0508-H-01. GPO. <http://www.nlm.nih.gov/pubs/resources.html>; <http://purl.access.gpo.gov/GPO/LPS536>.

> Content: bibliographies on biomedical topics generated from the National Library of Medicine's online databases.

Discussion

The National Library of Medicine publishes *Index Medicus*, the premiere index to the world's medical literature. This comprehensive index provides detailed access to medical literature for the serious researcher. Many of the sources cited will only be available in large libraries, in medical libraries, or through interlibrary loan. Although relevant U.S. government publications are included in these indexes, they are a small proportion of the overall content. For general coverage of government publications, the government publication indexes listed in the "Index" section below are the best choices.

Index Medicus indexes journal articles in more than 4,300 biomedical journals. It provides comprehensive coverage of medical and health care topics. Each monthly issue is published in two parts and contains a subject section, an author section, and a bibliography of medical reviews. A separate annual guide to subject headings, *Medical Subject Headings*, is included with the subscription, as is an annual *List of Journals Indexed*. A multivolume annual cumulation replaces the monthly issues. The annual cumulation also contains the subject index, author index, bibliography of medical reviews, medical subject headings, and list of journals indexed.

MEDLINE is the online database version of *Index Medicus* with some additional materials on nursing and dentistry added. The database contains more than 11 million records, and about 33,000 new citations are added each month. The National Library of Medicine offers two Web versions of *MEDLINE—PubMed* and *Internet Grateful Med*. The two versions have different search interfaces and options. A document delivery option is available for users who wish to order full-text copies of articles. *Internet Grateful Med* also provides access to several additional databases besides *MEDLINE*. These include *AIDSLINE, AIDSDRUGS,* and *AIDSTRIALS* discussed under the "Sources on Diseases" section earlier in this chapter; and *DIRLINE* mentioned under "General Health Sources" at the beginning of this chapter. Other databases available include *BIOETHICSLINE, ChemID, HealthSTAR* (health administration), *HISTLINE* (history of medicine), *HSRPROJ* (health services research projects in progress), *OLDMEDLINE* (1960–65), *POPLINE* (population information), *SDILINE* (current month from *MEDLINE*), *SPACELINE* (space life sciences), and *TOXLINE* (drug toxicology). *MEDLINE* is also available online from several commercial sources, including Ovid Technologies, Knight-Ridder Information (DataStar, DIALOG), CompuServe Information Service Knowledge Index, STN International, OCLC FirstSearch, and LEXIS-NEXIS. CD-ROM versions are available from Ovid Technologies, Aries Systems, EBSCO, and SilverPlatter.

The *MEDLINEplus* Web page provides links to additional resources on health and diseases, as well as links to *MEDLINE*. A health topics section contains a list of specific diseases or subject areas such as arthritis, cancer, depression, multiple sclerosis, and many others. For each topic a list of links to information resources, publications, and Web sites is provided arranged by categories such as general/overviews, diagnosis, clinical trials, disease management or treatment, organizations, and specific population groups such as women or children. Preconstructed searches of *MEDLINE* are offered as well as a link directly to *MEDLINE* for those who want to construct their own search statements. Other choices available from the main menu include dictionaries for definitions of medical terms, directories of doctors and hospitals, and other resources such as organizations, health libraries, publications/news, databases, and *MEDLINE*.

Current Bibliographies in Medicine is a series of individual bibliographies on medical topics. The bibliographies are generated from *MEDLINE* and other National Library of Medicine online databases. Bibliographies list journal articles, monographs, reports, government publications, and other materials on topics of interest. Data usually cover several years. Recent titles include *Zinc and Health* (no. 98-3, Web only), *Diagnosis and Treatment of Attention Deficit Hyperactivity Disorder* (HE 20.3615/2:98-2), and *Rehabilitation of Persons with Traumatic Brain Injury* (HE 20.3615/2:98-1).

INDEXES
Checklist

Catalog of United States Government Publications (MOCAT). WEB. 1994–. U.S. Government Printing Office. Superintendent of Documents. <http://www.gpo.gov/catalog>; <http://www.access.gpo.gov/su_docs/locators/cgp/index.html>; <http://purl.access.gpo.gov/GPO/LPS844>.

Monthly Catalog of United States Government Publications. CD-ROM. 1996–. U.S. Government Printing Office. Superintendent of Documents. GP 3.8/7: Item 0557-C. GPO.

Monthly Catalog of United States Government Publications (Condensed version). PRINT. (monthly) 1996–. U.S. Government Printing Office. Superintendent of Documents. GP 3.8/8: (Earlier full version, GP 3.8:, 1895-1995). Item 0557-D. GPO.

U.S. Government Online Bookstore. WEB. U.S. Government Printing Office. <http://bookstore.gpo.gov/>; <http://orders.access.gpo.gov/su_docs/sale/index.html>; <http://purl.access.gpo.gov/GPO/LPS851>.

American Statistics Index (ASI). PRINT. (monthly) 1973–. Bethesda, MD: Congressional Information Service.

Statistical Universe. WEB. Bethesda, MD: Congressional Information Service.

CIS/Index. PRINT. (monthly) 1970–. Bethesda, MD: Congressional Information Service.

Congressional Universe. WEB. Bethesda, MD: Congressional Information Service.

Discussion

The *Monthly Catalog* is the most comprehensive index for government publications. The complete version is available on the Web and on CD-ROM. For publications on health, search subject headings beginning with "Health" and under such headings as "Aged," "Alcoholism," "Drug Abuse," "Handicapped," "Mental Health," "Smoking,"

and specific diseases and programs. Commercial online and CD-ROM versions of the *Monthly Catalog* are also available. For more information, see Chapter 3, "The Basics of Searching."

The U.S. Government Online Bookstore provides access to the Sales Product Catalog, a searchable database of government publications currently available for sale. It can be searched by keyword, title, author, and other selected fields.

A comprehensive listing of statistical material can be found in *American Statistics Index (ASI)* by looking under such headings as "Health Condition," "Health Facilities and Services," "Aged and Aging," "Alcohol Abuse and Treatment," "Disabled and Handicapped Persons," "Drug Abuse and Treatment," "Mental Health and Illness," "Smoking," and specific diseases and programs. *Statistical Universe* includes a Web version of *ASI*.

Congressional publications can be found through *CIS/Index* under subject headings beginning with "Health" or "Medical" and under such headings as "Aged and Aging," "Alcohol Abuse and Treatment," "Diseases and Disorders," "Drug Abuse and Treatment," "Handicapped," "Mental Health and Illness," "Public Health," "Smoking," and specific diseases and programs. *Congressional Universe* includes a Web version of *CIS*.

RELATED MATERIAL
Within this Work

Chapter 28 Population Statistics

Chapter 29 Vital Statistics

Chapter 49 Technical Reports

GPO Subject Bibliographies. PRINT. WEB. GP 3.22/2:

<http://bookstore.gpo.gov/sb/about.html>.

No. 8 "Diseases"

No. 37 "Physically Challenged"

No. 39 "Aging"

No. 119 "Health Care"

No. 121 "Vital and Health Statistics"

No. 163 "Substance Abuse"

No. 167 "Mental Health"

Other

Consumer Information Catalog. PRINT. WEB. (quarterly) U.S. General Services Administration. Consumer Information Center. GS 11.9: Item 0580-B. <http://www.pueblo.gsa.gov/>; <http://purl.access.gpo.gov/GPO/LPS1527>.

CHAPTER 20
Education

Educational materials published by the U.S. government range from small pamphlets to massive statistical compilations. Their content also varies from curriculum materials to research reports. Most educational materials are issued by the Department of Education and its many divisions, such as the National Center for Education Statistics. Many educational publications are available on the Web.

SEARCH STRATEGY

This chapter shows a subject search strategy. Statistical materials dealing with education are also a large part of this chapter and can be found by applying a statistical search strategy. Steps in finding materials are

1. Check the major sources, series, and agency Web sites listed here;
2. Use the *Monthly Catalog* to locate additional materials on a given subject;
3. Check the *Digest of Education Statistics* and other statistical compilations if statistical materials are needed; and
4. Use *American Statistics Index (ASI)* to locate other statistical sources.

GENERAL PUBLICATIONS SERIES AND INFORMATION
Checklist

U.S. Department of Education Home Page. WEB. U.S. Department of Education. <http://www.ed.gov/>.
> Content: information about the Department of Education and its programs; publications and products; Department of Education offices; news and events; research and statistics; student financial assistance.

General Publications. PRINT. MF. WEB. (irregular) U.S. Department of Education. ED 1.2: Item 0455-B-02.

> Content: general publications dealing with education topics.

Handbooks, Manuals, Guides. PRINT. MF. (irregular) U.S. Department of Education. ED 1.8: Item 0461-B-01.
> Content: general guides on education topics.

General Publications. PRINT. MF. WEB. (irregular) U.S. Department of Education. Office of Educational Research and Improvement. National Center for Education Statistics. ED 1.102: Item 0461-A-01.
> Content: general publications on educational topics of interest to the National Center for Education Statistics.

PRINT. MF. (irregular) U.S. Department of Education. Office of Educational Research and Improvement. National Center for Education Statistics. ED 1.108: Item 0461-A-03.
> Content: general handbooks and guides on educational topics of interest to the National Center for Education Statistics.

General Publications. PRINT. MF. (irregular) U.S. Department of Education. Office of Special Education and Rehabilitative Services. ED 1.202: Item 0529.
> Content: general publications on educational topics of interest to the Office of Special Education and Rehabilitative Services.

Handbooks, Manuals, Guides. PRINT. MF. (irregular) U.S. Department of Education. Office of Special Education and Rehabilitative Services. ED 1.208: Item 0529-B.
> Content: general handbooks and guides on educational topics of interest to the Office of Special Education and Rehabilitative Services.

General Publications. PRINT. WEB. (irregular) U.S. Department of Education. Office of Educational Research and Improvement. ED 1.302: Item 0461-D-05.
> Content: general publications on educational topics of interest to the Office of Educational Research and Improvement.

Handbooks, Manuals, Guides. PRINT. MF. WEB. (irregular) U.S. Department of Education. Office of Educational Research and Improvement. ED 1.308: Item 0455-G-04.

Content: general handbooks and guides on educational topics of interest to the Office of Educational Research and Improvement.

General Publications. PRINT. (irregular) U.S. Department of Education. Office of Elementary and Secondary Education. ED 1.402: Item 0461-H.

Content: general publications on educational topics of interest to the Office of Elementary and Secondary Education.

Handbooks, Manuals, Guides. PRINT. (irregular) U.S. Department of Education. Office of Elementary and Secondary Education. ED 1.408: ITEM 0461-B-02.

Content: general handbooks and guides on educational topics of interest to the Office of Elementary and Secondary Education.

Discussion

The *Department of Education Home Page* includes extensive information about the Department of Education, its programs, services, publications, organization, and research activities. A "Topics from A to Z" listing, site map, and site search engine help to navigate the different areas and resources of the site. Major sections of the site include "President's and Secretary's Priorities," giving information on current major initiatives, "Funding Opportunities," with information on grants and contracts, "Student Financial Assistance," providing information for students and parents, and "Research and Statistics," with links to statistical publications and reports. Other major sections include "News and Events," "Programs and Services," "Publications and Products," and "ED Offices and Budget." The *Department of Education Home Page* is an excellent starting point for locating governmental education information.

The other series listed in this section are all *General Publications* and *Handbooks, Manuals, and Guides* series of the Department of Education and offices within the Department of Education. They include a variety of publications on general topics relating to the Department of Education or education in general. Many of these publications are also available on the Web. Since the individual URLs vary, they are not included in the series entries listed here.

Examples of publications from the overall Department of Education *General Publications* series includes *Principles and Recommendations for Early Childhood Assessments* (ED 1.2:C 43/25), *The National Educational Research Policy and Priorities Board: Its Role, Development, and Prospects* (ED 1.2:B 63), and *Ready Schools: A Report of the Goal 1 Ready Schools Resource Group* (ED 1.2:G 53/17). The *Handbooks, Manuals, and Guides* series of the overall Department of Education includes such titles as *Direct PLUS Loans: A Guide to Federal Education Loans for Parents* (ED 1.8:L 78/8), *Preventing Youth Hate Crime: A Manual for Schools and Communities* (ED 1.8:Y 8), and *Guide to Direct Consolidation Loans* (ED 1.8:L 78/5/998).

The other *General Publications* and *Handbooks, Manuals, and Guides* listed here include publications of similar scope, format, and subject of those of the overall Department of Education. For example, publications include *Indicators of School Crime and Safety, 1998* (ED 1.102:C 86), and *Handbook on Human Resources: Recordkeeping and Analysis* (ED 1.108:H 88) from the National Center for Education Statistics and *Basic Data Elements for Elementary and Secondary Education Information Systems* (ED1.102:EL 2) and *Technology for Students With Disabilities: A Decision Maker's Resource Guide* (ED 1.208:ST 9) from the Office of Special Education and Rehabilitative Services. Publications from the Office of Educational Research and Improvement include *National Educational Research and Development Centers* (ED 1.302:ED 8/15/998) and *A Pocket Guide to ERIC* (ED 1.308:ED 8/6/999). The Office of Elementary and Secondary Education includes *The New Title I: Helping Disadvantaged Children Meet High Standards* (ED 1.402:D 63), and *Harvests of Hope: Guide to the Program Services of the Office of Migrant Education* (ED 1.408:H 26)

DIRECTORIES
Checklist

Education Resource Organizations Directory. WEB. U.S. Department of Education. <http://www.ed.gov/Programs/EROD/>.

Content: searchable database of nationwide educational resource organizations, such as resource centers, state agencies, federal agencies, assistance centers, and many other organizations providing resources.

National Public School and School District Locator. WEB. U.S. Department of Education. Office of Educational Research and Improvement. National Center for Education Statistics.<http://nces.ed.gov/ccdweb/school/>.

Content: searchable database of public schools and public school districts.

Directory of Postsecondary Institutions. PRINT. WEB. (annual) U.S. Department of Education. Office of Educational Research and Improvement. National Center for Education Statistics. ED 1.111/4: Item 0461-A-21. ASI 4844-3. <http://nces.ed.gov/pubsearch/getpubcats.asp?sid=010>.

Content: comprehensive directory of over 10,000 U.S. postsecondary institutions, both degree and non-degree granting.

Directory of Public Elementary and Secondary Education Agencies. PRINT. WEB. U.S. Department of Education. Office of Educational Research and Improvement. National Center for Education Statistics. ED 1.111/2: Item 0460-B-01. ASI 4834-1. <http://nces.ed.gov/pubsearch/getpubcats.asp?sid=001>.

Content: listing of educational agencies.

Public Library Locator. WEB. U.S. Department of Education. Office of Educational Research and Improvement. National Center for Education Statistics. <http://nces.ed.gov/surveys/libraries/liblocator/default.asp>.

Content: searchable database of public libraries.

Discussion

The *Education Resource Organizations Directory* is a searchable database of over 2400 educational resource organizations at the national, regional, and state level. A search on the subject "reading," for example, returns entries for such organizations as the Center for the Study of Reading; the ERIC Clearinghouse on Reading, English, and Communication; and the Learning Research and Development Center. A simple search provides basic keyword searching and an advanced search feature allows field searching by "State(s)/Territory(ies)," "Subject(s)," "Title," "Description," "Audience(s)," "Service(s)," "Type of Organization," and "Geographic Scope."

The *National Public School and School District Locator* allows the user to search the *Common Core of Data (CCD)* database (the Department of Education's primary database on public elementary and secondary education in the United States) on a number of fields to locate public schools and school districts nationwide. The public schools interface allows field searching on "School District Name," "County where school district is located," "NCES Local Education Agency ID #," "School Name," "School Address," "City," "State," "Zip Code," "Area Code," and "Telephone Number." The school districts interface allows field searching on "School District Name," "County where school district is located," "NCES Local Education Agency ID #," "City," and "State."

The *Directory of Postsecondary Institutions* includes the institution's name, address, telephone number, fall enrollment, percent female enrollment, tuition and fees, room and board charges, and IPEDS and Office of Postsecondary Education code number. It also includes whether a public or private institution, religious affiliation, highest degree offered, Carnegie classification, academic calendar, programs offered, and accreditation. The directory is issued in two volumes, one for degree-granting institutions, and one for non-degree granting institutions. Data are taken from the Integrated Postsecondary Education Data System (IPEDS) Institutional Characteristics Survey.

The *Directory of Public Elementary and Secondary Education Agencies* is derived from the *Common Core of Data* database. It includes directory information for regular school districts; supervisory union administrative centers; regional education service agencies; state-operated agencies, federally operated, agencies, and any other agencies dealing with elementary and secondary education; and districts having student membership. Each entry includes state, name of agency, mailing address, telephone number, name of county, metropolitan status code, grade span, student membership, number of regular high school graduates, number of students with an Individual Education Program (IEP), number of teachers, and number of schools.

The *Public Library Locator* derives its information from the National Center for Education Statistics *Public Library Survey*. It provides an interface to search the database and find directory information about the library. Searchable fields include "Library Identification ID," "Library Name," "Street Address," "City," "County," "State," "Region," "Zip Code," and "Telephone Number." A similar search interface allows the user to locate information on public library service outlets, which includes such things as central library outlets, branch library outlets, and bookmobile outlets.

STATISTICAL SOURCES
Checklist

Digest of Education Statistics. PRINT. WEB. (annual) 1962–. U.S. Department of Education. Office of Educational Research and Improvement. National Center for Education Statistics. ED 1.326: (Earlier, ED 1.113:, HE 19.315:) Item 0461-D-09. ASI 4824-2. GPO. <http://nces.ed.gov/pubsearch/majorpub.asp>.

> Coverage: world, world regions, selected countries, U.S., regions, states, large school districts, selected colleges and universities.
>
> Content: comprehensive statistical compilation of statistics on all levels of education, including elementary and secondary, college and university, vocational and adult, federal programs, outcomes, international comparisons, and learning resources and technology.

The Condition of Education. PRINT. WEB. (annual) 1975–. U.S. Department of Education. Office of Educational Research and Improvement. National Center for Education Statistics. ED 1.109: (Earlier, HE 19.314:) Item 0461-A-12. ASI 4824-1, 4824-15. GPO. <http://nces.ed.gov/pubsearch/majorpub.asp>; <http://purl.access.gpo.gov/GPO/LPS4175>.

> Coverage: selected countries, U.S., regions, states.
>
> Content: statistical indicators on educational progress; educational performance; educational environment; social support; enrollment; educational attainment.

Education Statistics of the United States. PRINT. (annual) 1999–. Lanham, MD: Bernan Press.

> Coverage: U.S., regions, divisions, states, counties.
>
> Content: school enrollment by level and grade; educational attainment; data by age, race, sex, family characteristics, and labor force characteristics; state and county school characteristics and finances.

Projections of Education Statistics to [year]. PRINT. WEB. (annual) 1964–. U.S. Department of Education. Office of Educational Research and Improvement. National Center for Education Statistics. ED 1.120: (Earlier, HE 19.320:) Item 0460-A-10. ASI 4824-4. GPO. <http://nces.ed.gov/pubsearch/majorpub.asp>; <http://nces.ed.gov/pubsearch/getpubList.asp?L1=40&L2=0>.

> Coverage: U.S., regions, states.
>
> Content: enrollment; graduates; degrees; teachers; expenditures; school-age populations.

Education Statistics Quarterly. PRINT. WEB. (quarterly) Spring 1999–. U.S. Department of Education. Office of Educational Research and Improvement. National Center for Education Statistics. ED 1.328/13: Item 0455-G-20. <http://nces.ed.gov/pubsearch/majorpub.asp#quarterly>.

> Coverage: varies; U.S., states.

Content: statistical articles reporting on National Center for Education Statistics surveys, publications, and data products; summaries of recent products.

National Center for Education Statistics Web Site. WEB. U.S. Department of Education. National Center for Education Statistics. <http://nces.ed.gov/index.html>.
Content: publications, summary statistics, data files, survey and program information.

Dropout Rates in the United States: [year]. MF. WEB. (annual) 1988–. U.S. Department of Education. Office of Educational Research and Improvement. National Center for Education Statistics. ED 1.329: Item 0461-D-05. ASI 4834-23. GPO. <http://nces.ed.gov/pubsearch/majorpub.asp>.
Coverage: U.S., regions, states.
Content: high school dropout rates; characteristics of dropouts; high school completion rates.

Public Elementary and Secondary Education Statistics: School Year [years]. PRINT. WEB. U.S. Department of Education. Office of Educational Research and Improvement. National Center for Education Statistics. ED 1.328/12: (Title varies: *Early Estimates of Public Elementary and Secondary Education Statistics*) Item 0455-G-19. ASI 4834-19. <http://nces.ed.gov/pubsearch/getpubcats.asp?sid=001>; <http://nces.ed.gov/pubsearch/>.
Coverage: U.S., states.
Content: membership, teachers, high school graduates, revenue, expenditures.

E.D. TABS. MF. WEB. (irregular) U.S. Department of Education. Office of Educational Research and Improvement. National Center for Education Statistics. ED 1.328/3: Item 0455-G-09. ASI varies. GPO. <http://nces.ed.gov/pubsearch/>.
Coverage: varies; U.S., states.
Content: data reports on educational topics.

Statistics in Brief. PRINT. WEB. (irregular) U.S. Department of Education. Office of Educational Research and Improvement. National Center for Education Statistics. ED 1.328/4: Item 0455-G-11. ASI 4826-10. <http://nces.ed.gov/pubsearch/>.
Coverage: varies; U.S., regions, states.
Content: brief statistical analyses of educational topics.

Statistical Analysis Report. MF. WEB. (irregular) U.S. Department of Education. Office of Educational Research and Improvement. National Center for Education Statistics. ED 1.328/5: Item 0455-G-09. ASI varies. GPO. <http://nces.ed.gov/pubsearch/>.
Coverage: varies; U.S., regions, states.
Content: analytical survey reports on educational topics.

Survey Report. MF. WEB. (irregular) U.S. Department of Education. Office of Educational Research and Improvement. National Center for Education Statistics. ED 1.328: Item 0455-G-09. ASI varies. GPO. <http://nces.ed.gov/pubsearch/>.
Coverage: varies; U.S., states.
Content: statistical reports from surveys on educational topics.

Common Core of Data (CCD) School Years [years]. CD-ROM. U.S. Department of Education. Office of Educational Research and Improvement. National Center for Education Statistics. ED 1.334/2:C 73/. Item 0455-N-04. Related database, *National*

Public School and School District Locator: <http://nces.ed.gov/ccdweb/school/index.asp>.
Content: statistical database on elementary and secondary schools and school districts.

Integrated Postsecondary Education Data System: IPEDS. CD-ROM. WEB. (annual) 1990–. U.S. Department of Education. Office of Educational Research and Improvement. National Center for Education Statistics. ED 1.334/4: Item 0455-N-06. ASI 4844-22. GPO. <http://nces.ed.gov/ipeds/data.html>; Related database, *IPEDS College Opportunities Online*: <http://nces.ed.gov/ipeds/cool/>.
Content: statistical database on postsecondary institutions.

Public-Use Data: SASS 1987–88, 1990–91, 1993–94; TFS 1988–89, 1991–92, 1994–95. CD-ROM. (1998) U.S. Department of Education. Office of Educational Research and Improvement. National Center for Education Statistics. ED 1.334/2:SCH 6/CD. (Other titles: *Schools and Staffing Survey (SASS) and Teacher Followup Survey (TFS) CD-ROM, SASS and TFS CD-ROM*) Item 0455-N-04. GPO.
Content: survey data from the Schools and Staffing Survey and Teacher Followup Survey.

National Postsecondary Student Aid Study: NPSAS. CD-ROM. U.S. Department of Education. Office of Educational Research and Improvement. National Center for Education Statistics. ED 1.333: Item 0455-N-02. GPO.
Content: survey data on how students and their families pay for postsecondary education.

National Household Education Survey Data Files and Electronic Codebook. CD-ROM. U.S. Department of Education. Office of Educational Research and Improvement. National Center for Education Statistics. ED 1.334/5: Item 0455-N-07. GPO.
Content: survey data from the National Household Education Survey.

Discussion

The *Digest of Education Statistics* is the major source for educational statistics. It pulls together information from a variety of published and unpublished sources, providing information for all educational levels. Subjects such as enrollment, number of teachers, finances, degrees earned, educational attainment, federal support, and computer use are covered. A brief narrative overview explaining the tables and analyzing trends is included at the beginning of each major section. Recent editions of the *Digest* are available on the Web in both HTML and PDF formats. Figure 20.1 shows a sample table from the *Digest*.

The *Condition of Education* presently consists of two volumes: a main report and a volume of supplemental and standard error tables. The main report uses tables, charts, and textual analysis to show educational trends for selected indicators. The indicators selected are considered the most significant national measures of the condition and progress of U.S. education. An overview chapter presents a summary of the condition of education. Individual indicator data are grouped by broad areas including learner outcomes, quality of education environments, social support for learning, and educational participation and progress. A selection of supplemental tables is included.

196 HIGHER EDUCATION: ENROLLMENT

Table 172.—Total fall enrollment in institutions of higher education, by attendance status, sex of student, and control of institution: 1947 to 1996

Year	Total enrollment	Attendance status		Sex of student		Control of institution			
		Full-time	Part-time	Men	Women	Public	Private		
							Total	Nonprofit	Proprietary
1	2	3	4	5	6	7	8	9	10
				Institutions of higher education					
1947[1]	2,338,226	—	—	1,659,249	678,977	1,152,377	1,185,849	—	—
1948[1]	2,403,396	—	—	1,709,367	694,029	1,185,588	1,217,808	—	—
1949[1]	2,444,900	—	—	1,721,572	723,328	1,207,151	1,237,749	—	—
1950[1]	2,281,298	—	—	1,560,392	720,906	1,139,699	1,141,599	—	—
1951[1]	2,101,962	—	—	1,390,740	711,222	1,037,938	1,064,024	—	—
1952[1]	2,134,242	—	—	1,380,357	753,885	1,101,240	1,033,002	—	—
1953[1]	2,231,054	—	—	1,422,598	808,456	1,185,876	1,045,178	—	—
1954[1]	2,446,693	—	—	1,563,382	883,311	1,353,531	1,093,162	—	—
1955[1]	2,653,034	—	—	1,733,184	919,850	1,476,282	1,176,752	—	—
1956[1]	2,918,212	—	—	1,911,458	1,006,754	1,656,402	1,261,810	—	—
1957	3,323,783	—	—	2,170,765	1,153,018	1,972,673	1,351,110	—	—
1959	3,639,847	2,421,016	[2]1,218,831	2,332,617	1,307,230	2,180,982	1,458,865	—	—
1961	4,145,065	2,785,133	[2]1,359,932	2,585,821	1,559,244	2,561,447	1,583,618	—	—
1963	4,779,609	3,183,833	[2]1,595,776	2,961,540	1,818,069	3,081,279	1,698,330	—	—
1964	5,280,020	3,573,238	[2]1,706,782	3,248,713	2,031,307	3,467,708	1,812,312	—	—
1965	5,920,864	4,095,728	[2]1,825,136	3,630,020	2,290,844	3,969,596	1,951,268	—	—
1966	6,389,872	4,438,606	[2]1,951,266	3,856,216	2,533,656	4,348,917	2,040,955	—	—
1967	6,911,748	4,793,128	[2]2,118,620	4,132,800	2,778,948	4,816,028	2,095,720	—	—
1968	7,513,091	5,210,155	2,302,936	4,477,649	3,035,442	5,430,652	2,082,439	—	—
1969	8,004,660	5,498,883	2,505,777	4,746,201	3,258,459	5,896,868	2,107,792	—	—
1970	8,580,887	5,816,290	2,764,597	5,043,642	3,537,245	6,428,134	2,152,753	—	—
1971	8,948,644	6,077,232	2,871,412	5,207,004	3,741,640	6,804,309	2,144,335	—	—
1972	9,214,820	6,072,389	3,142,471	5,238,757	3,976,103	7,070,635	2,144,185	—	—
1973	9,602,123	6,189,493	3,412,630	5,371,052	4,231,071	7,419,516	2,182,607	—	—
1974	10,223,729	6,370,273	3,853,456	5,622,429	4,601,300	7,988,500	2,235,229	—	—
1975	11,184,859	6,841,334	4,343,525	6,148,997	5,035,862	8,834,508	2,350,351	—	—
1976	11,012,137	6,717,058	4,295,079	5,810,828	5,201,309	8,653,477	2,358,660	2,314,298	44,362
1977	11,285,787	6,792,925	4,492,862	5,789,016	5,496,771	8,846,993	2,438,794	2,386,652	52,142
1978	11,260,092	6,667,657	4,592,435	5,640,998	5,619,094	8,785,893	2,474,199	2,408,331	65,868
1979	11,569,899	6,794,039	4,775,860	5,682,877	5,887,022	9,036,822	2,533,077	2,461,773	71,304
1980	12,096,895	7,097,958	4,998,937	5,874,374	6,222,521	9,457,394	2,639,501	2,527,787	[3]111,714
1981	12,371,672	7,181,250	5,190,422	5,975,056	6,396,616	9,647,032	2,724,640	2,572,405	[3]152,235
1982	12,425,780	7,220,618	5,205,162	6,031,384	6,394,396	9,696,087	2,729,693	2,552,739	[3]176,954
1983	12,464,661	7,261,050	5,203,611	6,023,725	6,440,936	9,682,734	2,781,927	2,589,187	192,740
1984	12,241,940	7,098,388	5,143,552	5,863,574	6,378,366	9,477,370	2,764,570	2,574,419	190,151
1985	12,247,055	7,075,221	5,171,834	5,818,450	6,428,605	9,479,273	2,767,782	2,571,791	195,991
1986	12,503,511	7,119,550	5,383,961	5,884,515	6,618,996	9,713,893	2,789,618	2,572,479	[4]217,139
1987	12,766,642	7,231,085	5,535,557	5,932,056	6,834,586	9,973,254	2,793,388	2,602,350	[4]191,038
1988	13,055,337	7,436,768	5,618,569	6,001,896	7,053,441	10,161,388	2,893,949	2,673,567	220,382
1989	13,538,560	7,660,950	5,877,610	6,190,015	7,348,545	10,577,963	2,960,597	2,731,174	229,423
1990	13,818,637	7,820,985	5,997,652	6,283,909	7,534,728	10,844,717	2,973,920	2,760,227	213,693
1991	14,358,953	8,115,329	6,243,624	6,501,844	7,857,109	11,309,563	3,049,390	2,819,041	230,349
1992	14,487,359	8,162,118	6,325,241	6,523,989	7,963,370	11,384,567	3,102,792	2,872,523	230,269
1993	14,304,803	8,127,618	6,177,185	6,427,450	7,877,353	11,189,088	3,115,715	2,888,897	226,818
1994	14,278,790	8,137,776	6,141,014	6,371,898	7,906,892	11,133,680	3,145,110	2,910,107	235,003
1995	14,261,781	8,128,802	6,132,979	6,342,539	7,919,242	11,092,374	3,169,407	2,929,044	240,363
1996[5]	14,300,255	8,213,490	6,086,765	6,343,992	7,956,263	11,090,171	3,210,084	2,940,557	269,527
				Degree-granting institutions [6]					
1996[5]	14,367,520	8,302,953	6,064,567	6,352,825	8,014,695	11,120,499	3,247,021	2,942,556	304,465

[1] Degree-credit enrollment only.
[2] Includes part-time resident students and all extension students.
[3] Large increases are due to the addition of schools accredited by the Accrediting Commission of Career Schools and Colleges of Technology.
[4] Because of imputation techniques, data are not consistent with figures for other years.
[5] Preliminary data.
[6] Data are for 4-year and 2-year degree-granting higher education institutions that were eligible to participate in Title IV federal financial aid programs.
—Data not available.

NOTE.—Trend tabulations of institutions of higher education data are based on institutions that were accredited by an agency or association that was recognized by the U.S. Department of Education. The Department of Education no longer distinguishes between those institutions and other institutions that are eligible to participate in Title IV programs. The new degree-granting classification is very similar to the earlier higher education classification, except that it includes some additional, primarily 2-year colleges, and excludes a few higher education institutions that did not award degrees.

SOURCE: U.S. Department of Education, National Center for Education Statistics, Higher Education General Information Survey (HEGIS), "Fall Enrollment in Colleges and Universities" surveys; and Integrated Postsecondary Education Data System (IPEDS), "Fall Enrollment" surveys. (This table was prepared April 1998.)

Source: *Digest of Education Statistics*, 1998, p.196.

Figure 20.1: Sample Page from the *Digest of Education Statistics*.

The second volume includes additional statistical tables on the same topics. It also repeats the supplemental tables included in the main volume. Although the subject coverage is not as comprehensive as the *Digest of Education Statistics*, the selected indicators provide a different approach with emphasis on analyzing trends and progress. Recent editions of *The Condition of Education* are available on the Web in both HTML and PDF formats. The HTML version incorporates the supplemental tables from the second volume.

Education Statistics of the United States is a convenient compilation of education data gathered primarily from the Census Bureau and National Center for Education Statistics sources. Extensive national-level data are available for school enrollment and educational attainment. Some historical tables are included. A state-level section covers population, income, educational attainment, schools, student characteristics, dropouts, completions, student/teacher ratios, staff, assessment and test results, revenues, expenditures, and degrees conferred. A county-level section covers a smaller number of data items, including population, schools, characteristics of students, student/teacher ratios, staff, dropouts, graduates, revenues, and expenditures.

Projections of Education Statistics provides projections at three different levels of assumptions regarding the growth or decline of populations and educational enrollments. Besides providing individual statistical tables, it also includes a report and analysis of educational trends. Statistics from previous years are given along with the projections, usually providing at least 10 years of past data and 10 years of projections.

Education Statistics Quarterly contains articles based on National Center for Education Statistics publications and data. Each issue contains a feature article on a selected study with analyses from commentators. Numerous shorter articles are grouped by broad area such as elementary and secondary education, postsecondary education, and lifelong learning. Shorter articles have often been published previously in agency reports or as separate publications. A separate section on "Data Products, Other Publications, and Funding Opportunities" describes recent data files and publications including availability on the Web. Recent articles include "NAEP 1998 Civics Report Card for the Nation" (Vol. 1, No. 4), "Key Statistics on Public Elementary and Secondary Schools and Agencies: School Year 1995–96" (Vol. 1, No. 4), and "Enrollment Patterns of First-Time Beginning Postsecondary Students" (Vol. 1, No. 4).

The National Center for Education Statistics (NCES) is the primary agency involved in the collection of education statistics. The *National Center for Education Statistics Web Site* provides access to the agency's publications and data files. Main menu choices include "Electronic Catalog," "Survey & Program Areas," "Encyclopedia of ED Stats," "NCES Fast Facts," and "Search NCES." The "Electronic Catalog" provides several options for locating NCES publications and data products. Searches may be conducted by NCES publication number; keyword in title, author, or abstract; program area; product type; and date. Once a product has been located it can often be viewed online or downloaded. Other features include a "Subjects A–Z" listing, "Popular NCES Reports," "Data Access Tools" that search various data sets, and a database of Department of Education reports in the ERIC database since 1980. (See the "Educational Resources Information Center (ERIC) Sources" section for more information on ERIC.) The main menu option on "Survey & Program Areas" lists and describes survey categories such as "Elementary/Secondary Surveys" or "Postsecondary Surveys." Individual survey programs are listed in each survey area with links to background information and related databases, datafiles, and publications.

Dropout Rates in the United States is a comprehensive report focusing on the extent of the dropout problem and identification of students who are most likely to become dropouts. The appropriate statistical tables and textual explanation are grouped together under three areas: event dropout rates, status dropout rates, and high school completion rates. Supplemental tables and time series data are included in appendixes.

Public Elementary and Secondary Education Statistics: School Year [years] provides basic statistics on elementary and secondary schools on a relatively current basis. It contains a small number of tables of key statistics, including total students, teachers, and high school graduates by state. Total revenues and expenditures are also covered. Additional data include pupil/teacher ratio, per pupil revenue, and per pupil expenditure.

The National Center for Education Statistics publishes many statistical publication series. A selection of these series is listed here. The *E.D. TABS* series is designed to present tabular data from various surveys in a timely fashion with minimal analysis. The series includes recurring and individual titles in such areas as enrollments, degrees, libraries, staff, and salaries. Examples of titles include *Fall Enrollment in Postsecondary Institutions 1996* (ED 1.328/3:F 19 (MF)), *Characteristics of Stayers, Movers, and Leavers: Results from the Teacher Followup Survey: 1994–95* (ED 1.328/3:C 37/3/994-95 (MF)), and *Current Funds Revenues and Expenditures of Institutions of Higher Education* (ED 1.328/3:F 96/ (MF)). Recent publications in this series can be found on the Web by searching the NCES electronic catalog. Select "E.D. TAB" in the type of product box.

The *Statistics in Brief* series provides brief analyses and statistics on policy topics. Reports cover participation in specific types of courses and programs and basic educational topics such as enrollments and staff. A few titles are issued on a recurring basis. Sample titles include *Overview of Public Elementary and Secondary Schools and Districts: School Year [years]* (ED 1.328/4:EL 2/), *Public*

School Student, Staff, and Graduate Counts by State, School Year [years] (ED 1.328/4:ST 9/), *Service-Learning and Community Service in K-12 Public Schools* (ED 1.328/4:SCH 6/2), and *Student Interest in National News and its Relation to School Courses* (ED 1.328/4:ST 9/3). Publications in this series can be found on the Web by searching the NCES electronic catalog. Select "Statistics in Brief" in the type of product box.

The *Statistical Analysis Report* series contains analytical reports on individual surveys or on topics that may be covered by several surveys. Sample titles include *Characteristics of the 100 Largest Public Elementary and Secondary School Districts in the United States: [years]* (ED 1.328/5:C 37/2/ (MF)), *Characteristics of Children's Early Care and Education Programs* (ED 1.328/5:C 37/4 (MF)), *Parent Involvement in Children's Education: Efforts by Public Elementary Schools* (ED 1.328/5:P 21), and *Choosing a Postsecondary Institution* (ED 1.328/5:P 84/3 (MF)). Publications in this series can be found on the Web by searching the NCES electronic catalog. Select "Statistical Analysis Report" in the type of product box.

The *Survey Report* series contains statistical reports based on NCES surveys. As with many of the NCES series, it covers all levels of education with data on enrollments, staff, student characteristics, and libraries. One recurring title is *Key Statistics on Public Elementary and Secondary Schools and Agencies: School Year: [years]* (ED 1.328:ST 2/3/) that provides more detailed statistics than the *Public Elementary and Secondary Education Statistics: School Year [years]* early estimate report discussed above. Other titles issued in this series include *The Status of Academic Libraries in the United States: Results from the 1994 Academic Library Survey with Historical Comparisons* (ED 1.328:AC 1/2 (MF)), *Selected Data on Minority Participation in the Public Schools* (ED 1.328:M 66/2 (MF)), and *Use of Educational Research and Development Resources by Public School Districts* (ED 1.328:ED 8/2 (MF)). Publications in this series can be found on the Web by searching the NCES electronic catalog.

NCES conducts several regular surveys to collect educational data. The publications listed in this section are based on data from these surveys. Original datafiles and databases from the surveys are also available on the Web and on CD-ROM. The datafiles, CD-ROMs, and publications associated with a particular survey can be found on the Web through the "Survey & Program Areas" menu option on the *National Center for Education Statistics Web Site*. It lists and describes survey categories such as "Elementary/Secondary Surveys" or "Postsecondary Surveys." Individual survey programs are listed in each survey area with links to background information and related databases, datafiles, and publications. Selected CD-ROMs that are issued periodically are listed in this section. In some cases related Web databases are also available.

The *Common Core of Data (CCD) School Years [years]* CD-ROM contains five years of data from the NCES's primary database on elementary and secondary education. Data include school information and characteristics, school district information and characteristics, district-level demographic characteristics, staff, dropouts, revenue and expenditures, and state totals. A related Web database of school and school district addresses, *National Public School and School District Locator*, is available on the NCES Web site and is also cited in the "Directories" section of this chapter. It contains some basic statistics on total students and teachers for the district and for individual schools. School information includes number of students by grade and by race/ethnicity.

The *Integrated Postsecondary Education Data System: IPEDS* CD-ROM contains selected data from the IPEDS survey of postsecondary institutions. The survey covers enrollment, program completions, faculty and staff, finances, and libraries. The CD contains data on institutional information and characteristics, enrollment, revenues, expenditures, salaries, and completions. An interactive Web database is also available and data can be downloaded. Another related Web database, *IPEDS College Opportunities Online* (COOL), provides information to help students and their parents select a college. Users can search for a specific institution or search by location, programs, or degrees. Information given includes address, telephone numbers, type of institution, degrees, costs, enrollment, degrees awarded by program, percentage of students receiving financial aid, and average financial aid awards.

The *Public-Use Data: SASS 1987–88, 1990–91, 1993–94; TFS 1988–89, 1991–92, 1994–95* CD-ROM contains three cycles of survey data for the Schools and Staffing Survey (SASS) and the Teacher Followup Survey (TFS). These surveys cover public and private schools from K-12. They are designed to monitor teacher supply and demand, teacher and principal qualifications and characteristics, and school conditions. SASS covers teacher characteristics, education, and salaries and school characteristics. TFS covers teacher retention.

The *National Postsecondary Student Aid Study: NPSAS* CD-ROM provides data from a survey of undergraduate students, graduate students, and first-year professional students at all types of postsecondary institutions. The survey provides information on the cost of postsecondary education, distribution of financial aid, and the characteristics of students and families receiving and not receiving aid.

The *National Household Education Survey Data Files and Electronic Codebook* CD-ROM contains data from the National Household Education Survey (NHES). The survey collects information from U.S. households on educational activities. Each survey may cover a different topic. Topics covered in the past include adult education, early childhood education, school readiness, school safety and discipline, parent involvement in education, and civic involvement.

EDUCATIONAL RESOURCES INFORMATION CENTER (ERIC) SOURCES
Checklist

Educational Resources Information Center Web Site. WEB. U.S. Department of Education. Office of Educational Research and Improvement. Educational Resources Information Center. <http://www.accesseric.org/>.

> Content: general information about ERIC; ERIC sites; ERIC products; ERIC database; publications; FAQ's.

Resources. WEB. U.S. Department of Education. Office of Educational Research and Improvement. Educational Resources Information Center. <http://www.accesseric.org/resources/resources.html>.

> Content: listing and links to resources about the ERIC system; other ERIC resources.

ERIC Sites. WEB. U.S. Department of Education. Office of Educational Research and Improvement. Educational Resources Information Center. <http://www.accesseric.org/sites/barak.html>.

> Content: listing and links to ERIC Clearinghouses, Adjunct ERIC Clearinghouses; Affiliate ERIC Clearinghouses; ERIC support components; other publishers of ERIC materials.

Welcome to AskERIC. WEB. U.S. Department of Education. Office of Educational Research and Improvement. Educational Resources Information Center. <http://ericir.syr.edu/>.

> Content: clearinghouse providing educational information to teachers, librarians, counselors, administrators, parents, and others, including information on the ERIC system.

A Pocket Guide to ERIC. PRINT. WEB. (irregular) U.S. Department of Education. Office of Educational Research and Improvement. Educational Resources Information Center. ED 1.308:ED 8/6/year. Item 0455-G-04. <http://www.accesseric.org/resources/resources.html>.

> Content: brief description of the ERIC system.

All About ERIC. PRINT. WEB. (irregular) U.S. Department of Education. Office of Educational Research and Improvement. Educational Resources Information Center. ED 1.302:ED 8/2/year. Item 0461-D-05. <http://www.accesseric.org/resources/allabout/index.html>.

> Content: detailed descriptions and overview of the ERIC system, services, and products.

ERIC Annual Report. PRINT. WEB. U.S. Department of Education. Office of Educational Research and Improvement. Educational Resources Information Center. ED 1.301/2: Item 0461-D-21. <http://www.accesseric.org/resources/resources.html>.

> Content: annual report summarizing ERIC system accomplishments and future plans.

ERIC Review. PRINT. WEB. (3 timer per year.) 1990–. U.S. Department of Education. Office of Educational Research and Improvement. Educational Resources Center. ED 1.331: Item 0455-G-11. <http://www.accesseric.org/resources/ericreview/review.html>; <http://purl.access.gpo.gov/GPO/LPS2275>.

> Content: brief articles on educational programs and research; information on ERIC publications, products, and services.

Catalog of ERIC Clearinghouse Publications. PRINT. (irregular) U.S. Department of Education. Office of Educational Research and Improvement. Educational Resources Information Center. ED 1.302:C 58/year. Item 0461-D-05.

> Content: catalog of publications of ERIC Clearinghouses; includes index by Clearinghouse.

ERIC Digests. WEB. U.S. Department of Education. Office of Educational Research and Improvement. Educational Resources Information Center. ED 1.331/2: Item 0455-G-11. <http://www.ed.gov/databases/ERIC_Digests/index/>.

> Content: short reports on topics of current educational interest.

ERIC-Sponsored Internet Access to the ERIC Database. WEB. U.S. Department of Education. Office of Educational Research and Improvement. Educational Resources Information Center. <http://www.accesseric.org/earchdb/dbchart.html>.

> Content: links to publicly accessible ERIC sponsored versions of the ERIC Database; chart comparing search systems.

Resources in Education. PRINT. (monthly) 1966–. U.S. Department of Education. Office of Educational Research and Improvement. Educational Resources Information Center. ED 1.310: (Earlier title: *Research in Education*, HE 19.210:) Phoenix, AZ: Oryx Press (semiannual and annual cumulations only) Item 0466-A. GPO.

> Content: index and abstracts of ERIC documents.

Current Index to Journals in Education (CIJE). MF. PRINT. (monthly) U.S. Department of Education. Office of Educational Research and Improvement. Educational Resources Information Center. Phoenix, AZ: Oryx Press. (print monthly volumes and semiannual cumulations) ED 1.310/4: Item 0466-A-02.

> Content: index and abstract to periodical articles pertaining to education.

Thesaurus of ERIC Descriptors. PRINT. (1995) 13th Edition. Edited by James E. Houston. Phoenix, AZ: Oryx Press.

> Content: thesaurus used in the *ERIC Database*.

Database of U.S. Department of Education Publications in ERIC. WEB. 1980–. U.S. Department of Education. <http://www.ed.gov/pubs/pubdb.html>.

> Content: bibliographic database of Department of Education publications included in ERIC.

Welcome to ERIC Document Reproduction Services. WEB. U.S. Department of Education. Office of Educational Research and Improvement. Educational Resources Information Center. <http://www.edrs.com/default.cfm>.

> Content: information about EDRS products and services.

Directory of ERIC Resource Collections. WEB. ED 1.330/2: Item 0461-G-01. <http://ericae.net/derc.htm>; <http://www.ed.gov/BASISDB/EROD/eric/SF>.

> Content: searchable database of organizations with ERIC collections.

Education Documents Announced in RIE. MF. (irregular) U.S. Department of Education. Office of Educational Research and Improvement. Educational Resources Information Center. ED 1.310/2: Item 0466-A-03.

> Content: government-sponsored RIE reports.

Submitting Documents to ERIC: Frequently Asked Questions (FAQs). WEB. <http://ericfac.piccard.csc.com/submitting.html>.

> Content: information on submitting documents to the ERIC system.

Submitting Documents to ERIC: Educational Resources Information Center. PRINT. (1998) U.S. Department of Education. Office of Educational Research and Improvement. Educational Resources Information Center. ED 1.302:D 65/998. Item 0461-D-05.

> Content: information on submitting documents to the ERIC system.

National Educational Research and Development Centers: Research Literature. 1966–1997 CD-ROM. U.S. Department of Education. Office of Educational Research and Improvement. National Library of Education and ERIC Document Reproduction Service. (Nondepository)

> Content: database of bibliographic records for ERIC Documents produced by National Research and Development Centers; full text of ERIC Documents produced by National Research and Development Centers from 1980–1997.

Discussion

The Educational Resources Information Center (ERIC) is an educational information network that collects and disseminates educational information and research. ERIC was established in 1996 and has a long history of making information products available to users. A network of ERIC Clearinghouses covering specific subject areas collect, abstract, and index education materials, help users with information requests, and produce some publications in their respective areas. Examples of ERIC clearinghouses include the ERIC Clearinghouse on Elementary and Early Childhood Education, the ERIC Clearinghouse on Rural Education and Small Schools, and the ERIC Clearinghouse on Disabilities and Gifted Education. A major product of ERIC is the *ERIC Database*, which indexes and abstracts educational literature since 1966.

The *Educational Resources Information Center Web Site* is an excellent starting point for learning about the many aspects of ERIC, gaining access to the *ERIC Database*, locating ERIC publications in both full text and print and other formats, and linking to sites within the ERIC system. The *Resources* Web page within the site describes and links to publications describing the ERIC system, as well as other major resources. The *ERIC Sites* Web page describes and links to individual ERIC Clearinghouses, Adjunct ERIC Clearinghouses, Affiliate Clearinghouses, ERIC support components (such as the ERIC Document Reproduction Service (EDRS)), and other publishers of ERIC materials. It also links to the AskERIC Clearinghouse, which provides a wide range of educational information to users. This Clearinghouse provides information and help on using many of the ERIC resources described within this section of the chapter.

A Pocket Guide to ERIC concisely describes the ERIC system, explains how to use the ERIC system, and also describes the major ERIC products, publications, and other resources. It also covers how to obtain ERIC documents and journal articles, illustrates the use of the *ERIC Database* and other information services, and discusses how to submit documents to ERIC.

All About ERIC is a detailed and comprehensive 40-page plus guide to the ERIC system. It outlines the mission of ERIC, the use of the ERIC database, how to obtain ERIC documents and journal articles, and how to contribute to the ERIC database. It also describes other major ERIC publications and products, and the use of ERIC on the Internet. Also included is an ERIC system directory, and information on how to start an ERIC resource collection.

The *ERIC Annual Report* summarizes the work and accomplishments of the ERIC system during the previous year. Also included is some statistical information. This highly readable report is a quick way to gain an understanding of current developments and programs in the ERIC system. The *ERIC Review* is a periodical that provides information on ERIC products and services, and presents research results and articles on current educational trends and issues.

The *Catalog of ERIC Clearinghouse Publications* is a bibliography of over 1400 publications issued by ERIC Clearinghouses. Types of publications include parent brochures, directories and resource guides, *ERIC Digests,* and ERIC monographs/reports. An index by Clearinghouse name allows the publications of individual Clearinghouses to be easily identified.

ERIC Digests are short reports issued by ERIC Clearinghouses on educational topics of current interest. They are designed to give an overview of a topic and include references. The Web site for *ERIC Digests* provides a searchable database of the *ERIC Digests*. The full text of the *ERIC Digests* is accessible on the Web.

One of the major products of the ERIC system is the *ERIC Database*, the world's largest education database. The database began coverage in 1966. It includes over 980,000 entries and abstracts of documents and journal articles in education and related subject areas. An additional 30,000 new records are added each year. Included are bibliographic records for journal articles, research reports, curriculum and teaching guides, conference papers, and books. About 40 percent of the database is comprised of ERIC Documents, which include records for such non-journal items as books, research/technical reports, conference papers/speeches, project/program descriptions, opinion papers/essays, and teaching guides. The remainder of the database is composed of bibliographic records for journal articles. ERIC indexes and abstracts over 900 journals, some selectively, and some cover to cover.

Information included in ERIC Document entries includes such elements as the ERIC accession number, the

Clearinghouse accession number, the author(s), title, institution, sponsoring agency, contract or grant number, date published, ISBN (for published books), alternate source for obtaining document, descriptive note, ERIC Document Reproduction Service (EDRS) availability, publication type, descriptors, and abstract. Journal article entries include ERIC accession number, the Clearinghouse accession number, the author(s), article title, journal title, volume number, issue number, pages, publication date, major and minor descriptors, major and minor identifiers, annotation, and ISSN.

The *ERIC Database* is available in a number of different versions, both publicly accessible from ERIC, and in commercial versions from vendors. Depending on the version of the database, different combinations of these elements and others may be available for searching. Some databases provide fielded searching of individual record fields. Four versions of the *ERIC Database* publicly available through the ERIC system are listed at the *ERIC-Sponsored Internet Access to the ERIC Database* Web page. The page also provides information on what is included in each database, the searchable fields, the search engine used, and the search operators (Boolean, wild cards, sets, etc.) available.

The *ERIC Database* is also available from commercial vendors for a fee in Web and CD-ROM formats. Most versions of the database provide coverage from 1966-. Vendors include Dialog (Web and CD-ROM), OCLC FirstSearch (Web), and Ovid Technologies (Web). Both Web and CD-ROM versions are also available from SilverPlatter Inc., the National Information Services Corporation (NISC), and EBSCO Publishing.

Research in Education (RIE) is a print index and abstract version of the ERIC Document bibliographic records entered into the *ERIC Database*. Monthly issues of *RIE* are published by ERIC and distributed to depository libraries. Semiannual cumulations are published and made available for sale by a commercial publisher, The Oryx Press. *Current Index to Journals in Education (CIJE)* is a microfiche and print format index to the ERIC Journal bibliographic records. Monthly issues of *CIJE* are distributed to depository libraries in a microfiche format only. Print format monthly issues and annual cumulations of *CIJE* are also published commercially by Oryx Press. A print version of the *Thesaurus of ERIC Descriptors*, the thesaurus for the *ERIC Database*, is also published by Oryx Press. Some versions of the *ERIC Database* also provide ways of explicitly searching electronic versions of the *ERIC Thesaurus*.

The *Database of U.S. Department of Education Publications in ERIC* provides bibliographic records for all U.S. Department of Education publications entered into the ERIC system. A basic search interface and an advanced search interface that allows fielded searching on ERIC fields included in the document and journal entries is included. *Recent Department of Education Publications in*

ERIC provides a quarterly paper listing of similar publications.

The full collection of ERIC Documents are not distributed to depository libraries. ERIC Documents produced as government-sponsored reports are distributed to depository libraries in a microfiche format through the *Education Documents Announced in RIE* series. The ERIC Document Reproduction Services (EDRS) is the office responsible for making ERIC Documents available for sale. Many libraries and other organizations subscribe to the entire collection of ERIC Documents on microfiche. The searchable database *Directory of ERIC Resource Collections* can be used to identify those organizations with collections of ERIC documents. The EDRS is also beginning to make ERIC Documents available in electronic formats. Some libraries and other organizations subscribe to their E*Subscribe service, which provides access to the full-text of some 80% of the ERIC Documents from 1966-. EDRS also provides for the sale of individual documents in print, microfiche, and electronic (PDF) file versions. Information on submitting documents into the ERIC system can be found at the Web *Submitting Documents to ERIC: Frequently Asked Questions (FAQs)*. Consult the *Welcome to ERIC Document Reproduction Services* for information on EDRS products and services.

The *National Educational Research and Development Centers: Research Literature 1966–1997 CD-ROM* is a nondepository CD-ROM available for purchase from EDRS. It includes bibliographic records for 8,600 ERIC research documents from 1966–1997. It also includes the full text of 5,500 selected ERIC Documents from 1980–1997. These documents were produced by National Research and Development Centers sponsored by the Department of Education.

NATIONAL ASSESSMENT OF EDUCATIONAL PROGRESS (NAEP)
Checklist

National Assessment of Educational Progress Home Page. WEB. U.S. Department of Education. Office of Educational Research and Improvement. National Center for Education Statistics. <http://nces.ed.gov/nationsreportcard/site/home.asp>.
> Content: general information about the NAEP; links to resources arranged for specific audiences or by subject.

National Assessment of Educational Progress Products List. WEB. U.S. Department of Education. Office of Educational Research and Improvement. National Center for Education Statistics. <http://nces.ed.gov/pubsearch/getpubcats.asp?sid=031>.
> Content: listings of NAEP products by categories; descriptions of products; ordering information; links to the full text of products.

Directory of NAEP Publications. PRINT. WEB. (1999) ED 1.330:P 96. Item 0461-G. GPO. <http://nces.ed.gov/pubsearch/getpubcats.asp?sid=031>.
> Content: comprehensive listing of government-funded NAEP publications.

National Assessment of Educational Progress 1969–1983: A Bibliography of Documents in the ERIC Database. (1983) U.S. Department of Education. Office of Educational Research and Improvement. National Center for Education Statistics. Issued as ERIC Document ED 234 097.

> Content: reprint of citations to NAEP documents and journal articles in the ERIC database.

National Assessment of Educational Progress 1983–1987: A Bibliography of Documents in the ERIC Database. (1988) U.S. Department of Education. Office of Educational Research and Improvement. National Center for Education Statistics. ED 1.317:N 21/2. Item 0455-G-06. Issued as ERIC Document ED 302 580.

> Content: reprint of citations to NAEP documents and journal articles in the ERIC database.

NAEPfacts. PRINT. WEB. U.S. Department of Education. Office of Educational Research and Improvement. National Center for Education Statistics. ED 1.335: Item 0455-G-11. <http://nces.ed.gov/pubsearch/getpubcats.asp?sid=031>.

> Content: short summaries of NAEP assessments.

Focus on NAEP. PRINT. WEB. U.S. Department of Education. Office of Educational Research and Improvement. National Center for Education Statistics. ED 1.335/2: Item 0455-G-11. <http://nces.ed.gov/pubsearch/getpubcats.asp?sid=031>.

> Content: brief information sheets about NAEP developments.

Discussion

The National Assessment of Educational Progress (NAEP) has been conducted since 1969. It is often referred to as "The Nation's Report Card." A series of assessments gather information on the performance of students in the U.S. in elementary and secondary schools. Two series of assessments are carried out. The main assessments report on grades 4, 8, and 12. Areas covered are reading, mathematics, science, writing, U.S. history, civics, geography, the arts, and other subjects. The long-term trend assessments report on math, science, reading, and writing. They report on students ages 9, 13, and 17 in math, reading, and science and grades 4, 8, and 11 in writing. Some states also conduct their own individual state assessments. As a result of the NAEP, numerous reports and products are made available.

The *National Assessment of Educational Progress Home Page* is the best source to begin research on the NAEP. The page provides "starting points" for types of users, including administrators, policymakers, principals, and teachers. Another set of starting points are given by subject, including the arts, civics, geography, mathematics, reading, science, U.S. history, and writing. Once a starting point is selected, a page of resources particularly relevant to the type of user or subject selected appears. A typical page will provide news information, describe and link to the most relevant products, and highlight the most recent results. The *NAEP Home Page* also provides information about the NAEP in general, including sample questions and participation information.

From the *NAEP Home Page,* the user can also link to the *National Assessment of Educational Progress Products List.* This page includes the categories of "Arts," "Civics," "Data Products," "Geography," "Mathematics," "Reading," "Reports," "Science," "Shorter Publications," "Technical/Methodological," "U.S. History," "Working Papers," and "Writing." Once a category is selected, a listing of products in that category appears. Selecting an individual product provides a further descriptive page about the product, and links to the full text, if available. (Most products are available on the Web.) Ordering information for obtaining print and CD-ROM versions of products is also included. Many publications are available at no cost from the Education Publications Center (EDPubs), and a direct ordering system is linked with the product information pages.

The *Directory of NAEP Publications* is an extremely useful compilation of all government-funded NAEP publications published since the beginning of the NAEP program. Publications are listed by category, and arranged by year of publication within categories. Brief bibliographic information and the ERIC number if the publication is available through the ERIC system are given. The categories include "National Reports, "State Reports, "Abbreviated Documents," "Technical Reports," "Conference Proceedings and Commissioned Papers," "NAEP Evaluation Studies and Grant Publications," and "Subject Area Objectives, Frameworks, and Achievement Levels."

Two bibliographies of NAEP documents and journal articles that were included in the ERIC database are available. They are: *National Assessment of Educational Progress 1969–1983: A Bibliography of Documents in the ERIC Database,* and *National Assessment of Educational Progress 1983–1987: A Bibliography of Documents in the ERIC Database.*

Some NAEP publications have been distributed to depository libraries over the years under various SuDocs numbers and included in various series. For example, some NAEP publications have been distributed under the *General Publications* series of the Educational Research and Improvement Office (ED 1.302:) and in the *General Publications* (ED 1.102:) series of the Center for Education Statistics, cited in the "General Publications Series and Information" section of this chapter. Other publications issued as ERIC documents are included in the *Education Documents Announced in RIE* (ED 1.310/2:) series (see the "Educational Resources Information Center (ERIC) Sources" section of this chapter). The *Monthly Catalog* should be searched to determine whether an individual NAEP publication was distributed to depository libraries.

Two small titles of NAEP publications are presently being issued to depository libraries under individual SuDocs numbers, titled *NAEPfacts* and *Focus on NAEP.*

NAEPfacts provides brief summaries of the results of NAEP assessments. *Focus on NAEP* includes brief summaries of information about the ongoing development and implementation of NAEP. Sample titles of individual issues include *Long-Term Trends in Student Writing Performance* (ED 1.335:3/4), and *NAEP and Dance: Framework and Field Tests* (ED 1.335/2:3/1). These publications are also available on the Web from the *NAEP Home Page*.

STUDENT FINANCIAL AID SOURCES

Checklist

Student Financial Assistance. WEB. U.S. Department of Education. <http://www.ed.gov/finaid.html>.

  Content: information for students and parents; special initiatives; information for financial aid professionals.

Student Financial Assistance. WEB. U.S. Department of Education. Office of Student Financial Assistance Programs. <http://www.ed.gov/offices/OSFAP/Students/>.

  Content: general information about student financial aid; information on specific programs; application information.

The Student Guide. PRINT. WEB. (annual) U.S. Department of Education. ED 1.8/2:ST 9/5/year. Item 0461-B-01. <http://www.ed.gov/prog%5Finfo/SFA/StudentGuide/>; <http://purl.access.gpo.gov/GPO/LPS3842>.

  Content: comprehensive guide to student financial aid, including loans, work-study, and grants.

FAFSA on the Web. WEB. U.S. Department of Education. Office of Student Financial Assistance Programs. <http://www.fafsa.ed.gov/>.

  Content: electronic filing of the Free Application for Federal Student Aid form.

Funding Your Education. PRINT. WEB. (annual) U.S. Department of Education. Office of Student Financial Programs. ED 1.2:F 96/3/year. Item 0455-B-02. <http://www.ed.gov/prog_info/SFA/FYE/>; <http://purl.access.gpo.gov/GPO/LPS2830>.

  Content: overview of financial aid programs; how to apply for aid.

Information for Financial Aid Professionals. WEB. U.S. Department of Education. Office of Student Financial Assistance Programs. <http://ifap.ed.gov/dev_csb/new/home.nsf>.

  Content: site containing information needed by financial aid professionals in carrying out federal financial aid programs; includes publications and links to other related sites.

Welcome to the SFA Publication Listing. WEB. U.S. Department of Education. Office of Student Financial Assistance Programs. <http://ifap.ed.gov/csb_html/bookshlf.htm>.

  Content: listing and links to publications dealing with student financial aid program administration.

Student Financial Aid Handbook. PRINT. WEB. (annual) U.S. Department of Education. Office of Student Financial Assistance Programs. ED 1.45/4: Item 0461-B-04. <http://ifap.ed.gov/csb_html/fsfabknew.htm>; <http://purl.access.gpo.gov/GPO/LPS3883>.

  Content: comprehensive guide to federal financial aid requirements geared towards financial aid administrators.

Verification Guide. PRINT. WEB. U.S. Department of Education. Office of Student Financial Assistance Programs. ED 1.8:V 58/4/year. Item 0461-B-01. <http://ifap.ed.gov/csb_html/verifynew.htm>.

  Content: manual for the verification process for federal financial aid programs.

The Blue Book. PRINT. WEB. U.S. Department of Education. ED 1.2:B 62/year. Item 0455-B-02. <http://ifap.ed.gov/csb_html/bluebk.htm>.

  Content: manual for accounting, recordkeeping and reporting requirements.

Discussion

The first *Student Financial Assistance* page cited is part of the *U.S. Department of Education Home Page*. It provides some general information about student financial aid and gives links to some important pages for obtaining information for students and parents and for financial aid professionals. One of the pages it links to is also titled *Student Financial Assistance*, and this page serves as a gateway for information from the Office of Student Financial Assistance Programs. This page is geared toward students and their parents, and it comprehensively covers the information that students need to apply for financial aid. Major sections of the site include "Finding Out About Financial Aid," "Applying for Federal Student Aid," and "Paying Back Your Student Loan." Each topic includes a page of general information with links to more specific sites and information.

  Included at this site is the *Student Guide*, which is also issued in a print format. The *Student Guide* is a comprehensive guide to federal student financial aid. In addition to general information about federal student financial aid, the guide provides detailed information on major programs such as Pell Grants, Stafford Loans, and PLUS loans. It also describes the Federal Supplemental Educational Opportunity Grant (FSEOG) Program, the Federal Work-Study Program, and the Federal Perkins Loan Program. Application information and information about borrower responsibilities is also included. The *Student Guide* is one of the best sources for gaining an overall review of federal student aid programs. In addition to the Web version, a print version is also available.

  The *FAFSA on the Web* site makes it possible to electronically file the *Free Application for Federal Student Aid (FAFSA)*. The *FAFSA* is used to calculate an "Expected Family Contribution" (EFC) according to a formula set by Congress. This is used by schools to determine a student's eligibility for financial aid, including federal financial aid programs.

  Funding Your Education is aimed at prospective students and provides an overview of federal financial aid programs. It also covers the application process and eligibility requirements, and it includes lists of telephone numbers and URLs for further information. Its question-and-answer style provides an easy-to-read guide, particularly for high school students.

Information for Financial Aid Professionals contains detailed information for professionals involved in administering financial aid programs. It includes electronic versions of publications, forms, and manuals used by these professionals. The *Welcome to the SFA Publication Listing* page lists, describes, and links to the full text of these publications. Included among the publications at this site are three major manuals that are also distributed to depository libraries in a print format, and these are individually listed here. They include the *Student Financial Aid Handbook*, the *Verification Guide*, and *The Blue Book*. These manuals provide guidance for financial aid administrators in ensuring that the requirements of the federal financial aid programs are met.

EDUCATION PROGRAMS SOURCES

Checklist

Overview of ED Programs and Services. WEB. U.S. Department of Education. <http://www.ed.gov/Welcome/overview.html>.
 Content: summary of Department of Education programs.

Guide to U.S. Department of Education Programs and Services. WEB. U.S. Department of Education. <http://web99.ed.gov/ GTEP/Program2.nsf>.
 Content: catalog and detailed descriptions of U.S. Department of Education programs and services.

Biennial Evaluation Report. MF. WEB. U.S. Department of Education. ED 1.39: Item 0461-C-03. ASI 4804-5. <http:// www.ed.gov/programs.html>.
 Content: overview, evaluation, and summary of individual Department of Education programs.

Office of Inspector General Semi-Annual Report to Congress. MF. WEB. (semiannual) 1980–. U.S. Department of Education. Office of Inspector General. ED 1.26: Item 0455-L. ASI 4802-1. <http://www.vais.net/~edoig/sarpages.htm>.
 Content: report of investigatory activities of the Office of Inspector General.

Discussion

This section lists general sources that report on the programs of the Department of Education. The *U.S. Department of Education Home Page* (listed earlier) and individual Web sites of offices administering programs should also be consulted for information. The *Overview of ED Programs and Services* provides a concise summary and overview of the various programs of the Department of Education. Links for further information on specific programs are included within the text.

One of the best sources for obtaining information about U.S. Department of Education programs is the comprehensive Web-based catalog, the *Guide to U.S. Department of Education Programs and Services*. The interface allows the user to view program entries by categories. The categories included are "By Topical Heading," "By CFDA #" (*Catalog of Federal Domestic Assistance* number), "By Administering Office," "By Who May Apply," "By Education Level," "By Subject Index," and "By Assistance." Each entry includes basic information about the program, such as the title and administering office; appropriations information; awards information; a program details section that describes the program; and contact information.

The *Biennial Evaluation Report* provides an overview and evaluation of more than 150 programs administered by the Department of Education. It includes detailed descriptions, analysis, and evaluation of individual Department of Education programs. Descriptions may include statistical information, funding history, program effectiveness and progress, program goals and objectives, strategies to achieve goals, sources of evaluation studies, and contacts for obtaining further information about the program.

The *Office of Inspector General Semi-Annual Report to Congress* reports on the audit, investigation, and fraud control activities of the office. The Office of Inspector General is responsible for monitoring Department of Education programs.

INDEXES

Checklist

Catalog of United States Government Publications (MOCAT). WEB. 1994–. U.S. Government Printing Office. Superintendent of Documents. <http://www.gpo.gov/catalog>; <http:/ /www.access.gpo.gov/su_docs/locators/cgp/index.html>; <http://purl.access.gpo.gov/GPO/LPS844>.

Monthly Catalog of United States Government Publications. CD-ROM. 1996–. U.S. Government Printing Office. Superintendent of Documents. GP 3.8/7: Item 0557-C. GPO.

Monthly Catalog of United States Government Publications (Condensed version). PRINT. (monthly) 1996–. U.S. Government Printing Office. Superintendent of Documents. GP 3.8/8: (Earlier full version, GP 3.8:, 1895-1995) Item 0557-D. GPO.

American Statistics Index (ASI). PRINT. (monthly) 1973–. Bethesda, MD: Congressional Information Service.

Statistical Universe. WEB. Bethesda, MD: Congressional Information Service.

Discussion

The *Monthly Catalog* is the most comprehensive index to government publications. To find materials relating to education, search under headings and keywords beginning with "Education," and "Educational," "Adult Education," "Degrees, Higher Education," "Black Colleges," "Black Students," "Discrimination in Education," "Higher Education," "National Assessment of Educational Progress," "Public Schools," headings beginning with "School," "Schools," "Teachers," "Teaching," "Universities," "Colleges," and names of subjects subdivided by the term "Education." There are many other subject headings dealing with educational subjects. More specific aspects of education should be searched under the appropriate narrower subject term. The complete version of the *Monthly Catalog* is available on the Web and CD-ROM. Commercial online and CD-ROM versions of the *Monthly Catalog* are also available

To locate additional documents in *American Statistics Index (ASI)* search under headings such as those beginning with the term "Education," "Educational," "Adult education," "Curricula," "Degrees, higher education," "Black colleges," "Black students," "Discrimination in education," "Higher education," "Elementary and secondary education," "Federal aid to education," "Federal aid to higher education," "Federal aid to medical education," "Federal aid to vocational education," "National Assessment of Educational Progress," "Preschool education," "Private schools," and headings beginning with "School," "Special education," "Student aid," "Students," "Teachers," "Colleges and universities," and "Vocational education and training."

Statistical Universe includes a Web version of *ASI.*

For more information on these indexes, see Chapter 3, "The Basics of Searching."

GPO Subject Bibliographies. PRINT. WEB. GP 3.22/2:

<http://bookstore.gpo.gov/sb/about.html>

No. 83   "Educational Statistics"

No. 196 "Elementary and Secondary Education"

No. 217 "Higher Education"

Chapter 21
Geology

Most government publications and resources pertaining to geology are issued by the U.S. Geological Survey (USGS). The USGS issues a number of individual research publications within series of research reports. A great deal of geological information is also available online from USGS Web sites. This chapter cites and describes both technical sources and more general publications. Mineral and mineral industry information is specifically included as a separate section of this chapter. The Geological Survey also issues many geologic maps, and Chapter 16, "Maps," should also be consulted for geologic mapping.

SEARCH STRATEGY

This chapter shows a subject search strategy. Steps to follow are
1. Consult the listings of major series, publications, and online resources in this chapter;
2. Use the sources in the "Publication Listings and Databases" section of this chapter to locate specific USGS reports;
3. Search the *Monthly Catalog* for additional publications;
4. Use *American Statistics Index (ASI)* to search for statistical information relating to geology; and
5. Use the "Related Material" section to obtain additional information on geologic publications.

U.S. GEOLOGICAL SURVEY GENERAL PUBLICATIONS AND SOURCES

Checklist

U.S. Geological Survey Home Page. WEB. U.S. Department of the Interior. Geological Survey. <http://www.usgs.gov/>.
>   Content: general information about the USGS; products and data; browse by topics; news; audience tracks for information; links to other areas of the USGS Web site.

Geologic Information. WEB. U.S. Department of the Interior. Geological Survey. <http://geology.usgs.gov/index.shtml>.
>   Content: general information; earthquake information; research; products; regional information; ask-a-geologist.

Water Resources of the United States. WEB. U.S. Department of the Interior. Geological Survey. <http://water.usgs.gov/>.
>   Content: general information; news; water data; publications and products; programs; local information.

Annual Financial Report. MF. WEB. (annual) 1977–. U.S. Department of the Interior. Geological Survey. I 19.1: (Earlier title: *United States Geological Survey Yearbook*.) Item 0621-C. ASI 5664-8. <http://geology.usgs.gov/yrbooks.html>.
>   Content: annual review of USGS activities, programs, and finances.

General Publications. PRINT. MF. (irregular) U.S. Department of the Interior. Geological Survey. I 19.2: Item 0621.
>   Content: general publications pertaining to the USGS and geologic topics.

General Interest Publications [Online]. WEB. U.S. Department of the Interior. Geological Survey. <http://geology.usgs.gov/gip.html>.

Discussion

The United States Geological Survey (USGS) has a very well developed Web Site, and they use it effectively to provide information about their activities, programs, and products. Their home page is a good starting point for learning about the geologic resources that USGS has to offer. It offers a browse-by-topics approach; approaches for particular audience "tracks," such as scientists or teachers and students; and a large listing of links to major products and data. Two individual Web pages within the USGS Web site are of particular interest to those seeking geologic information and are cited here. They are titled *Geologic Information* and *Water Resources of the United States*.

The *Annual Financial Report* reviews USGS activities for the year. In a report full of photos and illustrations, information on the USGS in general and descriptions of specific programs are given. Financial information on funding for the USGS and information about the USGS structure are also included. This report is a good source for obtaining a concise overview of current developments in USGS programs.

The *General Publications* series of the USGS is made up of a large collection of miscellaneous publications. Some documents are guides to USGS publications, services, and programs, while others cover topics of a more general nature. Sample titles in this series include *Opportunities for Geologists and Geophysicists* (I 19.2:OP 5/2), *Aerial Photographs and Satellite Images* (I 19.2:AE 8/2/997), and *The Value of Metadata: National Spatial Data Infrastructure* (I 19.2:M 56/5/998).

The USGS has selected some of the most popular of its general interest publications and made electronic versions available on the Web at its *General Interest Publications [Online]* page. Included are such publications as *Acid Rain and Our Nation's Capital* <http://pubs.usgs.gov/gip/acidrain/>, *Fossils, Rocks, and Time* <http://pubs.usgs.gov/gip/fossils/>, and *Natural Gemstones* <http://pubs.usgs.gov/gip/gemstones/>.

U.S. GEOLOGICAL SURVEY REPORTS SERIES

U.S. Geological Survey Bulletin. PRINT. WEB. (irregular) 1883. U.S. Department of the Interior. Geological Survey. I 19.3: Item 0620. Selected publications: <http://greenwood.cr.usgs.gov/maps/bulletins.html>; <http://purl.access.gpo.gov/GPO/LPS2909>.

Content: results of geological studies.

U.S. Geological Survey Circular. PRINT. WEB. (irregular) 1933–. U.S. Department of the Interior. Geological Survey. I 19.4/2: Item 0620-A. <http://geo-www.er.usgs.gov/circular.html>.

Content: reports on geological studies.

U.S. Geological Survey Professional Paper. PRINT. WEB. (irregular) 1902–. U.S. Department of the Interior. Geological Survey. I 19.16: Item 0624. Selected publications: <http://geology.usgs.gov/profpaper.html>.

Content: formal reports of Geological Survey studies.

Open File Report. MF. WEB. (irregular) U.S. Department of the Interior. Geological Survey. I 19.76: Item 0624-H. Selected publications: <http://geology.usgs.gov/open-file/>; <http://purl.access.gpo.gov/GPO/LPS2141>.

Content: informal reports of Geological Survey studies and investigations.

U.S. Geological Survey Water-Supply Paper. PRINT. WEB. (irregular) 1896–. U.S. Department of the Interior. Geological Survey. I 19.13: Item 0625. Selected publications: <http://geology.usgs.gov/wsp.html>.

Content: reports on water resources research.

Water-Resources Investigations Report. PRINT. (irregular) 1973–. U.S. Department of the Interior. Geological Survey. I 19.42/4: Item 0624-B.

Content: informal reports of studies and investigations dealing with water resources.

Water Resources Data. [state]. MF. (annual) U.S. Department of the Interior. Geological Survey. I 19.53/2: Item 0619-E-01 to 53. ASI 5666-10,-12,-16, -20, -22. Alaska: <http://www-water-ak.usgs.gov/Publications/Water-Data/>.

Content: reports on water resources and quality for individual states.

National Water Conditions. WEB. (monthly) U.S. Department of the Interior. Geological Survey. I 19.42: Item 0624-B. <http://water.usgs.gov/nwc/>.

Content: monthly U.S. map and report of water conditions.

Discussion

The *U.S. Geological Survey Bulletin* series reports on the progress or results of various geological studies. Some *Bulletins* describe the USGS's methods and techniques. Maps often accompany the reports. Sample titles include *The Chemical Analysis of Argonne Premium Coal Samples* (I 19.3:2144), *Mineral Resource Potential and Teology of the San Juan National Forest, Colorado* (I 19.3:2127), and *Clastic Rocks Associated with the Midcontinent Rift System in Iowa* (I 19.3:1989-I). The *U.S. Geological Survey Circular* series reports on similar topics. However, reports are less formally presented, or are on a topic of more limited or temporary usefulness.

The *U.S. Geological Survey Professional Paper* series is made up of the formal reports of resource, topographic, hydrologic, paleontologic and geologic studies. Reports range in size from a few pages to book length. Reports often include various accompanying materials, such as photographs and maps. Sample titles include: *Geochemistry and Stratigraphic Relations of Middle Proterozoic Rocks of the New Jersey Highlands* (19.16:1565-C), *Structural Relationships of Pre-Tertiary Rocks In The Nevada Test Site Region, Southern Nevada* (I 19.16:P 1607), and *Ground-Water Hydrology and Simulated Effects of Development in The Milford Area, an Arid Basin in Southwestern Utah* (I 19.16:1409-G).

The *Open File Report* publications are an informal series of reports, maps, and other materials, such as slides, photographs, data sets, and other electronic products. Materials are placed in the *Open File Report* series in order to make them available for public use. They cover all aspects of the Geological Survey's work. Titles include *Nitrate and Pesticide Data for Waters of The Mid-Atlantic Region* (I 19.76:98-158), *Documentation for HYDMOD: A Program for Extracting and Processing Time-Series Data* (19.76:98-564), and *Leachate Chemistry Data for Solid Mine Waste Composite Samples from Silverton and Leadville, Colorado* (I 19.76:98-621).

The *U.S .Geological Survey Water Supply Paper* series consists of reports on geology, hydrology, and other topics related to water resources. Reports often cover specific streams, rivers, or geographic areas. Titles include *A Generalized Estimate of Ground-Water-Recharge Rates in the Lower Peninsula Of Michigan* (I 19.13:2437), *Ground-Water-Quality Assessment of the Central Oklahoma Aquifer, Oklahoma: Results of Investigations* (I 19.13:2357-A), and *Estimation of Roughness Coefficients for Natural Stream Channels with Vegetated Banks* (I 19.13:2441).

Water-Resources Investigations Reports is a series of informal reports dealing with various aspects of water resources. Titles in this series include *Water Resources of the Prairie Island Indian Reservation, Minnesota, 1994–97* (I 19.42/4:99-4069), *Reconfigured-Channel Monitoring and Assessment Program* (I 19.42/4:99-4111), and *Record Extension And Streamflow Statistics for the Pleasant River, Maine* (I 19.42/4:99-4078).

Reports in the *Water Resources Data. [state]* series are prepared cooperatively with state agencies and include records of stream flow, ground water levels, and quality of water. They also include a summary of hydrologic conditions for the state. The main portion of each report is a series of water quality and water discharge records for river basins throughout the state.

The *National Water Conditions* uses water resources data to create a monthly map and report of above normal, normal, and below normal streamflow conditions. Also included are data on water conditions in selected individual states, data on pH of precipitation, and data on daily streamflow conditions.

EARTHQUAKE DATA
Checklist

National Earthquake Information Center. WEB. U.S. Department of the Interior. Geological Survey. <http://neic.usgs.gov>.
> Content: general information; products and services; earthquake data; earthquake information sources.

Earthquake Search. WEB. U.S. Department of the Interior. Geological Survey. <http://neic.usgs.gov/neis/epic/epic.html>.
> Content: databases of information about earthquakes.

Preliminary Determination of Epicenters. MF. WEB. (monthly). U.S. Department of the Interior. Geological Survey. National Earthquake Information Center. I 19.66: Item 0192-C. (Web version includes the weekly *Preliminary Determination of Epicenters*, I 19.66/2:, Nondepository) <http://gldss7.cr.usgs.gov/site.html>; <http://purl.access.gpo.gov/GPO/LPS3194>.
> Content: listing and description of earthquake activity.

United States Earthquakes. PRINT. (annual) 1928–. U.S. Department of the Interior. Geological Survey. I 19.65/2: (Issued as part of the U.S. Geological Survey Bulletin series) (1986 is No. 2089) (Pre-1981 issues C 55.226:; issued jointly by the Department of Commerce and Department of the Interior.) Item 0208. ASI 5664-13.
> Content: describes all reported earthquakes in the United States.

Discussion

The National Earthquake Information Center (NEIC) is the national data center and archive for earthquake information. As part of its mission, it determines the location and size of all destructive earthquakes worldwide. In addition to collecting and disseminating data, NEIC also carries out various research initiatives. NEIC's Web site is one of the best places to begin locating earthquake information. Included at the site are constantly updated current and near-real-time earthquake information, general information and publications about earthquakes, and information about NEIC products and services.

Also included at the NEIC site is the *Earthquake Search* page, which allows the user to search a series of databases of earthquake information. The user has the option to select a specific database and the output file type. The search can also be limited to certain parameters such as date, magnitude, depth, and intensity.

Preliminary Determination of Epicenters gives a worldwide listing of all earthquakes detected, with the date and time of shock; location, depth and magnitude; and region in which the earthquake centered. The monthly version of this is distributed to depository libraries in microfiche. Both a weekly and monthly version are available as FTP files from the NEIC site. *Preliminary Determination of Epicenters* is also one of the databases searchable through the *Earthquake Database*.

United States Earthquakes includes a state-by-state description of all U.S. earthquakes, giving the origin time, epicenter, magnitude, and intensity. A table following the description provides summary information on U.S. earthquakes. Other sections of the report describe "Network Operations," "Miscellaneous Activities," and "Strong-Motion Seismographic Data." Publication of *United States Earthquakes* lags considerably—the 1986 volume was published in 1995.

SOURCES ON MINERALS
Checklist

Minerals Statistics and Information. WEB. U.S. Department of the Interior. Geological Survey. <http://minerals.usgs.gov/minerals/>.
> Content: general information; products; contacts; mineral statistics and information by commodity, country, and state.

Minerals Management Service Home Page. WEB. U.S. Department of the Interior. Minerals Management Service. <http://www.mms.gov/>.
> Content: general information; royalty programs; offshore programs; library; products and services.

Statistical Abstract of the United States. PRINT. WEB. (annual) 1878–. U.S. Department of Commerce. Economics and Statistics Administration. Bureau of the Census. C 3.134: Item 0150. ASI 2324-1. GPO. <http://www.census.gov/statab/www/>; <http://purl.access.gpo.gov/GPO/LPS2878>.
> Coverage: U.S. regions, divisions, states.
> Content: statistics on mining; mineral industries; mineral production, value, and prices; mineral commodities.

Statistical Abstract of the United States. CD-ROM. (annual) 1993–. U.S. Department of Commerce. Bureau of the Census. C 3.134/7: Item 0150-B. ASI 2324-14.

Content: CD-ROM version of the *Statistical Abstract*.

Historical Statistics of the United States: Colonial Times to 1970. Parts 1-2. PRINT. (1975) U.S. Department of Commerce. Bureau of the Census. C 3.134/2:H 62/789-970/pt.1-2. Item 0151. ASI (76) 2328-2. GPO.
    Content: historical statistics on mineral products and production.

Historical Statistics of the United States on CD-ROM: Colonial Times to 1970. CD-ROM. (1997) New York, NY: Cambridge University Press.
    Content: CD-ROM version of *Historical Statistics of the United States*

Minerals Yearbook. PRINT. WEB. (annual) 1932–. U.S. Department of the Interior. Geological Survey. I 19.165: (Earlier, I 28.37:. Issued since 1882 under other titles). Item 0639. ASI 5664-25, -26, -31. GPO. <http://minerals.usgs.gov/minerals/pubs/myb.html>; <http://purl.access.gpo.gov/GPO/LPS2120>.
    Coverage: countries, U.S.
    Content: production; consumption; trade; sales; prices; value; trends; developments.

Minerals and Materials Information. CD-ROM. 1994–. U.S. Department of the Interior. Geological Survey. I 19.120/4: Item 0639-J. ASI 5662-8.
    Content: *Minerals Yearbook* and other mineral publications.

Mineral Commodity Summaries. WEB. (annual) 1975–. U.S. Department of the Interior. Geological Survey. I 19.166: Item 0621-J. ASI 5664-22. GPO. <http://minerals.usgs.gov/minerals/pubs/mcs/>; <http://purl.access.gpo.gov/GPO/LPS5131>.
    Coverage: world, country groupings, selected countries, U.S.
    Content: compilation of brief mineral commodity profiles.

Mineral Industry Surveys. WEB. (frequencies and dates vary) U.S. Department of the Interior. Geological Survey. ASI 5662-5, 5662-6, 5664-21, 5664-23, 5664-24, 5664-30. <http://minerals.usgs.gov/minerals/pubs/commodity/mis.html>.
    Coverage: selected countries, U.S., states.
    Content: series of commodity reports; production; shipments, stocks; consumption; use; sales; prices; exports and imports; major events.

Annual Report on Alaska's Mineral Resources. PRINT. (annual) U.S. Department of the Interior. Geological Survey. Geological Survey Circular. I 19.4/4: Item 0620-A. ASI 5664-11.
    Content: information pertaining to minerals in Alaska gathered by various federal agencies.

Economic Census. PRINT. WEB. (quinquennial) 1997–. U.S. Department of Commerce. Economics and Statistics Administration. Census Bureau. (Formerly published as individual censuses for specific economic sectors.) ASI 2511, 2513, 2515, 2517. <http://www.census.gov/epcd/www/econ97.html>; <http://www.census.gov/mp/www/pub/ind/msind.html#Industry>; <http://www.census.gov/prod/www/abs/economic.html>.
    Coverage: U.S., states, offshore areas.

Content: number of establishments; number of employees; payroll; value added by mining; cost of supplies used; value of shipments and receipts; gross book value of depreciable/depletable assets; capital expenditures.

Economic Census. CD-ROM. (quinquennial) 1987–. U.S. Department of Commerce. Economics and Statistics Administration. Bureau of the Census. C 3.277: Item 0154-C.
    Coverage: U.S., states, counties, metropolitan areas, places of 2,500 or more, zip codes.
    Content: *Economic Census* reports.

American FactFinder. WEB. U.S. Department of Commerce. Bureau of the Census. <http://factfinder.census.gov/java_prod/dads.ui.homePage.HomePage>.
    Coverage: U.S., states, counties, metropolitan areas, places.
    Content: 1997 *Economic Census* data; other census products.

Census of Mineral Industries. PRINT. WEB. (quinquennial) 1954–1992. U.S. Department of Commerce. Bureau of the Census. C 3.216/ (Formerly included in the comprehensive decennial census.) Item 0158. ASI 2513. <http://www.census.gov/epcd/www/92result.html>; <http://www.census.gov/mp/www/pub/ind/msind.html>; <http://www.census.gov/prod/www/abs/manu-min.html>.
    Coverage: U.S., regions, divisions, states, counties.
    Content: economic census of mineral industry establishments.

Discussion

Most of the information on minerals is produced by the Geological Survey, with mineral industry information produced by the Bureau of the Census. Most of this information is now accessible on the Web, and in some cases is only available electronically. The *Minerals Statistics and Information* Web page of the Geological Survey is an excellent starting point for accessing mineral sources produced by the Survey. Links to information by commodity, state, or country make it easy to quickly locate relevant resources. Many of the publications included at the site are individually described later in this section. The Minerals Management Service (MMS) is involved with the management of leasing rights for the Outer Continental Shelf and the management of mineral revenue from Federal and Indian lands. Its Web site is also listed here.

Both the *Statistical Abstract of the United States* and *Historical Statistics of the United States* provide basic statistics on minerals and mineral industries. The full text of recent editions of the *Statistical Abstract* is available on the Census Bureau Web site as PDF files. The *Statistical Abstract* is also available on CD-ROM. A CD-ROM version of *Historical Statistics* is available from Cambridge University Press.

The *Minerals Yearbook* is a standard source for information on mineral industries and commodities. At present three volumes are published each year: *Metals and Minerals*, *Area Reports: Domestic*, and *Area Reports: International*. Volume 1, *Metals and Minerals*, consists of chapters on each commodity, which discuss and provide statistics on domestic production, consumption and uses, stocks, prices, and foreign trade. Each commodity chapter also often includes sections on legislation and government programs, world review, current research and technology, and outlook. Volume 2 contains reports on each state, which review the state's mineral commodities, the economic situation, the industry, and important events and issues affecting the industry. Specific companies may be mentioned. Volume 3 is issued in parts by region and contains country reports covering industry structure, production, trade, government policies, and a review of individual commodities produced by that country. The *Minerals Yearbook* is also available on the Web and on CD-ROM. (See Figure 21.1.)

The *Mineral Commodity Summaries* series includes a collection of brief profiles of over 80 nonfuel mineral commodities. Each profile includes statistics and data on such areas as domestic production and use, recycling, import sources, tariffs, world production and reserve base, and world resources. Although not as comprehensive as the *Minerals Yearbook*, it is a good source for a quick overview of a mineral commodity.

Mineral Industry Surveys consists of several individual reports on individual minerals. Reports are issued monthly or quarterly, with annual summaries. Annual summary information is also included within the *Minerals Yearbook*. Such minerals as manganese, copper, sulfur, tungsten, cobalt, platinum, and vanadium are covered by *Mineral Industry Surveys*. Reports include a brief summary of trends and events along with key statistics.

The *Annual Report on Alaska's Mineral Resources* is a recurring title in the *U.S. Geological Survey Circular* series that has been given a distinct SuDocs number. It provides an annual summary of information gathered by various federal agencies on Alaskan minerals.

The *Economic Census* is taken every five years, covering years ending in "2" and in "7." The data are collected in the year following the year of coverage (the 1997 census was conducted in 1998) and data may begin to appear in the year following that. It may take as long as three years after the census year for all publications and information to be made available. The exact content and component publications of the *Economic Census* have varied over the years. Major changes took place beginning with the 1997 *Economic Census* both in organization and in publishing formats. Previously, a separate *Census of Mineral Industries* title was produced. Most relevant mineral industry information in the 1997 Economic Census will be included in the mining sector. The definition of mining as used by the Census Bureau is "the extraction of naturally occurring mineral solids, such as coal and ores; liquid minerals, such as petroleum; and gases, such as natural gas. The term mining is used in the broad sense to include quarrying, well operations, beneficiating (e.g., crushing, screening, washing, and floatation), and other preparations customarily performed at the mine site or as part of the mining activities."

A series of industry, geographic area, and subject reports will be issued for the mining sector. Also beginning with 1997, data are published almost entirely on the Internet and on CD-ROM with only a small number of summary publications published in print format. A summary report will be issued in print, but most reports will be available on the Census Web site as PDF files or through the *American FactFinder* database, and on CD-ROM.

The geographic areas series will provide mineral statistics for the U.S. and states. It will contain general statistics on the number of establishments, sales or other revenue measure, payroll, and employment by kind of business or NAICS code. The industry series will include such reports as "Anthracite Mining," "Crushed and Broken Granite Mining and Quarrying," and "Lead Ore and Zinc Ore Mining." and include detailed industry statistics, product shipments by detailed product code, and materials consumed. U.S and state data are covered. Subject reports will also be issued.

The Census Bureau's *Economic Census* Web page lists reports from the 1997 census with links to the full text as they are released. A link is also available for the 1992 *Census of Mineral Industries* reports. General information about the *Census* is also available, including the *Guide to the 1997 Economic Census*.

American FactFinder is a Census Bureau Web database designed to provide access to data from the 1990 and 2000 *Census of Population and Housing*, the *American Community Survey*, and the 1997 *Economic Census*. It also contains a mapping feature and an option to search for information on Census Bureau products. 1997 *Economic Census* data are available in the "Industry and Business Facts" section as it is released. The Quick Industry Report option allows the user to select from a list of NAICS sectors and code numbers or to search by word to identify and display an industry report. Similarly, the Quick Geographic Report option can be used to display a geographic area report. A "Build a Query" option is also available.

PUBLICATION LISTINGS AND DATABASES
Checklist

Search Publications of the U.S. Geological Survey. WEB. 1880–. U.S. Department of the Interior. Geological Survey. <http://usgs-georef.cos.com/>.

Content: bibliographic database of all U.S. Geological Survey reports.

New Publications of the U.S. Geological Survey. PRINT. (quarterly) U.S. Department of the Interior. Geological Survey. I 19.14/4: Item 0622.

Content: quarterly listing of USGS publications.

New Publications of the U.S. Geological Survey. WEB. (monthly) U.S. Department of the Interior. Geological Survey. I 19.14/4-

COBALT

By Kim B. Shedd

Domestic survey data and tables were prepared by Jo-Ann S. Sterling, statistical assistant, and the world production tables were prepared by Ronald Hatch and Glenn J. Wallace, international data coordinators.

Cobalt is a strategic and critical metal used in many diverse industrial and military applications. The largest use of cobalt is in superalloys, which are used to make parts for gas turbine aircraft engines. Cobalt is also used to make magnets; corrosion- and wear-resistant alloys; high-speed steels; cemented carbides (also called hardmetals) and diamond tools; catalysts for the petroleum and chemical industries; drying agents for paints, varnishes, and inks; ground coats for porcelain enamels; pigments; battery electrodes; steel-belted radial tires; and magnetic recording media.

The United States is the world's largest consumer of cobalt. With the exception of negligible amounts of byproduct cobalt produced as intermediate products from some mining operations, the United States did not mine or refine cobalt in 1998. The U.S. Government maintained significant quantities of cobalt metal in the National Defense Stockpile (NDS) for military, industrial, and essential civilian use during a national emergency. Since 1993, sales of excess cobalt from the NDS have contributed to U.S. and world supplies.

World refined cobalt production continued to increase in 1998. Because no new sources of refined cobalt came into production, the increase was from existing producers. The annual rate of growth in world demand for refined cobalt decreased, primarily as a result of the economic recession in Asia and inventory reductions by consumers. The increase in availability, combined with a slowdown in demand, resulted in a significant decrease cobalt prices, particularly during the second half of the year (Cobalt Development Institute, 1999; Hawkins, 1999). The decrease in cobalt prices, as well as those of copper and nickel, resulted in delays in or postponements of various mining and refining projects that had been planning to produce cobalt. Certain projects in the Democratic Republic of the Congo [Congo (Kinshasa)] were also negatively affected by the ongoing civil war in that country.

Salient U.S. and world cobalt statistics for 1998 and the previous 4 years are listed in table 1. With the exception of prices and reported production from foreign countries, all quantity and value data in this report have been rounded to three significant digits. Totals and percentages were calculated from unrounded numbers.

Legislation and Government Programs

The Defense Logistics Agency (DLA) held monthly sealed-bid cobalt offerings during fiscal year 1998 (October 1, 1997, through September 30, 1998). During the fiscal year, the DLA sold 2,510 metric tons (t) of cobalt valued at nearly $102 million (table 2). This equaled 92% of the 2,720-t (6 million pounds) maximum allowed for sale under the 1998 Annual Materials Plan (AMP). The value of the cobalt sold represented 22% of the total value of all materials sold from the NDS that year. Cobalt has been the top selling material in terms of total dollar value for 4 of the 6 years since cobalt sales began. The AMP for fiscal year 1999 (October 1, 1998, through September 30, 1999) set the maximum allowable sale of cobalt at 2,720 t.

The DLA held 12 monthly cobalt offerings during calendar year 1998 and sold 1,950 t of cobalt valued at $77 million. On December 31, the total uncommitted cobalt inventory held by the DLA was 14,600 t, all of which was authorized for eventual disposal.

In August, the U.S. Environmental Protection Agency (EPA) issued a final rule that added spent hydrotreating and hydrorefining catalysts to a list of hazardous wastes under the Resource Conservation and Recovery Act. As a result of the ruling, these materials will be subject to management and treatment standards and to emergency notification requirements for releases of hazardous substances to the environment. The EPA's decision to classify these materials as hazardous was based on risks associated with their benzene and arsenic contents and on their potential to ignite spontaneously. In response to industry concern regarding the impact that the ruling might have on current catalyst regeneration, metal reclaiming, and recycling activities, the EPA stated that the decision was based primarily on the results of the risk assessment and that the potential impact of the decision on current (1998) catalyst-treatment practices was not a central issue in the decision (U.S. Environmental Protection Agency, 1998, p. 42110-42111, 42118-42121, 42154-42158).

Production

With the exception of negligible amounts of byproduct cobalt produced from some mining operations, the United States did not mine or refine cobalt in 1998. The U.S. Department of the Interior's Minerals Management Service (1999) reported sales of 44 t of cobalt valued at $101,000 from Federal lands in Missouri in 1998. Cobalt is present in the ores mined for platinum-group metals at the Stillwater Complex of southern Montana. At the Stillwater Mining Co.'s metallurgical complex in Columbus, MT, converter matte from the precious metals smelter was processed at the base metals refinery. Nickel-copper-cobalt sulfate solution from the refinery was sold to Westaim Corp. of Edmonton, Alberta, Canada. In 1998, Stillwater Mining began construction of a nickel-copper refining circuit as part of an expansion of the base metal refinery (Stillwater Mining Co., 1999, p. 9).

Source: *Minerals Yearbook*, 1998, Cobalt, p. T1.

Figure 21.1: Sample Page from *Minerals Yearbook*.

2: Item 0621-J. <http://pubs.usgs.gov/publications/>; <http://purl.access.gpo.gov/GPO/LPS1574>.
> Content: monthly listing of USGS publications.

Selected Water-Resources Abstracts. WEB. 1977–1997. U.S. Department of the Interior. Geological Survey. <http://water.usgs.gov/public/swra/index.html>.
> Content: bibliographic database of U.S. Geological Survey reports on water resources.

Discussion

The *Search Publications of the U.S. Geological Survey* Web database covers all USGS publications and non-USGS publications by USGS authors since 1983. The database is a subset of the American Geological Institute's *GeoRef* database. Some entries contain abstracts. The database can be searched by numerous fields including subject, title, author, keyword, journal or proceedings title, date, and type of map or document.

New Publications of the U.S. Geological Survey provides a listing of new USGS publications. Publications are arranged by categories and individual series of publications. The print version is produced quarterly, and the Web version monthly. The Web version also includes linked URLs as appropriate.

The *Selected Water-Resources Abstracts* Web database contains abstracts of USGS water resource publications compiled from several sources. Searches can be done by USGS series report numbers, keyword, author, hydrologic unit number, state, series, and year. The database presently ends with 1997. The help file indicates that the database will be added to as resources permit.

INDEXES
Checklist

Catalog of United States Government Publications (MOCAT). WEB. 1994–. U.S. Government Printing Office. Superintendent of Documents. <http://www.gpo.gov/catalog>; <http://www.access.gpo.gov/su_docs/locators/cgp/index.html>; <http://purl.access.gpo.gov/GPO/LPS844>.

Monthly Catalog of United States Government Publications. CD-ROM. 1996–. U.S. Government Printing Office. Superintendent of Documents. GP 3.8/7: Item 0557-C. GPO.

Monthly Catalog of United States Government Publications (Condensed version). PRINT. (monthly) 1996–. U.S. Government Printing Office. Superintendent of Documents. GP 3.8/8: (Earlier full version, GP 3.8:, 1895-1995). Item 0557-D. GPO.

American Statistics Index (ASI). PRINT. (monthly) 1973–. Bethesda, MD: Congressional Information Service.

Statistical Universe. WEB. Bethesda, MD: Congressional Information Service.

Discussion

The *Monthly Catalog* is a comprehensive index to government publications. The complete version is available on the Web and on CD-ROM. To find additional publications pertaining to geology, search subject headings and keywords beginning with "Geology," "Geomorphology," "Geophysics," "Geothermal Resources," "Mine," "Mines," "Mines and Mineral Resources," "Mining," "Hydrology," "Earthquakes," and "Mineral Industries."

American Statistics Index (ASI) is a comprehensive index to U.S. statistical information. To locate additional statistical information regarding geology, search under the following subject headings: "Geology," "Geological Survey," "Earthquakes," "Volcanoes," "Mineral Industry Surveys," "Mines and mineral resources," and the names of specific mineral commodities. The "Index by Categories" can also be searched "By Commodity," and "By Industry." *Statistical Universe* includes a Web version of *ASI*.

For more information on these indexes, see Chapter 3, "The Basics of Searching."

RELATED MATERIAL
Within this Work

Chapter 16 Maps

Chapter 18 Agriculture

Chapter 22 Environment

Chapter 31 Business and Industry Statistics

Chapter 41 Energy Statistics

Chapter 42 Projections

GPO Subject Bibliographies. PRINT. WEB. GP 3.22/2:

<http://bookstore.gpo.gov/sb/about.html>

No. 102 "Maps and Atlases"

No. 183 "Surveying and Mapping"

CHAPTER 22
Environment

Many materials relating to the environment are published by such government agencies as the Agriculture Department, Commerce Department, Energy Department, Environmental Protection Agency, and Interior Department. Congress also publishes many environmental materials. This chapter lists some basic resources that may be useful to consult at the beginning of a search on an environmental topic.

SEARCH STRATEGY

This chapter shows a subject search strategy. Suggested steps for searching are

1. Locate general overviews of environmental issues under the "General Environmental Sources" section in this chapter;
2. Use the "EPA Electronic Resources and Databases" to find full-text publications and local area environmental data on the Web;
3. Scan the specific environmental area sections for topics of interest: "Sources on Air," "Sources on Water," "Sources on Hazardous and Solid Waste," "Sources on Industry," "Sources on Fish and Wildlife," and "Sources on Public Lands";
4. Consult "Congressional Sources" for public policy and legislative discussion and analysis;
5. Consider the "EPA Publication Catalogs" for complete bibliographic listings of EPA publications, including non-depository materials; and
6. Consult the indexes and "Related Materials" section for more generally available publications in these and related areas.

GENERAL ENVIRONMENTAL SOURCES
Checklist

Environmental Quality. MF. WEB. (annual) 1970–. U.S. Executive Office of the President. Council on Environmental Qual-

ity. PREX 14.1: Item 0856-E-01. ASI 484-1. GPO.<http://ceq.eh.doe.gov/nepa/reports/reports.htm>.

> Coverage: world, world regions, U.S., regions, states, selected metropolitan areas.
> Content: survey of environmental conditions, trends, issues, national strategies, and programs; statistics on environmental economics, ecosystems, energy, water resources, air quality, land resources, pollution, transportation, and atmosphere.

Statistical Abstract of the United States. PRINT. WEB. (annual) 1878–. U.S. Department of Commerce. Economics and Statistics Administration. Bureau of the Census. C 3.134: Item 0150. ASI 2324-1. GPO.<http://www.census.gov/statab/www/>; <http://purl.access.gpo.gov/GPO/LPS2878>.

> Coverage: U.S., states, individual bodies of water.
> Content: land and water area; land ownership and use; water use; water quality violation rate; oil spills; air pollutant concentration and emissions; solid waste generation, disposal, and recovery; toxic chemical releases; hazardous waste sites; environmental industry revenue and employment; threatened and endangered species.

EPA United States Environmental Protection Agency Web Site. WEB. U.S. Environmental Protection Agency.<http://www.epa.gov/>.

> Content: agency information and news; full-text publications and databases.

General Publications. PRINT. MF. (irregular) U.S. Environmental Protection Agency. EP 1.2: Item 0431-I-01. GPO.

> Content: miscellaneous publications on the environment and EPA activities and programs.

Council on Environmental Quality Web Site. WEB. U.S. Council on Environmental Quality.<http://www.whitehouse.gov/CEQ/>.

> Content: agency news and information, National Environmental Policy Act guidance, selected full-text publications, environmental impact statement filings and statistics, environmental resource links.

Discussion

Environmental Quality is the annual report of the Council on Environmental Quality. It is one of the most important general sources published by the government on the environment. Chapters discuss national environmental goals and strategies, summarize accomplishments, and analyze special topics. Some of the reports survey all areas of the environment and some emphasize a particular theme. There is usually a chapter on the National Environmental Policy Act covering issues, selected court cases, and statistics on cases. A statistical section contains data on environmental conditions and trends. Statistics cover land ownership and use, energy production and consumption, water quality, air pollution emissions, wildlife populations, solid waste, and pollution control expenditures.

The *Statistical Abstract of the United States* contains basic environmental statistics in the "Geography and Environment" chapter. The full-text of recent editions of the *Statistical Abstract* is available on the Census Bureau Web site as PDF files. The *Statistical Abstract* is also available on CD-ROM. The CD uses Adobe Acrobat software and contains some additional geographic areas and time series in the form of spreadsheet files that are not in the printed version.

The *EPA United States Environmental Protection Agency Web Site* contains agency information, full-text publications, and databases. The main page offers a "Your Community" menu selection that can provide information from three databases for a particular zip code area. The databases are *Envirofacts*, *Enviromapper*, and *Surf Your Watershed*. *Envirofacts* provides information on Superfund sites, drinking water, air pollution, toxic releases, hazardous waste, and water discharge permits. *Enviromapper* produces a customized neighborhood map showing EPA regulated sites and key features. *Surf Your Watershed* provides an assessment of the watershed's condition and vulnerability.

The main page also offers an "Information Sources" menu option. This contains links to "Libraries & Information Centers," "Hotlines & Clearinghouses," "Dockets," "Publications," "Newsletters & Listservs," "FOIA Office," "Databases and Software," "Test Methods & Models," and "Frequently Asked Questions." The "Publications" area contains links to several publications-related sites such as the National Environmental Publications Internet Site, which contains a collection of 7,000 full-text documents, the National Service Center for Environmental Publications, and its *National Catalog*, which includes many free publications, and the publications pages of various EPA offices.

A "Laws & Regulations" main menu option offers the full text of major environmental laws and environmental regulations. Other main menu categories include "About the EPA," "In the News," "Browse EPA Topics," "Programs," and "Audience Groups," such as kids, students, concerned citizens, researchers, small businesses, and industry.

The Environmental Protection Agency's *General Publications* series is a general, comprehensive series of miscellaneous publications. The series is very large and contains many technical reports as well as more general publications. Examples of recent publications in this series include *EPA Action Plan for Beaches and Recreational Waters: Reducing Exposures to Waterborne Pathogens* (EP 1.2:AC 8/5); *Mid-Atlantic States: State of the Environment, 1998: the Challenge Ahead* (EP 1.2:C 35/3); *Managing for Results: Making a Difference in Environmental Protection* (EP 1.2:M 28/2); *Recycling, for the Future: It's Everybody's Business* (EP 1.2:R 24/14); and *An Overview of EPA's Strategic Plan* (EP 1.2:ST 8/12).

The *Council on Environmental Quality Web Site* provides news and information about the agency. A "NEPA Net" main menu option provides information, publications, and resources related to the National Environmental Policy Act (NEPA). These include the text of the law and related regulations, other related agency Web sites, and guidance information. A small number of full-text publications are available including studies on NEPA and recent *Environmental Quality* annual reports. A section on environmental impact analysis provides information on environmental impact statements including statistics, how to file, and listings of statements filed. An "Environmental Impact Analysis Data Links" option provides a list of environmental datasets available on the Internet.

EPA ELECTRONIC RESOURCES AND DATABASES
Checklist

National Environmental Publications Internet Site (NEPIS). WEB. U.S. Environmental Protection Agency.<http://www.epa.gov/ncepihom/nepishom/>.
> Content: full-text and images of over 7,000 archival and current EPA documents.

Digital Library of Environmental Quality. WEB. U.S. Environmental Protection Agency. Center for Environmental Information and Statistics.<http://www.epa.gov/ceisweb1/ceishome/digitallib/>.
> Content: selected full-text publications on the state of the environment by geographic areas and by theme.

Envirofacts Data Warehouse and Applications. WEB. U.S. Environmental Protection Agency.<http://www.epa.gov/enviro/index_java.html>.
> Content: data on air, chemicals, facilities, grant funding, hazardous waste, risk management plans, Superfund, toxic releases, water permits, drinking water, and drinking water contaminant occurrence.

Environmental Profiles. WEB. U.S. Environmental Protection Agency. Center for Environmental Information and Statistics.<http://tree2.epa.gov/ceis/ceis.nsf>.
> Content: county data on air quality, drinking water, surface water, hazardous waste, and toxic chemical releases.

Surf Your Watershed. WEB. U.S. Environmental Protection Agency.<http://www.epa.gov/surf/>.
> Content: comprehensive local area water and environmental information; assessments of watershed health; data on toxic releases, hazardous wastes, water, habitat, community groups, air emissions.

EnviroMapper. WEB. U.S. Environmental Protection Agency.<http://www.epa.gov/enviro/html/em/index.html>.
> Content: maps of environmental information including drinking water, toxic and air releases, hazardous waste, water discharge permits, and Superfund sites.

Environmental Atlas. WEB. U.S. Environmental Protection Agency. Center for Environmental Information and Statistics.<http://www.epa.gov/ceisweb1/ceishome/atlas/>.
> Content: online environmental map collection.

Discussion

The *National Environmental Publications Internet Site* contains a full-text database of more than 7,000 EPA publications. The simple search option retrieves page images based on a keyword search. An enhanced search option allows results to be viewed either as page images or as text. An EPA Web site search is also available. A complete list of publications available arranged by report number may also be displayed.

The *Digital Library of Environmental Quality* contains the full-text of selected state of the environment and environmental quality reports. The main page offers options to link to the full reports, to view summaries, or to do a search. The full report option provides a selection of theme categories or geographic areas. Examples of theme categories include air quality, climate change, water quality, toxics, waste, and living resources. Geographic area selections include cities and communities, states, regions, the United States, countries, and the world. Reports are available only for a small number of individual areas within each category. Reports are not limited to EPA reports, but include other general environmental quality reports available on the Internet. For each category, there is a list of selected titles with links to the full-text. The option to view summaries contains the same category and geographic listings that also display the titles available in each category. Selecting a title gives a description, table of contents, and URL from which the user can link to the full-text. The search option allows full-text searching of all the publications or of individual titles. The main page also includes a link to a listing of federal environmental statistics programs as published in the *Environmental Quality* annual report with links to data from each program that is available on the Internet.

The EPA *Envirofacts* database provides single-point access to several EPA databases. Users may search multiple databases or individual databases. Databases are grouped by broad categories including multisystem, maps, air, chemical information, facility information, grants/funding, hazardous waste, Superfund, risk management plans, Toxics Release Inventory, and water. Query forms are available for each database. The forms provide multiple ways of searching appropriate to each database, usually including facility, geography, and industry classification code. Descriptions of each database are included in the overview menu option.

The *Environmental Profiles* database provides county profiles. Users select a state and county or enter a zip code, then select the topic area of interest. Data available may vary depending on the county. The air quality profile contains a Pollutant Standards Index chart and graph and a pollutants emission graph. The drinking water profile contains charts on population served by community water sources in violation of safe standards and on community water systems with violations. The surface water profile lists individual watersheds in the county. Information on each watershed includes a map, list of areas served, assessments of the health of the watershed, environmental factors such as toxic releases, hazardous waste, and Superfund sites, and information on the bodies of water making up the watershed. The hazardous waste profile includes graphs on tons of hazardous waste generated and managed. The toxic chemicals releases profile contains a chart on total toxic releases. All profiles contain links to additional information.

Surf Your Watershed provides local area data on specific watersheds. Users select their area from a map or by entering a geographic name or zip code. Information on each watershed includes a map, list of areas served, assessments of the health of the watershed, environmental factors such as toxic releases, hazardous waste, and Superfund sites, and information on the bodies of water making up the watershed. Information on habitats and community groups is also included.

EnviroMapper provides local maps showing environmental features such as EPA-regulated facilities, Superfund sites, watershed characteristics, and toxic releases. It displays maps from the national level to the local level with feature identification and zoom and pan capabilities.

The *Environmental Atlas* offers online maps with environmental information. Main menu choices include USA maps and state and regional maps. USA maps are subdivided into air, land, or water. Individual maps are listed under each category. Maps come from various federal agencies and other sources. Examples of some of the specific maps available include total wetlands acres, pollutant loads discharged above permitted limits, and density map of carbon monoxide emissions by county. The state and regional map option allows the user to select a specific region or state and view a list of maps, including general base maps as well as those with environmental information. The main page also contains an interactive mapper option that links to the *EnviroMapper* Web site.

EPA PUBLICATION CATALOGS

Checklist

EPA National Publications Catalog. PRINT. WEB. 1994–. U.S. Environmental Protection Agency. Office of Administration and Resources Management. EP 1.21:P 96/5/. Item 0431-I-09. GPO.<http://www.epa.gov/ncepihom/catalog.html>;<http://purl.access.gpo.gov/GPO/LPS586>.

> Content: catalog of more than 5,000 current EPA publications.

OLS U.S. EPA Online Library System. WEB. U.S. Environmental Protection Agency.<http://www.epa.gov/natlibra/ols.htm>.

> Content: bibliographic citations to EPA reports and other materials in EPA libraries.

EPA Publications Bibliography: Quarterly Abstract Bulletin. PRINT. (quarterly) 1977–. U.S. Environmental Protection Agency. Center for Environmental Research Information. EP 1.21/7: Item 0431-I-39. ASI 9182-5. NTIS.

> Content: index and abstracts of reports from the Environmental Protection Agency and its contractors.

EPA Publications Bibliography. PRINT. 1977–1990. U.S. Environmental Protection Agency. EP 1.21/7-2: (Title varies). Item 0431-I-39. NTIS.

> Content: cumulated edition of the *Quarterly Abstract Bulletin.*

Discussion

The *EPA National Publications Catalog* lists more than 5,000 current Environmental Protection Agency (EPA) publications with ordering information. Publications are listed by sponsoring office, EPA number, and subject. The numeric listing gives the source for obtaining the publication. Many publications are available free from the National Service Center for Environmental Publications (NSCEP). These are highlighted throughout the *Catalog* for easy identification. Other publications are available from other EPA offices or for a fee from the National Technical Information Service (NTIS) or other sources. Sample order forms and instructions are included. A list of all the sources is given at the beginning of the *Catalog* with address, telephone and fax numbers, and Internet addresses. A searchable version of the *Catalog* is available on the Internet.

The *OLS U.S. EPA Online Library System* contains several databases for locating books, reports, and audiovisual materials. The "National Catalog" contains the holdings of most of the 28 EPA regional libraries and laboratories, as well as EPA reports available from the National Technical Information Service (NTIS). Other databases available include the National Service Center for Environmental Publications containing popular, free publications; an environmental financing database; an EPA enforcement training database; a subsurface remediation database; and some individual regional library databases. Searches can be done by title, keyword, author, corporate source, and report number. Advanced searching offers searching by year of publication, specific fields, and spe-

cific databases. Many publications found through *OLS* are available at EPA libraries. Some may be obtained for free from the National Service Center for Environmental Publications, and some may be purchased from NTIS.

EPA Publications Bibliography: Quarterly Abstract Bulletin lists all technical reports and journal articles submitted to NTIS by the Environmental Protection Agency. The final issue for each year contains cumulative annual indexes. There are seven indexes: title, keyword, sponsoring EPA office, corporate author, personal author, contract/grant number, and NTIS order/report number. The cumulative indexes give references to the issue number and the NTIS order number. The abstracts in each issue are arranged by the NTIS number.

EPA Publications Bibliography is a hardcover cumulation of the quarterly issues. Three sets have been published, each covering a seven-year period. These cumulations cover 1970–76, 1977–83, and 1984–90. The first set for 1970–1976 was titled *EPA Cumulative Bibliography*. It is the only set without a sponsoring EPA office index.

SOURCES ON AIR

Checklist

National Air Pollutant Emission Trends. MF. WEB. (annual) U.S. Environmental Protection Agency. Office of Air Quality Planning and Standards. EP 4.24: (Earlier, EP 4.2:AI 7/8/years). Item 0483-E-16. ASI 9194-13.<http://www.epa.gov/airtrends/>.

> Coverage: Europe, European countries, Canada, U.S., states.
> Content: trends for major air pollutants by source; top industries and plants emitting pollutants; pollutant density maps.

National Air Quality and Emissions Trends Report. MF. WEB. (annual) 1973–. U.S. Environmental Protection Agency. Office of Air Quality Planning and Standards. EP 4.22/2: (Title and frequency vary) Item 0483-E-15. ASI 9194-1.<http://www.epa.gov/airtrends/>.

> Coverage: U.S., EPA regions, counties, metropolitan areas.
> Content: air quality status; concentration of major pollutants.

AIRSData. WEB. U.S. Environmental Protection Agency. Office of Air Quality Planning and Standards. Information Transfer and Program Integration Division.<http://www.epa.gov/airsdata/>.

> Coverage: U.S., states, counties, individual facilities.
> Content: pollutant concentration and emissions for major pollutants.

AIRSExecutive Plus. CD-ROM. U.S. Environmental Protection Agency. Office of Air Quality Planning and Standards. Information Transfer and Program Integration Division. Information Transfer Group. EP 4.30: Item 0483-E-20. GPO. Related site:<http://www.epa.gov/airs/aeplus/>.

> Coverage: world, world regions, countries, selected world cities, U.S., EPA regions, states, counties, individual facilities.

Content: pollutant concentration and emissions for major pollutants.

AIRNOW. WEB. U.S. Environmental Protection Agency. Office of Air Quality Planning and Standards.<http://www.epa.gov/airnow/>.

Content: real-time air pollution data; ozone maps; ozone forecasts.

Office of Air and Radiation Web Page. WEB. U.S. Environmental Protection Agency. Office of Air and Radiation.<http://www.epa.gov/oar/>.

Content: agency information; full-text publications; air pollution information, activities, and resources.

Office of Air Quality Planning and Standards Web Page. WEB. U.S. Environmental Protection Agency. Office of Air Quality Planning and Standards.<http://www.epa.gov/oar/oaqps/>.

Content: agency information; full-text publications; air quality information, activities, resources, and standards.

Air CHIEF (ClearingHouse for Inventory and Emission Factors) CD-ROM. (annual) 1992–. U.S. Environmental Protection Agency. Office of Air Quality Planning and Standards. Emission Factor and Inventory Group. EP 1.109: Item 0431-T. GPO.

Content: data on air pollutants and emission sources; includes the publication *Compilation of Air Pollutant Emission Factors*, reports on specific hazardous air pollutant emission factors and methods for determining emissions, and the Factor Information Retrieval database (FIRE) with data on air pollutant emission factors, industry sources, and chemicals emitted.

Discussion

National Air Pollutant Emission Trends gives emissions estimates and trends for major pollutants, including particulate matter, sulfur dioxide, nitrogen oxide, volatile organic compounds, carbon monoxide, and lead. Statistics are given on the sources of each pollutant, such as on-road vehicles, non-road engines and vehicles, utility fuel combustion, industrial fuel combustion, and waste disposal. National emission density maps display emissions to the county level. Additional tables list the top 50 plants emitting each type of pollutant. Historical tables and graphs show emissions trends for selected years, generally since 1940. Additional chapters cover topics such as projections, biogenic emissions, air toxic emissions, greenhouse gas emissions, and international emissions. In some years, briefer online updates are issued in place of the full report.

National Air Quality and Emissions Trends Report contains trend data for major pollutants, including particulate matter, sulfur dioxide, nitrogen dioxide, carbon monoxide, ozone, and lead. A section on national trends gives an overview of each pollutant including concentration levels, emissions, nature and sources, health and environmental effects, national and regional trends, and air quality status. Other overview sections cover metropolitan trends, nonattainment areas, air toxics, visibility trends, and acid deposition. An appendix of data tables gives concentration and emission data for each pollutant for recent years. Data include maximum air quality concentrations by county and metropolitan area, number of days with the Pollutant Standards Index (PSI) greater than 100 for metropolitan areas, and a list of nonattainment areas.

AIRSData is a Web database containing a subset of data from the EPA's *Aerometric Information Retrieval System (AIRS)*. The *National Air Pollutant Emission Trends* report and the *National Air Quality and Emissions Trends Report* are produced from *AIRS*. *AIRSData* contains air quality measurements and pollutant emissions estimates. *AIRSData* options include "Sources," "Monitors," and "Maps." "Sources" displays annual emissions of air pollutants from major individual plants and factories. "Monitors" provides annual reports of air pollution measurements at particular sites. Several reports are available for this option including a values report (a summary of pollutant levels by year for each site), a trends report (annual pollutant level for multiple years), and a PSI report (county Pollutant Standards Index values). A direct query option is available for advanced users. "Maps" displays prepared maps showing the locations of air pollution monitoring sites, air pollution sources, areas that exceed air pollution standards, and the top 25 individual sources of air pollution. AIRS data is also available through *Envirofacts* discussed in the "EPA Electronic Resources and Databases" section of this chapter. The *AIRSExecutive Plus* CD-ROM also contains a subset of information from the AIRS database.

The *AIRNOW* Web site provides real-time air pollution data. An ozone map feature provides current and previous day regional maps showing ozone levels categorized from good to very unhealthy. Previous day peak value maps are also available. Ozone forecasts for the next day are given for selected states and metropolitan areas. Other features include links to real-time state and local Web sites, map archives for the current year, and a small selection of air pollution publications.

The *Office of Air and Radiation Web Page* contains menu options on organization, publications, and selected subject areas including the ozone layer, radiation, acid rain, vehicles/engines, air toxics, and indoor air. Publications cover general air pollution topics and specific pollutants. The subject area menu selections provide overviews and background information on the topic with links to selected publications and Web sites.

The *Office of Air Quality Planning and Standards Web Page* contains menu options on agency organization, projects, publications, and selected subject areas including air quality, air toxics, visibility, emissions, and education. Publications cover general air pollution topics and specific pollutants. The subject area menu selections provide overviews and background information on the topic with links to selected publications and Web sites. The main menu also includes a link to the TTNWeb Technology Transfer Network, a collection of Web sites on air pollution science and technology. Some of the Web sites included are *AMTIC* (Ambient Monitoring Technology Information Center), *CHIEF* (ClearingHouse for Inventories and Emission Factors), *OARP&G* (OAR Policy and Guidance Web site), and *UATW* (Unified Air Toxics Web site). *AMTIC* contains information and files on ambient air quality monitoring programs and methods, air quality trends, and regulations. *CHIEF* contains the publication *Compilation of Air Pollutant Emission Factors*, emissions trends reports, and tools and information on estimating emissions of air pollutants and performing air emission inventories. *OARP&G* provides access to regulations and policy and guidance information arranged by Clean Air Act title. Information includes *Federal Register* notices, reports, memoranda, and fact sheets. General documents are also available including the full-text of the Clean Air Act and general information about the Act. *UATW* provides information on air toxics including basic facts, health effects, regulations, sources, information resources, and related Web sites.

The *Air CHIEF* CD-ROM contains reports on air emission factors for estimating types and quantities of pollutants from a wide variety of sources. Reports are similar to those available on the *CHIEF* Web site discussed above. The CD includes the FIRE database of emission factors, sources, and chemicals, which is not available on the Web.

SOURCES ON WATER

Checklist

National Water Quality Inventory: [year] Report to Congress. PRINT. WEB. (biennial) 1974–. U.S. Environmental Protection Agency. Office of Water. EP 2.17/2: Item 0473-A-09. ASI 9204-6. <http://www.epa.gov/305b/>.
>   Coverage: U.S., states.
>   Content: water quality assessment by types of water bodies; extent of impairment; causes and sources of pollution; water pollution management programs.

Surf Your Watershed. WEB. U.S. Environmental Protection Agency.<http://www.epa.gov/surf/>.
>   Content: comprehensive local area water and environmental information; assessments of watershed health; data on toxic releases, hazardous wastes, water, habitat, community groups, air emissions.

Envirofacts Data Warehouse and Applications. WEB. U.S. Environmental Protection Agency.<http://www.epa.gov/enviro/index_java.html>.
>   Content: data on water discharge permits, safe drinking water, drinking water contaminant occurrence, and drinking water microbial and disinfection byproducts.

Providing Safe Drinking Water in America: National Public Water Systems Compliance Report and Update on Implementation of the 1996 Safe Drinking Water Act Amendments. PRINT. WEB. (annual) 1996–. U.S. Environmental Protection Agency. Office of Enforcement and Compliance Assurance. EP 1.2:SA 1/3. Item 0431-I-01. ASI 9204-18. GPO. <http://www.epa.gov/ogwdw/annual/>.
>   Coverage: U.S., states.
>   Content: public water systems compliance with drinking water standards; violations; drinking water programs and regulations.

General Publications. PRINT. MF. (irregular) U.S. Environmental Protection Agency. Office of Water. Water Programs Operations Office. EP 2.2: Item 0473-A-01. GPO.
>   Content: miscellaneous publications on water quality, programs, issues.

Office of Water Home Page. WEB. U.S. Environmental Protection Agency. Office of Water.<http://www.epa.gov/OW/>.
>   Content: national water programs, water topics, full-text publications, laws and regulations, information resources, agency information.

State of the Coast Web Site. WEB. U.S. Department of Commerce. National Oceanic and Atmospheric Administration.<http://state-of-coast.noaa.gov/>.
>   Content: topical essays on coastal environmental issues.

Water Resources Data. [state]. MF. (annual) U.S. Department of the Interior. Geological Survey. I 19.53/2: Item 0619-E-01 to 53. ASI 5666-10,-12,-16, -20, -22. Alaska:<http://www-water-ak.usgs.gov/Publications/Water-Data/>.
>   Coverage: individual monitoring stations.
>   Content: surface and groundwater measurements; streamflow, groundwater levels, water quality, discharge.

Water Resources of the United States. WEB. U.S. Department of the Interior. Geological Survey.<http://water.usgs.gov/>.
>   Content: water data, publications and resources, water programs.

Selected Water-Resources Abstracts. WEB. 1977–1997. U.S. Department of the Interior. Geological Survey.<http://water.usgs.gov/public/swra/index.html>.
>   Content: bibliographic database of U.S. Geological Survey reports on water resources.

Search Publications of the U.S. Geological Survey. WEB. 1880–. U.S. Department of the Interior. Geological Survey.<http://usgs-georef.cos.com/>.
>   Content: bibliographic database of all U.S. Geological Survey reports.

Discussion

The *National Water Quality Inventory: [year] Report to Congress* is based on state reports on water quality submitted to the EPA. The main report contains national summary findings for each water type with chapters on rivers and streams; lakes, ponds, and reservoirs; coastal resources; wetlands; and ground water. Chapters discuss the amount of water surveyed, whether the quality supports aquatic communities and human activities, leading pollutants and sources of pollutants, and percentage of water found to be impaired. Additional chapters cover public health and aquatic life concerns and water quality management programs. A state summary section contains two-page overviews on each state. Appendices contain state data tables on the extent of waters surveyed, whether waters fully support use or use is threatened or impaired, aquatic life support, amount of impaired water, and leading pollutants and sources. Recent reports and selected chapters from earlier reports are available on the Internet. Appendices are also available for downloading in Excel spreadsheet format.

Surf Your Watershed provides comprehensive local area data on specific watersheds. Main menu options include "Locate Your Watershed," "Index of Watershed Indicators," and "Environmental Websites." The "Locate Your Watershed" option allows users to select an area from a map or by entering a geographic name or zip code. Information on each watershed includes a map, list of places in the watershed, assessments of the health of the watershed, and environmental factors such as toxic releases, hazardous wastes, Superfund sites, and air emissions. A water information section covers the amount and types of water bodies making up the watershed, nonpoint source project grants, community water sources, water dischargers, U.S. Geological Survey (USGS) data on stream flow, science in your watershed covering USGS data and projects, historical water data, water use, and relevant USGS report abstracts. Information on habitats and community groups is also included. The main menu "Index of Watershed Indicators" option provides background information on the IWI, a major environmental indicator available in the individual watershed profiles. The "Environmental Websites" main menu option is a searchable database of hundreds of environmental Web sites. Search options include state, full text search, information type (data, maps, services, or text), and keyword.

The EPA *Envirofacts* database provides single-point access to several EPA databases. Users may search multiple databases or individual databases. Databases are grouped by broad categories including water. The Water Discharge Permits database provides permit information for individual facilities. The Safe Drinking Water database gives violation and enforcement information for local drinking water suppliers. The Drinking Water Occurrence database covers contaminant occurrence in individual systems or geographic areas. A database on drinking water microbial and disinfection byproducts covers sampling data for individual large water systems and for states and the U.S. Search options vary for each database, but generally include facility and geography. Descriptions of each database are included in the overview menu option.

Providing Safe Drinking Water in America summarizes annual state reports on public water system compliance with drinking water standards. The report provides a national overview on the safety of drinking water and background information on related laws and regulations. Individual state summaries cover the number of regulated systems and the number and category of violations. Violation categories include chemical contaminants, coliform, surface water treatment, and lead and copper.

The *General Publications* series of the Office of Water contains general and technical publications on water quality and EPA water program activities. Examples of recent titles include *Coral Reefs and Your Coastal Watershed* (EP 2.2:C 81), *Co-occurrence of Drinking Water Contamination: Primary and Secondary Constituents* (EP 2.2:P 93/2 (MF)), *Urbanization and Streams: Studies of Hydrologic Impacts* (EP 2.2:UR 1 (MF)), and *Marinas and Recreational Boating: Management Measures for Sources of Nonpoint Pollution in Coastal Waters* (EP 2.2:M 33 (MF)).

The *Office of Water Home Page* provides information on water topics and national water programs. Main menu options include program areas such as "Ground Water & Drinking Water" or "Wetlands, Oceans & Watersheds"; "Water Topics" such as water conservation, coral reefs, or ground water protection; "Water Where You Live"; "Publications"; "Databases and Software"; and "Laws and Regulations." The "Water Where You Live" option provides resource listings by state such as 305B water quality fact sheets, drinking water information, Index of Watershed Indicators, real time data, grants and projects, water not meeting quality standards, and environmental Web sites.

The *State of the Coast Web Site* offers essays on coastal environmental issues written by experts for a general audience. Main menu topics include "Pressure" (pressures on the coastal environment), "State" (state of the coastal environment), and "Response" (societal response). Each area includes an introduction and reports on specific topics. Some of the topics covered are "Ecological Effects of Fishing" (Pressure), "The Extent and Condition of U.S. Coral Reefs" (State), and "Restoring Coastal Habitats" (Response). A "National Dialogues" main menu option provides papers and reports from national commissions and workshops on coastal topics and a forum of views and perspectives on the future called "Coasts 2025."

Water Resources Data for each state contains hydrologic data gathered from monitoring stations along rivers, streams, lakes, and at wells. An overview section summarizes conditions for the state. Data are then given for individual monitoring stations. Station data vary depending on the nature of the station and the type of water being monitored. Examples of information available include station location, drainage area, daily discharge data, water level, and water quality. Water quality indicators include daily specific conductance, pH, temperature, dissolved oxygen, hardness, and concentrations of various substances.

The *Water Resources of the United States* Web page serves as a guide and access point for U.S. Geological Survey water data and publications. The "National Water Conditions" feature offers daily and monthly streamflow condition maps. The water data menu category offers real time streamflow condition maps and individual station data, historical streamflow data for individual stations, GIS data sources, water quality data, water use data, and acid rain data. The water quality data include individual station streamflow and water quality in ASCII format. The water use data include downloadable data for local areas. The acid rain data include national maps and individual site measurements. All these data areas also include background information and related publications. The *Water Resources* Web site also provides menu options for "Publications and Products," "Technical Resources," and "Programs." The "Publications and Products" option includes fact sheets summarizing USGS research and investigations arranged by subject area or state, news releases, education resources, a database of abstracts of USGS reports, memos, and online reports. The "Technical Resources" option supplies links to information resources for the topic areas of ground water, surface water, water quality software, and projects. The "Programs" option provides information on specific programs, such as the National Water Quality Assessment Program and the Toxic Substances Hydrology (Toxics) Program.

The *Selected Water-Resources Abstracts* Web database contains abstracts of USGS water resource publications compiled from several sources. Searches can be done by USGS series report numbers, keyword, author, hydrologic unit number, state, series, and year. The database presently ends with 1997, although the help file indicates that the database will be added to as resources permit.

The *Search Publications of the U.S. Geological Survey* Web database covers all USGS publications and non-USGS publications by USGS authors since 1983. The database is a subset of the American Geological Institute's *GeoRef* database. Some entries contain abstracts. The database can be searched by numerous fields including subject, title, author, keyword, journal or proceedings title, date, and type of map or document.

SOURCES ON HAZARDOUS AND SOLID WASTE

Checklist

Solid Waste Management (SW). MF. (irregular) U.S. Environmental Protection Agency. Office of Solid Waste and Emergency Response. EP 1.17: Item 0431-I-07.

Content: informational, educational, and technical publications on wastes and recycling.

Office of Solid Waste Home Page. WEB. U.S. Environmental Protection Agency. Office of Solid Waste.<http://www.epa.gov/osw/>.

Content: information on solid waste, recycling, waste disposal, and waste cleanup; full-text publications; information resources; agency information.

A Collection of Solid Waste Resources. CD-ROM. U.S. Environmental Protection Agency. Office of Solid Waste and Emergency Response. EP 1.104:C 68/. Item 0431-R.

Content: full-text publications on solid waste and recycling.

Welcome to Superfund: Cleaning up the Nation's Hazardous Waste Sites. WEB. U.S. Environmental Protection Agency. Office of Emergency and Remedial Response.<http://www.epa.gov/superfund/index.htm>.

Content: information on the Superfund program and related laws; database of hazardous waste sites.

National Biennial RCRA Hazardous Waste Report. WEB. (biennial) 1987–. U.S. Environmental Protection Agency. EP 1.104/3: Item 0431-R-02. ASI 9214-8.<http://www.epa.gov/epaoswer/hazwaste/data/#brs>.

Coverage: U.S., EPA regions, states.

Content: hazardous waste generated, number of waste generating facilities, largest waste generating facilities and managers, quantity of waste managed, management methods, hazardous waste shipments and receipts, number of shippers and receivers.

Discussion

The *Solid Waste Management* series contains publications on hazardous and solid waste and related issues. Examples of recent titles include *Solid Waste Funding: A Guide to Federal Assistance* (EP 1.17:530-F-97-027 (MF)), *Puzzled About Recycling's Value?: Look Beyond the Bin* (EP 1.17:530-K-97-008 (MF)), *Characterization of Municipal Solid Waste in the United States: 1996 Update* (EP 1.17:530-R-97-015 (MF)), and *RCRA in Focus: Printing: Regulatory Update, Reducing Waste, Hot off the Press* (EP 1.17:530-K-97-007 (MF)). Many of the publications in this series are also available on the Office of Solid Waste Web site and CD-ROM also listed in this section.

The *Office of Solid Waste Home Page* contains background information on solid waste and full-text publications. Topical information is grouped into three areas: "Industrial & Special Waste," "Municipal Solid Waste," and "Hazardous Waste." A list of subtopics is available for each area. Under "Municipal Solid Waste," for example, are such categories as "Basic Facts," "Composting," "Landfills," and "Recycling." These categories generally provide narrative overviews with links to additional information. Other menu selections cover categories such as "Publications," "RCRA Online," "Software & Databases," "Laws, Regulations & Policies" and "Students and Teachers." The "Publications" menu option contains the full-text of the agency's *Catalog of Hazardous and Solid Waste Publications* and an alphabetical title list of publications available in full-text on the Web. "RCRA Online" is a database of selected letters, memoranda, and questions and answers covering the management of waste under the Resource Conservation and Recovery Act. The "Software & Databases" menu choice provides a list of databases, software, and related resources. It includes a link to the *Municipal Solid Waste Factbook*, which can be viewed online or is available as application software that can be downloaded. The *Municipal Solid Waste Factbook* covers household waste management, federal and state municipal solid waste program information, facts and figures, inventories of solid waste facilities, and regulations.

A *Collection of Solid Waste Resources* CD-ROM contains full-text publications on solid waste topics similar to those in the *Solid Waste Management* series and on the *Office of Solid Waste Home Page*. Publication subject categories include composting, education, hazardous waste management, landfilling, municipal solid waste management, and recycling. The CD also includes an installable software version of the *Municipal Solid Waste Factbook*. Updated versions of the CD are issued periodically.

The *Welcome to Superfund* Web page provides information on the Superfund program and includes a database of hazardous waste sites. Main menu options include "About Superfund," "Site Information," "Programs," "Accomplishments," "Regions," and "Resources." Also available are an alphabetical listing of resources by topic ("Topics"), an alphabetical list of full-text publications ("Publications"), and a search option. The "Site Information" option provides various search options for retrieving information on specific waste sites. A "CERCLIS Sites by State" option allows the user to select a state, then a city or county, and see a list of hazardous waste sites. An alphabetical list by site name is also available. Information on specific sites includes name, address, National Priority List (NPL) status, and incident category. Links to additional information include actions, financial transactions, and abstracts of Records of Decision (RODs) that analyze the site's contamination and possible clean-up remedies and costs. Another option is "ROD Abstracts by State" which provides similar facility information and ROD abstracts. A "Basic Queries" search option allows the user to search by several fields, including name, geographic location, NPL status, contaminated media, and contaminants. An "Advanced Query Option" provides more detailed search options and customized output. Mapping features are also available. The Superfund database is also available through *Envirofacts*, discussed in the "EPA Electronic Resources and Databases" section of this chapter.

The *National Biennial RCRA Hazardous Waste Report* contains information on the generation, management, and disposition of hazardous wastes. The report includes a national analysis, state summary and detail analyses, and lists of large quantity generators and treatment, storage, and disposal facilities. The report is available in PDF format on the Web and the data files are also available for downloading. Individual facility data are also available through the *Envirofacts* database, discussed in the "EPA Electronic Resources and Databases" section of this chapter. To search in *Envirofacts*, select the "Biennial Report" database in the Hazardous Materials category. Data can be searched by facility name, geography (state, city, county, zip code), and Standard Industrial Classification (SIC) number.

SOURCES ON INDUSTRY

Checklist

Toxics Release Inventory (TRI) Web Page. WEB. U.S. Environmental Protection Agency. Office of Pollution Prevention and Toxics.<http://www.epa.gov/tri/>.

Content: background information, data products, and databases from the Toxics Release Inventory.

Envirofacts Data Warehouse and Applications. WEB. U.S. Environmental Protection Agency.<http://www.epa.gov/enviro/index_java.html>.

Content: Toxics Release Inventory database.

RTK NET TRI Search. WEB. 1987–. The Right-to-Know Network.<http://www.rtk.net/trisearch.html>.

Content: Toxics Release Inventory database.

TOXNET (Toxicology Data Network). WEB. U.S. National Library of Medicine.<http://toxnet.nlm.nih.gov/>.

Content: Toxics Release Inventory database.

Toxics Release Inventory Public Data Release. WEB. (annual) 1987–. U.S. Environmental Protection Agency. Office of Pollution Prevention and Toxics. (Title varies) EP 5.18/2: Item 0473-B-14. ASI 9234-6.<http://www.epa.gov/tri/>;<http://www.epa.gov/opptintr/chemrel.htm>.

Coverage: U.S., states.

Content: varies; summary and analysis of chemical releases; releases by chemical and industry; comparisons to previous years.

Toxics Release Inventory State Fact Sheets. WEB. (annual) 1989–. U.S. Environmental Protection Agency. Office of Pollution Prevention and Toxics. ASI 9234-8.<http://www.epa.gov/tri/>; <http://www.epa.gov/opptintr/chemrel.htm>.

Coverage: states.

Content: state rankings; quantity and rank of releases by category; top five chemical releases; top five facilities for releases; map of facility locations.

Toxics Release Inventory (TRI). CD-ROM. (annual) 1987–. U.S. Environmental Protection Agency. Office of Pollution Prevention and Toxics. EP 5.22/2: Item 0473-H. ASI 9234-7. GPO.<http://www.rtk.net/trisearch.html>; <purl.access.gpo.gov/GPO/LPS3702>.

Content: CD-ROM version of the Toxic Release Inventory database; includes *Public Data Release* and *State Fact Sheets* publications.

Sector Notebook Project series. PRINT. WEB. U.S. Environmental Protection Agency. Office of Enforcement and Compliance Assurance. Office of Compliance. EP 1.113: (Earlier, EP 1.2:P 94/, EP 1.2:SE 2/7) Item 0431-I-85. ASI 9186-10. GPO.<http://es.epa.gov/oeca/sector/>;<purl.access.gpo.gov/GPO/LPS459>.

Content: industry environmental profiles.

Discussion

The Toxics Release Inventory provides information on toxic chemicals used, manufactured, treated, transported, or released into the environment. The number of facilities reporting and the number of chemicals covered has increased over time. Presently more than 21,000 facilities report on more than 600 chemicals. Information reported includes basic information identifying each facility; contact person; environmental permits held; amounts of each TRI chemical released to the environment at the facility; amounts of each chemical shipped from the facility to other locations for recycling, energy recovery, treatment, or disposal; amounts of each chemical recycled, burned for energy recovery, or treated at the facility; maximum amount of chemical present onsite at the facility during the year; types of activities conducted at the facility involving the toxic chemical; and source reduction activities.

The *Toxics Release Inventory (TRI) Web Page* provides background information and access to TRI reports and databases. The "Accessing TRI Data" menu option includes the full-text of the annual *Public Data Release* and *State Fact Sheets* for recent years. State files in dBase format are also available for download. This menu option also includes links to online TRI databases available from EPA's *Envirofacts* database, the Right-to-Know Network, and the National Library of Medicine's *TOXNET*. The Web page also includes guidance documents and a "Policy, Regulations & Statute" category.

Envirofacts, also discussed under the "EPA Electronic Resources and Databases" section of this chapter, includes the "Toxics Releases Inventory" database. Options include a TRI facility query, state reports, E-Z Query, and Customized Query. Data are for the most recent year available. The facility query allows searching by facility name, geography, Standard Industrial Classification (SIC) number, and chemical name. Data retrieved include individual facility listings with location and identification information and the facility's chemical reports listing each TRI chemical transferred to other sites or released to the air, land surface, surface water, or underground injection. An option to map the facility location is available. The state report search option gives a state overview with data on total facilities, total releases by category (such as air emissions, surface water discharges), onsite waste management, offsite transfers for further waste management, top 10 chemical releases by category, and top 10 facilities with releases by category. The E-Z Query search option allows the user to build a tabular report for downloading. The user selects an interest area, specific columns or data elements, and search criteria. A Customized Query option for more advanced users is also available.

The Right-to-Know Network (*RTK NET*) offers TRI database searches by geographic area, facility information, industry, parent company, and offsite waste transfer. Data are available for all years since 1987. The National Library of Medicine's *TOXNET* system of databases also includes the TRI database. Coverage is presently for the most recent three years. Searches can be done by chemical name or registry number, facility information, or geographic location.

The *Toxics Release Inventory Public Data Release* report analyzes annual inventory findings. A national overview chapter gives the total quantity and percentage by release category (onsite, offsite, onsite waste management, transfers offsite for waste management) and by chemical and release category. The top 20 chemical releases are also identified. A year-to-year comparisons chapter gives quantity of releases and chemical data for selected years.

An industry chapter gives quantity of releases by broad industry category.

Toxics Release Inventory State Fact Sheets is a companion title to the *Toxics Release Inventory Public Data Release*. It contains state summary tables for each release category for recent years and a two-page fact sheet for each state. The summary tables list states by rank. The fact sheets show the state's rank in each category, a map of facility locations, quantities of releases in each category, the top five chemicals released, the top five facilities for onsite releases, and the top five facilities for both onsite and offsite releases.

The *Toxics Release Inventory* CD-ROM set contains the complete database for several years, reporting forms, chemical fact sheets, and the *Toxics Release Inventory Public Data Release* and *Toxics Release Inventory State Fact Sheets* reports. The database is searchable by more than 200 fields and includes the ability to map facility locations and show demographic census information.

The *Sector Notebook Project* series consists of environmental profiles for more than 30 major industries. Examples of specific titles and industries include *Profile of the Aerospace Industry* (EP 1.113:310-R-98-001), *Profile of the Textile Industry* (EP 1.113:310-R-97-009), and *Profile of the Metal Casting Industry* (EP 1.113:310-R-97-004). Each profile contains a general description of the industry, including economic trends and geographic distribution, a description of the industrial process, a chemical release profile, pollution prevention opportunities, summary of federal statutes and regulations, compliance and enforcement history, compliance assurance activities and initiatives, and contacts and resources. The chemical release data are from the Toxic Release Inventory and include chemicals released into the air, water, or ground; chemicals transferred; top ten facilities releasing chemicals; air pollutant releases by industry sector; and toxic releases by selected industries. Compliance data include number of inspections and enforcement actions and major enforcement cases. An overall update to the 1995 and 1997 sector notebooks was issued as *Sector Notebook Data Refresh–1997* (EP 1.2:SE 2/7).

SOURCES ON FISH AND WILDLIFE
Checklist

General Publications. PRINT. MF. (irregular) U.S. Department of the Interior. Fish and Wildlife Service. I 49.2: Item 0612.
> Content: brochures and publications on fish and wildlife subjects and programs.

Endangered Species Bulletin. PRINT. (bimonthly) 1976–. U.S. Department of the Interior. Fish and Wildlife Service. I 49.77: (Title and frequency vary) Item 0611-L. <http://endangered.fws.gov/bulinfo.html>; <http://purl.access.gpo.gov/GPO/LPS1662>; Boxscore:<http://ecos.fws.gov/tess/html/boxscore.html>.
> Content: articles on proposed and actual changes to the endangered species list; recovery and protection plans;

habitat conservation; issues relating to endangered species.

Report to Congress on the Recovery Program for Endangered and Threatened Species. PRINT. WEB. (biennial) 1990–. U.S. Department of the Interior. Fish and Wildlife Service. I 49.77/3: (Title varies) Item 0614-D. ASI 5504-35.<http://www.nctc.fws.gov/library/pubs3.html>.

    Content: status of listed species; percentage of recovery achieved and recovery priority for each species; possible delisting and reclassification actions.

Welcome to the Endangered Species Program Home Page. WEB. U.S. Department of the Interior. Fish and Wildlife Service. <http://endangered.fws.gov/>.

    Content: endangered species lists, news, and program information.

U.S. Fish & Wildlife Service Home Page. WEB. U.S. Department of the Interior. Fish and Wildlife Service.<http://www.fws.gov/>.

    Content: agency information and news; resources and full-text publications on fish and wildlife issues and programs.

Our Living Oceans: Report on the Status of U.S. Living Marine Resources. MF. WEB. U.S. Department of Commerce. National Oceanic and Atmospheric Administration. National Marine Fisheries Service. C 55.1/2: (Earlier, C 55.13/2:NMFS-F/SPO-1) Item 0250-E-26. ASI 2164-22.<http://www.st.nmfs.gov/st2/pdf.htm>;<http://purl.access.gpo.gov/GPO/LPS3031>.

    Coverage: U.S., regions.

    Content: biological status of U.S. fishery resources; harvest levels; degree of utilization; management issues.

Fisheries of the United States. PRINT. WEB. (annual) 1959–. U.S. Department of Commerce. National Oceanic and Atmospheric Administration. National Marine Fisheries Service. Current Fishery Statistics. C 55.309/2-2: (Earlier, C 55.309/2:) Item 0610-A. ASI 2164-1. GPO.<http://www.st.nmfs.gov/st1/publications.html>.

    Coverage: world, world regions, countries, U.S., regions, states, major U.S. ports.

    Content: fish landings; exports and imports; production and supply of fishery products; consumption.

Fishery Bulletin. PRINT. WEB. (quarterly) 1881–. U.S. Department of Commerce. National Oceanic and Atmospheric Administration. National Marine Fisheries Service. C 55.313: (Title and format vary) Item 0611. GPO.<http://fishbull.noaa.gov/>.

    Content: research articles in fishery science.

Discussion

The *General Publications* series of the Fish and Wildlife Service contains a variety of publications ranging from small brochures on topics of general interest to detailed research reports. Examples of recent titles include *Status Assessment and Conservation Plan for the Black Tern (Chlidonias Niger Surinamensis) in North America* (I 49.2:B 56 (MF)), *Environmental Contaminants Program: Looking Out for Wildlife* (I 49.2:C 76/12), *Giant Panda: Ailuropoda Melanoleuca* (I 49.2:P 19/998), *A Profile of Land Protection Actions by the U.S. Fish & Wildlife Service 1999* (I 49.2:P 94/3/999), *Feasibility Study on the*

Reintroduction of Gray Wolves to the Olympic Peninsula (I 49.2:R 27/2 (MF)), and *Teacher's Packet to Help Teachers and Students Learn More About Endangered Species* (I 49.2:T 22/2/PACK).

The *Endangered Species Bulletin* contains news articles on endangered species, their status and classification, habitat threats, and conservation and protection efforts. Articles regularly provide information on species proposed for or added to the endangered or threatened species list. A regular "Box Score" feature gives summary statistics on the number of endangered or threatened species and recovery plans by category. Regular departments include "Listing Actions" for proposed listings, final listings, and withdrawals from the endangered species list and "Regional News and Recovery Updates" with species and program news by region. Recent articles include "The Brown Bears of Kenai: A Population at Risk" (Vol. 24, No. 2), "Restoring Habitat Through Pesticide Management" (Vol. 24, No. 1), "South Florida Multi-Species Recovery Plan" (Vol. 23, No. 6), and "Native Trout Rebound in the Blackfoot River" (Vol. 23, No. 5). An index is published irregularly.

The *Report to Congress on the Recovery Program for Endangered and Threatened Species* reports on the progress made in arresting or reversing the decline of endangered or threatened species. A brief status report gives an overview and chart on the percentage of species that are stable and improving, declining, or uncertain. A list of species proposed for delisting or downlisting is given with reason for the action. An appendix provides information on each species' listing status, population status, existence of recovery plan, status of plan, percentage of recovery objectives achieved, and recovery priority.

The *Welcome to the Endangered Species Program Home Page* offers news items, species information, program information, and answers to frequently asked questions. The "Species Information" menu category includes a summary of listed species (boxscore identical to that published in the *Endangered Species Bulletin*), species lists by group and region with links to species profiles, state maps showing number of listed species per state, state lists, species proposed for the list, and listings from the *Federal Register*. The "What We Do" main menu option provides information on the endangered species program, including an overview, the text of the Endangered Species Act, history, policies, and specific program area information such as Habitat Conservation Plans or Recovery & Delisting Program. The "Questions" main menu option lists and answers frequently asked questions.

The *U.S. Fish & Wildlife Service Home Page* provides information and resources on fish and wildlife issues. Basic menu options include "Information," "Search," "Index," "Pictures," "Library," and "Species." The "Information" menu option is an online information clearinghouse with categories for wildlife species, publications, photos/images, videos, sound spots, maps, office directory, conservation history, and policies and notices. The

"Wildlife species" option provides a list of fact sheets for species of common interest as well as links to other resources. The "Publications" option provides an alphabetical title list of publications available online including a list of brochures on wildlife refuges. The Home Page main menu also includes a list of popular topics to select from such as "endangered species," "migratory birds," "invasive species," "refuges," and "wetlands." These choices go to subject pages or appropriate office pages that offer resources and publications on that topic.

Our Living Oceans: Report on the Status of U.S. Living Marine Resources is a periodic report on the status of fishery groups and species, selected nearshore species, marine mammals, and sea turtles. A national overview section provides U.S., regional, and species information on yield, stock levels, and degree of utilization. More detailed sections cover individual fishery groups such as "Northeast Demersal Fisheries" or "Atlantic Shark Fisheries." These sections describe the species, location, fishing methods, management concerns, economic issues, and progress made. Data given for each species include recent average yield, current potential yield, long-term potential yield, fishery utilization level, and stock level relative to long-term potential yield. Sections on marine mammals and sea turtles discuss population size and trends, status, issues, and progress.

Fisheries of the United States is a statistical report on fish caught and the production of fish products. A general review section summarizes key statistics under such headings as processed products, per capita consumption, foreign trade, other important facts, and important species. Detailed statistical tables give data on U.S. fish landings by species and area in which caught. Other tables cover the world commercial catch by species groups and country. Data on fishery products include the percentage of fish used for food or industrial purposes; production of fresh, frozen, canned, and other products by species; and per capita consumption.

Fishery Bulletin contains scientific articles on fish investigations. Each issue is substantial, containing 200 or more pages with approximately 20 research articles and technical notes. Examples of recent articles include "Habitat Selection and Diet of Juvenile Red Porgy, Pagrus Pagrus" (Vol. 97, No. 3), "Capture Rate as a Function of School Size in Pantropical Spotted Dolphins, Stenella Attenuata, in the Eastern Tropical Pacific Ocean" (Vol. 97, No. 3), and "Variability in Reactions of Pacific Harbor Seals, Phoca Vitulina Richardsi, to Disturbance" (Vol. 97, No. 2).

SOURCES ON PUBLIC LANDS AND FORESTS
Checklist

Public Land Statistics. PRINT. WEB. (annual) U.S. Department of the Interior. Bureau of Land Management. I 53.1/2: Item 0633-C. ASI 5724-1. <http://www.blm.gov/nhp/info/index.htm>.

Coverage: U.S., states.
Content: public lands; survey actions; land use; grazing; wetlands; land and habitat improvements; forest products; forest development; game; recreational use; wilderness; mineral leases; fires; finances.

General Publications. PRINT. MF. (irregular) U.S. Department of Agriculture. Forest Service. A 13.2: Item 0084. GPO.
Content: miscellaneous publications on the Forest Service, forest management and resources, individual national forests, plants and wildlife, and recreation.

USDA Forest Service Home Page. WEB. U.S. Department of Agriculture. Forest Service.<http://www.fs.fed.us/>.
Content: information on national forests and forest resource management; agency information and news.

Land Areas of the National Forest System. MF. WEB. (annual) U.S. Department of Agriculture. Forest Service. A 13.10: Item 0084-A. ASI 1204-2.<http://www.fs.fed.us/land/staff/lar/>.
Coverage: U.S., Forest service regions, states, congressional districts, individual national forests, and other Forest Service managed areas.
Content: land area of national forests, national grasslands, and other Forest Service managed areas.

Resource Bulletins. MF. (irregular) U.S. Department of Agriculture. Forest Service. A 13.80: Item 0083-B-05. ASI 1206-, 1208-.
Coverage: varies; states, substate regions, counties.
Content: reports on forest land ownership, forest resources, and statistics.

Forest Inventory and Analysis Database Retrieval Systems. WEB. U.S. Department of Agriculture. Forest Service.<http://www.srsfia.usfs.msstate.edu/wo/dbrs_setup.htm>.
Content: forest resource and timber databases.

Natural Resource Year in Review. MF. WEB. (annual) 1996–. U.S. Department of the Interior. National Park Service. Natural Resource Program Center. I 29.1/4: Item 0653-A-01.<http://www2.nature.nps.gov/pubs/yir/>;<purl.access.gpo.gov/GPO/LPS3940>.
Content: review of natural resource issues and studies in national parks.

ParkNet. WEB. U.S. Department of the Interior. National Park Service.<http://www.nps.gov/>.
Content: information on national parks and related natural resources.

Discussion

Public Land Statistics contains statistics related to public land management. Tables are grouped by program area such as "Land Resources and Information," "Healthy Productive Lands," and "Commercial Uses and Revenues Generated." There is a short introduction to each section. Statistics cover such subjects as the history of public land acquisition, acreage owned by the federal government in each state, number and type of big game animals, oil and gas activities on federal lands, amount of timber sales, and visitor hours spent on water sports. Lists of wilderness areas and wild, scenic, and recreational rivers on federal lands are also included.

The Forest Service *General Publications* series contains miscellaneous publications on Forest Service programs and national forests. Examples of titles in this series include *Camping and Picnicking on the National Forests of Utah* (A 13.2:C 15/21/999), *Charting Our Future—: A Nation's Natural Resource Legacy* (A 13.2:R 31/27), *Recreation Sites in Southwestern National Forests and Grasslands* (A 13.2:R 24/28/998), and *The Land We Cared For—: A History of the Forest Service's Eastern Region* (A 13.2:H 62/9).

The *USDA Forest Service Home Page* contains information on forest resources and agency news. Main menu category options include "Library," "News & Issues," and "Programs & Staffs." The "Library" option provides access to listings of publications by various categories such as issuing unit or agency reports. Categories are also available for "Data and Information Systems," "Software," "Maps," video categories, and photographs. The "Programs & Staffs" option provides listings of national forests by map, state, region, or name. Information or a Web site for each national forest is available. Other choices include "National Grasslands" and "Research and Development." The "Research and Development" option includes links to the Web sites of individual forest research stations. The main menu of the *USDA Forest Service Home Page* also includes topic boxes for four interest areas: opportunities, the outdoors, resource management, and administration. Various selections are available in each category. Some of these selections include volunteer (opportunities), campgrounds (the outdoors), forest health (resource management), and policy analysis (administration).

Land Areas of the National Forest System lists, by state, each national forest or other Forest Service-managed area and gives acreage. National forest land totals by region and congressional district are also provided. Tables also list the land area of other national areas including national wilderness areas, primitive areas, scenic areas, wild and scenic river areas, recreation areas, game refuges and wildlife preserves, national monument areas, and other areas. A historical table shows national forest acreage by year. A national map shows the locations of forest and grassland areas.

The *Resource Bulletins* series is subdivided into groups representing the various forest research stations that produce these publications. Each station has a set of identifying initials, such as NC for North Central, NE for Northeastern, RMRS for Rocky Mountain, and so on. Each station's publications contain information regarding that region and the states within that region. Publications often consist of inventories and assessments of forest and timber resources. Recent titles include *Forest Statistics for North Georgia, 1998* (A 13.80:SRS-35 (MF)), *Illinois Timber Industry: An Assessment of Timber Product Output and Use, 1996* (A 13.80:NC-192 (MF)), and *Comprehensive Inventory of Utah's Forest Resources, 1993* (A 13.80:RMRS-RB-1 (MF)).

The *Forest Inventory and Analysis Database Retrieval Systems* presently offers databases on forest resources. The *National FIA (Forest Inventory and Analysis) Database* offers data from state forest inventories. Users select the state, inventory year, all counties, or a specific county. The search may be further refined by specific forest attributes (such as ownership or forest type) or tree attributes (such as species or size). A standard set of tables is available or the user can customize the output. Inventory years available vary for each state. Data available include timberland area by forest type and ownership class, number of trees by species, volume of growing stock, and annual growth and removals. *The Timber Product Output (TPO) Database* provides information on trees harvested and logging residues. Users select a region, subregion, state, all counties, or specific county. The search may be further refined by timber removal attributes (such as product or species) or timber residue attributes (such as use or residue type). Data available include volume of roundwood products removed, volume of logging residues, all removals, and mill residues. Most data are given by species, source, and geographic area. Related databases also available include the Resource Planning Act (RPA) Assessment Database and the *Climate Change Atlas for 80 Forest Tree Species of the Eastern United States*.

Natural Resource Year in Review is an annual review of resource management issues in national parks. Brief "Year at a Glance" and "Year in Review" sections give an overview of National Park Service activities in natural resource management. Numerous brief articles cover specific activities, programs, and studies. Examples of recent articles include "Commercial Fishing Issues in Glacier Bay Resolved Through Legislation" (1998), "Riparian Monitoring Focused on Stream Recovery in Canyonlands" (1998), "Inventory of Biodiversity Takes Shape in the Smoky Mountains" (1998), and "Great Expectations for the Black-Footed Ferret at Badlands" (1998).

ParkNet is the main Web page for the National Park Service. A "Visit Your Parks" main menu option provides information on fees and reservations and individual park information and maps. The "NatureNet" main menu option covers natural resources. "NatureNet" menu options include "Air," "Biology," "Geology," "Social Science," "Water," "Data/Science," and "Publications." The subject area categories provide information on each program area. The "Air" category includes extensive information on individual park air quality programs and air quality data, especially under the "Parks and Refuges" park listings or through the "Searches" option. The "Biology" category includes brochures and fact sheets on national park plants and wildlife. The "Water" category provides fact sheets on water pollution and water quality in the national parks.

CONGRESSIONAL SOURCES

Many congressional committees publish materials on environmental programs and issues. Some of these include the Senate Committee on Energy and Natural Resources (Y 4.EN 2:), the Senate Committee on Environment and Public Works (Y 4.P 96/10:), the House Committee on Resources (Y 4.R 31/3:), and the House Committee on Science (Y 4.SCI 2:). Examples of recent titles from these and other committees include *Clean Air Act: Proposed Regional Haze Regulations* (Y 4.P 96/10:S.HRG.105-677), *Transborder Air Pollution, Including the Impact of Emissions from Foreign Transborder Commuter Vehicles on Air Quality in Border Regions* (Y 4.C 73/8:105-60), *Estuary Restoration and Coastal Water Conservation Legislation* (Y 4.P 96/10:S.HRG.105-819), *Hearing on the Implementation of the Endangered Species Act of 1973* (Y 4.R 31/3:105-80), and *Oversight Hearing on Arctic Snow Geese* (Y 4.R 31/3:105-81). For complete listings of congressional publications, consult the *Monthly Catalog* and *CIS/Index* listed in the "Indexes" section below.

INDEXES
Checklist

Catalog of United States Government Publications (MOCAT). WEB. 1994–. U.S. Government Printing Office. Superintendent of Documents.<http://www.gpo.gov/catalog>; <http://www.access.gpo.gov/su_docs/locators/cgp/index.html>; <http://purl.access.gpo.gov/GPO/LPS844>.

Monthly Catalog of United States Government Publications. CD-ROM. 1996–. U.S. Government Printing Office. Superintendent of Documents. GP 3.8/7: Item 0557-C. GPO.

Monthly Catalog of United States Government Publications (Condensed version). PRINT. (monthly) 1996–. U.S. Government Printing Office. Superintendent of Documents. GP 3.8/8: (Earlier full version, GP 3.8:, 1895-1995). Item 0557-D. GPO.

CIS/Index. PRINT. (monthly) 1970–. Bethesda, MD: Congressional Information Service.

Congressional Universe. WEB. Bethesda, MD: Congressional Information Service.

American Statistics Index (ASI). PRINT. (monthly) 1973–. Bethesda, MD: Congressional Information Service.

Discussion

The *Monthly Catalog* is the most comprehensive index for government publications. The complete version is available on the Web and on CD-ROM. Information related to the environment can be found under many subject headings including "Environmental Protection," "Environmental Policy," "Air-Pollution," "Water-Pollution," "Pollution," "Refuse and Refuse Disposal," "Recycling (Waste, etc.)," and headings beginning with "Waste Disposal." See also "Conservation of Natural Resources" and headings beginning with "Forest(s)," "Fish(es)," "Fishery," and "Wildlife." Commercial online and CD-ROM versions of the

Monthly Catalog are also available. For more information see Chapter 3, "The Basics of Searching."

CIS/Index indexes the many congressional publications on the environment. Several congressional committees have responsibilities for areas affecting the environment. Publications are indexed under such headings as "Environmental pollution and control," "Air pollution," "Water pollution," "Refuse and refuse disposal," and "Recycling of waste materials." See also "Conservation of natural resources," "Forests and forestry," and "Wildlife and wildlife conservation." *Congressional Universe* includes a Web version of *CIS*.

American Statistics Index (ASI) is a comprehensive statistical index that should be used to locate any environmental statistics. Material can be found under "Environmental pollution and control," "Air pollution," "Water pollution," "Refuse and refuse disposal," and "Recycling of waste materials." See also "Conservation of natural resources," "Forests and forestry," and "Wildlife and wildlife conservation." *Statistical Universe* includes a Web version of *ASI*.

RELATED MATERIAL
Within this Work

Chapter 14 Climate

Chapter 18 Agriculture

Chapter 21 Geology

Chapter 41 Energy Statistics

Chapter 49 Technical Reports

GPO SUBJECT BIBLIOGRAPHIES. PRINT. WEB. GP 3.22/2:

<http://bookstore.gpo.gov/sb/about.html>.

No. 46 "Air Pollution"

No. 50 "Water Management"

No. 86 "Trees, Forest Management and Products"

No. 88 "Environmental Protection"

No. 95 "Waste Management"

No. 116 "Wildlife Management"

No. 177 "Birds"

No. 209 "Aquatic Life"

No. 238 "Conservation"

No. 256 "Bureau of Land Management"

CHAPTER 23
Astronomy and Space

Many publications related to space sciences and exploration are published by the National Aeronautics and Space Administration and the Congress. This chapter discusses selected series of a general nature. (See Chapter 49, "Technical Reports," for additional technical series in this area.)

SEARCH STRATEGY

This chapter shows a subject search strategy. Suggested steps for searching are

1. See the "General Sources" section for general materials on space;
2. For additional general publications on a wide range of space-related topics, consult the "Selected NASA Publications Series" section;
3. See the "Multimedia Sources" section for audiovisual materials;
4. See the "Astronauts" section for information on astronauts;
5. If interested in astronomical events and planetary positions, see the "Almanacs" section;
6. Consult "Congressional Sources" for additional materials;
7. Consider the "Related Material" section; and
8. Search indexes for additional information.

GENERAL SOURCES
Checklist

Spinoff. MF. WEB. (annual) 1976–. U.S. National Aeronautics and Space Administration. Office of Aeronautics and Space Transportation Technology. Commercial Programs Division. NAS 1.1/4: Item 0830-A-01. GPO.<http://www.sti.nasa.gov/tto/online.html>;<purl.access.gpo.gov/GPO/LPS3744>; Database:<http://www.sti.nasa.gov/tto/spinselect.html>.

> Content: review of NASA centers and research programs; descriptions of beneficial commercial applications of NASA technology in a variety of economic sectors.

Aeronautics and Space Report of the President. PRINT. WEB. (annual) 1958–. U.S. National Aeronautics and Space Administration. NAS 1.52: (Earlier, PREX 5.9: and House Documents series) Item 0856-D. ASI 9504-9.<http://www.hq.nasa.gov/office/pao/History/presrep.htm>;<http://purl.access.gpo.gov/GPO/LPS726>.

> Content: summary reports on aeronautics and space activities of all federal agencies with relevant responsibilities; chronologies of launches; launch vehicles; budget data.

NASA Spacelink Web Site. WEB. U.S. National Aeronautics and Space Administration.<http://spacelink.nasa.gov/.index.html>.

> Content: instructional materials; educational services and contacts; agency news and information; information on NASA projects and space-related topics.

NASA Home Page. WEB. U.S. National Aeronautics and Space Administration.<http://www.nasa.gov/>.

> Content: NASA program information, news, and agency information.

Discussion

Spinoff is an annual review of the ways NASA technology has been used in commercial products and services. It contains three sections: "Aerospace Research and Development," "Technology Transfer and Commercialization," and "Commercial Benefits—Spinoffs." The "Aerospace Research and Development" section describes NASA's major aeronautical and space centers, including each center's activities and technological contributions. The "Technology Transfer and Commercialization" section describes activities in the transfer of technology to the commercial sector and highlights the work of a selected field center. The "Commercial Benefits—Spinoffs" section describes selected products and processes developed from NASA technology in such areas as health and medicine, transportation, public safety, environment and resource management, computer technology, industrial productivity, and consumer/home/recreation. Colorful illustrations are used throughout the book. The full text of recent issues is available on the Web. A *Spinoff* database is also available. Users may search for specific products. Information available includes the issue and page of *Spinoff* where the product was mentioned, the NASA center and program that developed it, the manufacturer, and a brief abstract describing the product.

The *Aeronautics and Space Report of the President* is an annual summary of federal government agency activities in aeronautics and space. Arranged by agency, it includes the activities of NASA, the Department of Defense, the Federal Aviation Administration, the Department of Commerce, the Department of Energy, the Department of the Interior, the Department of State, and several others. Appendixes include a list of successful U.S. launches for the year and historical lists of total successful and failed launches by year, total successful launches of other countries, and human space flights. A list of U.S. space launch vehicles and historical and current budget expenditures for space activities are also available.

The *NASA Spacelink Web Site* provides educational resources for teachers, but the general information about NASA activities and services is useful to anyone interested in space-related topics. Main menu categories include "The Library," "Hot Topics," and "Cool Picks." "The Library" area includes "Educational Services," "Instructional Materials," "NASA Overview," "NASA Projects," "NASA News," and "Frequently Asked Questions." "Instructional Materials" offers full-text publications and information on multimedia resources. The "NASA Overview" area includes fact sheets on NASA organization, history, products, and budget. The "NASA Projects" section offers a list of popular project topics such as astronauts, the Hubble space telescope, or the space shuttle. Users can also browse projects by broad topic area such as "Human Exploration and Development of Space" or "Space Science."

The *NASA Home Page* provides access to NASA program information and space-related resources. Main menu options include the agency's four program or enterprise areas: aero-space technology, human exploration and development of space, earth science, and space science. Other main menu options cover educational resources, history, news and information, organization and subject index, project home pages, scientific and technical information, and launch schedule. The news and information category includes the text of news releases, press kits, status reports, fact sheets, public reports, and biographies of astronauts and administrators. Project home pages provide links to Web pages on such projects as Compton Gamma Ray Observatory, GOES Project Science, Human Space Flight Web, Asteroid and Comet Impact Hazards, and Mars Missions. This page also includes a space calendar for space-related events and a tour of the solar system.

SELECTED NASA PUBLICATION SERIES
Checklist

General Publications. PRINT. MF. (irregular) U.S. National Aeronautics and Space Administration. NAS 1.2: Item 0830-C.
> Content: miscellaneous reports, booklets, and brochures on all aspects of NASA activities and programs.

NASA SP. PRINT. MF. WEB. (irregular) 1961–. U.S. National Aeronautics and Space Administration. Scientific and Technical Information Division. NAS 1.21: Item 0830-I. GPO. Selected titles:<http://www.hq.nasa.gov/office/pao/History/series95.html>.
> Content: book-length studies of an historic or scientific nature on NASA missions, space, and aeronautics.

NASA NP. PRINT. (irregular) U.S. National Aeronautics and Space Administration. NAS 1.83: Item 0830-I.
> Content: colorful booklets on NASA missions, programs, and activities.

NASA Facts. WEB. (irregular) U.S. National Aeronautics and Space Administration. NAS 1.20: Item 0830-H.<http://www.nasa.gov/newsinfo/fsheet_index.html>.
> Content: brief overviews of NASA programs and related subjects.

Jet Propulsion Laboratory: Publications. PRINT. (irregular) U.S. National Aeronautics and Space Administration. Jet Propulsion Laboratory. NAS 1.12/7: Item 0830-H-09.
> Content: miscellaneous publications on Jet Propulsion Laboratory missions, activities, programs, and facilities.

NASA Tech Briefs. MF. WEB. (monthly) April 1987–. U.S. National Aeronautics and Space Administration. NAS 1.29/3-2: (Non-commercial edition; commercial edition distributed to depository libraries through May 1987 under NAS 1.29/3:) Item 0830-L-02.<http://www.nasatech.com/Home/index.html>.
> Content: abstracts of new NASA technology available for commercial applications.

Discussion

Several NASA publication series contain attractive publications of a general and educational nature. The *General Publications* series contains a wide range of reports, booklets, and brochures on NASA missions and programs. The series includes scientific reports, committee reports, educational materials, information on NASA programs, and publications on aeronautics and space topics. Recent publications include *The Mars Millennium Project: Picture the Future: A National Arts, Sciences, and Technology Education Initiative* (NAS 1.2:M 35/9), *Communications Satellite: NASA's Advanced Communications Technology Satellite* (NAS 1.2:SA 8/11/999), *Implementing NASA's Strategies for the 21st Century* (NAS 1.2:ST 8/4), and *The Sun-Earth Connection: Report to the Associate Administrator, Office of Space Science* (NAS 1.2:SU 7/9).

The *NASA SP* series (Special Publications) consists of book-length histories and scientific studies on NASA missions and on aeronautics and space topics. The series is directed toward an educated public and scientists in other fields. Many of the titles contain space photography and have become NASA best-sellers. Many titles belong to the *NASA History* subseries and provide substantial historical information on particular programs. Examples of these include *This New Ocean: A History of Project Mercury* (NAS 1.21:4201/998), *The Space Shuttle Decision: NASA's Search for a Reusable Space Vehicle* (NAS 1.21:4221), and *Exploring the Unknown: Selected Documents in the History of the U.S. Civil Space Program* (NAS 1.21:4407/v.1-3). Other titles cover scientific subjects. Examples of these include *Passage to a Ringed World: The Cassini-Huygens Mission to Saturn and Titan* (NAS 1.21:533) and *Photographic Survey of the LDEF Mission* (NAS 1.21:531).

The *NASA NP* series contains colorful booklets on NASA programs. Topics covered include NASA history, specific programs, vehicles, satellites, and business resources. Recent titles include *Clouds and the Earth's Radiant Energy System: CERES: NASA's Earth Observing System* (NAS 1.83:1999-04-069-GSFC), *Discovering Jupiter* (NAS 1.83:1997-02-225-HG), and *The Next Generation Space Telescope: Visiting a Time When Galaxies Were Young* (NAS 1.83:1997(05)-016-GSFC/STSCLM-9701).

NASA Facts are brief educational pamphlets on NASA programs and space-related topics issued by NASA centers. The Web site lists the centers that issue fact sheets with links to each fact sheet list. NASA Headquarters, for example, issues fact sheets on such topics as the international space station, unidentified flying objects, and asteroids. The Jet Propulsion Laboratory fact sheets cover solar system exploration missions such as *Cassini to Saturn* or *Stardust to Comet Wild-2*.

The *Jet Propulsion Laboratory: Publications* series contains publications about the Jet Propulsion Laboratory and its programs and activities. The series also contains colorful mission booklets and mission photographs. Recent titles include *Roadmap: Fundamental Physics in Space* (NAS 1.12/7:400-808), *Mission to the Solar System: Exploration and Discovery* (NAS 1.12/7:97-12), and *The Cassini-Huygens Mission to Saturn and Titan Pocket Reference: Postlaunch Update* (NAS 1.12/7:400-711).

NASA Tech Briefs contains abstracts of new NASA technology that may be useful for industrial or other commercial applications. Each issue is arranged by broad subject areas, such as electronic components and circuits, physical sciences, computer programs, machinery, and life sciences. Each abstract describes the technology and includes a drawing. Information is given on who performed the work, whether the technology is owned or patented by NASA, and how to obtain licensing or other information. Depository libraries have received a condensed, noncommercial edition of *NASA Tech Briefs* since 1987. A non-depository commercial edition also exists.

MULTIMEDIA SOURCES
Checklist

Posters and Pictures. PRINT. (irregular) U.S. National Aeronautics and Space Administration. NAS 1.43: Item 0830-H-06.

> Content: posters, pictures, patches, and stickers showing missions, space scenes, crews, vehicles, satellites, and facilities.

NASA Multimedia Gallery Web Page. WEB. U.S. National Aeronautics and Space Administration.<http://www.nasa.gov/gallery/index.html>.

> Content: photo images and indexes; video and audio resources.

Discussion

The *Posters and Pictures* series contains picture materials of many sizes and types. This series contains large and small posters, wall charts, picture sets, individual photographs, crew patches, and decals. Examples of posters include *Mars Pathfinder: Roving on the Red Planet* (NAS 1.43:M 35/5), *One Small Step for A Man, One Giant Leap for Mankind, Apollo 11, 20, 1969–1989* (NAS 1.43:AP 4/5), and *Exploring Uranus* (NAS 1.43:UR 1/11). Examples of other materials include *Spacesuit* wall chart (NAS 1.43:SP 1/24), *Hubble Space Telescope* wall chart (NAS 1.43:H 86/6), *Crew of Space Shuttle Mission STS-88* picture (NAS 1.43:SP1/26), *Selections from the NASA Art Collection* poster set (NAS 1.43:SE 4), and *Columbia, Young, Crippen, 1981–1991, 10th Anniversary Decal* (NAS 1.43:C 72/4). The number of materials issued in this series has decreased in recent years.

The *NASA Multimedia Gallery Web Page* contains photo, video, audio, and arts gallery menu options. The "Photo Gallery" provides information on obtaining NASA images, a photo index of images available for purchase, the NASA Image Exchange database of online images, and links to other NASA Web sites containing images. The "Video Gallery" contains links to NASA video clips. The "Audio Gallery" provides information on NASA television mission broadcasts over the Internet. The "Arts Gallery" contains information on NASA art collections with sample reproductions.

ASTRONAUTS
Checklist

Astronauts and Cosmonauts Biographical and Statistical Data. PRINT. MF. (1994) U.S. Congress. House. Committee on Science, Space, and Technology. Y 4.SCI 2:103/I. Items 1025-A-01 or -02(MF).

> Content: biographies of U.S. astronauts and cosmonauts of the former Soviet Union.

NASA Astronauts Web Page. WEB. U.S. National Aeronautics and Space Administration.<http://www.hq.nasa.gov/office/pao/History/nauts.html>.

Content: astronaut biographies.

Discussion

Astronauts and Cosmonauts Biographical and Statistical Data contains biographical information for all participants in space missions of the U.S. and of the former Soviet Union. Part 1 contains an overview of the U.S. astronaut program and biographies of U.S. mission participants. The biographies are divided into three groups: astronauts, participants in flight programs that develop astronauts, and payload specialists and other passengers. Information on each individual includes a photograph and brief biographical data. Part 2 contains similar information on cosmonauts of the former Soviet Union and foreign cosmonaut-researchers. Photographs are not always available for cosmonauts. Summary tables in each biographical section list astronauts with information on rank, flights, and total space time. Part 3 contains comparative data on spaceflights of the United States and of the former Soviet Union.

The *NASA Astronauts Web Page* provides biographical information on current and former astronauts. The "Current Astronaut Biographies" option provides a list of current astronauts with detailed biographical information and a photograph for each. Other options available from this Web page include astronaut candidates, cosmonauts, payload specialists, and a "More about Astronauts" option that provides information on public appearances, becoming an astronaut, living and working in space, and links to other NASA human spaceflight Web resources. The "More about Astronauts" page also provides access to the PDF publication, *Astronaut Fact Book*. The *Astronaut Fact Book* provides brief biographical information on current and former astronauts. This source also includes a complete alphabetical list of astronauts with selection year, number of flights, and status; astronauts winning the Congressional Space Medal of Honor; educational institutions and service academies from which astronauts have earned degrees; astronaut birthplaces by state or country; astronauts' scouting records; current astronauts in active military service; and a U.S. human space flight log listing missions, crews, dates, mission time, and cumulative man-hours in space.

ALMANACS

Checklist

The Astronomical Almanac for the Year [year]: Data for Astronomy, Space Sciences, Geodesy, Surveying, Navigation and Other Applications. PRINT. (annual) 1981–. U.S. Department of the Navy. Naval Observatory. Nautical Almanac Office. D 213.8: (Issued earlier as two separate publications: *The American Ephemeris and Nautical Almanac* and *The Astronomical Ephemeris*) Item 0394. GPO.

Content: times, dates, locations of astronomical phenomena; calendars; daily positions of sun, moon, planet, and satellites.

The Nautical Almanac for the Year [year]. PRINT. (annual) 1855–. U.S. Department of the Navy. Naval Observatory. Nautical Almanac Office. D 213.11: Item 0395. GPO.

Content: positions of the sun, moon, stars, and planets.

The Air Almanac. PRINT. (annual) 1953–. U.S. Department of the Navy. Naval Observatory. Nautical Almanac Office. D 213.7: Item 0393. GPO.

Content: positions of the sun, moon, Aries, and selected planets.

Astronomical Applications Data Services Web Page. WEB. U.S. Department of the Navy. Naval Observatory.<http://aa.usno.navy.mil/AA/data/>.

Content: sunrise, sunset, moonrise, moonset, twilight, phases of the moon, eclipses, positions of the sun and moon, interactive computer almanac, celestial navigation data, seasonal dates.

Discussion

The Astronomical Almanac is published in advance of the year covered and contains information on the sun, moon, planets, and astronomical phenomena for the coming year. Information includes dates of the moon's phases, locations and dates of eclipses, planet visibility, sunrise and sunset times for each day, moonrise and moonset times, twilight times, calendars, and planet coordinates and locations for each day of the year.

The Nautical Almanac gives daily information needed for ocean navigation. It contains coordinates for the sun, moon, and planets for one-hour intervals plus additional information useful for navigation. Data include the Greenwich Hour Angle (G.H.A.) for Aries—vernal equinox, a point used in celestial navigation— and the G.H.A. and declination for the sun, moon, and four navigational planets. The times for twilight, sunrise, moonrise, and moonset are also given. Other sections cover phases of the moon, eclipses, and star charts.

The Air Almanac gives daily information needed for air navigation. The information is used to calculate the position of an astronomical body. Data are given for 10-minute intervals and include the Greenwich Hour Angle (G.H.A.) and declination for the sun, moon, Aries, and the three planets most suitable for observation at the specified time. Additional information useful for air navigation is also included, such as a star chart, sky diagrams, and sunrise, sunset, and twilight times.

The *Astronomical Applications Data Services Web Page* provides some basic astronomical data. Users may enter a specific date and location and obtain daily or yearly times for sunrise, sunset, moonrise, moonset, and twilight. Information on phases of the moon is available for a specific day or in yearly tables. Other options include recent and upcoming eclipses of the sun and moon, a lunar eclipse computer that provides specific timing of any eclipse by location, and altitude and azimuth of the sun and moon for a specified day. A "Multiyear Interactive Computer Almanac" for technical users performs common astronomical calculations from January 1 of the previous year to 30 days beyond the current date. Data include celestial coordinates, sidereal time, and lunar and planetary configurations. Also available are celestial navigation data and dates for earth's seasons.

CONGRESSIONAL SOURCES
Checklist

Hearings, Prints, and Miscellaneous Publications. PRINT. MF. U.S. Congress. House. Committee on Science. Y 4.SCI 2: Items 1025-A-01 or 02(MF). GPO. Committee home page:<http://www.house.gov/science/welcome.htm>.
> Content: committee hearings and research reports on space programs and issues.

Hearings, Prints, and Miscellaneous Publications. PRINT. MF. U.S. Congress. Senate. Committee on Commerce, Science, and Transportation. Y 4.C 73/7: Items 1041-A or -B(MF). GPO. Committee Space Web Page: <http://www.senate.gov/~commerce/issues/space.htm>.
> Content: committee hearings and research reports on space programs and issues.

Discussion

The House Committee on Science and the Senate Committee on Commerce, Science, and Transportation publish materials on a variety of scientific subjects, including space. Publications include transcripts of committee hearings on bills, programs, and issues, as well as studies and guides. Examples of recent House hearings include *NASA at 40, What Kind of Space Program Does America Need for the 21st Century?* (Y 4.SCI 2:105/90) and *U.S.-Russian Cooperation in Human Spaceflight, Parts I-V* (Y 4.SCI 2:105/79). Another report from the House committee of more historical interest is *Space Activities of the United States, Soviet Union and Other Launching Countries/Organizations: 1957-1993* (Y 4.SCI 2:103-K). The Senate committee publishes similar hearings and reports. Recent Senate hearings include *International Space Station* (Y 4.C 73/7:S.HRG.105-436) and *Commercialization of Space* (Y 4.C 73/7:S.HRG.105-912).

A limited number of congressional hearings are available on the Web. The House Science Committee Web page contains the text of statements submitted by witnesses for selected, recent hearings. The Senate Committee on Commerce, Science, and Transportation has a space-related Web page, which also has the text of statements submitted by witnesses for selected, recent hearings. This Web page also contains links to other committee information on space and links to selected other Web sites.

INDEXES
Checklist

Catalog of United States Government Publications (MOCAT). WEB. 1994–. U.S. Government Printing Office. Superintendent of Documents.<http://www.gpo.gov/catalog>; <http://www.access.gpo.gov/su_docs/locators/cgp/index.html>; <http://purl.access.gpo.gov/GPO/LPS844>.

Monthly Catalog of United States Government Publications. CD-ROM. 1996–. U.S. Government Printing Office. Superintendent of Documents. GP 3.8/7: Item 0557-C. GPO.

Monthly Catalog of United States Government Publications (Condensed version). PRINT. (monthly) 1996–. U.S. Government Printing Office. Superintendent of Documents. GP 3.8/8: (Earlier full version, GP 3.8:, 1895-1995). Item 0557-D. GPO.

CIS/Index. PRINT. (monthly) 1970–. Bethesda, MD: Congressional Information Service.

Congressional Universe. WEB. Bethesda, MD: Congressional Information Service.

Discussion

The *Monthly Catalog* is the most comprehensive index for government publications. For publications on space look for subject headings beginning with "Space," such as "Space Flight" or "Space Vehicles." Other relevant subject headings include "Outer Space," "Astronautics," "Astronauts," and "Astronomy." See also specific planets and programs. The complete version of the *Monthly Catalog* is available on the Web and CD-ROM. Commercial online and CD-ROM versions of the *Monthly Catalog* are also available.

Congressional publications can be found through *CIS/Index* under subject headings beginning with "Space." A smaller number of materials may be found under "Astronomy," "Astronautics," "Astronauts," and under specific programs. *Congressional Universe* includes a Web version of *CIS*.

For more information on these indexes, see Chapter 3, "The Basics of Searching."

RELATED MATERIAL
Within this Work

Chapter 49   Technical Reports

GPO SUBJECT BIBLIOGRAPHIES. PRINT. WEB. GP 3.22/2:

<http://bookstore.gpo/gov/sb/about.html>

No. 222 "Aerospace"

No. 297 "Space Exploration"

The Agency Search

The agency search can be used to answer such questions as "What are the requirements of the food stamp program?" "What assistance programs are available from the Department of Housing and Urban Development?" and "What are the responsibilities of the Federal Trade Commission?" A good starting point is to check the *United States Government Manual*, the *List of Classes*, or the *Catalog of Federal Domestic Assistance*.

Annual reports and general publications series often provide valuable information on agency activities. An integral part of such activities are agency regulations, which specify program details in depth and generally are found in the *Code of Federal Regulations*. Finally, indexes may be searched for more specific information.

This section contains a chapter on locating information on agency programs, two chapters relating to administrative regulations and decisions, and a chapter on a special "agency"—"The President"—which also partly relates to administrative actions.

CHAPTER 24
Government Programs and Grants

Information about specific agency programs and grant activities can be located in several different major sources and through the use of agency specific Web sites and resources. This chapter lists general sources that provide program and grant information. Many agencies also provide access to information through their agency Web sites and through agency publications such as annual reports, program annual reports or evaluations, grant guides, and other related sources. This chapter also includes a selection of agency specific information from selected agencies as examples of the types of information that is available. Information about programs and grants may also appear in congressional publications, particularly hearings, and in U.S. government budget reports. Consult Chapter 45, "Legislative History," for information on locating congressional sources, and Chapter 47, "Budget Analysis," for more detailed information on locating budget sources.

SEARCH STRATEGY

This chapter shows an agency search strategy. The steps to follow are

1. Use the *United States Government Manual* to locate background information on the agency and its programs;
2. Locate descriptions of specific agency programs and grants in the *Catalog of Federal Domestic Assistance*;
3. The *List of Classes* and *Guide to U.S. Government Publications* can be used to quickly identify program and grant-related series and major titles;
4. Search the *Code of Federal Regulations* and *Federal Register* for regulations and notices pertaining to the program or grant;
5. Scan the "Statistical Sources" section of this chapter to locate statistical sources relating to programs and grants;

6. Search *American Statistics Index (ASI)* for more detailed or additional statistics;
7. Use the sources listed in the "General Accounting Office (GAO) Publications and Information" section of this chapter to locate analyses and evaluations of programs;
8. If your agency is included, use the guides and Web sites listed in the "Individual Agency Grant Publications And Information" section of this chapter;
9. See the listings of agency Web sites in Chapter 9, "Directories," to locate additional relevant agency Web sites;
10. Search the *Monthly Catalog* to find additional publications on the program or grant; and
11. Search *CIS/Index* to locate any congressional hearings, committee prints, reports, or documents pertaining to the program or grant.

BASIC SOURCES
Checklist

United States Government Manual. PRINT. WEB. (annual) 1935–. U.S. National Archives and Records Administration. Office of the Federal Register. AE 2.108/2: (Earlier, GS 4.109:) Item 0577. GPO. <http://www.access.gpo.gov/nara/nara001.html>; <http://purl. access.gpo.gov/GPO/LPS2410>.
> Content: short descriptions of agencies and their programs and activities.

Catalog of Federal Domestic Assistance. PRINT. WEB. (annual, with annual update) 1965–. U.S. Executive Office of the President. Office of Management and Budget and General Services Administration. PREX 2.20: (Earlier title: *Catalog of Federal Assistance Programs*, PREX 10.2:P 94) Item 0853-A-01. ASI 104-5. GPO.<http://www.cfda.gov/>;<http://purl.access.gpo.gov/GPO/LPS1729>.
> Content: individual descriptions of agency assistance programs.

Catalog of Federal Domestic Assistance. CD-ROM. U.S. Executive Office of the President. Office of Management and Budget and General Services Administration. (Nondepository)

> Content: CD-ROM version of the *Catalog of Federal Domestic Assistance.*

Government Assistance Almanac. PRINT. (annual) 1986–. Detroit, MI: Omnigraphics, Inc.

> Content: commercial abridged edition of the *Catalog of Federal Domestic Assistance.*

Background Material and Data on Major Programs Within the Jurisdiction of the Committee on Ways and Means. PRINT. WEB. (biennial). U.S. Congress. House. Committee on Ways and Means. Y 4.W 36:10-4/year. (title often known as the *Green Book*) Items 1028-A or -B(MF). GPO.<http://www.access.gpo.gov/congress/wm001.html>;<http://purl.access.gpo.gov/GPO/LPS963>.

> Content: comprehensive compilation describing and analyzing individual government programs under the jurisdiction of the Committee on Ways and Means.

List of Classes of United States Government Publications Available for Selection by Depository Libraries. PRINT. WEB. (semiannual). U.S. Government Printing Office. Superintendent of Documents. Library Programs Service. Library Division. Depository Administration Branch. GP 3.24: Item 0556-C.<http://www.du.edu/~ttyler/locintro.htm#gtr00>;<http://govdoc.wichita.edu/ddm/GdocFrames.asp>;<http://www.access.gpo.gov/su_docs/fdlp/pubs/loc/index.html>;<http://fedbbs.access.gpo.gov/libs/CLASS.htm>;<http://purl.access.gpo.gov/GPO/LPS1480>.

> Content: depending on version, listing or database of depository series available for distribution.

Guide to U.S. Government Publications. PRINT. (annual) 1959–. Donna Batten, Editor. Farmington Hills, MI: Gale Group, Inc. (Earlier published by Documents Index.)

> Content: listing and description of agency series.

Discussion

The *United States Government Manual* gives a short overview of each agency's activities and programs. Authorizing laws and purposes of programs are often included. Program publications and agency contacts for further information are also provided. Using the *United States Government Manual* is a good first step in gathering program information. The Web version of the *Government Manual* provides keyword and phrase searching capabilities.

The *Catalog of Federal Domestic Assistance* is a massive guide to government assistance programs. It is available in both print and Web-based versions. Programs included, as defined in the introduction of the *Catalog*, are "...any function of a Federal agency that provides assistance or benefits for a State or States, territorial possession, county, city, other political subdivision, grouping, or instrumentality thereof; any domestic profit or nonprofit corporation, institution, or individual, other than an agency of the Federal government."

Individual program descriptions are arranged by agency. Descriptions may include several elements. (See Figure 24.1 for a sample program description.) Key elements include:

1. **Program Number, Title, and Popular Name.** Each program is assigned a five-digit program identification number. The first two digits identify the department or agency, and the last three identify the specific program. Thus, all programs listed under the Department of Health and Human Services begin with 93, such as program 93.178, "Nursing Education Opportunities for Individuals from Disadvantaged Backgrounds."
2. **Federal Agency.** Refers to the federal agency and subunit responsible for administering the program.
3. **Authorization.** Gives the legal authority for the program, such as acts, public laws, *U.S. Code*, executive orders, etc.
4. **Objectives.** A statement of what the program is intended to accomplish.
5. **Types of Assistance.** Indicates the grant form, such as project grants, formula grants, guaranteed insured loans, etc., in which the assistance is received.
6. **Uses and Use Restrictions.** Describes potential uses of the assistance and any specific restrictions on using the assistance.
7. **Eligibility Requirements.** Indicates who is eligible to receive the assistance.
8. **Application and Award Process.** Lists the procedures for the application and award of assistance.
9. **Assistance Considerations.** Gives the formula for calculating assistance and time period for which the assistance is available.
10. **Post-Assistance Requirements.** Lists any reports, audits, or records required.
11. **Financial Information.** Gives the budget account identification code; budget amounts obligated for the program for the past, current and estimated budget years; and the range and average amount of financial assistance available.
12. **Program Accomplishments.** Describes program results.
13. **Regulations, Guidelines, and Literature.** Lists *Code of Federal Regulations* citation and any other published guidelines, handbooks, or manuals regarding the program.
14. **Information Contacts.** Gives agency contact person, addresses, e-mail addresses, and telephone numbers needed to obtain further information.
15. **Related Programs.** Cites other closely related programs found in the *Catalog*.
16. **Examples of Funded Projects.** Examples of the types of projects funded by the program.
17. **Criteria for Selecting Proposals.** Describes criteria used to evaluate proposals.

14.181 SUPPORTIVE HOUSING FOR PERSONS WITH DISABILITIES
(Section 811)

FEDERAL AGENCY: HOUSING, DEPARTMENT OF HOUSING AND URBAN DEVELOPMENT

AUTHORIZATION: National Affordable Housing Act, Public Law 101-625, 42 U.S.C. 8013, 104 Stat. 4324, 4331.

OBJECTIVES: To provide for supportive housing for persons with disabilities.

TYPES OF ASSISTANCE: Direct Payments for Specified Use.

USES AND USE RESTRICTIONS: Capital advances may be used to construct, rehabilitate or acquire structures to be used as supportive housing for persons with disabilities. Project rental assistance is used to cover the difference between the HUD-approved operating costs of the project and the tenants' contributions toward rent (30 percent of adjusted income).

ELIGIBILITY REQUIREMENTS:

Applicant Eligibility: Nonprofit organizations with a Section 501(c)(3) tax exemption from the Internal Revenue Service.

Beneficiary Eligibility: Beneficiaries of housing developed under this program must be very low income physically disabled, developmentally disabled or chronically mentally ill persons (18 years of age or older).

Credentials/Documentation: The nonprofit sponsor and owner must receive certification of eligibility from HUD. The owner must submit financial statements to support its ability to provide a minimum capital investment of 1/2 of 1 percent of the capital advance amount, up to a maximum of $10,000. This program is excluded from coverage under OMB Circular No. A-87.

APPLICATION AND AWARD PROCESS:

Preapplication Coordination: Applicants must forward a copy of their applications to the appropriate state or local agency for a review of the supportive services plan and a completed certification from the agency as to whether the provision of services is well designed to meet the needs of the anticipated occupancy be included in the applicant's submission of its application to the HUD field office. This program is excluded from coverage under OMB Circular No. A-102. An environmental assessment is required for applications containing evidence of site control. This program is eligible for coverage under E.O. 12372, "Intergovernmental Review of Federal Programs." An applicant should consult the office or official designated as the single point of contact in his or her State for more information on the process the State requires to be followed in applying for assistance, if the State has selected the program for review.

Application Procedure: A Notice of Funding Availability is published in the Federal Register each fiscal year announcing the availability of funds to HUD Field Offices. Applicants must submit an application, including a Request for Fund Reservation using HUD Form 92016-CA, in response to the Notice of Fund Availability (or Funding Notification issued by the local HUD Field Office.) This program is excluded from coverage under OMB Circular No. A-110.

Award Procedure: Applications are reviewed and selected for funding within the funding allocation of the particular HUD Field Office. Those selected for funding must meet basic program requirements including, but not limited to: eligibility as a nonprofit entity, financial commitment and prior experience in housing or related service activities.

Deadlines: Applications must be submitted within the time period specified in the Notice of Fund Availability (or Funding Notification) usually 60 to 90 days.

Range of Approval/Disapproval Time: At the fund reservation stage, the sponsor usually is advised of the decision within 4 to 5 months from the end of the application period.

Appeals: Applicants are afforded the right to appeal HUD's determination of technical rejection.

Renewals: None.

ASSISTANCE CONSIDERATIONS:

Formula and Matching Requirements: This program has maintenance of effort (MOE) requirements; see funding agency for further details. Statistical factors used for fund allocation include a measure of the number of non-institutionalized persons age 16 or older with a work disability and a mobility or self-care limitation, and the number of non-institutionalized persons age 16 or older having a mobility or self-care limitation but having no work disability from the Census. Statistical factors used for eligibility do not apply for this program.

Length and Time Phasing of Assistance: The capital advance is not repayable if the project is available for very low income persons with disabilities for 40 years. Project Rental Assistance Contracts may not exceed 5 years. However, contracts are renewable based on availability of funds. Projects are expected to start construction within 18 months of the date of the fund reservation, with limited provision for extensions. Funds will be advanced on a monthly basis during construction for work in place.

POST ASSISTANCE REQUIREMENTS:

Reports: Any change in the owner during the 40-year period must be approved by HUD. All owners will be required to submit an annual financial statement to HUD.

Audits: HUD reserves the right to audit the accounts of the owners in order to determine compliance and conformance with HUD regulations and standards.

Records: Regular financial reports are required. Owners must service and maintain records in accordance with acceptable mortgage practices and HUD regulations. Owners also must supply those records necessary to indicate compliance with the project rental assistance contract.

FINANCIAL INFORMATION:

Account Identification: 86-0164-0-3-371; 86-4588-0-3-371; 86-0320-0-3-371.

Obligations: (Reservations) FY 98 $305,247,089; FY 99 est $220,806,690; and FY 00 est $194,000,000.

Range and Average of Financial Assistance: In fiscal year 1998, the average award was $821,070; the smallest, $213,000; the largest $1,650,200.

PROGRAM ACCOMPLISHMENTS: In fiscal year 1998, HUD funded 1,650 units. The Department anticipates a similar level of funding in fiscal year 1999.

REGULATIONS, GUIDELINES, AND LITERATURE: 24 CFR, 891; HUD Handbooks 4571.2.

INFORMATION CONTACTS:

Regional or Local Office: Contact the appropriate HUD field office listed in Appendix IV of the Catalog.

Headquarters Office: Office of Business Products, Department of Housing and Urban Development, Washington, DC 20410. Telephone: (202) 708-2866. Use the same number for FTS.

RELATED PROGRAMS: 14.157, Supportive Housing for the Elderly; 14.195, Section 8 Housing Assistance Payments.

EXAMPLES OF FUNDED PROJECTS: Not applicable.

CRITERIA FOR SELECTING PROPOSALS: Not applicable.

14.183 HOME EQUITY CONVERSION MORTGAGES
(255)

FEDERAL AGENCY: HOUSING, DEPARTMENT OF HOUSING AND URBAN DEVELOPMENT

AUTHORIZATION: National Housing Act, as amended; Housing and Community Development Act of 1987, Section 417, Public Law 100-242, 12 U.S.C. 1715z-20.

OBJECTIVES: To enable elderly homeowners to convert equity in their homes to monthly streams of income or lines of credit.

TYPES OF ASSISTANCE: Guaranteed/Insured Loans.

USES AND USE RESTRICTIONS: HUD insures lenders against loss on reverse mortgage loans. These loans may be used to provide monthly streams of income or lines of credit for older homeowners, 62 years of age or older.

ELIGIBILITY REQUIREMENTS:

Applicant Eligibility: Eligible borrowers are persons 62 years of age or older. Eligible properties include Single Family one-to-four unit owner-occupied dwelling units, condominiums and Planned Unit Developments, if they meet FHA standards, and manufactured homes, if they meet FHA standards.

Beneficiary Eligibility: Individuals.

Source: *Catalog of Federal Domestic Assistance*, 1999, p.261.

Figure 24.1: Sample Page from *Catalog of Federal Domestic Assistance*.

The Web version of the *Catalog of Federal Domestic Assistance* provides several ways of accessing the *Catalog*. In addition to keyword searching, the *Catalog* may be browsed by functional area, agency, sub-agency, alphabetically by program title, applicant eligibility, beneficiary, program deadline, type of assistance, and by programs requiring Executive Order 12372 review.

A CD-ROM version of the *Catalog* is nondepository, but is available for purchase from the General Service Administration's Federal Domestic Assistance Catalog Staff.

The *Government Assistance Almanac* is a commercially produced annual version of the *Catalog of Federal Domestic Assistance*. It provides a summary annotation for each program in the *Catalog of Federal Domestic Assistance*, using the same program identification numbers as the *Catalog of Federal Domestic Assistance*. Summary tables of program funding levels and an extensive directory of agency field office contacts are also included.

The *Background Material and Data on Major Programs Within the Jurisdiction of the Committee on Ways and Means*, commonly known as the *Green Book*, is an extremely valuable compilation of information on government programs that are under the jurisdiction of the Committee on Ways and Means. Such programs as the Old-Age and Survivors Insurance (OASI) program, Social Security, Medicare, trade adjustment assistance programs, child support enforcement programs, social services block grant programs, and child care programs are included. Descriptions contain numerous statistical charts and tables. Various appendices are also included, which contain detailed compilations on various related subjects such as "Demographic and Economic Characteristics of the Elderly," "Demographic, Economic, and Social Characteristics of Families with Children," and "Poverty, Income Distribution, and Antipoverty Effectiveness." (See Figure 24.2.)

The *List of Classes* provides information about the sources currently available for selection by selective depository libraries and received in entirety by regional depository libraries. Increasingly, the *List of Classes* also lists electronic versions of items accessible through the Web that are only available that way—and are not otherwise distributed to depository libraries or are not produced in any other format. The *List of Classes* is useful for quickly identifying annual reports of agencies and other relevant sources, such as grant handbooks and guides listed as series. Annual reports of an agency often provide program overviews, statistics, and trends.

The print version of the *List of Classes* is arranged by agency in SuDocs number order. For each class under an agency, the title, SuDocs number, item number, and often the frequency of the title is given. The format designations Print (P), Microfiche (MF), CD-ROM (CD-ROM), Electronic (E), and Electronic Library (EL) are also included. The print version includes an alphabetical list of government authors and a list of item numbers, giving

SECTION 11. CHILD PROTECTION, FOSTER CARE, AND ADOPTION ASSISTANCE

CONTENTS

Background
Federal Child Welfare Programs Today
  The Title IV-B Child Welfare Services Program
  The Title IV-E Foster Care Program
  The Title IV-E Adoption Assistance Program
  The Title IV-E Independent Living Program
Protections for Children in Foster Care
  Protections Linked to Title IV-B Child Welfare Services Funding
  Mandatory Protections for Foster Children Funded Under Title IV-E
  Reasonable Efforts Requirement
  State Compliance With Section 427 Child Protections
  Federal Financial Review Procedures Under Title IV-E
  New Conformity Review System Under Public Law 103-432
Recent Trends Affecting Child Welfare Populations and Programs
  Child Abuse and Neglect
  Child Abuse Fatalities
  Substance Abuse
  Trends in Foster Care Caseloads
  Increase in "Kinship" Care
  Family Preservation Programs
  National Data on Foster Care and Adoption Assistance
  Characteristics of Children in Substitute Care
  Reasons for Placement in Substitute Care
  Permanency Goals
  Living Arrangements of Children in Substitute Care
  Number and Duration of Placements While in Foster Care
  Outcomes for Children Leaving Care
  Characteristics of Children in Adoptive Care
  Trends in Child Welfare and Foster Care Costs
Foster Care and Adoption Information System
  Lack of Adequate Data
  OBRA 1993 and Final Rules for AFCARS and SACWIS
Legislative History
  Adoption Legislation in the 105th Congress
References

(727)

Figure 24.2: Sample Page from *Background Material and Data on Major Programs Within the Jurisdiction of the Committee on Ways and Means*.

SuDocs. The HTML version of the *List of Classes* at the *Basic Depository Library Documents* (*BDLD*) site provides a similarly formatted version, and also includes a list of government authors arranged by government author name, and a list of classes arranged by item number. A searchable version of the *List of Classes* is also available at the *Documents Data Miner*© Web site. This site allows boolean searching of the agency, item number, SuDocs stem, title, formats, and status fields. Truncated and wild card searching is also included. This version also allows you to easily display the libraries selecting the item for a particular class, according to user defined filters for the geographic areas of the depository libraries that should be included.

A GPO version of the *List of Classes* is made available through the *Federal Bulletin Board File Libraries* as ASCII comma delimited files. Although somewhat unwieldy to search and use, these files can be downloaded and manipulated. They also provide the data for the two versions of the *List of Classes* previously described.

The *Guide to U.S. Government Publications*, previously known as *Andriot* (for its original author), also provides a listing of classes in a SuDocs number arrangement. Entries include the SuDocs number, title, and item number if depository; other elements that are sometimes included are dates, frequency of publication, ISSN number; notes about title and SuDocs number changes, and descriptions of the title. Information about the creation, authority, and establishment dates of each individual agency is included at the beginning of an agency's listing. Entries are often annotated, and individual documents within a series are sometimes noted and annotated. An "Agency Class Chronology" section gives a historical SuDocs numbers listing for each agency, and an agency, title, and keyword in title index are included within the volume. In many ways The *Guide to U.S. Government Publications* can be used as an expanded *List of Classes*. The *Guide*, however, includes nondepository titles and discontinued classes, whereas the *List of Classes* includes current depository classes only.

REGULATIONS

Checklist

Code of Federal Regulations. PRINT. MF. WEB. (annual) 1938–. U.S. National Archives and Records Administration. Office of the Federal Register. AE 2.106/3: (*CFR Index and Finding Aids,* AE 2.106/3-2:). (Earlier, GS 4.108:, GS 4.108/4:) Items 0572, 0572-B or -C(MF). GPO.<http://www.access.gpo.gov/nara/cfr/index.html>;<http://purl.access.gpo.gov/GPO/LPS3384>.

> Content: all U.S. government regulations in force as of cover date, with a one-volume index.

CFR Index and Finding Aids. PRINT. (annual) U.S. National Archives and Records Administration. Office of the Federal Register. AE 2.106/3-2: (Earlier, GS 4.108/4:) (Accompanies the *Code of Federal Regulations*) Item 0572. GPO. Parallel table:<http://www.access.gpo.gov/nara/cfr/index.html>;<http://purl.access.gpo.gov/GPO/LPS3384>.

> Content: general subject and agency index to the *Code of Federal Regulations;* tables relating *United States Code* sections to *CFR* sections; outline of *CFR* titles and parts.

Index to the Code of Federal Regulations. PRINT. (annual with quarterly supplements) 1977–. Bethesda, MD: Congressional Information Service, Inc.

> Content: in-depth, multivolume subject, geographic, and CFR section number index.

Federal Register. PRINT. MF. WEB. (daily, Mon.-Fri., except holidays) 1936-. U.S. National Archives and Records Administration. Office of the Federal Register. AE 2.106: (Earlier, GS 4.107:) Items 0573-C, -D(MF), or –F(EL). GPO.<http://www.access.gpo.gov/su_docs/aces/aces140.html>;<http://purl.access.gpo.gov/GPO/LPS1756>.

> Content: regulations; proposed regulations; presidential proclamations and executive orders; background analyses relating to regulations; announcements regarding agency actions, hearings, grants, and publications.

The Federal Register Home Page. WEB. U.S. National Archives and Records Administration.<http://www.nara.gov/fedreg/>.

> Content: information about the Federal Register, indexes, and research tools.

Discussion

The *Code of Federal Regulations* provides the specific regulations that an agency uses for administering its programs. Sections may cover who is eligible for the program, how the program should be implemented, and any requirements for review of the program. Figure 24.3 reproduces, for example, a section of the *Code of Federal Regulations* describing the "Runaway and Homeless Youth Program."

The one-volume *CFR Index and Finding Aids* included in the print version of the *CFR* provides agency access and very general subject access to the regulations concerning a program. Congressional Information Service, Inc. publishes *Index to the Code of Federal Regulations,* a more detailed, multivolume annual index with quarterly updates. Online versions of the *CFR* provide full-text searching.

The *Code of Federal Regulations* is available on the Web from the Government Printing Office's *GPO Access* Web site (July 1996–). Online commercial services also include the *CFR,* including *CIS Congressional Universe* (current), *LEXIS-NEXIS* (1981–), *LEXIS-NEXIS Academic Universe* (current), *Westlaw* (1984–), and *CQ.com On Congress.* The *LEXIS* file is called CFR and is available in several libraries, including GENFED, CODES, and EXEC. The GENFED library offers the most options, including different editions of the *CFR.* Relevant titles of the *CFR* also appear in appropriate subject libraries. A CD-ROM version is available from West.

The *Federal Register* includes proposed regulations, new regulations, and agency notices regarding programs and grants. Figure 24.4 gives an example of a notice concerning the transmittal of grant applications for programs authorized under the Individuals with Disabilities Education Act (IDEA). The *Federal Register* is an essential source for keeping track of current agency program and grant activity. For the print version, a cumulative monthly index (culminating in an annual index) provides broad subject and agency access. *The Federal Register Home Page* also provides information about the content and use of the *Federal Register* and related index and research aids. The "Federal Register Indexes" provides table of contents listings for recent years, the current year-to-date index, and annual indexes for several years. The home page also provides links to the online *Federal Register* available from the Government Printing Office.

The *Federal Register* is available on the Web from the Government Printing Office's *GPO Access* Web site (1994–). It is also available from several commercial online services, including *LEXIS-NEXIS* (July 1, 1980–), *CIS Congressional Universe* (1980–), *Westlaw* (July 1, 1980–), *CQ.com On Congress* (1997–), and Dialog (1985–). The *LEXIS* file is called FEDREG and can be found in several libraries, including the GENFED and EXEC libraries. Dialog also offers a CD-ROM version. See Chapter 25, "Regulations and Administrative Actions," for more information on using the *Code of Federal Regulations* and the *Federal Register.*

SUBCHAPTER F—THE ADMINISTRATION FOR CHILDREN, YOUTH AND FAMILIES, FAMILY AND YOUTH SERVICES BUREAU

PART 1351—RUNAWAY AND HOMELESS YOUTH PROGRAM

Subpart A—Definition of Terms

Sec.
1351.1   Significant terms.

Subpart B—Runaway and Homeless Youth Program Grant

1351.10   What is the purpose of the Runaway and Homeless Youth grant?

1351.11   Who is eligible to apply for a Runaway and Homeless Youth Program grant?

1351.12   Who gets priority for the award of a Runaway and Homeless Youth Program grant?

1351.13   What are the Federal and non-Federal match requirements under a Runaway and Homeless Youth Program grant?

1351.14   What is the period for which a grant will be awarded?

1351.15   What costs are supportable under a Runaway and Homeless Youth Program grant?

1351.16   What costs are not allowable under a Runaway and Homeless Youth Program grant?

1351.17   How is application made for a Runaway and Homeless Youth Program grant?

1351.18   What criteria has HHS established for deciding which Runaway and Homeless Youth Program grant applications to fund?

1351.19   What additional information should an applicant or grantee have about a Runaway and Homeless Youth Program grant?

Subpart C—Additional Requirements

1351.20   What are the additional requirements under a Runaway and Homeless Youth Program grant?

AUTHORITY: 42 U.S.C. 5701.

SOURCE: 43 FR 55635, Nov. 28, 1978, unless otherwise noted.

EDITORIAL NOTE: For nomenclature changes to this part see 54 FR 20854, May 15, 1989, and 55 FR 5601, Feb. 16, 1990.

Subpart A—Definition of Terms

§ 1351.1   Significant terms.

For the purposes of this part:

(a) *Aftercare services* means the provision of services to runaway or otherwise homeless youth and their families, following the youth's return home or placement in alternative living arrangements which assist in alleviating the problems that contributed to his or her running away or being homeless.

(b) *Area* means a specific neighborhood or section of the locality in which the runaway and homeless youth project is or will be located.

(c) *Coordinated networks of agencies* means an association of two or more private agencies, whose purpose is to develop or strengthen services to runaway or otherwise homeless youth and their families.

(d) *Counseling services* means the provision of guidance, support and advice to runaway or otherwise homeless youth and their families designed to alleviate the problems which contributed to the youth's running away or being homeless, resolve intrafamily problems, to reunite such youth with their families, whenever appropriate, and to help them decide upon a future course of action.

(e) *Demonstrably frequented by or reachable* means located in an area in which runaway or otherwise homeless youth congregate or an area accessible to such youth by public transportation or by the provision of transportation by the runaway and homeless youth project itself.

(f) *Homeless youth* means a person under 18 years of age who is in need of services and without a place of shelter where he or she receives supervision and care.

(g) *Juvenile justice system* means agencies such as, but not limited to juvenile courts, law enforcement, probation, parole, correctional institutions, training schools, and detention facilities.

(h) *Law enforcement structure* means any police activity or agency with

299

Source: Code of Federal Regulations, Title 45, Subchapter F, Part 1351.

Figure 24.3: Sample Page from *Code of Federal Regulations*.

DEPARTMENT OF EDUCATION

Office of Special Education and Rehabilitative Services; Grant Applications under Part D, Subpart 2 of the Individuals with Disabilities Education Act Amendments of 1997

AGENCY: Department of Education.

ACTION: Notice inviting applications for new awards for fiscal year (FY) 2000.

SUMMARY: This notice provides closing dates and other information regarding the transmittal of applications for FY 2000 competitions under five programs authorized by the Individuals with Disabilities Education Act (IDEA), as amended. The five programs are: (1) Special Education—Research and Innovation to Improve Services and Results for Children with Disabilities (seven priorities); (2) Special Education—Personnel Preparation to Improve Services and Results for Children with Disabilities (four priorities); (3) Special Education—Technical Assistance and Dissemination to Improve Services and Results for Children with Disabilities (two priorities); (4) Special Education—Technology and Media Services for Individuals with Disabilities (five priorities); and (5) Special Education—Training and Information for Parents of Children with Disabilities (one priority).

This notice supports the National Education Goals by helping to improve results for children with disabilities.

Waiver of Rulemaking

It is generally the practice of the Secretary to offer interested parties the opportunity to comment on proposed priorities. However, section 661(e)(2) of IDEA makes the Administrative Procedure Act (5 U.S.C. 553) inapplicable to the priorities in this notice.

General Requirements

(a) Projects funded under this notice must make positive efforts to employ and advance in employment qualified individuals with disabilities in project activities (see section 606 of IDEA);

(b) Applicants and grant recipients funded under this notice must involve individuals with disabilities or parents of individuals with disabilities in planning, implementing, and evaluating the projects (see section 661(f)(1)(A) of IDEA);

(c) Projects funded under these priorities must budget for a two-day Project Directors' meeting in Washington, D.C. during each year of the project;

(d) In a single application, an applicant must address only one absolute priority in this notice; and (e) Part III of each application submitted under a priority in this notice, the application narrative, is where an applicant addresses the selection criteria that are used by reviewers in evaluating the application. An applicant must limit Part III to the equivalent of no more than the number of pages listed in the "Page Limits" section under the applicable priority in this notice. An applicant must use the following standards: (1) A "page" is 8½″ × 11″ (on one side only) with one-inch margins (top, bottom, and sides). (2) All text in the application narrative, including titles, headings, footnotes, quotations, references, and captions, as well as all text in charts, tables, figures, and graphs, must be double-spaced (no more than 3 lines per vertical inch). If using a proportional computer font, use no smaller than a 12-point font, and an average character density no greater than 18 characters per inch. If using a nonproportional font or a typewriter, do not use more than 12 characters to the inch.

The page limit does not apply to Part I—the cover sheet; Part II—the budget section (including the narrative budget justification); Part IV—the assurances and certifications; or the one-page abstract, resumes, bibliography, and letters of support. However, all of the application narrative must be included in Part III. If an application narrative uses a smaller print size, spacing, or margin that would make the narrative exceed the equivalent of the page limit, the application will not be considered for funding.

Note: The Department of Education is not bound by any estimates in this notice.

Information collection resulting from this notice has been submitted to OMB for review under the Paperwork Reduction Act and has been approved under control number 1820–0028, expiration date July 31, 2000.

Research and Innovation To Improve Services and Results for Children With Disabilities

Purpose of Program

To produce, and advance the use of, knowledge to: (1) Improve services provided under IDEA, including the practices of professionals and others involved in providing those services to children with disabilities; and (2) improve educational and early intervention results for infants, toddlers, and children with disabilities.

Eligible Applicants

State and local educational agencies; institutions of higher education; other public agencies; private nonprofit organizations; outlying areas; freely associated States; and Indian tribes or tribal organizations.

Applicable Regulations

(a) The Education Department General Administrative Regulations (EDGAR) in 34 CFR parts 74, 75, 77, 79, 80, 81, 82, 85, 86, and; (b) The selection criteria for the priorities under this program are drawn from the EDGAR general selection criteria menu. The specific selection criteria for each priority are included in the funding application packet for the applicable competition.

Note: The regulations in 34 CFR part 86 apply to institutions of higher education only.

Priority

Under 34 CFR 75.105(c)(3), we consider only applications that meet one of the following priorities:

Absolute Priority 1—Student—Initiated Research Projects (84.324B)

This priority provides support for short-term (up to 12 months) postsecondary student-initiated research projects focusing on special education and related services for children with disabilities and early intervention services for infants and toddlers, consistent with the purposes of the program, as described in Section 672 of the Act.

Projects must—

(a) Develop research skills in postsecondary students; and (b) Include a principal investigator who serves as a mentor to the student researcher while the project is carried out by the student.

Competitive Preferences:

Within this absolute priority, we will give the following competitive preference under section 606 of IDEA and 34 CFR 75.105(c)(2)(i), to applications that are otherwise eligible for funding under this priority:

Up to ten (10) points based on the extent to which an application includes effective strategies for employing and advancing in employment qualified individuals with disabilities in projects awarded under this absolute priority. In determining the effectiveness of such strategies, the Secretary will consider the applicant's success, as described in the application, in employing and advancing in employment qualified individuals with disabilities in the project.

For purposes of this competitive preference, applicants can be awarded

Figure 24.4: Sample *Federal Register* Notice.

STATISTICAL SOURCES

Checklist

Statistical Abstract of the United States. PRINT. WEB. (annual) 1878–. U.S. Department of Commerce. Economics and Statistics Administration. Bureau of the Census. C 3.134: Item 0150. ASI 2324-1. GPO. <http://www.census.gov/statab/www/>; <http://purl.access.gpo.gov/GPO/LPS2878>.

> Coverage: U.S., states.
> Content: statistics on money spent on government programs; most statistics are for broad subject categories of programs.

Statistical Abstract of the United States. CD-ROM. (annual) 1993–. U.S. Department of Commerce. Bureau of the Census. C 3.134/7: Item 0150-B. ASI 2324-14.

> Content: CD-ROM version of the *Statistical Abstract.*

Historical Statistics of the United States: Colonial Times to 1970. Parts 1-2. PRINT. (1975) U.S. Department of Commerce. Bureau of the Census. C 3.134/2:H 62/789-970/pt.1-2. Item 0151. ASI (76) 2328-2. GPO.

> Coverage: U.S.
> Content: basic historical statistics on amount of money spent for broad categories of programs.

Historical Statistics of the United States on CD-ROM: Colonial Times to 1970. CD-ROM. (1997) New York, NY: Cambridge University Press.

> Content: CD-ROM version of *Historical Statistics of the United States.*

Budget of the United States Government. PRINT. WEB. (annual) 1922–. U.S. Executive Office of the President. Office of Management and Budget. PREX 2.8: (Also issued as a House Document, Y 1.1/7:) Item 0853. ASI 104-2. GPO.<http://w3.access.gpo.gov/usbudget/>;<http://purl.access.gpo.gov/GPO/LPS2343>.

> Coverage: U.S.
> Content: detailed statistical information on budget outlays for agencies and programs.

Budget of the United States Government Fiscal Year [year]. CD-ROM. (annual) 1996–. U.S. Executive Office of the President. Office of Management and Budget. PREX 2.8/1: Item 0853-C.

> Content: CD-ROM version of the *Budget of the United States Government.*

Federal Assistance Awards Data System (FAADS). WEB. (quarterly) U.S. Department of Commerce. Bureau of the Census.<http://www.census.gov/govs/www/faads.html>.

> Coverage: U.S., states, counties, places.
> Content: federal expenditures or obligations for formula, project, and block grants; cooperative agreements; direct and guaranteed loans; direct payments for individuals; and insurance.

Consolidated Federal Funds Report: Fiscal Year [fiscal year] State and County Areas. PRINT. WEB. (annual) 1983–. U.S. Department of Commerce. Economics and Statistics Administration. Bureau of the Census. C 3.266/2: Item 0137-B. ASI 2464-3. GPO.<http://www.census.gov/ftp/pub/govs/www/cffr.html>.

> Coverage: U.S., states, counties
> Content: federal expenditures or obligations for the following; direct payments for retirement and disability; other direct payments; grants; procurement contracts; salaries and wages; direct loans; guaranteed or insured loans.

Consolidated Federal Funds Report. CD-ROM. (annual) U.S. Department of Commerce. Economics and Statistics Administration. Bureau of the Census. C 3.266/3: Item 0154-B-02.

> Coverage: U.S., states, counties, subcounty areas.
> Content: federal expenditures or obligations for the following: direct payments for retirement and disability; other direct payments; grants; procurement contracts; salaries and wages; direct loans; guaranteed or insured loans.

Federal Aid to States for Fiscal Year [fiscal year]. (annual) 1998–. PRINT. WEB. U.S. Department of Commerce. Economics and Statistics Administration. Bureau of the Census. C 3.266: Item 0137-B. ASI 2464-4. GPO. <http://www.census.gov/prod/www/abs/fas.html>; <http://purl.access.gpo.gov/GPO/LPS4561>.

> Coverage: U.S., states.
> Content: federal grant payments to state and local governments by agency and for selected programs.

Discussion

Both the *Statistical Abstract of the United States* and *Historical Statistics of the United States* provide some basic statistics on governmental financing of programs. Most statistics are only for broad groups of programs, such as "Health Research and Training," "Housing Assistance," or "Social Services." The full text of recent editions of the *Statistical Abstract* is available on the Census Bureau Web site as PDF files. The *Statistical Abstract* is also available on CD-ROM. The CD uses Adobe Acrobat software. *Historical Statistics of the United States: Colonial Times to 1970* covers the time period before 1970. A CD-ROM version of *Historical Statistics* is available from Cambridge University Press.

The *Budget of the United States Government* includes detailed statistics on outlays for agencies and their programs. Statistics are given by agency and then by specific programs and accounts within agencies. Statistics are usually given for the actual expenditures for the previous budget year, estimated expenditures for the current budget year, and estimated proposed expenditures for the forthcoming budget year. A CD-ROM version of the *Budget* is also available. The *Budget* is an excellent source for obtaining specific financial information on agency and grant funding programs.

The *Federal Assistance Awards Data System* is a quarterly set of data providing information on federal financial assistance awards. It seeks to cover assistance awards from all programs in the *Catalog of Federal Domestic Assistance*, as well as some additional assistance awards. The data are distributed at the Census Bureau's Web site, although the Office of Management and Budget provides policy oversight. Summaries of the data for the U.S. and each state may be viewed directly, but the full data files must be downloaded to obtain the more detailed data. Files are flat ASCII text files and the quarterly data sets are not cumulated. Entries are included for each assistance transaction and are also aggregated at the county level. Detailed information on each transaction is included. Some of the many data elements include: CFDA program number, recipient name, recipient city name, recipient county name, recipient state code, recipient zip code, type of recipient, recipient congressional district, federal funding amount, type of assistance transaction, principal place of performance, CFDA program title, and federal agency name. Although not particularly easy to use without search features, the *Federal Assistance Awards Data System* does provide some of the most detailed information available on individual assistance transactions.

The *Consolidated Federal Funds Report* gives statistics on federal government expenditures and obligations for federal government programs. While many of the items included are payments or expenditures to individuals, it also includes federal expenditures to state and local governmental units. The print version of the *Consolidated Federal Funds Report* (also available on the Web in a PDF format) includes data for only states and county areas. Data at more detailed geographic levels are available for viewing and as downloadable files from the Census Bureau Web site. A CD-ROM version of the *Consolidated Federal Funds Report* also includes the more detailed data.

Federal Aid to States is also issued as a result of the *Consolidated Federal Funds Reports* data collection. It gives data on Federal grants to state and local governments. Statistics are often shown by federal agency and program. Some historical data are also included in the report.

GENERAL ACCOUNTING OFFICE (GAO) PUBLICATIONS AND INFORMATION
Checklist

Reports to Congress by the Comptroller General of the United States. WEB. (irregular) U.S. General Accounting Office. GA 1.13: Item 0546-D. ASI 26104-26131.<http://www.access.gpo.gov/su_docs/aces/aces160.shtml>.
    Content: individual GAO reports.

GAO Reports and Testimony. WEB. U.S. General Accounting Office. <http://www.gao.gov/reports.htm>
    Content: includes links to GAO resources providing access to GAO reports and other publications.

GAO Month in Review. WEB. (monthly) U.S. General Accounting Office. GA 1.16/3: Item 0546-E.<http://www.gao.gov/reports.htm>;<http://purl.access.gpo.gov/GPO/LPS3307>.
    Content: listing of individual GAO reports by topic.

Abstracts of Reports and Testimony. WEB. (annual) U.S. General Accounting Office. GA 1.16/3-3: Item 0546-E. <http://www.gao.gov/reports.htm>.
    Content: annual index and abstracts of GAO reports.

Comptroller General's Annual Report. MF. (annual) 1922–. U.S. General Accounting Office. GA 1.1: Item 0543. ASI 26104-1.
    Content: overview of GAO activities.

Discussion

The General Accounting Office is responsible for auditing and evaluating government programs and activities. The reports compiled by GAO are distributed to depository libraries in a microfiche format, and are increasingly made available to the public on the Web. The URL cited here goes to a GPO Access search page. The search interface allows the user to search a database of all GAO reports released since fiscal year 1995, and provides a link to the full-text of reports (if available) in ASCII text and PDF formats.

GAO reports are an invaluable source of information for analyzing and evaluating government programs. Examples of report titles include: *Major Management Challenges and Program Risks: Social Security Administration* (GA 1.13:OCG-99-20), *Unmanned Aerial Vehicles: Progress Toward Meeting High Altitude Endurance Aircraft* (GA 1.13:NSIAD-99-29), *Social Security: Government and Commercial Use of the Social Security Number* (GA 1.13:HEHS-99-28), and *Welfare Reform: Status of Awards and Selected States' Use of Welfare-to-Work* (GA 1.13:HEHS-99-40).

The *GAO Reports and Testimony* Web page provides links to the resources and tools needed to access GAO publications. Included on this page are links to the *GAO Month in Review* described below, indexes, the GPO Access search page with the GAO database, GAO announcements, a new reports and testimony section, selected GAO correspondence, a special interest publications section, and order forms for requesting print format copies of GAO reports.

The *GAO Month in Review* lists and abstracts new GAO reports, grouped in broad topical areas such as "Income Security," "National Defense," "Education," and "Agriculture and Food." Direct links to electronic versions of the report are included, if available. *Abstracts of Reports and Testimony* provides indexing of GAO reports by broad subject category, subject/identifier term, title, and authoring division. Browsing and searching functions are both included. Once identified, abstracts of reports are included, with links to text and PDF versions of the full reports.

The *Comptroller General's Annual Report* gives a short overview of GAO programs and includes summaries of selected GAO reports issued during the year. Financial statements for the GAO are also included.

FEDRIP AND FEDIX
Checklist

Federal Research in Progress (FEDRIP) Database. WEB. U.S. National Technical Information Center. (GOV.Research_Center™) <http://grc.ntis.gov/fedrip.htm>.
    Content: database of information on ongoing federally funded projects in the fields of the physical sciences, engineering, and life sciences.

FEDIX. WEB. ScienceWise.com.<http://www.sciencewise.com/fedix/>.

Content: database of federal funding opportunities geared toward the research and educational community.

Discussion

Two general databases related to federal funding of grants and programs are available and cited here. NTIS makes available *FEDRIP*, a database of information on research in progress that comes from a number of different agencies. It includes research funded by the Department of Agriculture, Department of Energy, Department of Veterans Affairs, Environmental Protection Agency, Federal Highway Administration, National Institutes of Health, NASA, National Science Foundation, US Geological Survey, National Institute of Standards and Technology, Nuclear Regulatory Commission and the Small Business Innovation Research. *FEDRIP* is not available free-of-charge, and is most readily available from GOV.Research_Center™, which is a partnership between NTIS and National Information Services Corporation (NISC) that provides access to a number of governmentally produced databases. The *FEDRIP* database is also available through Dialog (File 266), Knowledge Express Data Systems, and NERAC, Inc.

The *FEDIX* database consists of funding opportunities from the following agencies: Agency for International Development, Air Force Office of Scientific Research, Department of Agriculture, National Aeronautics and Space Administration, National Institutes of Health, National Cancer Institute, National Institute of Allergy and Infectious Diseases, and Office of Naval Research. Opportunities listed are of special interest to researchers, faculty members, and students. The search interface allows the user to search all agencies at once, or individual agencies. Access to the database is free-of-charge. An e-mail alert service for new funding opportunities, *FEDIX Opportunity Alert*, is also available.

INDIVIDUAL AGENCY GRANT PUBLICATIONS AND INFORMATION

Department of Agriculture

Grants. WEB. U.S. Department of Agriculture. Cooperative State Research, Education, and Extension Service.<http://www.reeusda.gov/1700/programs/grants.htm>.

Content: information about individual grant programs funded by CSREES.

National Foundation on the Arts and Humanities

National Endowment for the Arts Guidelines and Applications. WEB. U.S. National Endowment for the Arts.<http://arts.endow.gov/guide/>.

Content: deadlines; applications; information on awards; information for NEA grantees and cooperators.

Grants and Applications. WEB. U.S. National Endowment for the Humanities.<http://www.neh.gov/grants/index.html>.

Content: upcoming deadlines; application guidelines; recent awards.

All About Grants and Awards. WEB. U.S. Institute of Museum and Library Services.<http://www.imls.gov/grants/index.htm>.

Content: deadlines, applications, descriptions of grant programs.

Department of Education

Grants Information. WEB. U.S. Department of Education. Office of the Chief Financial Officer.<http://ocfo.ed.gov/grntinfo.htm>.

Content: grant application announcements; grant award database; grant application forms and application packages; grants forecast; applicable laws and regulations; other related information.

Grant and Contract Awards. WEB. U.S. Department of Education. Office of the Chief Financial Officer.<http://ocfo.ed.gov/grntinfo/grntawd.htm>.

Content: searchable databases of grants and contracts awarded by the Department of Education.

Guide to U.S. Department of Education Programs and Resources. WEB. U.S. Department of Education.<http://web99.ed.gov/GTEP/Program2.nsf>.

Content: database of Department of Education programs; grant awards.

Department of Health and Human Services

Welcome to GrantsNet. WEB. U.S. Department of Health and Human Services. <http://www.os.dhhs.gov:80/progorg/grantsnet/>.

Content: general grants information; HHS grant administration; links to other information.

NIH Office of Extramural Research: Grants. WEB. U.S. Department of Health and Human Services. National Institutes of Health. Office of Extramural Research.<http://grants.nih.gov/grants/oer.htm>.

Content: funding opportunities; grants policy; awards data; receipt dates (deadlines).

CRISP. WEB. U.S. Department of Health and Human Services. National Institutes of Health. Office of Extramural Research. (full title of database is *Computer Retrieval of Information on Scientific Projects*)<https://www-commons.cit.nih.gov/crisp/>.

Content: database of federally funded biomedical research projects.

NIH Guide for Contracts and Research. WEB. Department of Health and Human Services. National Institutes of Health. Office of Extramural Research.<http://grants.nih.gov/grants/guide/index.html>.

Content: weekly publication that includes NIH notices; requests for applications; and program announcements.

Department of Housing and Urban Development

Grantees. WEB. U.S. Department of Housing and Urban Development. <http://grants.nih.gov/grants/guide/index.html>.

Content: collection of links to other HUD Web pages; includes information on grant programs; HUD resources; funding announcements.

Department of the Interior

U.S. Department of the Interior Financial Assistance (Grants). WEB. U.S. Department of the Interior.<http://www.doi.gov/non-profit/fax.html>.

Content: descriptions of Department of Interior grant programs; contact information; policies and regulations; other related links.

Department of Justice

Funding Opportunities at OJP. WEB. U.S. Department of Justice. Office of Justice Programs.<http://www.ojp.usdoj.gov/fundopps.htm>.

Content: application kits and solicitation; online grants management system; descriptions of programs and program offices.

Department of Labor

Grant Information and Resources. WEB. U.S. Department of Labor. Office of the Assistant Secretary for Administration and Management.<http://www.dol.gov/dol/oasam/public/grants/grants.htm>.

Content: general information about Department of Labor grants; forms; links to general federal government grants information.

National Aeronautics and Space Administration

NASA Research Opportunities Online. WEB. U.S. National Aeronautics and Space Administration.<http://www.nasa.gov/research.html>.

Content: information about NASA research grant programs; research announcements; deadlines; awards granted.

National Science Foundation

Grants and Awards. WEB. U.S. National Science Foundation.<http://www.nsf.gov/home/grants.htm>.

Content: funding opportunities; awards data; access to FastLane, NSF's electronic grant administration system; forms; deadlines and target dates; regulations, policies, and notices; links to other NSF offices and related resources.

Department of State

Grants Policy Information. WEB. U.S. Department of State. Secretary of State.<http://www.statebuy.gov/grants/gtpolicy.htm>.

Content: descriptions of programs; regulations and policies; forms.

Department of Transportation

Department of Transportation Grants and Cooperative Agreements: Information & Policy. WEB. U.S. Department of Transportation. <http://www.dot.gov/ost/m60/grant/>.

Content: grant regulations and directives; DOT grant related sites; grant information system; other related information.

Discussion

This section provides a sampling of agency Web sites and other resources dealing with grants and grants administration. It is not comprehensive, but provides resources from some of the departments and agencies most involved with grant awards. Because of the time-sensitive nature of much of this information, agencies increasingly use the Web to distribute such items as grant applications or program guidelines. While some of this information is available in print formats and is distributed to depository libraries in print or microfiche, depository distribution is often spotty or items are not always distributed quickly enough for current use. The most current information will be available from agency Web sites, and they should be consulted whenever possible. See Chapter 9, "Directories," for information on locating additional agency Web sites.

INDEXES
Checklist

Catalog of United States Government Publications (MOCAT). WEB. 1994–. U.S. Government Printing Office. Superintendent of Documents.<http://www.gpo.gov/catalog>;<http://www.access.gpo.gov/su_docs/locators/cgp/index.html>; <http://purl.access.gpo.gov/GPO/LPS844>.

Monthly Catalog of United States Government Publications. CD-ROM. 1996–. U.S. Government Printing Office. Superintendent of Documents. GP 3.8/7: Item 0557-C. GPO.

Monthly Catalog of United States Government Publications (Condensed version). PRINT. (monthly) 1996–. U.S. Government Printing Office. Superintendent of Documents. GP 3.8/8: (Earlier full version, GP 3.8:, 1895–1995). Item 0557-D. GPO.

CIS/Index. PRINT. (monthly) 1970–. Bethesda, MD: Congressional Information Service.

Congressional Universe. WEB. Bethesda, MD: Congressional Information Service.

American Statistics Index (ASI). PRINT. (monthly) 1973–. Bethesda, MD: Congressional Information Service.

Discussion

The *Monthly Catalog* is the most comprehensive index for government publications. The complete version is available on the Web and on CD-ROM. To locate additional publications on programs and grants in the *Monthly Catalog*, search under subject headings and keywords such as "Grants," "Grants-in-Aid," "Federal Aid to [name of subject]," "Block Grants," and names of specific programs and subject areas of interest. Commercial online and CD-ROM versions of the *Monthly Catalog* are also available.

For more information, see Chapter 3, "The Basics of Searching."

To locate program and grant information in *CIS/Index*, search subject headings under the terms "Federal aid programs," "Federal aid to [subject]," "Federal funding for research and development," "Grants and grants-in-aid," and the names of individual programs, agencies, or subject areas of interest. *Congressional Universe* includes a Web version of *CIS*.

To locate additional statistical information in *American Statistics Index (ASI)*, search the following subject headings: "Federal aid programs," "Federal aid to [subject]," "Federal funding for research and development" "Grants and grants-in-aid," and the names of specific programs, agencies, or subject areas of interest. *Statistical Universe* includes a Web version of *ASI*.

RELATED MATERIAL
Within this Work

GPO Subject Bibliographies. PRINT. WEB. GP 3.22/2:

<http://bookstore.gpo.gov/sb/about.html>

No. 258 "Grants and Awards"

CHAPTER 25
Regulations and Administrative Actions

Regulations are issued by various government agencies in response to congressional laws. These regulations are also a form of law and may be extremely detailed. The relationship between laws and regulations can be illustrated by the Food Stamp Act of 1964 (as amended) located in the *United States Code* (7 USC 2011+). This law establishes the basic guidelines for the food stamp program. It also directs the Secretary of Agriculture to issue more detailed regulations (7 *USC* 2013(c)). The regulations that were subsequently issued can be found in the Agriculture section of the *Code of Federal Regulations* (7 CFR 271+). (See Figure 25.1.)

All government agency rules and regulations appear first in the *Federal Register*. These regulations are then compiled annually and arranged by subject in the *Code of Federal Regulations*.

SEARCH STRATEGY

This chapter shows an agency search strategy. Finding a regulation itself may be the goal of a search strategy, or it may be part of an overall strategy to locate information regarding a particular government agency. The steps for locating regulations are

1. Begin with the *Code of Federal Regulations* (*CFR*) and its indexes, unless the regulation is recent;
2. For recent regulations (within approximately the last year), go first to the *Federal Register* and its indexes;
3. To find background information on regulations found in the *CFR*, go to the *Federal Register* references found at the end of each regulation and see the historical list of *Federal Register* changes appearing in the back of the *CFR* volume;
4. See the sources under "Updating and Finding Aids" in this chapter for updating a particular *CFR* section;
5. For background information and nonregulatory agency actions and notices found only in the *Federal Register*, consult the *Federal Register* indexes;
6. For information on regulations under development and regulatory policy, see the "Regulatory Agendas" section;
7. Consider "Departmental and Other Sources for Regulations";
8. For an overview of the indexes available, see the "Indexes" section; and
9. Consider the "Related Material" section.

THE *CODE OF FEDERAL REGULATIONS* AS A SOURCE
Checklist

Code of Federal Regulations. PRINT. MF. WEB. (annual) 1938–. U.S. National Archives and Records Administration. Office of the Federal Register. AE 2.106/3: (*CFR Index and Finding Aids,* AE 2.106/3-2:). (Earlier, GS 4.108:, GS 4.108/4:) Items 0572, 0572-B or -C(MF). GPO.<http://www.access.gpo.gov/nara/cfr/index.html>;<http://purl.access.gpo.gov/GPO/LPS3384>.
> Content: all U.S. government regulations in force as of cover date, with a one-volume index.

Index to the Code of Federal Regulations. PRINT. (annual with quarterly supplements) 1977–. Bethesda, MD: Congressional Information Service, Inc.
> Content: in-depth, multivolume subject, geographic, and *CFR* section number index.

Discussion

The *Code of Federal Regulations* contains all current regulations as of the date on the individual volume cover. Regulations are shown in their present form with all amendments incorporated. The *CFR* is divided into 50 subject categories called titles. Title 21, for example, is "Food and Drugs" and contains the regulations of the Food and Drug Administration, the Drug Enforcement Administration, and the Office of National Drug Control Policy. (This title arrangement is very similar to that of the *United States Code.*)

SUBCHAPTER C—FOOD STAMP AND FOOD DISTRIBUTION PROGRAM

PART 271—GENERAL INFORMATION AND DEFINITIONS

Sec.
271.1 General purpose and scope.
271.2 Definitions.
271.3 Delegations to FNS for administration.
271.4 Delegations to State agencies for administration.
271.5 Coupons as obligations of the United States, crimes and offenses.
271.6 Complaint procedure.
271.7 Allotment reduction procedures.
271.8 Information collection/record-keeping—OMB assigned control numbers.

AUTHORITY: 7 U.S.C. 2011–2032.

§ 271.1 General purpose and scope.

(a) *Purpose of the food stamp program.* The food stamp program is designed to promote the general welfare and to safeguard the health and well being of the Nation's population by raising the levels of nutrition among low-income households. Section 2 of the Food Stamp Act of 1977 states, in part:

Congress hereby finds that the limited food purchasing power of low-income households contributes to hunger and malnutrition among members of such households. Congress further finds that increased utilization of food in establishing and maintaining adequate national levels of nutrition will promote the distribution in a beneficial manner of the Nation's agricultural abundance and will strengthen the Nation's agricultural economy, as well as result in more orderly marketing and distribution of foods. To alleviate such hunger and malnutrition, a food stamp program is herein authorized which will permit low-income households to obtain a more nutritious diet through normal channels of trade by increasing food purchasing power for all eligible households who apply for participation.

(b) *Scope of the regulations.* Part 271 contains general information, definitions, and other material applicable to all parts of this subchapter. Part 272 sets forth policies and procedures governing State agencies which participate in the program. Part 273 describes the eligibility criteria to be applied by State agencies and related processing requirements and standards. Part 274 provides requirements for the issuance of coupons to eligible households and establishes related issuance responsibilities. Part 275 sets forth guidelines for monitoring the food stamp program, analyzing the results and formulating corrective action. Part 276 establishes State agency liability and certain Federal sanctions. Part 277 outlines procedures for payment of administrative costs of State agencies. Part 278 delineates the terms and conditions for the participation of retail food stores, wholesale food concerns, meal services, and insured financial institutions. Part 279 establishes the procedures for administrative and judicial reviews requested by food retailers, food wholesalers, and meal services. Part 280 explains procedures for issuing emergency coupon allotments to certain victims of disasters unable to purchase adequate amounts of food. Part 281 sets forth guidelines for designating Indian tribes as State agencies. Part 282 provides guidelines for initiation, selection, and operation of demonstration, research, and evaluation projects. Part 284 provides for a nutrition assistance program for the Commonwealth of the Northern Mariana Islands (CNMI). Part 285 describes the general terms and conditions under which grant funds are provided to the Commonwealth of Puerto Rico.

[Amdt. 132, 43 FR 47882, Oct. 17, 1982, as amended by Amdt. 216, 47 FR 23461, May 28, 1982; Amdt. 248, 48 FR 16832, Apr. 19, 1983; Amdt. 356, 59 FR 29713, June 9, 1994]

§ 271.2 Definitions.

Access device means any card, plate, code, account number, or other means of access that can be used alone, or in conjunction with another access device, to obtain payments, allotments, benefits, money, goods, or other things of value, or that can be used to initiate a transfer of funds under the Food Stamp Act of 1977, as amended.

Active case means a household which was certified prior to, or during, the

482

Source: Code of Federal Regulations: Agriculture, Title 7, part 271 (1999), p. 482.

Figure 25.1: Sample Page from the *Code of Federal Regulations.*

An alphabetical list of all agencies, as well as an outline of the titles, can be found at the end of any *CFR* volume. References to the *CFR* follow the general form of 21 *CFR* 131.206. This designates Title 21, part 131, section 206.

The one-volume *CFR Index and Finding Aids* provides agency access and very general subject access to regulations. It is possible to identify the sections covering color additives, for example, but not the exact location of a specific additive, such as caramel. To find such a specific reference, it is necessary to use the outlines provided at the beginning of each part in the color additives section of the *CFR* itself. Congressional Information Service, Inc., publishes *Index to the Code of Federal Regulations*, a more detailed, multivolume annual index with quarterly updates. With this index, specific names such as "caramel" can be located directly. Online versions of the *CFR* provide full-text searching.

The *Code of Federal Regulations* is available on the Web from the Government Printing Office's *GPO Access* Web site (July 1996–). Online commercial services also include the *CFR,* including *CIS Congressional Universe* (current), *LEXIS-NEXIS* (1981–), *LEXIS-NEXIS Academic Universe* (current), *Westlaw* (1984–), and *CQ.com On Congress* (links to *GPO Access*). The *LEXIS* file is called CFR and is available in several libraries, including GENFED, CODES, and EXEC. The GENFED library offers the most options, including different editions of the *CFR.* Relevant titles of the *CFR* also appear in appropriate subject libraries. A CD-ROM version is available from West.

Regulations cover a wide range of subjects in very specific detail. Some examples include standards for celery stalks, specifying midrib length of branches for different grades (7 *CFR* 51.595+); requirements for canned fruit cocktail (21 *CFR* 145.135); air pollution emission standards for kraft pulp mills (40 *CFR* 60.280+); radio frequency allocation (47 *CFR* 2.100+); performance standards for surface mining relative to topsoil, hydrologic balance, revegetation, etc. (30 *CFR* 816); and Occupational Safety and Health Administration standards for portable wood ladders (29 *CFR* 1910.25).

THE *FEDERAL REGISTER* AS A SOURCE

Checklist

Federal Register. PRINT. MF. WEB. (daily, Mon.-Fri., except holidays) 1936–. U.S. National Archives and Records Administration. Office of the Federal Register. AE 2.106: (Earlier, GS 4.107:) Items 0573-C, -D(MF), or –F(EL). GPO. <http://www.access.gpo.gov/su_docs/aces/aces140.html>; <http://purl.access.gpo.gov/GPO/LPS1756>.
    Content: regulations; proposed regulations; presidential proclamations and executive orders; background analyses relating to regulations; announcements regarding agency actions, hearings, grants, and publications.

CIS Federal Register Index. PRINT. 1984–1998. Bethesda, MD: Congressional Information Service, Inc.
    Content: in-depth index to the *Federal Register.*

The Federal Register: What It Is and How to Use It. PRINT. WEB. (1992) U.S. National Archives and Records Administration. Office of the Federal Register. AE 2.108:F 31/2. Item 0574-B. <http://www.nara.gov/fedreg/frtu/index.html>.
    Content: historical background, the rule-making process, using the *Code of Federal Regulations* and the *Federal Register.*

The Federal Register Home Page. WEB. U.S. National Archives and Records Administration. <http://www.nara.gov/fedreg/>.
    Content: information about the *Federal Register,* indexes, and research tools.

Discussion

New regulations appear first in the *Federal Register,* initially in draft form for public comment and eventually in final form. The *Federal Register* can be used to monitor proposed and final rules, to update the *Code of Federal Regulations,* and to trace the history and background of a regulation. References to the *Federal Register* follow the general form of 44 *FR* 16285, designating volume 44, page 16285.

A cumulative monthly index (culminating in an annual index) provides broad subject and agency access. The *CIS Federal Register Index* provides a much more detailed index for the time period it covers. Online versions provide full-text searching.

Each issue of the *Federal Register* has four basic sections: presidential documents, rules and regulations, proposed rules, and notices. A contents list at the beginning of each issue is arranged by agency with subheadings for rules, proposed rules, and notices. Sections may be set aside at the end of an issue for publication of major rules.

The final regulations that appear in the *Federal Register* will eventually be incorporated into the *Code of Federal Regulations.* The *Federal Register,* however, contains a great deal of material that will not appear in the *CFR,* including draft regulations, background analyses, other agency actions, and agency notices.

The *Federal Register: What It Is and How to Use It* is an excellent guide to the *Federal Register* and *Code of Federal Regulations,* illustrating with sample pages the relationships between these publications and laws, the types of information contained, finding aids, and search strategies. A Web tutorial version is also available.

The Federal Register Home Page also provides information about the content and use of the *Federal Register* and related index and research aids. Main menu options include "What is the Federal Register?," "Federal Register Indexes and Tables of Contents," and "Other Research Tools." "Federal Register Indexes and Table of Contents" provides table of contents listings for recent years, the current year-to-date index, and annual indexes for several years. "Other Research Tools" contains a list of public laws, a codification of presidential documents, an executive orders disposition table, thesaurus of indexing terms, purchasing information, changes in federal government agencies and functions, and frequently asked questions. The home page also provides links to the online *Federal Register* available from the Government Printing Office.

The *Federal Register* is available on the Web from the Government Printing Office's *GPO Access* Web site (1994–). It is also available from several commercial online services, including *LEXIS-NEXIS* (July 1, 1980–), *CIS Congressional Universe* (1980–), *Westlaw* (July 1, 1980–), *CQ.com On Congress* (1997–), and Dialog (1985–). The *LEXIS* file is called FEDREG and can be found in several libraries, including the GENFED and EXEC libraries. Dialog also offers a CD-ROM version.

THE FEDERAL REGISTER: *MORE THAN REGULATIONS*

The *Federal Register* provides a wealth of information on government agency actions beyond actual regulations. Particularly useful is the sometimes lengthy background material provided on proposed or final regulations. Figure 25.2 shows a final rule for a federal motor vehicle safety standard on child restraint systems. Appearing before the actual text of the rule is a "Supplementary Information" section giving background and discussing comments and issues that arose during consideration of the previously printed draft regulation. In other examples, the Food and Drug Administration published an extensive analysis of the scientific evidence that soy protein may reduce the risk of coronary heart disease (63 *FR* 62977); the Health Resources and Services Administration published an analysis of the organ transplant network covering such issues as broader geographic sharing of organs, waiting time, and socioeconomic barriers (64 *FR* 56650); and the Fish and Wildlife Service published an analysis of the threatened species, the Pecos sunflower, with information on its history, characteristics, locations, use, survival, habitat, and conservation measures (64 *FR* 56582).

Other types of material printed in the *Federal Register* include policy and interpretation statements and occasional administrative publications such as Office of Management and Budget *Circulars* or Securities and Exchange Commission *Staff Accounting Bulletins*. In addition, there are grant application instructions and deadlines; notices of hearings and meetings on regulatory issues; announcements of agency decisions, petitions received, and official actions; and notices on agency reorganizations, the establishment and termination of commissions, and the availability of information.

UPDATING AND FINDING AIDS
Checklist

Code of Federal Regulations. LSA, List of CFR Sections Affected. PRINT. MF. WEB. (monthly) 1977–. U.S. National Archives and Records Administration. Office of the Federal Register. AE 2.106/2: (Earlier, GS 4.108/3:) (Published prior to 1977 un-

der other titles) Items 0573-C or -D(MF). GPO.<http://www.access.gpo.gov/nara/lsa/aboutlsa.html>;<http://purl.access.gpo.gov/GPO/LPS3383>.

> Content: listing by *CFR* titles and parts of related material appearing in the *Federal Register* during the given time period.

"CFR Parts Affected During [month]." PRINT. MF. (In the *Federal Register* at the end of each issue) AE 2.106: (Earlier, GS 4.107:) Items 0573-C, -D(MF), -F(EL). GPO.

> Content: listing by *CFR* titles and parts of related material appearing in the *Federal Register* during the month.

Current List of CFR Parts Affected. WEB. U.S. National Archives and Records Administration. Office of the Federal Register.<http://www.access.gpo.gov/nara/lsa/curlist.html>.

> Content: Web version of "CFR Parts Affected During [month]."

"CFR Parts Affected in This Issue." PRINT. MF. (In the *Federal Register* at the beginning of each issue) AE 2.106: (Earlier, GS 4.107:) Items 0573-C, -D(MF), or –F(EL). GPO.

> Content: listing by *CFR* titles and parts of related material appearing in each individual issue of the *Federal Register*.

List of CFR Parts Affected Today. WEB. U.S. National Archives and Records Administration. Office of the Federal Register.<http://www.access.gpo.gov/nara/lsa/lsatoday.html>.

> Content: Web version of "CFR Parts Affected in This Issue."

CFR Index and Finding Aids. PRINT. (annual) U.S. National Archives and Records Administration. Office of the Federal Register. AE 2.106/3-2: (Earlier, GS 4.108/4:) (Accompanies the *Code of Federal Regulations*) Item 0572. GPO. Parallel table:<http://www.access.gpo.gov/nara/cfr/index.html>;<http://purl.access.gpo.gov/GPO/LPS3384>.

> Content: general subject and agency index to the *Code of Federal Regulations*; tables relating *United States Code* sections to *CFR* sections; outline of *CFR* titles and parts.

CIS Federal Register Index. PRINT. 1984–1998. Bethesda, MD: Congressional Information Service, Inc.

> Content: in-depth index to the *Federal Register*.

Discussion

To update a given section of the *Code of Federal Regulations* or to find regulations that correspond with a particular law, the above sources are needed. When using the *Code of Federal Regulations*, note the date on the cover of the volume. Changes or additions after that date will be in the *Federal Register*.

To locate these, first use the *Code of Federal Regulations. LSA, List of CFR Sections Affected.* Material is arranged by *CFR* title and part number and shows all entries in the *Federal Register* that affect that part since the latest cover date of that *CFR* volume. Periodically, there are annual cumulations of changes. As an example, if consulting Title 47, section 64.2005, in a *CFR* volume dated Oct. 1, 1998, check the latest monthly issue of *LSA* under that title and section. Figure 25.3 shows that a revision to

10786   Federal Register / Vol. 64, No. 43 / Friday, March 5, 1999 / Rules and Regulations

DEPARTMENT OF TRANSPORTATION

National Highway Traffic Safety Administration

49 CFR Parts 571 and 596

[Docket No. 98–3390, Notice 2]

RIN 2127–AG50

Federal Motor Vehicle Safety Standards; Child Restraint Systems; Child Restraint Anchorage Systems

AGENCY: National Highway Traffic Safety Administration (NHTSA), Department of Transportation.

ACTION: Final rule.

SUMMARY: This final rule establishes a new Federal motor vehicle safety standard that requires motor vehicle manufacturers to provide motorists with a new way of installing child restraints. In the future, vehicles will be equipped with child restraint anchorage systems that are standardized and independent of the vehicle seat belts.

The new independent system will have two lower anchorages, and one upper anchorage. Each lower anchorage will include a rigid round rod or "bar" unto which a hook, a jaw-like buckle or other connector can be snapped. The bars will be located at the intersection of the vehicle seat cushion and seat back. The upper anchorage will be a ring-like object to which the upper tether of a child restraint system can be attached. The new independent anchorage system will be required to be installed at two rear seating positions. In addition, a tether anchorage will be required at a third position. This final rule also amends the child restraint standard to require child restraints to be equipped with means for attaching to the new independent anchorage system.

This final rule is being issued because the full effectiveness of child restraint systems is not being realized. The reasons for this include design features affecting the compatibility of child restraints and both vehicle seats and vehicle seat belt systems. By requiring an easy-to-use anchorage system that is independent of the vehicle seat belts, this final rule makes possible more effective child restraint installation and will thereby increase child restraint effectiveness and child safety.

Issuance of this rule makes the United States the first country to adopt requirements for a complete universal anchorage system. To the extent consistent with safety, NHTSA has sought to harmonize its rule with requirements being considered by standard bodies and regulatory

authorities in Europe and elsewhere. The agency has harmonized with anticipated Economic Commission for Europe and Canadian regulations by requiring that bars be used as the lower anchorages for installing child restraints. The agency has also harmonized with Canadian and Australian regulations by expressly requiring tether anchorages in vehicles and indirectly requiring tethers on most child restraints.

For the convenience of the traveling public, DOT wants child restraints complying with this final rule to be usable in both aircraft and motor vehicles to the extent practicable. To that end, the agency is developing a proposal to ensure that the new child restraints are not designed in a way that might make them unsuitable for aircraft use. NHTSA expects to issue the proposal next spring.

DATES: The amendments made in this rule are effective September 1, 1999.

The incorporation by reference of the material listed in this document is approved by the Director of the Federal Register as of September 1, 1999.

Petitions for reconsideration of the rule must be received by April 19, 1999.

ADDRESSES: Petitions for reconsideration should refer to the docket number of this document and be submitted to: Administrator, Room 5220, National Highway Traffic Safety Administration, 400 Seventh Street S.W., Washington, D.C., 20590.

FOR FURTHER INFORMATION CONTACT: For nonlegal issues: George Mouchahoir, PhD. (202–366–4919), Office of Crashworthiness Standards, NHTSA.

For legal issues: Deirdre R. Fujita, Office of the Chief Counsel (202–366–2992), NHTSA.

Both of the above persons can be reached at the National Highway Traffic Safety Administration, 400 Seventh St., S.W., Washington, D.C., 20590.

SUPPLEMENTARY INFORMATION:

Table of Contents

Source: Federal Register, v. 64, no. 43, Mar. 5, 1999, p. 10786.

Figure 25.2: Sample Page from the *Federal Register.*

108　LSA—LIST OF CFR SECTIONS AFFECTED

CHANGES OCTOBER 1, 1999 THROUGH OCTOBER 29, 1999

TITLE 46　Chapter I—Con.

199.175 Table amended; (b)(21)(ii) removed; (b)(21)(i)(D), (E), (F) and (G) redesignated as (b)(21)(ii) introductory text, (A), (B) and (C) 53229
199.200 Amended 53229
199.220 (a)(2) amended 53229
199.260 Amended 53229
199.280 (b) and (e) amended 53229
199.610 (a) table, (b) Note and (c) amended 53229

Chapter II—Maritime Administration, Department of Transportation (Parts 200—399)

204 Authority citation revised........54782
204.4 (b) amended 54782
204.7 Revised..................................54783
204.8 Revised..................................54783

Proposed Rules:

5..53970
15..56720

TITLE 47—TELECOMMUNICATION

Chapter I—Federal Communications Commission (Parts 0—199)

Chapter I Order 54561
0.41 (k) revised...............................57585
0.251 (f) revised..............................57585
0.408 Revised (OMB numbers) 55425
0.442 (a) and (b) amended; (d)(1), (3) and (e) revised 55162
0.459 (d)(1) and (g) amended; (i) added 55163
　OMB number 56269
0.461 (i) revised 55163
1.923 (i) added; eff. 11-30-99 53238
1.927 (a) revised; eff. 11-30-99..........53238
1.928 Added; eff. 11-30-99 53238
1.929 (b)(2), (c)(4)(i), (iii), (v) and (d) revised; eff. 11-30-99.............53239
1.939 (b) amended; eff. 11-30-99........53240
1.947 (b) revised; eff. 11-30-99..........53240
1.955 (a)(1) and (b)(2) amended; eff. 11-30-99.............................53240
13.8 Added; eff. 11-30-99...................53240
13.10 Added; eff. 11-30-99 53240
20.6 Revised 54574
22.165 (e) amended; eff. 11-30-99
　...53240

22.529 Introductory text revised; (c) added; eff. 11-30-99 (effective date pending) 53240
22.709 (f) added (effective date pending in part)......................53240
22.803 (c) added (effective date pending in part)......................53240
22.929 Introductory text revised; (d) added; eff. 11-30-99 (effective date pending) 53241
22.942 Revised 54576
22.946 (a) amended; eff. 11-30-99
　...53241
22.953 (a)(5) removed; eff. 11-30-99
　...53241
64 Policy statement.......................55164
　Technical correction 57994
64.703 Regulation at 64 FR 47119 eff. 11-8-99 54577
64.2005 (b)(1) revised; (b)(3) removed; (d) added (effective date pending).........................53264
64.2007 (f)(4) removed (effective date pending)..........................53264
64.2009 (a), (b) and (e) revised (effective date pending)...............53264
64.2301—64.2345 (Subpart X) Added 53947
64.2400 Regulation at 64 FR 34497 eff. 11-12-99 55163
　Correctly designated 56177
64.2401 Regulation at 64 FR 34497 eff. 11-12-99 55163
　Correctly designated 56177
73 Actions on petitions..................55434
73.202 (b) table amended.......54224, 54225, 54783—54786, 55172—55175, 55435, 56704
73.3513 (c) revised...........................56978
73.3555 OMB number 54225
73.3564 (a)(2) revised; (a)(3) added
　...56978
80.59 (c)(2) amended; eff. 11-30-99
　...53241
87.25 (a) removed; eff. 11-30-99 53241
90.167 Heading revised; eff. 11-30-99...53241
90.693 (b), (c), (d)(1) and (2) amended; eff. 11-30-99 53241
95.5 Revised; eff. 11-30-99 53241
95.7 (a) amended; eff. 11-30-99 53241
95.29 (a) and (b) revised; (e) removed; eff. 11-30-99..................53241
95.101 (d) added; eff. 11-30-99 53242
95.103 (a) and (b) revised; eff. 11-30-99.......................................53242

NOTE: **Boldface page numbers indicate 1998 changes.**

Source: Code of Federal Regulations. LSA, List of CFR Sections Affected, Oct. 1999, p. 108.

Figure 25.3: Sample Page from *Code of Federal Regulations. LSA, List of CFR Sections Affected*.

that section appeared on page 53264 of the 1999 *Federal Register*.

To update the *LSA*, check the "CFR Parts Affected During [month]" section in the "Reader Aids" section in the back of the latest issue of the *Federal Register* to find changes for the current month to date. If using the Web version of the *LSA*, there is a direct link to the comparable Web version of this table. There is also a "CFR Parts Affected in This Issue" list located in the front of each issue of the *Federal Register* after the table of contents. This can be used to monitor changes on a daily or individual issue basis. This is also available from the *LSA* Web page. The *LSA* is available on the Web since 1997.

For a historical record of *Federal Register* changes from 1986 to the cover date, see the back of each *CFR* volume. Changes for that volume are listed in part number order. Earlier changes can be traced through the cumulated volumes of the *LSA*.

To find regulations relating to a particular law, it is helpful to know the *United States Code* (*USC*) reference for that law. This can be found by looking up the name of the law or the subject in the *United States Code* index. (The *United States Code* is discussed in more detail in Chapter 45, "Legislative History.") The *CFR Index and Finding Aids* contains a "Parallel Table of Authorities and Rules" arranged by the *United States Code* title and section numbers, showing corresponding *CFR* titles and parts. This table is also available on the Web.

The *CIS Federal Register Index* also has a *CFR* title and part index. References related to specific laws can also be found under the law name in the subject portion of the index.

Updating the *CFR* is less cumbersome with online databases. Many commercial online versions of the *Code of Federal Regulations* are updated every two weeks, including those on *LEXIS-NEXIS, LEXIS-NEXIS Academic Universe, CIS Congressional Universe,* and *Westlaw*. Online versions of the *Federal Register* can also be searched by *CFR* citation. Although the *GPO Access* version is not presently updated any more frequently than the print version, the Government Printing Office has announced plans to offer a daily updated version of the *CFR* in the near future.

REGULATORY AGENDAS
Checklist

"Unified Agenda of Federal Regulatory and Deregulatory Actions." PRINT. MF. WEB. (semiannual) (In the *Federal Register* in April and October) AE 2.106: (Earlier, GS 4.107:). Items 0573-C, -D(MF), or –F(EL). GPO.<http://www.access.gpo. gov/su_docs/aces/aaces002.html>;<http://purl.access. gpo.gov/GPO/LPS839>;<http://ciir.cs.umass.edu/ua/>.

> Content: comprehensive list of regulations under development.

Discussion

The "Unified Agenda of Federal Regulatory and Deregulatory Actions" is published in the *Federal Register* in April and October. It lists all government agency regulatory actions planned for the next 12 months. The agenda is organized by agency. Each agency provides a short introductory statement and contents list at the beginning of its agenda. Within each agency's section, rules are grouped according to their status in the regulatory process: prerule stage, proposed rule stage, final rule stage, long-term actions, and completed actions. A brief summary of each rule includes the title, priority, legal authority, *CFR* citation, deadline, a short abstract, timetable, and agency contact. The October issue also includes each agency's regulatory plan for the coming year. This is a more detailed statement of priorities and significant regulatory actions. Several indexes are provided. The Regulatory Flexibility Act Section 610 Review Index lists rules that have a substantial economic impact on small entities that are scheduled for a required periodic review in the coming year. The Regulatory Flexibility Analysis Index lists proposed actions that may have a substantial economic impact on small entities and that will require a regulatory flexibility analysis. The small entities index lists other planned regulations that may affect small businesses, small government jurisdictions, and small organizations. The government levels index lists regulations that may affect local, state, tribal, and federal governments. There is also a subject index. To locate the "Unified Agenda" in the *Federal Register* look in the *Federal Register Index* under "Regulatory Information Service Center." The "Unified Agenda" is also available on the Internet.

DEPARTMENTAL AND OTHER SOURCES FOR REGULATIONS
Checklist

List of Classes of United States Government Publications Available for Selection by Depository Libraries. PRINT. WEB. (semiannual). U.S. Government Printing Office. Superintendent of Documents. Library Programs Service. Library Division. Depository Administration Branch. GP 3.24: Item 0556-C.<http://www.du.edu/~ttyler/locintro.htm#gtr00>;<http://govdoc.wichita.edu/ddm/GdocFrames.asp>; <http://www.access.gpo.gov/su_docs/fdlp/pubs/loc/index.html>: <http://fedbbs.access.gpo.gov/libs/CLASS.htm>;<http://purl.access.gpo.gov/GPO/LPS1480>.

> Content: depending on version, listing or database of depository series available for distribution.

The Federal Web Locator. WEB. The Center for Information Law and Policy. Illinois Institute of Technology's Chicago-Kent College of Law.<http://www.infoctr.edu/fwl/>.

> Content: list of federal government agency Web sites.

U.S. Federal Government Agencies Directory. WEB. (Also titled: *Federal Agency Internet Sites*.) U.S. Government Printing Office. Superintendent of Documents and Louisiana State University Libraries.<http://www.access.gpo.gov/su_docs/locators/agency/index.html>;<http://purl.access.gpo.gov/GPO/LPS849>.

> Content: list of federal government agency Web sites.

Export Administration Regulations. PRINT. WEB. (looseleaf) U.S. Department of Commerce. Bureau of Export Administration. C 63.23: Item 0231-S-02. GPO.<http://w3.access.gpo.gov/bxa/>; By subscription:<http://bxa.fedworld.gov/>.

> Content: regulations on export licensing and the control of exports that have both civil and military applications.

Federal Acquisition Regulation: WEB. U.S. General Services Administration; Department of Defense; National Aeronautics and Space Administration. GS 1.6/10: Item 0559-K. GPO.<http://www.arnet.gov/far/>.

> Content: federal acquisition regulation on the procurement of supplies and services for government agencies.

Federal Acquisition Regulation System (Title 48, CFR). CD-ROM. (quarterly) U.S. Government Printing Office. GP 3.38/2: Item 552-D-01. GPO.

> Content: Title 48 of the *Code of Federal Regulations, Federal Register* updates, related circulars, forms, pricing guides, and other material.

OSHA CD-ROM. CD-ROM. (quarterly) 1991–. U.S. Department of Labor. Occupational Safety and Health Administration. L 35.26: (Alternate title: *OSHA Documents and Files*) Item 0744-G-01. GPO.

> Content: OSHA regulations, standards, interpretation letters and memos, *Federal Register* documents, compliance directives, compliance guides, review commission decisions (RCDs), news releases, fact sheets, hazard information bulletins, manuals, and other agency memos, letters, and documents.

OSHA Regulations and Compliance Links Web Page. WEB. U.S. Department of Labor. Occupational Safety and Health Administration.<http://www.osha.gov/comp-links.html>.

> Content: regulations, standards, *Federal Register* documents, interpretation letters and memos, compliance directives, compliance guides, review commission decisions (RCDs), news releases, fact sheets, hazard information bulletins, manuals, and other agency memos, letters, and documents.

Customs Regulations of the United States. PRINT. (loose-leaf) U.S. Department of the Treasury. Customs Service. T 17.9: Item 0948, 0948-A. GPO.

> Content: Customs Service regulations.

Rulings and Regulations Web Page. WEB. U.S. Department of the Treasury. Customs Service.<http://www.customs.treas.gov/impoexpo/rulings.htm>.

> Content: customs regulations, laws, and ruling letters.

Internal Revenue Bulletin. PRINT. WEB. (weekly) 1922–. U.S. Department of the Treasury. Internal Revenue Service. T 22.23: (Sample citation: 1999-34 I.R.B. 278) Item 0957. GPO.<http://www.irs.ustreas.gov/prod/bus_info/bullet.html>;<http://purl.access.gpo.gov/GPO/LPS1636>.

> Content: Internal Revenue Service rules and Treasury Decisions.

Tax Regs in Plain English Web Page. WEB. U.S. Department of the Treasury. Internal Revenue Service.<http://www.irs.ustreas.gov/prod/tax_regs/index.html>.

> Content: tax regulations listing with summaries and full-text; laws; link to Title 26 of the *Code of Federal Regulations* on *GPO Access;* link to the *Internal Revenue Bulletin.*

Federal Aviation Regulations. PRINT. (loose-leaf) U.S. Department of Transportation. Federal Aviation Administration. TD 4.6: Item 0431-C-13. GPO.

> Content: consists of several parts on airworthiness standards, certification of airmen, maintenance, air carrier operations, airports, and flight rules.

Title 14 Code of Federal Regulations (CFR) Web Page. WEB. U.S. Department of Transportation. Federal Aviation Administration. Flight Standards Service.<http://www.faa.gov/avr/AFS/FARS/far_idx.htm>.

> Content: federal aviation regulations.

United States Nuclear Regulatory Commission Rules and Regulations. PRINT. (loose-leaf) U.S. Nuclear Regulatory Commission. Y 3.N 88:6. Item 1052. GPO.

> Content: rules and regulations, policy statements, memoranda of understanding, and notices; covers licensing of nuclear power plants, radiation, by-products, environmental protection, waste disposal, and transportation.

Rulemaking Web Page. WEB. U.S. Nuclear Regulatory Commission.<http://www.nrc.gov/NRC/rule.html>.

> Content: rulemaking process; Title 10, Chapter I of the *Code of Federal Regulations*; and recent *Federal Register* documents.

Discussion

Some agencies publish departmental editions of their regulations. A selection of these is listed in this section. These regulations duplicate those appearing in the *Code of Federal Regulations* and the *Federal Register*, but in some cases they may contain additional interpretative material. Such editions can be more convenient and easier to use for someone interested in one particular agency or area.

Agencies that do not issue complete sets of their regulations may publish selected regulations and regulatory guides. Look in the *List of Classes of U.S. Government Publications Available for Selection by Depository Libraries* (GP 3.24:, discussed in Chapter 3, "The Basics of Searching") for a listing on "Regulations, Rules, Instructions" under the agency or consult the *Monthly Catalog* discussed in the "Indexes" section of this chapter. For a list of current subscriptions and loose-leaf services available from the Government Printing Office, see the *U.S. Government Subscriptions Catalog* (<http://bookstore.gpo.gov/subscriptions/index.html>; <purl.access.gpo.gov/GPO/LPS1787>) or *U.S. Government Subscriptions* (GP 3.9:).

Many regulatory agencies post selected regulations and *Federal Register* documents on their Web sites. *The Federal Web Locator* and the *U.S. Federal Government Agencies Directory* Web sites can be used to identify and link to an individual agency Web site.

Export Administration Regulations compiles regulations on the export licensing of selected commodities. Sections cover general information, steps for using the regulations, scope, general prohibitions, the commerce control list, country chart, control policy, and application processing. Additional materials include the text of the Export Administration Act of 1979, related executive orders, and forms. The Web version sponsored by the Government Printing Office offers viewing and downloading options, a search feature, and a list of related *Federal Register* citations with links to the full text. It does not, however, include the forms. A fee-based subscription Web version is also available.

The *Federal Acquisition Regulation* (*FAR*) contains the regulations governing the acquisition of supplies and services by government agencies. These regulations are also found in Title 48 of the *Code of Federal Regulations*. The Web site contains the full text of the current *FAR* plus the individual *Federal Acquisition Circulars* (*FAC*) that update the regulation. Also available are an index, a search option, currently proposed rules, forms, earlier editions of the *FAR*, and a small entity compliance guide. A CD-ROM version is also available.

The *OSHA CD-ROM* contains the regulations and *Federal Register* documents of the Occupational Safety and Health Administration (OSHA), as well as an extensive collection of other OSHA publications related to the regulations. These materials include standards interpretations, directives, the *OSHA Technical Manual*, compliance memos, settlement agreements, *Hazard Information Bulletins*, and congressional testimony. The *OSHA Regulations and Compliance Links Web Page* is similar to the CD-ROM, containing regulations, *Federal Register* documents, and selected compliance materials. Links to the Library and News Room provide additional publications.

Customs Regulations of the United States covers regulations of the U.S. Customs Service relating to the administration of customs laws. The Customs Service *Rulings and Regulations Web Page* offers a searchable version of Title 19 of the *Code of Federal Regulations* and Title 19 of the *United States Code* containing regulations and laws on customs duties. Ruling letters are also available for searching.

The *Internal Revenue Bulletin* contains the texts of new tax laws and regulations (the latter are referred to as Treasury Decisions [T.D.]). It is also the source for revenue rulings and revenue proceedings concerning specific tax matters and procedures not clearly covered in laws and regulations. The title is also available on the Web for recent years. The *Tax Regs in Plain English Web Page* provides a list of tax regulations issued since Aug. 1, 1995 with summaries and links to the full text. Current proposed regulations are also available for comment. This page also provides links to Title 26 (Internal Revenue) of the *Code of Federal Regulations* from the *GPO Access* Web site and to the *Internal Revenue Bulletin*.

Federal Aviation Regulations reproduces the regulations of the Federal Aviation Administration. The regulations are available in more than 30 individual parts, each part corresponding to a specific topic and part number in the *Code of Federal Regulations*. Examples of parts available include *Part 21, Certification Procedures for Products and Parts, Part 33, Airworthiness Standards: Aircraft Engines,* and *Part 91, General Operating and Flight Rules*. The *Title 14 Code of Federal Regulations (CFR) Web Page* lists all the parts in *Title 14, Aeronautics and Space,* that contain Federal Aviation Administration regulations. The list gives the most recent amendment number, date, and links to the full text.

United States Nuclear Regulatory Commission Rules and Regulations contains the rules regulating nuclear power from Title 10, Chapter 1, of the *Code of Federal Regulations*. Additional materials available include policy statements, memoranda of understanding, lists of regulatory guides, and brief summaries of selected General Notices issued by the commission. The Nuclear Regulatory Commission's *Rulemaking Web Page* menu options and links include "NRC Rulemaking Process," "NRC Rulemaking Web Site," and "10 CFR Chapter I." The "NRC Rulemaking Web Site" provides lists and texts of current rulemaking documents and the text of recent final rules. The "10 CFR Chapter I" link provides a full text version of Title 10, Chapter 1, that is updated weekly.

Commercial publishers such as the Bureau of National Affairs (BNA) and CCH Incorporated also publish extensive loose-leaf services, guides, and related electronic information services that cover relevant laws and regulations in particular subject areas. Examples of subject areas covered include health, taxation, securities, and labor. Many of the BNA and CCH products are also available through *LEXIS-NEXIS* and *Westlaw*. Dialog contains a *BNA Daily News from Washington* file covering BNA's daily business and legal news titles. Another company, IHS Health Information, provides health regulation products on either CD-ROM or via the Web, including the *Medicare/Medicaid Library, Healthcare Facilities Library,* and *Food Regulation Library*. These products contain the relevant sections from the *Code of Federal Regulations, Federal Register* documents, agency manuals, and other materials.

INDEXES

Checklist

CFR Index and Finding Aids. PRINT. (annual) U.S. National Archives and Records Administration. Office of the Federal Register. AE 2.106/3-2: (Earlier, GS 4.108/4:) (Accompanies the *Code of Federal Regulations*) Item 0572. GPO. Parallel table:<http://www.access.gpo.gov/nara/cfr/index.html>;<http://purl.access.gpo.gov/GPO/LPS3384>.

Federal Register Index. PRINT. MF. (monthly) U.S. National Archives and Records Administration. Office of the Federal Register. AE 2.106: (Earlier, GS 4.107:) (Accompanies the *Federal Register*) Items 0573-C, -D(MF), or –F(EL). GPO.

Index to the Code of Federal Regulations. PRINT. (annual with quarterly supplements) 1977–. Bethesda, MD: Congressional Information Service, Inc.

CIS Federal Register Index. PRINT. 1984–1998. Bethesda, MD: Congressional Information Service, Inc.

Catalog of United States Government Publications (MOCAT). WEB. 1994–. U.S. Government Printing Office. Superintendent of Documents. <http://www.gpo.gov/catalog>; <http://www.access.gpo.gov/su_docs/locators/cgp/index.html>; <http://purl.access.gpo.gov/GPO/LPS844>.

Monthly Catalog of United States Government Publications. CD-ROM. 1996–. U.S. Government Printing Office. Superintendent of Documents. GP 3.8/7: Item 0557-C. GPO.

Monthly Catalog of United States Government Publications (Condensed version). PRINT. (monthly) 1996–. U.S. Government Printing Office. Superintendent of Documents. GP 3.8/8: (Earlier full version, GP 3.8:, 1895-1995). Item 0557-D. GPO.

Discussion

Many of these indexes have been mentioned throughout this chapter. The first two indexes listed, *CFR Index and Finding Aids* and the *Federal Register Index* are the most readily available, as they are automatically received as part of the *CFR* and the *Federal Register*. These indexes provide basic subject and agency access. The CIS indexes provide much more thorough indexing, but must be purchased separately and may be available only in large libraries. Online versions of the *Code of Federal Regulations* and the *Federal Register*, such as those available through *GPO Access* and commercial sources mentioned in this chapter, allow direct full-text searching.

The *Monthly Catalog* does not index the contents of the *Federal Register* or *Code of Federal Regulations*, but can be useful for identifying agency editions of regulations and agency regulatory guides. Look under the specific subject of interest. Materials on the regulatory process itself may be found under such headings as "Delegated Legislation," "Administrative Law," and "Administrative Procedure." The complete version of the *Monthly Catalog* is available on the Web and CD-ROM. Commercial online and CD-ROM versions of the *Monthly Catalog* are also available.

RELATED MATERIAL
Within this Work

Chapter 7   Selling to the Government

Chapter 10   Tax Information

Chapter 26   Administrative Decisions

Chapter 45   Legislative History

GPO Subject Bibliographies. PRINT. WEB. GP 3.22/2:

<http://bookstore.gpo.gov/sb/about.html>.

No. 12   "Federal Aviation Regulations"

No. 129   "Procurement"

No. 141   "Federal Government"

No. 247   "General Services Administration"

Chapter 26
Administrative Decisions

Administrative decisions are those decisions, orders, and opinions issued by an administrative agency. They are legally grounded in the regulatory powers given to that agency. These administrative decisions are published by several different regulatory agencies, such as the Federal Communications Commission, the Securities and Exchange Commission, and the Federal Labor Relations Authority. This chapter lists major agency decisions and decision-related materials, such as digests and indexes, either recently received as depository documents or publicly available from agency or other Web sites. For the most part, it does not include commercially published material that must be purchased or requires an access fee to use. Other related agency administrative material is also often available from agency Web sites, and an agency's Web site should be consulted for possible additional information. Informal advisory opinions of an agency, for example, may be accessible from an agency site.

Many commercial publishers and vendors publish administrative decisions and the related digests, citators, explanatory material, etc., in print and electronic formats. In some cases, commercially produced sources are the only sources generally available to the user. Some agencies rely solely on a commercial source to disseminate their decisions. The commercial sources are often more current, provide better indexing or searching features, and include more information and analysis than the agency produced sources. These sources are often quite expensive, or require access to commercial vendors to use the electronic versions, but if available, may be much easier to use than the agency sources. This chapter does not individually list these numerous commercially published and produced sources. The two major legal database vendors, Westlaw and LEXIS-NEXIS, also include many administrative decisions databases among their libraries and files. The entries in this chapter for decisions available to depository libraries (either through depository distribution or a publicly accessible agency Web site) indicate whether an equivalent database is available from one of these two services.

USING DECISIONS
Citations

Legal citations (bibliographic references) to print administrative decisions often follow the general format of "volume, reporter abbreviation, page number or decision number." Thus the citation 7 E.A.D. 254 stands for the Environmental Protection Agency's decision found in the Volume 7, p. 254 volume of the *Environmental Administrative Decisions: Decisions of the United States Environmental Protection Agency*. (See Figure 26.1) Law dictionaries and legal research guides often include tables of legal abbreviations that aid in identifying the reporter indicated by a particular abbreviation. Sample citations are included within the bibliographic entries in this chapter where appropriate.

Indexes/Finding Aids

The types of decision indexes and finding aids available vary considerably from agency to agency. In some print versions, finding aids are issued as separate volumes, while others are included within the decisions-reporter volumes. Commercial sources will also include similar types of indexes and finding aids. Electronic versions of decisions often have search interfaces that allow the user to search for decisions in similar ways. A few agencies are also providing Web-accessible databases of decisions that allow for sophisticated searching. Most commonly, though, agency electronic versions are presently either PDF versions of the print publications or HTML versions of the decisions.

Digests are subject indexes to decisions. They may also contain numerical finding lists that relate the decisions to specific laws or regulations. In print formats, some digests are separately published, while others are included within each print reporter volume.

Many decisions have a compiled table of cases. Tables of cases will list the names of cases, followed by the appro-

254   ENVIRONMENTAL ADMINISTRATIVE DECISIONS

IN RE WOODKILN INC.

CAA Appeal No. 96-2

FINAL DECISION

———————

Decided July 17, 1997

———————

Syllabus

This appeal concerns a wood heater, "Model WK23G," designed by Woodkiln Inc. ("Woodkiln"), that is subject to the particulate matter ("PM") emission limits set forth in 40 C.F.R. Part 60, Subpart AAA. Subpart AAA, which is a new source performance standard ("NSPS") enacted by EPA under section 111 of the Clean Air Act, requires models of wood heaters to be tested for compliance with applicable PM emission limits under testing procedures that are specified by regulation; the set of testing procedures to be followed in a Subpart AAA certification test is known as "Method 28." Subpart AAA provides that if a wood heater meets the PM emission limits when tested under Method 28 procedures, EPA will issue a "certificate of compliance" to the product's manufacturer. Wood heater models lacking such a certificate cannot lawfully be manufactured or sold at retail.

Among other things, Method 28 requires the performance of at least one test run in which the rate of fuel consumption — the "burn rate" — is less than or equal to 1.00 kilogram per hour ("kg/hr"). The published regulatory history associated with Subpart AAA indicates that that is a burn rate at which wood heaters are sometimes operated by consumers in their homes and at which PM emissions, in the absence of effective regulatory controls, could become high owing to "incomplete combustion" of the fuel.

In October 1993, Woodkiln tested its Model WK23G for compliance with Subpart AAA. The tested unit did not, however, complete a test run with an average burn rate less than or equal to 1.00 kg/hr, as required by Method 28. EPA's Office of Air Quality Planning and Standards ("OAQPS") therefore informed Woodkiln that it was not entitled to a certificate of compliance for Model WK23G based on those results. Further testing in January 1994 failed to yield the necessary test run, and in May 1994, OAQPS issued a letter denying Woodkiln's request for a certificate of compliance for Model WK23G. Woodkiln then requested a hearing before an administrative law judge ("ALJ") pursuant to 40 C.F.R. § 60.539(a)(1).

Woodkiln continued to assert, as in its earlier correspondence with OAQPS, that consumers would be unlikely to operate Model WK23G at a burn rate less than or equal to 1.00 kg/hr, and that Method 28's 1.00 kg/hr burn rate requirement should therefore not apply to Model WK23G. The ALJ ruled, however, that Subpart AAA clearly makes all of the Method 28 requirements, including burn rate requirements, applicable to Model WK23G. He declined to reach the merits of Woodkiln's contention that it is unreasonable for Subpart AAA to impose Method 28 testing requirements upon all wood heaters (including Model WK23G) to which Subpart AAA applies, because he concluded that contentions of that nature were required to have been presented to EPA during the rulemaking process in which Subpart AAA was developed. Specifically, the ALJ looked to the statutory provision (Clean Air Act § 307(b), 42 U.S.C.

Source: Environmental Administrative Decisions: Decisions of the United States Environmental Protection Agency, Volume 7, p. 254.

Figure 26.1: Sample Administrative Decision.

priate citation. In the case of electronic versions of decisions, the ability to search by the names of cases is usually present, but tables of cases may also be made available for increased ease of use. Using tables of cases or searching by the name of a case can be extremely timesaving when compared with trying to locate a known decision by subject, especially when the exact time period is unknown or the subject is hard to pinpoint. Again, electronic sources will often have search commands that allow searching or retrieval by the names of cases or parties within the cases.

Citators provide the user with a list or referral to later cases citing a given case. This is useful for finding later related cases, on the assumption that the original case would not be cited unless it has some bearing or subject relationship to the case. Electronic versions of cases also often provide ways of quickly finding cases citing a particular case.

SEARCH STRATEGY

This chapter shows an agency search strategy. The steps to follow are

1. If commercially produced versions of the administrative decisions are available in print or electronic form, check those versions first for the easiest access to administrative decisions;
2. Check the agency listings given here to find the depository print and CD-ROM versions of decisions and related materials and any publicly-accessible agency Web sites with administrative decisions;
3. Use the *Federal Administrative Decisions & Other Actions* Web site to locate other administrative material available on the Web; and
4. Use the *Monthly Catalog* to locate additional administrative material titles.

AGENCY DECISIONS
Checklist

Federal Administrative Decisions & Other Actions. WEB. University of Virginia School of Law. <http://www.law.virginia.edu/admindec>.
    Content: directory of Web accessible administrative decisions and other administrative actions.

Administrative Decisions. WEB. U.S. Government Printing Office. Superintendent of Documents. <http://www.access.gpo.gov/su_docs/admin.html>.
    Content: GPO Access search page and links to selected administrative decisions on the Web.

Agriculture Department

Agriculture Decisions: Decisions of the Secretary of Agriculture under the Regulatory Laws Administered in the United States Department of Agriculture. PRINT. (semiannual) 1942–. U.S. Department of Agriculture. Secretary of Agriculture. A 1.58/A: (Sample citation: 50 Agric. Dec. 23 (1991)) Item 0002. LEXIS-NEXIS: USDA; WESTLAW: USDA.

Content: decisions of the secretary of agriculture or an officer authorized in the secretary's stead regarding matters arising under laws administered by the Department of Agriculture; includes selected court decisions arising under laws administered by the Department of Agriculture; includes selected court decisions concerning the Agriculture Department's regulatory programs, disciplinary decisions; reparation decisions, reparation default orders, and miscellaneous orders.

Energy Department

Federal Energy Guidelines. FERC Reports. PRINT. WEB. (quarterly loose-leaf volumes, with current updates) 1977-. U.S. Department of Energy. Federal Energy Regulatory Commission. E 2.17: (Sample Citation; 81 FERC <P> 61,103) Item 0438-C. LEXIS-NEXIS: FERC; WESTLAW: FEN-FERC. <http://cips.ferc.fed.us/cips/>
    Content: Federal Energy Regulatory Commission opinions, orders, and notices; office director orders; administrative law judge decisions and orders.

FERC Reports Archive. CD-ROM. (1998). U.S. Department of Energy. Federal Energy Regulatory Commission. E 2.17/2:PTS.1-2. Item 0438-C-03. LEXIS-NEXIS: FERC; WESTLAW: FEN-FERC.
    Content: compilation of *FERC Reports* from v. 1-v.84 (Nov. 1998).

Environmental Protection Agency

Environmental Administrative Decisions: Decisions of the United States Environmental Protection Agency. PRINT. WEB. 1972–. U.S. Environmental Protection Agency. Environmental Appeals Board. EP 1.2: D 35/[v.]. (Sample Citation: 7 E.A.D. 318) 0431-I-01. GPO. <http://www.epa.gov/eab/opinions.htm> LEXIS-NEXIS: EPAAPP; WESTLAW: FENV-EPA.
    Content: decisions of the Environmental Protection Agency.

Federal Communications Commission

FCC Record. U.S. Federal Communications Commission. PRINT. (semimonthly) 1986–. CC 1.12/3: (Sample Citation: 14 FCC Rcd 1 (1999)) Item 0284. GPO. LEXIS-NEXIS: FCC; WESTLAW: FCOM-FCC.
    Content: decisions; reports; public notices; memorandums; opinions; orders of the Federal Communications Commission.

Resources: Finding FCC Information. WEB. U.S. Federal Communications Commission. <http://www.fcc.gov/resources.html>.
    Content: links to electronic versions of orders.

Federal Labor Relations Authority

Report of Case Decisions. PRINT. U.S. Federal Labor Relations Authority. Y 3.F 31/21-3:9/. Item 1061-G-01. GPO. LEXIS-NEXIS: FLRA; WESTLAW: FLB-FLRA.
    Content: individual case decisions of the Federal Labor Relations Authority.

FSIP Releases. PRINT. WEB. (Print:1970–?; WEB:1995–) U.S. Federal Labor Relations Authority. Federal Service Impasses Panel. Y 3.F 31/21-3:14-3/. (Sample citation: Case No. 99 FSIP

69) Item 1061-G-01. GPO. <http://www.flra.gov/20.html> LEXIS-NEXIS: FSIP; WESTLAW: FLB-FSIP.

> Content: decisions and orders of the Federal Service Impasses Panel.

Decisions of the Federal Labor Relations Authority. MF. WEB. U.S. Federal Labor Relations Authority. Y 3.F 31/21-3:10-4/. (Sample Citation 55 F.L.R.A. 16) Item 1061-G-01. <http://www.flra.gov/page2.html>. LEXIS-NEXIS: FLRA; WESTLAW: FLB-FLRA.

> Content: decisions made under Executive Order 11491 and the Federal Service Labor-Management Relations Statute.

Administrative Law Judge Decisions Report. PRINT. Federal Labor Relations Authority. Y 3.F 31/21-3:9-3/. Item 1061-G-01. GPO. LEXIS-NEXIS: FLRA; WESTLAW: FLB-FLRA.

> Content: individual decisions and orders of the Federal Labor Relations Authority administrative law judges.

Citator of Decisions of the Federal Labor Relations Authority. PRINT. U.S. Federal Labor Relations Authority. Y 3.F 31/21-3:9-4/. Item 1061-G-01.

> Content: citator to decisions and interpretations of the Federal Labor Relations Authority.

Subject Matter Index of the Decisions of the Federal Labor Relations Authority. MF. U.S. Federal Labor Relations Authority. Y 3.F 31/21-3:10-3/. Item 0762-D-12.

> Content: subject index to decisions of the Federal Labor Relations Authority.

Federal Maritime Commission

Decisions of the Federal Maritime Commission. PRINT. WEB. (irregular) 1919– (earlier titles varied) U.S. Federal Maritime Commission. FMC 1.10: (Sample citation: 23 F.M.C. 135) Item 0233-A. Formal Docket Decisions: <http://www.fmc.gov/docket.htm>. WESTLAW: FMRT-FMC.

> Content: decisions of the Federal Maritime Commission.

Federal Mine Safety and Health Review Commission

Decisions. PRINT. WEB. (monthly) U.S. Federal Mine Safety and Health Review Commission. Y 3. M 66:9/. Item 1061-H-01. <http://www.fmshrc.gov/decisions/published.html>. LEXIS-NEXIS: FMSHRC; WESTLAW: FLB-FMSHRC.

> Content: decisions of the Federal Mine Safety and Health Review Commission; administrative law judge decisions.

Federal Mine Safety and Health Review Commission Index. PRINT. (quarterly) U.S. Federal Mine Safety and Health Review Commission. Y 3.M 66:9-2/. Item 1061-H-02.

> Content: index to decisions of the Federal Mine Safety and Health Review Commission.

Federal Trade Commission

Federal Trade Commission Decisions. PRINT. (annual) 1915–. U.S. Federal Trade Commission. Office of the Deputy Executive Director for Planning and Information. Information Management Branch. FT 1.11: (Sample citation: 114 F.T.C. 152) Item 0534. GPO. LEXIS-NEXIS: FTC; WESTLAW: FATR-FTC.

> Content: decisions; findings; opinions; orders; advisory opinions.

Formal Actions, Opinions, & Activities. WEB. U.S. Federal Trade Commission. <http://www.ftc.gov/ftc/formal.htm>. LEXIS-NEXIS: FTC; WESTLAW: FATR-FTC.

> Content: decisions and orders; final orders; advisory opinions.

General Accounting Office

Decisions of the Comptroller General of the United States. WEB. 1996–. U.S. General Accounting Office. Office of the Comptroller General. (Sample Citation: B-271136) <http://www.gao.gov/decisions/decision.htm>; <http://www.gao.gov/legal.htm>; <http://www.access.gpo.gov/su_docs/aces/aces170.shtml>. LEXIS-NEXIS: COMGEN; WESTLAW: CG.

> Content: decisions of the comptroller general; searchable databases of decisions.

Justice Department

Opinions of the Office of Legal Counsel of the United States Department of Justice. PRINT. (annual) 1977–. U.S. Department of Justice. Office of Legal Counsel. J 1.5/4: Item 0717-C-04. WESTLAW: USAG.

> Content: selected memorandum opinions of the Office of Legal Counsel.

Office of the Legal Counsel: Memorandum & Opinions. WEB. U.S. Department of Justice. Office of Legal Counsel. <http://www.usdoj.gov/olc/mem_ops.htm>. WESTLAW: USAG.

> Content: selected memorandum opinions available as downloadable WordPerfect files.

Interim Decisions. PRINT. WEB. (irregular). U.S. Department of Justice. Board of Immigration Appeals. J 21.11/2: (Sample citation: Int. Dec. No. 2951) Item 0723-A-05. GPO. <http://www.ins.usdoj.gov/graphics/lawsregs/biadec.htm>. LEXIS-NEXIS: BIA; WESTLAW: FIM-BIA.

> Content: decisions of the Board of Immigration Appeals.

Labor Department

Digest and Decisions of the Employees' Compensation Appeals Board. PRINT. (irregular) 1947–. U.S. Department of Labor. Employees' Compensation Appeals Board. L 28.9: (Sample citation: 43 ECAB 173) Item 0749-B. GPO. LEXIS-NEXIS; ECAB; WESTLAW: FLB-ECAB.

> Content: decisions of the Employees' Compensation Appeals Board under the Federal Employees' Compensation Act; digest index of decisions.

National Labor Relations Board

Decisions and Orders of the National Labor Relations Board. PRINT. WEB. (irregular) 1935–. U.S. National Labor Relations Board. LR 1.8: (Sample Citation: 321 NLRB No. 91) Item 0826. GPO. <http://www.nlrb.gov/decision.html>. LEXIS-NEXIS: NLRB; WESTLAW: FLB-NLRB.

> Content: decisions and orders of the Board.

Classified Index of the National Labor Relations Board Decisions and Related Court Decisions. PRINT. U.S. National Labor Relations Board. LR 1.8/6: Item 0826. GPO.

> Content: index to NLRB decisions.

Weekly Summary of NLRB Cases. PRINT. WEB. (weekly) U.S. National Labor Relations Board. LR 1.15/2: Item 0826-C. GPO. <http://www.nlrb.gov/weeklysum/weeksum.html>; <http://purl.access.gpo.gov/GPO/LPS3308>.

Content: summary of National Labor Relations Board cases.

Merit Systems Protection Board

Decision Database. WEB. U.S. Merit Systems Protection Board. <http://www.mspb.gov/decisions/decisions.html>; <http://fedbbs.access.gpo.gov/mspb01.htm>. LEXIS-NEXIS: MSPB; WESTLAW: FLB-MSPB.

National Transportation Safety Board

NTSB Opinions and Orders. WEB. 1992–. U.S. National Transportation Safety Board. <http://www.ntsb.gov/o_n_o/query.asp>. LEXIS-NEXIS: NTSB; WESTLAW: FLB-MSPB.

Content: opinions and orders of the National Transportation Safety Board.

Nuclear Regulatory Commission

Nuclear Regulatory Commission Issuances, Opinions and Decisions of the Nuclear Regulatory Commission with Selected Orders. MF. 1975–. U.S. Nuclear Regulatory Commission. Office of the Chief Information Officer. Y 3. N 88: 11/. (Sample citation: 34 NRC 297 (1991)). Item 1051-J. LEXIS-NEXIS: NRC; WESTLAW: FEN-NRC.

Content: issuances of the Nuclear Regulatory Commission, its Atomic Safety and Licensing Appeals Boards, and administrative law judge. LEXIS-NEXIS: NRC; WESTLAW: FEN-NRC

Nuclear Regulatory Commission Issuances. PRINT. (monthly) U.S. Nuclear Regulatory Commission. Office of the Chief Information Officer. Y 3.N 88:11-2/. Item 1051-J-01. GPO. LEXIS-NEXIS: NRC; WESTLAW: FEN-NRC.

Content: monthly preprints of the bound volumes.

NRC Public Electronic Reading Room. WEB. U.S. Nuclear Regulatory Commission. <http://www.nrc.gov/NRC/ADAMS/index.html>. LEXIS-NEXIS: NRC; WESTLAW: FEN-NRC.

Content: electronic system for accessing Nuclear Regulatory Commission publications: includes access to electronic versions of *Nuclear Regulatory Commission Issuances, Opinions and Decisions of the Nuclear Regulatory Commission with Selected Orders* and *Nuclear Regulatory Commission Issuances* through its "ADAMS" record management system.

Occupational Safety and Health Review Commission

OSHRC Administrative Law Judge and Commission Decisions. CD-ROM. 1993–. (quarterly) Y 3.OC 1:10-2/. (Sample Citation: 90 ISAHRC 43/C14) Item 1070-L-01. LEXIS-NEXIS: OSAHRC; WESTLAW: FLB-OSRC.

Content: commission and administrative law judge decisions of the Occupational Safety and Health Review Commission.

ALJ Decisions. WEB. 1993–. Y 3.OC 1:10-5/. Item 1070-L-02. <http://www.oshrc.gov/decisions/decisions.html>; <http://purl.access.gpo.gov/GPO/LPS434>. LEXIS-NEXIS: OSAHRC; WESTLAW: FLB-OSRC.

Content: administrative law judge decisions of the Occupational Safety and Health Review Commission.

Commission Decisions. WEB. 1981–. Y 3.OC 1:10-6/. (Sample Citation: 1999 OSHRC No. 8) Item 1070-L-02. <http://www.oshrc.gov/decisions/decisions.html>; <http://purl.access.gpo.gov/GPO/LPS2896>. LEXIS-NEXIS: OSAHRC; WESTLAW: FLB-OSRC.

Content: commission decisions of the Occupational Safely and Health Review Commission.

Postal Service

Administrative Decisions. WEB. 1957–. U.S. Postal Service. (Sample Citation: P.O.D. Docket No. 2/210) <http://usps.gov/judicial/ald.htm>.

Content: searchable database of decisions.

Securities and Exchange Commission

Decisions and Reports. PRINT. (irregular) 1934–. U.S. Securities and Exchange Commission. SE 1.11: (Sample citation: 48 S.E.C. 166 (1985)) Item 0908. GPO. LEXIS-NEXIS: SECREL; WESTLAW: FSEC-RELS.

Content: decisions of the Securities and Exchange Commission.

Social Security Administration

Rulings: Social Security Rulings and Acquiescence Rulings On Federal Old-Age, Survivors, Disability, Supplemental Security Income, and Black Lung Benefits. WEB. (irregular) 1960–. U.S. Social Security Administration. Office of Policy. (Sample citation: SSR 99-1p (4/14/99)). <http://www.ssa.gov/OP_Home/rulings/rulings.html>. LEXIS-NEXIS: SSRULE; WESTLAW: FGB-SSR.

Content: individual Social Security Rulings and Acquiescence Rulings; cumulative subject index; finding lists

Social Security Administration CD-ROM Publications. CD-ROM. U.S. Social Security Administration. SSA 1.8/4: Item 0516-X-01. GPO. LEXIS-NEXIS: SSRULE; WESTLAW: FGB-SSR.

Content: includes Social Security Rulings and Acquiescence Rulings.

Treasury Department

Customs Bulletin and Decisions: Regulations, Rulings, Decisions, and Notices Concerning Customs and Related Matters of the United States Court of Customs and Patent Appeals and the United States Customs Court. PRINT. (weekly) U.S. Department of Treasury. Customs Service. T 17.6/3-4: (Sample citation: T.D. 89-80 C.S.C. 89-6) Item 0950-D. GPO. WESTLAW: FINT-CUSTB.

Content: Treasury decisions; Customs Service decisions.

Customs Bulletin: Treasury Decisions under Customs and other Laws. MF. (irregular) 1867–. U.S. Department of the Treasury. Customs Service. T 17.6/3-5: (Sample citation: 23 Cust. B & DEC. 66) Item 0927. GPO. WESTLAW: FINT-CUSTB.

Content: Treasury decisions; Customs Service decisions.

Internal Revenue Bulletin. PRINT. WEB. (weekly) 1922–. U.S. Department of the Treasury. Internal Revenue Service. T 22.23: (Sample citation: 1999-34 I.R.B. 278) Item 0957. GPO. <http://www.irs.ustreas.gov/prod/bus_info/bullet.html>; <http://

purl.access.gpo.gov/GPO/LPS1636>. LEXIS-NEXIS: CB; WESTLAW: FTX-CB.

Content: official rulings and procedures (revenue rulings and revenue proceedings), Treasury decisions, executive orders, tax conventions, legislation, court decisions, and other tax-related items.

Federal Tax Products. CD-ROM. U.S. Department of the Treasury. Internal Revenue Service. T 22.51/4: Item 0923-B-01. GPO. NTIS. LEXIS-NEXIS: CB; WESTLAW: FTX-CB.

Content: most recent year of the *Internal Revenue Bulletin.*

Internal Revenue Cumulative Bulletin. PRINT. (semiannual) 1922–. U.S. Department of the Treasury. Internal Revenue Service. T 22.25: (Sample citation: 1991-1 C.B. 286). Item 0960. GPO.

Content: consolidation of items of a permanent nature from the weekly *Internal Revenue Bulletin.*

Quarterly Bulletin. MF. WEB. (quarterly) 1983–. U.S. Department of the Treasury. Bureau of Alcohol, Tobacco and Firearms. T 70.7: Item 0961-C. GPO. <http://www.atf.treas.gov/pub/index.htm>. WESTLAW: ATF.

Content: Treasury decisions and rulings on administrative matters concerning alcohol, tobacco, firearms, and explosives.

Veterans Affairs

Board of Veterans' Appeals Decisions. CD-ROM. WEB. (annual) VA 1.95/2: Item 0983-E-01. GPO. <www.va.gov/vbs/bva/index.htm>.

Content: decisions of the Board of Veterans Appeals.

LEXIS-NEXIS. <http://www.lexis-nexis.com/lncc/>.

Content: commercial legal database vendor; includes many administrative decisions.

Westlaw. <http://www.westlaw.com>.

Content: commercial legal database vendor; includes many administrative decisions.

Discussion

This listing cites major administrative decisions and related material currently being received by depository libraries or available free of charge from agency Web sites. Sample citations are included in the entries when appropriate. Depository administrative decision material is often sporadically received. Some administrative decision material lags far behind in being published, and the individual agency must sometimes be contacted to obtain current information. Increasingly, administrative material is not being issued in a print format, and is only available in an electronic version—often a commercial one.

The *Federal Administrative Decisions & Other Actions* Web site provides an agency by agency listing and links to the Web sites of many administrative decisions and other administrative related materials. It provides a good first step for locating administrative decisions available from agency Web sites. The *Administrative Decisions* Web site

from GPO Access provides access to a small number of agency administrative decisions.

As discussed in the introduction, many commercial publishers and vendors publish and provide access to administrative decisions in both print and electronic formats. Two of the most comprehensive of these are LEXIS-NEXIS and Westlaw, who include many administrative decisions. Access to LEXIS-NEXIS and Westlaw is provided by commercial vendors and is restricted by the licensing agreements of those vendors. Many libraries, educational institutions, legal firms, and other businesses purchase access to one or both of these systems. If access to these systems is available, they provide a timely and efficient way of obtaining administrative decision information.

The entries in the checklist indicate when these two systems include files for the administrative decisions in the listing. Decisions are often included in more than one file; only the most directly applicable file is indicated. Additional administrative decisions beyond the ones distributed to depository libraries or on publicly accessible Web sites are also included in LEXIS-NEXIS and Westlaw, but are not listed here. Consult the two Web sites cited here for more information on the administrative decisions included within LEXIS-NEXIS and Westlaw.

INDEXES
Checklist

Catalog of United States Government Publications (MOCAT). WEB. 1994–. U.S. Government Printing Office. Superintendent of Documents. <http://www.gpo.gov/catalog>; <http://www.access.gpo.gov/su_docs/locators/cgp/index.html>; <http://purl.access.gpo.gov/GPO/LPS844>.

Monthly Catalog of United States Government Publications. CD-ROM. 1996–. U.S. Government Printing Office. Superintendent of Documents. GP 3.8/7: Item 0557-C. GPO.

Monthly Catalog of United States Government Publications (Condensed version). PRINT. (monthly) 1996–. U.S. Government Printing Office. Superintendent of Documents. GP 3.8/8: (Earlier full version, GP 3.8:, 1895-1995). Item 0557-D. GPO.

Discussion

The *Monthly Catalog* is a comprehensive index to U.S. government publications. (See Chapter 3, "The Basics of Searching," for more information on using the *Monthly Catalog.*) The complete version is available on the Web and on CD-ROM. Commercial online and CD-ROM versions of the *Monthly Catalog* are also available. To locate additional decisions and related material, search the subject index under the heading format "[name of subject]-United States-Cases." The name of the agency can also be searched in the author index or as a keyword.

RELATED MATERIAL
Within this Work
Chapter 10 Tax Information

Chapter 25 Regulations and Administrative Actions

GPO Subject Bibliographies. PRINT. WEB. GP 3.22/2:

<http://bookstore.gpo.gov/sb/about.html>

No. 64   "Labor-Management Relations"

No. 66   "Internal Revenue Cumulative Bulletins"

No. 100   "Federal Trade Commission"

No. 246   "Alcohol, Tobacco, and Firearms"

No. 281   "Federal Communications Commission"

No. 295   "Securities and Investments"

CHAPTER 27
The President

This chapter deals with sources covering the official acts and statements of the Presidents of the United States. These consist of executive orders and proclamations, speeches to the public and Congress, press conferences, and other messages. Also covered are major reports and publications issued by the President's office.

SEARCH STRATEGY

The presidential search strategy may be considered as an agency search or as one part of a historical search. Either case involves the use of a unique strategy:

1. See the titles listed under the "Compilations of Presidential Documents and Speeches" and "Additional Sources for Presidential Documents" sections when looking for messages and speeches. In the latter category, *CQ Weekly* and *Congressional Quarterly Almanac* are convenient sources for major messages;

2. Check the "Executive Orders and Proclamations" section of this chapter for descriptions of sources for locating this specific type of document. The time period is important in selecting the right source for these materials. A separate timetable is included to show the time coverage of each source;

3. For publications issued by the Office of the President or for reports to the President, consult the "Annual Reports of the President" and "Selected Publication Series of the President" sections;

4. Look at the "Archives and Manuscript Sources" section of this chapter to locate information about unpublished sources available from the National Archives and the Library of Congress;

5. Check the "Additional Sources" section for biographical and specialized sources;

6. Consider the "Related Material" section; and

7. Search the "Indexes" for additional information.

COMPILATIONS OF PRESIDENTIAL DOCUMENTS AND SPEECHES
Checklist

Presidential Documents on NARA Web Sites Web Page. WEB. U.S. National Archives and Records Administration. <http://www.nara.gov/fedreg/presdoc.html#top>.
> Content: links to NARA web resources for presidential documents.

Weekly Compilation of Presidential Documents. PRINT. WEB. (weekly) 1965–. U.S. National Archives and Records Administration. Office of the Federal Register. AE 2.109: (Earlier, GS 4.114:) Item 0577-A. GPO. <http://www.access.gpo.gov/nara/nara003.html>; <http://purl.access.gpo.gov/GPO/LPS1769>.
> Content: presidential addresses; appointments and nominations; communications to Congress; other statements, messages, and remarks.

Public Papers of the Presidents of the United States. PRINT. WEB. 1957–. U.S. National Archives and Records Administration. Office of the Federal Register. AE 2.114: (Earlier, GS 4.113:). Item 0574-A. GPO. <http://www.gpo.gov/nara/pubpaps/srchpaps.html>; Bush: <http://bushlibrary.tamu.edu/papers/>.
> Content: presidential papers and messages covering 1929–33 and 1945–; covers the Hoover Administration and from the Truman Administration to the present.

White House Virtual Library. WEB. U.S. President. <http://www.whitehouse.gov/library/>.
> Content: press briefings, radio addresses, executive orders, publications from 1993.

A Compilation of the Messages and Papers of the Presidents, 1789–1897. PRINT. 10 vols. (1896–1899) (James D. Richardson) U.S. Congress. House. Miscellaneous Document No. 210 (53rd Congress, 2nd session). Serial Set 3265-1 to -10.
> Content: presidential papers and messages from 1789 to 1897; covers Washington through McKinley.

The Avalon Project at the Yale Law School: The Papers of the Presidents of the United States. WEB. Yale Law School. <http://www.yale.edu/lawweb/avalon/presiden/presiden.htm>.

Content: inaugural addresses, messages to congress, proclamations, state of the union addresses for selected presidents.

Inaugural Addresses of the Presidents of the United States from George Washington 1789 to George Bush 1989. PRINT. MF. WEB. (1989) (Bicentennial edition) U.S. Congress. Senate. Senate Document No. 101-10. Serial Set 13914. Y 1.1/2:13914. Items 0996-B(MF) or -C. <http://www.bartleby.com/124/index.html>; <http://www.yale.edu/lawweb/avalon/presiden/inaug/inaug.htm>.

Content: inaugural addresses.

Discussion

Many of the sources for presidential documents are published or maintained by the National Archives and Records Administration (NARA). The *Presidential Documents on NARA Web Sites Web Page* provides a consolidated listing of NARA presidential resources available on the Web. This page can serve as an overview of resources available and a convenient starting point for connecting to individual sources. Most of these sources are also listed and discussed individually in this chapter.

The *Weekly Compilation of Presidential Documents* is issued each Monday and contains the messages and statements of the President and related materials for the preceding week. This is the most comprehensive source of presidential materials. Figure 27.1 shows the contents of one weekly issue and illustrates the wide range of information provided. Categories of materials commonly listed include addresses and remarks, appointments and nominations, bill signings, bill vetoes, communications to Congress, communications to federal agencies, executive orders, interviews with the news media, meetings with foreign leaders, proclamations, and statements. Separate quarterly, semiannual, and annual indexes are issued. Indexes consist of a subject index, a name index, and a document categories list.

The *Weekly Compilation of Presidential Documents* is available on the Web from the Government Printing Office's *GPO Access* Web site (1993–). Several commercial online services also include the *Weekly Compilation*. *LEXIS-NEXIS* (March 24, 1979–) contains the text in several libraries including the EXEC, GENFED, LEGIS, and NEWS libraries. The file name is PRESDC. A related Web product, *LEXIS-NEXIS Academic Universe,* contains the same material in the General News category, the Newsletters subcategory. (To limit a search to just this title, use the "More Options" search form and enter the title *Public Papers of the Presidents* in the individual title search option box.) *Westlaw* (West Group) covers 1995 on.

The *Public Papers of the Presidents of the United States* contains the texts of presidential speeches, press conferences, messages, statements, and other documents. It is a hardcover compilation of the materials previously published in the *Weekly Compilation of Presidential Documents*. There are usually two volumes published per year.

Documents in the *Public Papers* are arranged chronologically with indexes at the end of each volume. For some years, cumulative annual indexes were included in the last volume of the year. Indexes presently consist of a subject index, a name index, and a document categories list. The document categories list provides access by type of document, such as addresses and remarks, communications to Congress, and meetings with foreign leaders and international officials.

Appendixes include a digest of other White House announcements, including the President's daily public schedule; a list of nominations submitted to Senate; a checklist of press releases not printed; and a list of presidential documents, including proclamations and executive orders. The texts of proclamations and executive orders are not presently included in the *Public Papers*, although they were included from 1977 through 1988. The list in the appendix gives references to the *Federal Register,* one of the sources where the full texts of proclamations and executive orders can be found. The texts are also included in the *Weekly Compilation of Presidential Documents*.

Before the *Public Papers* series, there was no systematic publication of presidential papers. Commercial publishers have, however, published various collections on individual presidents that sometimes contain some of these materials.

The *White House Virtual Library* was begun by the Clinton Administration and contains the full text of presidential statements and documents since 1993. Users may search the White House Web site, an archive of all presidential documents, or a specific category of documents, such as press briefings. Date ranges may be specified for document searches.

Richardson's *A Compilation of the Messages and Papers of the Presidents, 1789–1897* attempts to collect the papers of earlier presidents and contains texts of annual messages, special messages, veto messages, executive orders, and proclamations; however, it is not complete. Various commercial editions of Richardson's *Compilation* exist that contain materials for later administrations and end at varying dates.

The *Avalon Project at the Yale Law School: The Papers of the President of the United States* provides major presidential addresses and messages. Presently, coverage is limited to a small number of presidents.

Inaugural Addresses of the Presidents of the United States from George Washington 1789 to George Bush 1989 contains presidential inaugural addresses for the nation's first 200 years. The Bartleby Web site version is updated to include Clinton.

All of these sources are useful for answering questions about what a President said or wrote on a particular issue or in a given situation.

Contents

Addresses to the Nation

Military Technical Agreement on Kosovo—1074

Addresses and Remarks

Democratic Congressional Campaign Committee dinner—1077

Democratic National Committee dinner for Terence McAuliffe—1058

Hungary, state visit of President Goncz
State dinner—1064
Welcoming ceremony—1059

Law enforcement and communities, opening remarks at a roundtable discussion on trust—1065

Maryland, dedication ceremony for the Dale and Betty Bumpers Vaccine Research Center in Bethesda—1068

Military Technical Agreement on Kosovo—1070

National Association of Theatre Owners, remarks following meeting—1062

Radio address—1049

U.S. Conference of Mayors, exerpt of videotape remarks—1080

White House Conference on Mental Health—1052

World Series champion New York Yankees—1073

Communications to Congress

Albania, letter reporting decision to send certain U.S. forces—1050

Communications to Federal Agencies

Convention on Combating Bribery of Foreign Public Officials in International Business Transactions, memorandum—1074

Communications to Federal Agencies—Continued

Fairness in law enforcement, memorandum—1067

Executive Orders

Increasing Participation of Asian Americans and Pacific Islanders in Federal Programs—1056

Interviews With the News Media

Exchanges with reporters
Briefing Room—1070
Oval Office—1060
Roosevelt Room—1062

Meetings With Foreign Leaders

Hungary, President Goncz—1059, 1060, 1064

Resignations and Retirements

White House staff, Council of Economic Advisers Chair, statement—1064

Statements by the President

See also Resignations and Retirements
Death of Zachary Fisher—1049
Military Technical Agreement on Kosovo—1070

Supplementary Materials

Acts approved by the President—1083

Checklist of White House press releases—1083

Digest of other White House announcements—1081

Nominations submitted to the Senate—1082

Editor's Note: The President was at Whiteman Air Force Base, MO, on June 11, the closing date of this issue. Releases and announcements issued by the Office of the Press Secretary but not received in time for inclusion in this issue will be printed next week.

WEEKLY COMPILATION OF

PRESIDENTIAL DOCUMENTS

Published every Monday by the Office of the Federal Register, National Archives and Records Administration, Washington, DC 20408, the *Weekly Compilation of Presidential Documents* contains statements, messages, and other Presidential materials released by the White House during the preceding week.

The *Weekly Compilation of Presidential Documents* is published pursuant to the authority contained in the Federal Register Act (49 Stat. 500, as amended; 44 U.S.C. Ch. 15), under regulations prescribed by the Administrative Committee of the Federal Register, approved by the President (37 FR 23607; 1 CFR Part 10).

Distribution is made only by the Superintendent of Documents, Government Printing Office, Washington, DC 20402. The *Weekly Compilation of Presidential Documents* will be furnished by mail to domestic subscribers for $80.00 per year ($137.00 for mailing first class) and to foreign subscribers for $93.75 per year, payable to the Superintendent of Documents, Government Printing Office, Washington, DC 20402. The charge for a single copy is $3.00 ($3.75 for foreign mailing).

There are no restrictions on the republication of material appearing in the *Weekly Compilation of Presidential Documents*.

Source: *Weekly Compilation of Presidential Documents*, vol. 35, no. 23, June 14, 1999.

Figure 27.1: Sample Page from *Weekly Compilation of Presidential Documents*.

EXECUTIVE ORDERS AND PROCLAMATIONS
Checklist

Federal Register. PRINT. MF. WEB. (daily, Mon.-Fri., except holidays) 1936–. U.S. National Archives and Records Administration. Office of the Federal Register. AE 2.106: (Earlier, GS 4.107:). Items 0573-C, -D(MF), or –F(EL). GPO. <http://www.access.gpo.gov/su_docs/aces/aces140.html>; <http://purl.access.gpo.gov/GPO/LPS1756>.

    Content: proclamations; executive orders; other presidential documents.

Code of Federal Regulations. Title 3: The President. PRINT. MF. WEB. (annual) 1936–. U.S. National Archives and Records Administration. Office of the Federal Register. AE 2.106/3: (Earlier, GS 4.108/2:). Items 0572-B or -C(MF). GPO. <http://www.access.gpo.gov/nara/cfr/index.html>; <http://purl.access.gpo.gov/GPO/LPS3384>.

    Content: proclamations; executive orders; other presidential documents appearing in the *Federal Register*.

Codification of Presidential Proclamations and Executive Orders April 13, 1945–January 20, 1989. PRINT. WEB. (1989) U.S. National Archives and Records Administration. Office of the Federal Register. AE 2.113:945-89. Item 0574-A-01. GPO. <http://www.nara.gov/fedreg/codific/index.html#top>.

    Content: proclamations and executive orders in effect at time of publication, with amendments; arranged by broad subject.

Executive Orders Disposition Table Web Page. WEB. U.S. National Archives and Records Administration. <http://www.nara.gov/fedreg/eo.html#top>.

    Content: numerical list of executive orders by President from 1957 on, with date signed, *Federal Register* citation, and history of amendments and revocations.

United States Code Congressional and Administrative News. PRINT. (monthly) 1942–. (Title varies) St. Paul, MN: West Group.

    Content: proclamations and executive orders.

Proclamations and Executive Orders: Herbert Hoover March 4, 1929 to March 4, 1933. 2 vols. (1974) U.S. General Services Administration. National Archives and Records Service. Office of the Federal Register. GS 4.113/2:H 76/v.1-2. Item 0574-A.

    Content: collection of the proclamations and executive orders of Herbert Hoover.

United States Statutes at Large. (STAT) PRINT. WEB. (annual) 1789–. U.S. National Archives and Records Administration. Office of the Federal Register. AE 2.111: (Earlier, GS 4.111:; S 7.9:) (Title varies) Item 0576. GPO. Selected volumes: <http://lcweb2.loc.gov/ammem/amlaw/lwsl.html>.

    Content: proclamations.

Executive Orders. –1936. U.S. President. PR [no.].5:

    Content: individually issued executive orders, grouped by President number.

Proclamations. –1936. U.S. President. PR [no.].7:

    Content: individually issued proclamations, grouped by president number.

List and Index of Presidential Executive Orders: Unnumbered Series (1789–1941). PRINT. (1979) Clifford L. Lord, ed. (Originally published in 1944 by the Historical Records Survey, Works Project Administration, Newark, NJ) Wilmington, DE: Michael Glazier, Inc.

    Content: chronological list of unnumbered executive orders identifying topic and manuscript location or published source, if any.

Presidential Executive Orders: Numbered 1-8030, 1862–1938. PRINT. 2 vols. (1944) Clifford L. Lord, ed. (Reprint edition available from William S. Hein and Co., Inc., Buffalo, NY) New York: Books, Inc.

    Content: numerical list with dates of numbered executive orders and references to published sources, if any.

CIS Index to Presidential Executive Orders and Proclamations. PRINT. 22 vols. (1986–87) Bethesda, MD: Congressional Information Service, Inc.

    Content: index to executive orders and proclamations issued from 1789–1983.

Discussion

Since 1936, executive orders and proclamations have been published in the *Federal Register* and compiled annually in Title 3 of the *Code of Federal Regulations*. These two sources also contain other presidential documents, including presidential determinations, orders, memorandums, and reorganization plans. The *Code of Federal Regulations. Title 3, The President* volumes each contain a subject index. The *Federal Register* has a cumulative, monthly index for each year. Access is primarily by agency. Material from the President is listed under "Presidential Documents."

    The *Federal Register* is available on the Web from the Government Printing Office's *GPO Access* Web site (1994–). It is also available from several commercial online services, including *LEXIS-NEXIS* (July 1, 1980–), *CIS Congressional Universe* (1980–), *Westlaw* (July 1, 1980–), *CQ.com On Congress* (1997–), and *Dialog* (1985–). The *LEXIS* file is called FEDREG and can be found in several libraries, including the GENFED and EXEC libraries. Dialog also offers a CD-ROM version.

    The *Code of Federal Regulations* is also available on the Web from the Government Printing Office's *GPO Access* Web site (July 1996–). Online commercial services also include the *CFR*, including *CIS Congressional Universe* (current), *LEXIS-NEXIS* (1981–), *LEXIS-NEXIS Academic Universe* (current), *Westlaw* (1984–), and *CQ.com On Congress* (links to *GPO Access*). The *LEXIS* file is called *CFR* and is available in several libraries, including GENFED, CODES, and EXEC. The GENFED library offers the most options, including different editions of the *CFR*. Relevant titles of the *CFR* also appear in appropriate subject libraries. A CD-ROM version is available from West.

The *Codification of Presidential Proclamations and Executive Orders* is a subject arrangement of orders that had continuing legal effect as of 1989. Any amendments have been incorporated. Material from years before 1945 may be included if it was affected by later orders or proclamations. A numerical finding list in the back lists all orders and proclamations issued during this time period, any amendments, and their current status. If the document is included in the *Codification*, a location reference is given. A subject index is also provided.

The *Executive Orders Disposition Table Web Page* provides a numerical list of executive orders by President, beginning with Eisenhower. The lists give the title, date signed, location in the *Federal Register*, and related executive orders amended, amending, or revoked. This can be used to update, in part, the *Codification of Presidential Proclamations and Executive Orders*.

Some commercial sources, such as *U.S. Code Congressional and Administrative News*, also contain executive orders and proclamations.

Before 1936 (and for a while thereafter) executive orders and proclamations were issued as individual documents. Only one compilation has been issued for this time and it covers only 1929–33: *Proclamations and Executive Orders: Herbert Hoover March 4, 1929 to March 4, 1933*. Most of the proclamations appear in the *United States Statutes at Large*, but there is no one collection of executive orders. Some of the individually issued orders and proclamations were sent to depository libraries, particularly during the period from 1925 to 1936. These were assigned a SuDocs classification number based on the President issuing them. For example, the executive orders of Franklin D. Roosevelt, the thirty-second President, were numbered PR 32.5:, and his proclamations were given the number PR 32.7:.

Many orders issued before 1929 were not numbered or filed in any centralized location. Some earlier executive orders have been published in compilations on special subjects, such as Indians. Some may be found in Richardson's *Compilation*, in nongovernment collections of presidential papers, and in early Congressional proceedings and documents. Two indexes, *List and Index of Presidential Executive Orders* and *Presidential Executive Orders*, attempt to identify and list early published and unpublished executive orders. Orders are listed chronologically with citations to any published sources. Subject indexes are also provided.

The *CIS Index to Presidential Executive Orders and Proclamations* is the most comprehensive index of executive orders and proclamations. It consists of two multivolume parts. Part 1 covers 1789–1921; part 2 covers 1922–1983. Each part contains a reference bibliography that lists each document and provides a brief description. Each entry contains a source code indicating the location of the original publication. Some of the sources refer to printed publications, such as the *Federal Register*,

but many of the early orders are in the National Archives or in other unpublished files. Indexes provide access by subject, personal name, and site and document number. Other finding aids include a chronological list and a numerical list correlating interrelated orders and proclamations. A microfiche set of all of the orders and proclamations included in the index is also available from CIS.

See also the "Archives and Manuscript Sources" section in this chapter for information on sources of unpublished materials.

Executive Orders and Proclamations Time Table: Major Text Sources

1789–1983	*CIS Index to Presidential Executive Orders and Proclamations* microfiche set.
1791–	*United States Statutes at Large*, proclamations only.
c.1925–36	PR [no.].5:, PR [no.].7:
1929–33	*Proclamations and Executive Orders: Herbert Hoover.*
1936–	*Code of Federal Regulations. Title 3, The President.*
1936–	*Federal Register.*
1945–1989	*Codification of Presidential Proclamations and Executive Orders*, in effect at time of publication.
1965–	*Weekly Compilation of Presidential Documents.*
1977–1988	*Public Papers of the Presidents of the United States.*

ADDITIONAL SOURCES FOR PRESIDENTIAL DOCUMENTS
Checklist

Congressional Record. PRINT. MF. WEB. (daily when Congress in session) 1873–. U.S. Congress. X 1.1:, X 1.1/A: (Earlier, X, X/A) (Issued earlier as *Annals of Congress, Register of Debates,* and *Congressional Globe*) Items 0993-A(MF); 0993-A-01 (Regionals only, 1985–), 0993-B or -C(MF); 0994-B or -C(MF), 0994-D(EL). GPO. <http://www.access.gpo.gov/su_docs/aces/aces150.html>; <http://purl.access.gpo.gov/GPO/LPS1671>; <http://thomas.loc.gov/>.

Content: presidential messages and communications to Congress.

U.S. Congressional Serial Set. PRINT. MF. 1817–. U.S. Congress. Y 1.1/2: (Before 1817, see the *American State Papers*). Items 0996-B(MF) or -C; 1008-D(MF) or –E; 1008-F (105th Congress–, regional depository libraries only) Early volumes: <http://lcweb2.loc.gov/ammem/amlaw/lwss.html>; Individual documents and reports since 1995: <http://www.access.gpo.gov/su_docs/legislative.html>.

Content: presidential communications to Congress.

Journal of the House of Representatives of the United States. PRINT. MF. CD-ROM. WEB. (annual) 1789–. U.S. Congress. House. XJH. (Early journals issued in the *Serial Set*) (Reprint edition of 1789–1817 published by Michael Glazier, Wilmington, DE, 1977) Items 1030-A, -B(MF), or B-01(CD). Early volumes: <http://lcweb2.loc.gov/ammem/amlaw/lwhj.html>;

1991–: <http://www.access.gpo.gov/congress/cong018.html>; <http://purl.access.gpo.gov/GPO/LPS2564>.

Content: major addresses and messages to Congress.

Journal of the Senate of the United States of America. PRINT. MF. WEB. (annual) 1789–. U.S. Congress. Senate. XJS. (Early journals issued in the *Serial Set*) (Reprint edition of 1789-1817 published by Michael Glazier, Wilmington, DE, 1977) Items 1047-A or -B(MF). Early volumes: <http://lcweb2.loc.gov/ammem/amlaw/lwsj.html>; <http://purl.access.gpo.gov/GPO/LPS486>.

Content: major addresses and messages to Congress.

Presidential Vetoes, 1789-1988. PRINT. (1992) U.S. Congress. Senate. Y 1.3:S.PUB.102-12. (1989-1996 update is Y 1.3:S.PUB.102-13). Item 0998-A-01.

Content: list of vetoes with documentary references to veto actions and sources of veto messages.

Presidential Directives and Where to Find Them Web Page. WEB. U.S. Library of Congress. Newspaper & Current Periodical Reading Room. George Caldwell (Updated by Charles Bean and Lyle Minter.) <http://lcweb.loc.gov/rr/news/directives.html>.

Content: lists of sources for locating presidential directives.

Declassified Documents Catalog. PRINT. (quarterly) CD-ROM. (annual) 1975–. (Title varies) Woodbridge, CT: Primary Source Media (Gale Group), Inc.

Content: index to declassified materials; accompanied by full-text on microfiche.

World Government Documents Archive Online: Declassified Documents Reference System—United States. WEB. Gale Group.

Content: Web version of *Declassified Documents Catalog.*

Foreign Relations of the United States. PRINT. MF. WEB. (annual) 1818–. U.S. Department of State. Bureau of Public Affairs. Office of the Historian. S 1.1: (Earliest volumes issued in the *Serial Set*) Items 0872-B or -C(MF), 0872-D(MF). GPO. Selected volumes: <http://www.state.gov/www/about_state/history/frusonline.html>.

Content: official record of U.S. foreign policy with correspondence and papers on major policies and decisions, including occasional presidential directives.

CQ Weekly. PRINT. WEB. (weekly) 1946–. (Title varies. Earlier, *Congressional Quarterly Weekly Report*) Washington, D.C.: Congressional Quarterly, Inc. CQ Library: <http://libraryip.cq.com/>.

Content: major Presidential messages and activities.

Congressional Quarterly Almanac. PRINT. (annual) 1945–. Washington, D.C.: Congressional Quarterly, Inc.

Content: major Presidential messages and activities.

Discussion

The *Congressional Record* contains addresses to Congress and many presidential statements and messages. These can be found through the annual and biweekly indexes under "President of the United States" or by specific subject. The categories listed under "President" in the index have varied over the years. Some of the categories included are addresses, analyses, articles and editorials, bills and resolutions, executive orders (very selective), letters, memorandums, messages, press releases, proclamations (very selective), remarks in House, remarks in Senate, statements, transcripts (earlier broadcasts). Many of the entries under these headings are about the President and presidential policies rather than actual messages or remarks of the President. A separate index entry is also available for "Presidential Appointments" (earlier "Executive Nominations and Confirmations").

The *Congressional Record* is available on the Web from the Government Printing Office's *GPO Access* Web site (1994–; index, 1983–) and on the Library of Congress' *Thomas* Web site (1989–; index, 1994–). Commercial online services also offer the *Congressional Record*, including *CIS Congressional Universe* (1985–), *LEXIS-NEXIS* (1985–), *Westlaw* (1985–), and *CQ.com On Congress* (1987–). On *LEXIS* it is in several libraries, including GENFED and LEGIS. The file name for the complete *Congressional Record* since 1985 is RECORD. There are also files for individual congresses or sections.

The *U.S. Congressional Serial Set* contains some presidential messages also. These are usually issued as House or Senate documents or treaty documents. These messages are listed in the *Monthly Catalog* author index under "United States. President" or in the subject index by specific subject. They can also be found in *CIS/Index* under "Presidential communications and messages" and "Presidential vetoes," as well as by subject. For years before *CIS/Index* was published, the *CIS U.S. Serial Set Index* indexes these materials by subject or name of the President, or under "Presidential Message" or "Veto." All of these indexes are listed and discussed in the "Indexes" section at the end of this chapter. The full text of individual congressional documents since 1995 is available on the Government Printing Office's *GPO Access* Web site and on *CIS Congressional Universe.*

The *Journal of the House of Representatives* and the *Journal of the Senate* contain records of congressional action without the transcripts of debate that appear in the *Congressional Record*. The journals also print the texts of major presidential addresses to Congress, transmittals, and veto messages. Both journals have a general subject index that contains entries under the subject "President of the United States." Subheadings include appointments, messages, and reports filed. The *House Journal* is also available on CD-ROM beginning with 1991.

Presidential Vetoes lists all vetoes in chronological order by President and gives the bill number, purpose of the bill, and veto actions taken. References are given to House and Senate journals, House and Senate documents, the *Congressional Record*, and the *Weekly Compilation of Presidential Documents* where texts of veto messages or official records of actions can be found. A subject index is also included.

The *Presidential Directives and Where to Find Them Web Page* lists sources for locating presidential directives.

Presidential directives relate to national security and are issued by the National Security Council. These are classified, but many older directives have been declassified or obtained through Freedom of Information Act requests. Many of these materials have been compiled by commercial publishers and made available in microform sets and books. Major microform collections are available from Chadwyck-Healey and University Publications of America (CIS). The *Declassified Documents Catalog* also covers National Security Council documents such as presidential directives when they are declassified. *Foreign Relations of the United States* contains the full-text of selected directives, but is not published until many years after the original date.

CQ Weekly and *Congressional Quarterly Almanac* are major sources for congressional information and include the full text of selected presidential press conferences, major statements, messages, and speeches. These titles also provide information on presidential activities, positions, and policies. The *Almanac* is a compilation of the year's congressional activities and selected presidential addresses. Major speeches and other statements are usually compiled in a separate appendix named "Texts," or in earlier years "Presidential Messages." Materials can also be found by looking under the name of the President in the index. An index to *CQ Weekly* is available online at no charge from the *CQ Library* Web site. Look under the name of the President for topical references on presidential activities, policies, and major statements. The *CQ Library* Web service also offers the full text of *CQ Weekly* for a subscription fee.

ARCHIVES AND MANUSCRIPT SOURCES
Checklist

Guide to Federal Records in the National Archives of the United States. PRINT. WEB. (1995) U.S. National Archives and Records Administration. AE 1.108:G 94/v. Item 0569-B. <http://www.nara.gov/guide/>.
> Content: description of records in the National Archives, arranged by record group number, with subject index.

NARA Archival Information Locator (NAIL). WEB. U.S. National Archives and Records Administration. <http://www.nara.gov/nara/nail.html>.
> Content: prototype online information system of NARA archival and microfilm holdings, including selected digital images.

Information About the National Archives for Researchers. PRINT. (1994) U.S. National Archives and Records Administration. General Information Leaflet No. 30. AE 1.113:30/994. Item 0569.
> Content: basic information on the facilities of the National Archives and how to use them; addresses of regional archives and presidential libraries.

Presidential Libraries Web Page. WEB. U.S. National Archives and Records Administration. <http://www.nara.gov/nara/president/address.html>.
> Content: addresses, telephone numbers, Web links, and email addresses for presidential libraries.

Select List of Publications of the National Archives and Records Administration. PRINT. WEB. (1994) U.S. National Archives and Records Administration. General Information Leaflet No. 3. AE 1.113:3/994. Item 0569. <http://www.nara.gov/publications/gil3home.html>.
> Content: list of National Archives publications currently in print by series.

Presidential Library Finding Aids Web Page. WEB. U.S. National Archives and Records Administration. <http://www.nara.gov/research/all/presmats.html#faids>.
> Content: Web links to collection descriptions for presidential libraries.

Presidents' Papers Index. PRINT. (1960–) Library of Congress. Manuscript Division. LC 4.7: Item 0811-B.
> Content: indexes to microfilmed presidential papers in the Library of Congress by President.

Online Collections in American Memory. WEB. U.S. Library of Congress. Manuscript Division. <http://lcweb.loc.gov/rr/mss/ammem.html>.
> Content: list of online collections from the Manuscript Division, including selected presidential paper collections.

Discussion

The *Guide to Federal Records in the National Archives of the United States* describes the records in the National Archives. The category or record group called "General Records of the United States Government" (Record Group 11) includes executive orders, proclamations, and other presidential documents. The executive orders, proclamations, and some other materials from this record group have been microfilmed and are available for purchase from the National Archives. The category "Records of the White House Office" (Record Group 130) also includes some executive orders and proclamations, as well as messages, letters, and news releases for certain time periods.

The *NARA Archival Information Locator (NAIL)* is a prototype online database of holdings in Washington, D.C., regional archives, and presidential libraries. NAIL contains a selection of archival, microfilm, and audiovisual materials, including more than 100,000 full-text documents and images. Although it contains thousands of entries, these represent only a small portion of NARA holdings at this time. Separate searches for archival or microfilm materials are available. The archival search includes a standard and expert search option and an option to search the digital collection only.

Beginning with Herbert Hoover, Presidential papers have been housed in a system of Presidential libraries. *Information About the National Archives for Researchers* lists these libraries and their addresses. The *Presidential Libraries Web Page* also provides addresses, as well as links to the libraries' Web pages. The *Select List of Publications of the National Archives and Records Administration* lists guides and publications relating to each library that can be obtained from the libraries themselves. The *Presidential Library Finding Aids Web Page* provides Web links to online guides and finding aids for individual libraries. Occasionally publications from presidential libraries are sent to depository libraries, primarily in the *General Publications* series of the National Archives (AE 1.102:, Item 0569-B-02), but depository distribution has been undependable. Titles sent to depositories in recent years include: *Historical Materials in the Herbert Hoover Presidential Library* (AE 1.102:H 62/5), *Historical Materials in the John Fitzgerald Kennedy Library* (AE 1.102:H 62/3 or AE 1.102:H 62/2/993), *Historical Materials in the Franklin D. Roosevelt Library* (AE 1.102:H 62), and *Historical Materials in the Harry S Truman Library* (AE 1.102:H 62/3 (MF)).

The Library of Congress contains presidential papers for more than 20 presidents. These have been microfilmed and indexed. The *Presidents' Papers Index* series has been distributed to depository libraries, but the microfilm must be purchased separately from the Library of Congress. The *Online Collections in American Memory* Web page lists manuscript collections in the Library of Congress for which materials have been digitized and made available in the Library of Congress's *American Memory* Web collection. Presidential papers presently available include George Washington, Thomas Jefferson, and Abraham Lincoln.

ANNUAL REPORTS OF THE PRESIDENT
Checklist

Economic Report of the President Transmitted to the Congress. PRINT. WEB. (annual) 1947–. U.S. President. PR [no.].9: (SuDocs number varies with each President) Item 0848. ASI 204-1. GPO. <http://w3.access.gpo.gov/eop/index.html>.

 Coverage: U.S.
 Content: President's economic program and policies; assessment of the economic situation; administration economic strategies.

Budget of the United States Government. PRINT. WEB. (annual) 1922–. U.S. Executive Office of the President. Office of Management and Budget. PREX 2.8: (Also issued as a House Document, Y 1.1/7:) Item 0853. ASI 104-2. GPO. <http://w3.access.gpo.gov/usbudget/>; <http://purl.access.gpo.gov/GPO/LPS2343>.

 Coverage: U.S.
 Content: budget message of the President; budget themes and priorities; administration's proposed budget.

The Budget of the United States Government Fiscal Year [year]. CD-ROM. (annual) 1996–. U.S. Executive Office of the President. Office of Management and Budget. PREX 2.8/1: Item 0853-C. ASI 104-38. GPO.

 Content: CD-ROM version of the *Budget of the United States Government.*

[Year] Trade Policy Agenda and [year] Annual Report of the President of the United States on the Trade Agreements Program. PRINT. WEB. (annual) 1960–. U.S. Executive Office of the President. Office of the United States Trade Representative. PREX 9.11: (Earlier, PR 40.11:; PR 39.13:) Item 0857-G-01. ASI 444-1. GPO. <http://www.ustr.gov/reports/index.html>.

 Content: trade policy agenda for upcoming year; review of trade accomplishments and U.S. trade situation; trade negotiations and agreements; activities under U.S. trade laws.

Aeronautics and Space Report of the President. PRINT. WEB. (annual) 1958–. U.S. National Aeronautics and Space Administration. NAS 1.52: (Earlier, PREX 5.9: and House Documents series). Item 0856-D. ASI 9504-9. <http://www.hq.nasa.gov/office/pao/History/presrep.htm>; <http://purl.access.gpo.gov/GPO/LPS726>.

 Content: summary reports on aeronautics and space activities of all federal agencies with relevant responsibilities; chronologies of launches; launch vehicles; budget data.

Discussion

The *Economic Report of the President* describes the administration's domestic and international economic policy and provides a comprehensive review and assessment of the current economic situation. The first section of the report contains the President's economic report. This is a short message from the President containing an assessment of the present economic situation and describing the administration's policies and proposals for dealing with specific economic needs. Most of the *Economic Report* is devoted to the annual report of the Council of Economic Advisers. This is a much more in-depth look at the economy and provides the background for administration policies. Reports generally discuss recent economic trends, the administration's economic policies, recent developments and the economic outlook, the labor market, income, regulation, and global economic issues. A statistical appendix provides comprehensive, historical national statistics on national income, employment, productivity, business activity, prices, and finance.

The *Budget of the United States Government* is the President's proposed budget for the next fiscal year. It gives a strong reflection of the President's goals and priorities. At the beginning of the *Budget* is the President's budget message. This is a brief introduction to the year's budget. Introductory chapters review the budget situation in greater depth and present the administration's agenda and policies. An economic projections or assumptions section describes the projected economic outlook on which the budget is based. Additional chapters provide a detailed analysis of the administration's budget approach and priorities in specific program areas. Chapters may discuss such areas as education, children or families, research and development, health care, law enforcement, the environment, and national security. The largest portion of the *Budget* is the detailed agency-by-agency budget section, most often included in a separate appendix volume. This section contains a detailed listing of agency programs and expenditures with the President's proposed budget figures, as well as estimated and actual budget figures from the previous two years.

The *Trade Policy Agenda and Annual Report of the President of the United States on the Trade Agreements Program* describes the President's trade policies. The trade policy agenda portion of the report sets forth the agenda for the coming year. The agenda is organized around specific trade negotiations, countries or world regions, and products. Most of the report is devoted to the annual report on trade agreements. This contains a review of U.S. trade for the year and an extensive discussion of various trade negotiations with international groups and individual countries. Some statistics on exports and imports and trade balances are incorporated in the text. The annual report also includes a survey of activities relating to specific trade law provisions.

The *Aeronautics and Space Report of the President* is an annual summary of federal government agency activities in aeronautics and space. Arranged by agency, it includes the activities of NASA, the Department of Defense, the Federal Aviation Administration, the Department of Commerce, the Department of Energy, the Department of the Interior, the Department of State, and several others. Appendixes include a list of successful U.S. launches for the year and historical lists of total successful and failed launches by year, total successful launches of other countries, and human space flights. A list of U.S. space launch vehicles and historical and current budget expenditures for space activities are also available.

SELECTED PUBLICATION SERIES OF THE PRESIDENT

Checklist

General Publications. PRINT. (irregular) U.S. President. PR 42.2: (Earlier, PR 41.2:; SuDocs number varies with each President) Item 0850. GPO.

> Content: miscellaneous brochures and publications on Presidential programs.

Special Committees and Commissions. PRINT. (irregular) U.S. President. PR 42.8: (Earlier, PR 41.8:; SuDocs number varies with each President) Item 0851-J. GPO.

> Content: reports of Presidential commissions, task forces, and committees.

Discussion

The *General Publications* series of the U.S. President contains miscellaneous publications relating to the presidency. Publications relate to presidential policy initiatives or programs sponsored by the President's office. Examples of publications in this series include *The National AIDS Strategy: 1997* (PR 42.2:AC 7/997), *The President's Plan to Strengthen and Modernize Medicare for the 21st Century* (PR 42.2:M 46), and *One America in the 21st Century: the President's Initiative on Race: One America Dialogue Guide, Conducting a Discussion on Race* (PR 42.2:ON 2).

The *Special Committees and Commissions* series contains reports from presidential commissions and task forces.

Some of these include *America's Commitment: Federal Programs Benefiting Women and New Initiatives as Follow-Up to the UN Fourth World Conference on Women* (PR 42.8:W 84), *Towards a Sustainable America: Advancing Prosperity, Opportunity, and a Healthy Environment for the 21st Century* (PR 42.8:SU 8/AM 3/3), and *Final Report to President Clinton White House Commission on Aviation Safety and Security* (PR 42.8:AV 5/AV 5).

ADDITIONAL SOURCES

Checklist

Nomination and Election of the President and Vice President of the United States, 1992: Including the Manner of Selecting Delegates to National Party Conventions. PRINT. MF. (1992) U.S. Congress. Senate. Committee on Rules and Administration. Senate Document No. 102-14. Y 1.1/3:102-14. Items 0996-A or -B(MF).

> Content: federal and state laws and political party rules relating to the nomination and election of the President and Vice President.

Visits Abroad of the Presidents of the United States 1906–1989. PRINT. WEB. (1990) U.S. Department of State. S 1.2:V 82/4/906-89. Item 0876. <http://www.state.gov/www/about_state/history/prestravels2.html>.

> Content: list of official visits to foreign countries made by U.S. Presidents and Presidents-elect.

The Presidents of the United States of America. PRINT. WEB. (1995) White House Historical Association. (Nondepository) (Earlier, Y 3.H 62/4:2 P 92, Item 1089) <http://www.whitehouse.gov/WH/glimpse/presidents/html/presidents.html>.

> Content: color portraits and biographies of the Presidents.

The First Ladies. PRINT. WEB. (1995) White House Historical Association. (Nondepository) (Earlier, Y 3.H 62/4:2 F 51, Item 1089) <http://www.whitehouse.gov/WH/glimpse/firstladies/html/firstladies.html>.

> Content: color portraits and biographies of First Ladies.

The Presidents from the Inauguration of George Washington to the Inauguration of Jimmy Carter: Historic Places Commemorating the Chief Executives of the United States. PRINT. (1977) U.S. Department of the Interior. National Park Service. The National Survey of Historic Sites and Buildings. I 29.2:H 62/9/v.20/977. Item 0648.

> Content: color portraits and biographical sketches of Presidents; list and description of historic sites associated with Presidents.

The White House: The House of the People. PRINT. (1998?) U.S. President. PR 42.2:W 58/2. Item 0850.

> Content: history and description of the White House; biographical information on the Clintons and Gores.

The White House. PRINT. (1989) U.S. President. PR 41.2:W 58. Item 0850.

> Content: history and description of the White House; biographical information on George Bush; Bush family life.

The President's House. PRINT. (1984) U.S. President. Pr 40.2:H 81. Item 0850.

Content: history and description of the White House; a day in the life of the President and First Lady; the Reagan family; biographical information on Ronald Reagan.

Discussion

Nomination and Election of the President and Vice President of the United States, 1992 contains the text of constitutional provisions and federal laws relating to the election of the President. Federal and party rules related to the nominating convention and the selection of delegates are also included, along with a survey of significant court decisions. State laws on the election and on delegate selection are summarized. There is a list of important dates, including presidential primary dates, and tables listing all of the Presidents, their opponents, and their Vice-Presidents with brief biographical data, numbers of votes cast, and length of term served. Other tables give general statistics on votes cast for President by state and political party.

Visits Abroad of the Presidents of the United States 1906–1989 lists official presidential visits to other countries in chronological order, by President. Information given includes date, country, locale, and remarks concerning activities or purpose of the visit. The chronology begins with Theodore Roosevelt, whose 1906 visit to Panama was the first trip abroad for any U.S. President. Another listing arranged alphabetically by country visited is also included. The Web version is updated through 1997.

The Presidents of the United States of America and *The First Ladies* contain full-page color portraits of each President or first lady and give brief biographies. These are attractive and convenient sources for basic information on the Presidents and first ladies.

The Presidents from the Inauguration of George Washington to the Inauguration of Jimmy Carter: Historic Places Commemorating the Chief Executives of the United States also contains color portraits of the Presidents and longer biographical sketches. The second half of the book is a listing by state of National Park and historic landmark areas associated with Presidents, such as birthplaces, homes, monuments, and sites of historic occasions. Illustrations and descriptions of each area are provided. This book also contains an introductory survey of the historic role of Presidents and a summary of presidential characteristics derived from the biographical sketches.

The White House: The House of the People, The White House, and *The President's House* are similar in format, combining descriptive information about the White House with information on family life or behind the scenes life in the White House. The booklets describe the major rooms in the White House and give biographical information on the current President.

INDEXES
Checklist

Catalog of United States Government Publications (MOCAT). WEB. 1994–. U.S. Government Printing Office. Superintendent of Documents. <http://www.gpo.gov/catalog>; <http://www.access.gpo.gov/su_docs/locators/cgp/index.html>; <http://purl.access.gpo.gov/GPO/LPS844>.

Monthly Catalog of United States Government Publications. CD-ROM. 1996–. U.S. Government Printing Office. Superintendent of Documents. GP 3.8/7: Item 0557-C. GPO.

Monthly Catalog of United States Government Publications (Condensed version). PRINT. (monthly) 1996–. U.S. Government Printing Office. Superintendent of Documents. GP 3.8/8: (Earlier full version, GP 3.8:, 1895–1995). Item 0557-D. GPO.

CIS/Index. PRINT. (monthly) 1970–. Bethesda, MD: Congressional Information Service.

Congressional Universe. WEB. Bethesda, MD: Congressional Information Service.

CIS U.S. Serial Set Index, 1789–1969. PRINT. (1975–79) Washington, DC: Congressional Information Service, Inc.

Congressional Masterfile I. CD-ROM. Bethesda, MD: Congressional Information Service, Inc.

CIS Federal Register Index. PRINT. 1984–1998. Bethesda, MD: Congressional Information Service, Inc.

CIS Index to Presidential Executive Orders and Proclamations. PRINT. (1986–87) Bethesda, MD: Congressional Information Service, Inc.

Discussion

The *Monthly Catalog* is the most comprehensive index to government publications. Materials relating to the President can be found in the subject index under "Presidents" or under the name of particular Presidents and in the author index under "United States. President." The complete version of the *Monthly Catalog* is available on the Web and CD-ROM. Commercial online and CD-ROM versions of the *Monthly Catalog* are also available.

CIS/Index indexes congressional publications, some of which include presidential messages. Look under "Presidential communications and messages," "Presidential vetoes," "Presidential appointments," and the names of individual Presidents. *Congressional Universe* includes a Web version of *CIS.*

For more information on these two indexes, see Chapter 3, "The Basics of Searching."

The *CIS U.S. Serial Set Index, 1789–1969* provides access to historical congressional materials similar to those in *CIS/Index* that contain presidential messages. The use of this index and of *CIS* to locate presidential documents is discussed in this chapter's section on "Additional Sources for Presidential Documents."

Congressional Masterfile I is a compact disc version of several historical congressional indexes published by

Congressional Information Service, Inc., including the *CIS U.S. Serial Set Index*. It provides comprehensive coverage for congressional publications from 1789 through 1969. This index is also available online as an add-on subscription to *Congressional Universe*.

The *CIS Federal Register Index* is a detailed index to the contents of the *Federal Register*, including the executive orders, proclamations, and other presidential documents that appear in the *Federal Register*. Materials are indexed under the subject headings "Executive Orders" and "Presidential Documents," as well as under specific subjects. An "Index by CFR Section Numbers" lists presidential documents by type and number under Title 3. All index entries give date and page in the *Federal Register*. The *Federal Register* also has its own, more general, monthly index.

The *CIS Index to Presidential Executive Orders and Proclamations* indexes executive orders and proclamations from 1789 through 1983. It is discussed more thoroughly in this chapter's section on "Executive Orders and Proclamations."

RELATED MATERIAL
Within this Work

Chapter 4   Foreign Policy

Chapter 52 Historical Searches

Chapter 53 National Archives

GPO Subject Bibliographies. PRINT. WEB. GP 3.22/2:

<http://bookstore.gpo.gov/sb/about.html>.

No. 106 "Presidents"

Other

Encyclopedia of Governmental Advisory Organizations. PRINT. (1973–) Detroit: Gale Research.

Guide to the Presidential Advisory Commissions 1973–84. PRINT. (1987) Steven D. Zink. Alexandria, VA: Chadwyck-Healey, Inc.

Presidential Advisory Commissions: Truman to Nixon. PRINT. (1975) Thomas R. Wolanin. Madison: University of Wisconsin Press.

These sources provide assistance in identifying presidential commissions and their reports. The *Encyclopedia of Governmental Advisory Organizations* lists more than 7,000 government advisory committees, task forces, and commissions, including presidential commissions. Organizations are arranged by broad subject categories such as agriculture; business, economics, industry, and labor; and defense and military science. Each organization entry provides information on the name of the body, address, telephone number, email, Web site, key contact, history and authority, program, findings and recommendations, membership, meetings, and publications, if appropriate. Publication information is limited to title and date. No SuDocs numbers are provided. Indexes provide access by names of individuals, publication titles, President, and keyword.

Steven Zink's *Guide to the Presidential Advisory Commissions* lists presidential commissions, committees, and task forces established from 1973 through 1984. Commissions are listed by year. Information includes the commission name, establishment information, termination, functions, activities and recommendations, meetings, members, and publication information. SuDocs numbers are included when available. Indexes provide access by personal name, title, and subject.

Presidential Advisory Commissions: Truman to Nixon contains an appendix listing presidential commissions by President and giving report titles and dates. Another appendix on "Responses to the Recommendations of Commissions" contains bibliographical references to follow-up reports and activities.

The Statistical Search

The statistical search is used to answer such questions as "How many teenagers commit suicide?" "How many traffic accidents involve drunk driving?" and "What was the total number of department store sales in 1997?" The first step in answering such questions is to consult the *Statistical Abstract of the United States*.

There are other comprehensive statistical compendiums published by the Census Bureau that can be useful to check at the beginning of a statistical search. Additionally, there are the various censuses themselves and several statistical compilations on specific subject areas. Finally, search *American Statistics Index (ASI)* or the Web version, *Statistical Universe*, for detailed information on statistical sources.

The chapters in this section list important sources for selected, popular statistical topics. The object of these chapters is to provide a quick alternative to searching *ASI* by listing titles that are frequently used to answer questions in these areas. However, *ASI* must be searched for more detailed or specialized information and to locate materials not covered in these chapters.

CHAPTER 28
Population Statistics

The major source of U.S. population statistics is the information gathered through the decennial census conducted by the Census Bureau. The Census Bureau also provides other population statistics through its "Current Population Survey (CPS)" program, conducted cooperatively with the U.S. Bureau of Labor Statistics and the "Survey of Income and Program Participation (SIPP)." There are many government sources containing population data, but the majority of population statistics originate from these basic sources of data. This chapter cites basic population statistical sources for the United States. For information on population statistics for other countries, see the "Demographic Sources" section of Chapter 5, "Foreign Countries."

SEARCH STRATEGY

This chapter shows a statistical search strategy. The steps to follow are

1. Search the general statistical sources listed: many population questions can be answered through the use of these sources alone;
2. Use census materials in print or electronic formats (especially Web and CD-ROM) to obtain more detailed statistics or statistics for specific geographic areas; the *Census Bureau Web site* should be thoroughly searched;
3. Search *American Statistics Index (ASI)* for other population statistics, including descriptions of other individual *Current Population Reports*; and
4. Use the Census Bureau Guides and *Census Bureau Web Site* to find out how to obtain other electronic information not available through the Web but available on CD-ROMs, magnetic tapes, or other electronic formats.

GENERAL STATISTICAL SOURCES
Checklist

Statistical Abstract of the United States. PRINT. WEB. (annual) 1878–. U.S. Department of Commerce. Economics and Statistics Administration. Bureau of the Census. C 3.134: Item 0150. ASI 2324-1. GPO. <http://www.census.gov/statab/www/>; <http://purl.access.gpo.gov/GPO/LPS2878>.

> Coverage: U.S., divisions, regions, state, metropolitan areas, cities of 100,000 or more.
> Content: total population counts; various other population characteristics, including age, race, Hispanic origin, sex, marital status; household characteristics; other social and economic characteristics.

Statistical Abstract of the United States. CD-ROM. (annual) 1993–. U.S. Department of Commerce. Bureau of the Census. C 3.134/7: Item 0150-B. ASI 2324-14.

> Content: CD-ROM version of the *Statistical Abstract*.

Historical Statistics of the United States: Colonial Times to 1970. Parts 1-2. PRINT. (1975) U.S. Department of Commerce. Bureau of the Census. C 3.134/2:H 62/789-970/pt.1-2. Item 0151. ASI (76) 2328-2. GPO.

> Coverage: U.S., regions, states, metropolitan areas.
> Content: total population counts; population by characteristics such as sex, race, age, marital status, nativity; household and family characteristics.

Historical Statistics of the United States on CD-ROM: Colonial Times to 1970. CD-ROM. (1997) New York, NY: Cambridge University Press.

> Content: CD-ROM version of *Historical Statistics of the United States*.

County and City Data Book. PRINT. WEB. (quinquennial) 1947–. U.S. Department of Commerce. Economics and Statistics Administration. Bureau of the Census. C 3.134/2:C 83/2/year. Item 0151. ASI 2328-1. GPO. <http://fisher.lib.Virginia.EDU/ccdb/>.

> Coverage: U.S., regions, divisions, states, counties, cities of 25,000 or more, places of 2,500 or more.
> Content: total population counts; population by age and race.

County and City Data Book. CD-ROM. (quinquennial) 1988–. U.S. Department of Commerce. Bureau of the Census. C 3.134/2-1: (Earlier, C 3.134/2:C 83/2/). Item 0151-D-01. ASI 2328-1.

> Content: CD-ROM version of the *County and City Data Book.*

County and City Extra: Annual Metro, City, and County Data Book. PRINT. (annual) 1992–. Lanham, MD: Bernan Press.

> Coverage: U.S., states, counties, metropolitan areas, congressional districts, cities of 25,000 or more.
>
> Content: updated version of the *County and City Data Book.*

Places, Towns, and Townships. PRINT. (irregular) 1993–. Lanham, MD: Bernan Press.

> Coverage: incorporated places.
>
> Content: updated supplement to the *County and City Data Book.*

State and Metropolitan Area Data Book. PRINT. WEB. (irregular) 1979–. U.S. Department of Commerce. Economics and Statistics Administration. Bureau of the Census. C 3.134/5: Item 0150. ASI 2328-54. GPO. <http://www.census.gov/statab/www/smadb.html>.

> Coverage: U.S., states, metropolitan areas, central cities of metropolitan areas, component counties of metropolitan areas.
>
> Content: total population counts; population by race, Hispanic origin, and age; household characteristics.

State and Metropolitan Area Data Book. CD-ROM. (irregular) 1997/98–. U.S. Department of Commerce. Economics and Statistics Administration. Bureau of the Census. (Not distributed to depository libraries).

> Content: CD-ROM version of the *State and Metropolitan Area Data Book.*

USA Counties. CD-ROM. WEB. (irregular) 1992–. U.S. Department of Commerce. Economics and Statistics Administration. Bureau of the Census. C 3.134/6: Item 0150-C. ASI 2324-17. <http://govinfo.kerr.orst.edu/usaco-stateis.html>; <http://tier2.census.gov/usac/index.html-ssi>.

> Coverage: U.S., states, counties.
>
> Content: population counts; births, deaths, percent of population 65 years and over; education; labor force participation; personal income.

Discussion

All of these general statistical sources include some basic data on population statistics. These sources provide a first ready-reference step in locating population statistics and should be checked before consulting the more detailed sources listed in this chapter.

The *Statistical Abstract of the United States* includes an entire section on population statistics and is particularly good for locating information at the U.S. level. Many population statistical questions may be answered by using this source alone. The full-text of recent editions of the *Statistical Abstract* is available on the Census Bureau Web site as PDF files. The *Statistical Abstract* is also available on CD-ROM. The CD contains additional geographic areas, variables, or time series not in the printed version.

Historical Statistics of the United States: Colonial Times to 1970 provides a convenient historical compilation of population statistics. The *County and City Data Book* and the *State and Metropolitan Area Data Book* are especially useful for obtaining basic population information for geographic areas smaller than the United States.

The *County and City Data Book* is also available on CD-ROM. The University of Virginia Library Geospatial and Statistical Data Center also offers recent editions of the *County and City Data Book* on the Internet in their interactive data area. Users select the desired edition, geography, and variables to create a customized data display. The *State and Metropolitan Area Data Book* is available as a PDF file on the *Census Bureau Web site.* A CD-ROM edition is also available.

The *County and City Extra: Annual Metro, City, and County Data Book* is a commercially published book that is similar to the *County and City Data Book* but includes additional updated information. *Places, Towns, and Townships* is a companion title for smaller geographic areas.

The *USA Counties* CD-ROM contains county and state data from the last two or three issues of the *County and City Data Book* and the *State and Metropolitan Area Data Book* to provide several years of data in one source. The data are similar to that found in the two data books. The Oregon State University Government Information Sharing Project provides access to the current issue on the Internet. Users select a geographic area profile or an area comparison and then the desired geography. A subject area can then be selected or a keyword search conducted to display data. The *Census Bureau Web site* contains a similar version.

CENSUS OF POPULATION SOURCES
Checklist

Census of Population. PRINT. (decennial) 1950–. U.S. Department of Commerce. Economics and Statistics Administration. Bureau of the Census. (Format has changed over the years; titles listed below reflect current format. Before 1950 included in comprehensive decennial census.)

General Population Characteristics. C 3.223/6:; C 3.223/6-2:; C 3.223/6-3:; C 3.223/6-4: Items 0159-C-01 to 53, 0154-A-01-03.

> Coverage: U.S., states, counties, places of 1,000 or more; separate reports on metropolitan areas, urbanized areas, American Indian and Alaska Native areas.
>
> Content: total population; age; sex; race; Hispanic origin; marital status; household relationship characteristics.

Social and Economic Characteristics. C 3.223/7:; C 3.223/7-2:; C 3.223/7-3:; C3.223/7-4: (Earlier title: *General Social and Economic Characteristics*) Items 0159-C-01 to 53, 0154-A-01 to 03. ASI 2531-5.

> Coverage: U.S., states, counties, places of 2,500 or more, selected county subdivisions (MCDs) of 2,500 or more; separate reports on metropolitan areas, urbanized areas, American Indian and Alaska Native areas.

Content: population subjects such as income, education, and occupation.

Summary Population and Housing Characteristics. C 3.223/18: Item 0159-B-01 to 53. ASI 2551-1.

Coverage: U.S., states, counties, places, county subdivisions (MCDs), American Indian and Alaska Native areas.
Content: total population counts; summary statistics on age, sex, race, Hispanic origin, household relationships, families and family characteristics, population density, and group quarters.

Summary Social, Economic, and Housing Characteristics. C 3.223/23: Item 0156-M-01 to 53. ASI 2551-7.

Coverage: U.S., states, counties, places, county subdivisions (MCDs), American Indian and Alaska Native areas.
Content: disability; educational attainment; family type and presence of own children; income; labor force status; language spoken at home and ability to speak English; means of transportation to work; nativity; place of birth; poverty status; residence in 1985; school enrollment and type of school; veteran status.

Population and Housing Unit Counts. C 3.223/5: Item 0159-C-01 to 53. ASI 2551-2.

Coverage: U.S., regions, divisions, states, counties, county subdivisions, places, metropolitan areas, urbanized areas.
Content: total population counts.

Population and Housing Characteristics for Census Tracts and Block Numbering Areas. C 3.223/11: (Earlier title, *Census Tracts*). Item 0156-K-01 to 53. ASI 2551-3.

Coverage: metropolitan areas, census tracts in metropolitan areas, census tracts or block numbering areas in the nonmetropolitan area portions of each state, counties, places of 10,000 or more.
Content: total population counts; age; sex; race; Hispanic origin; marital status; household relationship characteristics; disability; educational attainment; family type and presence of own children; labor force status; language spoken at home and ability to speak English; means of transportation to work; nativity; place of birth; poverty status; residence in 1985; school enrollment and type of school; veteran status.

Population and Housing Characteristics for Congressional Districts of the 103rd Congress. PRINT. C 3.223/20: (Title varies; before 1980 data were published in *Congressional District Data Book*) Item 0159-C-01 to 53. ASI 2551-4.

Coverage: congressional districts, counties, minor civil divisions of 10,000 or more, places of 10,000 or more.
Content: population; sex; marital status; family and household characteristics; education; employment; occupation; income; vehicle availability; tenure; units in structure; value; rent; monthly owner costs; vacancy/occupancy status; number of rooms; number of bedrooms; condominium status; kitchen facilities; sewage disposal; year built; water source; heating fuel; telephone availability; plumbing facilities.

Population Subject Reports. PRINT. C 3.223/10: Item 0159-G. ASI 2533-.

Coverage: varies; U.S., regions, divisions.
Content: reports on special topics.

Supplementary Reports. PRINT. C 3.223/12: Item 0154. ASI 2535-[no.].

Coverage: varies; U.S., regions, divisions.
Content: reports on special topics.

1990 Census of Population and Housing Summary Tape File 1A. CD-ROM. WEB. U.S. Department of Commerce. Bureau of the Census. Data User Services Division. C 3.282: Item 0154-F. ASI 2551-9. <http://venus.census.gov/cdrom/lookup>; <http://sunsite.Berkeley.edu/GovData/info/>; <http://govinfo.kerr.orst.edu/stateis.html>.

Coverage: states, counties, places, county subdivisions, tracts, block numbering areas, block groups, congressional districts.
Content: population; age; race; sex; marital status; Hispanic origin; household type; household relationship; housing units; units in structure; number of rooms; tenure; value; rent; vacancy/occupancy status.

1990 Census of Population and Housing Block Statistics (Summary Tape File 1B). CD-ROM. U.S. Department of Commerce. Bureau of the Census. Data User Services Division. C 3.282/3: Item 0154-F. ASI 2551-16.

Coverage: states, metropolitan areas, urbanized areas, counties, places, county subdivisions, tracts, block numbering areas, block groups, blocks.
Content: population; race; Hispanic origin; persons under 18; persons over 65; household type; household relationship; housing units; units in structure; number of rooms; tenure; value; rent; vacancy/occupancy status.

1990 Census of Population and Housing Summary Tape File 1C. CD-ROM. WEB. U.S. Department of Commerce. Bureau of the Census. Data User Services Division. C 3.282: Item 0154-F. ASI 2551-17. <http://venus.census.gov/cdrom/lookup>; <http://sunsite.Berkeley.edu/GovData/info/>; <http://govinfo.kerr.orst.edu/stateis.html>.

Coverage: U.S., regions, divisions, states, metropolitan areas, urbanized areas, counties, places of 10,000 or more, selected minor civil divisions, congressional districts.
Content: population; age; race; sex; marital status; Hispanic origin; household type; household relationship; housing units; units in structure; number of rooms; tenure; value; rent; vacancy/occupancy status.

1990 Census of Population and Housing Summary Tape File 3A. CD-ROM. WEB. U.S. Department of Commerce. Bureau of the Census. Data User Services Division. C 3.282/2: Item 0154-F-01. ASI 2551-11. <http://venus.census.gov/cdrom/lookup>; <http://sunsite.Berkeley.edu/GovData/info/>; <http://govinfo.kerr.orst.edu/stateis.html>.

Coverage: states, counties, metropolitan areas, urbanized areas, county subdivisions, places, tracts, block numbering areas, block groups.
Content: population; age, race, sex, marital status, Hispanic origin; family type; household type, household relationship; language spoken at home; ancestry; birthplace; citizenship; means of transportation to work; educational attainment; school enrollment; disability, veteran/military status; employment; industry; occupation; income; poverty status; housing units; household income; vehicle availability; tenure; units in structure; value; rent; monthly owner costs; vacancy/occupancy status; number of rooms; number of bedrooms; condominium status; kitchen fa-

cilities; sewage disposal; water source; heating fuel; telephone availability; plumbing facilities.

1990 Census of Population and Housing Summary Tape File 3B. CD-ROM. WEB. U.S. Department of Commerce. Bureau of the Census. Data Users Services Division. C 3.282/2: Item 0154-F-01. ASI 2551-13. <http://venus.census.gov/cdrom/lookup>; <http://sunsite.Berkeley.edu/GovData/info/>.

> Coverage: zip codes.
> Content: population; age, race, sex, marital status, Hispanic origin; family type; household type, household relationship; language spoken at home; ancestry; birthplace; citizenship; means of transportation to work; educational attainment; school enrollment; disability; veteran/military status; employment; industry; occupation; income; poverty status; housing units; household income; vehicle availability; tenure; units in structure; value; rent; monthly owner costs; vacancy/occupancy status; number of rooms; number of bedrooms; condominium status; kitchen facilities; sewage disposal; water source; heating fuel; telephone availability; plumbing facilities.

1990 Census of Population and Housing Summary Tape File 3C. CD-ROM. WEB. U.S. Department of Commerce. Bureau of the Census. Data User Services Division. C 3.282/2: Item 0154-F-01. ASI 2551-14. <http://venus.census.gov/cdrom/lookup>; <http://sunsite.Berkeley.edu/GovData/info/>; <http://govinfo.kerr.orst.edu/stateis.html>.

> Coverage: U.S., regions, divisions, states, counties, selected county subdivisions, places of 10,000 or more, metropolitan areas, urbanized places.
> Content: population; age, race, sex, marital status, Hispanic origin, family type; household type, household relationship; language spoken at home; ancestry; birthplace; citizenship; means of transportation to work; educational attainment; school enrollment; disability; veteran/military status; employment; industry; occupation; income; poverty status; housing units; household income; vehicle availability; tenure; units in structure; value; rent; monthly owner costs; vacancy/occupancy status; number of rooms; number of bedrooms; condominium status; kitchen facilities; sewage disposal; water source; heating fuel; telephone availability; plumbing facilities.

1990 Census Lookup Web Page. WEB. U.S. Department of Commerce. Bureau of the Census. <http://venus.census.gov/cdrom/lookup>.

> Content: Web-based interface to STF data.

Congressional Districts of the United States Summary Tape File 1D; Summary Tape File 3D. CD-ROM. U.S. Department of Commerce. Bureau of the Census. C 3.282/4: Item 0154-F-05. ASI 2551-18. <http://www.census.gov/prod/www/abs/congprof.html>.

> Coverage: states, congressional districts, counties, places, American Indian areas.
> Content: population; age, race, sex, marital status, Hispanic origin; family type; household type, household relationship; language spoken at home; ancestry; birthplace; citizenship; means of transportation to work; educational attainment; school enrollment; disability; veteran/military status; employment; industry; occupation; income; poverty status; housing units; household income; vehicle availability; tenure; units in structure; value; rent; monthly

owner costs; vacancy/occupancy status; number of rooms; number of bedrooms; condominium status; kitchen facilities; sewage disposal; water source; heating fuel; telephone availability; plumbing facilities.

1990 Census of Population and Housing Subject Summary Tape Files. CD-ROM. WEB. U.S. Department of Commerce. Bureau of the Census. Data User Services Division. C 3.286: Item 0154-G. ASI 2551-12. <http://govinfo.kerr.orst.edu/earnstateis.html>; <http://sunsite.Berkeley.edu/GovData/info/>.

> Coverage: varies; U.S., regions, divisions, states, metropolitan areas, large counties and places.
> Content: specialized subject reports on various population and housing topics.

1990 Census of Population and Housing PL 94-171. CD-ROM. U.S. Department of Commerce. Bureau of the Census. C 3.281: Item 0154-B-01. ASI 2551-6.

> Coverage: U.S., states, counties, places, county subdivisions, tracts, block numbering areas, block groups, blocks, some voting districts.
> Content: population; age; race; Hispanic origin; housing units.

1990 Census of Population and Housing Census/Equal Employment Opportunity (EEO) Special File. CD-ROM. WEB. U.S. Department of Commerce. Bureau of the Census. C 3.283: Item 0154-F-02. ASI 2551-15. <http://tier2.census.gov/eeo/eeo.htm>; <http://govinfo.kerr.orst.edu/stateis.html>.

> Coverage: U.S., states, counties, metropolitan statistical areas, places and minor civil divisions of 50,000 or more.
> Content: age; sex; race; Hispanic origin; occupations; educational attainment.

1990 Census of Population and Housing. Special Tabulation on Aging. CD-ROM. U.S. Department of Commerce. Bureau of the Census. Data User Services. C 3.281/2:. Item 0154-B-03. (95) ASI 2551-19.

> Coverage U.S.; regions; divisions; states; counties; places and county subdivisions greater than 2500; census tracts; block numbering areas; metropolitan statistical areas; urbanized areas; American Indian areas; planning and service areas (PSAs) as constructed by State Agencies on Aging.
> Content: data are generally provided for persons and householders age 60 and over; population; age, race, sex, marital status, Hispanic origin, family type; household type, household relationship; language spoken at home; ancestry; birthplace; citizenship; means of transportation to work; educational attainment; school enrollment; disability; mobility and self-care limitation; veteran/military status; employment; industry; occupation; income; poverty status; housing units; household income; vehicle availability; tenure; units in structure; value; rent; monthly owner costs; vacancy/occupancy status; number of rooms; number of bedrooms; condominium status; kitchen facilities; sewage disposal; water source; heating fuel; telephone availability; plumbing facilities.

1990 Census of Population and Housing. Public Use Microdata Samples. CD-ROM. U.S. Department of Commerce. Bureau of the Census. Data User Services. C 3.285: Item 0154-F-04.

> Coverage: varies depending on the sample; county groups or smaller areas with 100,000 or more; metropolitan statistical areas and other large areas with 100,000 or more;

county (or county equivalent), groups of counties, places, or county/place parts of more than 200,000; MSAs, groups of MSAs, parts of MSAs when the MA is larger than 200,000 persons, and groups of nonmetropolitan areas.

Content: sample data of individual records of responses to questionnaires with unique identifiers removed.

1990 Census of Population and Housing. County-to-County Migration Flow Files, Special Project 312 (SP312). CD-ROM. U.S. Department of Commerce. Bureau of the Census. Data User Services. C 3.284: Item 0154-F-03.

Coverage: counties within states; some minor civil divisions.

Content: intrastate and interstate county-to-county migration; demographic characteristics of movers, including age, college enrollment, employment status, Hispanic origin, household type, income in 1989, industry, occupation, place of birth and citizenship, poverty status in 1989, race, sex, and tenure.

The American Community Survey Web Site. WEB. U.S. Department of Commerce. Bureau of the Census. <http://www.census.gov/acs/www/index.html>.

Content: description of American Community Survey and data products; selected data profiles from the survey.

The American Community Survey. CD-ROM. WEB. (annual) 1996–. U.S. Department of Commerce. Bureau of the Census. C 3.297: Item 0154-B-14. <http://www.census.gov/CMS/www/>; <http://www.census.gov/cms/www/index_c.htm>; <http://purl.access.gpo.gov/GPO/LPS1258>.

Coverage: selected counties and cities.

Content: household and family types; housing units; householder characteristics; housing characteristics (bedrooms, units in structure, water, sewage disposal, year built, heating fuel, air conditioning, telephones, vehicles available); vacant and occupied units; housing costs (rent, mortgage status, monthly owner costs, value); plumbing/kitchen facilities.

American FactFinder. WEB. U.S. Department of Commerce. Bureau of the Census. <http://factfinder.census.gov/java_prod/dads.ui.homePage.HomePage>.

Coverage: U.S., regions, divisions, states, counties, county subdivisions, congressional districts, metropolitan areas, urbanized areas, places, tracts, block numbering areas, block groups, zip codes, American Indian areas.

Content: 1990 census data; 2000 census data as it becomes available; American Community Survey data; other census products.

Bureau of the Census Web Site. WEB. U.S. Department of Commerce. Bureau of the Census <http://www.census.gov>.

Content: comprehensive Web site of Census information; includes data sets and PDF versions of Census publications.

Census 1990. WEB. U.S. Department of Commerce. Bureau of the Census. <http://www.census.gov/main/www/cen1990.html>.

Content: information and data from the 1990 census.

United States Census 2000. WEB. U.S. Department of Commerce. Bureau of the Census. <http://www.census.gov/dmd/www/2khome.htm>.

Content: information about the 2000 census.

Selected Historical Census Data: Population and Housing Counts. WEB. U.S. Department of Commerce. Bureau of the Census. <http://www.census.gov/population/www/censusdata/pop-hc.html>.

Content: historical population and housing counts from 1790–.

Population of States and Counties of the United States: 1790 to 1990, From the Twenty-One Decennial Censuses. PRINT. (1996) U.S. Department of Commerce. Bureau of the Census. C 3.2: P 81/26. Item 0146. ASI (97) 2328-105. GPO.

Coverage: states, counties.

Content: population counts for individual states and counties 1790–1990.

United States Historical Census Data Browser. WEB. University of Virginia Library. Geospatial and Statistical Data Center. <http://fisher.lib.virginia.edu/census/>.

Coverage: U.S., states, counties.

Content: interactive software allowing manipulation and graphing of data from decennial censuses from 1790–1970.

Discussion

Data from the Census of Population and Housing are composed of two types: 100-percent and sample. One hundred-percent data are obtained from questions asked of all persons, whereas sample data are obtained from questions asked of only a portion of the persons filling out census questionnaires. In general, 100-percent data are available for the smallest geographic areas, with sample data available for larger geographic areas. Figure 28.1 shows the areas covered by the 100-percent component and the sample component for the 1990 census. When dealing with geographic areas, the census uses specific terms, such as census tract, place, block, or urbanized area, to indicate the type of areas. Figure 28.2 shows and defines some of these geographic area terms.

The *Census of Population* reports vary from census to census but have tended to follow the same general format. Descriptions that follow are for the 1990 Census. *Census 2000* is anticipated to have fewer printed reports, and will mainly be distributed via the Web and CD-ROM products (see Figure 28.3). The Web product, *The American FactFinder*, will be extensively used to provide access to data cross-tabulations.

The *General Population Characteristics* reports are published with a U.S. summary, individual state reports, and reports for American Indian and Alaska Native areas, metropolitan areas, and urbanized areas. Data covered are 100 percent. The *Social and Economic Characteristics* volume is published with a similar number of reports. Data includes statistics on both 100-percent data and sample data.

Two summary volumes are also published. *Summary Population and Housing Characteristics* includes 100-percent data and covers geographic areas down to places. This title was new for 1990 and replaces in part the 1980

Figure 1.   1990 CENSUS CONTENT

100-PERCENT COMPONENT

Population
Household relationship
Sex
Race
Age
Marital status
Hispanic origin

Housing
Number of units in structure
Number of rooms in unit
Tenure—owned or rented
Value of home or monthly rent
Congregate housing (meals included in rent)
Vacancy characteristics

SAMPLE COMPONENT

Population

Social characteristics:
Education—enrollment and attainment
Place of birth, citizenship, and year of entry to U.S.
Ancestry
Language spoken at home
Migration (residence in 1985)
Disability
Fertility
Veteran status

Economic characteristics:
Labor force
Occupation, industry, and class of worker
Place of work and journey to work
Work experience in 1989
Income in 1989
Year last worked

Housing
Year moved into residence
Number of bedrooms
Plumbing and kitchen facilities
Telephone in unit
Vehicles available
Heating fuel
Source of water and method of sewage disposal
Year structure built
Condominium status
Farm residence
Shelter costs, including utilities

NOTE: Questions dealing with the subjects covered in
     the 100-percent component will be asked of all
     persons and housing units. Those covered by
     the sample component will be asked of a portion
     or sample of the population and housing units.

Source: Census '90 Basics, p.4.

Figure 28.1: 1990 Census Content.

report series called *Summary Characteristics for Governmental Units. Summary Social, Economic, and Housing Characteristics* gives summary data for 100-percent and sample data. These reports are issued for the U.S., each state, and the District of Columbia. Figure 28.4 reprints a table from the *Summary Population and Housing Characteristics* volume.

Population and Housing Unit Counts give 100-percent data for population and housing at small geographic levels. Data for previous censuses are also included. Reports for the United States, each state, and the District of Columbia were issued for 1990. *Population and Housing Characteristics for Census Tracts and Block Numbering Areas* contains information at the Census tract and block numbering area level. Census tracts are areas of about 4,000 people in a metropolitan area. A block numbering area is a similar area in a nonmetropolitan area. (The 2000

census will eliminate the term "block numbering area" and call all of these areas census tracts.) Reports in this series are issued for each metropolitan area and for each state. Maps showing tract boundaries and identifying each tract by number accompany the census tract reports. For the 1990 census, depository libraries were only able to receive the tract maps for their state. Maps for areas in other states are available in each state's regional depository library and can also be purchased from the Census Bureau or in microfiche from Congressional Information Service. (Before 1990, depository libraries could receive all tract maps.)

The Population and Housing Characteristics for Congressional Districts of the 103rd Congress provides 100-percent and sample data for congressional districts and areas within congressional districts. A report is issued for each state and for the District of Columbia. *Population*

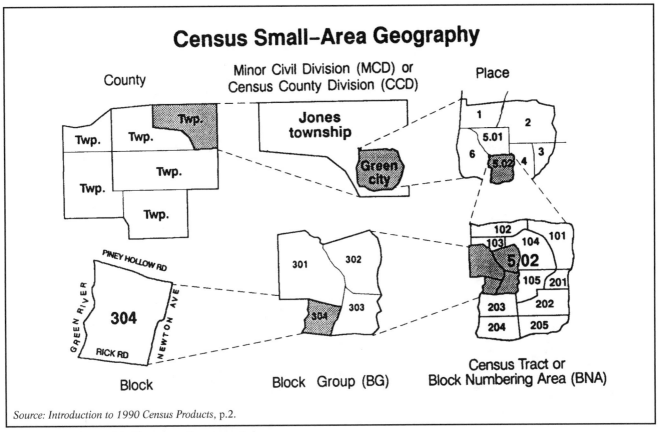

Census Small-Area Geography

Source: Introduction to 1990 Census Products, p.2.

Figure 28.2: 1990 Census Geography.

Subject Reports are issued as detailed reports on specific topics. Although the coverage varies, data have usually been provided primarily for the United States. Reports on various subject topics are also issued in the *Supplementary Reports* series. Sample titles from the 1990 census in this series include *Detailed Occupation and Other Characteristics from the EEO File for the U.S.* (C 3.223/12:1) and *Detailed Ancestry Groups for States*, (C 3.223/12:2).

The *1990 Census of Population and Housing Summary Tape File* CD-ROMs contain the data used to produce the printed census reports. The Summary Tape File 1 series contains data from the short questionnaire sent to everyone (100-percent data). It consists of subseries A, B, and C, which cover different geographic areas. Summary Tape File 1A contains basic population data for state and substate areas.

Summary Tape File 1B contains similar data for blocks, the smallest level of geography available in the census. Blocks are usually bounded by streets and average about 30 people. The data for such a small area as a block are limited. Before the 1990 census, block reports were available to depository libraries in microfiche (1980) or paper (1970 and earlier) and were accompanied by maps. 1990 block maps were not depository. Paper copies of 1990 block maps may be purchased from the Census Bureau. Summary Tape File 1C contains U.S. summary data

for population as well as data for other selected geographic areas.

The Summary Tape File 3 series includes sample population and housing characteristics. Summary Tape File 3A contains data from the long questionnaire sent only to a sample of the population (sample data). Summary Tape File 3C contains the same data tables, but covers different geographic areas, including United States summary data. Summary Tape File 3B contains zip code data. *Congressional Districts of the United States* contains both Summary Tape File 1 and 3 data for congressional districts. Information from STF 1 and 3 are also available as lookup tables for each congressional district from the Census Bureau Web site.

Census reports mentioned above that are generated from Summary Tape File 1 data include: *General Population Characteristics* and *Summary Population and Housing Characteristics*. Summary Tape File 3A corresponds to *Social and Economic Characteristics* and *Summary Social, Economic, and Housing Characteristics*. Tract reports contain a combination of data from both files. The data from some of these CDs are accessible from the Internet, either through the *Bureau of the Census Web site* or from other non-governmental sites, most notably the Government Information Sharing Project and the Berkeley Digital Library SunSITE. This checklist gives the STF CDs that were made available to depository libraries. Ad-

Finding Traditional 1990 Census Products in Census 2000		
1990	**Title**	**Description**	**2000**
Population and Housing Unit Counts	CPH-2 Reports	Historical population and housing totals with boundary and annexation information	Printed Reports
Population and Housing Characteristics for Census Tracts and Block Numbering	CPH-3 Reports	Both 100 percent and sample population and housing data published for each MSA/PMSA portion of each state	American FactFinder Summary Files & Quick Tables
Census of Population and Census of Housing Reports for Metropolitan Areas and Urbanized Areas	CP-1, CP-2 CH-1, CH-2	Population and housing for metro and urban areas	Printed Reports & Quick Tables
Subject Summary Tape Files and Subject Reports	SSTS CP-3 CH-3	Includes electronic files and some corresponding reports covering specific populations and housing subjects and subgroups	American FactFinder custom cross-tabula- tions
Equal Employment Opportunity (EEO)	Basic EEO File	Tabulations for detailed occupations, educational attainment, age, sex, race, and Hispanic origin	Census Bureau analysts working with federal agencies through reimbursable tabulation agreements
County-to-County Migration File	County-to-County Migration File	A reimbursable product preceded the release of the standard product	Census Bureau analysts working with reimbursable tabulations agreements
Zip Code File	STF3B	Census Bureau purchased equivalency ZIP Code file to produce STF3	American FactFinder

Census 2000, Frequently Asked Questions <http://www.census.gov/Census 2000, *Frequently Asked questions* <http://www.census.gov/dmd/www/genfaq.htm>

Figure 28.3: Finding Traditional 1990 Census Products in Census 2000.

Table 5. Household, Family, and Group Quarters Characteristics: 1990—Con.

[For definitions of terms and meanings of symbols, see text]

State County County Subdivision Place	Persons in households	All households	Family households — Total	Married-couple family	Female householder, no husband present	Nonfamily households — Total	Householder living alone — Total	65 years and over — Total	65 years and over — Female	Persons per — Household	Persons per — Family	Persons in group quarters — Total	Institutionalized persons	Other persons in group quarters
Howard County—Con.														
Jamestown township	679	265	184	162	14	81	76	46	33	2.56	3.20	–	–	–
Riceville city (pt.)	334	154	94	77	-11	60	57	40	30	2.17	2.85	–	–	–
New Oregon township	831	330	223	203	8	107	103	65	54	2.52	3.22	–	–	–
Protivin city	305	149	83	79	3	66	65	50	46	2.05	2.87	–	–	–
Oak Dale township	221	74	60	53	4	14	14	4	1	2.99	3.43	–	–	–
Paris township	384	141	106	101	2	35	29	13	6	2.72	3.23	–	–	–
Saratoga township	304	114	89	78	6	25	25	15	9	2.67	3.09	–	–	–
Vernon Springs township	4 198	1 786	1 183	1 025	118	603	558	335	263	2.35	2.96	174	174	–
Cresco city	3 530	1 556	987	842	112	569	530	320	253	2.27	2.92	139	139	–
Humboldt County	10 589	4 339	3 101	2 785	234	1 238	1 154	691	566	2.44	2.96	167	148	19
Avery township	359	135	106	93	6	29	26	16	10	2.66	3.04	–	–	–
Bradgate city	124	48	33	30	2	15	15	8	6	2.58	3.30	–	–	–
Gilmore City city (pt.)	–	–	–	–	–	–	–	–	–	–	–	–	–	–
Beaver township	329	132	97	87	5	35	30	12	8	2.49	2.94	–	–	–
Corinth township	430	150	131	126	4	19	18	10	7	2.87	3.12	–	–	–
Dakota City city	1 019	361	277	230	36	84	74	32	27	2.82	3.28	–	–	–
Delana township	555	236	166	151	7	70	65	43	34	2.35	2.84	5	–	5
Bode city	335	152	98	90	6	54	53	36	31	2.20	2.84	–	–	–
Grove township	272	99	82	81	1	17	16	4	1	2.75	3.10	–	–	–
Humboldt city	4 276	1 894	1 265	1 129	118	629	592	371	323	2.26	2.84	162	148	14
Humboldt township	645	267	179	157	14	88	86	58	44	2.42	3.08	–	–	–
Livermore city	436	194	119	100	13	75	73	51	41	2.25	2.99	–	–	–
Lu Verne city (pt.)	2	1	1	1	–	–	–	–	–	2.00	2.00	–	–	–
Lake township	262	109	83	78	4	26	25	17	13	2.40	2.81	–	–	–
Hardy city	47	22	15	13	2	7	7	6	4	2.14	2.67	–	–	–
Norway township	463	180	136	126	5	44	42	30	24	2.57	3.04	–	–	–
Thor city	205	84	61	57	2	23	23	17	11	2.44	2.95	–	–	–
Rutland township	529	194	153	140	8	41	34	19	12	2.73	3.09	–	–	–
Rutland city	149	60	41	36	5	19	15	6	5	2.48	3.07	–	–	–
Vernon township	545	236	168	149	13	68	64	35	27	2.31	2.80	–	–	–
Lu Verne city (pt.)	52	26	14	11	3	12	11	6	5	2.00	2.79	–	–	–
Renwick city	287	136	87	77	5	49	46	25	20	2.11	2.68	–	–	–
Wacousta township	301	104	86	80	2	18	16	8	4	2.89	3.27	–	–	–
Ottosen city	72	31	21	18	2	10	10	7	4	2.32	2.95	–	–	–
Weaver township	604	242	172	158	11	70	66	36	32	2.50	3.05	–	–	–
Gilmore City city (pt.)	319	148	91	79	10	57	54	32	30	2.16	2.82	–	–	–
Pioneer city	46	14	12	12	–	2	1	1	1	3.29	3.58	–	–	–
Ida County	8 164	3 222	2 317	2 121	140	905	849	541	453	2.53	3.09	201	188	13
Battle township	269	86	77	74	1	9	8	3	3	3.13	3.34	–	–	–
Blaine township	577	215	168	152	12	47	45	30	26	2.68	3.14	–	–	–
Arthur city	272	113	78	67	9	35	34	25	22	2.41	3.01	–	–	–
Corwin township	2 601	1 080	737	668	58	343	322	198	166	2.41	3.01	75	75	–
Ida Grove city	2 282	973	650	588	53	323	304	192	161	2.35	2.96	75	75	–
Douglas township	277	90	75	68	3	15	14	5	4	3.08	3.47	–	–	–
Galva township	626	255	180	165	8	75	70	52	44	2.45	3.01	–	–	–
Galva city	398	178	111	105	4	67	63	51	43	2.24	2.92	–	–	–
Garfield township	195	70	54	48	3	16	14	9	6	2.79	3.26	–	–	–
Grant township	247	75	67	67	–	8	8	1	1	3.29	3.57	–	–	–
Griggs township	1 641	699	464	424	31	235	219	155	129	2.35	2.97	59	59	–
Holstein city	1 390	606	391	354	29	215	202	149	126	2.29	2.94	59	59	–
Hayes township	270	84	77	73	–	7	7	3	3	3.21	3.38	–	–	–
Logan township	261	98	81	80	1	17	16	7	5	2.66	2.96	–	–	–
Maple township	1 021	403	285	255	20	118	113	76	64	2.53	3.13	67	54	13
Battle Creek city	751	320	212	189	17	108	103	75	63	2.35	2.99	67	54	13
Silver Creek township	179	67	52	47	3	15	13	2	2	2.67	3.10	–	–	–
Iowa County	14 348	5 713	4 126	3 663	342	1 587	1 425	818	675	2.51	3.02	282	236	46
Dayton township	264	94	81	78	3	13	12	7	5	2.81	3.06	–	–	–
English township	1 444	625	421	350	52	204	194	126	99	2.31	2.88	66	66	–
Millersburg city	188	87	53	44	6	34	30	19	12	2.16	2.75	–	–	–
North English city (pt.)	866	393	254	204	39	139	133	96	77	2.20	2.82	66	66	–
Fillmore township	499	190	135	119	11	55	47	23	15	2.63	3.17	–	–	–
Parnell city	209	89	52	43	7	37	33	14	10	2.35	3.12	–	–	–
Greene township	504	169	145	136	5	24	21	11	10	2.98	3.28	–	–	–
Hartford township	1 396	565	405	365	30	160	152	95	77	2.47	3.01	–	–	–
Ladora city (pt.)	273	112	75	65	8	37	35	21	18	2.44	3.11	–	–	–
Victor city (pt.)	842	350	243	222	18	107	103	68	56	2.41	2.99	–	–	–
Hilton township	755	260	219	199	9	41	34	16	11	2.90	3.20	–	–	–
Williamsburg city (pt.)	7	3	3	2	–	–	–	–	–	2.33	2.33	–	–	–
Honey Creek township	355	133	100	95	2	33	26	9	6	2.67	3.07	–	–	–
Iowa township	602	226	179	166	10	47	39	18	13	2.66	3.04	–	–	–
Lenox township	1 396	587	433	398	27	154	138	71	61	2.38	2.80	46	46	–
Lincoln township	255	84	70	66	2	14	14	7	4	3.04	3.40	–	–	–
Marengo township	2 314	999	636	541	71	363	324	199	168	2.32	2.96	80	80	–
Marengo city (pt.)	1 869	808	505	423	64	303	269	174	153	2.31	2.99	80	80	–
Pilot township	351	113	99	84	8	14	12	5	3	3.11	3.29	–	–	–
Sumner township	439	140	126	119	5	14	10	4	4	3.14	3.32	–	–	–
Ladora city (pt.)	35	11	10	9	1	1	–	–	–	3.18	3.30	–	–	–
Troy township	2 472	1 005	707	626	65	298	276	177	158	2.46	3.02	90	44	46
Williamsburg city (pt.)	2 123	880	595	520	62	285	263	169	151	2.41	3.03	44	44	–
Washington township	934	391	258	217	36	133	110	47	41	2.39	2.97	–	–	–
Marengo city (pt.)	321	139	86	67	16	53	48	21	18	2.31	2.99	–	–	–
York township	368	132	112	104	6	20	16	3	–	2.79	3.02	–	–	–
Jackson County	19 660	7 527	5 479	4 711	566	2 048	1 870	1 040	819	2.61	3.15	290	285	5
Bellevue township	2 830	1 075	765	674	63	310	289	185	147	2.63	3.23	54	54	–
Bellevue city	2 185	873	595	515	54	278	260	169	138	2.50	3.13	54	54	–
Brandon township	319	99	83	70	10	16	11	4	4	3.22	3.51	–	–	–
Butler township	315	105	83	71	6	22	20	12	8	3.00	3.48	–	–	–
Fairfield township	410	136	114	99	8	22	22	9	6	3.01	3.37	–	–	–
Sprogueville city (pt.)	36	12	11	8	2	1	1	1	1	3.00	3.18	–	–	–
Farmers Creek township	468	169	126	115	8	43	39	17	11	2.77	3.31	–	–	–
Iowa township	739	281	212	189	13	69	61	38	30	2.63	3.10	–	–	–
Miles city (pt.)	370	152	99	84	7	53	48	33	25	2.43	3.13	–	–	–
Jackson township	497	168	131	122	3	37	36	16	12	2.96	3.49	–	–	–
Springbrook city	116	41	30	30	–	11	11	4	4	2.83	3.50	–	–	–
Maquoketa township	2 991	1 229	822	664	123	407	367	179	129	2.43	3.06	20	16	4
Maquoketa city (pt.)	2 270	978	614	472	114	364	330	160	121	2.32	3.01	20	16	4

1990 Census of Population and Housing, Summary Population and Housing Characteristics, Iowa volume, p.130.

Figure 28.4: Sample Table from *Summary Population and Housing Characteristics*.

ditional STF products in electronic tape or CD-ROM formats are also available for purchase from the Bureau of the Census.

Data from STF1A, STF1C, and STF 3A, STF3B, and STF3C, are accessible through the *1990 Census Lookup*. An easy-to-use interface allows the searcher to select the geographic area and variables to be displayed. The entries for the STF CD-ROMs described earlier in this section include the URLs for the *1990 Census Lookup* for those STFs available from the *Lookup* page.

The *Subject Summary Tape Files (SSTF)* series includes both 100-percent and sample data. The printed *Population Subject Reports* correspond to SSTFs in this series, but provide less detailed data. Sample *Subject Summary Tape Files* CD-ROM titles include *Ancestry of Population of the United States* (SSTF 2), *Characteristics of the Asian and Pacific Islander Population in the United States* (SSTF 5), *Housing of the Elderly* (SSTF 8), *and Earnings by Occupation and Education* (SSTF 22). SSTF in tape formats are also available for purchase from the Census Bureau. A limited number of these files are accessible on the Internet.

PL 94-171 census data are data that were required for congressional redistricting purposes. They include statistics on total population, age, sex, race, Hispanic origin, and housing unit counts. States, counties, metropolitan areas, places, census tracts, block numbering areas, block groups and blocks, and voting districts are covered. The *1990 Census of Population and Housing Census/Equal Employment Opportunity (EEO) Special File* gives sample data relating to EEO and affirmative action uses, such as tabulations of occupation data by age and by educational attainment by age, cross-tabulated by sex, Hispanic origin, and race. The *1990 Census of Population and Housing. Special Tabulation on Aging* CD-ROM includes 100-percent and sample data with cross-tabulations primarily for persons 60 years of age and older.

The *1990 Census of Population and Housing. Public Use Microdata Samples (PUMS)* contains a sample of individual long-form census records with the individual identifying information removed. The *1990 Census of Population and Housing. County-to-County Migration Flow Files, Special Project 312 (SP312)* includes data at the state and county level on intrastate county-to-county migration and interstate county-to-county migration.

The *American Community Survey* is an ongoing monthly survey that is in its initial phases of development. When fully implemented (presently expected to be in 2003) this survey will replace the long form or sample data in the decennial census with more current annual estimates. The data available from the survey are presently similar to that found in Summary Tape File 3. Adjustments in the data collected may be made as needs change. During the development stage, data are collected only for a small number of test sites. Coverage will gradually be expanded and by 2004 coverage is expected to include all states,

counties, cities, metropolitan areas, and population groups of 65,000 people or more. By 2008 coverage for smaller areas, including census tracts, will become available.

American FactFinder is a Census Bureau Web database designed to provide access to data from the 1990 and 2000 *Census of Population and Housing*, the *American Community Survey*, and the 1997 *Economic Census*. It also contains a mapping feature and an option to search for information on Census Bureau products. Population data from the 1990 census are available in both the "Facts about My Community" section and the "Population and Housing Facts" section. Users make a series of selections from lists of geographic areas, tables, and/or sources or search by word to identify and display data. A general search option is also available.

The *Bureau of the Census Web Site* contains an extensive amount of data from the decennial censuses. PDF versions of some publications are also included. The site also includes descriptions and documentation for many of the products described in this chapter. The *Census 1990* and *United States Census 2000* Web pages provide links to data and information available on the Census Bureau Web site. The *Census 1990* site contains links to the *Summary Tape File* CD-ROMs and *American FactFinder*. The *United States Census 2000* site contains information on the development and progress of the 2000 census.

The *Selected Historical Census Data: Population and Housing Counts* Web page provides some historical census data in the form of basic population and housing counts, down to the county level for as far back in time as the county was formed. A corresponding print report is titled *Population of States and Counties of the United States: 1790 to 1990, From the Twenty-one Decennial Censuses*. Historical data from the decennial censuses from 1790-1970 are also available from the *United States Historical Census Data Browser*. This Web site is derived from data from the decennial census and other demographic, economic, and social data sources compiled originally by the Inter-University Consortium for Political and Social Research (ICPSR). The highly flexible interface allows the user to choose demographic variables for each census and to browse the data chosen. Up to fifteen variables can be displayed. Data are available at the U.S., state, and county level.

TIGER/LINE FILES
Checklist

TIGER: Topologically Integrated Geographic Encoding and Referencing System Web Site. WEB. U.S. Department of Commerce. Bureau of the Census. <http://www.census.gov/geo/www/tiger/index.html>.

> Content: descriptions of TIGER/LINE files; information on TIGER releases; links to TIGER related products and documentation; links to other related on-line mapping, cartographic and geographic resources.

TIGER/Line Census Files. CD-ROM. U.S. Department of Commerce. Bureau of the Census. C 3.279: Item 0154-E.

> Content: TIGER/Line files of coordinate-based geographic information.

TIGER/Census Tract Street Index. CD-ROM. U.S. Department of Commerce. Bureau of the Census. Geography Division. C 3.279/2: Item 0154-E-01.

> Content: street name/address data based on the TIGER database.

The Census Tract Street Locator. WEB. U.S. Department of Commerce. Bureau of the Census. <http://tier2.census.gov/ctsl/ctsl.htm>.

> Content: searchable site that locates the census tract associated with an address.

Discussion

The TIGER/LINE Census files are files that contain extracts of geographic and cartographic information. TIGER stands for "Topologically Integrated Geographic Encoding and Referencing System." TIGER files contain information such as geographic area codes, latitude/longitude coordinates of features and boundaries, and the name and type of feature for each individual feature (for example, an individual segment of a road). Used with Geographic Information System (GIS) software, these files can be used to create maps. The geographic and cartographic information from the TIGER files can also be combined with statistical data, such as STF data. TIGER/Line files are distributed to depository libraries in a CD-ROM format, but GIS software is not provided to depository libraries by the Census Bureau and must be obtained from commercial vendors or other sources. The TIGER/Line files are periodically revised, and new versions are produced.

The *TIGER: Topologically Integrated Geographic Encoding and Referencing System Web Site* includes an extensive amount of information about and documentation for the TIGER/Line files. The site also includes links to a wide variety of other related resources, including a searchable directory of companies providing services related to the TIGER/Line data or who use TIGER extract products.

The *TIGER/Census Tract Street Index* CD-ROM includes the data files needed to determine the 1990 census tract, congressional district, and zip code associated with a specific street address in the 50 states and the District of Columbia. *The Census Tract Street Locator* is a Census Bureau publicly accessible Web site that also allows users to identify the census tract associated with an address. *The Census Tract Street Locator* also provides a profile of data from the *1990 Census of Population and Housing Summary Tape File 3A CD-ROM* for each identified tract, and allows the user to compare data with other tracts.

CPS, SIPP, PEP, AND CURRENT POPULATION REPORTS
Checklist

Current Population Survey Main Page. WEB. U.S. Department of Commerce. Bureau of the Census. <http://www.bls.census.gov/cps/cpsmain.htm>.

> Content: overview of the CPS; links to publications and data from the CPS; methodology and documentation; history and concepts; basic monthly survey; supplements; related surveys and programs.

Technical Documentation: Current Population Survey Web Page. WEB. U.S. Department of Commerce. Bureau of the Census. <http://www.census.gov/apsd/techdoc/cps/cps-main.html>.

> Content: documentation for Current Population Survey data files.

Labor Force Statistics from the Current Population Survey Web Page. WEB. U.S. Department of Labor. <http://stats.bls.gov/cps_over.htm>.

> Content: overview of CPS and labor statistics available from it; methodology; links to news releases and related information.

Survey of Income Participation and Program Participation Web Page. WEB. U.S. Department of Commerce. Bureau of the Census. <http://www.sipp.census.gov/sipp/>.

> Content: overview of SIPP; links to publications and analyses; history and concepts, methodology and documentation.

FERRET (Federal Electronic Research and Review Extraction Tool). WEB. U.S. Department of Commerce. Bureau of the Census. <http://ferret.bls.census.gov/cgi-bin/ferret>.

> Content: view prepared tables or extract customized data from major surveys, including the Current Population Survey and the Survey of Income Participation and Program Participation .

The Data Extraction System (DES) Web Page. WEB. U.S. Department of Commerce. Bureau of the Census. <http://www.census.gov/DES/www/welcome.html>.

> Content: software tool for extracting records from public-use data files; can be used with Current Population Survey, Survey of Income Participation and Program Participation, and Decennial Census Public Use Microdata Samples through the Web-based interface.

Population Estimates Web Page. WEB. U.S. Department of Commerce. Bureau of the Census. <http://www.census.gov/population/www/estimates/popest.html>.

> Content: tables and links to full-text publications on national, state, county, place and subcounty divisions, and metropolitan area estimates of population.

Population Projections Web Page. WEB. U.S. Department of Commerce. Bureau of the Census. <http://www.census.gov/population/www/projections/popproj.html>.

> Content: tables and links to full-text publications on national, household, state, and voting-age population projections.

Income and Poverty. CD-ROM. (annual) 1993– . U.S. Department of Commerce. Bureau of the Census. C 3.224/12-2: Item 0155-C-01. ASI 2324-19.

Coverage: varies; U.S., divisions, regions, states, selected metropolitan areas.

Content: income of households, families, and persons by selected characteristics, including age, race, sex, and household type; poverty status by selected characteristics including age, race, sex, and education; Current Population Survey microdata files.

Current Population Reports. PRINT. WEB. (irregular) 1946–. U.S. Department of Commerce. Economics and Statistics Administration. Bureau of the Census. C 3.186:; C 3.186/. Items 0142-C, 0142-C-01 to 15. GPO. <http://www.census.gov/prod/www/abs/popula.html>; <http://www.census.gov/mp/www/pub/pop/mspop.html#CPR>.

Population Characteristics. (irregular) 1946–. U.S. Department of Commerce. Economics and Statistics Administration. Bureau of the Census. C 3.186:P-20/. Item 0142-C-01. ASI 2546-1. <http://www.census.gov/prod/www/abs/popula.html#pop>; <http://www.census.gov/mp/www/pub/pop/mspop01.html>.

Coverage: varies; usually U.S.

Content: statistical reports on population characteristics.

Voting and Registration in the Election of [date]. PRINT. WEB. (biennial). 1964–. Series P-20: Population Characteristics. C 3.186/3-2: (Earlier, C 3.186:P-20/). Item 0142-C-01. ASI 2546-1-[no.]. <http://www.census.gov/prod/www/abs/popula.html#pop>; <http://www.census.gov/mp/www/pub/pop/mspop01.html>; <http://www.census.gov/population/www/socdemo/voting.html>.

Coverage: U.S. regions, divisions (Web), states (Web).

Content: voting and registration by such characteristics as age, sex, race, Hispanic origin, school enrollment status, years of school completed, employment status, class of worker, major occupation group, voting and registration of family members, family income, duration of residence and tenure.

Marital Status and Living Arrangements: [date]. PRINT. WEB. (annual) Series P-20: Population Characteristics. C 3.186/6: Item 0142-C-01. ASI 2546-1-[no.] <http://www.census.gov/prod/www/abs/popula.html#pop>; <http://www.census.gov/mp/www/pub/pop/mspop01.html>; <http://www.census.gov/population/www/socdemo/ms-la.html>.

Coverage: U.S., regions.

Content: marital status and living arrangements by such characteristics as age, sex, race, Hispanic origin, presence of children, family relationships, characteristics of parents, and metropolitan residence.

Fertility of American Women: [date]. PRINT. WEB. (annual) Series P-20: Population Characteristics. C 3.186/10 . Item 0142-C-01. ASI 2546-1-[no.]. <http://www.census.gov/prod/www/abs/popula.html#pop>; <http://www.census.gov/mp/www/pub/pop/mspop01.html>; <http://www.census.gov/ population/ www/socdemo/fertility.html>.

Coverage: U.S., regions.

Content: births and birth expectations by such characteristics as race, age, marital status, children ever born, labor force status, occupation, family income, regions of residence, and metropolitan residence.

School Enrollment—Social and Economic Characteristics of Students. PRINT. WEB. (biennial with updates). Series P-20: Population Characteristics. C 3.186/12: Item 0142-C-01. ASI 2546-1-[no.]. <http://www.census.gov/prod/www/abs/popula.html#pop>; <http://www.census.gov/mp/www/pub/pop/mspop01.html>; <http://www.census.gov/prod/www/abs/school.html>; <http://www.census.gov/population/www/socdemo/school.html>; <http://purl.access.gpo.gov/GPO/LPS3278>.

Coverage: primarily U.S., regions.

Content: school enrollment by age, sex, race, income, educational attainment, marital status, type of school or college, family type, metropolitan-nonmetropolitan residence, employment status, and other characteristics; includes nursery school, kindergarten, elementary school, high school, and college and professional school.

The Hispanic Population in the United States: [date]. PRINT. WEB. (annual) Series P-20: Population Characteristics. C 3.186/14-2: Item 0142-C-01. ASI 2546-1-[no.]. <http://www.census.gov/population/www/socdemo/hispanic.html>; <http://www.census.gov/prod/www/abs/popula.html#pop>; <http://www.census.gov/mp/www/pub/pop/mspop01.html>.

Coverage: U.S.

Content: data for Hispanic origin population by detailed origin, with comparisons to black, white, and other non-Hispanic populations; includes characteristics such as age, education, and earnings; family and household characteristics; labor force; poverty status; and marital status.

Household and Family Characteristics: [date]. PRINT. WEB. (annual) Series P-20: Population Characteristics. C 3.186/17: Item 0142-C-01. ASI 2546-1-[no.]. <http://www.census.gov/population/www/socdemo/hh-fam.html>; <http://purl.access.gpo.gov/GPO/LPS4664>; <http://www.census.gov/prod/www/abs/popula.html#pop>; <http://www.census.gov/mp/www/pub/pop/mspop01.html>.

Coverage: U.S., regions, states.

Content: household and family characteristics by such items as type; race; Hispanic origin; marital status; size; metropolitan-nonmetropolitan residence; and age, presence, and type of children.

Geographical Mobility: [dates]. PRINT. WEB. (annual) Series P-20: Population Characteristics. C 3.186/18: Item 0142-C-01. ASI 2546-1-[no.]. <http://www.census.gov/prod/www/abs/popula.html#pop>; <http://www.census.gov/mp/www/pub/pop/mspop01.html>; <http://www.census.gov/population/www/socdemo/migrate.html>; <http://purl.access.gpo.gov/GPO/LPS4168>.

Coverage: varies; primarily U.S.

Content: geographic mobility by detailed characteristics such as race, Hispanic origin, sex, age, geographic region, years of school completed, labor force status, and household characteristics; migration flows between regions, divisions, states, MSAs.

Educational Attainment in the United States: [dates]. PRINT. WEB. (annual) Series P-20: Population Characteristics. C 3.186/23: Item 0142-C-10. ASI 2546-1-[no.] <http://www.census.gov/population/www/socdemo/educ-attn.html>; <http://www.census.gov/prod/www/abs/

popula.html#pop>; <http://www.census.gov/mp/www/pub/pop/mspop01.html>; <http://www.census.gov/population/www/socdemo/education.html>.

Coverage: U.S., regions, divisions, states.

Content: educational attainment by age, sex, race, Hispanic origin, geographic location, occupation, income, labor force status, earnings, and household relationship.

Special Studies. PRINT. WEB. (irregular) Series P-23: Special Studies. C 3.186: P-23. Item 0142-C-02. ASI 2546-2. <http://www.census.gov/prod/www/abs/popula.html#popspec>; <http://www.census.gov/mp/www/pub/pop/mspop03.html>.

Coverage: varies; usually U.S.

Content: reports on methods; demographic analyses; miscellaneous reports.

Population Profile of the United States [year]. PRINT. WEB. (biennial) Series P-23: Special Studies. C 3.186/8: Item 0142-C-02. ASI 2546-2-[no.]. <http://www.census.gov/prod/www/abs/popula.html#popspec>; <http://www.census.gov/mp/www/pub/pop/mspop03.html>.

    Coverage: U.S.

    Content: short summaries of selected demographic, social, and economic characteristics, including school enrollment, educational attainment, households and families, marital status and living arrangements, child care arrangements, need for assistance with everyday activities, labor force and occupation, money income, poverty, household wealth and asset ownership, and the elderly population.

Current Population Reports: Population Estimates and Projections. Series P-25. PRINT. WEB. U.S. Department of Commerce. Economics and Statistics Administration. Bureau of the Census. C 3.186:P-25/. Item 0142-C-03. GPO. ASI 2546-3. <http://www.census.gov/prod/www/abs/popula.html#popest>; <http://www.census.gov/mp/www/pub/pop/mspop05.html>.

    Coverage: varies; usually U.S.

    Content: reports on population projections and estimates.

Projections of the Number of Households and Families in the United States: [years]. PRINT. WEB (quinquennial) Series P-25: Population Estimates and Projections. C 3.186/15: Item 0142-C-03. ASI 2546-3. <http://www.census.gov/prod/www/abs/popula.html#popest>; <http://www.census.gov/population/www/projections/nathh.html>; <http://www.census.gov/mp/www/pub/pop/mspop05.html>; <http://www.census.gov/population/www/projections/popproj.html>.

    Coverage: U.S.

    Content: households by type, age of householder, race, and children under 18; number of persons living alone and marital status by age and sex; three alternative series of projections.

Projections of the Voting-Age Population for States: November [year]. PRINT. WEB. (biennial) Series P-25: Population Estimates and Projections. C 3.186/26: Item 0142-C-03. ASI 2542-1. <http://www.census.gov/prod/www/abs/popula.html#popest>; <http://www.census.gov/mp/www/pub/pop/mspop05.html>; <http://www.census.gov/population/www/socdemo/voting.html>.

    Coverage: U.S., regions, divisions, states.

Content: projections of population of voting age by age, sex, race, and Hispanic origin; estimates of percentage casting vote for President and U.S. representatives; participation in elections for President and U.S. representatives.

Current Population Reports: Consumer Income. Series P-60. PRINT. WEB. C 3.186:P-60/. Item 0142-C-07. ASI 2546-6. GPO. <http://www.census.gov/prod/www/abs/popula.html#income>; <http://www.census.gov/mp/www/pub/pop/mspop10.html>.

    Content: reports on income, poverty, and benefits, and related topics.

Poverty in the United States. PRINT. WEB. (annual) 1995–. C 3.186/22: (Issued earlier under other titles) Series P-60: Consumer Income. Item 0142-C-07. ASI 2546-6. <http://www.census.gov/hhes/www/poverty.html>; <http://www.census.gov/prod/www/abs/popula.html#income>; <http://www.census.gov/mp/www/pub/pop/mspop10.html>.

    Coverage: U.S., regions, states.

    Content: poverty status and ratio of family income to poverty level by selected characteristics; work experience; income type; tables often by age, race, sex, and household type.

Current Population Reports: Household Economic Studies. Series P-70. PRINT. WEB. C 3.186:P-70/2/. Item 0142-C-08. ASI 2546-20. GPO. <http://www.census.gov/prod/www/abs/popula.html#pophhes>; <http://www.census.gov/mp/www/pub/pop/mspop12.html>.

    Content: reports on the economic status of households, benefits received, and related social characteristics.

Subject Index to Current Population Reports and Other Population Report Series. PRINT. WEB. (1996) C 3.186:P-23/192. Item 0142-C-02. ASI (96) 2546-2.179. GPO. <http://www.census.gov/prod/2/pop/p23/p23-192.pdf>.

    Content: index to *Current Population Reports* series.

Population Paper Listings. MF. C 3.223/25: Item 0154-B-54.

    Content: unpublished tabulations and data relating to population.

Discussion

For more current statistics than the latest census or for statistics for years in between censuses, the Census Bureau conducts two major on-going surveys, the Current Population Survey (CPS) and the Survey of Income and Program Participation (SIPP). Selected data from these surveys are published in the agency's *Current Population Reports* series, on its Web site, and on CD-ROM. Researchers may also extract data from the complete surveys via the Web. Through its Population Estimates and Projections (PEP) program, the Census Bureau also provides estimates and projections of population, using as its basis the decennial census and a variety of other data.

The Current Population Survey (CPS) is a long-standing (over 50 years) monthly survey of a sampling of some 60,000 households in the U.S. The survey concentrates on collecting data on labor force participation (particularly for those 16 years of age and older) and is conducted by personal and telephone interviews. The Census Bureau conducts the Survey for the Bureau of Labor Statistics, and it takes place each month in the week that includes the 12th day of the month (Sunday through Saturday). Estimates obtained from the CPS include employment, unemployment, earnings, hours of work, and other employment indicators by age, sex, race, marital status, educational attainment, occupation, industry, and class of worker. Additional data pertaining to school enrollment, income, previous work experience, health, employee benefits, and work schedules are periodically collected as part of supplemental surveys to the basic monthly CPS. A demographic supplemental survey is added annually to the March monthly survey.

The *Current Population Survey Main Page* provides an extensive guide to the Current Population Survey Program, data collection, documentation, and data products and publications. A site with technical documentation for the CPS files is also available from the Census Bureau. Another site from the Bureau of Labor Statistics, *Labor Force Statistics from the Current Population Survey*, provides additional information and links to data from the CPS. It includes news releases, links to data sites, and search and display interfaces to some data. Some data files are available for download from this site. The *Survey of Income Participation and Program Participation Web Page* provides detailed information on the Survey of Income Participation and Program Participation (SIPP) program, including data access, methodology, and publications and analyses.

FERRET is a Web-based tool that allows users to work directly with original survey data to create their own tables, and that can be used with the Current Population Survey data. Users select from a list of specific surveys available, such as "CPS March Supplement 1992–1998." Background information on each survey is also available. After selecting the desired survey, users then have the option of viewing a set of already created tables or creating their own. To create tables, users select variables and output options. Some familiarity with the survey's contents, statistical terminology, and file formats is helpful for table creation.

The *Data Extraction System (DES) Web Page* allows users to extract records from a number of large publicly-accessible data files, including the Current Population Survey, Survey of Income Participation and Program Participation, and the Decennial Census Public Use Microdata Samples. The user can select the data files and variables that are to be extracted through a step-by-step Web interface. The files created can then be downloaded from a FTP site. *DES* does not allow the user to manipulate or display the extracted data—additional statistical analysis software or programming to access the data must be provided by the user.

The *Population Estimates Web Page* and *Population Projections Web Page* provide data from the Population Estimates program. The *Population Estimates Web Page* contains data on national population estimates by age, sex, race, and Hispanic origin for the United States. Included is the national population data series titled "Monthly Estimates of the United States Population," which is updated monthly. It also includes data on the state, county, place and county subdivision, and metropolitan population estimates constructed by the program. Information on methodology of the program and documentation are also included.

The *Population Projections Web Page* contains four categories that represent the areas of population projections available from the Census Bureau: national, state, households and families, and population of voting age. Each category provides relevant statistical tables and links to full-text editions of related publications, including *Current Population Reports*.

The *Income and Poverty* CD-ROM contains PDF files that include publications from the *Current Population Reports* P-60 series. Geographic coverage is generally national and regional with some limited data for states and large metropolitan areas. Original survey data (microdata) for the Current Population Survey is also available on the CD with CrossTab software for tabulating data. This file contains national, regional, state, and selected metropolitan area data. Software and file types vary on earlier CDs. The CD also includes files of income and poverty press releases and tables. The tables cover detailed income levels by a large number of demographic and household characteristics. Historical tables are also available.

Current Population Survey data, Survey of Income and Program Participation data, and data from the Population Estimates and Projections Program are also published in a series of statistical reports issued by the Census Bureau, called the *Current Population Reports*. Reports listed here are part of one of the following overall series: *Series P-20: Population Characteristics*; *Series P-23: Special Studies*; *Series P-25: Population Estimates and Projections*; *Series P-60: Consumer Income*, and *Series P-70: Household Economic Studies*. Series P-20, Series P-23, and Series P-60 are compiled from data from the CPS survey. Series P-70 are compiled from data from the Survey of Income and Program Participation data. Series P-25 reports are compiled from data from the Population Estimates and Projections Program. In the past, recurring titles within these series were given the SuDocs number of the overall series, but most are now assigned a unique SuDocs number for the individual report title.

Most reports are issued in a print format, but also have a Web version (usually PDF format) available on the *Census Bureau Web site*. Some of the reports are brief summary versions of the data collected, with fuller information available only on the *Census Bureau Web site*. Some data are also made available through the *Population Paper*

Listings series, which is distributed to depository libraries in a microfiche format. Many earlier editions of *Current Population Reports* publications are also included on the *Census Bureau Web site.* There are often several ways to access these *Current Population Reports* from the Census Bureau site, and URLs for some of the most direct approaches are included in the entries.

Current Population Reports cover a wide range of topics, and vary in length. Most reports cover large geographic areas, such as the United States and regions, although a few reports cover county and subcounty areas. *Current Population Reports* cover many of the same subject areas as the *Census of Population*, and can be used to update much of the data in the census. An older subject index to the reports, available in print format and a PDF Web version, is listed here.

CENSUS GUIDES

Product Catalog. WEB. U.S. Census Bureau. C 3.163/3: Item 0138. <http://www.census.gov/mp/www/censtore.html>.
   Content: descriptions and prices of Census Bureau products.

Census Catalog and Guide. CD-ROM. WEB. (annual) 1946–. U.S. Department of Commerce. Economics and Statistics Administration. Census Bureau. (CD-ROM not distributed to depository libraries) (Issued in print through 1998 under C 3.163/3:, Item 0138) (Title varies) <http://www.census.gov/mp/www/censtore.html>; <http://www.census.gov/prod/www/abs/catalogs.html>; <http://purl.access.gpo.gov/GPO/LPS3138>.
   Content: CD-ROM version of the Web *Product Catalog.*

Bureau of the Census Catalog of Publications 1790–1972. PRINT. (1974) C 56.222/2-2:790-972. ASI (75) 2308-1.
   Content: complete listing of publications in each census as well as all other Census Bureau publications, with histories and descriptions.

Monthly Product Announcement. PRINT. WEB. (monthly) U.S. Department of Commerce. Economics and Statistics Administration. Census Bureau. C 3.163/7: Item 0138-A-02. ASI 2302-6. <http://www.census.gov/mp/www/mpa.html#MPA>; <http://purl.access.gpo.gov/GPO/LPS1680>.

Census CD-ROM Products. WEB. (1997) U.S. Department of Commerce. Economics and Statistics Administration. Bureau of the Census. <http://www.census.gov/prod/3/97pubs/mso-9707.pdf>.
   Content: listing and description of census CD-ROMs, including geographical coverage, price, and availability.

Maps and More: Your Guide to Census Bureau Geography. PRINT. (1994) U.S. Department of Commerce. Economics and Statistics Administration. Bureau of the Census. C 3.2:G29/4/994. Item 0146.
   Content: geography; the TIGER system; code schemes and reference files; maps; geographic reporting in data products.

Census '90 Basics. PRINT. (1990) U.S. Department of Commerce. Bureau of the Census. C 3.2:B 29. Item 0146.

Content: basic guide to data collected, reports issued, and census geography.

1990 Census of Population and Housing: Guide. PRINT. (1992) U.S. Department of Commerce. Economics and Statistics Administration. Bureau of the Census. C 3.223/22:90-R-1A/pt. Item 0154. ASI (92, 93) 2555-1.
   Content: history, questionnaire content, data collection procedures, geography, data products, understanding the data, sources of assistance.

200 Years of U.S. Census Taking: Population and Housing Questions, 1790–1990. PRINT. (1989) U.S. Department of Commerce. Bureau of the Census. C 3.2:T 93. Item 0146.
   Content: instructions to enumerators for censuses; questions asked on each census.

Discussion

A number of census guides are available to help in understanding the census and the Census Bureau's data collection and programs. This section describes some of the most relevant ones when dealing with population statistics. The *Bureau of the Census Web Site* should also be consulted when searching for this kind of material, as the site includes many pages of explanatory text and user information.

The Census Bureau *Product Catalog* describes agency products and provides availability and ordering information. Products are listed by format and then by subject category or series. Individual title descriptions include prices, ordering information, formats, subject content, geographic coverage, and links to online data. The *Census Catalog and Guide* on CD-ROM contains the Web *Product Catalog* as of the specified date. The *Monthly Product Announcement* serves as an update to the catalog. It lists, but does not describe, publications released during the previous month. The cumulative catalog, *Bureau of the Census Catalog of Publications 1790–1972*, is a thorough historical guide to censuses and publication series.

Census CD-ROM Products is a concise listing of CD-ROMs currently available from the Census Bureau. It allows the user to quickly determine the basic content and geographic coverage of a particular CD-ROM. Included are many of the Census of Population CD-ROMs described earlier in this chapter.

Maps and More: Your Guide to Census Bureau Geography is a detailed guide to census geography. Printed in an oversize format, the publication includes numerous charts and examples of census geography and mapping products. The guide also discusses the TIGER system in detail. A section on code schemes and reference files is helpful in understanding the use of standard computerized codes with census data.

Census '90 Basics is a 19-page introductory guide to the 1990 Census of Population and Housing. It provides an overview of the census, information on census content and sample design, definitions of census geography, descriptions of census reports and products, and sources for obtaining additional information. Its clear charts and figures are especially useful.

The *1990 Census of Population and Housing: Guide* contains detailed information on the 1990 Census of Population and Housing. Important features include definitions of geographic areas used in the census and lists and descriptions of map series, printed reports, and other data products. One chapter also provides advice on understanding census statistics. An extensive appendix on sources of assistance includes a detailed list of Census Bureau contacts and a directory of State Data Centers and related organizations. The guide also provides information on census history and procedures.

200 Years of U.S. Census Taking: Population and Housing Questions, 1790–1990 reprints the instructions to enumerators and the questions asked for each census. An essay covering the historical background of each census and a section titled "Availability of Population Schedules" are also included.

INDEXES

Checklist

American Statistics Index (ASI). PRINT. (monthly) 1973–. Bethesda, MD: Congressional Information Service.

Statistical Universe. WEB. Bethesda, MD: Congressional Information Service.

Catalog of United States Government Publications (MOCAT). WEB. 1994–. U.S. Government Printing Office. Superintendent of Documents. <http://www.gpo.gov/catalog>; <http://www.access.gpo.gov/su_docs/locators/cgp/index.html>; <http://purl.access.gpo.gov/GPO/LPS844>.

Monthly Catalog of United States Government Publications. CD-ROM. 1996–. U.S. Government Printing Office. Superintendent of Documents. GP 3.8/7: Item 0557-C. GPO.

Monthly Catalog of United States Government Publications (Condensed version). PRINT. (monthly) 1996–. U.S. Government Printing Office. Superintendent of Documents. GP 3.8/8: (Earlier full version, GP 3.8:, 1895-1995). Item 0557-D. GPO.

Discussion

A comprehensive listing of material can be found in the *American Statistics Index (ASI)*. To find population data, look under subject headings "Population characteristics," "Population size," "Census of Population," "Census of Population and Housing," "Population projections," "Families and households," "Farm population," and other terms including "Population." *Statistical Universe* includes a Web version of *ASI*.

The *Monthly Catalog* may also be used to locate materials, but does not provide the depth of indexing for statistics that *ASI* does. Look under subject headings or keywords beginning with "Population" or keywords of other topics of interest. The complete version of the *Monthly Catalog* is available on the Web and CD-ROM. Commercial online and CD-ROM versions of the *Monthly Catalog* are also available.

For more information on these indexes, see Chapter 3, "The Basics of Searching."

RELATED MATERIAL

Within this Work

GPO Subject Bibliographies. PRINT. WEB. GP 3.22/2:

<http://bookstore.gpo.gov/sb/about.html>

No. 181 "Census of Population and Housing"

No. 311 "Census Tracts and Blocks (Publications)"

No. 312 "Census Tracts and Blocks (Maps)"

CHAPTER 29
Vital Statistics

The term "vital statistics" encompasses data on births; deaths; abortions; fetal deaths, including stillbirths; life expectancy; marriages; and divorces. This chapter covers those topics for the United States. The primary agency collecting this data is the National Center for Health Statistics (NCHS). Data are often collected at the state level by state vital statistics agencies. Some vital statistics are collected by the Bureau of the Census. Statistics on mortality and abortion are also compiled by the Centers for Disease Control and Prevention.

SEARCH STRATEGY

This chapter shows a statistical search strategy. The steps to follow are

1. Consult the general statistical sources listed in this chapter, especially the *Statistical Abstract*;
2. Use the *Vital Statistics of the United States* to obtain detailed information;
3. Consult the National Center for Health Statistics (NCHS) Web site;
4. Scan other sources listed in this chapter; and
5. If extensive data files are needed for research purposes, consult the "Catalogs" section, the electronic sources listed in various sections, and the *National Center for Health Statistics Web Site*, as the National Center for Health Statistics makes much of its data available in electronic form.

GENERAL STATISTICAL SOURCES
Checklist

Statistical Abstract of the United States. PRINT. WEB. (annual) 1878–. U.S. Department of Commerce. Economics and Statistics Administration. Bureau of the Census. C 3.134: Item 0150. ASI 2324-1. GPO. <http://www.census.gov/statab/www/>; <http://purl.access.gpo.gov/GPO/LPS2878>.
    Coverage: U.S., divisions, states.

    Content: births; deaths; abortions; fetal deaths; life expectancy; fertility; marriages; divorces.

Statistical Abstract of the United States. CD-ROM. (annual) 1993–. U.S. Department of Commerce. Bureau of the Census. C 3.134/7: Item 0150-B. ASI 2324-14.
    Content: CD-ROM version of the *Statistical Abstract*.

Historical Statistics of the United States: Colonial Times to 1970. Parts 1-2. PRINT. (1975) U.S. Department of Commerce. Bureau of the Census. C 3.134/2:H 62/789-970/pt.1-2. Item 0151. ASI (76) 2328-2. GPO.
    Coverage: U.S.
    Content: births; deaths; fetal deaths; life expectancy; fertility; marriages; divorces.

Historical Statistics of the United States on CD-ROM: Colonial Times to 1970. CD-ROM. (1997) New York, NY: Cambridge University Press.
    Content: CD-ROM version of *Historical Statistics of the United States*.

County and City Data Book. PRINT. (quinquennial) 1947–. U.S. Department of Commerce. Economics and Statistics Administration. Bureau of the Census. C 3.134/2:C 83/2/year. Item 0151. ASI 2328-1. GPO. <http://fisher.lib.Virginia.EDU/ccdb/>.
    Coverage: U.S., regions, divisions, states, counties, cities of 25,000 or more.
    Content: births; deaths; marriages; divorces.

County and City Data Book. CD-ROM. (quinquennial) 1988–. U.S. Department of Commerce. Bureau of the Census. C 3.134/2-1: (Earlier, C 3.134/2:C 83/2/). Item 0151-D-1. ASI 2328-1. GPO.

County and City Extra: Annual Metro, City, and County Data Book. PRINT. (annual) 1992–. Lanham, MD: Bernan Press.
    Coverage: states, counties, metropolitan areas.
    Content: updated supplement to the *County and City Data Book*.

Places, Towns, and Townships. PRINT. (irregular) 1993–. Lanham, MD: Bernan Press.
    Coverage: places, townships.

Content: updated supplement to the *County and City Data Book*.

USA Counties. CD-ROM. WEB. (irregular) 1992–. U.S. Department of Commerce. Economics and Statistics Administration. Bureau of the Census. C 3.134/6: Item 0150-B-01. ASI 2324-17. <http://govinfo.kerr.orst.edu/usaco-stateis.html>; <http://tier2.census.gov/usac/index.html-ssi>.

    Coverage: U.S., states, counties.
    Content: births, deaths, infant deaths, marriages, divorces.

State and Metropolitan Area Data Book. PRINT. WEB. (irregular) 1979–. U.S. Department of Commerce. Economics and Statistics Administration. Bureau of the Census. C 3.134/5: Item 0150. ASI 2328-54. GPO. <http://www.census.gov/statab/www/smadb.html>.

    Coverage: regions, divisions, states, metropolitan areas, counties, central cities.
    Content: births; deaths; abortions; marriages; divorces.

State and Metropolitan Area Data Book. CD-ROM. (irregular) 1997/98–. U.S. Department of Commerce. Economics and Statistics Administration. Bureau of the Census. (Not yet distributed to depository libraries).

    Content: CD-ROM version of the *State and Metropolitan Area Data Book*.

Health United States. PRINT. WEB. (annual) 1976–. U.S. Department of Health and Human Services. Centers for Disease Control and Prevention. National Center for Health Statistics. HE 20.7042/6: (Earlier, HE 20.6223:; HE 20.21:). Item 0483-A-19. ASI 4144-11. GPO. <http://www.cdc.gov/nchs/products/pubs/pubd/hus/2010/2010.htm>.

    Coverage: primarily U.S.; some regions, states.
    Content: births; deaths; death rates; abortions; fetal deaths; infant mortality; maternal mortality; life expectancy; fertility.

Discussion

All of these general statistical sources include some basic data on vital statistics. They provide a first ready-reference step in searching for vital statistics. More detailed sources should be searched only if a search of these sources has proved unsuccessful or if the geographic coverage needed is too detailed to be included in these sources.

    In particular, the *Statistical Abstract of the United States* provides a good overview of vital statistics for the United States as a whole. Many of the tables include statistics for several years of data. The full-text of recent editions of the *Statistical Abstract* is available on the Census Bureau Web site as PDF files. The *Statistical Abstract* is also available on CD-ROM. The CD uses Adobe Acrobat software and contains some additional geographic areas and time series in the form of spreadsheet files that are not in the printed version. *Historical Statistics of the United States* includes some historical series of data related to vital statistics.

    Data from the *County and City Data Book* give basic information on births, deaths, marriages, and divorces at the county level. The *County and City Extra* is similar to the *County and City Data Book*, but includes annually

updated information. *Places, Towns, and Townships* is a companion title for smaller geographic areas. *USA Counties* also includes basic vital statistics information at the county level. *The State and Metropolitan Area Data Book* is a good source of information for metropolitan areas. The *State and Metropolitan Area Data Book* is available as a PDF file on the Census Bureau Web site. A CD-ROM edition is also being published. *Health United States* is also a good source for basic fertility and birth rate data, although most statistics cover only the U.S. geographical area.

NATIONAL CENTER FOR HEALTH STATISTICS SOURCES

Checklist

Vital Statistics of the United States. PRINT. (annual) 1937–. U.S. Department of Health and Human Services. Centers for Disease Control and Prevention. National Center for Health Statistics. HE 20.6210: Item 0510. V.1 *Natality*. ASI 4144-1. V.2 *Mortality*. ASI 4144-2, 3. GPO.

  V.1 *Natality*
      Coverage: U.S., divisions, states, MSAs, counties, cities of 100,000 or more.
      Content: over 200 detailed tables on fertility, characteristics of live births, characteristics of mothers and parents, birth rates.

  V.2 *Mortality*
      Coverage: U.S., divisions, states, counties, MSAs, places of 10,000 or more.
      Content: over 100 detailed tables on mortality; causes of mortality; infant mortality; fetal mortality; accident mortality; perinatal deaths; life tables.

National Vital Statistics Reports. PRINT. WEB. (monthly) U.S. Department of Health and Human Services. Centers for Disease Control and Prevention. National Center for Health Statistics. HE 20.6217: (Earlier title: *Monthly Vital Statistics Report*.) Item 0508-B. ASI 4142-1. <http://www.cdc.gov/nchs/products/pubs/pubd/nvsr/nvsr.htm>; <http://purl.access.gpo.gov/GPO/LPS2365>.

    Coverage: U.S.
    Content: births; deaths; marriages; divorces.

Provisional Tables on Births, Marriages, Divorces, and Deaths. WEB. (irregular) U.S. Department of Health and Human Services. Centers for Disease Control and Prevention. National Center for Health Statistics. <http://www.cdc.gov/nchs/products/pubs/pubd/nvsr/nvsr.htm>.

    Coverage: divisions, states.
    Content: births; deaths; infant mortality; marriages; divorces.

National Vital Statistics Reports Supplements. PRINT. WEB. (irregular) U.S. Department of Health and Human Services. Centers for Disease Control and Prevention. National Center for Health Statistics. HE 20.6217: Item 0508-B. ASI 4146-5. <http://www2.cdc.gov/mmwr/mmwr_sup.html>.

    Coverage: U.S.
    Content: advance final data on births; deaths; marriages; divorces.

Vital and Health Statistics. PRINT. MF. WEB. (irregular) 1962–. U.S. Department of Health and Human Services. Centers for Disease Control and Prevention. National Center for Health Statistics. HE 20.6209:; HE 20.6209/. Item 0500-E. ASI 4147-. GPO. <http://www.cdc.gov/nchs/products/pubs/pubd/series/ser.htm>.

> Coverage: varies; U.S., regions, states.
> Content: statistics and special analyses on health and vital statistics topics.

Data on Mortality. PRINT. WEB. (irregular) U.S. Department of Health and Human Services. Centers for Disease Control and Prevention. Vital and Health Statistics Series 20. HE 20.6209:20 Item 0500-E. ASI 4147-20. GPO. <http://www.cdc.gov/nchs/products/pubs/pubd/series/sr20/ser20.htm>.

> Coverage: varies; U.S., regions, states.
> Content: statistics and special analyses on mortality.

NCHS CD-ROM Series 20. CD-ROM. (irregular) U.S. Department of Health and Human Services. Centers for Disease Control and Prevention. HE 20.6209/4-7:20/. Item 0500-E-07. ASI 4147-20. GPO.

> Coverage: varies; U.S. regions, states, metropolitan areas of 100,000 or more.
> Content: series of CD-ROM data sets with data on mortality; births; infant deaths; and fetal deaths.

Data on Natality, Marriage, and Divorce. PRINT. WEB. (irregular) U.S. Department of Health and Human Services. Centers for Disease Control and Prevention. Vital and Health Statistics Series 21. HE 20.6209:21. Item 0500-E. ASI 4147-21. GPO. <http://www.cdc.gov/nchs/products/pubs/pubd/series/sr21/ser21.htm>.

> Coverage: varies; U.S., regions, states.
> Content: statistics and special analyses on natality, marriage, and divorce.

NCHS CD-ROM Series 21. CD-ROM. (irregular) U.S. Department of Health and Human Services. Centers for Disease Control and Prevention. HE 20.6209/11: Item 0500-E-09. ASI 4147-21. GPO.

> Coverage: varies; U.S., regions, states.
> Content: series of CD-ROM data sets on natality, marriage, and divorce.

Data From the National Survey of Family Growth. PRINT. WEB. (irregular) U.S. Department of Health and Human Services. Centers for Disease Control and Prevention. Vital and Health Statistics Series 23. HE 20.6209:23. Item 0500-E. ASI 4147-23. GPO. <http://www.cdc.gov/nchs/products/pubs/pubd/series/sr23/ser23.htm>.

> Coverage: varies; U.S., regions.
> Content: statistics and special analyses on factors that affect birth rates, including fertility.

NCHS CD-ROM Series 23. CD-ROM. (irregular) U.S. Department of Health and Human Services. Centers for Disease Control and Prevention. HE 20.6209/10: Item 0500-E-08. ASI 4147-23. GPO.

> Coverage: varies; U.S., regions.
> Content: series of CD-ROMs with data sets from the National Survey on Family Growth; fertility, contraception, infertility, and other factors relating to childbearing.

Advance Data from Vital and Health Statistics of the Centers for Disease Control and Prevention, National Center for Health Statistics. PRINT. WEB. (irregular) 1976–. U.S. Department of Health and Human Services. Centers for Disease Control and Prevention. National Center for Health Statistics. HE 20.6209/3: Item 0500-E. ASI 4146-8. <http://www.cdc.gov/nchs/products/pubs/pubd/ad/ad.htm>; <http://purl.access. gpo.gov/GPO/LPS3741>.

> Coverage: varies; U.S.
> Content: advance data on mortality, natality, marriage, divorce.

Vital and Health Statistics Series: An Annotated Checklist and Index to the Publications of the "Rainbow Series." PRINT. (1991) Jim Walsh and A. James Bothmer. Westport, CT: Greenwood Press.

> Content: index and annotations of individual reports in the *Vital and Health Statistics Series.*

Atlas of United States Mortality. PRINT. WEB. (1996) U.S. Department of Health and Human Services. Centers for Disease Control and Prevention. National Center for Health Statistics. HE 20.6202:AT 6. Item 0508. ASI (97) 4148-35. GPO. <http://www.cdc.gov/nchs/data/atlasmet.pdf>.

> Coverage: U.S., health service areas (HSAs).
> Content: mortality; graphs and maps showing causes of deaths by sex and race.

Atlas of United States Mortality. CD-ROM. (1997) U.S. Department of Health and Human Services. Centers for Disease Control and Prevention. National Center for Health Statistics. HE 20.6209/12:1. Item 0508-W. GPO.

> Content: CD-ROM version of *Atlas of United States Mortality.*

Publications from the National Center for Health Statistics. CD-ROM. (annual) 1995–. Centers for Disease Control and Prevention. National Center for Health Statistics. HE 20.7042/7: Item 0483-A-20. GPO.

> Content: full text of selected publications including *Vital and Health Statistics* series reports; *Atlas of United States Mortality*; and *National Vital Statistics Reports.*

National Center for Health Statistics Web Site. WEB. U.S. Department of Health and Human Services. Centers for Disease Control and Prevention. National Center for Health Statistics. <http://www.cdc.gov/nchs/default.htm>.

> Content: full text of selected publications including *Health, United States*; *Vital and Health Statistics* series reports; and *National Vital Statistics Reports.*

Birth Data from the National Vital Statistics System. WEB. U.S. Department of Health and Human Services. Centers for Disease Control and Prevention. National Center for Health Statistics. <http://www.cdc.gov/nchs/births.htm>.

> Content: full text of publications on birth data; descriptions of data sets, data documentation, and data collection; data files; news releases; and statistical tables on birth data.

Mortality Data from the National Vital Statistics System. WEB. U.S. Department of Health and Human Services. Centers for Disease Control and Prevention. National Center for Health Statistics. <http://www.cdc.gov/nchswww/about/major/dvs/mortdata.htm>.

Content: full text of publications on mortality data; descriptions of data sets, documentation, and data collection; data files, news releases; and statistical tables on mortality data.

Fetal Deaths. WEB. U.S. Department of Health and Human Services. Centers for Disease Control and Prevention. National Center for Health Statistics. <http://www.cdc.gov/nchswww/about/major/fetaldth/abfetal.htm>.

Content: full text of publications on fetal death data; descriptions of data sets, data documentation, and data collection; data files; news releases; and statistical tables on fetal deaths data.

Discussion

Vital Statistics of the United States is the most detailed and comprehensive published report on U.S. vital statistics. It is issued in two volumes, with several sections within each volume. A geographic and subject guide to each section is also included. A third volume titled *Marriage and Divorce* discontinued publication with the 1988 volume. Figure 29.1 reproduces a sample page from a table of *Vital Statistics*. *Vital Statistics* is the first place to search for more detailed information than that given in the general statistical sources. Its main drawback is its time lag—volumes are usually published three to four years after the time period covered.

Vital Statistics of the United States is updated by the monthly *National Vital Statistics Reports*, which gives basic provisional data on births, deaths, marriages, and divorces for the U.S., regions, and states. These provisional tables are also conveniently gathered together at a Web site titled *Provisional Tables on Births, Marriages, Divorces, and Deaths. National Vital Statistics Reports* also include reports on vital statistics topics. Sample reports include "Mortality from Alzheimer's Disease: An Update" (Vol. 47, No. 20), "Trends in Twin and Triplet Births: 1980–97" (Vol. 47, No. 24), and "Trends in the Attendant, Place, and Timing of Births, and in the Use of Obstetric Interventions: United States, 1989–97" (Vol. 47, No. 27). *National Vital Statistics Report Supplements* provide more detailed advance data on natality, mortality, marriage, divorce, and other topics. All of these reports serve to announce data ahead of publication in the *Vital Statistics of the United States.*

The *Vital and Health Statistics* series provide statistics and data analysis of information collected from the National Center for Health Statistics' various data collection programs. Three subseries within the *Vital and Health Statistics* series deal directly with vital statistics. They are *Data on Mortality*, Series 20, *Data on Natality, Marriage, and Divorce*, Series 21, and *Data from the National Survey of Family Growth*, Series 23. The series contain special reports and statistical analyses on topics such as *Medical and Life-Style Risk Factors Affecting Fetal Mortality, 1989–90* (Series 20, No.31), *Mortality Trends for Alzheimer's Disease, 1979–91* (Series 20, No. 28), *Trip-*

let Births: Trends and Outcomes, 1971–94 (Series 21, No. 55), *Births to Unmarried Mothers: United States, 1980–92* (Series 21, No. 53), and *Fertility, Family Planning, and Women's Health: New Data From the 1995 National Survey of Family Growth* (Series 23, No. 19).

A series of CD-ROMs are also issued by NCHS that include public-use data sets from the data collection surveys themselves. *NCHS CD-ROM Series 20* includes CD-ROMs on mortality topics, particularly those concerning infant and fetal deaths. Sample titles include *1995 Perinatal Mortality Data File* (No.12), *1991 Birth Cohort Linked Birth/Infant Death Data Set* (No 7), and *1994 Multiple Cause-of-Death File* (No. 12A). *NCHS CD-ROM Series 21* includes the title *Marriage and Divorce Data, 1989–95* (No. 6). This data set includes data on marriage and divorce that were published previously in Volume 3 of the *Vital Statistics of the United States.* An annual title, *Natality Data Set,* is also published within this series. *NCHS CD-ROM Series 23* includes data from the National Survey of Family Growth (NSFG). *Advance Data* provides summary statistics and data from the National Center for Health Statistics' health and demographic surveys. Much of the data are later published as more detailed reports in the *Vital and Health Statistics* series.

The *Vital and Health Statistics Series: An Annotated Checklist and Index to the Publications of the "Rainbow Series"* is a comprehensive index to older publications within the *Vital and Health Statistics* series. It includes author, title, and subject indexes; annotations; and a listing of individual reports by series.

The *Atlas of United States Mortality* is available in both print and CD-ROM formats. The print version provides very detailed maps of 832 Health Service Areas (HSAs). The death rate for each area is portrayed, along with data by race, sex, and cause of death. A PDF version of the print atlas is also available on the Web. The CD-ROM version includes the same maps and data, but provides additional searching capabilities. The annual CD-ROM *Publications from the National Center for Health Statistics* includes the full text of a number of NCHS publications, including the *Atlas of United States Mortality.*

The *National Center for Health Statistics Web Site* also includes the full text of many of the agency's publications under the "Publications and Information Products" menu selection. Publications available in full text are similar to those included on the CD-ROM described above, but the Web site is more current. The Web site also provides more complete listings of all publications issued in each series with links to abstracts and full-text when available. Another feature of the Web site is the "Surveys and Data Collection Systems" menu choice, which pulls information together for each individual survey that the agency conducts. Three subsets of Web pages from this area are of particular interest for Vital Statistics use, and are individually cited here. They include *Birth Data from the Na-*

SECTION 1 - NATALITY - PAGE 9

Table 1-8. Monthly Indices and Seasonally Adjusted Birth Rates and Fertility Rates: United States, 1984-1993

[Monthly birth and fertility rates adjusted for seasonal variation are those that would have been observed if the characteristic seasonal pattern of births were eliminated. Rates on an annual basis per 1,000 estimated population for specified month. Birth rates based on total population; fertility rates based on women aged 15-44 years. For method of seasonal adjustment see Technical Appendix]

Month	1993	1992	1991	1990	1989	1988	1987	1986	1985	1984 [1]
MONTHLY INDEX [2]										
January	95.1	97.0	96.0	94.9	93.4	93.7	94.3	96.0	95.2	94.0
February	99.3	97.9	98.0	98.0	96.9	96.3	97.0	98.0	97.5	96.9
March	100.7	98.6	98.5	99.3	99.0	97.2	98.1	97.9	97.3	97.8
April	99.5	100.0	99.3	98.4	96.0	96.5	98.3	98.5	97.6	95.0
May	98.9	99.9	101.1	100.3	98.0	98.4	98.8	99.0	99.4	96.3
June	102.0	101.9	98.9	101.6	102.1	102.6	102.5	99.7	99.8	99.4
July	103.8	104.3	103.9	104.1	103.9	104.6	104.0	104.8	104.4	104.7
August	103.3	101.3	105.1	105.5	106.8	107.0	102.4	104.7	105.4	107.9
September	105.8	104.3	105.4	105.0	107.6	107.6	108.2	106.7	106.2	108.5
October	98.0	99.8	99.9	100.0	100.3	100.0	100.9	100.0	101.1	103.4
November	96.2	96.6	95.8	97.5	98.0	98.1	97.8	95.0	97.6	98.7
December	97.5	98.1	97.7	95.3	97.9	97.2	99.0	98.0	97.3	97.2
BIRTH RATE										
January	15.5	16.3	16.5	16.7	16.2	15.8	15.6	15.8	15.8	15.4
February	15.8	16.1	16.4	16.8	16.3	15.8	15.6	15.7	15.8	15.4
March	15.9	16.0	16.4	16.9	16.6	15.9	15.8	15.6	15.6	15.4
April	15.6	16.2	16.7	16.9	16.1	15.8	15.8	15.9	15.9	15.3
May	15.5	16.0	16.6	16.9	16.3	15.9	15.8	15.8	16.1	15.4
June	15.6	16.0	15.8	16.6	16.5	16.4	16.2	15.7	15.8	15.5
July	15.5	16.0	16.3	16.7	16.3	16.0	15.6	15.7	15.8	15.6
August	15.3	15.3	16.2	16.6	16.5	16.2	15.3	15.5	15.7	15.8
September	15.6	15.8	16.1	16.3	16.5	16.2	15.7	15.8	15.8	15.8
October	15.2	15.9	16.3	16.7	16.4	15.9	15.7	15.5	15.8	16.0
November	15.4	15.8	16.0	16.7	16.5	16.1	15.8	15.2	15.7	15.7
December	15.4	16.0	16.5	16.5	16.4	15.9	15.9	15.6	15.8	15.4
FERTILITY RATE										
January	67.3	70.0	70.4	70.9	68.1	66.2	65.2	66.1	66.4	64.8
February	68.8	69.1	69.8	71.1	68.8	66.4	65.4	65.7	66.2	64.8
March	69.1	69.0	69.7	71.5	70.0	66.7	65.9	65.5	65.3	65.0
April	68.0	69.8	71.0	71.6	68.1	66.2	66.1	66.3	66.9	64.6
May	67.4	69.2	71.0	71.7	68.8	67.0	66.1	66.2	67.7	64.9
June	67.8	69.0	67.5	70.6	69.6	69.1	67.6	65.4	66.4	65.3
July	67.5	69.0	69.0	70.8	69.1	67.4	65.4	65.6	66.3	65.5
August	66.8	66.2	69.0	70.4	69.9	68.2	64.0	66.0	65.8	66.3
September	66.5	66.8	69.8	71.0	69.5	67.0	65.6	64.6	66.2	67.3
October	67.4	68.7	68.7	71.0	69.7	67.7	66.1	66.1	65.9	65.9
November	67.4	69.6	70.7	70.3	69.4	66.9	66.6	65.4	66.1	64.7
December										

[1] Based on 100 percent of births in selected States and on a 50-percent sample of births in all other States; see Technical Appendix.
[2] Index is the ratio of the number of births in a given month to the average monthly number of births for the year (adjusted for the number of days in the month), multiplied by 100.

Source: Vital Statistics of the United States, 1993, V. 1, Natality, p.9.

Figure 29.1: Sample Page from *Vital Statistics of the United States*.

tional Vital Statistics System, Mortality Data from the National Vital Statistics System, and Fetal Deaths.

MORBIDITY AND MORTALITY WEEKLY REPORT (MMWR) SOURCES

Checklist

Morbidity and Mortality Weekly Report: MMWR. PRINT. WEB. (weekly) 1952–. U.S. Department of Health and Human Services. Centers for Disease Control and Prevention. HE 20.7009: (Title varies). Item 0508-A. ASI 4202-1. GPO. <http://www2.cdc.gov/mmwr/mmwr.html>; <http://purl.access.gpo.gov/GPO/LPS2051>.

> Coverage: 122 cities.
> Content: deaths.

Morbidity and Mortality Weekly Report: MMWR. CD-ROM. 1993–. Centers for Disease Control and Prevention. HE 20.7039/3: Item 0504-W-01. GPO.

> Content: full text of *MMWR* publications and selected other CDC publications.

Morbidity and Mortality Weekly Report. CDC Surveillance Summaries: MMWR. PRINT. WEB. (5 or 6 a year) U.S. Department of Health and Human Services. Centers for Disease Con-

trol and Prevention. HE 20.7009/2: Item 0508-A. ASI 4202-7. GPO. <http://www2.cdc.gov/mmwr/mmwr_ss.html>.

> Coverage: varies; countries, U.S., states, selected metropolitan areas.
> Content: summary analyses with statistics on topics involving mortality monitored by the Centers for Disease Control and Prevention.

Morbidity and Mortality Weekly Report: MMWR Web Site. WEB. U.S. Department of Health and Human Services. Centers for Disease Control and Prevention. National Center for Health Statistics. <http://www.cdc.gov/mmwr/>.

> Content: full text of *Morbidity and Mortality Weekly Report: MMWR, Morbidity and Mortality Weekly Report. CDC Surveillance Summaries: MMWR,* and other related publications and information.

Discussion

Morbidity and Mortality Weekly Report: MMWR is a current source of information on death and death rates. Especially useful are the current data on deaths in 122 U.S. cites. *MMWR* is available in a variety of formats—Web, print, and CD-ROM.

The Morbidity and Mortality Weekly Report. CDC Surveillance Summaries: MMWR contains articles reporting on areas studied and monitored by the Centers for Disease Control. While most of the articles are on disease-related topics, one recurring vital statistics title of interest is an article titled "Abortion Surveillance, United States [year]." It is the most comprehensive government report containing data on abortions, with tables detailing the number of abortions, abortion-related deaths, and characteristics of women receiving abortions, such as age, race, Hispanic origin, and marital status. Type of abortion procedure, weeks of gestation, and number of previous abortions and live births are included. Data are given for the states, the District of Columbia, and New York City. The publication of the yearly report lags several years from the time period of the data.

Articles on other vital statistics topics are also included in the *Morbidity and Mortality Weekly Report. CDC Surveillance Summaries: MMWR.* One example is the article "Postneonatal Mortality Surveillance, United States, 1980-1994" (v. 47(SS-2)), describing causes of deaths among infants aged 28-364 days.

The *Morbidity and Mortality Weekly Report: MMWR Web Site* provides PDF and HTML versions of the *MMWR* and other related publications.

CURRENT POPULATION REPORTS
Checklist

Population Profile of the United States [year]. PRINT. WEB. (biennial). U.S. Department of Commerce. Economics and Statistics Administration. Bureau of the Census. Current Population Reports: Special Studies, Series P-23. C3.186/8: Item 0142-C-02. ASI 2546-2-[no.]. GPO. <http://www.census.gov/prod/www/abs/popula.html#popspec>; <http://www.census.gov/mp/www/pub/pop/mspop03.html>.

> Coverage: U.S., states.
> Content: births; deaths; marital status; marriages; divorces; fertility.

Fertility of American Women. PRINT. WEB. (annual) U.S. Department of Commerce. Economics and Statistics Administration. Bureau of the Census. Current Population Reports: Population Characteristics, Series P-20. C 3.186/10: Item 0142-C-01. ASI 2546-1-[no.]. GPO. <http://www.census.gov/prod/www/abs/fertilty.html.>; <http://www.census.gov/population/www/socdemo/fertility.html>; <http://www.census.gov/mp/www/pub/pop/mspop01.html>. GPO.

> Coverage: U.S., regions, states.
> Content: fertility; births; birth projections.

Fertility of American Women Web Site. WEB. U.S. Department of Commerce. Economics and Statistics Administration. Bureau of the Census. <http://www.census.gov/population/www/socdemo/fertility.html>.

> Content: Census Bureau Web pages describing and linking to Current Population Survey publications and data tables on fertility.

Marital Status and Living Arrangements. PRINT. WEB. (annual) U.S. Department of Commerce. Economics and Statistics Administration. Bureau of the Census. Current Population Reports: Population Characteristics, Series P-20. C 3.186/6: Item 0142-C-01. ASI 2546-1.[no.]. GPO. <http://www.census.gov/prod/www/abs/marital.html>; <http://www.census.gov/prod/www/abs/popula.html#pop>; <http://www.census.gov/mp/www/pub/pop/mspop01.html>.

> Coverage: U.S., regions.
> Content: marital status.

Discussion

Current Population Reports are a series of reports that cover topics describing the U.S. population, such as population characteristics, consumer income and poverty, labor force participation, and population projections. (See Chapter 28, *Population Statistics*, for more information on *Current Population Reports*.) Typical vital statistics topics included are fertility, births, marriage, and divorce. Some vital statistics projections are also included. Three of the individual recurring publications within this series (which have their own individual SuDocs numbers) are included here. *Population Profile of the United States* summarizes basic population information and includes data for several years.

The *Fertility of American Women* report gives statistical data on such fertility-related topics as current fertility, birth expectations, and premarital childbearing. Tables such as "Fertility Indicators for Women 15 to 44 Years Old by State," "Fertility Indicators for Women 15 to 44 Years Old by Hispanic Origin," "Percent Childless and Births per 1,000 in the Last Year," and "Distribution of Women and Average Number of Children Ever Born, by Race, Age, and Marital Status," are typical of the types of information included. A related Bureau of the Census Web site, *Fertility of American Women Web Site*, includes the full-text of these reports, along with other historical tables and information.

The *Marital Status and Living Arrangements* series includes data on marital status and marriages, with cross-tabulations to items such as age, sex, race, and Hispanic Origin.

LIFE TABLES
Checklist

U.S. Decennial Life Tables. PRINT. WEB. (decennial) U.S. Department of Health and Human Services. Centers for Disease Control and Prevention. National Center for Health Statistics. HE 20.6215: (Earlier, FS 2.85/3:) Item 0500-E. ASI 4146-6; 4146-7.

> Coverage: U.S., states.
> Content: life tables by age, race, sex.

U.S. Decennial Life Table for 1989–91. PRINT. WEB. (1997–1998). U.S. Department of Health and Human Services. Centers for Disease Control and Prevention. National Center for Health Statistics. HE 20.6215: Item 0500-E. V.1 *U.S. Life Tables.* ASI (98) 4146-6. V.2 *State Life Tables.* ASI (98) 4146-7. GPO. <http://www.cdc.gov/nchs/products/pubs/pubd/lftbls/decenn/1991-89.htm>; <http://purl.access.gpo.gov/GPO/LPS3123>.

Guide to United States Life Tables, 1900–1959. PRINT. (1963). U.S. Department of Health, Education, and Welfare. Public Health Service. Public Health Bibliography Series No. 42. FS 2.21:42. Item 0481-A.

> Content: index and guide to published and unpublished life tables.

Vital Statistics of the United States, V. 2, Mortality, Part A, Section 6, Life Tables. PRINT. WEB. (annual) 1937–. U.S. Department of Health and Human Services. Centers for Disease Control and Prevention. National Center for Health Statistics. HE 20.6210: Item 0510. ASI 4144-2. GPO. <http://www.cdc.gov/nchs/products/pubs/pubd/lftbls/life/1966.htm>.

Discussion

U.S. Decennial Life Tables reports have been issued regularly since 1900. The tables for 1989–91 published in 1997–98, are the latest issued in the series. Volume 1 includes life tables for the U.S., while Volume 2 has life tables for each individual state. Life tables are used for comparing the longevity of different populations or subgroups of populations. A typical life table might give information, for example, on the life expectancy of a white 36-year-old female in Idaho. See figure 29.2 for an example of a life table. The *Guide to United States Life Tables, 1900–1959,* is a useful tool for historical research.

Life tables also appear in Volume 2, Part A, Section 6 of the *Vital Statistics of the United States,* cited earlier, but are calculated differently than the decennial tables. Preprints of this *Life Tables* section of the *Vital Statistics* have also been issued, with the most recent one occurring as a report in the *National Vital Statistics Report Supplement* series.

ELECTRONIC DATA FILES/PUBLICATION CATALOGS
Checklist

Catalog of Publications of the National Center for Health Statistics. MF. WEB. (annual) 1980–. U.S. Department of Health and Human Services. Centers for Disease Control and Prevention. National Center for Health Statistics. HE 20.6216/4: (Cumulative volumes are: 1962–1979; 1980–89). Item 0508-G. ASI 4124-1. <http://www.cdc.gov/nchswww/products/catalogs/catpub.htm>.

> Content: index to publications of the National Center for Health Statistics.

Catalog of Electronic Products. WEB. U.S. Department of Health and Human Services. Centers for Disease Control and Prevention. National Center for Health Statistics. <http://www.cdc.gov/nchswww/products/catalogs/catelec.htm>.

> Content: description of public-use data files and other electronic products of the National Center for Health Statistics.

Discussion

The *Catalog of Publications of the National Center for Health Statistics* gives ordering information and describes the center's publications. GPO stock numbers and NTIS order numbers are included for the publications when appropriate. Many of the publications are also available in PDF format from the National Center for Health Statistics Web site.

The National Center for Health Statistics makes available a wide variety of data sets and publications in electronic formats that include magnetic data tapes, CD-ROMs, diskettes, and files available directly from the Centers for Disease Control and Prevention FTP server. Most of the NCHS data collection programs issue corresponding public use data files on magnetic data tape available for use by researchers. These tapes require additional analytic software in order to use them. Some data sets are issued in a CD-ROM format that includes the Statistical Export and Tabulation System (SETS) retrieval software. Some data sets are also issued in a diskette format. Many of the sources and reports described earlier in this chapter are derived from data available in an electronic format listed in the *Catalog of Electronic Products.* The *Catalog* includes information on availability, prices, ordering information, data use restrictions and policies, and detailed descriptions of the files. A useful feature is the "Directory by Subject and Survey," which helps to identify the products associated with a particular data collection subject or broad subject category.

DIRECTORIES
Checklist

Where to Write for Vital Records, Births, Deaths, Marriages, and Divorces. PRINT. WEB. (irregular). U.S. Department of Health and Human Services. Public Health Service. Centers for Disease Control and Prevention. National Center for Health Statistics. HE 20.6210/2: Item 0510-A-01. ASI 4128-11. GPO. <http://www.cdc.gov/nchswww/howto/w2w/w2welcom.htm>; <http://purl.access.gpo.gov/GPO/LPS2642>.

> Coverage: states.
> Content: addresses, telephone numbers, URLs for state Web sites, and other information needed to obtain individual birth, death, marriage, and divorce records.

Discussion

Where to Write for Vital Records: Births, Deaths, Marriages, and Divorces provides a state-by-state directory of where and how to obtain these records. It is available in print, PDF, and HTML formats. Complete information for obtaining records from state offices are given in a state-by-state listing. These listings also indicate when records are available from county offices, but do not give individual county contact information. (See Figure 29.3.)

Table 5. Life table for white males: United States, 1989–91

Age interval	Proportion dying	Of 100,000 born alive		Stationary population		Average remaining lifetime
Period of life between two ages (1)	Proportion of persons alive at beginning of age interval dying during interval (2)	Number living at beginning of age interval (3)	Number dying during age interval (4)	In the age interval (5)	In this and all subsequent age intervals (6)	Average number of years of life remaining at beginning of age interval (7)
x to $x + t$	$_tq_x$	l_x	$_td_x$	$_tL_x$	T_x	$\overset{\circ}{e}_0$
Days						
0–1	.00302	100,000	302	273	7,271,574	72.72
1–7	.00134	99,698	134	1,638	7,271,301	72.93
7–28	.00100	99,564	99	5,725	7,269,663	73.01
28–365	.00329	99,465	327	91,684	7,263,938	73.03
Years						
0–1	.00862	100,000	862	99,320	7,271,574	72.72
1–2	.00066	99,138	66	99,105	7,172,254	72.35
2–3	.00049	99,072	48	99,049	7,073,149	71.39
3–4	.00037	99,024	37	99,005	6,974,100	70.43
4–5	.00032	98,987	31	98,972	6,875,095	69.45
5–6	.00028	98,956	27	98,943	6,776,123	68.48
6–7	.00026	98,929	26	98,915	6,677,180	67.49
7–8	.00024	98,903	24	98,891	6,578,265	66.51
8–9	.00022	98,879	22	98,868	6,479,374	65.53
9–10	.00019	98,857	18	98,848	6,380,506	64.54
10–11	.00016	98,839	16	98,831	6,281,658	63.55
11–12	.00017	98,823	17	98,815	6,182,827	62.56
12–13	.00024	98,806	23	98,794	6,084,012	61.58
13–14	.00039	98,783	38	98,764	5,985,218	60.59
14–15	.00059	98,745	59	98,716	5,886,454	59.61
15–16	.00081	98,686	80	98,646	5,787,738	58.65
16–17	.00102	98,606	100	98,555	5,689,092	57.70
17–18	.00118	98,506	116	98,448	5,590,537	56.75
18–19	.00127	98,390	126	98,327	5,492,089	55.82
19–20	.00132	98,264	130	98,199	5,393,762	54.89
20–21	.00136	98,134	133	98,068	5,295,563	53.96
21–22	.00141	98,001	139	97,931	5,197,495	53.04
22–23	.00145	97,862	142	97,791	5,099,564	52.11
23–24	.00148	97,720	144	97,648	5,001,773	51.18
24–25	.00150	97,576	146	97,503	4,904,125	50.26
25–26	.00151	97,430	147	97,357	4,806,622	49.33
26–27	.00153	97,283	149	97,208	4,709,265	48.41
27–28	.00156	97,134	151	97,058	4,612,057	47.48
28–29	.00162	96,983	157	96,904	4,514,999	46.55
29–30	.00169	96,826	164	96,744	4,418,095	45.63
30–31	.00177	96,662	172	96,576	4,321,351	44.71
31–32	.00185	96,490	179	96,401	4,224,775	43.78
32–33	.00193	96,311	186	96,219	4,128,374	42.86
33–34	.00201	96,125	193	96,028	4,032,155	41.95
34–35	.00210	95,932	201	95,831	3,936,127	41.03
35–36	.00219	95,731	210	95,626	3,840,296	40.12
36–37	.00230	95,521	220	95,411	3,744,670	39.20
37–38	.00240	95,301	228	95,187	3,649,259	38.29
38–39	.00250	95,073	238	94,954	3,554,072	37.38
39–40	.00260	94,835	247	94,711	3,459,118	36.48
40–41	.00271	94,588	257	94,459	3,364,407	35.57
41–42	.00283	94,331	267	94,198	3,269,948	34.66
42–43	.00298	94,064	281	93,924	3,175,750	33.76
43–44	.00317	93,783	297	93,634	3,081,826	32.86
44–45	.00341	93,486	319	93,327	2,988,192	31.96
45–46	.00370	93,167	345	92,994	2,894,865	31.07
46–47	.00404	92,822	376	92,634	2,801,871	30.19
47–48	.00441	92,446	407	92,243	2,709,237	29.31
48–49	.00479	92,039	441	91,818	2,616,994	28.43
49–50	.00518	91,598	474	91,381	2,525,176	27.57
50–51	.00564	91,124	515	90,867	2,433,815	26.71
51–52	.00620	90,609	561	90,328	2,342,948	25.86
52–53	.00683	90,048	615	89,741	2,252,620	25.02

Source: U.S. Decennial Life Table for 1989-91, volume 1, number 1, United States Life Tables, p. 20.

Figure 29.2: Sample Page from U.S. Decennial Life Tables.

Place of event	Cost of copy	Address	Remarks
Alabama			
Birth or Death	$12.00	Center for Health Statistics State Department of Public Health P.O. Box 5625 Montgomery, AL 36103-5625	State office has had records since January 1908. Additional copies at same time are $4.00 each. Fee for special searches is $10.00 per hour. Check or money order should be made payable to **Center for Health Statistics.** Personal checks are accepted. To verify current fees, the telephone number is **(334) 206-5418.**
Marriage	$12.00	Same as Birth or Death	State office has records since August 1936.
	Varies	See remarks	Contact Probate Court in county where license was issued.
Divorce	$12.00	Same as Birth or Death	State office has records since January 1950.
	Varies	See remarks	Contact Clerk of Circuit Court in county where divorce was granted.
Alaska			
Birth or Death	$10.00	Department of Health and Social Services Bureau of Vital Statistics P.O. Box 110675 Juneau, AK 99811-0675	State office has had records since January 1913. Money order should be made payable to **Bureau of Vital Statistics.** Personal checks are not accepted. To verify current fees, the telephone number is **(907) 465-3391.** This will be a **recorded** message.
Marriage	$10.00	Same as Birth or Death	State office has had records since 1913.
Divorce	$10.00	Same as Birth or Death	State office has had records since 1950.
	Varies	See remarks	Clerk of Superior Court in judicial district where divorce was granted. Juneau and Ketchikan (First District), Nome (Second District), Anchorage (Third District), Fairbanks (Fourth District).
American Samoa			
Birth or Death	$2.00	Registrar of Vital Statistics Vital Statistics Section Government of American Samoa Pago Pago, AS 96799	Registrar has had records since 1900. Money order should be made payable to **ASG Treasurer.** Personal checks are not accepted. To verify current fees, the telephone number is **(684) 633-1222, ext. 214.** Personal identification required before record will be sent.
Marriage	$2.00	Same as Birth or Death	
Divorce	$1.00	High Court of American Samoa Tutuila, AS 96799	

2

Source: Where to Write for Vital Records: Births, Deaths, Marriages, and Divorces, 1999, p. 2

Figure 29.3: Sample Page from *Where to Write for Vital Records: Births, Deaths, Marriages, and Divorces.*

INDEXES
Checklist

American Statistics Index (ASI). PRINT. (monthly) 1973–. Bethesda, MD: Congressional Information Service.

Statistical Universe. WEB. Bethesda, MD: Congressional Information Service.

Discussion

A comprehensive listing of material can be found in *ASI* by looking under such subject headings as "Vital statistics," "Births," "Deaths," "Fetal deaths," "Life expectancy," "Marriage and divorce," "Fertility," "Abortion," "Infant mortality," and "Child mortality." *Statistical Universe* includes a Web version of *ASI*. (See Chapter 3, "The Basics of Searching," for more information on *ASI*.)

RELATED MATERIAL
Within this Work

Chapter 19 Health

Chapter 28 Population Statistics

GPO Subject Bibliographies. PRINT. WEB. GP 3.22/2:

<http://bookstore.gpo.gov/sb/about.html>

No. 121 "Vital and Health Statistics"

CHAPTER 30
Economic Indicators

Economic indicators are such measures of the economy as gross national product, personal consumption expenditures, national income, personal income, productivity, industrial production, capacity utilization rate, money stock, consumer prices, producer prices, employment, and unemployment. These types of statistics provide a barometer to measure growth or changes in the economy.

This chapter provides sources for locating information on the major economic indicators. It includes some of the most basic sources, and also concentrates on describing sources from the Bureau of Economic Analysis (BEA), the agency most concerned with economic indicators. Some indicators are described in more detail in other chapters, and are not included in a comprehensive way in this chapter—consult the "Related Material" section for a listing of these chapters. Sources of information on economic indicators for other countries are described in the "Economic Sources" section of Chapter 5, "Foreign Countries."

SEARCH STRATEGY

This chapter shows a statistical search strategy. Search steps are

1. Search general statistical sources listed, such as the *Statistical Abstract of the United States*;
2. Consult the major titles listed here and grouped by subject;
3. Use *American Statistics Index (ASI)* for further searching; and
4. Examine the "Related Material" section, especially the listings of related chapters.

BASIC SOURCES
Checklist

Statistical Abstract of the United States. PRINT. WEB. (annual) 1878–. U.S. Department of Commerce. Economics and Statistics Administration. Bureau of the Census. C 3.134: Item 0150. ASI 2324-1. GPO. <www.census.gov/statab/www/>; <http://purl.access.gpo.gov/GPO/LPS2878>.

> Coverage: U.S., regions, divisions, states, selected metropolitan areas.
> Content: basic statistics on a wide range of economic indicators.

Statistical Abstract of the United States. CD-ROM. (annual) 1993–. U.S. Department of Commerce. Bureau of the Census. C 3.134/7: Item 0150-B. ASI 2324-14.

> Content: CD-ROM version of the *Statistical Abstract*.

Historical Statistics of the United States: Colonial Times to 1970. Parts 1-2. PRINT. (1975) U.S. Department of Commerce. Bureau of the Census. C 3.134/2:H 62/789-970/pt.1-2. Item 0151. ASI (76) 2328-2. GPO.

> Coverage: U.S., states.
> Content: basic historical statistics on a wide range of economic indicators.

Historical Statistics of the United States on CD-ROM: Colonial Times to 1970. CD-ROM. (1997) New York, NY: Cambridge University Press.

> Content: CD-ROM version of *Historical Statistics of the United States*.

Discussion

The *Statistical Abstract of the United States* includes several sections relating to economic indicators including "Income, Expenditures, and Wealth," "Prices," "Banking, Finance, and Insurance," and "Business Enterprise." The *Statistical Abstract* is also searchable in a CD-ROM format. *Historical Statistics of the United States: Colonial Times to 1970* includes most of the statistical series from the *Statistical Abstract* for years earlier than 1970. A CD-ROM version of *Historical Statistics* is available from Cambridge University Press. Many economic indicator-type questions can be answered by using these two basic sources.

BUREAU OF ECONOMIC ANALYSIS (BEA) PUBLICATIONS

Checklist

Survey of Current Business. PRINT. WEB. (monthly) 1921–. U.S. Department of Commerce. Bureau of Economic Analysis. C 59.11: Item 0228. ASI 2702-1. GPO. <http://www.bea. doc.gov/bea/pubs.htm>; <http://purl.access.gpo.gov/GPO/ LPS1730>.

> Coverage: U.S.; occasionally states and smaller geographic regions.
> Content: articles on business and economic conditions; detailed series of economic and business statistics.

Survey of Current Business. CD-ROM. (annual) 1994–. U.S. Department of Commerce. Economics and Statistics Administration. Bureau of Economic Analysis. C 59.11/1: Item 0228-A. GPO.

> Content: CD-ROM version of *Survey of Current Business.*

Business Statistics of the United States. PRINT (annual) 1995–. Lanham, MD: Bernan Press. (Continuation of *Business Statistics* published by the Bureau of Economic Analysis, 1951–1991, C 59.11/3:)

> Coverage: U.S.
> Content: economic and industry time series data; industry data on production, capacity utilization, shipments, inventories, orders, producer prices, employment, hours, earnings, sales.

National Income and Product Accounts of the United States, 1929–94. PRINT. 2 vols. (1998) U.S. Department of Commerce. Economics and Statistics Administration. Bureau of Economic Analysis. C 59.11/5:929-94/v.1-2. Item 0228-A-03. ASI (98) 2708-5. GPO.

> Coverage: U.S.
> Content: historical compilation of the monthly national income and product account statistics appearing in the *Survey of Current Business.*

National Income and Product Accounts of the United States, 1929–97. CD-ROM. (1999) U.S. Department of Commerce. Economics and Statistics Administration. Bureau of Economic Analysis. C 59.11/5-2:929-97. Item 0228-A-04.

> Content: CD-ROM version of *National Income and Product Accounts of the United States.*

REIS: Regional Economic Information System. CD-ROM. (annual) U.S. Department of Commerce. Economics and Statistics Administration. Bureau of Economic Analysis. C 59.24: Item 0130-U. ASI 2704-7. <http://govinfo.kerr.orst.edu/reis-stateis.html>; <http://fisher.lib.virginia.edu/reis/index.html>.

> Coverage: U.S., BEA regions, states, counties, metropolitan areas, BEA economic areas.
> Content: data on income, earnings, and employment.

STAT-USA Internet. WEB. U.S. Department of Commerce. C 1.91: Item 0128-P. <http://www.stat-usa.gov/>.

> Coverage: U.S., regions, states, counties, metropolitan areas.
> Content: current and historical economic press releases on National Income and Product Accounts; wide variety of other economic indicator data.

Bureau of Economic Analysis Web Site. WEB. U.S. Department of Commerce. Economics and Statistics Administration. Bureau of Economic Analysis. <http://www.bea.doc.gov/>.

> Content: agency information; data files; full-text publications and press releases.

Bureau of Economic Analysis Catalog of Products. WEB. U.S. Department of Commerce. Economics and Statistics Administration. Bureau of Economic Analysis. <http://www.bea. doc.gov/bea/uguide.htm>; <http://purl.access. gpo.gov/GPO/ LPS1879>.

> Content: catalog of products available via the Web, and CD-ROM, print, diskette, and downloadable files products.

BEA Recorded Telephone Messages. U.S. Department of Commerce. Economics and Statistics Administration. Bureau of Economic Analysis.

> Content: brief recorded telephone messages summarizing key estimates.
> Gross domestic product 202-606-5306
> Personal income and outlays 202-606-5303
> U.S. international transactions 202-606-5362

Discussion

The *Survey of Current Business* is a monthly report of many of the most important economic indicators for the United States. The first section of *Survey of Current Business* includes statistical articles on such topics as "State Personal Income," "Foreign Direct Investment in the United States," "Federal Budget Estimates," and "Gross State Product by Industry." The *Survey of Current Business* also contains a section on National Income and Product Accounts (NIPA) statistics on the nation's economic activity. NIPA statistics cover the Gross Domestic Product (GDP) and its components and the distribution of national income. Each issue of the *Survey of Current Business* contains a section called "BEA Current and Historical Data" that presents selected economic statistics. Much of the data for industry is given by broad sectors, such as manufacturing or retail trade. More specific industry categories are given for gross domestic product, compensation, and employment. Data are primarily for the United States. Trade data include some world region and country data. State data are limited to gross state product information. More extensive annual NIPA data appear in the August issue. Articles provide more detailed analyses and updates on specific topics. Each issue contains a regular feature called "Business Situation" which briefly describes the current trends in the GDP and corporate profits

Recent issues of the *Survey of Current Business* are also available from the *Bureau of Economic Analysis Web Site* and from the *STAT-USA* Web site. The BEA site lists recent months with links to the full text of articles and tables. Files are a combination of PDF and HTML formats. Subject guides are available for years since 1995. *STAT-USA* lists articles since 1997 and makes them available as PDF files. Articles can also be retrieved through the search feature in the "State of the Nation Library" area. A CD-ROM version contains PDF files for the year with selected previous articles dating from 1987.

Business Statistics of the United States contains a wide range of economic and industry statistics compiled from government sources, as well as from some private sources. Part I is the most relevant to this chapter, and contains general economic statistics with sections on such areas as gross domestic product and cyclical indicators; consumer income and spending; and U.S. foreign trade and finance. Some sections in this part include breakdowns by industry: industrial production and capacity utilization; business sales, inventories and investment; prices; employment costs, productivity and profits; and employment, hours and earnings. Part II is arranged by industry group and provides several years of data for each industry. The type of data varies slightly from industry to industry, reflecting what is most appropriate for that industry. Part III contains additional historical data for selected series. A notes section provides information on sources of data, definitions, revisions, availability, and references for additional information.

The *REIS: Regional Economic Information System* includes a series of data on personal and farm income and employment. Detailed statistics by industry are included. *REIS* is issued in a CD-ROM format by the BEA, and two searchable Web versions of the database are also available.

The *STAT-USA Internet* site is divided into two areas: State of the Nation and Globus & NTDB. The State of the Nation area contains domestic economic statistical releases. Current versions of the top 50 releases are organized by categories. Data files for the Consumer Price Index, Producer Price Index, Gross Domestic Product, and National Income and Product Accounts (NIPA) are included. Other data related to housing and construction, employment, manufacturing and industry, monetary statistics, and economic policy are also available. Some parts of *STAT-USA* are only available to subscribers, but federal depository libraries may register for free access for two workstations. The option to purchase individual reports is also made available.

The *Bureau of Economic Analysis Web Site* includes many full text publications, articles, statistical tables, and data files available for downloading or viewing. The site should particularly be consulted if more detailed information on BEA produced economic indicators or information on BEA methodology is needed. Also included within the site is the *Bureau of Economic Analysis Catalog of Products*. The BEA also provides recorded telephone messages for selected economic indicators

ADDITIONAL SOURCES
Checklist

Handbook of International Economic Statistics. PRINT. WEB. (annual) 1992–. U.S. Central Intelligence Agency. Directorate of Intelligence. PREX 3.16: (Issued earlier as *Handbook of Economic Statistics*, PREX 3.10/7-5:) Item 0856-A-09. ASI 9114-4. GPO. <http://www.cia.gov/cia/di/products/hies/index.html>; <http://purl.access.gpo.gov/GPO/LPS2917>.

> Coverage: world, world regions, country groupings, selected countries, U.S.
> Content: broad range of selected economic indicators, including gross domestic product; prices; foreign debt; unemployment rates; energy; agriculture; foreign trade and aid; environment.

Economic Report of the President Transmitted to the Congress. PRINT. WEB. (annual) 1947–. U.S. President. PR [no.].9: (SuDocs number varies with each President). Item 0848. ASI 204-1. GPO. <http://w3.access.gpo.gov/eop/index.html>.

> Coverage: U.S.
> Content: varies; economic outlook; gross domestic product; consumer price index; prices; unemployment rate; interest rate; government finance; agriculture.

Economic Indicators. PRINT. WEB. (monthly) 1948–. U.S. Congress. Joint Economic Committee. Y4.EC 7:EC 7/ Item 0997. ASI 23842-1. GPO. <http://www.access.gpo.gov/congress/cong002.html>; <http://purl.access.gpo.gov/GPO/LPS1458>.

> Coverage: U.S.
> Content: total output, income and spending; employment, unemployment, and wages; production and business activity; prices; money, credit, and security markets; federal finance; international statistics.

Rural Conditions and Trends. PRINT. WEB. (3 times per year) 1990–. U.S. Department of Agriculture. Economic Research Services. A 93.41/3: Item 0021-N-08. ASI 1502-8. <http://www.ers.ag.gov/epubs/pdf/rcat/rcat.htm>; <http://purl.access.gpo.gov/GPO/LPS1396>.

> Coverage: varies; primarily U.S.
> Content: varies; includes articles on such topics as macroeconomic conditions, employment and unemployment, industrial structure, earnings and income, poverty, and population.

Handbook of U.S. Labor Statistics: Employment, Earnings, Prices, Productivity, and Other Labor Data. PRINT. (annual) 1997–. Lanham, MD: Bernan Press. (Continuation of *Handbook of Labor Statistics* published by the Bureau of Labor Statistics, 1924-1989, L 2.3/5:, L 2.3:)

> Coverage: selected countries, U.S., states.
> Content: number in labor force, employed, and unemployed; unemployment rate; data by age, race, sex, marital status, occupation, industry, family characteristics, and educational attainment.

Bureau of Labor Statistics Web Site. WEB. U.S. Department of Labor. Bureau of Labor Statistics. <http://stats.bls.gov/>.

> Content: includes a wide variety of statistical data, publications, methodology, research data, and other information; particularly pertaining to employment and unemployment; prices and living conditions; compensation and working conditions; productivity and technology.

Recorded Telephone Summaries. (202-606-7828) (telephone hotline). U.S. Department of Labor. Bureau of Labor Statistics. Content: frequently updated recorded telephone summaries of information about: Consumer Price Index (CPI); Producer Price Index (PPI); Employment Situation; Employment Cost Index (ECI); and Publication Information.

Discussion

The *Handbook of International Economic Statistics* provides a series of tables portraying various economic statistics. Statistics on gross national product, consumer prices, industrial production and other related topics are included. The *Handbook* is especially useful for making economic comparisons between the United States and other countries. The Web version also includes downloadable Excel (.xls) files of the data included in the tables of the report.

The *Economic Report of the President Transmitted to the Congress* provides a thorough annual analysis of the U.S. economic situation. It is prepared by the Council of Economic Advisors. It includes in an appendix a series of over 100 tables of economic indicators, such as national income, wages, production, prices, money stock, and government finances. These tables are downloadable as Excel (.xls) files from the Web site. Most tables include historical annual statistics as well as current statistics. The Web site features the ability to search the full-text of several years worth of the title, and also includes PDF versions of the full-text of earlier years of the title. The *Economic Report of the President* is a basic tool for tracking U.S. economic policy.

Economic Indicators is prepared by the Council of Economic Advisors for the Joint Economic Committee. It consists of graphs and statistical tables with such titles as "Implicit Price Deflators for Gross Domestic Product," "Sources of Personal Income," "Selected Unemployment Rates," "Manufacturers' Shipments, Inventories, and Orders," and "Interest Rates and Bond Yields." Data are usually given annually for several years, along with monthly and quarterly data for the past two to three years. (See Figure 30.1). The Web version provides both PDF format and ASCII text versions of the title. It also includes a searchable interface to issues from April 1995 and forward.

Each issue of *Rural Conditions and Trends* contains several articles on U.S. rural economics. Articles are primarily statistically based and are often accompanied by charts, tables, and graphs. Analysts in the Economic Research Service generally prepare articles, and contact information for further information from the analysts is included. Economic indicator information is often included or analyzed within the articles. This publication is an excellent source for tracking economic information for rural areas.

The *Handbook of Labor Statistics* is a convenient compilation of statistics, including some economic indicators such as productivity, consumer prices, producer prices, employment, and unemployment. Historical statistics are also included for many of the indicators. *The Bureau of Labor Statistics Web Site* also includes some economic indicator statistics, most notably employment and unemployment data and price data. The BLS also maintains 24 hour a day, 7 days a week telephone hotlines for recorded summaries of economic information.

FEDERAL RESERVE PUBLICATIONS
Checklist

Federal Reserve Bulletin. PRINT. (monthly) 1915–. U.S. Board of Governors of the Federal Reserve System. FR 1.3: (nondepository) (Copies available for sale by the Board of Governors of the Federal Reserve System). ASI 9362-1. Selected articles: <http://www.bog.frb.fed.us/pubs/bulletin/default.htm>.

> Coverage: world, world regions, country groupings, countries, U.S.
> Content: financial statistics and articles; money stock; bank credit; federal reserve banks; bank loans; bank assets and liabilities; interest rates; stock market; federal finances; corporate profits; mortgages; consumer credit; flow of funds; capacity utilization; industrial production; housing and construction; price indexes; gross domestic product (GDP); personal income; international transactions; foreign liabilities and claims; exchange rates.

Statistics: Releases and Historical Data Web Page. WEB. U.S. Board of Governors of the Federal Reserve System. <http://www.federalreserve.gov/releases/>.

> Coverage: primarily U.S.
> Content: current and historical statistical series; includes data on interest rates; current paper rates and outstandings; money stock; assets and liabilities of commercial banks; foreign exchange rates; and other related statistics.

FRED™: Federal Reserve Economic Data. WEB. U.S. Federal Reserve Bank of St. Louis. <http://www.stls.frb.org/fred/index.html>.

> Coverage: varies; primarily U.S.; some Federal Reserve Bank of St. Louis regional and state data.
> Content: historical and current economic data; employment and population data; commercial banking data; monetary data; gross domestic product; consumer price indexes; interest rate; producer price indexes; monthly reserves data.

Discussion

The *Federal Reserve Bulletin* includes articles on finance, business, and banking that often include economic indicator statistics. The *Bulletin* also includes monthly compilations of financial and business statistics. Statistics are grouped under the following topics: "Domestic Financial Statistics," "Domestic Nonfinancial Statistics," "International Statistics," "Intermittent Tables," and "Annual Tables." Tables are quite detailed, and often include weekly and monthly data.

While the Web version of the *Federal Reserve Bulletin* only includes selected articles and does not include all of

SOURCES OF PERSONAL INCOME

Personal income rose $35.4 billion (annual rate) in November, following an increase of $100.4 billion in October. Wages and salaries increased $13.6 billion in November, following an increase of $27.9 billion in October. Personal income for November and October was affected by several special factors. In November and October personal income was boosted by Federal farm subsidy payments and union contract signing bonuses. Personal income in October was also boosted by the effects of Hurricane Floyd, which had reduced personal income in September. Excluding special factors, personal income increased $39.7 billion in November and $48.9 billion in October.

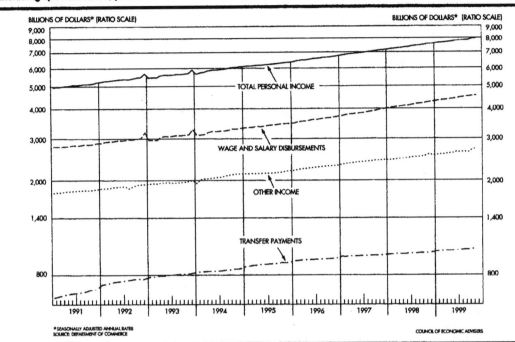

*SEASONALLY ADJUSTED ANNUAL RATES
SOURCE: DEPARTMENT OF COMMERCE

COUNCIL OF ECONOMIC ADVISERS

[Billions of dollars; monthly data at seasonally adjusted annual rates]

Period	Total personal income	Wage and salary disbursements [1]	Other labor income [1][2]	Proprietors' income [3] Farm	Proprietors' income [3] Nonfarm	Rental income of persons [3]	Personal dividend income	Personal interest income	Transfer payments [6]	Less: Personal contributions for social insurance
1990	4,903.2	2,754.6	390.0	31.1	349.9	49.1	165.4	772.4	594.4	203.7
1991	5,085.4	2,824.2	415.6	26.4	357.8	56.4	178.3	771.8	669.9	215.1
1992	5,390.4	2,982.6	449.5	32.7	401.7	63.3	185.3	750.1	751.7	226.6
1993	5,610.0	3,085.2	482.8	30.1	431.7	90.9	203.0	725.5	798.6	237.8
1994	5,888.0	3,236.7	507.5	31.9	444.6	110.3	234.7	742.4	833.9	254.1
1995	6,200.9	3,424.7	497.0	22.2	475.5	117.9	254.0	792.5	885.9	268.8
1996	6,547.4	3,626.5	490.0	34.3	510.5	129.7	297.4	810.6	928.8	280.4
1997	6,951.1	3,888.9	500.9	29.5	549.1	130.2	333.4	854.9	962.4	298.1
1998	7,358.9	4,186.0	515.7	25.1	581.0	137.4	348.3	897.8	983.6	315.9
1998: Nov	7,556.5	4,301.1	522.1	60.0	595.3	150.9	351.9	906.3	991.1	322.2
Dec	7,554.5	4,318.8	523.6	33.7	600.3	146.7	353.2	906.2	995.1	323.1
1999: Jan	7,599.0	4,350.7	526.1	33.6	603.7	147.6	354.6	905.8	1,004.7	327.7
Feb	7,636.4	4,377.9	528.1	33.7	608.0	148.8	356.0	906.8	1,006.6	329.3
Mar	7,655.3	4,385.8	529.8	30.1	610.8	149.3	357.6	909.6	1,012.0	329.6
Apr	7,692.7	4,410.4	531.3	30.1	618.4	148.6	359.3	914.3	1,011.3	331.1
May	7,721.8	4,432.1	533.0	27.3	619.4	147.3	361.2	921.0	1,013.0	332.3
June	7,783.3	4,455.4	534.8	45.0	625.8	150.5	363.0	926.2	1,016.4	333.7
July [r]	7,806.0	4,491.4	536.7	23.5	630.2	144.9	364.9	932.4	1,017.8	335.7
Aug [r]	7,840.0	4,508.2	538.6	21.4	636.4	143.6	367.0	938.8	1,022.6	336.6
Sept [r]	7,848.1	4,528.5	540.3	18.0	632.5	128.5	369.0	945.3	1,023.6	337.8
Oct [r]	7,948.5	4,556.4	542.0	47.1	642.1	148.7	371.1	952.2	1,028.3	339.3
Nov [p]	7,983.9	4,570.0	543.8	49.3	648.9	150.6	373.1	958.8	1,029.5	340.0

[1] The total of wage and salary disbursements and other labor income differs from compensation of employees (see p. 4) in that it excludes employer contributions for social insurance and the excess of wage accruals over wage disbursements.

[2] Consists primarily of employer contributions to private pension and private welfare funds.

[3] With inventory valuation and capital consumption adjustments.
[4] With capital consumption adjustment.
[6] Consists mainly of social insurance benefits, direct relief, and veterans payments.

Source: Department of Commerce, Bureau of Economic Analysis.

5

Source: Economic Indicators, December 1999, p. 5.

Figure 30.1: Sample Page from *Economic Indicators*.

the statistical tables provided in the print version, some statistical tables are available from the Board of Governors of the Federal Reserve system *Statistics: Releases and Historical Data Web Page.*

FRED™: Federal Reserve Economic Data, is a quite comprehensive site that provides access to detailed financial and economic data, often spanning long periods of time. Coverage is for the United States, and for the geographic region encompassing the states of Arkansas, Illinois, Indiana, Kentucky, Mississippi, Missouri, and Tennessee. Data series from twelve categories of information are included: "Business/Fiscal Data," "Exchange Rate, Balance of Payments and Trade Data," "Monthly Commercial Banking Data," "Monthly Employment and Population Data," "Monthly Monetary Data," "Daily/Weekly U.S. Financial Data," "Gross Domestic Product and Components," "Monthly Consumer Price Indexes," "Monthly Interest Rates," "Monthly Producer Price Indexes," and "Monthly Reserves Data." Large data files of historical series are also available for download in zipped and compressed file formats.

PRICE INDEXES
Checklist

CPI Detailed Report. PRINT. (monthly) 1974–. U.S. Department of Labor. Bureau of Labor Statistics. L 2.38/3: (Issued earlier as *Consumer Price Index*) Item 0768-F. ASI 6762-2. GPO.
> Coverage: U.S., regions, selected metropolitan areas.
> Content: consumer price index for all urban consumers and for urban wage earners and clerical workers, total and by categories; percentage change; average energy and food prices.

Consumer Price Index. WEB. (monthly) U.S. Department of Labor. Bureau of Labor Statistics. L 2.38/3-2: Item 0768-F. ASI 6762-1. <http://www.bls.gov/news.release/cpi.toc.htm>; <http://www.bls.gov/bls_news/archives/cpi_nr.html>; <http://purl.access.gpo.gov/GPO/LPS3314>.
> Coverage: U.S., regions, selected metropolitan areas.
> Content: consumer price index for all urban consumers and for urban wage earners and clerical workers by general expenditure category; percentage change.

Consumer Price Indexes Web Page. WEB. U.S. Department of Labor. Bureau of Labor Statistics. <http://www.bls.gov/cpihome.htm>.
> Content: full-text news releases, selected data tables, and background information for the consumer price index.

PPI Detailed Report. PRINT. (monthly with annual supplement) 1996–. U.S. Department of Labor. Bureau of Labor Statistics. L 2.61: (Annual Supplement, L 2.61/11:) (Issued earlier under other titles: *Producer Price Indexes, Producer Prices and Price Indexes, Wholesale Prices and Price Indexes*). Item 0771-B. ASI 6762-6, 6764-2. GPO.
> Coverage: U.S.
> Content: price index and percentage change by stage of processing, commodity groupings, selected industries and their products, and individual items.

Producer Price Index. WEB. (monthly) U.S. Department of Labor. Bureau of Labor Statistics. L 2.61/10:. Item 0771-B. ASI 6762-5. <http://www.bls.gov/news.release/ppi.toc.htm>; <http://www.bls.gov/bls_news/archives/ppi_nr.htm>.
> Coverage: U.S.
> Content: price index and percentage change by stage of processing, selected commodity groupings, and major industry groups.

Producer Price Indexes Web Page. WEB. U.S. Department of Labor. Bureau of Labor Statistics. <http://www.bls.gov/ppihome.htm>; <http://purl.access.gpo.gov/GPO/LPS1881>.
> Content: full-text news releases, selected data tables, and background information for the producer price index.

STAT-USA Internet. WEB. U.S. Department of Commerce. C 1.91: Item 0128-P. <http://www.stat-usa.gov/>.
> Coverage: U.S., regions, divisions, states, metropolitan areas.
> Content: *Consumer Price Index* and *Producer Price Index* press releases.

Handbook of U.S. Labor Statistics: Employment, Earnings, Prices, Productivity, and Other Labor Data. PRINT. (annual) 1997–. Lanham, MD: Bernan Press. (Continuation of *Handbook of Labor Statistics* published by the Bureau of Labor Statistics, 1924-1989, L 2.3/5:, L 2.3:)
> Coverage: U.S., regions, selected metropolitan areas.
> Content: producer price indexes by state of processing, commodity group, and selected industries; consumer price index by major group.

Discussion

The consumer price index (CPI) is a measure of the change in prices over time and is widely used as a measure of inflation. The index only measures the effects of price changes on the cost of living; it does not measure changes in the total amount spent for living expenses. There are now two major forms of the CPI commonly used: CPI-U and CPI-W. The CPI-U is the "Consumer Price Index for All Urban Consumers" and is used more often than the CPI-W, the "Consumer Price Index for Urban Wage Earners and Clerical Workers." The CPI measures price change from a designated date period, with most charts now using the 1982–84 period as a base.

The *CPI Detailed Report* gives information on the consumer price index by detailed expenditure category showing price changes for selected items in the categories of food and beverages, housing, apparel, transportation, medical care, recreation, and other goods and services. Less detailed subcategories are given for regions and metropolitan areas. The metropolitan areas covered differ from month to month. Three cities — Chicago, Los Angeles, and New York — appear monthly. Eleven additional metropolitan areas are divided into two groups published bimonthly in alternating issues. Another group of 12 cities is covered in semiannual tables in the January and July issues and in annual average tables in the January issue. (See Figure 30.2.) Historical tables provide U.S. consumer price index data for several years.

Table 7. Consumer Price Index for Urban Wage Earners and Clerical Workers (CPI-W): Seasonally adjusted U.S. city average, by expenditure category and commodity and service group -Continued

(1982-84=100, unless otherwise noted)

Item and group	Seasonally adjusted indexes				Seasonally adjusted annual rate percent change for					
					3 months ended—				6 months ended—	
	June 1999	July 1999	Aug. 1999	Sep. 1999	Dec. 1998	Mar. 1999	June 1999	Sep. 1999	Mar. 1999	Sep. 1999
Expenditure category										
Recreation [2]	101.4	101.4	101.3	100.8	-0.4	0.4	2.0	-2.3	0.0	-0.2
Video and audio [1] [2]	100.4	100.3	100.6	100.0	-1.2	-2.7	-.4	-1.6	-2.0	-1.0
Education and communication [2]	101.4	101.6	101.7	101.7	.8	2.0	.0	1.2	1.4	.6
Education [2]	107.7	108.2	108.3	108.6	4.7	6.3	5.4	3.4	5.5	4.4
Educational books and supplies	266.1	266.9	268.6	269.3	8.2	3.9	4.8	4.9	6.0	4.8
Tuition, other school fees, and childcare	302.8	304.1	304.4	305.2	4.6	6.5	5.3	3.2	5.6	4.3
Communication [1] [2]	96.4	96.3	96.5	96.2	-2.8	-1.6	-4.0	-.8	-2.2	-2.4
Information and information processing [1] [2]	96.0	96.0	96.1	95.8	-2.8	-2.4	-4.5	-.8	-2.6	-2.7
Telephone services [1] [2]	99.9	99.7	99.9	99.7	-1.6	.0	-2.0	-.8	-.8	-1.4
Information and information processing other than telephone services [1] [5]	30.8	31.1	30.8	30.3	-21.1	-25.0	-28.5	-6.3	-23.1	-18.2
Personal computers and peripheral equipment [1] [2]	54.0	52.5	50.6	49.4	-26.0	-37.5	-18.9	-30.0	-32.0	-24.6
Other goods and services	259.4	262.4	261.4	267.7	23.9	5.0	5.3	13.4	14.1	9.3
Tobacco and smoking products	345.2	357.0	352.0	374.8	88.1	5.4	10.1	39.0	40.8	23.7
Personal care [1]	161.3	161.3	161.6	161.9	1.5	5.2	2.5	1.5	3.3	2.0
Personal care products [1]	153.3	152.7	153.1	153.7	-1.3	5.5	4.6	1.0	2.0	2.8
Personal care services [1]	171.2	171.8	172.2	172.4	2.9	3.9	2.4	2.8	3.4	2.6
Miscellaneous personal services	242.4	243.2	243.8	244.5	4.1	4.3	2.5	3.5	4.2	3.0
Commodity and service group										
Commodities	143.9	144.6	145.2	146.4	2.3	-.6	4.3	7.1	.8	5.7
Food and beverages	163.5	163.8	164.1	164.6	2.8	1.5	1.7	2.7	2.1	2.2
Commodities less food and beverages	132.2	133.1	133.8	135.4	1.9	-1.8	6.0	10.0	.0	8.0
Nondurables less food and beverages	136.5	138.3	139.6	141.8	2.8	1.2	10.3	16.5	2.0	13.3
Apparel	130.0	129.1	128.4	130.1	-.6	-7.4	3.5	.3	-4.1	1.9
Nondurables less food, beverages, and apparel	144.8	147.3	150.2	152.9	5.4	5.6	14.1	24.3	5.5	19.1
Durables	125.6	125.8	126.0	126.7	-.3	-5.5	.6	3.5	-3.0	2.1
Services	185.0	185.6	185.7	186.2	2.4	2.7	2.0	2.6	2.5	2.3
Rent of shelter [4]	174.7	174.9	175.3	175.8	3.5	1.6	2.8	2.5	2.6	2.7
Tenants' and household insurance [1] [2]	102.3	102.2	102.3	102.5	3.7	1.2	6.9	.8	2.4	3.8
Gas (piped) and electricity [3]	118.3	119.0	119.4	120.4	.0	1.4	-1.7	7.3	.7	2.7
Water and sewer and trash collection services [2]	103.9	103.9	104.0	104.2	2.8	2.4	1.9	1.2	2.6	1.6
Household operations [1] [2]	104.8	104.8	105.4	105.7	3.6	3.1	2.7	3.5	3.3	3.1
Transportation services	187.1	188.5	188.0	188.0	.9	4.4	-1.3	1.9	2.6	.3
Medical care services	254.7	255.3	255.8	256.7	2.6	3.6	3.9	3.2	3.1	3.5
Other services	219.6	220.1	220.5	220.5	2.1	3.4	2.6	1.6	2.7	2.1
Special indexes										
All items less food	162.3	163.0	163.4	164.3	2.0	1.0	3.5	5.0	1.5	4.3
All items less shelter	157.4	158.1	158.6	159.5	2.1	.5	3.4	5.4	1.3	4.4
All items less medical care	158.6	159.2	159.6	160.4	2.3	1.0	3.1	4.6	1.7	3.8
Commodities less food	133.9	134.7	135.5	137.0	1.8	-1.8	6.2	9.6	.0	7.9
Nondurables less food	138.5	140.1	141.4	143.7	2.7	1.5	10.1	15.9	2.1	13.0
Nondurables less food and apparel	146.3	148.6	151.2	153.7	5.3	4.7	14.0	21.8	5.0	17.8
Nondurables	150.5	151.4	152.3	153.6	2.2	1.9	6.1	8.5	2.1	7.3
Services less rent of shelter [4]	173.6	174.2	174.7	175.0	1.4	2.1	1.9	3.3	1.8	2.6
Services less medical care services	179.2	179.7	180.0	180.4	2.5	1.8	2.3	2.7	2.2	2.5
Energy	103.3	105.7	108.7	110.7	-5.9	7.1	15.2	31.9	.4	23.3
All items less energy	171.0	171.3	171.4	172.1	2.9	.7	2.4	2.6	1.8	2.5
All items less food and energy	173.1	173.5	173.6	174.3	2.8	.5	2.3	2.8	1.6	2.6
Commodities less food and energy commodities	141.1	144.3	144.1	145.4	4.0	-3.8	2.5	3.7	.0	3.1
Energy commodities	96.4	100.4	105.7	108.6	-12.0	13.6	37.0	61.1	.0	48.6
Services less energy services	192.7	193.2	193.4	193.7	2.6	2.8	2.3	2.1	2.7	2.2

[1] Not seasonally adjusted.
[2] Indexes on a December 1997=100 base.
[3] This index series was calculated using a Laspeyres estimator. All other item stratum index series converted to a geometric means estimator in January, 1999.
[4] Indexes on a December 1984=100 base
[5] Indexes on a December 1988=100 base.
NOTE: Index applies to a month as a whole, not to any specific date.

28

Source: CPI Detailed Report, September 1999, p.28.

Figure 30.2: Sample Page from *CPI Detailed Report*.

Consumer Price Index is a monthly press release. It is more current than the *CPI Detailed Report* and contains tables similar to the general tables in that report. It does not, however, contain the more detailed expenditure category tables. The regional and metropolitan area data are limited to the overall, all items consumer price index with no expenditure category data.

The *Consumer Price Indexes Web Page* contains links to the full-text of the *Consumer Price Index* press release and related data files including the most frequently requested consumer price index data series and historical data. Publications about the consumer price index are also included on this page.

The *PPI Detailed Report* contains indexes that measure price changes at the producer or wholesale level. The indexes are given by industry, commodity group, and individual items. Commodity and product coverage is quite detailed. Indexes are available for such items as fresh strawberries, chewing gum, spark plugs, and sofas. The annual supplement contains similar tables showing monthly and annual data for the year.

Producers Price Index is a monthly press release that is available to depository libraries in electronic form only. It is more current than the *PPI Detailed Report* and contains tables similar to the general tables in that report. It does not, however, contain the more detailed industry and commodity tables.

The *Producer Price Indexes Web Page* contains links to the full-text of the *Producer Price Index* press release and related data files, including the most frequently requested producer price index data series. Publications about the consumer price index are also included on this page.

The *STAT-USA Internet* site is divided into two areas: State of the Nation and Globus & NTDB. *STAT-USA Internet* is a fee-based service, but federal depository libraries may register for free access for two workstations. The State of the Nation area contains domestic economic statistical releases. Current versions of the top 50 releases are organized by categories. The current editions of the *Consumer Price Index* and *Producer Price Index* press releases are available under the "General Economic Indicators" category. Additional files, including earlier data, are available in the State of the Nation Library. These files are also arranged by category names, including a "Price & Productivity" category for price index data. A search option for the State of the Nation Library is also available.

The *Handbook of U.S. Labor Statistics* compiles many years of basic price indexes in one convenient source. The "Prices and Living Conditions" section contains producer price indexes by broad commodity group and selected industries. Consumer price indexes are given by broad expenditure category. The regional and metropolitan area data are limited to the overall, all items consumer price index with no expenditure category data.

INDEXES
Checklist

American Statistics Index (ASI). PRINT. (monthly) 1973–. Bethesda, MD: Congressional Information Service.

Statistical Universe. WEB. Bethesda, MD: Congressional Information Service.

Discussion

A comprehensive listing of material can be found in *ASI* by looking under subject terms such as "Business assets and liabilities"; "Business and industry"; "Business income and expenses"; "Business inventories"; "Capital investments"; "Consumer Price Index (CPI)"; "Credit"; "Earnings, general"; "Economic and econometric models"; "Economic Indicators," "Employment and unemployment, general"; "Flow-of-funds accounts"; "Gross Domestic Product"; "Gross National Product"; "Housing costs and financing"; "Housing sales"; "Industrial capacity and utilization"; "Industrial production"; "Industrial production indexes"; "Inflation"; "Job creation"; "Job vacancy"; "Labor productivity"; "Labor turnover"; "Money supply"; "National income and product accounts"; "Personal and household income"; "Personal consumption"; "Prices"; and "Producer Price Index. (PPI)." *Statistical Universe* includes a Web version of *ASI*. (See Chapter 3, "The Basics of Searching," for more information on *ASI*.)

RELATED MATERIAL
Within this Work

GPO Subject Bibliographies. PRINT. WEB. GP 3.22/2:

<http://bookstore.gpo.gov/sb/about.html>

No. 97   "The Economy"

No. 204 "Economic Policy"

CHAPTER 31
Business and Industry Statistics

A large number of business and economic statistics are published by the federal government. This chapter concentrates on describing sources that give statistics on specific types of businesses and industries, such as the automobile industry, dairy industry, or retail clothing stores. Other chapters in this book cover areas of interest to business, such as the chapters on "Economic Indicators," "Foreign Countries," or "Foreign Trade Statistics." For a complete list, see the "Related Material" section at the end of this chapter.

One of the major sources of business data is the U.S. Census Bureau; its *Economic Census* is one of the main components of this chapter. The Census Bureau is prohibited by law from publishing any data that might reveal the identity or activities of any specific firm; thus, all census data are given for an industry as a whole, and small geographic area data may not be available in all cases. Other government agencies' publications may occasionally mention specific companies, but in general the government publishes little information on individual companies. (See the "Individual Company Information" section of this chapter for additional discussion on this topic.)

SEARCH STRATEGY

This chapter shows a statistical search strategy. The suggested steps for locating information on a specific business or industry are

1. Begin with the *U.S. Industry & Trade Outlook* in the "General Business Sources" section to obtain an overview, basic statistics, and references to additional sources;
2. Locate additional general statistics in the titles listed in the "General Statistical Sources" section and in the other titles in the "General Business Sources" section;
3. Find the North American Industry Classification (NAICS) code number(s) relating to the industry as

discussed in the "Industrial Classification Sources" section;
4. Consult the appropriate census as determined from the NAICS chart in Figure 31.2;
5. Consult the current sources or updates that relate to the appropriate census;
6. Try the guides listed under the "Census Guides" section for additional assistance with the census and related publications;
7. Consider titles listed in the "Other Sources," "Selected Industry Reports", and "Individual Company Information" sections of this chapter;
8. Consider any relevant "Related Material"; and
9. Look for other specific industry reports in the indexes listed in the "Indexes" section.

GENERAL STATISTICAL SOURCES
Checklist

Statistical Abstract of the United States. PRINT. WEB. (annual) 1878–. U.S. Department of Commerce. Economics and Statistics Administration. Bureau of the Census. C 3.134: Item 0150. ASI 2324-1. GPO. <http://www.census.gov/statab/www/>; <http://purl.access.gpo.gov/GPO/LPS2878>.

> Coverage: varies; world, world regions, selected countries, U.S., regions, states, selected metropolitan areas.
> Content: chapters on "Banking, Finance and Insurance," "Business Enterprise," "Manufactures," "Domestic Trade and Services," "Communications," "Transportation," and "Industrial Outlook," giving a variety of basic information.

Statistical Abstract of the United States. CD-ROM. (annual) 1993–. U.S. Department of Commerce. Bureau of the Census. C 3.134/7: Item 0150-B. ASI 2324-14.

> Content: CD-ROM version of the *Statistical Abstract*.

Historical Statistics of the United States: Colonial Times to 1970. Parts 1-2. PRINT. (1975) U.S. Department of Commerce. Bureau of the Census. C 3.134/2:H 62/789-970/pt.1-2. Item 0151. ASI (76) 2328-2. GPO.

> Coverage: U.S.
> Content: chapters on "Manufactures," "Business Enterprise," "Distribution and Services," "Financial Markets and Institutions," and other specific areas such as "Minerals," "Transportation," and "Communications," giving pre-1970 basic statistics.

Historical Statistics of the United States on CD-ROM: Colonial Times to 1970. CD-ROM. (1997) New York, NY: Cambridge University Press.

> Content: CD-ROM version of *Historical Statistics of the United States.*

County and City Data Book. PRINT. WEB. (quinquennial) 1947–. U.S. Department of Commerce. Economics and Statistics Administration. Bureau of the Census. C 3.134/2:C 83/2/year. Item 0151. ASI 2328-1. GPO. <http://fisher.lib.Virginia.EDU/ccdb/>.

> Coverage: U.S., regions, divisions, states, counties, cities of 25,000 or more.
> Content: number of establishments, earnings, employees, payroll, value of shipments or sales for manufacturing, retail and wholesale trade, and services; bank deposits and savings.

County and City Data Book. CD-ROM. (quinquennial) 1988–. U.S. Department of Commerce. Bureau of the Census. C 3.134/2-1: (Earlier, C 3.134/2:C 83/2/) Item 0151-D-01. ASI 2328-103.

> Content: CD-ROM version of the *County and City Data Book.*

County and City Extra: Annual Metro, City, and County Data Book. PRINT. (annual) 1992–. Lanham, MD: Bernan Press.

> Coverage: U.S., states, counties, metropolitan areas, cities of 25,000 or more.
> Content: updated version of the *County and City Data Book.*

Places, Towns, and Townships. PRINT. (irregular) 1993–. Lanham, MD: Bernan Press.

> Coverage: incorporated places of 2,500 or more.
> Content: number of establishments, employees, payroll, value of shipments or sales for manufacturing, retail and wholesale trade, and services.

State and Metropolitan Area Data Book. PRINT. WEB. (irregular) 1979–. U.S. Department of Commerce. Economics and Statistics Administration. Bureau of the Census. C 3.134/5: Item 0150. ASI 2328-54. GPO. <http://www.census.gov/statab/www.smadb.html>.

> Coverage: U.S., states, metropolitan areas, central cities of metropolitan areas, component counties of metropolitan areas.
> Content: number of establishments, earnings, employees, payroll, value of shipments or sales for each economic sector; bank assets and deposits; women and minority-owned firms; business failures and starts.

State and Metropolitan Area Data Book. CD-ROM. (irregular) 1997/98–. U.S. Department of Commerce. Economics and Statistics Administration. Bureau of the Census. (Not distributed to depository libraries)

> Content: CD-ROM version of the *State and Metropolitan Area Data Book.*

USA Counties. CD-ROM. WEB. (irregular) 1992–. U.S. Department of Commerce. Economics and Statistics Administration. Bureau of the Census. C 3.134/6: Item 0150-B-01. ASI 2324-17. <http://govinfo.kerr.orst.edu/usaco-stateis.html>; <http://tier2.census.gov/usac/index.html-ssi>.

> Coverage: U.S., states, counties.
> Content: time series data for number of establishments, earnings, employees, payroll, value of shipments or sales for each economic sector and for selected types of business in the retail trade and services sectors.

Discussion

The *Statistical Abstract of the United States* contains basic statistics on many businesses, industries, and products. Checking the index under subjects beginning with "Apparel," for instance, provides references to manufacturing data (earnings, employees, shipments), retail stores data (establishments, earnings, employees, sales), and other items such as foreign trade and consumer expenditures. The majority of data is for the United States as a whole.

Statistics are compiled from many of the more detailed sources covered later in this chapter. Source notes at the end of each table can direct the user to more current or more detailed sources for the information in that table. The full text of recent editions of the *Statistical Abstract* is available on the Census Bureau Web site as PDF files. The *Statistical Abstract* is also available on CD-ROM. The CD uses Adobe Acrobat software and contains some additional geographic areas and time series in the form of spreadsheet files that are not in the printed version. *Historical Statistics of the United States* provides similar data for years before 1970. A CD-ROM version of *Historical Statistics* is available from Cambridge University Press.

County and City Data Book and *State and Metropolitan Area Data Book* concentrate on smaller geographic areas but give less specific information. The *County and City Data Book* gives data for economic sectors as a whole, such as manufacturing or retail trade, rather than for individual industries or businesses. The *State and Metropolitan Area Data Book* includes similar information at the state level, plus some additional information by business types for the retail trade and services categories. The metropolitan data give sector totals only for a smaller number of variables (number of establishments, employment, and earnings) and cover a smaller number of sectors. The *County and City Data Book* is also available in CD-ROM from the Census Bureau. The University of Virginia Library Geospatial and Statistical Data Center offers recent editions of the *County and City Data Book* on the Internet in their interactive data area. Users select the desired edition, geography, and variables to create a customized data display. The *State and Metropolitan Area Data Book* is available as a PDF file on the Census Bureau Web site and on CD-ROM.

County and City Extra is a commercially produced annual version of the *County and City Data Book*. The business data are similar to that in the *County and City Data Book* with a small number of additional data items. *Places, Towns, and Townships* provides similar data for cities.

The *USA Counties* CD-ROM contains county and state data from the last two or three issues of the *County and City Data Book* and the *State and Metropolitan Area Data Book* to provide several years of data in one source. The data are similar to that found in the two data books. The Oregon State University Government Information Sharing Project provides access to the current issue on the Internet. Users select a geographic area profile or an area comparison and then the desired geography. A subject area can then be selected or a keyword search conducted to display data. The Census Bureau Web site contains a similar version.

GENERAL BUSINESS SOURCES
Checklist

U.S. Industry & Trade Outlook. PRINT. CD-ROM. (annual) 1998–. The McGraw-Hill Companies and U.S. Department of Commerce. International Trade Administration. C 61.48: (Earlier, C 61.34:, C 62.17:; C 57.18:) (Continuation of *U.S. Industrial Outlook* issued by the International Trade Administration, 1960-1994) Item 0215-L-08. NTIS.

> Coverage: U.S.
> Content: economic and trade review and outlook for industries; statistical tables and charts on trends, forecasts, and trade; references to additional sources of information.

Survey of Current Business. PRINT. WEB. (monthly) 1921–. U.S. Department of Commerce. Bureau of Economic Analysis. C 59.11: Item 0228. ASI 2702-1. GPO. <http://www.bea.doc.gov/bea/pubs.htm>; <http://purl.access.gpo.gov/GPO/LPS1730>.

> Coverage: world regions, country groupings, selected countries, U.S., divisions, states.
> Content: gross domestic product; compensation; employment; exports and imports; business inventories and sales; corporate profits; U.S. and foreign direct investment and affiliates; gross state product.

Survey of Current Business. CD-ROM. (annual) 1994–. U.S. Department of Commerce. Economics and Statistics Administration. Bureau of Economic Analysis. C 59.11/1: Item 0228-A. GPO.

> Content: CD-ROM version of *Survey of Current Business*.

Business Statistics of the United States. PRINT. (annual) 1995–. Lanham, MD: Bernan Press. (Continuation of *Business Statistics* published by the Bureau of Economic Analysis, 1951-1991, C 59.11/3:)

> Coverage: U.S.
> Content: economic and industry time series data; industry data on production, capacity utilization, shipments, inventories, orders, producer prices, employment, hours, earnings, sales.

STAT-USA Internet. WEB. U.S. Department of Commerce. C 1.91: Item 0128-P. <http://www.stat-usa.gov/>.

> Coverage: countries, U.S., regions, divisions, states, metropolitan areas.
> Content: economic and industry statistics; sales, shipments, inventories, orders, production, capacity utilization, financial data, international market research reports.

National Trade Data Bank: The Export Connection. WEB. CD-ROM. (monthly) Oct. 1990–. U.S. Department of Commerce. STAT-USA. C 1.88: (Depository distribution of CD-ROM discontinued with Oct. 2000 disc) Item 0128-L. ASI 2002-6. <http://www.stat-usa.gov/tradtest.nsf>; <http://purl.access.gpo.gov/GPO/LPS1777>.

> Coverage: countries, U.S.
> Content: international trade resources; international marketing research reports.

Discussion

These sources all provide basic business and industry statistics. The most valuable and most specific of these sources is the *U.S. Industry & Trade Outlook*. When gathering data on a specific industry, this source is a good starting point. Each chapter covers a major industry group such as "Chemicals and Allied Products" or "Computer Software and Networking." Chapters begin with an industry definition followed by an overview of the industry and sections on selected sub-industries within the group. Industry discussions vary depending on the nature of the industry, but generally cover global and domestic trends, international trade, outlook, and future prospects. Chapters often conclude with a list of selected references for additional information. A "Trends and Forecasts" table gives value of shipments or sales, employment, and trade information. Most chapters also have a trade patterns table showing trade with top regions and countries. A page of graphs at the beginning of each chapter usually shows U.S. international trade; world export market share; export dependence and import penetration; and output and output per worker. Graphs may vary depending on the industry. A CD-ROM version is also available for purchase, although not available through the depository library program.

The *Survey of Current Business* contains National Income and Product Accounts (NIPA) statistics on the nation's economic activity. NIPA statistics cover the Gross Domestic Product (GDP) and its components and the distribution of national income. Each issue of the *Survey of Current Business* contains a section called "BEA Current and Historical Data" that presents selected economic statistics. Much of the data for industry is given by broad sectors, such as manufacturing or retail trade. More specific industry categories are given for gross domestic product, compensation, and employment. Data are primarily for the United States. Trade data include some world region and country data. State data are limited to gross state product information. More extensive annual NIPA data appear in the August issue. Articles provide more detailed analyses and updates on specific topics. Each issue contains a regular feature called "Business Situation" which briefly describes the current trends in the GDP and corporate profits. A quarterly report, "Real Inventories, Sales, and Inventory Sales Ratios for Manufacturing and Trade," gives statistics on inventories and sales by industry sector. Examples of other recent articles relating to industry include "U.S. Multinational Companies: Operations in 1996" (Vol. 78, No. 9), "Motor Vehicles, Model Year 1998" (Vol. 78, No. 11), and "Manufacturing Earnings in BEA Component Economic Areas, 1996" (Vol. 78, No. 11). Recent issues of the *Survey of Current Business* are also available from the Bureau of Economic Analysis Web site and from the *STAT-USA* Web site. The BEA site lists recent months with links to the full text of articles and tables. Files are a combination of PDF and HTML. Subject guides are available for years since 1995. *STAT-USA* lists articles for recent months. The articles are available as PDF files. Articles can also be retrieved through the search feature in the State of the Nation Library area. A CD-ROM version contains PDF files for the year with selected previous articles dating from 1987.

Business Statistics of the United States contains a wide range of economic and industry statistics compiled from government sources, as well as from some private sources. Part I contains general economic statistics with sections on such areas as gross domestic product and cyclical indicators; consumer income and spending; and U.S. foreign trade and finance. Some sections in this part include breakdowns by industry: industrial production and capacity utilization; business sales, inventories and investment; prices; employment costs, productivity and profits; and employment, hours and earnings. Part II is arranged by industry group and provides several years of data for each industry. The type of data varies slightly from industry to industry, reflecting what is most appropriate for that industry. Construction data, for example, include housing starts and building permits issued. Data are given monthly for recent years and annually for many years. Part III contains additional historical data for selected series. A notes section provides information on sources of data, definitions, revisions, availability, and references for additional information.

STAT-USA Internet is a fee-based service, but federal depository libraries may register for free access for two workstations. The *STAT-USA Internet* site is divided into two areas: State of the Nation and Globus & NTDB. The State of the Nation area contains domestic economic statistical releases. Current versions of the top 50 releases are organized by the following categories: General Economic Indicators; Housing and Construction; Employment; Manufacturing and Industry; Monetary Statistics; and Economic Policy. The releases in the Manufacturing and Industry section contain United States statistics on retail sales; wholesale sales; manufacturer's shipments, inventories, and orders; industrial production and capacity utilization; and financial data. Additional files, includ-

ing earlier data, are available in the State of the Nation Library. These files are also arranged by categories such as Industry Statistics, Regional Economic Stats, and Survey of Current Business. A search option for the State of the Nation Library is also available. The Globus & NTDB area emphasizes trade statistics and international market research. Market research reports analyze international trends for selected industries and countries.

The *National Trade Data Bank* is available as part of the *STAT-USA Internet* site. A CD-ROM is also produced but not distributed to depository libraries after Oct. 2000. It contains publications and statistics related to international trade and international marketing research reports for selected industries in relation to specific countries.

INDUSTRIAL CLASSIFICATION SOURCES
Checklist

North American Industry Classification System United States, 1997. PRINT. CD-ROM. (1998) U.S. Executive Office of the President. Office of Management and Budget. PREX 2.6/2:IN 27/997 and /CLOTH. Item 0854-A. ASI 108-4. GPO. NTIS. Lanham, MD: Bernan Press.
  Content: industry classification system and industry definitions.

North American Industry Classification System (NAICS) Web Page. WEB. U.S. Census Bureau. <http://www.census.gov/epcd/www/naics.html>.
  Content: background, updates, NAICS search, NAICS and SIC correspondence tables, implementation schedules, products, effect on users.

Standard Industrial Classification Manual 1987. (1987) U.S. Executive Office of the President. Office of Management and Budget. PREX 2.6/2:IN 27/987. Item 0854-A. ASI (87) 108-4. GPO. <http://www.osha.gov/oshstats/sicser.html>; <http://www.lib.virginia.edu/socsci/sic.html>.
  Content: industry classification system and industry definitions.

Numerical List of Manufactured and Mineral Products. PRINT. WEB. (quinquennial) 1958–. U.S. Department of Commerce. Economics and Statistics Administration. Bureau of the Census. C 3.24/2:P 94/5/. (Title varies) Item 0135. ASI 2628-10. <http://www.census.gov/prod/ec97/97numlist/97numlist.html>; <http://www.census.gov/prod/www/abs/manu-min.html#mm>.
  Content: product codes used in the *Economic Census* and *Current Industrial Reports* for the manufacturing and mineral sectors.

Discussion

The *North American Industry Classification System United States, 1997* (NAICS) is the official economic classification system used for collecting and reporting Federal industry statistics. Many government statistical reports with industry data, especially Census Bureau reports, are arranged by the NAICS system. The system is also used by businesses, commercial publishers, and other organizations. NAICS uses a six-digit code to classify establishments by type of economic activity. Industries are first grouped into 20 broad sectors, such as manufacturing; retail trade; accommodation and food services; and health care and social assistance. Each sector is assigned a two-digit code number. Sectors are further subdivided into subsectors (addition of a third digit), industry group (fourth digit), industry (fifth digit), and U.S. industry (sixth digit). Part I of the *North American Industry Classification System* outlines this numerical hierarchy with definitions of each sector, subsector, and industry. In some cases the definition includes illustrative examples of industries fitting the definition. Cross-references to related classifications are also provided. Part II is a condensed numerical listing with short industry titles. Part III contains appendices that match the NAICS classification system to the previously used Standard Industrial Classification System (SIC) and vice versa. Part IV is an alphabetical index.

The *North American Industry Classification System (NAICS) Web Page* provides background and information on NAICS. A "NAICS Search" box searches the *North American Industry Classification System* by keyword, NAICS number, or SIC number. Search results include NAICS industry definitions, corresponding SIC (or NAICS) numbers, and links to basic data tables from the *Economic Census*. A separate "NAICS to SIC/SIC to NAICS" menu box is also available. This provides conversion information in tabular form. Information is also available on the development of NAICS, how it will affect users, and agency implementation schedules.

The *Standard Industrial Classification Manual* defines and outlines the SIC system, the classification system used prior to the implementation of NAICS. The SIC system uses a four-digit code to classify establishments.

The Census Bureau has developed a product classification code based directly on the NAICS code (or SIC code in earlier years) to allow for the collection and reporting of more detailed product information. This code expands the six-digit NAICS industry code to a ten-digit number for product. The *Numerical List of Manufactured and Mineral Products*, issued with each new economic census, is a list of these product codes. The list is arranged by industry group (NAICS subsectors). For each specific product code, information is given on the type of data collected (such as value of shipments) and any related *Current Industrial Reports* series numbers. Appendices list *Current Industrial Reports* series, product codes included in selected *Current Industrial Reports*, and product code comparability between the current and previous *Economic Census*.

The *Economic Census* parallels the broad industry sectors of the NAICS code, with reports issued for each sector. Figure 31.2 shows the NAICS numbers for each sector. Some industry areas are not covered in the census. Using this chart, one can quickly determine which sector reports to use for any given NAICS industry code.

ECONOMIC CENSUS
Checklist

Economic Census. PRINT. WEB. (quinquennial) 1997–. U.S. Department of Commerce. Economics and Statistics Administration. Census Bureau. (Formerly published as individual censuses for specific economic sectors.) ASI 2311, 2355, 2373, 2390, 2397, 2405, 2451, 2493, 2513, 2573, 2575, 2597, 2605, 2615, 2635, 2645, 2665, 2685. <http://www.census.gov/epcd/www/econ97.html>; <http://www.census.gov/mp/www/pub/ind/msind.html#Industry>; <http://www.census.gov/prod/www/abs/economic.html>.

> Coverage: varies by sector; U.S., states, counties, metropolitan areas, places of 2,500 or more, zip codes.
> Content: number of establishments; number of employees; payroll; sales, receipts or value of shipments/construction work done; some sectors also contain data on expenses, capital expenditures, assets, and inventories.

Economic Census. CD-ROM. (quinquennial) 1987–. U.S. Department of Commerce. Economics and Statistics Administration. Bureau of the Census. C 3.277: Item 0154-C.

> Coverage: U.S., states, counties, metropolitan areas, places of 2,500 or more, zip codes.
> Content: *Economic Census* reports.

American FactFinder. WEB. U.S. Department of Commerce. Bureau of the Census. <http://factfinder.census.gov/java_prod/dads.ui.homePage.HomePage>.

> Coverage: U.S., states, counties, metropolitan areas, places.
> Content: 1997 *Economic Census* data; other census products.

Discussion

The *Economic Census* is taken every five years covering years ending in "2" and in "7." The data are collected in the year following the year of coverage (the 1997 census was conducted in 1998) and data may begin to appear in the year following that. It may take as long as three years after the census year for all publications and information to be made available. Data from the *Economic Census* are used by businesses, governments, researchers, and students to measure potential markets, gauge the general economic situation, measure trends, analyze sales, calculate and compare business costs, study the feasibility of a new business, and to plan store or plant locations.

The *Economic Census* answers questions such as the number of companies in a particular line of business or manufacturing field and their geographic locations; sales or value of shipments; and financial and operating statistics. An outline of the basic information items in the 1997 *Economic Census* is shown in Figure 31.1. Explanations and definitions are included in the introduction to each report and in appendices.

The exact content and component publications of the *Economic Census* have varied over the years. The descriptions in this chapter are based on a combination of early reports and pre-publication information for the 1997 *Eco-*

Table 4.
Major Data Items Published in the 1997 Economic Census

(Legend: ● All areas (see Table 3), except ZIP Codes; Z ZIP and States; M MAs, states, and National; S States and Natic N National only; e National data only in Business Expenses[1]

	Manu-facturing	Mining	Con-struction	Retail Trade	Whole-sale Trade	Management of companies	All other sectors
NUMBER OF ESTABLISHMENTS AND FIRMS							
Establishments with payroll	●,Z	S	S	●,Z	●	●	●,Z
Establishments without payroll (nonemployers)			S	S			S
Single-unit and multi-unit establishments	N	N	N	N	N	N	N
Establishments by legal form of organization	N	N	N	N	N	N	N
Firms	N	N		N	N	N	N
EMPLOYMENT							
All employees	●	S	S	●	●	●	●
Production (construction) workers/hours	●	S	S				
Employment size of establishment	●,Z	N	S	N,Z	N	N	N,Z[2]
LABOR COSTS							
Payroll, entire year	●	S	S	●	●	●	●
Payroll, first-quarter				●	●	●	●
Worker wages	●	S	S				
Supplemental costs	S	S	S	e	e	e	e
Cost of contract labor				e	e	e	e
SALES, RECEIPTS, VALUE OF SHIPMENTS, OR VALUE OF CONSTRUCTION WORK DONE							
Establishments with payroll	●	S	S	●	●	●	●
By specific product, line, or type of construction	S	S	S	M	M[3]		S[2]
Sales/receipts size of establishment			S	N,Z	N		N,Z[2]
Class of customer				N	N		N
Type of structure			N				
EXPENSES							
Total						N	N
Cost of materials, etc	●	S	S		e	e	e
Cost of fuels	S	S					
Energy consumed	S	S					
Cost of electricity	S	S	S		e	e	e
Cost of other utilities					e	e	e
Products bought for resale		S	S			e	
Taxes and license fees					e	e	e
Cost of office supplies					e	e	e
Depreciation charges	S	S			e	e	e
Commission expense					e		
Purchased services:							
Advertising	N				e	e	e
Rental payments	S	S	S		e	e	e
Legal services	N				e	e	e
Accounting services	N				e	e	e
Data processing services	N				e	e	e
Refuse removal	N						
Communications services	N	S	S		e	e	e
Purchased repairs	N	S	S		e	e	e
Cost of contract work	S	S			e		
ASSETS, CAPITAL EXPENDITURES, INVENTORIES							
Capital expenditures, total	S	S	S				
Depreciable assets, gross value	S	S	S				
Value of inventories	S	S	S	e	●		

[1] The Business Expenses report covers auxiliary establishments classified in manufacturing, mining, and construction under the old SIC; and all establishments in retail and wholesale trade and service industries, also as defined under the old SIC.

[2] National data only for utilities, trucking and warehousing, finance and insurance, and real estate and rental and leasing.
[3] 15 selected states and 15 selected metro areas only.

Source: *Preview to the 1997 Economic Census,* p. 6-7.

Figure 31.1: Major Data Items in the 1997 Economic Census.

nomic Census. Major changes took place beginning with the 1997 *Economic Census* both in organization and in publishing formats. The implementation of the NAICS classification system reorganized and increased industry coverage resulting in data being published for 18 economic sectors. (See Figure 31.2.) The previous economic census for 1992, based on the SIC classification system, was organized into eight sectors. (The agriculture sector is partially covered by the *Census of Agriculture* discussed in Chapter 18, Agriculture). Also beginning with 1997, data are published almost entirely on the Internet and on CD-ROM with only a small number of summary publications published in print format.

Data series are published for each economic sector. All sectors have a geographic area series (statistics by state and smaller geographic units if applicable) and a subject series. The manufacturing, mining, and construction sectors also have an industry series. Zip code statistics are available for selected sectors. Reports are available on the Census Web site as PDF files or through the *American FactFinder* database and on CD-ROM. One summary report for each sector will be issued in print format. A small

Table 2.
**NAICS Sectors and Their Coverage
in the 1997 Economic Census**

NAICS codes	Economic Sector
11	**Agriculture, Forestry, Fishing, and Hunting** (Separate census of agriculture, conducted by the Department of Agriculture, covers farming but excludes agricultural services, forestry, and fisheries)
21	**Mining**
22	**Utilities**
23	**Construction**
31-33	**Manufacturing**
42	**Wholesale Trade**
44-45	**Retail Trade**
48-49	**Transportation and Warehousing** (Census excludes U.S. Postal Service, large certificated passenger air transportation, and all rail transportation)
51	**Information**
52	**Finance and Insurance** (Census excludes funds and trusts)
53	**Real Estate and Rental and Leasing**
54	**Professional, Scientific, and Technical Services** (Census excludes landscape architecture and veterinary services)
55	**Management of Companies and Enterprises**
56	**Administrative and Support, Waste Management, and Remediation Services** (Census excludes landscaping services)
61	**Educational Services** (Census excludes elementary and secondary schools, colleges, and professional schools)
62	**Health Care and Social Assistance**
71	**Arts, Entertainment, and Recreation**
72	**Accommodation and Foodservices**
81	**Other Services (Except Public Administration)** (Census excludes pet care; labor, political, and religious organization; and private households)
92	**Public Administration** (Separate census of governments does not present data according to NAICS or SIC systems)

Source: Preview to the 1997 Economic Census, p. 3.

Figure 31.2: NAICS Sectors and Their Coverage in the 1997 Economic Census.

number of economy-wide reports will also be issued, including a comparative statistics report and bridge tables between SIC and NAICS.

The geographic area reports are available for all sectors and contain general statistics on the number of establishments, sales or other revenue measure, payroll, and employment by kind of business or NAICS code. This series gives United States totals, as well as data on the smallest geographic areas available. For several sectors this includes states, metropolitan areas, counties, and places of 2,500 or more. A few sectors have state and metropoli-

tan area data only; mining, construction, and management of companies and enterprises have state data only.

Subject series reports are also issued for all sectors, although the reports vary from sector to sector. Subject reports most frequently issued are on revenue lines or sources of receipts, establishment and firm size, and miscellaneous subjects. A merchandise line sales report for retail trade and a commodity line sales report for wholesale trade give information on general product lines sold by type of business. Mining and manufacturing have a subject report on materials consumed. Subject reports contain primarily national data, with some limited state and metropolitan area data.

The industry series reports issued for mining, manufacturing, and construction give detailed industry statistics, product shipments by detailed product code, and materials consumed. Industry series reports give national and state data.

Zip code statistics published for several sectors give data on number of establishments by employment size and sometimes by size of sales or receipts. Data are given by state and five-digit zip code.

The Census Bureau's *Economic Census* Web page lists reports from the 1997 census with links to the full text as they are released. A link is also available for the 1992 reports. General information about the *Census* is also available, including the *Guide to the 1997 Economic Census*.

American FactFinder is a Census Bureau Web database designed to provide access to data from the 1990 and 2000 *Census of Population and Housing*, the *American Community Survey*, and the 1997 *Economic Census*. It also contains a mapping feature and an option to search for information on Census Bureau products. 1997 *Economic Census* data are available in the "Industry and Business Facts" section as it is released. The Industry Quick Reports option allows the user to select from a list of NAICS sectors and code numbers or to search by word to identify and display a basic industry report. The industry reports show number of establishments, number of employees, annual payroll, and shipments/sales/receipts by state. Similarly, the Geography Quick Reports option can be used to display a geographic area report. The geographic report shows similar data items to the industry report for all industries at the two-digit NAICS sector level for the selected area. A "Build a Query" option is also available. This option allows the user to search for or select specific data sets for display.

CENSUS GUIDES

Checklist

Product Catalog. WEB. U.S. Census Bureau. C 3.163/3: Item 0138. <http://www.census.gov/mp/www/censtore.html>.
    Content: descriptions and prices of Census Bureau products.

Census Catalog and Guide. CD-ROM. WEB. (annual) 1946–. U.S. Department of Commerce. Economics and Statistics Administration. Census Bureau. (CD-ROM not distributed to depository libraries) (Issued in print through 1998 under C 3.163/3:, Item 0138) (Title varies) <http://www.census.gov/mp/www/censtore.html>; <http://www.census.gov/prod/www/abs/catalogs.html>; <http://purl.access.gpo.gov/GPO/LPS3138>.

  Content: CD-ROM version of the Web *Product Catalog.*

Bureau of the Census Catalog of Publications 1790–1972. PRINT. (1974) U.S. Department of Commerce. Social and Economic Statistics Administration. Bureau of the Census. C 56.222/2-2:790-972. ASI (75) 2308-1.

  Content: complete listing of publications in each census as well as all other Census Bureau publications, with histories and descriptions.

Monthly Product Announcement. PRINT. WEB. (monthly) U.S. Department of Commerce. Economics and Statistics Administration. Census Bureau. C 3.163/7: Item 0138-A-02. ASI 2302-6. <http://www.census.gov/mp/www/mpa.html#MPA>; <http://purl.access.gpo.gov/GPO/LPS1680>.

  Content: new products issued each month.

Guide to the 1997 Economic Census. WEB. U.S. Census Bureau. <http://www.census.gov/epcd/www/guide.html>.

  Content: publication schedule, reports available, industry classification, geography, content, types of reports.

Discussion

Some of the Census Bureau guides that are of help in using the *Economic Census* and related census publications are listed above.

  The Census Bureau *Product Catalog* describes agency products and provides availability and ordering information. Products are listed by format and then by subject category or series. Individual title descriptions include prices, ordering information, formats, subject content, geographic coverage, and links to online data. The *Census Catalog and Guide* on CD-ROM contains the Web *Product Catalog* as of the specified date. The *Monthly Product Announcement* serves as an update to the catalog. It lists, but does not describe, publications released during the previous month. The cumulative catalog, *Bureau of the Census Catalog of Publications 1790–1972*, is a thorough historical guide to censuses and publication series.

  The *Guide to the 1997 Economic Census* describes the reports issued and gives general information on the NAICS industry classification system, geographic coverage, data content, and publication formats. The *Guide* includes a chart of data items contained in the census with associated geographic coverage arranged by sector; descriptions of publication series; lists of reports by sector, with geographic coverage, format, and publication schedule; and a list of reports that have been issued by series with links to the full text.

CURRENT CENSUS SOURCES
Checklist

County Business Patterns. WEB. (annual) 1946–. U.S. Department of Commerce. Economics and Statistics Administration. Bureau of the Census. C 3.204/3-(nos.): (Earlier, C 3.204:). (Print discontinued after 1997 issues) Item 0133-A-01 to 53. ASI 2326-6, -8. GPO. <http://www.census.gov/epcd/cbp/view/cbpview.html>; <http://purl.access.gpo.gov/GPO/LPS2877>; <http://tier2.census. gov/cbp/cbp_sts.htm>; <http://www.census.gov/mp/www/pub/bus/msbus28.html>; <http://www.census.gov/prod/www/abs/cbptotal.html>; <http://purl.access.gpo.gov/GPO/LPS547>; <http://fisher.lib.virginia.edu/cbp/home.html>.

  Coverage: U.S., states, counties.
  Content: number of establishments, employees, and payroll by industry and by employment-size class.

County Business Patterns. CD-ROM. (annual) U.S. Department of Commerce. Bureau of the Census. C 3.204/4: Item 0133-E.

  Content: CD-ROM version of *County Business Patterns.*

Zip Code Business Patterns. WEB. CD-ROM. U.S. Department of Commerce. Bureau of the Census. C 3.298: Item 0154-B-13. <http://tier2.census.gov/zbp/zbp.htm>.

  Coverage: zip codes.
  Content: total number of establishments, employees, and payroll; specific industry data limited to number of establishments and establishments by employment-size class.

Annual Survey of Manufactures. PRINT. WEB. (annual) 1949–. U.S. Department of Commerce. Economics and Statistics Administration. Bureau of the Census. C 3.24/9-[no.] (Earlier, C 3.24/9:; C 3.24/9-2:). Item 0134-A. ASI 2506-14, -15. GPO. <http://www.census.gov/econ/www/manumenu.html>; <http://tier2.census.gov/asm/asm.htm>; <http://purl.access.gpo.gov/GPO/LPS2593>; <http://www.census.gov/mp/www/pub/mfg/msmfg.html#mas>; <http://www.census.gov/prod/www/abs/manu-min.html#mm>.

  Coverage: U.S., states.
  Content: number of establishments, employees, payroll, production workers, hours, value added by manufacture, cost of materials, value of shipments, capital expenditures, inventories, labor costs, and fuels and electric energy used by industry.

Current Industrial Reports. WEB. (frequencies and dates vary) U.S. Department of Commerce. Economics and Statistics Administration. Bureau of the Census. C 3.158: Item 0142-A. ASI 2506-3 through -12. GPO. <http://www.census.gov/econ/www/manumenu.html>; <http://purl.access.gpo.gov/GPO/LPS2593>; <http://www.census.gov/econ/www/ind_num.html>.

  Coverage: varies; U.S., regions, divisions, selected states.
  Content: series of more than 60 reports on industries in the following major groups: food products; textiles, apparel and footwear; building materials; chemicals and related products; glass products; primary metals; electronics; consumer durables; industrial equipment, heavy machinery; and aerospace; data on production, shipments, consumption, inventories, orders, and trade for products.

Current Industrial Reports Manufacturing Profiles. PRINT. WEB. (annual) 1992–. U.S. Department of Commerce. Economics and Statistics Administration. Bureau of the Census. C 3.158/

4: Item 0142-A-01. ASI 2504-2. <http://www.census.gov/econ/www/manumenu.html>; <http://purl.access.gpo.gov/GPO/LPS2593>; <http://www.census.gov/prod/www/abs/mfg-prof.html>.

  Coverage: U.S., regions, divisions, selected states.
  Content: annual compilation of individual *Current Industrial Reports*.

Current Business Reports. U.S. Department of Commerce. Economics and Statistics Administration. Bureau of the Census.

Monthly Retail Trade Survey. WEB. (monthly) 1952-. C 3.138/3: (Title varies. Earlier print title, *Monthly Retail Trade Sales and Inventories*). Item 0147-B. <http://www.census.gov/mrts/www/mrts.html>; <http://purl.access.gpo.gov/GPO/LPS1684>; <http://www.census.gov/mp/www/pub/bus/msbus19b.html>.

  Coverage: U.S.
  Content: retail sales by kind of business, percent change in sales, inventories, inventories/sales ratios.

Annual Benchmark Report for Retail Trade. PRINT. WEB. (annual) 1987/96-. U.S. Department of Commerce. Economics and Statistics Administration. Bureau of the Census. C 3.138/3-8: (Earlier, C 3.138/3-7; title varies) Item 0147-B-02. ASI 2413-5. <http://www.census.gov/prod/www/abs/br_month.html>; <http://www.census.gov/mp/www/pub/bus/msbus19c.html>.

  Coverage: U.S.
  Content: retail sales by kind of business, inventories, sales/inventories ratios, purchases, gross margin, gross margin as percent of sales, accounts receivable by type of account, per capita sales.

Monthly Wholesale Trade Sales and Inventories. WEB. (monthly) 1936-. C 3.133: (Title varies). Item 0147-C. ASI 2413-7. GPO. <http://www.census.gov/svsd/www/mwts.html>; <http://purl.access.gpo.gov/GPO/LPS1531>; <http://www.census. gov/econ/www/retmenu.html#WHOL>; <http://www. census.gov/mp/www/pub/bus/msbus21a.html>; <http://www.census.gov/prod/www/abs/bw_month.html>.

  Coverage: U.S.
  Content: sales, inventories, and inventories/sales ratios of merchant wholesalers by kind of business; percent change in sales and inventories.

Annual Benchmark Report for Wholesale Trade. PRINT. WEB. (annual) 1987/97-. C 3.133/5: (Earlier, C 3.133/4:; title varies) Item 0147-C-01. ASI 2413-13. <http://www.census.gov/svsd/www/mwts.html>; <http://purl.access.gpo.gov/GPO/LPS1531>; <http://www.census.gov/econ/www/retmenu.html#WHOL>; <http://www.census.gov/prod/www/abs/bw_month.html>; <http://www.census.gov/mp/www/pub/bus/msbus21c.html>; <http://purl.access.gpo.gov/GPO/LPS3283>.

  Coverage: U.S.
  Content: sales, inventories, inventories/sales ratios, purchases, gross margins, and gross margins/sales ratios by kind of business.

Service Annual Survey. WEB. (annual) 1982-. C 3.138/3-4: Item 0147-B. ASI 2413-8. <http://www.census.gov/prod/www/abs/services.html>; <http://purl.access.gpo.gov/GPO/LPS3288>; <http://www.census.gov/pub/svsd/www/sas.html>; <http://purl.access.gpo.gov/GPO/LPS3529>;

<http://www.census.gov/ftp/pub/mp/www/pub/bus/msbus25.html>.

  Coverage: U.S.
  Content: receipts, percent change, expenses for selected service industries; source of receipts and per capita receipts for some industries; some data given by taxable and tax-exempt firms.

Annual Survey of Communication Services. WEB. (annual) 1990-. C 3.138/3-6: Item 0147-B. ASI 2413-15. GPO. <http://www.census.gov/svsd/www/ascs.html>; <http://purl. access.gpo.gov/GPO/LPS3285>; <http://www. census.gov/prod/www/abs/comm-ser.html>; <http://www.census.gov/mp/www/pub/bus/msbus24.html>; <http://www.census.gov/econ/www/servmenu.html>.

  Coverage: U.S.
  Content: revenue and expenses for telephone, television, radio, and other communications services.

Annual Transportation Survey. WEB. (annual) 1985-. C 3.138/3-5: (Earlier title, *Motor Freight Transportation and Warehousing Survey*) Item 0147-B-01. ASI 2413-14. <http://www.census.gov/pub/svsd/www/tas.html>; <http://purl.access.gpo.gov/GPO/LPS3293>; <http://www.census.gov/econ/www/servmenu.html>; <http://www.census.gov/mp/www/pub/bus/msbus26x.html>.

  Coverage: U.S.
  Content: trucking and courier services operating revenue and operating expense components by type of carrier; size of shipments, and commodities handled; truck inventories; public warehousing revenue and operating expenses.

Discussion

These sources all supplement the *Economic Census*, giving more current, although less detailed, data. They give basic statistics on particular businesses and industries.

County Business Patterns covers most areas of economic activity. The industry groups covered are agricultural services; forestry and fishing; mining; construction; manufacturing; transportation and public utilities; wholesale trade; retail trade; finance, insurance, real estate; and services. Information on the total number of establishments, number of establishments by employment size, number of employees, and payroll is given by industries. Industries are arranged by SIC number through 1997 and by NAICS number beginning with 1998. For each year, there is a U.S. summary report and reports for each state that give state and county data. This title is available on the Internet for recent years (PDF, spreadsheet, and searchable formats) and on CD-ROM. A zip code version is also available as a searchable database on the Internet and on CD-ROM.

The *Annual Survey of Manufactures* and *Current Industrial Reports* update some of the statistics in the *Economic Census* for the manufacturing sector. The *Annual Survey* presently consists of three regular reports each year. (The number of reports per year has decreased over the years). The three reports are *Statistics for Industry Groups and Industries* (C 3.24/9-7:), *Value of Product Shipments*

(C 3.24/9-6:), and *Geographic Area Statistics* (C 3.24/9-9:). The first two reports give national statistics, while the *Geographic Area Statistics* report gives state statistics. The *Annual Survey* contains data very similar to the data found in the *Economic Census* for the manufacturing sector and is issued for every year in which there is no census.

The *Current Industrial Reports* series consists of individual reports on selected manufacturing industries. Beginning with 1993 these reports have been published online with a less current annual compilation, *Current Industrial Reports Manufacturing Profiles*, available in print. Each report has a series number beginning with M (for manufactures) and a letter designating the frequency of the report. MA is an annual report, MQ is quarterly, and M alone is monthly. The number following the letters is based on the SIC number. MA20D, for example, indicates an annual report covering selected products in SIC major group 20. Reports are now also assigned a NAICS series code. Series MA20D is also MA311D. Many reports give data by product codes. The complete product code list and a correlation to *Current Industrial Reports* series can be found in the *Numerical List of Manufactured and Mineral Products* discussed under "Industrial Classification Sources" above. A list of *Current Industrial Reports* can also be found in this title (Figure 31.3) and in an appendix of the *Annual Survey of Manufactures* report, *Value of Product Shipments*. The Census Bureau Web site provides a list of reports by report number and by subject with links to the full text of recent issues. The information in each report varies but is most frequently on the quantity and value of shipments, production, consumption, stocks, and trade. Most data are for the United States; a few reports include other geographic areas.

A small number of general purpose reports are also issued in the *Current Industrial Reports* series, most notably *Manufacturers' Shipments, Inventories, and Orders* (M3-1), which covers all manufacturing industry groups. This title continues to be published monthly in print format along with multi-year cumulations of revised data.

The titles in the series and their frequencies have varied over the years. Some of the titles can be traced as far back as the 1920s; others began in the 1960s or later. For the history of any report, consult editions of the *Census Catalog and Guide* (including the 1790–1972 cumulative catalog) listed under "Census Guides" in this chapter.

The *Current Business Reports* series supplements the *Economic Census* for selected sectors. The retail sales reports consist of a monthly report and an annual report with revised data. The *Monthly Retail Trade Sales and Inventories* report has been published only electronically beginning in 1998. It contains United States data only. Data for selected states and selected metropolitan areas were reported in the print publication through 1996 and are available on the *Census Bureau Web site* from 1986-1996 in spreadsheet format. The annual series covers ten years of data in each report with the figures revised and updated. Monthly and annual totals are reported for sales and inventories. Annual totals are also given for some additional data items not in the monthly report. As with the monthly report, smaller geographic areas were included in some earlier years through 1996.

The wholesale trade reports consist of a monthly report and an annual report with revised data similar to the retail trade series. The *Annual Benchmark Report for Wholesale Trade* covers ten years of data in each report with the figures revised and updated. The annual, as with the retail trade annual, contains a small number of additional data items not included in the monthly series. Both reports are also available on the *Census Bureau Web site* for recent years. The monthly report is available only on the Web after 1999.

The *Service Annual Survey* gives estimated annual receipts for a variety of service industries for a ten-year period. An overview chapter is followed by chapters on specific industry areas such as travel and lodging services or health services. Some subareas are singled out for additional tables including personnel supply/temporary help services, computer programming/data processing, and the arrangement of passenger transportation. One additional data item included for these areas is receipts by source. Prior to the beginning of the annual survey in 1982 there was a monthly report called *Monthly Selected Services Receipts* (C 3.239:).

Annual Survey of Communication Services gives data on sources of revenue and types of expenses for communication services. There is an overview table and a section on each major industry area, such as telephone communications or radio and television broadcasting services. Examples of data available include telephone industry revenues from long-distance service, cable company revenues from pay and premium services, or television and radio broadcasting expenses for broadcast rights.

The *Annual Transportation Survey* provides current revenue and expense information for the trucking and public warehousing industries. A summary table gives total revenue, operating expenses, and payroll for the industries in this category. Separate chapters give more detailed data for trucking and courier services and for public warehousing. Trucking data is the most detailed with such information as revenue from agricultural and food product shipments or inventories of truck-tractors.

For a complete publishing history of any of these series, see the *Census Catalog and Guide* and related titles listed under "Census Guides" in this chapter.

ADDITIONAL CURRENT SOURCES
Discussion

The Census Bureau publishes several current series for the construction sector. These are discussed in Chapter 32, Housing and Construction Statistics. Current statistics relating to the mining sector are available from the U.S. Geological Survey. See Chapter 21, Geology. Cur-

Appendix A.
Current Industrial Reports Survey Names and Titles

NAICS survey name	SIC survey name	Survey title	Publication period
M311A	M20A	Flour Milling	monthly
M311J	M20J	Fats and Oils: Oilseed Crushings	monthly
M311K	M20K	Fats and Oils: Production, Consumption, and Stocks	monthly
MA311D	MA20D	Confectionery	annual
M313P	M22P	Consumption on the Cotton System	monthly
MQ313D	MQ22D	Consumption on the Woolen System	quarterly
MQ313T	MQ22T	Broadwoven Fabrics	quarterly
MA313F	MA22F	Yarn Production	annual
MA313K	MA22K	Knit Fabric Production	annual
MQ314X	MQ23X	Bed and Bath Furnishings	quarterly
MA314Q	MA22Q	Carpets and Rugs	annual
MQ315A	MQ23A	Apparel	quarterly
MA315D	MA23D	Gloves and Mittens	annual
MA316A	MA31A	Footwear	annual, quarterly
MA321T	MA24T	Lumber Production and Mill Stocks	annual
M325AT	M28AT	Titanium Dioxide	monthly
MA325A	MA28A	Inorganic Chemicals	annual, quarterly
MA325B	MA28B	Fertilizer Materials	annual, quarterly
MA325C	MA28C	Industrial Gases	annual, quarterly
MA325F	MA28F	Paint and Allied Products	annual, quarterly
MA325G	MA28G	Pharmaceutical Preparations	annual
M327G	M32G	Glass Containers	monthly
MQ327D	MQ32D	Clay Construction Products	quarterly
MA327A	MA32A	Flat Glass	annual
MA327C	MA32C	Refractories	annual
MA327E	MA32E	Glassware	annual
M331D	M33D	Aluminum Ingot and Mill Products	monthly
M331J	M33J	Inventories of Steel Producing Mills	monthly
MA331A	MA33A	Iron and Steel Castings	annual
MA331B	MA33B	Steel Mill Products	annual
MA331E	MA33E	Nonferrous Castings	annual
MQ332E	MQ34E	Plumbing Fixtures	quarterly
MA332K	MA34K	Steel Shipping Drums and Pails	annual
MA332Q	MA35Q	Antifriction Bearings	annual
MQ333W	MQ35W	Metalworking Machinery	quarterly
MA333A	MA35A	Farm Machinery and Lawn and Garden Equipment	annual
MA333D	MA35D	Construction Machinery	annual
MA333F	MA35F	Mining Machinery	annual
MA333J	MA35J	Industrial Air Pollution Control Equipment	annual
MA333L	MA35L	Internal Combustion Engines	annual
MA333M	MA35M	Refrigeration, Air Conditioning, and Warm Air Heating Equipment ...	annual
MA333N	MA35N	Fluid Power Products	annual
MA333P	MA35P	Pumps and Compressors	annual
MA334B	MA38B	Measurement Instruments and Related Products	annual
MA334M	MA36M	Consumer Electronics	annual
MA334P	MA36P	Communication and Other Electronic Equipment	annual
MA334Q	MA36Q	Semiconductors and Electronic Components	annual
MA334R	MA35R	Computers and Office Machines	annual
MA334S	MA38R	Electromedical and Irradiation Equipment	annual
MQ335C	MQ36C	Fluorescent Lamp Ballasts	quarterly
MA335A	MA36A	Switchgear and Industrial Controls	annual
MA335E	MA36E	Electric Housewares and Fans	annual
MA335F	MA36F	Major Household Appliances	annual
MA335H	MA36H	Motors and Generators	annual
MA335J	MA33L	Insulated Wire and Cable	annual
MA335K	MA36K	Wiring Devices and Supplies	annual
MA335L	MA36L	Electric Lighting Fixtures	annual
M336G	M37G	Civil Aircraft and Aircraft Engines	monthly
M336L	M37L	Truck Trailers	monthly

APPENDIX A   A–1

Source: 1997 Economic Census Numerical List of Manufactured and Mineral Products, p. A-1.

Figure 31.3: List of Current Industrial Reports Series.

rent statistics relating to agriculture, as well as the *Census of Agriculture*, are discussed in Chapter 18, Agriculture.

OTHER SOURCES

Checklist

Survey of Minority-Owned Business Enterprises. MF. WEB. (quinquennial) 1969–. U.S. Department of Commerce. Economics and Statistics Administration. Bureau of the Census. C 3.258: Item 0160-E(MF). ASI 2326-10. <http://www.census.gov/csd/mwb/>; <http://purl.access.gpo.gov/GPO/LPS3294>.

> Coverage: U.S., states, selected metropolitan areas, selected counties, selected places.
> Content: number of firms; sales; employees; payroll; data by industry, race, sex, legal form of organization, size of receipts, and employment size.

Women-Owned Businesses. MF. WEB. (quinquennial) 1972–. U.S. Department of Commerce. Economics and Statistics Administration. Bureau of the Census. C 3.250: Item 0132(MF). ASI 2328-9. <http://www.census.gov/csd/mwb/>; <http://purl.access.gpo.gov/GPO/LPS3294>.

> Coverage: U.S., states, selected metropolitan areas, selected counties, selected places.
> Content: number of firms; sales; employees; payroll; data by industry, legal form of organization, size of receipts, and employment size.

Characteristics of Business Owners. PRINT. WEB. (quinquennial) 1982–. U.S. Department of Commerce. Economics and Statistics Administration. Bureau of the Census. C 3.2:C 37/. Item 0146. ASI 2328-59. <http://www.census.gov/csd/cbo/>.

> Coverage: U.S.
> Content: characteristics of business owners and businesses; demographic data; acquisition; financing; income; profit and loss; percent minority employees and customers.

Quarterly Financial Report for Manufacturing, Mining, and Trade Corporations. MF. WEB. (quarterly) 1947–. U.S. Department of Commerce. Economics and Statistics Administration. Bureau of the Census. C 3.267: (Earlier, FT 1.18:) Item 0536-A. ASI 2502-1. (Earlier, 9402-1) GPO. <http://www.census.gov/prod/www/abs/qfr-mm.html>; <http://www.census.gov/mp/www/pub/mfg/msmfg13a.html>; <http://purl.access.gpo.gov/GPO/LPS1832>.

> Coverage: U.S.
> Content: income statements and balance sheets for industry groups; income or loss; assets and liabilities; operating and balance sheet ratios; rates of change in sales and profits; profits per dollar of sales; annual rates of profit on stockholders' equity; rates of return.

Federal Reserve Bulletin. PRINT. (monthly) 1915–. U.S. Board of Governors of the Federal Reserve System. FR 1.3: (nondepository) (Copies available for sale by the Board of Governors of the Federal Reserve System) ASI 9362-1. Selected articles: <http://www.bog.frb.fed.us/pubs/bulletin/default.htm>.

> Coverage: world, world regions, country groupings, countries, U.S.
> Content: financial statistics and articles; money stock; bank credit; federal reserve banks; bank loans; bank assets and liabilities; interest rates; stock market; federal finances; corporate profits; mortgages; consumer credit; flow of

funds; capacity utilization; industrial production; housing and construction; price indexes; gross domestic product (GDP); personal income; international transactions; foreign liabilities and claims; exchange rates.

Foreign Direct Investment in the United States: Operations of U.S. Affiliates of Foreign Companies. PRINT. WEB. (annual) 1981–. U.S. Department of Commerce. Economics and Statistics Administration. Bureau of Economic Analysis. C 59.20: (Includes both preliminary and revised estimates) Item 0130-D-07. ASI 2704-4. GPO. <http://www.bea.doc.gov/bea/ai/12-99.htm#FDIUS>.

> Coverage: world, world regions, country groupings, countries, U.S., regions, states.
> Content: financial and operating data; balance sheets; property, plant, and equipment; income statements; gross product; employment and compensation of employees; trade; interest and dividends.

U.S. Direct Investment Abroad: Operations of U.S. Parent Companies and Their Foreign Affiliates. PRINT. WEB. (annual) 1983–. U.S. Department of Commerce. Economics and Statistics Administration. Bureau of Economic Analysis. C 59.20/2: Item 0130-D-06. ASI 2704-5. GPO. <http://www.bea.doc.gov/bea/ai/12-99.htm#USDIA>.

> Coverage: world, world regions, country groupings, countries, U.S.
> Content: balance sheets; property, plant, and equipment; income statements; sales; gross product; employment and compensation of employees; trade.

Statistics of Income: Corporation Income Tax Returns. PRINT. WEB. (annual) 1916–. U.S. Department of the Treasury. Internal Revenue Service. T 22.35/5: (Earlier, T 22.35/2:C 81/year. Earlier title, *Statistics of Income*, T 22.35:). Item 0964. ASI 8304-4. GPO. <http://www.irs.ustreas.gov/prod/tax_stats/soi/corp_id.html>.

> Coverage: U.S.
> Content: data by industry on number of returns, assets, liabilities, receipts, deductions, net income, taxable income, credits.

Source Book Statistics of Income: Active Corporation Income Tax Returns. PRINT. (annual) 1928–. U.S. Department of the Treasury. Internal Revenue Service. Statistics of Income Division. T 22.35/5-2: (Earlier, T 22.35/2:C 81/year/SB). Item 0964. ASI 8304-21.

> Coverage: U.S.
> Content: balance sheet and income statement data for major and minor industries and by asset size; number of returns; assets; liabilities; receipts; deductions; net income; taxable income; income tax; credits.

Statistics of Income (SOI) Bulletin. PRINT. WEB. (quarterly) 1981–. U.S. Department of the Treasury. Internal Revenue Service. T 22.35/4: Item 0964-C. ASI 8302-2. GPO. <http://www.irs.ustreas.gov/prod/tax_stats/soi/soi_bul.html>; <http://purl.access.gpo.gov/GPO/LPS3363>.

> Coverage: U.S., states; occasionally world, world regions, country groupings, selected countries.
> Content: earliest published statistics on income tax returns of corporations, partnerships, and sole proprietorships; number of returns, assets, receipts, deductions, net income, tax by broad industry sector; articles on tax return statistics.

Discussion

The Census Bureau publishes some additional five-year surveys associated with the *Economic Census*. The *Survey of Minority-Owned Business Enterprises* consists of four reports on specific minority groups and a summary report. The minority group reports cover Blacks; Hispanics; Asians and Pacific Islanders; and American Indians and Alaska natives. (The latter two groups were issued in one publication before 1997). The greatest detail is given at the national level where it is possible to find such information as the number of food stores in the United States owned by Mexicans. At the state and metropolitan level there is less industry and nationality detail. No industry or nationality detail is available for counties and places. *Women-Owned Businesses* is a single report in similar format. Data from both these reports are also available on the *Economic Census* CD-ROM and on the Census Bureau Web site.

Characteristics of Business Owners provides demographic and financial data on business owners and their businesses. Data are given for businesses owned by Hispanics, Blacks, women, and other minorities, as well as for nonminority male-owned businesses. Examples of data given include age of owner by broad industry division, educational level of owner by business receipts size, and sources of borrowed capital by industry division. This report was not funded for 1997.

Quarterly Financial Report for Manufacturing, Mining, and Trade Corporations contains financial statistics for all manufacturing industries and for large mining, wholesale trade, and retail trade corporations. Manufacturing statistics are given for industry groups, such as electrical and electronic equipment or lumber and wood products, as well as for manufacturing as a whole. Data are presented by asset size class. Mining industry statistics are reported in total with no data on individual industries. Wholesale trade data are given for durable and nondurable goods. Retail trade data are given for general merchandise stores, food stores, and all other stores. Totals for each sector are also reported. Data given for an industry such as iron and steel include cash and demand deposits; net property, plant and equipment; loans from banks; stockholders' equity; inventory ratios; income; and annual rate of profit.

Federal Reserve Bulletin contains statistics and articles on finance. The "Financial and Business Statistics" section contains extensive data on money, credit, and banks. Examples of data available include interest rates, the prime rate, the condition of Federal Reserve Banks, commercial bank loans and deposits, foreign exchange rates, and basic economic indicators. An index to the statistical tables is provided. Each issue also has one or two feature articles and sections on statements to Congress, announcements, and legal developments. Examples of recent articles include "Industrial Production and Capacity Utilization: 1998 Annual Revision" (Jan. 1999); "Trends in Home Purchase Lending: Consolidation and the Com-

munity Reinvestment Act" (Feb. 1999); and "Monetary Policy Report to the Congress" (Mar. 1999).

Foreign Direct Investment in the United States and *U.S. Direct Investment Abroad* contain similar data. The first title reports data on foreign companies with affiliates in the United States, while the second reports on United States companies with affiliates in other countries. Data are given by industry sector and selected industries. Examples of information available include sales of rubber goods industry companies with French ownership or total insurance industry assets of U.S. affiliates in Canada. These titles can be downloaded from the agency's Web site.

The Internal Revenue Service publishes statistical reports based on income tax returns. *Statistics of Income: Corporation Income Tax Returns* contains data on returns, balance sheet items, income, and tax items by industry. Figure 31.4 shows the table with the most detailed industry breakdown. Other tables contain greater financial detail for assets, liabilities, receipts, and deductions, but with less industry detail. Recent years of this title can be downloaded from the IRS Web site in Excel format, but cannot be viewed directly on the site. The *Source Book Statistics of Income: Active Corporation Income Tax Returns* gives similar balance sheet and income data but contains more detailed industry coverage. The 1980 *Source Book* was the first sent to depository libraries.

The *Statistics of Income (SOI) Bulletin* serves as an update to these and other IRS statistical reports based on income tax returns. Summary reports on corporation income tax returns appear here prior to publication of *Statistics of Income: Corporate Income Tax Returns*. Summary data are also published for the tax returns from partnerships and sole proprietorships. Each issue contains a section of tables called "Selected Historical and Other Data" which gives summary data on corporation income tax returns by broad industry sector for selected years. Examples of recent articles include "Foreign-Controlled Domestic Corporations, 1995" (Fall 1998); "Corporate Foreign Tax Credit, 1994" (Fall 1998); and "Sole Proprietorships Returns, 1996" (Summer 1998).

SELECTED INDUSTRY REPORTS

Checklist

Food Marketing Review. MF (biennial) 1985–. U.S. Department of Agriculture. Economic Research Service. Agricultural Economic Report series. A 1.107/3: (Sometimes classed A1.107:; 1989–90 classed A 1.107: 639). Item 0042-C. ASI 1544-22.

> Coverage: world, selected countries, U.S.
> Content: overview of food manufacturing, wholesaling, retailing, and service industries; number of establishments in each category; sales by industry segment and product category; sales of top companies in each category; shipments; employment and earnings; price indexes; profits and profit margins; advertising; mergers; new products; food expenditures; income and balance sheet data; foreign investment.

Food Market Indicators Briefing Room. WEB. U.S. Department of Agriculture. Economic Research Service. <http://www.ers/usda/gov/Briefing/foodmark/>.

> Content: food expenditures; retail food prices; food cost review; food consumer price index forecasts; food markets; food baseline; publications; subject specialists.

Statistics of Communications Common Carriers. MF. WEB. (annual) 1939–. Federal Communications Commission. CC 1.35: (Title prior to 1957 is *Statistics of the Communications Industry in the United States*). Item 0288. ASI 9284-6. GPO. <http://www.fcc.gov/Bureaus/Common_Carrier/Reports/FCC-State_Link/socc.html>; <http://purl.access.gpo.gov/GPO/LPS292>; <http://purl.access.gpo.gov/GPO/LPS3640>.

> Coverage: world regions, countries, U.S., states, individual companies.
> Content: financial data for telephone and telegraph companies and the Communications Satellite Corporation; number of carriers; assets and liabilities; revenues and expenses; facilities and equipment; kilometers of wire and cable; access lines; selected ratios; households with telephone service; number of calls and minutes billed; overseas calls/messages; rates; historical trends.

100 Contractors Receiving the Largest Dollar Volume of Prime Contract Awards for Research, Development, Test, and Evaluation Fiscal Year. WEB. (annual) U.S. Department of Defense. Washington Headquarters Services. Directorate for Information Operations and Reports. D 1.57/2: Item 0310-E-16. ASI 3544-4. <http://web1.whs.osd.mil/PEIDHOME/PROCSTAT/procstat.HTM>; <http://purl.access.gpo.gov/GPO/LPS663>.

> Content: ranked listing of top 100 contractors with location of work, value of awards, and total awards; divided into business firms, educational and nonprofit institutions, and foreign contractors.

Annual Procurement Report. WEB. (annual) National Aeronautics and Space Administration. NAS 1.30: (Title varies). Item 0830-A-03. ASI 9504-13. (Earlier, 9502-6, 9532-6, 9504-3). <http://www.hq.nasa.gov/office/procurement/>.

> Coverage: countries, U.S., states.
> Content: procurement awards by type of contractor, type of contract, product or service; top 100 business firms, educational and non-profit institutions and value of awards.

Performance Profiles of Major Energy Producers. MF. WEB. (annual) 1977–. U.S. Department of Energy. Energy Information Administration. Office of Energy Markets and End Use. E 3.37: Item 0435-K. ASI 3164-44. GPO. <http://www.eia.doe.gov/bookshelf/finance.html>; <http://tonto.eia.doe.gov/bookshelf/index.html>; <http://purl.access.gpo.gov/GPO/LPS3492>.

> Coverage: world, world regions, selected countries, U.S.
> Content: finances and operations of major energy companies; revenue and income; taxation; profits; assets; liabilities; investment; exploration and development expenses.

Financial Statistics of Major U.S. Investor-Owned Electric Utilities. MF. WEB. (annual) 1937–. U.S. Department of Energy. Energy Information Administration. Office of Coal, Nuclear, Electric and Alternate Fuels. E 3.18/4-2: (Earlier, E 3.18/2:, FP 1.21:. Title varies.). Item 0435-E-01. ASI 3164-23. (Earlier, 9354-2). GPO. <http://www.eia.doe.gov/bookshelf/electric.html>; <http://tonto.eia.doe.gov/bookshelf/index.html>; <http://purl.access.gpo.gov/GPO/LPS3492>.

> Coverage: U.S., individual utilities.
> Content: income; expenses; earnings; ratios; assets; liabilities; cash flow; number of consumers; sales; sources and disposition of energy.

Financial Statistics of Major U.S. Publicly Owned Electric Utilities. MF. WEB. (annual) 1943–. U.S. Department of Energy. Energy Information Administration. Office of Coal, Nuclear, Electric and Alternate Fuels. E 3.18/4-3: (Earlier, E 3.18/4:, E 3.18/3:, FP 1.21:. Title varies.). Item 0435-E-01. ASI 3164-24. (Earlier, 9354-3). GPO. <http://www.eia.doe.gov/bookshelf/electric.html>; <http://tonto.eia.doe.gov/bookshelf/index.html>; <http://purl.access.gpo.gov/GPO/LPS3492>.

> Coverage: U.S., individual utilities.
> Content: income; expenses; assets; liabilities; number of consumers; sales; sources and disposition of energy.

Sector Notebook Project series. PRINT. WEB. U.S. Environmental Protection Agency. Office of Enforcement and Compliance Assurance. Office of Compliance. EP 1.113: (Earlier, EP 1.2:P 94/, EP 1.2:SE 2/7) Item 0431-I-85. ASI 9186-10. GPO. <http://es.epa.gov/oeca/sector/>; <http://purl.access.gpo.gov/GPO/LPS459>.

> Content: industry environmental profiles.

Minerals Yearbook. PRINT. WEB. (annual) 1932–. U.S. Department of the Interior. Geological Survey. I 19.165: (Earlier, I 28.37:. Issued since 1882 under other titles) Item 0639. ASI 5664-25, -26, -31. GPO. <http://minerals.usgs.gov/minerals/pubs/myb.html>; <http://purl.access.gpo.gov/GPO/LPS2120>.

> Coverage: world, world regions, countries, U.S., states.
> Content: production; shipments; value; consumption; trade; stocks; prices; trends; outlook.

Minerals and Materials Information. CD-ROM. 1994–. U.S. Department of the Interior. Geological Survey. I 19.120/4: Item 0639-J. ASI 5662-8.

> Content: *Minerals Yearbook* and other mineral publications.

Industry & Trade Summary series. MF. WEB. (irregular) 1991–. U.S. International Trade Commission. Office of Industries. ITC 1.33: Item 0978-A-01. ASI 9885-. <http://www.usitc.gov/332s/332index.htm#INDUSTRY & TRADE SUMMARIES>.

> Coverage: world, selected world regions, selected country groupings, selected countries, U.S.
> Content: reports on selected products imported into or exported from the U.S.; industry trends in consumption, production, and trade; product uses and consumer characteristics.

Air Carrier Financial Statistics Quarterly. MF. (quarterly) Sept. 1984–. U.S. Department of Transportation. Bureau of Transportation Statistics. Office of Airline Information. TD 12.15/3: (Earlier, TD 10.9/4:, CAB 1.17:; C 31.240:) (Title varies) Item 0982-N-03. ASI 7312-3.

> Coverage: U.S., individual air carriers.
> Content: income and balance sheet data for individual carriers; operating revenues and expenses by category; profits; income; assets; liabilities; stockholders' equity.

Airline Quarterly Financial Review. WEB. (quarterly) 1995–. U.S. Department of Transportation. Office of Aviation Analysis. Economic and Financial Analysis Division. ASI 7302-14. <http://ostpxweb.dot.gov/aviation/finance.htm>.

> Coverage: major passenger and cargo airlines.

1995 Corporation Returns - Basic Tables

RETURNS OF ACTIVE CORPORATIONS

Table 1--Number of Returns, Selected Receipts, Cost of Goods Sold, Net Income, Deficit, Income Subject to Tax, Total Income Tax, Selected Credits, Total Assets, Net Worth, Depreciable Assets, Depreciation Deduction, and Coefficients of Variation, by Minor Industry--Continued

[All figures are estimates based on samples--money amounts are in thousands of dollars]

Minor Industry	Foreign tax credit	U.S. possessions tax credit	Nonconventional source fuel credit	General business credit	Prior year minimum tax credit	Total income tax after credits	Total assets	Net worth	Depreciable assets	Depreciation deduction
	(31)	(32)	(33)	(34)	(35)	(36)	(37)	(38)	(39)	(40)
Transportation and public utilities --Continued										
Communication	0.21	(²)	0.01	0.25	0.46	0.22	0.11	0.32	0.16	0.18
Telephone, telegraph, and other communication services	0.31	(²)	(²)	0.17	0.43	0.23	0.13	0.29	0.16	0.18
Radio and television broadcasting	(²)	-	7.31	1.06	4.46	0.79	0.34	1.27	0.90	0.96
Electric, gas, and sanitary services	0.11	-	0.01	0.16	0.12	0.11	0.06	0.11	0.09	0.18
Electric services	0.19	-	(²)	0.05	(²)	0.06	0.06	0.06	0.04	0.11
Gas production and distribution	(²)	-	0.02	0.35	0.18	0.31	0.18	0.25	0.20	0.45
Combination utility services	(²)	-	(²)	(²)	0.01	0.12	0.07	0.06	0.06	0.11
Water supply and other sanitary services	(²)	-	0.07	24.21	17.96	1.74	1.05	1.39	1.65	1.93
Wholesale and retail trade	0.93	(²)	0.10	1.50	0.57	0.41	0.14	0.49	0.36	0.35
Wholesale trade	(²)	0.09	2.77	0.99	0.79	0.23	0.63	0.69	0.47	(²)
Groceries and related products	44.57	(²)	-	24.35	9.48	2.53	1.48	2.89	2.21	2.13
Machinery, equipment, and supplies	39.07	(²)	7.01	7.17	5.19	2.62	1.33	3.09	2.51	2.52
Miscellaneous wholesale trade	0.96	(²)	0.09	2.55	1.00	0.89	0.24	0.91	0.77	0.45
Motor vehicles and automotive equipment	8.39	-	-	0.15	0.35	2.30	0.66	1.51	0.59	0.25
Furniture and home furnishings	7.31	-	-	14.56	9.08	12.56	7.72	11.55	10.29	10.37
Lumber and construction materials	86.11	(²)	-	48.78	31.99	7.50	3.72	6.02	4.91	5.78
Sporting, recreational, photographic, and hobby goods, toys and supplies	3.15	-	-	4.25	30.33	4.00	2.99	5.26	4.67	3.48
Metals and minerals, except petroleum and scrap	3.52	(²)	7.31	30.21	1.65	3.72	2.13	4.41	4.40	4.50
Electrical goods	6.16	-	(²)	3.06	4.30	2.30	1.11	2.62	1.63	1.60
Hardware, plumbing, and heating equipment and supplies	9.51	-	-	38.61	31.63	6.44	3.61	4.74	4.61	6.65
Other durable goods	19.49	-	91.14	25.32	6.07	2.80	1.68	3.12	3.09	3.22
Paper and paper products	45.91	-	-	62.31	41.21	7.32	2.11	2.21	4.62	2.61
Drugs, drug proprietaries, and druggists' sundries	4.05	(²)	-	5.24	2.94	4.10	1.82	3.70	2.96	3.35
Apparel, piece goods, and notions	1.33	-	-	2.55	9.22	2.58	2.76	4.96	5.42	6.73
Farm-product raw materials	(²)	-	(²)	6.63	13.47	2.40	1.32	1.84	2.65	2.63
Chemicals and allied products	3.62	-	-	19.34	3.69	9.46	4.21	6.76	6.59	6.96
Petroleum and petroleum products	1.53	-	0.07	1.11	13.33	3.21	0.41	1.81	3.67	3.85
Alcoholic beverages	(²)	-	-	63.07	16.44	6.62	3.69	6.26	6.67	6.13
Miscellaneous nondurable goods; wholesale trade not allocable	0.98	(²)	-	24.62	17.95	3.80	1.97	6.36	5.90	3.64
Retail trade	(²)	20.24	1.79	0.99	0.43	0.22	0.69	0.42	0.64	(²)
Building materials, garden supplies, and mobile home dealers	0.21	-	-	1.17	19.11	1.61	1.43	2.64	2.06	2.16
Building material dealers	0.21	-	-	0.55	19.20	1.65	1.91	2.38	2.31	2.54
Hardware stores	-	-	-	24.16	-	13.14	6.54	10.05	6.86	6.69
Garden supplies and mobile home dealers	-	-	-	97.33	34.33	4.45	4.75	19.03	7.84	7.16
General merchandise stores	0.19	(²)	96.49	0.99	0.08	0.30	0.14	0.30	0.23	0.21
Food stores	1.30	-	-	2.65	3.21	0.75	0.63	1.67	0.63	0.91
Grocery stores	1.35	-	-	2.53	2.96	0.66	0.61	1.59	0.77	0.84
Other food stores	(²)	-	-	13.96	21.22	8.63	5.03	10.71	6.44	6.46
Automotive dealers and service stations	61.17	(²)	-	13.49	7.00	2.67	0.76	2.91	1.61	2.11
Motor vehicle dealers	71.51	-	-	19.58	6.43	3.99	1.02	4.26	1.78	2.45
Gasoline service stations	40.64	-	-	26.54	43.79	10.17	4.61	6.79	6.15	6.67
Other automotive dealers	-	(²)	-	21.26	24.55	4.06	3.05	4.99	3.95	6.00
Apparel and accessory stores	0.47	(²)	-	0.62	1.20	1.25	1.11	1.66	1.22	1.37
Furniture and home furnishings stores	3.66	-	-	1.67	7.41	3.69	2.17	3.25	2.69	5.70
Eating and drinking places	0.41	(²)	-	3.61	19.24	1.40	0.72	2.42	1.26	1.36
Miscellaneous retail stores	1.26	(²)	4.56	4.24	6.20	1.61	0.75	1.66	1.53	1.70
Drug stores and proprietary stores	17.00	-	-	0.67	7.78	3.06	1.41	2.00	1.73	1.31
Liquor stores	-	-	94.43	97.03	-	21.06	6.79	16.66	12.06	13.51
Other retail stores	1.26	(²)	(²)	6.94	6.52	1.90	0.96	2.14	1.62	2.13
Wholesale and retail trade not allocable	66.66	66.66	66.66	70.38	26.29	10.76	19.20	11.77	16.96	(²)
Finance, insurance, and real estate	0.06	(²)	1.14	0.47	0.34	0.30	0.62	0.06	0.43	0.30
Banking	(²)	(²)	(²)	0.10	0.24	0.56	0.02	0.32	0.05	0.06
Mutual savings banks	1.27	-	-	0.91	2.06	0.19	0.20	1.96	0.33	0.24
Bank holding companies	(²)	-	(²)	0.06	0.26	0.06	0.03	0.17	0.04	0.02
Banks, except mutual savings banks and bank holding companies	0.06	-	(²)	2.20	0.55	6.62	0.36	7.41	0.62	1.13
Credit agencies other than banks	0.11	(²)	6.53	0.13	0.10	0.18	0.06	1.17	0.65	0.66
Savings and loan associations	0.02	(²)	(²)	0.42	0.10	0.09	0.07	6.93	0.12	0.09
Personal credit institutions	(²)	(²)	-	(²)	(²)	0.46	0.22	0.47	1.74	1.43
Business credit institutions	(²)	(²)	-	0.74	0.37	0.17	0.16	0.90	1.73	1.40
Other credit agencies; finance not allocable	0.13	(²)	6.62	0.10	0.31	0.51	0.10	0.65	2.21	1.63
Security, commodity brokers and services	0.30	-	(²)	0.27	0.66	2.20	0.06	1.14	1.00	-8.96
Security brokers, dealers, and flotation companies	0.29	-	(²)	0.07	0.66	0.39	0.04	1.23	0.86	0.94

Footnotes at end of table section. Detail may not add to total because of rounding. See text for "Explanation of Terms" and "Description of the Sample and Limitations of the Data."

35

Source: 1995 *Statistics of Income: Corporation Income Tax Returns*, p. 35.

Figure 31.4: Sample Page from *Statistics of Income: Corporation Income Tax Returns*.

Content: total operating revenues and expenses; profits; net income; traffic; yield and unit cost; financial ratios and percentages; passenger load factor; employment and productivity.

Economic Data for Class 1 Railroads. WEB. U.S. Department of Transportation. Surface Transportation Board. <http://www.stb.dot.gov/infoex1.htm>.

Coverage: U.S., individual class 1 railroads.
Content: assets; liabilities; operating income and expenses; cash flow; equipment; employment; wages.

FDIC Statistics on Banking. MF. WEB. (annual) 1981–. Federal Deposit Insurance Corporation. Y 3.F 31/8:1-2/year. (Title varies. Previously part of Annual Report, Y 3.F 31/8:1/year). Item 1061-K. ASI 9294-4. <http://www.fdic.gov/bank/statistical/statistics/index.html>.

Coverage: U.S., states.
Content: number and types of banks; number of new and closed banks; assets, deposits, and liabilities; income and expenses.

Bank & Thrift Branch Office Data Book: Office Deposits and Addresses of FDIC-Insured Institutions Summary of Deposits. PRINT. MF. WEB. (annual) 1997–. Federal Deposit Insurance Corporation. Y 3.F 31/8:22/ (Issued earlier under other titles: *Data Book Operating Banks and Branches, Banks and Branches Data Book, Summary of Accounts and Deposits in All Commercial and Mutual Savings Banks.* Irregular prior to 1980) Item 1061-K. ASI 9295-3. <http://www2.fdic.gov/sod/>; <http://purl.access.gpo.gov/GPO/LPS381>.

Coverage: U.S., states, counties, metropolitan areas, individual banks and branches.
Content: number of banks and branches by type; deposits.

Discussion

Occasionally the government publishes reports on specific industries, especially in areas that are regulated by the government. Many of these reports fall in the areas of banking, energy, trade, and transportation. Selected recurring reports are listed above.

Food Marketing Review is a comprehensive analysis of the food industry covering manufactures, retail and wholesale trade, and services. Sales statistics and after-tax profits are given for specific top companies in each area. Advertising expenditures for a small number of leading food advertisers are also given. The *Food Market Indicators Briefing Room* Web site provides access to data and publications of the Economic Research Service. The "Food Markets" menu category contains the latest data tables from the *Food Marketing Review.* (See also Chapter 18, "Agriculture," for other related sources.)

The Federal Communications Commission regulates interstate and foreign communication. Its report, *Statistics of Communications Common Carriers,* covers telephone and telegraph companies and COMSAT (Communications Satellite Corporation). Detailed income and balance sheet data are given for individual companies, as well as other statistics on the domestic and international communications industry.

The Defense Department publishes several reports on contractors that identify major contractors and the amount of awards. *100 Contractors Receiving the Largest Dollar Volume of Prime Contract Awards* names the top 100 contractors with awards over $25,000. (For more on contractor reports, see Chapter 40, "Defense and Military Statistics.") NASA also publishes a report identifying major contractors. The *Annual Procurement Report* contains a list of the top 100 business firms and the top 100 educational and nonprofit institutions contracting with NASA and the amount of the award. Tables also give total awards by state and total awards being performed in other countries by country. Although this report is a depository item it has not been distributed to depository libraries for many years. Recent years are available on the Internet.

Many of the Energy Department's statistical publications cover energy industries. *Performance Profiles of Major Energy Producers* summarizes data from annual financial reports that more than 20 major energy companies are required to file with the Department of Energy. The narrative portion of the report analyzes activities and trends in the industry. A statistical appendix provides more detailed tables. Some general information on individual companies is included, especially in the area of mergers and acquisitions. Most statistics, however, are for the companies as a group. The two *Financial Statistics* reports on electric utilities provide detailed data on individual utilities. (For more sources related to energy industries see Chapter 41, "Energy Statistics.")

The *Sector Notebook Project* series consists of environmental profiles for more than 30 major industries. Examples of specific titles and industries include *Profile of the Aerospace Industry* (EP 1.113:310-R-98-001), *Profile of the Textile Industry* (EP 1.113:310-R-97-009), and *Profile of the Metal Casting Industry* (EP 1.113:310-R-97-004). Each profile contains a general description of the industry, including economic trends and geographic distribution, a description of the industrial process, a chemical release profile, pollution prevention opportunities, summary of federal statutes and regulations, compliance and enforcement history, compliance assurance activities and initiatives, and contacts and resources. An overall update to the 1995 and 1997 sector notebooks was issued as *Sector Notebook Data Refresh – 1997* (EP 1.2:SE 2/7).

The *Minerals Yearbook* is a standard source for information on mineral industries and commodities. At present three volumes are published each year: *Metals and Minerals, Area Reports: Domestic,* and *Area Reports: International.* Volume 1, *Metals and Minerals,* consists of chapters on each commodity, which discuss and provide statistics on domestic production, consumption and uses, stocks, prices, and foreign trade. Each commodity chapter also often includes sections on legislation and government programs, world review, current research and technology, and outlook. Volume 2 contains reports on each state, which review the state's mineral commodities, the economic situation, the industry, and important events and issues affecting the industry. Specific companies may be mentioned. Volume 3 is issued in parts by region and contains country reports covering industry structure, production, trade, government policies, and a review of individual commodities produced by that country. The *Minerals Yearbook* is also available on the Web and on CD-ROM.

The International Trade Commission publishes reports on trade issues. The *Industry & Trade Summary* series covers selected products such as nonalcoholic beverages (ITC 1.33:N 73), fertilizers (ITC 1.33:F 41), or synthetic rubber (ITC 1.33:SY 7/2). Each report discusses industry structure and trends, the U.S. market, U.S. trade, and foreign industry. Basic statistics on shipments, production, and trade are included.

The Transportation Department collects economic data on transportation industries, such as airlines and railroads. Of the two airline reports listed above, *Air Carrier Financial Statistics Quarterly* covers more airlines and gives more detailed categories for revenues and expenses. *Airline Quarterly Financial Review* contains charts and brief narrative highlights of trends, as well as statistical tables. It also includes traffic information and some additional financial items not included in the first report. *Economic Data for Class I Railroads* is a Web resource that provides annual railroad financial data, quarterly earnings reports, monthly employment data, and annual wage statistics. (For more on transportation sources see Chapter 44, "Transportation Statistics.")

The Federal Deposit Insurance Corporation publishes summary statistics on banking based on financial reports filed by federally insured banks. *FDIC Statistics on Banking* gives statistics on insured commercial banks and savings institutions. The *Bank & Thrift Branch Office Data Book* consists of a set of regional reports with individual bank data arranged by state and county. There is also a national summary report. The regional reports list each bank and branch, its address, and deposits. There are county and state totals. The national report gives totals for the United States, states, counties, and metropolitan areas. Although this report is listed as available to depository libraries, distribution has been sporadic. Both of these FDIC reports are available on request from the agency and are on the agency's Web site. The agency will also provide a report on a specific bank for a small fee.

INDIVIDUAL COMPANY INFORMATION
Checklist

EDGAR Database of Corporate Information. WEB. 1994–. U.S. Securities and Exchange Commission. <http://www.sec.gov/edgarhp.htm>.
　　Content: company reports required to be filed with the SEC, including 10-K, 10-Q, 8-K reports; registration reports; and proxy statements.

Discussion

Individual company information in government publications is limited. The Census Bureau, a source of many industry statistics, is required by law to keep individual company data confidential. Some company information is available in areas where the government has oversight or regulatory responsibilities. Several examples of these kinds of reports are listed in the "Selected Industry Reports" section. Even in cases where certain companies are required to file reports with regulatory agencies, the data may not be published by the government. Such files may be available for inspection at the agency, or photocopies can be requested for a fee. Some government publications may list companies in a specific industry area or mention information of a generally public nature, such as mergers and acquisitions. Congressional hearings may sometimes contain company information if there has been an investigation of an industry.

The largest government source of individual company information is the Securities and Exchange Commission (SEC). Public companies are required to file numerous reports with the commission, including comprehensive annual 10-K reports. These reports generally include the company name, address, telephone number, state of incorporation, description of the business and its products, officers, ownership, sales, financial data from balance sheets and income statements, stock prices, and dividends. These reports are not available as part of the depository library program. The SEC has implemented an electronic filing system for these reports called EDGAR (Electronic Data Gathering, Analysis, and Retrieval). EDGAR was phased-in over a period of time with all companies required to participate by May 6, 1996. Reports since 1994 are available on the SEC's Web site. A commercial source, Disclosure, Inc., provides online and CD-ROM products containing SEC company reports. The Disclosure databases are also available from many other vendors, including America Online, Compuserve, Dow Jones, Knight Ridder (DataStar, DIALOG), LEXIS/NEXIS, OCLC (FirstSearch), and SilverPlatter. Commercial versions may provide more historical coverage, more sophisticated searching, and additional company information from non-SEC sources.

INDEXES
Checklist

American Statistics Index (ASI). PRINT. (monthly) 1973–. Bethesda, MD: Congressional Information Service.

Statistical Universe. WEB. Bethesda, MD: Congressional Information Service.

Catalog of United States Government Publications (MOCAT). WEB. 1994–. U.S. Government Printing Office. Superintendent of Documents. <http://www.gpo.gov/catalog>; <http://www.access.gpo.gov/su_docs/locators/cgp/index.html>; <http://purl.access.gpo.gov/GPO/LPS844>.

Monthly Catalog of United States Government Publications. CD-ROM. 1996–. U.S. Government Printing Office. Superintendent of Documents. GP 3.8/7: Item 0557-C. GPO.

Monthly Catalog of United States Government Publications (Condensed version). PRINT. (monthly) 1996–. U.S. Government Printing Office. Superintendent of Documents. GP 3.8/8: (Earlier full version, GP 3.8:, 1895-1995). Item 0557-D. GPO.

CIS/Index. PRINT. (monthly) 1970–. Bethesda, MD: Congressional Information Service.

Congressional Universe. WEB. Bethesda, MD: Congressional Information Service.

Discussion

A comprehensive listing of material can be found in the *American Statistics Index (ASI)* by looking under such general headings as "Business assets and liabilities, specific industry" or "Business income and expenses, specific industry." Look also under specific types of industries (such as "Electronics industry and products," "Glass and glass industry," "Liquor and liquor industry," or "Sugar industry and products") or under specific financial or business topics (such as "Business inventories," "Capital investments, specific industry," or "Operating ratios"). The *ASI* category indexes "By Industry" and "By Individual Company or Institution" are also valuable for locating business statistics. *Statistical Universe* includes a Web version of *ASI*.

The *Monthly Catalog* may also be used to locate materials, but does not provide the depth of indexing for statistics that *ASI* does. Look under subject headings beginning with "Business," specific topics such as "Inventories," or specific industries. Reports that are exclusively statistical are often indexed under the subheading "Statistics," such as "Corporations-United States-Statistics" or "Glass Manufacture-United States-Statistics." The complete version of the *Monthly Catalog* is available on the Web and CD-ROM. Commercial online and CD-ROM versions of the *Monthly Catalog* are also available.

CIS/Index can be used to identify congressional hearings on an industry and testimony from company representatives on issues related to an industry. Individual company information may sometimes be included in hearings. Look also under the subject heading "Statistical data: industry and commerce." *Congressional Universe* includes a Web version of *CIS*.

For more information on these indexes, see Chapter 3, "The Basics of Searching."

RELATED MATERIAL
Within this Work

Chapter 5   Foreign Countries

Chapter 7   Selling to the Government

Chapter 8   Business Aids

Chapter 18   Agriculture

Chapter 24   Government Programs and Grants

Chapter 25   Regulations and Administrative Actions

Chapter 28   Population Statistics

Chapter 30   Economic Indicators

Chapter 32   Housing and Construction Statistics

Chapter 33   Income

Chapter 34   Earnings

Chapter 35   Employment

Chapter 36   Prices

Chapter 37   Consumer Expenditures

Chapter 38   Foreign Trade Statistics

Chapter 40   Defense and Military Statistics

Chapter 41   Energy Statistics

Chapter 42   Projections

Chapter 44   Transportation Statistics

Chapter 50   Patents and Trademarks

Chapter 51   Standards and Specifications

GPO Subject Bibliographies. PRINT. WEB. GP 3.22/2:

<http://bookstore.gpo.gov/sb/about/html>.

No. 4   "Business"

No. 125   "Marketing"

No. 128   "Financial Institutions"

No. 146   "Census of Manufactures"

No. 149   "Census of Transportation"

No. 151   "Minerals"

No. 152   "Census of Business"

No. 157   "Census of Construction"

No. 216   "Construction Industry"

No. 277   "Census of Agriculture"

No. 295   "Securities and Investments"

No. 307   "Small Business"

No. 310   "Census of Mineral Industries"

CHAPTER 32
Housing and Construction Statistics

Housing statistics are one indicator of the nation's economy. They also have specific application to many businesses and industries involved in construction, building supplies, energy, household services, furnishings, and appliances.

SEARCH STRATEGY

This chapter shows a statistical search strategy. The suggested steps for locating information on housing and construction are

1. Consult the *Statistical Abstract of the United States* and other titles listed in the "General Statistical Sources" and "General Housing Sources" section of this chapter for basic statistics;
2. For the most detailed housing statistics consult the "Census of Housing Sources" and the more current related sources under "Current Census Sources: Housing";
3. For the most detailed construction industry statistics see the "Economic Census Sources" section and the more current sources under "Current Census Sources: Construction";
4. For assistance with using census sources, consult the titles in the "Census Guides" section;
5. Consider the "Related Material" section; and
6. Search the indexes listed at the end of the chapter for thorough coverage of the resources available.

GENERAL STATISTICAL SOURCES
Checklist

Statistical Abstract of the United States. PRINT. WEB. (annual) 1878–. U.S. Department of Commerce. Economics and Statistics Administration. Bureau of the Census. C 3.134: Item 0150. ASI 2324-1. GPO. <http://www.census.gov/statab/www/>; <http://purl.access.gpo.gov/GPO/LPS2878>.

Coverage: U.S., regions, states, selected metropolitan areas.
Content: number of construction industry establishments and employees; price indexes; value of new construction; construction contracts; new and existing housing units and their characteristics; sales and financing; vacancy rates; commercial buildings and their characteristics.

Statistical Abstract of the United States. CD-ROM. (annual) 1993–. U.S. Department of Commerce. Bureau of the Census. C 3.134/7: Item 0150-B. ASI 2324-14.
Content: CD-ROM version of the *Statistical Abstract*.

Historical Statistics of the United States: Colonial Times to 1970. Parts 1-2. PRINT. (1975) U.S. Department of Commerce. Bureau of the Census. C 3.134/2:H 62/789-970/pt.1-2. Item 0151. ASI (76) 2328-2. GPO.
Coverage: U.S.
Content: value of construction; cost and activity indexes; housing starts; number and characteristics of residential structures; vacancy rates.

Historical Statistics of the United States on CD-ROM: Colonial Times to 1970. CD-ROM. (1997) New York, NY: Cambridge University Press.
Content: CD-ROM version of *Historical Statistics of the United States*.

County and City Data Book. PRINT. WEB. (quinquennial) 1947–. U.S. Department of Commerce. Economics and Statistics Administration. Bureau of the Census. C 3.134/2:C 83/2/year. Item 0151. ASI 2328-1. GPO. <http://fisher.lib.Virginia.EDU/ccdb/>.
Coverage: U.S., regions, divisions, states, counties, cities of 25,000 or more.
Content: housing units and their characteristics; median value or rent; building permits.

County and City Data Book. CD-ROM. (quinquennial) 1988–. U.S. Department of Commerce. Bureau of the Census. C 3.134/2-1: (Earlier, C 3.134/2:C 83/2/) Item 0151-D-01. ASI 2328-1.
Content: CD-ROM version of the *County and City Data Book*.

County and City Extra: Annual Metro, City, and County Data Book. PRINT. (annual) 1992–. Lanham, MD: Bernan Press.

Coverage: U.S., states, counties, metropolitan areas, congressional districts, cities of 25,000 or more.

Content: updated version of the *County and City Data Book*.

Places, Towns, and Townships. PRINT. (irregular) 1993–. Lanham, MD: Bernan Press.

Coverage: incorporated places.

Content: number and value of new residential construction units authorized by building permits; occupied housing units; median value or rent.

State and Metropolitan Area Data Book. PRINT. WEB. (irregular) 1979–. U.S. Department of Commerce. Economics and Statistics Administration. Bureau of the Census. C 3.134/5: Item 0150. ASI 2328-54. GPO. <http://www.census.gov/statab/www.smadb.html>.

Coverage: U.S., states, metropolitan areas, central cities of metropolitan areas, component counties of metropolitan areas.

Content: housing starts; home sales; vacancy rates; homeownership rate; construction employment, earnings, establishments, contracts; building permits.

State and Metropolitan Area Data Book. CD-ROM. (irregular) 1997/98–. U.S. Department of Commerce. Economics and Statistics Administration. Bureau of the Census. (Not distributed to depository libraries)

Content: CD-ROM version of the *State and Metropolitan Area Data Book*.

USA Counties. CD-ROM. WEB. (irregular) 1992–. U.S. Department of Commerce. Economics and Statistics Administration. Bureau of the Census. C 3.134/6: Item 0150-C. ASI 2324-17. <http://govinfo.kerr.orst.edu/usaco-stateis.html>; <http://tier2.census.gov/usac/index.html-ssi>.

Coverage: U.S., states, counties.

Content: time series data; number, units in structure, and value of new housing units authorized by building permits; value of additions, alterations, and non-residential construction; number and characteristics of housing units; vacant units; median value or rent; median monthly owner costs.

Discussion

The *Statistical Abstract of the United States* contains statistics on the construction industry and the characteristics of housing. Construction industry data are available by specific industry subcategories such as general building contractors for single family houses; highway and street construction; plumbing, heating, and air conditioning; and electrical work. Housing characteristics covered include units in structure, stories, foundation, year built, main heating equipment, air conditioning, source of water, sewage disposal, rooms, lot size, square footage, and appliances.

Statistics are compiled from many of the more detailed sources covered later in this chapter. Source notes at the end of each table can direct the user to more current or more detailed sources for the information in that table. The full text of recent editions of the *Statistical Abstract* is available on the Census Bureau Web site as PDF files. The *Statistical Abstract* is also available on CD-ROM. The CD contains additional geographic areas, variables or time series not in the printed version. *Historical Statistics of the United States* provides similar data for years before 1970. A CD-ROM version of *Historical Statistics* is available from Cambridge University Press.

County and City Data Book and *State and Metropolitan Area Data Book* concentrate on smaller geographic areas but give less specific information. The *County and City Data Book* gives data on housing unit characteristics such as units in structure, age, water source, sewage disposal, owner-occupied, renter-occupied, median value or rent, telephone, and heating fuel. Information on number of new housing units authorized by building permits is also given. The *State and Metropolitan Area Data Book* provides a different group of data items at the state level. The metropolitan tables are limited to information on building permits. The *County and City Data Book* is also available in CD-ROM from the Census Bureau. The University of Virginia Library Geospatial and Statistical Data Center offers recent editions of the *County and City Data Book* on the Internet in their interactive data area. Users select the desired edition, geography, and variables to create a customized data display. The *State and Metropolitan Area Data Book* is available as a PDF file on the Census Bureau Web site. A CD-ROM edition is also available.

County and City Extra is a commercially produced annual version of the *County and City Data Book*. Data is similar to that in the *County and City Data Book* with some variations. The *County and City Data Book* has a larger number of data items in the area of housing characteristics. *Places, Towns, and Townships* provides a small number of data items for cities.

The *USA Counties* CD-ROM contains county and state data from the last two or three issues of the *County and City Data Book* and the *State and Metropolitan Area Data Book* to provide several years of data in one source. The data are similar to that found in the two data books. The Oregon State University Government Information Sharing Project provides access to the current issue on the Internet. Users select a geographic area profile or an area comparison and then the desired geography. A subject area can then be selected or a keyword search conducted to display data. The Census Bureau Web site contains a similar version.

GENERAL HOUSING SOURCES
Checklist

Housing Statistics of the United States. PRINT. (irregular) 1997–. Washington, D.C.: Bernan Press.

Coverage: U.S., regions, states.

Content: number and characteristics of housing units; new housing units authorized, started, completed; characteristics of new housing units; value of construction; new and existing home sales; median asking price and sales price; price indexes; vacancy rates; homeownership rates; housing problems; selected housing costs; affordability status; mortgage characteristics; federal housing assistance.

U.S. Housing Market Conditions. PRINT. WEB. (quarterly) 1993, 4th quarter–. U.S. Department of Housing and Urban Development. Office of Policy Development and Research. HH 1.120/2: Item 0581-K-01. ASI 5182-2. <http://www.huduser.org/periodicals/ushmc.html>; <http://purl.access.gpo.gov/GPO/LPS2473>.

Coverage: U.S., regions, HUD regions, states, selected metropolitan areas.

Content: housing permits, starts, under construction, completions, mobile home shipments and placements, sales, prices, affordability, apartment absorptions, builders' views of market activity, mortgages, residential fixed investment and gross domestic product, value of new construction, number of households by type and householder characteristics, housing stock, vacancy rates, homeownership rates.

Discussion

Housing Statistics of the United States is a commercial publication that collects several years of housing statistics in one convenient source. Much of the data comes from government sources, including many Census Bureau publications, several of which are listed later in this chapter. Some data from private sources is included as well. Chapters cover demographics and housing demand; housing stock, production, and investment; market outcomes; housing finance; and federal housing assistance. Appendices include detailed notes on tables and descriptions of data sources. An index is included.

U.S. Housing Market Conditions gives national and regional summaries of the current housing industry situation with current and historical statistical tables. Current national data tables give statistics for the latest quarter, previous quarter, same quarter previous year, and percent change. A regional activity section summarizes trends for HUD regions, often including a section on one metropolitan area in the region. Regional statistics are given on building permits. An historical data section provides annual data and monthly data for recent months. Data is similar to that in the current national data section, but with some additional variables. Issues since 1994, 4th quarter, are also available on the Internet.

CENSUS OF HOUSING SOURCES

Checklist

Census of Housing. PRINT. (decennial) 1950–. U.S. Department of Commerce. Economics and Statistics Administration. Bureau of the Census. (Format has changed over the years; titles listed below reflect current format. Before 1950 included in the comprehensive decennial census.)

General Housing Characteristics. C 3.224/3:; C 3.224/3-2: to 3-4: Items 0156-B-01 to 53, 0155-A-01 to 03. ASI 2471-1.

Coverage: states, counties, places of 1,000 or more, selected county subdivisions (MCDs); separate reports on metropolitan areas, urbanized areas, and American Indian and Alaska Native areas.

Content: housing units; age and race of householder; units in structure; value; rent; number of rooms; persons per room or unit; tenure; vacancy characteristics.

Detailed Housing Characteristics. C 3.224/3:; C 3.224/3-5: to 3-7: Items 0156-B-01 to 53, 0155-A-01 to 03. ASI 2471-2.

Coverage: states, counties, places of 2,500 or more, selected county subdivisions (MCDs); separate reports on metropolitan areas, urbanized areas, and American Indian and Alaska Native areas.

Content: year moved in; number of bedrooms; plumbing and kitchen facilities; telephone; vehicles available; heating fuel; water source; sewage disposal; year built; costs of utilities; housing costs.

Metropolitan Housing Characteristics. C 3.224/4-2: Item 0146-T. ASI 2471-5.

Coverage: U.S.

Content: units in structure; year built; year householder moved in; person in unit; persons per room; household income; telephone; kitchen/plumbing facilities; condominium; poverty level; mortgage status; monthly owner costs; value or rent.

Residential Finance. C 3.224/13: Item 0155-A-04. ASI 2471-6. <http://www.census.gov/prod/www/abs/decenial.html>.

Coverage: U.S., regions.

Content: number of units; manner of acquisition; source of downpayment; year acquired; building and land acquisition; new or previously owned; year built; price; value or rental receipts; type and source of property benefits; owner age, race, sex, income; real estate tax; rental vacancy losses; type of mortgage; mortgage insurance; mortgage status.

Population and Housing Characteristics for Census Tracts and Block Numbering Areas. C 3.223/11: (Earlier title, *Census Tracts*) Item 0156-K-01 to 53. ASI 2551-3.

Coverage: metropolitan areas, census tracts in metropolitan areas, census tracts or block numbering areas in the nonmetropolitan area portions of each state, counties, places of 10,000 or more.

Content: units in structure; value; rent; number of rooms; tenure; vacancy characteristics; year moved in; number of bedrooms; plumbing and kitchen facilities; telephone; vehicles available; heating fuel; water source; sewage disposal; year built; housing costs.

Summary Population and Housing Characteristics. C 3.223/18: Item 0159-B-01 to 53. ASI 2551-1.

Coverage: U.S., states, counties, places, county subdivisions (MCDs), American Indian and Alaska Native areas.

Content: housing units; race of householder; units in structure; value; rent; number of rooms; persons per unit or room; tenure; vacancy characteristics.

Summary Social, Economic, and Housing Characteristics. C 3.223/23: Item 0156-M-01 to 53. ASI 2551-7.

Coverage: U.S., states, counties, places, county subdivisions (MCDs), American Indian and Alaska Native areas. Content: year built; bedrooms; condominium status; plumbing and kitchen facilities; sewage disposal; water source; heating fuel; vehicles available; telephone; year moved in; mortgage status; owner costs.

Population and Housing Unit Counts. C 3.223/5: Item 0159-C-01 to 53. ASI 2551-2.

Coverage: U.S., regions, divisions, states, counties, county subdivisions, places, metropolitan areas, urbanized areas. Content: total housing unit counts, density.

Population and Housing Characteristics for Congressional Districts of the 103rd Congress. PRINT. C 3.223/20: (Title varies; before 1980 data were published in *Congressional District Data Book*) Item 0159-C-01 to 53. ASI 2551-4.

Coverage: congressional districts, counties, minor civil divisions of 10,000 or more, places of 10,000 or more. Content: household type; householder characteristics; vehicle availability; tenure; units in structure; value; rent; monthly owner costs; vacancy/occupancy status; number of rooms; number of bedrooms; condominium status; kitchen facilities; sewage disposal; year built; water source; heating fuel; telephone availability; plumbing facilities.

1990 Census of Population and Housing Summary Tape File 1A. CD-ROM. WEB. U.S. Department of Commerce. Bureau of the Census. Data User Services Division. C 3.282: Item 0154-F. ASI 2551-9. <http://venus.census.gov/cdrom/lookup>; <http://sunsite.Berkeley.edu/GovData/info/>; <http://govinfo.kerr.orst.edu/stateis.html>.

Coverage: states, counties, places, county subdivisions, tracts, block numbering areas, block groups, congressional districts. Content: household type; housing units; units in structure; number of rooms; tenure; value; rent; vacancy/occupancy status.

1990 Census of Population and Housing Block Statistics Summary Tape File 1B. CD-ROM. U.S. Department of Commerce. Bureau of the Census. Data User Services Division. C 3.282/3: Item 0154-F. ASI 2551-16.

Coverage: states, metropolitan areas, urbanized areas, counties, places, county subdivisions, tracts, block numbering areas, block groups, blocks. Content: household type; housing units; units in structure; mean number of rooms; tenure; mean value; mean rent; persons per unit or room; vacancy/occupancy status.

1990 Census of Population and Housing Summary Tape File 1C. CD-ROM. WEB. U.S. Department of Commerce. Bureau of the Census. Data User Services Division. C 3.282: Item 0154-F. ASI 2551-17. <http://venus.census.gov/cdrom/lookup>; <http://sunsite.Berkeley.edu/GovData/info/>; <http://govinfo.kerr.orst.edu/stateis.html>.

Coverage: U.S., regions, divisions, states, metropolitan areas, urbanized areas, counties, places of 10,000 or more, selected minor civil divisions, congressional districts.

Content: household type; housing units; units in structure; number of rooms; tenure; value; rent; vacancy/occupancy status.

1990 Census of Population and Housing Summary Tape File 3A. CD-ROM. WEB. U.S. Department of Commerce. Bureau of the Census. Data User Services Division. C 3.282/2: Item 0154-F-01. ASI 2551-11. <http://venus.census.gov/cdrom/lookup>; <http://sunsite.Berkeley.edu/GovData/info/>; <http://govinfo.kerr.orst.edu/stateis.html>.

Coverage: states, counties, metropolitan areas, urbanized areas, county subdivisions, places, tracts, block numbering areas, block groups. Content: family type; household type; housing units; householder characteristics; vehicle availability; tenure; units in structure; value; rent; monthly owner costs; vacancy/occupancy status; number of rooms; number of bedrooms; condominium status; kitchen facilities; sewage disposal; year built; water source; heating fuel; telephone availability; plumbing facilities.

1990 Census of Population and Housing Summary Tape File 3B. CD-ROM. WEB. U.S. Department of Commerce. Bureau of the Census. Data Users Services Division. C 3.282/2: Item 0154-F-01. ASI 2551-13. <http://venus.census.gov/cdrom/lookup>; <http://sunsite.Berkeley.edu/GovData/info/>.

Coverage: zip codes. Content: family type; household type; housing units; householder characteristics; vehicle availability; tenure; units in structure; value; rent; monthly owner costs; vacancy/occupancy status; number of rooms; number of bedrooms; condominium status; kitchen facilities; sewage disposal; year built; water source; heating fuel; telephone availability; plumbing facilities.

1990 Census of Population and Housing Summary Tape File 3C. CD-ROM. WEB. U.S. Department of Commerce. Bureau of the Census. Data User Services Division. C 3.282/2: Item 0154-F-01. ASI 2551-14. <http://venus.census.gov/cdrom/lookup>; <http://sunsite.Berkeley.edu/GovData/info/>; <http://govinfo.kerr.orst.edu/stateis.html>.

Coverage: U.S., regions, divisions, states, counties, selected county subdivisions of 10,000 or more, metropolitan areas, urbanized places, places of 10,000 or more. Content: family type; household type; housing units; householder characteristics; vehicle availability; tenure; units in structure; value; rent; monthly owner costs; vacancy/occupancy status; number of rooms; number of bedrooms; condominium status; kitchen facilities; sewage disposal; year built; water source; heating fuel; telephone availability; plumbing facilities.

Congressional Districts of the United States Summary Tape File 1D; Summary Tape File 3D. CD-ROM. U.S. Department of Commerce. Bureau of the Census. C 3.282/4: Item 0154-F-05. ASI 2551-18. <http://www.census.gov/prod/www/abs/congprof.html>.

Coverage: states, congressional districts, counties, places, American Indian areas.

Content: household and family types; housing units; householder characteristics; vehicle availability; tenure; units in structure; value; rent; monthly owner costs; vacancy/occupancy status; number of rooms; number of bedrooms; condominium status; kitchen facilities; sewage disposal; year built; water source; heating fuel; telephone availability; plumbing facilities.

1990 Census of Population and Housing Subject Summary Tape Files. CD-ROM. U.S. Department of Commerce. Bureau of the Census. Data User Services Division. C 3.286: Item 0154-G. ASI 2551-12.

Coverage: varies; U.S., regions, divisions, states, metropolitan areas.

Content: data on selected topics including metropolitan housing characteristics, housing of the elderly, characteristics of new housing units, mobile homes, and condominiums.

The American Community Survey. CD-ROM. WEB. (annual) 1996–. U.S. Department of Commerce. Bureau of the Census. C 3.297: Item 0154-B-14. <http://www.census.gov/CMS/www/index_c.htm>; <http://www.census.gov/CMS/www/>; <http://purl.access.gpo.gov/GPO/LPS1258>.

Coverage: selected counties and cities.

Content: household and family types; housing units; householder characteristics; housing characteristics (bedrooms, units in structure, water, sewage disposal, year built, heating fuel, air conditioning, telephones, vehicles available); vacant and occupied units; housing costs (rent, mortgage status, monthly owner costs, value); plumbing/kitchen facilities.

1990 Housing Highlights. PRINT. U.S. Department of Commerce. Economics and Statistics Administration. Bureau of the Census. C 3.224/3-8: Item 0140-A-06. ASI 2326-21, 2328-83.

Coverage: U.S., states.

Content: total housing inventory; owner-occupied units; renter-occupied units; vacant units; race of householder; median value or rent.

Census of Housing Web Page. WEB. U.S. Department of Commerce. Bureau of the Census. <http://www.census.gov/hhes/www/censushousing.html>.

Content: overview of the census with links to selected data and information.

American FactFinder. WEB. U.S. Department of Commerce. Bureau of the Census. <http://factfinder.census.gov/java_prod/dads.ui.homePage.HomePage>.

Coverage: U.S., regions, divisions, states, counties, county subdivisions, congressional districts, metropolitan areas, urbanized areas, places, tracts, block numbering areas, block groups, zip codes, American Indian areas.

Content: 1990 census data; 2000 census data as it becomes available; American Community Survey data; other census products.

Discussion

The *Census of Housing* provides in-depth information on the number of houses in existence and their use, structure, financial characteristics, and equipment. Information on housing values in a given area, water source and sewer availability, fuel and heating equipment and costs, and mortgage data can be valuable to local planners, businesses interested in potential markets and new locations, utilities, banks, and many other researchers.

The two basic series of publications are *General Housing Characteristics* and *Detailed Housing Characteristics*. Each of these series consists of a U.S. summary volume, individual state reports, and (beginning with the 1990 Census) three additional reports on American Indian and Alaska Native areas, metropolitan areas, and urbanized areas. As with most census volumes there are table-finding guides at the beginning of each report that list topics covered and correlate them with table numbers. There are also reports on *Metropolitan Housing Characteristics*, and *Residential Finance*.

Using the small area data available in *Population and Housing Characteristics for Census Tracts and Block Numbering Areas*, it is possible to obtain statistics on a portion of a city or a county. Census tracts are areas with an average population of 4,000 in a metropolitan area. A block numbering area is a similar area in a nonmetropolitan area. (The 2000 census will eliminate the term "block numbering area" and call all of these areas census tracts). The census tract/block numbering area reports are issued for each metropolitan area and for the nonmetropolitan area of each state. Maps showing tract boundaries and identifying each tract by number are available for each census tract report. For the 1990 census, depository libraries were only able to receive tract maps for their state. Maps for areas in other states are available in each state's regional depository library and can also be purchased from the Census Bureau or in microfiche from Congressional Information Service. (Before 1990, depository libraries could receive all tract maps.)

Population and Housing Unit Counts, Summary Population and Housing Characteristics and *Summary Social, Economic, and Housing Characteristics* present less detailed housing data than the *General* and *Detailed Housing Characteristics* reports, but cover smaller places and county subdivisions. The latter two reports do not, however, cover metropolitan areas. *Population and Housing Characteristics for Congressional Districts of the 103rd Congress* covers a wide range of housing data for congressional districts.

The *1990 Census of Population and Housing Summary Tape File* CD-ROMs contain the data used to produce the printed census reports. The Summary Tape File 1 series contains data from the short questionnaire sent to everyone (100-percent data). It consists of subseries A, B, and C which cover different geographic areas. Summary Tape File 1A contains basic housing data for state and substate areas.

Summary Tape File 1B contains similar data for blocks, the smallest level of geography available in the census. Blocks are usually bounded by streets and average about 30 people. The data for such a small area as a block are limited. Before the 1990 census, block reports were available to depository libraries in microfiche (1980) or paper (1970 and earlier) and were accompanied by maps. 1990 block maps were not depository. Paper copies of 1990 block maps may be purchased from the Census Bureau. *Summary Tape File 1C* contains U.S. summary data for housing as well as data for other selected geographic areas.

Summary Tape File 3A contains data from the long questionnaire sent only to a sample of the population (sample data). *Summary Tape File 3C* contains the same data tables, but covers different geographic areas, including United States summary data. *Summary Tape File 3B* contains zip code data. *Congressional Districts of the United States* contains both *Summary Tape File 1 and 3* data for congressional districts.

Census reports mentioned above that are generated from *Summary Tape File 1* data include: *General Housing Characteristics* and *Summary Population and Housing Characteristics*. *Summary Tape File 3A* corresponds to *Detailed Housing Characteristics* and *Summary Social, Economic, and Housing Characteristics*. Tract reports contain a combination of data from both files. Data from several of these CDs are also available on the Internet.

The American Community Survey is an ongoing monthly survey that is in its initial phases of development. When fully implemented (presently expected to be in 2003) this survey will replace the long form or sample data in the decennial census with more current annual estimates. The data available from the survey are presently similar to that found in *Summary Tape File 3*. Adjustments in the data collected may be made as needs change. During the development stage, data are collected only for a small number of test sites. Coverage will gradually be expanded and by 2004 coverage is expected to include all states, counties, cities, metropolitan areas, and population groups of 65,000 people or more. By 2008 coverage for smaller areas including census tracts will become available.

1990 Housing Highlights is a series of one-page fact sheets for the United States and each state plus one fact sheet on financial facts. The fact sheets summarize data from the 1990 census. The state and U.S. fact sheets contain a brief narrative analysis of housing trends in homeownership, household size, vacancy rates, one-family homes, and value or rent. Charts show number of housing units, one-family homes, and median value and rent. There is also a table on occupied units by race of householder. The *Financial Facts* title is four pages in length and describes trends in home values and rents. Tables rank states and regions for median home value and rent. Maps illustrate the percent change in median value and rent since 1980.

The *Census of Housing Web Page* contains background information on the *Census of Housing* and links to 1990 census data, 2000 census information, and selected historical data. The 1990 link provides access to selected *Summary Tape File* CD-ROMs through the Lookup feature. *Summary Tape Files 3A, 3B, 3C, 1A,* and *1C* are available. Also available under the 1990 link are selected data tables and the *American FactFinder* database.

American FactFinder is a Census Bureau Web database designed to provide access to data from the 1990 and 2000 *Census of Population and Housing*, the *American Community Survey*, and the 1997 *Economic Census*. It also contains a mapping feature and an option to search for information on Census Bureau products. Housing data from the 1990 census are available in both the "Facts about My Community" section and the "Population and Housing Facts" section. Users make a series of selections from lists of geographic areas, tables, and/or sources or search by word to identify and display data. A general search option is also available.

The 2000 census is expected to have fewer print products than the 1990 census. Data will be disseminated primarily through the Web, *American FactFinder*, and CD-ROMs.

ECONOMIC CENSUS SOURCES
Checklist

Economic Census. PRINT. WEB. (quinquennial) 1997–. U.S. Department of Commerce. Economics and Statistics Administration. Census Bureau. (Formerly published as individual censuses for specific economic sectors.) ASI 2373. <http://www.census.gov/epcd/www/econ97.html>; <http://www.census.gov/mp/www/pub/ind/msind.html#Industry>; <http://www.census.gov/prod/www/abs/economic.html>.

> Coverage: U.S., states, counties.
> Content: construction industry data; number of establishments; number of employees; payroll; value of construction work done; expenses, capital expenditures; assets; and inventories.

Census of Construction Industries. PRINT. WEB. (quinquennial) 1967–1992. U.S. Department of Commerce. Bureau of the Census. C 3.245/ Item 0133-D-02. ASI 2371, 2373, 2375, 2377. 1992 census reports: <http://www.census.gov/epcd/www/92result.html>; <http://www.census.gov/mp/www/pub/ind/msind.html#con>; <http://www.census.gov/prod/www/abs/cons-hou.html#contsvy>.

> Coverage: U.S., regions, states, metropolitan areas of 500,000 or more.
> Content: SIC groups 15-17, 6552; kinds of industries, number of establishments, value of construction, payroll, employment, operating expenses, capital expenditures, depreciation, inventories, type of operation and legal form of organization.

Economic Census. CD-ROM. (quinquennial) 1987–. U.S. Department of Commerce. Economics and Statistics Administration. Bureau of the Census. C 3.277: Item 0154-C.

> Coverage: U.S., states, counties, metropolitan areas, places of 2,500 or more, zip codes.
> Content: *Economic Census* reports.

American FactFinder. WEB. U.S. Department of Commerce. Bureau of the Census. <http://factfinder.census.gov/java_prod/dads.ui.homePage.HomePage>.

> Coverage: U.S., states, counties.
> Content: 1997 *Economic Census* as it becomes available; other census products.

Discussion

The *Economic Census* is taken every five years covering years ending in "2" and in "7." The data are collected in the year following the year of coverage (the 1997 census was conducted in 1998) and data may begin to appear in the year following that. Major changes took place beginning with the 1997 *Economic Census* both in organization and in publishing formats. The implementation of the NAICS classification system reorganized and increased industry coverage resulting in data being published for 18 economic sectors, one of which is construction. The previous economic census for 1992, based on the SIC classification system, was organized into eight sectors, also including construction. Also beginning with 1997, data are published almost entirely on the Internet and on CD-ROM with only a small number of summary publications published in print format.

The 1997 *Economic Census* reports for the construction sector include an industry series, a geographic area series (statistics by state), and a subject series. The subject series consists of two summary reports, one for the industry series and one for the geographic series. These two reports will be the only ones published in print.

The Census Bureau's *Economic Census* Web page lists reports from the 1997 census with links to the full text as they are released. A link is also available for the 1992 reports. General information about the census is also available, including the *Guide to the 1997 Economic Census*.

American FactFinder is a Census Bureau Web database designed to provide access to data from the 1990 and 2000 *Census of Population and Housing*, the *American Community Survey*, and the 1997 *Economic Census*. It also contains a mapping feature and an option to search for information on Census Bureau products. 1997 *Economic Census* data are available in the "Industry and Business Facts" section as it is released. The Industry Quick Reports option allows the user to select from a list of NAICS sectors and code numbers or to search by word to identify and display a basic industry report. The industry reports show number of establishments, number of employees, annual payroll, and shipments/sales/receipts by state. Similarly, the Geography Quick Reports option can be used to display a geographic area report. The geographic report shows similar data items to the industry report for all industries at the two-digit NAICS sector level for the selected area. A "Build a Query" option is also available. This option allows the user to search for or select specific data sets for display.

CENSUS GUIDES
Checklist

Product Catalog. WEB. U.S. Census Bureau. C 3.163/3: Item 0138. <http://www.census.gov/mp/www/censtore.html>.

Content: descriptions and prices of Census Bureau products.

Census Catalog and Guide. CD-ROM. WEB. (annual) 1946–. U.S. Department of Commerce. Economics and Statistics Administration. Census Bureau. (CD-ROM not distributed to depository libraries) (Issued in print through 1998 under C 3.163/3:, Item 0138) (Title varies) <http://www.census.gov/mp/www/censtore.html>; <http://www.census.gov/prod/www/abs/catalogs.html>; <http://purl.access.gpo.gov/GPO/LPS3138>.

Content: CD-ROM version of the Web *Product Catalog*.

Bureau of the Census Catalog of Publications 1790–1972. PRINT. (1974) U.S. Department of Commerce. Social and Economic Statistics Administration. Bureau of the Census. C 56.222/2-2:790-972. ASI (75) 2308-1.

Content: complete listing of publications in each census as well as all other Census Bureau publications, with histories and descriptions.

Monthly Product Announcement. PRINT. WEB. (monthly) U.S. Department of Commerce. Economics and Statistics Administration. Census Bureau. C 3.163/7: Item 0138-A-02. ASI 2302-6. <http://www.census.gov/mp/www/mpa.html#MPA>; <http://purl.access.gpo.gov/GPO/LPS1680>.

Content: new products issued each month.

1990 Census of Population and Housing: Guide. PRINT. (1992) U.S. Department of Commerce. Economics and Statistics Administration. Bureau of the Census. C 3.223/22:90-R-1A/pt. Item 0154. ASI (92, 93) 2555-1.

Content: history, questionnaire content, data collection procedures, geography, data products, understanding the data, sources of assistance.

Guide to the 1997 Economic Census. WEB. U.S. Census Bureau. <http://www.census.gov/epcd/www/guide.html>.

Content: publication schedule, reports available, industry classification, geography, content, types of reports.

Discussion

Some of the Census Bureau guides that are of help in using the *Census of Housing* and the *Economic Census* and related census publications are listed above.

The Census Bureau *Product Catalog* describes agency products and provides availability and ordering information. Products are listed by format and then by subject category or series. Individual title descriptions include prices, ordering information, formats, subject content, geographic coverage, and links to online data. The *Census Catalog and Guide* on CD-ROM contains the Web *Product Catalog* as of the specified date. The *Monthly Product Announcement* serves as an update to the catalog. It lists, but does not describe, publications released during the previous month. The cumulative catalog, *Bureau of the Census Catalog of Publications 1790–1972*, is a thorough historical guide to censuses and publication series.

The *1990 Census of Population and Housing: Guide* contains detailed information on the 1990 Census of Population and Housing. Important features include definitions of geographic areas used in the census and lists and descriptions of map series, printed reports, and other data products. One chapter also provides advice on understanding census statistics. An extensive appendix on sources of assistance includes a detailed list of Census Bureau contacts and a directory of State Data Centers and related organizations. The guide also provides information on census history and procedures.

The *Guide to the 1997 Economic Census* describes the reports issued and gives general information on the NAICS industry classification system, geographic coverage, data content, and publication formats. The *Guide* includes a chart of data items contained in the census with associated geographic coverage arranged by sector; descriptions of publication series; lists of reports by sector, with geographic coverage, format, and publication schedule; and a list of reports that have been issued by series with links to the full text.

CURRENT CENSUS SOURCES: HOUSING

Checklist

Current Housing Reports. U.S. Department of Commerce. Economics and Statistics Administration. Census Bureau.

American Housing Survey for the United States. PRINT. WEB. (biennial) 1973–. C 3.215:H-150/. (Earlier, C 3.215/18-) (Titled *Annual Housing Survey* before 1985) (Supplements, C 3.215:H-151/). Item 0141-A. ASI 2485-12. (Supplements, ASI 2485-13,-14). GPO. <http://www.census.gov/mp/www/pub/con/mscho.html#ahs>; <http://www.census.gov/prod/www/abs/cons-hou.html#house>; <http://www.huduser.org/datasets/ahs.html>.
> Coverage: U.S., regions.
> Content: physical and financial housing characteristics; household composition and income; housing value and costs; neighborhood characteristics; previous unit of recent movers and reasons for move; data by owner-occupied or renter-occupied housing and by Black, Hispanic, and elderly householders.

American Housing Survey for the [name] Metropolitan Area in [year]. PRINT. WEB. (annual) 1974–. C 3.215:H-170/. (Earlier, C 3.215/17) (Titled *Annual Housing Survey* before 1984) (Supplements, C 3.215/16:) Item 0141-A. ASI 2485-6. (Supplement, 2485-8) <http://www.census.gov/mp/www/pub/con/mscho.html#ahs>; <http://www.census.gov/prod/www/abs/cons-hou.html#house>; <http://www.huduser.org/datasets/ahs.html>.
> Coverage: selected metropolitan areas, selected subareas (counties, places).
> Content: physical and financial housing characteristics; household composition and income; housing value and costs; neighborhood characteristics; previous unit of recent movers and reasons for move; data by owner-occupied or renter-occupied housing and by Black and Hispanic householders.

American Housing Survey. CD-ROM. 1985–89–. C 3.215/19: Item 0156-P.

> Content: microdata files from the *American Housing Survey.*

Housing Vacancies and Homeownership. WEB. (quarterly) 1955–. C 3.215:H-111/. (Title varies) Item 0141-A. ASI 2482-1, 2484-1. <http://www.census.gov/hhes/www/hvs.html>; <http://purl.access.gpo.gov/GPO/LPS1377>.
> Coverage: U.S., regions, states (in annual data), selected metropolitan areas (in annual data).
> Content: vacancy rates by selected physical and financial characteristics; homeownership rates by age of householder; housing inventory; selected physical and financial characteristics of vacant units by units in structure; type of vacant units.

Market Absorption of Apartments. PRINT. WEB. C 3.215:H-130/. Item 0141-A. ASI 2482-2, 2484-2. GPO. <http://www.census.gov/hhes/www/soma.html>; <http://www.census.gov/mp/www/pub/con/mscho17a.html>; <http://www.census.gov/prod/www/abs/apart.html>.
> Coverage: U.S., regions.
> Content: absorption rates of completed apartments and condominiums; selected characteristics of apartments and condominiums rented or sold.

Characteristics of Apartments Completed. PRINT. WEB. C 3.215:H 131/. Item 0141-A. ASI 2484-3. <http://www.census.gov/mp/www/pub/con/mscho18a.html>; <http://www.census.gov/prod/www/abs/h131apt.html>; <http://purl.access.gpo.gov/GPO/LPS3600>.
> Coverage: U.S., regions.
> Content: selected financial and physical characteristics of apartments and condominiums completed.

Housing Characteristics. PRINT. WEB. (irregular) 1955–. C 3.215:H 121/. Item 0141-A. ASI 2486-1. <http://www.census.gov/mp/www/pub/con/mscho15a.html>.
> Coverage: varies; U.S., regions.
> Content: reports on housing topics.

Discussion

The *Current Housing Reports* series includes *American Housing Survey* reports that supplement the *Census of Housing.* Many of the data items found in the *Census of Housing* are found in the *American Housing Survey* reports, but some of the data are unique to this series. The *American Housing Survey for the United States* and *American Housing Survey for the [name] Metropolitan Area in [year]* are similar in content. Statistics cover such housing characteristics as number of rooms, size of unit and lot, heating equipment, plumbing facilities, appliances, and garages. There is also information on the number and characteristics of occupants, including age, marital status, education, and income. Financial data such as mortgages and monthly housing costs are included, as well as indicators of quality such as number of toilet breakdowns, holes in roof, and trash accumulation. The national report differs from the metropolitan areas report in that the national report has separate chapters on elderly householders and on housing in central cities, suburbs, and outside metropolitan areas. The metropolitan series does incorporate some data on the elderly in other tables. Before 1985 the national report was issued in several separate parts each year. Due to the redesign of the survey in 1985, comparisons over the years may not be accurate. The metropolitan series covers 46 areas of which a varying number are published each year on a rotating basis. The number of metropolitan areas covered has varied over the years.

A supplement is issued for both the United States and metropolitan *American Housing Survey* reports. The *Supplement to the American Housing Survey for the United States* provides a selection of data items from the main report classified by family type, such as married couple or female householder, no husband present. Some additional data on neighborhood quality is available, including the role of public elementary schools, public transportation, and neighborhood shopping. Data on the journey to work is also available. The *Supplement to the American Housing Survey for Selected Metropolitan Areas in [year]* is similar in content except it does not cover journey to work.

The *American Housing Survey* CD-ROMs contain microdata files (original survey responses) for the national and metropolitan area surveys. No software is included on the CDs. Use of these files requires additional statistical analysis software.

Additional titles in the *Current Housing Reports* series cover vacancy rates and characteristics of apartments. *Housing Vacancies and Homeownership* gives number of vacant apartments and homes by various characteristics such as number of bedrooms, year built, and rent or value. The annual data covers smaller geographic areas than the quarterly data. This publication was issued in print through 1994. *Market Absorption of Apartments* provides information on how many new apartments and condominiums are rented or sold within specified time periods and the rent or price and number of bedrooms of those rented or sold. The annual issue includes additional features of rented apartments such as swimming pools, dishwashers, and utilities. *Characteristics of Apartments Completed* is very similar to the annual issue for *Market Absorption of Apartments*. It covers number of apartments and condominiums completed by number of bedrooms, rent, and availability of selected features. The absorption data is less detailed. The *Housing Characteristics* series consists of a small number of special studies issued irregularly, such as *What We Have Learned About Properties, Owners, and Tenants from the 1995 Property Owners and Managers Survey* (C 3.215:H 121/98-1) and *Moving to America – Moving to Homeownership* (C 3.215:H 121/97-2).

CURRENT CENSUS SOURCES: CONSTRUCTION

Checklist

STAT-USA Internet. WEB. U.S. Department of Commerce. C 1.91: Item 0128-P. <http://www.stat-usa.gov/>.

Coverage: U.S., regions, divisions, states, metropolitan areas.
Content: number and value of housing units authorized; housing starts; building permits; housing units completed; vacancies; homeownership rates; new construction; new home sales.

Current Construction Reports. PRINT. WEB. U.S. Department of Commerce. Economics and Statistics Administration. Census Bureau. (Titles vary). <http://www.census.gov/const/www/index.html>; <http://www.census.gov/prod/www/abs/conshou.html#contsvy>; <http://www.census.gov/mp/www/pub/ind/msind.html#tion>.

Housing Starts. PRINT. WEB. (monthly) 1959–. C 3.215/2:C 20/. Item 0140-A-01. ASI 2382-1. GPO. <http://www.census.gov/ftp/pub/const/www/c20index.html>; <http://www.census.gov/mp/www/pub/con/mscho04a.html>; <http://www.census.gov/prod/www/abs/c20.html>.

Coverage: U.S., regions.
Content: new privately owned housing units started and authorized; units in structure; purpose or intended use; time from authorization to start; time from start to completion; mobile home placements, average sales price, inventories, and shipments.

Housing Completions. PRINT. WEB. (monthly) 1970–. C 3.215/13:C 22/. Item 0140-A-08. ASI 2382-2. GPO. <http://www.census.gov/ftp/pub/const/www/c22index.html>; <http://www.census.gov/mp/www/pub/con/mscho06a.html>; <http://www.census.gov/prod/www/abs/c22.html>.

Coverage: U.S., regions.
Content: new privately owned housing units completed; number of units in structure; housing units under construction; physical characteristics of completed houses/buildings.

New One-Family Houses Sold. PRINT. WEB. (monthly) 1962–. C 3.215/9:C 25/. Item 0140-A-06. ASI 2382-3. GPO. <http://www.census.gov/ftp/pub/const/www/c25index.html>; <http://www.census.gov/mp/www/pub/con/mscho07a.html>; <http://www.census.gov/prod/www/abs/c25.html>.

Coverage: U.S., regions.
Content: houses sold and for sale total, by stage of construction, by median number of months on market, and by type of financing; supply available; houses sold by sales price; median and average sales price overall and by type of financing; price indexes.

Characteristics of New Housing. PRINT. WEB. (annual) 1963–. C 3.215/9-3: Item 0140-A-06. ASI 2384-1. GPO. <http://www.census.gov/ftp/pub/const/www/c25index.html>; <http://www.census.gov/mp/www/pub/con/mscho07b.html>.

Coverage: U.S., regions.
Content: purpose of construction; physical and financial characteristics for completed and sold housing and mobile homes; type of financing; sales price; construction/design features; floor area.

Value of Construction Put in Place. PRINT. WEB. (monthly) 1959–. C 3.215/3:C 30/. Item 0140-A-02. ASI 2382-4. GPO. <http://www.census.gov/ftp/pub/const/www/c30index.html>; <http://www.census.gov/mp/www/pub/

con/mscho09a.html>; <http://www.census.gov/prod/www/abs/c30.html>.

> Coverage: U.S., regions, divisions.
> Content: value of private and public construction by type.

Housing Units Authorized by Building Permits. WEB. (monthly) 1959–. C 3.215/4:C 40/. Item 0140-A-03. ASI 2382-5, 2384-2. <http://www.census.gov/ftp/pub/const/www/c40index.html>; <http://www.census.gov/pub/const/www/C40/c40text.html>.

> Coverage: U.S., regions, divisions, states, metropolitan areas, permit-issuing places.
> Content: number of housing units authorized; value; units in structure.

Expenditures for Residential Improvements and Repairs. PRINT. WEB. (quarterly) 1961–. C 3.215/8:C 50/. Item 0140-A-05. ASI 2382-7. GPO. <http://www.census.gov/ftp/pub/const/www/c50index.html>; <http://www.census.gov/mp/www/pub/con/mscho12a.html>; <http://www.census.gov/prod/www/abs/c50.html>.

> Coverage: U.S., regions.
> Content: expenditures for maintenance and repairs, additions and alterations, and major replacements; expenditures by property type, by year built, and by payments to contractors or materials purchased; annual data by job category and selected household characteristics.

Discussion

STAT-USA Internet is a fee-based service, but federal depository libraries may register for free access for two workstations. The *STAT-USA Internet* site is divided into two areas: State of the Nation and Globus & NTDB. The State of the Nation area contains domestic economic statistical releases. Current versions of the top 50 releases are organized into subject areas including Housing and Construction. Releases in this category include *Census Construction Review, Census State Housing Permits, Housing Starts and Building Permits, Housing Units Completed, New Construction,* and *New Home Sales.* Additional files, including earlier data, are available in the State of the Nation Library. These files are also arranged by categories with the housing and construction data under the Economic Indicators category. A search option for the State of the Nation Library is also available.

The *Current Construction Reports* series provides a variety of monthly, quarterly, and annual statistics on new housing and construction. All of the information in this series of reports centers around the number, type, characteristics, value, sales, and price of new housing and construction or on improvements and repairs.

Housing Starts contains statistics on new privately owned housing and construction and mobile homes. A standard set of monthly tables is supplemented by additional quarterly and annual tables in various issues throughout the year on purpose or intended use of new housing units and more detailed mobile home data. Annual supplements also appear on the length of time from authorization to start of construction and from start to completion.

Housing Completions provides statistics on housing units completed and under construction by number of units in structure. A standard set of monthly tables is supplemented by additional quarterly tables on selected characteristics of completed housing. Examples of characteristics covered include type of heating system, air conditioning, parking facilities, bedrooms, floor area, type of foundation, and exterior wall material.

New One-Family Houses Sold gives data on number of houses sold and sales price. A standard set of monthly tables is supplemented by additional quarterly tables on prices by region, type of financing, and price indexes.

Characteristics of New Housing is the annual issue for *New One-Family Houses Sold.* The annual provides more detail on the characteristics of one-family housing units both completed and sold. Data cover such characteristics as central air conditioning, number of bathrooms and bedrooms, number of fireplaces, type of heating system and fuel, and number of stories. Price data for houses sold include total, average, and median price; price by type of financing; price per square foot; and price by selected physical characteristics. A smaller number of tables also cover multifamily housing, contractor-built houses started, and mobile home placements. A supplement covers types and characteristics of new apartments and condominiums.

Value of Construction Put in Place contains statistics on the value of private and public construction by type. Types of construction include residential; industrial; office; hotels and motels; religious; educational; hospital and institutional; public utilities; highways and streets; military facilities; conservation and development; sewer systems; and water supply facilities. Annual supplemental tables appearing in various issues cover total time and monthly progress from start to completion and provide additional data for regions and divisions. The May issue includes revised monthly and annual data.

Housing Units Authorized by Building Permits contains the smallest geographic area data in the *Current Construction Reports* series. It gives statistics on the number of housing units authorized and value by number of units in structure. This title was discontinued in print format at the end of 1995.

Expenditures for Residential Improvements and Repairs gives statistics on expenditures for maintenance and upkeep. Additional annual tables appear in the last issue for the year and give data on expenditures by job category. Examples of job categories include decks and porches; fences; plumbing; roofing; painting and papering; kitchen remodeling; and windows and doors. The annual tables also include expenditures for owner-occupied one-unit properties by selected characteristics such as property value, year unit acquired, and income and age of householder. More detailed regional data by property type are also included in the annual tables.

INDEXES
Checklist

American Statistics Index (ASI). PRINT. (monthly) 1973–. Bethesda, MD: Congressional Information Service.

Statistical Universe. WEB. Bethesda, MD: Congressional Information Service.

Catalog of United States Government Publications (MOCAT). WEB. 1994–. U.S. Government Printing Office. Superintendent of Documents. <http://www.gpo.gov/catalog>; <http://www.access.gpo.gov/su_docs/locators/cgp/index.html>; <http://purl.access.gpo.gov/GPO/LPS844>.

Monthly Catalog of United States Government Publications. CD-ROM. 1996–. U.S. Government Printing Office. Superintendent of Documents. GP 3.8/7: Item 0557-C. GPO.

Monthly Catalog of United States Government Publications (Condensed version). PRINT. (monthly) 1996–. U.S. Government Printing Office. Superintendent of Documents. GP 3.8/8: (Earlier full version, GP 3.8:, 1895-1995). Item 0557-D. GPO.

CIS/Index. PRINT. (monthly) 1970–. Bethesda, MD: Congressional Information Service.

Congressional Universe. WEB. Bethesda, MD: Congressional Information Service.

Discussion

A comprehensive listing of material can be found in the *American Statistics Index (ASI)* by looking under such headings as "Construction industry," "Housing condition and occupancy," "Housing construction," "Housing costs and financing," "Housing sales," and other headings beginning with "Housing." *Statistical Universe* includes a Web version of *ASI*.

The *Monthly Catalog* may also be used to locate materials, but does not provide the depth of indexing for statistics that *ASI* does. Look under subject headings beginning with "Housing" or "Construction Industry." Reports that are exclusively statistical are often indexed under the subheading "Statistics," such as "Housing-United States-Statistics." The complete version of the *Monthly Catalog* is available on the Web and CD-ROM. Commercial online and CD-ROM versions of the *Monthly Catalog* are also available.

CIS/Index can be used to identify congressional hearings and reports on housing and construction issues. Statistical data may sometimes be included. Look under "Construction industry," "Housing," and subjects beginning with "Housing." See also "Statistical data: housing and construction." *Congressional Universe* includes a Web version of *CIS*.

For more information on these indexes, see Chapter 3, "The Basics of Searching."

RELATED MATERIAL
Within this Work

Chapter 28 Population Statistics

Chapter 31 Business and Industry Statistics

GPO Subject Bibliographies. PRINT. WEB. GP 3.22/2:

<http://bookstore.gpo.gov/sb/about.html>.

No. 157 "Census of Construction"

No. 181 "Census of Population and Housing"

No. 216 "Construction Industry"

No. 280 "Housing and Development"

No. 311 "Census Tracts and Blocks (Publications)"

No. 312 "Census Tracts and Blocks (Maps)"

CHAPTER 33
Income

Income statistics originate from one of three agencies: the Census Bureau, the Bureau of Economic Analysis (BEA), and the Internal Revenue Service. Each of these agencies collects the data in different ways and uses different definitions of income. Data from one agency are not comparable to data from another.

SEARCH STRATEGY

This chapter shows a statistical search strategy. The steps to follow are

1. Consult ready-reference sources listed in the "General Statistical Sources" section of this chapter (these provide quite a bit of information on income);
2. Try the *Census of Population* itself, which also contains extensive income statistics;
3. Examine other statistical compendiums listed under "Additional Census-Related Sources," the "Bureau of Economic Analysis (BEA) Sources," and the "Internal Revenue Service (IRS) Sources" sections;
4. Search *American Statistics Index (ASI)* or the Web version, *Statistical Universe*, for additional information; and
5. Check for any "Related Material."

GENERAL STATISTICAL SOURCES
Checklist

Statistical Abstract of the United States. PRINT. WEB. (annual) 1878–. U.S. Department of Commerce. Economics and Statistics Administration. Bureau of the Census. C 3.134: Item 0150. ASI 2324-1. GPO. <http://www.census.gov/statab/www/>; <http://purl.access.gpo.gov/GPO/LPS2878>.

    Coverage: U.S., regions, states, selected metropolitan areas.

    Content: national income; total personal income; per capita income; money income of households by level and selected characteristics; mean and median income; persons below poverty level.

Statistical Abstract of the United States. CD-ROM. (annual) 1993–. U.S. Department of Commerce. Bureau of the Census. C 3.134/7: Item 0150-B. ASI 2324-14.

    Content: CD-ROM version of the *Statistical Abstract.*

Historical Statistics of the United States: Colonial Times to 1970. Parts 1-2. PRINT. (1975) U.S. Department of Commerce. Bureau of the Census. C 3.134/2:H 62/789-970/pt.1-2. Item 0151. ASI (76) 2328-2. GPO.

    Coverage: U.S., states.

    Content: national income (total personal income, per capita income); percent distribution of families by income level; median money income; correlation of income and demographic variables such as race, age, family characteristics.

Historical Statistics of the United States on CD-ROM: Colonial Times to 1970. CD-ROM. (1997) New York, NY: Cambridge University Press.

    Content: CD-ROM version of *Historical Statistics of the United States.*

State and Metropolitan Area Data Book. PRINT. WEB. (irregular) 1979–. U.S. Department of Commerce. Economics and Statistics Administration. Bureau of the Census. C 3.134/5: Item 0150. ASI 2328-54. GPO. <http://www.census.gov/statab/www.smadb.html>.

    Coverage: U.S., states, metropolitan areas, component cities and counties of metropolitan areas.

    Content: total and per capita personal income; percent of personal income attributable to earnings by industry sector; median household income; persons below poverty level.

State and Metropolitan Area Data Book. CD-ROM. (irregular) 1997/98–. U.S. Department of Commerce. Economics and Statistics Administration. Bureau of the Census. (Not distributed to depository libraries)

    Content: CD-ROM version of the *State and Metropolitan Area Data Book.*

County and City Data Book. PRINT. WEB. (quinquennial) 1947–. U.S. Department of Commerce. Economics and Statistics Administration. Bureau of the Census. C 3.134/2:C 83/2/year. Item 0151. ASI 2328-1. GPO. <http://fisher.lib.Virginia.EDU/ccdb/>.

> Coverage: U.S., regions, divisions, states, counties, cities of 25,000 or more, places of 2,500 or more.
> Content: total and per capita personal income; percent of personal income attributable to earnings by industry sector; per capita money income; median family and household income; families and persons below poverty level; percentage of households within an income range; rankings.

County and City Data Book. CD-ROM. (quinquennial) 1988–. U.S. Department of Commerce. Bureau of the Census. C 3.134/2-1: (Earlier, C 3.134/2:C 83/2/) Item 0151-D-01. ASI 2328-103.

> Content: CD-ROM version of the *County and City Data Book.*

County and City Extra: Annual Metro, City, and County Data Book. PRINT. (annual) 1992–. Lanham, MD: Bernan Press.

> Coverage: U.S., states, counties, metropolitan areas, cities of 25,000 or more, congressional districts.
> Content: updated version of the *County and City Data Book.*

USA Counties. CD-ROM. WEB. (irregular) 1992–. U.S. Department of Commerce. Economics and Statistics Administration. Bureau of the Census. C 3.134/6: Item 0150-B-01. ASI 2324-17. <http://govinfo.kerr.orst.edu/usaco-stateis.html>; <http://tier2.census.gov/usac/index.html-ssi>.

> Coverage: U.S., states, counties.
> Content: personal income; per capita personal and money income; median family and household money income; number of families and households in specified income ranges; persons and families below poverty level.

Discussion

Census Bureau statistical compendiums provide quick and easy access to income information. The choice of which source to use should be based on currency or geographic coverage, as well as content. The data are not drawn exclusively from the Census Bureau's own surveys — a wide range of sources has often been used. All provide excellent source notes, which can lead the user to other potential references that might provide more detail or cover different time periods.

The *Statistical Abstract of the United States* has a section on "Income, Expenditures, and Wealth" and answers most basic income questions, such as Kentucky's per capita income and state rank, the number of Black households in the $50,000–$74,999 income bracket, or the median income of college graduates. Statistics are selected from many of the more detailed sources covered in this chapter. Source notes at the end of each table can direct the user to more current or more detailed sources for the information in that table. This source is the most current and has the greatest range of detail of the sources listed in this section, but it does not cover small geographic areas. The full-text of recent editions of the *Statistical Abstract* is available on the Census Bureau Web site as PDF files. The *Statistical Abstract* is also available on CD-ROM. The CD uses Adobe Acrobat software and contains some additional geographic areas and time series in the form of spreadsheet files that are not in the printed version.

Historical Statistics of the United States: Colonial Times to 1970 has a national income and a consumer income section in part 1 and provides income statistics for the time period before 1970. A CD-ROM version of *Historical Statistics* is available from Cambridge University Press.

For smaller geographic areas, the *State and Metropolitan Area Data Book* and *County and City Data Book* give basic income information. The *State and Metropolitan Area Data Book* contains income data for metropolitan areas and their component cities and counties and states. The state section contains one data item not available at the other geographic levels: median household income. The state section, however, does not give personal income earnings by industry sector. The *State and Metropolitan Area Data Book* is available as a PDF file on the Census Bureau Web site. A CD-ROM version is also available. The *County and City Data Book* is divided into geographic sections: states, counties, cities, and places. Only median and per capita money income is available at the place level. The *County and City Data Book* is also available in CD-ROM from the Census Bureau. The University of Virginia Library Geospatial and Statistical Data Center offers recent editions of the *County and City Data Book* on the Internet in their interactive data area. Users select the desired edition, geography, and variables to create a customized data display.

County and City Extra is a commercially produced annual version of the *County and City Data Book.* The income data is similar to that in the *County and City Data Book*, with slightly fewer variables.

The *USA Counties* CD-ROM contains county and state data from the last two or three issues of the *County and City Data Book* and the *State and Metropolitan Area Data Book* to provide several years of data in one source. The data are similar to that found in the two data books. The Oregon State University Government Information Sharing Project provides access to the current issue on the Internet. Users select a geographic area profile or an area comparison and then the desired geography. A subject area can then be selected or a keyword search conducted to display data. The Census Bureau Web site contains a similar version.

CENSUS OF POPULATION SOURCES
Checklist

Census of Population. PRINT. (decennial) 1950–. U.S. Department of Commerce. Economics and Statistics Administration. Bureau of the Census. (Format has changed over the years; titles listed below reflect current format. Before 1950 included in comprehensive decennial census.)

Social and Economic Characteristics. C 3.223/7:, C 3.223/7-2:, C 3.223/7-3:, C 3.223/7-4: (Earlier title: *General Social and Economic Characteristics*) Items 0159-C-01 to 53, 0154-A-01 to 03. ASI 2531-5.

Coverage: U.S., states, counties, places of 2,500 or more, selected county subdivisions (MCDs) of 2,500 or more; separate reports on metropolitan areas, urbanized areas, American Indian and Alaska Native areas.

Content: median household and family income; per capita income; persons and families below poverty level; race and ancestry; income type; levels of income; family characteristics.

Population and Housing Characteristics for Census Tracts and Block Numbering Areas. C 3.223/11: (Earlier title, *Census Tracts*) Item 0156-K-01 to 53. ASI 2551-3.

Coverage: metropolitan areas, census tracts in metropolitan areas, census tracts or block numbering areas in the nonmetropolitan area portions of each state, counties, places of 10,000 or more.

Content: income levels; mean and median income; per capita income; family type; persons below poverty level.

Summary Social, Economic, and Housing Characteristics. C 3.223/23: Item 0156-M-01 to 53. ASI 2551-7.

Coverage: U.S., states, counties, places, county subdivisions (MCDs), American Indian and Alaska Native areas.

Content: per capita income; median family and household income; poverty status; children and elderly below poverty level.

Population and Housing Characteristics for Congressional Districts of the 103rd Congress. PRINT. C 3.223/20: (Title varies; before 1980 data were published in *Congressional District Data Book*) Item 0159-C-01 to 53. ASI 2551-4.

Coverage: congressional districts, counties, places of 10,000 or more, minor civil divisions of 10,000 or more.

Content: income and poverty status.

1990 Census of Population and Housing Summary Tape File 3A. CD-ROM. WEB. U.S. Department of Commerce. Bureau of the Census. Data User Services Division. C 3.282/2: Item 0154-F-01. ASI 2551-11. <http://venus.census.gov/cdrom/lookup>; <http://sunsite.Berkeley.edu/GovData/info/>; <http://govinfo.kerr.orst.edu/stateis.html>.

Coverage: states, counties, metropolitan areas, urbanized areas, county subdivisions, places, tracts, block numbering areas, block groups.

Content: total and median household income; type of income; total and median family income; per capita income; poverty status; some data by age, race, sex, household or family type.

1990 Census of Population and Housing Summary Tape File 3B. CD-ROM. WEB. U.S. Department of Commerce. Bureau of the Census. Data Users Services Division. C 3.282/2: Item 0154-F-01. ASI 2551-13. <http://venus.census.gov/cdrom/lookup>; <http://sunsite.Berkeley.edu/GovData/info/>.

Coverage: zip codes.

Content: total and median household income; type of income; total and median family income; per capita income; poverty status; some data by age, race, sex, household or family type.

1990 Census of Population and Housing Summary Tape File 3C. CD-ROM. WEB. U.S. Department of Commerce. Bureau of the Census. Data User Services Division. C 3.282/2: Item 0154-F-01. ASI 2551-14. <http://venus.census.gov/cdrom/lookup>; <http://sunsite.Berkeley.edu/GovData/info/>; <http://govinfo.kerr.orst.edu/stateis.html>.

Coverage: U.S., regions, divisions, states, counties, selected county subdivisions, metropolitan areas, urbanized places, places of 10,000 or more.

Content: total and median household income; type of income; total and median family income; per capita income; poverty status; some data by age, race, sex, household or family type.

Congressional Districts of the United States Summary Tape File 1D; Summary Tape File 3D. CD-ROM. U.S. Department of Commerce. Bureau of the Census. C 3.282/4: Item 0154-F-05. ASI 2551-18. <http://www.census.gov/prod/www/abs/congprof.html>.

Coverage: states, congressional districts, counties, places, American Indian areas.

Content: total and median household income; type of income; total and median family income; per capita income; poverty status; some data by age, race, sex, household or family type.

The American Community Survey. CD-ROM. WEB. (annual) 1996–. U.S. Department of Commerce. Bureau of the Census. C 3.297: Item 0154-B-14. <http://www.census.gov/CMS/www/index_c.htm>; <http://www.census.gov/CMS/www/>; <http://purl.access.gpo.gov/GPO/LPS1258>.

Coverage: selected counties and cities.

Content: household and family income; median income; per capita income; income type; poverty status.

Census 1990. WEB. U.S. Department of Commerce. Bureau of the Census. <http://www.census.gov/main/www/cen1990.html>.

Content: information and data from the 1990 census.

United States Census 2000. WEB. U.S. Department of Commerce. Bureau of the Census. <http://www.census.gov/dmd/www/2khome.htm>.

Content: information about the 2000 census.

American FactFinder. WEB. U.S. Department of Commerce. Bureau of the Census. <http://factfinder.census.gov/java_prod/dads.ui.homePage.HomePage>.

Coverage: U.S., regions, divisions, states, counties, county subdivisions, congressional districts, metropolitan areas, urbanized areas, places, tracts, block numbering areas, block groups, zip codes, American Indian areas.

Content: 1990 census data; 2000 census data as it becomes available; American Community Survey data; other census products.

Discussion

The *Census of Population* provides the most detailed income statistics available and the most complete geographic coverage. Most census reports contain a table-finding guide at the beginning that allows the user to match a subject, such as income, with the desired geographic area and find appropriate table numbers. Income statistics are given in relation to various demographic, educational, and employment characteristics.

The most detailed data are available in *Social and Economic Characteristics*, which consists of a U.S. summary report, individual state reports, and (beginning in 1990) three separate reports on metropolitan areas, urbanized areas, and American Indian and Alaska Native areas. *Population and Housing Characteristics for Census Tracts and Block Numbering Areas* contains the smallest geographic area information. Census tracts are areas of about 4,000 people in a metropolitan area. A block numbering area is a similar area in a nonmetropolitan area. (The 2000 census will eliminate the term "block numbering area" and call all of these areas census tracts). Reports in this series are issued for each metropolitan area and for each state. Maps showing tract boundaries and identifying each tract by number accompany the census tract reports. For the 1990 census, depository libraries were only able to receive the tract maps for their state. Maps for areas in other states are available in each state's regional depository library and can also be purchased from the Census Bureau or in microfiche from Congressional Information Service. (Before 1990, depository libraries could receive all tract maps.)

Summary Social, Economic, and Housing Characteristics gives summary data for small areas, like county subdivisions, that are not available elsewhere. This title was new for 1990 and replaces in part the 1980 report series called *Summary Characteristics for Governmental Units*. *Population and Housing Characteristics for Congressional Districts of the 103rd Congress* contains basic income and poverty data for congressional districts.

The *1990 Census of Population and Housing Summary Tape File 3A* CD-ROM contains census data for geographic levels down to the tract and block group level. Data include detailed economic, social, and housing information. *Summary Tape Files 3B and 3C* contain the same data tables, but cover different geographic areas. These *Summary Tape Files* are also available on the Internet. The *Congressional Districts of the United States* contains the same data for congressional districts. Many of the *Census of Population* reports mentioned in this chapter are generated from this file.

The *American Community Survey* is an ongoing monthly survey that is in its initial phases of development. When fully implemented (presently expected to be in 2003) this survey will replace the long form or sample data in the decennial census with more current annual estimates. The data available from the survey is presently similar to that found in *Summary Tape File 3*. Adjustments in the data collected may be made as needs change. During the development stage, data are collected only for a small number of test sites. Coverage will gradually be expanded and by 2004 coverage is expected to include all states, counties, cities, metropolitan areas, and population groups of 65,000 people or more. By 2008, coverage for smaller areas including census tracts will become available.

The *Census 1990* and *United States Census 2000* Web pages provided links to data and information available on the Census Bureau Web site. The *Census 1990* site contains links to the *Summary Tape File* CD-ROMs and *American FactFinder*. The *United States Census 2000* site contains information on the development and progress of the 2000 census.

American FactFinder is a Census Bureau Web database designed to provide access to data from the 1990 and 2000 *Census of Population and Housing*, the *American Community Survey*, and the 1997 *Economic Census*. It also contains a mapping feature and an option to search for information on Census Bureau products. Income data from the 1990 census is available in both the "Facts about My Community" section and the "Population and Housing Facts" section. Users make a series of selections from lists of geographic areas, tables, and/or sources or search by word to identify and display data. A general search option is also available.

The 2000 census is expected to have fewer print products than the 1990 census. Data will be disseminated primarily through the Web, *American FactFinder*, and CD-ROMs.

ADDITIONAL CENSUS-RELATED SOURCES
Checklist

Current Population Reports: Consumer Income. Series P-60. PRINT. WEB. U.S. Department of Commerce. Economics and Statistics Administration. Bureau of the Census. C 3.186:P-60/. Item 0142-C-07. GPO. ASI 2546-6. GPO. <http://www.census.gov/prod/www/abs/popula.html#income>; <http://www.census.gov/mp/www/pub/pop/mspop10.html>.
> Content: reports on income, poverty, and benefits, and related topics.

Money Income in the United States. PRINT. WEB. (annual) 1995–. C 3.186:P-60/ (Issued earlier under other titles) <http://www.census.gov/hhes/www/income.html>.
> Coverage: U.S., regions, states.
> Content: total income; levels of income; mean and median income; source of income; income distribution; data often by selected characteristics including age, race, sex, number of earners, work experience, size and type of family or household, education, occupation.

Poverty in the United States. PRINT. WEB. (annual) 1995–. C 3.186/22: (Issued earlier under other titles) <http://www.census.gov/hhes/www/poverty.html>.
> Coverage: U.S., regions, states.
> Content: poverty status and ratio of family income to poverty level by selected characteristics; work experience; income type; tables often by age, race, sex, and household type.

Current Population Reports: Special Studies. Series P-23. PRINT. WEB. U.S. Department of Commerce. Economics and Statistics Administration. Bureau of the Census. C 3.186:P-23/. Item 0142-C-02. GPO. ASI 2546-6. <http://www.census.gov/prod/www/abs/popula.html#popspec>; <http://www.census.gov/mp/www/pub/pop/mspop03.html>.

Content: reports on methods, concepts, and various demographic topics.

Subject Index to Current Population Reports and Other Population Report Series. PRINT. WEB. (1996) C 3.186:P-23/192. ASI (96) 2546-2.179. GPO. <http://www.census.gov/prod/2/pop/p23/p23-192.pdf>.

Content: index to *Current Population Reports* series.

Current Population Reports: Household Economic Studies. Series P-70. PRINT. WEB. U.S. Department of Commerce. Economics and Statistics Administration. Bureau of the Census. C 3.186:P-70/2/. Item 0142-C-08. ASI 2546-20. GPO. <http://www.census.gov/prod/www/abs/popula.html#pophhes>; <http://www.census.gov/mp/www/pub/pop/mspop12.html>.

Content: reports on the economic status of households, benefits received, and related social characteristics.

Income and Poverty. CD-ROM. (annual) 1993–. U.S. Department of Commerce. Bureau of the Census. C 3.224/12-2: Item 0155-C-01. ASI 2324-19.

Coverage: varies; U.S., divisions, regions, states, selected metropolitan areas.

Content: income of households, families, and persons by selected characteristics, including age, race, sex, and household type; poverty status by selected characteristics including age, race, sex, and education; Current Population Survey microdata files.

Small Area Income and Poverty Estimates Intercensal Estimates for States, Counties, and School Districts. WEB. U.S. Department of Commerce. Bureau of the Census. <http://www.census.gov/hhes/www/saipe.html>.

Coverage: states, counties, school districts.

Content: median household income; poverty status.

Income Web Page. WEB. U.S. Department of Commerce. Bureau of the Census. <http://www.census.gov/hhes/www/income.html>.

Content: data and full-text publications from the Census Bureau on income.

Poverty Web Page. WEB. U.S. Department of Commerce. Bureau of the Census. <http://www.census.gov/hhes/www/poverty.html>.

Content: data and full-text publications from the Census Bureau on poverty.

CPS Publications Income. WEB. U.S. Department of Labor. Bureau of Labor Statistics. U.S. Department of Commerce. Bureau of the Census. <http://www.bls.census.gov/cps/pub/pubincrn.htm>.

Content: press releases and detailed statistical tables from the Current Population Survey.

CPS Publications Poverty. WEB. U.S. Department of Labor. Bureau of Labor Statistics./U.S. Department of Commerce. Bureau of the Census. <http://www.bls.census.gov/cps/pub/pubpov.htm>.

Content: press releases and detailed statistical tables from the Current Population Survey.

FERRET (Federal Electronic Research and Review Extraction Tool). WEB. U.S. Department of Commerce. Bureau of the Census. <http://ferret.bls.census.gov/cgi-bin/ferret>.

Content: view prepared tables or extract customized data from major surveys, including the Current Population Survey and the Survey of Income and Program Participation.

American Housing Survey for the United States. PRINT. WEB. (biennial) 1973–. C 3.215:H-150/. (Earlier, C 3.215/18-) (Titled *Annual Housing Survey* before 1985) (Supplements, C 3.215:H-151/). Item 0141-A. ASI 2485-12. (Supplements, ASI 2485-13,-14). GPO. <http://www.census.gov/mp/www/pub/con/mscho.html#ahs>; <http://www.census.gov/prod/www/abs/cons-hou.html#house>; <http://www.huduser.org/datasets/ahs.html>.

Coverage: U.S., regions.

Content: household and family/individual income; median income; income sources; savings and investments; food stamps; data by household characteristics, race, and age 65 or over.

American Housing Survey for the [name] Metropolitan Area in [year]. PRINT. WEB. (annual) 1974–. C 3.215:H-170/. (Earlier, C 3.215/17) (Titled *Annual Housing Survey* before 1984) (Supplements, C 3.215/16:). Item 0141-A. ASI 2485-6. (Supplement, 2485-8). <http://www.census.gov/mp/www/pub/con/mscho.html#ahs>; <http://www.census.gov/prod/www/abs/cons-hou.html#house>; <http://www.huduser.org/datasets/ahs.html>.

Coverage: selected metropolitan areas, selected subareas (counties, places).

Content: household and family/individual income; median income; income sources; savings and investments; food stamps; data by household characteristics, race, and age 65 or over.

American Housing Survey. CD-ROM. 1985–89–. C 3.215/19: Item 0156-P.

Content: microdata files from the *American Housing Survey.*

Income of the Population 55 and Older. WEB. (biennial) 1976–. U.S. Social Security Administration. Office of Research, Evaluation and Statistics. HE 3.75: (Earlier, HE 3.2:IN 2/4, HE 3.56:). Item 0516-M. ASI 9954-7. (Earlier, 4744-26) GPO. <http://www.ssa.gov/policy/pubs/pages/IncomeoftheAged.htm>; <http://purl.access.gpo.gov/GPO/LPS2697>.

Coverage: U.S.

Content: detailed data on income sources received; total money income; amount from particular sources; relative importance of sources; proportions below the poverty line; most data by age, sex, race, marital status, and social security beneficiary status.

Discussion

For more current statistics than the latest census or for statistics for years in between censuses, the Census Bureau conducts two major on-going surveys, the Current Population Survey (CPS) and the Survey of Income and Program Participation (SIPP). Selected data from these surveys are published in the agency's *Current Population Reports* series, on its Web site, and on CD-ROM. Researchers may also extract data from the complete surveys via the Web.

The *Current Population Reports* series provides more current, although less detailed, data than the *Census of Population*. Several reports in these series contain income data. A complete list of previous reports arranged by subject, including income, can be found in *Subject Index to Current Population Reports and Other Population Report Series*. Recent reports are available on the *Census Bureau Web site*.

The *Current Population Reports: Consumer Income* series contains two major annual reports related to income, as well as occasional other income reports. *Money Income in the United States* contains detailed national statistics on income. Most data are national or regional, with one state table on median household income in the introductory text. An example of the type of data available is the number of married-couple families, with two or more children with both spouses working, that have an income between $45,000 and $49,999. An appendix provides definitions of terms such as the difference between a household and a family and what is included in "income."

Poverty in the United States contains tables on the number and percentage of persons below the poverty level and the ratio of their income to poverty level. Most data are national or regional, with one state table on the percentage of people in poverty in the introductory text. Examples of the type of data available include the number of families with a female householder receiving food stamps that were under 1.50 of poverty level and the percentage of women in metropolitan areas age 18–24 under .50 of poverty level. One table gives percentage of people in poverty under fourteen different definitions of income.

Examples of other recent titles in the P-60 series include *Measuring 50 Years of Economic Change* (C 3.186:P-60/203), a historical chartbook with time series tables on income, and *A Brief Look at Postwar U.S. Income Inequality* (C 3.186:P-60/191).

Both the *Current Population Reports: Special Studies* series and the *Current Population Reports: Household Economic Studies* series contain occasional reports related to income. Recent titles in the P-23 series include *Changes in Median Household Income: 1969 to 1996* (C 3.186:P-23/196) and *How We're Changing Demographic State of the Nation: 1997* (C 3.186:P-23/193), which discusses recent trends, including income. Recent titles in the P-70 series include *Dynamics of Economic Well-Being, Poverty 1993-94: Trap Door? Revolving Door? Or Both?* (C 3.186:P-70/2/63) and *Dynamics of Economic Well-Being: Income, 1993 to 1994 Moving Up and Down the Income Ladder* (C 3.186:P-70/2/65).

The *Income and Poverty* CD-ROM contains HTML and PDF files of income and poverty press releases and tables. Offline browser software and Adobe Acrobat software are included on the CD. HTML files were taken from the *Census Bureau Web site,* but are not identical to current Web site contents. Tables cover detailed income levels by a large number of demographic and household characteristics. Historical tables are also available. PDF files include publications from the *Current Population Reports* P-60 series. Geographic coverage for the HTML and PDF files is generally national and regional with some limited data for states and large metropolitan areas. Original survey data (microdata) for the Current Population Survey is also available on the CD with CrossTab software for tabulating data. This file contains national, regional, state, and selected metropolitan area data. Software and file types vary on earlier CDs.

The *Small Area Income and Poverty Estimates Intercensal Estimates for States, Counties, and School Districts* Web page contains the most recent small area income data. These data are not published in print format. The tables available for states and counties give number and percentage of people of all ages in poverty, people under age 18 in poverty, related children 5–17 in families in poverty, and median household income. School district data contain information on the number of poor children in each school district, but no specific income information.

The Census Bureau's *Income* and *Poverty Web Pages* provide a guide to Census Bureau data on income and poverty with links to related data and publications. The pages list Current Population Survey resources, *Census of Population* resources, other survey data, historical data, and related sites. The *Poverty Web Page* also includes poverty definitions and thresholds.

The *CPS Publications Income* and *CPS Publications Poverty* Web pages provide press releases and listings of tables from the Current Population Survey related to the *Current Population Reports: Consumer Income* (P-60) series. The tables are similar in content to those in the two annual reports *Money Income in the United States* and *Poverty in the United States*, but contain a larger number of data categories (such as more detailed income ranges) or combine a larger number of variables.

FERRET is a Web-based tool that allows users to work directly with original survey data to create their own tables. Users select from a list of specific surveys available, such as "CPS March Supplement 1992–1998." Background information on each survey is also available. After selecting the desired survey, users then have the option of viewing a set of already created tables or creating their own. To create tables, users select variables and output options. Some familiarity with the survey's contents, statistical terminology, and file formats is helpful for table creation.

The two *American Housing Survey* series contain almost identical data. The metropolitan series covers 46 areas of which a varying number are published each year on a rotating basis. These reports give number of households in an income range and correlate income with various household characteristics such as number of bathrooms, presence of children, presence of spouse, or type of heating equipment.

The *American Housing Survey* CD-ROMs contain microdata files (original survey responses) for the national and metropolitan area surveys. No software is included on the CDs. Use of these files requires additional statistical analysis software.

Income of the Population 55 and Older, although published by the Social Security Administration, is based on the Census Bureau's Current Population Survey. This source gives information on how much of the income of the elderly comes from earnings, veterans' benefits, interest and dividends, public assistance, and other sources. Tables show percentage of units (similar to households) at various income levels and give median income data. The relative importance of various income sources is shown: for example, what proportion of income comes from social security or from assets.

BUREAU OF ECONOMIC ANALYSIS (BEA) SOURCES

Checklist

National Income and Product Accounts of the United States, 1929–94. PRINT. 2 vols. (1998) U.S. Department of Commerce. Economics and Statistics Administration. Bureau of Economic Analysis. C 59.11/5:929-94/v.1-2. Item 0228-A-03. ASI (98) 2708-5. GPO.

> Coverage: U.S.
> Content: national income, total personal income and its disposition, personal income by type of income.

National Income and Product Accounts of the United States, 1929–97. CD-ROM. (1999) U.S. Department of Commerce. Economics and Statistics Administration. Bureau of Economic Analysis. C 59.11/5-2:929-97. Item 0228-A-04.

> CD-ROM version of *National Income and Product Accounts of the United States.*

Survey of Current Business. PRINT. WEB. (monthly) 1921–. U.S. Department of Commerce. Bureau of Economic Analysis. C 59.11: Item 0228. ASI 2702-1. GPO. <http://www.bea.doc.gov/bea/pubs.htm>; <http://purl.access.gpo.gov/GPO/LPS1730>.

> Coverage: U.S., regions, states, metropolitan areas, counties.
> Content: national income, personal income.

Survey of Current Business. CD-ROM. (annual) 1994–. U.S. Department of Commerce. Economics and Statistics Administration. Bureau of Economic Analysis. C 59.11/1: Item 0228-A. GPO.

> Content: CD-ROM version of *Survey of Current Business.*

Business Statistics of the United States. PRINT. (annual) 1995–. Lanham, MD: Bernan Press. (Continuation of *Business Statistics* published by the Bureau of Economic Analysis, 1951-1991, C 59.11/3:)

> Coverage: U.S.. states.
> Content: economic time series data, including national and personal income; median income; and poverty status.

STAT-USA Internet. WEB. U.S. Department of Commerce. C 1.91: Item 0128-P. <http://www.stat-usa.gov/>.

> Coverage: U.S., regions, states, counties, metropolitan areas.

Content: current and historical economic press releases on National Income and Product Accounts; personal income.

Local Area Personal Income. PRINT. (quinquennial) 1969–. U.S. Department of Commerce. Economics and Statistics Administration. Bureau of Economic Analysis. C 59.18: (Earlier, C 59.2:IN 2/year). Item 0130-D-04. ASI 2708-49. (Earlier, 2704-2)

> Coverage: U.S., regions, states, counties, metropolitan areas.
> Content: total personal income, per capita personal income.

REIS: Regional Economic Information System. CD-ROM. (annual) U.S. Department of Commerce. Economics and Statistics Administration. Bureau of Economic Analysis. C 59.24: Item 0130-U. ASI 2704-7. <http://govinfo.kerr.orst.edu/reis-stateis.html>; <http://fisher.lib.virginia.edu/reis/index.html>.

> Coverage: U.S., BEA regions, states, counties, metropolitan areas, BEA economic areas.
> Content: per capita personal income and total personal income by major source.

SPI: State Personal Income. CD-ROM. (annual) 1969–95–. U.S. Department of Commerce. Economics and Statistics Administration. Bureau of Economic Analysis. C 59.25: Item 0130-U-02. ASI 2704-9. <http://fisher.lib.virginia.edu/spi/>.

> Coverage: U.S., states.
> Content: per capita personal income and total personal income by major source.

Bureau of Economic Analysis Web Site. WEB. U.S. Department of Commerce. Economics and Statistics Administration. Bureau of Economic Analysis. <http://www.bea.doc.gov/>.

> Content: agency information, data files, full-text publications and press releases.

Discussion

Sources from the Bureau of Economic Analysis use different statistical methods and categories than Census Bureau sources.

National Income and Product Accounts of the United States provides national income data and national totals on personal income and its composition and disposition. National income is reported by type of income (such as compensation of employees, proprietors' income, rental income, and corporate profits) and by sector (such as domestic business, households and institutions, and general government). Personal income is reported by type of income (such as wages and salaries by sector, proprietors' income, rental income, personal dividend income, and personal interest income) and its disposition (such as tax payments, personal consumption expenditures, and personal saving). Figures are also given for disposable income and per capita disposable income. A more current edition of this title is available on CD-ROM. These tables are updated monthly or quarterly in the *Survey of Current Business'* "BEA Current and Historical Data" section. An annual update article is published in the August issue. Several years of annual, quarterly, and monthly national and personal income tables can also be found in *Business Statistics of the United States*. This title also contains several years of annual data on median income and poverty status, including state data.

STAT-USA Internet is a fee-based service, but federal depository libraries may register for free access for two workstations. The *STAT-USA Internet* site is divided into two areas: State of the Nation and Globus & NTDB. The State of the Nation area contains domestic economic statistical releases. Current versions of the top 50 releases are organized by categories. The "Gross Domestic Product" and "Personal Income and Outlays" releases in the General Economic Indicators category contain the most current national and personal income data. Additional files, including earlier data, are available in the State of the Nation Library. These files are also arranged by category. The "NIPA Information" category includes additional files on national and personal income. The "Regional Economic Stats" category contains personal income files for smaller geographic areas. A search option for the State of the Nation Library is also available.

Local area personal income statistics are available in several sources. They are published in the *Survey of Current Business*, on CD-ROMs, on the Internet, and in occasional print compilations.

The most current print source is the *Survey of Current Business*. Basic data is published in its regular statistical section, "BEA Current and Historical Data." A regional data section gives total and per capita personal income for states and metropolitan areas. Articles provide more detailed quarterly and annual updates that include components and derivation of personal income and county data. *Local Area Personal Income* compiles many years of basic small area data in one source, but is far less current.

The CD-ROM titles also contain several years of personal income data. *REIS* is the most comprehensive title, covering all available geographic areas. The table selections that contain the most personal income data are CA05.1 (PI & Earnings-short), CA05.2 (PI & Earnings-long), CA30 (Economic Profile), and BEARFACTS. The PI & Earnings tables (both short and long) contain total personal income, per capita income, and derivation or source of personal income (such as earnings, dividends, transfer payments). The Economic Profile table contains more detailed derivation and per capita income figures. BEARFACTS produces a short narrative summary for a specified geographic area, covering per capita personal income, total personal income, and components of total personal income. (See Figure 33.1.) The "Other Tables" menu selection also contains personal income data. The State Quarterly Personal Income table provides several years of quarterly data on total personal income for the U.S., regions, and states. The County Summary table compares all the counties in a state for specified variables, including personal income, personal income percentage change, per capita personal income, and per capita per-

sonal income as a percentage of the U.S. A County Rankings table ranks the 250 highest and lowest counties for per capita income, giving rank number, per capita income, and percentage of national average.

The *SPI* CD-ROM contains data similar to that in the *REIS* basic tables, but it covers only the U.S. and states. It does, however, cover many more years than *REIS*. It contains state versions of the Personal Income & Earnings table, the Economic Profile table, and BEARFACTS.

The *Bureau of Economic Analysis Web Site* provides information on the agency, agency data and full-text publications, and access to many downloadable files. Full-text publications include recent issues of the *Survey of Current Business* and press releases containing economic statistics. Users may also select data by geographic area: national, international, and regional. For each area users can select a data category for lists of viewable tables and downloadable files or an article category for a list of full-text articles from the *Survey of Current Business*. The regional data area includes personal income tables and the BEARFACTS regional fact sheets (Figure 33.1.) The national area includes National Income and Product Accounts tables and articles.

INTERNAL REVENUE SERVICE (IRS) SOURCES
Checklist

Statistics of Income: Individual Income Tax Returns. PRINT. WEB. (annual) 1916–. U.S. Department of the Treasury. Internal Revenue Service. T 22.35/8: (Earlier, T 22.35/2:IN 2/year, T 22.35:) (Title varies) Item 0964. ASI 8304-2. GPO. <http://www.irs.ustreas.gov/prod/tax_stats/soi/ind_gss.html>.

    Coverage: U.S.
    Content: number and characteristics of returns by size of adjusted gross income; sources of income; exemptions and deductions; amount of tax; some data by marital status.

Statistics of Income (SOI) Bulletin. PRINT. WEB. (quarterly) 1981–. U.S. Department of the Treasury. Internal Revenue Service. T 22.35/4: Item 0964-C. ASI 8302-2. GPO. <http://www.irs.ustreas.gov/prod/tax_stats/soi/soi_bul.html>; <http://purl.access.gpo.gov/GPO/LPS3363>.

    Coverage: U.S., states; occasionally world, world regions, country groupings, selected countries.
    Content: earliest published statistics on income tax returns of individuals; tax return statistics; periodic or special tax studies; historical data.

Discussion

Analysis of tax returns by the IRS gives a different perspective on income data. *Statistics of Income: Individual Income Tax Returns* gives statistics on the number of tax returns in each adjusted gross income category, as well as various characteristics of these returns. Income groups are analyzed by source of income and by other tax return items, such as deductions and exemptions. Examples of

```
                    BEARFACTS 1996-1997--Butler, Ohio [39017]
                                    BEARFACTS

                                  Butler, Ohio
                                    1996-97

        Butler is one of the 88 counties in Ohio.  It is part of the
        Hamilton-Middletown Metropolitan Area. Its 1997 population of 327,081 ranked
        8th in the State.

     PER CAPITA PERSONAL INCOME
        In 1997, Butler had a per capita personal income (PCPI) of $23,309. This
        PCPI ranked 19th in the State, and was 96 percent of the State average,
        $24,163, and 92 percent of the national average, $25,288. The 1997 PCPI
        reflected an increase of 5.1 percent from 1996. The 1996-97 State change was
        4.8 percent and the national change was 4.7 percent.

     TOTAL PERSONAL INCOME
        In 1997, Butler had a total personal income (TPI) of $7,624,086*.  This TPI
        ranked 8th in the State and accounted for 2.8 percent of the State total.
        The 1997 TPI reflected an increase of 6.2 percent from 1996. The 1996-97
        State change was 5.0 percent and the national change was 5.7 percent.

     COMPONENTS OF TOTAL PERSONAL INCOME
        Total personal income (TPI) includes the earnings (wages and salaries, other
        labor income, proprietors' income); dividends, interest, and rent; and
        transfer payments received by the residents of Butler.  In 1997, earnings
        were 71.2 percent of TPI; dividends, interest, and rent were 13.8 percent;
        and transfer payments were 15.0 percent. From 1996 to 1997, earnings
        increased 7.4 percent; dividends, interest, and rent increased 3.5 percent;
        and transfer payments increased 3.6 percent.

     EARNINGS BY INDUSTRY
        Earnings by persons employed in Butler increased from $3,864,311* in 1996 to
        $4,198,273* in 1997, an increase of 8.6 percent.  The largest industries in
        1997 were durable goods manufacturing, 19.8 percent of earnings; services,
        18.8 percent; and state and local government, 12.6 percent.  Of the
        industries that accounted for at least 5 percent of earnings in 1997, the
        slowest growing from 1996 to 1997 was durable goods manufacturing, which
        increased 1.8 percent; the fastest was finance, insurance, and real estate
        (6.7 percent of earnings in 1997), which increased 54.3 percent.

     * All income estimates, with the exception of PCPI, are in thousands of
       dollars.

                                     Regional Economic Information System
                                     Bureau of Economic Analysis
```

Source: REIS: Regional Economic Information System 1969-1997, BEARFACTS 1996-1997 table.

Figure 33.1: BEARFACTS County Summary.

data available include the number of returns in a specific income range, the number of returns taking advantage of the child care credit or the number of returns with adjusted gross income of a million dollars or more that reported receiving alimony.

Preliminary statistics for the above report appear in the *Statistics of Income (SOI) Bulletin*. The *SOI Bulletin* also contains a "Selected Historical and Other Data" section featuring statistics on such items as individual income tax returns by adjusted gross income range.

INDEXES
Checklist

American Statistics Index (ASI). PRINT. (monthly) 1973–. Bethesda, MD: Congressional Information Service.

Statistical Universe. WEB. Bethesda, MD: Congressional Information Service.

Discussion

A comprehensive listing of material can be found in *ASI* by looking under "Personal and household income." *Statistical Universe* includes a Web version of *ASI*. (See Chapter 3, "The Basics of Searching," for more information on *ASI*.)

RELATED MATERIAL
Within this Work

Chapter 30 Economic Indicators

Chapter 34 Earnings

GPO Subject Bibliographies. **PRINT. WEB. GP 3.22/2:**

<http://bookstore.gpo.gov/sb/about.html>.

No. 181 "Census of Population and Housing"

No. 311 "Census Tracts and Blocks (Publications)"

No. 312 "Census Tracts and Blocks (Maps)"

CHAPTER 34
Earnings

Earnings refers to that portion of income derived from wages and salaries. Data on earnings are collected and published primarily by the Bureau of Labor Statistics (BLS). Earnings data are gathered through several different survey programs, each of which has its own distinctive characteristics. The most commonly used data originate from the Current Population Survey (CPS), conducted by the Census Bureau for BLS, and from the Current Employment Statistics (CES) survey of cooperating state agencies and voluntarily participating establishments in nonagricultural industries.

Earnings tables are often categorized as to whether they represent data collected from participating establishments in the Current Employment Statistics survey (CES or "establishment" data) or from the Current Population Survey (CPS or "household" data). Establishment earnings data provide greater industry detail; CPS data correlate earnings to demographic characteristics and provide distribution and median information not available in establishment data.

Sources from other BLS surveys containing earnings data, as well as sources from the Census Bureau and the Bureau of Economic Analysis, are also covered in this chapter.

SEARCH STRATEGY

This chapter shows a statistical search strategy. The steps to follow proceed from general sources to the more specific:

1. Consult the "General Statistical Sources" section of this chapter for basic information sources;
2. Consult the titles in the "Current Sources" section for more current, comprehensive data;
3. Locate additional detailed and historical statistics through sources listed in the "Labor Statistics Compilations" section;
4. Find additional data by occupations in the "Occupational Survey Sources" section;
5. Consider the "Census Bureau Sources" section for additional earnings data;
6. Locate industry earnings data in "Bureau of Economic Analysis (BEA) Sources;"
7. Search the index *ASI* or its Web counterpart, *Statistical Universe*, for areas not covered in this chapter; and
8. Consider the related material.

GENERAL STATISTICAL SOURCES
Checklist

Statistical Abstract of the United States. PRINT. WEB. (annual) 1878–. U.S. Department of Commerce. Economics and Statistics Administration. Bureau of the Census. C 3.134: Item 0150. ASI 2324-1. GPO. <http://www.census.gov/statab/www/>; <http://purl.access.gpo.gov/GPO/LPS2878>.
>   Coverage: U.S., states, selected metropolitan areas.
>   Content: average hourly earnings by industry; average hourly and weekly earnings by industry group; median weekly earnings by occupation, sex, and race; average annual pay.

Statistical Abstract of the United States. CD-ROM. (annual) 1993–. U.S. Department of Commerce. Bureau of the Census. C 3.134/7: Item 0150-B. ASI 2324-14.
>   Content: CD-ROM version of the *Statistical Abstract.*

Historical Statistics of the United States: Colonial Times to 1970. Parts 1-2. PRINT. (1975) U.S. Department of Commerce. Bureau of the Census. C 3.134/2:H 62/789-970/pt.1-2. Item 0151. ASI (76) 2328-2. GPO.
>   Coverage: U.S.
>   Content: average annual, monthly, weekly, and daily earnings for selected industries and occupations.

Historical Statistics of the United States on CD-ROM: Colonial Times to 1970. CD-ROM. (1997) New York, NY: Cambridge University Press.

Content: CD-ROM version of *Historical Statistics of the United States*.

State and Metropolitan Area Data Book. PRINT. WEB. (irregular) 1979–. U.S. Department of Commerce. Economics and Statistics Administration. Bureau of the Census. C 3.134/5: Item 0150. ASI 2328-54. GPO. <http://www.census.gov/statab/www.smadb.html>.
    Coverage: U.S., states, metropolitan areas.
    Content: average annual pay total and by broad industry; industry earnings by sector; average hourly earnings for manufacturing production workers; annual payroll per employee by industry sector.

State and Metropolitan Area Data Book. CD-ROM. (irregular) 1997/98–. U.S. Department of Commerce. Economics and Statistics Administration. Bureau of the Census. (Not distributed to depository libraries)
    Content: CD-ROM version of the *State and Metropolitan Area Data Book*.

County and City Data Book. PRINT. WEB. (quinquennial) 1947–. U.S. Department of Commerce. Economics and Statistics Administration. Bureau of the Census. C 3.134/2:C 83/2/year. Item 0151. ASI 2328-1. GPO. <http://fisher.lib.Virginia.EDU/ccdb/>.
    Coverage: U.S., regions, divisions, states, counties.
    Content: total earnings by industry sector.

County and City Data Book. CD-ROM. (quinquennial) 1988–. U.S. Department of Commerce. Bureau of the Census. C 3.134/2-1: (Earlier, C 3.134/2:C 83/2/) Item 0151-D-01. ASI 2328-103.
    Content: CD-ROM version of the *County and City Data Book*.

County and City Extra: Annual Metro, City, and County Data Book. PRINT. (annual) 1992–. Lanham, MD: Bernan Press.
    Coverage: U.S., states, counties, metropolitan areas, cities of 25,000 or more.
    Content: industry earnings total and by sector; average wages of manufacturing production workers; total average payroll per employee.

Places, Towns, and Townships. PRINT. (irregular) 1993–. Lanham, MD: Bernan Press.
    Coverage: incorporated places of 2,500 or more.
    Content: averages wages of manufacturing production workers.

USA Counties. CD-ROM. WEB. (irregular) 1992–. U.S. Department of Commerce. Economics and Statistics Administration. Bureau of the Census. C 3.134/6: Item 0150-B-01. ASI 2324-17. <http://govinfo.kerr.orst.edu/usaco-stateis.html>; <http://tier2.census.gov/usac/index.html-ssi>.
    Coverage: U.S., states, counties.
    Content: industry earnings total and by sector.

Discussion

The *Statistical Abstract of the United States* contains a small number of tables on earnings in its "Labor Force, Employment, and Earnings" section and can answer basic questions such as average hourly earnings in the flat glass industry or average weekly earnings in the construction industry. The data available for states and metropolitan areas are limited to total average annual pay, with no industry or occupational breakdown. Statistics are selected from many of the more detailed sources covered in this chapter. Source notes at the end of each table can direct the user to more current or more detailed sources for the information in that table. The full text of recent editions of the *Statistical Abstract* is available on the Census Bureau Web site as PDF files. The *Statistical Abstract* is also available on CD-ROM. The CD uses Adobe Acrobat software and contains some additional geographic areas and time series in the form of spreadsheet files that are not in the printed version.

Historical Statistics of the United States: Colonial Times to 1970 contains a section on "Earnings, Hours and Working Conditions" with tables on such specific subjects as the daily wage rates of artisans from 1785 to 1830 or the daily wage rates on the Erie Canal from 1828 to 1881, as well as more standard earnings information for industries. A CD-ROM version of *Historical Statistics* is available from Cambridge University Press.

The *State and Metropolitan Area Data Book* provides basic earnings data for metropolitan areas and states. The states table is the most detailed. It gives average annual pay by broad industry sector. For the manufacturing sector, there are also data on average hourly earnings of production workers. Annual payroll per employee is given for most industry sectors. The metropolitan area table contains only information on total average annual pay and total industry earnings by sector. The *State and Metropolitan Area Data Book* is available as a PDF file on the *Census Bureau Web site*. A CD-ROM edition is also available.

The *County and City Data Book* contains only data on total industry earnings by broad industry sector. The *County and City Data Book* is also available in CD-ROM from the Census Bureau. The University of Virginia Library Geospatial and Statistical Data Center offers recent editions of the *County and City Data Book* on the Internet in their interactive data area. Users select the desired edition, geography, and variables to create a customized data display.

County and City Extra is an updated version of the *County and City Data Book* with a small number of additional data items for earnings. Information for cities is limited to average wages of manufacturing production workers. *Places, Towns, and Townships* is a companion title for smaller cities also covering only average wages of manufacturing production workers.

USA Counties contains several years of data on industry earnings. Data are similar to that found in the *County and City Data Book*. The Oregon State University Government Information Sharing Project provides access to the current issue on the Internet. Users select a geographic area profile or an area comparison and then the desired geography. A subject area can then be selected or a keyword search conducted to display data. The Census Bureau Web site contains a similar version.

CURRENT SOURCES
Checklist

Employment and Earnings. PRINT. WEB. (monthly) 1954–. U.S. Department of Labor. Bureau of Labor Statistics. L 2.41/2: Item 0768-B. ASI 6742-2. GPO. Current monthly establishment tables: <http://stats.bls.gov/cesee.htm>; Current CPS tables: <http://stats.bls.gov/cpshome.htm>.
> Coverage: U.S., states, selected metropolitan areas.
> Content: median weekly earnings by age, race, sex, and occupation; average hourly and weekly earnings by major industry group and detailed industry.

Monthly Labor Review. PRINT. WEB. (monthly) 1915–. U.S. Department of Labor. Bureau of Labor Statistics. L2.6: Item 0770. ASI 6722-1. GPO. <http://stats.bls.gov/opub/mlr/mlrhome.htm>; <http://purl.access.gpo.gov/GPO/LPS806>.
> Coverage: U.S.
> Content: total average hourly compensation; average hourly and weekly earnings by major industry and major manufacturing group.

Compensation and Working Conditions. PRINT. WEB. (quarterly) May 1991–. U.S. Department of Labor. Bureau of Labor Statistics. L 2.44/4: (Earlier, L 2.44:) Item 0768-D. ASI 6782-1. GPO. <http://stats.bls.gov/opub/cwc/cwchome.htm>.
> Coverage: selected metropolitan areas.
> Content: mean hourly earnings by selected occupations and by occupational group and level.

The Employment Situation. PRINT. WEB. (monthly) U.S. Department of Labor. Bureau of Labor Statistics. L 2.53/2: Item 0768-T. ASI 6742-5. <http://stats.bls.gov/news.release/empsit.toc.htm>; <http://purl.access.gpo.gov/GPO/LPS1637>; <http://stats.bls.gov/bls_news/archives/empsit_nr.htm>.
> Coverage: U.S.
> Content: average hourly and weekly earnings of production or nonsupervisory workers by major industry and major manufacturing group.

Usual Weekly Earnings of Wage and Salary Workers. PRINT. WEB. (quarterly) 2nd qtr. 1987–. L 2.126: Item 0769-M. ASI 6742-20. <http://stats.bls.gov/news.release/wkyeng.toc.htm>; <http://purl.access.gpo.gov/GPO/LPS1793>; <http://stats.bls.gov/bls_news/archives/all_nr.htm#WKYENG>.
> Coverage: U.S.
> Content: median weekly earnings by age, race, sex, occupation, and educational attainment.

Real Earnings. PRINT. WEB. (monthly) U.S. Department of Labor. Bureau of Labor Statistics. L 2.115: Item 0768-T-02. ASI 6742-3. <http://stats.bls.gov/news.release/realer.toc.htm>; <http://purl.access.gpo.gov/GPO/LPS1794>; <http://stats.bls.gov/bls_news/archives/realer_nr.htm>.
> Coverage: U.S.
> Content: total average weekly and hourly earnings; total real average weekly earnings; average hourly and weekly earnings of production or nonsupervisory workers by major industry.

Average Annual Pay by State and Industry. PRINT. WEB. (annual) U.S. Department of Labor. Bureau of Labor Statistics. L 2.120/2-3: Item 0769-P. ASI 6784-17.1. <http://stats.bls.gov/news.release/annpay.toc.htm>; <http://purl.access.gpo.gov/GPO/LPS2725>; <http://stats.bls.gov/bls_news/archives/all_nr.htm#ANNPAY>.
> Coverage: U.S., states.
> Content: total average annual pay and average annual pay by industry sector.

Average Annual Pay Levels in Metropolitan Areas. PRINT. WEB. (annual) U.S. Department of Labor. Bureau of Labor Statistics. L 2.120/2-4: Item 0769-P. ASI 6784-17.2. <http://stats.bls.gov/news.release/anpay2.toc.htm>; <http://purl.access.gpo.gov/GPO/LPS3670>; <http://stats.bls.gov/bls_news/archives/all_nr.htm#ANNPAY2>.
> Coverage: metropolitan areas.
> Content: total average annual pay and rank.

Employment and Average Annual Pay for Large Counties. PRINT. WEB. (annual) U.S. Department of Labor. Bureau of Labor Statistics. L 2.120/2-17: (Earlier, L 2.120: (1996 is 98-443)) Item 769-P-02. <http://stats.bls.gov/news.release/eaapc.toc.htm>; <http://stats.bls.gov/bls_news/archives/all_nr.htm#EAAPC>.
> Coverage: large counties.
> Content: total average annual pay and rank.

Employment and Unemployment Web Page. WEB. U.S. Department of Labor. Bureau of Labor Statistics. <http://stats.bls.gov/proghome.htm#OEUS>.
> Content: data from the Current Population Survey and Current Employment Statistics survey including earnings tables.

STAT-USA Internet. WEB. U.S. Department of Commerce. C 1.91: Item 0128-P. <http://www.stat-usa.gov/>.
> Coverage: U.S., regions, states, counties, metropolitan areas.
> Content: current and historical economic press releases on National Income and Product Accounts; personal income.

General Wage Determinations Issued Under the Davis-Bacon and Related Acts. Vols. 1-7. PRINT (loose-leaf) U.S. Department of Labor. Employment and Standards Administration. Wage and Hour Division. L 36.211: Item 0777-B-04 through 0777-B-10. GPO.
> Coverage: counties.
> Content: prevailing wage rates for construction-related occupations.

FedWorld Davis Bacon Wage Determination Decisions. WEB. U.S. Department of Commerce. National Technical Information Service. <http://davisbacon.fedworld.gov/>
> Content: online version of *General Wage Determinations.*

Discussion

The periodical *Employment and Earnings* consists almost entirely of statistics and is the most detailed current source for earnings information. A basic group of tables appears every month, with additional tables appearing quarterly. The tables are divided into "Household Data" and "Establishment Data" to represent the two types of data collected. Annual averages and revisions appear in various issues throughout the year. National household data annual averages appear in January, and state and area establishment data annual averages appear in May.

The median weekly earnings tables are part of the "household" data and appear only quarterly. These tables contain national data. The establishment data are published monthly and are more detailed. These tables give hourly and weekly earnings by industry for the United States and overall average hourly and weekly earnings (not broken down by industry) for states and selected metropolitan areas. Average earnings for a specific industry, such as frozen food and vegetables, can be found for the United States but not for smaller geographic areas. The national household annual averages that appear in the January issue differ slightly from the comparable quarterly tables. The annual data contain more detailed occupational information.

The *Monthly Labor Review* contains articles as well as a monthly "Current Labor Statistics" section. The earnings statistics found in this section are similar to the establishment data tables that appear in *Employment and Earnings* but are more limited. An annual index is published in the December issue for the articles in that volume.

Compensation and Working Conditions contains articles as well as a statistical section called "Technical Notes and Tables." The statistics include a section on the National Compensation Survey with earnings data by occupation for a small number of metropolitan areas. The metropolitan areas vary in each issue based on what areas were recently surveyed. This is the only source in this section with data from the National Compensation Survey. More detailed sources based on the National Compensation Survey are covered later in this chapter in the "Occupational Survey Sources" section.

Press releases are the most current sources of information and are available on the Internet as soon as released on the BLS Web site or on *STAT-USA*. Print versions can also be more current than the data in *Employment and Earnings* and *Monthly Labor Review*. The *Employment Situation* is a press release containing establishment earnings data very similar to that in the *Monthly Labor Review*. The *Usual Weekly Earnings of Wage and Salary Workers* contains earnings data from the Current Population Survey. *Real Earnings* gives earnings adjusted for inflation. The earnings by industry data are given in current and constant dollars.

The three *Average Annual Pay* press releases contain data from state employment agencies on workers covered by unemployment insurance. In addition to the basic average annual pay figure, all of these titles include the percentage change in pay from the previous year. These titles are not as current as the other titles in this section.

The *Employment and Unemployment Web Page* brings together data and press releases from the Bureau of Labor Statistics' employment surveys. Earnings data are included in some of these surveys. The "Labor Force Statistics from the Current Population Survey" menu choice links to a list of full-text press releases, most requested series, other data, and the current CPS tables published in *Employment and Earnings*. The two "Nonfarm Payroll Statistics from the Current Employment Statistics" menu choices link to national or state and area establishment data press releases, most requested series, and other data. The national section includes the current national establishment data tables published in *Employment and Earnings*. Both of these sections also contain an FTP link for historical timeseries data equivalent to the *Employment, Hours, and Earnings* titles discussed in the "Labor Statistical Compilations" section of this chapter.

STAT-USA Internet is a fee-based service, but federal depository libraries may register for free access for two workstations. The *STAT-USA Internet* site is divided into two areas: State of the Nation and Globus & NTDB. The State of the Nation area contains domestic economic statistical releases. Current versions of the top 50 releases are organized by categories. The current edition of *The Employment Situation* press release is available under the "Employment" category. The *Real Earnings* release is in the "General Economic Indicators" section. Additional files, including earlier data, are available in the State of the Nation Library. These files are also arranged by similar category names. A search option for the State of the Nation Library is also available.

Construction projects funded or assisted under the Davis-Bacon Act and related statutes require payment of minimum wages based on locally prevailing rates. *General Wage Determinations Issued Under the Davis-Bacon and Related Acts* specifies the current wage rates for individual construction-related occupations for most counties. The Government Printing Office plans to make this title available as a Web database on *GPO Access* in the near future. The *FedWorld* database is a fee-based subscription service with free accounts available for federal depository libraries upon application.

LABOR STATISTICS COMPILATIONS
Checklist

Handbook of U.S. Labor Statistics: Employment, Earnings, Prices, Productivity, and Other Labor Data. PRINT. (annual) 1997–. Lanham, MD: Bernan Press. (Continuation of *Handbook of Labor Statistics* published by the Bureau of Labor Statistics, 1924-1989, L 2.3/5:, L 2.3:)

    Coverage: U.S., states.

    Content: median annual earnings by age, sex, race, broad occupation, educational attainment; average hourly and weekly earnings of production workers by industry.

Employment, Hours, and Earnings, United States, 1909–94. PRINT. (1994) U.S. Department of Labor. Bureau of Labor Statistics. Bulletin No. 2445. L 2.3:2445/v.1-2. Item 0768-A-01. ASI (94) 6744-4. GPO.

    Coverage: U.S.

Content: average weekly and hourly earnings by SIC industry.

Employment, Hours, and Earnings, United States, 1988–96. PRINT. (1996) U.S. Department of Labor. Bureau of Labor Statistics. Bulletin No. 2481. L 2.3:2481. Item 0768-A-01. ASI (96) 6744-4.
    Coverage: U.S.
    Content: average weekly and hourly earnings by SIC industry.

Employment, Hours, and Earnings, States and Areas, 1939–82. PRINT. (1984) U.S. Department of Labor. Bureau of Labor Statistics. Bulletin No. 1370-17. L 2.3:1370-17/v.1-2. Item 0768-A-01. ASI (84) 6744-5.
    Coverage: states, selected metropolitan areas.
    Content: average weekly and hourly earnings by SIC industry.

Employment, Hours, and Earnings, States and Areas, 1972–87. PRINT. (1989) U.S. Department of Labor. Bureau of Labor Statistics. Bulletin No. 2320. L 2.3:2320/v.1-5. Item 0768-A-01. ASI (89) 6748-81.
    Coverage: states, selected metropolitan areas.
    Content: average weekly and hourly earnings by SIC industry.

Employment, Hours, and Earnings, States and Areas, 1988–94. PRINT. (1994) U.S. Department of Labor. Bureau of Labor Statistics. Bulletin No. 2454. L 2.3:2454. Item 0768-A-01. ASI (95) 6748-81.
    Coverage: states, selected metropolitan areas.
    Content: average weekly and hourly earnings for the manufacturing sector.

Employment and Wages Annual Averages. MF. (annual) 1975–. U.S. Department of Labor. Bureau of Labor Statistics. L 2.104/2: Item 0768-D. ASI 6744-16. GPO.
    Coverage: U.S., states.
    Content: total annual wages, annual wages per employee, and average weekly wages by 4-digit Standard Industrial Classification (SIC) and by level of government for selected industries.

Labor Force Statistics Derived from the Current Population Survey, 1948–87. PRINT. (1988) U.S. Department of Labor. Bureau of Labor Statistics. Bulletin No. 2307. L 2.3:2307. Item 0768-A-01. ASI (88) 6748-72.
    Coverage: U.S.
    Content: median hourly and weekly earnings by age, sex, race, family characteristics, and occupation; median annual earnings by age, sex, race, and occupation.

Discussion

The *Handbook of U.S. Labor Statistics* compiles many years of labor statistics in one convenient source. Median annual earnings data can be found in "Part 1: Population, Labor Force, and Employment Status" under the subcategories for work experience and special survey data. Industry earnings data are in "Part 2: Employment, Hours, and Earnings, Nonagricultural Payrolls." The industry data are the only data available by state.

The *Employment, Hours, and Earnings* titles are useful for obtaining more detailed industry or smaller area data. The *United States* titles, *States and Areas, 1939–82*, and *States and Areas, 1972–87* contain average weekly earnings and average hourly earnings for production and nonsupervisory workers by industry. Industries are arranged by Standard Industrial Classification (SIC) number (see Chapter 31, "Business and Industry Statistics," for more information on SIC.) The *Employment, Hours, and Earnings, United States* titles give more detailed industry breakdowns (three- or four-digit SIC numbers) than the *States and Areas* reports. (See Figure 34.1.) The *States and Areas* reports provide the most geographic detail, giving such information as average earnings in the electrical and electronic equipment industry in St. Louis. The *States and Areas* report for 1988–94 is, however, more limited in industry coverage. Earnings data are available only for the manufacturing sector as a whole and for the manufacturing groups of durable and nondurable goods. Both the 1972–87 and the 1988–94 *States and Areas* reports provide monthly statistics as well as annual data. The *Employment, Hours, and Earnings* timeseries are also available via FTP from the BLS Web site. See the *Employment and Unemployment Web Page* discussed in the "Current Sources" section. More recent information is available in *Employment and Earnings* also discussed in the "Current Sources" section.

Employment and Wages Annual Averages gives wages for workers covered by unemployment insurance laws. It covers more than 97% of the total wage and salary civilian employment in nearly all sectors of the economy. This source contains the most detailed industry data giving both national and state wages at the four-digit SIC level. Unlike the other sources in this category, there is limited data for previous years.

Labor Force Statistics Derived from the Current Population Survey contains historical demographic and occupational data, but not industry data. Similar, but more recent statistics are found in *Employment and Earnings* listed in the "Current Sources" section of this chapter. Section B of *Labor Force Statistics* contains several tables under the category "Hourly and Weekly Earnings." The earliest year data are available for earnings in this source is 1979. Somewhat similar, earlier data (back to 1967) can be found in the previous 1982 edition (*Labor Force Statistics Derived from the Current Population Survey: A Databook*, L 2.3:2096/v.1-2). This source gives such information as median earnings for men compared to women in sales occupations or median earnings of Blacks compared to Whites.

OCCUPATIONAL SURVEY SOURCES
Checklist

National Compensation Surveys. PRINT. WEB. (annual) 1950–. U.S. Department of Labor. Bureau of Labor Statistics. Bulletin series. L 2.121/(no.): (Earlier, L 2.3:; L 2.3/2:. Earlier titles,

MANUFACTURING | **SIC 3949**

SIC 3942,4—DOLLS, GAMES, TOYS, AND CHILDREN'S VEHICLES

ALL EMPLOYEES—IN THOUSANDS

Year	Ann. Avg.	Jan.	Feb.	Mar.	Apr.	May	June	July	Aug.	Sept.	Oct.	Nov.	Dec.
1988	45.4	42.3	44.6	46.0	45.7	41.7	42.4	41.3	46.5	47.1	47.3	46.6	42.9
1989	44.4	41.3	42.8	43.9	44.4	44.3	44.8	44.1	46.8	46.9	47.3	44.9	41.4
1990	42.3	41.1	42.6	42.1	41.4	41.7	42.4	41.3	42.9	44.3	44.2	42.9	40.3
1991	41.8	39.8	41.4	41.2	41.1	40.8	41.1	41.0	42.3	43.4	44.4	44.0	41.5
1992	42.7	41.4	42.6	41.4	42.7	42.1	42.2	41.7	43.0	43.4	44.5	44.7	41.7
1993	43.3	40.7	42.2	42.2	42.0	42.2	42.7	42.8	44.0	45.0	45.9	46.2	43.6
1994	43.0	42.4	42.9	42.8	42.8	42.8	42.4	41.5	43.3	44.2	44.5	44.3	42.8
1995	41.7	40.8	41.0	41.0	41.2	41.4	41.9	40.7	42.5	42.1	42.7	43.1	41.8
1996		40.3	41.0	41.1									

WOMEN EMPLOYEES—IN THOUSANDS

Year	Ann. Avg.	Jan.	Feb.	Mar.	Apr.	May	June	July	Aug.	Sept.	Oct.	Nov.	Dec.
1988	26.0	23.9	25.7	26.5	25.9	26.0	26.0	26.5	26.8	26.9	27.2	26.6	24.1
1989	25.1	22.7	23.9	24.9	25.1	25.7	25.0	25.8	27.0	27.3	25.8	23.2	
1990	23.5	23.0	23.6	23.5	23.2	23.2	23.8	22.9	23.8	24.7	24.5	23.6	21.8
1991	22.2	21.3	22.3	22.0	22.0	21.5	21.9	21.5	22.5	23.0	23.6	23.3	22.0
1992	22.0	21.4	22.2	21.9	22.2	21.8	21.3	21.3	22.0	22.5	23.0	23.1	21.1
1993	22.1	20.8	21.8	21.7	21.4	21.4	21.7	21.6	22.3	23.0	23.5	23.5	22.1
1994	21.9	21.4	21.5	21.3	21.3	21.1	21.3	21.3	22.1	22.8	23.2	23.1	21.8
1995	21.3	20.7	20.8	21.0	20.9	20.9	21.5	20.7	21.6	21.7	22.0	22.3	21.3

PRODUCTION WORKERS—IN THOUSANDS

Year	Ann. Avg.	Jan.	Feb.	Mar.	Apr.	May	June	July	Aug.	Sept.	Oct.	Nov.	Dec.
1988	32.8	29.9	32.4	33.7	33.3	32.7	32.7	32.7	34.0	34.4	34.3	33.6	29.6
1989	31.3	28.0	29.5	30.6	31.2	31.2	31.8	31.1	33.6	33.8	34.0	32.4	28.9

PRODUCTION-WORKER AVERAGE WEEKLY HOURS

Year	Ann. Avg.	Jan.	Feb.	Mar.	Apr.	May	June	July	Aug.	Sept.	Oct.	Nov.	Dec.
1988	38.2	39.0	38.1	38.6	37.9	37.4	37.4	37.0	38.2	38.9	38.9	39.4	36.9
1989	38.3	38.5	37.8	37.7	38.4	38.1	38.7	37.6	38.4	38.7	39.1	39.8	37.1
1990	39.0	38.0	38.4	38.6	38.9	39.4	38.7	38.6	39.7	40.0	40.7	40.9	38.6
1991	38.8	38.0	39.5	39.5	38.8	39.0	39.0	38.4	40.2	41.1	40.7	41.0	40.4
1992	38.6	38.9	39.7	39.4	38.8	38.8	39.5	39.5	40.0	39.2	40.9	40.4	39.1
1993	38.7	39.2	39.0	38.5	38.5	38.1	39.3	38.0	38.5	38.9	39.8	39.1	38.7
1994	38.6	37.7	37.0	38.8	38.5	38.7	38.0	38.0	39.3	39.4	39.3	39.6	38.3
1995	38.7	35.9	39.0	38.8	37.4	38.3	37.6	36.9	38.8	40.1	40.1	40.7	

PRODUCTION-WORKER AVERAGE WEEKLY OVERTIME HOURS

Year	Ann. Avg.	Jan.	Feb.	Mar.	Apr.	May	June	July	Aug.	Sept.	Oct.	Nov.	Dec.
1988	1.6	2.3	1.6	1.6	1.4	1.2	1.2	1.2	1.4	2.2	2.2	1.9	.8
1989	1.7	1.4	1.4	1.5	1.3	1.7	1.7	1.2	1.3	2.0	2.5	2.4	1.9
1990	2.2	1.6	1.9	2.0	2.0	1.7	2.6	1.7	2.6	2.6	3.0	3.2	2.6
1991	2.6	2.5	2.5	2.8	2.5	2.4	2.4	2.2	3.1	3.6	3.6	3.5	3.2
1992	2.8	2.8	2.8	2.8	2.1	2.0	2.1	2.0	2.8	2.8	4.0	3.5	2.6
1993	2.3	2.7	2.3	1.9	2.0	1.6	2.5	1.8	3.1	3.0	3.1	2.7	2.2
1994	2.4	1.9	1.9	2.0	2.0	2.0	1.8	2.1	2.1	3.5	3.2	3.1	2.2
1995	2.5	2.5	2.2	2.1	1.8	2.0	2.0	1.9	2.9	3.7	3.0	3.5	2.2

SIC 3942,4—DOLLS, GAMES, TOYS, AND CHILDREN'S VEHICLES (Con.)

PRODUCTION-WORKER AVERAGE HOURLY EARNINGS—IN CURRENT DOLLARS

Year	Ann. Avg.	Jan.	Feb.	Mar.	Apr.	May	June	July	Aug.	Sept.	Oct.	Nov.	Dec.
1988	7.05	7.25	7.12	7.05	7.04	7.03	6.97	6.97	6.98	6.98	7.00	7.08	7.25
1989	7.41	7.50	7.50	7.46	7.39	7.41	7.40	7.40	7.24	7.27	7.30	7.52	7.59
1990	7.80	7.69	7.69	7.90	7.77	7.80	7.94	7.65	7.72	7.70	7.78	7.89	7.96
1991	8.00	8.14	8.06	8.04	7.95	7.84	7.94	7.93	7.92	7.97	7.83	8.06	8.21
1992	8.23	8.12	8.12	8.14	8.14	8.56	8.25	8.27	8.25	8.26	8.30	8.28	8.33
1993	8.51	8.36	8.40	8.46	8.58	8.56	8.47	8.45	8.45	8.61	8.52	8.55	8.73
1994	8.65	8.87	8.63	8.63	8.63	8.65	8.65	8.77	8.61	8.68	8.66	8.83	8.84
1995	9.16	9.28	9.18	9.19	9.32	9.08	9.08	8.95	9.08	9.03	9.12	9.16	9.30
1996		9.16	9.25										

PRODUCTION-WORKER AVERAGE WEEKLY EARNINGS—IN CURRENT DOLLARS

Year	Ann. Avg.	Jan.	Feb.	Mar.	Apr.	May	June	July	Aug.	Sept.	Oct.	Nov.	Dec.
1988	269.31	272.75	271.27	275.13	266.82	262.92	262.77	257.89	265.87	270.74	272.30	278.16	267.53
1989	283.60	298.75	283.50	281.24	283.78	282.32	286.38	278.24	278.02	281.35	285.43	299.30	281.59
1990	304.20	299.82	300.67	303.38	286.71	282.63	304.17	296.82	302.63	306.00	311.20	322.70	308.86
1991	318.40	317.46	318.37	317.58	314.03	309.66	315.22	304.51	316.36	327.57	318.68	330.48	331.68
1992	325.91	323.99	322.38	320.72	318.55	320.10	326.67	320.10	331.20	323.79	339.47	333.70	325.70
1993	329.34	327.71	327.60	325.71	330.33	326.22	332.88	317.72	325.48	334.93	329.10	334.31	337.85
1994	341.61	334.40	333.71	343.77	330.42	330.64	342.88	333.26	340.23	350.27	348.20	349.67	337.85
1995	354.49	358.21	358.02	356.57	349.57	353.13	341.41	330.28	352.30	350.77	365.71	372.61	340.81
1996		328.84	357.98										356.19

SIC 3949—SPORTING AND ATHLETIC GOODS, NEC

ALL EMPLOYEES—IN THOUSANDS

Year	Ann. Avg.	Jan.	Feb.	Mar.	Apr.	May	June	July	Aug.	Sept.	Oct.	Nov.	Dec.
1988	57.9	55.7	56.4	57.9	58.6	58.6	59.0	58.5	57.9	57.9	58.3	57.9	58.6
1989	59.8	58.7	59.5	60.1	60.8	60.2	61.3	60.0	59.2	58.8	58.8	59.9	59.0
1990	61.4	60.4	60.9	61.5	61.8	62.1	62.1	61.8	61.0	62.2	61.9	62.2	61.1
1991	61.8	60.9	61.2	61.2	60.8	60.8	61.8	61.8	62.4	62.7	63.3	63.3	63.3
1992	65.2	63.1	63.6	64.5	64.7	66.0	66.2	67.1	66.9	65.9	66.4	66.4	66.8
1993	67.6	66.0	67.1	66.2	66.0	66.8	66.5	67.4	67.4	67.4	67.4	68.1	68.5
1994	72.4	69.8	70.0	71.0	71.4	72.1	72.0	72.8	72.9	72.9	74.5	75.5	75.5
1995	76.4	76.0	77.3	77.4	77.5	77.5	77.1	74.7	73.4	74.5	76.0	77.8	77.6

WOMEN EMPLOYEES—IN THOUSANDS

Year	Ann. Avg.	Jan.	Feb.	Mar.	Apr.	May	June	July	Aug.	Sept.	Oct.	Nov.	Dec.
1988	26.6	25.3	26.0	26.9	27.2	27.0	26.8	26.3	26.4	28.4	28.8	28.7	28.4
1989	27.4	27.2	27.6	27.7	27.9	27.7	27.9	27.3	27.9	28.8	28.9	28.9	27.7

PRODUCTION WORKERS—IN THOUSANDS

Year	Ann. Avg.	Jan.	Feb.	Mar.	Apr.	May	June	July	Aug.	Sept.	Oct.	Nov.	Dec.
1988	44.3	42.9	43.7	44.8	45.1	45.1	45.2	45.2	45.1	45.6	43.9	43.7	44.5
1989	44.9	44.5	45.2	45.5	45.5	46.2	44.7	44.8	45.5	45.6	43.8	44.6	44.7
1990	45.8	45.0	45.6	46.0	46.1	46.1	46.3	45.1	45.5	45.8	48.2	48.8	48.6
1991	45.6	45.3	45.1	45.1	45.1	45.1	44.7	45.0	45.6	45.6	45.1	48.6	48.3
1992	48.2	47.0	47.5	48.0	48.0	48.3	48.1	48.3	46.8	48.2	48.4	48.0	48.2
1993	48.3	48.2	48.5	50.1	50.0	50.5	50.2	47.3	48.5	48.4	49.1	49.6	49.8
1994	53.3	50.0	51.1	52.8	52.6	53.0	53.8	53.6	54.0	53.6	55.0	55.9	55.7

Source: Employment, Hours, and Earnings, United States, 1988-96, p. 155.

Figure 34.1: Sample Page from *Employment, Hours, and Earnings, United States*.

See footnotes at end of tables.

Occupational Compensation Surveys, Area Wage Surveys). Item 0768-B-01 to 53. ASI 6785-16, -17. (Earlier, 6785-11,-12). GPO. <http://stats.bls.gov/comhome.htm>.

> Coverage: selected metropolitan areas.
> Content: mean and median hourly, weekly, and annual earnings for selected occupations; mean hourly earnings by selected occupation and level.

National Compensation Surveys, Summaries. PRINT. WEB. (irregular) U.S. Department of Labor. Bureau of Labor Statistics. L 2.122/(no.): (Earlier, L 2.113:. Earlier titles, *Occupational Compensation Surveys, Summaries; Area Wage Survey, Summaries*). Item 0768-B-01 to 53. ASI 6785-3. <http://stats.bls.gov/comhome.htm>.

> Coverage: selected states, portions of states, metropolitan areas.
> Content: mean and median hourly, weekly, and annual earnings for selected occupations; mean hourly earnings by occupational group and levels.

National Compensation Survey: Occupational Wages in the United States. PRINT. WEB. (annual) 1993–. U.S. Department of Labor. Bureau of Labor Statistics. Bulletin series. L 2.3: (1997 is L 2.3:2529) (Earlier title, *Occupational Compensation Survey, National Summary*) Item 0768-A-01. ASI 6785-18. <http://stats.bls.gov/comhome.htm>.

> Coverage: U.S., divisions, ten largest metropolitan areas.
> Content: mean hourly earnings and mean weekly hours by occupation, occupational levels, major industry, establishment size, and metropolitan or nonmetropolitan area.

Occupational Employment and Wages. PRINT. (annual) 1996–. U.S. Department of Labor. Bureau of Labor Statistics. Bulletin series. L 2.3: (1997 is L 2.3:2516) Item 0768-A-01. ASI 6744-26. GPO.

> Coverage: U.S.
> Content: percentage of workers in specified earnings ranges by industry; mean wage for ten largest occupations by industry.

Occupational Employment Statistics Web Page. WEB. U.S. Department of Labor. Bureau of Labor Statistics. <http://stats.bls.gov/oeshome.htm>.

> Content: full-text news releases and data on wages by occupation.

Discussion

The *National Compensation Surveys* began to replace the former *Occupational Compensation Surveys* in late 1996. The new series covers a broader range of occupations. Data on benefits, included periodically in the previous survey, will be added as the new survey develops. Selected metropolitan areas are surveyed on a periodic basis. Reports begin with a brief narrative overview. The most extensive data are given for hourly earnings. Hourly earnings tables by occupation give data for all industries; private industry as compared to state and local government; and full-time workers as compared to part-time. In addition to mean and median (50% percentile range) figures, hourly earnings are given for other percentile ranges (such as 10% or 90%). Weekly and annual earnings figures are limited to mean and median for full-time workers in all industries. Mean hourly earnings are also given for occupations by level. Levels indicate increasing degrees of job difficulty and responsibility. The sales occupation group, for example, may show earnings for eight different levels. *National Compensation Survey: Occupational Wages in the United States* is an annual summary report on the survey.

National Compensation Surveys, Summaries contain similar data, but have less detailed occupational coverage. They are available, however, for additional geographic areas not covered by the fuller reports. This series became available to depository libraries in 1985. Lists of the areas covered by both *National Compensation Survey* series can be found in most issues of either title and on the Internet, which also provides the full text.

Occupational Employment and Wages contains data from another BLS survey, the Occupational Employment Statistics (OES) survey. Wage data was added to this survey in 1996. More current and more detailed geographic area data from this survey are available on the *Occupational Employment Statistics Web Page*. National, state, and metropolitan area tables are available with more detailed occupation and wage distribution information.

CENSUS BUREAU SOURCES

Checklist

Census of Population. PRINT. (decennial) 1950–. U.S. Department of Commerce. Economics and Statistics Administration. Bureau of the Census. (Format has changed over the years; titles listed below reflect current format. Before 1950 included in comprehensive decennial census.)

Social and Economic Characteristics. C 3.223/7:, C 3.223/7-2:, C 3.223/7-3:, C 3.223/7-4: (Earlier title: *General Social and Economic Characteristics*) Items 0159-C-01 to 53, 0154-A-01 to 03. ASI 2531-5.

> Coverage: U.S., states, counties, places of 2,500 or more, selected county subdivisions (MCD's) of 2,500 or more; separate reports on metropolitan areas, urbanized areas, American Indian and Alaska Native areas.
> Content: number of households with earnings and mean earnings by race.

Population and Housing Characteristics for Census Tracts and Block Numbering Areas. C 3.223/11: (Earlier title, *Census Tracts*). Item 0156-K-01 to 53. ASI 2551-2.

> Coverage: metropolitan areas, census tracts in metropolitan areas, census tracts or block numbering areas in the nonmetropolitan area portions of each state, counties, places of 10,000 or more.
> Content: number of households with earnings and mean earnings by race.

1990 Census of Population and Housing. Earnings by Occupation and Education. CD-ROM. U.S. Department of Commerce. Bureau of the Census. Data User Services Division. Subject Summary Tape File 22A-C. C 3.286:CD 90 SSTF 22 A-22 C. Item 0154-G. ASI (95) 2551-12.5. <http://govinfo.kerr.orst.edu/earn-stateis.html>.

Coverage: U.S., states, metropolitan areas.

Content: aggregate earnings and mean hourly and annual earnings by sex, age group, detailed occupation, and educational attainment.

The American Community Survey. CD-ROM. WEB. (annual) 1996–. U.S. Department of Commerce. Bureau of the Census. C 3.297: Item 0154-B-14. <http://www.census.gov/CMS/www/index_c.htm>; <http://www.census.gov/CMS/www/>; <http://purl.access.gpo.gov/GPO/LPS1258>.

Coverage: selected counties and cities.

Content: number of households with wage and salary income; mean wage and salary income.

Census 1990. WEB. U.S. Department of Commerce. Bureau of the Census. <http://www.census.gov/main/www/cen1990.html>.

Content: information and data from the 1990 census.

United States Census 2000. WEB. U.S. Department of Commerce. Bureau of the Census. <http://www.census.gov/dmd/www/2khome.htm>.

Content: information about the 2000 census.

American FactFinder. WEB. U.S. Department of Commerce. Bureau of the Census. <http://factfinder.census.gov/java_prod/dads.ui.homePage.HomePage>.

Coverage: U.S., regions, divisions, states, counties, county subdivisions, congressional districts, metropolitan areas, urbanized areas, places, tracts, block numbering areas, block groups, zip codes, American Indian areas.

Content: 1990 census data; 2000 census data as it becomes available; American Community Survey data; other census products.

Discussion

Census Bureau statistics are often based on "income" rather than on "earnings." Income is a broader term, encompassing earnings but also including money received from sources other than wages and salaries (such as Social Security). This section discusses census sources that do specifically cover earnings.

The *Census of Population* includes some earnings data. The *Social and Economic Characteristics* series consists of a U.S. summary report, individual state reports, and (beginning in 1990) three separate reports on metropolitan areas, urbanized areas, and American Indian and Alaska Native areas. The income tables in these reports include a category for type of income. The breakdown by type includes earnings and gives mean earnings. Most census reports contain a table-finding guide at the beginning that allows the user to match a subject, such as income, with the desired geographic area and find appropriate table numbers.

Population and Housing Characteristics for Census Tracts and Block Numbering Areas contains the smallest geographic area information. Census tracts are areas of about 4,000 people in a metropolitan area. A block numbering area is a similar area in a nonmetropolitan area. (The 2000 census will eliminate the term "block numbering area" and call all of these areas census tracts.) Reports in this series are issued for each metropolitan area and for each state. Maps showing tract boundaries and identifying each tract by number accompany the census tract reports. For the 1990 census, depository libraries were only able to receive the tract maps for their state. Maps for areas in other states are available in each state's regional depository library and can also be purchased from the Census Bureau or in microfiche from Congressional Information Service. (Before 1990, depository libraries could receive all tract maps.) The 1990 reports contain several tables that begin with the heading "Occupation, Income in 1989, and Poverty Status in 1989 ...." These give number of households with earnings and mean earnings.

The *Earnings by Occupation and Education* CD-ROM contains the most detailed 1990 census data on earnings. Although it doesn't cover smaller geographic areas, it provides earnings data by detailed occupation and several other variables.

The American Community Survey is an ongoing monthly survey that is in its initial phases of development. When fully implemented (presently expected to be in 2003), this survey will replace the long form or sample data in the decennial census with more current annual estimates. Data available on earnings are similar to that found in the 1990 census reports. During the development stage, data are collected only for a small number of test sites. Coverage will gradually be expanded and by 2004 coverage is expected to include all states, counties, cities, metropolitan areas, and population groups of 65,000 people or more. By 2008, coverage for smaller areas including census tracts will become available.

The *Census 1990* and *United States Census 2000* Web pages provided links to data and information available on the Census Bureau Web site. The *Census 1990* site contains links to selected data tables, some of which contain basic earnings data similar to that in the printed reports. Users can also link to *American FactFinder.* The *United States Census 2000* site contains information on the development and progress of the 2000 census.

American FactFinder is a Census Bureau Web database designed to provide access to data from the 1990 and 2000 *Census of Population and Housing,* the *American Community Survey,* and the 1997 *Economic Census.* It also contains a mapping feature and an option to search for information on Census Bureau products. Users make a series of selections from lists of geographic areas, tables, and/or sources or search by word to identify and display data. A general search option is also available. A search on the word "earnings" retrieves tables from the 1990 census and the *American Community Survey.*

The 2000 census is expected to have fewer print products than the 1990 census. Data will be disseminated primarily through the Web, *American FactFinder,* and CD-ROMs.

BUREAU OF ECONOMIC ANALYSIS (BEA) SOURCES

Checklist

REIS: Regional Economic Information System. CD-ROM. (annual) U.S. Department of Commerce. Economics and Statistics Administration. Bureau of Economic Analysis. C 59.24: Item 0130-U. ASI 2704-7. <http://govinfo.kerr.orst.edu/reis-stateis.html>; <http://fisher.lib.virginia.edu/reis/index.html>.

> Coverage: U.S., BEA regions, states, counties, metropolitan areas, BEA economic areas.
> Content: total earnings by industry; average earnings per job.

SPI: State Personal Income. CD-ROM. (annual) 1969–95–. U.S. Department of Commerce. Economics and Statistics Administration. Bureau of Economic Analysis. C 59.25: Item 0130-U-02. ASI 2704-9. <http://fisher.lib.virginia.edu/spi/>.

> Coverage: U.S., states.
> Content: total earnings by industry; average earnings per job.

Bureau of Economic Analysis Web Site. WEB. U.S. Department of Commerce. Economics and Statistics Administration. Bureau of Economic Analysis. <http://www.bea.doc.gov/>.

> Content: agency information, data files, full-text publications and press releases.

Discussion

Bureau of Economic Analysis sources deal primarily with total earnings as a component of personal income and national income. The most detailed data report earnings by industry and geographic area.

The *REIS* CD-ROM contains data on total earnings and earnings by industry for several geographic areas. The PI & Earnings table (long version) contains the most detailed industry listing. The Economic Profile table gives average earnings per job. BEARFACTS produces a short narrative summary for a specified geographic area with a short summary on earnings by industry. (See Figure 33.1.)

The *SPI* CD-ROM contains data similar to that in the *REIS* basic tables, but it covers only the U.S. and states. It does, however, cover many more years than *REIS*. It contains state versions of the Personal Income & Earnings table, the Economic Profile table, and BEARFACTS.

The *Bureau of Economic Analysis Web Site* provides information on the agency, agency data and full-text publications, and access to many downloadable files. Full-text publications include press releases containing economic statistics. Releases on personal income often contain total earnings statistics. Users may also select data by geographic area: national, international, and regional. For each area users can select a data category for lists of viewable tables and downloadable files or an article category for a list of full-text articles. The regional data area includes wage and salary tables and the BEARFACTS regional fact sheets.

INDEXES

Checklist

American Statistics Index (ASI). PRINT. (monthly) 1973–. Bethesda, MD: Congressional Information Service.

Statistical Universe. WEB. Bethesda, MD: Congressional Information Service.

Catalog of United States Government Publications (MOCAT). WEB. 1994–. U.S. Government Printing Office. Superintendent of Documents. <http://www.gpo.gov/catalog>; <http://www.access.gpo.gov/su_docs/locators/cgp/index.html>; <http://purl.access.gpo.gov/GPO/LPS844>.

Monthly Catalog of United States Government Publications. CD-ROM. 1996–. U.S. Government Printing Office. Superintendent of Documents. GP 3.8/7: Item 0557-C. GPO.

Monthly Catalog of United States Government Publications (Condensed version). PRINT. (monthly) 1996–. U.S. Government Printing Office. Superintendent of Documents. GP 3.8/8: (Earlier full version, GP 3.8:, 1895-1995). Item 0557-D. GPO.

Discussion

A comprehensive listing of material can be found in *ASI* by looking under "Earnings, general," "Earnings, specific industries," "Earnings, local and regional," or individual industries and occupations. *Statistical Universe* includes a Web version of *ASI*.

The *Monthly Catalog* can also be used to identify general statistical publications on earnings, but does not provide the in-depth indexing of statistics that *ASI* does. Try subject headings beginning with "Wages" and look for the subheading "Statistics." General publications may also contain statistical information. The complete version of the *Monthly Catalog* is available on the Web and CD-ROM. Commercial online and CD-ROM versions of the *Monthly Catalog* are also available.

For more information on these indexes, see Chapter 3, "The Basics of Searching."

RELATED MATERIAL

Within this work

GPO Subject Bibliographies. PRINT. WEB. GP 3.22/2:

<http://bookstore.gpo.gov/sb/about.html>

No. 181 "Census of Population and Housing"

No. 311 "Census Tracts and Blocks (Publications)"

No. 312 "Census Tracts and Blocks (Maps)"

Other

Major Programs of the Bureau of Labor Statistics. PRINT. (annual) 1969–. U.S. Department of Labor. Bureau of Labor Statistics. L 2.125: Item 0768-G(MF). Related site: <http://stats.bls.gov/proghome.htm>

Major Programs of the Bureau of Labor Statistics provides an overview of each survey or program of the Bureau. Programs are grouped by broad topic. Sections on "Employment and Unemployment Statistics" and "Compensation and Working Conditions" describe programs related to earnings. For each program there is a brief outline of data available, coverage, sources of data, forms of publication, and uses. A list of selected publications is provided at the end of each topic section.

CHAPTER 35
Employment

The government publishes a tremendous amount of material on employment. Only some of the many available publications will be mentioned here. For additional sources, consult the *American Statistics Index (ASI)* or its Web version, *Statistical Universe*.

Employment, in the context of this chapter, refers to statistics on the labor force and its characteristics, unemployment rates, and employment by occupation or industry. These statistics are primarily gathered and reported by the Bureau of Labor Statistics (BLS) and the Census Bureau.

As with earnings data, many employment statistics are collected by the Bureau of Labor Statistics through two surveys: the Current Population Survey (CPS) and the Current Employment Statistics (CES) survey of cooperating state agencies and voluntarily participating establishments. CPS data are more demographically oriented (age, race, sex characteristics), while the establishment data from participating industries contain more detailed industry analysis. The two types of data are not directly comparable.

Sources from other BLS surveys containing employment data, as well as sources from the Census Bureau, are also covered in this chapter.

SEARCH STRATEGY

This chapter shows a statistical search strategy. The searcher should follow these steps:

1. Consult ready-reference sources such as the *Statistical Abstract of the United States* and other titles listed in the "General Statistical Sources" section of this chapter;
2. Consult the periodical *Employment and Earnings* and the other titles presented in the "Current Sources" section for more current and detailed information;
3. Consider the "Bureau of Labor Statistics (BLS) Annual Sources;"
4. Try other statistical compendiums listed under "Labor Statistics Compilations";
5. Try the "Census Bureau Sources" for demographic data on the employed and unemployed, small geographic area detail, and industry employment;
6. Consult the "Additional Sources" section for more specialized employment data;
7. Check the "Related Material" section; and
8. Search the indexes listed at the end of this chapter for more thorough coverage of the sources available.

GENERAL STATISTICAL SOURCES
Checklist

Statistical Abstract of the United States. PRINT. WEB. (annual) 1878–. U.S. Department of Commerce. Economics and Statistics Administration. Bureau of the Census. C 3.134: Item 0150. ASI 2324-1. GPO. <http://www.census.gov/statab/www/>; <http://purl.access.gpo.gov/GPO/LPS2878>.

> Coverage: U.S., states, selected metropolitan areas.
> Content: number and characteristics of labor force; number and characteristics of employed/unemployed; unemployment rate; employment by school enrollment, marital status, occupation, industry, and educational attainment; many tables by age, race, and sex.

Statistical Abstract of the United States. CD-ROM. (annual) 1993–. U.S. Department of Commerce. Bureau of the Census. C 3.134/7: Item 0150-B. ASI 2324-14.

> Content: CD-ROM version of the *Statistical Abstract*.

Historical Statistics of the United States: Colonial Times to 1970. Parts 1-2. PRINT. (1975) U.S. Department of Commerce. Bureau of the Census. C 3.134/2:H 62/789-970/pt.1-2. Item 0151. ASI (76) 2328-2. GPO.

> Coverage: U.S., states.
> Content: labor force and its components; number employed/unemployed; age, race, sex, and marital charac-

teristics; unemployment rate; unemployment rate by broad industry; employment by industry and occupations.

Historical Statistics of the United States on CD-ROM: Colonial Times to 1970. CD-ROM. (1997) New York, NY: Cambridge University Press.

Content: CD-ROM version of *Historical Statistics of the United States.*

State and Metropolitan Area Data Book. PRINT. WEB. (irregular) 1979–. U.S. Department of Commerce. Economics and Statistics Administration. Bureau of the Census. C 3.134/5: Item 0150. ASI 2328-54. GPO. <http://www.census.gov/statab/www.smadb.html>.

Coverage: U.S., states, metropolitan areas and component counties.

Content: total labor force; number unemployed; unemployment rate; employment by broad industry; state data by sex.

State and Metropolitan Area Data Book. CD-ROM. (irregular) 1997/98–. U.S. Department of Commerce. Economics and Statistics Administration. Bureau of the Census. (Not distributed to depository libraries)

Content: CD-ROM version of the *State and Metropolitan Area Data Book.*

County and City Data Book. PRINT. WEB. (quinquennial) 1947–. U.S. Department of Commerce. Economics and Statistics Administration. Bureau of the Census. C 3.134/2:C 83/2/year. Item 0151. ASI 2328-1. GPO. <http://fisher.lib.Virginia.EDU/ccdb/>.

Coverage: U.S., regions, divisions, states, counties, cities of 25,000 or more.

Content: total labor force; number unemployed; unemployment rate; employment by broad industry; some data by sex.

County and City Data Book. CD-ROM. (quinquennial) 1988–. U.S. Department of Commerce. Bureau of the Census. C 3.134/2-1: (Earlier, C 3.134/2:C 83/2/) Item 0151-D-01. ASI 2328-103.

Content: CD-ROM version of the *County and City Data Book.*

County and City Extra: Annual Metro, City, and County Data Book. PRINT. (annual) 1992–. Lanham, MD: Bernan Press.

Coverage: U.S., states, counties, metropolitan areas, cities of 25,000 or more, congressional districts.

Content: updated version of the *County and City Data Book.*

Places, Towns, and Townships. PRINT. (irregular) 1993–. Lanham, MD: Bernan Press.

Coverage: incorporated places of 2,500 or more.

Content: total civilian employment; number of employees in selected industry sectors.

USA Counties. CD-ROM. WEB. (irregular) 1992–. U.S. Department of Commerce. Economics and Statistics Administration. Bureau of the Census. C 3.134/6: Item 0150-B-01. ASI 2324-17. <http://govinfo.kerr.orst.edu/usaco-stateis.html>; <http://tier2.census.gov/usac/index.html-ssi>.

Coverage: U.S., states, counties.

Content: labor force; unemployment; unemployment rate; employment by industry and occupation; some data by sex.

Discussion

These sources compile selected data from many of the more detailed sources mentioned elsewhere in this chapter. The *Statistical Abstract of the United States*, for example, reproduces data that appear in *Employment and Earnings* and the *Monthly Labor Review*. The information is, therefore, similar to that of other sources but is sometimes less detailed and less current. It is very convenient, however, to begin with the *Statistical Abstract* when looking for any kind of employment data. Source notes at the end of each table can direct users to more current or more detailed sources for the information in that table. The full text of recent editions of the *Statistical Abstract* is available on the Census Bureau Web site as PDF files. The *Statistical Abstract* is also available on CD-ROM. The CD uses Adobe Acrobat software and contains some additional geographic areas and time series in the form of spreadsheet files that are not in the printed version. *Historical Statistics of the United States: Colonial Times to 1970* covers the time period before 1970. A CD-ROM version of *Historical Statistics* is available from Cambridge University Press.

The *State and Metropolitan Area Data Book* and the *County and City Data Book* include a small number of employment facts for the smaller geographic areas. Both titles are available in CD-ROM from the Census Bureau. The *State and Metropolitan Area Data Book* is also available as a PDF file on the Census Bureau Web site. The University of Virginia Library Geospatial and Statistical Data Center offers recent editions of the *County and City Data Book* on the Internet in their interactive data area. Users select the desired edition, geography, and variables to create a customized data display.

County and City Extra is a commercially produced annual version of the *County and City Data Book*. The earnings data is similar to that in the *County and City Data Book* with a small number of variations. The congressional district data, unlike the other geographic area sections, does not include earnings by industry sector. *Places, Towns, and Townships* provides similar data for cities. Total civilian employment is available only for places with a population of 10,000 or more. Number of employees in manufactures, retail trade, and services are the only data available for places of 2,500 or more.

The *USA Counties* CD contains several years of state and county statistics on employment. The Oregon State University Government Information Sharing Project provides access to the current issue on the Internet. Users select a geographic area profile or an area comparison and then the desired geography. A subject area can then be selected or a keyword search conducted to display data. The Census Bureau Web site contains a similar version.

CURRENT SOURCES
Checklist

Employment and Earnings. PRINT. WEB. (monthly) 1954–. U.S. Department of Labor. Bureau of Labor Statistics. L 2.41/2: Item 0768-B. ASI 6742-2. GPO. Current monthly establishment tables: <http://stats.bls.gov/cesee.htm>; Current CPS tables: <http://stats.bls.gov/cpshome.htm>.
> Coverage: U.S., regions, divisions, states, selected metropolitan areas.
> Content: number and characteristics of persons in the labor force, employed, and unemployed; unemployment rate; data by age, race, sex, marital status, educational attainment, industry, occupation.

Monthly Labor Review. PRINT. WEB. (monthly) 1915–. U.S. Department of Labor. Bureau of Labor Statistics. L2.6: Item 0770. ASI 6722-1. GPO. <http://stats.bls.gov/opub/mlr/mlrhome.htm>; <http://purl.access.gpo.gov/GPO/LPS806>.
> Coverage: selected countries, U.S., states.
> Content: labor force; employment and unemployment by age, race, sex, and industry; unemployment rates.

Local Area Unemployment Statistics Home Page. WEB. U.S. Department of Labor. Bureau of Labor Statistics. <http://stats.bls.gov/lauhome.htm>.
> Content: news releases and data from the Local Area Unemployment Statistics program; small area data on labor force, employment, unemployment, and unemployment rate.

The Employment Situation. PRINT. WEB. (monthly) U.S. Department of Labor. Bureau of Labor Statistics. L 2.53/2: Item 0768-T. ASI 6742-5. <http://stats.bls.gov/news.release/empsit.toc.htm>; <http://purl.access.gpo.gov/GPO/LPS1637>; <http://stats.bls.gov/bls_news/archives/empsit_nr.htm>.
> Coverage: U.S.
> Content: number in labor force, number employed/unemployed, and unemployment rate by age, sex, race, educational attainment, occupation, and industry.

Metropolitan Area Employment and Unemployment. PRINT. WEB. (monthly) 1998–. U.S. Department of Labor. Bureau of Labor Statistics. L 2.111/5: (Issued since 1976 under earlier title, *State and Metropolitan Area Employment and Unemployment*) Item 0768-T-01. ASI 6742-25. <http://stats.bls.gov/news.release/metro.toc.htm>; <http://purl.access.gpo.gov/GPO/LPS1801>; <http://stats.bls.gov/bls_news/archives/metro_nr.htm>.
> Coverage: states, metropolitan areas.
> Content: number in labor force; number unemployed; unemployed as percent of labor force; employees on nonfarm payrolls.

Regional and State Employment and Unemployment. PRINT. WEB. (monthly) 1998–. U.S. Department of Labor. Bureau of Labor Statistics. L 2.111/7: Item 0768-T-03. ASI 6742-26. <http://stats.bls.gov/news.release/laus.toc.htm>; <http://purl.access.gpo.gov/GPO/LPS1802>; <http://stats.bls.gov/bls_news/archives/laus_nr.htm>.
> Coverage: regions, divisions, states.
> Content: number in labor force; number unemployed; unemployed as percent of labor force; employees by industry division.

State and Regional Unemployment, [year] Annual Averages. PRINT. WEB. (annual) U.S. Department of Labor. Bureau of Labor Statistics. L 2.120/2: Item 0769-P. ASI 6726-1. <http://stats.bls.gov/news.release/srgune.toc.htm>; <http://purl.access.gpo.gov/GPO/LPS2718>; <http://stats.bls.gov/bls_news/archives/all_nr.htm#SRGUNE>.
> Coverage: regions, divisions, states.
> Content: number in labor force; number employed/unemployed; unemployment rate.

Employment Characteristics of Families. PRINT. WEB. (annual) 1996–. U.S. Department of Labor. Bureau of Labor Statistics. L 2.118/2: Item 0769-L. ASI 6744-24. <http://stats.bls.gov/news.release/famee.toc.htm>; <http://stats.bls.gov/bls_news/archives/all_nr.htm#FAMEE>.
> Coverage: U.S.
> Content: employment/unemployment by race, sex, marital status, family type, and age of children.

STAT-USA Internet. WEB. U.S. Department of Commerce. C 1.91: Item 0128-P. <http://www.stat-usa.gov/>.
> Coverage: U.S., regions, divisions, states, metropolitan areas.
> Content: selected BLS news releases and files.

Surveys & Program Web Page. WEB. U.S. Department of Labor. Bureau of Labor Statistics. <http://stats.bls.gov/proghome.htm>.
> Content: data from the Current Population Survey, Current Employment Statistics survey, Local Area Unemployment Statistics program, and other employment surveys.

Discussion

Employment and Earnings is the most comprehensive source for employment data. Statistical tables are divided into "Household" data and "Establishment" data. The household data are from the Current Population Survey and contain national statistics on employment and on the demographic characteristics of the employed and unemployed. In addition to monthly data, a set of quarterly household tables is published each quarter. Establishment tables contain national, state, and selected area data on employment by industry. Regional, state, and selected area labor force and unemployment statistics from another BLS program, the Local Area Unemployment Statistics program, are also included. Annual averages and revisions appear in various issues throughout the year. National household data annual averages appear in January, and state and area establishment data annual averages appear in May. *Employment and Earnings* can answer such questions as "What is the unemployment rate for women by marital status?," "How many people work in the metal can industry?," and "What is the unemployment rate in Ann Arbor, Michigan?"

Most of the data relating to employment in the statistical portion of the *Monthly Labor Review* can also be found in *Employment and Earnings. Monthly Labor Review* contains less detail but often covers a longer range of years. Many of the articles are also statistical and can provide additional data on various aspects of employment. An annual index is published in the December issue and the articles are also indexed in *ASI*.

The *Local Area Unemployment Statistics Home Page* provides access to full-text press releases and data from the Local Area Unemployment Statistics program. Data choices include most requested series, selective access, and FTP options. The data available consist of four items: number of employed, number in the labor force, number unemployed, and unemployment rate. The most requested series option provides data for states. One of the most requested series options is for a geographic profile by state that provides additional data by age, race, and sex. The selective access option allows the user to select smaller areas, including metropolitan areas, counties, and cities of 25,000 or more.

Press releases are the most current sources of information and are available on the Internet as soon as released on the BLS Web site or on *STAT-USA*. Print versions can also be more current than the data in *Employment and Earnings* and *Monthly Labor Review*. The *Employment Situation* is a press release containing a selection of household and establishment employment data that can also be found in *Employment and Earnings*.

The *Metropolitan Area Employment and Unemployment*, *Regional and State Employment and Unemployment*, and *State and Regional Unemployment, [year] Annual Averages* press releases contain basic data from the Local Area Unemployment Statistics program and (except for the *Annual Averages* title) the Current Employment Statistics survey (establishment data).

Employment Characteristics of Families contains data from the Current Population Survey on employment by family characteristics. This information is not found in the other BLS titles discussed in this section.

STAT-USA Internet is a fee-based service, but federal depository libraries may register for free access for two workstations. The *STAT-USA Internet* site is divided into two areas: State of the Nation and Globus & NTDB. The State of the Nation area contains domestic economic statistical releases. Current versions of the top 50 releases are organized by categories. The current editions of *The Employment Situation, Metropolitan Area Employment and Unemployment*, and *Regional and State Employment and Unemployment* press releases are available under the "Employment" category. Additional files, including earlier data, are available in the State of the Nation Library. These files are also arranged by similar category names, including an "Employment Statistics" category. A search option for the State of the Nation Library is also available.

The *Surveys & Programs Web Page* includes an "Employment & Unemployment" section that brings together data and press releases from the Bureau of Labor Statistics' employment surveys. The "Labor Force Statistics from the Current Population Survey" menu choice links to a list of full-text press releases, most requested series, other data, and the current CPS tables published in *Employ-*

ment and Earnings. The two "Nonfarm Payroll Statistics from the Current Employment Statistics" menu choices link to national or state and area establishment data press releases, most requested series, and other data. The national section includes the current national establishment data tables published in *Employment and Earnings*. Both of these sections also contain an FTP link for historical time series data equivalent to the *Employment, Hours, and Earnings* titles discussed in the "Labor Statistical Compilations" section of this chapter.

BUREAU OF LABOR STATISTICS (BLS) ANNUAL SOURCES
Checklist

Employment and Wages Annual Averages. MF. (annual) 1975–. U.S. Department of Labor. Bureau of Labor Statistics. L 2.104/2: Item 0768-D. ASI 6744-16. GPO.
> Coverage: U.S., states.
> Content: average annual employment by four-digit SIC industry and by level of government for selected industries.

Geographic Profile of Employment and Unemployment. MF. WEB. (annual) 1971–. U.S. Department of Labor. Bureau of Labor Statistics. Bulletin series. L 2.3/12: (Earlier, L 2.3:; L 2.71:) Item 0768-A-06. ASI 6744-7. GPO. <http://www.bls.gov/opub/gp/laugp.htm>.
> Coverage: U.S., regions, divisions, states, 50 large metropolitan areas, 17 central cities.
> Content: civilian labor force; number of persons employed/unemployed; unemployment rate; most data by age, race, sex, occupation, and industry.

Occupational Employment and Wages. PRINT. (annual) 1996–. U.S. Department of Labor. Bureau of Labor Statistics. Bulletin series. L 2.3: (1996 is L 2.3:2506) Item 0768-A-01. ASI 6744-26. GPO.
> Coverage: U.S.
> Content: employment by industry; employment by ten largest occupations in each industry.

Discussion

Employment and Wages Annual Averages gives annual average employment data for workers covered by unemployment insurance laws. It covers more than 97% of the total wage and salary civilian employment in nearly all sectors of the economy. This source contains the most detailed industry data available giving both national and state data by four-digit SIC industry.

The *Geographic Profile of Employment and Unemployment* contains the widest variety of statistics for states and areas but covers a smaller number of geographic areas than *Employment and Earnings* or the *Local Area Unemployment Statistics* Web page listed in the "Current Sources" section of this chapter. *Geographic Profile* gives unemployment rates, data on demographic characteristics of the employed and unemployed, and data by occupation and industry. Occupation and industry categories are quite broad at the state and metropolitan level. Types of data include the number of people employed in service occupations in Alabama, the number of women unemployed in Nebraska, or the unemployment rate for service occupations in Indianapolis.

Occupational Employment and Wages provides national data from the Occupational Employment Statistics survey on employment by industry and occupation. The total number of persons employed in a variety of occupations such as child care workers, motion picture projectionists, and primary metal industry furnace operators is given.

LABOR STATISTICS COMPILATIONS

Checklist

Handbook of U.S. Labor Statistics: Employment, Earnings, Prices, Productivity, and Other Labor Data. PRINT. (annual) 1997–. Lanham, MD: Bernan Press. (Continuation of *Handbook of Labor Statistics* published by the Bureau of Labor Statistics, 1924–1989, L 2.3/5:, L 2.3:)
> Coverage: selected countries, U.S., states.
> Content: number in labor force, employed, and unemployed; unemployment rate; data by age, race, sex, marital status, occupation, industry, family characteristics, and educational attainment.

Employment, Hours, and Earnings, United States, 1909–94. PRINT. (1994) U.S. Department of Labor. Bureau of Labor Statistics. Bulletin No. 2445. L 2.3:2445/v.1-2. Item 0768-A-01. ASI (94) 6744-4. GPO.
> Coverage: U.S.
> Content: number of employees by four-digit SIC industry; number of women employees and production or nonsupervisory employees.

Employment, Hours, and Earnings, United States, 1988–96. PRINT. (1996) U.S. Department of Labor. Bureau of Labor Statistics. Bulletin No. 2481. L 2.3:2481. Item 0768-A-01. ASI (96) 6744-4.
> Coverage: U.S.
> Content: number of employees by four-digit SIC industry; number of women employees and production or nonsupervisory employees.

Employment, Hours, and Earnings, States and Areas, 1939–82. PRINT. (1984) U.S. Department of Labor. Bureau of Labor Statistics. Bulletin No. 1370-17. L 2.3:1370-17/v.1-2. Item 0768-A-01. ASI (84) 6744-5.
> Coverage: states, selected metropolitan areas.
> Content: number of employees by broad SIC industry.

Employment, Hours, and Earnings, States and Areas, 1972–87. PRINT. (1989) U.S. Department of Labor. Bureau of Labor Statistics. Bulletin No. 2320. L 2.3:2320/v.1-5. Item 0768-A-01. ASI (89) 6748-81.
> Coverage: states, selected metropolitan areas.
> Content: number of employees by broad SIC industry.

Employment, Hours, and Earnings, States and Areas, 1988–94. PRINT. (1994) U.S. Department of Labor. Bureau of Labor Statistics. Bulletin No. 2454. L 2.3:2454. Item 0768-A-01. ASI (95) 6748-81.
> Coverage: states, selected metropolitan areas.
> Content: number of employees by broad SIC industry.

Labor Force Statistics Derived from the Current Population Survey, 1948–87. PRINT. (1988) U.S. Department of Labor. Bureau of Labor Statistics. Bulletin No. 2307. L 2.3:2307. Item 0768-A-01. ASI (88) 6748-72.
> Coverage: U.S.
> Content: number in labor force; number of employed/unemployed; unemployment rates; work experience; marital and family characteristics; school enrollment and educational attainment; much of the data are by age, race, sex, industry, and occupation.

Discussion

The *Handbook of U.S. Labor Statistics* compiles many years of labor statistics in one convenient source. Employment data by demographic characteristics from the Current Population Survey can be found in "Part 1: Population, Labor Force, and Employment Status." Establishment employment data by industry are in "Part 2: Employment, Hours, and Earnings, Nonagricultural Payrolls." The industry data are the only data available by state.

The *Employment, Hours, and Earnings* titles provide many years of employment data by industry and cover smaller geographic areas than the other titles in this section. The national report has a more detailed industry breakdown and includes separate categories for women and production or nonsupervisory workers, which the state reports do not. (See Figure 34.1.) The *States and Areas* report for 1988–94 is more limited in industry coverage than the earlier state reports. Both the 1972–87 and the 1988–94 *States and Areas* reports provide monthly statistics as well as annual data. Industries are arranged by Standard Industrial Classification (SIC) number. (See Chapter 31, "Business and Industry Statistics," for additional information on SIC.) The *Employment, Hours, and Earnings* time series are also available via FTP from the BLS Web site. See the *Surveys & Programs Web Page* discussed in the "Current Sources" section. More recent information is available in *Employment and Earnings* also discussed in the "Current Sources" section.

Labor Force Statistics Derived from the Current Population Survey is a historical compilation of much of the data collected from the Current Population Survey over the years since the survey began. The data are similar to those published in *Employment and Earnings* and the *Monthly Labor Review*, where the most current data can be found. The compilation consists of three sections: monthly data not seasonally adjusted, annual averages, and special labor force data. Kinds of information found in this source include number of unemployed workers in sales occupations, number of unemployed Hispanic females 25 years and older, employment status of divorced persons, and employment status of school dropouts.

CENSUS BUREAU SOURCES

Checklist

Census of Population. PRINT. (decennial) 1950–. U.S. Department of Commerce. Economics and Statistics Administration. Bureau of the Census. (Format has changed over the years; titles listed below reflect current format. Before 1950 included in comprehensive decennial census.)

Social and Economic Characteristics. C 3.223/7:, C 3.223/7-2:, C 3.223/7-3:, C 3.223/7-4: (Earlier title: *General Social and Economic Characteristics*) Items 0159-C-01 to 53, 0154-A-01 to 03. ASI 2531-5.

> Coverage: U.S., states, counties, places of 2,500 or more, selected county subdivisions (MCDs) of 2,500 or more; separate reports on metropolitan areas, urbanized areas, American Indian and Alaska Native areas.
> Content: labor force and work status; labor force status by family characteristics and school enrollment; occupation; industry; class of worker; data by age, race, and sex.

Summary Social, Economic, and Housing Characteristics. C 3.223/23: Item 0156-M-01 to 53. ASI 2551-7.

> Coverage: U.S., states, counties, places, county subdivisions (MCDs), American Indian and Alaska Native areas.
> Content: labor force; percent unemployed; parents in the labor force with children under six.

Population and Housing Characteristics for Census Tracts and Block Numbering Areas. C 3.223/11: (Earlier title, *Census Tracts*). Item 0156-K-01 to 53. ASI 2551-2.

> Coverage: metropolitan areas, census tracts in metropolitan areas, census tracts or block numbering areas in the nonmetropolitan area portions of each state, counties, places of 10,000 or more.
> Content: labor force status; occupations and selected industries; workers in family.

1990 Census of Population and Housing Summary Tape File 3A. CD-ROM. WEB. U.S. Department of Commerce. Bureau of the Census. Data User Services Division. C 3.282/2: Item 0154-F-01. ASI 2551-11. <http://venus.census.gov/cdrom/lookup>; <http://sunsite.Berkeley.edu/GovData/info/>; <http://govinfo.kerr.orst.edu/stateis.html>.

> Coverage: states, counties, metropolitan areas, urbanized areas, county subdivisions, places, tracts, block numbering areas, block groups.
> Content: employment status by sex, race, and presence of children; work status by sex; employment by industry and occupation; class of worker.

1990 Census of Population and Housing Summary Tape File 3B. CD-ROM. WEB. U.S. Department of Commerce. Bureau of the Census. Data Users Services Division. C 3.282/2: Item 0154-F-01. ASI 2551-13. <http://venus.census.gov/cdrom/lookup>; <http://sunsite.Berkeley.edu/GovData/info/>.

> Coverage: zip codes
> Content: employment status by sex, race, and presence of children; work status by sex; employment by industry and occupation; class of worker.

1990 Census of Population and Housing Summary Tape File 3C. CD-ROM. WEB. U.S. Department of Commerce. Bureau of the Census. Data User Services Division. C 3.282/2: Item 0154-F-01. ASI 2551-14. <http://venus.census.gov/cdrom/lookup>; <http://sunsite.Berkeley.edu/GovData/info/>; <http://govinfo.kerr.orst.edu/stateis.html>.

> Coverage: U.S., regions, divisions, states, counties, selected county subdivisions of 10,000 or more, metropolitan areas, urbanized places, places of 10,000 or more.
> Content: employment status by sex, race, and presence of children; work status by sex; employment by industry and occupation; class of worker.

Congressional Districts of the United States Summary Tape File 1D; Summary Tape File 3D. CD-ROM. U.S. Department of Commerce. Bureau of the Census. C 3.282/4: Item 0154-F-05. ASI 2551-18. <http://www.census.gov/prod/www/abs/congprof.html>.

> Coverage: states, congressional districts, counties, places, American Indian areas.
> Content: employment status by sex, race, and presence of children; work status by sex; employment by industry and occupation; class of worker.

1990 Census of Population and Housing Census/Equal Employment Opportunity (EEO) Special File. CD-ROM. WEB. U.S. Department of Commerce. Bureau of the Census. C 3.283: Item 0154-F-02. ASI (94) 2551-15. <http://tier2.census.gov/eeo/eeo.htm>; <http://govinfo.kerr.orst.edu/eeo-stateis.html>.

> Coverage: U.S., states, counties, metropolitan areas, places and minor civil divisions of 50,000 or more.
> Content: occupation by sex and race; educational attainment by age, sex, and race.

1990 Census of Population and Housing Subject Summary Tape Files. CD-ROM. U.S. Department of Commerce. Bureau of the Census. Data User Services Division. C 3.286: Item 0154-G. ASI 2551-12.

> Coverage: U.S., states.
> Content: data on selected topics including employment status and employment by occupation and industry.

The American Community Survey. CD-ROM. WEB. (annual) 1996–. U.S. Department of Commerce. Bureau of the Census. C 3.297: Item 0154-B-14. <http://www.census.gov/CMS/www/index_c.htm>; <http://www.census.gov/CMS/www/>; <http://purl.access.gpo.gov/GPO/LPS1258>.

> Coverage: selected counties and cities.
> Content: number of persons in labor force, employed, and unemployed by sex; parents in the labor force by age of children; employment by occupation and class of worker.

Census 1990. WEB. U.S. Department of Commerce. Bureau of the Census. <http://www.census.gov/main/www/cen1990.html>.

> Content: information and data from the 1990 census.

United States Census 2000. WEB. U.S. Department of Commerce. Bureau of the Census. <http://www.census.gov/dmd/www/2khome.htm>.

> Content: information about the 2000 census.

American FactFinder. WEB. U.S. Department of Commerce. Bureau of the Census. <http://factfinder.census.gov/java_prod/dads.ui.homePage.HomePage>.

> Coverage: U.S., regions, divisions, states, counties, county subdivisions, congressional districts, metropolitan areas, urbanized areas, places, tracts, block numbering areas, block groups, zip codes, American Indian areas.
> Content: 1990 census data; 2000 census data as it becomes available; American Community Survey data; other census products.

Economic Census. PRINT. WEB. (quinquennial) 1997–. U.S. Department of Commerce. Economics and Statistics Administration. Bureau of the Census. (Formerly published as individual censuses for specific economic sectors.) ASI 2311, 2355, 2373, 2390, 2397, 2405, 2451, 2493, 2513, 2573, 2575, 2597, 2605, 2615, 2635, 2645, 2665, 2685. <http://www.census.gov/epcd/www/econ97.html>; <http://www.census.gov/mp/www/pub/ind/msind.html#Industry>; <http://www.census.gov/prod/www/abs/economic.html>.

> Coverage: varies by sector; U.S., states, counties, metropolitan areas, places of 2,500 or more.
> Content: number of employees by detailed industry.

Economic Census. CD-ROM. (quinquennial) 1987–. U.S. Department of Commerce. Economics and Statistics Administration. Bureau of the Census. C 3.277: Item 0154-C.

> Coverage: U.S., states, counties, metropolitan areas, places of 2,500 or more, zip codes.
> Content: *Economic Census* reports.

Annual Survey of Manufactures. PRINT. WEB. (annual) 1949–. U.S. Department of Commerce. Economics and Statistics Administration. Bureau of the Census. C 3.24/9-[no.] (Earlier, C 3.24/9:; C 3.24/9-2:). Item 0134-A. ASI 2506-14,-15. GPO. <http://www.census.gov/econ/www/manumenu.html>; <http://tier2.census.gov/asm/asm.htm>; <http://purl.access.gpo.gov/GPO/LPS2593>; <http://www.census.gov/mp/www/pub/mfg/msmfg.html#mas>; <http://www.census.gov/prod/www/abs/manu-min.html#mm>.

> Coverage: U.S., states.
> Content: number of employees and number of production workers for manufacturing industries.

County Business Patterns. PRINT. WEB. (annual) 1946–. U.S. Department of Commerce. Economics and Statistics Administration. Bureau of the Census. C 3.204/3-(nos.): (Earlier, C 3.204:). (Print discontinued after 1997 issues) Item 0133-A-01 to 53. ASI 2326-6,-8. GPO. <http://www.census.gov/epcd/cbp/view/cbpview.html>; <http://purl.access.gpo.gov/GPO/LPS2877>; <http://tier2.census.gov/cbp/cbp_sts.htm>; <http://www.census.gov/mp/www/pub/bus/msbus28.html>; <http://www.census.gov/prod/www/abs/cbptotal.html>; <http://purl.access.gpo.gov/GPO/LPS547>; <http://fisher.lib.virginia.edu/cbp/home.html>.

> Coverage: U.S., states, counties.
> Content: number of employees by industry.

County Business Patterns. CD-ROM. (annual) U.S. Department of Commerce. Bureau of the Census. C 3.204/4: Item 0133-E.

> Content: CD-ROM version of *County Business Patterns.*

Zip Code Business Patterns. WEB. CD-ROM. U.S. Department of Commerce. Bureau of the Census. C 3.298: Item 0154-B-13. <http://tier2.census.gov/zbp/zbp.htm>.

> Coverage: zip codes.
> Content: total number of employees.

Discussion

The *Census of Population* is the most geographically detailed source but may not be as current as other titles. Many of the census reports contain table-finding guides at the front that list topics covered and geographic areas available for each topic. The categories of industries and occupations used for employment data are based on the Census Bureau's own occupational classification system and are not comparable to BLS categories.

The most detailed data are available in *Social and Economic Characteristics,* which consists of a U.S. summary report, individual state reports, and (beginning in 1990) three separate reports on metropolitan areas, urbanized areas, and American Indian and Alaska Native areas. The reports in this series contain data on the number of persons in the labor force, the number employed and unemployed, and labor force status by various demographic variables. Information available includes such items as number of single parents with children under six who are in the labor force, number of males age 20 to 24 who are unemployed, and number of people employed in chemicals and allied products.

Summary Social, Economic, and Housing Characteristics gives summary data for small areas, like county subdivisions, that are not available elsewhere. This title was first issued with the 1990 census and replaces in part the 1980 report series called *Summary Characteristics for Governmental Units.* It contains very basic data on employment status and the labor force.

Population and Housing Characteristics for Census Tracts and Block Numbering Areas contains the smallest geographic area information. Census tracts are areas of about 4,000 people in a metropolitan area. A block numbering area is a similar area in a nonmetropolitan area. (The 2000 census will eliminate the term "block numbering area" and call all of these areas census tracts.) Reports in this series are issued for each metropolitan area and for each state. Maps showing tract boundaries and identifying each tract by number accompany the census tract reports. For the 1990 census, depository libraries were only able to receive the tract maps for their state. Maps for areas in other states are available in each state's regional depository library and can also be purchased from the Census Bureau or in microfiche from Congressional Information Service. (Before 1990, libraries could receive all tract maps.)

The *1990 Census of Population and Housing Summary Tape File 3A* CD-ROM contains census data for geographic levels down to the tract and block group level. Data include detailed economic, social, and housing information. *Summary Tape Files 3B* and *3C* contain the same data tables, but cover different geographic areas. Data from these *Summary Tape Files* are also available on the Internet. The *Congressional Districts of the United States* contains the same data for congressional districts. Many of the *Census of Population* reports mentioned in this chapter are generated from this file.

The *1990 Census of Population and Housing Census/Equal Employment Opportunity (EEO) Special File* CD contains detailed occupational data by sex and race and educational attainment data by age, sex, and race for counties, metropolitan areas, and places of 50,000 or more.

The CD is designed to assist in affirmative action planning for equal employment opportunity.

The *1990 Census of Population and Housing Subject Summary Tape Files* CD-ROM series contains two titles with employment data. *Education in the United States/ Employment Status, Work Experience, and Veteran Status* (C 3.286:CD 90 SSTF 06/CD 90 SSTF 12) contains two reports on one CD. The *Employment Status, Work Experience, and Veteran Status* report gives number of persons in the labor force, number of employed, and number unemployed by numerous demographic and economic variables including age, sex, race, household type, presence and age of children, marital status, school enrollment, occupation, class of worker, and income. *Occupation and Industry: Industry by Occupation Alphabetical Index* CD (C 3.286:CD 90 SSTF 14) gives information on the number of persons employed in detailed occupations by industry and in industries by occupation.

The American Community Survey is an ongoing monthly survey that is in its initial phases of development. When fully implemented (presently expected to be in 2003) this survey will replace the long form or sample data in the decennial census with more current annual estimates. The data available from the survey are presently similar to that found in *Summary Tape File 3*. Adjustments in the data collected may be made as needs change. During the development stage, data are collected only for a small number of test sites. Coverage will gradually be expanded and by 2004 coverage is expected to include all states, counties, cities, metropolitan areas, and population groups of 65,000 people or more. By 2008 coverage for smaller areas including census tracts will become available.

The *Census 1990* and *United States Census 2000* Web pages provide links to data and information available on the Census Bureau Web site. The *Census 1990* site contains links to the *Summary Tape File* CD-ROMs and *American FactFinder*. The *United States Census 2000* site contains information on the development and progress of the 2000 census.

American FactFinder is a Census Bureau Web database designed to provide access to data from the 1990 and 2000 *Census of Population and Housing*, the *American Community Survey*, and the 1997 *Economic Census*. It also contains a mapping feature and an option to search for information on Census Bureau products. Employment data from the 1990 census are available in both the "Facts about My Community" section and the "Population and Housing Facts" detailed tables section. Users make a series of selections from lists of geographic areas, tables, and/or sources or search by word to identify and display data. A general search option is also available.

The 2000 census is expected to have fewer print products than the 1990 census. Data will be disseminated primarily through the Web, *American FactFinder*, and CD-ROMs.

The *Economic Census* gives information on total number of employees in an industry. Beginning with the 1997 census, industries are arranged by NAICS code. A series of reports are issued for each of 18 different economic sectors. Before 1997 there were separate censuses covering eight sectors and arranged by SIC code. All sectors have a geographic area series (statistics by state and smaller geographic units if applicable). The manufacturing, mining, and construction sectors also have an industry series with detailed industry breakdowns. Reports are available on the Census Web site as PDF files or through the *American FactFinder* database and on CD-ROM. One summary report for each sector will be issued in print format. A small number of economy-wide reports will also be issued, including a comparative statistics report and bridge tables between SIC and NAICS.

The *Annual Survey of Manufactures* updates some of the statistics in the *Economic Census* for the manufacturing sector. The *Annual Survey* presently consists of three regular reports each year. The three reports are *Statistics for Industry Groups and Industries* (C 3.24/9-7:), *Value of Product Shipments* (C 3.24/9-6:), and *Geographic Area Statistics* (C 3.24/9-9:). *Statistics for Industry Groups and Industries* gives number of employees by detailed industry. *Geographic Area Statistics* contains employee data for smaller areas, but has less industry detail. The *Annual Survey of Manufactures* is issued for every year in which there is no census.

County Business Patterns also gives number of employees by industry. It covers all economic sectors, however, not just manufacturing. There is an annual report for each state and a U.S. summary report. *County Business Patterns* is available on the Internet and on CD-ROM. *Zip Code Business Patterns* gives only total employees in a zip code area with no industry breakdown.

ADDITIONAL SOURCES

Checklist

Federal Civilian Workforce Statistics: Employment and Trends. MF. WEB. (bimonthly) May 1986–. U.S. Office of Personnel Management. PM 1.15: (Issued earlier under variant titles, CS 1.55/2:) Item 0293-E. <http://www.opm.gov/feddata/html/ empt.htm>; <http://purl.access.gpo.gov/GPO/LPS918>.

> Coverage: world, U.S., Washington, D.C. metropolitan area, government branch, individual federal agencies.
> Content: federal civilian employment and payroll by branch, geographic area, agency; types of appointments; pay system; accessions and separations.

Federal Employment Statistics Web Page. WEB. U.S. Office of Personnel Management. <http://www.opm.gov/feddata/ main.htm>.

> Content: publications and statistics on the federal civilian workforce.

Selected Manpower Statistics, [fiscal year]. WEB. (annual) U.S. Department of Defense. Washington Headquarters Services. Directorate for Information Operations and Reports. D 1.61/

4: Item 0310-E-09. ASI 3544-1. <http://web1.whs.osd.mil/mmid/pubs.htm>; <http://purl.access.gpo.gov/GPO/LPS2692>; <http://purl.access.gpo.gov/GPO/LPS2601>.

> Coverage: world regions, countries, U.S., states, Washington, D.C. metropolitan area.
> Content: Department of Defense military and civilian personnel by branch of service, area of assignment, and grade; some data by sex, family characteristics, educational levels, and age.

Expenditure and Employment Statistics. WEB. U.S. Department of Justice. Bureau of Justice Statistics. <http://www.ojp.usdoj.gov/bjs/eande.htm>.

> Content: links to data and publications on criminal justice employment; summary statistics; codebooks and datasets; related links.

Justice Expenditure and Employment Extracts, [FY]: Data from the Annual General Finance and Employment Surveys. PRINT. WEB. (irregular) U.S. Department of Justice. Office of Justice Programs. Bureau of Justice Statistics. J 29.11/2-2: Item 0968-H-13. ASI 6064-4. <http://www.ojp.usdoj.gov/bjs/eande.htm>.

> Coverage: U.S., states, 68 individual large county governments, 49 large city governments.
> Content: justice expenditures, employment, and payrolls by type of government and activity.

Discussion

Federal Civilian Workforce Statistics: Employment and Trends contains statistics on federal government employment. Data cover such items as total full-time employment, overseas employment of U.S. and non-U.S. citizens, legislative branch employment, or employment of individual agencies, such as the Marine Mammal Commission. Occasional special features cover such topics as occupations, work years, or a profile of the typical employee.

The *Federal Employment Statistics Web Page* lists full-text publications and statistics relating to the federal civilian workforce. Publications include *Employment and Trends* discussed above, *The Fact Book* with information on demographic characteristics of federal workers, and *Occupations of Federal White-Collar and Blue-Collar Workers.* A category for statistical tables provides data from the Central Personnel Data File on selected topics such as women and minorities and occupations.

Selected Manpower Statistics provides detailed data on military employment. It contains five sections covering total personnel, active duty military personnel, civilian personnel, other, and reserve personnel. The most detailed data are provided for active duty military personnel. Statistics give information on the number and characteristics of personnel in each branch of the service. Many of the tables include historical data.

The Justice Department collects various information on justice employment. The *Expenditures and Employment Statistics* Web Page provides links to relevant publications, links to selected statistics, links to codebooks and

datasets, links to related employment and expenditure data, and a description of the data collection.

The *Justice Expenditure and Employment Extracts* title provides a series of statistical tables documenting trends in justice employment and expenditures at the state and local level. Employment data are given for federal, state, and local governments in the areas of police protection, judicial and legal, and corrections. The Web version of the *Justice Expenditures and Employment Extracts* provides a PDF format file, ASCII text files, and spreadsheet format files.

INDEXES
Checklist

American Statistics Index (ASI). PRINT. (monthly) 1973–. Bethesda, MD: Congressional Information Service.

Statistical Universe. WEB. Bethesda, MD: Congressional Information Service.

Catalog of United States Government Publications (MOCAT). WEB. 1994–. U.S. Government Printing Office. Superintendent of Documents. <http://www.gpo.gov/catalog>; <http://www.access.gpo.gov/su_docs/locators/cgp/index.html>; <http://purl.access.gpo.gov/GPO/LPS844>.

Monthly Catalog of United States Government Publications. CD-ROM. 1996–. U.S. Government Printing Office. Superintendent of Documents. GP 3.8/7: Item 0557-C. GPO.

Monthly Catalog of United States Government Publications (Condensed version). PRINT. (monthly) 1996–. U.S. Government Printing Office. Superintendent of Documents. GP 3.8/8: (Earlier full version, GP 3.8:, 1895–1995). Item 0557-D. GPO.

Discussion

A comprehensive listing of material can be found in *ASI* by looking under "Employment and unemployment, general," "Employment and unemployment, local and regional," "Employment and unemployment, specific industries," or individual industries and occupations. *Statistical Universe* includes a Web version of *ASI.*

The *Monthly Catalog* can also be used to identify general statistical publications on employment, but does not provide the in-depth indexing of statistics that *ASI* does. Try subject headings beginning with "Labor Supply," "Unemployment," and "Employment" and look for the subheading "Statistics." General publications may also contain statistical information. The complete version of the *Monthly Catalog* is available on the Web and CD-ROM. Commercial online and CD-ROM versions of the *Monthly Catalog* are also available.

For more information on these indexes, see Chapter 3, "The Basics of Searching."

RELATED MATERIAL
Within this Work

Chapter 30 Economic Indicators

Chapter 33 Income

Chapter 34 Earnings

Chapter 43 State and Local Government Statistics

GPO Subject Bibliographies. PRINT. WEB. GP 3.22/2:

<http://bookstore.gpo.gov/sb/about.html>

No. 44   "Employment and Occupations"

No. 181 "Census of Population and Housing"

No. 311 "Census Tracts and Blocks (Publications)"

No. 312 "Census Tracts and Blocks (Maps)"

Other

Major Programs of the Bureau of Labor Statistics. PRINT. (annual) 1969–. U.S. Department of Labor. Bureau of Labor Statistics. L 2.125: Item 0768-G(MF). Related site: <http://stats.bls.gov/proghome.htm>.

Major Programs of the Bureau of Labor Statistics provides an overview of each survey or program of the Bureau. Programs are grouped by broad topic. A section on "Employment and Unemployment Statistics" describes programs related to employment. For each program there is a brief outline of data available, coverage, sources of data, forms of publication, and uses. A list of selected publications is provided at the end of each topic section.

CHAPTER 36
Prices

The sources in this chapter cover actual prices of individual commodities or products and price indexes. The consumer price index, one of the best known economic measures, is discussed. Most other price data from the government fall into two general categories: (1) energy and (2) agriculture or food prices. Sources included in this chapter are those covering more than one product.

SEARCH STRATEGY

This chapter shows a statistical search strategy. The steps in the search are

1. Consult the "General Statistical Sources" section of this chapter to locate titles containing basic data;
2. Try sources in the "Prices and Price Indexes" section for the most comprehensive price information;
3. Locate more specialized sources under "Energy Prices," "Agricultural and Food Prices," and "Miscellaneous Sources"; and
4. Consider the "Indexes" and "Related Material" sections for locating additional information.

GENERAL STATISTICAL SOURCES
Checklist

Statistical Abstract of the United States. PRINT. WEB. (annual) 1878–. U.S. Department of Commerce. Economics and Statistics Administration. Bureau of the Census. C 3.134: Item 0150. ASI 2324-1. GPO. <http://www.census.gov/statab/www/>; <http://purl.access.gpo.gov/GPO/LPS2878>.
> Coverage: country groupings, selected countries, U.S., regions, selected metropolitan areas.
> Content: consumer price indexes by category; producer price indexes of selected commodities and industries; average prices of selected mineral products; food prices; average fuel prices; housing; other price indexes.

Statistical Abstract of the United States. CD-ROM. (annual) 1993–. U.S. Department of Commerce. Bureau of the Census. C 3.134/7: Item 0150-B. ASI 2324-14.
> Content: CD-ROM version of the *Statistical Abstract*.

Historical Statistics of the United States: Colonial Times to 1970. Parts 1-2. PRINT. (1975) U.S. Department of Commerce. Bureau of the Census. C 3.134/2:H 62/789-970/pt.1-2. Item 0151. ASI (76) 2328-2. GPO.
> Coverage: U.S.
> Content: wholesale prices of selected commodities; retail prices of selected foods; price indexes.

Historical Statistics of the United States on CD-ROM: Colonial Times to 1970. CD-ROM. (1997) New York, NY: Cambridge University Press.
> Content: CD-ROM version of *Historical Statistics of the United States.*

State and Metropolitan Area Data Book. PRINT. WEB. (irregular) 1979–. U.S. Department of Commerce. Economics and Statistics Administration. Bureau of the Census. C 3.134/5: Item 0150. ASI 2328-54. GPO. <http://www.census.gov/statab/www.smadb.html>.
> Coverage: U.S., states.
> Content: average hospital cost per day and per stay.

State and Metropolitan Area Data Book. CD-ROM. (irregular) 1997/98–. U.S. Department of Commerce. Economics and Statistics Administration. Bureau of the Census. (Not distributed to depository libraries)
> Content: CD-ROM version of the *State and Metropolitan Area Data Book.*

Discussion

Some limited price data are available in the standard statistical reference sources. The *Statistical Abstract of the United States* contains a "Prices" section with energy and food prices and tables on consumer and producer price indexes. See also the index under "Prices" and under individual commodities. Statistics are selected from many of the more detailed sources covered in this chapter. Source notes at the end of each table can direct the user to more current or more detailed sources for the information in that table. The full text of recent editions of the *Statistical Abstract* is available on the Census Bureau Web site as PDF files. The *Statistical Abstract* is also available on CD-ROM. The CD uses Adobe Acrobat software and contains some additional geographic areas and time series in the form of spreadsheet files that are not in the printed version. *Historical Statistics of the United States: Colonial Times to 1970* contains older, more limited data. Price information is in the "Prices and Price Indexes" section of Chapter D, "Labor." Also check the index under specific commodities as additional price data are scattered throughout the source. A CD-ROM version of *Historical Statistics* is available from Cambridge University Press.

The *State and Metropolitan Area Data Book* contains one cost-related item. The *State and Metropolitan Area Data Book* is available as a PDF file on the Census Bureau Web site and on CD-ROM.

PRICES AND PRICE INDEXES
Checklist

CPI Detailed Report. PRINT. (monthly) 1974–. U.S. Department of Labor. Bureau of Labor Statistics. L 2.38/3: (Issued earlier as *Consumer Price Index*) Item 0768-F. ASI 6762-2. GPO.
>   Coverage: U.S., regions, selected metropolitan areas.
>   Content: consumer price index for all urban consumers and for urban wage earners and clerical workers, total and by categories; percentage change; average energy and food prices.

Consumer Price Index. WEB. (monthly) U.S. Department of Labor. Bureau of Labor Statistics. L 2.38/3-2: Item 0768-F. ASI 6762-1. <http://www.bls.gov/news.release/cpi.toc.htm>; <http://www.bls.gov/bls_news/archives/cpi_nr.htm>; <http://purl.access.gpo.gov/GPO/LPS3314>.
>   Coverage: U.S., regions, selected metropolitan areas.
>   Content: consumer price index for all urban consumers and for urban wage earners and clerical workers by general expenditure category; percentage change.

Consumer Price Indexes Web Page. WEB. U.S. Department of Labor. Bureau of Labor Statistics. <http://www.bls.gov/cpihome.htm>; <http://purl.access.gpo.gov/GPO/LPS3314>.
>   Content: full-text news releases, selected data tables, and background information for the consumer price index.

PPI Detailed Report. PRINT. (monthly with annual supplement) 1996–. U.S. Department of Labor. Bureau of Labor Statistics. L 2.61: (Annual Supplement, L 2.61/11:) (Issued earlier under other titles: *Producer Price Indexes, Producer Prices and Price Indexes, Wholesale Prices and Price Indexes*) Item 0771-B. ASI 6762-6, 6764-2. GPO.
>   Coverage: U.S.
>   Content: price index and percentage change by stage of processing, commodity groupings, selected industries and their products, and individual items.

Producer Price Index. WEB. (monthly) U.S. Department of Labor. Bureau of Labor Statistics. L 2.61/10: Item 0771-B. ASI 6762-5. <http://www.bls.gov/news.release/ppi.toc.htm>; <http://www.bls.gov/bls_news/archives/ppi_nr.htm>.

>   Coverage: U.S.
>   Content: price index and percentage change by stage of processing, selected commodity groupings, and major industry groups.

Producer Price Indexes Web Page. WEB. U.S. Department of Labor. Bureau of Labor Statistics. <http://www.bls.gov/ppihome.htm>; <http://purl.access.gpo.gov/GPO/LPS1881>.
>   Content: full-text news releases, selected data tables, and background information for the producer price index.

STAT-USA Internet. WEB. U.S. Department of Commerce. C 1.91: Item 0128-P. <http://www.stat-usa.gov/>.
>   Coverage: U.S., regions, divisions, states, metropolitan areas.
>   Content: *Consumer Price Index* and *Producer Price Index* press releases.

Handbook of U.S. Labor Statistics: Employment, Earnings, Prices, Productivity, and Other Labor Data. PRINT. (annual) 1997–. Lanham, MD: Bernan Press. (Continuation of *Handbook of Labor Statistics* published by the Bureau of Labor Statistics, 1924–1989, L 2.3/5:, L 2.3:)
>   Coverage: U.S., regions, selected metropolitan areas.
>   Content: producer price indexes by state of processing, commodity group, and selected industries; consumer price index by major group.

Discussion

The consumer price index (CPI) is a measure of the change in prices over time and is widely used as a measure of inflation. The *CPI Detailed Report* gives information on the consumer price index by detailed expenditure category showing price changes for selected items in the categories of food and beverages, housing, apparel, transportation, medical care, recreation, and other goods and services. Less detailed subcategories are given for regions and metropolitan areas. The metropolitan areas covered differ from month to month. Three cities — Chicago, Los Angeles, and New York — appear monthly. Eleven additional metropolitan areas are divided into two groups published bimonthly in alternating issues. Another group of 12 cities are covered in semiannual tables in the January and July issues and in annual average tables in the January issue. Historical tables provide U.S. consumer price index data for several years. In addition to the many price index tables, there are also four tables at the end of the report that give actual prices for selected items. Average prices for utility natural gas, electricity, fuel oil, and gasoline are given for the U.S., regions, and selected metropolitan areas. Average retail food prices for specific items are given for the U.S. and regions. Examples of data available include the price of a pound of chocolate chip cookies in the Midwest region and the price of electricity in Atlanta. Before 1986 these price tables were published in a separate news release titled *Consumer Prices: Energy and Food* (L 2.38/7:).

Consumer Price Index is a monthly press release available on the Internet. It is more current than the *CPI De-*

tailed Report and contains tables similar to the general tables in that report. It does not, however, contain the more detailed expenditure category tables. The regional and metropolitan area data are limited to the overall, all items consumer price index with no expenditure category data.

The *Consumer Price Indexes Web Page* contains links to the full text of the *Consumer Price Index* press release and related data files including the most frequently requested consumer price index data series and historical data. Publications about the consumer price index are also included on this page.

The *PPI Detailed Report* contains indexes that measure price changes at the producer or wholesale level. The indexes are given by industry, commodity group, and individual items. Commodity and product coverage is quite detailed. Indexes are available for such items as fresh strawberries, chewing gum, spark plugs, and sofas. The annual supplement contains similar tables showing monthly and annual data for the year.

Producers Price Index is a monthly press release that is available to depository libraries in electronic form only. It is more current than the *PPI Detailed Report* and contains tables similar to the general tables in that report. It does not, however, contain the more detailed industry and commodity tables.

The *Producer Price Indexes Web Page* contains links to the full text of the *Producers Price Index* press release and related data files, including the most frequently requested producer price index data series. Publications about the consumer price index are also included on this page.

STAT-USA Internet is a fee-based service, but federal depository libraries may register for free access for two workstations. The *STAT-USA Internet* site is divided into two areas: State of the Nation and Globus & NTDB. The State of the Nation area contains domestic economic statistical releases. Current versions of the top 50 releases are organized by categories. The current editions of the *Consumer Price Index* and *Producer Price Index* press releases are available under the "General Economic Indicators" category. Additional files, including earlier data, are available in the State of the Nation Library. These files are also arranged by category names, including a "Price & Productivity" category for price index data. A search option for the State of the Nation Library is also available.

The *Handbook of U.S. Labor Statistics* compiles many years of basic price indexes in one convenient source. The "Prices and Living Conditions" section contains producer price indexes by broad commodity group and selected industries. Consumer price indexes are given by broad expenditure category. The regional and metropolitan area data are limited to the overall, all items consumer price index with no expenditure category data.

ENERGY PRICES
Checklist

Annual Energy Review. MF. WEB. (annual) 1977–. U.S. Department of Energy. Energy Information Administration. Office of Energy Markets and End Use. E 3.1/2: (Earlier, E 3.1: year/v.2) Item 0429-J-01. ASI 3164-74. GPO. <http://www.eia.doe.gov/aer/>; <http://tonto.eia.doe.gov/bookshelf/index.html>; <http://purl.access.gpo.gov/GPO/LPS3492>.

> Coverage: selected countries, U.S., states.
> Content: prices for fossil fuel production, crude oil, selected petroleum products, motor gasoline, natural gas, coal, electricity, and photovoltaic cells; consumer energy prices by type.

Monthly Energy Review. PRINT. WEB. (monthly) 1974–. U.S. Department of Energy. Energy Information Administration. Office of Energy Markets and End Use. E 3.9: Item 0434-A-02. ASI 3162-24. GPO. <http://www.eia.doe.gov/emeu/mer/contents.html>; <http://purl.access.gpo.gov/GPO/LPS1714>; <http://tonto.eia.doe.gov/bookshelf/index.html>; <http://purl.access.gpo.gov/GPO/LPS3492>.

> Coverage: country groupings, selected countries, U.S., selected states.
> Content: prices for crude oil, motor gasoline, petroleum products, electricity, and natural gas.

Historical Monthly Energy Review 1973–1992. MF. WEB. (1994) U.S. Department of Energy. Energy Information Administration. Office of Energy Markets and End Use. E 3.2:H 62/2/973-92. Item 0429-T-11. ASI (94) 3168-123. <http://www.eia.doe.gov/bookshelf/multi.html>; <http://www.eia.doe.gov/historic.html>; <http://tonto.eia.doe.gov/bookshelf/index.html>; <http://purl.access.gpo.gov/GPO/LPS3492>.

> Coverage: country groupings, selected countries, U.S., selected states.
> Content: historical monthly data series corresponding to the tables in the *Monthly Energy Review*; prices by energy source.

State Energy Price and Expenditure Report. MF. WEB. (annual) 1980–. U.S. Department of Energy. Energy Information Administration. Office of Energy Markets and End Use. E 3.42/3: (Earlier, E 3.2: P93/4/970-) Item 0435-E-24. ASI 3164-64. GPO. <http://www.eia.doe/gov/emeu/seper/contents.html>; <http://www.eia.doe.gov/bookshelf/state.html>; <http://tonto.eia.doe.gov/bookshelf/index.html>; <http://purl.access.gpo.gov/GPO/LPS3492>.

> Coverage: U.S., states.
> Content: prices by energy source and end-user sector; state rankings by prices for each energy source.

International Energy Annual. MF. WEB. (annual) 1979–. U.S. Department of Energy. Energy Information Administration. Office of Energy Markets and End Use. E 3.11/20: Item 0435-H. ASI 3164-50. GPO. <http://www.eia.doe.gov/emeu/iea/contents.html>; <http://purl.access.gpo.gov/GPO/LPS3018>; <http://tonto.eia.doe.gov/bookshelf/index.html>; <http://purl.access.gpo.gov/GPO/LPS3492>.

> Coverage: selected countries, U.S.
> Content: prices of crude oil and petroleum products.

Petroleum Marketing Monthly. WEB. MF. 1983–. (monthly) U.S. Department of Energy. Energy Information Administration.

Office of Oil and Gas. E 3.13/4: Item 0434-A-20. ASI 3162-11. GPO. <http://www.eia.doe.gov/oil_gas/petroleum/data_publications/petroleum_marketing_monthly/pmm.html >; <http://purl.access.gpo.gov/GPO/LPS1645>; <http://tonto.eia.doe.gov/bookshelf/index.html>; <http://purl.access.gpo.gov/GPO/LPS3492>.

> Coverage: country groupings, selected countries, U.S., Petroleum Administration for Defense (PAD) districts, states.
> Content: prices of crude oil and petroleum products.

Petroleum Marketing Annual. WEB. (annual) 1985–. U.S. Department of Energy. Energy Information Administration. Office of Oil and Gas. E 3.13/4-2: Item 0434-A-20. ASI 3164-85. <http://www.eia.doe.gov/oil_gas/petroleum/data_publications/petroleum_marketing_annual/pma_historical.html>; <http://purl.access.gpo.gov/GPO/LPS2324>; <http://tonto.eia.doe.gov/bookshelf/index.html>; <http://purl.access.gpo.gov/GPO/LPS3492>.

> Coverage: country groupings, selected countries, U.S., Petroleum Administration for Defense (PAD) districts, states.
> Content: prices of crude oil and petroleum products.

Energy Prices at a Glance Web Page. WEB. U.S. Department of Energy. Energy Information Administration. <http://www.eia.doe.gov/price.html>.

> Content: price data by energy source.

State Energy Information at a Glance Web Page. WEB. U.S. Department of Energy. Energy Information Administration. <http://www.eia.doe.gov/emeu/states/_states.html>.

> Coverage: states.
> Content: prices by energy source and end-use sector.

Energy Prices (International) Web Page. WEB. U.S. Department of Energy. Energy Information Administration. <http://www.eia.doe.gov/emeu/international/prices.html>.

> Coverage: world, country groupings, selected countries, U.S.
> Content: prices by energy source.

Energy InfoDisc. CD-ROM. (quarterly) 1996–. U.S. Department of Energy. Energy Information Administration. E 3.60: Item 0429-K-08. ASI 3162-47. <http://tonto.eia.doe.gov/bookshelf/index.html>; <http://purl.access.gpo.gov/GPO/LPS3492>; Related site: <http://www.eia.doe.gov/infodisc.html>.

> Content: full-text energy publications and database applications.

Discussion

Annual Energy Review contains primarily U.S. statistics arranged by type of energy source. Chapters on each energy source contain price tables with annual historical data. In addition to the energy source chapters, an "Energy Overview" chapter contains a table on state-level prices for all energy sources combined. A chapter on "Financial Indicators" contains tables on fossil fuel production prices and price estimates for each energy source. An "International Energy" chapter contains tables on crude oil and gasoline prices in selected countries. Most tables are illustrated by graphs or charts. The Web version provides a combination of formats including HTML, PDF, spreadsheet files, and an interactive query option.

The *Monthly Energy Review* contains an "Energy Prices" section with tables on major energy sources. Annual averages are shown for years since the late 1970s with monthly data given for the last two to three years. Country data are limited to crude oil prices and state data are limited to distillate prices. The Web site provides a combination of formats including HTML, PDF, spreadsheet files, a database version, and downloadable database applications. The *Historical Monthly Energy Review* provides monthly (as well as annual) historical data from 1973 on that correspond to that in the *Monthly Energy Review*. It also contains previously unpublished revisions to *Monthly Energy Review* data and provides a more accurate, one-stop source for older statistics.

The *State Energy Price and Expenditure Report* contains a U.S. section and sections for each state. Each section gives prices for specific fuels both overall and by end-use sector. Data are given for many years. This title is published about three years after the last year of coverage and is not as current as the other titles in this section.

International Energy Annual contains a small number of international price tables in a "Prices" section. Prices are given for crude oil and petroleum products.

Petroleum Marketing Monthly and *Petroleum Marketing Annual* contain detailed price statistics on petroleum and petroleum products. The tables in the annual correspond directly to those in the monthly publication but have been updated and corrected since first published. Several prices are given for crude oil, including domestic first purchase price, FOB (free on board) and landed cost of imports, and refiner acquisition cost. Detailed petroleum product data cover refiner and retailer prices to end users and the prices of each product by state and month, such as the July price of premium gasoline in South Dakota. Many of the tables in the annual publication cover several years of annual data and cover monthly data for the most recent three years.

The *Energy Information Administration Web site* has several pages related to prices. The *Energy Prices at a Glance Web Page* lists price tables by energy source. For each source there is a chart showing types of prices, the data frequencies available, and geographic levels available with links to the tables and to the table of contents of the original publication source. The *State Energy Information at a Glance Web Page* provides a guide to a wide variety of energy data available at the state level. Users may select an individual state from a map, then select from a range of topics, some of which relate to prices. Some price data can be displayed in various formats including charts, graphs, and tables. The state page also has a general "Prices & Expenditures" menu selection which links to the full text of the *State Energy Price and Expenditure Report*. The *Energy Prices (International) Web Page* contains international price graphs and tables for each energy source. Data range from weekday crude oil spot prices to annual household electricity prices.

The *Energy InfoDisc* CD-ROM contains PDF files for the full text of recent editions of Energy Information Administration publications including those mentioned in this section. The agency's Web site includes a publications database search feature to locate these publications on the Web site. Users may search by words in the title, description, author, or year.

AGRICULTURAL AND FOOD PRICES
Checklist

Agricultural Statistics. PRINT. WEB. (annual) 1936–. U.S. Department of Agriculture. National Agricultural Statistics Service. A 1.47: Item 0001. ASI 1004-1. GPO. <http://www.usda.gov/nass/pubs/agstats.htm>; <http://purl.access.gpo.gov/GPO/LPS1063>.
>   Coverage: U.S., states, selected market cities.
>   Content: farm product prices; prices received and paid by farmers.

Agricultural Statistics. CD-ROM. (annual) 1994–. U.S. Department of Agriculture. A 1.47/2: Item 0001-A. GPO.
>   Content: CD-ROM version of *Agricultural Statistics*.

Agricultural Outlook. PRINT. WEB. (10 issues a year) 1975–. U.S. Department of Agriculture. Economic Research Service. A 93.10/2: Item 0042-M. ASI 1502-4. GPO. <http://www.ers.usda.gov/epubs/pdf/agout/ao.htm>; <http://purl.access.gpo.gov/GPO/LPS4107>; <http://usda.mannlib.cornell.edu/reports/erssor/economics/ao-bb/>; <http://purl.access.gpo.gov/GPO/LPS1093>.
>   Coverage: U.S.
>   Content: commodity market outlook; farm product prices; prices received by farmers; consumer and producer price indexes; farm-retail price spreads.

Food Consumption, Prices, and Expenditures. MF. WEB. (annual) U.S. Department of Agriculture. Economic Research Service. Statistical Bulletin series. A 1.34/4: (Earlier, A 1.34:) Item 0015. ASI 1544-4. <http://www.ers.usda.gov/prodsrvs/reptfd.htm#consumption>; <http://purl.access.gpo.gov/GPO/LPS3832> 1970-97 edition: <http://www.ers.usda.gov/epubs/pdf/sb965/>.
>   Coverage: U.S.
>   Content: average retail food prices for individual items; consumer price index for food items.

Food Cost Review. MF. WEB. (annual) U.S. Department of Agriculture. Economic Research Service. Agricultural Economic Report series. A 1.107/2: (Earlier, A 1.107:) (Earlier title: *Developments in Farm to Retail Price Spreads for Food Products*) Item 0042-C. ASI 1544-9. Tables: <http://www.ers.usda.gov/briefing/foodmark/cost/cost.htm>; <http://www.ers.usda.gov/Prodsrvs/rept-fd.htm#costs>; <http://purl.access.gpo.gov/GPO/LPS3833>.
>   Coverage: U.S.
>   Content: food price developments; consumer price index; retail food prices for individual items; farm-retail price spreads.

Commodity Situation and Outlook Reports. MF. WEB. (frequency varies; two to twelve issues a year) (Dates and titles vary) U.S. Department of Agriculture. Economic Research Service. <http://www.ers.usda.gov/prodsrvs/periodic.htm#SandO)>.
>   Coverage: varies; world, U.S., regions, states, selected market cities.
>   Content: various price data; prices received by farmers; wholesale and retail prices; spot prices; price indexes.

Cotton and Wool Outlook. WEB. (monthly) A 93.24/2: Item 0021-M. ASI 1561-1. <http://usda.mannlib.cornell.edu/reports/erssor/field/cws-bb/>.

Feed Outlook. WEB. (monthly) A 93.11/2: Item 0021-E. ASI 1561-4. <http://usda.mannlib.cornell.edu/reports/erssor/field/fds-bb/>; <http://purl.access.gpo.gov/GPO/LPS1100>.

Fruit and Tree Nuts Situation and Outlook. MF. WEB. (three issues a year) A 93.12/3: Item 0021-K. ASI 1561-6. GPO. <http://usda.mannlib.cornell.edu/reports/erssor/specialty/fts-bb/>; <http://purl.access.gpo.gov/GPO/LPS3327>.

Livestock, Dairy, and Poultry Situation and Outlook. WEB. (monthly) A 93.46/3: Item 0024-C. ASI 1561-19. <http://usda.mannlib.cornell.edu/reports/erssor/livestock/ldp-mbb/>; <http://purl.access.gpo.gov/GPO/LPS2552>.

Oil Crops Outlook. WEB. (monthly) A 93.23/2: Item 0021-D. ASI 1561-3. <http://usda.mannlib.cornell.edu/reports/erssor/field/ocs-bb/>; <http://purl.access.gpo.gov/GPO/LPS1105>.

Rice Outlook. WEB. (monthly) A 93.11/3: Item 0021-P. ASI 1561-8. <http://usda.mannlib.cornell.edu/reports/erssor/field/rcs-bb/>.

Sugar and Sweetener. MF. WEB. (two issues a year) A 93.31/3: Item 0024-R. ASI 1561-14. GPO. <http://usda.mannlib.cornell.edu/reports/erssor/specialty/sss-bb/>; <http://purl.access.gpo.gov/GPO/LPS1109>.

Tobacco Situation and Outlook. MF. WEB. (three issues a year) A 93.25: Item 0024-D-01. ASI 1561-10. GPO. <http://usda.mannlib.cornell.edu/reports/erssor/specialty/tbs-bb/>; <http://purl.access.gpo.gov/GPO/LPS1110>; <http://www.ers.usda.gov/briefing/tobacco/index.htm>.

Vegetables and Specialties Situation and Outlook. MF. WEB. (three issues a year) A 93.12/2: Item 0021-L. ASI 1561-11. GPO. <http://usda.mannlib.cornell.edu/reports/erssor/specialty/vgs-bb/>; <http://purl.access.gpo.gov/GPO/LPS3325>.

Wheat Outlook. WEB. (monthly) A 93.11: Item 0021-I. ASI 1561-12. <http://usda.mannlib.cornell.edu/reports/erssor/field/whs-bb/>; <http://purl.access.gpo.gov/GPO/LPS1112>.

Agricultural Prices. WEB. (monthly, annual summary) U.S. Department of Agriculture. Agricultural Statistics Board. National Agricultural Statistics Service. A 92.16:; A 92.16/2: Item 0018-C. ASI 1629-1,-5. <http://usda.mannlib.cornell.edu/reports/nassr/price/pap-bb/>; <http://usda.mannlib.cornell.edu/reports/nassr/price/zap-bb/>; <http://purl.access.gpo.gov/GPO/LPS3074>.
>   Coverage: U.S., states, regions.
>   Content: indexes of prices received and paid by farmers; prices received; prices paid.

Crop Values: [year] Summary. WEB. (annual) U.S. Department of Agriculture. National Agricultural Statistics Service. A 92.24/3: Item 0020-B-05. ASI 1621-2. <http://usda.mannlib.cornell.edu/reports/nassr/price/zcv-bb/>; <http://purl.access.gpo.gov/GPO/LPS3076>.

> Coverage: U.S., states.
> Content: average prices for individual crops.

Discussion

Agricultural Statistics contains a farm product price table in the chapter on "Farm Resources, Income and Expenses" that gives marketing year average price received by farmers for several different products. Other tables in this section cover prices paid by farmers for selected commodities, price components of a market basket of farm food products, and related price indexes. Price data are also included in the individual commodity sections and can be located by checking the index under specific commodities. These tables are more detailed, covering several years, and often give prices by state.

Agricultural Outlook is a current source for general price information. In the "Briefs" section broad commodity areas such as field crops or livestock, poultry and dairy are surveyed and price outlook is sometimes covered. A "Statistical Indicators" section contains tables on prices received by farmers, price indexes, and prices for specific livestock and crop products.

Food Consumption, Prices, and Expenditures contains a price section with one table on prices and several tables on the consumer price index. Average retail prices are given for specific items such as white bread, frankfurters, or coffee. The price index tables give the consumer price index for food items. Data are given for several years.

Food Cost Review is a narrative report with numerous statistical tables. There is an overview section and sections on "Market Basket Prices," and "Price Spreads for Selected Foods." The market basket price tables give retail prices, farm value, and farm value share of retail prices for specific food items. Related price indexes are given for broad food groups. The price spread tables give retail price, wholesale value, price spreads, and farm value share for selected food items.

The *Commodity Situation and Outlook Reports* contain a narrative overview and outlook for selected commodities. Reports analyze production, stocks, trade, and prices and sometimes contain an article on a special topic. Statistical tables and graphs are included in the narrative report. There is also a section of more detailed statistical tables at the end of the report. Price data are usually discussed in the narrative report and covered in the statistical tables. A recent issue of *Wheat Outlook*, for example, contains a short narrative analysis of wheat price trends and tables covering the average farm price for recent years and recent monthly prices of types of wheat in selected market cities.

Agricultural Prices covers prices received by farmers, rather than retail prices. It also includes prices paid by farmers for such items as feed, fuels, farm supplies, and fertilizer. The prices paid information in the monthly issues is limited to price indexes. Actual prices paid by region and more specific product listings are found in the annual summary issue. Both the monthly and annual issues contain prices received by farmers for specific commodities. The annual summary contains more detailed commodity listings and provides a greater range of historical data, often by month.

Crop Values gives average marketing year prices. It gives a unit price for more than 100 crops and state price data for major crops. Data cover the most recent three years.

MINERAL SOURCES
Checklist

Minerals Yearbook. PRINT. WEB. (annual) 1932–. U.S. Department of the Interior. Geological Survey. I 19.165: (Earlier, I 28.37:. Issued since 1882 under other titles) Item 0639. ASI 5664-25, -26, -31. GPO. <http://minerals.usgs.gov/minerals/pubs/myb.html>; <http://purl.access.gpo.gov/GPO/LPS2120>.

> Coverage: world, U.S.
> Content: prices for mineral commodities.

Minerals and Materials Information. CD-ROM. 1994–. U.S. Department of the Interior. Geological Survey. I 19.120/4: Item 0639-J. ASI 5662-8.

> Content: *Minerals Yearbook* and other mineral publications.

Metal Prices in the United States Through 1998. PRINT. WEB. (1999) U.S. Department of Interior. Geological Survey. I 19.2:M 56/7. Item 0621. <http://minerals.usgs.gov/minerals/pubs/metal_prices/>.

> Coverage: U.S.
> Content: historical metal prices, significant events affecting prices, overview of metal's history.

Discussion

Volume 1 of the *Minerals Yearbook* covers "Metals and Minerals" and contains a chapter on each mineral. One section of each chapter covers prices in a narrative description. A statistical table on prices is also sometimes included. Examples of data available include the price of a pound of lithium fluoride or average monthly prices for heavy melting steel. The *Minerals Yearbook* is also available on the *Minerals and Materials Information* CD-ROM.

Metal Prices in the United States Through 1998 contains two- to three-page profiles of individual metals arranged alphabetically by the name of the metal. Each profile includes a graph of current and constant prices from 1959 through 1998, a table listing annual average price by year for as far back as it could be obtained, a list of significant events affecting prices, and a narrative overview of the history of the metal. Bibliographic references for each metal are also included.

INDEXES
Checklist

American Statistics Index (ASI). PRINT. (monthly) 1973–. Bethesda, MD: Congressional Information Service.

Statistical Universe. WEB. Bethesda, MD: Congressional Information Service.

Catalog of United States Government Publications (MOCAT). WEB. 1994–. U.S. Government Printing Office. Superintendent of Documents. <http://www.gpo.gov/catalog>; <http://www.access.gpo.gov/su_docs/locators/cgp/index.html>; <http://purl.access.gpo.gov/GPO/LPS844>.

Monthly Catalog of United States Government Publications. CD-ROM. 1996-. U.S. Government Printing Office. Superintendent of Documents. GP 3.8/7: Item 0557-C. GPO.

Monthly Catalog of United States Government Publications (Condensed version). PRINT. (monthly) 1996–. U.S. Government Printing Office. Superintendent of Documents. GP 3.8/8: (Earlier full version, GP 3.8:, 1895-1995). Item 0557-D. GPO.

Discussion

ASI is a comprehensive index to government statistics. Data on prices can be found under such subject headings as "Prices," "Energy prices," "Food prices," "Agricultural prices," "Consumer Price Index," and "Producer Price Index." See also the names of individual products and commodities. *Statistical Universe* includes a Web version of *ASI*.

The *Monthly Catalog* may also be used to locate material, but does not provide the depth of indexing for statistics that *ASI* does. Look under subject headings beginning with "Prices," and for the subdivision "Statistics" as in "Prices-United States-Statistics." See also "Consumer Price Indexes," "Price Indexes," and "Agricultural Prices." "Prices" is also used as a subdivision under specific products and industries such as "Automobiles-Prices" or "Cement Industries-Prices-United States." The complete version of the *Monthly Catalog* is available on the Web and CD-ROM. Commercial online and CD-ROM versions of the *Monthly Catalog* are also available.

For more information on these indexes, see Chapter 3, "The Basics of Searching."

RELATED MATERIAL
Within this Work

Chapter 5   Foreign Countries

Chapter 30   Economic Indicators

Chapter 37   Consumer Expenditures

Chapter 41   Energy Statistics

Chapter 42   Projections

GPO Subject Bibliographies. PRINT. WEB. GP 3.22/2:

<http://bookstore.gpo.gov/sb/about.html>

No. 226 "Cost of Living"

Other

Major Programs of the Bureau of Labor Statistics. PRINT. (annual) 1969–. U.S. Department of Labor. Bureau of Labor Statistics. L 2.125: Item 0768-G. Related site: <http://stats.bls.gov/proghome.htm>.

Major Programs of the Bureau of Labor Statistics provides an overview of each survey or program of the Bureau. Programs are grouped by broad topic. A section on "Prices and Living Conditions" describes programs related to prices. For each program there is a brief outline of data available, coverage, sources of data, forms of publication, and uses. A list of selected publications is provided at the end of each topic section.

CHAPTER 37
Consumer Expenditures

Consumer expenditures, or personal consumption expenditures for goods and services, is a major component of the gross domestic product (GDP) and gross national product (GNP). Data on such expenditures are usually found in detailed GDP and GNP tables. There is also a major consumer expenditure survey published by the Bureau of Labor Statistics. Government sources on this topic, however, are somewhat limited.

SEARCH STRATEGY

This chapter shows a statistical search strategy. The steps to follow are

1. Consult the "General Statistical Sources" section of this chapter for sources of basic data;
2. Look at the "National Income and Product Accounts" sources in this chapter for the most detailed GDP tables;
3. See the *Consumer Expenditure Survey* for the most detailed information on expenditures for specific items;
4. For additional information on specific subjects, see the "Additional Sources" section;
5. Consider the sources listed in the "Related Material" section of this chapter; and
6. Search the indexes for more specific information.

GENERAL STATISTICAL SOURCES
Checklist

Statistical Abstract of the United States. PRINT. WEB. (annual) 1878–. U.S. Department of Commerce. Economics and Statistics Administration. Bureau of the Census. C 3.134: Item 0150. ASI 2324-1. GPO.<http://www.census.gov/statab/www/>; <http://purl.access.gpo.gov/GPO/LPS2878>.
> Coverage: selected countries, U.S., regions, selected metropolitan areas.

Content: personal consumption expenditures (total and by major categories); average annual expenditures by category and household characteristics.

Statistical Abstract of the United States. CD-ROM. (annual) 1993–. U.S. Department of Commerce. Bureau of the Census. C 3.134/7: Item 0150-B. ASI 2324-14.
> Content: CD-ROM version of the *Statistical Abstract*.

Historical Statistics of the United States: Colonial Times to 1970. Parts 1-2. PRINT. (1975) U.S. Department of Commerce. Bureau of the Census. C 3.134/2:H 62/789-970/pt.1-2. Item 0151. ASI (76) 2328-2. GPO.
> Coverage: U.S.
> Content: personal consumption expenditures (total and by major category); historical expenditure data by type of family and income class for major categories.

Historical Statistics of the United States on CD-ROM: Colonial Times to 1970. CD-ROM. (1997) New York, NY: Cambridge University Press.
> Content: CD-ROM version of *Historical Statistics of the United States*.

Discussion

Some basic consumer expenditure data can be found in the *Statistical Abstract of the United States*. Many of the tables are in the "Income, Expenditures, and Wealth" section, but other tables are scattered throughout the book. Look in the index under "Personal consumption expenditures" and under "Consumer — expenditures." Statistics are selected from many of the more detailed sources covered in this chapter. Source notes at the end of each table can direct the user to more current or more detailed sources for the information in that table. The full text of recent editions of the *Statistical Abstract* is available on the Census Bureau Web site as PDF files. The *Statistical Abstract* is also available on CD-ROM. The CD uses Adobe Acrobat software and contains some additional geographic areas and time series in the form of spreadsheet files that are not in the printed version. *Historical Statistics of the United States: Colonial Times to 1970* contains a chapter on "Consumer Income and Expenditures" with historical expenditure tables. A CD-ROM version of *Historical Statistics* is available from Cambridge University Press.

NATIONAL INCOME AND PRODUCT ACCOUNTS

Checklist

Survey of Current Business. PRINT. WEB. (monthly) 1921–. U.S. Department of Commerce. Bureau of Economic Analysis. C 59.11: Item 0228. ASI 2702-1. GPO.<http://www.bea.doc.gov/bea/pubs.htm>;<http://purl.access.gpo.gov/GPO/LPS1730>.
    Coverage: U.S.
    Content: monthly national income and product accounts tables; annual tables in every August issue; personal consumption expenditures by type of expenditure.

Survey of Current Business. CD-ROM. (annual) 1994–. U.S. Department of Commerce. Economics and Statistics Administration. Bureau of Economic Analysis. C 59.11/1: Item 0228-A. GPO.
    Content: CD-ROM version of *Survey of Current Business.*

National Income and Product Accounts of the United States, 1929–94. PRINT. 2 vols. (1998) U.S. Department of Commerce. Economics and Statistics Administration. Bureau of Economic Analysis. C 59.11/5:929-94/v.1-2. Item 0228-A-03. ASI (98) 2708-5. GPO.
    Coverage: U.S.
    Content: national income, total personal income and its disposition, personal income by type of income.

National Income and Product Accounts of the United States, 1929–97. CD-ROM. (1999) U.S. Department of Commerce. Economics and Statistics Administration. Bureau of Economic Analysis. C 59.11/5-2:929-97. Item 0228-A-04.
    Content: CD-ROM version of *National Income and Product Accounts of the United States.*

Business Statistics of the United States. (annual) 1995–. Lanham, MD: Bernan Press. (Continuation of *Business Statistics* published by the Bureau of Economic Analysis, 1951-1991, C 59.11/3:)
    Coverage: U.S.. states.
    Content: economic time series data, including national and personal income; median income; and poverty status.

STAT-USA Internet. WEB. U.S. Department of Commerce. C 1.91: Item 0128-P.<http://www.stat-usa.gov/>.
    Coverage: U.S., regions, states, counties, metropolitan areas.
    Content: current and historical economic press releases on National Income and Product Accounts; personal income.

Bureau of Economic Analysis Web Site. WEB. U.S. Department of Commerce. Economics and Statistics Administration. Bureau of Economic Analysis.<http://www.bea.doc.gov/>.
    Content: agency information, data files, full-text publications and press releases.

Discussion

National income and product accounts tables contain data on consumer expenditures. Basic monthly, quarterly, and annual tables on personal consumption expenditures can be found in any issue of the *Survey of Current Business* in the "BEA Current and Historical Data" section. Total expenditures can be found in Table 1.1 (Gross Domestic Product) and Table B.2 (The Disposition of Personal Income). More detailed data for major product categories and selected products can be found in Table B.4 (Personal Consumption Expenditures by Type of Expenditure). (See Figure 37.1.) Some additional tables are published with the latest annual estimates in the August issues of the *Survey of Current Business.* A historical compilation of data from 1929 to 1994 is also available in *National Income and Product Accounts of the United States.* A more current edition is available on CD-ROM. *Business Statistics of the United States* also contains several years of personal consumption expenditure tables.

    STAT-USA Internet is a fee-based service, but federal depository libraries may register for free access for two workstations. The *STAT-USA Internet* site is divided into two areas: State of the Nation and Globus & NTDB. The State of the Nation area contains domestic economic statistical releases. Current versions of the top 50 releases are organized by categories. The "Gross Domestic Product" and "Personal Income and Outlays" releases in the General Economic Indicators category contain the most current personal consumption expenditure data. Additional files, including earlier data, are available in the State of the Nation Library. These files are also arranged by category. The "NIPA Information" category includes additional National Income and Product Account files and earlier gross domestic product and personal income releases. A search option for the State of the Nation Library is also available.

    The *Bureau of Economic Analysis Web Site* provides information on the agency, agency data, full-text publications, and access to many downloadable files. Full-text publications include recent issues of the *Survey of Current Business* and press releases containing economic statistics. Users may also select data by geographic area: national, international, and regional. For each area users can select a data category for lists of viewable tables and downloadable files or an article category for a list of full-text articles from the *Survey of Current Business.* The national area includes National Income and Product Accounts tables and articles.

CONSUMER EXPENDITURE SURVEY

Checklist

Consumer Expenditure Survey. PRINT. (biennial) 1984–. U.S. Department of Labor. Bureau of Labor Statistics. Bulletin series. L 2.3: (1994-95 is L 2.3:2492) Item 0768-A-01. (Title

January 2000 SURVEY OF CURRENT BUSINESS *National Data • D-31*

Table B.4.—Personal Consumption Expenditures by Type of Expenditure

	Billions of dollars			Billions of chained (1996) dollars		
	1996	1997	1998	1996	1997	1998
Personal consumption expenditures	**5,237.5**	**5,524.4**	**5,848.6**	**5,237.5**	**5,433.7**	**5,698.6**
Food and tobacco	**834.1**	**866.3**	**907.4**	**834.1**	**846.2**	**866.2**
Food purchased for off-premise consumption (n.d.)	476.7	489.5	509.4	476.7	480.5	494.0
Purchased meals and beverages [1] (n.d.)	300.5	318.5	334.7	300.5	309.8	317.6
Food furnished to employees (including military) (n.d.)	8.2	8.5	8.8	8.2	8.3	8.4
Food produced and consumed on farms (n.d.)	.5	.5	.5	.5	.5	.5
Tobacco products (n.d.)	48.2	49.3	54.0	48.2	47.1	45.8
Addenda: Food excluding alcoholic beverages (n.d.)	689.1	715.2	745.2	689.1	699.7	716.5
Alcoholic beverages purchased for off-premise consumption (n.d.)	56.1	58.3	61.3	56.1	57.4	60.0
Other alcoholic beverages (n.d.)	40.7	43.5	46.9	40.7	42.0	44.1
Clothing, accessories, and jewelry	**333.3**	**348.2**	**367.9**	**333.3**	**348.8**	**375.8**
Shoes (n.d.)	38.8	40.0	41.6	38.8	40.1	42.0
Clothing and accessories except shoes [2]	219.5	230.9	244.4	219.5	230.7	249.8
Women's and children's (n.d.)	140.8	147.7	155.6	140.8	148.0	160.6
Men's and boys' (n.d.)	78.6	83.2	88.8	78.6	82.7	89.2
Standard clothing issued to military personnel (n.d)	.3	.3	.3	.3	.3	.3
Cleaning, storage, and repair of clothing and shoes (s.)	12.7	13.5	13.4	12.7	13.2	12.9
Jewelry and watches (d.)	40.3	41.2	44.2	40.3	42.8	47.7
Other [3] (s.)	21.7	22.3	24.0	21.7	21.8	23.2
Personal care	**71.6**	**76.1**	**80.5**	**71.6**	**75.1**	**78.2**
Toilet articles and preparations (n.d.)	48.0	50.6	53.8	48.0	50.5	52.9
Barbershops, beauty parlors, and health clubs (s.)	23.5	25.5	26.8	23.5	24.6	25.4
Housing	**772.5**	**809.8**	**855.9**	**772.6**	**786.5**	**805.6**
Owner-occupied nonfarm dwellingsspace rent [4] (s.)	555.4	585.5	622.6	555.4	569.0	586.6
Tenant-occupied nonfarm dwellingsrent [5] (s.)	180.6	186.0	193.6	180.6	180.9	182.6
Rental value of farm dwellings (s.)	6.2	6.4	6.6	6.2	6.0	5.9
Other [6] (s.)	30.2	31.9	33.1	30.2	30.6	30.5
Household operation	**589.2**	**617.5**	**646.5**	**589.2**	**611.2**	**643.7**
Furniture, including mattresses and bedsprings (d.)	50.9	54.1	57.0	50.9	54.2	57.2
Kitchen and other household appliances [7] (d.)	30.0	30.9	32.3	30.0	31.0	32.9
China, glassware, tableware and utensils (d.)	25.4	27.1	29.2	25.4	27.3	28.9
Other durable house furnishings [8] (d.)	50.5	53.4	57.6	50.5	53.1	57.1
Semidurable house furnishings [9] (n.d.)	31.0	32.6	34.6	31.0	33.3	36.2
Cleaning and polishing preparations, and miscellaneous household supplies and paper products (n.d)	49.8	51.5	54.3	49.8	51.0	52.9
Stationery and writing supplies (n.d.)	18.8	20.0	21.3	18.8	19.1	19.9
Household utilities	185.0	188.6	186.8	185.0	184.6	187.1
Electricity (s.)	93.3	93.8	95.9	93.3	93.3	99.3
Gas (s.)	35.5	36.6	32.2	35.5	34.2	30.7
Water and other sanitary services (s.)	40.7	43.0	45.4	40.7	42.0	42.9
Fuel oil and coal (n.d.)	15.6	15.2	13.2	15.6	15.1	14.5
Telephone and telegraph (s.)	97.1	103.9	113.1	97.1	103.7	114.6
Domestic service (s.)	13.6	13.8	16.0	13.6	13.5	15.2
Other [10] (s.)	37.1	41.6	44.2	37.1	40.4	42.1
Medical care	**932.3**	**977.6**	**1,032.3**	**932.3**	**956.6**	**987.4**
Drug preparations and sundries [11] (n.d.)	100.3	108.1	116.8	100.3	106.5	112.6
Ophthalmic products and orthopedic appliances (d.)	17.6	19.4	21.2	17.6	19.1	20.5
Physicians (s.)	199.1	206.9	219.6	199.1	204.1	212.2
Dentists (s.)	48.4	52.0	54.8	48.4	49.7	50.2
Other professional services [12] (s.)	119.7	125.1	131.8	119.7	120.4	123.8
Hospitals and nursing homes [13]	390.8	408.5	428.4	390.8	400.8	410.4
Hospitals	327.6	341.9	357.1	327.6	336.5	344.3
Nonprofit (s.)	213.5	221.3	230.6	213.5	216.9	219.8
Proprietary (s.)	38.7	41.6	43.3	38.7	41.3	42.7
Government (s.)	75.4	79.0	83.2	75.4	78.3	81.9
Nursing homes (s.)	63.2	66.7	71.3	63.2	64.3	66.2
Health insurance	56.6	57.6	59.8	56.6	56.0	57.9
Medical care and hospitalization [14] (s.)	45.3	46.9	49.7	45.3	45.0	46.3
Income loss [15] (s.)	1.0	1.2	1.4	1.0	1.0	1.1
Workers' compensation [16] (s.)	10.3	9.6	8.7	10.3	10.0	10.5
Personal business	**435.1**	**488.3**	**528.6**	**435.1**	**477.5**	**505.5**
Brokerage charges and investment counseling (s.)	43.2	50.9	59.2	43.2	51.1	60.9
Bank service charges, trust services, and safe deposit box rental (s.)	42.9	47.9	55.7	42.9	45.7	51.7
Services furnished without payment by financial intermediaries except life insurance carriers (s.)	177.0	203.3	218.4	177.0	203.1	215.5
Expense of handling life insurance and pension plans [17] (s.)	81.3	89.0	91.3	81.3	84.5	82.4
Legal services (s.)	51.5	55.0	58.5	51.5	52.9	53.8
Funeral and burial expenses (s.)	14.5	15.3	16.0	14.5	14.6	14.7
Other [18] (s.)	24.8	26.9	29.5	24.8	26.0	27.6
Transportation	**594.6**	**623.7**	**647.4**	**594.6**	**616.4**	**653.8**
User-operated transportation	550.2	575.6	598.0	550.2	570.3	606.1
New autos (d.)	81.9	82.8	90.6	81.9	82.7	91.2
Net purchases of used autos (d.)	51.4	53.4	55.5	51.4	54.8	57.6
Other motor vehicles (d.)	84.3	87.2	101.4	84.3	86.4	100.6
Tires, tubes, accessories, and other parts (d.)	38.7	39.7	41.7	38.7	39.9	42.3
Repair, greasing, washing, parking, storage, rental, and leasing (s.)	134.2	145.9	153.8	134.2	143.9	149.0
Gasoline and oil (n.d.)	124.2	126.2	112.9	124.2	126.2	127.7
Bridge, tunnel, ferry, and road tolls (s.)	3.7	4.0	4.4	3.7	3.9	3.9
Insurance [19] (s.)	31.8	36.3	37.8	31.8	32.5	33.6
Purchased local transportation	11.2	11.8	12.1	11.2	11.6	12.0
Mass transit systems (s.)	7.7	8.1	8.4	7.7	8.0	8.3
Taxicab (s.)	3.5	3.7	3.7	3.5	3.6	3.7
Purchased intercity transportation	33.3	36.3	37.2	33.3	34.5	35.7
Railway (s.)	.6	.7	.7	.6	.7	.7
Bus (s.)	1.8	1.8	2.0	1.8	1.8	1.8
Airline (s.)	26.2	29.0	29.5	26.2	27.4	28.3
Other [20] (s.)	4.7	4.7	5.1	4.7	4.6	4.9
Recreation	**429.6**	**457.8**	**494.7**	**429.6**	**464.6**	**512.2**
Books and maps (d.)	24.9	26.6	27.8	24.9	26.3	26.8
Magazines, newspapers and sheet music (n.d.)	27.6	29.5	31.9	27.6	29.2	30.9
Nondurable toys and sport supplies (n.d.)	50.6	53.7	57.7	50.6	54.2	61.1
Wheel goods, sports and photographic equipment, boats, and pleasure aircraft (d.)	40.5	43.2	47.1	40.5	43.4	47.9
Video and audio goods, including musical instruments, and computer goods (d.)	80.0	84.0	92.6	80.0	97.0	124.5
Video and audio goods, including musical instruments (d.)	56.4	57.8	62.2	56.4	60.3	68.2
Computers, peripherals, and software (d.)	23.6	26.2	30.4	23.6	38.1	63.9
Radio and television repair (s.)	3.7	3.9	3.9	3.7	3.8	3.8
Flowers, seeds, and potted plants (n.d.)	14.9	15.6	16.5	14.9	16.1	16.8
Admissions to specified spectator amusements	20.7	22.2	23.8	20.7	21.6	22.6
Motion picture theaters (s.)	5.8	6.4	6.8	5.8	6.2	6.5
Legitimate theaters and opera, and entertainments of nonprofit institutions (except athletics) (s.)	8.0	8.7	9.4	8.0	8.4	8.9
Spectator sports [21] (s.)	6.9	7.1	7.6	6.9	6.9	7.2
Clubs and fraternal organizations [22] (s.)	14.0	14.4	14.9	14.0	14.1	14.1
Commercial participant amusements [23] (s.)	48.3	52.3	56.2	48.3	51.1	53.8
Pari-mutuel net receipts (s.)	3.5	3.6	3.7	3.5	3.5	3.5
Other [24] (s.)	100.8	109.0	118.6	100.8	105.1	110.8
Education and research	**122.3**	**130.7**	**139.2**	**122.3**	**126.1**	**130.1**
Higher education [25] (s.)	66.1	69.2	71.8	66.1	66.7	66.7
Nursery, elementary, and secondary schools [26] (s.)	27.4	29.0	30.1	27.4	28.1	28.3
Other [27] (s.)	28.8	32.4	37.3	28.8	31.4	35.2
Religious and welfare activities [28] (s.)	**146.8**	**150.3**	**163.5**	**146.8**	**145.9**	**154.7**
Foreign travel and other, net	**−24.1**	**−21.8**	**−15.3**	**−24.1**	**−20.7**	**−11.8**
Foreign travel by U.S. residents [29] (s.)	57.6	63.4	68.2	57.6	62.3	68.5
Expenditures abroad by U.S. residents (n.d.)	2.2	2.9	3.7	2.2	3.3	4.1
Less: Expenditures in the United States by nonresidents [30] (s.)	82.4	86.5	85.4	82.4	84.7	82.7
Less: Personal remittances in kind to nonresidents (n.d.)	1.5	1.6	1.6	1.5	1.6	1.6
Residual	....	....	....	.1	−3.2	−17.3

1. Consists of purchases (including tips) of meals and beverages from retail, service, and amusement establishments, hotels, dining and buffet cars, schools, school fraternities, institutions, clubs, and industrial lunchrooms. Includes meals and beverages consumed both on- and off-premise.
2. Includes luggage.
3. Consists of watch, clock, and jewelry repairs, costume and dress suit rental, and miscellaneous personal services.
4. Consists of rent for space and for heating and plumbing facilities, water heaters, lighting fixtures, kitchen cabinets, linoleum, storm windows and doors, window screens, and screen doors, but excludes rent for appliances and furniture and purchases of fuel and electricity.
5. Consists of space rent (see footnote 4) and rent for appliances, furnishings, and furniture.
6. Consists of transient hotels, motels, clubs, schools, and other group housing.
7. Consists of refrigerators and freezers, cooking ranges, dishwashers, laundry equipment, stoves, room air conditioners, sewing machines, vacuum cleaners, and other appliances.
8. Includes such house furnishings as floor coverings, comforters, quilts, blankets, pillows, picture frames, mirrors, art products, portable lamps, and clocks. Also includes writing equipment and hand, power, and garden tools.
9. Consists largely of textile house furnishings, including piece goods allocated to house furnishing use. Also includes lamp shades, brooms, and brushes.
10. Consists of maintenance services for appliances and house furnishings, moving and warehouse expenses, postage and express charges, premiums for fire and theft insurance on personal property less benefits and dividends, and miscellaneous household operation services.
11. Excludes drug preparations and related products dispensed by physicians, hospitals, and other medical services.
12. Consists of osteopathic physicians, chiropractors, private duty nurses, chiropodists, podiatrists, and others providing health and allied services, not elsewhere classified.
13. Consists of (1) current expenditures (including consumption of fixed capital) of nonprofit hospitals and nursing homes, and (2) payments by patients to proprietary and government hospitals and nursing homes.
14. Consists of (1) premiums, less benefits and dividends, for health, hospitalization, and accidental death and dismemberment insurance provided by commercial insurance carriers, and (2) administrative expenses (including consumption of fixed capital) of nonprofit and self-insured health plans.
15. Consists of premiums, less benefits and dividends, for income loss insurance.
16. Consists of premiums, less benefits and dividends, for privately administered workers' compensation.
17. Consists of (1) operating expenses of commercial life insurance carriers, (2) administrative expenses of private noninsured pension plans and publicly administered government employee retirement plans, and (3) premiums, less benefits and dividends, of fraternal benefit societies. For commercial life insurance carriers, excludes expenses for accident and health insurance and includes profits of stock companies and services furnished without payment by banks, credit agencies, and investment companies. For pension and retirement plans, excludes services furnished without payment by banks, credit agencies, and investment companies.
18. Consists of current expenditures (including consumption of fixed capital) of trade unions and professional associations, employment agency fees, money order fees, spending for classified advertisements, tax return preparation services, and other personal business services.
19. Consists of premiums, less benefits and dividends, for motor vehicle insurance.
20. Consists of baggage charges, coastal and inland waterway fares, travel agents' fees, and airport bus fares.
21. Consists of admissions to professional and amateur athletic events and to racetracks.
22. Consists of dues and fees excluding insurance premiums.
23. Consists of billiard parlors; bowling alleys; dancing, riding, shooting, skating, and swimming places; amusement devices and parks; golf courses; sightseeing buses and guides; private flying operations; casino gambling; and other commercial participant amusements.
24. Consists of net receipts of lotteries and expenditures for purchases of pets and pet care services, cable TV, film processing, photographic studios, sporting and recreation camps, video cassette rentals, and recreational services, not elsewhere classified.
25. For private institutions, equals current expenditures (including consumption of fixed capital) less receipts—such as those from meals, rooms, and entertainments—accounted for separately in consumer expenditures, and less expenditures for research and development financed under contracts or grants. For government institutions, equals student payments of tuition.
26. For private institutions, equals current expenditures (including consumption of fixed capital) less receipts—such as those from meals, rooms, and entertainments—accounted for separately in consumer expenditures. For government institutions, equals student payments of tuition. Excludes child day care services, which are included in religious and welfare activities.
27. Consists of (1) fees paid to commercial, business, trade, and correspondence schools and for educational services, not elsewhere classified, and (2) current expenditures (including consumption of fixed capital) by research organizations and foundations for education and research.
28. For nonprofit institutions, equals current expenditures (including consumption of fixed capital) of religious, social welfare, foreign relief, and political organizations, museums, libraries, and foundations. The expenditures are net of receipts such as those from meals, rooms, and entertainments accounted for separately in consumer expenditures, and excludes relief payments within the United States and expenditures by foundations for education and research. For proprietary and government institutions, equals receipts from users.
29. Beginning with 1981, includes U.S. students' expenditures abroad; these expenditures were $0.3 billion in 1981.
30. Beginning with 1981, includes nonresidents' student and medical care expenditures in the United States; student expenditures were $2.2 billion and medical expenditures were $0.4 billion in 1981.

NOTE.—Consumer durable goods are designated (d.), nondurable goods (n.d.), and services (s.).

Chained (1996) dollar series are calculated as the product of the chain-type quantity index and the 1996 current-dollar value of the corresponding series, divided by 100. Because the formula for the chain-type quantity indexes uses weights of more than one period, the corresponding chained-dollar estimates are usually not additive. The residual line is the difference between the first line and the sum of the most detailed lines.

Source: *Survey of Current Business*, v. 80, no. 1, January 2000, p. D-31.

Figure 37.1: Sample Page from *Survey of Current Business*.

varies) ASI 6764-5. GPO. Tables:<http://stats.bls.gov/csxhome.htm>.

> Coverage: U.S., regions, selected metropolitan areas.
> Content: average annual expenditures by category and household characteristics including income, age, size and composition of household, number of earners, tenure, race, occupation, and educational attainment.

Consumer Expenditures in [year]. PRINT. (annual) 1991–. U.S. Department of Labor. Bureau of Labor Statistics. Report series. L 2.71: (1997 is L 2.71:927) ASI 6764-6.

> Coverage: U.S., regions.
> Content: average annual expenditures by category and household characteristics including income, age, size and composition of household, number of earners, tenure, race, occupation, and educational attainment.

Consumer Expenditures in [year]. PRINT. WEB. (annual) U.S. Department of Labor. Bureau of Labor Statistics. L 2.120/2-5: (Earlier title, *Consumer Expenditure Survey Results from [year]*) Item 0769-P. ASI 6726-1.[no.].<http://stats.bls.gov/news.release/cesan.toc.htm>;<http://stats.bls.gov/bls_news/archives/all_nr.htm#CESAN>; <http://purl.access.gpo.gov/GPO/LPS2727>.

> Coverage: U.S.
> Content: average annual expenditures by broad category.

Consumer Expenditure Surveys Web Page. WEB. U.S. Department of Labor. Bureau of Labor Statistics.<http://stats.bls.gov/csxhome.htm>.

> Content: Consumer Expenditure Survey tables, news releases, and information.

Handbook of U.S. Labor Statistics: Employment, Earnings, Prices, Productivity, and Other Labor Data. PRINT. (annual) 1997–. Lanham, MD: Bernan Press. (Continuation of *Handbook of Labor Statistics* published by the Bureau of Labor Statistics, 1924-1989, L 2.3/5:, L 2.3:)

> Coverage: U.S., regions.
> Content: average annual expenditures by category and household characteristics including income, age, size and composition of household, number of earners, tenure, race.

Discussion

The *Consumer Expenditure Survey* was originally published approximately every 10 years beginning with an 1888–91 survey. It became a continuous, ongoing survey in 1980. The survey is conducted in two parts—an interview survey and a diary survey. Separate publications were often issued for each type of survey. Integrated survey data for the years 1984 on have been published in *Consumer Expenditure Survey.* The report contains an introductory summary of results and a basic set of tables giving household characteristics and average annual expenditures by category. These tables are repeated for different classifications: income quintiles, income range, age of householder, size of household, composition of household, number of earners, housing tenure and race of householder, region, occupation, education, shares of average annual expenditures, and aggregate expenditure shares. Additional

tables combine income ranges with age of householder, region, and size of household. Examples of data available from the basic tables include fresh fruit expenditures of one-person households, gasoline and motor oil expenditures of husband-and-wife households with the oldest child between six and 17, entertainment fees and admissions expenditures of service workers, and expenditures on health care in Cincinnati. From the tables that combine income with other variables it is possible to get such data as expenditures on beef for four-person households in the $15,000 to $19,999 income range. Comparable, more current tables are available on the Internet.

Consumer Expenditures in [year] is an annual publication issued in the *Report* series that is more current, but less detailed than the *Consumer Expenditure Survey.* This title contains the same basic set of tables, but has less detailed expenditure categories and does not include the additional cross-tabulations that are available in the *Consumer Expenditure Survey.*

Consumer Expenditures in [year] is an annual press release summarizing data from the consumer expenditure survey. It contains a brief narrative summary and a single table on total annual expenditures by broad category for recent years.

The *Consumer Expenditure Surveys Web Page* contains detailed tables from several years of the Consumer Expenditure Survey. These tables are similar to those published in the *Consumer Expenditure Survey* report, but are more current. The Web page also gives information on other data available and includes a link to the annual press release, *Consumer Expenditures in [year].*

The *Handbook of U.S. Labor Statistics* contains basic tables from the most recent Consumer Expenditure Survey available at the time of publication. The tables are similar to those published in *Consumer Expenditures in [year]* in the *Report* series, but not as current and without the occupation and educational attainment data.

ADDITIONAL SOURCES

Checklist

Food Consumption, Prices, and Expenditures. MF. WEB. (annual) U.S. Department of Agriculture. Economic Research Service. Statistical Bulletin series. A 1.34/4: (Earlier, A 1.34:) Item 0015. ASI 1544-4.<http://www.ers.usda.gov/prodsrvs/reptfd.htm#consumption>; <http://purl.access.gpo.gov/GPO/LPS3832>; 1970–97 edition:<http://www.ers.usda.gov/epubs/pdf/sb965/>.

> Coverage: selected countries, U.S.
> Content: food expenditures as share of all disposable personal income; percentage of food expenditures by income range; percentage of personal consumption expenditures for food and alcoholic beverages; total expenditures for food and alcoholic beverages at home and away from home; food expenditures by source of funds.

Agricultural Outlook. PRINT. WEB. (10 issues a year) 1975–. U.S. Department of Agriculture. Economic Research Service.

A 93.10/2: Item 0042-M. ASI 1502-4. GPO.<http://www.ers.usda.gov/epubs/pdf/agout/ao.htm>;<http://purl.access.gpo.gov/GPO/LPS4107>; <http://usda.mannlib.cornell.edu/reports/erssor/economics/ao-bb/>; <http://purl.access.gpo.gov/GPO/LPS1093>.

    Coverage: U.S.

    Content: personal consumption expenditures; total food expenditures at home and away from home.

Family Economics and Nutrition Review. MF. WEB. (quarterly) 1995–. U.S. Department of Agriculture. Food and Consumer Service. A 98.20: (Earlier, A 77.245:) (Issued since 1957 as *Family Economics Review*) Item 0074-A-09. ASI 1362-17. GPO.<http://www.usda.gov/cnpp/FENR.htm>.

    Coverage: U.S., regions.

    Content: average cost per week and month for food at four cost levels by family size and age groups; periodic feature on expenditures on a child by age and category for three income levels.

Official USDA Food Plans: Cost of Food at Home at Four Levels. WEB. (monthly) U.S. Department of Agriculture. Food and Consumer Service. A 98.19/2: Item 0074-A-08.<http://www.usda.gov/cnpp/using3.htm>;<http://purl.access.gpo.gov/GPO/LPS1848>.

    Coverage: U.S.

    Content: average cost per week and month for food at four cost levels by family size and age groups.

Expenditures on Children by Families. MF. WEB. (annual) U.S. Department of Agriculture. Food and Consumer Service. A1.38:1528-. Item 0013-A. ASI 1364-20.<http://www.usda.gov/cnpp/using2.htm>; <http://purl.access.gpo.gov/GPO/LPS4534>.

    Coverage: U.S., regions.

    Content: expenditures on a child by age and category for three income levels.

Food Cost Review. MF. WEB. (annual) U.S. Department of Agriculture. Economic Research Service. Agricultural Economic Report series. A 1.107/2: (Earlier, A 1.107:) (Earlier title: *Developments in Farm to Retail Price Spreads for Food Products*) Item 0042-C. ASI 1544-9. Tables:<http://www.ers.usda.gov/briefing/foodmark/cost/cost.htm>; <http://www.ers.usda.gov/Prodsrvs/rept-fd.htm#costs>; <http://purl.access.gpo.gov/GPO/LPS3833>.

    Coverage: U.S.

    Content: marketing bill and farm value components of consumer expenditures; food expenditures as share of disposable personal income; annual food expenditures by income range and food product.

Food Review: The Magazine of Food Economics. PRINT. WEB. (quarterly) 1978–. U.S. Department of Agriculture. Economic Research Service. A 93.16/3: (Earlier, A 105.15:) (Before 1991 titled *National Food Review*) Item 0021-H. ASI 1541-7. GPO.<http://www.ers.usda.gov/epubs/pdf/foodrevw/foodrevw.htm>.

    Coverage: U.S.

    Content: annual issue on the food system; food spending at home and away from home; personal consumption expenditures by category; annual food expenditures by size of household, income group, race, age of household head.

A Look at Residential Energy Consumption in 1997. PRINT. WEB. (1999) U.S. Department of Energy. Energy Information Administration. Office of Energy Markets and End Use. E 3.2:R 31/10. Item 0429-T-11. <http://www.eia.doe.gov/emeu/recs/contents.html>.

    Coverage: U.S., regions.

    Content: total household energy expenditures; expenditures for space-heating, air-conditioning, water-heating, and appliances; data by year of construction, household income, type of housing unit, and region.

Residential Energy Consumption Survey Web Page. WEB. U.S. Department of Energy. Energy Information Administration. <http://www.eia.doe.gov/emeu/recs/contents.html>.

    Coverage: U.S., regions, divisions, four most populated states.

    Content: survey background, data tables, publications, and data files; tables cover average household energy expenditures for space heating, air-conditioning, water heating, and appliances by selected household characteristics including climate zone, year of construction, household income, type of housing unit, size of household, age and race of householder, floor space, temperature settings, and insulation.

Health Care Financing Review. PRINT. (quarterly) Summer 1979–. U.S. Department of Health and Human Services. Health Care Financing Administration. Office of Strategic Planning. HE 22.512: (Earlier, HE 22.18:) Item 0512-A-10. ASI 4652-1. GPO. Article abstracts:<http://www.hcfa.gov/pubforms/ordpub.htm>; Health expenditures:<http://www.hcfa.gov/stats/NHE-OAct/>.

    Coverage: U.S.

    Content: annual health expenditures article; total and per capita health expenditures; expenditures by type of service; hospital revenues; source of funds.

Discussion

These sources contain expenditure data in specific areas. Most of them deal with food expenditures. Others cover energy and health expenditures.

    Food Consumption, Prices, and Expenditures contains some tables on food expenditures. Statistics give total food expenditures for food and alcoholic beverages at home or away from home. Additional tables for each of these categories indicate where the money was spent. For example, the away-from-home food table gives expenditures for food at eating and drinking places, hotels and motels, retail stores, recreational places, or schools and colleges. Additional tables give food expenditures by source of funds, such as families or governments, and compare food expenditures for selected countries. Expenditures for specific food items are not given in this source.

    Agricultural Outlook provides current, more limited statistics on food expenditures in its "Statistical Indicators" section. A table on food expenditures covers total food sales at home and away from home. This table updates the more detailed annual tables in *Food Consumption, Prices, and Expenditures.* There is also a table on the gross domestic product that gives personal consumption expenditures for very broad categories such as durable goods or food.

Family Economics and Nutrition Review contains a regular table on cost of food at home. It gives the weekly and monthly cost of food at four different levels ranging from a thrifty plan to a liberal plan. Information is given for families of two, families of four, and for individuals by age group and sex. This table, *Official USDA Food Plans: Cost of Food at Home at Four Levels*, also appears monthly on the agency's Web site. A periodic article with tables on expenditures for a child by husband-wife families and by single-parent families also appears. The husband-wife tables are the most detailed. They give expenditures by age of the child for the U.S. and regions. Data are given by expenditure categories such as clothing or food. The data are repeated for lower, middle, and higher income families. Similar data are also issued in the annual report, *Expenditures on Children by Families*, on the agency's Web site.

The *Food Cost Review* is a narrative report with a few tables on food expenditures. One table relates food expenditures to disposable income, giving such information as the amount and proportion of income spent for food at home or away from home. (A similar table is also available in *Food Consumption, Prices, and Expenditures*.) There are also data on food expenditures by food group, such as the amount of expenditures on poultry or eggs. Other tables cover the amount of food expenditures attributable to farm value and marketing costs.

The *Food Review* publishes an annual issue on the U.S. food system (in recent years it has been issue number three). This issue contains general articles that review trends in several food areas including food spending. The food spending article(s) contain basic statistical tables and charts.

A Look at Residential Energy Consumption in 1997 presents data from the 1997 Residential Energy Consumption Survey covering household characteristics, energy consumption, and energy expenditures. The survey has been conducted periodically since 1978 and data from previous surveys have been published in a variety of different publication titles. An appendix on related publications lists the publications and products from current and previous surveys. The report includes an energy overview section, a survey of changes since 1978, brief reports on special topics, and detailed data tables. Data on expenditures include a special topic report on percentiles for household energy costs and data tables on total energy expenditures, space-heating expenditures, electric air-conditioning expenditures, water-heating expenditures, and appliances expenditures. More detailed tables are available on the Internet.

The *Residential Energy Consumption Survey Web Page* provides access to data and information from the Residential Energy Consumption Survey of household energy use. It includes the full-text of the current survey report, *A Look at Residential Energy Consumption in 1997*. More detailed expenditure tables are available in the "Detailed Data Tables" category under the heading "Household Energy Consumption and Expenditures 1997." The HTML format option allows users to retrieve tables by selecting a topic, a characteristic, and expenditure or consumption tables. Examples of data available include amount spent on electricity for refrigerators in households with income between $25,000 and $49,999 and space heating expenditures for households that set the temperature lower during sleeping hours. Full-text reports and data files from previous surveys are also available from the main menu page.

Health Care Financing Review contains an annual article titled "National Health Expenditures, [year]." The issue containing the article varies, although it is often in the fall issue (No. 1). The article analyzes developments in health expenditures and contains several charts and tables. Expenditures are given for different categories of health care such as hospital care, physician services, prescription drugs, or nursing home care. Key expenditure measures are given such as per capita expenditures, percent of gross domestic product, and annual growth. Data on sources of funding for health expenditures are given including such information as the amount of home health care expenditures paid for by private health insurance, out-of-pocket, or by the federal government. Other articles cover detailed aspects of medical care financing. The full text of articles is not presently available on the Internet. However, abstracts of the articles and tables similar to those in the annual health expenditures article are available.

INDEXES
Checklist

American Statistics Index (ASI). PRINT. (monthly) 1973–. Bethesda, MD: Congressional Information Service.

Statistical Universe. WEB. Bethesda, MD: Congressional Information Service.

Catalog of United States Government Publications (MOCAT). WEB. 1994–. U.S. Government Printing Office. Superintendent of Documents.<http://www.gpo.gov/catalog>;<http://www.access.gpo.gov/su_docs/locators/cgp/index.html>; <http://purl.access.gpo.gov/GPO/LPS844>.

Monthly Catalog of United States Government Publications. CD-ROM. 1996–. U.S. Government Printing Office. Superintendent of Documents. GP 3.8/7: Item 0557-C. GPO.

Monthly Catalog of United States Government Publications (Condensed version). PRINT. (monthly) 1996–. U.S. Government Printing Office. Superintendent of Documents. GP 3.8/8: (Earlier full version, GP 3.8:, 1895-1995). Item 0557-D. GPO.

Discussion

ASI is a comprehensive index to government statistical data. Look under the subject headings "Personal consumption," "Cost of living," "Family budgets," and "Consumer Expenditure Survey" for general expenditure sources. See also specific topics such as "Medical Costs."

The *Monthly Catalog* may also be used to locate material, but does not provide the depth of indexing for statistics that *ASI* does. Look under "Consumption (Economics)," "Cost and Standard of Living," and more specific topics, such as "Food Consumption," or "Medical Care, Cost of." Statistical materials are usually found under the subdivision "Statistics," as in "Cost and Standard of Living-United States-Statistics." The complete version of the *Monthly Catalog* is available on the Web and CD-ROM. Commercial online and CD-ROM versions of the *Monthly Catalog* are also available.

For more information on these indexes, see Chapter 3, "The Basics of Searching."

RELATED MATERIAL
Within this Work

GPO Subject Bibliographies. PRINT. WEB. GP 3.22/2:

<http://bookstore.gpo.gov/sb/about.html>

No. 2   "Consumer Information"

No. 226 "Cost of Living"

CHAPTER 38
Foreign Trade Statistics

The U.S. government publishes many resources on foreign trade; the major statistical sources are covered in this chapter. The U.S. Department of Commerce is the original collector of all trade data. Other agencies may supplement Commerce data with sources of their own or reorganize it to suit their own needs.

All the sources in this chapter give statistics on value and/or quantity of exports and imports. They vary in the level of commodity and geographic detail presented and in the ways the data are combined. Most sources cover U.S. trade and discuss other countries in relation to the U.S. Very little information on other countries' non-U.S. trade is available through U.S. government sources.

SEARCH STRATEGY

This chapter shows a statistical search strategy. The strategy is as follows:

1. Begin with the "General Statistical Sources" section of this chapter, particularly the *Statistical Abstract of the United States*;
2. For additional general level data go to the "Bureau of Economic Analysis (BEA) Sources";
3. Go to the "General Foreign Trade Sources" for more specific country, industry, and commodity data;
4. Use the "STAT-USA Sources" to obtain extensive trade data ranging from the basic to the detailed;
5. For other approaches to both general and detailed data see the "Census Bureau Sources" and the "International Trade Commission Sources";
6. Use the "Guides and Classifications" section of this chapter for help with definitions and commodity classification systems;
7. For a more specialized subject approach consider the reports in "Agricultural Trade Sources," and "Other Subject Sources"; and
8. Consult the "Indexes" and the "Related Material" sections of this chapter for additional help.

GENERAL STATISTICAL SOURCES
Checklist

Statistical Abstract of the United States. PRINT. WEB. (annual) 1878–. U.S. Department of Commerce. Economics and Statistics Administration. Bureau of the Census. C 3.134: Item 0150. ASI 2324-1. GPO. <http://www.census.gov/statab/www/>; <http://purl.access.gpo.gov/GPO/LPS2878>.

> Coverage: world, world regions, country groupings, countries, U.S., states, customs districts.
> Content: total value of U.S. exports and imports; trade balance; value of exports and imports by country and selected commodities; value of exports by state of origin; value of exports and imports by custom district.

Statistical Abstract of the United States. CD-ROM. (annual) 1993–. U.S. Department of Commerce. Bureau of the Census. C 3.134/7: Item 0150-B. ASI 2324-14.

> Content: CD-ROM version of the *Statistical Abstract*.

Historical Statistics of the United States: Colonial Times to 1970. Parts 1-2. PRINT. (1975) U.S. Department of Commerce. Bureau of the Census. C 3.134/2:H 62/789-970/pt.1-2. Item 0151. ASI (76) 2328-2. GPO.

> Coverage: world regions, selected countries, U.S., customs districts.
> Content: total value of exports and imports for U.S.; value by class (manufactured, crude materials, etc.), geographic area, and end-use categories; exports and imports of selected products.

Historical Statistics of the United States on CD-ROM: Colonial Times to 1970. CD-ROM. (1997) New York, NY: Cambridge University Press.

> Content: CD-ROM version of *Historical Statistics of the United States*.

State and Metropolitan Area Data Book. PRINT. WEB. (irregular) 1979–. U.S. Department of Commerce. Economics and Statistics Administration. Bureau of the Census. C 3.134/5: Item 0150. ASI 2328-54. GPO.<http://www.census.gov/statab/www.smadb.html>.

> Coverage: metropolitan areas.
> Content: export sales.

State and Metropolitan Area Data Book. CD-ROM. (irregular) 1997/98–. U.S. Department of Commerce. Economics and Statistics Administration. Bureau of the Census. (Not distributed to depository libraries)

> Content: CD-ROM version of the *State and Metropolitan Area Data Book.*

County and City Extra: Annual Metro, City, and County Data Book. PRINT. (annual) 1992–. Lanham, MD: Bernan Press.

> Coverage: U.S., states.
> Content: exports by state of origin for manufactured and nonmanufactured goods.

Handbook of International Economic Statistics. PRINT. WEB. (annual) 1992–. U.S. Central Intelligence Agency. Directorate of Intelligence. PREX 3.16: (Issued earlier as *Handbook of Economic Statistics*, PREX 3.10/7-5:) Item 0856-A-09. ASI 9114-4.GPO.<http://www.cia.gov/cia/di/products/hies/index.html>;<http://purl.access.gpo.gov/GPO/LPS2917>.

> Coverage: world, world regions, country groupings, selected countries, U.S.
> Content: total value of exports and imports; direction of trade; exports and imports by commodity.

Discussion

All of these sources provide basic export and import data. The *Statistical Abstract of the United States* contains a chapter on "Foreign Commerce and Aid," a portion of which covers U.S. exports and imports. Tables give data on exports and imports separately by country and selected commodities. There are no tables in this section that combine country and commodity data. The "Comparative International Statistics" chapter contains one table that combines country and commodity data, but only for wheat, rice, and corn. This section also has one table showing source of imports and destination of exports by region for selected countries. Additional export and import data can also be found on individual commodities by looking up the specific commodity in the book's index. Agricultural commodities are discussed in the "Agriculture" chapter, for instance, and minerals are examined in the "Natural Resources" chapter. The full-text of recent editions of the *Statistical Abstract* is available on the Census Bureau Web site as PDF files. The *Statistical Abstract* is also available on CD-ROM. The CD uses Adobe Acrobat software and contains some additional geographic areas and time series in the form of spreadsheet files that are not in the printed version.

Historical Statistics of the United States: Colonial Times to 1970 contains historical data for some of the information found in the *Statistical Abstract*. It also has a "Foreign Commerce" section and, as with the *Statistical Abstract*, individual commodities may be mentioned in other related chapters. A CD-ROM version of *Historical Statistics* is available from Cambridge University Press.

The *State and Metropolitan Area Data Book* contains one data item related to trade—export sales for metropolitan areas. This title is available as a PDF file on the Census Bureau Web site, and on CD-ROM.

County and City Extra, a commercially produced statistical compilation, gives exports by state of origin. The value of total exports, manufactured exports, and nonmanufactured exports is given with no specific commodity breakdown.

The *Handbook of International Economic Statistics* contains a section on "Foreign Trade and Aid." This source is particularly good for data on China and the Big Seven countries: U.S., Japan, Germany, France, the United Kingdom, Italy, and Canada. Commodity information is given primarily at a very broad level for the Big Seven, but in more detail for China. There is also good information on direction of trade. Many tables show trade between selected regions or country groupings, such as a series of tables on European Union exports to various world regions.

BUREAU OF ECONOMIC ANALYSIS (BEA) SOURCES

Checklist

National Income and Product Accounts of the United States, 1929–94. 2 vols. (1998) PRINT. U.S. Department of Commerce. Economics and Statistics Administration. Bureau of Economic Analysis. C 59.11/5:929-94/v.1-2. Item 0228-A-03. ASI (98) 2708-5. GPO.

> Coverage: U.S.
> Content: total value of exports and imports of goods and services; value by broad product category.

National Income and Product Accounts of the United States, 1929–97. CD-ROM. (1999) U.S. Department of Commerce. Economics and Statistics Administration. Bureau of Economic Analysis. C 59.11/5-2:929-97. Item 0228-A-04.

> CD-ROM version of *National Income and Product Accounts of the United States.*

Survey of Current Business. PRINT. WEB. (monthly) 1921–. U.S. Department of Commerce. Bureau of Economic Analysis. C 59.11: Item 0228. ASI 2702-1. GPO.<http://www.bea.doc.gov/bea/pubs.htm>;<http://purl.access.gpo.gov/GPO/LPS1730>.

> Coverage: world regions, country groupings, selected countries, U.S.
> Content: total value of exports and imports of goods and services; value by broad product category and selected geographic area.

Survey of Current Business. CD-ROM. (annual) 1994–. U.S. Department of Commerce. Economics and Statistics Administration. Bureau of Economic Analysis. C 59.11/1: Item 0228-A. GPO.

> Content: CD-ROM version of *Survey of Current Business.*

Bureau of Economic Analysis Web Site. WEB. U.S. Department of Commerce. Economics and Statistics Administration. Bureau of Economic Analysis.<http://www.bea.doc.gov/>.

> Content: agency information, data files, full-text publications and press releases.

Discussion

National Income and Product Accounts of the United States contains basic export and import data in gross domestic product tables and foreign transaction tables. A more current edition of this title is available on CD-ROM. These tables are updated quarterly in the *Survey of Current Business'* "BEA Current and Historical Data" section. An annual update article is published in the August issue.

The *Survey of Current Business* "BEA Current and Historical Data" section also contains a "Transactions Tables" section that gives trade data by world region and selected countries for total goods and broad service categories. A quarterly feature article on U.S. international transactions includes additional analysis of the trade situation and more detailed commodity tables.

The *Bureau of Economic Analysis Web Site* provides information on the agency, agency data and full-text publications, and access to many downloadable files. Full-text publications include recent issues of the *Survey of Current Business* and press releases containing economic statistics. Users may also select data by geographic area: national, international, and regional. For each area users can select a data category for lists of viewable tables and downloadable files or an article category for a list of full-text articles from the *Survey of Current Business*. The international data area includes a basic international transactions tables with total export and import data, tables from the joint Census Bureau and BEA press release, *U.S. International Trade in Goods and Services*, discussed in the "Census Bureau Sources" section, and basic trade in goods and services tables by world region and selected countries. The international articles category includes the international transactions articles from the *Survey of Current Business*.

GENERAL FOREIGN TRADE SOURCES

Checklist

Foreign Trade of the United States: Including Exports by State and Metro Area Export Data. PRINT. 1999–. Washington, D.C.: Bernan Press.

> Coverage: world, world regions, country groupings, countries, U.S., states, metropolitan areas.
> Content: total value of exports and imports; percentage of gross domestic product; trade balance; trade in services by broad category and region; trade in goods by end-use category and industry; trade in goods by country and broad category; state exports by destination and industry category; metropolitan area exports by destination and industry category.

U.S. Industry & Trade Outlook. PRINT. CD-ROM. (annual) 1998–. The McGraw-Hill Companies and U.S. Department of Commerce. International Trade Administration. C 61.48: (Earlier, C 61.34:, C 62.17:; C 57.18:). (Continuation of *U.S. Industrial Outlook* issued by the International Trade Administration, 1960-1994). Item 0215-L-08. NTIS.

> Coverage: U.S.
> Content: trade review and outlook for industries; value of imports and exports; trade patterns.

Country Reports on Economic Policy and Trade Practices. PRINT. MF. WEB. (annual) 1989–. U.S. Congress. House. Committee on International Relations. Or U.S. Congress. Senate. Committee on Foreign Relations. (Report is published in alternate years by the two committees) Y 4.IN 8/16:C 83/year or Y 4.F 76/2:S.PRT.(no.) (1997 is Y 4.F 76/2:S.PRT.105-51; 1999 report is Y 4.IN 8/16:C 83/999) Items 1017-A-01 or -B-01(MF); 1039-A or -B(MF). ASI 21464-2; ASI 25384-2. GPO.<http://www.state.gov/www/issues/economic/trade_reports/index.html>;<http://purl.access.gpo.gov/GPO/LPS2637>.

> Coverage: countries.
> Content: total value of exports and imports; value of exports and imports with the U.S.; trade balance; trade balance with the U.S.

U.S. Foreign Trade Highlights. WEB. (annual) 1984–. U.S. Department of Commerce. International Trade Administration. C 61.28/2: Item 0231-B-14. ASI 2044-37.<http://www.ita.doc.gov/td/industry/otea/usfth/>;<http://purl.access.gpo.gov/GPO/LPS3685>.

> Coverage: world, world regions, country groupings, countries, U.S.
> Content: total value of exports and imports and trade balances by country; top trade partners; top purchasers and suppliers; total exports and imports by commodity; leading commodity exports and imports by country.

International Trade Administration Web Site. WEB. U.S. Department of Commerce. International Trade Administration. <http://www.ita.doc.gov/>.

> Content: trade statistics, agency information, sources and links for trade assistance.

Discussion

Foreign Trade of the United States compiles trade data from the Bureau of Economic Analysis, Bureau of the Census, and the International Trade Administration. Part A, "Highlights of U.S. International Transactions," provides several years of data on the total value of exports and imports, total trade in goods and services, and the trade balance. Part B, "U.S. Foreign Trade in Services," gives trade data for specific types of services by world region and selected countries. Part C, "U.S. Foreign Trade in Goods," gives total trade by end-use category and industry. Exports and imports are also given by country, but the commodity categories are limited to all goods, agriculture, and manufactures. Part D, "State Exports of Goods," gives total value of exports for each state, total value by world regions and selected countries, and total value by industry category. Country and industry data are not correlated. Part E, "Metropolitan Area Exports of Goods," gives total exports for each metropolitan area, total exports by industry category, and total exports by world region and selected countries. Again, country and industry data are not correlated.

U.S. Industry & Trade Outlook contains industry profiles with basic trade data. Each chapter covers a major industry group such as "Chemicals and Allied Products" or "Computer Software and Networking." Chapters begin with an industry definition followed by an overview of the industry and sections on selected sub-industries within the group. Industry discussions vary depending on the nature of the industry, but generally cover international trade. A "Trends and Forecasts" table gives value of exports and imports. Most chapters also have a trade patterns table showing trade with top regions and countries. A page of graphs at the beginning of each chapter usually shows U.S. international trade; world export market share; and export dependence and import penetration. Graphs may vary depending on the industry. A CD-ROM version is also available for purchase, although not available through the depository library program.

Country Reports on Economic Policy and Trade Practices is prepared by the Department of State for the guidance of Congress. Brief reports on each country begin with key economic indicators, followed by a narrative overview of economic and trade topics. The key economic indicators include basic export and import statistics. The report has been issued alternately by the House and the Senate and the SuDocs number has varied accordingly.

U.S. Foreign Trade Highlights is an excellent source for U.S. commodity trade statistics by country and general statistics on U.S. exports and imports. Tables are grouped into three sections. The first contains aggregate trade totals by commodity categories or by countries. The other two sections contain more detailed data on commodity trade by world and region and by country. For each country or region there are tables showing total U.S. imports and exports by broad commodity category and for leading individual commodities. This title was distributed to depository libraries in print format through 1996.

The *International Trade Administration Web Site* provides access to trade statistics and information resources. The main menu offers an "ITA Trade Statistics" option. This area contains *U.S. Foreign Trade Highlights* discussed above and "U.S. Foreign Monthly Trade Data" with spreadsheet files of monthly figures on the value of total trade for goods and services, trade by end-use category, trade by world area and selected countries, and trade by industry sector. Also in the "ITA Trade Statistics" area is a "Reports on U.S. Trade" section. One of the reports in this section is a *Monthly Trade Update* newsletter with narrative highlights and charts on current regional and sector trade trends. Other resources available in this area include state and metropolitan area export databases and links to international and country trade sites. The state and metropolitan area databases give exports by product sector and selected regions and countries. In addition to the "ITA Trade Statistics" area, the main menu page also offers resources for "Countries and Regions," "Industries and Sectors," and "Answers to Your Export Questions" from the Trade Information Center.

STAT-USA SOURCES
Checklist

STAT-USA Internet. WEB. U.S. Department of Commerce. C 1.91: Item 0128-P. <http://www.stat-usa.gov/>.

Coverage: world, world regions, country groupings, countries, U.S., states.
Content: *National Trade Data Bank*; exports and imports by country and commodity; press releases; country commercial guides; country and industry market research reports; trade leads; trade contacts; trade publications.

National Trade Data Bank: The Export Connection. WEB. CD-ROM. (monthly) Oct. 1990–. U.S. Department of Commerce. STAT-USA. C 1.88: (Depository distribution of CD-ROM discontinued with Oct. 2000 disc) Item 0128-L. ASI 2002-6. <http://www.stat-usa.gov/tradtest.nsf>; <http://purl.access.gpo.gov/GPO/LPS1777>.

Coverage: world, world regions, country groupings, countries, U.S.
Content: country commercial guides; country and industry market research reports; trade leads; trade contacts; trade publications.

USA Trade Online. WEB. U.S. Department of Commerce. STAT-USA. and Census Bureau. Foreign Trade Division. <http://www.usatradeonline.gov/>.

Coverage: world, countries, U.S., customs districts.
Content: value and quantity of exports and imports by detailed commodity, country, and customs district; fee-based subscription.

National Trade Data Bank: USA Trade. CD-ROM. (monthly) 1998–. U.S. Department of Commerce. Census Bureau and STAT-USA. C 1.88/3: (Depository distribution to be discontinued). Item 0128-L-01.

Coverage: world, countries, U.S., customs districts.
Content: value and quantity of exports and imports by detailed commodity, country, and customs district.

Discussion

STAT-USA products are a comprehensive source of international trade information available on the Internet and on CD-ROMs. These products provide detailed export and import statistics by country and commodity, international market research reports, and trade-related press releases and publications from several government agencies.

The *STAT-USA Internet* site is a fee-based service, but federal depository libraries may register for free access for two workstations. *STAT-USA* is divided into two areas: State of the Nation and Globus & NTDB. The Globus & NTDB area contains international trade and marketing resources. Resources are grouped into several categories, including Current and Historical Trade Leads, Market and Country Research, International Trade Statistics, Current Press Releases, and Contacts. Some files are updated daily. There are options to search the entire NTDB or do a country map search which executes preformatted searches to retrieve all data related to the selected country. An International Trade Library option includes full-text publications that can be searched or browsed by title.

The International Trade Statistics category offers four historical files from Census Bureau databases: U.S. Exports by Commodity, U.S. Exports by Country, U.S. Imports by Commodity, and U.S. Imports by Country. The commodity files provide detailed commodity listings and give quantity and value of exports or imports for each by country. The country files give value of exports or imports by broad commodity category and for the 100 top individual commodities for each country. Files cover five to seven years of data through 1999. Current data are provided through the *USA Trade Online* service and the *National Trade Data Bank: USA Trade* CD-ROM. Eventually these titles will replace the historical tables.

The Current Press Releases category includes *U.S. International Trade in Goods and Services*, a monthly press release from the Census Bureau with the latest statistics on exports and imports by commodity and selected countries and the balance of trade. Most of the country and commodity data are not correlated.

The Market and Country Research category includes *Country Commercial Guides*, extensive country overviews with chapters on such topics as economic trends, marketing U.S. products, leading sectors for U.S. exports, trade regulations, and trade statistics. Also available are *Industry Sector Analysis Reports* and *International Marketing Insight Reports*. The *Industry Sector Analysis Reports* are in-depth profiles of a selected industry in a particular country. *International Marketing Insight Reports* are profiles of specific foreign market conditions, projects, or opportunities in specific countries or regions.

The *National Trade Data Bank* CD-ROM contains much of the same data found on the *STAT-USA Internet* site. Some files on the *National Trade Data Bank* CD-ROM, however, are not as current as those on the Internet, particularly the press releases and trade leads. The CD offers three search options—browsing the table of contents, a full-text quick search option with Boolean operators, and an advanced, fielded search.

Detailed export and import statistics by country and commodity are available through the *USA Trade Online* service and the *National Trade Data Bank: USA Trade* CD-ROM. Both formats are fee-based subscriptions not available through the depository library program. Some early issues of the CD-ROM were distributed to depository libraries. The *USA Trade* titles contain export and import databases for different time periods, including monthly, year-to-date, and annual. The data in each database are similar and include quantity and value for more than 18,000 commodities by country and customs district. Commodities are available at different levels of detail ranging from two-digit Harmonized System Codes to 10-digit. Data are displayed in tables that can be manipulated, sorted, and exported. Some historical data in a different format continue to be available temporarily on the *STAT-USA Internet* site in the International Trade Statistics category.

CENSUS BUREAU SOURCES
Checklist

U.S. International Trade in Goods and Services. MF. WEB. (monthly) 1994–. U.S. Department of Commerce. Economics and Statistics Administration. Bureau of the Census. Foreign Trade Division. FT 900. C 3.164:900-. (Monthly supplement also issued). (Issued earlier under other titles). Item 0144-A-06. <http://www.census.gov/foreign-trade/www/press.html>;<http://purl.access.gpo.gov/GPO/LPS1830>.
> Coverage: world regions, country groupings, countries, U.S., states.
> Content: trade balance; value of exports and imports; exports and imports by broad end-use commodity category, by SITC commodity groupings and sections, by SIC-based product code, and by country; petroleum exports and imports; origin of exports by state.

U.S. Merchandise Trade: Selected Highlights. MF. (monthly) U.S. Department of Commerce. Bureau of the Census. FT 920. C3.164:920/. Item 0144-A-06.
> Coverage: world, world regions, countries, U.S., customs districts.
> Content: value, shipping weight, and method of transportation for exports and imports; duty value for imports.

U.S. Imports of Merchandise: International Harmonized System Commodity Classification (HTSUSA) by Country, by Customs District. CD-ROM. (monthly) April 1990–. U.S. Department of Commerce. Bureau of the Census. Foreign Trade Division. C 3.278/2: (Earlier, C 3.278:IM 7/(yr.-mo.)/CD) Item 0154-D. ASI 2422-14.
> Coverage: countries, U.S., customs districts.
> Content: value, quantity, and method of transportation for imports by commodity and country; duty and import charges; shipping weight.

U.S. Exports of Merchandise: International Harmonized System Commodity Classification (HS-Based Schedule B) by Country, by Customs District. CD-ROM. (monthly) April 1990–. U.S. Department of Commerce. Bureau of the Census. Foreign Trade Division. C 3.278/3: (Earlier, C 3.278:EX 7/(yr.-mo.)/CD) Item 0154-D. ASI 2422-13.
> Coverage: countries, U.S., customs districts.
> Content: value, quantity, and method of transportation for exports by commodity and country; shipping weight.

U.S. Exports History: Historical Summary [years]: International Harmonized System Commodity Classification (HS-Based Schedule B) by Country, by Customs District. CD-ROM. WEB. (annual) 1989–92–. U.S. Department of Commerce. Bureau of the Census. C 3.278/3: Item 0154-D.<http://govinfo.kerr.orst.edu/impexp.html>;<http://fisher.lib.virginia.edu/trade/>.
> Coverage: countries, U.S., customs districts.
> Content: value and quantity of exports by commodity and country.

U.S. Imports History: Historical Summary [years]: International Harmonized System Commodity Classification (HTSUSA) by Country, by Customs District. CD-ROM. WEB. (annual) 1989–92–. U.S. Department of Commerce. Bureau of the Census. C 3.278/2: Item 0154-D. <http://govinfo.kerr.orst.edu/impexp.html>;<http://fisher.lib.virginia.edu/trade/>.
> Coverage: countries, U.S., customs districts.

Content: value and quantity of imports by commodity and country.

Country by 1-digit SITC Commodity Trade Data Web Page. WEB. (monthly) U.S. Department of Commerce. Bureau of the Census. Foreign Trade Division.<http://www.census.gov/foreign-trade/sitc1/>.

Coverage: countries, U.S.

Content: value of exports and imports for broad commodity by country.

U.S. International Trade Statistics Web Site. WEB. (monthly) U.S. Department of Commerce. Bureau of the Census.<http://tier2.census.gov/sitc/sitcpage.htm>.

Coverage: world, countries, U.S.

Content: value of exports and imports by commodity and country.

Foreign Trade Statistics Your Key to Trade. WEB. U.S. Department of Commerce. Bureau of the Census. Foreign Trade Division.<http://www.census.gov/foreign-trade/www/>.

Content: foreign trade statistics, information, and services.

Discussion

U.S. International Trade in Goods and Services, a monthly press release, is the most general of these titles. It pro-

vides information on the trade balance and the value of exports and imports. Data are given for export and import totals, exports and imports by broad commodity categories, and exports and imports by countries. Commodity and country data are not correlated. The monthly supplement contains data by SIC-based product code, exports by state, and more detailed country data.

U.S. Merchandise Trade: Selected Highlights gives information on the total value and the value by vessel or air of all exports and imports for the current month and the year to date. Shipping weight is given by customs district and country. Duty free and dutiable value is given for imports, as well as the value and percentage of duty. This report contains no commodity data.

The *U.S. Exports of Merchandise* and *U.S. Imports of Merchandise* CD-ROMs contain the Census Bureau's entire foreign trade database. These data are the most detailed available providing detailed commodity statistics by country and customs district. The user selects a commodity from a series of increasingly detailed commodity classification lists. Information on value, quantity, and method of transportation is given for each commodity for the current month and year to date. For imports,

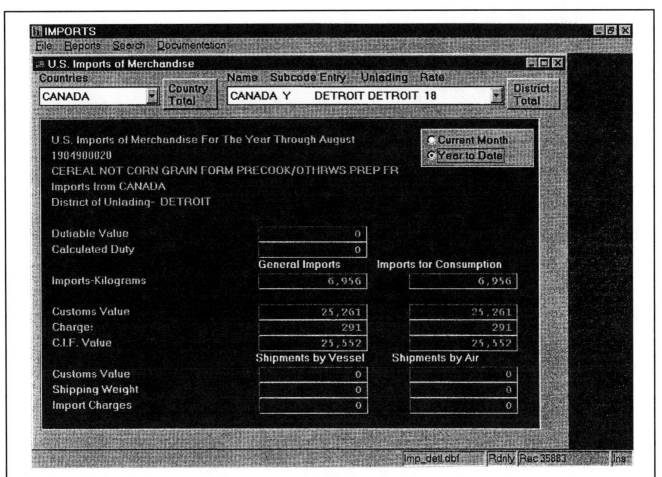

Source: U.S. Imports of Merchandise: International Harmonized System Commodity Classification (HTSUSA) by Country by Customs District CD-ROM, August 1999.

Figure 38.1: *U.S. Imports of Merchandise* **CD-ROM.**

duty and import charges are also given. Figure 38.1 shows the country data screen for imports of a specific commodity. It is not possible, however, to search by country to obtain a list of all commodities for a single country. An annual summary disc is issued for each of these two series. These are titled *U.S. Exports History* and *U.S. Imports History*. Each disc contains annual data for five years. The annual title does not contain method of transportation information. The most recent issue of both of these titles is also available on the Web from the Oregon State University Government Information Sharing Project. Earlier editions are available at the University of Virginia Geospatial & Statistical Data Center.

The *Country by 1-digit SITC Commodity Trade Data Web Page* gives the value of exports and imports by broad commodity group for each country. Data are available by month or year for recent years. Users select a year, a country, then a particular month or year-to-date.

The *U.S. International Trade Statistics Web Site* is a database application based on the same data used for the *Country by 1-digit SITC Commodity Trade Data Web Page*, but with more detail and flexibility. Users may select a country and view data by two- or three-digit SITC commodities. Monthly or annual data can be selected. Users may also begin by selected a two- or three-digit commodity to view total information for that commodity. A list of all countries for that commodity can then be selected, as shown in Figure 38.2.

Foreign Trade Statistics Your Key to Trade is the main page of the Census Bureau's Foreign Trade Division and

---

U.S. Census Bureau
Standard International Trade Classification

|Census Home Page|Database Apps on the Web|SITC Page|Country Page|

For different month, year ⌷ November ▾ ⌷ 1999 ▾ ⌷ Go ⌷

For SITC Commodity Groupings ⌷ Go ⌷

Value of Exports, General Imports, And Imports for Consumption by SITC Commodity by Country
111 - Nonalcoholic Beverages, N.e.s.

[In Thousands of Dollars.(-) represents zero.(Z)-represents less than 0.05.]

Country Name	Code	November 99 Exports F.A.S. Value Basis	November 99 General Imports Customs Value Basis	November 99 General Imports C.I.F. Value Basis	Cumulative Year to Date through November 99 Exports F.A.S. Value Basis	Cumulative Year to Date through November 99 General Imports Custom Value Basis	Cumulative Year to Date through November 99 General Imports C.I.F. Value Basis
CANADA	1220	13,990	16,398	17,126	162,061	257,515	266,791
MEXICO	2010	1,165	9,564	9,999	22,717	105,253	109,657
GUATMAL	2050	82	-	-	1,483	-	-
BELIZE	2080	4	-	-	139	-	-
SALVADR	2110	9	2	2	238	77	83
HONDURA	2150	3	11	13	50	123	148
NICARAG	2190	-			127	-	-
C RICA	2230	47	22	23	357	108	119
PANAMA	2250	26	-	-	697	-	-
BERMUDA	2320	392	-	-	2,871	-	-
BAHAMAS	2360	331			3,143	-	-
JAMAICA	2410	134	72	80	1,573	805	887
TURK IS	2430	62	-	-	756	-	-
CAYMAN	2440	259	-	-	3,874	-	-
HAITI	2450	56	-	-	1,265	-	-
DOM REP	2470	200	36	39	2,200	214	231
ANGLLA	2481	7	-	-	203	-	-
B VIRGI	2482	82	-	-	737	-	-
ST K N	2483	19	-	-	107	-	-

Source: U.S. International Trade Statistics Web Site.<http://tier2.census.gov/sitc/sitcpage.htm>

Figure 38.2: *U.S. International Trade Statistics Web Site*: Commodity by Country.

provides a gateway to the agency's trade information. The "Statistics" menu category provides links to current and previous issues of the *U.S. International Trade in Goods and Services* FT900 press release and the *Country by 1-digit SITC* data. Other links in this category provide tables on trade balances, top trading partners, and trade highlights. Another feature of the main page is an Index option that lists items and topics alphabetically. A search engine for the Schedule B commodity export classification system is also available.

Most trade data use specialized terminology. Definitions are often included in the source. Imports are reported in terms of customs value or C.I.F. value. Customs value is the value of imports as appraised by the U.S. Customs Service and is the price actually paid for the merchandise, excluding duties, freight, and other charges. C.I.F. value is the customs value plus import charges, except for duties. Exports are reported in terms of F.A.S. value, which is based on transaction price, freight to the port, and other charges. Imports are frequently divided into the categories "general imports" and "imports for consumption." "General imports" is a more comprehensive term and reflects total arrivals. The term "imports for consumption" refers only to those items available for immediate consumption and does not include imports that are warehoused or held in customs custody.

The commodity classification systems used with many of these data are based on the Harmonized System (HS) adopted by the United States in January 1989. Prior to that time a different series of reports existed based on different classification systems. Comparison of detailed commodity statistics collected after 1989 with statistics from previous years may result in inaccuracies. Some data are also reported by the Standard International Trade Classification (SITC) system.

For guides to foreign trade data and the classification schedules, see the "Guides and Classifications" section later in this chapter.

INTERNATIONAL TRADE COMMISSION SOURCES

Checklist

The Year in Trade: Operation of the Trade Agreements Program During [year]. PRINT. WEB. (annual) 1934/48–. U.S. International Trade Commission. ITC 1.24: (Title and SuDocs vary) Item 0980-A. ASI 9884-5.<http://www.usitc.gov/332s/332index.htm#SECTION 332>.

> Coverage: country groupings, selected countries, U.S.
> Content: trade agreement activities; trade relations and issues with major trading partners; trade law administration; value of exports and imports by broad commodity and leading exports and imports for selected areas.

Shifts in U.S. Merchandise Trade. MF. WEB. (annual) 1981–. U.S. International Trade Commission. ITC 1.15/2: (Title and frequency vary) Item 0980-E-07. ASI 9884-27.<http://www.usitc.gov/332s/332index.htm#SECTION 332>.

> Coverage: world regions, country groupings, selected countries, U.S.
> Content: value of exports and imports and trade balances by broad commodity and selected countries; value of exports and imports by detailed commodity; number of establishments, employees, capacity utilization, production, and consumption by detailed industry group.

Recent Trends in U.S. Services Trade. MF. WEB. (annual) 1996–. U.S. International Trade Commission. ITC 1.15/3: (Title varies) Item 908-E-12. ASI 9884-31.<http://www.usitc.gov/332s/332index.htm#SECTION 332>.

> Coverage: country groupings, selected countries, U.S.
> Content: value of exports and imports and trade balances for service industries.

United States International Trade Commission Web Site. WEB. U.S. International Trade Commission.<http://www.usitc.gov/>.

> Content: full-text publications, databases, statistical tables, and agency information relating to international trade.

Discussion

The International Trade Administration publishes many trade analyses on specific products and issues. These are some of the more general statistical titles and resources.

The Year in Trade is primarily a narrative analysis of annual trade activities and developments. A statistical appendix gives export and import data for major trading partners.

Shifts in U.S. Merchandise Trade provides an overview of trade by major commodity sectors such as agricultural products or minerals and metals. Chapters on each commodity sector contain tables on exports, imports, and trade balances for the sector by selected country and country groups. A more detailed table gives the same data for detailed commodities, but without the country information. An appendix of industry group profiles combines trade data with industry data such as number of establishments and employees. This title also analyzes major trade changes for the year by commodity and country.

Recent Trends in U.S. Services Trade is a companion title to *Shifts in U.S. Merchandise Trade* covering the service sector. Chapters discuss the current trade situation for each service sector, including distribution, education, financial, professional, telecommunications, transportation, and travel and tourism. Almost all data are presented in the form of charts and graphs. Charts show value of exports and imports and trade balances by major trading partners.

All three of these reports are available on the Internet. The URL listed provides a list of recent reports from the International Trade Commission. Users can scroll through the list to locate the latest edition of a particular report. A search option at the top of the page allows searching all reports, including archived earlier editions of these reports.

United States International Trade Commission Web Site provides access to international trade data and publications. Menu options of particular interest for statistics include "Publications and reports," "DataWeb," and "Miscellaneous." "Publications and reports" offers the full text of recent agency publications, including those discussed in this section. Users can scroll through a list of current reports or use the search option for a complete list, including earlier editions. "DataWeb" provides access to several trade databases. The *ITC Trade DataWeb* export and import database is being offered as a pilot project to assess costs. Users enter a commodity code (HTS, SIC, STIC) and select type of data, time period, frequency, and country or area. Several display options are available. Data includes quantity and value of exports and imports and trade balance for recent years. Registration is required to use the database, but there is no fee. Also available is the *ITC Tariff Database*. Users can search by word or HTS code to retrieve data. Data include customs value of recent imports by country and detailed tariff treatment information. (For more information on commodity classification codes, see the "Guides and Classifications" section.) The *Summary U.S. Trade by World Region* database provides country trade data. Users select type of data and world region. Tables display region total, appropriate country groupings, and countries. Data available include exports, imports, and trade balance. Additional data by broad commodity is available by clicking on individual country total values. Another option is *U.S. Trade by Partner Country* that gives trade balance by country with total export and import figures. Data by broad commodity is available by clicking on the individual country total values. The "Miscellaneous" main menu option offers some downloadable trade statistics files.

GUIDES AND CLASSIFICATIONS

Checklist

Guide to Foreign Trade Statistics. PRINT. WEB. (1992) U.S. Department of Commerce. Economics and Statistics Administration. Bureau of the Census. C 3.6/2:F 76/992. Item 0146-A. ASI (93) 2428-11.<http://www.census.gov/foreign-trade/guide/index.html>.
> Content: background and definitions; data products available; information locator guide; samples of tables from each product (print edition only).

Product Catalog. WEB. U.S. Census Bureau. C 3.163/3: Item 0138.<http://www.census.gov/mp/www/censtore.html>.
> Content: descriptions and prices of Census Bureau products.

Census Catalog and Guide. CD-ROM. WEB. (annual) 1946–. U.S. Department of Commerce. Economics and Statistics Administration. Census Bureau. (CD-ROM not distributed to depository libraries) (Issued in print through 1998 under C 3.163/3:, Item 0138) (Title varies) <http://www.census.gov/mp/www/censtore.html>;<http://www.census.gov/prod/www/abs/catalogs.html>;<http://purl.access.gpo.gov/GPO/LPS3138>.
> Content: CD-ROM version of the Web *Product Catalog*.

Schedule B: Statistical Classification of Domestic and Foreign Commodities Exported from the United States. 1996 edition.

PRINT. WEB. (Loose-leaf; updated with transmittals) U.S. Department of Commerce. Bureau of the Census. C 3.150:B/996/v.1-2. Item 0148. ASI 2428-5. GPO.<http://www.census.gov/foreign-trade/schedules/b/index.html>.
> Content: schedule B commodity classification for exports; schedule C classification for countries; schedule D classification for customs districts and ports.

U.S. Exports Commodity Classification International Harmonized System Commodity Classification (HS-Based Schedule B). CD-ROM. WEB. (annual) 1992–. U.S. Department of Commerce. Economics and Statistics Administration. Census Bureau. Foreign Trade Division. C 3.6/2.C 73/3/. Item 0154-B-01. <http://www.census.gov/foreign-trade/schedules/b/index.html>.
> Content: CD-ROM version of schedule B.

Harmonized Tariff Schedule of the United States. PRINT. WEB. (irregular) 1963–. U.S. International Trade Commission. ITC 1.10: Item 0982-B-02. ASI 9886-13. GPO.<http://www.usitc.gov/taffairs.htm>;<http://purl.access.gpo.gov/GPO/LPS2145>.
> Content: commodity listing by classification number with rates of duty for imports; classification schedules C and D.

Harmonized Tariff Schedule of the United States. CD-ROM. WEB. U.S. International Trade Commission. ITC 1.10/4: Item 0982-B-03. GPO.<http://www.usitc.gov/taffairs.htm>;<http://purl.access.gpo.gov/GPO/LPS2145>.
> Content: CD-ROM version of the *Harmonized Tariff Schedule*.

Commodity Indexes for the Standard International Trade Classification, Revision 3. PRINT. United Nations. Department for Economic and Social Information and Policy Analysis. Statistical Division. Statistical Papers Series M, No. 38/Rev. 2, Vol. I&II. UN Number: ST/ESA/STAT/SER.M/38/Rev.2 (Vol.). New York: United Nations, 1994.
> Content: international commodity classification system; item and alphabetical indexes.

Discussion

These guides and classifications are of use when using foreign trade data. The *Guide to Foreign Trade Statistics* is a comprehensive guide to Census Bureau resources. Although it is out-of-date in regard to many published reports that have since been discontinued, it is still valuable for background information, terminology, types of information collected, and historical data.

The Census Bureau *Product Catalog* describes agency products and provides availability and ordering information. Products are listed by format and then by subject category or series, including foreign trade. Individual title descriptions include prices, ordering information, formats, subject content, geographic coverage, and links to online data. The *Census Catalog and Guide* on CD-ROM contains the Web *Product Catalog* as of the specified date.

If one is looking up data on a specific commodity, having the classification numbers for that commodity will make the task easier. Schedule B is a detailed commodity classification used with export statistics in the *U.S. Exports of Merchandise* CD-ROM discussed in the "Census

Bureau Sources" section. *Schedule B: Statistical Classification of Domestic and Foreign Commodities Exported from the United States* outlines the schedule and contains an alphabetical commodity index. Every commodity is assigned a unique 10-digit code. Data may be reported at broader categories, such as two-, four-, or six-digit code levels. *Schedule B* also contains Schedules C and D used for countries and customs districts. Schedule B is also available on the Web. It can be browsed by chapter, searched by keyword, or downloaded. The *U.S. Exports Commodity Classification International Harmonized System* is a CD-ROM version of Schedule B.

The *Harmonized Tariff Schedule of the United States* classifies commodities for the purpose of assessing duty on imports and for tabulating statistics. Included are an alphabetical index to the classification system and Schedules C and D. The *Harmonized Tariff Schedule* classification is used in the *U.S. Imports of Merchandise* CD-ROM discussed in the "Census Bureau Sources" section and by many of the International Trade Commission sources. The International Trade Commission offers downloadable and PDF versions on their Web site.

Commodity Indexes for the Standard International Trade Classification, Revision 3 is issued by the United Nations. It contains a corrected and amended version of the Standard International Trade Classification (SITC). A numerical item index lists representative commodities for each classification. An alphabetical index is also available. This classification system is used in the two Census Bureau Web sites, *Country by 1-digit SITC Commodity Trade Data* and *U.S. International Trade Statistics*, and in some of the tables in the Census Bureau press release, *U.S. International Trade in Goods and Services*. These titles are discussed in the "Census Bureau Sources" section.

AGRICULTURAL TRADE SOURCES

Checklist

Agricultural Statistics. PRINT. WEB. (annual) 1936–. U.S. Department of Agriculture. National Agricultural Statistics Service. A 1.47: Item 0001. ASI 1004-1. GPO.<http://www.usda.gov/nass/pubs/agstats.htm>;<http://purl.access.gpo.gov/GPO/LPS1063>.

> Coverage: country groupings, countries, U.S.
> Content: value and quantity of agricultural exports and imports by commodity and country; exports by government program.

Agricultural Statistics. CD-ROM. (annual) 1994–. U.S. Department of Agriculture. A 1.47/2: Item 0001-A. GPO.

> Content: CD-ROM version of *Agricultural Statistics.*

U.S. Agricultural Trade Update. MF. WEB. (monthly) U.S. Department of Agriculture. Economic Research Service. A 93.17/7-5: Item 0042-E. ASI 1522-7.<http://usda.mannlib.cornell.edu/reports/erssor/trade/fau-bb/>;<http://purl.access.gpo.gov/GPO/LPS1111>.

> Coverage: world, country groupings, selected countries, U.S., occasionally selected states.
> Content: quantity and value of exports and imports by commodity; quantity of exports to leading countries by major commodities; trade balance.

Foreign Agricultural Trade of the United States (FATUS) Calendar Year Supplement. MF. (annual) U.S. Department of Agriculture. Economic Research Service. A 93.17/7-3: Item 0042-E. ASI 1522-4. GPO. Selected tables: <http://www.ers.usda.gov/briefing/AgTrade/htm/Data.htm>.

> Coverage: world, world regions, country groupings, countries, U.S.
> Content: value and quantity of agricultural exports and imports for commodities, countries, and commodities by country; balance of trade.

Foreign Agricultural Trade of the United States—Briefing Room. WEB. U.S. Department of Agriculture. Economic Research Service.<http://www.ers.usda.gov/briefing/AgTrade/>.

> Coverage: world, world regions, country groupings, countries, U.S.
> Content: Foreign Agricultural Trade of the United States (FATUS) database; quantity and value of agricultural exports and imports by commodity and country.

Agricultural Outlook. PRINT. WEB. (10 issues a year) 1975. U.S. Department of Agriculture. Economic Research Service. A 93.10/2: Item 0042-M. ASI 1502-4. GPO.<http://www.ers.usda.gov/epubs/pdf/agout/ao.htm>;<http://purl.access.gpo.gov/LPS4107>;<http://usda.mannlib.cornell.edu/reports/erssor/economics/ao-bb/>;<http://purl.access.gpo.gov/GPO/LPS1093>.

> Coverage: world, world regions, selected countries, U.S.
> Content: quantity and value of agricultural exports and imports by selected commodities; value of agricultural exports by region.

Outlook for U.S. Agricultural Trade. WEB. (quarterly) 1982–. U.S. Department of Agriculture. Economic Research Service and Foreign Agricultural Service. A 93.43: Item 0006-C. (Earlier title, *Outlook for U.S. Agricultural Exports*) ASI 1542-4. GPO.<http://usda.mannlib.cornell.edu/reports/erssor/trade/aes-bb/>;<http://purl.access.gpo.gov/GPO/LPS1107>.

> Coverage: world regions, country groupings, countries, U.S.
> Content: agricultural trade balance; value of agricultural exports and imports by commodity and region; quantity of exports and imports by commodity; forecasts for next fiscal year.

BICO Reports: U.S. Export/Import Statistics for Bulk, Intermediate and Consumer-Oriented (BICO) Foods and Beverages. WEB. U.S. Department of Agriculture. Foreign Agricultural Service.<http://www.fas.usda.gov/scriptsw/bico/bico_frm.idc>.

> Coverage: world, country groupings, countries, U.S.
> Content: value of agricultural exports and imports by broad commodity and area.

Discussion

The Agriculture Department publishes extensively on agricultural trade. A selection of these resources is listed above.

Agricultural Statistics contains a section of tables on basic agricultural trade statistics. Many of the individual commodity tables also include data on exports and imports. To locate trade data on a specific commodity, look for the subheadings "exports" or "imports" in the index under the name of the commodity.

U.S. Agricultural Trade Update is a newsletter on current agricultural trade trends and statistics. A brief narrative overview summarizes the current month's trends in exports and imports. Statistical tables give exports and imports for detailed agricultural commodities. Occasionally a special feature is included. One recurring feature covers state agricultural exports, giving the total value of exports for all states and value of exports by commodity group for leading states.

Foreign Agricultural Trade of the United States (FATUS) contains detailed statistical tables on agricultural trade. There are some summary tables on total trade, some historical tables, and a set of detailed tables for both exports and imports. The detailed tables include commodity by country data for the last two years.

The *Foreign Agricultural Trade of the United States—Briefing Room* Web site provides access to the Foreign Agricultural Trade of the United States (FATUS) database. Both a search option and preformatted tables are available. With the search option, users may select exports and imports, then either a commodity or a country/region. The individual commodity reports list exports or imports for all geographic areas. The country/region reports list all commodities for that area. An option to produce more customized reports is also available. The preformatted tables are available in downloadable spreadsheet and HTML formats. Links are also provided to publications and other Web sites.

Agricultural Outlook contains some trade-related articles and statistics. Recurring departments include "World Agriculture and Trade" and "Commodity Spotlight" which contain current news on specific commodities and trade developments. The "Statistical Indicators" section contains a "U.S. Agricultural Trade" section and sections on livestock and crops that contain trade data.

Outlook for U.S. Agricultural Trade is a narrative report with statistical tables. A brief forecast for exports and imports is given. More detailed sections discuss commodity highlights, the economic outlook, regional highlights for specific countries or areas, and agricultural export programs. Tables provide basic trade data on exports and imports by major commodity and region.

BICO Reports is a Web database for agricultural commodity trade data. Users may select a commodity group or a geographic area. Export and import tables are available by fiscal year or calendar year. Commodity tables display world, world region, and top country data for the most recent five years. Country or region tables display data for broad commodity categories for the same time period.

OTHER SUBJECT SOURCES
Checklist

World Military Expenditures and Arms Transfers. WEB. (annual) 1965–. U.S. Department of State. Bureau of Arms Control. S 22.116: (Earlier, AC 1.16:) Item 0900-H-01. ASI 9824-1. GPO.<http://www.state.gov/www/global/arms/bureau_ac/reports_ac.html>; <http://purl.access.gpo.gov/GPO/LPS4526>.

> Coverage: world, world regions, country groupings, countries.
> Content: value of total and arms exports and imports; value of arms transfers by major supplier and recipient; number of arms delivered by selected supplier, recipient region, and major weapon type.

Annual Energy Review. MF. WEB. (annual) 1977–. U.S. Department of Energy. Energy Information Administration. Office of Energy Markets and End Use. E 3.1/2: (Earlier, E 3.1: year/v.2) Item 0429-J-01. ASI 3164-74. GPO.<http://www.eia.doe.gov/aer/>;<http://tonto.eia.doe.gov/bookshelf/index.html>;<http://purl.access.gpo.gov/GPO/LPS3492>.

> Coverage: world, world regions, country groupings, selected countries, U.S.
> Content: quantity of energy-related exports and imports by type; value of fossil fuel exports and imports.

International Energy Annual. MF. WEB. (annual) 1979–. U.S. Department of Energy. Energy Information Administration. Office of Energy Markets and End Use. E 3.11/20: Item 0435-H. ASI 3164-50. GPO.<http://www.eia.doe.gov/emeu/iea/contents.html>;<http://purl.access.gpo.gov/GPO/LPS3018>;<http://tonto.eia.doe.gov/bookshelf/index.html>;<http://purl.access.gpo.gov/GPO/LPS3492>.

> Coverage: world, world regions, countries, U.S.
> Content: quantity of exports and imports for energy type by country.

Minerals Yearbook. PRINT. WEB. (annual) 1932–. U.S. Department of the Interior. Geological Survey. I 19.165: (Earlier, I 28.37:. Issued since 1882 under other titles). Item 0639. ASI 5664-25, -26, -31. GPO.<http://minerals.usgs.gov/minerals/pubs/myb.html>.

> Coverage: countries, U.S.
> Content: value and quantity of mineral commodity exports and imports, usually by country.

Minerals and Materials Information. CD-ROM. 1994–. U.S. Department of the Interior. Geological Survey. I 19.120/4: Item 0639-J. ASI 5662-8.

> Content: *Minerals Yearbook* and other mineral publications.

Discussion

Reports on trade in other specific areas are also published. Many of the Energy Department's statistical publications deal with trade in energy-related products. Trade data on minerals is available from the Mines Bureau. A selection of these publications is listed above.

World Military Expenditures and Arms Transfers contains statistics on the arms trade. It begins with a highlights section that includes an overview of arms transfers.

The discussion covers world trade and import and export trends by region and includes statistics and colorful graphs. A country ranking section ranks countries by value of arms imports and exports and percentage of total trade. Statistical tables provide data on exports and imports of arms by region and country for several years and information on source and recipient countries and weapon types.

Annual Energy Review is a detailed, comprehensive overview of energy statistics. A narrative overview chapter analyzes energy history and trends. The other chapters are statistical with graphs and charts illustrating each table. An "Energy Overview" section includes summary statistics on trade. The "Financial Indicators" section contains tables on the value of fossil fuel imports and exports by type of fuel. Other sections are devoted to each major energy source. The sections on petroleum, natural gas, and coal each contain trade tables. Country data are given only for crude oil, petroleum, and natural gas. Data cover many years. The URLs listed cover the current edition and a publication search form that can retrieve any editions available on the Web site. The Web version of the current edition provides a combination of formats including HTML, PDF, spreadsheet files, and an interactive query option.

International Energy Annual also contains chapters on major energy topics. The chapters on individual energy sources contain basic export and import data for each country for the most recent year. The URLs listed cover the current edition and a publication search form that can retrieve any editions available on the Web site.

The *Minerals Yearbook* contains trade data by commodity in Volume I, "Metals and Minerals." Each commodity chapter consists of a narrative overview and statistical tables. Although content varies for each mineral, the narrative analysis often contains a brief section and trade and the statistical tables often give export and import data by country. The *Minerals Yearbook* is also available on the *Minerals and Materials Information* CD-ROM.

INDEXES
Checklist

American Statistics Index (ASI). PRINT. (monthly) 1973–. Bethesda, MD: Congressional Information Service.

Statistical Universe. WEB. Bethesda, MD: Congressional Information Service.

Discussion

A comprehensive listing of material can be found in *ASI* by looking under "Foreign trade," "Agricultural exports and imports," "Energy exports and imports," "Arms trade," specific countries, or specific products. The category index for statistics "By Foreign Country" can also be useful. *Statistical Universe* includes a Web version of *ASI*. (For more information, see Chapter 3, "The Basics of Searching.")

RELATED MATERIAL
Within this Work

Chapter 4   Foreign Policy

Chapter 5   Foreign Countries

Chapter 8   Business Aids

Chapter 18 Agriculture

Chapter 30 Economic Indicators

Chapter 31 Business and Industry Statistics

Chapter 41 Energy Statistics

Chapter 44 Transportation Statistics

GPO Subject Bibliographies. PRINT. WEB. GP 3.22/2:

<http://bookstore.gpo.gov/sb/about.html>

No. 123 "International Trade"

No. 317 "Export/Import"

CHAPTER 39
Crime and Criminal Justice Statistics

Most crime and law enforcement statistics are available from the Justice Department and the judiciary branch of government. There are several publications and series that report on crime, prisons, and the court system.

SEARCH STRATEGY

This chapter is an example of a statistical search strategy. The steps for finding statistics are

1. Check the "General Statistical Sources" section of this chapter for basic statistical sources;
2. Examine the listings in the "General Criminal Statistics Sources" section for more detailed basic reference sources that specialize in criminal statistics;
3. Consider sources listed in the "Other Criminal Statistics Sources" for additional material on specific areas;
4. For more specialized topics, see the sections on "Sources on Prisons and Prisoners," "Court Statistics Sources," "Drugs," or "Terrorism";
5. See the "National Criminal Justice Reference Service (NCJRS)" section for information on a comprehensive criminal justice database;
6. Search the indexes for additional sources; and
7. Consider the "Related Material" section.

GENERAL STATISTICAL SOURCES
Checklist

Statistical Abstract of the United States. PRINT. WEB. (annual) 1878–. U.S. Department of Commerce. Economics and Statistics Administration. Bureau of the Census. C 3.134: Item 0150. ASI 2324-1. GPO.<http://www.census.gov/statab/www/>;<http://purl.access.gpo.gov/GPO/LPS2878>.
　　Coverage: U.S., states, selected cities.
　　Content: types of crime and crime rates; crime characteristics; victim characteristics and victimization rates; arrests; law enforcement agencies and personnel; court cases;

child abuse; number and characteristics of prisoners; correctional facilities; probation and parole.

Statistical Abstract of the United States. CD-ROM. (annual) 1993–. U.S. Department of Commerce. Bureau of the Census. C 3.134/7: Item 0150-B. ASI 2324-14.
　　Content: CD-ROM version of the *Statistical Abstract.*

Historical Statistics of the United States: Colonial Times to 1970. Parts 1-2. PRINT. (1975) U.S. Department of Commerce. Bureau of the Census. C 3.134/2:H 62/789-970/pt.1-2. Item 0151. ASI (76) 2328-2. GPO.
　　Coverage: U.S.
　　Content: types of crime and crime rates; homicides; arrests; criminal justice system expenditures; court cases filed; prisoners and executions.

State and Metropolitan Area Data Book. PRINT. WEB. (irregular) 1979–. U.S. Department of Commerce. Economics and Statistics Administration. Bureau of the Census. C 3.134/5: Item 0150. ASI 2328-54. GPO.<http://www.census.gov/statab/www.smadb.html>.
　　Coverage: U.S., states, metropolitan areas.
　　Content: number and types of crimes; crime rate; law enforcement employment; number of prisoners; prisoners executed; prisoners under death sentence.

State and Metropolitan Area Data Book. CD-ROM. (irregular) 1997/98–. U.S. Department of Commerce. Economics and Statistics Administration. Bureau of the Census. (Not distributed to depository libraries)
　　Content: CD-ROM version of the *State and Metropolitan Area Data Book.*

County and City Data Book. PRINT. WEB. (quinquennial) 1947–. U.S. Department of Commerce. Economics and Statistics Administration. Bureau of the Census. C 3.134/2:C 83/2/year. Item 0151. ASI 2328-1. GPO.<http://fisher.lib.Virginia.EDU/ccdb/>.
　　Coverage: U.S., regions, divisions, states, counties, cities of 25,000 or more.
　　Content: number of serious crimes known; crime rate; number of violent crimes.

County and City Data Book. CD-ROM. (quinquennial) 1988–. U.S. Department of Commerce. Bureau of the Census. C 3.134/

2-1: (Earlier, C 3.134/2:C 83/2/) Item 0151-D-01. ASI 2328-103.

> Content: CD-ROM version of the *County and City Data Book*.

County and City Extra: Annual Metro, City, and County Data Book. PRINT. (annual) 1992–. Lanham, MD: Bernan Press.

> Coverage: U.S., states, counties, metropolitan areas, cities of 25,000 or more.
> Content: updated version of the *County and City Data Book*.

Places, Towns, and Townships. PRINT. (irregular) 1993–. Lanham, MD: Bernan Press.

> Coverage: incorporated places of 10,000 or more.
> Content: number and rate of serious crimes; number of violent and property crimes.

USA Counties. CD-ROM. WEB. (irregular) 1992–. U.S. Department of Commerce. Economics and Statistics Administration. Bureau of the Census. C 3.134/6: Item 0150-B-01. ASI 2324-17.<http://govinfo.kerr.orst.edu/usaco-stateis.html>;<http://tier2.census.gov/usac/index.html-ssi>.

> Coverage: U.S., states, counties.
> Content: serious crimes known to police; types of crimes; crime rate for serious crimes.

Discussion

The *Statistical Abstract of the United States* contains a section on "Law Enforcement, Courts, and Prisons" that summarizes a wide range of statistical data. Information includes murder victims by weapons used; incidence of specific crimes, such as pocket picking; arson arrests by age and sex; and prisoners under sentence of death. Statistics are selected from many of the more detailed sources covered in this chapter. Source notes at the end of each table can direct the user to more current or more detailed sources for the information in that table. The full text of recent editions of the *Statistical Abstract* is available on the Census Bureau Web site as PDF files. The *Statistical Abstract* is also available on CD-ROM. The CD uses Adobe Acrobat software and contains some additional geographic areas and time series in the form of spreadsheet files that are not in the printed version. *Historical Statistics of the United States: Colonial Times to 1970* has a "Crime and Correction" chapter with earlier, but more limited, statistics.

> *State and Metropolitan Area Data Book* contains a variety of crime and related statistics for states. For metropolitan areas, the information available is limited to the number of serious crimes, the percentage that are violent, and the serious crime rate. The *State and Metropolitan Data Book* is available as a PDF file on the Census Bureau Web site and on CD-ROM.

> *County and City Data Book* covers smaller geographic areas. There are three basic data items given for each geographic level: number of serious crimes known to police, crime rate, and number of violent crimes. For cities, there is one additional data item on number of serious crimes

per police officer. Data are for the most recent year available at publication. The *County and City Data Book* is also available on CD-ROM from the Census Bureau. The University of Virginia Library Geospatial and Statistical Data Center offers recent editions of the *County and City Data Book* on the Internet in their interactive data area. Users select the desired edition, geography, and variables to create a customized data display.

> *County and City Extra* is a commercially produced annual version of the *County and City Data Book*. The crime data is very similar to that in the *County and City Data Book* with minor variation. *Places, Towns, and Townships* provides similar data for cities.

> The *USA Counties* CD contains several years of basic crime data. The Oregon State University Government Information Sharing Project provides access to the current issue on the Internet. Users select a geographic area profile or an area comparison and then the desired geography. A subject area can then be selected or a keyword search conducted to display data. The Census Bureau Web site offers a similar version.

GENERAL CRIMINAL STATISTICS SOURCES
Checklist

Sourcebook of Criminal Justice Statistics. PRINT. WEB. (annual) 1973–. U.S. Department of Justice. Office of Justice Programs. Bureau of Justice Statistics. J 29.9/6: (Earlier, J 29.9:SD-SB-) Item 0968-H-06. ASI 6064-6. GPO.<http://www.albany.edu/sourcebook/>;<http://purl.access.gpo.gov/GPO/LPS2497>.

> Coverage: U.S., regions, divisions, states, cities over 100,000.
> Content: characteristics of the criminal justice system; public attitudes toward crime topics; nature and distribution of known offenses; characteristics and distribution of persons arrested; judicial processing of defendants; persons under correctional supervision.

Sourcebook of Criminal Justice Statistics. CD-ROM. 1994–. U.S. Department of Justice. Office of Justice Programs. Bureau of Justice Statistics. J 29.9/6-2: Item 0968-H-31. GPO.

> Content: CD-ROM version of the *Sourcebook of Criminal Justice Statistics*.

Crime in the United States: Uniform Crime Reports. PRINT. WEB. (annual) 1930–. U.S. Department of Justice. Federal Bureau of Investigation. J 1.14/7: Item 0722. ASI 6224-2. GPO.<http://www.fbi.gov/ucr.htm>;<http://purl.access.gpo.gov/GPO/LPS3082>.

> Coverage: U.S., regions, divisions, states, metropolitan areas, selected counties, cities, individual universities and colleges.
> Content: number and types of offenses; crime index; crime rate; offenses cleared by arrest; number and characteristics of persons arrested; number of law enforcement personnel.

Crime in the United States: Uniform Crime Reports. CD-ROM. 1995–. U.S. Department of Justice. Federal Bureau of Investigation. J 1.14/7-8: Item 0722-A-03. GPO.

Content: CD-ROM version of *Crime in the United States*.

Discussion

Sourcebook of Criminal Justice Statistics is an excellent, comprehensive reference source for locating crime-related data. The criminal justice system section covers the number and type of criminal justice agencies, criminal justice employment and expenditures, and tables summarizing state laws on alcohol use and driving and gun control. There are numerous tables on public attitudes towards such topics as abortion, capital punishment, gun control, alcohol, drugs, police, and courts. Other sections cover the number and type of crimes, crime victimization, drug and alcohol use, arrests, court cases and dispositions, and prisoners. Data given for cities are primarily for type of offense and for violent crime rate. Other features available include an annotated list of sources and an index. Examples of data available include the number of burglaries in Raleigh, North Carolina, the prevalence of crack use by age or race, the victimization rate for robbery, the average sentence in U.S. district courts for auto theft, and the number of weapons detected by airline passenger screening. The Web version of the *Sourcebook* is updated on an ongoing basis. The CD-ROM version contains multiple, recent editions of the *Sourcebook*.

Crime in the United States is based on voluntary reports from state and local law enforcement agencies to the FBI on crime and arrests. At the beginning of the report is a summary analysis for each type of offense. The offenses covered are murder and nonnegligent manslaughter, forcible rape, robbery, aggravated assault, burglary, larceny-theft, motor vehicle theft, and arson. Detailed tables contain statistics on crime rates and indexes, number of offenses, and trends for geographic areas. The crime index gives statistics on number of crimes and the rate per 100,000 people, with geographic coverage down to the metropolitan area level. The data on number of offenses cover smaller geographic areas including cities and towns of 10,000 or more, selected counties, and individual universities and colleges. Additional sections cover offenses cleared by arrest, persons arrested, and law enforcement personnel. Arrest data are by age, race, sex, and type of crime with no data below the state level. The law enforcement personnel section contains the most detailed geographic coverage with data for cities and counties. The CD-ROM version contains multiple recent editions of *Crime in the United States*.

OTHER CRIMINAL STATISTICS SOURCES
Checklist

Bureau of Justice Statistics Web Site. WEB. U.S. Department of Justice. Office of Justice Programs. Bureau of Justice Statistics.<http://www.ojp.usdoj.gov/bjs/>.
> Content: crime and justice system statistics; full-text publications; data files; agency information.

Criminal Victimization [year]: Changes [years] with Trends [years]. PRINT. WEB. (annual) U.S. Department of Justice. Office of Justice Programs. Bureau of Justice Statistics. J 29.11/10: (Earlier, J 29.11:) Item 0968-H-13. ASI 6066-3.[no.]<http://www.ojp.usdoj.gov/bjs/pubalp2.htm#Criminal Victimization>.
> Coverage: U.S., regions.
> Content: number and rate of crime victimization by type of crime; victimization rate by victim characteristics including age, race, sex, income, and marital status; victim and offender relationship; use of weapons; reporting of crime to police.

Hate Crime Statistics. WEB. U.S. Department of Justice. Federal Bureau of Investigation. ASI 6224-9.<http://www.fbi.gov/ucr.htm>;<http://purl.access.gpo.gov/GPO/LPS3082>.
> Coverage: U.S., states, selected counties, cities, universities and colleges, state police agencies, other agencies.
> Content: number of incidents and nature of offense by type of bias; number and type of victims.

Bureau of Justice Statistics Special Report. PRINT. WEB. (irregular) 1983–. U.S. Department of Justice. Office of Justice Programs. Bureau of Justice Statistics. J 29.13: Item 0968-H-16. ASI 6066-19.<http://www.ojp.usdoj.gov/bjs/pubalp2.htm>.
> Coverage: varies; U.S., states.
> Content: varies; reports on crime topics.

Compendium of Federal Justice Statistics. PRINT. WEB. (annual) 1984–. U.S. Department of Justice. Office of Justice Programs. Bureau of Justice Statistics. J 29.20: Item 0968-H-16. ASI 6064-29.<http://www.ojp.usdoj.gov/bjs/pubalp2.htm#Compendium of Federal Justice Statistics>.
> Coverage: U.S.
> Content: prosecution of suspects by offense; pretrial release or detention; disposition of cases; length and type of sentences; appeals; probation and parole; prison admissions; average time served.

Law Enforcement Officers Killed and Assaulted. PRINT. WEB. (annual) 1982–. U.S. Department of Justice. Federal Bureau of Investigation. J 1.14/7-6: (Formerly issued as two publications: *Assaults on Federal Officers*, J 1.14/7-3:, and *Law Enforcement Officers Killed*, J 1.14/7-5:) Item 0722-A. ASI 6224-3.<http://www.fbi.gov/ucr.htm>;<http://purl.access.gpo.gov/GPO/LPS3082>; <http://purl.access.gpo.gov/GPO/LPS700>.
> Coverage: U.S., regions, divisions, states, agencies.
> Content: number of law enforcement officers killed; location; type of weapon; time of day; type of assignment; profile of victims; profile and disposition of offenders; circumstances; summaries of incidents; accidental deaths; assaults on law officers and federal agency officers.

Bombing Incidents. MF. WEB. (annual) U.S. Department of Justice. Federal Bureau of Investigation. Bomb Data Center. General Information Bulletin. J 1.14/7-7: (Earlier, J 1.14/8-2:, J 1.14/7-4:B 63/) Item 0722-A. ASI 6224-5.<http://www.fbi.gov/library.htm>.
> Coverage: U.S., regions, states.
> Content: number of bombings, injuries, and deaths; type of targets; amount of damage; time of day and quarter of year; bomb characteristics; type of offender; motivation; hoaxes.

Arson and Explosives National Repository. WEB. U.S. Department of the Treasury. Bureau of Alcohol, Tobacco and Firearms.<http://ows.atf.treas.gov:9999/>.

Content: database on arson and explosives incidents.

Discussion

The *Bureau of Justice Statistics Web Site* provides access to statistics, full-text publications, and datasets on crime. Statistical data are available by topics including crime and victims, criminal offenders, and the justice system. A "Key Facts at a Glance" menu option offers charts showing crime and justice system trends. A "Publications" category lists publications alphabetically by title with abstracts, full text, related press releases, spreadsheets, and datasets. Datasets are also available from the main menu under the "Data for Analysis" category. The "Crime & Justice Electronic Data Abstracts" option under this category offers spreadsheet data for downloading. The "Online tabulations, datasets & codebooks" option offers datasets from the National Archive of Criminal Justice Data and the Federal Justice Statistics Resource Center.

Criminal Victimization [year]: Changes [years] with Trends [years] is a brief summary report on criminal victimization rates and trends. Data are from the National Crime Victimization Survey that surveys sample households across the United States. It covers selected personal crimes (rape or sexual assault, robbery, assault, and theft) and selected property crimes (burglary, motor vehicle theft, and theft). This survey reflects both reported and unreported crimes, which is an advantage over some other sources. The report includes narrative analysis, a highlights box, statistical tables, and charts. Tables cover number and rate of crime by type and more general crime category data by sex, age, race, household income, marital status, region, and urban, suburban or rural residence. A trends table gives victimization rate by type of crime for recent years.

Hate Crime Statistics reports on number and type of crimes motivated by bias. Categories of bias covered include racial, religious, sexual-orientation, ethnicity/national origin, and disability. National level data includes number of incidents and victims by specific bias (anti-Black, anti-Jewish), location of incidents (e.g., number of sexual-orientation incidents in parking lots/garages), and number of offenses (e.g., aggravated assault motivated by anti-male homosexual bias). Data for smaller geographic areas are limited to number of incidents by broad bias category.

The *Bureau of Justice Statistics Special Report* series contains brief reports on individual topics. Reports include narrative analysis, a highlights box, statistical tables, and charts. Recent titles include "Carjackings in the United States, 1992–96" (J 29.13:C 19), "DWI Offenders Under Correctional Supervision" (J 29.13:D 83), "Workplace Violence, 1992–96" (J 29.13:W 89), and "Juvenile Felony Defendants in Criminal Courts" (J 29.13:J 98).

Recent titles are included on the *Bureau of Justice Statistics Web Site* under the publications category, listed alphabetically by title.

The *Compendium of Federal Justice Statistics* provides an overview of federal criminal case processing, from the prosecution of suspects through imprisonment. Chapters cover prosecution, pretrial release, adjudication, sentencing, appeals, and corrections. Each chapter consists of a narrative overview, charts, and statistical tables. Information is available on such topics as offenders on parole who commit new crimes, the age and race of convicted offenders, conviction rate by offense, and suspects prosecuted by offense.

Law Enforcement Officers Killed and Assaulted gives detailed statistics on officers killed, including specific local agency for which they worked, type of weapon used, location of wounds, and characteristics of victims and offenders. There is a narrative summary of each incident arranged by state. Similar but less detailed data are given for assaults on law officers and federal officers. Information on federal officers is shown by government department and agency. Types of information available include number of officers killed while handling family quarrels, number of officers killed on Thursdays, and number of assaults on Internal Revenue Service officers.

The *Bombing Incidents* report covers bombing incidents reported to the FBI by federal, state, and local agencies. A brief comments section highlights key findings. More detailed data are presented in tables and charts. Information includes total incidents, injuries, and deaths for recent years. Other types of topics covered include types of targets, such as restaurants or academic facilities, characteristics of people involved, such as juvenile or domestic/love triangle, and motivation, such as revenge or mischief.

The *Arson and Explosives National Repository* provides access to Web databases on arson, explosives, and fire incidents. The AEXIS database covers arson and explosives incidents. Users can select from a list of standard data tables, do a query by date range, or see a five-year incident summary for a selected state. Standard data tables cover the most recent year available and provide information on explosive incidents by type, target type, incidents by state, fatalities and injuries by target type, motives, pipe bomb incidents, and arson incidents. The same data are available for a range of years in the query by date range option. The state summary option lists types of incidents. Also available are church arson statistics and the NFIRS (National Fire Information Reporting System) database.

SOURCES ON PRISONS AND PRISONERS
Checklist

Correctional Populations in the United States. PRINT. WEB. (annual) 1985–. U.S. Department of Justice. Office of Justice Programs. Bureau of Justice Statistics. J 29.17: (Data available earlier in other titles) Item 0968-H-24. ASI 6064-26.<http://www.ojp.usdoj.gov/bjs/pubalp2.htm#Correctional Populations in the United States>;<http://purl.access.gpo.gov/GPO/LPS2863>.

> Coverage: U.S., regions, states.
> Content: jail inmates; probation; prisoners; parole; capital punishment; number of persons in each category by various characteristics including sex, race, type of offense, sentence length, and type of release; capacity and condition of correctional facilities.

Prisoners in [year]. PRINT. WEB. (annual) U.S. Department of Justice. Office of Justice Programs. Bureau of Justice Statistics. Bulletin. J 29.11/7: (Earlier, J 29.11:) Item 0968-H-13. ASI 6066-25.[no.]<http://www.ojp.usdoj.gov/bjs/pubalp2.htm#Prisoners>; <http://purl.access.gpo.gov/GPO/LPS2497>.

> Coverage: U.S., regions, states.
> Content: number of inmates; type of facility; prison capacities; prisoners by race, sex, age, and offense; time served.

Capital Punishment. PRINT. WEB. (annual) U.S. Department of Justice. Office of Justice Programs. Bureau of Justice Statistics. Bulletin. J 29.11/3: Item 0968-H-13.<http://www.ojp.usdoj.gov/bjs/pubalp2.htm#Capital Punishment>.

> Coverage: U.S., regions, states.
> Content: number of executions; number of prisoners under sentence of death by race, sex, age, and other characteristics.

Historical Corrections Statistics in the United States, 1850–1984. PRINT. (1986) U.S. Department of Justice. Bureau of Justice Statistics. J 29.2:C 81/850-984. Item 0717-R-01. ASI (87) 6068-213.

> Coverage: U.S., regions, divisions, states.
> Content: capital punishment; prisoners; prison facilities; jail inmates; jail facilities; juvenile correctional facilities; parole; probation.

Discussion

Correctional Populations in the United States gives statistics on persons in jails and prisons and on probation or parole. Chapters cover trends, jail inmates, probation, prisoners, parole, capital punishment, and military corrections. The jail inmates section gives average daily jail population, sex and race of inmates, and information on jail capacity. The probation section gives statistics on adults entering and leaving probation, on probation and supervision status, and on sex, race, type of sentence, and type of offense. The prisoners section covers sentence length, sex and race of prisoners, type of admission, and type of release. The parole tables give data on adults entering and leaving parole, supervision status, sex, race, and sentence length. Capital punishment statistics cover the age, race, sex, education, marital status, and felony history of prisoners under sentence of death. This section also includes information on the status of the death penalty in each state and the number of executions by year and offense. Data on military corrections include number of prisoners by

branch of service, race, sex, offense, sentence length, and officer or enlisted status. Often there is an additional section on a special topic, such as local jail inmates or state and federal correctional facilities, which varies from year to year. *Correctional Populations in the United States* combines four previously separate reports: *Prisoners in State and Federal Institutions, Capital Punishment, Characteristics of Persons Entering Parole,* and *Parole in the United States.*

Prisoners in [year] is a more current summary report on prisoners. The report includes narrative analysis, a highlights box, and statistical tables. Tables cover such topics as the number of prisoners by sex and race, the states with the highest and lowest prison population, prison capacities, and trends in releases.

Capital Punishment covers executions and prisoners under sentence of death. Information is given by state on capital offenses, method of execution, and minimum age for capital punishment. Statistics cover demographic characteristics of prisoners under sentence of death, criminal history, and time under sentence of death.

Historical Corrections Statistics in the United States, 1850–1984 covers many of the same areas as *Correctional Populations in the United States,* but contains historical data. Each chapter contains statistical tables for a particular subject area such as "State and Federal Prison Statistics" or "Parole and Probation Statistics," and includes an overview of the history of data collection in that area and the sources available. Types of data available include illegal lynchings from 1880–1962, median sentences by offense for 1923–81, characteristics of persons in jail 1910–83, characteristics and offenses of juvenile offenders, and liquor law violators 1901–35.

COURT STATISTICS SOURCES
Checklist

Judicial Business of the United States Courts. MF. WEB. U.S. Administrative Office of the United States Courts. JU 10.1/4: (Also included in JU 10.1/2:) Item 0728-C-01. ASI 18204-2. GPO.<http://www.uscourts.gov/publications.html>;<http://purl.access.gpo.gov/GPO/LPS2715>.

> Coverage: U.S., individual court circuits and districts.
> Content: number and disposition of cases by court; cases commenced, terminated, and pending by type; origin of appeals; time involved; number and length of trials; length of sentences; federal probation system; bankruptcy petitions; jurors selected.

Federal Judicial Caseload Statistics. PRINT. (annual) U.S. Administrative Office of the United States Courts. JU 10.21: (Earlier title, *Federal Judicial Workload Statistics*) Item 0729-D. ASI 18204-11. GPO.

> Coverage: U.S., individual court circuits and districts.
> Content: number and type of federal court cases filed, pending, and terminated; jurors selected; persons on parole or probation.

Statistical Tables for the Federal Judiciary. PRINT. (semiannual) U.S. Administrative Office of the United States Courts. JU 10.21/2: (Earlier title, *Statistical Tables for the Twelve Month Period Ended...*) Item 0729-D-01.

> Coverage: U.S., individual court circuits and districts.
> Content: number and type of federal court cases filed, pending, and terminated; jurors selected; persons on parole or probation.

Federal Court Management Statistics. MF. (annual) U.S. Administrative Office of the United States Courts. JU 10.14: (Earlier title, *Management Statistics for United States Courts*) Item 0717-X. ASI 18204-3.

> Coverage: U.S., individual U.S. appellate and district courts.
> Content: caseload profiles for individual courts; filings, terminations, and pending cases; judgeships; actions per judgeship; median times; types of cases; national profiles; court rankings.

Juvenile Court Statistics. MF. WEB. (annual) 1927–. U.S. Department of Justice. Office of Justice Programs. Office of Juvenile Justice and Delinquency Prevention. J 32.15: (Earlier issuing agencies and call numbers vary) Item 0717-B-04. ASI 6064-12.<http://ojjdp.ncjrs.org/pubs/court.html>.

> Coverage: U.S., states, selected counties.
> Content: number of cases by type, age, sex, race; disposition.

Discussion

Judicial Business of the United States Courts contains extensive federal court statistics. Sections cover the U.S. Supreme Court, U.S. courts of appeals, U.S. district courts (civil and criminal cases, trials), the federal probation system, bankruptcy courts, other federal courts, and related matters. This source gives detailed data on cases filed, pending, and terminated. Examples of statistics available include number of appeals to the fourth circuit court of appeals from each district, number of appeals involving criminal proceedings terminated by procedural judgments, and number of civil cases pending in the Southern Ohio district involving motor vehicle personal injury.

Federal Judicial Caseload Statistics is a much more condensed version of the statistics found in *Judicial Business of the United States Courts*. It contains a brief narrative overview and an appendix of selected tables identical to some of those available in *Judicial Business of the United States Courts*. Tables cover 12-month periods running from April 1 through March 31. Before 1989 this report was issued quarterly.

Statistical Tables for the Federal Judiciary contains identical tables to those in *Federal Judicial Caseload Statistics*, but covers 12-month periods ending in June and December. This title does not contain the narrative overview that is included in *Federal Judicial Caseload Statistics*.

Federal Court Management Statistics contains one- to two-page profiles on the activities of each appellate and district court for the past six years. Data include number of cases handled, caseload per judge, median times from filing to disposition, and, for the current year, types of suits and offenses. Data are slightly different for the two types of courts. There is more case detail for district courts, and there are statistics on juror selection.

Juvenile Court Statistics has been published by many different agencies over the years. From 1975 to 1981 it was published privately. This title contains national estimates of delinquency cases and of petitioned status offense cases. Status offenses are acts that are crimes only when committed by a juvenile. Chapters on each of these two topics consist of narrative analysis, charts, and tables illustrating type of offense, source of referral, detention, disposition, and demographic characteristics of offenders. An appendix lists number of cases by state and selected counties. Examples of data available include percentage of property offenses resulting in out-of-home placement, percentage of female delinquents, and percentage of cases involving twelve year olds.

DRUGS
Checklist

The NNICC Report [year]: The Supply of Illicit Drugs to the United States. WEB. (annual) 1978–. National Narcotics Intelligence Consumers Committee. J 24.22: Item 1093. ASI 6284-2.<http://www.usdoj.gov/dea/pubs/intel.htm>;<http://purl.access.gpo.gov/GPO/LPS3379>.

> Coverage: world regions, selected countries, U.S.
> Content: availability and use of cocaine, heroin, methamphetamine, cannabis, and other dangerous drugs; quantities available; prices; purity; cultivation and production; trafficking; seizures; sources.

Annual Report on Drug Use Among Adult and Juvenile Arrestees. PRINT. WEB. (annual) 1987–. U.S. Department of Justice. Office of Justice Programs. National Institute of Justice. J 28.15/2-3: (Title and frequency vary. Earlier, J 28.15/2-2:D 84/7/) Item 0717-J-01. ASI 6064-44. (Earlier, 6062-3)<http://www.adam-nij.net/report.htm>;<http://www.ojp.usdoj.gov/nij/drugdocs.htm>;<http://purl.access.gpo.gov/GPO/LPS2993>.

> Coverage: selected metropolitan areas.
> Content: drug use among persons arrested by type of drug, type of crime, sex, age, race.

International Narcotics Control Strategy Report. PRINT. WEB. (annual) 1984–. U.S. Department of State. Bureau for International Narcotics and Law Enforcement Affairs. S 1.146: (Earlier, S 1.2:N 16/3/year) Item 0876-A-06. ASI 7004-17. GPO.<http://www.state.gov/www/global/narcotics_law/narc_reports_mainhp.html>;<http://purl.access.gpo.gov/GPO/LPS3635>.

> Coverage: world, world regions, countries.
> Content: production, cultivation, and eradication of specific drugs; refining; seizures; arrests; labs destroyed; consumption; users.

National Household Survey on Drug Abuse. PRINT. WEB. (annual) 1971–. U.S. Department of Health and Human Services. Substance Abuse and Mental Health Services Administration.

Office of Applied Studies. (Title and frequency vary) ASI 4096-3 (Earlier, 4094-3, 4494-5, 4498-4) GPO.<http://www.samhsa.gov/OAS/p0000016.htm>;<http://purl.access.gpo.gov/GPO/LPS3753>.

Main Findings. PRINT. WEB. HE 20.417/3: (Earlier, HE 20.402:D 84/, HE 20.8202:H 81/, HE 20.8202: Su7/) Item 0497-D-26.

> Coverage: U.S., regions.
> Content: prevalence, trends, and frequency of drug use for marijuana, cocaine, inhalants, hallucinogens, heroin, psychotherapeutic drugs, alcohol, cigarettes, and smokeless tobacco; by age group, sex, race, education, employment status; problems associated with drug use; use patterns; perceptions of risk; availability.

Population Estimates. PRINT. WEB. HE 20.417/2: (Earlier, HE 20.402:D 84/, HE 20.2:H 81/, HE 20.8202:H 81/2/) Item 0497-D-24.

> Coverage: U.S., regions.
> Content: prevalence and frequency of drug use by sex, race, age group.

Summary of Findings from the [year] National Household Survey on Drug Abuse. PRINT. WEB. 1992–. HE 20.417/5: (Title varies. Earlier, HE 20.417/4:, HE 20.417/2:, HE 20.421:) Item 0497-D-39.

> Coverage: U.S., regions, divisions.
> Content: prevalence and frequency of drug use by sex, race, age group and other characteristics.

National Survey Results on Drug Use from the Monitoring the Future Study. PRINT. (annual) 1975– . U.S. Department of Health and Human Services. Public Health Service. National Institutes of Health. National Institute on Drug Abuse. HE 20.3968: (Earlier, HE 20.3952:D 84/) Item 0467-A-32. ASI 4494-4. GPO. Selected data:<http://monitoringthefuture.org/data/data.html>.

> Coverage: U.S., regions.
> Content: prevalence and frequency of drug use for various drugs, alcohol, and tobacco; differences in use by sex, race, and selected socioeconomic factors; grade of first use; degree and duration of highs; attitudes and beliefs; social milieu.

Discussion

The *NNICC Report* is prepared by a committee of government agencies that deal with drug law enforcement, policy, and research. Some of the agencies involved include the Drug Enforcement Administration, the Central Intelligence Agency (CIA), the Federal Bureau of Investigation (FBI), the National Institute on Drug Abuse, the Customs Service, the Defense Department, and the State Department. Chapters on each major drug discuss domestic availability and use, foreign sources, and trafficking. Statistics are incorporated into the text. Occasional tables give statistics on production and seizures. Developments in specific world regions and countries are discussed. Examples of information available include estimated cocaine cultivation in Peru or clandestine laboratory seizures of PCP.

Annual Report on Drug Use Among Adult and Juvenile Arrestees contains statistics on drug use by persons arrested. Sample data are collected from voluntary participants in 35 cities. Two-page profiles for adult arrestees are given for each city. One-page profiles for a smaller number of cities are given for juvenile arrestees. The adult profiles give number of people in the sample and selected demographic characteristics. Tables cover percentage of persons testing positive for selected drugs by sex, age, race, and offense category. Self-reported drug information includes age at first use, prior treatment, ever injected drugs, and drug use in the past 30 days. The juvenile profiles give sample size by age and race and percentage testing positive for selected drugs by sex, age, race, offense category, and school status. Both profiles also include a historic trends chart.

The *International Narcotics Control Strategy Report* is a primarily narrative report on international narcotics control efforts. It summarizes program annual activities, developments, and future plans. A large part of the report is devoted to country summaries. These are divided into such sections as "Status of Country," "Country Actions Against Drugs," and "U.S. Policy Initiatives and Programs." The "Country Actions" section covers such areas as policy initiatives, accomplishments, law enforcement efforts, corruption, agreements and treaties, drug flow, and domestic programs. For many countries there is a statistical table covering cultivation, eradication, and seizure of specific drugs.

The *National Household Survey on Drug Abuse Main Findings* covers the U.S. household population aged 12 and up and is a comprehensive report on the prevalence and frequency of drug use. The report contains a trends chapter and chapters for each type of drug. Each chapter contains a narrative overview and statistical tables. Statistics show percentage of persons who have ever used drugs, used drugs during the past year, or used drugs during the past month by demographic characteristics for each drug. Additional chapters cover problems associated with use, use patterns, and special topics. These provide data in such areas as age at first use, multiple drug use, dependence, and binge alcohol use. The *Population Estimates* report is entirely statistical. It contains a set of prevalence tables for each drug giving the percentage and number of persons who have ever used the drug, used it in the past year, or in the past month. Tables are broken down by sex and age group with separate tables for each race category and region. A similar set of tables show frequency of use during the past year. The *Summary of Findings* report provides early estimates from the survey and covers the same type of data as the other two reports. The first part of the report gives narrative highlights illustrated with graphs and charts. An appendix contains detailed tables of preliminary data on percentages of people reporting lifetime, past year, or past month use; number reporting first use each year and age at first use; availability; and perceptions of risk.

Another drug use survey of secondary school students, college students, and young adults is also conducted annually. *National Survey Results on Drug Use from the Monitoring the Future Study* also covers prevalence and frequency of use, but contains slightly different variables than the household survey above. Drug use data are analyzed in relation to college attendance plans and the level of parental education. Information is also collected on the grade in which drugs were first used, the degree and duration of the high, and attitudes and social factors involved. The latter two areas involve beliefs regarding the harmfulness of drugs, extent of disapproval of drugs, attitudes toward legality, and perceived attitudes of friends. Volume 1 covers secondary school students; volume 2 covers college students and young adults. Selected data from recent surveys are available on the Internet.

TERRORISM
Checklist

Terrorism in the United States. PRINT. WEB. 1981–. (annual) U.S. Department of Justice. Federal Bureau of Investigation. National Security Division. Counterterrorism Threat Assessment and Warning Unit. J 1.14/22: Item 0717-C-17. ASI 6224-6.<http://www.fbi.gov/library/terror/terroris.htm>;<http://purl.access.gpo.gov/GPO/LPS2826>.

> Coverage: U.S., locales of specific incidents.
> Content: number of incidents; suspected incidents and preventions; terrorist groups; summary of specific incidents for current year; multi-year list of incidents.

Patterns of Global Terrorism. PRINT. WEB. (annual) 1976–. U.S. Department of State. Office of the Secretary of State. Office of the Coordinator for Counterterrorism. S 1.138: (Earlier, PREX 3.10/7:) (Title varies) Item 0876-A-06. ASI 7004-13.<http://www.state.gov/www/global/terrorism/annual_reports.html#patterns>;<http://www.usis.usemb.se/terror/index.html>;<http://purl.access.gpo.gov/GPO/LPS1488>.

> Coverage: world, world regions, countries.
> Content: terrorist attacks by type of facility, type of victim, type of event; number wounded and killed.

Discussion

Terrorism in the United States gives an overview and analysis of terrorist incidents in the U.S. A chart shows number of incidents, suspected incidents, and preventions for several years. Narrative text summarizes the year's incidents, suspected incidents, and preventions. Significant events, major issues, and the current situation are analyzed. A multi-year list of incidents gives date, location, type of incident, and the group to whom it was attributed.

Patterns of Global Terrorism covers terrorist incidents around the world. This primarily narrative source analyzes the year's terrorist incidents by region and country.

A "Statistical Review" appendix contains a small number of colorful graphs and charts illustrating numbers and types of incidents by world region. This source also includes a chronology of significant events and background information on terrorist groups.

NATIONAL CRIMINAL JUSTICE REFERENCE SERVICE (NCJRS)
Checklist

National Criminal Justice Reference Service NCJRS Abstracts Database. WEB. CD-ROM. 1972–. U.S. Department of Justice. National Institute of Justice. J 28.31/2: Item 0718-D-01. GPO.<http://www.ncjrs.org/database.htm>;<http://purl.access.gpo.gov/GPO/LPS523>.

> Content: bibliographic information and abstracts for criminal justice books, reports, articles, and documents.

NCJRS Catalog. PRINT. WEB. (bimonthly) Nov./Dec. 1991–. U.S. Department of Justice. Office of Justice Programs. National Criminal Justice Reference Service. J 28.14/2: Item 0968-H-10.<http://www.ncjrs.org/catalog.htm>;<http://purl.access.gpo.gov/GPO/LPS1533>.

> Content: information on new criminal justice publications available from NCJRS and other sources.

Dialog. WEB.<http://www.dialog.com/>.

> Content: comprehensive online data provider; NCJRS database.

Discussion

The National Criminal Justice Reference Service (NCJRS) is an information clearinghouse for criminal justice research. NCJRS collects and disseminates research findings to assist policymakers, law enforcement professionals, and researchers in improving the criminal justice system. NCJRS maintains an extensive database of criminal justice literature, operates specialized clearinghouses such as the Bureau of Justice Statistics Clearinghouse, and provides various related information services.

The *National Criminal Justice Reference Service NCJRS Abstracts Database* contains bibliographic information and abstracts for more than 150,000 books, reports, articles, and government documents on law enforcement and criminal justice. Availability information is included in the record. The Web version includes links to the full text of publications when available online (generally for publications published by Justice Department agencies since 1995). Publications of Justice Department agencies may also be available from the NCJRS at no charge or for a small fee. All publications in the database are also available from NCJRS through interlibrary loan. Some libraries may have the NCJRS microfiche collection that was available through 1995. Some of the titles published by Department of Justice agencies are available to depository libraries. The NCJRS database is also available through Dialog. Researchers may also contact NCJRS directly for a search.

The *NCJRS Catalog* contains information on new criminal justice resources. A "Just In" section describes selected new titles added to the NCJRS collection. Entries contain bibliographic and availability information and an abstract. Other sections cover key articles in professional journals, Internet sites, criminal justice news, older publications of continuing interest, and recent grant awards. An order form for materials available from NCJRS is also included.

INDEXES
Checklist

American Statistics Index (ASI). PRINT. (monthly) 1973–. Bethesda, MD: Congressional Information Service.

Statistical Universe. WEB. Bethesda, MD: Congressional Information Service.

Catalog of United States Government Publications (MOCAT). WEB. 1994–. U.S. Government Printing Office. Superintendent of Documents. <http://www.gpo.gov/catalog>;<http://www.access.gpo.gov/su_docs/locators/cgp/index.html>; <http://purl.access.gpo.gov/GPO/LPS844>.

Monthly Catalog of United States Government Publications. CD-ROM. 1996–. U.S. Government Printing Office. Superintendent of Documents. GP 3.8/7: Item 0557-C. GPO.

Monthly Catalog of United States Government Publications (Condensed version). PRINT. (monthly) 1996–. U.S. Government Printing Office. Superintendent of Documents. GP 3.8/8: (Earlier full version, GP 3.8:, 1895-1995). Item 0557-D. GPO.

Discussion

American Statistics Index (ASI) is a comprehensive index to government statistics. Possible subject headings to look under for crime statistics include "Crime and criminals," "Correctional institutions," "Prisoners," "Parole and probation," "Courts," and "Law enforcement." Materials can also be found under specific crimes such as "Homicide" or "Rape" and under more specialized headings such as "Police," "Juvenile delinquency," or "Terrorism." *Statistical Universe* includes a Web version of *ASI*.

The *Monthly Catalog* can also be used to locate materials, but does not provide the in depth indexing of statistics that *ASI* does. Look under such general subject headings as "Crime and Criminals," "Criminals," and "Criminal Statistics." For materials on the criminal justice system look under such headings as "Criminal Justice, Administration of," "Courts," "Prisoners," "Parole," "Probation," and "Correctional Institutions." Many other specific subjects are used including "Juvenile Delinquency" and "Terrorism." The complete version of the *Monthly Catalog* is available on the Web and CD-ROM. Commercial online and CD-ROM versions of the *Monthly Catalog* are also available.

For more information on these indexes, see Chapter 3, "The Basics of Searching."

RELATED MATERIAL
GPO Subject Bibliographies. PRINT. WEB. GP 3.22/2:

<http://bookstore.gpo.gov/sb/about/html>

No. 36 "Criminal Justice"

CHAPTER 40
Defense and Military Statistics

Although very specific statistics on a particular defense project may be buried in an appropriations hearing or a technical report, there are a number of detailed statistical reports published in the defense and military area. Statistics available cover a wide range of subjects, from military property to the number of enlisted Army women. Most of these reports originate directly from the Department of Defense. This chapter covers statistics about the U.S. military. Military assistance to other countries is covered in Chapter 4, "Foreign Policy."

SEARCH STRATEGY

This chapter is an example of a statistical search strategy. The strategy is as follows:

1. Try the general sources listed in this chapter, especially the *Statistical Abstract of the United States* and the *Historical Statistics of the United States: Colonial Times to 1970*;
2. Consult the *Budget of the United States Government* if searching for specific budgetary or program information;
3. Check general and specific defense departmental reports listed in this chapter;
4. Search other appropriate sources listed within this chapter; and
5. Search *American Statistics Index (ASI)* for further defense and military statistics.

GENERAL SOURCES
Checklist

Statistical Abstract of the United States. PRINT. WEB. (annual) 1878–. U.S. Department of Commerce. Economics and Statistics Administration. Bureau of the Census. C 3.134: Item 0150. ASI 2324-1. GPO.<http://www.census.gov/statab/www/>;<http://purl.access.gpo.gov/GPO/LPS2878>.
   Coverage: primarily U.S; some countries, states.

Content: federal budget outlays; defense spending; defense contract awards; military sales and assistance to foreign governments; major military forces; military personnel; veterans.

Statistical Abstract of the United States. CD-ROM. (annual) 1993–. U.S. Department of Commerce. Bureau of the Census. C 3.134/7: Item 0150-B. ASI 2324-14.
   Content: CD-ROM version of the *Statistical Abstract*.

Historical Statistics of the United States: Colonial Times to 1970. Parts 1-2. PRINT. (1975) U.S. Department of Commerce. Bureau of the Census. C 3.134/2:H 62/789-970/pt.1-2. Item 0151. ASI (76) 2328-2. GPO.
   Coverage: U.S.
   Content: historical statistics on federal budget outlays; defense spending; military personnel; veterans.

Historical Statistics of the United States on CD-ROM: Colonial Times to 1970. CD-ROM. (1997) New York, NY: Cambridge University Press.
   Content: CD-ROM version of *Historical Statistics of the United States*.

Budget of the United States Government. PRINT. WEB. (annual) 1922–. U.S. Executive Office of the President. Office of Management and Budget. PREX 2.8: (Also issued as a House Document, Y 1.1/7:) Item 0853. ASI 104-2. GPO.<http://w3.access.gpo.gov/usbudget/>;<http://purl.access.gpo.gov/GPO/LPS2343>.
   Coverage: U.S.
   Content: overview of defense and military programs and expenditures.

The Budget of the United States Government Fiscal Year [year]. CD-ROM. (annual) 1996–. U.S. Executive Office of the President. Office of Management and Budget. PREX 2.8/1: Item 0853-C. ASI 104-38. GPO.
   Content: CD-ROM version of *The Budget of the United States*.

Discussion

The *Statistical Abstract of the United States* includes an entire chapter on "National Defense and Veterans Affairs" and is the first source to check for military and defense statistics. One especially useful feature is its condensation of statistics from the *Budget of the United States Government*. The *Statistical Abstract* is also available in a CD-ROM version.

The *Historical Statistics of the United States: Colonial Times to 1970* provides series of data from many of the tables included within the current *Statistical Abstract*. Series Y849-1031 is an entire section on "Armed Forces and Veterans," but many of the budget series pertaining to the military are included in Series Y272-848, "Government Employment and Finances."

The *Budget of the United States Government* provides an overview of proposed defense spending, and in the appendix volume, detailed statistics regarding proposed defense spending. The actual amounts spent on defense for the preceding year are given, along with estimates for the fiscal year in progress and the next approaching year. The statistics include a number of categories, such as "Military Personnel," "Procurement," and "Military Construction."

GENERAL DEPARTMENT OF DEFENSE SOURCES

Checklist

DefenseLINK. WEB. U.S. Department of Defense.<http://www.defenselink.mil/>.
    Content: general information about the Department of Defense, including some statistical information; links to Department of Defense Web sites.

DoD Almanac. WEB. U.S. Department of Defense. American Forces Information Service.<http://www.defenselink.mil/pubs/almanac/>.
    Content: wide range of statistical information including budget information; military personnel; civilian personnel; weapons; facilities; procurement; contracts; and research and development.

Report of the Secretary of Defense to the President and the Congress. MF. WEB. (annual) 1948–. U.S. Department of Defense. D 1.1: Item 0306-A-02. ASI 3544-2. GPO.<http://www.dtic.mil/execsec/adr_intro.html>.
    Content: comprehensive report covering Department of Defense budget summaries, programs, personnel, and policies.

Atlas/Data Abstract for the United States and Selected Areas. MF. WEB. (annual) 1986–. U.S. Department of Defense. Washington Headquarters Services. Directorate for Information Operations and Reports. D 1.58/4: Item 0310-E-22. ASI 3544-29.GPO.<http://web1.whs.osd.mil/MMID/PUBS.HTM>;<http://purl.access.gpo.gov/GPO/LPS2601>.
    Coverage: selected countries, U.S., states, U.S. territories and possessions, individual military sites.

Content: Department of Defense personnel; payroll outlays; prime contracts over $25,000.

Directorate for Information Operations and Reports Web Site. WEB. U.S. Department of Defense. Washington Headquarters Services. Directorate for Information Operations and Reports.<http://web1.whs.osd.mil/diorhome.htm>.
    Content: general information about the DIOR and its programs; statistical information; links to full-text sources; downloadable standard tabulation files.

Catalog of DIOR Reports. WEB. D 1.33/4: Item 0304-D. U.S. Department of Defense. Washington Headquarters Services. Directorate for Information Operations and Reports.<http://web1.whs.osd.mil/DIORCAT.HTM>.
    Content: electronic catalog of DIOR publications, including links to the full-text of publications when available.

Discussion

The *DefenseLINK Web* site provides general information about the Department of Defense, including some statistical information. The site also includes links to other Department of Defense Web sites, which can be useful for identifying agency sites that may include statistics on a particular topic. The site also includes the *DoD Almanac*, which includes basic current statistics on a wide range of military and defense-related topics. The *Almanac* is well organized and easy to navigate, and is an excellent ready-reference source for finding statistical information.

The *Report of the Secretary of Defense to the President and the Congress* is one of the best places to begin a search for statistical information on the Department of Defense's programs. Using text, tables, and graphs, the report comprehensively describes the entire Department of Defense budget and programs. Areas covered include policy, programs, personnel, and budgets. Projections for later fiscal years are often included within the report. The Web version of the report provides a search interface to search keywords and topics within either a single year of the report or across several of the most recent years of the report.

The *Atlas/Data Abstract for the United States and Selected Areas* includes maps for each state, territory, U.S. possession, or selected country, which pinpoint military installations and plant locations. Accompanying the maps are statistical tables showing the number of personnel in the area and payroll outlays, including active duty military pay, civilian pay, reserve and National Guard pay, and retired military pay. Also included are statistics on prime contract awards over $25,000. The top five contractors receiving the largest dollar volume of prime contract awards in the area are also listed.

The Directorate for Information Operations and Reports (DIOR) is the Department of Defense agency most involved with collecting statistical information for the Department of Defense. The DIOR's Web site provides links to a wide range of data involving personnel and procurement. The full-text of many of the sources cited later in this chapter is included on this Web site. The site also includes downloadable standard tabulations of data in PCL4 (HP Printer Control Language) formats (meant for the output to be printed) for contract and procurement statistical information. The DIOR Web site also has a link to the *Catalog of DIOR Reports*, which provides a summary of DIOR publications, ordering information, and links to the full-text Web versions of the reports when available.

DEPARTMENTAL WEB SITES

Checklist

U.S. Army Homepage. WEB. U.S. Department of the Army.
Content: general information about the Army; links to other Army Web sites. <http://www.army.mil>.

The United States Navy: Welcome Aboard. WEB. U.S. Department of the Navy.<http://www.navy.mil/>.
Content: general information about the Navy, links to other Navy Web sites.

Air Force Link. WEB. U.S. Department of the Air Force.
Content: general information about the Air Force, links to other Air Force sites. <http://www.af.mil/>.

Discussion

In addition to the more general *DefenseLINK* Web site described in the previous section, the home pages of individual Department of Defense departments and the offices, bureaus, and other subagencies beneath them can be important resources for locating statistical information. While it may not always be obvious on the Web sites where statistical information is located, the Web sites often provide more current information and are usually frequently updated. Cited here are the home pages for the Army, Navy, and Air Force. *DefenseLINK* can also be used to identify additional Department of Defense Web sites.

SOURCES ON MILITARY PERSONNEL

Checklist

Selected Manpower Statistics, [fiscal year]. WEB. (annual) U.S. Department of Defense. Washington Headquarters Services. Directorate for Information Operations and Reports. D 1.61/4: Item 0310-E-09. ASI 3544-1.<http://web1.whs.osd.mil/MMID/PUBS.HTM>;<http://purl.access.gpo.gov/GPO/LPS2601>; <http://purl.access.gpo.gov/GPO/LPS2692>.
Coverage: world, world regions, countries, U.S., states, Washington D.C. metropolitan area.
Content: current and historical military personnel statistics for the Department of Defense, Army, Navy, Marine Corps, and Air Force.

Military Manpower Statistics. WEB. (quarterly) 1978–. U.S. Department of Defense. Washington Headquarters Services. Directorate for Information Operations and Reports. D 1.61: Item 0310-E-08. ASI 3542-14.<http://web1.whs.osd.mil/

mmid/military/miltop.htm>;<http://purl.access.gpo.gov/GPO/LPS3056>.
Coverage: world regions; U.S.; countries.
Content: total military personnel; civilian personnel; active duty personnel; reserve personnel; female personnel; reenlistment rates.

Civilian Manpower Statistics. WEB. (quarterly) U.S. Department of Defense. Washington Headquarters Services. Directorate for Information Operations and Reports. D 1.61/2: Item 0310-E-06. ASI 3542-16.<http://web1.whs.osd.mil/MMID/PUBS.HTM>;<http://purl.access.gpo.gov/GPO/LPS2601>.
Coverage: world, countries, U.S., Washington, D.C. metropolitan area.
Content: Department of Defense civilian employment.

Worldwide Manpower Distribution by Geographical Area. WEB. (quarterly) 1979–. U.S. Department of Defense. Washington Headquarters Services. Directorate for Information Operations and Reports. D 1.61/3: Item 0310-E-07. ASI 3542-20.<http://web1.whs.osd.mil/MMID/PUBS.HTM>;<http://purl.access.gpo.gov/GPO/LPS2692>.
Coverage: world, world regions, countries.
Content: geographic distribution of Department of Defense military and civilian personnel and their dependents.

Distribution of Personnel by State and by Selected Locations. WEB. (annual) U.S. Department of Defense. Washington Headquarters Services. Directorate for Information Operations and Reports. D 1.61/5: Item 0310-E-14. ASI 3544-7. <http://web1.whs.osd.mil/MMID/PUBS.HTM>;<http://purl.access.gpo.gov/GPO/LPS2601>.
Coverage: state, cities, installation sites.
Content: Department of defense military and civilian personnel.

Worldwide U.S. Active Duty Military Personnel Casualties. WEB. (quarterly) 1984–. U.S. Department of Defense. Washington Headquarters Services. Directorate for Information Operations and Reports. D 1.61/6. Item 0310-E-15. ASI 3544-40.<http://web1.whs.osd.mil/mmid/pubs.htm>.
Coverage: U.S., states.
Content: detailed categorized statistics on active duty casualties, including deaths, personnel captured, and missing personnel.

Official Guard and Reserve Manpower Strengths and Statistics. PRINT. (annual) 1989–. U.S. Department of Defense. Office of the Secretary of Defense. (nondepository) ASI 3544-38.
Coverage: U.S. states
Content: detailed statistics on reserve strengths, profiles of personnel by such characteristics as sex, ethnicity, race, age, grade, and years of service; accessions, attritions, and retentions.

Reserve Manpower Statistics. MF. (annual) 1989–. U.S. Department of Defense. Washington Headquarters Services. Directorate for Information Operations and Reports. D 1.61/7: Item 0310-E-08. ASI 3542-4. GPO.
Coverage: U.S.
Content: basic statistics on reserve strengths and characteristics.

Reserve Component Programs FY [year]: Annual Report of the Reserve Forces Policy Board. MF. U.S. Department of Defense.

Office of the Secretary of Defense. Reserve Forces Policy Board. D 1.1/3-2: Item 0306-A-01. ASI 3544-31.

> Content: review of reserve forces; Army National Guard; Marine Corps Reserve; Air National Guard; Air Force Reserve; Coast Guard Reserve.

Population Representation in the Military Service. WEB. U.S. Department of Defense. Office of the Secretary of Defense. Office of the Assistant Secretary of Defense for Force Management Policy. ASI 3544-41.<http://dticaw.dtic.mil/prhome/das_mpp.html>.

> Coverage: U.S., regions, states.
> Content: demographic, socioeconomic, and service characteristics of active military personnel and selected reserve personnel.

Discussion

Most of the reports in this section come from the Directorate for Information Operations and Reports (DIOR). The DIOR now distributes most of its publications electronically from its Web site, and those URLs are given in the entries. Depository libraries generally no longer receive print or microfiche versions of DIOR reports, and most publications are no longer available for sale from GPO. NTIS does distribute some DIOR sources, particularly data sets in electronic formats.

Selected Manpower Statistics, [fiscal year] consists of a series of tables describing various Department of Defense personnel. Sections of the report cover active duty, military, civilian, reserve, and retired personnel. Many of the tables provide historical data, with a few selected tables giving data from 1789 to the present.

Military Manpower Statistics and *Civilian Manpower Statistics* provide current quarterly data, which are later included in the *Selected Manpower Statistics*. *Worldwide Manpower Distribution by Geographical Area* details the worldwide locations of military and civilian personnel and their dependents, while the *Distribution of Personnel by State and by Selected Locations* does the same for personnel within the United States.

Worldwide U.S. Active Duty Military Personnel Casualties gives a variety of statistics on deaths occurring among active duty personnel. Information included is from 1979 to the present. Sample tables include "Nonhostile Deaths by Manner per 100,000 Strength," "By Place of Casualty and Military Service," "By Pay Grade and Race," and "Deaths Resulting from Hostile Action."

Official Guard and Reserve Manpower Strengths and Statistics is a detailed annual report on the characteristics of guard and reserve personnel. The Army, Navy, Air Force, Coast Guard, Marine Corps Reserves, and Army and Air National Guard are all covered. Statistical tables describe the strength of the forces, gains and losses, demographic profiles, and information on reenlistments/extensions, continuation rates, and retirees. *Reserve Manpower Statistics* is a much less complete summary report of reserve strengths and selected characteristics, covering

the U.S. only. *Reserve Component Programs FY [year]: Annual Report of the Reserve Forces Policy Board* also includes statistical information on reserve personnel. Tables and charts are interspersed with text narrative. One chapter of the report is devoted specifically to personnel issues.

Population Representation in the Military Service is a very detailed annual report that provides a continuing analysis of the characteristics of military personnel. Narrative text is combined with statistical tables and charts in looking at such characteristics as age, race, ethnicity, sex, educational attainment, marital status, Armed Forces Qualification Test (AFQT) category, and occupational area. Both active personnel and reserve personnel are included. Some longitudinal data are also included.

DEPARTMENT OF DEFENSE CONTRACT REPORTS
Checklist

Department of Defense Prime Contract Awards. WEB. (semiannual) U.S. Department of Defense. Washington Headquarters Services. Directorate for Information Operations and Reports. D 1.57/3: Item 0310-E-13. ASI 3542-1.<http://web1.whs.osd.mil/peidhome/procstat/procstat.htm>.

> Content: number and net value of military prime contract awards of $25,000 or more.

100 Companies Receiving the Largest Dollar Volumes of Prime Contract Awards. WEB. (annual) U.S. Department of Defense. Washington Headquarters Services. Directorate for Information Operations and Services. D 1.57: Item 0310-E-16. ASI 3544-5.<http://web1.whs.osd.mil/peidhome/procstat/procstat.htm>;<http://purl.access.gpo.gov/GPO/LPS663>.

> Content: statistics on the top 100 defense contractors and their subsidiaries; listings of the individual companies and parent companies.

100 Contractors Receiving the Largest Dollar Volume of Prime Contract Awards for Research, Development, Test, and Evaluation Fiscal Year. WEB. (annual) U.S. Department of Defense. Washington Headquarters Services. Directorate for Information Operations and Reports. D 1.57/2: Item 0310-E-16. ASI 3544-4.<http://web1.whs.osd.mil/peidhome/procstat/procstat.htm>;<http://purl.access.gpo.gov/GPO/LPS663>.

> Content: statistics on top 100 contractors; listing of the individual companies in alphabetical and rank order.

Prime Contract Awards by Region and State. WEB. (annual) U.S. Department of Defense. Washington Headquarters Services. Directorate for Information Operations and Reports. D 1.57/5: Item 0310-E-13. ASI 3544-11.<http://web1.whs.osd.mil/peidhome/geostats/geostat.htm>.

> Coverage: regions, states.
> Content: statistics on prime contract awards over $25,000 by category and contractor type.

Prime Contract Awards by State. WEB. MF. (annual) U.S. Department of Defense. Washington Headquarters Services. Directorate for Information Operations and Reports. D 1.57/6: Item 0310-E-13. ASI 3544-45.<http://web1.whs.osd.mil/peidhome/geostats/geostat.htm>.

AUTHORIZED PERSONNEL STRENGTH IN THE PENTAGON BUILDING

FISCAL YEARS 1945 THROUGH PRESENT

YEAR A/	TOTAL	MILITARY	CIVILIAN
1945	29,178	10,809	18,369
1951	28,827	10,413	18,414
1952	28,786	10,516	18,270
1953	29,263	11,324	17,939
1954	27,199	9,895	17,304
1955	28,049	10,021	18,028
1956	27,317	9,795	17,522
1957	26,691	10,055	16,636
1958	25,608	9,950	15,658
1959	25,251	9,913	15,338
1960	24,538	9,414	15,124
1961	25,329	10,912	14,417
1962	24,863	10,651	14,212
1963	24,757	11,106	13,651
1964	24,518	11,548	12,970
1965	26,057	11,884	14,173
1966	27,172	12,353	14,819
1967	29,737	13,313	16,424
1968	28,945	13,501	15,444
1969	27,482	13,498	13,984
1970	24,726	11,783	12,943
1971	25,939	12,150	13,789
1972	25,338	12,178	13,160
1973	24,103	11,718	12,385
1974	22,632	10,667	11,965
1975	22,879	10,904	11,975
1976	22,547	10,438	12,109

Prepared by: Washington Headquarters Services
Directorate for Information Operations and Reports

17

Source: *Selected Manpower Statistics*, FY 1998, p. 17.

Figure 40.1: Sample Table from *Selected Manpower Statistics*.

Coverage: states, counties.

Content: statistics on total value of contracts by type of contracts.

Educational and Nonprofit Institutions Receiving Prime Contract Awards for Research, Development, Test and Evaluation. WEB. (annual) U.S. Department of Defense. Washington Headquarters Services. Directorate for Information Operations and Reports. D 1.57/8: Item 0310-E-21. ASI 3544-17.<http://web1.whs.osd.mil/peidhome/procstat/procstat.htm>.

Coverage: individual institutions and agencies.

Content: listing of contract awards of $25,000 or more issued to U.S. and foreign educational and nonprofit institutions and government agencies.

Prime Contract Awards by Service Category and Federal Supply Classification. WEB. (annual) U.S. Department of Defense. Washington Headquarters Services. Directorate for Information Operations and Reports. D 1.57/4: Item 0310-E-13. ASI 3544-18.<http://web1.whs.osd.mil/peidhome/prodserv/prodserv.htm>.

Coverage: U.S.

Content: prime contract awards of $25,000 or more arranged by detailed procurement categories.

Prime Contract Awards, Size Distribution. MF. WEB. (annual) U.S. Department of Defense. Washington Headquarters Services. Directorate for Information Operations and Reports. D 1.57/3-5: Item 0310-E-13. ASI 3544-19.<http://web1.whs.osd.mil/peidhome/procstat/procstat.htm>.

Coverage: U.S.

Content: statistics on number and net value of prime contract awards of $25,000 or more arranged by size.

Companies Participating in the Department of Defense Subcontracting Program. WEB. (semiannual) U.S. Department of Defense. Washington Headquarters Services. Directorate for Information Operations and Reports. D 1.57/9: Item 0310-E-18. ASI 3542-17.<http://web1.whs.osd.mil/peidhome/procstat/procstat.htm>.

> Coverage: U.S., states.

> Content: summary statistics on subcontracting programs and commitments to small and disadvantaged business firms.

Standard Tabulations. WEB. (annual) U.S. Department of Defense. Washington Headquarters Services. Directorate for Information Operations and Reports.<http://web1.whs.osd.mil/peidhome/procstat/procstat.htm>.

> Content: series of downloadable data files providing detailed contract and procurement data.

ST01. Prime Contractors with Awards Over $25,000 by Name, Locations, and Contract Number.

> Content: individual name listings of contractors, with location, contract number, and dollar amount of contract.

ST06. Dollar Summary of Federal Supply Classification and Service Category by Company.

> Content: individual name listings of contractors, with location and dollar amount of contract, by Federal Supply Classification and Service Category (Army, Navy, Air Force, etc.).

ST08. Prime Contract Awards Over $25,000 by Weapon System, Contractor, and Work Performance.

> Content: individual name listings of contractors with state or country location, Federal Supply Classification, and dollar amount of contract.

ST11. Geographic List of Prime Contract Awards.

> Content: individual name listings, by city, state and country location.

ST18. Alphabetical List of Prime Contract Awards.

> Content: individual name listings arranged alphabetically, with city, state, and country location.

ST19. DoD Prime Contract Awards Over $25,000 by Contractor, State, and City.

> Content: individual name listings of contractors, with city, state and country location, and by Service Category (Army, Navy, Air Force, etc.).

ST24. Prime Contract Awards Over $25,000 by State, City, Place, and Contractor.

> Content: individual name listings of contractors, with state, city, and place.

ST25. Dollar Summary of Prime Contract Awards by State, County, Contractor and Place.

> Content: individual name listings of contractors, by state, county, place, and by Service Category (Army, Navy, Air Force, etc.).

ST26. Dollar Summary of Prime Contract Awards with Principle Place of Performance Outside the U.S., by Country and Contractor.

> Content: individual name listings of contractors by country.

ST27. DoD Prime Contractor Places with Awards Totaling $5 Million or More by Locations — Three Year Comparison.

> Content: individual name listings of contractors by state, county, and place; includes program and amount of awards for last three years.

ST28. Prime Contract Awards of $25,000 or More by FSC/SVC and Purchasing Office.

> Content: total dollar amounts of awards and number of awards by department; purchasing office; state; city; U.S. Business and Small Business categories; and by Federal Supply Classification and Service Category.

DMS/FI Contract Awards. WEB. Dialog.<www.dialog.com>.

> Content: prime contract awards of $25,000 or more.

Federal Prime Contracts Data Base. CD-ROM. (formerly titled *ICAR CD-ROM*) Fairfax City, VA: Eagle Eye Publishers.

> Content: prime contract awards of $25,000 or more.

Discussion

The Directorate for Information Operations and Reports (DIOR) collects and disseminates information on contract awards and procurement activities of the Department of Defense. Several of these reports are listed here. As in the case of the DIOR reports cited earlier, most are available from the DIOR Web site, with some data sources also available for purchase from NTIS.

Department of Defense Prime Contract Awards is one of the more basic reports in the series, giving aggregate figures on the net value and distribution of prime contract awards of $25,000 or more. *100 Companies Receiving the Largest Dollar Volumes of Prime Contract Awards* and *100 Contractors Receiving the Largest Dollar Volume of Prime Contract Awards for Research, Development, Test, and Evaluation, [fiscal year]* are two similar reports that are useful for obtaining individual company data on the largest defense contractors. A series of similar reports are also listed here that give information on prime contracts by various features—by region and state, state, educational and nonprofit institutional status, by service category and federal supply classification, and by size distribution.

Companies Participating in the Department of Defense Subcontracting Program gives summary statistics for Department of Defense subcontracting programs to small business firms, small disadvantaged business firms, historically black colleges and universities/minority institutions, and women owned small business firms. Dollar amounts and distribution percentages are included, as well as listing awards by location. Individual company listings by branch of service are also included in the report.

The DIOR also makes available a series of data sets called *Standard Tabulations.* From their Web site, these tabulations can be downloaded in PCL 4 (HP Printer Control Language) format and printed on a printer. A sample of each *Standard Tabulation* is included at the site so the *Standard Tabulation* may be previewed before it is downloaded. DIOR also makes many of these data sets available for purchase from NTIS.

The *Standard Tabulations* currently available from the Web site are listed here. They provide detailed information on contracts and procurement activities. Most provide data on individual companies or contractors, and are particularly useful when searching for the individual company or contractor data or when searching for contracts by detailed geographic locations.

Two commercial databases of prime contract awards data are also included here. The *DMS/FI Contract Awards* is available through Dialog as File 588. It includes non-classified prime contract awards of $25,000 or more. *Federal Prime Contracts Data Base* covers similar contract award information, in a CD-ROM format.

INDEXES
Checklist

American Statistics Index (ASI). PRINT. (monthly) 1973–. Bethesda, MD: Congressional Information Service.

Statistical Universe. WEB. Bethesda, MD: Congressional Information Service.

Discussion

American Statistics Index (ASI) is a comprehensive index to government statistics, available in both a print and electronic format. (For more information on *ASI*, see Chapter 3, "The Basics of Searching.") To find more information on defense and military statistics, search subject headings beginning with "Military" and "Defense, " and the headings "National defense," "Armed services," "Military personnel," "Defense contracts and procurement," "Government contracts and procurement," the names of individual units of the Department of Defense, and the names of individual weapons.

CHAPTER 41
Energy Statistics

The primary source of government energy statistics is the Energy Information Administration located within the Department of Energy. Energy-related statistics can also be found in many of the economic censuses, particularly in relation to specific industries.

SEARCH STRATEGY

This chapter is an example of the statistical search strategy. The strategy is as follows:

1. Examine the *Statistical Abstract of the United States* and other sources listed in the "General Statistical Sources" section of this chapter for quick, basic statistics;
2. Locate more detailed statistics in the comprehensive sources listed in the "Energy Statistical Sources" section;
3. See the sections in this chapter relating to major energy sources if interested in a specific energy source;
4. Use census publications to locate statistics on energy consumption by specific industries and data on energy-related housing characteristics; and
5. See also the indexes and related materials listed at the end of this chapter.

GENERAL STATISTICAL SOURCES
Checklist

Statistical Abstract of the United States. PRINT. WEB. (annual) 1878–. U.S. Department of Commerce. Economics and Statistics Administration. Bureau of the Census. C 3.134: Item 0150. ASI 2324-1. GPO.<http://www.census.gov/statab/www/>;<http://purl.access.gpo.gov/GPO/LPS2878>.
> Coverage: world, world regions, country groupings, selected countries, U.S., states.

Content: fuel resources; energy production and consumption; expenditures and prices; trade; electricity; utilities; nuclear power.

Statistical Abstract of the United States. CD-ROM. (annual) 1993–. U.S. Department of Commerce. Bureau of the Census. C 3.134/7: Item 0150-B. ASI 2324-14.
> Content: CD-ROM version of the *Statistical Abstract*.

Historical Statistics of the United States: Colonial Times to 1970. Parts 1-2. PRINT. (1975) U.S. Department of Commerce. Bureau of the Census. C 3.134/2:H 62/789-970/pt.1-2. Item 0151. ASI (76) 2328-2. GPO.
> Coverage: U.S.
> Content: fuel consumption; electricity production; electric utility plants and characteristics.

Historical Statistics of the United States on CD-ROM: Colonial Times to 1970. CD-ROM. (1997) New York, NY: Cambridge University Press.
> Content: CD-ROM version of *Historical Statistics of the United States.*

State and Metropolitan Area Data Book. PRINT. WEB. (irregular) 1979–. U.S. Department of Commerce. Economics and Statistics Administration. Bureau of the Census. C 3.134/5: Item 0150. ASI 2328-54. GPO.<http://www.census.gov/statab/www.smadb.html>.
> Coverage: U.S., states.
> Content: energy consumption by type and end-use sector; energy expenditures by selected source and end-use sector; electric and gas utility sales and revenues; electricity generation.

State and Metropolitan Area Data Book. CD-ROM. (irregular) 1997/98–. U.S. Department of Commerce. Economics and Statistics Administration. Bureau of the Census. (Not distributed to depository libraries)
> Content: CD-ROM version of the *State and Metropolitan Area Data Book.*

Discussion

The *Statistical Abstract of the United States* has a chapter on energy that contains some basic statistics. The index should also be checked under individual types of energy or fuels, as data may also be found in other chapters such as "Natural Resources." Statistics are selected from many of the more detailed sources covered in this chapter. Source notes at the end of each table can direct the user to more current or more detailed sources for the information in that table. The full text of recent editions of the *Statistical Abstract* is available on the Census Bureau Web site as PDF files. The *Statistical Abstract* is also available on CD-ROM. The CD uses Adobe Acrobat software and contains some additional geographic areas and time series in the form of spreadsheet files that are not in the printed version. Similar (although more limited) statistics for earlier years can be found in *Historical Statistics of the United States: Colonial Times to 1970*. A CD-ROM version of *Historical Statistics* is available from Cambridge University Press.

The *State and Metropolitan Area Data Book* gives statistics at the state and national level for basic consumption and expenditures and for utilities. The *State and Metropolitan Area Data Book* is available as a PDF file on the Census Bureau Web site and on CD-ROM.

ENERGY STATISTICAL SOURCES
Checklist

Annual Energy Review. MF. WEB. (annual) 1977–. U.S. Department of Energy. Energy Information Administration. Office of Energy Markets and End Use. E 3.1/2: (Earlier, E 3.1: year/v.2) Item 0429-J-01. ASI 3164-74. GPO.<http://www.eia.doe.gov/aer/>;<http://tonto.eia.doe.gov/bookshelf/index.html>;<http://purl.access.gpo.gov/GPO/LPS3492>.

> Coverage: world, world regions, country groupings, countries, U.S., regions, states.
> Content: energy consumption and resources; production, trade, supply, and prices for each energy source.

Monthly Energy Review. PRINT. WEB. (monthly) 1974–. U.S. Department of Energy. Energy Information Administration. Office of Energy Markets and End Use. E 3.9: Item 0434-A-02. ASI 3162-24. GPO.<http://www.eia.doe.gov/emeu/mer/contents.html>;<http://purl.access.gpo.gov/GPO/LPS1714>;<http://tonto.eia.doe.gov/bookshelf/index.html>;<http://purl.access.gpo.gov/GPO/LPS3492>.

> Coverage: world, world regions, country groupings, countries, U.S., limited divisions and states.
> Content: consumption, production, supply, trade, prices by energy source.

Historical Monthly Energy Review 1973–1992. MF. WEB. (1994) U.S. Department of Energy. Energy Information Administration. Office of Energy Markets and End Use. E 3.2:H 62/2/973-92. Item 0429-T-11. ASI (94) 3168-123.<http://www.eia.doe.gov/bookshelf/multi.html>; <http://www.eia.doe.gov/historic.html>;<http://tonto.eia.doe.gov/bookshelf/index.html>.;<http://purl.access.gpo.gov/GPO/LPS3492>.

> Coverage: country groupings, selected countries, U.S., selected states.
> Content: historical monthly data series corresponding to the tables in the *Monthly Energy Review*; consumption, production, supply, trade, prices for major energy sources.

Annual Energy Outlook. MF. WEB. (annual) 1977–. U.S. Department of Energy. Energy Information Administration. Office of Integrated Analysis and Forecasting. E 3.1/4: (Earlier, E 3.1:year/v.3) Item 0429-J-01. ASI 3164-75. GPO.<http://www.eia.doe.gov/oiaf/aeo.html>;<http://tonto.eia.doe.gov/bookshelf/index.html>;<http://purl.access.gpo.gov/GPO/LPS3492>.

> Coverage: world, world regions, country groupings, selected countries, U.S.
> Content: analysis of energy demand and supply trends; projection tables for production, consumption, exports, imports, and prices for various energy sources under different growth assumptions; consumption and prices by end-use sector; gross domestic product; disposable personal income.

International Energy Annual. MF. WEB. (annual) 1979–. U.S. Department of Energy. Energy Information Administration. Office of Energy Markets and End Use. E 3.11/20: Item 0435-H. ASI 3164-50. GPO.<http://www.eia.doe.gov/emeu/iea/contents.html>;<http://purl.access.gpo.gov/GPO/LPS3018>;<http://tonto.eia.doe.gov/bookshelf/index.html>;<http://purl.access.gpo.gov/GPO/LPS3492>.

> Coverage: world, world regions, country groupings, countries, U.S.
> Content: production, consumption, supply, trade, prices by energy source.

State Energy Data Report [year] Consumption Estimates. MF. WEB. (annual) U.S. Department of Energy. Energy Information Administration. Office of Energy Markets and End Use. E 3.42: Item 0435-E-24. ASI 3164-39. GPO.<http://www.eia.doe.gov/emeu/states/_states.html>.(Select Consumption data from the menu);<http://tonto.eia.doe.gov/bookshelf/index.html>;<http://purl.access.gpo.gov/GPO/LPS3492>.

> Coverage: U.S., states.
> Content: time series data on energy consumption by source and end-use sector.

Energy Information Administration Home Page. WEB. U.S. Department of Energy. Energy Information Administration. <http://www.eia.doe.gov/>.

> Content: full-text energy publications, tables, and databases arranged by energy source, topic or geographic level.

Energy InfoDisc. CD-ROM. (quarterly) 1996–. U.S. Department of Energy. Energy Information Administration. E 3.60: Item 0429-K-08. ASI 3162-47.<http://tonto.eia.doe.gov/bookshelf/index.html>;<http://purl.access.gpo.gov/GPO/LPS3492>; Related site:<http://www.eia.doe.gov/infodisc.html>.

> Content: full-text energy publications and database applications.

Discussion

These publications are some of the most popular and most comprehensive sources from the Energy Information Administration (EIA). *Annual Energy Review* is a detailed, comprehensive overview of energy statistics. A narrative overview chapter analyzes energy history and trends. The other chapters are statistical with graphs and charts illustrating each table. An "Energy Overview" section gives summary statistics on production, consumption, and trade. An "End-Use Energy Consumption" section covers energy use by end-use sector, such as residential or commercial. Tables cover household energy use, motor vehicle efficiency, commercial building energy use, and manufacturing energy use. Other sections are devoted to each major energy source, such as petroleum, natural gas, or nuclear energy. There are also sections on "Energy Resources," "Financial Indicators," and "International Energy." Statistics center on production, consumption, trade, and price data for the various energy sources. The Web version provides a combination of formats including HTML, PDF, spreadsheet files, and an interactive query option.

The *Monthly Energy Review* also provides detailed, comprehensive statistics on energy resources and is more current than the *Annual Energy Review*. This periodical is almost entirely statistical. It gives annual data for several years and monthly data for the last two or three years. An overview section is followed by sections on each major energy source. Other sections cover energy consumption, energy prices, and international energy. A very brief summary introduces each section, followed by a page of graphs and charts illustrating key data items. The Web site provides a combination of formats including HTML, PDF, and spreadsheet files, a database version, and downloadable database applications. The *Historical Monthly Energy Review* provides monthly (as well as annual) historical data from 1973 through 1992 that correspond to that in the *Monthly Energy Review*. It contains previously unpublished revisions to *Monthly Energy Review* data and provides a more accurate, one-stop source for older statistics.

The *Annual Energy Outlook* analyzes trends in energy supply and demand. A narrative section with graphs and charts summarizes trends and issues affecting supply and demand and analyzes the market outlook for specific fuel sources. More detailed projections tables in appendices present five scenarios based on different variables such as differing oil prices and different levels of growth. These tables cover supply and disposition, prices, production, consumption, and trade for each energy source. Consumption data are given by end-use sector, such as residential or commercial, and covers the amount of energy used for specific applications such as heating, dishwashers, or refrigeration. International coverage is limited to petroleum. This title gives guidance on what energy sources may be most predominant in the future, what the primary uses of energy will be, and what the supply of each source is likely to be. Supplemental tables are available on the Web site in the same location as the main report. These tables provide more detailed projections by census division and end-

use sector. A data query option is also available for consumption and price data from the supplement.

The *International Energy Annual* is a comprehensive source for international energy information. Sections cover world energy consumption, world energy production, prices, energy reserves, and each type of energy source. This title gives information on such things as Malaysia's oil production or the natural gas consumption of Poland.

The *State Energy Data Report* covers the time period 1960 to date and provides consistent, historical consumption trends by state. Tables for each state cover consumption by energy source and by end-use sector (residential, commercial, industrial, transportation, and electric utilities).

The *Energy Information Administration Home Page* provides full-text access to energy publications including all those discussed in this chapter. The home page menu provides a variety of different options for locating information. Users may select a particular energy source (e.g. petroleum, natural gas), selected topic areas (e.g. energy users, finance, historical data), or geographic levels (international or state data). Each category page lists the data sources available in that area, including tables, publications, and databases. The home page also includes a "Bookshelf" option to go directly to publication listings.

The *Energy InfoDisc* CD-ROM contains PDF files for the full text of recent editions of Energy Information Administration publications including those mentioned in this chapter. Database applications from which some of the publications are generated are also included. Some of these databases include *Annual Energy Outlook*, *Monthly Energy Review*, *State Energy Data*, and *World Energy Database*. Several of the databases require Microsoft Access, an additional database software application. The agency's Web site includes a publications database search feature to locate these publications on the Web site. Users may search by words in the title, description, author, or year.

SOURCES ON COAL
Checklist

Quarterly Coal Report. MF. WEB. (quarterly) 1982–. U.S. Department of Energy. Energy Information Administration. Office of Coal, Nuclear, Electric and Alternate Fuels. E 3.11/9: Item 0435-G. ASI 3162-37. GPO.<http://www.eia.doe.gov/bookshelf/coal.html>;<http://www.eia.doe.gov/cneaf/coal/quarterly/qcr_sum.html>;<http://purl.access.gpo.gov/GPO/LPS1251>;<http://tonto.eia.doe.gov/bookshelf/index.html>;<http://purl.access.gpo.gov/GPO/LPS3492>.

> Coverage: world, world regions, countries, U.S., divisions, states, coal-producing regions, customs districts, individual utility plants.
> Content: coal production; exports and imports; average price of exports and imports; receipts and average price by end-use sector; consumption by end-use sector; stocks; coke production, trade, consumption, and stocks; cost, quality, origin, and destination of coal received.

Coal Industry Annual. MF. WEB. (annual) 1993–. U.S. Department of Energy. Energy Information Administration. Office of Coal, Nuclear, Electric and Alternate Fuels. E 3.11/7-3: (Issued earlier under other titles) Item 0435-E-02. ASI 3164-104. GPO.<http://www.eia.doe.gov/bookshelf/coal.html>;<http://tonto.eia.doe.gov/bookshelf/index.html>;<http://purl.access.gpo.gov/GPO/LPS3492>.

> Coverage: world, world region, countries, U.S., divisions, customs districts, coal-producing regions, states, counties.
> Content: coal production; consumption; distribution; stocks; quality; trade; number, characteristics, and list of mines; average mine and delivered prices; productivity and employment; recoverable reserves.

Weekly Coal Production. WEB. (weekly) U.S. Department of Energy. Energy Information Administration. Office of Coal, Nuclear, Electric, and Alternate Fuels. (Earlier, E 3.11/4:, MF) ASI 3162-1.<http://www.eia.doe.gov/cneaf/coal/weekly/weekly_html/wcppage.htm>.

> Coverage: U.S., states, coal-producing regions.
> Content: coal production.

Coal Information at a Glance Web Page. WEB. U.S. Department of Energy. Energy Information Administration.<http://www.eia.doe.gov/fuelcoal.html>.

> Content: statistical tables and full-text publications relating to coal.

Discussion

Quarterly Coal Report is the most general and comprehensive periodical on coal. It contains brief statistical chapters for each of the following areas: production, exports and imports, receipts, consumption, and stocks. Data are for recent quarters, current and previous year, and selected earlier years. An appendix provides additional detailed information on coal imports to the individual utility level.

Coal Industry Annual gives detailed statistics on mine production covering mine type, mining methods, mine production range, mine capacity, and production of major individual mines. Other areas covered include reserves; distribution by origin, destination, and method of transportation; major distributors and consumers; consumption by end-use sector; prices; and coal quality. An appendix contains one-page profiles of each state with basic coal statistics for recent years.

The *Weekly Coal Production* Web site is the most current source of data. One basic table is available for each week giving total production by state and region. Monthly and semiannual versions of the table are also available.

The Energy Information Administration's *Coal Information at a Glance Web Page* provides a guide and access to the agency's coal data. A data table menu lists basic topics such as imports, exports, prices, or production with links to annual or quarterly statistical tables and summary information. Users can also select a publications option that provides a list of full-text publications on coal, including the titles discussed in this section, and additional titles, such as *State Coal Profiles*.

SOURCES ON PETROLEUM AND NATURAL GAS

Checklist

Petroleum Supply Monthly. MF. WEB. (monthly) 1982–. U.S. Department of Energy. Energy Information Administration. Office of Oil and Gas. E 3.11/5: (Formerly published under other titles) Item 0435-J-01. ASI 3162-6. GPO.<http://www.eia.doe.gov/oil_gas/petroleum/data_publications/petroleum_supply_monthly/psm.html>;<http://tonto.eia.doe.gov/bookshelf/index.html>;<http://purl.access.gpo.gov/GPO/LPS3492>.

> Coverage: world, country groupings, countries, U.S., Petroleum Administration for Defense (PAD) districts, refining districts, states.
> Content: supply and disposition, production, refinery operations, exports and imports, stocks, product movements.

Petroleum Supply Annual. MF. WEB. (annual) 1981–. U.S. Department of Energy. Energy Information Administration. Office of Oil and Gas. E 3.11/5-5: Item 0435-J-01. ASI 3164-2. GPO. Vol. 1:<http://www.eia.doe.gov/oil_gas/petroleum/data_publications/petroleum_supply_annual/psa_volume1/psa_volume1.html>;<http://purl.access.gpo.gov/GPO/LPS2326>; Vol. 2:<http://www.eia.doe.gov/oil_gas/petroleum/data_publications/petroleum_supply_annual/psa_volume2/psa_volume2.html>;<http://purl.access.gpo.gov/GPO/LPS2327>;<http://tonto.eia.doe.gov/bookshelf/index.html>;<http://purl.access.gpo.gov/GPO/LPS3492>.

> Coverage: world, country groupings, countries, U.S., Petroleum Administration for Defense (PAD) districts, refining districts, states, refineries.
> Content: supply and disposition; production; stocks; exports and imports; refinery operations and capacity; product movements.

Weekly Petroleum Status Report. MF. WEB. (weekly) 1979–. U.S. Department of Energy. Energy Information Administration. E 3.32: Item 0429-T-58. ASI 3162-32. GPO.<http://www.eia.doe.gov/oil_gas/petroleum/data_publications/weekly_petroleum_status_report/wpsr.html>.

> Coverage: world, country groupings, countries, U.S., Petroleum Administration for Defense (PAD) districts.
> Content: supply, production, stocks, imports, and prices.

International Petroleum Monthly. MF. WEB. (monthly) Mar. 1989–. U.S. Department of Energy. Energy Information Administration. Energy Markets and Contingency Information Division. E 3.11/5-6: (Earlier title, *International Petroleum Statistics Report*) Item 0435-J-01. ASI 3162-42. GPO.<http://www.eia.doe.gov/emeu/ipsr/contents.html>;<http://purl.access.gpo.gov/GPO/LPS1643>;<http://www.eia.doe.gov/bookshelf/oil.html>;<http://tonto.eia.doe.gov/bookshelf/index.html>;<http://purl.access.gpo.gov/GPO/LPS3492>.

> Coverage: world, country groupings, countries, U.S.
> Content: production, supply, demand, imports, and stocks.

Natural Gas Annual. MF. WEB. (annual) 1976–. U.S. Department of Energy. Energy Information Administration. Office of Oil and Gas. E 3.11/2-2: (Title varies) Item 0429-K-03. ASI 3164-4. GPO.<http://www.eia.doe.gov/oil_gas/natural_gas/data_publications/natural_gas_annual/nga.html>;<http://

tonto.eia.doe.gov/bookshelf/index.html>;<http://
purl.access.gpo.gov/GPO/LPS3492>.

> Coverage: selected countries, U.S., divisions, states, leading natural gas companies.
> Content: supply, transmission, consumption, and consumer prices.

Historical Natural Gas Annual. WEB. (annual) U.S. Department of Energy. Energy Information Administration. Office of Oil and Gas. (Issued earlier as v. 2 of *Natural Gas Annual*) ASI 3164-4.<http://www.eia.doe.gov/oil_gas/natural_gas/data_publications/historical_natural_gas_annual/hnga.html>;<http://purl.access.gpo.gov/GPO/LPS2308>.

> Coverage: U.S., divisions, states.
> Content: historical supply and disposition data; production, consumption, storage, movements, prices, deliveries.

Natural Gas Monthly. MF. WEB. (monthly) 1977–. U.S. Department of Energy. Energy Information Administration. Office of Oil and Gas. E 3.11: Item 0435-E-10. ASI 3162-4. GPO.<http://www.eia.doe.gov/oil_gas/natural_gas/data_publications/natural_gas_monthly/ngm.html>;<http://purl.access.gpo.gov/GPO/LPS2309>;<http://tonto.eia.doe.gov/bookshelf/index.html>;<http://purl.access.gpo.gov/GPO/LPS3492>.

> Coverage: selected countries, U.S., states.
> Content: production; supply and disposition; consumption; deliveries by end-use sector; exports and imports; storage; prices.

U.S. Crude Oil, Natural Gas, and Natural Gas Liquids Reserves. MF. WEB. (annual) 1977–. U.S. Department of Energy. Energy Information Administration. Office of Oil and Gas. E 3.34: Item 0429-K-02. ASI 3164-46. GPO. <http://www.eia.doe.gov/oil_gas/natural_gas/data_publications/nat_data_publications.html>; <http://www.eia.doe.gov/oil_gas/petroleum/data_publications/pet_data_publications.html>; <http://www.eia.doe.gov/bookshelf/oil.html>.

> Coverage: world, country groupings, selected countries, U.S., states, state subdivisions, top oil and gas fields.
> Content: reserves; production; exploration and development activities.

U.S. Petroleum Information at a Glance Web Page. WEB. U.S. Department of Energy. Energy Information Administration. <http://www.eia.doe.gov/oil_gas/petroleum/pet_frame.html>;<http://purl.access.gpo.gov/GPO/LPS1645>.

> Content: full-text publications and resources on petroleum.

U.S. Natural Gas Information at a Glance Web Page. WEB. U.S. Department of Energy. Energy Information Administration. <http://www.eia.doe.gov/oil_gas/natural_gas/nat_frame.html>.

> Content: full-text publications and resources on natural gas.

Discussion

Petroleum Supply Monthly contains supply and disposition data on petroleum and petroleum products. For each product, data are provided on production, stocks, and exports and imports. Refinery inputs, production, and stocks are also covered, as are movements of crude oil and petroleum products by various means of transportation. This title answers such questions as how much kerosene was produced by refineries or how much crude oil was imported from Angola.

The *Petroleum Supply Annual* is issued in two volumes. Volume 1 contains final annual data corresponding to the monthly tables in *Petroleum Supply Monthly*. An additional section on refinery capacity is included that gives capacity and production for individual refineries. Volume 2 contains the final month-by-month tables replacing those originally published in individual issues of *Petroleum Supply Monthly*.

The *Weekly Petroleum Status Report* contains current information on the supply of crude oil, motor gasoline, and other petroleum products. There are several tables on the stocks and prices of each type of product, as well as tables on imports.

International Petroleum Monthly provides current and historical statistics on international oil supply and demand. Section 1 contains monthly and annual time series on production, supply, demand, and stocks. Section 2 gives statistics on the oil supply and demand balance for the world. Section 3 covers oil imports. Data in this section show imports from one country or country grouping to another. Section 4 contains historical series for several years.

The *Natural Gas Annual* contains extensive data on the supply and disposition of natural gas. It contains an introductory overview and sections on supply, transmission, consumption, and consumer prices. Each section begins with a short narrative summary. Supply data cover total withdrawals, offshore withdrawals, number of wells, and wellhead value. Transmission tables show interstate movements, imports and exports, and storage data. Consumption tables show total consumption and consumption by end-use. The consumer prices section gives average city gate prices, average delivered prices, and information on leading suppliers. A large portion of the publication is devoted to summary statistics tables for each census division and state. *Historical Natural Gas Annual* is a companion volume providing national historical data since 1930 and state historical data since 1967.

Natural Gas Monthly contains a brief narrative overview and statistical tables covering supply, production, consumption, storage, and prices. Examples of information given include the amount of natural gas produced in each state, the amount of natural gas delivered to residential consumers in each state, and its average price.

U.S. Crude Oil, Natural Gas, and Natural Gas Liquids Reserves is a more specialized source. It gives data on total reserves, changes in reserves, and production. An overview section summarizes notable developments. Individual sections discuss crude oil, natural gas, and natural gas liquids. An appendix provides historical statistics on reserves.

The Energy Information Administration maintains Web pages on petroleum and natural gas that provide full-text access to the agency's publications. The *U.S. Petroleum Information at a Glance Web Page* lists topics such as resources/reserves, stocks, petroleum overview, and specific petroleum products. For each topic there is a list of data tables and publications. Data tables are listed by frequency, such as annual or weekly. Weekly reports provide basic current data for several petroleum products. A selection of monthly and annual reports is also available, including most of the petroleum publications discussed in this section. Additional main menu options provide access to data publications, analysis publications, feature articles, and presentations. The *U.S. Natural Gas Information at a Glance Web Page* is identical in format, listing topics with data tables by frequency. Additional main menu options include data publications, analysis publications, feature articles, and presentations. All of the natural gas publications discussed in this section, as well as additional publications, are available in full text.

SOURCES ON ELECTRICITY

Checklist

Electric Power Monthly. MF. WEB. (monthly) 1980–. U.S. Department of Energy. Energy Information Administration. Office of Coal, Nuclear, Electric and Alternate Fuels. E 3.11/17-8: Item 0435-E-18. ASI 3162-35. GPO.<http://www.eia.doe.gov/cneaf/electricity/epm/epm_sum.html>; <http://www.eia.doe.gov/bookshelf/electric.html>;<http://tonto.eia.doe.gov/bookshelf/index.html>;<http://purl.access.gpo.gov/GPO/LPS3492>.

 Coverage: U.S., North American Electric Reliability Council (NERC) regions, divisions, states, individual utilities.
 Content: electricity generation; fuel consumption to produce electricity; fuel receipts, costs, and stocks; sales and revenue.

Electric Power Annual. MF. WEB. (annual) 1981–. U.S. Department of Energy. Energy Information Administration. Office of Coal, Nuclear, Electric and Alternate Fuels. E 3.11/17-10: Item 0435-E-18. ASI 3164-11. GPO. Vol. 1:<http://www.eia.doe.gov/cneaf/electricity/epav1/epav1_sum.html>; Vol. 2:<http://www.eia.doe.gov/cneaf/electricity/epav2/epav2_sum.html>;<http://www.eia.doe.gov/bookshelf/electric.html>;<http://tonto.eia.doe.gov/bookshelf/index.html>;<http://purl.access.gpo.gov/GPO/LPS3492>.

 Coverage: U.S., North American Electric Reliability Council (NERC) regions, divisions, states.
 Content: electricity generation and generating capacity; fuel sources, consumption, stocks, receipts, and costs; electricity sales and revenue; utility finances; environmental statistics.

Inventory of Electric Utility Power Plants in the United States. MF. WEB. (annual) 1975–. U.S. Department of Energy. Energy Information Administration. Office of Coal, Nuclear, Electric and Alternate Fuels. E 3.29: (Earlier title, *Inventory of Power Plants in the United States*) Item 0429-T-59. ASI 3164-36. GPO.<http://www.eia.doe.gov/cneaf/electricity/ipp/ipp_sum.html>;<http://www.eia.doe.gov/bookshelf/electric.html>;<http://tonto.eia.doe.gov/bookshelf/index.html>;<http://purl.access.gpo.gov/GPO/LPS3492>.

 Coverage: U.S., federal regions, North American Electric Reliability Council (NERC) regions, divisions, states, individual utilities.
 Content: electrical generating capacity by fuel source; existing and planned electric generating units with data on primary energy source and capacity rating.

Electricity Information at a Glance Web Page. WEB. U.S. Department of Energy. Energy Information Administration. <http://www.eia.doe.gov/fuelelectric.html>

 Content: full-text publications and resources on electricity.

Discussion

Electric Power Monthly presents summary data directed to a general audience on electricity generation, the fuel consumed or energy source used in producing electricity, sales, and revenues. Each issue begins with a monthly update and summary of industry developments. More detailed chapters cover net generation; consumption of fossil fuels; stocks of fossil fuels; receipts and cost of fossil fuels; sales, revenue, and average revenue per kilowatthour; and plant data. This source can tell the user how much electricity is generated by nuclear power versus coal or what the average revenue per kilowatthour is from the residential sector. For each individual utility information is given on generation by fuel source, fuel consumption, and receipts and cost of fuel.

The *Electric Power Annual* covers the same areas in greater detail, providing more data on generating capacity. There is also more information on utility finances and environmental factors, such as emissions. The annual does not, however, provide data on individual utilities. The annual consists of two volumes. Volume 1 contains a comprehensive industry review and outlook with a statistical appendix. Volume 2 contains an industry overview with additional chapters on retail sales and revenue, financial statistics, environmental statistics, power transactions, demand-side management, and nonutility power producers. Each chapter contains a narrative analysis and statistical tables.

Inventory of Electric Utility Power Plants in the United States lists each individual power plant by state. The name and location of each unit is given plus its primary energy source, capacity rating, and date placed in service. Separate tables list units added during the year, units retired during the year, proposed unit changes, and projected additions for the next 10 years. Summary statistical tables provide data on present and planned capacity and fuel sources.

The *Electricity Information at a Glance Web Page* provides access to data tables and other information on electricity. Topics included in the data tables menu section include electricity generation, financial statistics, and retail electricity sales. A featured topics menu section includes "Quick Data Links" for frequently requested information such as lists of plants and utilities, electricity generation, prices, and expenditures. The main menu also offers state profiles, publications, databases, and monthly and annual industry overviews.

OTHER SOURCES
Checklist

Renewable Energy Annual. PRINT. WEB. (annual) 1995–. U.S. Department of Energy. Energy Information Administration. Office of Coal, Nuclear, Electric and Alternate Fuel. E 3.19/2: Item 0429-T-20. ASI 3164-112. GPO.<http://www.eia.doe.gov/cneaf/solar.renewables/rea_data/rea_sum.html>;<http://www.eia.doe.gov/bookshelf/renew.html>;<http://tonto.eia.doe.gov/bookshelf/index.html>;<http://purl.access.gpo.gov/GPO/LPS3492>.

> Coverage: world regions, selected countries, U.S., regions, states.
> Content: consumption by sector and source; electricity generation and capacity; solar and geothermal industry shipments and exports.

Renewable Fuels Information at a Glance Web Page. WEB. U.S. Department of Energy. Energy Information Administration. <http://www.eia.doe.gov/fuelrenewable.html>.

> Content: full-text publications and profiles on renewable energy sources.

Nuclear and Uranium Information at a Glance Web Page. WEB. U.S. Department of Energy. Energy Information Administration.<http://www.eia.doe.gov/fuelnuclear.html>.

> Content: summary data and full-text publications on nuclear energy and the uranium industry; basic data on individual nuclear reactors.

Discussion

Renewable Energy Annual covers biomass, geothermal, wind, and solar energy sources. Chapters are a combination of narrative and statistical tables. An overview chapter covers renewable energy use and capability with consumption statistics. Additional chapters cover the solar energy industry and the geothermal heat pump industry. These industry chapters give statistics on number of companies in the industry and analyze shipments. Types of data available include destination or distribution of shipments, value of shipments, and average price.

The *Renewable Fuels Information at a Glance Web Page* lists types of energy sources and other topics and provides profiles on each from the *Renewable Energy Annual.* The page also contains a publications menu option that lists publications with links to the full text, including a link to the *Renewable Energy Annual.*

The *Nuclear and Uranium Information at a Glance Web Page* contains a menu options for U.S. nuclear reactors that lists nuclear reactors by name or state. Information on individual nuclear reactors includes location, capacity, reactor type, and electricity produced. The Web page also provides a daily nuclear power plant status report. Main menu options related to the uranium industry include an overview and selections on such topics as uranium mining, production, marketing, and inventories. A publications menu choice lists nuclear and uranium industry publications with links to the full-text.

CENSUS BUREAU PUBLICATIONS
Checklist

Economic Census. PRINT. WEB. (quinquennial) 1997–. U.S. Department of Commerce. Economics and Statistics Administration. Census Bureau. (Formerly published as individual censuses for specific economic sectors.) ASI 2311, 2355, 2373, 2390, 2397, 2405, 2451, 2493, 2513, 2573, 2575, 2597, 2605, 2615, 2635, 2645, 2665, 2685.<http://www.census.gov/epcd/www/econ97.html>;<http://www.census.gov/mp/www/pub/ind/msind.html#Industry>;<http://www.census.gov/prod/www/abs/economic.html>.

> Coverage: U.S., states.
> Content: cost of fuel and electricity for manufacturing, mining, and construction industries; quantity of electricity purchased for manufacturing and mining industries; industry data for mining and energy-related manufacturing industries.

Economic Census. CD-ROM. (quinquennial) 1987–. U.S. Department of Commerce. Economics and Statistics Administration. Bureau of the Census. C 3.277: Item 0154-C.

> Coverage: U.S., states.
> Content: *Economic Census* reports.

American FactFinder. WEB. U.S. Department of Commerce. Bureau of the Census.<http://factfinder.census.gov/java_prod/dads.ui.homePage.HomePage>.

> Coverage: U.S., states, counties, metropolitan areas, places.
> Content: 1997 *Economic Census* data; other census products.

Annual Survey of Manufactures. PRINT. WEB. (annual) 1949–. U.S. Department of Commerce. Economics and Statistics Administration. Bureau of the Census. C 3.24/9-[no.] (Earlier, C 3.24/9:; C 3.24/9-2:). Item 0134-A. ASI 2506-14,-15. GPO.<http://www.census.gov/econ/www/manumenu.html>;<http://tier2.census.gov/asm/asm.htm>;<http://purl.access.gpo.gov/GPO/LPS2593>;<http://www.census.gov/mp/www/pub/mfg/msmfg.html#mas>;<http://www.census.gov/prod/www/abs/manu-min.html#mm>.

> Coverage: U.S., states.
> Content: cost of purchased fuels; cost and quantity of electric energy purchased.

American Housing Survey for the United States. PRINT. WEB. (biennial) 1973–. C 3.215:H-150/. (Earlier, C 3.215/18-) (Titled *Annual Housing Survey* before 1985) (Supplements, C 3.215:H-151/). Item 0141-A. ASI 2485-12. (Supplements, ASI 2485-13,-14). GPO.<http://www.census.gov/mp/www/pub/con/mscho.html#ahs>;<http://www.census.gov/prod/www/abs/cons-hou.html#house>;<http://www.huduser.org/datasets/ahs.html>.

> Coverage: U.S., regions.
> Content: energy-related housing characteristics; type of fuel; fuel costs; heating and air conditioning equipment.

American Housing Survey for the [name] Metropolitan Area in [year]. PRINT. WEB. (annual) 1974–. C 3.215:H-170/. (Earlier, C 3.215/17) (Titled *Annual Housing Survey* before 1984) (Supplements, C 3.215/16:) Item 0141-A. ASI 2485-6. (Supplement, 2485-8)<http://www.census.gov/mp/www/pub/con/mscho.html#ahs>;<http://www.census.gov/prod/www/abs/

cons-hou.html#house>;<http://www.huduser.org/datasets/ahs.html>.

> Coverage: selected metropolitan areas, selected subareas (counties, places).
> Content: energy-related housing characteristics; type of fuel; fuel costs; heating and air conditioning equipment.

American Housing Survey. CD-ROM. 1985–89–. C 3.215/19: Item 0156-P.

> Content: microdata files from the *American Housing Survey.*

Discussion

Energy-related information can be extracted from the *Economic Census*. The *Economic Census* is taken every five years, covering years ending in "2" and in "7." The data are collected in the year following the year of coverage (the 1997 census was conducted in 1998) and data may begin to appear in the year following that. Major changes took place beginning with the 1997 *Economic Census* both in organization and in publishing formats. The implementation of the NAICS classification system reorganized and increased industry coverage resulting in data being published for 18 economic sectors. The previous economic census for 1992, based on the SIC classification system, was organized into eight sectors. Also beginning with 1997, data are published almost entirely on the Internet and on CD-ROM with only a small number of summary publications published in print format.

The reports for the manufacturing, mining, and construction sectors contain data on the cost of fuels and electricity at the national level in each industry report and a state total in the geographic area series reports. Quantity of electricity purchased is also available for manufacturing and mining. The mineral industry series reports give additional information on fuels consumed by type. Construction industry series data on cost of fuels are the only industry data that include a breakdown by type of fuel. Some of the industries covered are themselves energy-related, such as mining of energy minerals or certain manufacturing industries, such as petroleum refining. For these industries, additional basic data are available such as number of establishments, employment, payroll, value of shipments, expenses, assets, capital expenditures, and inventories. These industry data are available for smaller geographic levels such as counties, metropolitan areas, and selected places depending on the sector. The Census Bureau's *Economic Census* Web page lists reports from the 1997 census with links to the full text as they are released. A link is also available for the 1992 reports.

American FactFinder is a Census Bureau Web database designed to provide access to data from the 1990 and 2000 *Census of Population and Housing*, the *American Community Survey*, and the 1997 *Economic Census*. It also contains a mapping feature and an option to search for information on Census Bureau products. 1997 *Eco-nomic Census* data are available in the "Industry and Business Facts" section as it is released. The Industry Quick Reports option allows the user to select from a list of NAICS sectors and code numbers or to search by word to identify and display a basic industry report. The industry reports show number of establishments, number of employees, annual payroll, and shipments/sales/receipts by state. Similarly, the Geography Quick Reports option can be used to display a geographic area report. The geographic report shows similar data items to the industry report for all industries at the two-digit NAICS sector level for the selected area. A "Build a Query" option is also available. This option allows the user to search for or select specific data sets for display.

The *Annual Survey of Manufactures* updates the *Economic Census* reports for the manufacturing sector. The *Annual Survey* consists of three annual reports. One, *Statistics for Industry Groups and Industries* (C 3.24/9-7:), gives cost of fuels and electric energy by industry for the United States. Another report, *Geographic Area Statistics* (C 3.24/9-9:), gives the same information by state without industry detail.

The *American Housing Survey for the United States* gives information on housing characteristics. Energy-related statistics include air conditioning and heating equipment, fuel types used, and monthly cost of electricity, gas, and fuel oil. Data are given for owner-occupied housing and renter-occupied housing and for Black, Hispanic, and elderly householders. Sample data include total number of housing units using wood for heating fuel or median monthly cost of fuel oil for housing with Hispanic householders.

The *American Housing Survey for the [name] Metropolitan Area in [year]* covers 46 areas of which a varying number are published each year on a rotating basis. The number of metropolitan areas covered has varied over the years. The data are almost identical to that in the national report.

The *American Housing Survey* CD-ROMs contain microdata files (original survey responses) for the national and metropolitan area surveys. No software is included on the CDs. Use of these files requires additional statistical analysis software.

INDEXES
Checklist

American Statistics Index (ASI). PRINT. (monthly) 1973–. Bethesda, MD: Congressional Information Service.

Statistical Universe. WEB. Bethesda, MD: Congressional Information Service.

Discussion

A comprehensive listing of statistical material can be found in *ASI* by looking under subject headings beginning with

"Energy," such as "Energy resources and consumption," "Energy reserves," and "Energy prices." Also see headings for specific types of energy sources, such as those beginning with "Coal," "Natural gas," or "Petroleum." *Statistical Universe* includes a Web version of *ASI*. (See Chapter 3, "The Basics of Searching," for more information.)

RELATED MATERIAL
Within this Work

GPO Subject Bibliographies. PRINT. WEB. GP 3.22/2:

<http://bookstore.gpo.gov/sb/about.html>

No. 9   "Solar Energy"

No. 200 "Nuclear Power"

No. 303 "Energy"

CHAPTER 42
Projections

The government publishes many projections, ranging from general discussions of trends to detailed statistical tables. These are often sought by businesses, government officials, educators, and planners.

Projections are only as valid as the underlying assumptions on which they are based. Most publications explain the assumptions and methodology used. Often more than one set of projections is presented. These alternate sets are sometimes based on high, medium, and low estimates or sometimes on differing methodologies. Many projections are not statements of what will actually happen but guidelines on what might happen if present conditions continue unchanged.

Population, economic, budget, and energy projections are the most heavily represented in government publications. This chapter emphasizes recurring titles or ongoing series containing projections. Individual reports on specific topics and articles in government periodicals may also contain projections.

SEARCH STRATEGY

This chapter is an example of the statistical search strategy. The basic strategy is

1. Check the *Statistical Abstract* and other sources under "General Statistical Sources";
2. Search for relevant sources in this chapter by subject area of interest; and
3. Search *American Statistics Index* (*ASI*) to find more detailed or specialized projections and projections on subject areas not covered by this chapter.

GENERAL STATISTICAL SOURCES
Checklist

Statistical Abstract of the United States. PRINT. WEB. (annual) 1878–. U.S. Department of Commerce. Economics and Statistics Administration. Bureau of the Census. C 3.134: Item 0150. ASI 2324-1. GPO. <http://www.census.gov/statab/www/>; <http://purl.access.gpo.gov/GPO/LPS2878>.

   Coverage: selected countries, U.S., states.
   Content: population by age, sex, race; households by type and householder age and race; total personal income; birth, death, and fertility rates; life expectancy; school enrollment; teachers; degrees; employment by occupation and industry; labor force by age, sex, race; energy supply.

Statistical Abstract of the United States. CD-ROM. (annual) 1993–. U.S. Department of Commerce. Bureau of the Census. C 3.134/7: Item 0150-B. ASI 2324-14.

   Content: CD-ROM version of the *Statistical Abstract*.

State and Metropolitan Area Data Book. PRINT. WEB. (irregular) 1979–. U.S. Department of Commerce. Economics and Statistics Administration. Bureau of the Census. C 3.134/5: Item 0150. ASI 2328-54. GPO. <http://www.census.gov/statab/www.smadb.html>.

   Coverage: U.S., states, metropolitan areas.
   Content: population by age group; total and per capita personal income.

State and Metropolitan Area Data Book. CD-ROM. (irregular) 1997/98–. U.S. Department of Commerce. Economics and Statistics Administration. Bureau of the Census. (Not distributed to depository libraries)

   Content: CD-ROM version of the *State and Metropolitan Area Data Book*.

Discussion

The *Statistical Abstract of the United States* contains summary projections on population, vital statistics, education, employment, and energy. Statistics are selected from many of the more detailed sources covered in this chapter. Source notes at the end of each table can direct the user to more current or more detailed sources for the information in that table. To locate statistics on projections, look in the index under "Projections." The full text of recent editions of the *Statistical Abstract* is available on the Census Bureau Web site as PDF files. The *Statistical Abstract* is also available on CD-ROM. The CD uses Adobeâ Acrobatâ software and contains some additional geographic areas and time series in the form of spreadsheet files that are not in the printed version.

The *State and Metropolitan Area Data Book* contains population projections for the state and national level and personal income projections for metropolitan areas. The *State and Metropolitan Area Data Book* is available as a PDF file on the Census Bureau Web site and on CD-ROM.

POPULATION PROJECTIONS

Checklist

Current Population Reports: Population Estimates and Projections. Series P-25. PRINT. WEB. U.S. Department of Commerce. Economics and Statistics Administration. Bureau of the Census. C 3.186:P-25/. Item 0142-C-03. GPO. ASI 2546-3. <http://www.census.gov/prod/www/abs/popula.html#popest>; <http://www.census.gov/mp/www/pub/pop/mspop05.html>.
  Content: reports on population projections and estimates.

Population Projections of the United States by Age, Sex, Race, and Hispanic Origin: [years]. C 3.186:P-25/. (1995–2050 is C 3.186:P-25/1130)
  Coverage: U.S.
  Content: detailed population projections by age, sex, and race under middle fertility, life expectancy, and immigration assumptions; some data for low and high assumptions.

Projections of the Number of Households and Families in the United States: [years]. C 3.186/15: <http://www.census.gov/population/www/projections/nathh.html>.
  Coverage: U.S.
  Content: households by type, age of householder, race, and children under 18; number of persons living alone and marital status by age and sex; three alternative series of projections.

Population Projections: States, [years]. C 3.186:P-25/. (1995–2025 is C 3.186:P-25/1131)
  Coverage: U.S., regions, divisions, states.
  Content: total population, net change, births, deaths, interstate migration, and immigration.

Projections of the Voting-Age Population for States: November [year]. (biennial) C 3.186/26: <http://www.census.gov/population/www/socdemo/voting.html>.
  Coverage: U.S., regions, divisions, states.
  Content: voting age population by age group, sex, and race; election participation.

Population Projections Web Page. WEB. U.S. Department of Commerce. Census Bureau. <http://www.census.gov/population/www/projections/popproj.html>.
  Content: tables and links to full-text publications on national, state, household, and voting-age population projections.

Social Security Area Population Projections. WEB. (annual) 1981–. U.S. Social Security Administration. Office of the Chief Actuary. Actuarial Studies. SSA 1.25/2: (Earlier, HE 3.19:)

(1997 report is SSA 1.25/2:112) Item 0516-X-03. ASI 9936-2.[no.]. <http://www.ssa.gov/OACT/NOTES/actstud.html>.
  Coverage: U.S.
  Content: fertility, birth, marriage, divorce, and death rates and numbers; life expectancy; population by age group, sex, and marital status.

World Population Profile: [year]. PRINT. (biennial) 1985–. U.S. Department of Commerce. Economics and Statistics Administration. Bureau of the Census. C 3.205/3:WP(year). (Issued earlier under other titles) Item 0146-F. ASI 2324-9. GPO. <http://www.census.gov/ipc/www/world.html>; <http://www.census.gov/ipc/www/publist.html>; <purl.access.gpo.gov/GPO/LPS2698>.
  Coverage: world, world regions, country groupings, countries, U.S.
  Content: population; population by sex and age group; growth rates; women of reproductive age; fertility; life expectancy.

World Population Information Web Page. WEB. U.S. Department of Commerce. Bureau of the Census. <http://www.census.gov/ipc/www/world.html>.
  Content: tables, charts, publications, and databases on world population.

Discussion

The *Current Population Reports: Population Estimates and Projections* P-25 series is a major source for population projections. Most of these reports are updated periodically.

Population Projections of the United States by Age, Sex, Race, and Hispanic Origin provides projections for more than 50 years into the future. Basic data on growth rate and population are given for each year of the projected time period by race. Birth, death, and immigration rates and numbers are included. Population by age, sex, and race combined is given for selected years. Less detailed age, race, and sex data are also given for alternative projection series.

Projections of the Number of Households and Families in the United States gives alternate series of projections for households by type and householder characteristics. Types of households include married couple families, female or male householder families, and nonfamily households.

Population Projections: States is a summary report with projections of total population, births, deaths, and migration for selected years. Charts illustrate key trends such as the fastest growing states. More detailed tables for states are available through the Census Bureau's *Population Projections* Web page.

Projections of the Voting-Age Population for States projects the voting age population by sex, race, and age group. Tables also show historical and current data on the number and percentage of people who voted in particular elections. This report is usually issued near the beginning of election years.

The *Population Projections Web Page* contains four categories that represent the areas of population projections available from the Census Bureau: national, state, households and families, and population of voting age. These categories also correspond to the four *Current Population Reports* series titles discussed above. Each category provides relevant statistical tables and links to full-text editions of related publications, including most of the *Current Population Reports* titles listed above.

The Social Security Administration publishes *Social Security Area Population Projections*, which gives U.S. projections for the population by age group, sex, and marital status. There are also tables on fertility rates, birth rates by age, death rates by age group and sex, life expectancy by sex, and marriage and divorce rates. Most data are given for three alternative levels of assumptions.

World Population Profile consists of a narrative analysis of world population trends followed by an appendix of more detailed tables on population and factors affecting population growth. Several of the tables contain projections.

The *World Population Information Web Page* includes a link to the full-text of the *World Population Profile*, a world population table with projections and related graphs, and the International Data Base with demographic summary tables for individual countries that include projections.

ECONOMIC PROJECTIONS
Checklist

U.S. Industry & Trade Outlook. PRINT. CD-ROM. (annual) 1998–. The McGraw-Hill Companies and U.S. Department of Commerce. International Trade Administration. C 61.48: (Earlier, C 61.34:, C 62.17:; C 57.18:). (Continuation of *U.S. Industrial Outlook* issued by the International Trade Administration, 1960-1994) Item 0215-L-08. NTIS.

> Coverage: U.S.
> Content: industry profiles; trends and prospects; short-term forecasts for shipments, production, revenues, employment, and trade; general economic outlook.

The Economic and Budget Outlook for Fiscal Years [years]. PRINT. WEB. (annual) 1986–1990–. U.S. Congress. Congressional Budget Office. Y 10.13: (Update, Y 10.17:) Item 1005-F. ASI 26306-7. (Earlier, 26304-3) GPO. <http://www.cbo.gov/byclasscat.cfm?class=0&cat=0>; <http://purl.access.gpo.gov/GPO/LPS755>.

> Coverage: U.S.
> Content: economic and budget projections; gross domestic product; consumer price index; unemployment rate; interest rates; budget revenues and outlays; budget deficit/surplus.

Budget of the United States Government. PRINT. WEB. (annual) 1922–. U.S. Executive Office of the President. Office of Management and Budget. PREX 2.8: (Also issued as a House Document, Y 1.1/7:) Item 0853. ASI 104-2. GPO. <http://w3.access.gpo.gov/usbudget/>; <http://purl.access.gpo.gov/GPO/LPS2343>.

> Coverage: U.S.
> Content: varies; economic assumptions; gross domestic product; consumer price index; unemployment rate; interest rates; budget receipts and outlays.

The Budget of the United States Government Fiscal Year [year]. CD-ROM. (annual) 1996–. U.S. Executive Office of the President. Office of Management and Budget. PREX 2.8/1: Item 0853-C. GPO.

> Content: CD-ROM version of *The Budget of the United States*.

Analysis of the President's Budgetary Proposals for Fiscal Year [year]. PRINT. WEB. (annual) 1977–. U.S. Congress. Congressional Budget Office. Y 10.19: (Earlier, Y 10.2:B 85/) (Title varies) Item 1005-K. GPO. <http://www.cbo.gov/byclasscat.cfm?class=0&cat=1>; <http://purl.access.gpo.gov/GPO/LPS2121>.

> Coverage: U.S.
> Content: economic and budget projections; gross domestic product; consumer price index; unemployment rate; interest rates; budget revenues and outlays; budget deficit/surplus.

Economic Report of the President Transmitted to the Congress. PRINT. WEB. (annual) 1947– . U.S. President. PR [no.].9: (SuDocs number varies with each President) Item 0848. ASI 204-1. GPO. <http://w3.access.gpo.gov/eop/>.

> Coverage: U.S.
> Content: varies; economic outlook; gross domestic product; consumer price index; unemployment rate; interest rates.

Employment Outlook. PRINT. (biennial) 1957–. U.S. Department of Labor. Bureau of Labor Statistics. Bulletin series. L 2.3: (1998 edition is L 2.3:2502) (Title varies) Item 0768-A-01. ASI 6744-19. (Earlier, 6748-91, 6728-29). GPO.

> Coverage: U.S.
> Content: economic and employment projections for the labor force, gross domestic product, employment by industry and occupation, and employment change.

Occupational Projections and Training Data. MF. (biennial) 1971–. U.S. Department of Labor. Bureau of Labor Statistics. Bulletin series. L 2.3/4-2: (Earlier, L 2.3:) Item 0768-A-10. ASI 6744-3.

> Coverage: U.S.
> Content: projected employment, employment change, annual average openings, and replacement rates by occupation.

Employment Projections Web Page. WEB. U.S. Department of Labor. Bureau of Labor Statistics. <http://stats.bls.gov/emphome.htm>.

> Content: selected data tables on employment projections by occupation, industry, education, and earnings; publication information.

FAA Aerospace Forecasts Fiscal Years [years]. MF. (annual) U.S. Department of Transportation. Federal Aviation Administration. Office of Aviation Policy and Plans. TD 4.57/2: (Earlier, TD 4.57:; TD 4.32/11:; TD 4.2:AV 5/) (Title varies. Earlier title, *FAA Aviation Forecasts*) Item 0431-C-27. ASI 7504-6. <http://api.hq.faa.gov/apo_pubs.htm>.

> Coverage: world, world regions, U.S.

Content: economic and industry review; gross domestic product; consumer price index; fuel prices; passenger and cargo revenues; trip length; capacity and load factors; fuel consumption; type of aircraft; airborne hours; pilots; aircraft operations.

Terminal Area Forecast (TAF) System. WEB. U.S. Department of Transportation. Federal Aviation Administration. (Earlier, TD 4.57:) <http://api.hq.faa.gov/apo_pubs.htm>.
> Coverage: U.S., FAA regions, states, individual airports.
> Content: database and summary tables with projections for enplanements and aircraft operations.

Discussion

U.S. Industry & Trade Outlook is a standard source for locating information on industry trends. Issued early each year, it gives the outlook for the coming year. Each chapter covers a major industry group such as "Chemicals and Allied Products" or "Computer Software and Networking." Chapters begin with an industry definition followed by an overview of the industry and sections on selected subindustries within the group. Industry discussions vary depending on the nature of the industry, but generally cover global and domestic trends, outlook, and future prospects. A "Trends and Forecasts" table gives value of shipments or sales, employment, and trade information for past years and a forecast for the coming year. Introductory chapters discuss the outlook for the general economy. A CD-ROM version is also available for purchase, although not available through the depository library program.

The Economic and Budget Outlook analyzes the economic and budget situation and gives projections for several years. It is a narrative report with numerous tables and charts. An economic outlook chapter discusses the economic situation including the economic forecast with projections for basic economic indicators. Other chapters cover the outlook for the budget, revenue, and spending. These contain projections for budget outlays, revenues, and the surplus or deficit. A midyear update titled *The Economic and Budget Outlook: An Update* is also issued.

The *Budget of the United States Government* also makes projections concerning basic economic indicators and budget totals. These usually differ from those of the Congressional Budget Office. Near the beginning of the annual budget there is usually a chapter on the economic situation that includes economic assumptions. Other chapters discuss specific federal program areas and often include budget projections. Detailed budget tables also show outlays by function and estimate revenues and expenditures for the next few years. The *Budget* can answer such questions as whether inflation (as measured by the consumer price index) or unemployment is expected to go up or down or how much may be spent on the space program in the next few years.

An Analysis of the President's Budgetary Proposals analyzes and compares the economic and budget forecasts of the Administration, the Congressional Budget Office (CBO), and the Blue Chip independent survey. The CBO projections are similar to those in *The Economic and Budget Outlook* and the Administration figures are based on the *Budget of the United States Government*. Tables compare short-term forecasts and medium-term projections from all three sources for major economic indicators. An appendix contains CBO baseline budget projections on budget revenue, outlays, and the deficit/surplus. Other chapters and tables analyze specific federal program areas or more specialized aspects of the budget and also include projections.

The *Economic Report of the President* contains an in-depth review of the economy including a section on the economic outlook. Forecasts of basic economic indicators are projected for about five years.

Employment Outlook 1996–2006 contains economic projections and projections of employment by occupation and industry. It summarizes more detailed articles that appeared in the agency's periodical, *Monthly Labor Review* (L 2.6:). The subtitle of this report, and sometimes the title, change with each edition. Narrative analysis summarizes trends and issues in employment. Detailed tables on employment by industry and by occupation give statistics on current and projected employment and on projected employment change.

Occupational Projections and Training Data contains information on current and projected employment by detailed occupation. Occupations are also ranked from very high to very low for expected rate of employment change and annual average job openings.

The *Employment Projections Web Page* provides access to the Bureau of Labor Statistics' most popular tables on employment and occupation projections. A menu of data items covers "Most Requested Tables" and specific topics such as "Occupational," "Industry," "Labor Force (demographic)," and "State occupational employment projections." Each topic choice offers statistical tables, recent articles, datafiles, and related information sources. An "Education and training" option includes a "Compare occupations" feature that allows searching by occupation or level of education to retrieve specified tables on employment and projected change or growth.

FAA Aerospace Forecasts contains some general economic projections and projections on the aviation industry. Narrative chapters with graphs summarize trends for the economic environment and specific types of carriers such as commercial air carriers or regionals/commuters. Another chapter provides more detailed tables with yearly historical and projected statistics on revenue and traffic measures.

The *Terminal Area Forecast (TAF) System* contains historical and projected aviation activity for individual airports. This Web title includes a PDF version of the publication *Terminal Area Forecasts Fiscal Years [years]*, which is now only published electronically. This title covers more than 400 airports and gives projections for air carrier and commuter enplanements, itinerant and local aircraft operations, and instrument operations. A more extensive database and accompanying software for downloading are also included under this Web entry.

EDUCATION PROJECTIONS
Checklist

Projections of Education Statistics to [year]. PRINT. WEB. (annual) 1964–. U.S. Department of Education. Office of Educational Research and Improvement. National Center for Education Statistics. ED 1.120: (Earlier, HE 19.320:) Item 0460-A-10. ASI 4824-4. GPO. <http://nces.ed.gov/pubsearch/getpubList.asp?L1=40&L2=0>.

> Coverage: U.S., regions, states.
> Content: enrollment; graduates; degrees; teachers; expenditures; school-age populations.

Discussion

Projections of Education Statistics is a basic, comprehensive source for education projections. Chapters on each topic area contain a narrative introduction with graphs and charts, followed by statistical tables. Three alternative projections are usually given for each topic. Data for previous years are also given. Enrollment projections are given for elementary, secondary, and higher education. The higher education figures are particularly detailed. Tables cover two- and four-year institutions, undergraduates, and graduate students, and give data by sex and sometimes by age. Other tables give number of degrees by type, number of teachers, pupil-teacher ratios, expenditures, and average salaries. State data are limited to elementary and secondary school enrollment and number of high school graduates. An appendix of supplementary tables gives projections for school-age population, average daily attendance, disposable personal income, education revenue, the consumer price index, and tax payments. This source answers such questions as "Is college enrollment dropping?" or "Are pupil-teacher ratios increasing?"

ENERGY PROJECTIONS
Checklist

Annual Energy Outlook. MF. WEB. (annual) 1977–. U.S. Department of Energy. Energy Information Administration. Office of Integrated Analysis and Forecasting. E 3.1/4: (Earlier, E 3.1:year/v.3) Item 0429-J-01. ASI 3164-75. GPO. <http://www.eia.doe.gov/oiaf/aeo.html>; <http://tonto.eia.doe.gov/bookshelf/index.html>; <http://purl.access.gpo.gov/GPO/LPS3492>.

> Coverage: world, world regions, country groupings, selected countries, U.S.
> Content: analysis of energy demand and supply trends; projection tables for production, consumption, exports, imports, and prices for various energy sources under different growth assumptions; consumption and prices by

end-use sector; gross domestic product; disposable personal income.

Short-Term Energy Outlook. PRINT. WEB. (quarterly) 1979–. U.S. Department of Energy. Energy Information Administration. Office of Energy Markets and End Use. E 3.31: Item 0429-K-01. ASI 3162-34. GPO. <http://www.eia.doe.gov/emeu/steo/pub/contents.html>; <http://purl.access.gpo.gov/GPO/LPS1651>; <http://tonto.eia.doe.gov/bookshelf/index.html>; <http://purl.access.gpo.gov/GPO/LPS3492>.

> Coverage: world, country groupings, selected countries, U.S.
> Content: supply and demand for petroleum and petroleum products, natural gas, coal, and electricity; prices.

International Energy Outlook. MF. WEB. (annual) 1986–. U.S. Department of Energy. Energy Information Administration. Office of Integrated Analysis and Forecasting. E 3.11/20-3: Item 0435-H. ASI 3164-84. GPO. <http://www.eia.doe.gov/oiaf/ieo.html>; <http://purl.access.gpo.gov/GPO/LPS2970>; <http://tonto.eia.doe.gov/bookshelf/index.html>; <http://purl.access.gpo.gov/GPO/LPS3492>.

> Coverage: world, world regions, country groupings, selected countries, U.S.
> Content: consumption by energy type and region; world oil prices; production; reserves; capacity; trade; gross domestic product.

Energy InfoDisc. CD-ROM. (quarterly) 1996–. U.S. Department of Energy. Energy Information Administration. E 3.60: Item 0429-K-08. ASI 3162-47. <http://tonto.eia.doe.gov/bookshelf/index.html>; <http://purl.access.gpo.gov/GPO/LPS3492>; Related site: <http://www.eia.doe.gov/infodisc.html>.

> Content: full-text publications and database applications.

Forecasting Information at a Glance Web Page. WEB. U.S. Department of Energy. Energy Information Administration. <http://www.eia.doe.gov/oiaf/forecasting.html>.

> Content: forecasts for several energy sources and topics; links to full-text publications.

Discussion

The *Annual Energy Outlook* analyzes trends in energy supply and demand. This is the most comprehensive of the energy outlook publications available. A narrative section with graphs and charts summarizes trends and issues affecting supply and demand and analyzes the market outlook for specific fuel sources. More detailed projections tables in appendices present five scenarios based on different variables such as differing oil prices and different levels of growth. These tables cover supply and disposition, prices, production, consumption, and trade for each energy source. Consumption data are given by end-use sector, such as residential or commercial, and covers the amount of energy used for specific applications such as heating, dishwashers, or refrigeration. International coverage is limited to petroleum. This title gives guidance on what energy sources may be most predominant in the future, what the primary uses of energy will be, and what the supply of each source is likely to be. Supplemental tables are available on the Web site in the same location as the main report. These tables provide more detailed projections by census division and end-use sector. A data query option is also available for consumption and price data from the supplement.

Short-Term Energy Outlook predicts the supply, demand, and price situation for the current year and following year and gives some data for previous years. A narrative section discusses the current situation, prices, and economic assumptions on which the forecasts are based and summarizes the outlook for each energy source. Statistical tables provide detailed projections for each energy source, as well as for economic and weather factors. More detail is provided for petroleum, including international data, than for other energy sources. The Web site provides a variety of formats including HTML, PDF, spreadsheets, PowerPoint presentations, and a query system.

International Energy Outlook analyzes world trends in energy consumption. Narrative chapters with graphs and charts discuss each energy source. Appendices include more detailed projection tables. Alternative projections for high or low economic growth are also provided. Data are usually given for recent years with projections for five-year intervals. The data and models used to produce this report, called the *World Energy Projection System*, are available in spreadsheet form and can be downloaded from the agency's Web site at the same location as the main report.

The *Energy InfoDisc* CD-ROM contains PDF files for the full text of recent editions of Energy Information Administration publications including those mentioned in this section.

The *Forecasting Information at a Glance Web Page* provides forecast information arranged by category, including coal, electricity, energy consumption/prices, and energy demand sectors. Under each category are relevant current data tables from the *Annual Energy Outlook*, *Short-Term Energy Outlook*, and other sources. The main menu also offers a publications category that leads to the full-text of all the publications in this section as well as additional related information.

AGRICULTURE
Checklist

USDA Agricultural Baseline Projections to [year]. MF. WEB. (annual) U.S. Department of Agriculture. Office of the Chief Economist. World Agricultural Outlook Board. A93.44:WAOB-. Item 0042-W=01. ASI 1524-13. <http://www.ers.usda.gov/Briefing/baseline/>.

Coverage: world, world regions, country groupings, selected countries, U.S.

Content: gross domestic product; disposable personal income; price indexes; crop acreage, yields, supply and use, stocks, trade, production, prices, costs and returns; livestock stocks, production, trade, prices, inventory, costs and returns; farm receipts, expenses, and income; food expenditures.

International Agricultural Baseline Projections to [year]. MF. WEB. (annual) U.S. Department of Agriculture. Economic Research Service. Market and Trade Economics Division. Agricultural Economic Report. (Earlier, A 1.107:) ASI 1524-15. <http://www.ers.usda.gov/briefing/baseline/1999/internat.htm>.

Coverage: world, world regions, country groupings, countries, U.S.

Content: gross domestic product; prices; crop and livestock trade and supply and use; yield, production, consumption, and stocks.

Discussion

USDA Agricultural Baseline Projections to [year] analyzes the general economic and agricultural policy situation and provides projections on crops, livestock, farm income and farm financial conditions, food prices and expenditures, and agricultural trade. Each area consists of a narrative overview and statistical tables.

International Agricultural Baseline Projections to [year] is a companion publication with more detailed country data. It also contains a narrative summary on the general economy and agricultural policies with chapters on individual major crops and livestock. The crop and livestock chapters include a detailed trade projections table and a supply and use projections table. Tables include figures for some previous years as well. Each chapter includes graphs on historical and projected prices. The crop chapters have additional graphs on historical and projected area and yield or supply and use.

INDEXES
Checklist

American Statistics Index (ASI). PRINT. (monthly) 1973–. Bethesda, MD: Congressional Information Service.

Statistical Universe. WEB. Bethesda, MD: Congressional Information Service.

Discussion

A comprehensive listing of material can be found in *ASI* by looking under the subjects "Projections and forecasts," "Energy projections," "Population projections," or specific topics of interest. *Statistical Universe* includes a Web version of *ASI*. (See Chapter 3, "The Basics of Searching," for more information on *ASI*.

CHAPTER 43
State and Local Government Statistics

The federal government compiles and makes available a number of statistical materials relating to state and local governments. The major provider of information is the Bureau of the Census, particularly through the quinquennial *Census of Governments*. Many of the sources are now accessible through the Web, and data are often available for viewing or downloading from the Web.

SEARCH STRATEGY

This chapter is an example of a statistical search strategy. The steps to follow are

1. Consult the basic sources listed in the first section of this chapter;
2. Locate more detailed statistics in the comprehensive sources listed in the "Census Bureau Sources," and "Other Sources" sections, particularly resources from the *Census of Governments*; and
3. Search *American Statistics Index (ASI)* to obtain additional statistical sources.

GENERAL STATISTICAL SOURCES
Checklist

Statistical Abstract of the United States. PRINT. WEB. (annual) 1878–. U.S. Department of Commerce. Economics and Statistics Administration. Bureau of the Census. C 3.134: Item 0150. ASI 2324-1. GPO. <http://www.census.gov/statab/www/>; <http://purl.access.gpo.gov/GPO/LPS2878>.
    Coverage: U.S., divisions, states, selected metropolitan areas.
    Content: state revenues, expenditures, debt outstanding, and tax collections; state income taxes; local government general revenues; state aid to local governments; federal aid to state and local governments; county and city government revenues, expenditures, and debt outstanding; state and local government employment and payrolls.

Statistical Abstract of the United States. CD-ROM. (annual) 1993–. U.S. Department of Commerce. Bureau of the Census. C 3.134/7: Item 0150-B. ASI 2324-14.
    Content: CD-ROM version of the *Statistical Abstract*.

Historical Statistics of the United States: Colonial Times to 1970. Parts 1-2. PRINT. (1975) U.S. Department of Commerce. Bureau of the Census. C 3.134/2:H 62/789-970/pt.1-2. Item 0151. ASI (76) 2328-2. GPO.
    Coverage: U.S.
    Content: state and local payrolls; state and local government employment; state and local government revenue, expenditures, and debt (often classified by function).

Historical Statistics of the United States on CD-ROM: Colonial Times to 1970. CD-ROM. (1997) New York, NY: Cambridge University Press.
    Content: CD-ROM version of *Historical Statistics of the United States*.

County and City Data Book. PRINT. WEB. (quinquennial) 1947–. U.S. Department of Commerce. Economics and Statistics Administration. Bureau of the Census. C 3.134/2:C 83/2/year. Item 0151. ASI 2328-1. GPO. <http://fisher.lib.Virginia.EDU/ccdb/>.
    Coverage: U.S., regions, divisions, states, counties, cities of 25,000 or more.
    Content: state revenues and expenditures; state and local government employment; local government revenues and expenditures.

County and City Data Book. CD-ROM. (quinquennial) 1988–. U.S. Department of Commerce. Bureau of the Census. C 3.134/2-1: (Earlier, C 3.134/2:C 83/2/). Item 0151-D-01. ASI 2328-1.
    Content: CD-ROM version of the *County and City Data Book*.

County and City Extra: Annual Metro, City, and County Data Book. PRINT. (annual) 1992–. Lanham, MD: Bernan Press.
    Coverage: U.S., states, counties, metropolitan areas, congressional districts, cities of 25,000 or more.
    Content: updated version of the *County and City Data Book*.

Places, Towns, and Townships. PRINT. (irregular) 1993–. Lanham, MD: Bernan Press.

Coverage: incorporated places.

Content: updated supplement to the *County and City Data Book*.

State and Metropolitan Area Data Book. PRINT. WEB. (irregular) 1979–. U.S. Department of Commerce. Economics and Statistics Administration. Bureau of the Census. C 3.134/5: Item 0150. ASI 2328-54. GPO. <http://www.census.gov/statab/www.smadb.html>.

Coverage: U.S., states, metropolitan areas, central cities of metropolitan areas, component counties of metropolitan areas.

Content: revenues; expenditures; tax collections; state government employment; state payrolls.

State and Metropolitan Area Data Book. CD-ROM. (irregular) 1997/98–. U.S. Department of Commerce. Economics and Statistics Administration. Bureau of the Census. (Not distributed to depository libraries).

Content: CD-ROM version of the *State and Metropolitan Area Data Book*.

USA Counties. CD-ROM. WEB. (irregular) 1992–. U.S. Department of Commerce. Economics and Statistics Administration. Bureau of the Census. C 3.134/6: Item 0150-B-01. ASI 2324-17. <http://govinfo.kerr.orst.edu/usaco-stateis.html>; <http://tier2.census.gov/usac/index.html-ssi>.

Coverage: U.S., states, counties.

Content: state and local government employment and earnings; local government finances and employment.

Discussion

These general sources derive much of their data from the more detailed sources listed later in this chapter. In particular, the *Statistical Abstract of the United States* includes a number of tables giving state and local government statistics. A recurring section of the *Statistical Abstract* is titled "State and Local Government Finances and Employment." A CD-ROM version of the *Statistical Abstract* is also available. The *State and Metropolitan Data Book* includes a lesser number of statistical series but provides more detailed geographic coverage. The *County and City Data Book* provides information on employment, revenues, and expenditures, and is available in print, CD-ROM, and as a Web version.

The *County and City Extra: Annual Metro, City, and County Data Book* is similar to the *County and City Data Book*, but includes additional data and more updated information. *Places, Towns, and Townships* is a companion title for smaller geographic areas. *Historical Statistics of the United States* gives a number of historical series, but information is only included at the aggregate U.S. level.

CENSUS BUREAU SOURCES
Checklist

Census of Governments. (quinquennial) 1957–. (Titles of individual volumes vary) U.S. Department of Commerce. Economics and Statistics Administration. Bureau of the Census. C 3.145/4: Item 0148-A. ASI 2450-1 to 2460-1. GPO. <http://www.census.gov/prod/www/abs/govern.html>; <http://www.census.gov/mp/www/pub/gov/msgov.html>.

Government Organization. (Vol. 1, *Government Organization*, No. 1)

Coverage: U.S., states, counties, municipalities, townships, school districts, special districts, public school systems, governmental units.

Content: number of state and local governments; number of governments by state, type of government, size, and county location; description of local government structure by state.

Popularly Elected Officials. (Vol. 1, *Government Organization*, No. 2)

Coverage: U.S., regions, states, counties, municipalities, townships, school districts, special districts, public school systems, governmental units.

Content: number and characteristics of elected officials, including sex, race, and ethnic origin.

Assessed Valuations for Local General Property Taxation. (Vol. 2, *Taxable Property Values*, No. 1)

Coverage: U.S., states, counties, selected major cities.

Content: gross and net assessed value of property subject to local general property taxation by class of property and state; property tax revenue of state and local governments; assessed value of property subject to local general property taxation for counties and selected cities.

Employment of Major Local Governments. (Vol. 3, *Public Employment*, No. 1)

Coverage: states, counties, and municipal governments; township governments with 25,000 or more population; special district governmental units of 100 or more full-time employees; individual school systems enrolling 5,000 or more pupils.

Content: employment; employment in selected functions; payrolls; average earnings.

Compendium of Public Employment (Vol. 3, *Public Employment*, No. 2)

Coverage: U.S.; states; counties; and municipal, township, school district, and special district governmental units; individual county areas.

Content: employment and payrolls by level, type of government, function, and population-size and employment-size groups.

Public Education Finances (Vol. 4, *Government Finances*, No. 1)

Coverage: U.S., states, public school systems of 5,000 or more enrollment.

Content: federal, state, and local government expenditures for education; elementary-secondary public-school system finances; local public school system finances; state and local government expenditures for higher education; individual public school system finances of districts of 5,000 or more enrollment; state relational statistics and rankings.

Finances of Special Districts (Vol. 4, *Government Finances*, No. 2)

Coverage: U.S., states, special districts, individual large special district governments.

Content: revenues; expenditures; indebtedness and debt transactions; cash and security holdings; revenues by type, source, and function; expenditures by function and character and object; detailed finances for individual large special district governments.

Finances of County Governments. (Vol. 4, *Government Finances*, No. 3)

Coverage: U.S., states, county governments.

Content: revenues; expenditures; indebtedness and debt transactions; cash and security holdings; revenue by source; expenditures by function and character and object; finances by county population-size groups; finances of individual county governments.

Finances of Municipal and Township Governments. (Vol. 4, *Government Finances*, No. 4)

Coverage: U.S; states; population-size groups of municipalities, townships, Northeast township governments, individual municipal governments and Northeast township governments of 25,000 or greater population.

Content: revenues by source and function; expenditures by function, character, and object; indebtedness and debt transactions; cash and security holdings; finances for population-size groups of municipalities and Northeast townships; finances of municipally operated utilities and liquor stores; finances of individual municipal and Northeast township governments with 25,000 or greater population.

Compendium of Government Finances. (Vol. 4, *Government Finances*, No. 5)

Coverage: U.S; states; counties; municipal, township, school district, and special district governmental units; population-size groups of county areas; individual county areas.

Content: revenues; expenditures by function, level, character and object; tax revenues; local government intergovernmental revenue from federal and state governments; finances of utilities; indebtedness and debt transactions; cash and security holdings; state and local government employee retirement system finances; state and local government finances per capita and per $1,000 of personal income; local government finances by type of government; population-size groups of county areas; individual county areas.

Employee Retirement Systems of State and Local Governments. (Vol. 4, *Government Finances*, No. 6)

Coverage: U.S., states, individual state and local government employee retirement systems with cash and investment holdings of $20 million or more.

Content: summary statistics; revenues and expenditures; cash and investment holdings; system receipts and payments; beneficiaries and monthly payments; statistics by membership-size group and type of employees covered; individual finances of state and local government employee retirement systems with cash and investment holdings of $20 million or more.

Governments. WEB. U.S. Department of Commerce. Economics and Statistics Administration. Bureau of the Census. <http://www.census.gov/govs/www/index.html>.

Content: information about government structure and data collection; links to individual Web pages of governmental data.

State Government Finance Data, by State. WEB. (annual) U.S. Department of Commerce. Economics and Statistics Adminis-

tration. Bureau of the Census. <http://www.census.gov/govs/www/state.html>.

Coverage: U.S., states.

Content: revenues, expenditures, indebtedness and debt transactions; cash and security holdings.

Finance Data for the Largest Cities in the U.S. WEB. (annual) U.S. Department of Commerce. Economics and Statistics Administration. Bureau of the Census. <http://www.census.gov/govs/www/city50.html>.

Coverage: city governments of 500,000 or more.

Content: revenues, expenditures, indebtedness and debt transactions; cash and security holdings.

Finance Data for the Largest Counties in the U.S. WEB. (annual) U.S. Department of Commerce. Economics and Statistics Administration. Bureau of the Census. <http://www.census.gov/govs/www/cou50.html>.

Coverage: individual counties of 1,000,000 population or more.

Content: revenue by type; expenditures by function; debt; cash and security holdings.

State Government Tax Collections Data by State. WEB. (annual) U.S. Department of Commerce. Economics and Statistics Administration. Bureau of the Census. <http://www.census.gov/govs/www/statetax.html>.

Coverage: U.S., states.

Content: detailed statistics on tax collections; including property taxes; sales and gross receipts; license taxes; individual income; corporate net income; death & gift; documentary & stock transfer; severance

Public Elementary-Secondary Education Finance Data. WEB. (annual) U.S. Department of Commerce. Economics and Statistics Administration. Bureau of the Census. <http://www.census.gov/govs/www/school.html>.

Coverage: U.S., state, individual school districts with enrollments of 15,000 or more.

Content: revenue from federal, state, and local governmental sources used for education; current spending and expenditures; per pupil expenditure; indebtedness; state rankings; detailed finances of individual school districts with enrollments of 15,000 or more.

State Government Employment and Payroll Data. WEB. (annual). U.S. Department of Commerce. Economics and Statistics Administration. Bureau of the Census. <http://www.census.gov/govs/www/apesst.html>.

Coverage: U.S., states.

Content: number of employees; gross payrolls by government function for state governments.

State and Local Government Employment and Payroll Data. WEB. (annual) U.S. Department of Commerce. Economics and Statistics Administration. Bureau of the Census. <http://www.census.gov/govs/www/apesstl.html>.

Coverage: U.S., states.

Content: number of employees; gross payrolls by government function for state and local governments.

Local Government Employment and Payroll Data. WEB. (annual) U.S. Department of Commerce. Economics and Statistics Administration. Bureau of the Census. <http://www.census.gov/govs/www/apesloc.html>.

Content: numbers of employees and gross payrolls by government function for local governments.

Federal Assistance Awards Data System (FAADS). WEB. (quarterly) U.S. Department of Commerce. Bureau of the Census. <http://www.census.gov/govs/www/faads.html>.

Coverage: U.S., states, counties, places.

Content: federal expenditures or obligations for formula, project, and block grants; cooperative agreements; direct and guaranteed loans; direct payments for individuals; and insurance.

Consolidated Federal Funds Report: Fiscal Year [fiscal year] State and County Areas. PRINT. WEB. (annual) 1983–. U.S. Department of Commerce. Economics and Statistics Administration. Bureau of the Census. C 3.266/2: Item 0137-B. ASI 2464-3. GPO. <http://www.census.gov/ftp/pub/govs/www/cffr.html>; <http://tier2.census.gov/cffr/cffr.htm>.

Coverage: U.S., states, counties

Content: federal expenditures or obligations for the following; direct payments for retirement and disability; other direct payments; grants; procurement contracts; salaries and wages; direct loans; guaranteed or insured loans.

Consolidated Federal Funds Report. CD-ROM. (annual) U.S. Department of Commerce. Economics and Statistics Administration. Bureau of the Census. C 3.266/3: Item 0154-B-02.

Coverage: U.S., states, counties, subcounty areas.

Content: federal expenditures or obligations for the following: direct payments for retirement and disability; other direct payments; grants; procurement contracts; salaries and wages; direct loans; guaranteed or insured loans.

Federal Aid to States for Fiscal Year [fiscal year]. (annual) 1998–. PRINT. WEB. U.S. Department of Commerce. Economics and Statistics Administration. Bureau of the Census. C 3.266: Item 0137-B. ASI 2464-4. <http://www.census.gov/prod/www/abs/fas.html>; <http://purl.access.gpo.gov/GPO/LPS4561>.

Coverage: U.S., states.

Content: federal grant payments to state and local governments by agency and for selected programs.

Quarterly Summary of State and Local Tax Revenue. PRINT. WEB. (quarterly) 1963–. U.S. Department of Commerce. Economics and Statistics Administration. Bureau of the Census. C 3.145/6: Item 0146-E. ASI 2462-3. <http://www.census.gov/govs/www/qtax.html>.

Coverage: U.S., states.

Content: total tax collections; collection by type of tax including income, property, corporate net income, motor fuel sales, tobacco product sales, alcoholic beverage sales, motor vehicle and operators' license; other license fee and tax revenue from various sources.

Finances of Selected Public Employee Retirement Systems. PRINT. WEB. (quarterly) 1968–. U.S. Department of Commerce. Economics and Statistics Administration. Bureau of the Census. C 3.242: Item 0148-E. ASI 2462-2. <http://www.census.gov/govs/www/qpr.html>; <http://purl.access.gpo.gov/GPO/LPS1837>.

Coverage: aggregate total figures for 104 selected major public employee retirement systems.

Content: cash and security holdings; receipts, benefits, and withdrawal payments; percent distribution of cash and security holdings; percent distribution of receipts.

State and Local Government Finance Estimates, by State. WEB. 1988–. U.S. Department of Commerce. Economics and Statistics Administration. Bureau of the Census. <http://www.census.gov/govs/www/estimate.html>.

Coverage: U.S., states.

Content: revenues; expenditures; debt; cash and security holdings.

Discussion

The *Census of Governments* is conducted every five years and provides the most detailed data on federal, state, and local governments. The level of geographic detail varies. Most tables provide information at the aggregate U.S. and state levels, and many tables provide statistics at the county, township, municipal, school district, and special district level. Data are also often given by population-size of the governmental units. Data for some individual large governmental units are also included.

The individual volumes of the *Census of Governments* listed here generally reflect the volumes published for the 1992 Census. There is generally a lag of several years before all the data are compiled and volumes are published. Individual titles published may vary from census to census. Volume 1, Number 2, *Popularly Elected Officials*, is only issued every 10 years. Reports consist primarily of statistical tables, with introductory text. Figure 43.1 reprints a typical page from the *Census of Governments*.

The *Governments* page provides a starting point for locating additional Census Bureau data on governmental finance and employment. It provides information on the data being gathered and links to other Web pages. Most of the data are collected annually, and Web pages provide several years worth of data. The most relevant of these Web pages are listed individually here. Until around 1992, much of this data was published in a print format in two series, the *Government Finances* series (C 3.191/2- and the *Government Employment* series (C 3.140/2-).

State Government Finance Data, by State provides a state by state summary of the most significant finance data. U.S. totals and individual state data can be viewed online, and files can also be downloaded in ASCII text and spreadsheet formats. *Finance Data for the Largest Cities in the U.S.* and *Finance Data for the Largest Counties in the U.S.* provide detailed data, but cover only a small number of the largest cities and counties. *State Government Tax Collections Data by State* gives tax revenue information for both the U.S. and individual states. Data on these three pages are also viewable online or available for downloading in text or spreadsheet formats. *Public Elementary-Secondary Education Finance Data* gives detailed statistics on state and local government spending on elementary and secondary education. Data for selected large individual school districts are also included. Statistical tables in PDF format provide a convenient method to view the data online, and various options for downloading the data are included.

Table 50. Local Government Finances for Individual County Areas by State: 1991-92—Con.

[Thousand dollars. Duplicative intergovernmental transactions are excluded. Detail may not add to total because of rounding. For meaning of abbreviations and symbols, see introductory text]

Geographic area	Transportation — Highways (24)	Transportation — Other transportation (25)	Public safety — Police protection (26)	Public safety — Fire protection (27)	Public safety — Correction (28)	Public safety — Protective inspection and regulation (29)	Environment and housing — Natural resources (30)	Environment and housing — Parks and recreation (31)	Environment and housing — Housing and community development (32)	Environment and housing — Sewerage (33)	Environment and housing — Sanitation other than sewerage (34)
TEXAS—Con.											
1 Montague	2 105	–	1 016	490	404	–	53	315	531	3 313	414
2 Montgomery	16 028	333	17 268	3 281	4 563	–	735	1 258	507	9 169	948
3 Moore	3 238	348	1 906	522	366	51	470	155	65	220	558
4 Morris	191	–	877	68	307	–	–	6	159	223	337
5 Motley	103	–	18	9	28	–	7	–	–	1	–
6 Nacogdoches	5 257	348	3 641	2 188	1 041	135	489	692	1 428	1 379	1 961
7 Navarro	5 456	101	3 241	1 592	1 460	42	103	617	1 258	1 319	1 232
8 Newton	1 178	3	285	31	171	–	26	58	69	22	91
9 Nolan	1 242	35	1 451	736	85	–	81	230	338	378	861
10 Nueces	20 717	42 190	32 618	13 820	9 201	1 214	758	15 990	9 766	13 279	7 682
11 Ochiltree	400	6	1 464	330	–	5	78	365	–	266	345
12 Oldham	209	6	350	77	6	–	66	12	–	29	50
13 Orange	3 079	2 931	4 962	730	2 469	207	1 906	386	379	2 315	2 319
14 Palo Pinto	1 465	313	1 609	339	751	101	462	404	846	6 192	646
15 Panola	4 749	24	1 586	228	1 398	19	108	151	588	–	322
16 Parker	5 696	–	5 484	1 216	–	75	6	675	1 651	7 245	827
17 Parmer	124	–	364	83	189	–	30	57	–	77	211
18 Pecos	1 517	32	1 669	228	461	–	271	1 349	854	4	880
19 Polk	3 093	354	2 555	506	661	32	–	63	590	554	1 112
20 Potter	7 270	1 993	21 355	7 664	1 640	1 105	70	5 166	4 872	3 384	5 608
21 Presidio	329	12	215	40	265	–	14	98	118	164	80
22 Rains	819	–	293	75	194	–	18	–	–	88	84
23 Randall	1 759	–	2 849	270	670	103	98	228	38	773	325
24 Reagan	419	1	116	18	57	–	105	5	–	97	123
25 Real	56	2	22	2	12	–	19	–	–	33	117
26 Red River	1 443	–	771	208	213	–	69	19	261	57	56
27 Reeves	835	15	1 265	274	6 132	28	29	372	–	140	602
28 Refugio	843	–	443	102	13	3	78	112	–	418	129
29 Roberts	362	3	138	26	34	–	14	17	–	24	75
30 Robertson	4 666	4	1 273	346	194	35	3	243	654	464	230
31 Rockwall	7 938	131	3 583	551	1 130	102	289	2 150	160	1 116	1 141
32 Runnels	799	–	667	36	389	–	22	32	78	87	437
33 Rusk	3 301	–	2 481	729	827	51	99	168	253	554	737
34 Sabine	1 213	–	365	12	4	–	–	44	180	812	116
35 San Augustine	486	1	439	95	53	–	3	11	–	98	87
36 San Jacinto	1 487	27	771	103	310	–	256	–	–	333	245
37 San Patricio	4 113	658	5 310	685	1 373	193	2 145	604	897	1 939	2 366
38 San Saba	361	–	176	20	115	–	15	36	85	126	146
39 Schleicher	820	–	101	53	37	–	9	4	328	176	69
40 Scurry	1 189	–	1 511	413	294	–	70	227	–	412	438
41 Shackelford	260	–	171	45	22	–	–	56	–	119	137
42 Shelby	1 519	–	1 849	288	37	–	16	55	179	540	764
43 Sherman	208	–	208	31	26	–	16	16	–	44	54
44 Smith	14 047	2 675	11 904	5 704	8 178	283	194	3 397	2 684	3 499	4 162
45 Somervell	827	76	219	13	164	–	25	490	132	181	99
46 Starr	4 877	4	2 379	94	1 353	–	287	128	289	172	474
47 Stephens	965	3	672	247	215	–	30	12	–	217	292
48 Sterling	86	–	121	59	1	–	103	7	–	37	9
49 Stonewall	615	12	426	5	149	–	14	19	61	–	–
50 Sutton	687	–	729	198	48	–	149	135	–	222	182
51 Swisher	992	13	587	85	3	–	74	132	6	116	219
52 Tarrant	118 383	36 062	134 020	70 219	51 044	8 788	247	61 184	45 504	128 961	23 039
53 Taylor	7 006	576	9 736	6 227	2 831	399	106	5 282	3 479	3 148	3 211
54 Terrell	–	–	67	4	–	–	1	–	–	–	–
55 Terry	1 580	82	1 199	324	375	43	100	369	–	202	480
56 Throckmorton	674	–	219	36	25	–	36	7	40	42	79
57 Titus	3 408	136	2 011	854	473	93	384	257	270	5 689	2 384
58 Tom Green	5 104	1 375	8 632	4 870	1 598	335	388	2 401	1 337	2 106	89
59 Travis	60 981	15 331	69 282	37 238	31 510	1 320	4 246	56 815	23 014	62 397	14 323
60 Trinity	1 990	2	863	119	17	–	33	37	–	207	1
61 Tyler	1 509	6	947	29	397	–	28	–	179	358	207
62 Upshur	2 034	–	1 258	297	515	–	8	78	189	119	326
63 Upton	832	6	516	102	54	–	143	513	–	30	125
64 Uvalde	1 002	76	1 476	286	267	120	19	889	450	362	706
65 Val Verde	2 415	127	3 291	1 458	1 160	104	70	531	3 244	1 100	713
66 Van Zandt	3 284	–	1 313	170	2 302	–	60	38	221	321	455
67 Victoria	10 503	1 321	11 466	3 677	313	505	787	2 004	2 862	3 606	2 887
68 Walker	3 235	134	3 334	758	1 133	151	64	2 048	1 048	79 849	1 253
69 Waller	5 609	–	1 906	119	1 726	–	661	219	–	854	209
70 Ward	577	12	1 337	99	867	–	148	728	851	708	594
71 Washington	3 035	–	2 312	288	–	38	154	288	100	223	429
72 Webb	16 107	6 964	12 876	7 276	8 341	401	91	3 773	2 343	3 252	2 609
73 Wharton	5 052	55	3 171	238	851	686	1 750	1 025	383	988	1 224
74 Wheeler	775	–	540	91	122	–	45	16	–	28	187
75 Wichita	8 994	185	11 221	5 768	2 330	625	988	3 050	1 895	7 629	5 899
76 Wilbarger	1 496	220	863	570	232	12	155	297	598	269	268

See footnotes at end of table.

TIPSII [UPF] DCOP50 GOVTS 68137200 01/29/97 3:39 PM MACHINE: D DATA:NONE TAPE: NONE FRAME: 163
TSF:GOVTS*92. 01/29/97 15:27:01 UTF:GOVTS*93. 01/29/97 15:27:01 META:GOVTS*98. 01/29/97 15:34:26

Source: 1992 *Census of Governments*, vol. 4, *Government Finances*, no. 5, *Compendium of Government Finances*, Table 50, "Local Government Finances for Individual County Areas by State: 1991-92."

Figure 43.1: Sample Page from the *Census of Governments*.

Three similar Web sites from the Bureau of the Census provide data on state and local government employment. They are titled *State Government Employment and Payroll Data*, *State and Local Government Employment and Payroll Data*, and *Local Government Employment and Payroll Data*. Each site includes summary tables for viewing, downloadable ASCII text files, and data files in Lotus 123 spreadsheet format. Data are collected on an annual basis for the month of March. *The State Government Employment and Payroll Data* site includes data for state governments on the number of employees and the gross payroll of state governments. The *State and Local Government Employment and Payroll Data* site gives similar information for state, local, and state plus local aggregates. The *Local Government Employment and Payroll Data* gives this data for local governments (counties, municipalities, townships, special districts, and school districts).

The *Federal Assistance Awards Data System* is a quarterly set of data providing information on federal finanical assistance awards. It seeks to cover assistance awards from all programs in the *Catalog of Federal Domestic Assistance*, as well as some additional assistance awards. It includes assistance to states and local governments. The data are distributed at the Census Bureau's Web site, although the Office of Management and Budget provides policy oversight. Summaries of the data for the U.S. and each state may be viewed directly, but the full data files must be downloaded to obtain the more detailed data. Files are flat ASCII text files and the quarterly data sets are not cumulated. Entries are included for each assistance transaction and are also aggregated at the county level. Detailed information on each transaction is included. Some of the many data elements include: CFDA program number, recipient name, recipient city name, recipient county name, recipient state code; recipient zip code, type of recipient, recipient congressional district, federal funding amount, type of assistance transaction, principal place of performance, CFDA program title, and federal agency name. Although not particularly easy to use without search features, the *Federal Assistance Awards Data System* does provides some of the most detailed information available on individual assistance transactions.

The *Consolidated Federal Funds Report* gives statistics on federal government expenditures and obligations. While many of the items included are payments or expenditures to individuals, it also includes federal expenditures to state and local governmental units. The print version of the *Consolidated Federal Funds Report* (also available on the WEB in a PDF format) includes data for only states and county areas. Data at more detailed geographic levels are available for viewing and as downloadable files from the Census Bureau Web site. A CD-ROM version of the *Consolidated Federal Funds Report* also includes the more detailed data.

Federal Aid to States is also issued as a result of the *Consolidated Federal Funds Reports* data collection. It gives data on Federal grants to state and local governments. Statistics are often shown by federal agency and program. Some historical data are also included in the report.

The *Quarterly Summary of State and Local Tax Revenue* is a long-standing survey that collects data at the state level for state and local tax revenues from a variety of sources. Three tables are included—the Web version of the *Quarterly Summary* includes both a text viewable version and a spreadsheet format file for downloading. Table 1 is "National Totals of State and Local Tax Revenue, by Type of Tax," and includes quarterly and annual summary data by broad category of tax revenue. Table 2 is titled "National Totals of State Tax Revenue, by Type of Tax," and gives similar information for state tax revenue. Table 3, "State Tax Collections by State and Type of Tax," gives statistics on over 25 different forms of tax revenues collected in each state, as well as summary statistics for each state.

The *Finances of Selected Public Employee Retirement Systems* publishes information from a quarterly survey of 104 of the largest public employee retirement systems. These data have been collected since 1968. The four tables provide a summary of these systems' finances and represent 87 percent of the total assets of the public employee retirement systems covered by the *Census of Governments*. This is a good source for a current representative look at the finances of public employee retirement systems.

The State and Local Government Finance Estimates, by State Web page provides a series of viewable tables and downloadable files in ASCII text and spreadsheet formats. Statistics are available as a national summary and for each state. Statistics on revenues, expenditures, debt, and cash and security holdings are included for each state. Statistics by level of government—state, local, and state plus local, are also included.

ADDITIONAL SOURCES
Checklist

Budget Information for States, Fiscal Year [year]. PRINT. WEB. (annual). PREX 2.8: [date]/INFO. Item 0853. ASI 104-30. GPO. <http://w3.access.gpo.gov/usbudget/index.html>; <http://purl.access.gpo.gov/GPO/LPS862>.

> Coverage: U.S., states
> Content: statistical tables depicting federal obligations to state and local governments.

Expenditure and Employment Statistics. WEB. U.S. Department of Justice. Bureau of Justice Statistics. <http://www.ojp.usdoj.gov/bjs/eande.htm>.

> Content: links to data and publications; summary statistics; codebooks and datasets; related links.

Justice Expenditure and Employment Extracts, [FY]: Data from the Annual General Finance and Employment Surveys. PRINT. WEB. (irregular) U.S. Department of Justice. Office of Justice Programs. Bureau of Justice Statistics. J 29.11/2-2: Item 0968-H-13. ASI 6064-4. <http://www.ojp.usdoj.gov/bjs/eande.htm>.

Coverage: U.S., states, 68 individual large county governments, 49 large city governments.

Content: justice expenditures, employment, and payrolls; statistics by state, character, and type of government; detailed statistics on 68 individual large county governments and 49 large city governments.

Job Patterns for Minorities and Women in State and Local Government. PRINT. (annual) U.S. Equal Employment Opportunity Commission. Y 3.EQ 2:12-4/year. Item 1059-A-01. ASI 9244-6.

Coverage: U.S., states.

Content: statistics on employment by race, ethnic group, sex, type of government, job category, and function; salaries.

Discussion

Budget Information for States includes data compiled during the federal budgetary process by the Office of Management and Budget. The report details federal obligations to state and local governments for major Federal formula grant programs, such as the National School Lunch Program and Adult Employment and Training Grants. Tables include summary tables, data by program, and data by state.

The Justice Department collects various information on justice expenditures and employment. The *Expenditure and Employment Statistics* Web Page provides links to relevant publications, links to selected statistics, links to codebooks and datasets, links to related employment and expenditure data, and a description of the data collection. This page provides an excellent entry point to obtaining state and local information.

The *Justice Expenditure and Employment Extracts* title provides a series of statistical tables documenting trends in justice employment and expenditures at the state and local level. Of particular interest are the detailed statistics provided for 68 individual large county governments and 49 large city governments. The Web version of the *Justice Expenditures and Employment Extracts* provides a PDF format file, ASCII text files, and spreadsheet format files.

Job Patterns for Minorities and Women in State and Local Government presents a series of statistical tables that compare salaries and employment by race, ethnic group, and sex. Most tables include statistics on male and female Whites, Blacks, Hispanics, Asians or Pacific Islanders, and American Indians or Alaskan Natives. Data are collected through a survey that covers state and local governments with 15 or more full-time employees.

INDEXES
Checklist

American Statistics Index (ASI). PRINT. (monthly) 1973–. Bethesda, MD: Congressional Information Service.

Statistical Universe. WEB. Bethesda, MD: Congressional Information Service.

Catalog of United States Government Publications (MOCAT). WEB. 1994–. U.S. Government Printing Office. Superintendent of Documents. <http://www.gpo.gov/catalog>; <http://www.access.gpo.gov/su_docs/locators/cgp/index.html>; <http://purl.access.gpo.gov/GPO/LPS844>.

Monthly Catalog of United States Government Publications. CD-ROM. 1996–. U.S. Government Printing Office. Superintendent of Documents. GP 3.8/7: Item 0557-C. GPO.

Monthly Catalog of United States Government Publications (Condensed version). PRINT. (monthly) 1996–. U.S. Government Printing Office. Superintendent of Documents. GP 3.8/8: (Earlier full version, GP 3.8:, 1895-1995). Item 0557-D. GPO.

Discussion

A comprehensive listing of material relating to state and local governmental statistics can be found in the *American Statistics Index (ASI)* by searching such headings as "Local government," "Census of Governments," "City and town planning," "Federal aid to local areas," "Federal-local relations," "School districts," "Cities," "Counties," "Special districts," "State and local employees," "Government employees," "State and local employees pay," "State and local taxes," "State funding for local areas," "Federal aid to States," "State government," "State government spending," "State funding for economic development," "State funding for education," "State funding for health and hospitals," "State funding for higher education," "State-local relations," "State funding for local areas," "State funding for natural resources and conservation," "State funding for public safety," "State funding for social welfare," "State funding for transportation," "Medicaid," "Medical assistance," "Unemployment insurance," "Workers compensation," "Police," "Fire departments" "State police," "Officials," "Teachers," "Educational employees pay," "State and local taxes," "Excise tax," "Fuel tax," "Property tax," "Revenue sharing," "Sales tax," and "Severance taxes." *Statistical Universe* includes a Web version of *ASI*.

The *Monthly Catalog* can also be used to identify general statistical publications on state and local government statistics, but does not provide the in-depth indexing of statistics that *ASI* does. Try subject headings beginning with "State Governments" "[Names of States]-Politics and Government" (i.e. "Oregon-Politics and Government"), "Municipal Government," "County Government," "Metropolitan Government," "Local Government," "Local Officials and Employees," "County Officials and Employees," "Municipal Officials and Employees," "Local Finance," "Municipal Finance," and "Special Districts." The complete version of the *Monthly Catalog* is available on the Web and CD-ROM. Commercial online and CD-ROM versions of the *Monthly Catalog* are also available.

RELATED MATERIAL
Within this Work

Chapter 24 Government Programs and Grants

Chapter 47 Budget Analysis

GPO Subject Bibliographies. PRINT. WEB. GP 3.22/2:

<http://bookstore.gpo.gov/sb/about.html>

No. 156 "Census of Governments"

No. 211 "Intergovernmental Relations"

CHAPTER 44
Transportation Statistics

Transportation statistics are primarily available from the Transportation Department and the Census Bureau. A large proportion of the statistics available deal with aviation and with accidents for all modes of transportation. The Census Bureau publishes statistics on the journey to work. Many sources that give statistics by industry include data for the transportation industry. Some of these sources are discussed in such chapters as Chapter 31, "Business and Industry Statistics" or Chapter 35, "Employment."

SEARCH STRATEGY

This chapter is an example of a statistical search strategy. The strategy is as follows:

1. Consult "General Statistical Sources" for a broad selection of basic statistics;
2. Examine the titles under "General Transportation Statistics" for more comprehensive information;
3. For more in depth coverage of a specific transportation mode or industry, check the sections on "Air Transportation," "Water Transportation," or "Other Transportation Industry Sources";
4. If interested in transportation accidents, consider the sources in the "Accidents" section;
5. For data on transportation to work, consult "Journey to Work Sources";
6. Search the indexes to locate additional sources of information; and
7. Consider the "Related Material" section.

GENERAL STATISTICAL SOURCES
Checklist

Statistical Abstract of the United States. PRINT. WEB. (annual) 1878–. U.S. Department of Commerce. Economics and Statistics Administration. Bureau of the Census. C 3.134: Item 0150. ASI 2324-1. GPO. <http://www.census.gov/statab/www/>; <http://purl.access.gpo.gov/GPO/LPS2878>.

> Coverage: world, selected countries, U.S., major waterways, states, selected metropolitan areas, top airports.
> Content: land, air, and water transportation; transportation industry establishments and revenues by industry; passenger and freight traffic; commodity shipments; transportation accidents; highway mileage and finances; number of motor vehicles; motor vehicle registrations, sales, ownership costs, travel miles; fuel consumption; public transit; railroads; airports; aircraft; merchant vessels.

Statistical Abstract of the United States. CD-ROM. (annual) 1993–. U.S. Department of Commerce. Bureau of the Census. C 3.134/7: Item 0150-B. ASI 2324-14.

> Content: CD-ROM version of the *Statistical Abstract*.

Historical Statistics of the United States: Colonial Times to 1970. Parts 1-2. PRINT. (1975) U.S. Department of Commerce. Bureau of the Census. C 3.134/2:H 62/789-970/pt.1-2. Item 0151. ASI (76) 2328-2. GPO.

> Coverage: world, U.S., regions.
> Content: highway, rail, water, and air transportation; revenues; passenger and freight traffic; highway mileage and finances; motor vehicle sales, registrations, travel miles, and accidents; fuel consumption; railroad equipment, traffic, and finances; vessels; shipbuilding; air carrier revenues and expenses; airports; aircraft; pilots.

State and Metropolitan Area Data Book. PRINT. WEB. (irregular) 1979–. U.S. Department of Commerce. Economics and Statistics Administration. Bureau of the Census. C 3.134/5: Item 0150. ASI 2328-54. GPO. <http://www.census.gov/statab/www.smadb.html>.

> Coverage: U.S., states.
> Content: highway mileage; motor vehicle registrations; driver licenses; traffic fatalities; alcohol-related crashes.

State and Metropolitan Area Data Book. CD-ROM. (irregular) 1997/98–. U.S. Department of Commerce. Economics and Statistics Administration. Bureau of the Census. (Not distributed to depository libraries)

> Content: CD-ROM version of the *State and Metropolitan Area Data Book*.

County and City Data Book. PRINT. WEB. (quinquennial) 1947–. U.S. Department of Commerce. Economics and Statistics Administration. Bureau of the Census. C 3.134/2:C 83/2/year. Item 0151. ASI 2328-1. GPO. <http://fisher.lib.Virginia.EDU/ccdb/>.

> Coverage: U.S., regions, divisions, states, counties, cities of 25,000 or more.
> Content: journey to work.

County and City Data Book. CD-ROM. (quinquennial) 1988–. U.S. Department of Commerce. Bureau of the Census. C 3.134/2-1: (Earlier, C 3.134/2:C 83/2/). Item 0151-D-01. ASI 2328-103.

> Content: CD-ROM version of the *County and City Data Book.*

USA Counties. CD-ROM. WEB. (irregular) 1992–. U.S. Department of Commerce. Economics and Statistics Administration. Bureau of the Census. C 3.134/6: Item 0150-B-01. ASI 2324-17. <http://govinfo.kerr.orst.edu/usaco-stateis.html>; <http://tier2.census.gov/usac/index.html-ssi>.

> Coverage: U.S., states, counties.
> Content: journey to work.

Discussion

The *Statistical Abstract of the United States* contains two chapters on transportation: "Transportation—Land" and "Transportation—Air and Water." The land chapter covers highways, motor vehicles, public transit, trucking, railroads, and pipelines. The air and water chapter covers air carriers, the aerospace industry, water transportation and commerce, merchant vessels, and shipyards. Statistics are selected from many of the more detailed sources covered in this chapter. Source notes at the end of each table can direct the user to more current or more detailed sources for the information in that table. The broad range of statistics provides an excellent overview of transportation and can answer many basic statistical questions. Examples of specific data items include miles of interstate highways by state; age of cars in use; speeding-related traffic fatalities; railroad income and expenses; passengers enplaned at top airports; and U.S. flag merchant vessels active in foreign trade. The full text of recent editions of the *Statistical Abstract* is available on the Census Bureau Web site as PDF files. The *Statistical Abstract* is also available on CD-ROM. The CD uses Adobe Acrobat software and contains some additional geographic areas and time series in the form of spreadsheet files that are not in the printed version.

Historical Statistics of the United States contains a chapter on "Transportation" with sections on each type: highway, rail, water, and air. Statistics are similar to those in the *Statistical Abstract* but cover the earliest years available through 1970.

The *State and Metropolitan Area Data Book* provides statistics on motor vehicle transportation topics at the state and national level. This title is available as a PDF file on the Census Bureau Web site and on CD-ROM edition.

The *County and City Data Book* contains journey to work data that cover selected means of transportation to work and average travel time. The *County and City Data Book* is also available in CD-ROM from the Census Bureau. The University of Virginia Library Geospatial and Statistical Data Center offers recent editions of the *County and City Data Book* on the Internet in their interactive data area. Users select the desired edition, geography, and variables to create a customized data display.

The *USA Counties* CD contains data on the journey to work, including number of workers working outside their county of residence, means of transportation to work, and travel time to work. The Oregon State University Government Information Sharing Project provides access to the current issue on the Internet. Users select a geographic area profile or an area comparison and then the desired geography. A subject area can then be selected or a keyword search conducted to display data. The Census Bureau Web site contains a similar version.

GENERAL TRANSPORTATION STATISTICS
Checklist

Transportation Statistics Annual Report. MF. WEB. (annual) 1994–. U.S. Department of Transportation. Bureau of Transportation Statistics. TD 12.1: Item 0982-N. ASI 7314-3. GPO. <http://www.bts.gov/programs/transtu/tsar/prod.html>.

> Coverage: U.S., limited regions, states, metropolitan areas.
> Content: assessment of the state of the transportation system, its economic impacts, and its consequences for safety, energy, and the environment; each issue also features sections on a special theme.

National Transportation Statistics. WEB. (annual) 1977–. U.S. Department of Transportation. Bureau of Transportation Statistics. TD 12.1/2: (Earlier, TD 10.9:) (Issued in MF through 1997; Web only 1998–) (Issued before 1977 under other titles) Item 0982-K-01. ASI 7314-1. (Earlier, 7304-2) <http://www.bts.gov/btsprod/nts/>; <http://purl.access.gpo.gov/GPO/LPS673>.

> Coverage: world, countries, U.S., top airports, top ports.
> Content: statistics on transportation system and each type of transportation; physical network; travel and goods movement; vehicle, aircraft, and vessel inventories; condition and performance of the system; consumer and government expenditures; industry employment and productivity; safety; energy use; pollution.

Bureau of Transportation Statistics Web Site. WEB. U.S. Department of Transportation. Bureau of Transportation Statistics. <http://www.bts.gov/>.

> Content: publications and data on transportation statistics.

Highway Statistics. MF. WEB. (annual) 1945–. U.S. Department of Transportation. Federal Highway Administration. Office of Highway Information Management. TD 2.23: (Historical summary under TD 2.23/2:) Item 0265-B. ASI 7554-1. <http://www.fhwa.dot.gov/ohim/ohimstat.htm>.

> Coverage: selected countries, U.S., states, urbanized areas, county and municipal toll facilities.
> Content: motor fuel use and taxes; vehicle registration and taxes; drivers' licenses by sex and age group; govern-

ment highway finance; mileage by type of road and road characteristics; vehicle miles of travel; fatalities and injuries; household and personal travel.

Discussion

The *Transportation Statistics Annual Report* is a comprehensive overview of the transportation system. Narrative chapters analyze trends and highlight key statistics. Chapters are illustrated with charts and include a small number of statistical tables. A chapter on the transportation system analyzes trends in passenger travel, freight transportation, the transportation network, and the system's condition and performance. A chapter on transportation and the economy discusses the role of transportation in the national economy, consumer expenditures, government expenditures and revenues, and transportation employment. A chapter on transportation safety reports on recent crashes, fatality rates for different modes of transportation, and causes of crashes. Another chapter discusses transportation, energy, and the environment. Chapters are also devoted to a selected theme, such as long distance travel and freight movement in the 1998 report. Each chapter includes bibliographic references.

National Transportation Statistics is a companion volume to the *Transportation Statistics Annual Report* containing detailed statistical tables. It brings together statistics from many government and private sources and covers all types of transportation. Chapters parallel those in the *Transportation Statistics Annual Report* and cover the transportation system; transportation and the economy; transportation safety; and transportation, energy, and the environment. Examples of data included are revenue passenger-miles for transportation modes, retail sales of passenger cars, highway condition, air carrier delays, fatalities by mode, personal consumption expenditures on transportation categories, and fuel consumption and travel by type of vehicle, fuel efficiency, and vehicle emission rates. An appendix called "Modal Profiles" provides an overview of each type of transportation (for example, air carrier profile, highway profile). These summarize data in four categories: financial, inventory, performance, and safety. This title also includes extensive source references, a glossary of terms, and a bibliography. It is the best single source for a wide range of transportation statistics. Tables are available on the Web for viewing or downloading in Excel format.

The *Bureau of Transportation Statistics Web Site* contains extensive transportation data and resources. Main menu options include "Airline Information," "American Travel Survey," "Commodity Flow Survey," "Databases," "Geographic Information Services," "International Transportation," "National Transportation Library," "Product Information & Services," and "Transportation Studies." The "Airline Information" option contains selected statistical data and information on other sources of information. The "American Travel Survey" provides tables, pub-

lications, and maps on long-distance travel at the national, state, and metropolitan area level. The "Commodity Flow Survey" provides reports and maps on commodity shipments for manufacturing and selected other sectors at the national and state level. The "Databases" option lists transportation databases from various government agencies. Links may include information about the database, related products and publications, and sometimes Web versions of the database. "Geographic Information Services" contains information on geo-spatial datasets and includes maps that can be viewed or downloaded. The "International Transportation" option contains reports and statistics on North American border travel and freight transportation, Latin American transportation fact sheets, and international air travel and tourism. The "National Transportation Library" contains documents and databases from various public and private organizations. The library is searchable or can be browsed by subject category. The "Product Information & Services" option searches or displays Bureau of Transportation Statistics publications and products. The "Transportation Studies" option lists major transportation reports and studies available on the Web primarily from the Bureau of Transportation Statistics.

Highway Statistics is a compilation of statistics on highway use, finance, and physical characteristics. Most of the data are for the current year. A separate report contains historical data. The most recent historical report is *Highway Statistics Summary to 1995* (TD 2.23/2:995). Statistics relating to motor vehicles include use of gasoline by month and state, number and type of vehicle registrations, and number and type of driver's licenses by state. More extensive statistics are available for highway finance and highway use and characteristics. The highway finance section covers federal, state, and local government receipts and disbursements. Highway characteristics include mileage, traffic volume, lane width, access control, jurisdiction, type of surface, and pavement condition. Data are by state and type of highway (interstate, principal or minor arterials), not by specific highways. Questions that can be answered by this source include "How many miles of roads are there in Houston or Texas?," "Which state has the most vehicle-miles of travel?" (California), and "How many licensed male drivers under 19 years of age are there in Ohio?"

AIR TRANSPORTATION
Checklist

FAA Statistical Handbook of Aviation. MF. WEB. (annual) U.S. Department of Transportation. Federal Aviation Administration. TD 4.20: Item 0431-C-14. ASI 7504-1. <http://api.hq.faa.gov/apo_pubs.htm >; <http://www.api.faa.gov/apo_pubs.htm>; <http://www.bts.gov/ntda/shafaa/>.

> Coverage: U.S., FAA regions, states, top airports, hubs, air carriers.
> Content: air traffic, airports, passengers, departures, aircraft, revenue ton-miles, revenue passenger miles, oper-

ating revenues and expenses, pilots, accidents, aircraft production.

Air Travel Consumer Report. MF. WEB. (monthly) Nov. 1987–. U.S. Department of Transportation. Office of Aviation Enforcement and Proceedings. TD 1.54: Item 0982-C-29. ASI 7302-11. <http://www.dot.gov/airconsumer/index1.htm>; <http://purl.access.gpo.gov/GPO/LPS4338>; <http://www.dot.gov/ost/oge/subject/consumer/aviation/data/atcr/index.html>; <http://purl.access.gpo.gov/GPO/LPS1712>.

> Coverage: U.S., large airports, large air carriers.
> Content: percentage of on-time arrivals and departures; number of mishandled baggage reports; number of boardings denied due to oversales; number and category of consumer complaints; airline rankings.

Domestic Airline Fares Consumer Report. WEB. (quarterly) 1996, 3rd quarter–. U.S. Department of Transportation. ASI 7302-13. <http://ostpxweb.dot.gov/aviation/domfares/domfares.htm>.

> Coverage: large city-pair markets
> Content: average fare; largest and lowest fare carriers and their percentage of market; markets with largest percentage increase and decrease.

Air Carrier Financial Statistics Quarterly. MF. (quarterly) Sept. 1984–. U.S. Department of Transportation. Bureau of Transportation Statistics. Office of Airline Information. TD 12.15/3: (Earlier, TD 10.9/4:, CAB 1.17:; C 31.240:) (Title varies) Item 0982-N-03. ASI 7312-3.

> Coverage: U.S., individual air carriers.
> Content: income and balance sheet data for individual carriers; operating revenues and expenses by category; profits; income; assets; liabilities; stockholders' equity.

Airline Quarterly Financial Review. WEB. (quarterly) 1995–. U.S. Department of Transportation. Office of Aviation Analysis. Economic and Financial Analysis Division. ASI 7302-14. <http://ostpxweb.dot.gov/aviation/finance.htm>.

> Coverage: major passenger and cargo airlines.
> Content: total operating revenues and expenses; profits; net income; traffic; yield and unit cost; financial ratios and percentages; passenger load factor; employment and productivity.

Air Carrier Traffic Statistics Monthly. MF. (monthly) Sept. 1984–. U.S. Department of Transportation. Bureau of Transportation Statistics. Office of Airline Information. TD 12.15/2: (Earlier, TD 10.9/3:, CAB 1.13:; C 31.241:) (Title varies) Item 0982-N-02. ASI 7312-2.

> Coverage: U.S., individual air carriers.
> Content: revenue passenger-miles; revenue ton-miles; available seat-miles; capacity and load factors; revenue passenger enplanements; aircraft revenue miles and hours.

APO Data System. WEB. U.S. Department of Transportation. Federal Aviation Administration. Aviation Policy and Plans. <http://www.apo.data.faa.gov/>.

> Coverage: regions, states, airports, FAA facilities.
> Content: air traffic activity database; departures; overflights; itinerant or local; instrument operations; approach operations; flight services.

Airport Activity Statistics of Certificated Air Carriers. MF. (annual) 1962–. U.S. Department of Transportation. Bureau of

Transportation Statistics. Office of Airline Information. TD 4.14: (Earlier, C 31.251:) Item 0177-A. ASI 7314-9.

> Coverage: U.S., states, individual airlines, individual airports.
> Content: aircraft departures, enplaned passengers, freight, and mail.

Enplanement and All-Cargo Statistics. WEB. U.S. Department of Transportation. Federal Aviation Administration. Office of Airports. <http://www.faa.gov/arp/A&D-stat.htm>; Download related Excel files: <http://www.faa.gov/arp/410home.htm>.

> Coverage: U.S., states, airports.
> Content: cargo landed weight, passenger enplanements.

Office of Airline Information Home Page. WEB. U.S. Department of Transportation. Bureau of Transportation Statistics. Office of Airline Information. <http://www.bts.gov/programs/oai/>.

> Content: airline statistics and information resources.

FAA Aerospace Forecasts Fiscal Years [years]. MF. (annual) U.S. Department of Transportation. Federal Aviation Administration. Office of Aviation Policy and Plans. TD 4.57/2: (Earlier, TD 4.57:, TD 4.32/11:, TD 4.2:Av5/) (Title varies) (Earlier title, *FAA Aviation Forecasts*) Item 0431-C-27. ASI 7504-6. Selected tables: <http://api.hq.faa.gov/apo_pubs.htm>; <http://www.api.faa.gov/apo_pubs.htm>.

> Coverage: world, world regions, U.S.
> Content: economic and industry review; gross domestic product; consumer price index; fuel prices; passenger and cargo revenues; trip length; capacity and load factors; fuel consumption; type of aircraft; airborne hours; pilots; aircraft operations.

Terminal Area Forecast (TAF) System. WEB. U.S. Department of Transportation. Federal Aviation Administration. (Earlier, TD 4.57:) <http://api.hq.faa.gov/apo_pubs.htm>; <http://www.api.faa.gov/apo_pubs.htm>.

> Coverage: U.S., FAA regions, states, individual airports.
> Content: database and summary tables with projections for enplanements and aircraft operations.

Discussion

The *FAA Statistical Handbook of Aviation* contains a wide range of air transportation statistics. Air traffic activity tables give number of flights handled for top airports, regions, and states. Data on aircraft departures are given by air carrier and state. This includes statistics on number of enplaned passengers and enplaned revenue tons. Other tables list aircraft in operation by model or by air carrier and type. A section on operating data gives revenue and expenses for large certificated air carriers as a group. Additional sections cover airports, general aviation aircraft, pilots, accidents, and aeronautical production and trade. This title summarizes data from many of the more detailed publications of the FAA and the Department of Transportation.

Air Travel Consumer Report contains information on the quality of service provided by the airlines. Data are given for individual major airlines. The largest section is on flight delays. Tables give summary data on on-time flights and data for selected large airports. Airlines are ranked according to their performance. Other data include overall percentage of on-time flights at each airport by time of day and a list of specific flights that arrive late 80% of the time or more. A section on mishandled baggage gives number of baggage reports per 1000 passengers. Oversales statistics cover voluntary and involuntary denied boardings and involuntary denied boardings per 1000 passengers. Statistics are also given on number and types of consumer complaints. Sample questions that can be answered with this title include "What percentage of Delta's flights arrive on time?" and "What percentage of evening flights into Atlanta are on time?"

The *Domestic Airline Fares Consumer Report* covers average prices paid by consumers in approximately the top 1000 city-pair markets in the contiguous United States. The most detailed table (Table 1) groups city-pairs by mileage block and gives the nonstop distance, passengers per day, average one-way fare, and largest and lowest fare carriers with their percentage of market share and average one-way fare. A more detailed fare table is given for highest and lowest fare markets under 750 miles with information on the percentage of passengers paying the lowest and highest fare intervals. An expanded version of Table 1 covering all domestic markets is also available in comma-delimited format.

Air Carrier Financial Statistics Quarterly provides income and balance sheet data for air carrier groups arranged by size and for individual air carriers. The size groups are majors, nationals, large regionals, and medium regionals. Medium regionals are only included on a semiannual basis in the June and December issues. Each group or carrier is subdivided into categories for domestic and international (if applicable). International categories may be further subdivided by world region. Specific data elements available include revenue sources, such as first-class passenger revenues or mail revenues, expenses for such items as flying operations and maintenance, assets in cash or property, and liabilities such as current obligation under capital leases or long-term debt. Data are given for the current quarter and last 12 months with comparisons to the previous year. Questions that can be answered with this source include "What is American Airlines' recent net income or loss?" "How much did Delta take in in passenger revenues?" and "How much did Continental spend for maintenance?"

Airline Quarterly Financial Review gives data on the financial condition of major airlines. Summary tables give financial and traffic review totals for all airlines covered and for major passenger airlines for systems operations, domestic operations, and international operations. Financial and traffic review data are then given for each major individual airline. Each section contains charts and brief narrative highlights of trends, as well as statistical tables. This title covers fewer individual airlines than *Air Carrier Financial Statistics Quarterly* and contains less detail on revenues and expenses subcategories. It does, however, include traffic information and some additional financial items not included in the first report.

Air Carrier Traffic Statistics Monthly contains a variety of performance measures that are given for carrier groups and for individual carriers. The groups are the same as with *Air Carrier Financial Statistics Quarterly*. Data are similarly divided into domestic and international operations with international operations often subdivided by world region. Statistics are given for scheduled services, nonscheduled services, and all services. Examples of data available for each airline include revenue passenger-miles from first-class passengers, revenue ton-miles from air express, total revenue load factor, aircraft revenue departures performed, revenue passenger per aircraft mile, available seats per aircraft mile, and on-flight passenger trip length.

The *APO Data System* provides access to the Air Traffic Activity Data System (ATADS) and other databases. ATADS search categories include Centers (Air Route Traffic Control Centers), Towers (Airport Traffic Control Towers), Instrument Operations, Approach Operations, and Flight Service Stations. Users may usually select a region, state, or individual facility; desired data year; monthly or annual data; and an activity or ranking report. Data are usually presented by aircraft category: air carrier, air taxi, general aviation, and military.

Airport Activity Statistics of Certificated Air Carriers contains summary tables and detailed individual airport tables with data on aircraft departures, enplaned revenue passengers, and enplaned revenue tons of cargo and mail. Specific airline data are included at the overall summary level and at the airport level.

The *Enplanement and All-Cargo Statistics* Web page also covers airport activity data. It contains tables listing cargo landed weight and enplanements by airport category, by state, or by rank. Individual airports are listed in most tables. Some tables give data for several years.

The *Office of Airline Information Home Page* provides access to air transportation statistical resources. Main menu choices include "On-Time Statistics," "BTS Transportation Indicators," "FAA Statistical Handbook of Aviation," and "Sources of Air Carrier Aviation Data." The "On-Time Statistics" option provides a description of the program, links to related products, including the *Air Travel Consumer Report*, and a searchable database of on-time data for specific routes, multiple airport combinations, and specific flights. The "BTS Transportation Indicators" option provides summary charts and tables for domestic and international traffic and financial measures. Data available include overall totals for revenue passenger and ton-miles, available seat and ton-miles, and operating finances. More detailed tables can be viewed or downloaded. The "Sources of Air Carrier Aviation Data" option lists agencies and businesses offering aviation resources.

FAA Aerospace Forecasts gives an overview of the aviation industry and the outlook for aviation activity. Narrative chapters discuss the economic environment and each segment of aviation, including air carriers, regionals and commuters, and general aviation. A statistical chapter gives annual forecasts for about 11 years. Tables are grouped into sections dealing with the economy, air carriers, regionals and commuters, general aviation, and FAA workload. Representative data available include number of commercial pilots in 10 years, number of revenue passenger enplanements, and fuel consumption.

The *Terminal Area Forecast (TAF) System* contains historical and projected aviation activity for individual airports. This Web title includes a PDF version of the publication *Terminal Area Forecasts Fiscal Years [years]*, which is now only published electronically. This title covers more than 400 airports and gives projections for air carrier and commuter enplanements, itinerant and local aircraft operations, and instrument operations. A more extensive database and accompanying software are also included under this Web entry for downloading.

WATER TRANSPORTATION

Checklist

MARAD [year]: The Annual Report of the Maritime Administration. (annual) 1950–. U.S. Department of Transportation. Maritime Administration. TD 11.1: (Earlier, C39.201:) Item 0233. ASI 7704-14. <http://www.marad.dot.gov/publications/index.html>; <http://purl.access.gpo.gov/GPO/LPS857>; <http://purl.access.gpo.gov/GPO/LPS4097>.
  Coverage: countries, U.S.
  Content: shipbuilding; merchant marine fleets; waterborne trade; shipping subsidies; maritime employment.

U.S. Merchant Marine Data Sheet. WEB. (quarterly) U.S. Department of Transportation. Maritime Administration. ASI 7702-1. <http://www.marad.dot.gov/publications/index.html>; <http://purl.access.gpo.gov/GPO/LPS857>; <http://purl.access. gpo.gov/GPO/LPS4097>.
  Coverage: U.S.
  Content: U.S.-flag merchant fleet by type of ship, ownership, and deployment; subsidized vessels; employment; ship construction.

Merchant Fleets of the World: Oceangoing Self-Propelled Vessels of 1000 Gross Tons and Above as of [date]. WEB. (quarterly) 1923–. U.S. Department of Transportation. Maritime Administration. TD 11.14: Item 0236-B. ASI 7702-4. <http://www.marad.dot.gov/publications/index.html>; <http://purl.access.gpo.gov/GPO/LPS857>; <http://purl.access.gpo.gov/GPO/LPS4097>.
  Coverage: world, countries, U.S.
  Content: number of ships and weight by country of registry and type.

Waterborne Commerce of the United States. MF. WEB. (annual) 1942–. U.S. Department of the Army. Corps of Engineers. Water Resources Support Center. D 103.1/2: Item 0334. ASI 3754-3. <http://www.wrsc.usace.army.mil/ndc/wcsc.htm>.
  Coverage: U.S., states, coastal areas, Great Lakes, and individual waterways, harbors, and ports.
  Content: domestic and foreign freight traffic by commodity and type.

NDC Publications and U.S. Waterway Data CD. CD-ROM. U.S. Department of the Army. Corps of Engineers. Water Resources Support Center. Navigation Data Center. D 103.135:P 96/. Item 0337-B-20.
  Content: CD-ROM version of *Waterborne Commerce of the United States* and other waterway information.

Waterborne Commerce Statistics Center. WEB. U.S. Department of the Army. Corps of Engineers. Navigation Data Center. <http://www.wrsc.usace.army.mil/ndc/wcsc.htm>.
  Content: waterborne transportation statistics; tonnage indicators; commodity movements database; *Waterborne Commerce of the United States.*

U.S. Foreign Waterborne Transportation Statistics Quarterly Report. WEB. (quarterly) U.S. Department of Transportation. Maritime Administration and U.S. Army Corps of Engineers. Navigation Data Center. TD 11.35: (Earlier, C 3.164:985/) Item 0235-B-03. ASI 7702-5. <http://www.marad.dot.gov/statistics/usfwts/index.html>.
  Coverage: selected countries, U.S., coastal districts, customs districts, ports.
  Content: imports and exports by value and weight; type and nationality of vessels; leading commodities; top trading partners.

Discussion

The *MARAD* annual report contains summary statistics on the merchant marine fleet. Information on the U.S. oceangoing merchant marine includes number and type of ships, such as the number of privately owned general cargo ships engaged in noncontiguous domestic trade. A list of major world merchant fleets shows number and tonnage of ships for the top 15 countries. Other tables cover amount and value of waterborne trade, the U.S. Great Lakes fleet, and government-sponsored cargoes.

Two other titles provide information on the merchant fleet. *U.S. Merchant Marine Data Sheet* contains data on the U.S. merchant marine fleet. Data include number and weight of ships by type, such as tanker, dry bulk, or containership and whether engaged in U.S. foreign trade, foreign-to-foreign trade, or domestic trade. Tables also cover related employment and ship construction contracts. *Merchant Fleets of the World* contains basic statistics on the merchant fleets of all maritime countries. Data are given for the number and types of ships, including tankers, dry bulk, and cruise/passenger. Gross tons and deadweight tons are also given for each ship category.

Waterborne Commerce of the United States gives detailed statistics on the movement of goods on coastal and inland waterways and on the Great Lakes. The report is divided into five parts. The first four parts each deal with a specific region: Atlantic Coast; Gulf Coast, Mississippi River System and Antilles; Great Lakes; and Pacific Coast, Alaska and Hawaii. Part 5 contains national summaries. The regional reports list each waterway and port and give total traffic for recent years and freight traffic by commodity and type, such as domestic, foreign, or internal. The national report gives summary data for the U.S., commodities, and for selected major waterways, states, and ports. Regional reports give such data as tons of corn outbound (and either upbound or downbound) on the Illinois River; tons of wood chip foreign export traffic at Mobile Harbor, Alabama; or total freight traffic (upbound or downbound) on the Missouri River from Omaha to Kansas City. National data include such information as total tons of wheat for domestic use moved lakewise, total overseas imports moving through the Great Lakes, or tons of coal shipped through the Ohio River System. A CD-ROM version, *NDC Publications and U.S. Waterway Data CD*, is also available. The CD also includes several other publications and databases on commodity movements, locks, ports, the U.S. waterway system, and waterborne transportation lines.

The *Waterborne Commerce Statistics Center* Web site offers a variety of data on waterborne commerce, including the full text of recent years of *Waterborne Commerce of the United States*. "Internal U.S. Waterway Monthly Tonnage Indicators" gives monthly data for recent years for total tons shipped as well as tons of coal, petroleum and chemicals, and food and farm products. "Domestic U.S. Waterborne Traffic" gives comparisons and percentage change by year and for the most recent six months for tonnage shipped by broad commodity category and for major waterways. "Commodity Movements from the Public Domain Database" show commodities moved by region or state of origin and destination. Reports are available by commodity, by destination, and by origin. "Waterborne Tonnage for Principal U.S. Ports and all 50 States and U.S. Territories" gives tonnage totals for foreign, imports, exports, and domestic for selected ports by port name or in ranked order. Tonnage data by state name or rank are also available for domestic and foreign shipping and receiving.

U.S. Foreign Waterborne Transportation Statistics Quarterly Report gives data on U.S. foreign trade exported or imported by vessel. Value and weight of exports and imports is given by customs district and port and by type of service (liner, tanker, or tramp). Tables also list total U.S. leading imported commodities by weight and principal trading partners by weight. Commodity and country data are not correlated. Additional data include principal ports handling containerized cargo and the top five commodities in each coastal district. Each issue also features a selected port, giving leading commodities and top trading partners for that specific port.

OTHER TRANSPORTATION INDUSTRY SOURCES
Checklist

Economic Census. PRINT. WEB. (quinquennial) 1997–. U.S. Department of Commerce. Economics and Statistics Administration. Bureau of the Census. (Formerly published as individual censuses for specific economic sectors.) ASI 2569, 2570, 2573,

2575, 2579. <http://www.census.gov/epcd/www/econ97.html>; <http://www.census.gov/mp/www/pub/ind/msind.html#Industry>; <http://www.census.gov/prod/www/abs/economic.html>; <http://www.census.gov/prod/www/abs/transpor.html#trans>.
> Coverage: U.S., states, metropolitan areas.
> Content: number of establishments; number of employees; payroll; revenue; number and characteristics of trucks; commodity transportation.

Census of Transportation, Communications, and Utilities. PRINT. WEB. 1992. U.S. Department of Commerce. Economics and Statistics Administration. Bureau of the Census. C 3.292: Item 0160-D-01. ASI 2569, 2570, 2573, 2575, 2579. <http://www.census.gov/prod/www/abs/transpor.html#trans>; <http://www.census.gov/epcd/www/92result.html>; <http://www.census.gov/mp/www/pub/ind/msind.html#trans>.
> Coverage: U.S., states, metropolitan areas.
> Content: railroad, passenger, water, and air transportation; trucking and warehousing; transportation services; number of establishments; number of employees; payroll; sales, receipts or value of shipments/construction work done; number and characteristics of trucks; commodity transportation.

Economic Census. CD-ROM. (quinquennial) 1987–. U.S. Department of Commerce. Economics and Statistics Administration. Bureau of the Census. C 3.277: Item 0154-C.
> Coverage: U.S., states, counties, metropolitan areas, places of 2,500 or more, zip codes.
> Content: *Economic Census* reports.

American FactFinder. WEB. U.S. Department of Commerce. Bureau of the Census. <http://factfinder.census.gov/java_prod/dads.ui.homePage.HomePage>.
> Coverage: U.S., states, counties.
> Content: 1997 *Economic Census* as it becomes available; other census products.

Annual Transportation Survey. WEB. (annual) 1985–. C 3.138/3-5: (Earlier title, *Motor Freight Transportation and Warehousing Survey*) Item 0147-B-01. ASI 2413-14. <http://www.census.gov/pub/svsd/www/tas.html>; <http://purl.access.gpo.gov/GPO/LPS3293>; <http://www.census.gov/econ/www/servmenu.html>; <http://www.census.gov/mp/www/pub/bus/msbus26x.html>.
> Coverage: U.S.
> Content: trucking and courier services operating revenue and operating expense components by type of carrier; size of shipments, and commodities handled; truck inventories; public warehousing revenue and operating expenses.

Motor Carriers of Passengers. WEB. (quarterly) 1994–95–. U.S. Department of Transportation. Bureau of Transportation Statistics. ASI 7312-5. <http://www.bts.gov/mcs/prod.html>.
> Coverage: U.S., individual carriers.
> Content: financial and operating data for Class I bus companies; revenue; expenses; income; revenue passengers.

Motor Carriers of Property. WEB. (annual) 1994–95–. U.S. Department of Transportation. Bureau of Transportation Statistics. ASI 7314-11. <http://www.bts.gov/mcs/prod.html>.
> Coverage: U.S., individual carriers.
> Content: financial and operating data for large Class I trucking companies; revenues; expenses; income.

Economic Data for Class I Railroads. WEB. U.S. Department of Transportation. Surface Transportation Board. (Previously issued in *Transport Statistics in the United States,* IC 1.25:) <http://www.stb.dot.gov/infoex1.htm>.

> Coverage: U.S., individual Class I railroads.
> Content: financial and operating data for Class I railroads; assets; liabilities; income; cash flow; operating expenses; depreciation; equipment; employment; wages.

National Transit Database. WEB. (annual) 1978–79–. U.S. Department of Transportation. Federal Transit Administration. (Title varies) TD 7.11/2-2: (Earlier, TD 7.11/2:) Item 0982-H-08. ASI 7884-4. <http://www.fta.dot.gov/ntl/database.html>.

> Coverage: U.S., individual transit agencies.
> Content: financial and operating data for transit agencies; passenger and vehicle revenue miles; average trips; vehicles; sources of operating and capital funds; operating expenses; performance ratios; injuries; crime; employment.

Discussion

The *Economic Census* is taken every five years covering years ending in "2" and in "7." The data are collected in the year following the year of coverage (the 1997 census was conducted in 1998) and data may begin to appear in the year following that. Major changes took place beginning with the 1997 *Economic Census* both in organization and in publishing formats. The implementation of the NAICS classification system reorganized and increased industry coverage resulting in data being published for 18 economic sectors, one of which is transportation and warehousing. The previous economic census for 1992, based on the SIC classification system, was organized into eight sectors, one of which was transportation, communications, and utilities. Also beginning with 1997, data are published almost entirely on the Internet and on CD-ROM, with only a small number of summary publications published in print format.

The 1997 *Economic Census* reports for the transportation and warehousing sector include a geographic area series (statistics by states and metropolitan areas), a subject series, and a summary report. The subject series consists of three reports on revenue lines, establishment and firm size, and miscellaneous subjects. The summary report will be the only one published in print. Two surveys are also issued for the transportation sector: Vehicle Industry and Use Survey (formerly Trucking Inventory and Use) and Commodity Flow Survey. The Vehicle Industry and Use Survey covers the number of trucks and their physical characteristics. Some of the data available include annual miles, major use, body type, vehicle size, year model, truck type, products carried, weight, maintenance, and engine size. The Commodity Flow Survey covers transportation of commodities. Data on the value, tons, and ton-miles of shipments are given by modes of transportation, distance shipped, size of shipment, broad commodity category, and state of destination.

The Census Bureau's Web site lists reports from the 1997 census with links to the full text as they are released. 1992 reports and general information about the *Census* are also available, including the *Guide to the 1997 Economic Census.*

American FactFinder is a Census Bureau Web database designed to provide access to data from the 1997 *Economic Census.* It also contains a mapping feature and an option to search for information on Census Bureau products. 1997 *Economic Census* data are available in the "Industry and Business Facts" section as it is released. The Industry Quick Reports option allows the user to select from a list of NAICS sectors and code numbers or to search by word to identify and display a basic industry report. The industry reports show number of establishments, number of employees, annual payroll, and shipments/sales/receipts by state. Similarly, the Geography Quick Reports option can be used to display a geographic area report. The geographic report shows similar data items to the industry report for all industries at the two-digit NAICS sector level for the selected area. A "Build a Query" option is also available. This option allows the user to search for or select specific data sets for display.

The *Annual Transportation Survey* provides current revenue and expense information for the trucking and public warehousing industries. A summary table gives total revenue, operating expenses, and payroll for the industries in this category. Separate chapters give more detailed data for trucking and courier services and for public warehousing. Trucking data are the most detailed with such information as revenue from agricultural and food product shipments or inventories of truck-tractors.

Motor Carriers of Passengers and *Motor Carriers of Property* both contain financial data for motor carriers. The quarterly issues of the *Motor Carriers of Passengers* report gives total data for all carriers on revenue and revenue passengers by category, such as intercity regular route or charter or special. Operating expenses, operating income, net income, and operating ratio are also given. An annual issue gives similar data for individual carriers. The *Motor Carriers of Property* report gives operating revenues, operating expenses, net carrier operating income, and net carrier income for individual carriers and in total.

Economic Data for Class I Railroads contains several reports that give summary and individual railroad financial data. Reports available include "Annual Railroad Financial Data," "Quarterly Selected Earnings Reports for Class I Railroads," "Employment Data," "Class I Railroads' Price Index," and "Wage Statistics." "Annual Railroad Financial Data" contains detailed financial information and is available for viewing or downloading. Reports are available for industry totals and for large railroad companies. Data include miles of road operated, number of cars by type, repairs and maintenance expenses, tons and ton-miles of freight, passenger income, and many financial items. "Quarterly Selected Earnings Reports for Class

I Railroads" gives operating revenues, operating income, net income, and revenue ton-miles of freight for individual railroads and in total. "Employment Data" gives number of railroad employees and percentage change by category and total employees for individual railroads. "Wage Statistics" contains overall totals on service hours and compensation by employee category.

The *National Transit Database* consists of three reports: *Transit Profiles, Data Tables,* and *National Transit Summaries and Trends. National Transit Summaries and Trends* is a narrative overview of the mass transit industry with key statistics. A "National Transit Profile" chapter gives summary financial and operational characteristics for the industry. Other chapters summarize trends in capital funding, operating funding and expenses, service supplied and consumed, safety, and reliability and maintenance effectiveness. A chapter on key modal characteristics gives data for selected individual agencies. *Data Tables* consists of statistical tables with data for individual agencies. Tables cover transit revenues and expenses, operating data, performance indicators, employment, vehicle maintenance, energy consumption, mileage, safety, and age of vehicle inventory. *Transit Profiles* consists of two reports — one for transit agencies in urbanized areas with a population of more than 200,000 and one for agencies in urbanized areas with a population of less than 200,000. Each agency has a single page profile covering general information on the urbanized area and service area, service supplied and consumed, vehicles operated, sources of operating funds, operating expenses, and performance measures.

ACCIDENTS
Checklist

MOTOR VEHICLES

Traffic Safety Facts [year]: A Compilation of Motor Vehicle Crash Data from the Fatality Analysis Reporting System and the General Estimates System. PRINT. WEB. (annual) 1992–. U.S. Department of Transportation. National Highway Traffic Safety Administration. TD 8.27: Item 0982-D-19. ASI 7764-24. <http://www.nhtsa.dot.gov/people/ncsa/TSF97.html>; <http://purl.access.gpo.gov/GPO/LPS2874>; <http://www.nhtsa.dot.gov/people/ncsa/>.
> Coverage: U.S., states, selected cities.
> Content: automobile crashes; number and rates of fatalities and injuries; alcohol involvement; restraint use; day and time; circumstances of crash; speed limit; type of vehicle; age and sex of victims; motorcycle helmet usage; emergency medical services response time.

Traffic Safety Facts [year]: [topic]. PRINT. WEB. (annual) U.S. Department of Transportation. National Highway Traffic Safety Administration. National Center for Statistics and Analysis. TD 8.27: (Earlier, TD 8.2:T 67/) Item 0982-D-19. ASI 7766-15. <http://www.nhtsa.dot.gov/people/ncsa/factsheet.html>; <http://www.nhtsa.dot.gov/people/ncsa/>.
> Coverage: U.S., states.

> Content: fact sheets on different aspects of traffic accident fatalities and injuries.

State Traffic Safety Information. PRINT. WEB. (annual) 1998–. U.S. Department of Transportation. National Highway Traffic Safety Administration. TD 8.62: Item 0982-D-45. ASI 7764-28. <http://www.nhtsa.dot.gov/people/ncsa/stateinfo/index.htm>; <http://www.nhtsa.dot.gov/people/ncsa/>.
> Coverage: U.S., states.
> Content: traffic fatalities and fatality rate; economic cost of crashes; alcohol involvement; restraint use; speed; highway safety program funds; key legislative issues; motorcycle helmets.

Fatality Analysis Reporting System (FARS). WEB. (annual) 1994–. U.S. Department of Transportation. National Highway Traffic Safety Administration. <http://www-fars.nhtsa.dot.gov/>.
> Coverage: U.S., states, counties, cities.
> Content: searchable database of fatal accident reports.

Traffic Safety CD-ROM. CD-ROM. 1996. U.S. Department of Transportation. Bureau of Transportation Statistics. TD 1.56:T 67/996. Item 0982-L. ASI (97) 7314-10.
> Content: Fatal Accident Reporting System (FARS), General Estimates System (GES), *Traffic Safety Facts, Traffic Safety* fact sheets.

Motor Carrier Safety Statistics Web Page. WEB. U.S. Department of Transportation. Federal Highway Administration. Office of Motor Carrier and Highway Safety. <http://mchs.fhwa.dot.gov/factsfigs/mchsstats.htm>.
> Coverage: U.S., limited states.
> Content: fact sheets, overviews, and reports on large truck crashes.

Safety Management Information Statistics (SAMIS) Annual Report. MF. WEB. (annual) 1990–. U.S. Department of Transportation. Federal Transit Administration. Office of Safety and Security. TD 7.11/2: Item 0982-H-08. ASI 7884-13. Selected data: <http://transit-safety.volpe.dot.gov/Data/Reports.stm>.
> Coverage: U.S., FTA regions.
> Content: mass transit system accidents, casualties, and crime incidents.

National Highway Traffic Safety Administration Home Page. WEB. U.S. Department of Transportation. National Highway Traffic Safety Administration. <http://www.nhtsa.dot.gov/>.
> Content: publications, data, and program information related to car safety and people safety; agency news and information.

RAILROAD

Federal Railroad Administration Office of Safety Analysis Web Site. WEB. U.S. Department of Transportation. Federal Railroad Administration. Office of Safety Analysis. <http://safetydata.fra.dot.gov/officeofsafety/>.
> Coverage: U.S., states, individual railroads.
> Content: railroad accident databases and reports.

AIR

Annual Review of Aircraft Accident Data: U.S. Air Carrier Operations. MF. WEB. (annual) National Transportation Safety Board. TD 1.113/5: Item 0982-I-06. ASI 9614-2. <http://www.ntsb.gov/Publictn/A_Stat.htm>.
> Coverage: U.S.

Content: commercial air carrier accidents; fatalities; injuries; aircraft damages; list of individual accidents with basic data; type of person injured and degree of injury; first occurrence (problem) and phase of flight; causes and factors.

Annual Review of Aircraft Accident Data: U.S. General Aviation. MF. WEB. (annual) National Transportation Safety Board. TD 1.113: Item 0982-I-06. ASI 9614-3. <http://www.ntsb.gov/Publictn/A_Stat.htm>.

Coverage: U.S., states.

Content: general aviation accidents; fatalities; injuries; aircraft type; kind of flying; first occurrence (problem); phase of flight; causes and factors; type of person injured and degree of injury; pilot characteristics.

Aviation Web Page. WEB. National Transportation Safety Board. <http://www.ntsb.gov/aviation/aviation.htm>.

Content: accident synopses database; aviation accident statistics; publications.

Aviation Safety Data Web Page. WEB. U.S. Department of Transportation. Federal Aviation Administration. <http://nasdac.faa.gov/internet/>.

Content: aviation safety databases; accidents; incidents; safety recommendations; safety reports; near midair collisions.

WATER

Boating Statistics. MF. WEB. (annual) 1959–. U.S. Department of Transportation. Coast Guard. TD 5.11: Item 0941-A. ASI 7404-1. <http://www.uscgboating.org/saf/saf_stats199x.asp>.

Coverage: U.S., states.

Content: numbered boats; fatalities and fatality rates; injuries; property damage; accidents by type; age of victims; alcohol involvement; causes; operation/activity at time of accident; type of vessel; operator characteristics; weather and water conditions; time; month; day.

Discussion

Some statistics on accidents are available in the sources listed under "General Statistical Sources" and "General Transportation Statistics." Some titles in other sections include some accident statistics, such as the *FAA Statistical Handbook of Aviation* listed under "Air Transportation" and the *National Transit Database* in the "Other" section. The sources listed in this section provide more detailed accident data.

Traffic Safety Facts provides detailed statistics on motor vehicle accidents. Chapters cover trends, crashes, vehicles, people, and states. The trends chapter gives data for several years for fatality and injury rates, alcohol involvement, and restraint use. The remaining chapters present data for the current year. The chapter on crashes covers time, location, circumstances, and alcohol. The vehicles chapter gives statistics on types of vehicles involved in crashes, including passenger cars, light trucks, large trucks, motorcycles, and buses. The people chapter covers drivers, passengers, pedestrians, and others involved in crashes. The states chapter covers fatalities, alcohol, and state laws. This source answers such questions as

"How many accidents involve alcohol?," "What age-group or sex has the most accidents?," "How many accidents involve passing?," and "What state has the highest fatality rate?"

An annual series of fact sheets is also issued under the title *Traffic Safety Facts.* Each fact sheet is on a specific topic, such as alcohol, children, occupant protection, motorcycles, speeding, or young drivers. Fact sheets contain the most current crash statistics and are issued in advance of the annual publication. Most range from four to six pages and contain a narrative overview with charts and statistical tables.

State Traffic Safety Information gives two page state profiles on traffic accidents. Boxes and charts highlight key statistics, including the state fatality rate compared to the national rate, speed-related fatalities, and alcohol-related fatalities. Statistics on the use of safety belts, child safety seats, and motorcycle helmets include a figure for current lives saved and number potentially savable at 100% use.

The *Fatality Analysis Reporting System (FARS)* is a database of motor vehicle crashes resulting in fatalities. The database dates back to 1975, but the Web version presently covers 1994 on. The *Traffic Safety Facts* reports and the *State Traffic Safety Information* report are partly based on *FARS* data. The main *FARS* Web page provides links to information about *FARS*, a "Query FARS Data" option, a "Query Wizard" option, and a "Reports Library" option. Data may also be FTP'd. The "Query FARS Data" option is the most complex, providing interactive access to the full database. A workbook with instructions and examples can be viewed. Users select the year and then individual data items from a comprehensive list categorized by persons, crashes, vehicles, or drivers. A series of more specific variable selections is offered leading to the final report options, which include univariate tabulation (single variable), cross tab (two variables), case listing (individual case reports), or download. The "Query Wizard" option offers a list of predefined searches. The user selects a table, then the year and geographic level (state, county, city). The "Reports Library" option allows searching or browsing reports on crashes. Users may search by a specific year and keyword or browse the topic categories of fact sheets, trends, crashes, vehicles, people, and states.

The *Traffic Safety CD-ROM* 1996 edition contains the text *Traffic Safety Facts 1994* and the 1994 *Traffic Safety* fact sheets. Software on the CD provides access to these publications. The CD also contains ASCII format data from the Fatal Accident Reporting System (FARS) for 1975-1994 and the General Estimates System (GES) for 1988-1994. FARS contains data on fatal traffic accidents. GES contains sample data on police-reported crashes. These files require additional spreadsheet, database, or statistical application software.

The *Motor Carrier Safety Statistics Web Page* contains resources on large truck crashes. A "Large Truck Crash

Overview" is a brief overview of trends in fatal and injury crashes, vehicle characteristics, driver characteristics, and the crash environment. Key statistics are illustrated by charts. A more substantial report, "Large Truck Crash Profile," is also available. It covers similar topic areas, but provides more detailed statistical tables. Chapters cover trends in crashes, fatalities, and injuries; vehicle characteristics; drivers; environment; and crash characteristics.

The *Safety Management Information Statistics (SAMIS) Annual Report* covers accidents and crime on mass transit systems. A trends section contains a chart and table for each topic covered, including incidents, fatalities, injuries, collisions, derailments/buses going off road, personal casualties, fires, property damage, vehicles, vehicle miles, passenger miles, and passengers. This section is also available on the agency's Web site. A section of tables covers each of these topics in more detail including whether the persons involved were patrons or employees and where the event took place (parking facility, inside vehicle, etc.). The tables also cover crime offenses by region. Data given for each crime category include whether the victim was a patron or employee, where the crime took place, and where arrests were made.

The *National Highway Traffic Safety Administration Home Page* groups main menu options by the categories of car safety, people safety, and popular information. The car safety category includes menu options for vehicle and equipment information, problems and issues, testing results, regulations and standards, and research and development. People safety covers traffic safety/occupant issues, injury prevention, communications and outreach, driver performance, and crash information. Popular topics include such options as air bags, child passenger safety, crash tests, recalls, and school buses. A site search option is also available.

The *Federal Railroad Administration Office of Safety Analysis Web Site* provides statistics, publications, and databases on railroad accidents. The main menu options include "Quick Stats," "Accident/Incident Details," "Annual Report," "FRA Publications," and "Query FRA Safety Databases." The "Quick Stats" option contains basic statistics on number of train accidents, accidents per million train miles, casualties, trespasser fatalities, employee casualties, and highway-rail crossing incidents and fatalities. The "Accident/Incident Details" option provides more detailed data for recent years, including data for states and individual railroads. Data include type of incident and type of person involved and causes by broad category. The "Annual Report" option provides the full text of recent issues of the *Railroad Safety Statistics Annual Report*. This is an extensive statistical report with an overview chapter covering trends for several years, a chapter summarizing the current year's data, and chapters on casualties, employee casualties, train accidents, highway-rail incidents, and trespassers. State and individual railroad data are included. Examples of data available include number of accidents caused by brake defects on train cars,

types of accidents caused by failure to comply with a fixed signal, derailments caused by snow, ice, or other material on the tracks, and railroad employee days absent due to nervous shock. The "FRA Publications" option includes the *Railroad Safety Statistics Annual Report* and two of its predecessors, *Rail-Highway Crossing Inventory Bulletin* and *Accident/Incident Bulletin*. The "Query FRA Safety Databases" option provides access to the accident/incident database. Users select from categories, including overview, casualty, accidents, and highway-rail. Within each category additional options are available such as maps, tables, and different reports. Users may often specify individual railroad, state, county, and time period.

The *Annual Review of Aircraft Accident Data: U.S. Air Carrier Operations* contains detailed statistics on air carrier accidents. Statistics are divided into three groups based on regulatory categories: large commercial aircraft, scheduled air taxi and commuter operations, and non-scheduled air taxi and commuter operations. Summary data are given on number of accidents, degree of injury, fatalities by type of person, and aircraft damage. A list of individual accidents gives information on date, location, type of operation, carrier, aircraft type, aircraft damage, degree of injury, and first occurrence. First occurrence refers to the initial problem such as in flight encounter with weather or airframe/component/system failure/malfunction. Summary statistics are given for all accidents on first occurrences, flight phase in which problem arose (takeoff, cruising), and causes. An appendix lists detailed causes and factors with the number of accidents for the year attributed to each cause/factor. Examples of questions that could be answered with this source include "What percentage of accidents are caused by the pilot?" and "How many accidents occur during takeoff?"

Annual Review of Aircraft Accident Data: U.S. General Aviation provides detailed data on general aviation aircraft accidents by type of aircraft, purpose of flight (for example, personal or business), injuries and fatalities, and circumstances and cause. General aviation covers fixed-wing aircraft, rotorcraft, gliders, and balloons. Sample data available include accidents caused by in-flight loss of control and accidents caused by specific weather conditions such as crosswind.

The *Aviation Web Page* provides access to a database of accident synopses, current accident statistics, and publications. The accident synopses database contains accident report and selected incident summaries since 1983. Searches can be done by date, city, state, severity, aircraft category, amateur built, aircraft make, model, registration, operation, airline, and NTSB accident number. A list of reports by month can also be browsed. An aviation accident statistics category gives the most recent statistics, as well as data for earlier years, for accidents, fatalities, injuries, and accident rates. Tables give overall totals and totals by type of air carrier operation. A list of specific fatal accidents for several years is also available. A publications category lists National Transportation Safety Board accident reports and studies. Recent publications are available in full text.

The *Aviation Safety Data Web Page* provides access to aviation safety databases. These include the National Transportation Safety Board Aviation Accident/Incident Database, the FAA Incident Data System, Aviation Safety Reporting System, and Near Midair Collisions System. The National Transportation Safety Board Aviation Accident/Incident Database is the most comprehensive, covering accident reports and selected incidents since 1983. This is the same database available on the *Aviation Web Page*, but with complete report information rather than just a synopsis. Searches can be done by keyword, report number, date range, event type, state, registration number, aircraft make/model, operator (airline), and airport. Data available include location information, aircraft information, operator information, narrative, sequence of events, findings, injury, summary, weather/environmental information and pilot information. The FAA Incident Data System covers incidents (events where damage or injury is insufficient to qualify as an accident) since 1978. Search options and data available are generally similar to the National Transportation Safety Board database. The Aviation Safety Reporting System contains voluntary, confidential reports by aviation personnel regarding safety incidents since 1988. The Near Midair Collisions System database covers reports of near midair collisions since 1992.

Boating Statistics covers recreational boating accidents. Data cover accidents, fatalities, injuries, and property damage and analyze accident circumstances. Examples of information given include number of fatal accidents involving capsizing, number of accidents involving falling overboard in Missouri, fatalities from being struck by boat or propeller, and accidents while skiing/tubing.

JOURNEY TO WORK SOURCES

Checklist

American Housing Survey for the United States. PRINT. WEB. (biennial) 1973–. U.S. Department of Commerce. Economics and Statistics Administration. Census Bureau. C 3.215:H-150/. (Earlier, C 3.215/18-) (Titled *Annual Housing Survey* before 1985) (Supplements, C 3.215:H-151/). Item 0141-A. ASI 2485-12. (Supplements, ASI 2485-13,-14). GPO. <http://www.census.gov/mp/www/pub/con/mscho.html#ahs>; <http://www.census.gov/prod/www/abs/cons-hou.html#house>; <http://www.huduser.org/datasets/ahs.html>.

> Coverage: U.S., regions.
> Content: cars and trucks available by household characteristics; use and availability of public transportation; transportation to work, distance, and travel time.

American Housing Survey for the [name] Metropolitan Area in [year]. PRINT. WEB. (annual) 1974–. U.S. Department of Commerce. Economics and Statistics Administration. Census Bureau. C 3.215:H-170/. (Earlier, C 3.215/17) (Titled *Annual*

Housing Survey before 1984) (Supplements, C 3.215/16:). Item 0141-A. ASI 2485-6. (Supplement, 2485-8). <http://www.census.gov/mp/www/pub/con/mscho.html#ahs>; <http://www.census.gov/prod/www/abs/cons-hou.html#house>; <http://www.huduser.org/datasets/ahs.html>.

> Coverage: selected metropolitan areas, selected subareas (counties, places).
> Content: cars and trucks available by household characteristics; transportation to work, distance, and travel time.

American Housing Survey. CD-ROM. 1985–89–. U.S. Department of Commerce. Economics and Statistics Administration. Bureau of the Census. C 3.215/19: Item 0156-P.

> Content: microdata files from the *American Housing Survey*.

Census of Housing. PRINT. (decennial) 1950–. U.S. Department of Commerce. Economics and Statistics Administration. Bureau of the Census. (Format has changed over the years; titles listed below reflect current format. Before 1950 included in the comprehensive decennial census.)

Detailed Housing Characteristics. C 3.224/3:; C 3.224/3-5: to 3-7: Items 0156-B-01 to 53, 0155-A-01 to 03. ASI 2471-2.

> > Coverage: states, counties, places of 2,500 or more, selected county subdivisions (MCDs); separate reports on metropolitan areas, urbanized areas, and American Indian and Alaska Native areas.
> > Content: number of vehicles available.

Census of Population. PRINT. (decennial) 1950–. U.S. Department of Commerce. Economics and Statistics Administration. Bureau of the Census. (Format has changed over the years; titles listed below reflect current format. Before 1950 included in comprehensive decennial census.)

Social and Economic Characteristics. C 3.223/7:, C 3.223/7-2:, C 3.223/7-3:, C 3.223/7-4: (Earlier title: *General Social and Economic Characteristics*) Items 0159-C-01 to 53, 0154-A-01 to 03. ASI 2531-5.

> > Coverage: U.S., states, counties, places of 2,500 or more, selected county subdivisions (MCDs) of 2,500 or more; separate reports on metropolitan areas, urbanized areas, American Indian and Alaska Native areas.
> > Content: journey to work; place of work; means of transportation; travel time.

Summary Social, Economic, and Housing Characteristics. C 3.223/23: Item 0156-M-01 to 53. ASI 2551-7.

> > Coverage: U.S., states, counties, places, county subdivisions (MCDs), American Indian and Alaska Native areas.
> > Content: means of transportation to work; vehicles available.

Population and Housing Characteristics for Census Tracts and Block Numbering Areas. C 3.223/11: (Earlier title, *Census Tracts*) Item 0156-K-01 to 53. ASI 2551-3.

> > Coverage: metropolitan areas, census tracts in metropolitan areas, census tracts or block numbering areas in the nonmetropolitan area portions of each state, counties, places of 10,000 or more.
> > Content: journey to work; number of vehicles available.

Population and Housing Characteristics for Congressional Districts of the 103rd Congress. PRINT. C 3.223/20: (Title varies; before 1980 data were published in *Congressional District Data Book*) Item 0159-C-01 to 53. ASI 2551-4.

 Coverage: congressional districts, counties, minor civil divisions of 10,000 or more, places of 10,000 or more.
 Content: journey to work; number of vehicles available.

1990 Census of Population and Housing Summary Tape File 3A. CD-ROM. WEB. U.S. Department of Commerce. Bureau of the Census. Data User Services Division. C 3.282/2: Item 0154-F-01. ASI 2551-11. <http://venus.census.gov/cdrom/lookup>; <http://sunsite.Berkeley.edu/GovData/info/>; <http://govinfo.kerr.orst.edu/stateis.html>.

 Coverage: states, counties, metropolitan areas, urbanized areas, county subdivisions, places, tracts, block numbering areas, block groups.
 Content: place of work; transportation to work; travel time to work; time leaving to go to work; vehicles available.

1990 Census of Population and Housing Summary Tape File 3B. CD-ROM. WEB. U.S. Department of Commerce. Bureau of the Census. Data Users Services Division. C 3.282/2: Item 0154-F-01. ASI 2551-13. <http://venus.census.gov/cdrom/lookup>; <http://sunsite.Berkeley.edu/GovData/info/>.

 Coverage: zip codes
 Content: place of work; transportation to work; travel time to work; time leaving to go to work; vehicles available.

1990 Census of Population and Housing Summary Tape File 3C. CD-ROM. WEB. U.S. Department of Commerce. Bureau of the Census. Data User Services Division. C 3.282/2: Item 0154-F-01. ASI 2551-14. <http://venus.census.gov/cdrom/lookup>; <http://sunsite.Berkeley.edu/GovData/info/>; <http://govinfo.kerr.orst.edu/stateis.html>.

 Coverage: U.S., regions, divisions, states, counties, selected county subdivisions, metropolitan areas, urbanized places, places of 10,000 or more.
 Content: place of work; transportation to work; travel time to work; time leaving to go to work; vehicles available.

Congressional Districts of the United States Summary Tape File 1D; Summary Tape File 3D. CD-ROM. U.S. Department of Commerce. Bureau of the Census. C 3.282/4: Item 0154-F-05. ASI 2551-18. <http://www.census.gov/prod/www/abs/congprof.html>.

 Coverage: states, congressional districts, counties, places, American Indian areas.
 Content: place of work; transportation to work; travel time to work; time leaving to go to work; number of vehicles available.

1990 Census of Population and Housing Subject Summary Tape Files: Journey to Work in the United States. CD-ROM. (1995) U.S. Department of Commerce. Bureau of the Census. Data User Services Division. C 3.286:CD 90 SSTF 20. Item 0154-G. ASI (96) 2551-12.15.

 Coverage: U.S., metropolitan areas.
 Content: transportation to work; time leaving to go to work; travel time to work; private vehicle occupancy; place of work; vehicles available; most data by various characteristics including age, race, sex, household type, educational attainment, earnings, industry, and occupation.

1990 Census Transportation Planning Package. CD-ROM. U.S. Department of Transportation. Bureau of Transportation Statistics. TD 1.56/2: (TransVU software on separate floppy diskette, TD 1.56/2:C 33/floppy) Item 0982-L-02. ASI (94) 7318-1.

 Coverage: states, counties, metropolitan areas, urbanized areas, places of 2,500 or more.
 Content: worker characteristics; vehicles available; transportation to work; time of departure/arrival; travel time to work; place of work.

The American Community Survey. CD-ROM. WEB. (annual) 1996–. U.S. Department of Commerce. Bureau of the Census. C 3.297: Item 0154-B-14. <http://www.census.gov/CMS/www/index_c.htm>; <http://www.census.gov/CMS/www/>; <http://purl.access.gpo.gov/GPO/LPS1258>.

 Coverage: selected counties and cities.
 Content: transportation to work; mean travel time to work.

American FactFinder. WEB. U.S. Department of Commerce. Bureau of the Census. <http://factfinder.census.gov/java_prod/dads.ui.homePage.HomePage>.

 Coverage: U.S., regions, divisions, states, counties, county subdivisions, congressional districts, metropolitan areas, urbanized areas, places, tracts, block numbering areas, block groups, zip codes, American Indian areas.
 Content: 1990 census data; 2000 census data as it becomes available; *American Community Survey*; other census products.

Discussion

Statistics relating to transportation are available in several census publications. The *Census of Housing, Census of Population*, and related updates contain journey to work and vehicle ownership data.

The *American Housing Survey for the United States* contains one transportation-related element. It gives information on cars and trucks available to households, such as the number of elderly householders with two cars. The supplement to the U.S. report contains additional statistics on public transportation and journey to work. Information on public transportation includes whether it is available and how frequently it is used. For example, data are available on what percentage of urban households use public transportation at least weekly. Journey to work data covers the method of transportation, travel time, distance, and departure time. Examples of information available include how many people in metropolitan suburbs carpool or how many people in the Midwest walk to work. The *American Housing Survey for the [name] Metropolitan Areas* series contains the same table on cars and trucks available to households that is mentioned for the U.S. report above. The metropolitan series also has a supplement that contains data on public transportation similar to that in the U.S. report, but there is no journey to work data. The supplements to both reports are published a few years after the main reports. The *American Housing Survey* is also available on CD-ROM. The CD contains microdata files (original survey responses) for the national and metropolitan area surveys. No software is included.

Use of these files requires additional statistical analysis software.

The *Census Housing* and the *Census of Population* contain data similar to the *American Housing Survey*, but cover more geographic areas. The *Census of Housing* report series titled *Detailed Housing Characteristics* gives information on the number of vehicles available, such as the number of urban households with two vehicles. The *Census of Population* report series on *Social and Economic Characteristics* gives information on the journey to work, including number of people working in or outside their area of residence, means of transportation to work, carpooling, and travel time. The *Summary Social, Economic, and Housing Characteristics* series contains less detailed data, but covers smaller geographic areas. Data on transportation to work give the percentage of the population using motor vehicles, carpools, or public transportation. Other tables indicate the number of households with no vehicles available, those with one vehicle, and those with two or more. All of these series consist of a U.S. summary volume, reports for each state, and reports for metropolitan areas, urbanized areas, and American Indian and Alaska Native areas.

Population and Housing Characteristics for Census Tracts and Block Numbering Areas combines data from both censuses, covering both journey to work and vehicles available. Place of work data are more detailed than in other reports, showing the specific city or area of employment.

Population and Housing Characteristics for Congressional Districts of the 103rd Congress contains basic data on means of transportation to work, travel time, and vehicles available for congressional districts.

The *1990 Census of Population and Housing Summary Tape File* CD-ROMs contain the statistics from which the Census of Population and Housing reports listed in this chapter were produced. Data include detailed economic, social, and housing data. *Summary Tape Files* 3A, 3B, 3C, and 3D contain the same data tables, but cover different geographic areas.

The *1990 Census of Population and Housing Subject Summary Tape Files: Journey to Work in the United States* CD-ROM gives data on number and characteristics of workers by means of transportation to work, time leaving home to go to work, travel time to work, private vehicle occupancy, and place of work. Some tables also correlate time leaving for work and travel time with the means of transportation.

The *1990 Census Transportation Planning Package* contains special tabulations of place of work and transportation data on a set of 12 discs grouped by state. Data are grouped by place of residence, place of work, and journey to work. Users may select from a list of tables for each group. Tables cover worker characteristics, mode of transportation to work, time of departure/arrival, and travel time to work.

The American Community Survey is an ongoing monthly survey that is in its initial phases of development. During the development stage, data are collected only for a small number of test sites. Coverage will gradually be expanded and by 2004 coverage is expected to include all states, counties, cities, metropolitan areas, and population groups of 65,000 people or more. By 2008, coverage for smaller areas including census tracts will become available. The survey covers means of transportation to work and travel time to work.

American FactFinder is a Census Bureau Web database designed to provide access to data from the 1990 and 2000 *Census of Population and Housing*. It also contains a mapping feature and an option to search for information on Census Bureau products. Data from the 1990 census are available in both the "Facts about My Community" section and the "Population and Housing Facts" section. Users make a series of selections from lists of geographic areas, tables, and/or sources or search by word to identify and display data. A general search option is also available.

INDEXES
Checklist

American Statistics Index (ASI). PRINT. (monthly) 1973–. Bethesda, MD: Congressional Information Service.

Statistical Universe. WEB. Bethesda, MD: Congressional Information Service.

Catalog of United States Government Publications (MOCAT). WEB. 1994–. U.S. Government Printing Office. Superintendent of Documents. <http://www.gpo.gov/catalog>; <http://www.access.gpo.gov/su_docs/locators/cgp/index.html>; <http://purl.access.gpo.gov/GPO/LPS844>.

Monthly Catalog of United States Government Publications. CD-ROM. 1996–. U.S. Government Printing Office. Superintendent of Documents. GP 3.8/7: Item 0557-C. GPO.

Monthly Catalog of United States Government Publications (Condensed version). PRINT. (monthly) 1996–. U.S. Government Printing Office. Superintendent of Documents. GP 3.8/8: (Earlier full version, GP 3.8:, 1895-1995) Item 0557-D. GPO.

Discussion

A comprehensive listing of statistical material on transportation can be found in *American Statistics Index (ASI)* by looking under the subject headings "Transportation and transportation equipment," "Federal aid to transportation," and "Urban transportation." See also specific types of transportation such as "Automobiles," "Air Travel," or "Railroads." For statistics on accidents, see headings such as "Traffic Accidents and Safety," "Driving While Intoxicated," "Aviation Accidents and Safety," or "Transportation Accidents and Safety." *Statistical Universe* includes a Web version of *ASI*.

The *Monthly Catalog* may also be used to locate materials, but does not provide the depth of indexing for statistics that *ASI* does. Look under subject headings beginning with "Transportation" or under specific methods such as "Railroads," "Automobiles," or "Aeronautics, Commercial." Reports that are exclusively statistical are often indexed under the subheading "Statistics," such as "Trucks-United States-Statistics." There is also a subheading for "Accidents," as in "Transportation-United States-Accidents." See also specific types of accidents such as "Traffic Accidents." The complete version of the *Monthly Catalog* is available on the Web and CD-ROM. Commercial online and CD-ROM versions of the *Monthly Catalog* are also available.

RELATED MATERIAL
Within this Work

GPO Subject Bibliographies. **PRINT. WEB. GP 3.22/2:**

<http://bookstore.gpo.gov/sb/about.html>

No. 18   "Aviation"

No. 40   "Transportation"

No. 49   "Motor Vehicles"

No. 149 "Census of Transportation"

No. 181 "Census of Population and Housing"

No. 311 "Census Tracts and Blocks (Publications)"

No. 312 "Census Tracts and Blocks (Maps)"

Special Techniques

There are several areas within government publications that do not fit in with the basic subject, agency, or statistical search strategies. These areas require different strategies or procedures for uncovering information. Generally, these strategies do not rely heavily on the basic government publication indexes, but rather on special indexes or materials available as part of the U. S. government collection or from commercial sources.

The chapters in this section set forth strategies and key sources for historical, legislative, budgetary, technical, and specialized report areas.

CHAPTER 45
Legislative History

It is often necessary to trace the actions of Congress on a particular bill or area of legislation. As congressional action is taken, certain specific types of documents are created. Increasingly, the full-text of these sources are provided to the public on the Web free of charge. This chapter describes these sources and provides the search strategy needed to located this documentation, using both publicly available and some specialized commercially produced sources. It does not attempt to explain all of the intricacies of the legislative process. However, several documents that do explain the legislative process in great detail are listed in the first section of this chapter, "General Guides to the Legislative Process."

SEARCH STRATEGY

This chapter is an example of a special technique search. The search strategy for finding specific sources or following the legislative process can be described in the following search steps, using a bill originating in the House as an example. The search strategy is keyed to the individual sections of this chapter. Each search step indicates the section of this chapter to consult for more information.

1. A bill is introduced by a congressperson. (See "Major Comprehensive Legislative Resources" and "Congressional Sources—Bills and Resolutions.");
2. The bill is referred to a congressional committee. At this point, action may stop on the bill;
3. Committee reports, documents, and hearings may be generated as the committee deliberates. (See "Major Comprehensive Legislative Resources," "Congressional Sources—Reports and Documents," and "Congressional Sources—Hearings and Committee Prints.");
4. If the committee votes to report the bill, a committee report is written. (See "Major Comprehensive Legis-

lative Resources," "Congressional Sources—Reports and Documents.");
5. The report is brought to the House, and amendments may be taken from the floor. (See "Congressional Record and House and Senate Journals" for a record of congressional activities on the floor of the House and Senate.);
6. The bill is passed by the House and is referred to the appropriate Senate committee;
7. The committee reports the bill to the Senate;
8. Amendments may be added on the Senate floor;
9. If approved by the Senate, the bill is returned to the House;
10. If amendments are not substantial, the bill may be approved by the House with the amendments. If there is disagreement between the two houses, a conference with the Senate may be necessary. The houses will then report their activities in a conference report. (See "Major Comprehensive Legislative Resources," and "Congressional Sources—Reports and Documents.");
11. When the bill has been agreed to by both the House and Senate, it is sent to the President;
12. The President approves or vetoes the bill. If the President does nothing, the bill becomes law after 10 days. If the President vetoes the bill, it is sent back to Congress where it either passes with a two-thirds majority or it fails;
13. After the bill has been approved, it is issued in print form as a slip law. Individual laws are also made available electronically. (See "Statutory Sources."); and
14. Print slip laws are compiled into bound *Statutes at Large* volumes, then later compiled into the *United States Code*. Electronic versions of the *Statutes at Large* and *United States Code* are also made available. (See "Statutory Sources.")

GENERAL GUIDES TO THE LEGISLATIVE PROCESS

Checklist

Enactment of a Law: Procedural Steps in the Legislative Process. WEB. (1997) Robert B. Dove. U.S. Congress. Senate. Y 1.3:98016021. Item 0998-A-01. <http://thomas.loc.gov/home/enactment/enactlawtoc.html>.
> Content: step-by-step explanation of legislative procedure with examples.

How the Senate Works. WEB. U.S. Congress. Senate. <http://www.senate.gov/learning/index.cfm>.
> Content: includes explanations of Senate rules, process, and a section on frequently asked questions.

How Our Laws Are Made. WEB. (irregular) U.S. Congress. House. Issued as a House Document. Y 1.1/7: (2000 is Y 1.1/7:106-197). Items 0996-A or –B(MF). <http://thomas.loc.gov/home/lawsmade.toc.html>.
> Content: detailed explanation of legislative process and congressional actions.

Discussion

These three guides provide more detailed explanations of the legislative process. They can be consulted to provide an explanation of a specific congressional action or to gain a broad overview of the legislative process and its various steps.

MAJOR COMPREHENSIVE LEGISLATIVE RESOURCES

Checklist

THOMAS: Legislative Information on the Internet. WEB. U.S. Library of Congress. <http://thomas.loc.gov/>.
> Content: in-depth current coverage of legislative activities; some retrospective coverage.

GPO Access: Legislative. WEB. U.S. Government Printing Office. Superintendent of Documents. <http://www.access.gpo.gov/su_docs/legislative.html>.
> Content: searchable databases of many primary legislative materials; some retrospective coverage of materials.

CIS/Index. PRINT. (monthly) 1970–. Bethesda, MD: Congressional Information Service, Inc.
> Content: index to laws, reports, documents, hearings, legislative history.

Congressional Universe. WEB. Bethesda, MD: Congressional Information Service. <http://www.lexis-nexis.com/cispubs/Catalog/Universe/Congressional%20Universe/index.htm>.
> Content: comprehensive coverage of legislative activities, with full-text of many of the legislative sources.

CQ.com On Congress. WEB. Congressional Quarterly, Inc. <http://www.cq.com/>.
> Content: comprehensive legislative information system.

Congressional Index. PRINT. (biennial with loose-leaf updates) Washington, D.C.: Commerce Clearing House, Inc.
> Content: index to bills; history of legislation.

Calendar of United States House of Representatives and History of Legislation. PRINT. WEB. (daily) U.S. House. Y 1.2/2: Item 0998-A. GPO. <http://www.access.gpo.gov/congress/cong003.html>.
> Content: index to bills; history of legislation.

The U.S. House of Representatives: The Legislative Process. WEB. U.S. Congress. House of Representatives. <http://www.house.gov/house/Legproc.html>.
> Content: links to House legislative information, such as roll call votes, text of bills, status of bills, committee reports, and the *Congressional Record*.

Legislative Activities. WEB. U.S. Congress. Senate. <http://www.senate.gov/legislative/legis_act.html>.
> Content: links to Senate legislative information; roll call votes; Senate legislative calendar; calendar of committee actions.

LEXIS-NEXIS. <http://www.lexis-nexis.com/lncc/>.
> Content: legislative and legal databases.

Westlaw. <http://www.westlaw.com>.
> Content: legislative and legal databases.

Discussion

THOMAS provides publicly available free of charge legislative information. For most users, *THOMAS* is an excellent starting point for tracing legislative history. Much of the information available from *THOMAS* goes back retrospectively to the 93rd Congress (1973). *THOMAS* provides a "Bill Summary & Status" section that allows for multiple ways of searching bill information, including "Word/Phrase," "Subject Term," "Bill/Amendment No.," "Stage in Legislative Process," "Date of Introduction," "Sponsor/Cosponsor," and "Committee." The "Bill Summary and Status" section may also be browsed by the categories "Legislation," "Public Laws," "Private Laws," "Vetoed Bills," and "Sponsors/Cosponsors." *THOMAS* also includes the searchable full text of bills and public laws, and indexing of major legislation that includes listings by topic, by popular/short title, by bill number/type, and by whether the bill was enacted in law. (See Figure 45.1.)

THOMAS also includes the full text of the *Congressional Record*, and listings of House and Senate roll call votes. The full text of committee reports are also included on the site. Information on house hearings schedules and some hearings transcripts are also included.

THOMAS also includes information about members of Congress and some historical documents.

The *GPO Access: Legislative* site includes a series of full-text searchable databases. The *GPO Access* site and *THOMAS* overlap in some respects, although each includes some unique items. They also provide different searching interfaces and finding aids, with *THOMAS* in general providing a more sophisticated and easy-to-use searching interface. Included on the *GPO Access* site are the full text of bills from the 103rd Congress forward and *Public*

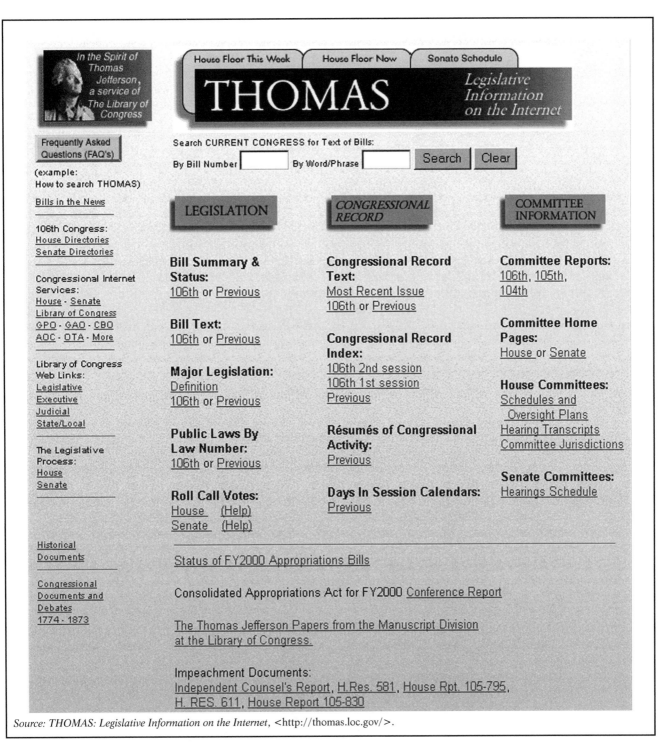

Figure 45.1: THOMAS Web Site.

Laws from the 104th Congress forward. The full text of Senate, House, and Treaty Documents and House, Senate, and Senate Executive Reports from the 104th Congress forward are also available. Basic boolean searching of keywords and phrases of the full text of all of these items is provided. The *History of Bills and Resolutions* section of the *Congressional Record Index* from 1983– is also available at the site. The entry for each bill or resolu-

tion lists actions reported in the *Congressional Record* and gives the *Congressional Record* citation. The full text of the *Congressional Record* from 1994– and of the *Congressional Record Index* from 1983– are also included at the *GPO Access* site.

The full text of a limited number of congressional hearings and committee prints from the 105th Congress forward are available. Other notable titles available from

GPO Access include the full text of the House and Senate *Calendars* from the 104th Congress forward and the text of the current edition of the *U.S. Code.*

CIS/Index is a comprehensive index and abstract for legislative materials. It is available in a print format, and is also included as part of the Web-based *Congressional Universe.* (See Chapter 3, "The Basics of Searching," for more complete descriptions of both of these sources.)

The print version of *CIS/Index* provides indexing and abstracts for all congressional materials except bills. Two sections of the print index are particularly useful for tracing legislative history. They are the "Legislative Histories" volume, and the "Index of Bill Numbers."

Entries in the "Legislative Histories" volume describe public laws and list the sources available relating to a public law's legislative history. Sources listed include slip laws, House and Senate hearings, House and Senate Reports, and House and Senate committee prints. Citations to the *Congressional Record* and the *Weekly Compilation of Presidential Documents* are also included.

The "Index of Bill Numbers" provides easy access to all entries associated with a particular bill number. Unlike the "Legislative Histories" volume, which only includes public laws, the "Index of Bill Numbers" includes all items associated with any bill, whether or not the bill became law.

Congressional Universe is a comprehensive information system covering all aspects of congressional activity. One major component of *Congressional Universe* is an electronic version of the *CIS/Index,* providing coverage back to 1970. In addition, *Congressional Universe* includes the full text of many congressional publications, and also includes the full text of the *Congressional Record,* the *Statutes at Large, Public Laws,* and the *United States Code Service.* It also includes sources of information about congressional members and analysis of congressional activities, such as the full-text of the periodicals the *National Journal* and the twice a day updated *CongressDaily.*

Congressional Universe also includes the full text of bills, and provides extensive bill tracking information. Bill information may be searched by keyword, sponsor, or bill number. Bill tracking entries provide a digest of the bill and detail all significant actions to date on the bill. The full text of bills may also be searched. A "Hot Bills" section highlights some of the most important bills being currently considered, and a "Hot Topics" section lists current important bills by subject area.

Similar to the print *CIS/Index, Congressional Universe* also includes a separate "Legislative Histories" section that provides in detail the legislative history information for all bills enacted in a congressional session. Links to the full text of available materials are also included within each entry. Legislative History entries can be searched by law or bill number, *Statutes at Large* citation, or by keyword. (See Figure 45.2.)

CQ.com On Congress is a comprehensive congressional information system. As part of its congressional news coverage, it includes the full text of the *CQ Daily Monitor* (daily news) and *CQ Weekly Reports.* It also provides transcripts of press conferences and news conferences, along with political news editorial reporting and analysis.

CQ.com On Congress's, "CQ BillTrack" and "CQ BillWatch" services provide constantly up-dated bill tracking and analysis, along with the full text of bills. *CQ.com On Congress* also provides voting analysis and the full text of the *Congressional Record.* Links to the full text of House and Senate Reports are also included.

The *Congressional Index* is a loose-leaf format index to bills. All bills on a given subject or by a given sponsor can be found using this index. The history and status of any particular bill can also be determined. The *Congressional Index* is issued in two volumes for each Congress and is updated periodically. Volume 1 contains a subject and author index for both House and Senate bills, along with sections of information on Senate bills. Volume two contains the other sections for House bills.

There are several sections within the *Congressional Index.* Of most relevance to the legislative history process are the "Status of Senate Bills" and "Status of House Bills" sections. The status section lists any action taken on a bill. It gives the date of introduction and any committee actions, lists any reports and dates of hearings, and provides information on votes and presidential actions. The "Senate Bills," "House Bills," Senate Resolutions," and "House Resolutions" sections each give a description of the bill or resolution, the sponsors of a bill, and the name of the committee that it has been sent to.

The "Voting Records on Senate Bills" and the "Voting Records on House Bills" sections record all roll-call votes. Votes are arranged so that it is possible to determine how an individual voted on any given legislation. The "Author Index" indexes the names of sponsors of bills or resolutions. The "Subject Index" indexes under broad, pre-established major subject categories and specific terms taken from the bill. Indexing is also done under the popular name of the bill or resolution.

The *Calendar of United States House of Representatives and History of Legislation* is another source of legislative history information. It includes sections listing bills in conference, bills through conference, calendars, public laws, private laws, and numerical listings of bills along with their legislative history. The calendar also includes a "Status of Major Bills" chart. The calendar indexes legislation in both the House and the Senate. It is issued daily, and each issue is cumulative. The Web version provides phrase and keyword searching.

The *U.S. House of Representatives: The Legislative Process* Web site provides links to House legislative information, most of it provided by *THOMAS.* Some information available from the site is compiled by the House Office of the Clerk, including House roll call votes from the

CIS Legislative Histories
Copyright © 1998, Congressional Information Service, Inc.

98 CIS PL 105374; 105 CIS Legis. Hist. P.L. 374

LEGISLATIVE HISTORY OF: P.L. 105-374

TITLE: Child Custody and Visitation

CIS-NO: 98-PL105-374
CIS-DATE: December, 1998
DOC-TYPE: **Legislative History**
DATE: Nov. 12, 1998
LENGTH: 2 p.
ENACTED-BILL: 105 H.R. 4164 Retrieve Bill Tracking report
STAT: 112 Stat. 3383
CONG-SESS: 105-2
ITEM-NO: 575

SUMMARY:
"To amend title 28, United States Code, with respect to the enforcement of child custody and visitation orders."

Clarifies that State courts must recognize grandparents' visitation rights granted by a court in another State in interstate child custody and visitation cases.

Prohibits State courts from modifying a visitation order issued by a court in another State unless that court no longer has jurisdiction to modify the order or has declined to exercise jurisdiction to modify the order.

CONTENT-NOTATION: Child custody and visitation rights, clarification

BILLS: 105 H.R. 1690 CHILDREN; STATE COURTS; FAMILIES; INTERSTATE RELATIONS; FEDERAL-STATE RELATIONS;JURISDICTION; CIVIL PROCEDURE

REFERENCES:

DEBATE:

144 Congressional Record, 105th Congress, 2nd Session - 1998
  July 14, House consideration and passage of H.R. 4164, p. H5437.
  Oct. 21, Senate consideration and passage of H.R. 4164 with an amendment, p. S12941.
  Oct. 21, House concurrence in the Senate amendment to H.R. 4164, p. H11699.

REPORTS:

105th Congress

H. Rpt. 105-546 on H.R. 1690, "Child Custody and Visitation Determinations," May 21, 1998.
  CIS NO: 98-H523-21
  LENGTH: 12 p.
  SUDOC: Y1.1/8:105-546

HEARINGS:

105th Congress

Hearings on H.R. 1690 before the Subcommittee on Courts and Intellectual Property, House Judiciary Committee, Apr. 23, 1998. (Not available at time of publication.)

Figure 45.2: Sample Legislative History from *Congressional Universe*.

101st Congress to the present and a summary of the current House floor proceedings. The *Legislative Activities* Web site of the Senate provides similar, but less comprehensive, information and links. It also includes Senate roll call votes.

LEXIS-NEXIS and *Westlaw* include many files of relevance to the legislative process. Both contain the text of the *Congressional Record* and the *U.S. Code. Westlaw* also includes access to the *United States Code Annotated* and a file of current and historical public laws. Its "BILLCAST" files includes access to the text of both current and historical bills, and bill tracking files and files describing the members of Congress are also available.

LEXIS-NEXIS includes the *United States Code Service, Statutes at Large,* and public law files. A bill tracking file, BLTRCK, and files containing the full text of bills are also included. *LEXIS-NEXIS* also tracks floor votes and committee votes and includes various files profiling congresspersons. It also includes a version of the *CIS/Index Legislative Histories,* and a file of the full text of House and Senate Documents. Most of the files of relevant interest can be found in the LEGIS library.

CONGRESSIONAL RECORD AND HOUSE AND SENATE JOURNALS

Checklist

Congressional Record. PRINT. MF. WEB. (daily when Congress in session) 1873–. U.S. Congress. X 1.1:, X 1.1/A: (Earlier, X, X/A) (Issued earlier as *Annals of Congress, Register of Debates,* and *Congressional Globe*). Items 0993-A(MF); 0993-A-01 (Regionals only, 1985-), 0993-B or -C(MF); 0994-B or -C(MF), 0994-D(EL). GPO. <http://www.access.gpo.gov/su_docs/aces/aces150.html>; <http://purl.access.gpo.gov/GPO/LPS1671>; <http://thomas.loc.gov/>.

    Content: verbatim record of the proceedings and debates of Congress.

Journal of the House of Representatives of the United States. PRINT. MF. CD-ROM. WEB. (annual) 1789–. U.S. Congress. House. XJH. (Early journals issued in the *Serial Set*) (Reprint edition of 1789-1817 published by Michael Glazier, Wilmington, DE, 1977) Items 1030-A, -B(MF), or B-01(CD). Early volumes: <http://lcweb2.loc.gov/ammem/amlaw/lwhj.html>; 1991– <http://www.access.gpo.gov/congress/cong018.html>; <http://purl.access.gpo.gov/GPO/LPS2564>.

    Content: record of the activities of the House.

Journal of the Senate of the United States of America. PRINT. MF. WEB. (annual) 1789–. U.S. Congress. Senate. XJS. (Early journals issued in the *Serial Set*) (Reprint edition of 1789-1817 published by Michael Glazier, Wilmington, DE, 1977) Items 1047-A or -B(MF). Early volumes: <http://lcweb2.loc.gov/ammem/amlaw/lwsj.html>; <http://purl.access.gpo.gov/GPO/LPS5486>.

    Content: official record of Senate proceedings.

Discusssion

The *Congressional Record* is a substantially verbatim record of the activities of Congress on the floor of each house. While both the House and Senate also are covered live by the C-SPAN television channel, some actions are not covered by C-SPAN. For example, the reading of a bill that might be truncated on the floor to save time is reprinted in full within the *Congressional Record.* The *Congressional Record* also includes any corrections to remarks that a Congressperson might make and the addition of the extension of some remarks that are spoken on the floor.

The *Congressional Record* is issued in daily volumes, which in the print version, are later cumulated into bound volumes. Each daily issue of the *Congressional Record* includes a section for the proceedings of the House, a section for the proceedings of the Senate, an "Extension of Remarks" section, and a "Daily Digest" section. (See Figure 45.3 for an excerpt from the *Congressional Record.*) The "Extension of Remarks" section includes a wide variety of materials such as letters from constituents or newspaper or magazine articles that congresspersons ask to be added to the *Congressional Record.* In the case of the House, it also includes additional remarks from congresspersons not actually spoken on the floor. In the case of the Senate, these types of remarks are added in a special section of the proceedings of the Senate, titled "Additional Statements."

The *Daily Digest* includes a summary of actions taken for that day. The Web version of the *Congressional Record* from *THOMAS* includes links to the appropriate full-text pages of the *Congressional Record* for the actions digested. It also includes links to the full-text of bills and laws as they are cited in the *Daily Digest.* This makes the *THOMAS* Web version of the daily *Congressional Record* an extremely useful version of the *Congressional Record.*

Semimonthly indices to the daily versions of the *Congressional Record* are published in both print and in a Web format available through *THOMAS.* The index provides access by names and subjects and includes a "History of Bills and Resolutions" section. This section is the most useful for tracking the legislative process, as references are given to pages of the *Congressional Record* that have action on a particular bill. The final bound volume also includes a similar index to the final version of the *Congressional Record,* which differs in pagination from the daily versions.

THOMAS also makes available a final index to the *Congressional Record* for each session of Congress. Word and phrase searching of the text of the *Congressional Record* are made available. It is also possible to browse a listing of index topics, which link to the full-text of the relevant page. *GPO Access* also provides keyword and phrase searching of the *Congressional Index* from 1983 to the present. The "History of Bills and Resolutions" section is searchable as a separate database on *GPO Access.*

bring this bill to the floor at this time. The bill would provide relief to Federal employees who through no fault of their own were placed in the wrong Federal retirement plan. Some Federal agencies mistakenly placed thousands of Federal employees into the Civil Service Retirement System, or CSRS, when the employees should have been placed in the Federal Employees Retirement System, FERS. Often this error has not been discovered until an employee is on the verge of retirement. Once discovered, the employee faces a severe erosion of his retirement security.

I am going to come back to the two employees that the gentleman from Florida mentioned who work at the Portsmouth Naval Shipyard in Kittery, Maine. They were very surprised to discover this error, and they face a serious deterioration of their retirement reserves unless Congress passes this bill. These two employees were placed in CSRS 14 years ago but only recently did they discover that they should have been placed in FERS. Once they learned that, they were then required involuntarily to switch from FERS to CSRS, and, since they had not been making their Social Security payments, all their CSRS resources were transferred to Social Security to make up for what they would otherwise have been paying in FICA taxes. For one of the men, his $30,000 CSRS investment was all used to pay so-called back FICA taxes. Furthermore, these employees will likely have to pay FICA tax not withheld for overtime, awards and other compensation for which they had legitimately not paid FICA tax because they were in CSRS which did not require it. This may total another $10,000 to $15,000.

Finally, the FERS plan consists of three components, Social Security, a small defined benefit plan, and a Thrift Savings Plan contribution plan. Consequently, these employees will need to make substantial catch-up contributions to the Thrift Savings Plan if they want any sort of nest egg for retirement. These heavy TSP contributions and FICA tax payments quickly consume the paychecks of these employees. As a result, one employee will delay his retirement by 3 years and the other may have trouble financing his child's college education.

□ 1315

Mr. Speaker, H.R. 416 will offer vital relief to these employees by making the agency responsible for their mistakes. The agency made the mistakes; the agency should be responsible. The bill requires the agency to make up both the agency's and the employee's lost contributions to the TSP.

These hard-working employees do not deserve to have their retirement plans wiped out by a employer's mistake. H.R. 416 offers relief for a problem they did not cause.

I want to thank both the gentleman from Florida (Mr. SCARBOROUGH) and

the gentleman from Maryland (Mr. CUMMINGS) for their work on this and leadership on this issue, and I urge my colleagues to support the bill.

Mr. CUMMINGS. Mr. Speaker, I yield myself such time as I may consume.

Mr. Speaker, a little earlier I mentioned Mr. Garcia, and Mr. Garcia had been placed, of course, in the wrong retirement system, and like numerous other federal employees, he had been forced to rearrange his life and his financial plans to address this problem.

Many without financial means have had to work beyond their retirement dates to build a full annuity. The Federal Retirement System was created to prevent just that, employees working into what should be their golden years, the years they rest, the years they travel, the years they take time out to spend with their grandchildren. The Federal Retirement Coverage Corrections Act would essentially permit those who have been the victims of an enrollment error to remain in the retirement system they were mistakenly placed in or to be covered by the system they should have been in. It would also hold the government financially responsible for making whole an effected employee's thrift savings account. Together these provisions would end the harm now being done by the existing rules governing the correction of these errors. To address my concern that the unanticipated costs of making an employee whole might cause agencies to rif its employees, I included a provision in the bill requiring that offsetting savings be realized through attrition and limitations on hiring.

There has been much debate over the cost to the government of making effected employees whole. The IRS Code requires that private sector employers bear the cost of correcting retirement errors. The Senate bill leaves it to the victimized employee to come up with the money to make themselves whole. That simply is not right. Our approach mirrors the private sector and is the fairest way to handle these problems. The longer it takes to enact this legislation, the more it is going to cause all effected parties. Federal employees who are in the wrong retirement system should not have to spend another year worrying about a problem that their agency created for them.

Mr. Speaker, I am committed to working with the Senate to reach agreement on the legislation that addresses all parties' concerns. These employees are waiting for us to act. Let us do so today, and again I want to thank the gentleman from Florida (Mr. SCARBOROUGH) and all the members of our subcommittee, our chairman, the gentleman from Indiana (Mr. BURTON), our ranking member of our full committee, the gentleman from California (Mr. WAXMAN).

Mr. Speaker, I have no further requests for time, and I yield back the balance of my time.

Mr. SCARBOROUGH. Mr. Speaker, I yield myself such time as I may consume.

Mr. Speaker, thousands of Federal employees, retirees and their families whose lives have been disrupted by bureaucratic errors are going to look again to this Congress to fix this problem. Many of them have suffered emotionally as well as financially, and I think it is time that we enact meaningful and fair relief during this Congress.

Mr. Speaker, H.R. 416 is strongly supported by the following employee organizations:

The American Federation of Government Employees,

The American Foreign Service Association,

The Federal Managers Association,

The Federally Employed Women,

The International Brotherhood of Boilermakers,

The National Association of Government Employees,

The National Federation of Federal Employees,

The Seniors Executives Association, and

The Social Security Managers' Association.

This is a bill that needs to pass in the best interests of every single Federal employee. It is the right thing to do, it is fair, and it is time that this House and, hopefully, this Senate, will step forward and do what is right.

The SPEAKER pro tempore (Mr. BASS). The question is on the motion offered by the gentleman from Florida (Mr. SCARBOROUGH) that the House suspend the rules and pass the bill, H.R. 416, as amended.

The question was taken; and (two-thirds having voted in favor thereof) the rules were suspended and the bill, as amended, was passed.

A motion to reconsider was laid on the table.

REMOVAL OF NAME OF MEMBER AS COSPONSOR OF H.R. 434

Mr. SHOWS. Mr. Speaker, I ask unanimous consent to remove my name as a cosponsor of H.R. 434.

The SPEAKER pro tempore. Is there objection to the request of the gentleman from Mississippi?

There was no objection.

SENSE OF HOUSE REGARDING FAMILY PLANNING PROGRAMS

Mr. CHABOT. Mr. Speaker, I move to suspend the rules and agree to the resolution (H. Res. 118) reaffirming the principles of the Programme of Action of the International Conference on Population and Development with respect to the sovereign rights of countries and the right of voluntary and informed consent in family planning programs.

The Clerk read as follows:

H. RES. 118

Whereas the United Nations General Assembly has decided to convene a special session from June 30 to July 2, 1999, in order to review and appraise the implementation of

---

Source: Congressional Record, March 23, 1999, Vol 145, p. H1510.

Figure 45.3: Sample *Congressional Record* Page.

The *Congressional Record* is available on the Web from the Government Printing Office's *GPO Access* Web site (1994–; index, 1983–) and on the Library of Congress' *Thomas* Web site (1989–; index, 1994–). Commercial online services also offer the *Congressional Record*, including *CIS Congressional Universe* (1985–), *LEXIS-NEXIS* (1987–), *Westlaw* (1985–), and *CQ.com On Congress* (1995–). On *LEXIS* it is in several libraries, including GENFED and LEGIS. The file name for the complete *Congressional Record* since 1985 is RECORD. There are also files for individual congresses or sections.

The House and Senate *Journals* are published annually at the end of a session. They are not verbatim, but cover each chamber's actions, vetos, procedures, motions, etc. Bill history sections are also included. The *House Journal* from 1991– is available in a searchable database edition on the Web from *GPO Access*.

CONGRESSIONAL SOURCES

The following sections describe the types of specialized documents and sources that are produced as a result of the legislative process. *THOMAS, GPO Access*, and *Congressional Universe* provide Web access to the full text of many of these sources. *LEXIS-NEXIS* and *Westlaw* also include some databases with the full text of sources. The depository system also distributes these publications in print and microfiche formats to depository libraries. Within each section, the items distributed to depository libraries are listed.

CONGRESSIONAL SOURCES: BILLS AND RESOLUTIONS

THOMAS: Bill Text. WEB. 1989–. U.S. Congress. (THOMAS) <http://thomas.loc.gov/>.
> Content: full text of bills from the 101st Congress to the present.

Congressional Bills. WEB. 1993–. U.S. Congress. (GPO Access) <http://www.access.gpo.gov/congress/cong009.html>; <http://purl.access.gpo.gov/GPO/LPS3503>.
> Content: full text of bills from the 103rd Congress to the present.

Senate Bills. MF. U.S. Congress. Senate. Y 1.4/1: Item 1006-A.
> Content: microfiche copies of Senate Bills.

Senate Resolutions. MF. U.S. Congress. Senate. Y 1.4/2: Item 1006-A.
> Content: microfiche copies of Senate Resolutions.

Senate Joint Resolutions. MF. U.S. Congress. Senate. Y 1.4/3: Item 1006-A.
> Content: microfiche copies of Senate Joint Resolutions.

Senate Concurrent Resolutions. MF. U.S. Congress. Senate. Y 1.4/4: Item 1006-A.
> Content: microfiche copies of Senate Concurrent Resolutions.

Senate Printed Amendments. MF. U.S. Congress. Senate. Y 1.4/5: Item 1006-A.
> Content: microfiche copies of Senate Printed Amendments.

House Bills. MF. U.S. Congress. House. Y 1.4/6: Item 1006-A.
> Content: microfiche copies of House Bills.

House Resolutions. MF. U.S. Congress. House. Y 1.4/7: Item 1006-A.
> Content: microfiche copies of House Resolutions.

House Joint Resolutions. MF. U.S. Congress. House. Y 1.4/8: Item 1006-A.
> Content: microfiche copies of House Joint Resolutions.

House Concurrent Resolutions. MF. U.S. Congress. House. Y 1.4/9: Item 1006-A.
> Content: microfiche copies of House Concurrent Resolutions.

Final Cumulative Finding Aid, House and Senate Bills. PRINT. (annual) U.S. Government Printing Office. Superintendent of Documents. GP 3.28: Item 0553-A.
> Content: finding aid to location of bills on microfiche.

Discussion

Bills are the form most commonly used to pass legislation. The bill itself includes the information needed by congresspersons to consider passage of the bill to become law. Bills may be introduced in either house. A joint resolution is very similar to a bill and may originate in either house. Resolutions are commonly used for passing matters concerning only one House. Concurrent resolutions are used for matters affecting the operation of both houses. Neither are acted upon by the President when passed. Resolutions and concurrent resolutions are used primarily for expressing facts, principles, opinions, and purposes of the two houses. (See Figure 45.4 for an example of a bill.)

THOMAS and *GPO Access* both provide access to the full-text of current bills. Bills are also presently distributed to depository libraries in a microfiche format, and those items are listed here, along with an entry for their finding aid. Microfiched distribution of bills to depository libraries will end with the 106th Congress. The full-text of bills are also available from many of the commercial vendors and products previously discussed, such as *Congressional Universe, CQ.com On Congress, LEXIS-NEXIS,* and *Westlaw*.

CONGRESSIONAL SOURCES—REPORTS AND DOCUMENTS
Checklist

THOMAS: Committee Reports. WEB. 1995–. U.S. Congress. (THOMAS) <http://thomas.loc.gov/>.
> Content: searchable database of the full text of House and Senate Reports from the 104th Congress to the present.

```
106TH CONGRESS
1ST SESSION       H. R. 301

To amend title XIX of the Social Security Act to reduce infant mortality
   through improvement of coverage of services to pregnant women and
   infants under the Medicaid Program.


          IN THE HOUSE OF REPRESENTATIVES

                  JANUARY 6, 1999
  Mr. TOWNS introduced the following bill; which was referred to the Committee
                      on Commerce


                   A BILL

To amend title XIX of the Social Security Act to reduce
   infant mortality through improvement of coverage of
   services to pregnant women and infants under the Medic-
   aid Program.

1       Be it enacted by the Senate and House of Representa-
2  tives of the United States of America in Congress assembled,
3  SECTION 1. SHORT TITLE.
4       This Act may be cited as the "Medicaid Infant Mor-
5  tality Amendments of 1999".
```

Source: H.R. 301, 106th Congress, 1st Session.

Figure 45.4: Sample Bill.

Senate, House, and Executive Reports. WEB. 1995–. U.S. Congress. (GPO Access) <http://www.access.gpo.gov/congress/cong005.html>.
> Content: searchable database of the full text of Senate, House, and Executive Reports from the 104th Congress to the present.

Senate, House, and Treaty Documents. WEB. 1995–. U.S. Congress (GPO Access) <http://www.access.gpo.gov/congress/cong006.html>.
> Content: searchable database of the full text of Senate, House, and Treaty Documents from the 104th Congress to the present.

Senate Reports. PRINT. MF. (irregular) U.S. Congress. Senate. Y 1.1/5: Items 1008-C or -D(MF).
> Content: individual print and microfiche copies of Senate Reports.

Senate Executive Reports. PRINT. MF. (irregular) U.S. Congress. Senate. Y 1.1/6: Items 1008-C or -D(MF).
> Content: individual print and microfiche copies of Senate Executive Reports.

Senate Documents. PRINT. MF. (irregular) U.S. Congress. Senate. Y 1.1/3: Items 0996-A or -B(MF).
> Content: individual print and microfiche copies of Senate Documents.

Senate Treaty Documents. PRINT. MF. U.S. Congress. Senate. Y 1.1/4: Items 0996-A or -B(MF).
> Content: individual print and microfiche copies of Senate Treaty Documents.

House Reports. PRINT. MF. U.S. Congress. House. Y 1.1/8: Items 1008-C or -D(MF).
> Content: individual print and microfiche copies of House Reports.

House Documents. PRINT. MF. U.S. Congress. House. Y 1.1/7: Items 0996-A or -B(MF).
> Content: individual print and microfiche copies of House Documents.

U.S. Congressional Serial Set. PRINT. MF. WEB. 1817–. U.S. Congress. Y 1.1/2: (Before 1817, see the *American State Papers*). Items 0996-B(MF) or -C; 1008-D(MF) or –E; 1008-F (105th Congress –, regional depository libraries only) Early volumes: <http://lcweb2.loc.gov/ammem/amlaw/lwss.html>; Individual documents and reports since 1995: <http://www.access.gpo.gov/su_docs/legislative.html>.
> Content: historical compilation of legislative sources that includes House and Senate Reports, House and Senate Documents, Senate Treaty Documents, and Senate Executive Reports.

Discussion

House and Senate reports are issued by the individual congressional committees. Reports most often contain recommendations to the entire Senate or House regarding legislation that the committee has considered. Reports may also be issued as "conference reports," which reconcile differences in similar legislation passed by the House and Senate. These reports will be issued by the conference committee (made up of members of both the Senate and House). Reports may also be issued on other matters not directly tied to a specific piece of legislation.

House and Senate documents make up a miscellaneous group of publications. They may include texts of presidential messages or agency annual and special reports submitted to Congress. Congressional special studies and reports are also included within the documents series. *Senate Executive Reports* and *Senate Treaty Documents* are special publications produced in conjunction with the ratification of treaties and conventions.

House and Senate reports and documents were historically issued individually, then compiled into a set known as the *Serial Set*. (See Chapter 52, "Historical Searches," for additional information on using the *Serial Set* and its finding aids.)

THOMAS provides access to the full-text of House and Senate reports. *THOMAS* also provides links to "Bill Digest" summaries and the full text of bills associated with a particular report. *GPO Access* provides access to House and Senate reports, Senate executive reports, House and Senate documents, and Senate treaty documents. These reports and documents are also distributed to depository libraries in a print or microfiche format, and those items are listed here. The full text of some of these reports and documents are also available from some of the commercial vendors and products previously discussed, such as *Congressional Universe* and *CQ.com On Congress*.

CONGRESSIONAL SOURCES—HEARINGS AND COMMITTEE PRINTS

House Committee Hearing Transcripts. WEB. 1995–. U.S. Congress. (THOMAS) <http://thomas.loc.gov/home/hhearing.html>.

> Content: links to House committee Web sites that provide transcripts of hearing testimony.

Congressional Hearings. WEB. 1997–. U.S. Congress. (GPO Access) <http://www.access.gpo.gov/congress/cong017.html>.

> Content: searchable database of a limited number of hearings available in full text.

Congressional Committee Prints. WEB. 1997–. U.S. Congress. (GPO Access) <http://www.access.gpo.gov/congress/cpsrch.html>.

> Content: searchable database of a limited number of committee prints available in full text.

Discussion

Hearings are held by congressional committees to provide an opportunity for interested parties to present testimony and other information to members of Congress. Hearings may be held on specific legislation, proposed or existing; as an overview of a subject or topical area; or as a hearing on appropriations. Hearings often reprint articles, reports, photographs, citizens' letters, etc. The testimony and material submitted as part of a hearing are often quite lengthy and the text of hearings can create a large document. *CIS/Index* and *Congressional Universe* serve as a major point of access to hearings, and *Congressional Universe* includes the full text of the hearing transcripts (written statements of witnesses and Q&A transcripts) for many hearings. A few hearings are becoming available through *THOMAS* and *GPO Access*, but access is still quite limited. Some committee Web sites also include selected testimony from hearings. The *House Committee Hearing Transcripts* Web site provides links to the available House transcripts.

Depository libraries receive hearings in either print or microfiche formats. Hearings are assigned SuDocs numbers beginning with Y 4, with the subsequent part of the class stem of the SuDocs determined by the committee involved. For example, hearings of the House Judiciary Committee all begin with the SuDocs number Y 4. J89/1: .

Committee prints are reports or studies prepared for the use of a committee. Prints are often prepared by the Congressional Research Service at the request of a congressional committee. Prints provide background and analysis to aid congresspersons in making legislative decisions. Committee prints are extremely useful in providing information and research on a wide range of topics.

As with hearings, the full text of a few prints are available from *GPO Access*. *Congressional Universe* also includes the full text of selected committee prints. Depository libraries also receive prints in either print or microfiche formats.

STATUTORY SOURCES
Checklist

Public Laws by Law Number. WEB. 1975–. U.S. Congress. (THOMAS) <http://thomas.loc.gov>.

> Content: electronic full text of public laws of the U.S.

Public Laws. WEB. 1995–. U.S. National Archives and Records Administration. Office of the Federal Register. (GPO Access) <http://www.access.gpo.gov/nara/nara005.html>.

> Content: electronic full text of public laws of the U.S.

Slip Laws. PRINT. (irregular) U.S. National Archives and Records Administration. Office of the Federal Register. AE 2.110: Item 575. GPO.

> Content: individual print copies of public laws of the U.S.

Private Laws. PRINT. (irregular) U.S. National Archives and Records Administration. Office of the Federal Register. AE 2.110/2: Item 0575-A. GPO.

> Content: individual print copies of private laws of the U.S.

United States Statutes at Large. PRINT. WEB. (annual) 1789–. U.S. National Archives and Records Administration. Office of the Federal Register. AE 2.111: (Earlier, GS 4.111:; S 7.9:) (Title varies) Item 0576. GPO. Selected volumes: <http://lcweb2.loc.gov/ammem/amlaw/lwsl.html>.

> Content: compilation of laws in chronological order.

United States Code. PRINT. CD-ROM. WEB. (annual supplements; revised every 6 years) 1926–. U.S. Congress. House. Y 1.2/5:, Y 1.2/5-2: (CD) (Annotated commercial editions also available) Items 0991-A or -B(CD). GPO. <http://www.access.gpo.gov/congress/cong013.html>; <http://uscode.house.gov/uscode.htm>; <http://purl.access.gpo.gov/GPO/LPS2873>; <http://www4.law.cornell.edu/uscode/>.

United States Code. WEB. Cornell Law School. Legal Information Institute. <http://www4.law.cornell.edu/uscode/>.

> Content: searchable version of *United States Code*.

United States Code Annotated. PRINT. WEB. 1927–. (updated periodically with supplements) St. Paul, MN: West Group. (Web version available from commercial vendors)

> Content: compilation by subject of current laws in effect with added notes and annotations.

United States Code Service. PRINT. WEB. 1972–. (updated periodically with supplements) Rochester, NY: Lawyer's Cooperative Publishing Company. (Web version available from commercial vendors)

> Content: compilation by subject of current laws in effect with added notes and annotations.

Discussion

Laws are first issued in print form as individual documents called slip laws. These individual slip laws are later bound chronologically into the *Statutes at Large* volumes.

113 STAT. 1032   PUBLIC LAW 106–71—OCT. 12, 1999

Public Law 106–71
106th Congress

An Act

Oct. 12, 1999
[S. 249]

To provide funding for the National Center for Missing and Exploited Children,
to reauthorize the Runaway and Homeless Youth Act, and for other purposes.

*Be it enacted by the Senate and House of Representatives of
the United States of America in Congress assembled,*

Missing,
Exploited, and
Runaway
Children
Protection Act.
42 USC 5601
note.

SECTION 1. SHORT TITLE.

This Act may be cited as the "Missing, Exploited, and Runaway
Children Protection Act".

SEC. 2. NATIONAL CENTER FOR MISSING AND EXPLOITED CHILDREN.

(a) FINDINGS.—Section 402 of the Missing Children's Assistance
Act (42 U.S.C. 5771) is amended—
 (1) in paragraph (7), by striking "and" at the end;
 (2) in paragraph (8), by striking the period at the end
and inserting a semicolon; and
 (3) by adding at the end the following:
 "(9) for 14 years, the National Center for Missing and
Exploited Children has—
  "(A) served as the national resource center and
 clearinghouse congressionally mandated under the provisions of the Missing Children's Assistance Act of 1984;
 and
  "(B) worked in partnership with the Department of
 Justice, the Federal Bureau of Investigation, the Department of the Treasury, the Department of State, and many
 other agencies in the effort to find missing children and
 prevent child victimization;
 "(10) Congress has given the Center, which is a private
nonprofit corporation, access to the National Crime Information
Center of the Federal Bureau of Investigation, and the National
Law Enforcement Telecommunications System;
 "(11) since 1987, the Center has operated the National
Child Pornography Tipline, in conjunction with the United
States Customs Service and the United States Postal Inspection
Service and, beginning this year, the Center established a
new CyberTipline on child exploitation, thus becoming 'the
911 for the Internet';
 "(12) in light of statistics that time is of the essence in
cases of child abduction, the Director of the Federal Bureau
of Investigation in February of 1997 created a new NCIC child
abduction ('CA') flag to provide the Center immediate notification in the most serious cases, resulting in 642 'CA' notifications
to the Center and helping the Center to have its highest

Source: Public Law 106-71, October 12, 1999.

Figure 45.5: Sample Public Law.

On the Web, individual public laws are available from both *THOMAS* and the National Archives and Records Administration (the publisher of the *Statutes at Large*). (See Figure 45.5.)

All current laws are also arranged by subject into "titles" and republished in the *United States Code*. The official *United States Code* volumes are published in a print format every six years, with supplements issued between editions of the *Code*. It is important to note that the *United States Code* is composed only of those laws currently in effect and that subsequent amendments to an original law will be incorporated into the *United States Code*. A CD-ROM version is also produced. A Web version of the *United States Code* is available from the House Office of Law Revision. This full-text version is fully searchable by keyword and by *U.S. Code* citations. A downloadable text version of the *U.S. Code* is also made available to users from this site. The "Classification Tables" included on this site allow the user to identify sections of the *U.S. Code* amended by current laws, and to also identify the section of the *Code* where the new laws will appear. Tables for each session of Congress are available sorted by *Public Law* order and by *U.S. Code* order. Web versions of the code are also available from several other non-governmental sites. The Legal Research Institute at Cornell University is one of the most popular of the legal meta-sites, and the *U.S. Code* found there is also cited.

Two commercial print editions of the *United States Code*, the *United States Code Annotated* and the *United States Code Service*, provide more current updating by the use of supplements and pocket parts. These two versions also include additional supplementary material in the form of extensive notes and annotations. These versions are also available in electronic formats.

Several commercial online services provide access to one or more versions of the *U.S. Code*, or subsets of the *U.S. Code* by year or topic. These include *LEXIS-NEXIS*, *LEXIS-NEXIS Academic Universe*, *CIS Congressional Universe*, *Westlaw*, and *CQ.com On Congress*. In particular, various subsets of the *United States Code Annotated* are available from *Westlaw*, and *LEXIS-NEXIS* and *LEXIS-NEXIS Academic Universe* include electronic versions of the *United States Code Service*.

OTHER LEGISLATIVE HISTORY AIDS
Checklist

CQ Weekly. PRINT. WEB. (weekly) 1946–. (Title varies. Earlier, *Congressional Quarterly Weekly Report*) Washington, D.C.: Congressional Quarterly, Inc. CQ Library: <http://libraryip.cq.com/>.
> Content: summary of congressional activities and votes.

Congressional Quarterly Almanac. PRINT. (annual) 1945–. Washington, D.C.: Congressional Quarterly, Inc.
> Content: votes; lobby registrations; presidential messages; listing of public laws.

Congressional Roll Call. PRINT. (annual) Washington, D.C: Congressional Quarterly, Inc.
> Content: record and analysis of congressional votes.

United States Code Congressional and Administrative News. PRINT. (monthly) 1942–. (Title varies) St. Paul, MN: West Publishing.
> Content: reprint of public laws, along with a selected reprinting of important legislative history items.

Discussion

Three reports published by Congressional Quarterly Inc., provide assistance in tracing legislative histories. *CQ Weekly* is a current periodical devoted to covering the actions of Congress, and available in both a print and Web version. The Web version provides a powerful searching tool that allows searching of the full-text archives of *CQ Weekly* back to 1983. *CQ Weekly* reports on important legislative action, floor action, analyzes issues, and also records any votes taken in Congress.

Congressional Quarterly Almanac is a massive annual volume that provides a summary of each congressional session's legislative activities. It provides legislative history information on every bill that *CQ Weekly* reported on during the year. It also includes roll call votes and voting analysis, along with other analyses of the legislative activities of the year. The *Congressional Roll Call* volume compiles and analyzes all of the voting records for each Congress. It is a convenient and easy source to consult for voting records for each Congress.

United States Code Congressional and Administrative News is another source that provides legislative history information. It is divided into two parts, with one section reprinting public laws and the other section providing a legislative history of the law. It also reprints excerpts of the entire document for selected items such as House and Senate Reports or Documents.

RELATED MATERIAL
Within this Work

Chapter 27 The President

GPO Subject Bibliographies. PRINT. WEB. GP 3.22/2:

<http://bookstore.gpo.gov/sb/about.html>

No. 197 "United States Code"

No. 201 "Congress"

CHAPTER 46
Judicial Reports

This chapter covers sources on federal court decisions with emphasis on the titles that are available through the depository library program. In addition to the decisions themselves, other selected titles and series relating to federal courts are included.

Court decisions or opinions are published in sets of books called "reporters" or "reports." Some of these case reports are published by government agencies, but many are published only by commercial publishers. Commercial publishers are also the primary sources for indexes to court decisions. Selected commercial titles have been included in this chapter.

Citations are needed to locate a specific court decision. Citations can be obtained from indexes and may also be included in bibliographic references found in books and journal articles. The following is an example of a case citation: 486 U.S. 249. The first number, 486, specifies a volume number. The abbreviation, U.S., indicates a specific reporter. In this example, the reference is to *United States Reports*. The second number, 249, is the page number. A complete bibliographic reference would also include the name of the case, the circuit or district for lower federal courts, and the date, as in *Satterwhite v. Texas*, 486 U.S. 249 (1988) or *U.S. v. Saunders*, 951 F.2d 1065 (9th Cir. 1991). A sample citation is included in the bibliographic entry for each case reporter listed in this chapter.

SEARCH STRATEGY

This chapter is an example of a special technique strategy. Special indexes are needed to locate individual court decisions. The steps for locating court decisions are

1. If the citation is not known, consult the indexes in the "Federal Court Decision Indexes" section of this chapter or use one of the online databases listed in the "Legal Databases" section;

2. When a citation has been obtained, match it to the appropriate federal case reporter (See "Supreme Court Decisions," "Appellate and District Court Decisions," and "Specialized Federal Court Decisions" sections.) to locate the specific case or view the full text in one of the "Legal Databases";

3. Selected, usually recent, decisions can also be located on the Internet. See the Web sites listed in the appropriate federal court sections of this chapter;

4. For other information on federal courts consult the "Court Rules," "Additional Sources," and "Indexes" sections; and

5. Consider the "Related Material" section.

SUPREME COURT DECISIONS
Checklist

United States Reports: Cases Adjudged in the Supreme Court. PRINT. (irregular) 1754–. U.S. Supreme Court. JU 6.8: (Title varies) (Sample citation: 486 U.S. 249) Item 0741. GPO.
  Content: U.S. Supreme Court decisions; final bound set.

Official Reports of the Supreme Court; Preliminary Print. PRINT. (irregular) U.S. Supreme Court. JU 6.8/A: Item 0740-B. GPO.
  Content: U.S. Supreme Court decisions; preliminary prints replaced by bound volumes of *United States Reports*.

Slip Opinions. PRINT. WEB. (irregular) U.S. Supreme Court. JU 6.8/B: Item 0740-A. GPO. <http://fedbbs.access.gpo.gov/court01.htm>; <http://purl.access.gpo.gov/GPO/LPS1858>.
  Content: individual U.S. Supreme Court decisions; replaced by *Official Reports of the Supreme Court; Preliminary Prints.*

West's Supreme Court Reporter. PRINT. CD-ROM. (semimonthly while court in session) 1882–. (Title varies) (Sample citation: 108 S.Ct. 1792) St. Paul, MN: West Group.
  Content: U.S. Supreme Court decisions.

United States Supreme Court Reports, Lawyers' Edition. PRINT. CD-ROM. (twice monthly while court in session) 1790–. (Title varies) (Sample citation: 100 L.Ed.2d 284) Charlottesville, VA: LEXIS Law Publishing.

Content: U.S. Supreme Court decisions.

FindLaw: U.S. Supreme Court Opinions Web Page. WEB. FindLaw. <http://www.findlaw.com/casecode/supreme.html>.

Content: Supreme Court decisions since 1893.

Supreme Court Collection Web Site. WEB. Legal Information Institute. Cornell Law School. <http://supct.law.cornell.edu/supct/>.

Content: Supreme Court decisions from 1990–; selected historical decisions; court calendar; court rules; biographies of current and former justices.

GPO Access: Judicial Web Site. WEB. U.S. Government Printing Office. <http://www.access.gpo.gov/su_docs/judicial.html>.

Content: Supreme Court decisions, 1937–1975, 1992–.

FLITE – Supreme Court Decisions 1937–1975 Web Site. WEB. U.S. Department of Commerce. National Technical Information Service. <http://www.fedworld.gov/supcourt/index.htm>.

Content: Supreme Court Decisions 1937-1975.

U.S. Supreme Court Multimedia Database: The Oyez Project. WEB. Northwestern University. <http://oyez.nwu.edu/>.

Content: oral arguments for leading constitutional law cases.

Supreme Court of the United States Web Site. WEB. U.S. Supreme Court. <http://www.supremecourtus.gov/>.

Content: Supreme Court decisions for the current term; court schedule; court rules; court information and history; biographies of justices.

USSC+. CD-ROM. WEB. InfoSynthesis, Inc. <http://www.ussscplus.com/index.htm>.

Content: Supreme Court decisions from the current term; database of the top 1000 most cited Supreme Court decisions; fee-based products for Supreme Court decisions since 1922 with selected historical decisions.

Discussion

The United States Supreme Court is the highest court in the federal system. Decisions may be appealed to the Supreme Court from U.S. appellate courts and from state supreme courts. The Supreme Court agrees to hear only a small number of the cases submitted to it. The importance of Supreme Court decisions is reflected in the number of reporters available for the Supreme Court. Three editions of Supreme Court decisions are published — one by the government and two by commercial publishers.

United States Reports is the official bound government edition of Supreme Court decisions and is available to depository libraries. Before the bound volumes are issued, Supreme Court decisions are published individually as *Slip Opinions*. The individual *Slip Opinions* are then superceded by softbound compilations called preliminary prints or advance sheets. These preliminary prints are titled *Official Reports of the Supreme Court.* The *Official Reports* are in turn superceded by the final, bound volumes

of *United States Reports*. There is a span of a few years between the date of the decision and its appearance in the bound volumes.

Two commercial publishers also issue sets of Supreme Court decisions. These decisions are no different from those published in *United States Reports*, but the publishers add additional annotations and research aids. These two titles are *West's Supreme Court Reporter* and *United States Supreme Court Reports, Lawyers' Edition.* Both of these titles are updated with advance sheets that are eventually replaced by bound volumes.

Supreme court decisions are also available from online legal databases (see the "Legal Databases" section of this chapter) and on the Web. The Supreme Court instituted a program beginning with the 1990–91 term to provide the full text of Supreme Court opinions to the public electronically shortly after their release. Called Project Hermes, the program distributes decisions electronically to selected participants. These decisions are available from several Web sites, often supplemented with older decisions from other sources.

The *FindLaw: U.S. Supreme Court Opinions Web Page* covers decisions since 1893. It offers searching by *U.S. Reports* citation, party name, and full text. Decisions can also be browsed by *U.S. Reports* volume number and year. A listing of recent cases and current year cases is also available.

Cornell's *Supreme Court Collection Web Site* contains decisions since 1990 plus more than 600 important historical decisions. The site provides several options for viewing decisions. Users may display current month, current term, or previous term decisions listed by date. Lists of orders are also available for the current month and term. A highlights section for the previous term lists key cases by topic and provides brief summaries. Topic lists for all cases covered and lists of all cases by name are also available. A quick search feature is also offered. Other features include a searchable database of orders in pending cases, court calendar, oral argument schedule, a list of questions presented in cases scheduled to be heard, historical cases by opinion author, and justice biographies with links to selected opinions written.

The *GPO Access: Judicial Web Site* offers two Supreme Court decision databases. One provides a list of decisions for viewing or downloading beginning with 1992. The other is a searchable database of decisions covering 1937–1975 made available by the U.S. Air Force from its *Federal Legal Information Through Electronics (FLITE)* database. Decisions can be searched by full text, case name, or case number. This database has not been authenticated by the Supreme Court.

Another version of the *FLITE* database is available from the National Technical Information Services' FedWorld Web site. The *FLITE – Supreme Court Decisions 1937–1975 Web Site* offers searching by case name and full text.

The *U.S. Supreme Court Multimedia Database: The Oyez Project* provides RealAudio recordings of the oral arguments for leading constitutional law cases. Cases may be searched by title, citation, subject, or date. Other features include biographical information on justices and a virtual tour of the Supreme Court building.

The *Supreme Court of the United States Web Site* contains opinions from the current term and provides information on the publishing process and a list of sources for obtaining Supreme Court opinions in various formats. General information and background on the Supreme Court are also provided.

USSC+ is a commercial service offering both a Web and CD-ROM product for a subscription fee. The Web site offers some free services. The text of cases from the current term and a database of the top 1000 cited cases are available at no charge.

APPELLATE AND DISTRICT COURT DECISIONS
Checklist

West's Federal Reporter: Cases Argued and Determined in the United States Courts of Appeals and Temporary Emergency Court of Appeals. PRINT. CD-ROM. (weekly) 1880–. (Title varies) (Sample citation: 951 F.2d 1065) St. Paul, MN: West Group.
> Content: U.S. appellate court decisions.

West's Federal Supplement. PRINT. CD-ROM. (weekly) 1932–. (Title varies) (Sample citation: 779 F.Supp. 614) St. Paul, MN: West Group.
> Content: selected U.S. district court decisions.

FindLaw: Federal Courts of Appeal Web Page. WEB. FindLaw. <http://www.findlaw.com/10fedgov/Judicial/Appeals_courts.html>.
> Content: search appellate court cases on FindLaw; link to individual court Web pages.

FindLaw: Federal District Courts Web Page. WEB. FindLaw. <http://www.findlaw.com/10fedgov/Judicial/district_courts.html>.
> Content: links to individual district court Web pages.

Federal Law Materials – Judicial Opinions Web Page. WEB. Legal Information Institute. Cornell Law School. <http://www.law.cornell.edu/federal/opinions.html#appeals>.
> Content: search court of appeals decisions available on the Internet; link to individual court Web pages.

Federal Court Locator. WEB. Villanova University School of Law. <http://vls.law.vill.edu/Locator/fedcourt.html>.
> Content: links to federal court Web pages.

Discussion

Federal appellate and district court decisions are not published by the government and are not available through the depository library program. The reporters for these courts are available through West Group, a major legal publisher. The appellate court system is one step below the U.S. Supreme Court. The United States is divided into 12 geographical circuits with one appellate court in each circuit. An additional appellate court for the Federal Circuit has jurisdiction for specific types of cases. Geographic circuits are further divided into districts. Each state has at least one district court. Large states have more than one. The district courts are the trial courts of the federal court system, where cases are first presented. The district courts determine the facts of the situation and apply the law accordingly. Most district court decisions are not published. Those deemed significant are published in *West's Federal Supplement*. District court cases may be appealed to the appellate court representing that district. The appeal is usually based on the interpretation of the law, not on the facts as determined by the district court. Appellate court decisions are published in *West's Federal Reporter*. Appellate court decisions may be appealed to the U.S. Supreme Court.

Appellate and district court decisions are also available from online legal databases (see the "Legal Databases" section of this chapter). Many recent appellate court decisions are available on the Web. Although the coverage varies for each individual court, decisions generally began being made available in the mid-1990s. Availability of district court decisions is much more limited. *FindLaw* has separate search pages for the appellate and district courts. The appellate court page has a general search option and links to the court decisions for each individual court. Cases for each individual court are listed by year, and sometimes month. Search options are available by docket number, party name, and full text. Links to the individual court Web pages are also listed with annotations on the type of information available from each. The district court page has links to individual court pages with annotations on the information available. Cornell's *Federal Law Materials – Judicial Opinions Web Page* provides a general search option for appellate decisions available on the Internet and links to individual court Web sites for appellate and district courts. *Federal Court Locator* is another listing of federal court Web sites.

FEDERAL COURT DECISION INDEXES
Checklist

United States Supreme Court Digest. PRINT. (annual updates) 1754–. St. Paul, MN: West Group.
> Content: digests of all Supreme Court decisions arranged by subject; indexes by subject, case name, and defendant name.

West's Federal Practice Digest. PRINT. CD-ROM. (annual updates with bimonthly supplements) 1961–. (Presently in 4th series; previous titles provide coverage prior to 1961: *Modern Federal Practice Digest* covers 1939–1961 and *Federal Digest* covers decisions from the earliest times to 1939) St. Paul, MN: West Group.

Content: digests of all published federal court decisions arranged by subject; indexes by subject, case name, and defendant name.

Discussion

The government does not publish comprehensive indexes to federal court decisions. The West digests listed above are the most commonly available indexes to federal decisions. *United States Supreme Court Digest* indexes all Supreme Court decisions. *West's Federal Practice Digest* indexes all federal decisions, including those of the Supreme Court. Digests are multivolume sets arranged alphabetically by broad subject areas, such as "Constitutional Law" or "Negligence." Outwardly, they are similar in appearance to encyclopedias. Each broad subject area is further subdivided into detailed subtopics. Relevant decisions are listed under each topic with a brief "digest" of each case. Digests also include a "Descriptive Word Index" for more specific subject access, a "Table of Cases" for access by case name, and a "Defendant-Plaintiff Table" for access by name of the defendant.

Individual volumes of case reporters also include subject indexes and listings of case names. It is possible to locate decisions by searching individual reporter volumes if the specific court and approximate date of the decision is known. This method of locating decisions, however, is much more difficult.

Online legal databases provide full-text searching (see the "Legal Databases" section of this chapter), as do some of the Web sites cited in this chapter for cases that are available on the Web.

SPECIALIZED FEDERAL COURT DECISIONS
Checklist

United States Court of International Trade Reports. PRINT. (annual) 1980–. U.S. Court of International Trade. JU 9.5/2: (Earlier title: *United States Customs Court Reports*, JU 9.5:) (Sample citation: 13 CIT 1) Item 0736. GPO. Current slip opinions: <http://www.uscit.gov/slip-op.html>.

Content: Court of International Trade decisions.

Trade Cases Adjudged in the U.S. Court of Appeals for the Federal Circuit. PRINT. (annual) 1982–. U.S. Court of Appeals (Federal Circuit). JU 7.5/2: (Sample citation: 6 Fed.Cir.(T)). Item 0733. GPO.

Content: trade decisions of the Court of Appeals for the Federal Circuit.

Reports of the United States Tax Court. PRINT. WEB. (semiannual) 1942–. U.S. Tax Court. JU 11.7: (Title varies) (Monthly advance sheets titled *Reports*, JU 11.7/A 2:) (Sample citation: 95 T.C. 1) Item 0742. GPO. <http://www.ustaxcourt.gov/UstcInOp/asp/HistoricOptions.asp>.

Content: U.S. Tax Court decisions.

T.C. Memo. MF. WEB. (irregular) U.S. Tax Court. JU 11.7/2: Item 0742-B. <http://www.ustaxcourt.gov/UstcInOp/asp/HistoricOptions.asp>.

Content: individual U.S. Tax Court memorandum decisions.

Slip Opinions. MF. WEB. U.S. Court of Appeals for Veterans Claims. JU 15.9: Item 0742-D. <http://www.vetapp.uscourts.gov/>.

Content: individual decisions of the U.S. Court of Appeals for Veterans Claims.

Opinions of the United States Court of Federal Claims. WEB. U.S. Department of Commerce. Office of General Counsel. <http://www.contracts.ogc.doc.gov/fedcl/cofc.html>.

Content: U.S. Court of Federal Claims decisions.

Discussion

The decisions of some specialized federal courts are published by the government and are available through the depository library program. The U.S. Court of International Trade makes decisions regarding customs duties, classification of merchandise for customs, and appraisal of merchandise. This court was called the U.S. Customs Court until 1981. The court's decisions are published in *United States Court of International Trade Reports*. Selected decisions are also published in *West's Federal Supplement*. Decisions of this court may be appealed to the Court of Appeals for the Federal Circuit.

The Court of Appeals for the Federal Circuit handles appeals in the specific subject areas of customs, patents, and claims against the United States. These cases are appealed from the Court of International Trade, the U.S. Court of Federal Claims, the Court of Veterans Appeals, the Patent and Trademark Office, and other government agencies. This court assumed the duties of the former U.S. Court of Customs and Patent Appeals, as well as the appellate responsibilities of the former Court of Claims. The trade decisions of the present court are published in *Trade Cases Adjudged in the U.S. Court of Appeals for the Federal Circuit*. These, as well as other decisions of this court, are also published in *West's Federal Reporter*.

The U.S. Tax Court handles cases involving taxpayer disputes over tax deficiencies assessed by the Internal Revenue Service. Taxpayers need not pay the disputed amount ahead of time when filing suit with the U.S. Tax Court. Tax Court decisions are published in *Reports of the United States Tax Court*. The Tax Court also publishes memorandum decisions, which do not establish new legal principles, but are primarily determinations of facts. Tax Court cases may be appealed to U.S. appellate courts. Tax cases involving claims for refunds of monies already paid are handled by the U.S. district courts and the U.S. Court of Federal Claims. Recent Tax Court decisions and memorandum decisions are available on the Web.

The Court of Veterans Appeals was created in 1988 and began hearing cases in October 1989. The name was changed to Court of Appeals for Veterans Claims in 1999. The court handles appeals from the Board of Veterans'

Appeals dealing with benefits and disability claims. The individual slip opinions are available to depository libraries. A bound reporter is published by West titled *West's Veterans Appeals Reporter*.

The *Opinions of the United States Court of Federal Claims* Web page contains recent decisions of the U.S. Court of Federal Claims.

Specialized federal court decisions not available through the depository program include *Federal Claims Reporter* (formerly *United States Claims Court Reporter*) (West) (Cl.Ct.); *West's Bankruptcy Reporter* (B.R.); *West's Military Justice Reporter* (M.J.); *West's Veterans Appeals Reporter* (Vet.App.); and *West's Federal Rules Decisions* (F.R.D.).

COURT RULES
Checklist

Rules of the Supreme Court of the United States. PRINT. WEB. (irregular) U.S. Supreme Court. JU 6.9: Item 0739. <http://www.law.cornell.edu/rules/supct/overview.html>.
> Content: Supreme Court rules.

Federal Rules of Appellate Procedure With Forms. PRINT. MF. WEB. (annual) U.S. Congress. House. Committee on the Judiciary. Y 4.J 89/1-10: Items 1020-A or -B(MF). GPO. <http://www.house.gov/judiciary/docs105.htm>.
> Content: procedures for appeals to appellate courts.

Federal Rules of Civil Procedure With Forms. PRINT. MF. WEB. (annual) U.S. Congress. House. Committee on the Judiciary. Y 4.J 89/1-11: Items 1020-A or -B(MF). GPO. <http://www.house.gov/judiciary/docs105.htm>; <http://www.law.cornell.edu/rules/frcp/overview.htm>.
> Content: district court procedures for civil cases.

Federal Rules of Criminal Procedure. PRINT. MF. WEB. (annual) U.S. Congress. House. Committee on the Judiciary. Y 4.J 89/1-12: Items 1020-A or -B(MF). GPO. <http://www.house.gov/judiciary/docs105.htm>; <http://www.law.ukans.edu/research/frcriml.htm>.
> Content: rules for criminal proceedings in district courts.

Federal Rules of Evidence. PRINT. MF. WEB. (annual) U.S. Congress. House. Committee on the Judiciary. Y 4.J 89/1-13: Items 1020-A or -B(MF). GPO. <http://www.house.gov/judiciary/docs105.htm>; <http://www.law.cornell.edu/rules/fre/overview.html>.
> Content: rules of evidence for U.S. courts.

United States Code. Title 28. PRINT. CD-ROM. WEB. (annual supplements; revised every 6 years) 1926–. U.S. Congress. House. Y 1.2/5:, Y 1.2/5-2: (CD) (Annotated commercial editions also available) (Sample citation: 28 USC 2255) Items 0991-A or -B(CD). GPO. <http://www.access.gpo.gov/congress/cong013.html>; <http://purl.access.gpo.gov/GPO/LPS2873>; <http://uscode.house.gov/uscode.htm>; <http://www4.law.cornell.edu/uscode/>.
> Content: federal rules of civil procedure; federal rules of evidence; rules of individual U.S. Courts of Appeals; federal rules of appellate procedure; rules of the Supreme

Court; rules of the U.S. Court of Federal Claims; rules of the U.S. Court of International Trade.

Discussion

Many of the rules and procedures governing federal courts are available individually. The rules are also compiled as an appendix to Title 28 of the *United States Code*. Rules cover all aspects of the trial and appeals process. Examples of topics covered include the format of appellant briefs (*Federal Rules of Appellate Procedure*, Rule 28); taking of testimony (*Federal Rules of Civil Procedure*, Rule 43); and search and seizure (*Federal Rules of Criminal Procedure*, Rule 41).

LEGAL DATABASES
Checklist

LEXIS-NEXIS. <http://www.lexis-nexis.com/lncc/>.
> Content: comprehensive online collection of legal databases, including full-text federal court decisions and rules.

LEXIS-NEXIS Academic Universe. <http://www.lexis-nexis.com/cispubs/Catalog/Universe/Academic%20Universe/index.htm>.
> Content: full-text legal databases, including federal court decisions.

Westlaw. <http://www.westlaw.com/>.
> Content: comprehensive online collection of legal databases including full-text federal court decisions and rules.

Discussion

LEXIS-NEXIS and *Westlaw* are major legal databases. Both contain the full texts of the federal court decisions and rules listed in this chapter. On *LEXIS-NEXIS*, federal court decisions are found in the GENFED library. Both services also contain libraries on selected subject areas, such as taxation or communications. *LEXIS-NEXIS Academic Universe* contains a more selective group of legal databases, also including the full texts of federal court decisions.

ADDITIONAL SOURCES
Checklist

United States Court Directory. MF. (annual) U.S. Administrative Office of the United States Courts. JU 10.17: Item 0717-Y-02. GPO.
> Content: names and addresses of judges and other court officials for all federal courts and related agencies.

Understanding the Federal Courts. PRINT. WEB. (1996?) U.S. Administrative Office of the United States Courts. JU 10.2:C 83/3/996. Item 0729. <http://www.uscourts.gov/UFC99.pdf>.
> Content: organization of the federal court system.

Discussion

The *United States Court Directory* is arranged by court, beginning with the Supreme Court. Judges are listed for each court with addresses and telephone numbers. Other personnel are also listed including clerks, staff attorneys, librarians, and chief probation officers. At the end of the book is an alphabetical name index, giving position and court or agency.

Understanding the Federal Courts gives background information on the structure of the U.S. court system. This title covers the Constitutional origin of the judicial system, judicial powers, and the hierarchical court structure. The responsibilities of specific courts are summarized. Charts show the federal judicial circuits and outline the trial process. Also included are a directory of appellate and district courts and a glossary of important judicial terms.

INDEXES
Checklist

Catalog of United States Government Publications (MOCAT). WEB. 1994–. U.S. Government Printing Office. Superintendent of Documents. <http://www.gpo.gov/catalog>; <http://www.access.gpo.gov/su_docs/locators/cgp/index.html>; <http://purl.access.gpo.gov/GPO/LPS844>.

Monthly Catalog of United States Government Publications. CD-ROM. 1996–. U.S. Government Printing Office. Superintendent of Documents. GP 3.8/7: Item 0557-C. GPO.

Monthly Catalog of United States Government Publications (Condensed version). PRINT. (monthly) 1996–. U.S. Government Printing Office. Superintendent of Documents. GP 3.8/8: (Earlier full version, GP 3.8:, 1895-1995). Item 0557-D. GPO.

Discussion

The *Monthly Catalog* provides access to sets of decisions, but not to individual decisions. (For indexes to individual decisions, see the "Federal Court Decision Indexes" section.) The *Monthly Catalog* is a comprehensive index to United States publications and can be used to identify sets of case reporters, publications of court rules, and miscellaneous publications about the federal court system. Relevant subject headings include "Courts," "Court Rules," and names of specific courts, such as "United States. Supreme Court." The complete version of the *Monthly Catalog* is available on the Web and CD-ROM. Commercial online and CD-ROM versions of the *Monthly Catalog* are also available. For more information, see Chapter 3, "The Basics of Searching."

RELATED MATERIAL
Within this Work

Chapter 10 Tax Information

Chapter 26 Administrative Decisions

GPO Subject Bibliographies. PRINT. WEB. GP 3.22/2:

<http://bookstore.gpo.gov/sb/about.html>

No. 25 "United States Reports"

No. 27 "Customs, Immunization and Passport Publications"

No. 36 "Criminal Justice"

No. 67 "Tax Court Reports"

CHAPTER 47
Budget Analysis

The budget process involves two of the three branches of the government: the executive and legislative branches. The President's budget is submitted by the Executive Office of the President to the Congress, which must decide whether to actually appropriate and authorize the spending of the money. A set timetable is provided for this budgetary process. As the different stages are carried out, a variety of documents are produced, with both the Office of Management and Budget in the Executive Office of the President and the Congressional Budget Office providing budget information. This chapter describes the basic materials published during the budgetary process and illustrates the basic steps of the budget process.

SEARCH STRATEGY

While the search strategy is a special technique, other strategies may be used as subsearches. The general search strategy can be summarized as follows:

1. Check the sources, such as the *Statistical Abstract*, in the "Basic Sources" section to obtain general budget information;
2. Consult the *Budget of the United States Government*, available in print, Web, and CD-ROM versions;
3. If searching for congressional publications associated with the budget process, search *CIS/Index*; and
4. Search *ASI* to identify additional statistical sources.

BASIC SOURCES
Checklist

Statistical Abstract of the United States. PRINT. WEB. (annual) 1878–. U.S. Department of Commerce. Economics and Statistics Administration. Bureau of the Census. C 3.134: Item 0150. ASI 2324-1. GPO. <www.census.gov/statab/www/>; <http://purl.access.gpo.gov/GPO/LPS2878>.
　　Content: summary of budget figures.

Statistical Abstract of the United States. CD-ROM. (annual) 1993–. U.S. Department of Commerce. Bureau of the Census. C 3.134/7: Item 0150-B. ASI 2324-14.
　　Content: CD-ROM version of the *Statistical Abstract*.

Historical Statistics of the United States: Colonial Times to 1970. Parts 1-2. PRINT. (1975) U.S. Department of Commerce. Bureau of the Census. C 3.134/2:H 62/789-970/pt.1-2. Item 0151. ASI (76) 2328-2. GPO.
　　Content: historical budget statistics.

Historical Statistics of the United States on CD-ROM: Colonial Times to 1970. CD-ROM. (1997) New York, NY: Cambridge University Press.
　　Content: CD-ROM version of *Historical Statistics of the United States*.

CQ Weekly. PRINT. WEB. (weekly) 1946–. (Title varies. Earlier, *Congressional Quarterly Weekly Report*) Washington, D.C.: Congressional Quarterly, Inc. CQ Library: <http://libraryip.cq.com/>.
　　Content: articles and statistics on the budget and the budget process.

Congressional Quarterly Almanac. PRINT. (annual) 1945–. Washington, D.C.: Congressional Quarterly, Inc.
　　Content: overview of the budget and congressional activity surrounding the budget process.

Discussion

The *Statistical Abstract of the United States* includes basic budget statistics. In particular, the chapter on "Federal Government Finance and Employment" is useful for gaining a quick overview of the federal budget. The full text of recent editions of the *Statistical Abstract* is available on the Census Bureau Web site as PDF files. The *Historical Statistics of the United States: Colonial Times to 1970* contains several series of budget statistics, which are helpful for making comparisons over a long period of time. The *Statistical Abstract* is also available on CD-ROM. A CD-

ROM version of *Historical Statistics* is available from Cambridge University Press.

Congressional Quarterly, Inc. publishes a number of sources related to Congress and congressional activities. The two titles listed here are the most significant titles that provide information on the budget and the congressional activity surrounding the budget process. *CQ Weekly*, available in both a print and Web version, comprehensively covers and analyzes the workings of Congress. It is an excellent source for obtaining information on current budget activities. The *Congressional Quarterly Almanac* is an annual volume that summarizes the year's congressional activities. It provides a good analysis of past budgets and budget activity.

OFFICE OF MANAGEMENT AND BUDGET (OMB) SOURCES
Checklist

OMB Home Page. WEB. U.S. Executive Office of the President. Office of Management and Budget. <http://www.whitehouse.gov/OMB/>.

> Content: Web site for the Office of Management and Budget; includes links to Budget publications; general information about OMB's activities.

Budget of the United States Government. PRINT. WEB. (annual) 1922–. U.S. Executive Office of the President. Office of Management and Budget. PREX 2.8: (Also issued as a House Document, Y 1.1/7:) Item 0853. ASI 104-2. GPO. <http://w3.access.gpo.gov/usbudget/>; <http://purl.access.gpo.gov/GPO/LPS2343>.

> Content: budget message of the President; budget themes and priorities; administration's proposed budget; detailed budget statistics; budget concepts; guide to the budget.

The Budget of the United States Government Fiscal Year [year]. CD-ROM. (annual) 1996–. U.S. Executive Office of the President. Office of Management and Budget. PREX 2.8/1: Item 0853-C. ASI 104-38. GPO.

> Content: CD-ROM version of *The Budget of the United States*.

Budget Information for States, Fiscal Year [year]. PRINT. WEB. (annual). PREX 2.8: [date]/INFO. Item 0853. ASI 104-30. GPO. <http://w3.access.gpo.gov/>; <http://purl.access.gpo.gov/GPO/LPS862>.

> Content: statistical tables depicting federal obligations to state and local governments.

Federal Credit Supplement. PRINT. WEB. (annual) 1993–. U.S. Executive Office of the President. Office of Management and Budget. PREX 2.8:/[date]/CREDIT. Item 0853. ASI 104-40. <http://w3.access.gpo.gov/usbudget/>.

> Content: statistical tables on federal direct loan and loan guarantee programs.

Object Class Analysis. PRINT. WEB. (annual) U.S. Executive Office of the President. Office of Management and Budget. Budget Review and Concepts Division. Budget Concepts Branch. PREX 2.8:/[date]/OBJECT. Item 0853. ASI 104-9. NTIS. <http://w3.access.gpo.gov/usbudget/>.

> Content: agency obligations by object class; object class obligations by agency; other obligations.

Object Class Analysis Detail. WEB. (annual) U.S. Executive Office of the President. Office of Management and Budget. Budget Review and Concepts Division. Budget Concepts Branch. <http://w3.access.gpo.gov/usbudget/>.

> Content: detailed object class obligations by agency.

Balances of Budget Authority. PRINT. WEB. (annual) U.S. Executive Office of the President. Office of Management and Budget. Budget Review and Concepts Division. Budget Concepts Branch. PREX 2.8:/[date]/BAL. Item 0853. ASI 104-8. NTIS. <http://w3.access.gpo.gov/usbudget/>.

> Content: report on agency unexpended balances of budget authorities.

Mid-Session Review of the Budget. PRINT. WEB. (annual) U.S. Executive Office of the President. Office of Management and Budget. PREX 2.31: Item 0853. ASI 104-7. GPO. <http://w3.access.gpo.gov/usbudget/>.

> Content: midsession review of the budget; statistical tables.

OMB Sequestration Update Report to the President and the Congress for FY [year]. WEB. (annual) U.S. Executive Office of the President. Office of Management and Budget. ASI 104-27. <http://w3.access.gpo.gov/usbudget/>.

> Content: OMB estimates of whether sequestration is necessary.

OMB Final Sequestration Report to the President and the Congress for FY [year]. PRINT. WEB. (annual) U.S. Executive Office of the President. Office of Management and Budget. Y 1.1/7: (Issued as a House Document, fiscal year 2000 is Y 1.1/7: 106-82) Items 0996-A or -B(MF). ASI 104-27. <http://w3.access.gpo.gov/usbudget/>.

> Content: final report on whether sequestration is required for the fiscal year.

Discussion

The Office of Management and Budget (OMB) is the primary agency involved in formulating, preparing, and overseeing the President's budget. OMB plays a large role in evaluating agency program effectiveness and setting spending priorities. The OMB Web site provides information about the OMB's organization, policies, and major responsibilities. One of the OMB's biggest responsibilities is the annual preparation and publication of the President's budget, the *Budget of the United States Government*.

The *Budget of the United States Government* presents the President's budget for the upcoming fiscal year. The report itself has been issued in various formats over the years, and the number and individual titles of the sections of the report has varied. The most recent budget for fiscal year 2001 included the following document titles: *Budget of the United States Government*; an *Appendix* volume titled: *Detailed Budget Estimates*; *Analytical Perspectives*; *Historical Tables*; *Budget System and Concepts*; and *A Citizen's Guide to the Budget Process*. The report is available in print, Web, and CD-ROM versions.

The *Budget of the United States Government* is the President's proposed budget for the next fiscal year and a strong reflection of the President's goals and priorities. At the beginning of the *Budget* is the President's budget message. This is a brief introduction to the year's budget. Introductory chapters review the budget situation in greater depth and present the administration's agenda and policies. An economic projections or assumptions section describes the projected economic outlook on which the budget is based. Additional chapters provide a detailed analysis of the administration's budget approach and priorities in specific program areas. Chapters may discuss such areas as education, children or families, research and development, health care, law enforcement, the environment, and national security.

The largest section of the *Budget* is the detailed agency-by-agency budget section included in the *Appendix* volume. This section contains a detailed listing of agency programs and expenditures with the President's proposed budget figures, as well as estimated and actual budget figures from the previous two years. The *Appendix* is a truly massive document, and is the best source of detailed information on specific agencies and their programs. Figure 47.1 shows an example of the level of detail included in the *Appendix*.

Analytical Perspectives highlights and analyzes specific budget areas, such as "Research and Development Funding," "Aid to State and Local Governments," and "Strengthening Federal Statistics," three recent areas included in *Analytical Perspectives*. This volume also provides detailed accounting and economic analyses on such topics as federal receipts and collections, federal borrowing and debt, federal spending, and current services estimates (budget information presented based on current laws enacted). Other detailed technical analyses of budget accounting are also included.

The *Historical Tables* is a compilation of data that provides budget information over long periods of time. Most data series begin in fiscal year 1940 or earlier, with projections for the upcoming five years. Examples of typical sections of the report include: "Federal Outlays by Function," "Federal Outlays by Agency," "Federal Debt," "Federal Government Payments to Individuals," "Social Security and Medicare," and "Federal Health Spending." Most data series are comparable over time.

The *Budget System and Concepts* section of the report explains some of the underlying concepts used to formulate the President's budget. It provides a fairly detailed look at the formulation of the President's budget, congressional action on the budget, and execution of the budget. A glossary of budget terms is also included in this volume.

A Citizen's Guide to the Budget Process aims to provide the average citizen with a basic understanding of the budget itself and the budget process. A series of charts, graphs, and tables are interspersed with text in an attempt to clearly illustrate budget concepts. A typical pie chart is titled: "The Federal Government Dollar—Where it Comes From," and illustrates the revenues received from major sources (mostly taxes).

A series of additional budget-related reports are presently being issued by the OMB and are also cited in this section. *Budget Information for States* details federal obligations to state and local governments for major Federal formula grant programs, such as the National School Lunch Program and Adult Employment and Training Grants. Tables include summary tables, data by program, and data by state. *Federal Credit Supplement* gives an analysis of Federal direct loan and loan guarantee programs covered by the Federal Credit Reform Act of 1990, as amended by the Balanced Budget Act of 1997. Typical tables from this report include, "Loan Guarantees: Subsidy Rates, Commitments, and Average Loan Size," "Direct Loans: Assumptions Underlying the FY 2001 Subsidy Estimates," and "Direct Loan Program Disbursement Rates in the FY 2001 Budget."

The *Object Class Analysis* and *Object Class Analysis Detail* reports provide information on obligations by object class. Object classes provide a system of uniformly describing financial transactions of the Federal government. Object class data allow the user to determine the types of services or products that the federal government has obligations to purchase. A typical object class is Object Class 25.5, Research and Development Contracts. *Object Class Analysis* provides summary information on agency obligations by object class and object class obligations by agency. The *Object Class Analysis Detail* report gives very detailed information on agency obligations by object class.

The *Balances of Budget Authority* reports on agency unexpended balances of budget authorities. These balances are those budget authorities that have been approved in a previous fiscal year, but remain unexpended. Various tables detailing the unexpended balances by department are included in the report.

The *Mid-Session Review of the Budget* is required by the *U.S. Code*, and is issued by the President to Congress. It contains revised estimates of budget receipts, outlays, and budget authority. Text, statistical tables, and charts are used to update and revise the President's initial budget. This report is a good summary of the current budgetary environment at the time it is written.

Sequestration reports determine whether sequestration (additional cutting of spending) are required in the budget. The two OMB sequestration reports cited here are required as a result of the Budget Enforcement Act of 1990 (BEA) as amended. They report on both discretionary programs (funded through the appropriations process) and pay-as-you go programs (direct spending programs). The *Update* report reviews the current status of spending and provides statistical tables and narrative analysis of the two areas of expenditures. *The OMB Final Sequestration*

942   Trust Funds—Continued

THE BUDGET FOR FISCAL YEAR 2001

HAZARDOUS SUBSTANCE SUPERFUND—Continued

(INCLUDING TRANSFER OF FUNDS)—Continued

Program and Financing (in millions of dollars)—Continued

Identification code 20–8145–0–7–304	1999 actual	2000 est.	2001 est.
72.95 From Federal sources: Receivables and unpaid, unfilled orders	80	79	79
72.99 Total unpaid obligations, start of year	2,642	2,488	2,904
73.10 Total new obligations	1,765	2,095	1,650
73.20 Total outlays (gross)	−1,715	−1,679	−1,627
73.40 Adjustments in expired accounts (net)	−1		
73.45 Adjustments in unexpired accounts	−201		
Unpaid obligations, end of year:			
74.40 Obligated balance, end of year	2,409	2,825	2,848
74.95 From Federal sources: Receivables and unpaid, unfilled orders	79	79	79
74.99 Total unpaid obligations, end of year	2,488	2,904	2,927
Outlays (gross), detail:			
86.90 Outlays from new discretionary authority	262	564	577
86.93 Outlays from discretionary balances	1,455	1,115	1,050
87.00 Total outlays (gross)	1,715	1,679	1,627
Offsets:			
Against gross budget authority and outlays:			
88.00 Offsetting collections (cash) from: Federal sources	−140	−200	−200
Against gross budget authority only:			
88.95 From Federal sources: Change in receivables and unpaid, unfilled orders	1		
Net budget authority and outlays:			
89.00 Budget authority	1,492	1,400	1,450
90.00 Outlays	1,577	1,479	1,427
Memorandum (non-add) entries:			
92.01 Total investments, start of year: U.S. securities: Par value	5,296	4,593	4,625
92.02 Total investments, end of year: U.S. securities: Par value	4,593	4,625	6,190

Summary of Budget Authority and Outlays

(in millions of dollars)

	1999 actual	2000 est.	2001 est.
Enacted/requested:			
Budget Authority	1,492	1,400	1,450
Outlays	1,577	1,479	1,427
Legislative proposal, subject to PAYGO:			
Budget Authority			150
Outlays			39
Total:			
Budget Authority	1,492	1,400	1,600
Outlays	1,577	1,479	1,466

This appropriation provides funds for the implementation of the Comprehensive Environmental Response, Compensation and Liability Act of 1980, as amended (CERCLA) including activities under the Working Capital Fund. Funding for activities in this account for the Office of Research and Development are included in the 21st Century Research Fund. This appropriation supports core Agency programs and a number of the Agency's ten goals. Specifically in 2001, emphasis will be placed on the following:

Better Waste Management, Restoration of Contaminated Waste Sites, and Emergency Response.—EPA will complete cleanups at 75 sites and conduct 275 removal actions. Through 1999, cleanups had been completed at 670 sites, and 5,929 removal actions had been taken at 4,258 sites. EPA will also work to maximize responsible parties' participation in site cleanups while promoting fairness in the enforcement process, and pursue greater recovery of EPA's cleanup costs. In addition, EPA will fund supplemental brownfields site assessments in 50 communities, resulting in a cumulative total of 2,100 sites assessed, the generation of 5,400 jobs, and the leveraging of $1.8 billion in cleanup and redevelop-

ment funds, and will fund brownfields cleanup revolving loan funds in 70 communities. EPA will allocate funds from its appropriation to other Federal agencies to carry out the Act. Legislation will be proposed to extend the taxes supporting the trust fund.

Sound Science, Improved Understanding of Environmental Risk, and Greater Innovation to Address Environmental Problems.—EPA will develop methods to assess and control the potential health and environmental risks posed by contaminated waste sites. EPA will also conduct risk management research which focuses on the remediation of surface and subsurface contaminated soils, sludge, sediments, buildings, debris, and groundwater.

A Credible Deterrent to Pollution and Greater Compliance With the Law.—EPA will investigate and refer for prosecution criminal violations of the Comprehensive Environmental Response, Compensation, and Liability Act of 1980 (CERCLA), and increase Regional support to criminal investigations in the field.

Effective Management.—EPA will work to ensure fiscal responsibility in support of site cleanups. EPA will continue to implement performance-based service contracts instead of the traditional cost-plus, level-of-effort contracts, and will improve the quality and availability of information on the status and use of resources.

Selected Annual Site Cleanup Targets

	1999 actual	2000 est.	2001 est.
NPL Site Cleanups Completed	670	755	830
Removal Action Starts	5,929	6,204	6,479

Status of Funds (in millions of dollars)

Identification code 20–8145–0–7–304	1999 actual	2000 est.	2001 est.
Unexpended balance, start of year:			
0100 Uninvested balance	68	38	38
U.S. Securities:			
0101 Par value	5,296	4,593	4,625
0102 Unrealized discounts	−221	−188	−244
0199 Total balance, start of year	5,144	4,443	4,419
Cash income during the year:			
Governmental receipts:			
0200 Excise taxes, Hazardous substance superfund, EPA	11		
0201 Corporate Income Tax, Hazardous substance superfund, EPA	10		
0202 Fines and penalties, Hazardous substance superfund, EPA	4	4	5
0203 Excise taxes, legislative proposal		204	942
0204 Corporate Income Tax, legislative proposal			1,115
Proprietary receipts:			
0220 Recoveries, Hazardous substance superfund, EPA	320	275	225
Intragovernmental transactions:			
0240 Interest and profits on investments, Hazardous substance superfund, EPA	207	198	179
0241 Interfund transactions, Hazardous substance superfund, EPA	325	700	250
0242 Interest and profits on investments, legislative proposal		74	203
Offsetting collections:			
0280 Offsetting collections	140	200	200
0297 Income under present law	1,017	1,377	859
0298 Income under proposed legislation		278	2,260
0299 Total cash income	1,017	1,655	3,119
Cash outgo during year:			
0500 Cash outgo during the year, legislative proposal (−)	−1,715	−1,679	−1,627
0502 Legislative proposal, subject to PAYGO			−39
0597 Outgo under present law (−)	−1,715	−1,679	−1,627
0598 Outgo under proposed legislation (−)			−39
0599 Total cash outgo (−)	−1,715	−1,679	−1,666
0650 Other adjustments	−1		
Unexpended balance, end of year:			
0700 Uninvested balance	38	38	38
U.S. Securities:			
0701 Par value	4,593	4,625	6,190
0702 Unrealized discounts	−188	−244	−356
0799 Total balance, end of year	4,443	4,419	5,872

Budget of the United States Government, Appendix, FY 2001, p. 942.

Figure 47.1: Sample Page from the *Appendix*.

Report to the President and the Congress for FY [year] also covers discretionary and pay-as-you go programs. It is issued at the end of a congressional session, and determines whether any final sequester is required. A third sequestration report is included as part of the *Budget of the United States Government*.

CONGRESSIONAL BUDGET OFFICE (CBO) PUBLICATIONS
Checklist

Congressional Budget Office Home Page. WEB. U.S. Congress. Congressional Budget Office. <http://www.cbo.gov/>.
> Content: links to CBO publications; news releases; statistical tables and charts.

The Economic and Budget Outlook for Fiscal Years [years]. PRINT. WEB. (annual) 1986–1990–. U.S. Congress. Congressional Budget Office. Y 10.13: (Update, Y 10.17:) Item 1005-F. ASI 26306-7.[no]. (Earlier, 26304-3.[no.]) GPO. <http://www.cbo.gov/byclasscat.cfm?class=0&cat=0>; <http://purl.access.gpo.gov/GPO/LPS755>.
> Content: analysis of the state of the economy; budget projections; background information for the major areas of the budget; statistical tables and charts.

Maintaining Budgetary Discipline: Spending and Revenue Options. PRINT. WEB. (1999) U.S. Congress. Congressional Budget Office. Y 10.2: D 63/2: Item 1005-C. ASI (99) 26306-7.2. <http://www.cbo.gov/howdoc.cfm?index=1222&sequence=0&from=1>.
> Content: describes and analyzes budgetary options for reducing expenditures and increasing revenues.

The Economic and Budget Outlook: An Update. PRINT. WEB. (annual) U.S. Congress. Congressional Budget Office. Y 10.17: Item 1005-F ASI 26306-7.[no]. (Earlier, 26304-3.[no.]) GPO.
> Content: mid-year analysis of the budget. <http://www.cbo.gov/byclasscat.cfm?class=0&cat=0>.

Sequestration Preview Report for Fiscal Year [year]. WEB. (annual) U.S. Congressional Budget Office. ASI 26304-6. <http://www.cbo.gov/byclasscat.cfm?class=0&cat=4>.
> Content: CBO preview sequestration report.

Sequestration Update Report for Fiscal Year [year]. WEB. (annual) U.S. Congressional Budget Office. ASI 26304-6. <http://www.cbo.gov/byclasscat.cfm?class=0&cat=4>.
> Content: CBO midyear update sequestration report.

Final Sequestration Report for Fiscal Year [year]. PRINT. WEB. Y 1.1/7: (FY 2000 is Y 1.1/7:106-168) (title varies) Items 0996-A or -B(MF). ASI 26304-6. <http://www.cbo.gov/byclasscat.cfm?class=0&cat=4>; <http://www.access. gpo.gov/congress/cong006.html>.
> Content: CBO final sequestration report.

An Analysis of the President's Budgetary Proposals for Fiscal Year [year]. PRINT. WEB. (annual) 1977–. U.S. Congress. Congressional Budget Office. Y 10.19: (Earlier, Y 10.2:B 85/) (Title varies). Item 1005-K. ASI 26304-2. <http://www.cbo.gov/byclasscat.cfm?class=0&cat=1>.
> Content: analysis of the President's budget assumptions; budgetary projections.

CBO Documents. WEB. U.S. Congress. Congressional Budget Office. <http://www.cbo.gov/docs.shtml>.
> Content: full text of studies and reports; cost estimates; testimony; other documents.

General Publications. PRINT. (irregular) U.S. Congress. Congressional Budget Office. Y 10.2: Item 1005-C. ASI 26306-6.
> Content: studies and papers on specific areas affected by budgetary and economic policies.

Monthly Budget Review. WEB. (monthly) U.S. Congress. Congressional Budget Office. Y 10.21/2: Item 1005-C-01. <http://www.cbo.gov/byclasscat.cfm?class=0&cat=35>.
> Content: CBO analysis of current status of budget.

Discussion

The Congressional Budget Office's (CBO) mission "is to provide the Congress with the objective, timely, nonpartisan analyses needed for economic and budget decisions and with the information and estimates required for the Congressional budget process." The CBO is mandated by law to provide several reports to Congress during the course of the budget process, as well as producing reports and compiling information about a broad range of budgetary issues. The *Congressional Budget Office Home Page* is a well-organized link to information about the CBO and its many publications. Many of the CBO's reports and documents are available in full-text at the site in a variety of formats including HTML, PDF, Postscript, and WordPerfect file formats.

The *Report to the Senate and House Committees on the Budget* series consists of reports required by Public Law 93-344, and includes detailed, comprehensive reports that describe and analyze the economy and the budget. The format of the report has varied over the years, and the report has been issued under various parts and titles. The most recent report has been issued in two parts, which are cited here, the first titled *The Economic and Budget Outlook FY [years]*, and *Maintaining Budgetary Discipline: Spending and Revenue Options*. *Economic and Budget Outlook* reviews the current economic situation and discusses economic trends and developments. It includes 5-year baseline projections of the budget. *Maintaining Budgetary Discipline: Spending and Revenue Options* includes 50 options for reducing expenditures or increasing revenues, presented in an impartial manner by the CBO. *The Economic and Budget Outlook: An Update* is issued as a midyear update. It looks at the economic and budget outlook based on the developments in the first half of the fiscal year.

Publication of the Congressional Budget Office sequestration reports is required by law. These reports determine if additional cutting of spending is needed. The *Final Sequestration Report* is available on the Web, and is also issued as a House Document. The *Preview Sequestration Report* and the *Sequestration Update Report* are also available from the CBO Web Site.

An Analysis of the President's Budgetary Proposals for Fiscal Year [year] analyzes and compares the President's budget with the proposals and estimates of the Congressional Budget Office. Detailed rationale and policy are given by the CBO in analyzing and explaining the differences between the President's and the CBO's budget estimates.

The Congressional Budget Office produces a wide range of documents and reports dealing with budgetary analysis and the analysis of the costs of governmental programs and policies. Many of these reports are available from the *CBO Documents* Web page. In the "Studies and Reports" section are mandated reports, studies, papers, and memorandums. Mandated reports are those required by law, such as the sequestration reports. Studies are analyses of programmatic or policy issues that relate to the budget. Papers respond to requests from Congress or relate to work being done by Congress. Memorandums also are published as a result of requests from Congress, but are more narrowly focused or more technical in nature than the papers.

The *CBO Documents Web* page also includes a section on cost estimates. When a bill is ordered reported by a full committee of Congress, the CBO prepares a cost estimate of the cost of the provisions of the bill if it is enacted into law. A third section titled "Testimony" provides the text of testimony that CBO employees have provided at congressional hearings. The last section of the page, "Other Documents," includes any other documents produced at the request of Congress, primarily more informal documents, such as letters. The *General Publications* series distributes many of the CBO documents to depository libraries in a print format.

The *Monthly Budget Review* provides a monthly analysis of Treasury receipts and outlays and determines the current surplus or deficit. Statistics on current outlays and budget projections are also included.

Discussion

Tracing the Budget Process

The previous sections list the major publications produced by the Office of Management and Budget and the Congressional Budget Office. A third group of documents includes the publications issued by Congress during its work on the budget. To locate the bills, reports, documents, hearings, committee prints, and other materials produced during the budgetary process, it is often necessary to carry out a legislative search as explained in Chapter 45, "Legislative History."

An interrelated area of the budget process is that of the appropriation bills and appropriation hearings. Whereas the budget sets out broad areas of spending, appropriations define the allocation of money for very specific programs and items. The appropriation process is carried out simultaneously as the budget process is going

on. These bills and hearings can be located by using the sources described in Chapter 45, "Legislative History."

The simplified steps of the basic budget process are:

Five days before the President submits his budget to Congress. CBO sequestration preview report is submitted.

Between the 1st Monday in January and the 1st Monday in February. The President submits his budget. See the "Office Of Management And Budget (OMB) Sources" section of this chapter for a description of the President's budget.

Same day the President submits his budget. OMB sequestration preview report is submitted. This report is included in the *Budget of the United States Government.*

February 15th. Congressional Budget Office submits report to Budget Committees. Within six weeks after the President submits his budget. Committees submit views and estimates to budget committees. All standing committees of the House and Senate submit their views and recommendations to their respective budget committees. These reports contain estimates and recommendations for the next fiscal year of outlays needed by programs under the jurisdiction of the Committees preparing the reports.

April 1. Senate Budget Committee reports concurrent resolution on the budget.

April 15th. Congress completes action on the concurrent resolution on the Budget. The concurrent budget resolution is drafted by the House and Senate budget committees. As a concurrent resolution, it is effective as soon as it has been agreed upon and passed by both the House and Senate. Each budget committee also submits a report to its respective chamber. These reports provide an analysis and overview of the budget by function. A conference report is submitted by the House or Senate committee to accompany this resolution. In developing the first concurrent resolution, the House and Senate committees on the budget hold hearings to receive testimony from congresspersons as well as the general public.

May 15th. Annual appropriation bills may be considered in the House.

June 10th. House Appropriation Committee reports last annual appropriation bill.

June 15th. Congress completes action on reconciliation legislation.

End of previous session until June 30th. House completes action on annual appropriation bills.

July 15th. The President submits to Congress the *Mid-Session Budget Review.*

August 10th. Notification regarding military personnel. The President may exempt the military from sequestration or lower the percentage of reduction, but in order to use this authority, he must notify Congress by August 10th.

August 15th. CBO sequestration update report is issued.

August 20th. OMB sequestration update report is issued.

October 1. Fiscal year begins.

10 days after end of session. CBO final sequestration report is issued.

15 days after end of session. OMB final sequestration report is issued. Presidential order is issued. If OMB estimates that sequestration is required, the President issues a Presidential order to federal agencies implementing the sequestration.

45 days after end of session. GAO compliance report is issued. This report is issued by the GAO and reports on the extent that the Presidential order and the OMB and CBO reports comply with the requirements of the Gramm-Hollings Act.

MISCELLANEOUS SOURCES
Checklist

The Congressional Budget Process—An Explanation. WEB. U.S. Senate. Committee on the Budget. <http://www.senate.gov/~budget/republican/reference/cliff_notes/clifftoc.htm>.
> Content: detailed guide to congressional budget process; including budget process timetable and history of budget laws.

BudgetNet. WEB. U.S. Chief Financial Officers Council. <http://www.financenet.gov/financenet/fed/budget/>.
> Content: gateway to federal budget information; links to budget publications and agency Web sites.

Discussion

The *Congressional Budget Process—An Explanation*, is an excellent guide to the budgetary process. It is a good source for examining the process from the congressional viewpoint. Particularly valuable is the "History of Budget Law" section which briefly summarizes major laws with an effect on the budget process. The "Budget Timetable," "Basic Budget Concepts," and "Budget Glossary" are also helpful aids in understanding the budget process.

BudgetNet provides links to a wide range of information, including many of the sources and Web sites cited and described in this chapter. *BudgetNet* is designed for professionals working with budget information, both inside government and outside of government. Sample relevant sections of *BudgetNet* are "Budget Issues," "Budget Trends," Budget Process," "Budget Agencies," "Timeline," and "OMB Functions."

INDEXES
Checklist

American Statistics Index (ASI). PRINT. (monthly) 1973–. Bethesda, MD: Congressional Information Service.

Statistical Universe. WEB. Bethesda, MD: Congressional Information Service.

Catalog of United States Government Publications (MOCAT). WEB. 1994–. U.S. Government Printing Office. Superintendent of Documents. <http://www.gpo.gov/catalog>; <http://www.access.gpo.gov/su_docs/locators/cgp/index.html>; <http://purl.access.gpo.gov/GPO/LPS844>.

Monthly Catalog of United States Government Publications. CD-ROM. 1996–. U.S. Government Printing Office. Superintendent of Documents. GP 3.8/7: Item 0557-C. GPO.

Monthly Catalog of United States Government Publications (Condensed version). PRINT. (monthly) 1996–. U.S. Government Printing Office. Superintendent of Documents. GP 3.8/8: (Earlier full version, GP 3.8:, 1895-1995). Item 0557-D. GPO.

CIS/Index. PRINT. (monthly) 1970–. Bethesda, MD: Congressional Information Service.

Congressional Universe. WEB. Bethesda, MD: Congressional Information Service.

Discussion

The *Monthly Catalog* is a comprehensive index to government publications. The complete version of the *Monthly Catalog* is available on the Web and CD-ROM. Commercial online and CD-ROM versions of the *Monthly Catalog* are also available. To find other publications relating to the budgetary process, search subject headings and keywords beginning with the term "Budget."

American Statistics Index (ASI) is a comprehensive statistical index that can be used to locate additional statistical publications relating to the budgetary process. Search under the subject headings: "Budget of the U.S.," "Defense budgets and appropriations," "Fiscal policy," "Government revenues," and "Government spending," *Statistical Universe* includes a Web version of *ASI*.

CIS/Index is a comprehensive index to congressional publications. To locate additional materials associated with the budgetary process, search the following subject headings: "Budget of the U.S." "Congressional committee budget estimates reports," "Defense budgets and appropriations," "Fiscal policy," "Government spending," "Sequestration of appropriated funds," and names of specific departments, agencies, and offices. *Congressional Universe* includes a Web version of *CIS*.

For more information on these indexes, see Chapter 3, "The Basics of Searching."

RELATED MATERIAL
Within this Work

Chapter 45 Legislative History

GPO Subject Bibliographies. PRINT. WEB. GP 3.22/2:

<http://bookstore.gpo.gov/sb/about.html>

No. 97   "The Economy"

No. 204   "Economic Policy"

CHAPTER 48
Treaties

U.S. treaties and international agreements are published or made available in several forms, both before they are approved and after ratification. Several unique finding aids, indexes, databases, and approaches provide access to these treaties. This chapter provides information on how to locate the text of U.S. treaties and international agreements and on using the specialized sources and searches needed to do so. It concentrates on providing information about U.S. treaties, and does not attempt to include all the sources available that provide access to non-U.S. treaties. Although this chapter concentrates on identifying sources distributed through the depository program or available for public access on the Web, many of the sources listed are commercially produced and require either purchase or a fee to use them. The process of searching for a treaty will to some extent be shaped by what sources are available to the searcher.

Treaties must be approved by the Senate through a treaty ratification process similar to passing a law. This chapter discusses the steps of the treaty ratification process and the documents generated as a result. Sources for locating information on current treaty actions are also given. Chapter 45, *Legislative History*, should be consulted for more detail on this aspect of the search process.

SEARCH STRATEGY

Treaty searches are one example of a special technique search strategy. Specialized indexes, databases, and finding aids must be used to locate specific treaties or treaties on a particular subject.

1. If a treaty is believed to still be in force, try identifying it through one of the versions of *Treaties in Force*;
2. Use sources available to you and listed under "Databases, Indexes, and Finding Aids" to locate the treaty, matching the sources to the time period of your search. The *Quick U.S. Treaties Index* is available on the Web

free of charge, if you do not have access to any of the other sources;
3. Use the sources available to you and listed in the "Texts of Treaties" section of this chapter to locate the actual texts of the treaties, again matching the time period covered by the sources to the date of the treaty;
4. If you need information on current treaty activity, use the sources listed in "Current Treaty Actions and Congressional Treaty Actions";
5. If you need to find congressional sources (especially Senate sources) produced as a part of the treaty ratification process, see the sources listed in "Current Treaty Actions and Congressional Treaty Actions." *THOMAS* and the *CIS/Index* in print or electronic formats are particularly good sources for tracking the status of treaty action within Congress; and
6. If you need information on Native American treaties or tax treaties, see the two specialized sections pertaining to these sources.

TEXTS OF TREATIES
Checklist

United States Statutes at Large. (STAT) PRINT. WEB. (annual) 1789–. U.S. National Archives and Records Administration. Office of the Federal Register. AE 2.111: (Earlier, GS 4.111:; S 7.9:) (Title varies) Item 0576. GPO. Selected volumes: <http://lcweb2.loc.gov/ammem/amlaw/lwsl.html>.
   Content: texts of treaties before 1950.

Treaties and Other International Agreements of the United States of America, 1776–1949. (Bevans) PRINT. (1968–76) U.S. Department of State. Compiled by Charles I. Bevans. S 9.12/2: Item 0899-A.
   Content: compilation of texts of treaties and other international agreements of the United States from 1776-1950.

Unperfected Treaties of the United States, 1776–1976. PRINT. (1976) Christian L. Wiktor. Dobbs Ferry, NY: Oceana Publications, Inc.
   Content: text of treaties not ratified from 1776–1976.

Treaty Series. (TS). PRINT. (18??–1948) U.S. Department of State. S 9.5/2.

> Content: pamphlets of individual treaties and agreements from the 1800s to 1929; treaties only from 1929–48.

Executive Agreement Series. (EAS.) PRINT. (1929–1945) U.S. Department of State. S 9.8:

> Content: text of international agreements from 1929–1945.

Treaties and Other International Acts Series. (TIAS.) PRINT. (irregular) 1946–. U.S. Department of State. S 9.10: Item 0899. GPO.

> Content: text of individual treaties and international agreements.

United States Treaties and Other International Agreements. (UST). PRINT. 1950–. U.S. Department of State. S 9.12: Item 0899-A. GPO.

> Coverage: texts of treaties and other international agreements of the U.S. from 1950 to the present.

Consolidated Treaties & International Agreements. Current Document Service. PRINT. 1990–. Dobbs Ferry, NY: Oceana Publications.

> Content: text of U.S. treaties and international agreements to which the United States is a signatory.

Hein's United States Treaties and Other International Agreements. MF. 1991–. Buffalo, NY: W.S. Hein and Co., Inc.

> Content: ongoing service providing the text of recent U.S. treaties and agreements.

TIARA™ U.S. Treaties Researcher. (Treaties & International Agreements Researcher's Archive). WEB. Oceana Publications. <http://www.oceanalaw.com>.

> Content: text of U.S. treaties and international agreements from 1783–.

United Nations Treaty Series. (UNTS). PRINT. WEB. 1946/47– United Nations. Office of Legal Affairs. Treaty Section. <http://untreaty.un.org/English/treaty.asp>.

> Content: text of all treaties registered with the United Nations, including treaties to which the U.S. is a party.

Texts of Recently Deposited Multilateral Treaties. WEB. United Nations. Office of Legal Affairs. Treaty Section. <http://untreaty.un.org/English/treaty.asp>.

> Content: text of treaties registered with the United Nations but not yet included in the *United Nations Treaty Series*.

LEXIS-NEXIS. <http://www.lexis-nexis.com/lncc/>.

> Content: text of treaties; other databases dealing with treaties.

Westlaw. <http://www.westlaw.com>.

> Content: text of treaties; other databases dealing with treaties.

Discussion

Treaties ratified before 1950 were officially published in the *United States Statutes at Large*. Volume 8 of the *Statutes at Large* contains a compilation of treaties published from 1776–1845. Volume 64, part 3 (1950–51) includes a list of all treaties and agreements in volumes 1– 64. The *Treaties and other International Agreements of the United States of America, 1776–1949*, often known as *Bevans*, compiles and reprints the texts of these pre-1950 treaties, which saves searching the individual *U.S. Statutes at Large* volumes. A general index to the treaties, which includes subject and country indexing, is included. *Unperfected Treaties of the United States, 1776–1975*, is a compilation of the texts of unratified treaties from 1776–1976.

Individual treaties and agreements were also published individually in pamphlet format in the *Treaty Series (TS)*. This series started during the 1800s, as an unnumbered series. Treaties began to be numbered in 1908. After 1929, the series includes only treaties, and agreements began to be issued in the *Executive Agreement Series (EAS)*. Since 1950, treaties have been issued individually in the *Treaties and other International Acts Series* (TIAS) and compiled into bound volumes in the *United States Treaties and Other International Agreements* (UST). Treaties are first assigned a *TIAS* number, such as TIAS 10603, and then also cited by the bound *UST* volume, such as 34 UST 4383. Both of these citations refer to an agreement with India on a project loan agreement for rural electrification. (See Figure 48.1).

Two commercial publishers, W.S. Hein and Co. Inc., and Oceana Publications, are major providers of treaty information, and several of their sources are described within this chapter. If these sources are available, they can in many cases make the treaty search process much easier and quicker. Oceana's *Consolidated Treaties & International Agreements. Current Document Service* is a current subscription service that provides the full text of U.S. treaties and international agreements in a print version. *Hein's United States Treaties and Other International Agreements* is a similar service that provides microfiche copies of the treaties and international agreements. Both services provide the texts of the treaties much sooner than they are published in the official *TIAS*.

Oceana's *TIARA U.S. Treaties Researcher* (*Treaties & International Agreements Researcher's Archive*) is a comprehensive electronic source for U.S. treaties and international agreements ratified from 1783 to the present, and includes the searchable full-text of over 10,000 treaties. Accessible from the Web, *TIARA* allows searching by twelve different fields: "Full-Text Search," "Country," "Subject," "Parallel Citations," "Treaty Name," "CTIA Number," "Date in Force," "In Force," "Termination Date," and "Treaty Type." The database is updated monthly, and is available as an annual subscription to academic and governmental institutions. The database is also available for access at an hourly rate, payable online with a credit card.

U.S. treaties are also published as part of the *United Nations Treaty Series*, which is available in both a print and Web version. Access to the Web version is part of a U.N. subscription service called *United Nations Treaty Collection ON-LINE*. The Web version of *Texts of Multi-*

3910   *U.S. Treaties and Other International Agreements*   [35 UST

AIR TRANSPORT AGREEMENT
BETWEEN THE GOVERNMENT OF THE
UNITED STATES OF AMERICA
AND
THE REPUBLIC OF COSTA RICA

The Government of the United States of America and the Government of The Republic of Costa Rica,

Desiring to promote an international air transport system based on competition among airlines in the marketplace with minimum governmental interference and regulation,

Desiring to facilitate the expansion of international air transport opportunities,

Desiring to make it possible for airlines to offer the traveling and shipping public a variety of service options at the lowest prices that are not predatory or discriminatory and do not represent abuse of monopoly power, and wishing to encourage individual airlines to develop and implement innovative and competitive prices,

Desiring to ensure the highest degree of safety and security in international air transport and reaffirming their grave concern about acts or threats against the security of aircraft, which jeopardize the safety of persons or property, adversely affect the operation of air transportation, and undermine public confidence in the safety of civil aviation,

Being Parties to the Convention on International Civil Aviation opened for signature at Chicago on December 7, 1944, [1]

Desiring to conclude an agreement covering all forms of air transportation,

Have agreed as follows:

ARTICLE 1

Definitions

For the purposes of this Agreement, unless otherwise stated, the term:

(a) "Aeronautical authorities" means, in the case of the United States, the Civil Aeronautics Board or the Department of Transportation, whichever has jurisdiction, or their successor agencies, and in the case of Costa Rica, Ministerio de Obras Publicas y Transportes, Consejo Tecnico de Aviación Civil, Dirección de Transporte Aereo y Dirección General de Aviación Civil, or its successor agency;

(b) "Agreement" means this Agreement, its Annexes, and any amendments thereto;

(c) "Air transportation" means any operation performed by aircraft for the public carriage of traffic in passengers, baggage, cargo and mail, separately or in combination, for remuneration or hire;

---

[1] TIAS 1591; 61 Stat. 1180.

TIAS 10894

Source: United States Treaties and Other International Agreements, vol. 34, part 4, 1981-82, p. 4383.

Figure 48.1: Sample Page from *UST*.

lateral Treaties Deposited with the Secretary-General Not Yet Published in the UNTS provides access to the most current treaties, and is also available as part of the United Nations Treaty Collection ON-LINE subscription.

LEXIS-NEXIS and Westlaw both include files of the full-text of treaties. LEXIS-NEXIS includes the Oceana Treaties database in its USTRTY file, which includes the text of ratified treaties from 1783 to the present. LEXIS-NEXIS also includes a number of specialized databases dealing with treaties in particular subject areas such as environmental law or tax treaties. Westlaw includes the USTREATIES database, which is a database of the full-text of treaties as received in TIAS format from 1979 to the present. Westlaw also provides a version of the full-text Oceana Treaties and International Agreements Researcher's Archive in its OCEANA-TIA database. Westlaw also includes some additional specialized databases related to treaties and international agreements.

DATABASES, INDEXES, AND FINDING AIDS
Checklist

Treaties in Force. PRINT. WEB. (annual) U.S. Department of State. Office of the Legal Advisor. Treaty Affairs. S 9.14: Item 0900-A ASI 7004-1. GPO. <http://www.state.gov/www/global/legal_affairs/tifindex.html>; <http://purl.access.gpo.gov/GPO/SPS4126>.
> Content: index and summary of all U.S. treaties currently in force.

Guide to the United States Treaties in Force. PRINT. (irregular) Igor I. Kavass. Buffalo, NY: W. S. Hein and Co., Inc.
> Content: numerical, subject, and chronological indexing of all treaties still in force; updated by supplements.

United States Treaty Index: 1776–1990 Consolidation. PRINT. (1991) Igor I. Kavass. Buffalo, NY: W.S. Hein and Co., Inc.
> Content: index to treaties and other international agreements from 1776 to 1990.

Current Treaty Index. (semi-annual) PRINT. 1992–. Igor I. Kavass. Buffalo, NY: W.S. Hein and Co., Inc.
> Content: indexes slip treaties and agreements and treaties and agreements not published in TIAS but publicized by the Department of State and other sources.

Hein's U.S. Treaties Index on CD-ROM. CD-ROM. 1976–. Buffalo, NY: W.S. Hein & Co., Inc.
> Content: index to treaties and other international agreements from 1976-present.

Index to International Treaties and Agreements. PRINT. 1994–. Erwin C. Surrency. Dobbs Ferry, NY: Oceana Publications, Inc.
> Content: index of treaties and international agreements to which the United States is a signatory from 1783 to the present.

TIARA U.S. Treaties Index. WEB. Oceana Publications. <http://www.oceanalaw.com>.
> Content: index to U.S. treaties and international agreements.

Quick U.S. Treaties Index. WEB. Oceana Publications.

> Content: index to U.S. treaties and international agreements. <http://www.oceanalaw.com>

Catalog of United States Government Publications (MOCAT). WEB. 1994–. U.S. Government Printing Office. Superintendent of Documents. <http://www.gpo.gov/catalog>; <http://www.access.gpo.gov/su_docs/locators/cgp/index.html>; <http://purl.access.gpo.gov/GPO/LPS844>.
> Content: index to current treaties being issued in TIAS form.

Monthly Catalog CD-ROM, WEB, and online versions. 1976–. (See Chapter 3, "The Basics of Searching" for more information.)
> Content: index to current treaties being issued in TIAS form.

American Foreign Policy and Treaty Index. PRINT. (quarterly) 1993–. Bethesda, MD: Congressional Information Service.
> Content: index and individual abstracts of current treaties being issued in TIAS form.

World Treaty Index. PRINT. (1983) Peter H. Rohn. 2d ed. Santa Barbara, CA: ABC-Clio, Inc.
> Content: index to worldwide treaties, 1899–1980; includes some UST and TIAS citations.

Discussion

Treaties in Force provides an annual listing of all treaties and other international agreements of the United States currently in force as of January 1 of the year. It is arranged in two parts; bilateral treaties and multilateral treaties. Both a print and a Web version in PDF format are available.

Part 1, "Bilateral Treaties and Other Agreements" lists each country or political entity (such as the United Nations) that the United States has a treaty or agreement with. Treaties are arranged by subject subheading underneath each country heading. (See Figure 48.2.) Entries include the name of the treaty or agreement, the date and place of signature, the date entered into force, and the citations of the treaty (UST, TIAS, etc).

Part 2, "Multilateral Treaties and Other Agreements," is a listing by subject of all multilateral agreements to which the United States is a party. An appendix lists the presidential proclamations, treaties, and conventions by which the United States has established copyright relations with other countries. The Guide to the United States Treaties in Force is a commercially published version of the Treaties in Force, which includes more detailed indexing and is more frequently updated.

Treaties and international agreements from 1776 to 1990 are indexed by United States Treaty Index: 1776–1990 Consolidation. This index includes a numerical listing, chronological index, country index, and subject index. It is updated by the Current Treaty Index. The Hein's U.S. Treaties Index on CD-ROM also provides similar indexing for treaties and international agreements from 1776 to the present in a CD-ROM format.

6   TREATIES IN FORCE

ARGENTINA (Cont'd)

ronment Program, with appendices. Signed at Buenos Aires June 28, 1995; entered into force June 28, 1995.
TIAS

EXTRADITION

Treaty on extradition.[1] Signed at Washington January 21, 1972; entered into force September 15, 1972.
23 UST 3501; TIAS 7510.

NOTE:
[1] Applicable to all territories.

FINANCE

Agreement relating to investment guaranties under section 413(b)(4) of the Mutual Security Act of 1954, as amended. Signed at Buenos Aires December 22, 1959; entered into force provisionally December 22, 1959; definitively May 5, 1961.
12 UST 955; TIAS 4799; 411 UNTS 41.

Agreement regarding the consolidation and rescheduling of certain debts owed to, guaranteed by or insured by the United States Government and its agencies, with annexes. Signed at Buenos Aires April 8, 1986; entered into force May 19, 1986.
NP

Swap agreement between the United States Treasury and the Central Bank of the Argentine Republic/Government of the Argentine Republic, with related letter and amendment. Signed at Washington and Buenos Aires February 23, 1988; entered into force February 23, 1988.
TIAS

Swap agreement between the United States Treasury, the Central Bank of the Argentine Republic/Government of the Argentine Republic, with memorandum of understanding. Signed at Washington and Buenos Aires October 19, 1988; entered into force October 19, 1988.
TIAS

Agreement regarding the consolidation and rescheduling or refinancing of certain debts owed to, guaranteed by, or insured by the United States Government and its agencies, with annexes. Signed at Buenos Aires December 14, 1989; entered into force January 22, 1990.
NP

Agreement regarding the consolidation and rescheduling of certain debts owed to, guaranteed by, or insured by the United States Government and its agencies, with annexes. Signed

at Buenos Aires December 5, 1990; entered into force January 16, 1991.
NP

Agreement regarding the consolidation and rescheduling or refinancing of certain debts owed to, guaranteed by or insured by the United States Government´ and its agencies, with annexes. Signed at Washington December 6, 1991; entered into force February 10, 1992.
NP

Agreement regarding the reduction of certain debts related to foreign assistance owed to the Government of the United States and its agencies, with appendices. Signed at Washington and Buenos Aires January 13 and 15, 1993; entered into force February 14, 1993.
NP

INVESTMENT

Treaty concerning the reciprocal encouragement and protection of investment, with protocol. Signed at Washington November 14, 1991; entered into force October 20, 1994.
TIAS

Amendment:
August 24 and November 6, 1992.

JUDICIAL ASSISTANCE

Treaty on mutual legal assistance in criminal matters, with attachments. Signed at Buenos Aires December 4, 1990; entered into force February 9, 1993.
TIAS

MAPPING

Memorandum of understanding relating to cooperation and mutual assistance in mapping, charting and geodesy, with annex. Signed at Buenos Aires June 23, 1981; entered into force June 23, 1981.
33 UST 2097; TIAS 10175; 1529 UNTS 299.

Agreement relating to cooperation and mutual assistance in cartography and geodesy, with annex. Signed at Buenos Aires July 11, 1983; entered into force July 11, 1983.
TIAS 10730.

Agreement concerning nautical cartography and geodesy, with annexes. Signed at Buenos Aires and Fairfax November 28, 1990 and June 18, 1991; entered into force June 18, 1991.
NP

MARITIME MATTERS

Agreement relating to the transfer to Argentina of certain United States naval vessels. Exchange of notes at Washington January 4 and

8, 1951 with memorandum of understanding dated January 11, 1951; entered into force January 8, 1951.
3 UST 2735; TIAS 2442; 165 UNTS 89.

Memorandum of understanding regarding certain maritime matters. Signed at Buenos Aires March 31, 1978; entered into force January 30, 1979.
30 UST 1054; TIAS 9239; 1152 UNTS 227.

MISSIONS, MILITARY

Agreement for a United States Air Force Mission to the Argentine Republic. Signed at Buenos Aires October 3, 1956; entered into force October 3, 1956.[1]
7 UST 2571; TIAS 3652; 279 UNTS 13.

Amendment:
October 16, 1959 (10 UST 1978; TIAS 4363; 361 UNTS 358).

Agreement relating to the appointment of officers to constitute a United States Army Mission to Argentina. Signed at Buenos Aires August 2, 1960; entered into force August 2, 1960.
11 UST 1964; TIAS 4546; 384 UNTS 105.

Amendment:
January 8 and June 7, 1962 (13 UST 1376; TIAS 5098; 458 UNTS 354).

NOTE:
[1] Article 17 suspended by agreement of November 27, 1972 (24 UST 279; TIAS 7550).

NARCOTIC DRUGS

Memorandum of understanding on cooperation in the narcotics field. Signed at Buenos Aires September 15, 1972; entered into force September 15, 1972.
23 UST 2620; TIAS 7450; 852 UNTS 97.

NAVIGATION

Treaty for the free navigation of the rivers Parana and Uruguay. Signed at San Jose de Flores July 10, 1853; entered into force December 20, 1854.
10 Stat. 1001; TS 3; 5 Bevans 58.

PEACE CORPS

Agreement establishing a Peace Corps program in Argentina. Exchange of notes at Buenos Aires July 18 and August 30, 1991; entered into force August 30, 1991.
TIAS 12102.

Figure 48.2: Sample Page from *Treaties in Force*.

The *Index to International Treaties and Agreements* is a loose-leaf index to treaties and international agreements to which the United States is a signatory. It includes indexing by a country list with subjects within each country category; subjects; and date signed. Access by treaty citations (UNTS, UST, TS, etc.) is also included.

Oceana provides several versions of treaty indexes. The *TIARA U.S. Treaties Index* is accessible via the Web as a subscription service, and provides detailed field indexing similar to that included in the *TIARA U.S. Treaties Researcher* cited earlier in the "Texts of Treaties" section. If the full *TIARA U.S. Treaties Researcher* database is available, it provides even greater access, as it also includes full-text searching. The *Quick U.S. Treaties Index* provides much more limited searching by only the four fields of "Country," "Subject," "Treaty Name," and "Date Signed," but it is available free of charge to anyone who registers at the Oceana site.

The *Catalog of United States Government Publications (MOCAT)*, and the other print, electronic, and CD-ROM versions of the *Monthly Catalog* include records and entries for each individual treaty in the *Treaties and Other International Acts Series*. The *American Foreign Policy and Treaty Index* also individually indexes and abstracts each individual treaty in the *Treaties and Other International Acts Series*.

There are also numerous other indexes and databases that cover worldwide treaties that also include U.S. treaties. Both *LEXIS-NEXIS* and *Westlaw* cited earlier can be used to locate some of these databases. One well-known and widely available print index, the *World Treaty Index*, is included here as an example of this type of source. It covers worldwide treaties from 1900-1980, and provides detailed indexing. The primary citations are to the *United Nations Treaty Series*, but citations to *UST* and *TIAS* are also sometimes included.

NATIVE AMERICAN TREATIES

Checklist

Treaties between the United States and the Indian Tribes. (1846) *Statutes at Large of the United States*, Volume 7. U.S. Congress. S 7.9:7.

    Content: Indian treaties, 1789–1842.

List of Indian Treaties: Memorandum and Accompanying Information. [1778–1889 with References to U.S. Statutes.] (1964) U.S. House. Committee on Interior and Insular Affairs. Subcommittee on Indian Affairs. Y 4.IN 8/14:IN 2/11. (Nondepository)

    Content: listing of treaties between the U.S. and Native Americans.

Kappler's Indian Affairs: Laws and Treaties. V. 2. PRINT. (1979) U.S. Department of the Interior. I 1.107:2. Item 627-J. Reprint and expanded edition of: *Indian Affairs: Laws and Treaties. Vol. II Treaties.* (1904) Charles J. Kappler. U.S. Senate. Committee on Indian Affairs. Y 4.IN 2/2:L 44. Also issued as *Serial Set* volume 4624 (v.2).

    Content: ratified and unratified treaties between the U.S. and Native Americans, 1778–1871.

Indian Affairs: Laws and Treaties. Vol. II (Treaties). WEB. Oklahoma State University Library. <http://digital.library.okstate.edu/kappler/>.

    Content: full text of selected treaties from *Kappler's Indian Affairs: Laws and Treaties.*

The Avalon Project at the Yale Law School: Treaties Between the United States and Native Americans. WEB. The Yale Law School. <http://www.yale.edu/lawweb/avalon/ntreaty/ntreaty.htm>.

    Content: full text of treaties between the U.S. and Native Americans from 1778–1868.

Early American Indian Documents: Treaties and Laws 1607–1789. PRINT. 1979–. Alden T. Vaughan, ed. Bethesda, MD: University Publications of America.

    Content: text of treaties between Native Americans and colonial, state, and national governments before 1789.

Discussion

There are several sources that list treaties between the U.S. government and Native American tribes, especially treaties of the 19th century. Treaties from 1789 to 1842 were compiled in volume 7 of the *Statutes at Large*, and later treaties were also printed within the *Statutes at Large*. The *List of Indian Treaties, Memorandum and Accompanying Information* was issued as a congressional committee print. The first section of the print is a "Chronological Treaty List" taken from the *Annual Report* of the Bureau of Indian Affairs, 1903, which lists the number, the date of the treaty the *Statutes at Large* citation, and the name of the tribe. The second part lists treaties alphabetically by tribe or nation. A third section reprints the index from *Kappler's Indian Affairs: Laws and Treaties.*

Volume 2 of Kappler's *Indian Affairs: Laws and Treaties* was published in 1904 and reprints all Native American treaties from 1778 to 1871, when a law was passed prohibiting treaties with Native American nations or tribes. Since 1871, agreements with Native American tribes have been passed as laws. An index of tribal names is also included in the Kappler volume. A later edition of this title was reprinted by the Department of Interior and distributed to depository libraries in a print format. The full text of *Indian Affairs: Laws and Treaties* has also been digitized and made available on the Web by the Oklahoma State University Library.

The *Avalon Project at the Yale Law School* makes available the text of treaties between the U.S. and Native Americans from 1778–1868, primarily deriving text from *Kappler's Indian Affairs: Laws and Treaties.* Pre-1789 treaties between Native Americans and colonial, state, and national governments are being collected and published as part of a 20 volume research set titled *Early American Indian Documents: Treaties and Laws 1607–1789.*

CURRENT TREATY ACTIONS AND CON-GRESSIONAL TREATY ACTIONS

Checklist

CIS/Index. PRINT. (monthly) 1970–. Bethesda, MD: Congressional Information Service.

> Content: comprehensive indexing and abstracting of congressional publications.

Congressional Universe. WEB. Bethesda, MD: Congressional Information Service. <http://www.lexis-nexis.com/cispubs/catalog/universe/congressional%20universe/index.html>.

> Content: comprehensive indexing and abstracting of congressional publications; also includes full-text of some publications, depending on subscription selection.

THOMAS: Legislative Information on the Internet. WEB. U.S. Library of Congress. <http://thomas.loc.gov/>.

> Content: publicly accessible site that tracks congressional actions and provides full-text access to many congressional publications.

Senate Treaty Documents. PRINT. MF. U.S. Congress. Senate. Y 1.1/4: Items 0996-A or -B(MF).

> Content: text of treaties proposed by the President for ratification by the Senate.

Senate Executive Reports. PRINT. MF. U.S. Congress. Senate. Y 1.1./6: Items 1008-C or -D(MF).

> Content: reports from the Senate Foreign Relations Committee on individual treaties.

Senate, House, and Treaty Documents. WEB. 1994–. U.S. Congress. (GPO Access Web Site) <http://www.access.gpo.gov/congress/cong006.html>.

> Content: searchable full-text *Senate Treaty Documents*.

Senate, House, and Executive Reports. WEB. 1994–. U.S. Congress. (GPO Access Web Site) <http://www.access.gpo.gov/congress/cong005.html>.

> Content: searchable full-text *Senate Executive Reports*.

U.S. Congressional Serial Set. PRINT. MF. 1817–. U.S. Congress. Y 1.1/2: (Before 1817, see the *American State Papers*). Items 0996-B(MF) or -C; 1008-D(MF) or –E; 1008-F (105th Congress -, regional depository libraries only) Individual documents and reports since 1995: <http://www.access.gpo.gov/su_docs/legislative.html>.

> Content: includes *Senate Treaty Documents* and *Senate Executive Reports*.

Congressional Record. PRINT. MF. WEB. (daily when Congress in session) 1873–. U.S. Congress. X 1.1:, X 1.1/A: (Earlier, X, X/A) Items 0993-A(MF); 0993-A-01 (Regionals only, 1985-), 0993-B or -C(MF); 0994-B or -C(MF), 0994-D(EL). GPO. <http://www.access.gpo.gov/su_docs/aces/aces150.html>; <http://purl.access.gpo.gov/GPO/LPS1671>; <http://thomas.loc.gov/>.

> Content: official transcript of congressional proceedings.

Journal of the Executive Proceedings of the Senate of the United States of America. PRINT. MF. WEB. 1789–. U.S. Congress. Senate. Y 1.3/4: (Earlier, Y 1.3:Ex 3/) (Title varies) (Reprint edition of early journals published by Johnson Reprint Corp., NY, 1969) Items 1047-C or -D(MF). Early volumes: <http://lcweb2.loc.gov/ammem/amlaw/lwej.html>.

> Content: text of treaty messages.

Weekly Compilation of Presidential Documents. PRINT. WEB. (weekly) 1965–. U.S. National Archives and Records Administration. Office of the Federal Register. AE 2.109: (Earlier, GS 4.114:) Item 0577-A. GPO. <http://www.access.gpo.gov/nara/nara003.html>; <http://purl.access.gpo.gov/GPO/LPS1769>.

> Content: text of treaty messages.

Congressional Index. PRINT. (biennial with loose-leaf updates) Washington, D.C.: Commerce Clearing House, Inc.

> Content: index to pending treaties and treaties ratified during the congressional session.

American Foreign Policy and Treaty Index. PRINT. (quarterly) 1993–. Bethesda, MD: Congressional Information Service.

> Content: indexes and abstracts presidential, congressional, and executive agency publications relating to treaty ratification.

United States Senate: Legislative Activities: Treaties. WEB. U.S. Senate. <http://www.senate.gov/legislative/legis_act_treaties.html>.

> Content: description and tracking of current Congress Senate treaty activity.

Current Treaty Actions. WEB. U.S. Department of State. Office of the Legal Advisor. <http://www.state.gov/www/global/legal_affairs/legal_adviser.html>.

> Content: listing and description of current treaty actions.

Discussion

A two-thirds majority of the Senate must vote in favor of a U.S. treaty before it can be ratified. The process of ratification is very similar to the legislative process, as reports and hearings may be issued during the treaty ratification process. Three major resources used for tracing the legislative process and in some cases providing the full text of the bills, reports, documents, and hearings generated are listed here. They include *CIS/Index, Congressional Universe,* and *THOMAS.* See Chapter 45, "Legislative History," for the details of using these sources.

Two unique types of Senate publications are produced during the treaty ratification process—*Senate Treaty Documents* and *Senate Executive Reports.* A *Senate Treaty Document* is published after a treaty has been submitted to the Senate by the President. A treaty is then printed as a *Senate Treaty Document* and sent to the Senate Foreign Relations Committee. *Senate Executive Reports* are the recommendations received from the Foreign Relations Committee for consideration by the rest of the Senate. They may contain the President's submittal message, text of the treaty, and additional committee analysis. These reports are available to depository libraries in both print and microfiche formats, and are also available as searchable full-text documents on the Web from the GPO Access site. *Senate Treaty Documents* and *Senate Executive Reports* have also been included as part of the *Serial Set,* and this is a particularly good source for obtaining the older titles.

The *Congressional Record, Journal of Executive Proceedings of the Senate of the United States of America,* and the *Weekly Compilation of Presidential Documents* contain the text of all treaty messages as they are received by the Senate. The *Congressional Record* is available on the Web from the Government Printing Office's *GPO Access* Web site (1994–; index, 1983–) and on the Library of Congress's *Thomas* Web site (1989–; index, 1994–). Commercial online services also offer the *Congressional Record*, including *CIS Congressional Universe* (1985–), *LEXIS-NEXIS* (1985–), *Westlaw* (1985–), and *CQ.com On Congress* (1987–). On *LEXIS* it is in several libraries, including GENFED and LEGIS. The file name for the complete *Congressional Record* since 1985 is RECORD. There are also files for individual congresses or sections.

The *Weekly Compilation of Presidential Documents* is available on the Web from the Government Printing Office's *GPO Access* Web site (1993–). Several commercial online services also include the *Weekly Compilation*. *LEXIS-NEXIS* (March 24, 1979–) contains the text in several libraries including the EXEC, GENFED, LEGIS, and NEWS libraries. The file name is PRESDC. A related Web product, *LEXIS-NEXIS Academic Universe,* contains the same material in the General News category, the Newsletters subcategory. (To limit a search to just this title use the "More Options" search form and enter the title *Public Papers of the Presidents* in the individual title search option box.) *Westlaw* (West Group) covers 1995 on.

The *Congressional Index*, a comprehensive loose-leaf guide to current congressional activities, includes a separate section dealing with pending treaties and treaties ratified during the current session. It includes a subject index and summary section. Each entry in the summary section gives the treaty document number, the dates of any action already taken, and a description of the treaty. Unlike other congressional actions, treaties may be held from one Congress to another awaiting action, so treaties from several Congresses are listed as still pending.

Congressional Information Service (CIS) publishes the *American Foreign Policy and Treaty Index*, a comprehensive index to key foreign policy documents produced by the executive branch, Congress, and independent agencies. A wide range of both depository and nondepository documents are included. In format, the index is similar to CIS's other products, and it includes extensive abstracts. CIS also produces an accompanying microfiche set of the full text of the publications described in the index. As part of its coverage, the *American Foreign Policy and Treaty Index* comprehensively covers sources related to the treaty process. Included in its indexing are *Senate Treaty Documents*, *Senate Executive Reports*, any other congressional documents related to the treaty process, and, as described earlier, the individual treaties listed in the *Treaties and International Acts Series*. Also indexed is the *Weekly Compilation of Presidential Documents*.

The *United States Senate: Legislative Activities: Treaties* Web site tracks treaty action occurring during the current Congress. A listing of treaties received identifies any treaties received from the President as well as any committee actions. Another section lists treaties approved during the Congress, along with the text of the treaty resolution. The "Treaties Actions" section lists any treaties with Senate floor action, along with the date and description of the action. The "Treaties on Executive Calendar" section identifies any treaties that have been reported out by the Foreign Relations Committee, and placed on the Executive Calendar as being ready for floor action.

The *Current Treaty Actions* Web page from the Department of State gives a monthly listing of new treaty actions. Included is information on the dates signed, dates entered into force, and citations to Senate Treaty Documents. This source is one of the most convenient sources for tracking current treaty actions.

TAX TREATY PUBLICATIONS
Checklist

Income Tax Treaties. WEB. U.S. Department of the Treasury. Internal Revenue Service. <http://www.irs.gov/ind_info/treaties.html>.

    Content: text of income tax treaties of over 30 countries.

Certification for Reduced Tax Rates in Tax Treaty Countries. PRINT. WEB. (irregular) U.S. Department of the Treasury. Internal Revenue Service. Publication 686. T 22.44/2:686/year. Item 0964-B. <http://www.irs.ustreas.gov/prod/forms_pubs/pubs/p686toc.htm>.

    Content: description of procedures for obtaining certification for reduced tax rates as a result of tax treaties.

Tax Guide for U.S. Citizens and Resident Aliens Abroad. PRINT. WEB. (irregular) U.S. Department of the Treasury. Internal Revenue Service. Publication 54. T 22.44/2:54/year. Item 0964-B. <http://www.irs.ustreas.gov/forms_pubs/pubs/p54toc.htm>; <http://purl.access.gpo.gov/GPO/LPS815>.

    Content: general tax guide.

Witholding of Tax on Nonresident Aliens and Foreign Corporations. PRINT. WEB. U.S. Department of the Treasury. Internal Revenue Service. Publication 515. T 22.44/2:515/year. Item 0964-B. <http://www.irs.ustreas.gov/forms_pubs/pubs/p515toc.html>; <http://purl.access.gpo.gov/GPO/LPS1225>.

    Content: includes tables listing U.S. tax treaties and treaty provisions that affect withholding.

U.S. Tax Treaties. PRINT. WEB. (irregular) U.S. Department of the Treasury. Internal Revenue Service. Publication 901. T 22.44/2:901/year. Item 0964-B. <http://www.irs.ustreas.gov/prod/forms_pubs/pubs/p901toc.htm>.

    Content: guide for residents of tax treaty countries who receive income from the United States.

Information on the United States-Canada Income Tax Treaty. PRINT. WEB. (irregular) U.S. Department of the Treasury. Internal Revenue Service. Publication 597. T 22.44/2:597/year. Item 0964-B. <http://www.irs.ustreas.gov/forms_pubs/pubs/p597toc.htm>.

    Content: description and text of U.S.-Canada income tax treaty.

Discussion

A series of tax treaties affect the tax rates that U.S. citizens and residents pay in other countries. These treaties also apply to people from other countries who are in the U.S. and affect their tax rates. Foreign workers and students are especially interested in the tax consequences of these treaties. The text of these treaties is made available at the *Income Tax Treaties* Web site.

The IRS publications cited in this section are useful in locating countries with which the United States has tax treaties and for analyzing the consequences of those treaties. *LEXIS-NEXIS* and *Westlaw*, the two major online legal systems, both include databases that provide the text of these IRS publications, along with numerous tax-related databases that discuss the implications of these treaties.

RELATED MATERIAL
Within this Work

Chapter 27 The President

Chapter 45 Legislative History

GPO *Subject Bibliographies*. PRINT. WEB. GP 3.22/2:

<http://bookstore.gpo.gov/sb/about.html>

No. 191 " Treaties and Other International Agreements of the United States"

CHAPTER 49
Technical Reports

Government technical reports consist primarily of U.S. government-sponsored research, development, and engineering reports. These reports are usually prepared by government contractors and grantees (such as universities, research organizations, or corporations) and consist of progress reports and final reports on projects. Most of these reports have not been made available to depository libraries. They are indexed and sold by the National Technical Information Service (NTIS), a federal agency required by law to be self-sustaining. Proposals to transfer the services of NTIS to other agencies have been proposed, and the long term status of NTIS is uncertain at this point.

Nearly three million reports and other information products in a variety of formats (including paper, microfiche, diskettes, CD-ROM, electronic tape, and additional formats) are available for sale by NTIS. Large libraries and technical libraries often subscribe to selected subject categories of NTIS publications in microfiche through NTIS's SRIM (Selected Research in Microfiche) program. Other libraries may subscribe to individual series or purchase selected products of interest. A small percentage of the reports and products available from NTIS have been made available to depository libraries. Some agencies (most notably the Department of Energy) have also begun to make the full-text of their reports accessible via the Web. The reports of the Department of Energy (DOE), the National Aeronautics and Space Administration (NASA), the Department of Defense (DOD), and the Environmental Protection Agency (EPA) are particularly well represented in the *NTIS Database*. Many other reports and products from a variety of sources, including publications sponsored by other federal agencies, state and local agencies, private contractors, and foreign governments are also made available by NTIS.

This chapter discusses the indexes and databases used to access the federal technical report literature, information about NTIS, relevant agency sites, and sources of the full-text of technical reports.

SEARCH STRATEGY

Locating technical reports uses a special techniques strategy. The major steps for locating technical reports are as follows:

1. For general information about the National Technical Information Search Service (NTIS), see the *NTIS* Web site;
2. To locate specific technical reports available for sale from NTIS, use the *NTIS Database*, if available, or the more limited listings of publications for sale at the *NTIS* Web site;
3. If interested in reports from a specific agency, see the individual sections for those agencies; and
4. Use the *Monthly Catalog* if interested in locating reports distributed through the depository program.

The sources used in a technical report search will depend somewhat on what is available to the searcher and whether the searcher is trying to locate reports distributed to depository libraries, reports available for sale by NTIS, or reports available online in full-text. Libraries that receive significant numbers of technical reports often classify and arrange them by the NTIS or report numbers, but many technical reports received through the depository system may be classified by the SuDocs number. The *NTIS Database*, the major indexing source for technical reports, only includes SuDocs numbers on a limited basis.

NTIS SOURCES
Checklist

National Technical Information Service Web Site. WEB. U.S. Department of Commerce. National Technical Information Service. <http://www.ntis.gov/>.

Content: general information about NTIS; product and collection information; ordering information.

NTIS Products—Catalogs.. WEB. U.S. Department of Commerce. National Technical Information Service. <http://www.ntis.gov/catalogs.htm>.

Content: PDF format catalogs of NTIS products.

NTIS Database. WEB. 1964–. GOV.Research_Center. <http://grc.ntis.gov/>.

Content: database of bibliographic records and abstracts of research, technical reports, and other products made available through NTIS.

NTIS Product Search. WEB. 1990–. U.S. Department of Commerce. National Technical Information Service. <http://www.ntis.gov/search.htm>.

Content: title search to NTIS reports issued since 1990.

NTIS OrderNow. WEB. U.S. Department of Commerce. National Technical Information Service. <http://www.fedworld.gov/onow/>.

Content: ordering information for the last 90 days of NTIS reports and products.

NTIS Customer Support. WEB. U.S. Department of Commerce. National Technical Information Service. <http://www.ntis.gov/support/index.html>.

Content: information on placing orders, contact information, deposit accounts, and order forms.

Government Reports Announcements and Index (GRAI). PRINT. (semimonthly) 1975–1996. U.S. Department of Commerce. National Technical Information Service. C51.9/3:; C59/9/4: (Issued since 1946 under other titles) Item 0270.

Content: historical index and abstracting service for NTIS government-sponsored research reports.

Discussion

The *National Technical Information Service Web Site* provides extensive information about NTIS products. In addition to technical and research reports, NTIS also sells a number of other products and provides subscriptions to various products and services. NTIS also provides services for other government agencies. The *National Technical Information Service Web Site* allows the user to identify various products and to browse listings and descriptions of product categories and collections. *The NTIS Products-Catalogs* Web page includes PDF versions of catalogs of NTIS products. Included is the most recent version of the *NTIS Catalog of Products,* which describes some of the most popular products, subscriptions, and services of NTIS. Other titles available at the *NTIS Products—Catalogs* Web page include *Catalog of Educational Multimedia Products* (PR-1047), *Fire & Emergency Services Training Packages* (PR-986), *Catalog of Multimedia and Training Products* (PR-1001), *Search Guide for the NTIS Database,* and *Video Training for Law Enforcement Agencies* (PR-1000).

The *NTIS Database* is a major indexing and abstracting source for reports handled by NTIS, and is one of the most comprehensive sources to use for identifying technical reports. Many libraries and other organizations subscribe to the *NTIS Database,* but it is not available through the depository library program. Coverage of the database begins with 1964, and it includes over 2 million bibliographic records. Topics covered represent a broad range of subject areas including agriculture, biotechnology, business, communication, energy, engineering, the environment, health and safety, medicine, research and development, science, space technology; and transportation. The database includes primarily U.S. government-sponsored research, but research from some foreign governments and other research organizations is also included.

NTIS provides access to the *NTIS Database* via *GOV.Research_Center,* created by a partnership between NTIS and the National Information Services Corporation. The database uses the BiblioLine search system, and provides different levels of searching interfaces (basic, advanced, and expert). Searching in the basic interface allows the user to search by keywords/phrase in the author, title, abstracts, and index fields. Searches may be limited by author, performing organization, or source agency. The expert mode provides the ability to search by field tags and combine search result sets. Searchable fields include "Accession Number," "Author," "Subject," "Institutional Author," "Index Terms," "Language," "Major Topic," "NTIS Journal Announcement," "Number," "Performing Organization," "Publication Place," "Publication Year," "Source," "Source Agency," "Sponsor," and "Title." A number of options are available for the display of results. Records retrieved include bibliographic citations and accompanying abstracts. Records may be saved to file, printed, or e-mailed. The user also has the option of ordering NTIS reports directly from the search results. In addition to various subscription options, "Day Passes" for one-time use are also available.

The *NTIS Database* is also available from a number of other commercial vendors including Cambridge Scientific Abstracts (1964–), Ovid Technologies (1970–) Dialog (Web:1964–), (CD-ROM: 1980–.), Silverplatter (Web and CD-ROM 1983–), STN International (1964–), and Questel-Orbit (1964–). NTIS database abstracts are also available from Northern Light as part of its *usgovsearch* service.

The *NTIS* Web site also provides free access to a less comprehensive database of some 400,000 NTIS products (including technical reports) published since 1990 at the *NTIS Product Search* page. This database allows the user to do simple title searches only. Abstracts are not included. The *NTIS Order-Now* database provides access to citations and some full-text documents for the last 90-day period. It is searchable by keywords, country of publication, source, title, subject, personal author, performing organization, document type, language, and words within an abstract. *The NTIS OrderNow* database also allows for direct online ordering of NTIS products.

The *NTIS Customer Support* page provides information on various options for ordering NTIS publications and products. It explains the use of the *NTIS OrderNow* online ordering system, telephone orders, fax orders, and e-mail orders. It also explains deposit account and billing options, and provides shipping information and copies of order forms.

Once a report has been identified, it may be ordered directly from NTIS, using the ordering resources previously described. Some libraries have collections of technical reports, often arranged and classified by technical report numbers. Technical reports distributed through the depository system will have SuDocs numbers assigned to them. Some technical report series distributed to depository libraries are identified in the following sections, although increasingly reports are being made available on the Web. For example, depository libraries previously received many technical reports in a microfiche format from the Department of Energy. These reports are now being distributed in electronic format on the Web and are not otherwise distributed to depository libraries.

The *Government Reports Announcement and Index (GRAI)* is a historical index and abstract that was produced in a print format. The *NTIS Database* includes records for the items that were included in *GRAI* from 1964. The equivalent of *GRAI* was produced in various titles since 1946, and the historical volumes will need to be consulted for items older than 1964. *Government Reports Announcements and Index* was discontinued in 1996.

NASA SOURCES

Checklist

NASA Scientific and Technical Information. WEB. U.S. National Aeronautics and Space Administration. Scientific and Technical Information Program. <http://www.sti.nasa.gov/>.

> Content: information about NASA's STI programs; links to databases and products; descriptions of products.

Scientific and Technical Aerospace Reports. (STAR). WEB. (semimonthly) 1963–. (Web version 1996–; print version from 1963–1995.) (Earlier, NAS 1.9/4:; NAS 1.9/5:; Item 0820-K) U.S. National Aeronautics and Space Administration. <http://www.sti.nasa.gov/Pubs/star/Star.html>.

> Content: index and abstracts of reports from NASA, NASA contractors, and other agencies covering aeronautics and related sciences.

CASI Technical Report Server. WEB. 1962–. U.S. National Aeronautics and Space Administration. <http://www. sti.nasa.gov/RECONselect.html>.

> Content: database of technical report bibliographic citations and abstracts.

NASA Technical Reports Server. WEB. U.S. National Aeronautics and Space Administration. <http://techreports.larc.nasa.gov/cgi-bin/NTRS>.

Content: search interface for technical report databases from a number of NASA agencies; includes access to some full-text technical reports.

Aerospace Database. WEB. CD-ROM. 1962-. Dialog. <www.dialog.com>.

Aerospace Database. WEB. 1962-. STN. <http://www.cas.org/stn.html>.

Aerospace Database. WEB. Cambridge Scientific Abstracts. 1986–. <http://www.csa.com/>.

NASA Technical Memorandum. MF. NAS 1.15: Item 0830-D.

NASA EP Series. MF. NAS 1.19 : Item 0830-G.

NASA SP Series. MF. NAS 1.21: Item 0830-I.

NASA Contractor Reports. MF. NAS 1.26: Item 0830-H-14.

NASA Conference Publications. MF. NAS 1.55: Item 0830-H-10.

NASA Technical Papers. MF. NAS 1.60: Item 0830-H-15.

NASA Reference Publications. MF. NAS 1.61: Item 0830-H-11.

NASA Patents Applications. MF. NAS 1.71: Item 0830-J-10.

Discussion

NASA carries out a Scientific and Technical Information (STI) program to help manage its information activities and to ensure that the results of its research are disseminated. The *NASA Scientific and Technical Information* Web site describes this STI program, and some of the databases and products produced as a result of the program. It also provides links to the databases and STI products and services, some of which relate to technical report literature and are further described in this section. This page is a good place to gain a basic understanding of NASA's STI program.

NASA issues numerous technical reports dealing not only with aeronautics and space, but with related aerospace aspects of earth resources, energy, and the environment. The most comprehensive index to NASA reports is the *Scientific and Technical Aerospace Reports (STAR)*. *STAR* was issued in print from 1963–1995, but issues of *STAR* are available on the Web in a PDF format only from January 1996 on. *STAR* abstracts and indexes NASA reports, reports of NASA contractors and grantees, and relevant reports from other government agencies and non-governmental institutions. There is considerable overlap in coverage between *STAR* and the *NTIS Database*, and most reports included in *STAR* are also indexed by NTIS and are available for sale from NTIS.

Abstracts in *STAR* are arranged in 10 major subject divisions, which are further divided into 76 specific subject subcategories. There are two indexes in each issue of *STAR*: subject and personal author. (See Figure 49.1.)

Source: *Scientific and Technical Aerospace Reports*, Volume 37,

04
AIRCRAFT COMMUNICATIONS AND NAVIGATION

Includes digital and voice communication with aircraft; air navigation systems (satellite and ground based); and air traffic control. For related information see also 17 Space Communications, Spacecraft Communications, Command and Tracking and 32 Communications and Radar.

19990114887 Federal Aviation Administration, Technical Center, Atlantic City, NJ USA
Air Traffic Control System Baseline Methodology Guide
Allendorefer, Kenneth R.; Galushka, Joseph; Jun. 1999; 88p; In English
Report No.(s): AD-A367892; DOT/FAA/CT-TN99/15; No Copyright; Avail: CASI; A05, Hardcopy; A01, Microfiche
　　The Air Traffic Control System Baseline Methodology Guide serves as a reference in the design and conduct of baseline studies. Engineering research psychologists are the intended audience for the Methodology Guide, which focuses primarily on techniques for studying the interaction between ATC systems and the controllers who use them. The Methodology Guide provides the following information: (a) descriptions of and references to past baselines that have successfully used the methodology, (b) detailed descriptions of the baseline operational constructs and corresponding objective and subjective measures, (c) a description of the overall baseline methodology, (d) other recommendations and lessons learned regarding the successful conduct of system baselines, and (e) a discussion of the role of system baselines in the ATC system acquisition process.
DTIC
Methodology; Management Information Systems; Air Traffic Control

19990115884 National Aerospace Lab., Structures Div., Tokyo, Japan
Confirmation Tests of ALFLEX Vibration Characteristics
Kanda, A.; Sotozaki, T.; Ueda, T.; Dec. 1998; 26p; In Japanese; Portions of this document are not fully legible
Report No.(s): PB99-164972; NAL-TR-1370; Copyright; Avail: National Technical Information Service (NTIS), Hardcopy
　　Ground vibration tests of ALFLEX were carried out by using the Dynamic Displacement Measurement System which enables automatic data acquisition. After structural improvements and flight experiments, vibration characteristics of ALFLEX were confirmed by ground tests. Modal measurements for local vibrations were also conducted by the hammer-impact method. The vibration problem that occurred in the pitch rate of IMU (Inertial Measurement Unit) the flight experiments was considered.
NTIS
Vibration Tests; Displacement Measurement; Automatic Landing Control; Structural Vibration

19990115909 Federal Aviation Administration, Cambridge, MA USA
Guidelines for the Use of Color in ATC Displays *Final Report*
Cardosi, Kim, Federal Aviation Administration, USA; Hannon, Dan, Federal Aviation Administration, USA; Jun. 1999; 60p; In English
Contract(s)/Grant(s): FA9L1/A9112
Report No.(s): AD-A367984; DOT-VNTSC-FAA-98-5; DOT/FAA/AR-99/52; No Copyright; Avail: CASI; A01, Microfiche; A04, Hardcopy
　　Color is probably the most effective, compelling, and attractive method available for coding visual information on a display. However, caution must be used in the application of color to displays for air traffic control (ATC), because it is easy to do more harm than good. The only thing that is truly obvious about the use of color on displays is that its benefits and drawbacks depend upon the task. This paper offers general guidelines on how color should, and should not, be used, but does not define a specific color-coding scheme. These guidelines are based on what is known about human vision, display capabilities, the knowledge gained from the lessons learned from the uses of color in the cockpit and ATC environments, and human factors "best practices." The report also discusses a series of experiments that examined color production capabilities within and across five Sony DDM-2801C monitors and selected and validated an "ideal" color set for this monitor.
DTIC
Visual Perception; Monitors; Air Traffic Control; Color Coding; Human Performance

19990116761 European Organization for the Safety of Air Navigation, Brussels, Belgium
Air Traffic Management Capacity Constraints on and Around Airports
Griffin, F. E. Martin, European Organization for the Safety of Air Navigation, Belgium; The Potential of Rotorcraft to Increase Airport Capacity: Proceedings; 1999, pp. 9.1 - 9.5; In English; See also 19990116754; Copyright; Avail: Issuing Activity, Hardcopy

14

December 1999, p.14.

Figure 49.1: Sample Page from *STAR*.

NASA also provides an additional way of accessing technical report citations through its *CASI Technical Report Server*. At this site, an option for selecting the *NASA Technical Reports Server* is available. Bibliographic data included in the database are derived from the *Scientific and Technical Aerospace Reports (STAR) File*, the same database that is the basis for producing the PDF *STAR*. In addition to keyword searching, field searching is available for "Title," "Author," "Abstract," "Report number," "Subject term," "Category," "Contract number," Accession number," "Journal-meeting title," "Language," "Publisher," "Corporate source," and " Publication date."

The *STAR Database* is also distributed by several commercial vendors as part of the American Institute of Aeronautics and Astronautics' *Aerospace Database*. The *Aerospace Database* also includes the *International Aerospace Abstracts*, which covers journal articles, conference proceedings, and monographs in the same subject areas as the *STAR Database*.

The *NASA Technical Reports Server* provides a search interface to the separate technical report databases of a number of NASA research centers, including the Ames Research Center, the Goddard Space Center, and the Langley Research Center. The user can select one or more databases to search. The search interface provides simple keyword and phrase searching. The coverage of the databases varies, since each database is created separately by its respective research center. Some centers also include access to the full-text of technical reports from their centers. This site also includes two databases pertaining to the technical report literature of NASA's predecessor, the National Advisory Committee for Aeronautics (NACA). An abstracts database covers reports published from 1915–1960. A database providing access to the full-text of a limited number of NACA reports is also available.

Some series of NASA technical reports have been issued to depository libraries over the years, primarily in microfiche formats. Several series currently or recently distributed to depository libraries are listed here.

DEPARTMENT OF ENERGY SOURCES
Checklist

Virtual Library of Energy Science and Technology. WEB. U.S. Department of Energy. Office of Scientific and Technical Information. <http://apollo.osti.gov/html/osti/ostipg.html>.
    Content: information about OSTI; descriptions of databases and resources; links to information resources.

DOE Reports Bibliographic Database. WEB. 1994–. U.S. Department of Energy. Office of Scientific and Technical Information. E 1.17/2: Item 0429-X. <http://apollo.osti.gov/dra/dra.html>.
    Content: bibliographic information and abstracts for reports issued by the Department of Energy and its contractors.

Energy Research Abstracts. PRINT. (monthly) 1977–1993. U.S. Department of Energy. Office of Scientific and Technical Information. E 1.17: (Issued semimonthly before 1991) Item 0474-A-06.

Content: historical index and abstracts for reports from the Department of Energy, its contractors, and other sources on all aspects of energy.

Energy Science and Technology. WEB. 1974–1993. Dialog. <www.dialog.com>.
    Content: online version of *Energy Research Abstracts*.

DOE Information Bridge. WEB. U.S. Department of Energy. Office of Scientific and Technical Information. E 1.137: Item 0429-X-19. <http://www.osti.gov/bridge/home.html>.
    Content: full-text of energy related technical reports.

Discussion

The Office of Science and Technical Information (OSTI) in the Department of Energy is responsible for providing direction and coordinating the dissemination of scientific and technical information. OSTI's Web site describes many of these efforts, as well as describing the major databases and products for which it has responsibility.

The *DOE Reports Bibliographic Database* contains citations and abstracts for all Department of Energy sponsored scientific and technical reports from the period of 1994 to the present. Most reports included in the database are also included in the *NTIS Database* and are available for purchase from NTIS. Some earlier reports (prior to 1997) in the database were also distributed to depository libraries in a microfiche format under the E 1.99: SuDocs number, and this will be designated in the record. Keyword searching of the text of bibliographic records is available, as well as title and personal author/affiliation field searches. A fielded keyword search and search by Department of Energy and Government Printing Office subject codes are also available.

The predecessor to the *DOE Reports Bibliographic Database* is the print *Energy Research Abstracts*, which provides coverage of the Department of Energy technical report literature from 1977–1993. Depository libraries received many Department of Energy reports covered by this index in a microfiche format, as well as some paper format reports. An electronic version of this database, titled *Energy Science and Technology*, is available from Dialog.

The DOE is now distributing the full text of its technical reports on the Web, through its *DOE Information Bridge*. The *DOE Information Bridge* includes the full-text and bibliographic records of DOE-sponsored report literature received and processed by DOE since January 1995. This includes a growing collection of over 3 million searchable pages in 49,000 reports. Pages may be viewed in GIF or TIFF formats. Search options in the "Easy Search" mode include author, title, or keyword searching of the OCR full text of the report or the OCR text of the bibliographic citation and abstract. The "Advanced Search" interface allows fielded searching of the OCR text and bibliographic citation and abstract, the OCR text of the bibliographic information only, the title, author, identifying number, laboratory, sponsoring agency, subject, keywords, author affiliation, distribution category, publication date, document type, and entry date. (See Figure 49.2.)

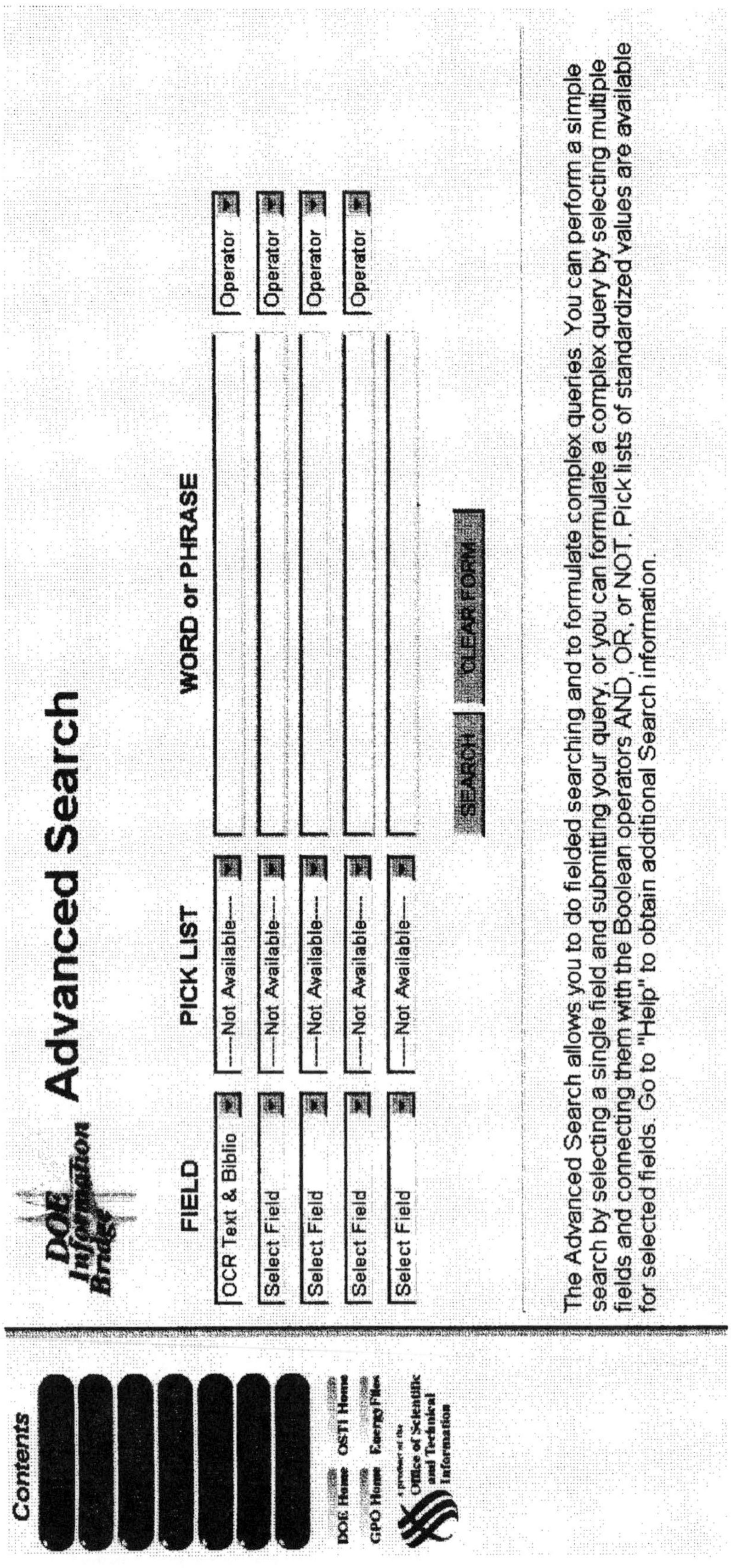

Source: DOE Information Bridge, <http://gpo.osti.gov:901/dds/advanced.html>.

Figure 49.2: *DOE Information Bridge Advanced Search.*

ENVIRONMENTAL PROTECTION AGENCY
Checklist

EPA Publications Bibliography: Quarterly Abstract Bulletin. PRINT. (quarterly) 1977–. U.S. Environmental Protection Agency. Center for Environmental Research Information. EP 1.21/7: Item 0431-I-39. ASI 9182-5. NTIS.
　　Content: index and abstracts of reports from the Environmental Protection Agency and its contractors.

EPA Publications Bibliography. PRINT. 1977–1990. U.S. Environmental Protection Agency. EP 1.21/7-2: (Title varies). Item 0431-I-39. NTIS.
　　Content: cumulated edition of the *Quarterly Abstract Bulletin.*

OLS U.S. EPA Online Library System. WEB. U.S. Environmental Protection Agency. <http://www.epa.gov/natlibra/ols.htm>.
　　Content: bibliographic citations to EPA reports and other materials in EPA libraries, including technical reports.

EPA National Publications Catalog. PRINT. WEB. 1994–. U.S. Environmental Protection Agency. Office of Administration and Resources Management. EP 1.21:P 96/5/. Item 0431-I-09. GPO. <http://www.epa.gov/ncepihom/catalog.html>; <http://purl.access.gpo.gov/GPO/LPS586>.
　　Content: catalog of more than 5,000 current EPA publications, including some technical reports.

National Environmental Publications Internet Site (NEPIS). WEB. U.S. Environmental Protection Agency. <http://www.epa.gov/ncepihom/nepishom/>.
　　Content: full-text and images of over 6,000 archival and current EPA documents, including some technical reports.

Solid Waste Management Series. MF. U.S. Environmental Protection Agency. EP 1.17: Item 0431-I-07.

Environmental Research Brief. PRINT. U.S. Environmental Protection Agency. EP 1.96: Item 0431-I-81.

Miscellaneous. MF. U.S. Environmental Protection Agency. EP 1.23/6: Item 0431-J.

Discussion

The Environmental Protection Agency issues numerous technical and research reports. Some of these reports are beginning to become available in full-text formats. Many EPA reports have also been distributed to depository libraries over the years and some libraries have large collections of EPA technical reports.

EPA Publications Bibliography: Quarterly Abstract Bulletin lists all technical reports and journal articles submitted to NTIS by the Environmental Protection Agency. The final issue for each year contains cumulative annual indexes. There are seven indexes: title, keyword, sponsoring EPA office, corporate author, personal author, contract/grant number, and NTIS order/report number. The cumulative indexes give references to the issue number and the NTIS order number. The abstracts in each issue are arranged by the NTIS number. Most reports included

in the *EPA Publications Bibliography* are also included in the *NTIS Database.*

EPA Publications Bibliography is a hardcover cumulation of the quarterly issues. Three sets have been published, each covering a seven-year period. These cumulations cover 1970–76, 1977–83, and 1984–90. The first set for 1970–1976 was titled *EPA Cumulative Bibliography.* It is the only set without a sponsoring EPA office index.

The *OLS U.S. EPA Online Library System* contains several databases for locating books, reports, and audiovisual materials. The "National Catalog" contains the holdings of most of the 28 EPA regional libraries and laboratories, and many of these libraries include technical report literature among their collections. A database of EPA reports available from the National Technical Information Service (NTIS) is also included. Searches can be done by title, keyword, author, corporate source, and report number. Advanced searching offers searching by year of publication, specific fields, and specific databases.

The *EPA National Publications Catalog* lists more than 5,000 current Environmental Protection Agency (EPA) publications with ordering information. Publications are listed by sponsoring office, EPA number, and subject. The numeric listing gives the source for obtaining the publication. Many publications are available free from the National Service Center for Environmental Publications (NSCEP). These are highlighted throughout the *Catalog* for easy identification. Other publications are available from other EPA offices or for a fee from the National Technical Information Service (NTIS) or other sources. Sample order forms and instructions are included. A list of all the sources is given at the beginning of the *Catalog* with address, telephone and fax numbers, and Internet addresses. A searchable version of the *Catalog* is available on the Internet that provides searching by title, EPA number, and subject. Some technical reports are included in the publications covered by the *EPA National Publications Catalog.*

The *National Environmental Publications Internet Site* contains a full-text database of over 6,000 EPA publications. The simple search option retrieves page images based on a keyword search. An enhanced search option allows results to be viewed either as page images or as text. An EPA Web site search is also available. A complete list of publications available arranged by report number may also be displayed. Selected technical reports are included in the database.

Many series of EPA technical reports have been issued to depository libraries over the years. Three series of technical reports currently being received are included here as examples.

Discussion

Nuclear Regulatory Commission

NRC Technical Reports in the NUREG Series. WEB. U.S. Nuclear Regulatory Commission. <http://www.nrc.gov/NRC/NUREGS/indexnum.html>.

> Content: full-text of a limited number of NUREG reports.

Discussion

The Nuclear Regulatory Commission (NRC) issues technical reports on nuclear energy and related issues. Depository libraries have received some of these reports over the years. A small number of NRC technical reports are available in full text from the NRC site.

DEFENSE TECHNICAL INFORMATION CENTER

Checklist

Scientific and Technical Information Network. WEB. U.S. Department of Defense. Defense Information Systems Agency. Defense Technical Information Center. <http://stinet.dtic.mil/>.

> Content: information about the public and secure versions of the Scientific and Technical Information Network (STINET).

Quick Search, Scientific and Technical Documents. WEB. U.S. Department of Defense. Defense Information Systems Agency. Defense Technical Information Center. <http://stinet.dtic.mil/str/index.html>.

> Content: interface to the DTIC *Technical Reports Collection* database.

Discussion

The Defense Technical Information Center (DTIC) makes Department of Defense-related information available to government agencies and government contractors. The *Scientific and Technical Information Network* Web page describes the information available to the public on the *Public STINET* and information only available to the DoD community (including government contractors) through the *Secure STINET* service. One of the databases available through *STINET* is the *DTIC Technical Reports Database*. The public portion of this database is available at the *Quick Search, Scientific and Technical Documents* page. It provides indexing and abstracting for unclassified technical reports from late 1974 to the present. A simple search form and a more advanced search form that provides fielded searching is available. Searchable fields include: "Accession Number," "Title," "Personal Author,"

"Corporate Author," "Source Code," "Descriptors," "Report Date," "Abstract," "Subject Categories," "Contract Number" "Descriptive Note," and "Identifiers." Included are reports on defense-related research, including some reports on basic sciences such as biological and medical sciences, environmental pollution and control, and behavioral and social sciences. Reports in the database are made available to DoD authorized DTIC users; they may be purchased by the general public from NTIS.

INDEXES

Checklist

Catalog of United States Government Publications (MOCAT). WEB. 1994–. U.S. Government Printing Office. Superintendent of Documents. <http://www.gpo.gov/catalog>; <http://www.access.gpo.gov/su_docs/locators/cgp/index.html>; <http://purl.access.gpo.gov/GPO/LPS844>.

Monthly Catalog of United States Government Publications. CD-ROM. 1996–. U.S. Government Printing Office. Superintendent of Documents. GP 3.8/7: Item 0557-C. GPO.

Monthly Catalog of United States Government Publications (Condensed version). PRINT. (monthly) 1996–. U.S. Government Printing Office. Superintendent of Documents. GP 3.8/8: (Earlier full version, GP 3.8:, 1895-1995). Item 0557-D. GPO.

Discussion

Technical reports sent through the depository library system are included in *the Monthly Catalog*. Most of the technical reports included in the *Monthly Catalog* are also included in the *NTIS Database*, but most technical reports are not depository, and are not included in the *Monthly Catalog*. Search the *Monthly Catalog* by keyword or subject to locate technical reports. The complete version of the *Monthly Catalog* is available on the Web and CD-ROM. Commercial online and CD-ROM versions of the *Monthly Catalog* are also available. For more information on the *Monthly Catalog*, see Chapter 3, "The Basics of Searching."

RELATED MATERIAL

Within this Work

CHAPTER 50
Patents and Trademarks

The United States patent system has its origins in the U.S. Constitution, which authorizes the government to grant inventors the exclusive rights to their inventions for a limited period of time (Article I, Section 8, Clause 8). The purpose of the patent system is to promote useful inventions by providing for the public disclosure of inventions and rewarding inventors. In return for public disclosure and future rights to use the invention, the government protects the inventor's exclusive rights for the lifetime of the patent.

Patents are an important source of current and historical technical and scientific information. Patents grant inventors the right to control the use of their inventions for 20 years (utility and plant patents; 14 years for design patents). The most obvious reason to search patents is to see if something has already been patented in preparation for making an application, but patents are also searched to find technical information, to study the history of technology, to monitor the activities of companies, or to locate inventions in the public domain. Each patent includes background information on the technology involved, references to related patents, and drawings. A detailed description of the invention covers its purpose, benefits, operation, and the ways in which it differs from other similar devices.

More than six million patents have been issued since the first numbered patent in 1836. (Patents have been issued since 1790.) The majority of patents are issued for new and useful processes, machines, manufactured articles, or chemical compositions. These are called utility patents. There are also design patents covering the appearance of a manufactured article, and plant patents for new varieties of asexually reproduced plants.

Trademarks are issued by the same office (the U.S. Patent and Trademark Office), but are quite different. Trademarks are symbols and/or words used for identification of goods or services in commercial transactions. A trademark identifies a product as being exclusively associated with a particular company. Trademark registrations are for periods of 10 years and can be renewed indefinitely as long as the mark continues to be used.

The Patent and Trademark Office administers the Patent and Trademark Depository Library Program. This program is separate from the Government Printing Office Federal Depository Library Program. While larger federal depository libraries may have some of the patent searching tools listed in this chapter, patent depository libraries are more likely to have full-text patent collections and more extensive patent-related resources. Patent library staff also receive specialized training in the use of these resources. Patent depository libraries are listed on the agency's Web site and in many of the Patent and Trademark Office publications, including *General Information Concerning Patents*. (See the "General Information" section of this chapter.)

SEARCH STRATEGY

This chapter is an example of a special technique search. For patent and trademark searches, follow these steps:

1. For background and reference information on patents and trademarks, consult the sources in the "General Information" section of this chapter;
2. To locate patents by subject find the proper classification and subclass codes for the subject, using the titles listed under the "Patent Classification Guides" section of this chapter. Searching by word in patent databases listed in the "Patent Search Sources" section can also help in identifying possible related patents and their classifications;
3. Once classes and subclasses have been identified, do class and subclass searches in the databases listed in the "Patent Search Sources" section — these will provide a list of patent numbers assigned to the selected classes and subclasses and, in some cases, abstracts or full text;

4. If abstracts or full text have not already been found in step 3, look up specific patent numbers in the *Official Gazette* to locate summaries of the patents, including a drawing. For those patents that are determined to be relevant, examine the actual patents in full-text databases listed in the "Patents: Abstracts and Texts" section or in patent depository libraries. Copies of patents may also be ordered from the Patent and Trademark Office;

5. If searching for patents by assignee, patent number, or other data elements, use the sources in the "Patent Search Sources" section;

6. Commercial vendors also offer patent databases and patent delivery options. Consult the "Commercial Patent Databases" section for information on these;

7. For trademark searches consult the sources in the "Trademark Search Sources" section;

8. See the "Commercial Trademark Sources and Databases" section for information on commercial trademark databases and other products;

9. To locate general publications about patents and trademarks search the indexes in the "Indexes" section; and

10. Consult the listings under "Related Material" for additional sources of information.

GENERAL INFORMATION

Checklist

General Information Concerning Patents. PRINT. WEB. (irregular) U.S. Department of Commerce. Patent and Trademark Office. C 21.26/2: Item 0256-A-02. GPO. <http://www.uspto.gov/web/offices/pac/doc/general/>.

> Content: definitions; what can be patented; publications; search room and patent searching; application procedures; fees; list of patent and trademark depository libraries.

Complete PTDL List. WEB. U.S. Department of Commerce. Patent and Trademark Office. <http://www.uspto.gov/go/ptdl/ptdlib_1.html>.

> Content: list of patent and trademark depository libraries by state.

Attorneys and Agents Registered to Practice Before the U.S. Patent and Trademark Office. MF. WEB. U.S. Department of Commerce. Patent and Trademark Office. C21.9/2: Item 0262-A. <http://www.uspto.gov/web/offices/dcom/olia/oed/roster/>.

> Content: attorneys and agents licensed to represent inventors before the Patent and Trademark Office.

U.S. Patent and Trademark Office Products and Service Catalog. PRINT. WEB. (annual) 1997–. U.S. Department of Commerce. Patent and Trademark Office. Information Dissemination Organizations. C 21.30: Item 0254-B-01. <http://www.uspto.gov/web/offices/ac/ido/oeip/catalog/index.html>; <http://purl.access.gpo.gov/GPO/LPS574>.

> Content: listing of patent and trademark products and services in all formats including Web and FTP; prices and ordering information.

Basic Facts About Trademarks. PRINT. WEB. (irregular) U.S. Department of Commerce. Patent and Trademark Office. C 21.2:T 67/4/. Item 0254. GPO. <http://www.uspto.gov/web/offices/tac/doc/basic/>.

> Content: definitions, application procedures, fees, and forms.

United States Patent and Trademark Office Web Site. WEB. U.S. Department of Commerce. Patent and Trademark Office. <http://www.uspto.gov/>.

> Content: general information on patents and trademarks; databases; printable forms; fee information; online ordering of patents and trademarks; agency information and news.

Discussion

General Information Concerning Patents is the basic government guide to patent information. It explains what a patent is, types of patents, what can be patented, and the rights of a patent holder. There is a discussion of the application format, process, review procedure, and information on who may apply. Also covered are the major publications of the office, the use of the Patent and Trademark Office's Search Room, patent depository libraries, patent attorneys and agents, and fees.

The *Complete PTDL List* is a Web version of the list that is also available in *General Information Concerning Patents.* Libraries are listed by state. Information includes the city, library name, telephone number, and a link to the library's Web site.

The preparation and presentation of a patent application requires knowledge of patent law and Patent and Trademark Office practices. Most inventors will require the assistance of a patent attorney or agent. *Attorneys and Agents Registered to Practice Before the U.S. Patent and Trademark Office* is a directory of authorized attorneys and agents. Part 1 is an alphabetical listing by name, with city and state information. Part 2 is a geographical listing by state with more complete address and telephone information. A Web database is also available. It may be searched by keyword, such as name or city. A list by state can also be displayed. Information includes name, address, telephone, registration number, and whether the person is an attorney or agent.

The *U.S. Patent and Trademark Office Products and Service Catalog* provides an overall guide to patent and trademark resources. The *Catalog* contains general information on contacting the agency, obtaining copies of patents and trademarks, patent and trademark depository libraries, and agency search facilities. Separate sections on patent products and trademark products describe each product, providing complete information on formats and how each may be obtained, including Web availability.

Basic Facts About Trademarks is the basic guide to trademarks. It covers the definition of a trademark, establishing trademark rights, maintaining a registration, the application process, and fees. Sample applications are also included.

The *U.S. Patent and Trademark Office Web Site* offers patent and trademark information and databases, including all of the resources listed in this section. Select either "Patents" or "Trademarks" from the main menu to view a list of resources in each area. The "Independent Inventor Resources" option provides basic information for inventors on such questions as "What can and cannot be patented?" "How do I know if my invention is patentable?" and "Do I need to hire a lawyer or agent?" Other main menu items include "Searchable Databases," "Printable Forms," "Order Copies," and "Fee Information."

PATENT CLASSIFICATION GUIDES
Checklist

Index to the U.S. Patent Classification System. PRINT. WEB. (annual) U.S. Department of Commerce. Patent and Trademark Office. C 21.12/2: Item 0257. GPO. <http://www.uspto.gov/web/offices/ac/ido/oeip/taf/c_index/index.htm>.
> Content: alphabetical index to the classes and subclasses of the patent classification system.

Manual of Classification. PRINT. WEB. (loose-leaf, updated with semiannual transmittals) U.S. Department of Commerce. Patent and Trademark Office. Search and Information Resources. C 21.12: Item 0258. GPO. <http://www.uspto.gov/web/offices/ac/ido/oeip/taf/moc/index.htm>.
> Content: numerical list of all class and subclass numbers in the patent classification system with descriptive titles.

Patent Classification Definitions. MF. WEB. (irregular) U.S. Department of Commerce. Patent and Trademark Office. Documentation Organizations. C 21.3/2: Item 0252-A. GPO. <http://www.uspto.gov/web/offices/ac/ido/oeip/taf/def/index.htm>.
> Content: detailed definitions of classes.

Patents ASSIST. DVD-ROM. (quarterly) U.S. Department of Commerce. Patent and Trademark Office. Office for Patent and Trademark Information. C 21.31/5: Item 0154-H-06.
> Content: full text of patent search tools; includes *Index to the U.S. Patent Classification System, Manual of Classification,* and *Patent Classification Definitions.*

Discussion

These titles provide access to the patent classification system at increasing levels of complexity. Any attempt to locate patents by subject area must begin with the identification of a general class and a more specific subclass within this system. The classification system is based on the use or function of the invention involved. There are more than 400 broad classes and more than 200,000 subclasses. The classification system is continuously revised and updated.

The *Index to the U.S. Patent Classification System* is the best source to use to begin this process. The *Index* is a guide to the classification system as published in the *Manual of Classification.* Subject headings include keywords, product terms, and commonly used words that are easier to work with than the functional terminology used in the classification itself. There is an alphabetical listing of main classes at the beginning, which serves as an overview of the classification system. *Index* entries identify a class and usually a subclass. A plus sign after the subclass means all subclasses indented under the named subclass are also relevant. Figure 50.1 shows that the class for nursing bottle supports is 248, and the subclass is 102 and its subentries in the *Manual.* All possible terms should be checked in the *Index.* A complete patent search usually involves the identification of several possible classes and subclasses, as patents are often assigned more than one class. The "original classification" is based on the primary function. "Cross reference" classifications cover additional functions. All are equally important, and all must be searched.

The *Manual of Classification* provides a more detailed look at the subclasses and gives a better idea of the subject coverage of each one. Once the *Index* provides an entry point, the *Manual* should be consulted to confirm the exact classes. Figure 50.2 shows a page from class 248, Supports, the class identified from the *Index* above. Subclass 102 is for nursing bottles, with further delineation of particular types in subclasses 103 to 107.

For further assistance in determining the proper class or subclass of a patent, *Patent Classification Definitions* (arranged by class number) should be consulted. Definitions cover the scope of each class, what is included and excluded, and referrals to related classes and subclasses. Each subclass is also defined.

All of these sources are available on the *Patent and Trademark Office Web site.* The Web version of the *Index to the U.S. Patent Classification System* includes links to the *Manual of Classification* entries. The *Manual of Classification* entries link to the *Patent Classification Definitions.* These titles are also included on the *Patents ASSIST* DVD. Some of the sources listed in the "Commercial Patent Databases" section also include electronic versions of some of these titles.

PATENT SEARCH SOURCES
Checklist

Patents BIB and Patents SNAP. DVD-ROM. (bimonthly) 1969–. U.S. Department of Commerce. Patent and Trademark Office. Office for Patent and Trademark Information. C 21.31/16: (Earlier, C 21.31/2:) Item 0154-H-01.
> Content: bibliographic information for utility patents from 1969 and for other types of patents from 1977; patent title; current classifications; assignee at time of issue; date of issue; state/country of first listed inventor's residence; status; patent image locations on *USAPAT* CDs since 1994; patent abstracts; concordance of application serial numbers to U.S. patent numbers.

Patents CLASS. DVD-ROM. (bimonthly) 1790–. U.S. Department of Commerce. Patent and Trademark Office. Office for Patent and Trademark Information. C 21.31/3: Item 0154-H-04.
> Content: current classifications for all patents; produces list of all patents in a class and subclass; identifies class and subclass of a particular patent number.

Booster		INDEX TO CLASSIFICATION			Bowl	
	Class	Subclass			Class	Subclass

Booster

	Class	Subclass
Booster fluid in conveyor	406	93
Brakes, anti-lock type valve system	303	113.1+
For tilting dump vehicle	298	19 B
Boot (See Shoes)	36	
Anti-slipping devices	36	59 R+
Design	D02	962
Design, protective	D30	146+
Blowout	152	367
Cleaner and cleaning	15	
Demonstration devices	434	397
Foot elevators	36	81
Footwear	36	
Hook	D02	643
Horse	54	82
Design	D30	146+
Jack	223	114+
Design	D02	642
Laces	24	712+
Design	D02	978
Making	12	
Forms	12	128 R+
Heel machines	12	42 R+
Jigging	12	DIG. 3
Lasting machines	12	7+
Dash pots	12	DIG. 2
Fluid activated	12	DIG. 1
Processes	12	142 R+
Sole machines	12	17 R+
Toe and heel stiffening	12	61 R+
Tools	12	103+
Upper machines	12	51+
Welt and rand machines	12	67 R+
Mold	425	119
Mold	425	393
Polish	106	3+
Protectors	36	72 R+
Putting on or removing	223	113+
Design	D02	641+
Quarter boots	D30	146+
Rack	211	34+
Retaining	36	58.5+
Riding	36	131
Shoe covering	D02	909+
Ski	36	117.1+
Sole gauges	33	3 R
Tree holders	12	123.5
Treeing machines	12	53.2
Vehicle body	296	76
Booth	52	261+
Article supporting	52	27+
Collapsible	52	64+
Design	D25	16
Guard	109	9
Illuminated	52	28
Ordnance shield type	89	36.14
Spray coating	118	300+
Ventilated spray booth	454	50+
Spray washing	134	
Bootstrap Amplifier	330	156
Boranes	423	294
Explosive compositions	149	22
Organo boranes	568	1+
Borate Esters	558	286+
Borax	423	277+
Recovery	423	179
Borders		
Coating	427	284
Coping for vertical structures	52	300
Earth supported	52	102
Garden	47	33
Printing elements for	101	400
Borehole Exploration		
Compressional wave type	367	86
Core permeability testing	73	38
Earth boring combined	175	40+
Formation logging	73	152.02
Inclinometer	33	304+
Ore detection electric	568	1+
Seismic acoustical	181	
Sounding	33	713+
Test electric	324	323+
Borescope		
Optical (incl	356	241.1+
Boring (See Auger; Bit)		
Bar	408	199+
Drilling and	408	
Earth	175	
Measuring & testing during boring	73	152.42+
Earth boring compositions	507	100+
Embroidering machine	112	89

	Class	Subclass
Pattern controlled	112	85
Head	408	199+
Lathe drill holders	408	238+
Metal cutters rotary	407	103+
Wood	408	
Augers	408	199+
Borneol	568	820
Boron and Compounds		
Acid and acid anhydride	423	277
Binary compounds	423	276+
Borates	423	
Carbide	423	291
Carbocyclic or acyclic compounds	568	1+
Cleaning or detergents compositions containing	510	345
Cleaning or detergents compositions containing	510	465
Elemental	423	298
Esters containing	423	277
Explosive or thermic composition containing	149	22
Fuels containing	44	314+
Nuclear fuel containing	252	636+
Bosom Shirt	2	118+
Machine	223	2+
Botany	47	
Bottle (See Carboy; Receptacles)	215	
Advertising indicia	40	310+
Design	D20	37
Atomizer	215	91.1
Attachments	215	386+
Baby bottle warmer	D07	326
Bail stopper bottle filling apparatus	53	265
Breakers	241	99
Brushes internal	15	164+
Cap seal	425	809*
Capping	53	287+
Caps	215	316+
Case or holder	206	139
Design	D09	455
Cleaning	15	
Filling combined	141	85+
Liquid contact	134	
Processes	134	
Closures	215	200+
Cap type	215	316+
Childproof	215	201+
Content indicating	215	365+
Cooled receptacle for	62	457.4
Liquid contacting bottle	62	373+
Cooler of inverted bottle type	165	132
Design	D09	
Dispensers	221	92+
Dispensing from	222	
Dynamic dispensing means	D09	300
Filling	141	
Inspection optical	356	239.4+
inspection optical	356	240.1
With rotation	356	428
Making		
Glass	65	
Molding and label applying	425	500+
Plastic	425	522+
Nursing	215	11.1+
Design	D24	197+
Nipple appliers	29	235.5
Openers		
Cap combined	215	228
Design	D08	33+
Hand manipulated types	81	3.07+
Mounts or supports	81	3.25+
Non manual operation	81	3.2
Other tools combined	7	151+
Plural or combined	81	3.09+
Stopper combined	215	228
Stopper removal facilitated	215	295+
Pressurized	D09	300
Pull stopper bottle filling apparatus	53	264
Rack supports for	211	74+
Shape	215	400
Nesting	215	10
Siphon bottle filling apparatus	141	14+
Stand, rack or tray for	D07	701+
Sterilizer	219	429+
Stoppers or plugs	215	355+
Supports for nursing	248	102+
Tap		
Cutter and or punch	222	80+
Thermos t m	215	12.1+
Warmer	126	261+
Chemical reaction	126	263.01+

	Class	Subclass
Electric	219	429+
Wipers internal	15	211+
Wrapper for	229	89+
Bougie Surgical	606	191+
Medicator, soluble	604	288
Methods of introducing	604	514+
Bouillon Cube	426	589
Meat containing	426	641+
Bouquet		
Imitation	428	17+
Supports	248	27.8
For personal wear	24	5+
For personal wear design	D02	624+
With holder	428	23
Bourdon Tube		
Gauge fluid pressure	73	732+
Making	29	890.14
Switch electric	200	81.8
Thermometer	374	203
Boutonniere	D11	117+
Bow	124	23.1
Apparel trim	2	244+
Making	223	46
Arrow projector	124	23.1+
Carrier for bow or arrow	224	916*
Compound	124	23.1
Pulley	124	900*
Decorative	428	4+
Dental bite impression device	433	44
Design	D22	107
Garment support combined	2	300
Hair ribbon fastener	132	275
Land vehicle top	296	98
Necktie	2	144+
Design	D02	606
Ox	54	77
Piano	84	256+
Ribbon	132	275
Saws	30	507+
Sight	33	265
String on bridge truss	14	9+
Thrusters, ship	114	151
Violin	84	282
Guides	84	283
Bow Tie	D02	606
Bowden Wire (See Shaft, Flexible)	74	500.5+
Link and lever system combined	74	500.5+
Mechanical movement combined	74	82
Bowling	8	139
Bowl (See Basin; Pot; Receptacles)		
Arenas	472	92+
Basins	4	619+
Closet		
Closures	4	253
Covers	4	234+
Disinfection	4	222+
Drip catcher	4	251.1
Obstruction remover	4	255.01
Support, coupling, seal or	4	252.1+
Ventilation	4	216
Compartment	D07	555
Dry closet	4	420+
Fish	D30	101+
Household article	D07	500+
Kitchen	220	
Lamp	362	154+
Reflector	362	341+
Lavatory	4	650+
Nut bowl	D07	500+
Railway amusement ride	104	68
Roundabouts	472	40+
Separator, imperforate bowl centrifugal	494	43+
Shaving	220	
Smoking pipe	131	226
Cleaners	131	246
Detachable from neck cup	131	222
Detachable from neck cup smoke treating type	131	214
Feeder	131	180
Lined or coated	131	220
Lined or coated material traps	131	204
Reversible	131	221
Spaced inner bowl	131	196
Storage means	131	180
Water closet		
Bowl	4	420+
Design	D23	295+
Plunger	4	420+
Seat combined	4	234+
Side receptacle	4	341+

24

Source: Index to the U.S. Patent Classification System, December 1998, p. 24.

Figure 50.1: Sample Page from *Index to the U.S. Patent Classification System*.

248-4

CLASS 248   SUPPORTS

DECEMBER 1996

	HOSE AND/OR NOZZLE TYPE
89	.Racks
90	..Folded hose
91	...Link supported
92	....Swinging or folding link
93	.....Simultaneously movable
94	STRAINER OR FUNNEL TYPE
95	BAG HOLDERS
96	.Golf bag
97	.Stands
98	..Wheeled
99	.Mouth holding frames
100	..Prong or hook type
101	..With clamp
102	NURSING BOTTLE TYPE
103	.Bracket
104	..Flexible
105	.Stands
106	..Adjustable
107	..Of wire
108	PASTE TUBE TYPE
109	.Stands
110	BRUSH AND BROOM
111	.Socket type
112	..Of wire
113	.Clasp type
114	WATCH AND CLOCK
115	.Brackets
116	.Stands
117.1	FLATIRON OR SOLDERING IRON
117.2	.Stand or base
117.3	..Insulated
117.4	...With clamp or hold-down
117.5	..Inverted
117.6	..With clamp or hold-down
117.7	.With clamp or hold-down
118	ARMREST OR HEADREST
118.1	.Armrest for writer
118.3	..Adjustable height
118.5	..Traveling
121	STAND AND BRACKET
122.1	.Having adjustable bracket
123.11	..Counterbalanced
123.2	...Via a counterweight
124.1	..Vertically and horizontally
124.2	...Via a single device (e.g., one two-way clamp)
125.1	..Vertically
125.2	...Bracket moved by mechanical operator (e.g., spring, threaded shaft, pulley and rope)
125.3	...In fixed increments
125.7	..Bracket specifically designed to rotate about a stand vertical axis
125.8	.Having vertically adjustable stand (e.g., telescoping rods)
125.9	..And bracket rotatable
126	STAND OR BRACKET ALTERNATIVE
127	STAND
	.Receptacle
128	..Movable receptacle
129	...Wheeled

130	...Rotating, horizontal axis
131	...Rotating, vertical axis
132	...Vertically
133	...Tilting
134	....Closure operating
135	....Casing and support convertible
136	....With foldable stand
137	....With axis intersecting receptacle
138	....Double horizontal axis
139	....Tilting cradle
140	.....With tilting or latch means
141	.....Axis intersecting receptacle
142	......With tilting or latch means
143	....Rocker stand
144	...Swinging base
145	...Swinging about a vertical standard
145.3	...Inverted receptacle pickup
145.6	...Handle
146	..Stationary receptacle
147	...With closure operator
148	...For sloping surface
149	...Adjustable
150	...Knockdown or folding
151	...Attached and detachable legs
152	...Of sheet material
153	...Of wire
154	...With clamp or hold-down
155	.Convertible to cane
155.1	..Handle becomes support surface
155.2	..Radially hinged support arms
155.3	...Slidable extensor
155.4	..Foldable or detachable longitudinal sections
155.5	..Intermediately pivoted sections
156	.Ground inserted
370	.Stand-mounted depending links carry support surface
371	.Tilting support surface
372.1	..Biased
393	..With incremental horizontal adjustment
394	...Ends raised differentially
395	...Concurrent with tilting
396	...Ends raised differentially
397	..With incremental adjustment about fixed horizontal pivot
398	..Tiltable with understructure
158	.Standard type
160	..Flexible
161	..Adjustable vertically
162.1	...Counterbalanced
404	...With force multiplying means
405	....Screw and nut
406.1	.....With rotation prevention disabler
406.2	......Weight or load responsive
407	...Notch or cavity engaging latch
408	....Biased latch
409	.....Support carried release
410	...Canted clutch collar
411	...Settable clamp
412	....Wedge actuated
413	....Set screw actuated

Source: Manual of Classification, December 1996, p. 248-3.

Figure 50.2: Sample Page from *Manual of Classification*.

Patents ASSIST. DVD-ROM. (quarterly) U.S. Department of Commerce. Patent and Trademark Office. Office for Patent and Trademark Information. C 21.31/5: Item 0154-H-06.

> Content: full text of patent search tools; includes *Index to the U.S. Patent Classification System, Manual of Classification, Patent Classification Definitions, Attorneys and Agents Registered to Practice Before the U.S. Patent and Trademark Office, U.S. Patent and Trademark Office Products and Service Catalog,* a Patentee-Assignee Index, and other tools.

Patents ASSIGN and Trademarks ASSIGN. DVD-ROM. (bi-monthly) U.S. Department of Commerce. Patent and Trademark Office. Office for Patent and Trademark Information. C 21.31/13: (Earlier, C 21.31/4:, C 21.31/9:) Item 0154-H-02.

> Content: patent assignments recorded since August 1980.

USPTO Web Patent Databases. WEB. U.S. Department of Commerce. Patent and Trademark Office. <http://www.uspto.gov/patft/index.html>.

> Content: full-text and bibliographic patent databases from 1976.

IBM Intellectual Property Network. WEB. IBM. <http://www.patents.ibm.com/>.

> Content: bibliographic patent database from 1971; full-text images from 1974.

Automated Patent System (APS). (weekly) U.S. Department of Commerce. Patent and Trademark Office.

> Content: text and image databases; text database contains full-text of patents since 1971 with sophisticated search options; image database contains all patent images since 1790; available only at the Patent and Trademark Office and selected Patent and Trademark Depository Libraries.

Index of Patents Issued from the United States Patent and Trademark Office. PRINT. MF. (annual) 1920–. U.S. Department of Commerce. Patent and Trademark Office. C 21.5/2: (Earlier, C 21.1/1:; I 23.1/1:) (Before 1920, issued in *Annual Report of the Commissioner of Patents*) Items 0255-A or -B(MF). GPO.

> Content: list of patent numbers by class and subclass; name index of patentees and assignees.

Official Gazette of the United States Patent and Trademark Office: Patents. PRINT. MF. (weekly) 1872–. U.S. Department of Commerce. Patent and Trademark Office. C 21.5: (Earlier, I 23.8:) (Title varies) Items 0260-A or -B(MF). GPO.

> Content: indexes by patentee and class; abstracts of all patents issued each week.

Discussion

Once the classification and subclass numbers have been determined, the above sources can be used to find actual patent numbers assigned to the class/subclass. Several of these sources provide other searching options as well.

Patents BIB and Patents SNAP, Patents CLASS, Patents ASSIST, and *Patents ASSIGN and Trademarks ASSIGN* are part of the Patent and Trademark Office's *CASSIS* (Classification and Search Support Information System) CD-ROM/DVD-ROM series, a comprehensive set of patent and trademark information tools. The Patent and Trademark Office is in the midst of a transition from CD-ROM to DVD-ROM. Some previous CD titles will be combined and coverage on some may be extended. Descriptions in this chapter are based on preliminary information.

Patents BIB and *Patents CLASS* can both be searched by class and subclass. Although *Patents BIB* does not cover as great a time span, it provides more extensive information. It contains bibliographic information on patents since 1969 and patent abstracts that make this a useful next step for a subject search. The CD-ROM version contains abstracts for the most recent two and one-half years. The DVD-ROM version will contain abstracts since 1988.

Reviewing other classification codes assigned and abstracts, when available, can help in determining the most relevant classifications. To complete the list of patent numbers for a particular class/subclass for the time period before 1969, use *Patents CLASS.* Figure 50.3 shows the list of patent numbers under class 248, subclass 102 from *Patents CLASS.* If a patent in the subject area is already known, either of these titles can identify that patent's classification codes. These can then be used to generate lists of other patents. The Patent and Trademark Office will also provide a list of patents in specified classes and subclasses for a small fee. Consult *U.S. Patent and Trademark Office Products and Service Catalog* for more information. For information on how to locate abstracts and complete patents for patent numbers found, see the "Patents: Abstracts and Texts" section.

The *USPTO Web Patent Databases* site consists of a full-text database and a bibliographic database. Both of these can also be searched by class/subclass, but do not go back as far as *Patents BIB* and *Patents CLASS.* The bibliographic database contains current classifications that reflect all classification changes. The classifications in the full-text database have not been updated and are the original classifications at time of issue. Full-text and images are also accessible from the bibliographic database by clicking on individual patent numbers in the search results. An additional TIFF plug-in is required, however, to view images.

The *IBM Intellectual Property Network* Web database allows searching or browsing by class and provides the full text and images. Although originating from a commercial source, it is listed in this category because it is a major database offered at no charge. As with the *USPTO Web Patent Databases* this database does not go back as far as *Patents BIB* and *Patents CLASS.*

The *Automated Patent System (APS)* is the Patent and Trademark Office's own automated system. It is available at the Patent and Trademark Office Search Facilities in Arlington, VA and at selected Patent and Trademark Depository Libraries. Several patent depository libraries have access to the text database, but the image database is accessible only from a smaller number of partnership sites. A list of patent depository libraries and their capabilities is available in many agency publications, including *General*

```
Classification: 248/102     ORs: 103      XRs: 101       Total: 204

5873551 O 5871184 O 5820084 O 5794898 O 5769367 O 5765225 X 5727842 X
5711500 O 5707031 X 5702039 X 5685447 X 5664745 X 5624090 O 5613657 O
5582335 X 5573153 X 5513885 X 5459903 X 5456432 O 5421496 X 5217192 O
5188320 X 5183229 O 5178291 X 5116275 X 5072843 X 4984697 X 4953816 O
4951997 X 4946119 O 4943017 O 4941579 X 4932566 X 4902261 X 4895327 O
4869381 X 4865239 X 4809938 O 4799636 O 4776546 O 4759963 X 4754903 X
4750696 O 4726551 O 4723801 X 4722713 X 4718623 O 4655715 X 4630793 O
4564957 X 4513935 X 4498613 X 4473907 X 4416438 O 4405106 O 4315654 X
4296902 O 4227270 X 4220302 O 4121797 O 4101042 X 4096977 X 4062510 O
4050600 X 3978610 X 3977638 O 3905571 O 3850393 O 3773287 O 3635430 O
3543976 X 3424547 X 3365153 O 3332563 X 3197099 X 3165219 X 3163194 X
3157303 X 3144230 O 3143374 X 3125984 X 3125484 X 3117759 X 3085612 X
3081895 X 3065944 O 3058708 O 3039159 X 3016221 O 2991032 X 2955382 X
2953337 O 2893672 X 2880950 O 2815909 O 2789002 X 2785503 X 2772801 X
2764376 O 2761580 X 2755051 O 2739320 X 2733883 X 2711052 X 2673705 X
2651485 O 2637515 O 2631288 X 2628802 X 2579701 O 2577849 X 2529173 X
2526121 O 2522120 X 2518862 X 2517829 X 2514134 O 2511864 O 2510953 O
2500846 O 2494632 O 2490207 X 2485461 O 2470379 X 2465015 O 2462187 X
2428724 X 2409820 X 2402820 X 2399320 X 2389390 X 2362020 O 2359452 X
2353678 X 2311397 X 2310515 X 2303728 X 2267113 O 2214882 O 2199869 O
2182164 X 2134746 O 2111724 O 2096961 X 2084243 O 2060194 O 2050841 O
2033296 O 1900691 O 1863163 O 1826810 O 1778545 X 1750672 X 1749432 X
1723731 X 1669061 X 1635789 O 1634162 X 1630167 O 1617944 X 1617213 X
1567225 O 1559740 O 1520839 X 1509940 X 1501080 O 1464525 X 1454530 X
1439255 X 1438272 X 1429198 X 1375917 O 1369928 O 1336898 X 1325860 O
1301886 O 1292631 O 1287125 O 1281948 O 1192170 O 1188904 X 1187845 O
1136529 O 1030744 O 1014004 O 1013221 O 0997614 O 0978892 X 0936293 O
0871622 O 0815815 O 0814574 O 0788859 O 0784914 X 0783423 O 0747025 X
0717995 O 0712184 O 0651647 O 0608053 O 0602991 O 0546033 O 0530435 O
0485098 X
```

Source: Patents CLASS, April 1999.

Figure 50.3: Sample Patent Classification and Subclass Listing.

Information Concerning Patents and other titles in the "General Information" section of this chapter.

The *Index of Patents Issued from the United States Patent and Trademark Office* has two parts: "List of Patentees" and "Index to Subjects of Inventions." Part 2, "Index to Subjects of Inventions" is the class number index. As with the preceding sources, patent numbers are listed under each class and subclass. There are two major disadvantages to using this index. First, each year must be searched individually. There may be many years in which no patents are issued in a given subclass. Second, patents will be listed as originally classed. The classification system has changed considerably over the years. Classes and subclasses identified from current sources may be different from those used in earlier years. The other sources in this section are updated to eliminate this problem.

To update the *CASSIS* DVDs and the *Index of Patents*, check current issues of the *Official Gazette of the United States Patent and Trademark Office: Patents*. There is a classification index in the back of each issue covering the patents for that week.

Many of the sources in this section can be used for other types of searches besides the subject search by class and subclass. *Patents BIB*, *USPTO Web Patent Databases*, and *IBM Intellectual Property Network* databases can search many patent fields by word. *Patents BIB* is limited to bibliographic fields and abstracts. The *USPTO Web Patent Databases* can search full text and specific fields such as the abstract, claims, and description/specification fields. *IBM Intellectual Property Network* can search the abstract, claims fields, and full text. Word searching can be useful for identifying classification codes, but only a classification search will locate all relevant patents. Other elements or fields of a patent are also searchable including patent number, patentee (inventor), and assignee. The assignee is the company or party to whom the inventor assigns the right to use the patent.

Other sources for patentee or assignee information include *Patents ASSIST* and *Patents ASSIGN and Trademarks ASSIGN*. *Patents ASSIST* includes a patentee-assignee index based on the assignee at time of issue. Assignee information is available for utility patents since 1969 and other patents since 1977. Patentee information is included since 1975. The index can be searched by patent number, assignment type, assignee name, inventor name, and inventor address. *Patents ASSIGN and Trademarks ASSIGN* includes patent assignments recorded at the Patent and Trademark Office after August 1980, both initially and later reassignments. This index can be searched by assignee name, assignor name, and patent number.

The *Index of Patents Issued from the United States Patent and Trademark Office*, Part 1, "List of Patentees," is an alphabetical name index of inventors and assignees at the time of issue. To update this annual index, check the weekly issues of the *Official Gazette*. Each *Official Gazette* issue contains a patentee index.

Many commercial online services and database vendors offer fee-based patent databases. See the "Commercial Patent Databases" section of this chapter for more information on these.

PATENTS: ABSTRACTS AND TEXTS
Checklist

Official Gazette of the United States Patent and Trademark Office: Patents. PRINT. MF. (weekly) 1872–. U.S. Department of Commerce. Patent and Trademark Office. C 21.5: (Earlier, I 23.8:) (Title varies) Items 0260-A or -B(MF). GPO.
> Content: abstracts of all patents issued each week; indexes by patentee and class.

USAPAT: Facsimile Images of United States Patents. DVD-ROM. (weekly) 1994–. U.S. Department of Commerce. Patent and Trademark Office. Office for Patent and Trademark Information. C 21.31: Item 260-E.
> Content: full patent images.

USPTO Web Patent Databases. WEB. U.S. Department of Commerce. Patent and Trademark Office. <http://www.uspto.gov/patft/index.html>.
> Content: full-text of patents from 1976.

IBM Intellectual Property Network. WEB. IBM. <http://www.patents.ibm.com/>.
> Content: full-text patent images from 1974.

Discussion

Once a patent number has been identified, it can be used to locate an abstract or summary of the patent or copies of the actual patent. The abstracts, found in the *Official Gazette*, are a good starting point. The abstract can assist in determining which patents are the most relevant. Each issue of the *Official Gazette* groups abstracts of utility patents granted that week into three categories: general and mechanical, chemical, and electrical. There are also sections for plant and design patents. The overall arrangement is by patent number.

Each abstract is identified by the patent number and contains basic information, including the patent title, name and address of the patent holder, date filed, class and subclass, a drawing, and a brief description. The abstract for patent 4,296,902, identified through the earlier subject search example on nursing bottle supports, is shown in Figure 50.4. Each issue of the *Official Gazette* also contains notices; reissue patents, which involve corrections to previous patents; reexaminations involving questions of legitimacy of particular patents; and indexes by patentee, classification, and geographical residence of inventors.

Complete patents can be obtained in several ways. Patent depository libraries maintain backfiles of patents on microfilm. The extent of the backfiles varies from library to library. Many patent depository libraries also offer fee-based delivery services. The *Official Gazette* lists patent depository libraries, as do several of the sources in the "General Information" section of this chapter.

The *USAPAT* DVD-ROM contains complete patents since 1994. These are in the form of page images and are not searchable. Patents are retrievable by a document number available from a cumulative index on the disc or from *Patents BIB*. The Patent and Trademark Office is also issuing backfiles for this title covering all patents from 1790. *USPTO Web Patent Databases* contains a full-text database of patents since 1976. The *IBM Intellectual Property Network* Web site has full images since 1974.

Patents can also be ordered directly from the Patent and Trademark Office (present cost as of this printing is $3.00 for a utility patent). Ordering information is on the first page of any *Official Gazette* issue and can also be found in the *U.S. Patent and Trademark Office Products and Services Catalog* and on the *U.S. Patent and Trademark Office Web Site* listed in the "General Information" section of this chapter. Ordering can also be done through the Web site. Many commercial vendors and online services offer full-text patents or patent delivery services, including the *IBM Intellectual Property Network* Web site. See the "Commercial Patent Databases" section of this chapter for more information.

COMMERCIAL PATENT DATABASES
Checklist
Web Sites

Chemical Patents Plus. WEB. 1975–. Chemical Abstracts Service. <http://casweb.cas.org/chempatplus/>.
> Content: full-text of all patents from 1975; partial coverage 1971–1974; complete patent page images from 1995; free searching and viewing of patent title and abstract; registration required; viewing of other fields, full-text, and chemical structures for a fee.

PatentWeb. WEB. MicroPatent. <http://www.micropat.com/0/patentweb9809.html>.
> Content: search full-text and bibliographic information, 1976-; download complete patents, 1964–.

PatentMiner. WEB. Manning & Napier Information Services. <https://www.patentminer.com/LIVE/cgi-bin/pm.cgi?zzz=www.patents.ibm.com>.
> Content: free search of bibliographic information from 1971; view full-text or download PDF versions of patents from 1974 at no charge; registration required; search full-text from 1974 and obtain PDF patent copies from 1790 for a fee.

sageway for boundary layer air on an aircraft having a laminar flow control means comprising:

- a removable cover plate having an upper and a lower surface; and
- a pair of sidewall members each including an upper surface removably bonded to the lower surface of said cover plate with a first adhesive and spaced apart a predetermined

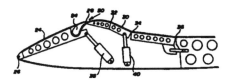

distance so as to form a continuous longitudinal slot of uniform width therebetween for passage of boundary layer air to said laminar flow control means, said removable cover plate providing means for maintaining a fixed spacing between said sidewalls and having sufficient transverse rigidity for maintaining a coplanar relationship between the respective upper surfaces of said sidewalls.

4,296,900
AIRFOIL CONSTRUCTION
Kenneth M. Krall, Arlington, Tex., assignor to Vought Corporation, Dallas, Tex.
Filed Apr. 23, 1979, Ser. No. 32,438
Int. Cl.³ B64C 3/48
U.S. Cl. 244—219   4 Claims

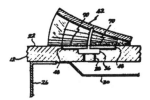

1. An airfoil construction, comprising:

(a) upper and lower surface structure which connects leading and trailing edges so as to form a relatively thin profile which is adapted to foster high speed flight, with one portion of the upper surface structure being pivotable upward about a hinge line that coincides generally with the leading edge of the airfoil, for increasing the thickness of the airfoil, and the chordwise length of said pivotable portion being substantially less than the chord length;

(b) a connecting section which forms part of the airfoil upper surface structure immediately aft of the pivotable portion, and said section being positionable for presenting a substantially continuous and rigid surface to the air moving over the upper surface structure during such times as the pivotable portion is being pivoted upward and downward, and the connecting section cooperating with the remainder of the airfoil upper surface when the connecting section is lowered to establish an elongated convex cross section for high speed fight, and the connecting section also cooperating with the remainder of the airfoil upper surface when the connecting section is fully raised to establish a compound curvature having both concave and convex portions for fostering low speed flight;

(c) a rearwardly directed nozzle located adjacent the aft edge of the pivotable portion and oriented such that it can discharge a gaseous fluid over the connecting section;

(d) a source of pressurized fluid adapted to be connected with said nozzle; and

(e) control means for adjusting the discharge of fluid from said source over the connecting section.

4,296,901
TRANSPORTATION SYSTEMS
Francis C. Perrott, The Manor House, South Cerney, Cirencester, Gloucestershire, England
Filed Jan. 2, 1980, Ser. No. 109,182
Claims priority, application United Kingdom, Jan. 2, 1979, 00046/79; Apr. 27, 1979, 14658/79; Sep. 29, 1979, 33865/79
Int. Cl.³ B61L 3/00
U.S. Cl. 246—167 R   12 Claims

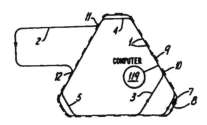

1. A transportation system comprising a track, driven vehicles movable along the track, and control means for generating control signals effectively defining a series of spaced control areas movable along the track, each control area being of such length as to be capable of accommodating a plurality of vehicles simultaneously, wherein each vehicle is provided with on-board detection means responsive to the control signals for maintaining the vehicle within the confines of a control area, and the control means includes vehicle closing means for sensing the presence of gaps between a plurality of vehicles confined within a single control area and for causing relative movement of said vehicle with respect to one another to close up the gaps.

4,296,902
BABY BOTTLE SUPPORT JIG
William G. Dachtler, 1021 Emory, Imperial Beach, Calif. 92032
Filed Sep. 10, 1979, Ser. No. 74,004
Int. Cl.³ A47D 15/00
U.S. Cl. 248—102   5 Claims

1. A baby bottle support jig comprising:

(a) a soft strap to loop over the head and pass behind the neck of a baby in a reclining position;

(b) a pair of substantially rigid support arms having ends lying alongside the opposite sides of the neck and being connected respectively to the ends of said strap, passing down in contact with the baby's chest, and extending to upper ends spaced from the baby's face and chest; and

(c) a bottle-holding cradle mounted to the upper ends of said support arms, whereby a baby bottle with the nipple thereof in the baby's mouth can be supported at its upper portion in said cradle.

Source: Official Gazette of the United States Patent and Trademark Office: Patents, v. 1011, no. 4, Oct. 27, 1981, p. 1473.

Figure 50.4: Sample Abstract from *Official Gazette of the United States Patent and Trademark Office: Patents.*

QPAT-US. WEB. 1974–. Questel/Orbit. <http://www.qpat.com/>.

>Content: search full-text; view text and images; free search of front page (bibliographic and abstract) information with registration.

U.S. Patents. WEB. 1975–. Community of Science. <http://patents.cos.com/>.

>Content: bibliographic database searchable by all fields; trace previous patents cited and subsequent citations to a specific patent; meta-database query to the *Manual of Classification*.

Online Information Providers

LEXIS-NEXIS. <http://www.lexis-nexis.com/lncc/>.

>Content: comprehensive online data provider; full-text of utility patents since 1975; partial coverage 1971–1974; full-text of design and plant patents since Dec. 1976; patent numbers by classification since 1790; *Manual of Classification*; *Index to the U.S. Patent Classification System.*

LEXIS-NEXIS Academic Universe. <http://www.lexis-nexis.com/cispubs/Catalog/Universe/Academic%20Universe/index.htm>.

>Content: full-text of utility patents since 1975; partial coverage 1971-1974; full-text of design and plant patents since Dec. 1976; patent numbers by classification since 1790; *Manual of Classification.*

Dialog. <http://www.dialog.com/>.

>Content: comprehensive online data provider; U.S. bibliographic and full-text patent databases; international databases.

Questel-Orbit. <http://www.questel.orbit.com/>.

>Content: comprehensive online data provider; more than 30 patent databases covering U.S. and international sources.

STN International. <http://www.cas.org/stn.html>.

>Content: comprehensive online data provider; U.S. bibliographic and full-text patent databases; international databases.

PATDATA. 1975–. Ovid Technologies.

>Content: bibliographic citations and abstracts for U.S. patents.

CD-ROMs

U.S. Patent Search+. CD-ROM. (monthly) 1975–. East Haven, CT: MicroPatent.

>Content: bibliographic information and abstracts; searchable on multiple fields.

U.S. FullText. CD-ROM. (monthly) 1975–. East Haven, CT: MicroPatent.

>Content: full-text patents; searchable by several fields.

U.S. PatentImages. CD-ROM. (weekly) 1964–. East Haven, CT: MicroPatent.

>Content: full-text patent images.

PatentBible. CD-ROM. (semiannual) East Haven, CT: MicroPatent.

>Content: full-text of *Manual of Classification, Index to the U.S. Patent Classification System, Classification Definitions*, and other patent tools.

OG+. CD-ROM. (weekly or monthly) 1990–. Alexandria, VA: Derwent Information.

>Content: full-text of the *Official Gazette*; bibliographic information and abstracts.

Discussion

Many fee-based commercial databases on patents are available. These may offer additional search enhancements, more historical information, and document delivery services. A selection of commercial Web sites are listed above. A few of the Web databases offer some free services.

Several online information service providers offer collections of databases, including patent databases, through online dial-up services and the Internet. *LEXIS-NEXIS* contains a patent library (LEXPAT) with the full-text of patents since 1971 (selected coverage from 1971-1974) and a classification number file listing patent numbers by classification. Other files cover plant and design patents, reexamination certificates, reissue patents, assignees, and the *Manual of Classification*. A related Web product, *LEXIS-NEXIS Academic Universe*, also includes the full-text of utility, plant, and design patents for the same time period, the classification number file, and the *Manual of Classification*.

Dialog patent databases include the IFI/Plenum Data Corporation *CLAIMS* databases. This set of databases covers bibliographical information on chemical patents since 1950, mechanical and electrical patents since 1963, and design and plant patents since December 1976. Companion databases cover reassignments and reexaminations, reference files such as the *Manual of Classification*, and a citation file for tracing cited and citing patent numbers. *Dialog* also offers full-text patent files since 1974, with partial coverage for 1971–1973. Other specialized and international patent files are also available.

Questel-Orbit, producer of the *QPAT-US* Web site, also offers the IFI/Plenum Data Corporation *CLAIMS* databases covering the classification system, patent listings by classification, bibliographic data searching, and reassignments. Derwent patent databases containing bibliographic data, text of claims, citation and class searching, and patent status information are also available. *Questel-Orbit* also offers international databases and specialized databases in selected subject areas.

STN International includes the IFI/Plenum *CLAIMS* databases and full-text U.S. patents since 1975, with partial coverage for 1971–1974, and page images from 1996. *STN* also offers international patent databases and specialized subject databases.

MicroPatent, producer of the *PatentWeb* Web site, also provides several patent CD-ROM products. Derwent offers the text of the *Official Gazette* on CD-ROM.

TRADEMARK SEARCH SOURCES
Checklist

U.S. Trademark Electronic Search System (TESS). WEB. U.S. Department of Commerce. Patent and Trademark Office. <http://www.uspto.gov/web/menu/tm.html>; <http://www.uspto.gov/web/menu/search.html>.
> Content: full-text of registered, pending, abandoned, cancelled, and expired trademarks with images, status history.

Trademarks REGISTERED and Trademarks PENDING. DVD-ROM. (bimonthly) 1884–. U.S. Department of Commerce. Patent and Trademark Office. Office for Patent and Trademark Information. C 21.31/14: (Earlier, C 21.31/7:, C 21.31/8:) Item 0154-H-03.
> Content: text of all registered trademarks; text of trademark applications filed but not yet approved; searchable by several fields including word mark, owner, class, and description of goods and services.

Patents ASSIGN and Trademarks ASSIGN. DVD-ROM. (bimonthly) U.S. Department of Commerce. Patent and Trademark Office. Office for Patent and Trademark Information. C 21.31/13: (Earlier, C 21.31/4:, C 21.31/9:) Item 0154-H-02.
> Content: trademark assignment records.

Trademarks ASSIST. DVD-ROM. (irregular) U.S. Department of Commerce. Patent and Trademark Office. Office for Patent and Trademark Information. C 21.31/10: Item 0154-H-05.
> Content: full-text of the *Trademark Manual of Examining Procedure*, the *Goods and Services Manual*, the *U.S. Patent and Trademark Office Products and Services Catalog*, and other trademark manuals and guides.

USAMark: Facsimile Images of Registered United States Trademarks. DVD-ROM. (monthly) 1870–. U.S. Department of Commerce. Patent and Trademark Office. Office for Patent and Trademark Information. C 21.31/11: Item 0260-E-01.
> Content: page images of U.S. registered trademarks.

Official Gazette of the United States Patent and Trademark Office: Trademarks. PRINT. MF. (weekly) 1971–. U.S. Department of Commerce. Patent and Trademark Office. C 21.5/4: (Title varies) (Formerly issued as part of *Official Gazette*, C 21.5:) Items 0260-C or -D(MF). GPO.
> Content: reproductions of trademarks requested; list of approved trademarks; registrants name index.

Index of Trademarks Issued from the United States Patent and Trademark Office. PRINT. MF. (annual) 1927–. U.S. Department of Commerce. Patent and Trademark Office. C 21.5/3: (Formerly included in *Annual Report of the Commissioner of Patents*, C 21.1/1:; I 23.1/1:) Items 0256-C or -D(MF). GPO.
> Content: name index of companies or organizations receiving trademarks.

Acceptable Identification of Goods and Services Manual. PRINT. WEB. 1997–. (loose-leaf) U.S. Department of Commerce. Patent and Trademark Office. C 21.14/2:G 62. Item 0254-A. GPO. <http://www.uspto.gov/web/offices/tac/doc/gsmanual/>.
> Content: list and definition of classes in the International Classification system; alphabetical and class listing of goods and services.

Discussion

The *U.S. Trademark Electronic Search System (TESS)* contains the full-text, images, and status history for registered, pending, and inactive trademarks. The database is updated daily, Tuesday through Saturday. Search options include a structured search form, free form search for advanced users, and a browse dictionary. The structured search form allows users to enter a search term, to select specific fields to search from a list (or select all fields), and to select Boolean and other logical operators from a list. The browse dictionary option lists terms in a dictionary display that shows similar nearby words and the number of occurrences of each term. Information for each trademark includes image (if available), word mark, goods and services category, mark drawing code, serial number, filing date, owner, and whether live or dead. A "check status" link shows current status, date of status, *Official Gazette* publication date, and prosecution history (if any).

Trademarks REGISTERED and Trademarks PENDING is the DVD-ROM version of the Patent and Trademark Office's trademark database. The Patent and Trademark Office is in the midst of a transition from CD-ROM to DVD-ROM. The descriptions in this chapter are based on preliminary information. The *Trademarks REGISTERED and Trademarks PENDING* DVD also contains the full text of registered trademarks and pending applications. It is searchable by several fields including word mark, mark combined search, design search code, owner, class, and description of goods and services. The Patent and Trademark Office also plans to include expired, cancelled, and abandoned trademarks on the DVD version.

Patents ASSIGN and Trademarks ASSIGN contains assignment records for trademarks. Records are searchable by several fields including word, assignee, assignor, and registration number.

The *Trademarks ASSIST* DVD contains the text of procedure manuals on the trademark application and appeals process. Also included is the *Goods and Services Manual*, which lists goods and services alphabetically and by classification. This title may be combined with *Trademarks REGISTERED and Trademarks PENDING* when issued on DVD.

USAMark contains facsimile page images of registered trademarks.

The *Official Gazette of the United States Patent and Trademark Office: Trademarks* publishes trademark requests "for opposition," giving persons an opportunity to file objections to particular trademarks before they are issued. Although it does not list all marks that are in pending applications, it can be used to some extent as an update to the *USPTO Web Trademark Database* and the *Trademarks REGISTERED and Trademarks PENDING* DVD. Trademark requests are arranged by more than 40 subject classes, such as chemicals, clothing, or wines, spirits and liqueurs. An outline of the classes can be found in the *Code of Federal Regulations* (37 *CFR* 6.1). There are also lists of approved registrations, renewals, and cancellations. There is a name index to approved registrants in each *Official Gazette* issue, including those making renewals, cancellations, and amendments. Drawings of trademarks are only shown at initial claim when published for opposition, not when listed as approved at a later date.

The annual *Index of Trademarks Issued from the United States Patent and Trademark Office* is an index of registrants — that is, an alphabetical index to companies, organizations, or persons registering trademarks for that year. Registrants renewing, canceling, and amending trademarks during the year are also included. The information for each registrant includes registration number, publication date, International Class, and type of action.

The *Acceptable Identification of Goods and Services Manual*, often called the *Goods and Services Manual*, begins with a brief overview of the International Classification system used for trademarks. Separate, detailed alphabetical listings for goods and services provide the class number for specific products. Listings of goods and services by class number are also included. The *Manual* is useful for identifying a particular class for trademark searching or for preparing trademark applications. It is also available on the *Trademarks ASSIST* DVD and in a searchable Web version.

COMMERCIAL TRADEMARK SOURCES AND DATABASES
Checklist

The Trademark Register of the United States. PRINT. (annual) 1884–. Washington, D.C.: The Trademark Register.
> Content: trademarks registered and pending applications; alphabetical list of trademarks arranged by class; registration number and date.

Trademark Register. WEB. (weekly) 1884–. The Trademark Register. <http://www.trademarkregister.com/>.
> Content: registered federal trademarks; published and unpublished pending applications; expired and cancelled trademarks

LEXIS-NEXIS. <http://www.lexis-nexis.com/lncc/>.
> Content: federal trademarks active since 1884; inactive trademarks since 1887.

Trademarkscan-U.S. Federal. 1884–. Dialog.
> Content: active federal trademark registrations and pending applications; images.

SAEGIS. WEB. 1884–. Thomson & Thomson. <http://www.thomson-thomson.com/>.
> Content: Web version of *Trademarkscan-U.S. Federal* and other trademark databases.

Dialog OnDisc: Trademarkscan-U.S. Federal. CD-ROM. (monthly) 1884–. Mountain View, CA: Knight-Ridder Information, Inc.
> Content: CD-ROM version of *Trademarkscan-U.S. Federal*.

Trademark.com. WEB. 1884–. MicroPatent. <http://www.micropat.com/0/trademarkweb9809.html>.
> Content: MarkSearch databases; active federal trademark registrations and applications.

MarkSearch. CD-ROM. (monthly) 1884–. East Haven, CT: MicroPatent.
> Content: full-text and images of all registered trademarks.

Discussion

Many fee-based trademark sources and databases are also available. The *Trademark Register of the United States* lists trademarks alphabetically within each class by the first word. There is no overall index. A more comprehensive Web database is also available. Purchase of the print title includes a year's free access to the database. Separate fee-based access is also available.

Some comprehensive online data providers offer trademark databases. *LEXIS-NEXIS* includes a trademark library (TRDMRK) with the full-text of federal trademarks, as well as individual state trademark registration files. Dialog offers *Trademarkscan-U.S. Federal* covering federal trademark registrations, as well as several other *Trademarkscan* databases covering states and other countries. *Trademarkscan-U.S. Federal* includes the trademark, design images, registration number, classification numbers, description of the product or service, current status, date of publication in the *Official Gazette,* date of first use, and ownership history. A CD-ROM version is also available.

Thomson & Thomson, the producer of the *Trademarkscan* databases offered through Dialog, also offers its own electronic version of those databases, the *SAEGIS* Web database.

MicroPatent offers its MarkSearch trademark databases via *Trademark.com* and CD-ROM.

INDEXES
Checklist

Catalog of United States Government Publications (MOCAT). WEB. 1994–. U.S. Government Printing Office. Superintendent of Documents. <http://www.gpo.gov/catalog>; <http://www.access.gpo.gov/su_docs/locators/cgp/index.html>; <http://purl.access.gpo.gov/GPO/LPS844>.

Monthly Catalog of United States Government Publications. CD-ROM. 1996–. U.S. Government Printing Office. Superintendent of Documents. GP 3.8/7: Item 0557-C. GPO.

Monthly Catalog of United States Government Publications (Condensed version). PRINT. (monthly) 1996–. U.S. Government Printing Office. Superintendent of Documents. GP 3.8/8: (Earlier full version, GP 3.8:, 1895-1995). Item 0557-D. GPO.

CIS/Index. PRINT. (monthly) 1970–. Bethesda, MD: Congressional Information Service.

Congressional Universe. WEB. Bethesda, MD: Congressional Information Service.

Discussion

These indexes provide access to publications about patents and trademarks and related issues, but not to specific patents or trademarks. The *Monthly Catalog* is the most comprehensive index. Look under "Patents," "Trademarks," and headings beginning with these words. The complete version of the *Monthly Catalog* is available on the Web and CD-ROM. Commercial online and CD-ROM versions of the *Monthly Catalog* are also available.

CIS/Index covers congressional publications. The same subject headings may be used as for the *Monthly Catalog*. *Congressional Universe* includes a Web version of *CIS*.

For more information on these indexes, see Chapter 3, "The Basics of Searching."

RELATED MATERIAL
Within this Work

Chapter 13 Copyright Information

GPO Subject Bibliographies. PRINT. WEB. GP 3.22/2:

<http://bookstore.gpo.gov/sb/about.html>

No. 21 "Patents and Trademarks"

CHAPTER 51
Standards and Specifications

Standards and specifications provide instructions or recommend how goods or services are to be manufactured, tested, designed, handled, or carried out. Specifications are used to set requirements for specific cases, whereas standards are used for more general applications. Several governmental agencies are involved in issuing standards and specifications. While standards produced by governmental agencies are primarily mandatory, some agencies, such as the National Institute of Standards, are also involved in developing voluntary standards. This chapter does not attempt to describe all of the standardization activities of the U.S. government. It concentrates on describing the procurement standards and specifications of the General Services Administration and the Department of Defense.

SEARCH STRATEGY

This chapter shows a special technique search strategy. The steps to follow are

1. If searching for Federal and Military procurement standards and specifications and related documentation, use the *Index of Federal Specifications, Standards, and Commercial Item Descriptions*, the *Department of Defense Index of Specifications and Standards*, or the publicly available Web-based Department of Defense system, *Assist Online*, to identify specific documents;
2. Use *Assist Online* to obtain the full-text of documents contained in its database, use print copies obtained by depository libraries, or use ordering information given in this chapter to obtain individual documents; and
3. If available to you, use one of the Information Handling Service's comprehensive Federal and Military standardization systems to identify and use the full-text of standardization documents.

GENERAL SERVICES ADMINISTRATION (GSA)/DEPARTMENT OF DEFENSE (DOD) SOURCES

Checklist

Federal Specifications. PRINT. (irregular) U.S. General Services Administration. Federal Supply Service. GS 2.8: Item 0563.
> Content: procurement specifications used by the General Services Administration.

Federal Standards. PRINT. (irregular) U.S. General Services Administration Federal Supply Service. GS 2.8/3: Item 0563.
> Content: standards used by the General Services Administration.

Federal Test Method Standards. PRINT. (irregular) U.S. General Services Administration. Federal Supply Service. GS 2.8/7: Item 0563.
> Content: standards describing testing methods.

Index of Federal Specifications, Standards, and Commercial Item Descriptions. PRINT. WEB. (annual with cumulated bimonthly supplements) U.S. General Services Administration. Federal Supply Service. GS 2.8/2: Item 0565. GPO. <http://pub.fss.gsa.gov/pub/fed-specs.cfm>.
> Content: index to Federal Specifications, Federal Standards, Commercial Item Descriptions, Federal Qualified Products Lists, and Institutional Meat Purchase Specifications.

Military Standards. PRINT. (irregular) U.S. Department of Defense. D 7.10: Item 0314-J.
> Content: procurement standards used by the Department of Defense.

Military Specifications. PRINT. (irregular) U.S. General Services Administration. Federal Supply Service. GS 2.8/3-2: Item 0563-A.
> Content: procurement specifications used by the Department of Defense.

Department of Defense Single Stock Point for MilSpecs and Standards Web Site. WEB. U.S. Department of Defense. Defense Automation and Production Service. <http://www.dodssp.daps.mil/>.

Content: distribution point for DOD standardization documents; information about standardization documents; acquisition and ordering information.

ASSIST Online. WEB. U.S. Department of Defense. Defense Automation and Production Service. <http://astimage.daps.dla.mil/online/>.

Content: comprehensive online system providing access to information about military specifications and standards; includes full-text of some items.

Department of Defense Index of Specifications and Standards. PRINT. WEB. (annual with cumulative bimonthly supplements) U.S. Department of Defense. D 1.76: Item 0314-G. GPO. <http://www.dtic.mil/str/dodiss4_field.html>.

Content: index to Department of Defense specifications and standards.

NSSN: A National Resource for Global Standards. WEB. American National Standards Institute. <http://www.nssn.org/>.

DOD Standardization Service. CD-ROM. Englewood, CO: Information Handling Services.

Content: comprehensive set of Federal and Military Specifications, Standards, Commercial Item Descriptions, Qualified Products Lists, Qualified Manufacturing Lists, and other related standardization documentation.

IHS Specs and Standardization Service. WEB. Information Handling Services. <http://www.ihsengineering.com/products/military_dod.html>.

Content: comprehensive set of Federal and Military Specifications, Standards, Commercial Item Descriptions, Qualified Products Lists, Qualified Manufacturing Lists, and other related standardization documentation; also includes nongovernmental standards.

IHS International Standards and Specifications. WEB. Dialog. <www.dialog.com>.

Content: index to Military and Federal specifications and standards.

Discussion

Federal Specifications gives detailed descriptions of the requirements for specific products. Each specification describes such areas as materials, processing techniques, physical requirements, quality assurance provisions, packaging, examinations and testing procedures, and labeling and marketing. (See Figure 51.1.) Specifications are issued for almost any product the government might possibly purchase, including "Bouillon (Soup and Gravy Bases)"; "Toothpicks (Wood)"; "Grinder, Electric, Portable"; "Napkins, Table, Paper," and "Oranges, Canned (Mandarin)." *Federal Specifications* are assigned individual document numbers beginning with two groups of letters followed by a number, i.e. *Federal Specification RR-T-64D,* the specification for "Tray, Medicine."

Federal Standards provides standard data that are referred to in the federal specifications. They include packaging, marking, and material identification standards. These include such standards as "Closing, Sealing, and Reinforcing of Fiberboard Shipping Boxes" and "Tape, Video, Magnetic, Recording, Formats for." *Federal Test Method Standards* are developed for such areas as "Cable and Wire, Insulated Methods of Testing"; "Textile Test Methods"; and "Plastics: Methods of Testing." *Federal Standards* and *Federal Test Method Standards* are identified by a one-to-three digit number, such as *Federal Standard STD 358, Sampling Procedures.*

The *Index of Federal Specifications, Standards, and Commercial Item Descriptions* is an index to these standardization documents. The print version includes individual sections of alphabetic and numeric listings for standards, specifications, and commercial item products. A numeric list of *Federal Qualified Products Lists* is also included. A listing of these documents by Federal Supply Classification (FSC) is also made available. The Web version of the *Index* provides a search interface that allows searching by title, document number, and federal supply classification. Presorted lists of items include the following: "Numeric List of Commercial Item Descriptions & Federal Specifications," "Numeric List of Federal Standards," "Numeric List of Federal Qualified Products (QPLs)," "Numeric List of U.S. Department of Agriculture (USDA) Institutional Meat Purchase Specifications," "Numeric List of Canceled/Superseded Commercial Item Descriptions, Federal Specifications & Standards," "Alphabetical List of Commercial Item Descriptions and Federal Specifications Containing Recycled Materials," "Alphabetical List of Federal Specifications & Commercial Item Descriptions," and "Alphabetical List of Federal Standards."

Commercial Item Descriptions and *Qualified Product Lists* are items used in conjunction with *Federal Specifications* and *Federal Standards. Qualified Product Lists* indicates specific products and individual plants producing items conforming to specification requirements. *Qualified Product Lists* numbers start with QPL, such as QPL-TT-P-2118-3, the *Federal Qualified Product List* for "Paint, Tree Marking." *Commercial Item Descriptions* are used for the procurement of readily available items, such as shaving cream, rubber bands, steak sauce, and padlocks. *Commercial Item Descriptions* are numbered A-A-1 through A-A-99999.

Ordering instructions and current prices of all of these standardization documents may be obtained by calling (202) 619-8925, or by fax to (202) 619-8978.

The Department of Defense (DOD) has its own specifications and standards, similar to the GSA specifications and standards. *Military Standards* are designated by document numbers such as *MIL-STD 188/200,* the standard for "*System Design and Engineering Standards for Tactical Communications.*" *Military Specifications* are similarly

| INCH-POUND |

WW-W-2845
April 15, 1994

FEDERAL SPECIFICATION

WATER PURIFICATION UNIT, FRAME MOUNTED DIATOMITE TYPE

This specification is approved by the Commissioner, Federal
Supply Service, General Services Administration, for the use
of all Federal agencies.

1.   SCOPE AND CLASSIFICATION

1.1   Scope.   This specification covers a diesel-engine-driven,
self-contained, frame mounted diatomaceous earth-type, water purification unit,
with a capacity of 50 gallons per minute (gpm)/3000 gallons per hour (gph)(3.15
liters per second (L/s)/189 liters per hour).

2.   APPLICABLE DOCUMENTS

2.1   Government documents.

2.1.1   Specifications, standards, and handbooks.   The following
specifications, standards, and handbooks form a part of this document to the
extent specified herein.   Unless otherwise specified, the issues of these
documents are those listed in the issue of the Department of Defense Index of
Specifications and Standards (DODISS) and supplement thereto, cited in the
solicitation (see 6.2).

Federal Specifications

        FF-B-575   - Bolts, Hexagon and Square
        FF-N-836   - Nut: Square, Hexagon, Cap, Slotted, Castle Knurled, Welding
                      and Single Ball Seat
        TT-P-664   - Primer Coating, Alkyd, Corrosion-Inhibiting, Lead and
                      Chromate Free, VOC-Compliant

───
|Beneficial comments (recommendations, additions, deletions) and any pertinent|
|data which may be of use in improving this document should be addressed to: |
|Commanding Officer (Code 156), Naval Construction Battalion Center, |
|1000 23rd Avenue, Port Hueneme, CA 93043-4301, by using the Standardization |
|Document Improvement Proposal (DD Form 1426) appearing at the end of this |
|document or by letter. |
───

AMSC N/A   FSC 4610

DISTRIBUTION STATEMENT A.   Approved for public release; distribution is
unlimited.

Source: Federal Specification for Water Purification Unit, Frame Mounted Diatomite Type, WW-W-2845, April 15, 1994.

Figure 51.1. Sample Federal Specification.

numbered, such as *MIL-H-12225H*, the specification for "Hood, Gas Mask, Toxicological Agents Protective: M-3."

The Department of Defense Single Stock Point for MilSpecs and Standards (DODSSP) is the central point of access for information about military specifications and standards and related standardization documents, and for obtaining military specification and standards. The DODSSP states, "The responsibilities of the DODSSP include electronic document storage, indexing, cataloging, maintenance, publish-on-demand, distribution, and sale of Military Specifications, Standards, and related standardization documents and publications comprising the DODSSP Collection." The *DODSSP Web Site* provides the detailed information needed to access this information.

Included as part of the *DODSSP Web Site* is the *ASSIST Online* system. *ASSIST Online* is a comprehensive Web-based system that provides information relating to Military and Federal standards and specifications and other related standardization documents. It provides public access to the downloadable full-text of many of the documents; included in the system are over 88,000 document images in PDF format. While the system concentrates on providing access to military standards, specifications, and documentation, other items are included if they have been entered into the system. *Assist Online*, then, is a source for the full-text of not only military standardization documentation, but also Federal Standards and Specifications and Commercial Item Descriptions. Some nongovernmental standards are also included in the system, but access to the full-text of these documents is restricted to Department of Defense usage. Documents not available digitally can be easily ordered through the *ASSIST Online System*. The *DODSSP Web Site* also includes information and copies of order forms for those wishing to order documents by mail, fax, or telephone.

The *Department of Defense Index of Specifications and Standards (DODISS)* is a catalog of Department of Defense standardization documents available in both a print and Web format. It includes information for Military/Performance/Detail Specifications;

Military Standards; DOD-adopted Non-Government/Industry Specifications and Standards; Federal Specifications and Standards; Military Handbooks; Qualified Products/Manufacturers Lists (QPL/QMLs); Commercial Item Descriptions (CIDs);

Air Force/Navy Aeronautical Standards/Design Standards; and Air Force Specifications Bulletins. The print *DODISS* consists of four parts. Part I includes a listing of current standardization documents listed alphabetically by the titles of the document. Part II is a numerical listing by document identifier number of all current documents and documents cancelled since the last edition of *DODISS*. Part III lists the documents within their Federal Supply Class (FSC). Part IV is a listing of cancelled documents since 1964. The Web version of *DODISS* allows for key-

word searching of all fields of a record, title searching, limiting by date and status, and searching by Federal Supply Classification (FSC) code. Results from the online *DODISS* link to any full-text documents available through *ASSIST Online*.

NSSN: A National Resource for Global Standards is produced by the American National Standards Institute (ANSI), and provides a free search engine to active standardization documents used by the Department of Defense and entered into the *ASSIST* database. *NSSN* refers the user back to *ASSIST Online* to download any full-text documents available from *ASSIST*.

The Information Handling Service (IHS) produces both a CD-ROM version and Web version of a product that comprehensively provides the full-text of Military and Federal Standards and Specifications and related documentation. Besides current documents, the services provide access to the full-text of cancelled and superceded documents. *The IHS International Standards and Specifications,* available through Dialog, also provides bibliographic references, but not the full-text, to Military and Federal Standards and Specifications and other related standardization documents.

CODE OF FEDERAL REGULATIONS
Checklist

Code of Federal Regulations. PRINT. MF. WEB. (annual) 1938–. U.S. National Archives and Records Administration. Office of the Federal Register. AE 2.106/3: (*CFR Index and Finding Aids*, AE 2.106/3-2:). (Earlier, GS 4.108:, GS 4.108/4:) Items 0572, 0572-B or -C(MF). GPO. <http://www.access.gpo.gov/nara/cfr/index.html>; <http://purl.access.gpo.gov/GPO/LPS3384>.

> Content: includes text of some mandatory and voluntary standards; references to standards.

Index to the Code of Federal Regulations. PRINT. (annual with quarterly supplements) 1977–. Bethesda, MD: Congressional Information Service, Inc.

> Content: in-depth, multivolume subject, geographic, and CFR section number index.

Discussion

Mandatory standards produced by government agencies are included within the *Code of Federal Regulations (CFR)*. Standards included within the *CFR* cover a wide range of subjects, activities, and agencies. Figure 51.2 displays a Consumer Product Safety Commission standard titled "Standard for the Flammability of Children's Sleepwear: Sizes 7 through 14," which is included in Title 16, Part 1616 of the *CFR*. Standards produced by nongovernmental agencies, such as the American National Standards Institute (ANSI) and Underwriter's Laboratories (UL), are often made mandatory by inclusion within the *CFR*. The full text of the standard may be included, or more typically, a reference to the standard in the text is given.

Pt. 1616

(d) Retailers, distributors, and wholesalers, as well as manufacturers, importers, and other persons (such as converters) introducing a fabric or garment into commerce which does not meet the requirements of the flammability standards for children's sleepwear, have an obligation not to promote or sell such fabric or garment for use as an item of children's sleepwear. Also, retailers, distributors, and wholesalers are advised not to advertise, promote, or sell as an item of children's sleepwear any item which a manufacturer, importer, or other person (such as a converter) introducing the item into commerce has indicated by label, invoice, or otherwise, does not meet the requirements of the children's sleepwear flammability standards and is not intended or suitable for use as sleepwear. Additionally, retailers are advised:

(1) To segregate, by placement in different parts of a department or store, fabrics and garments covered by the children's sleepwear standards from all fabrics and garments that are beyond the scope of the children's sleepwear standards but which resemble items of children's sleepwear;

(2) To utilize store display signs indicating the distinction between types of fabrics and garments, for example by indicating which are sleepwear items and which are not; and

(3) To avoid the advertisement or promotion of a fabric or garment that does not comply with the children's sleepwear flammability standard in a manner that may cause the item to be viewed by the consumer as an item of children's sleepwear.

(Sec. 5, Pub.L. 90–189, 81 Stat. 569, 15 U.S.C. 1194; sec. 30(b), Pub.L. 92–573, 86 Stat. 1231, 15 U.S.C. 2079(b); 5 U.S.C. 553)

[49 FR 10250, Mar. 20, 1984]

PART 1616—STANDARD FOR THE FLAMMABILITY OF CHILDREN'S SLEEPWEAR: SIZES 7 THROUGH 14 (FF 5–74)

Subpart A—The Standard

Sec.
1616.1 Scope and application.
1616.2 Definitions.
1616.3 General requirements.

1616.4 Sampling and acceptance procedures.
1616.5 Test procedure.
1616.6 Labeling requirements.

Subpart B—Rules and Regulations

1616.31 Labeling, recordkeeping, retail display and guaranties.
1616.32 Method for establishment and use of alternate laundering procedures under section 5(c)(4)(ii) of the standard.
1616.35 Use of alternate apparatus, procedures, or criteria for testing under the standard.
1616.36 Use of alternate apparatus or procedures for tests for guaranty purposes.

Subpart C—Interpretations and Policies

1616.61 Enforcement policy.
1616.62 Policy regarding retail display requirement for items.
1616.63 Policy regarding garment production unit identification.
1616.64 Policy regarding recordkeeping requirements.
1616.65 Policy scope of the standard.

SOURCE: 40 FR 59917, Dec. 30, 1975, unless otherwise noted.

Subpart A—The Standard

AUTHORITY: Sec. 4, 67 Stat. 112, as amended, 81 Stat. 569–70; 15 U.S.C. 1193.

§ 1616.1 Scope and application.

(a) This Standard provides a test method to determine the flammability of children's sleepwear, sizes 7 through 14 and fabric or related material intended or promoted for use in such children's sleepwear.

(b) All sleepwear items as defined in § 1616.2(c), are subject to the requirements of this Standard.

(c) Children's sleepwear items which meet all the requirements of the Standard for the Flammability of Children's Sleepwear: Sizes 0 through 6X (FF 3–71) (subpart A of part 1615 of this chapter) are in compliance with this Standard. FF 3–71 was issued July 29, 1971 (36 FR 14062), and amended July 21, 1972 (37 FR 14624).

(d) As used in this Standard, *pass* and *fail* refer to the test criteria for specimens while *accept* and *reject* refer to the acceptance or rejection of a production unit under the sampling plan.

(e) The flammability standards for clothing textiles and vinyl plastic film, parts 1610 and 1611 of this chapter, are

622

Source: Code of Federal Regulations, Title 16, Part 1616.

Figure 51.2. Sample Section of the *Code of Federal Regulations*.

The *Code of Federal Regulations* in print format includes its own index, and a commercial print index to the *CFR* is also available. Online versions of the *CFR* include various searching capabilities.

The *Code of Federal Regulations* is available on the Web from the Government Printing Office's *GPO Access* Web site (July 1996–). Online commercial services also include the *CFR*, including *CIS Congressional Universe* (current), *LEXIS-NEXIS* (1981–), *LEXIS-NEXIS Academic Universe* (current), *Westlaw* (1984–), and *CQ.com On Congress*. The *LEXIS* file is called CFR and is available in several libraries, including GENFED, CODES, and EXEC. The GENFED library offers the most options, including different editions of the *CFR*. Relevant titles of the *CFR* also appear in appropriate subject libraries. A CD-ROM version is available from West.

NATIONAL INSTITUTE OF STANDARDS AND TECHNOLOGY (NIST) SOURCES
Checklist

National Institute of Standards and Technology Web Site. WEB. U.S. Department of Commerce. National Institute of Standards and Technology. <http://www.nist.gov/>.
> Content: general information about NIST and its activities and programs.

FIPS Home Page. WEB. U.S. Department of Commerce. National Institute of Standards and Technology. <http://www. itl.nist.gov/fipspubs/>.
> Content: full-text of *Federal Information Processing Standards Publications (FIPS)*; *FIPS* search tools and listings.

Federal Information Processing Standards Publications (FIPS). PRINT. (irregular) U.S. Department of Commerce. National Institute of Standards and Technology. C 13.52: Item 0248-D.
> Content: Federal Government Information Processing Standards Publications.

Discussion

The National Institute of Standards (NIST) is involved with many aspects of standardization activities. The *NIST Web Site* provides a good entry point into the laboratories, programs, and services of NIST. One important set of standards produced by NIST are the *Federal Information Processing Standards Publications (FIPS)*. These standards are used government-wide and address such issues as the interoperability of different systems, portability of data and software, and computer security. The full-text of most *FIPS* publications are available for use at the *FIPS Home Page*.

INDEXES
Checklist

Catalog of United States Government Publications (MOCAT). WEB. 1994–. U.S. Government Printing Office. Superintendent of Documents. <http://www.gpo.gov/catalog>; <http://www.access.gpo.gov/su_docs/locators/cgp/index.html>; <http://purl.access.gpo.gov/GPO/LPS844>.

Monthly Catalog of United States Government Publications. CD-ROM. 1996–. U.S. Government Printing Office. Superintendent of Documents. GP 3.8/7: Item 0557-C. GPO.

Monthly Catalog of United States Government Publications (Condensed version). PRINT. (monthly) 1996–. U.S. Government Printing Office. Superintendent of Documents. GP 3.8/8: (Earlier full version, GP 3.8:, 1895-1995). Item 0557-D. GPO.

Discussion

The *Monthly Catalog* is the most comprehensive index to government publications. To locate additional publications relating to standards and specifications, search the following subject headings: "Standardization"; "Specifications"; "Standards, Engineering"; and "Testing." The terms "Standards," "Specifications," and "Testing" can also be used as subdivisions with subjects, e.g. "Trucks-Specifications." The complete version of the *Monthly Catalog* is available on the Web and CD-ROM. Commercial online and CD-ROM versions of the *Monthly Catalog* are also available. For more information on the *Monthly Catalog*, see Chapter 3, "The Basics of Searching."

RELATED MATERIAL
GPO Subject Bibliographies. PRINT. WEB. GP 3.22/2:

<http://bookstore.gpo.gov/sb/about.html>

No. 231 "Government Specifications and Standards"

No. 290 "National Institute of Standards and Technology"

CHAPTER 52
Historical Searches

Government publications are a rich source of U.S. historical information. Government publications provide original documentation on federal government activities. The sources discussed in this chapter generally cover materials published since the first Congress in 1789. Types of publications include congressional proceedings, investigative reports, scientific surveys, and agency reports.

Most government publications can be considered primary resources—that is, materials produced during the time of the events or situations involved. Government agencies also publish secondary resource materials, such as agency and military histories. There are also many nongovernmental sources of information on events in U.S. history that summarize and even reproduce selected government documents, as well as give extensive background information and analysis. These can provide the needed context for locating primary resource materials in government publications. They will give the researcher an idea of what to look for and can provide information on specific events, names, dates, and bibliographic references.

Government publications may be divided into three categories: congressional, executive, and judicial. For many years after the formation of the federal government, congressional publications were the predominant type of government publication. Most of these materials were published in the *U.S. Congressional Serial Set*. As the federal government grew, the volume of executive publications grew as well, but there is no comparable uniform set of executive publications. Judicial publications represent a smaller portion of government publishing and are discussed in Chapter 46, "Judicial Reports."

This chapter discusses the major indexes needed to identify and locate historical government publications. Chapter 3, "The Basics of Searching," discusses the primary indexes to U. S. government publications in use today. Those indexes can also be used to locate historical materials to varying degrees. The indexes discussed here, however, cover earlier time periods. This chapter also includes a section on the *U.S. Congressional Serial Set*, a brief discussion of the availability of historical digital and microform materials, and a discussion of selected secondary historical resources, such as military and biographical sources.

SEARCH STRATEGY

A historical search involves a special technique search strategy. A historical search may include a known item, subject, agency, or statistical search, but it may require different indexes. The steps to follow are

1. Select indexes that cover the appropriate time period from those listed in the "General Indexes" section of this chapter. The *Catalogue of the Public Documents of the (53rd–76th) Congress and of All Departments of the Government of the United States* is the best of these, followed by the *CIS* indexes;
2. After identifying a document through an index, consult additional guides to find SuDocs numbers or *Serial Set* volume numbers if they are not given in the index. (See the sections "Locating Congressional Reports in the *Serial Set*" and "Locating SuDocs Numbers When Not Given in Index," both of which can have application to more current searches as well);
3. Consider the sources listed in the "Historical Sets" section;
4. For biographical information, see the "Biographical Directories" section;
5. If interested in military history, see the sections on "Military History Series" and "Vietnam Series"; and
6. Consider the "Related Material" section.

U.S. CONGRESSIONAL SERIAL SET
Checklist

U.S. Congressional Serial Set. PRINT. MF. WEB. 1817–. U.S. Congress. Y 1.1/2: (Before 1817, see the *American State Pa-*

pers). Items 0996-B(MF) or -C; 1008-D(MF) or –E; 1008-F (105th Congress -, regional depository libraries only) Early volumes: <http://lcweb2.loc.gov/ammem/amlaw/lwss.html>; Individual documents and reports since 1995: <http://www.access.gpo.gov/su_docs/legislative.html>.

Content: bound collection of congressional publications consisting of the numbered series of House and Senate reports and House and Senate documents.

Discussion

One of the main sources of historical government publications is the *U.S. Congressional Serial Set*, an ongoing series of volumes containing the reports and documents of the House and Senate. These consist not only of congressional publications, but also of reports submitted to Congress by other government agencies and commissions. The complete set, from 1817 to the present, consists of more than 14,000 volumes. A complete microfiche set is available from Congressional Information Service, Inc. Selected early volumes are being made available on the Web as part of the Library of Congress American Memory project. The following sample documents found in the *Serial Set* illustrate the range of topics: *Affairs of the Mexican Kickapoo Indians, Hearings* (Serial 5247); *Future of Commerce* (Serial 5241); *The Brownsville Affray* (Serial 5252); *Swamp Lands of U.S.* (Serial 5265); and *Care of Insane Persons in Alaska* (Serial 5559).

It will be difficult, if not impossible, to do historical research in U.S. government publications without having the *Serial Set* available. Large, longstanding depository libraries will be most likely to have the *Serial Set*; libraries can also sometimes borrow materials not owned.

GENERAL INDEXES
Checklist
COMPREHENSIVE

1774–1881   *Descriptive Catalogue of the Government Publications of the United States, Sept. 5, 1774-March 4, 1881.* PRINT. (1885) U.S. Congress. Senate. Senate Miscellaneous Document No. 67, 48th Congress, 2nd Session. Serial Set 2268. (Commonly known as "Poore" for the author, Ben Perley Poore) New York: Johnson Reprint Corporation, 1970.

1789–1909   *Checklist of United States Public Documents, 1789–1909.* PRINT. (1911) U.S. Government Printing Office. Superintendent of Documents. GP 3.2:C 41/2 (Commonly known as the "1909 Checklist") New York: Kraus Reprint Corp., 1962.

1881–93   *Comprehensive Index to the Publications of the United States Government.* PRINT. (1905) U.S. Congress. House of Representatives. House Document No. 754, 58th Congress, 2nd Session. Serial Set 4745-4746. (Commonly known as

"Ames" for the author, John Griffith Ames) New York: Johnson Reprint Corporation, 1970.

1885–94   *United States Government Publications: A Monthly Catalog.* PRINT. 6 vols. (Commonly known as Hickcox's *Monthly Catalog* for the editor, John H. Hickcox) Reprinted with Superintendent of Documents classification numbers added. Arlington, VA: Carrollton Press, Inc.

1893–1940   *Catalogue of the Public Documents of the (53rd–76th) Congress and of All Departments of the Government of the United States for the Period from March 4, 1893 to Dec. 31, 1940.* PRINT. 25 vols. (biennial) U.S. Government Printing Office. Superintendent of Documents. GP 3.6: or Serial Set. (Commonly known as the *Document Catalogue*)

1895–   *Monthly Catalog of United States Government Publications.* PRINT. MF. (monthly) 1895–. (Title varies) U.S. Government Printing Office. Superintendent of Documents. GP 3.8: Items 0557-A or -B(MF). GPO.

Cumulative Subject Index to the Monthly Catalog of U.S. Government Publications, 1900–1971. PRINT. 15 vols. (1973–75) Arlington, VA: Carrollton Press, Inc.

Cumulative Subject Index to the Monthly Catalog of U.S. Government Publications, 1895–1899. PRINT. 2 vols. (1977) Arlington, VA: Carrollton Press, Inc.

Cumulative Title Index to United States Public Documents, 1789–1976. PRINT. 16 vols. (1979-82) Arlington, VA: United States Historical Documents Institute, Inc.

United States Government Publications Monthly Catalog: Quinquennial Cumulative Personal Author Index. PRINT. (Title varies) 1941–1975. Ann Arbor, MI: Pierian Press, 1971–1979.

CONGRESSIONAL ONLY

1789–1817   Public *Documents of the First Fourteen Congresses, 1789–1817: Papers Relating to Early Congressional Documents.* PRINT. (1900) U.S. Congress. Senate. Senate Document No. 428, 56th Congress, 1st Session. Serial Set 3879. (Commonly known as "Greeley" for the author, Adolphus Washington Greeley) New York: Johnson Reprint, 1963.

1789–1969   *CIS U.S. Serial Set Index, 1789–1969.* PRINT. (1975-79) Washington, DC: Congressional Information Service, Inc.

1817–93   *Tables of and Annotated Index to the Congressional Series of United States Public Documents.* PRINT. (1902) U.S. Government Printing Office. Superintendent of Documents. GP 3.2:P 96. Item 0551.

c.1830–1969 *CIS U.S. Congressional Committee Prints Index Through 1969.* (1980) Washington, DC: Congressional Information Service, Inc.

c.1833–1969 *CIS U.S. Congressional Committee Hearings Index.* (1981–85) Washington, DC: Congressional Information Service, Inc.

1789–1972 *Congressional Masterfile 1.* CD-ROM. Bethesda, MD: Congressional Information Service.

1789– *Congressional Universe.* WEB. Bethesda, MD: Congressional Information Service. Related information: <http://www.lexis-nexis.com/cispubs/Catalog/Universe/Congressional%20Universe/index.htm>.

EXECUTIVE ONLY

1789–1909 *CIS Index to U.S. Executive Branch Documents, 1789–1909: Guide to Documents Listed in Checklist of U.S. Public Documents, 1789–1909, Not Printed in the U.S. Serial Set.* PRINT. (1990–1995) Bethesda, MD: Congressional Information Service, Inc.

1910–1932 *CIS Index to U.S. Executive Branch Documents, 1910–1932: Guide to Documents Not Printed in the U. S. Serial Set.* PRINT. (1996–) In progress. Bethesda, MD: Congressional Information Service, Inc.

c.1945– *Declassified Documents Catalog.* PRINT. (quarterly) CD-ROM. (annual) 1975–. (Title varies) Woodbridge, CT: Primary Source Media (Research Publications), Inc.

c.1945– *World Government Documents Archive Online: Declassified Documents Reference System - United States.* WEB. Gale Group.

Discussion

These indexes provide access to early U.S. government publications. Indexes may overlap in some time periods. As each index has its own strengths and weaknesses, it is sometimes desirable to use more than one to completely cover the time period. Figure 52.1 illustrates the time period coverage of each index.

As a general guideline, if documents sought are from the time period 1893–1940, the first index to consult would be the *Document Catalogue*. This index has the most thorough coverage and provides the most complete information of all of the indexes available. The *Monthly Catalog* and the various *CIS* indexes are also good choices.

Many of the early government-produced indexes do not provide SuDocs classification numbers or *Serial Set* volume information. The *CIS* indexes do have that advantage. If using an index that does not provide this information, see the sections in this chapter titled "Locating Congressional Reports in the *Serial Set*" and "Locating SuDocs Numbers When Not Given in Index" for additional assistance.

For additional help in using some of the individual indexes, a brief description of each is given below.

Document Catalogue

The *Document Catalogue* dictionary format allows the user to go directly to the desired subject and locate complete

---

ISTHMIAN CANAL COMMISSION, 1899–1902. Report, [June 15] 1899– [Nov. 16] 1901. 1901–02. [2 pts.] 263 pp. 1 il. and 535 pp. il. 44 pl. 2 maps. (S. doc. 54, 2 pts., 57th Cong. 1st sess. In v. 7; 4225.) [Atlas and part of appendixes not yet printed.]

Source: *Document Catalogue*, 1901-03, p. 590.

Figure 52.2: Sample Entry from *Document Catalogue*.

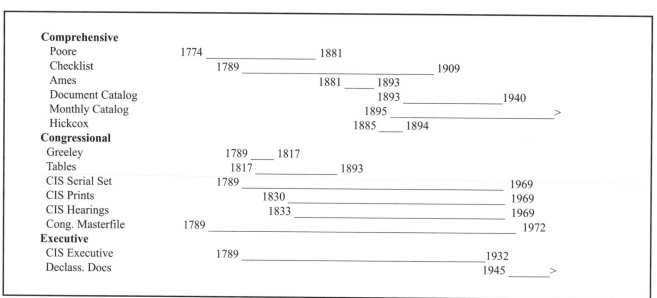

Comprehensive					
Poore	1774 _____ 1881				
Checklist	1789 _____ 1909				
Ames	1881 _____ 1893				
Document Catalog	1893 _____ 1940				
Monthly Catalog	1895 _____ >				
Hickcox	1885 _____ 1894				
Congressional					
Greeley	1789 _____ 1817				
Tables	1817 _____ 1893				
CIS Serial Set	1789 _____ 1969				
CIS Prints	1830 _____ 1969				
CIS Hearings	1833 _____ 1969				
Cong. Masterfile	1789 _____ 1972				
Executive					
CIS Executive	1789 _____ 1932				
Declass. Docs	1945 _____ >				

Figure 52.1: Historical Indexes: Time Period Coverage.

information, unlike most other government indexes, which require two or even three additional steps before complete information can be acquired. Figure 52.2 singles out an entry on a proposed Nicaraguan canal. This publication is a Senate document located in volume 4225 of the *Serial Set*. (The "v. 7" number has no direct bearing on locating the report.) For references that do not give *Serial Set* locations, it may be necessary to locate SuDocs numbers. (See the section on "Locating SuDocs Numbers When Not Given in Index" in this chapter.)

Monthly Catalog

The *Monthly Catalog* is the standard index for locating government publications in use today. It provides the longest-running comprehensive coverage of government publications. Before 1925 it did not include SuDocs classification numbers for the publications listed. A reprint edition from Carrollton Press, known as the "Classes Added" edition, has rectified this omission. If this "Classes Added" set is not available, see the section titled "Locating SuDocs Numbers When Not Given in Index" in this chapter. References to congressional reports do not include *Serial Set* volume numbers. To locate these, refer to the section titled "Locating Congressional Reports in the *Serial Set*" in this chapter.

Cumulative and related indexes for the *Monthly Catalog* include the *Monthly Catalog*'s own 10-year (later 5-year) cumulative indexes which begin in 1941, plus several commercially produced indexes.

Hickcox's *Monthly Catalog* was an early predecessor of the *Monthly Catalog*. It was not published by the government.

Checklist of United States Public Documents

The *Checklist of United States Public Documents, 1789–1909* lists documents in SuDocs number order. There is also a list of *Serial Set* volumes with information on the report and document numbers in each volume. There is an agency index, but no subject or title index. When an agency is known, however, scanning that agency's publications in the *Checklist* can be very valuable. Other indexes provide subject and title access for this time period: *CIS U.S. Serial Set Index*, *CIS Index to U.S. Executive Branch Documents, 1789–1909*, and *Cumulative Title Index to United States Public Documents, 1789–1976*.

CIS U.S. Serial Set Index

The *CIS U.S. Serial Set Index* covers only the *Serial Set*, whereas the *Document Catalogue* and the *Monthly Catalog* include executive department publications as well. Since so many historical publications are in the *Serial Set*, this is a valuable index. It covers a very long span and includes all of the information needed to locate a publica-

tion in the *Serial Set*. CIS also provides a full-text microfiche edition of the *Serial Set* to accompany the index.

The index is divided into parts, each of which covers a limited number of years. Shown in Figure 52.3 are sample entries from Part 5, covering 1897–1903. After each entry are listed the House or Senate report or document number, the Congress and session number in parentheses, and the volume of the *Serial Set* in which the report is located. This index is most valuable for years not covered by the *Documents Catalogue*. *Congressional Masterfile 1* is a CD-ROM version of several historical congressional indexes published by Congressional Information Service, Inc. The *CIS U.S. Serial Set Index* is included, along with the *CIS Congressional Committee Prints Index Through 1969* and the *CIS U.S. Congressional Committee Hearings Index*, discussed in the "Other Congressional Indexes" section of this chapter. *Congressional Masterfile 1* also includes some additional indexes to unpublished congressional materials that are not discussed in this chapter. This same group of historical indexes is available online in *Congressional Universe*, as an additional add-on subscription.

CIS Index to U.S. Executive Branch Documents, 1789–1909 and 1910–1932.

The *CIS Index to U.S. Executive Branch Documents, 1789–1909* indexes the executive agency publications listed in the *Checklist of United States Public Documents*. The 1910–1932 set continues where the *Checklist* leaves off. *CIS Index to U.S. Executive Branch Documents* covers only publications that are not in the *Serial Set*. *Serial Set* publications are covered by *CIS U.S. Serial Set Index*. The 1910–1932 executive branch index is being published over several years.

The indexes are divided into parts, each of which covers an agency or group of agencies. Part 1 of the 1789–1909 set, for example, covers the Treasury Department and the Commerce and Labor Departments. Each part consists of several volumes, including a reference bibliography, index by subjects and names, and supplementary indexes. The supplementary indexes cover SuDocs number, title, and agency report numbers. Indexes give accession numbers that must be looked up in the reference bibliography volumes, where bibliographic information and SuDocs numbers can be found.

Other Congressional Indexes

Two other CIS indexes provide thorough coverage of other congressional publications, from the earliest publications known to exist through 1969. One index is for committee prints, and one is for committee hearings. Both of these indexes are also available on *Congressional Universe* (as an add-on subscription) and on the *Congressional Masterfile 1* CD-ROM. There are also two older, less so-

NICARAGUA CANAL

Annual report of Maritime Canal Company of Nicaragua, 1898, p. 1029
H.doc. 5 (55-3) 3758

Annual report of Maritime Canal Company of Nicaragua, 1899, p. 555
H.doc. 5 (56-1) 3917

Annual report of Nicaragua Maritime Canal Co., 1897
S.doc. 10 (55-2) 3590

Annual report of Nicaragua Maritime Canal Co., 1898
S.doc. 13 (55-3) 3725

Annual report of Nicaragua Maritime Canal Co., 1899
S.doc. 13 (56-1) 3844

Annual report of Nicaragua Maritime Canal Co., 1900
S.doc. 28 (56-2) 4029

Annual report of Nicaragua Maritime Canal Co., 1901
S.doc. 27 (57-1) 4220

Annual report of Nicaragua Maritime Canal Co., 1902
S.doc. 8 (57-2) 4417

Article from 1881 on construction of Nicaragua Canal, by U. S. Grant
S.doc. 207 (57-1) 4234

Canal or fort? paper on neutralization of Nicaragua Canal
S.doc. 47 (56-2) 4033

Certificate of incorporation of Nicaragua Company
S.doc. 400 (56-1) 3877

Chronological statement as to Nicaragua Maritime Canal Co.
S.rp. 1417 (55-3) 3739

Construction of Nicaragua Canal
S.rp. 114 (56-1) 3886

Construction of Nicaragua Canal [Reprint of pt. 1, H. rp. 351, 56th Cong., 1st sess.]
H.rp. 15 (57-1) 4399

Construction of Nicaragua Canal, with minority report
H.rp. 351 (56-1) 4022

Convention with Great Britain for construction of Nicaragua Canal
S.doc. 160 (56-1) 3852; S.doc. 268 (56-1) 3868

Correspondence and papers relating to Nicaragua Canal
S.doc. 161 (56-1) 3853

Dream of navigators (Nicaragua Canal), paper by A. S. Crowninshield
S.doc. 263 (55-2) 3611

Estimate for continuing survey of Nicaragua Canal
S.doc. 249 (55-2) 3611

Hearings on New Panama Canal Co., Maritime Canal Co., and Nicaragua Canal Company
S.doc. 50 (56-1) 3848

Information regarding Nicaragua and other interoceanic canals
S.rp. 34 (56-1) 3886

Memorial to King of Spain in 1791 on Nicaragua Canal
S.doc. 157 (56-2) 4039

Nicaragua Canal, pts. 1 and 2
S.rp. 1337 (56-1) 3894

Nicaragua Canal, pts. 3-6
S.rp. 1337 (56-2) 4063

Preliminary report of Nicaragua Canal Commission
S.doc. 52 (55-3) 3728

Proposition to transfer stock of Nicaragua Maritime Canal Co. to U.S.
S.doc. 289 (55-2) 3611

Statements of members of Nicaragua Canal Comn., June 15-17, 1898
S.doc. 341 (55-2) 3615

To construct Nicaragua Canal
H.rp. 2104 (55-3) 3841

Treaties and concessions regarding Nicaragua Canal
S.doc. 291 (55-2) 3615

U.S. to assume charter of Nicaragua Maritime Canal Co.
S.rp. 1265 (55-2) 3627; S.rp. 1418 (55-3) 3739

NICARAGUA (SHIP)

Appeal for indemnity by owners of S.S. Nicaragua
S.doc. 301 (57-1) 4239

Correspondence relating to owners, etc., of steamer Nicaragua
H.doc. 162 (55-2) 3667

Papers relating to indemnity for steamship Nicaragua
S.doc. 17 (56-1) 3844

Relief of owners of Norwegian steamship Nicaragua
H.rp. 1829 (57-1) 4405

NICKERSON (SHIP)

Claims growing out of seizure of British schooners E. R. Nickerson, etc.
S.doc. 396 (57-1) 4245

NIGHT

Fixing pay of customs inspectors for night services
H.rp. 873 (56-1) 4024

To pay employees of Customs Service for night services
S.rp. 879 (56-1) 3890

NILES FERRY

To legalize bridge over Little Tennessee River at Niles Ferry, Tennessee
S.rp. 529 (57-1) 4259; H.rp. 575 (57-1) 4401

NINETEENTH STREET

To omit extension of Kalorama ave., D.C., from Columbia road to 19th st.
S.rp. 1939 (57-1) 4264

To widen 19th street northwest, D.C.
S.rp. 1216 (55-2) 3627

To widen 19th street northwest, Washington, D.C.
S.rp. 1527 (55-3) 3739; H.rp. 1752 (55-3) 3840

NIOBRARA

To sell part of Fort Niobrara military reservation to Valentine, Nebr.
S.rp. 661 (57-1) 4260; H.rp. 2101 (57-1) 4406

NIUCHWANG

Appropriation for consulate at Niuchwang, China
S.doc. 74 (56-2) 4033

NOME

see also Cape Nome

Bridge across Snake River at Nome, Alaska
S.rp. 2664 (57-2) 4411; H.rp. 3702 (57-2) 4415

Cape Nome Transportation, Bridge and Development Co. to bridge Snake River at Nome, Alaska
H.rp. 542 (56-1) 4023

NOMENCLATURE

American Republics Bureau; Commercial nomenclature, English Spanish, Portugese
S.doc. 178 (55-2) 3602

American Republics Bureau; Commercial nomenclature, Portugese, Spanish, English
S.doc. 178 (55-2) 3604

American Republics Bureau; Commercial nomenclature, Spanish, English, Portugese
S.doc. 178 (55-2) 3603

NOMINATIONS

Compilation of reports of Committee on Foreign Relations, 1789-1901, vol. 4: Mediterranean commerce, etc.; Nominations; Authorizations to accept decorations; International exhibitions and conferences, Maritime canals, Pacific cables, and Railroads; Foreign commerce; Tariff restrictions on swine products
S.doc. 231 (56-2) 4050

Report touching brevet nominations of Army
S.doc. 195 (57-2) 4430

NONCOMMISSIONED OFFICERS

see also Petty officers

Retired noncommissioned officers to assist in military training in schools
S.rp. 2860 (57-2) 4411; H.rp. 3705 (57-2) 4415

To regulate pay of noncommissioned officers in Army
S.rp. 87 (55-1) 3570

NONCONCURRENCE

Nonconcurrence in Senate amendments to war revenue bill
H.rp. 1516 (55-2) 3722

NONCONTIGUOUS

Statistics of trade between United States and its noncontiguous territory
S.rp. 220 (57-1) 4257

Statistics of trade between U.S. and its noncontiguous territory
H.rp. 1700 (57-1) 4404

Figure 52.3: Sample Entries from *CIS U.S. Serial Set Index*.

phisticated indexes that cover congressional publications. These are Greeley's *Public Documents of the First Fourteen Congresses, 1789–1817* and *Tables of and Annotated Index to the Congressional Series of United States Public Documents*.

The *CIS U.S. Congressional Committee Prints Index* covers the staff research reports, background studies, and Library of Congress research reports prepared at Congress's request on national issues and options. Many of the committee prints listed in this index were not sent to depository libraries. (Committee prints began to become available to depositories in the mid-1970s.) They are available, however, as a microfiche set from CIS. Many of these publications do not appear in any other index. A subject index gives the user an accession number to look up in volumes of the reference bibliography, where full bibliographic information is given. SuDocs numbers are included when available.

The *CIS U.S. Congressional Committee Hearings Index* covers congressional hearings. Many of these publications were made available to depository libraries. This index is issued in eight parts, each of which covers a particular time span. Each part contains a subject index, title index, bill number index, SuDocs number index, and names index. Indexes give accession numbers that must be looked up in the reference bibliography volumes, where full bibliographic information, a list of witnesses, and SuDocs numbers can be found. The hearings can also be purchased in microfiche for each part or as an entire set.

Greeley's *Public Documents* and *Tables* also cover congressional documents, but not as well as the *CIS U.S.*

Serial Set Index. In *Public Documents*, materials are listed chronologically. There is a name index, but no subject index. *Tables* continues where Greeley leaves off. It has a subject index, but only selective coverage of congressional materials.

Ames's and Poore's

Two other indexes—Ames's *Comprehensive Index to the Publications of the United States Government* and Poore's *Descriptive Catalogue of the Government Publications of the United States*—are frequently used because they are nearly the only government-produced indexes representative of their time periods.

Ames's is arranged in dictionary format. The sample entries in Figure 52.4 show listings under "Nicaragua Canal." The abbreviations in the right column indicate what kind of congressional report each title is (Senate miscellaneous report, Senate executive report) with Congress and session numbers, as well as report number. As with the *Monthly Catalog*, the exact *Serial Set* volume is not given. (To find *Serial Set* volume locations, see the section titled "Locating Congressional Reports in the *Serial Set*" in this chapter.)

Poore contains a subject index that refers the user to appropriate pages. However, it is necessary to search through all of the entries on a page in order to find the desired document. Congressional report information is given, but not the *Serial Set* volume location. (See the section titled "Locating Congressional Reports in the *Serial Set*" in this chapter.)

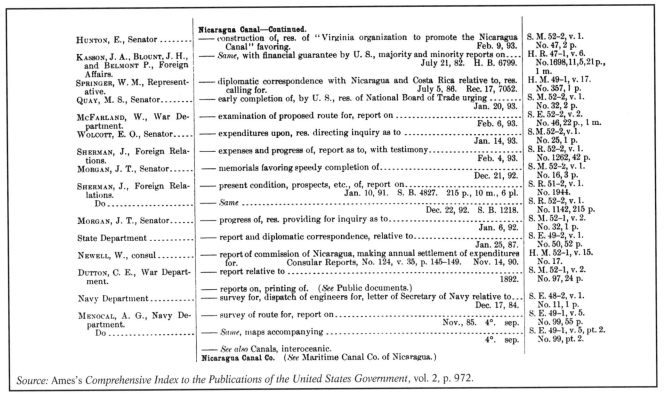

Source: Ames's *Comprehensive Index to the Publications of the United States Government*, vol. 2, p. 972.

Figure 52.4: Sample Entries from Ames's *Comprehensive Index*.

Declassified Documents Catalog

Declassified Documents Catalog is a commercial index to thousands of post-World War II U.S. government documents which were formerly classified but have since been released under an executive order requiring mandatory review. Most of the documents originate from the Central Intelligence Agency, the State Department, and the Defense Department, but other agencies are also represented, such as the National Security Council and the White House. Documents range from telegrams to substantial background studies on recent American history. The materials are indexed as they are declassified, so the year of the print index has no bearing on the dates of the material listed. The index gives the user an abstract number; each abstract gives a very brief summary and lists the issuing agency, type of document, date, date released, and classification level. The documents themselves can only be accessed by purchasing the accompanying microfiche set or subscribing to the Web index with full text. The index is also available on CD-ROM.

LOCATING CONGRESSIONAL REPORTS IN THE *SERIAL SET*

Checklist

1789–1909 *Checklist of United States Public Documents, 1789–1909*. PRINT. (1911) U.S. Government Printing Office. Superintendent of Documents. GP 3.2:C 41/2. (Commonly known as the "1909 Checklist") New York: Kraus Reprint Corp., 1962.

1789–1969 *CIS U.S. Serial Set Index, 1789–1969*. PRINT. (1975–79) Washington, DC: Congressional Information Service, Inc.

1897–1933 *Index to the Reports and Documents of the [no.] Congress, with Numerical Lists and Schedules of Volumes*. PRINT. U.S. Government Printing Office. Superintendent of Documents. GP 3.7: (Commonly known as *Document Index*).

1933–1980 *Numerical Lists and Schedules of Volumes*. U.S. Government Printing Office. Superintendent of Documents. GP 3.7/2: Item 0553. Buffalo, NY: William S. Hein & Co., Inc. 1983.

1981–1982 *Monthly Catalog of United States Government Publications: United States Congressional Serial Set Supplement*. PRINT. MF. U.S. Government Printing Office. Superintendent of Documents. GP 3.8/6: Item 0557-A or 0557-B(MF).

1983–84– *United States Congressional Serial Set Catalog: Numerical Lists and Schedule of Volumes*. PRINT. MF. U.S. Government Printing Office. Superintendent of Documents. Library Programs Service. Library Division. GP 3.34: Item 0557-A or 0557-B(MF).

Discussion

The *Monthly Catalog*, Ames, and Poore all contain references to congressional reports, but do not give the report location in the *Serial Set*. The indexes in this section should be used to find the exact location of such reports.

Checklist of United States Public Documents

At the beginning of the *Checklist* is a section titled "Congressional Tables." Tables are arranged by Congress number and session. To locate a specific report, such as Senate Executive Document No. 44 (32nd Congress, 2nd session), first find the section for the desired Congress and session. (See Figure 52.5.) Locate the Senate executive documents listing in the "Series" column. Look for number 44 in the "Document no." column. Follow this line back to column one for the *Serial Set* volume number, 665.

CIS U.S. Serial Set Index

The *CIS U.S. Serial Set Index* is divided into parts, each of which covers a group of Congresses or years. The last volume of each part is called "Finding Lists." These lists are arranged by Congress number, then by session, and lastly by type of document. The *Serial Set* volume number is given to the right of each document.

Index to the Reports and Documents of the (no.) Congress, with Numerical Lists and Schedules of Volumes (Document Index)

The *Document Index* generally contains an individual volume for each session of Congress. The first part of each volume is a subject index; the second part is a numerical list section. The numerical list section is arranged by type of publication (House report, Senate document, etc.). The reports are listed in numerical order with the *Serial Set* volume given in the last column.

Numerical Lists and Schedules of Volumes and Its Successors

The *Numerical Lists and Schedules of Volumes* consists of a numerical listing of each report type, the title of the report, and the *Serial Set* volume number. It is the successor to the *Document Index* and is similar in format, but does not contain a subject index. The title and format changed with the 1981–82 volume, which was issued as a supplement to the *Monthly Catalog of United States Government Publications*. Beginning with 1983–84 the publication was issued as a separate title, *United States Congressional Serial Set Catalog*. This version contains a numerical listing of each report type, bibliographic records in SuDocs number order, author index, title index, subject index, series/report index, and bill number index.

26

32d CONGRESS, 2d SESSION

Dec. 6, 1852—Mar. 3, 1853

Serial no.	Vol.	Part	Series	Document no.	Notes
657	....	....	S. journal.....	....	Also proceedings special sess. Senate, 33d Cong., Mar. 4–Apr. 11, 1853, p. 327.
658	1	....	S. ex. docs....	1.............	Message and Interior, 1852.
659	2	....	.....do........	1.............	War, Navy, and Post-Office, 1852.
660	3	....	.....do........	2, 3, 5–21, 23–40	Except 36, in serial nos. 663 and 664.
661	4	....	.....do........	4.............	Louisiana land claims, De Bastrop grant.
662	5	....	.....do........	22.............	Treasury rp. 1852, with Sabine's historical Report on fisheries of American seas, 1504–1852.
				Unnumbered .	Commerce and navigation, 1852.
663	6	1	.....do........	36.............	Exploration of valley of the Amazon, pt. 1, by Herndon.
664	6	2	.....do........	36.............	Same, pt. 2, by Gibbon.
665	7	....	.....do........	41–53, 56, 57....	52 is Foreign commercial regulations.
666	8	....	.....do........	54.............	Exploration of Red River of Louisiana, by Marcy.
667	9	....	.....do........	55.............	Patent Office, 1852, pt. 1, Arts; pt. 2, Agriculture.
668	10	....	.....do........	59.............	Zuni and Colorado River expedition, by Sitgreaves.
669	11	....	.....do........	58.............	Coast Survey, 1852.
670	....	....	S. misc. docs..	1–53.............	53 is Smithsonian Institution, 1852.
671	....	....	S. reports.....	358–432.........	
672	....	....	H. journal.....	....	
673	1	1	H. ex. docs....	1.............	Message and Interior, 1852.
674	1	2	.....do........	1.............	War, Navy, and Post-Office, 1852.
675	2	....	.....do........	2–6.............	2 is estimates for 1854; 6 is Treasurer's accts., 1852.
676	3	....	.....do........	7–23.............	23, Treasury rp., contains Sabine's historical Report on fisheries of American seas, 1504–1852.
677	4	....	.....do........	24–42.............	
678	5	....	.....do........	43.............	Exploration of valley of the Amazon, pt. 1, by Herndon. Pt. 2 is in serial no. 722.
679	6	....	.....do........	44–63.............	Except 62, in serial no. 680.
680	7	....	.....do........	62.............	Mail contracts, etc., 1852.
681	8	....	.....do........	64.............	Coast Survey, 1852.
682	9	1	.....do........	65.............	Patent Office, 1852, pt. 1: Arts and manufactures.
683	9	2	.....do........	65.............	Same, pt. 2: Agriculture.
684¹	10	....	.....do........	66–69.........	Condition of State banks; etc.
684²	11	....	.....do........	Unnumbered .	Commerce and navigation, 1852.
685	....	....	H. misc. docs..	2–24.............	No. 1 not printed.
686	....	....	[H. misc. docs.]	Unnumbered .	7th census of United States, 1850.
687	....	....	H. reports.....	1–7.............	Gardiner Mexican claim investigation; etc.

33d CONGRESS, SPECIAL SESSION SENATE

Mar. 4—Apr. 11, 1853

Serial no.	Vol.	Part	Series	Document no.	Notes
.....	....	....	S. journal.....	....	*See* serial no. 657, p. 327.
688	....	....	S. misc. docs..	1–3.............	
			S. reports.....	1, 2.............	Fraud investigations; etc.
			S. ex. docs....	1–8.............	4 is Indian affairs in California; 6 is Mexican Boundary.

Source: Checklist of United States Public Documents, 1789-1909, p. 26.

Figure 52.5: Sample Page from *Checklist of United States Public Documents*.

LOCATING SUDOCS NUMBERS WHEN NOT GIVEN IN INDEX

Checklist

Checklist of United States Public Documents, 1789–1909. PRINT. (1911) U.S. Government Printing Office. Superintendent of Documents. GP 3.2:C 41/2. (Commonly known as the "1909 Checklist") New York: Kraus Reprint Corp., 1962.

CIS Index to U.S. Executive Branch Documents, 1789–1909: Guide to Documents Listed in Checklist of U.S. Public Documents, 1789–1909, Not Printed in the U.S. Serial Set. PRINT. (1990–1995) Bethesda, MD: Congressional Information Service, Inc.

CIS Index to U.S. Executive Branch Documents, 1910–1932: Guide to Documents Not Printed in the U.S. Serial Set. PRINT. (1996–) In progress. Bethesda, MD: Congressional Information Service, Inc.

Guide to U.S. Government Publications. PRINT. (annual) 1959–. Donna Batten, Editor. Farmington Hills, MI: Gale Group, Inc. (Earlier published by Documents Index.)

Cumulative Title Index to United States Public Documents, 1789–1976. PRINT. 16 vols. (1979–82) Arlington, VA: United States Historical Documents Institute, Inc.

Discussion

In using the *Document Catalogue*, the "original" *Monthly Catalog* (rather than the "Classes Added" edition), Ames, or Poore, references to noncongressional publications will appear, but no SuDocs numbers will be given. The indexes in this section are useful for locating SuDocs numbers for such titles.

The easiest source to use is the *Cumulative Title Index*. In this index, the SuDocs number is listed following each title. If the publication is a recurring title or part of a series (such as an annual report, a periodical, or a numbered series), the *Guide to U.S. Government Publications* can be used. This is arranged by SuDocs classification number and lists the series name that corresponds to each SuDocs stem. The *Guide* lists series titles such as the *Research Monograph* series, but not the individual titles in the series. A series title index allows the user to look up the series name and obtain the SuDocs number.

The *Checklist of United States Public Documents, 1789–1909* is also a SuDocs series listing, but unlike the *Guide to U.S. Government Publications*, it does list individual titles in each series. Unfortunately, there is no title index. It is necessary to browse through the titles under the appropriate agency. (The *CIS Index to U.S. Executive Branch Documents, 1789–1909* can also be used as a title and subject index to these materials.) As an example, the *Checklist of United States Public Documents* can be used to locate a SuDocs number for a publication titled the *Monthly Bulletin*, issued by the American Republics Bureau, and dated 1902. The *Checklist* is arranged by SuDocs number with an agency index in the back. Looking in the

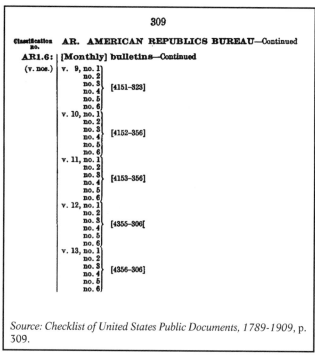

Source: *Checklist of United States Public Documents, 1789-1909*, p. 309.

Figure 52.6: Sample SuDocs Series Listing in *Checklist of United States Public Documents*.

index under the American Republics Bureau, the user is directed to the AR classification number in the SuDocs number section. Scanning this section leads the researcher to AR 1.6:, the number for the *Monthly Bulletin*. (See Figure 52.6.)

Often a government publication is issued by both an executive agency and by Congress. An important feature of the *Checklist* is the listing of both a SuDocs number for the agency edition and a *Serial Set* volume for the congressional edition. Most libraries will have only one of these editions. To the right of each volume of the *Monthly Bulletin* listed in the illustration is a bracketed number, the first part of which is the *Serial Set* volume.

The *CIS Index to U.S. Executive Branch Documents, 1789–1909* provides a title index to the executive agency publications listed in the *Checklist*. Each part covers a different agency or group of agencies. Part 1, for example, covers the publications of the Treasury Department and the Commerce and Labor Department. A title index is included in the supplementary indexes volume of each part. The title index gives an entry number that must be looked up in the accompanying reference bibliography. The bibliographic entry includes the SuDocs number. The availability of this index will make it unnecessary to browse through the agency publication listings in the *Checklist* to locate a SuDocs number for a particular title, as in the *Monthly Bulletin* example above.

HISTORICAL SETS

Checklist

American Archives. PRINT. 9 vols. (1837-53) Z 1.1:
  Content: colonial papers and documents for the period 1774–76 on colonial affairs and the American Revolution.

American State Papers. PRINT. (1832–61) U.S. Congress. Serial Set 01-038.
  Content: executive and legislative documents of the first 14 congresses, 1789–1823, grouped by subject categories such as foreign affairs, Indian affairs, military affairs, and public lands.

Decennial Census. PRINT. (decennial) 1790–1940. U.S. Department of Commerce. Bureau of the Census. C 3.940-5: (Earlier, C 3.37/5:; C 3.28/5:; C 3.16:; I [2 to 13].5:) (Agency varies) (Issued later as individual censuses) Selected data: <http://fisher.lib.virginia.edu/census/>.
  Coverage: varies; U.S., regions, divisions, states, territories, counties, townships, cities, wards.
  Content: varies; demographic, social, and economic statistics; population, manufactures, agriculture, vital statistics, mining, and other special topics.

Foreign Relations of the United States. PRINT. MF. WEB. (annual) 1818–. U.S. Department of State. Bureau of Public Affairs. Office of the Historian. S 1.1: (Earliest volumes issued in the *Serial Set*) Items 0872-B or -C(MF), 0872-D(MF). GPO. Selected volumes: <http://www.state.gov/www/about_state/history/frusonline.html>.
  Content: official record of U.S. foreign policy with correspondence and papers on major policies and decisions.

Historical Statistics of the United States: Colonial Times to 1970. Parts 1-2. PRINT. (1975) U.S. Department of Commerce. Bureau of the Census. C 3.134/2:H 62/789-970/pt.1-2. Item 0151. ASI (76) 2328-2. GPO.
  Content: statistical chapters on such subjects as population, vital statistics, labor, prices, consumer income, land, climate, agriculture, business and manufacturing, communication, and energy.

Historical Statistics of the United States on CD-ROM: Colonial Times to 1970. CD-ROM. (1997) New York, NY: Cambridge University Press.
  Content: CD-ROM version of *Historical Statistics of the United States.*

Journals of the Continental Congress, 1774–88. PRINT. WEB. (1777–1823) 13-34 vols. Various editions. Z 2.5:; Z 2.6:; Z 2.7:; LC 4.5: <http://lcweb2.loc.gov/ammem/amlaw/lwjc.html>.
  Content: proceedings of the Continental Congress.

Naval Documents of the American Revolution. PRINT. 1964–. U.S. Department of the Navy. Naval History Division. D 207.12: Item 0399-D. GPO.
  Content: original documents and letters on naval operations from 1774 to 1777.

Official Records of Union and Confederate Navies in War of Rebellion. PRINT. WEB. 22 vols. (1894–1927) U.S. Department of the Navy. Library and Naval War Records Office. N 16.6: or Serial Set. <http://moa.cit.cornell.edu/MOA/MOA-JOURNALS/OFRE.html>; Guide to volumes in the *Serial Set:*
  <http://www.access.gpo.gov/su_docs/fdlp/pubs/techsup/ts120197.html>.
  Content: letters, documents, reports regarding naval operations during the Civil War.

Revolutionary Diplomatic Correspondence, 1775–85. PRINT. (1889) 5 vols. Z 2.4: or Serial Set 2585-2589.
  Content: correspondence relating to foreign affairs and diplomacy during the American Revolution.

Territorial Papers of the United States. PRINT. 28 vols. (1934–1975) U.S. General Services Administration. National Archives and Records Service. GS 4.13: (Earlier, S 1.36:). Item 0571.
  Content: documents and correspondence relating to the constitutional and political beginnings and administration of territorial areas prior to statehood.

Treaties and Other International Agreements of the United States of America, 1776–1949. PRINT. (1968–76) U.S. Department of State. Compiled by Charles I. Bevans. S 9.12/2: Item 0899-A.
  Content: compilation of texts of treaties and other international agreements of the U.S.

Trial of the Major War Criminals before the International Military Tribunal, Nuremberg. PRINT. WEB. 42 vols. (1947–49) U.S. War Department. International Military Tribunal. W 1.2:C 86/v. <http://www.yale.edu/lawweb/avalon/imt/imt.htm>; <http://www.holocaust-history.org/works/imt/htm/intro001.htm>.
  Content: proceedings and documentary evidence of war criminal trials following World War II.

Trials of War Criminals before the Nuernberg Military Tribunals under Control Council Law No. 10. PRINT. 15 vols. (1949–53) U.S. Department of the Army. Adjutant General's Office. Nuernberg Military Tribunals. D 102.8:
  Content: selected records from the war crimes trials; statements; extracts from arguments; evidence; indictments; judgments; sentences.

United States Army in the Korean War. PRINT. WEB. 1961–. U.S. Department of the Army. Center of Military History. D 114.2:K 84/2/v., K 84/5. Item 0344. Selected volumes: <http://www.army.mil/cmh-pg/collections/USAKW.htm>.
  Content: history of combat operations in the Korean War and special topics.

United States Army in the World War, 1917–1919. PRINT. 17 vols. (1988–1992) U.S. Department of the Army. Center of Military History. D 114.8: (Reprint; earlier, M 103.9:) Item 0345.
  Content: correspondence; memorandums; reports; statistics on military organization and operations during World War I.

The United States Army in World War I. CD-ROM. (1998) U.S. Department of the Army. Center of Military History. D 114.21:W 19/v.1-3/CD. Item 0344-J. GPO.
  Content: CD-ROM version of *United States Army in the World War, 1917-1919,* plus all other agency publications on World War I including *Learning Lessons in the American Expeditionary Forces, Order of Battle of the United States Land Forces in the World War, American Armies and Battlefields in Europe,* and *Army Art of World War I.*

United States Army in World War II. PRINT. WEB. (1947–) U.S. Department of Defense. Army. Center of Military History.

D 114.7: Item 0345. Selected volumes: <http://www.army.mil/cmh-pg/collections/usaww2/USAWW2.htm>.

> Content: history of the Army in World War II with volumes on various theaters of operations, the War Department, technical services, and special studies on such topics as women and Blacks.

United States Statutes at Large. (STAT) PRINT. WEB. (annual) 1789–. U.S. National Archives and Records Administration. Office of the Federal Register. AE 2.111: (Earlier, GS 4.111:; S 7.9:) (Title varies) Item 0576. GPO. Early volumes: <http://lcweb2.loc.gov/ammem/amlaw/lwsl.html>.

> Content: laws; treaties before 1950; presidential proclamations.

Congressional Universe. WEB. Bethesda, MD: Congressional Information Service. Related information: <http://www.lexis-nexis.com/cispubs/Catalog/Universe/Congressional%20Universe/index.htm>.

> Content: includes add-on subscription for *United States Statutes at Large,* 1789–.

United States Treaties and Other International Agreements. PRINT. 1950–. U.S. Department of State. S 9.12: 0899-A.

> Coverage: texts of treaties and other international agreements of the U.S.

War of the Rebellion. Official Records of the Union and Confederate Armies. PRINT. WEB. 130 vols. (1880–1901) U.S. War Department. W 45.5: or Serial Set. <http://moa.cit.cornell.edu/MOA/MOA-JOURNALS/WARO.html>; Guide to volumes in the *Serial Set:* <http://www.access.gpo.gov/su_docs/fdlp/pubs/techsup/ts12097.html>.

> Content: military records; reports; letters; orders on the Civil War arranged by campaign and theaters of operation.

Army Official Records. Official Records of the Union and Confederate Armies. CD-ROM. (1995) Wilmington, NC: Broadfoot Publishing Co.

> Content: CD-ROM version of the *War of the Rebellion.*

CONGRESSIONAL PROCEEDINGS

Annals of Congress. PRINT. WEB. 1780–1824. X 1-X 42. <http://lcweb2.loc.gov/ammem/amlaw/lwac.html>.

Register of Debates. PRINT. WEB. 1824–37. X 43-X 71. <http://lcweb2.loc.gov/ammem/amlaw/lwrd.html>.

Congressional Globe. PRINT. WEB. 1833–73. X 72-X 180. <http://lcweb2.loc.gov/ammem/amlaw/lwcg.html>.

> Content: summary of congressional proceedings; predecessors to the *Congressional Record.*

Congressional Record. PRINT. MF. WEB. (daily when Congress in session) 1873–. U.S. Congress. X 1.1:; X 1.1/A: (Earlier, X, X/A) Items 0993-A(MF); 0993-A-01 (Regionals only, 1985-), 0993-B or -C(MF), 0994-B or -C(MF), 0994-D(EL). GPO. <http://www.access.gpo.gov/su_docs/aces/aces150.html>; <http://purl.access.gpo.gov/GPO/LPS1671>; <http://thomas.loc.gov/>.

> Content: official transcript of congressional proceedings.

Journal of the House of Representatives of the United States. PRINT. MF. CD-ROM. WEB. (annual) 1789–. U.S. Congress. House. XJH. (Early journals issued in the *Serial Set*) (Reprint edition of 1789–1817 published by Michael Glazier, Wilmington, DE, 1977) Items 1030-A, -B(MF), or B-01(CD). Early volumes: <http://lcweb2.loc.gov/ammem/amlaw/lwhj.html>; 1991- <http://www.access.gpo.gov/congress/cong018.html>; <http://purl.access.gpo.gov/GPO/LPS2564>.

> Content: official record of House proceedings.

Journal of the Senate of the United States of America. PRINT. MF. WEB. (annual) 1789–. U.S. Congress. Senate. XJS. (Early journals issued in the *Serial Set*) (Reprint edition of 1789–1817 published by Michael Glazier, Wilmington, DE, 1977) Items 1047-A or -B(MF). Early volumes: <http://lcweb2.loc.gov/ammem/amlaw/lwsj.html>; <http://purl.access.gpo.gov/GPO/LP5486>.

> Content: official record of Senate proceedings.

Journal of the Executive Proceedings of the Senate of the United States of America. PRINT. MF. WEB. 1789–. U.S. Congress. Senate. Y 1.3/4: (Earlier, Y 1.3:EX 3/) (Title varies) (Reprint edition of early journals published by Johnson Reprint Corp., NY, 1969) Items 1047-C or -D(MF). Early volumes: <http://lcweb2.loc.gov/ammem/amlaw/lwej.html>.

> Content: record of secret Senate meetings, published by Senate order usually after a period of time has passed.

Discussion

These titles are examples of major sets of historical materials compiled and published by the government. Some of the titles are available, at least in part, on the Internet. Although federal government publications begin in 1789, a few of the sets in this list contain materials from the pre-federal period. The *Checklist of United States Public Documents, 1789–1909,* discussed earlier, does include a small number of such materials under the SuDocs number Z. Z 1 was assigned to colonial documents and Z 2 to Continental Congress documents. These early collections were printed by various private printers and often in more than one edition.

Some of these series were issued in the *Serial Set* as well as by the executive department. *Official Records of the Union and Confederate Navies in War of Rebellion,* for example, was issued by the Navy under N 16.6: and as part of the *Serial Set.* Most libraries that have the *Official Records* will have one or the other of these editions, but not both. For complete bibliographic information on sets published before 1909, see the *Checklist of United States Public Documents* under the SuDocs number for that title.

DIGITAL AND MICROFORM SOURCE COLLECTIONS
Checklist

A Century of Lawmaking for a New Nation: U.S. Congressional Documents and Debates 1774–1873. WEB. Library of Congress. <http://lcweb2.loc.gov/ammem/amlaw/lawhome.html>.

> Content: full-text historical Congressional proceedings, documents, journals, and laws.

The Avalon Project at the Yale Law School: Documents in Law, History and Diplomacy. WEB. Yale Law School. <http://www.yale.edu/lawweb/avalon/avalon.htm>.

> Content: full-text historical resources including selected presidential messages and papers, selected statutes and treaties, and selected documents on foreign relations.

The National Security Archive. WEB. George Washington University. Gelman Library. The National Security Archive. <http://www.gwu.edu/~nsarchiv/>.

> Content: collections of declassified and other documents in selected areas of international relations.

CIS History Universe. WEB. Bethesda, MD: Congressional Information Service. Information: <http://www.lexisnexis.com/cispubs/Catalog/Universe/History%20Universe/index.htm>.

> Content: subject collections of primary resources and related secondary materials.

Discussion

Several projects are underway to make selected full-text historical source material available on the Internet. Selected Web sites containing U.S. government resources are listed in this section. *A Century of Lawmaking for a New Nation: U.S. Congressional Documents and Debates 1774–1873* is part of the Library of Congress's *American Memory Historical Collections* Web site. *American Memory* is a multimedia online resource for primary source materials on American history and culture. *A Century of Lawmaking for a New Nation* is a collection of the records of Congress that begins with 1774 and will cover up to 1873 when completed. It contains the records of the Continental Congress, the Constitutional Convention, and early Congresses. Titles available include the *Journals of the Continental Congress, 1774–1789, The Records of the Federal Convention of 1787 (Farrand's Records), The Debates in the Several State Conventions on the Adoption of the Federal Constitution, as Recommended by the General Convention at Philadelphia in 1787 (Elliot's Debates), Journal of the House of Representatives of the United States, Journal of the Senate of the United States of America, Journal of the Executive Proceedings of the Senate of the United States of America, Annals of Congress, Register of Debates, Congressional Globe, Journal of William Maclay, United States Senator from Pennsylvania, 1789–1991, Statutes at Large,* and the *Serial Set.* Future additions will include the *American State Papers.*

The Avalon Project at the Yale Law School: Documents in Law, History and Diplomacy provides selected primary resources in law, history, economics, politics, diplomacy, and government. Some of the major collection areas include "The American Constitution – a Documentary Record," "American Diplomacy: Bilateral Treaties 1778–1999," "Annual Messages of the Presidents," "Presidential Papers," and "United States Statutes." Each area contains a selection of individual documents. Materials can be listed by century, title, subject, major collection, and author. A general search option is also available.

The National Security Archive Web site contains collections of declassified documents on international relations obtained through Freedom of Information Act requests. The "Electronic Briefing Books" menu option offers collections of full-text documents in selected areas such as "The United States, China, and the Bomb," "The Contras, Cocaine, and Covert Operations," and "CIA and Assassinations: The Guatemala 1954 Documents."

CIS History Universe is a subscription Web database of primary source materials in selected subject areas. Initial subject areas covered are African American Studies, guides to selected University Publications of America microform collections, and Women's Studies. Examples of materials available include federal legislation, U.S. Supreme Court decisions, reference works, biographies, and manuscript collections.

Several other publishers also make available collections of primary U.S. government publications in various formats. Congressional Information Service (CIS) publishes microfiche collections of all of the materials indexed in CIS indexes, as well as other microfiche sets. Also available through CIS are the products of University Publications of America (UPA), a CIS imprint. University Publications of America publishes extensive microform research collections, many of which contain U.S. government materials. Examples include *Major Studies and Issue Briefs of the Congressional Research Service* (index also available on CD-ROM), FBI documents, Presidential papers and files, and State Department files on international relations from the National Archives.

Other selected publishers include Chadwyck-Healey, Primary Source Media, and Scholarly Resources. Chadwyck-Healey publishes microfiche collections of declassified material from the National Security Archive in a series of documentary collections on contemporary foreign policy areas. In addition to the microfiche collections, Chadwyck-Healey offers a Web version of the collections and a CD-ROM index. Primary Source Media offers such collections as Census microfilm, the *Declassified Documents* index and Web collection mentioned in the "General Indexes" section of this chapter, and CD-ROM collections on U.S. history topics. Scholarly Resources provides collections of National Archives materials on international relations, some FBI files, and manuscript collections.

BIOGRAPHICAL DIRECTORIES

Checklist

The Presidents of the United States of America. PRINT. WEB. (1995) White House Historical Association. (Nondepository) (Earlier, Y 3.H 62/4:2 P 92, Item 1089) <http://www.whitehouse.gov/WH/glimpse/presidents/html/presidents.html>.

> Content: color portraits and biographies of the Presidents.

The First Ladies. PRINT. WEB. (1995) White House Historical Association. (Nondepository) (Earlier, Y 3.H 62/4:2 F 51, Item

1089) <http://www.whitehouse.gov/WH/glimpse/firstladies/html/firstladies.html>.

> Content: color portraits and biographies of First Ladies.

The Presidents from the Inauguration of George Washington to the Inauguration of Jimmy Carter: Historic Places Commemorating the Chief Executives of the United States. PRINT. (1977) U.S. Department of the Interior. National Park Service. The National Survey of Historic Sites and Buildings. I 29.2:H 62/9/v.20/977. Item 0648.

> Content: color portraits and biographical sketches of Presidents; list and description of historic sites associated with Presidents.

Vice Presidents of the United States, 1789–1993. PRINT. MF. (1997) U.S. Congress. Senate. Senate Document No. 104-26. Y 1.1/2:14332. Items 0996-B(MF) or –C. GPO.

> Content: biographies of vice presidents.

The Supreme Court of the United States: Its Beginnings and Its Justices 1790–1991. PRINT. (1992) U.S. Commission on the Bicentennial of the United States Constitution. Y 3.B 47/2:2 SU 7. Item 1089. Site based on information from this source: <http://supct.law.cornell.edu/supct/cases/judges.htm>.

> Content: color portraits and biographies of Supreme Court justices.

Federal Judges Biographical Database. WEB. 1789–. Federal Judiciary Center. <http://air.fjc.gov/history/judges_frm.html>.

> Content: biographical information on federal judges.

Biographical Directory of the United States Congress: 1774–2000. PRINT. (2000) Lanham, MD: Bernan.

> Content: updated commercial version of the *Biographical Directory of the United States Congress.*

Biographical Directory of the United States Congress 1774–1989. PRINT. MF. (1989) U.S. Congress. Senate. Senate Document No. 100-34. (Bicentennial edition) Y 1.1/2:13849. Items 0996-B(MF) or -C. GPO.

> Content: biographies of all individuals who have served in Congress.

Biographical Directory of the United States Congress 1774–Present. WEB. U.S. Congress. <http://bioguide.congress.gov/biosearch/biosearch.asp>.

> Content: database of biographies of all individuals who have served in Congress; links to related research collections and bibliographies when available.

Biographical Directory of the Federal Judiciary, 1779–2000. PRINT. (2000) Lanham, MD: Bernan.

> Content: basic biographical information on all federal judges.

Women in Congress, 1917–1990. PRINT. MF. (1991) U.S. Congress. House. Office of the Historian. House Document No. 101-238. Y 1.1/2:14004. Items 0996-B(MF) or -C.

> Content: biographies of women who have served in the House or Senate.

Black Americans in Congress, 1870–1989. PRINT. MF. (1990) U.S. Congress. House. Office of the Historian. House Document No. 101-117. Y 1.1/2:13947. Items 0996-B(MF) or -C.

> Content: biographies of African-Americans who have served in the House or Senate.

A Guide to Research Collections of Former Members of the United States House of Representatives 1789–1987. PRINT. MF. WEB. (1988) U.S. Congress. House. Office for the Bicentennial. House Document No. 100-171. Y 1.1/2:13874. Items 0996-B(MF) or -C. <http://bioguide.congress.gov/biosearch/biosearch.asp>.

> Content: directory of manuscript collections containing the papers of former members of the House.

Guide to Research Collections of Former United States Senators 1789–1995. PRINT. MF. WEB. (1995) U.S. Congress. Senate. Senate Document No. 103-35. Y 1.1/2:14218. Items 0996-B(MF) or -C. <http://bioguide.congress.gov/biosearch/biosearch.asp>.

> Content: directory of manuscript collections containing the papers of former members of the Senate.

Senators of the United States: A Historical Bibliography: A Compilation of Works By and About Members of the United States Senate 1789–1995. PRINT. MF. WEB. (1995) U.S. Congress. Senate. Senate Document No. 103-34. Y 1.1/2:14217. Items 0996-B(MF) or –C. GPO. <http://bioguide.congress.gov/biosearch/biosearch.asp>.

> Content: selected bibliographic references for members of Senate with emphasis on materials relating to their Senate terms.

Librarians of Congress 1802–1974. PRINT. (1977) U.S. Library of Congress. LC 1.2:L 61/16/802-974. Item 0786.

> Content: biographical articles on librarians of Congress with emphasis on career accomplishments and events.

Soldier-Statesmen of the Constitution. PRINT. (1987) U.S. Department of Defense. Army. Center of Military History. D 114.19:C 76. Item 0344-G.

> Content: biographies of Revolutionary War veterans who also played a role in developing the Constitution.

Signers of the Declaration: Historic Places Commemorating the Signing of the Declaration of Independence. PRINT. (1975) U.S. Department of the Interior. National Park Service. The National Survey of Historic Sites and Buildings. I 29.2:H 62/9/v.18/975. Item 0648.

> Content: biographies and portraits of the signers of the Declaration of Independence; historical background; historic sites.

Secretaries of War and Secretaries of the Army: Portraits and Biographical Sketches. PRINT. (1992) U.S. Department of Defense. Army. Center of Military History. D 114.2:SE 2/992. Item 0344.

> Content: biographies and portraits of secretaries of war and secretaries of the army.

Commanding Generals and Chiefs of Staff 1775–1995: Portraits & Biographical Sketches of the United States Army's Senior Officers. PRINT. WEB. (1999) U.S. Department of the Army. Center of Military History. D 114.2:G 28/775-95. Item 0344. GPO. <http://www.army.mil/cmh-pg/books/cg&csa/cg-toc.htm>.

> Content: biographies and portraits of army commanding generals and chiefs of staff.

The Chairmanship of the Joint Chiefs of Staff. PRINT. WEB. (1995) U.S. Office of the Chairman of the Joint Chiefs of Staff. Joint History Office. D 5.2:C 34/2. Item 0315. GPO. <http://www.dtic.mil:80/jcs/core/history.html>.

> Content: analysis of evolving role of the chairman; biographies.

The Sergeants Major of the Army. PRINT. (1995) U.S. Department of the Army. Center of Military History. D 114.2:SE 6/2. Item 0344.

　　Content: biographies and portraits of army sergeants major.

The Secretaries of State: Portraits and Biographical Sketches. PRINT. (1978) U.S. Department of State. Office of Public Communication. Bureau of Public Affairs. Department and Foreign Service Series. S 1.69:162. Item 0863.

　　Content: portraits and biographies of secretaries of state.

Attorneys General of the United States 1789–1985. PRINT. (1985) U.S. Department of Justice. J 1.2:AT 8/6/789-85. Item 0717.

　　Content: portraits and biographies of attorneys general.

A Biographical Directory of the United States Customs Service, 1771–1989. 2 vols. (1985–86) U.S. Department of the Treasury. Customs Service. Historical Study series, nos. 4 & 5. T 17.15/2:B 52/771-989/v.1-2. Item 0948-B-01.

　　Content: biographies of customs commissioners, chiefs, collectors, officers, surveyors, and other employees.

Astronauts and Cosmonauts Biographical and Statistical Data. PRINT. MF. (1994) U.S. Congress. House. Committee on Science, Space, and Technology. Y 4.SCI 2:103/I. Items 1025-A-01 or -02(MF).

　　Content: biographies of U.S. astronauts and cosmonauts of the former Soviet Union.

Discussion

Biographical directories for government leaders and politicians are sometimes published by U.S. government agencies. Many of these are historical directories, spanning many years. This section lists some of the major directories available from U.S. government agencies. Many nongovernmental biographical sources are also available in these areas.

The Presidents of the United States of America and *The First Ladies* contain full-page color portraits of each President or first lady and give brief biographies. These are attractive and convenient sources for basic information on the Presidents and first ladies.

The Presidents from the Inauguration of George Washington to the Inauguration of Jimmy Carter: Historic Places Commemorating the Chief Executives of the United States also contains color portraits of the Presidents and longer biographical sketches. The second half of the book is a listing by state of National Park and historic landmark areas associated with Presidents, such as birthplaces, homes, monuments, and sites of historic occasions. Illustrations and descriptions of each area are provided. This book also contains an introductory survey of the historic role of Presidents and a summary of presidential characteristics derived from the biographical sketches.

Vice Presidents of the United States contains biographies for each vice president. Biographies provide basic background information with emphasis on the role of vice president, including selection for the position, major national issues, relationship with the president, and contributions in the position. Black and white portraits are included. An appendix lists major party presidential and vice-presidential candidates in each election year. Bibliographic references are included.

The Supreme Court of the United States contains full-page color portraits and one-page biographies of the Supreme Court justices from 1790 through 1991. Other sections cover the buildings and locations of the Supreme Court and the texts of remarks made at a bicentennial commemoration ceremony. A chronological list of the justices gives place and date of birth, date of judicial oath, age at which oath was taken, ending date of service, cause of termination, number of years of service, date of death, and the name of the appointing President. A bibliography is also included. Biographical information from this source has been incorporated into the Legal Information Institute Web site at Cornell Law School.

The *Federal Judges Biographical Database* is available on the Web as part of the Federal Judiciary Center's *History of the Federal Judiciary* Web site. The database provides brief biographical information on each federal judge's service record, date and place of birth and death, education, professional career, race or ethnicity, and gender. The service record includes date of nomination and nominating president. Users can search by name or list judges alphabetically by first letter of last name. Searches can also be done on selected criteria including court, nominating president, race, nomination date, and termination reason. The Web site provides additional historical information on courts, landmark judicial legislation, and selected topics such as impeachment.

The *Biographical Directory of the United States Congress 1774–1989* contains brief biographies for the more than 11,000 persons who have served in Congress. Entries are arranged alphabetically by name and contain basic data on office held, state represented, birthplace and date of birth, education, employment, other political offices, place and date of death, and place of burial. Occasional bibliographic references are included. A chronological section lists the members of each congress by date, beginning with the Continental Congress. A similar section lists officers of the executive branch chronologically by administration.

The *Biographical Directory of the United States Congress 1774–Present* is a searchable Web database based on the print publication of the same name, but updated to the present. Searches may be done by name, position, and state. Biographies include links to listings of research collections from *A Guide to Research Collections of Former Members of the United States House of Representatives* and *Guide to Research Collections of Former United States Senators* discussed in this section. Links to bibliographies for senators are also included from *Senators of the United States: A Historical Bibliography* also discussed in this section.

Women in Congress contains brief biographies with pictures of 115 representatives and 16 senators. Entries are alphabetically arranged and include office held, dates of office, political party membership, state represented, political career, education, family background, and major accomplishments.

Black Americans in Congress contains brief biographies with pictures of 65 Black Americans who have served in Congress. Entries are alphabetically arranged and include office held, dates of office, political party membership, state represented, background, and information on the person's political career. A small number of references for further reading are also provided.

A Guide to Research Collections of Former Members of the United States House of Representatives identifies public repositories and private collections containing the papers of former members of the House of Representatives. Such papers may consist of personal letters, diaries, office correspondence, scrapbooks, photographs, and other historical materials. The *Guide* is arranged alphabetically by representative's name. The representative's birth and death dates are given, as well as the state represented. Repositories are listed under each representative with information about the dates covered by the collection, the size of the collection, and a brief description. A list of the repositories by state is also included. Information from this source is incorporated in the Web version of the *Biographical Directory of the United States Congress,* also discussed in this section.

The *Guide to Research Collections of Former United States Senators* is similar in concept to the guide for representatives. It is arranged alphabetically by senator's name with the senator's birth and death dates, dates of Senate service, state represented, and party affiliation. Under each name is a list of libraries, historical societies, or other collections containing personal papers. A brief notation indicates time span, often the size of the collection or number of items, and content. Collections may contain personal papers, family papers, staff papers, correspondence, or oral history interview transcripts. Appendixes list senators by state, senators for whom no collections were found, and repository addresses by state. Information from this source is incorporated in the Web version of the *Biographical Directory of the United States Congress,* also discussed in this section.

Senators of the United States: A Historical Bibliography contains an alphabetical listing of senators who served from 1789 through January 1995 with selected bibliographic references on their lives and Senate careers. Basic information given for each senator includes date of birth, date of death, state, dates of service, and party. Bibliographic references are included for 1,164 of the 1,817 individuals listed. References include monographs, journal articles, and dissertations. An appendix lists senators by state. Information from this source is incorporated in

the Web version of the *Biographical Directory of the United States Congress,* also discussed in this section.

Librarians of Congress is a collection of articles on each of the first 12 librarians of Congress. In-depth articles survey the life and career of each librarian and include portraits and other illustrations.

Soldier-Statesmen of the Constitution contains biographical studies of 23 signers of the Constitution who also served in the Revolutionary War. An introduction provides an overview of the period and the role of the army in the founding of the United States. Each biography contains three sections: "The Patriot," "The Soldier," and "The Statesman." These discuss the development and career of each individual. A portrait is also included. Briefer biographical information is provided on nonmilitary signers of the Constitution. A selection of historical documents relating to the origin and development of the early military organization is also included. Appendixes provide lists of delegates to the Constitutional Convention, statistics on military service during the Revolution, a more complete list of soldiers who held national offices, and a list of selected further readings.

Signers of the Declaration is in the same series as *The Presidents from the Inauguration of George Washington to the Inauguration of Jimmy Carter* and is similar in format. Part 1 is a survey of the historical background of the Declaration of Independence. Part 2 contains biographical sketches arranged alphabetically by name. Each sketch is two to three pages long and includes a small portrait. Part 3 is a listing and description, by state, of historical sites and buildings associated with the signers. These include National Park Service areas, National Historic Landmarks, and other historical sites. Photographs are included. An appendix contains the text of the Declaration of Independence and a history of the document with suggested reading.

Secretaries of War and Secretaries of the Army contains full-page portraits and brief biographical sketches of secretaries of war and secretaries of the army. Entries are arranged chronologically. An introduction provides an overview of the creation of the War Department and the later Army Department, an overview of the secretaries, and a history of the secretaries' headquarters buildings. Appendixes provide a list of ad interim and acting secretaries and a chronological list of Presidents and secretaries. A general bibliography and a bibliography of individual secretaries and portrait artists are also included.

Commanding Generals and Chiefs of Staff contains full-page portraits and brief biographies of army chiefs of staff or, as the position was called in earlier days, commanding generals. Entries are arranged in chronological order. An introduction provides extensive historical background on the development of the position and the operation of the office. An appendix provides a chronological list of Presidents, secretaries of war or secretaries of the army, and commanding generals or chiefs of staff. A general bibliography and a bibliography by individual senior officer are also included.

The Chairmanship of the Joint Chiefs of Staff contains biographies of 12 officers who have served as chairman and two who have served as vice chairman. Biographies are arranged chronologically and range from five to seven pages in length. A list of promotions, assignments, and decorations is also included with each biography. Photographs or illustrations are included. A narrative section discusses the evolving role of the chairman. Appendixes contain the texts of relevant laws and a chronological listing of Presidents, secretaries of defense, and chairmen.

The Sergeants Major of the Army contains biographies and full-page portraits of army sergeants major. Biographies include a list of assignments and selected decorations and awards. The first part of the book describes the origin and development of the office. An appendix provides a chronological list of Presidents, secretaries of the army, chiefs of staff, and sergeants major.

The Secretaries of State contains full-page portraits and brief biographical information on secretaries of state. Entries are arranged chronologically. Appendixes list ad interim secretaries and provide a chronological list of Presidents, secretaries for foreign affairs, and secretaries of state.

Attorneys General of the United States contains full-page portraits and a brief biographical sketch of each attorney general. Entries are arranged chronologically with an alphabetical name index.

A Biographical Directory of the United States Customs Service contains over 1,000 brief biographical entries for Customs Service officers. Volume 1 is an alphabetical dictionary of names with information on office held; dates of office; birth and death dates; education, political, military or literary activity; predecessor and successor; and family. Volume 2 contains entries for lesser-known individuals identified after completion of volume 1. Entries are alphabetically arranged with one entry per page. Information provided is usually more limited than in volume 1. A note on source of information is included.

Astronauts and Cosmonauts Biographical and Statistical Data contains biographical information for all participants in space missions of the U.S. and of the former Soviet Union. Part 1 contains an overview of the U.S. astronaut program and biographies of U.S. mission participants. The biographies are divided into three groups: astronauts, participants in flight programs that develop astronauts, and payload specialists and other passengers. Information on each individual includes a photograph and brief biographical data. Part 2 contains similar information on cosmonauts of the former Soviet Union and foreign cosmonaut-researchers. Photographs are not always available for cosmonauts. Summary tables in each biographical section list astronauts with information on rank, flights, and total space time. Part 3 contains comparative data on space flights of the United States and of the former Soviet Union.

MILITARY HISTORY SERIES
Checklist
Army

U.S. Army Center of Military History Web Site. WEB. U.S. Department of the Army. Center of Military History. <http://www.army.mil/cmh-pg/default.htm>.

> Content: full-text publications; publication catalog; artworks and photographs; agency information.

A Guide to the Study and Use of Military History. PRINT. (1979) U.S. Department of the Army. Center of Military History. D 114.12:ST 9. Item 0344-F. GPO.

> Content: nature, use, and methods of military history; guide to major military history sources.

General Publications. PRINT. (irregular) U.S. Department of the Army. Center of Military History. D 114.2: Item 0344. GPO.

> Content: miscellaneous monographs on army history.

The U.S. Army Campaigns of World War II. PRINT. WEB. (irregular) 1992–. U.S. Department of the Army. Center of Military History. D 114.7/5: Item 0344-G. GPO. Selected titles: <http://www.army.mil/cmh-pg/online/Bookshelves/WW2-List.htm>.

> Content: booklets on individual campaigns.

American Forces in Action Series. PRINT. (irregular) U.S. Department of the Army. Center of Military History. D 114.9: Item 0344-G. GPO. Selected titles: <http://www.army.mil/cmh-pg/collections/AFIA.htm>.

> Content: studies on World War II operations.

Army Historical Series. PRINT. (irregular) U.S. Department of the Army. Center of Military History. D 114.19: Item 0344-G. GPO.

> Content: studies on army history.

Navy

Dictionary of American Naval Fighting Ships. PRINT. (1959–) U.S. Department of the Navy. Naval Historical Center. D 207.10: Item 0399-A. GPO.

> Content: alphabetical listing of navy ships with history and description.

General Publications. PRINT. (irregular) U.S. Department of the Navy. Naval Historical Center. D 221.2: (Some historical monographs previously issued under D 207.10/2:) Item 0415-D-04. GPO.

> Content: miscellaneous publications on naval history.

Contributions to Naval History. PRINT. (1988–) U.S. Department of the Navy. Naval Historical Center. D 221.19: (Earlier, D 207.10/4:) Item 0399-A-04. GPO.

> Content: studies on naval history.

Naval Historical Center Web Site. WEB. U.S. Department of the Navy. Naval Historical Center. <http://www.history.navy.mil/index.html>.

> Content: naval history resources, publication listings, bibliographies, agency information.

Marine Corps

Historical Publications. PRINT. (irregular) U.S. Marine Corps. History and Museums Division. D 214.13: Item 0383-B. GPO.
> Content: studies on the history of the Marines.

Marines in World War II Commemorative Series. PRINT. U.S. Marine Corps. D 214.14/4: Item 0383-C. GPO.
> Content: pamphlet histories on the marines in World War II.

Air Force

The Army Air Forces in World War II. PRINT. WEB. (irregular) U.S. Department of Defense. Air Force. Office of Air Force History. D 301.82: Item 0422-M. <http://www.airforcehistory.hq.af.mil/online/index.htm>.
> Content: history of the Army air forces; action and events in World War II.

The U.S. Air Service in World War I. PRINT. 4 vols. (1978–79) U.S. Air Force. Office of Air Force History. Albert F. Simpson Historical Research Center. D 301.82/2: Item 0422-M.
> Content: documents and reports related to U.S. air activities in Europe during World War I.

The United States Air Force General Histories. PRINT. (irregular) U.S. Air Force. Office of Air Force History. D 301.82/3: Item 0422-M.
> Content: general historical monographs on Air Force history.

United States Air Force Special Studies. PRINT. (irregular) U.S. Air Force. Office of Air Force History. D 301.82/4: Item 0422-M-01.
> Content: historical monographs on special topics relating to the Air Force.

United States Air Force Reference Series. PRINT. (irregular) U.S. Air Force. Office of Air Force History. D 301.82/5: Item 0422-M-01. GPO.
> Content: reference titles on air force history.

Air Staff Historical Study. PRINT. (irregular) U.S. Air Force. Office of Air Force History. D 301.82/6: Item 0422-M-02.
> Content: monographs on Air Force history.

Air Force History and Museums Program Publications. PRINT. U.S. Air Force. Air Force History and Museums Program. D 301.82/7: Item 0422-M-01. GPO.
> Content: general and topical histories.

USAF Warrior Studies. PRINT. (irregular) U.S. Air Force. Office of Air Force History. D 301.96: Item 0422-M-01.
> Content: historical Air Force studies on military history, combat leadership, and principles of war.

General Publications. PRINT. (irregular) U.S. Air Force. D 301.2: Item 0424. GPO.
> Content: historical Air Force studies.

United States Air Force History Support Office Web Site. WEB. U.S. Air Force. Air Force History Support Office. <http://www.airforcehistory.hq.af.mil/>.
> Content: publications list, selected full-text publications, links to Web resources on military history.

Discussion

Government agencies publish many secondary historical studies such as agency histories. Any agency may publish such a study, but the Defense Department in particular produces a large number of historical series. Selected military series are listed and discussed in this section.

The army's Center of Military History publishes many books and pamphlets on army history. These include major multivolume histories of World War I, World War II, the Korean War, and Vietnam. The World War I and II sets and the Korean War set are listed in the "Historical Sets" section of this chapter. The Vietnam series is listed and discussed in the "Vietnam" section of this chapter. Other monographs and series cover many subjects in U.S. military history and include general survey texts and detailed studies of specific departments, battles, and operations. A selection of these series is discussed here.

The *U.S. Army Center of Military History Web Site* provides the full-text of selected agency publications. The "Online Bookshelves" main menu option offers works published online arranged by time period or collection (series). Most of the series from this agency discussed in this chapter are represented with at least one online title. The "CMH Publications" menu choice links to *Publications of the U.S. Army Center of Military History,* the agency's catalog of publications in print. Main menu options also include "Artworks and Images," containing selections of art and photographs arranged by broad subject or artist.

The center's *A Guide to the Study and Use of Military History* provides an introduction to the field of military history and a guide to important bibliographic sources. The book is divided into four parts. Part 1 discusses the nature, value, and study of military history. Part 2 is the largest section and consists of several bibliographic essays for different time periods. Each essay discusses the major military history sources covering that time period and provides a bibliography. Parts 3 and 4 discuss the army's military history program and the programs of other military branches.

A variety of monographs from the Center of Military History are issued in the *General Publications* series. These publications range from a multivolume set on the *Order of Battle of the United States Land Forces in the World War* (D 114.2:B 32/v.) to a soldier-statesman series of brief biographical pamphlets on Revolutionary War veterans who contributed to the founding of the republic. Examples of other studies include *Black Soldier, White Army: The 24th Infantry Regiment in Korea* (D 114.2:B 56); *Lucky War: Third Army in Desert Storm* (D 114.2:D 45); *United States Army Logistics, 1775–1992: An Anthology* (D 114.2:L 82/4/v.1-3); and *The Inspectors General of the United States Army 1777–1903* (D 114.2:IN 7).

The *U.S. Army Campaigns of World War II* series, also from the Center of Military History, contains short booklets on individual campaigns. Examples of titles include *India-Burma* (D 114.7/5:IN 2) and *Philippine Is-*

lands (D 114.7/5:P 53). Booklets contain sections on the strategic setting, operations, analysis, and suggestions for further reading. Maps and photographs are also included.

The *American Forces in Action Series* consists of studies on World War II operations. Studies summarize major campaigns and battles, drawing on combat interviews and primary sources. Examples of titles include *Anzio Beachhead, 22 January – 25 May, 1944* (D 114.9:AN 9); *Guam: Operations of the 77th Division, 21 July – 10 August, 1944* (D 114.9:G 93); and *Merrill's Marauders, February – May 1944* (D 114.9:M 55). A small number of the titles in this series are available on the Web.

The *Army Historical Series* also contains historical studies. The series includes *American Military History* (D 114.19:M 59/2), a textbook for ROTC courses, and *Soldier-Statesmen of the Constitution* (D 114.19:C 76), a compilation of patriot biographies and significant documents of the period. Selected chapters from *American Military History* are included on the *U.S. Army Center of Military History Web Site* under "Online Bookshelves" in the published works by time period listings. Other titles in this series include *Combat Actions in Korea* (D 114.19:C 73); *The Role of Federal Military Forces in Domestic Disorders, 1789–1878* (D 114.19:R 64); *The Women's Army Corps, 1945–1978* (D 114.19:W 84); and *Getting the Message Through: A Branch History of the U.S. Army Signal Corps* (D 114.19:M 56).

The *Dictionary of American Naval Ships* is an eight-volume set listing ships alphabetically by name. Information is provided on the historical setting and contribution of each ship, as well as on its physical characteristics. Illustrations are sometimes included. Many of the volumes include appendixes on specific classes of ships, such as aircraft ships, battleships, amphibious assault ships, or cruisers.

The Naval Historical Center's *General Publications* series includes a small number of publications on naval history. Titles include *United States Naval Aviation, 1910–1995* (D 221.2:AV 5); *Shield and Sword: The United States Navy and the Persian Gulf War* (D 221.2:G 95); and *A Century of U.S. Naval Intelligence* (D 221.2:IN 8). Earlier historical monographs from this agency were published in a now discontinued *Historical Publications* series under D 207.10/2:.

The *Contributions to Naval History* series, also from the Naval Historical Center, consists of a small number of studies on various historical topics. Examples of titles include *Black Shoes and Blue Water: Surface Warfare in the United States Navy, 1945–1975* (D 221.19:6); *"Damn the Torpedoes:" A Short History of U.S. Naval Mine Countermeasures, 1777–1991* (D 207.10/4:4); and *On Course to Desert Storm: The United States Navy and the Persian Gulf* (D 207.10/4:5).

The *Naval Historical Center Web Site* contains basic information on naval history and on the agency's publications and resources. A main menu option on "Wars and Conflicts of the U.S. Navy" provides a short history of the navy, chronologies of events, statistics on casualties, and listings of resources by time period. The resources available include brief histories of the navy's involvement in particular wars or conflicts, bibliographies, descriptions of medals, selected officer listings, and selected articles and excerpts from publications. Other main menu options include "Traditions of the Naval Service," "Naval History Bibliography Series," "Publications (ordering info)," "Naval History-related web sites," and links to individual Naval Historical Center branches.

The Marine Corps' *Historical Publications* series contains studies on combat operations, missions, general histories, specific unit histories, and histories of Marine Corps bases. This series contains a major set on the *U.S. Marines in Vietnam* (D 214.13:V 67/) consisting of chronological volumes covering the span of Marine Corps involvement in Vietnam. Supplemental titles on Vietnam are also published including *The Marines in Vietnam 1954–1973: An Anthology and Annotated Bibliography* (D 214.13:V 67/954-73/985) and studies on chaplains (D 214.13:V 67/962-71) and military law (D 214.13:V 67/3). Examples of other titles include *U.S. Marines in Lebanon 1982–1984* (D 214.13:L 49); *Marines in the Revolution: A History of the Continental Marines in the American Revolution 1775–1783* (D 214.13:R 32/775-83); and *A History of the Women Marines, 1946–1977* (D 214:13:W 84/2).

The *Marines in World War II Commemorative Series* is a series of 8 ½ x 11 booklets of 30–40 pages on the U.S. marines in World War II. Examples of titles include *The Right to Fight: African-American Marines in World War II* (D 214.14/4:AF 8); *Infamous Day: Marines at Pearl Harbor, 7 December 1941* (D 214.14/4:IN 3); and *From Shanghai to Corregidor: Marines in the Defense of the Philippines* (D 214.14/4:SH 1).

The *Army Air Forces in World War II* series includes a seven-volume history of air operations in World War II also called *Army Air Forces in World War II*. The history discusses early plans and operations, combat operations in Europe and the Pacific, the organization of air services, weapons, recruitment and training, and support services. A separate related report titled *Army Air Forces in World War II: Combat Chronology 1941–1945* (D 301.82:C 73) was also issued. Several other individual reports have been issued under the title *U.S. Army Air Forces in World War II* with individual subtitles. Many of these later reports are available on the Web, although images are not included.

The U.S. Air Service in World War I is a collection of original documents on U.S. air activities during World War I. The four-volume set includes the final report on air activities in Europe; a tactical history; documents illustrating concepts and ideas on the use of air service at the time; operational reports, orders, and documents relating to the Battle of St. Mihiel; selected reports analyzing the air effort following the war; and a report on the effects of Allied bombing during the war.

There are a few small historical series from the air force that contain monographs on various topics. *The United States Air Force General Histories* series contains a small number of titles including *Prelude to the Total Force: The Air National Guard 1943–1969* (D 301.82/3:AI 7/943-969); *The United States Army Air Arm: April 1861 to April 1917* (D 301.82/3:AR 5); and *The Development of Ballistic Missiles in the United States Air Force 1945–1960* (D 301.82/3:B 21).

The *United States Air Force Special Studies* series is another small series of publications on more specific topics. Sample titles include *The Development of Air Doctrine in the Army Air Arm 1917–1941* (D 301.82/4:AI 7); *Air Warfare and Air Base Air Defense 1914-1973* (D 301.82/4:AI 7/2); and *Case Studies in the Achievement of Air Superiority* (D 301.82/4:SU 7).

The *United States Air Force Reference Series* contains a small number of reference titles on Air Force history. It contains two volumes of the *Encyclopedia of U.S. Air Force Aircraft and Missile Systems: Post-World War II Fighters 1945–1973* (D 301.82/5:F 45) and *Post-World War II Bombers 1945–1973* (D 301.82/5:B 63). Other titles include *Air Force Combat Wings Lineage and Honors Histories 1947–1977* (D 301.82/5:C 71/947-77), which contains brief histories of Air Force organizations, and *The United States Air Force and Humanitarian Airlift Operations, 1947–1994* (D 301.82/5:H 88).

The *Air Staff Historical Study* series contains *The United States Air Force: Basic Documents on Roles and Missions* (D 301.82/6:D 65), a compilation of significant legislation, executive orders, Department of Defense memorandums and directives, and military department executive directives and agreements. Other titles deal with case studies in cooperation between the air force and the army (D 301.82/6:IN 5) and technology forecasting (D 301.82/6:SCI 2).

Air Force History and Museums Program Publications is a larger series containing general air force histories and histories on broad themes, as well as more specific topics. General histories include *Winged Shield, Winged Sword: A History of the United States Air Force* (D 301.82/7:H 62/v.1-2) and *A Concise History of the U.S. Air Force* (D 301.82/7:H 62/2). Other titles include *Air Force Roles and Missions: A History* (D 301.82/7:H 62/3); *To Save a City: The Berlin Airlift, 1948–1949* (D 301.82/7:B 45); and *Defending the West: The United States Air Force and European Security, 1946–1998* (D 301.82/7:D 36).

The *USAF Warrior Studies* series is designed to promote military history education and encourage Air Force personnel to learn from the past. Sample titles include *Strategic Air Warfare: An Interview with Generals Curtis E. LeMay, Leon W. Johnson, David A. Burchinal, and Jack J. Catton* (D 301.96:ST 8/2); *Makers of the United States Air Force* (D 301.96:M 28); and *General Kenney Reports: A Personal History of the Pacific War* (D 301.96:P 11).

The *General Publications* series of the air force also contains many historical publications. These studies are from the Office of Air Force History and from historical offices of specific air force organizations and bases. Publications include general histories, histories of specific commands and units, and histories of specific air force bases. Examples of titles available include *Aviation in the U.S. Army 1919–1939* (D 301.2:AV 5); *The United States Air Force in Korea 1950–1953* (D 301.2:K 84/2/991); *Vezzano to Desert Storm: History of Fifteenth Air Force 1943–1991* (D 301.2:H 62/20); *Historical Highlights of Andrews AFB 1942–1989* (D 301.2:H 62/17); and *Anything, Anywhere, Anytime: An Illustrated History of the Military Airlift Command 1941–1991* (D 301.2:M 59/4).

The *United States Air Force History Support Office Web Site* provides a "Publications" option that lists the Office's publications and an "Online Publications" option with selected publications available in full text. The main menu also offers "Subjects of Interest" which provides brief information or Web resources on popular topics such as World War II, Tuskegee Airmen, and specific aircraft and operations. A "Links" section provides Web links to air force and other organizations relating to military history.

VIETNAM SERIES
Checklist

United States Army in Vietnam. PRINT. 1983–. U.S. Department of the Army. Center of Military History. D 114.7/3: Item 0345.

> Content: history of the army's role in Vietnam and special topics.

Vietnam Studies. PRINT. WEB. 1972–1982. U.S. Department of the Army. D 101.74: Item 0322-F. Selected titles: <http://www.army.mil/cmh-pg/collections/VN-Studies.htm>.

> Content: monographs on military operations in Vietnam.

The United States Navy and the Vietnam Conflict. PRINT. 1976–. U.S. Department of the Navy. Naval History Division. D 207.10/3: Item 0399-A-01.

> Content: official history of Navy operations in Vietnam.

United States Air Force in Southeast Asia. PRINT. 1982–. U.S. Air Force. Office of Air Force History. D 301.86/2: Item 0422-J. GPO.

> Content: historical studies on Air Force operations in Vietnam.

Discussion

There are several series of publications devoted to the military in Vietnam. The *United States Army in Vietnam* is a comprehensive history of the army in Vietnam. It includes a set on the army's efforts to advise the South Vietnamese: *Advice and Support: The Early Years 1941–1960* (D 114.7/3:AD 9/941-60) and *Advice and Support: The*

Final Years 1965–1973 (D 114.7/3:AD 9/941-60). Other titles on special subjects include *Images of a Lengthy War* (D 114.7/3:IM 1), *Combat Operations: Taking the Offensive, October 1966 to October 1967* (D 114.7/3:OF 3), and *Public Affairs: The Military and the Media 1968-1973* (D 114.7/3:P 96/996). Other studies cover communications. Studies planned for the future will cover additional battle histories, logistics, army headquarters activities, and an additional volume in the *Advice and Support* series.

Vietnam Studies is a series of monographs on different topics written closer to the time of the conflict than the official history above. Studies are based on official records, selected secondary materials, debriefing reports, and interviews. Examples of titles in the series include *Airmobility 1961–1971* (D 101.74:AI 7/961-71); *Command and Control 1950–1969* (D 101.74:C 73/2/950-69); *Riverine Operations 1966–1969* (D 101.74:R 52/966-69); and *U.S. Army Special Forces 1961–1971* (D 101.74:SP 3/961-71).

The United States Navy and the Vietnam Conflict is the title of a multivolume history of navy operations in Vietnam. Two volumes have been issued to date. Volume 1 covers the background and beginning of the conflict through 1959. Volume 2 covers 1959–1965.

The *United States Air Force in Southeast Asia* series contains histories of air force involvement in Vietnam. Examples of titles published include *Development and Employment of Fixed-Wing Gunships 1962–1972* (D 301.86/2:G 99/962-72); *Tactical Airlift* (D 301.86/2:AI 7); and *The War in South Vietnam: The Years of the Offensive 1965–1968* (D 301.86/2:V 67).

The Marine Corps has also published a major series on its role in Vietnam. The set is part of its *Historical Publications* series and is discussed under that series in the "Military History Series" section of this chapter.

RELATED MATERIAL
Within this Work

GPO Subject Bibliographies. PRINT. WEB. GP 3.22/2:

<http://bookstore.gpo.gov/sb/about.html>

No. 98   "Military History"

No. 144 "American Revolution"

No. 192 "Civil War"

No. 236 "Naval History"

Other

Directory of Federal Historical Programs and Activities. 6th ed. (1998) Washington, D.C.: Society for History in the Federal Government.

The *Directory of Federal Historical Programs and Activities* contains a list and description of federal agency historical programs. The program listing is arranged by agency and includes agency historical offices, programs, museums, individual military units, and individual national park and historical sites. Information provided includes the program name, program description, the head of the program, address, telephone and fax numbers, e-mail addresses, Web sites, and key personnel. A section on federal historical resources covers agencies whose primary mission is historical, including the National Archives and Records Administration and the Smithsonian and provides a list of documentary projects related to federal history. An index of individuals is also available.

CHAPTER 53
National Archives

The National Archives and Records Administration is responsible for preserving important government agency records. It publishes guides to its materials, makes important research material available on microfilm, and can provide copies of records for a fee. Presidential papers and collections are preserved through a system of presidential libraries. The National Archives also is responsible for publishing laws, regulations, and presidential documents. These materials are discussed in Chapter 25, "Regulations and Administrative Actions"; Chapter 27, "The President"; and Chapter 45, "Legislative History."

National Archives records are grouped by agency, and each such group is called a record group (RG). This collection constitutes a central depository for items of historic national value, such as State Department records on diplomatic relations, military records, land records, Native American records, and census records. These materials are used most by historians and genealogists.

Selected portions of the records have been microfilmed and are available for purchase. Many large libraries have some National Archives microfilm. Many materials, however, are only available at the National Archives itself. Limited, specific requests may be answered by mail.

SEARCH STRATEGY

Searching National Archives material may be considered an adjunct of the historical search that has its own special technique search strategy. The steps to follow are

1. Determine whether the National Archives contains any relevant material by consulting the *Guide to Federal Records in the National Archives of the United States* listed under the "General Guides" section of this chapter;

2. Pursue references given in the *Guide to Federal Records in the National Archives of the United States* to related publications (such as those listed in the "Record Group Guides" section) or microfilm collections;

3. For additional detail on microfilm collections consult the "Microfilm Catalogs" section;

4. Consult guides on special subjects, if any are relevant. (See the "Subject Guides" section of this chapter.);

5. See the "Regional Archives" section to identify facilities that may own the desired material; and

6. Consult the "Indexes" and "Related Material" for additional information.

GENERAL GUIDES
Checklist

Guide to Federal Records in the National Archives of the United States. PRINT. WEB. (1995) U.S. National Archives and Records Administration. AE 1.108:G 94/v. Item 0569-B. <http://www.nara.gov/guide/>.

> Content: description of records in the National Archives, arranged by record group number, with subject index.

NARA Archival Information Locator (NAIL). WEB. U.S. National Archives and Records Administration. <http://www.nara.gov/nara/nail.html>.

> Content: prototype online information system of NARA archival and microfilm holdings, including selected digital images.

Information About the National Archives for Researchers. PRINT. (1994) U.S. National Archives and Records Administration. General Information Leaflet No. 30. AE 1.113:30/994. Item 0569.

> Content: basic information on the facilities of the National Archives and how to use them; addresses of regional archives and presidential libraries.

Select List of Publications of the National Archives and Records Administration. PRINT. WEB. (1994) U.S. National Archives and Records Administration. General Information Leaflet No. 3. AE 1.113:3/994. Item 0569. <http://www.nara.gov/publications/gil3home.html>.

> Content: list of National Archives publications currently in print by series.

General Information Leaflets. PRINT. U.S. National Archives and Records Administration. AE 1.113: Item 0569.

> Content: small pamphlets on the National Archives, its resources, facilities, and services.

National Archives and Records Administration Web Site. WEB. U.S. National Archives and Records Administration. <http://www.nara.gov/>.

> Content: guides to material in the National Archives; how to do research; locations and hours of research facilities; publication catalogs; classroom activities; general agency information.

Discussion

The *Guide to Federal Records in the National Archives of the United States* describes the holdings of the National Archives. The chapters, arranged by record group, give brief descriptions of the content and amount of material in each group, agency organizational history, information on printed guides, microform availability, and any use restrictions (see Figure 53.1). An alphabetical list of agencies is included at the beginning of Vol. 1. Vol. 3 is an index by subject and name. A Web version of the guide offers keyword and record group number searching. The Web version is updated regularly.

Entries in the *Guide* may list related publications that give more detailed information on a particular record group, such as publications from the series listed under the "Record Group Guides" section of this chapter. The *Select List of Publications of the National Archives and Records Administration*, also discussed in this section, can also help identify more detailed publications on a particular record group.

The *Guide* may indicate that some material is available for purchase in microfilm. The "Microfilm Catalogs" listing in this chapter can also be checked for information on records available in microfilm, as well as ordering information. Some microfilm records may be available in large libraries. Otherwise the researcher may need to visit the National Archives to use the materials. Some microfilm records and regional records may also be consulted at regional archives branches. (See the section on "Regional Archives" for guides to locations and materials available.)

The *NARA Archival Information Locator (NAIL)* is a prototype online database of holdings in Washington D.C., regional archives, and presidential libraries. *NAIL* contains a selection of archival, microfilm, and audiovisual materials, including more than 100,000 full-text documents and images. Although it contains thousands of entries, these represent only a small portion of NARA holdings at this time. Separate searches for archival or microfilm materials are available. The archival search includes a standard and expert search option and an option to search the digital collection only.

Information on using the National Archives in person can be found in *Information About the National Archives for Researchers*, which contains information on hours, application and use procedures, and addresses of branches and presidential libraries.

The *Select List of Publications of the National Archives and Records Administration* provides a list of publications currently in print and available from the National Archives. Publications are listed by series or category, including a "General Interest" category. The Web version is more current than the paper edition.

The *General Information Leaflet* series includes small brochures that provide a good introduction to the National Archives and its services. Brochures provide a general overview of the National Archives (AE 1.113:1/998), information on specific branches and collections, and information on services. Examples of topics covered include military service records (AE 1.113:7), citing records in the National Archives (AE 1.113:17/997), the cartographic and architectural branch (AE 1.113:26), and electronic records (AE 1.113:37/998).

The *National Archives and Records Administration Web Site* provides information on doing research at the National Archives, digital classroom materials, online exhibits, and information on records management, grants, and archival preservation. A "Quick Links" menu includes links to "Nationwide Facilities: Locations, Hours & Accessibility" and "NARA Publications." The main menu includes "The Research Room" which provides information for researchers on facilities, how to do research, and guides to holdings. Holdings information includes a link to the *Guide to Federal Records in the National Archives of the United States* and holdings arranged by federal government organization, media, location, and selected topic. Also available is the *NARA Archival Information Locator (NAIL)* database.

MICROFILM CATALOGS

Checklist

Microfilm Resources for Research: A Comprehensive Catalog. PRINT. WEB. (1996) U.S. National Archives and Records Administration. AE 1.102:M 58/2/996. Item 0569-B-02. (Print copy nondepository; available from National Archives Trust Fund Board or Scholarly Resources, Inc.) <http://www.nara.gov/publications/microfilm/comprehensive/compcat.html>.

> Content: list of microfilmed records available for sale; arranged by agency and record group.

SELECT CATALOGS

Military Service Records: A Select Catalog of National Archives Microfilm Publications. PRINT. WEB. (1985) U.S. National Archives and Records Administration. National Archives Trust Fund Board. (Nondepository; available from National Archives Trust Fund Board or Scholarly Resources, Inc.) <http://www.nara.gov/publications/microfilm/military/service.html>.

> Content: description of microfilmed military records; arranged by broad area and record group with microfilm reel listings.

RECORDS OF THE AMERICAN COMMISSION TO NEGOTIATE PEACE

(RECORD GROUP 256)
1914–31
258 CU. FT.

256.1 ADMINISTRATIVE HISTORY

Established: By, and under the immediate supervision of, President Woodrow Wilson, following the signing of the Armistice ending World War I (Nov. 11, 1918).

Functions: Negotiated formal treaties ending World War I.

Abolished: December 1919.

Successor Agencies: Department of State as custodian of its records.

Finding Aids: Sandra K. Rangel, comp., *Records of the American Commission to Negotiate Peace*, Inv. 9 (1974).

Related Records:
General Records of the Department of State, RG 59.
Records of the Foreign Service Posts of the Department of State, RG 84.
Duplicates of some commission documents at the Library of Congress, Washington, DC, and at the Hoover Institution on War, Revolution and Peace, Stanford University, Palo Alto, CA.

Subject Access Terms: League of Nations; Paris Peace Conference; Treaty of Versailles; World War I agency.

256.2 RECORDS OF THE INQUIRY
1914-19
68 lin. ft.

History: "The Inquiry" organized as a research group by Col. Edward M. House at the request of President Wilson in the autumn of 1917 to investigate geographical, ethnological, economic, historic, and political problems of Europe in preparation for the anticipated peace conference. Ceased to exist effective with the convening of the peace conference in January 1919.

Textual Records: General correspondence, 1917-18. Administrative files, 1917-19. Special reports and studies, 1917-19, with index. Newspaper clippings, 1914-18, with index. Subject digest of declarations and proposals, 1915-18. Digest of statements by Allied and Entente spokesmen, 1914-17. Statistical card files on Central Powers' religions and languages, and Austria-Hungary's industry and population density, n.d. Reports, correspondence, and other records of the Economic Division, 1917-18, and the Latin American Division, 1918.

Microfilm Publications: M1107.

256.3 RECORDS OF THE AMERICAN COMMISSION TO NEGOTIATE PEACE
1918-31
277 lin. ft.

History: Commission participated in the peace negotiations at Versailles, January 18-December 9, 1919. The peace conference was superseded by the Conference of Ambassadors, 1920-31, which was organized to deal with various political questions.

Textual Records: General records, 1918-31 (537 vols., 158 ft.), including minutes of meetings of various councils, plenary sessions, committees, and commissions of the peace conference, 1918-19; reports of peace conference committees and commissions, 1918-19; letters and telegrams sent and received by the American commission, 1918-19; instructions to and reports from field missions of the American commission, 1918-19; memorandums, publications, and pamphlets, 1918-19; and minutes of meetings of the Conference of Ambassadors, 1920-31, with card index (102 ft.), classification manual, one-volume "key" to records, and document lists.

Microfilm Publications: M820.

256.4 CARTOGRAPHIC RECORDS (GENERAL)
1917-19
1,237 items

Maps: Europe, Africa, Asia, South and Central America, and the Middle East, depicting such subjects as mineral deposits, crop distribution, ethnology, linguistics, religion, terrain, boundaries, and transportation facilities, 1917-19.

RECORD TYPES	RECORD LOCATIONS	QUANTITIES
Textual Records	Washington Area	250 cu. ft.
Maps and Charts	College Park	1,237 items

Source: Guide to Federal Records in the National Archives of the United States, p. 256-1.

Figure 53.1: Sample Page from *Guide to Federal Records in the National Archives of the United States*.

Black Studies: A Select Catalog of National Archives Microfilm Publications. PRINT. WEB. (1984) U.S. General Services Administration. National Archives Trust Fund Board. (Nondepository; available from National Archives Trust Fund Board or Scholarly Resources, Inc.) <http://www.nara.gov/publications/microfilm/blackstudies/blackstd.html>.

> Content: description of microfilmed records relating to African-Americans; arranged by record group with microfilm reel listings.

Immigrant and Passenger Arrivals: A Select Catalog of National Archives Microfilm Publications. PRINT. WEB. 2d ed. (1991) U.S. General Services Administration. National Archives Trust Fund Board. (Nondepository; available from National Archives Trust Fund Board or Scholarly Resources, Inc.) <http://www.nara.gov/publications/microfilm/immigrant/immpass.html>.

> Content: description of microfilmed records of the U.S. Customs Service and the Immigration and Naturalization Service; arranged by port with microfilm reel listings.

Genealogical and Biographical Research: A Select Catalog of National Archives Microfilm Publications. PRINT. WEB. (1983) U.S. General Services Administration. National Archives Trust Fund Board. (Nondepository; available from National Archives Trust Fund Board or Scholarly Resources, Inc.) <http://www.nara.gov/publications/microfilm/biographical/genbio.html>.

> Content: description of microfilmed records useful for genealogical and biographical research; arranged by broad area and record group with microfilm reel listings.

American Indians: A Select Catalog of National Archives Microfilm Publications. PRINT. WEB. (1995) U.S. National Archives and Records Administration. National Archives Trust Fund Board. (Nondepository; available from National Archives Trust Fund Board or Scholarly Resources, Inc.) <http://www.nara.gov/publications/microfilm/amerindians/indians.html>.

> Content: description of microfilmed records relating to Native Americans; arranged by broad area and record group with microfilm reel listings.

Diplomatic Records: A Select Catalog of National Archives Microfilm Publications. PRINT. WEB. (1986) U.S. National Archives and Records Administration. National Archives Trust Fund Board. (Nondepository; available from National Archives Trust Fund Board or Scholarly Resources, Inc.) <http://www.nara.gov/publications/microfilm/diplomatic/>.

> Content: description of microfilmed diplomatic records from the Department of State, Foreign Service posts, and various commissions; arranged by record group, State Department decimal file, country, and microfilm publication number.

Federal Court Records: A Select Catalog of National Archives Microfilm Publications. PRINT. (1987) U.S. National Archives and Records Administration. National Archives Trust Fund Board. (Nondepository; available from National Archives Trust Fund Board or Scholarly Resources, Inc.)

> Content: description of microfilmed federal court records of the Supreme Court, circuit and district courts, and U.S. Court of Claims.

CENSUS CATALOGS

The 1790–1890 Federal Population Censuses: Catalog of National Archives Microfilm. PRINT. WEB. (1997) U.S. National Archives and Records Administration. National Archives Trust Fund Board. (Nondepository; available from National Archives Trust Fund Board or Scholarly Resources, Inc.) <http://www.nara.gov/publications/microfilm/census/1790-1890/17901890.html>.

> Content: microfilmed census schedules by year, state, and county.

1900 Federal Population Census: Catalog of National Archives Microfilm. PRINT. WEB. (1996) U.S. National Archives and Records Administration. National Archives Trust Fund Board. (Nondepository; available from National Archives Trust Fund Board or Scholarly Resources, Inc.) <http://www.nara.gov/publications/microfilm/census/1900/1900.html>.

> Content: microfilmed census schedules by state and county.

The 1910 Federal Population Census: A Catalog of Microfilm Copies of the Schedules. PRINT. WEB. (1982) National Archives Trust Fund Board. (Nondepository; available from National Archives Trust Fund Board or Scholarly Resources, Inc.) <http://www.nara.gov/publications/microfilm/census/1910/1910.html>.

> Content: microfilmed census schedules by state and county.

The 1920 Federal Population Census: Catalog of National Archives Microfilm. PRINT. WEB. 2d ed. (1992) U.S. National Archives and Records Administration. National Archives Trust Fund Board. (Nondepository; available from National Archives Trust Fund Board or Scholarly Resources, Inc.) <http://www.nara.gov/publications/microfilm/census/1920/1920.html>.

> Content: microfilmed census schedules by state and county.

How to Use NARA's Census Microfilm Catalogs Web Page. WEB. U.S. National Archives and Records Administration. <http://www.nara.gov/genealogy/microcen.html>.

> Content: information on how to use the census microfilm catalogs and microfilm soundex indexes; link to information on the microfilm rental program.

Discussion

Microfilm Resources for Research: A Comprehensive Catalog is a general catalog of National Archives records available in microfilm from the National Archives or from Scholarly Resources, Inc., an authorized vendor for National Archives microfilm. This microfilm provides facsimile reproductions of original (often handwritten) records judged to have high research value. The microfilm is not available through the depository library program, but must be purchased separately. The catalog is arranged numerically by record group. There is a subject index, an alphabetical list of record groups, and a numerical list of microfilm publication numbers.

A series of select catalogs on popular subject areas provides more detailed descriptions and reel listings for microfilm in these areas. All microfilmed records have been surveyed for material that relates to the selected subject. Background information and descriptions of the records in the subject area are provided, as well as detailed microfilm reel listings.

The census catalogs provide detailed reel listings for the more than 35,000 rolls of film that reproduce original census forms and related indexes. This microfilm allows users to find information on specific individuals, such as occupation, birthplace, and names of children. It is an important source of information for genealogists and historians. Census data are released only from the older censuses to protect individual privacy. Catalogs list the reels for each census by state and then by county. They give ordering information and may also serve as guides to locating specific rolls in a census microfilm collection.

The *How to Use NARA's Census Microfilm Catalogs Web Page* provides information on using the census microfilm catalogs, using the microfilm soundex indexes, and using the microfilm rental program.

Most of the catalogs listed in this section may be purchased for a small fee from the National Archives or from Scholarly Resources, Inc. Another commercial publisher, University Publications of America (Congressional Information Service), produces microfilm from selected National Archives records that have not been filmed through the National Archives' own program.

SUBJECT GUIDES
Checklist

Black History: A Guide to Civilian Records in the National Archives. PRINT. (1984) U.S. General Services Administration. National Archives Trust Fund Board. (Nondepository; for sale by the National Archives Trust Fund Board)

Content: description of civilian records relating to African-Americans arranged by agency.

Guide to Cartographic Records in the National Archives. PRINT. (1971) U.S. General Services Administration. National Archives and Records Service. National Archives. GS 4.6/2:C 24. Item 0569-B.

Content: description of maps and aerial photography in the National Archives by agency.

Guide to Materials on Latin America in the National Archives of the United States. PRINT. (1987) U.S. National Archives and Records Administration. (Nondepository; earlier edition GS 4.6/2:L 34 A/974)

Content: description of materials relating to Latin America arranged by agency.

Guide to Pre-Federal Records in the National Archives. PRINT. (1989) U.S. National Archives and Records Administration. (Nondepository; for sale by the National Archives Trust Fund Board)

Content: description of records pertaining to the United States and the new world before March 4, 1789, the date the Constitution went into effect; arranged by broad subject area.

Guide to Records in the National Archives of the United States Relating to American Indians. PRINT. (1981) U.S. General Services Administration. National Archives and Records Service. GS 4.6/2:AM 3. Item 0569-B.

Content: description of National Archives records on Native Americans by agency.

Guide to the Holdings of the Still Picture Branch of the National Archives. PRINT. (1991) U.S. National Archives and Records Administration. (Nondepository; for sale by the National Archives Trust Fund Board)

Content: description of photographs, negatives, transparencies, posters, and other visual image material in the National Archives.

The Trans-Mississippi West, 1804–1912: A Guide to Records of the [agency] for the Territorial Period. PRINT. 4 pts. (1993–1997) U.S. National Archives and Records Administration. (Nondepository; for sale by the National Archives Trust Fund Board)

Content: guide to materials on the American West in the National Archives; parts cover the records of the Department of State, Department of Justice, Department of Agriculture, and Department of the Interior.

CIVIL AND WORLD WARS

The Union: A Guide to Federal Archives Relating to the Civil War. PRINT. (1986) U.S. National Archives and Records Administration. National Archives Trust Fund Board. (Reprint of 1962 edition, GS 4.6/2:C 49).

Content: description of Civil War records by agency.

The Confederacy: A Guide to the Archives of the Government of the Confederate States of America. PRINT. (1986) U.S. National Archives and Records Administration. (Reprint of 1968 edition, GS 4.6/2:C 76)

Content: description of records relating to the Confederacy by agency.

A Guide to Civil War Maps in the National Archives. PRINT. (1986) U.S. National Archives and Records Administration. (Nondepository; for sale by the National Archives Trust Fund Board)

Content: guide to Civil War maps in the National Archives.

Handbook of Federal World War Agencies and Their Records, 1917–1921. PRINT. (1943) U.S. National Archives. AE 1.6:W 19/917-21. Item 0835.

Content: alphabetical listing of World War I agencies, their functions, and records.

Guide to Records Relating to U.S. Military Participation in World War II. PRINT. 2 pts. (1996–1998) U.S. National Archives and Records Administration. (Nondepository; for sale by the National Archives Trust Fund Board)

Content: description of records of military agencies in the areas of policy planning, administration, supply, and support.

Federal Records of World War II. PRINT. 2 vols. (1950–51) U.S. General Services Administration. National Archives and Records Service. National Archives. GS 4.2:R 25/2/v.1-2. Item 0569.

Content: guide to records available by agency and their location; volume 1 covers civilian agencies and volume 2 covers military agencies.

CONGRESS

Guide to the Records of the United States House of Representatives at the National Archives, 1789–1989. PRINT. MF. (1989) U.S. Congress. House of Representatives. House Document No. 100-245. Y 1.1/2:13886. (Bicentennial edition) Items 0996-B(MF) or -C.

> Content: history, organization, and types of House records in the National Archives; research strategies; descriptions of records arranged by committee.

Guide to the Records of the United States Senate at the National Archives, 1789–1989. PRINT. MF. (1989) U.S. Congress. Senate. Senate Document No. 100-42. Y 1.1/2:13853. (Bicentennial edition) Items 0996-B(MF) or -C.

> Content: history, organization, and types of Senate records in the National Archives; research strategies; descriptions of records arranged by committee.

GENEALOGY

Guide to Genealogical Research in the National Archives. PRINT. (1985) U.S. National Archives and Records Administration. (Nondepository; for sale by the National Archives Trust Fund Board)

> Content: genealogical materials available and how to use them, with chapters on population and immigration records, military records, women, Blacks, Native Americans, land, and other areas; includes references to additional published materials.

Using Records in the National Archives for Genealogical Research. PRINT. (1990) U.S. National Archives and Records Administration. AE 1.113:5/990. Item 0569.

> Content: brief guide to the types of records of interest to genealogists, such as census schedules, land records, naturalization records, service records, and others.

Discussion

In addition to the general *Guide to Federal Records in the National Archives of the United States*, there are several book-length guides devoted to specific subject areas. Some of these are listed. These guides describe agency record groups in the National Archives that contain materials related to the specific subject area. Most of them are similar in format, explaining the history and nature of the records with detailed descriptions of the material in each record group. A small number of titles also provide assistance with research methodology. The *Guide to Genealogical Research in the National Archives* is a guide to doing genealogical research, as well as a description of available records. The guides to the House and Senate also include a chapter on research strategy. *Using Records in the National Archives for Genealogical Research* is a small pamphlet with basic information on genealogical materials available.

RECORD GROUP GUIDES
Checklist

National Archives Microfilm Publications Pamphlet Describing [microfilm publication number]. PRINT. U.S. National Archives and Records Administration. (Nondepository; earlier AE 1.119:, GS 4.20:)

> Content: microfilm roll listings and content guides for microfilmed record sets.

Inventories. PRINT. 1970–. U.S. National Archives and Records Administration. (Nondepository; earlier GS 4.10/2:)

> Content: each inventory covers one record group; brief statement on the history and functions of the agency generating the records and description of arrangement and content of each record series within the group.

Preliminary Inventories. PRINT. 1941–. U.S. National Archives and Records Administration. (Nondepository; earlier GS 4.10:)

> Content: same as *Inventories* series but prepared before collection was thoroughly analyzed, so it may be less detailed.

Special Lists. MF. 1942–. U.S. National Archives and Records Administration. AE 1.115: (Earlier, GS 4.7:) Item 0570-A.

> Content: listings of individual records or data items in a specific area, such as a list of Black servicemen in the Revolutionary War or a list of population and mortality schedules.

Reference Information Papers. PRINT. (1942–) U.S. National Archives and Records Administration. AE 1.124: (Earlier, GS 4.15:) Item 0569.

> Content: descriptions of materials on specific topics from multiple record groups.

Guides to German Records Microfilmed at Alexandria, VA. MF. 1958–. U.S. National Archives and Records Administration. AE 1.112: (Earlier, GS 4.18:). Item 0570-C-01.

> Content: guides to National Archives microfilm of seized German records from German central, regional, and local government agencies, military commands and units, and the Nazi party from approximately 1920–45.

Index, The Papers of the Continental Congress 1774–1789. PRINT. 5 vols. (1978) U.S. General Services Administration. National Archives and Records Service. GS 4.2:C 76/3/774-89/v.1-5. Item 0569.

> Content: index to National Archives microfilm of Continental Congress papers.

Discussion

The National Archives often publishes guides relating to individual record groups. Most of these are published in the series listed. The *National Archives Microfilm Publications Pamphlet* series contains individual pamphlets for many of the microfilm sets of National Archives records. These sets correspond to particular record groups or portions of record groups. The pamphlets include a general introduction to the microfilm set and a list of rolls with content descriptions. These pamphlets are also supplied to anyone ordering the microfilm. The *Microfilm Resources for Research: a Comprehensive Catalog*, mentioned under

"Microfilm Catalogs" section of this chapter, indicates the availability of these pamphlets with a "DP" note. The NARA Archival Information Locator (NAIL) database on NARA's Web site also indicates the availability of descriptive pamphlets. Pamphlets may be requested from the National Archives.

Inventories and *Preliminary Inventories* have been done for selected record groups. These titles describe the contents of individual record groups and are similar in format. Each related group of files within the record groups is listed and described. An introduction gives information on the history and functions of the agency that produced the records. *Preliminary Inventories* are done before the materials in the record group have been analyzed and organized. *Inventories* are done after the materials have been thoroughly analyzed.

Special Lists are more detailed than inventories. A *Special List* contains information on individual record items in a particular group or series rather than the general description provided in an inventory.

Publications on a particular record group, including titles from these series, can be identified through the *Select List of Publications of the National Archives and Records Administration* or the *Guide to Federal Records in the National Archives of the United States* mentioned in the "General Guides" section. Figure 53.1, a sample page from the *Guide*, indicates that some of the records of the American Commission to Negotiate Peace have been microfilmed in the "Microfilm Publications" note at the end of subsections 256.2 and 256.3. The "Finding Aids" category in the administrative history section (256.1) also indicates that there is an *Inventory* available. The *Select List of Publications* contains a list of publications available by record group number, also indicating that there is an inventory for record group 256.

The *Reference Information Papers* series describes specific topics that may involve several record groups. Recent titles include *Records Relating to Personal Participation in World War II: "The American Soldier" Surveys* (AE 1.124:78) and *Records Relating to American Prisoners of War and Missing in Action from the Vietnam War* (AE 1.124:90).

One large record group (RG 242) that has been microfilmed covers foreign documents seized by the United States, particularly World War II German records. *Guides to German Records Microfilmed at Alexandria, VA* is an entire series devoted to part of this record group. Another record group (RG 360) containing papers of the Continental Congress has its own five-volume index, *Index, The Papers of the Continental Congress 1774–1789*.

These detailed guides give a more complete description of the contents of the records so that a researcher can further determine how helpful the material would be. The guides are also helpful when actually using the microfilm or records.

REGIONAL ARCHIVES

Checklist

The Regional Archives System of the National Archives. PRINT. (1993) U.S. National Archives and Records Administration. AE 1.113:22/993. Item 0569.
> Content: brief introduction to the system and its services; addresses of regional archives branches.

Guide to Records in the National Archives [area] Region. PRINT. (1989) U.S. National Archives and Records Administration. AE 1.108:R24/3/(area). Item 0569-B.
> Content: series of guides to the records and services of regional archives branches.

Regional Records Services Facilities Web Page. WEB. U.S. National Archives and Records Administration. <http://www.nara.gov/regional/nrmenu.html>.
> Content: addresses, telephone numbers, email, and Web sites for regional archives facilities; links to selected finding aids by regional facility.

Discussion

The *Regional Archives System of the National Archives* describes the regional archives system. Regional archives house materials of local and regional interest and maintain large collections of National Archives microfilm publications. This brochure briefly describes regional services and includes a list of the regional archives with addresses and telephone numbers.

The *Guide to Records in the National Archives [area] Region* series contains guides for each regional archives. Each guide contains a brief introduction, an index of agencies and subjects, and descriptions of each record group. There is also information on microfilm resources and services.

The *Regional Records Services Facilities Web Page* lists National Archives facilities by state. Information on each facility includes address, telephone number, fax number, email address link, Web page link, and a brief note about holdings.

INDEXES

Checklist

Catalog of United States Government Publications (MOCAT). WEB. 1994–. U.S. Government Printing Office. Superintendent of Documents. <http://www.gpo.gov/catalog>; <http://www.access.gpo.gov/su_docs/locators/cgp/index.html>; <http://purl.access.gpo.gov/GPO/LPS844>.

Monthly Catalog of United States Government Publications. CD-ROM. 1996–. U.S. Government Printing Office. Superintendent of Documents. GP 3.8/7: Item 0557-C. GPO.

Monthly Catalog of United States Government Publications (Condensed version). PRINT. (monthly) 1996–. U.S. Government Printing Office. Superintendent of Documents. GP 3.8/8: (Earlier full version, GP 3.8:, 1895-1995). Item 0557-D. GPO.

CIS/Index. PRINT. (monthly) 1970–. Bethesda, MD: Congressional Information Service.

Congressional Universe. WEB. Bethesda, MD: Congressional Information Service.

Discussion

General informational publications about the National Archives can be found through these basic indexes, which are discussed in more detail in Chapter 3, "The Basics of Searching." Materials from the National Archives may be found in the *Monthly Catalog* author index under "United States. National Archives and Records Administration." The same heading may be used in the subject index for publications about the National Archives. The complete version of the *Monthly Catalog* is available on the Web and CD-ROM. Commercial online and CD-ROM versions of the *Monthly Catalog* are also available.

CIS/Index indexes congressional publications on National Archives appropriations, operations, programs, and issues under the heading "National Archives and Records Administration." *Congressional Universe* includes a Web version of *CIS*.

RELATED MATERIAL
Within this Work

APPENDIX
Selected Nongovernment Addresses

The following is a list of addresses and telephone numbers for nongovernment publishers whose products and services are cited in this book.

ABC-CLIO, Inc.
130 Cremona Drive
Santa Barbara, CA 93117
Toll Free: 800-368-6868
Fax: 1-805-685-9685
E-Mail: sales@abc-clio.com
URL: <http://www.abc-clio.com>

ALLCENSUS
P.O. BOX 206
Green Creek, NJ 08219
E-Mail: Comments@allcensus.com
URL: <http://www.allcensus.com>

America Online, Inc.
8619 Westwood Center Drive
Vienna, VA 22182-2285
Phone: 703-448-8700
Toll Free: 800-827-6364
URL: <http://www.aol.com>

American National Standards Institute
11 West 42nd Street
New York, NY 10036
Phone: 212-642-4980
Fax: 212-302-1286
E-Mail: quote@ansi.org
URL: <http://www.ansi.org>

Arco Books
Peterson's
P.O. Box 2123
Princeton, NJ 08543-2123
Phone: 609-243-9111
Fax: 609-243-9150
Toll Free: 800-338-3282
URL: <http://www.petersons.com/arco/>

Aries Systems Corp.
200 Sutton Street
North Andover, MA 01845-1656
Phone: 508-975-7570
Fax: 508-975-3811
E-Mail: kfinder@ariessys.com
URL: <http://www.KFinder.com>

Auto-Graphics, Inc.
3201 Temple Avenue
Pomona, CA 91768
Phone: 909-595-7204
Toll Free: 800-776-6939
Fax: 909-595-3506
E-Mail: info@auto-graphics.com
URL: <http://www.auto-graphics.com>

Bernan Press
4611-F Assembly Drive
Lanham, MD 20706-4391
Phone: 301-459-2255
Toll Free: 800-274-4447
Fax Toll Free: 800-865-3450
E-Mail: bpress@bernan.com
URL: <http://www.bernan.com/BernanPress.asp>

Broadfoot Publishing Company
1907 Buena Vista Circle
Wilmington, NC 28411
Phone: 910-686-4816 (General Information)
Phone: 910-686-9591 (Orders)
Fax: 910-686-4379
E-Mail: bropubco@wilmington.net
URL: <http://broadfoot.wilmington.net>

Bureau of National Affairs, Inc. (BNA)
1231 25th Street NW
Washington, D.C. 20037
Phone: 202-452-4200
Toll Free: 800-372-1033
icustrel@bna.com
URL: <http://www.bna.com>

Cambridge University Press
110 Midland Avenue
Port Chester, NY 10573-4930
Phone: 914-937-9600
Toll Free: 800-872-7423
URL: <http://www.cup.org/>

CCH Inc.
4025 W. Peterson Avenue
Chicago, IL 60646-6085
Phone: 773-583-8500
Toll Free: 800-835-5224
Fax: 773-866-3895
E-Mail: cust_serv@cch.com
URL: <http://www.cch.com>

Chadwyck-Healey Ltd.
1101 King Street
Alexandria, VA 22314
Phone: 703-683-4890
Fax: 703-683-7589
E-Mail: info@chadwyck.com
URL: <http://www.chadwyck.com>

Census View
P.O. Box 39
Ripley, OK 74062
Phone: 918-372-4624
E-mail: censusvu@galstar.com
URL: <http://www.galstar.com/~censusvu>

CompuServe Information Service - Knowledge Index
5000 Arlington Centre Boulevard
P.O. Box 20212
Columbus, OH 43220
Phone: 614-457-8600
Toll Free: 800-848-8990
Fax: 614-457-0348

Congressional Information Service, Inc.
4520 East-West Highway
Bethesda, MD 20814
Phone: 301-654-1550
Toll Free: 800-638-8380
Fax: 301-654-4033
URL: <www.cispubs.com>

Congressional Quarterly, Inc.
1414 22nd Street, N.W.
Washington, D.C. 20037
Phone: 202-887-8500
Toll Free: 800-432-2250
Fax: 202-728-1862
E-Mail: online@cq.com; printcsvc.cq.com
URL: <http://www.cq.com>

CQ Directories, A Division of Congressional Quarterly, Inc.
815 Slaters Lane
Alexandria, VA 22314
Phone: 703-739-0900
Toll Free: 800-638-1710
Fax: 800-380-3810
E-Mail: staffdir@staffdirectories.com
URL: <http://store.yahoo.com/cq-press/cqdirectories.html>

Derwent Information
1725 Duke Street, Suite 250
Alexandria, VA 22314
Phone: 703-706-4220
Toll Free: 800-DER-WENT
Fax: 703-519-5838
E-Mail: info@derwent.com
URL: <http://www.derwent.com/index.html>

The Dialog Corporation
11000 Regency Parkway, Suite 400
Cary, NC 27511
Phone: 919-462-8600
Toll Free: 800-334-2564
Fax: 919-468-9890
URL: <http://www.dialog.com>

Disclosure, Inc.
5161 River Road
Bethesda, MD 20816
Phone: 301-951-1753
Toll Free: 800-754-9690; 800-236-6997
E-Mail: info@disclosure.com
URL: <http://www.disclosure.com>

Dow Jones & Company, Inc.
P.O. Box 300
Princeton, NJ 08543-0300
Phone: 609-520-4000
Toll Free: 800-832-1234
Fax: 609-520-4660
URL: <http://www.dowjones.com/corp/index.html>

Eagle Eye Publishers, Inc.
10560 Main Street, PH 18
Fairfax City, VA 22030-7182
Phone: 702-359-8980
Toll Free: 800-875-4201
Fax: 703-359-8981
E-Mail: tyeaney@eagleeyeinc.com
URL: <http://www.eagleeyeinc.com>

EBSCO Publishing
10 Estes Street
Ipswich, MA 01938
Phone: 978-356-6500
Toll Free: 800-653-2726
Fax: 978-356-6565
E-Mail: ep@epnet.com
URL: <http://www.epnet.com>

Federal Domestic Assistance Catalog Staff
300 7th Street, SW, Reporters Building, Room 101
Washington, DC 20407
Phone: 202-708-5126
Fax: 202-401-8233
URL: <http://www.cfda.gov/public/cat-order.htm>

Gale Group
World Headquarters
27500 Drake Road
Farmington Hills, MI 48331

Phone: 248-699-4253
Toll Free: 800-877-4153
Fax: 800-414-5043
E-Mail: galeord@galegroup.com
URL: <http://www.gale.com>

Greenwood Publishing Group, Inc.
88 Post Road West, P.O. Box 5007
Westport, CT 06881-5007
Phone: 203-226-3571, ext. 720
Fax: 203-222-1502
E-Mail: customer-service@greenwood.com

William S. Hein & Co., Inc.
1285 Main Street
Buffalo, NY 14209
Phone: 716-882-2600
Toll Free: 800-828-7571
Fax: 716-883-8100
E-mail: mail@wshein.com
URL: <http://www.wshein.com>

Hydrosphere Data Products, Inc.
1002 Walnut Street, Suite 200
Boulder, CO 80302
Phone: 303-443-7839
Toll Free: 800-949-4937
Fax: 303-442-0616
E-Mail: sales@hydrosphere.com
URL: <http://www.hydrosphere.com>

IHS Health Information
15 Inverness Way East
Englewood, CO 80112-5776
Phone: 303-267-1573
Toll Free: 800-525-5539
Fax: 303-267-1334
URL: <http://www.ihshealth.com/>

Information Handling Services: Engineering Products
15 Inverness Way East
Englewood, CO 80112
Toll Free: 800-716-3447
Fax: 800-716-6447
E-Mail: info@ihs.com
URL: <http://www.ihsengineering.com>

Information Today, Inc.
43 Old Marlton Pike
Medford, NJ 08055-8750
Phone: 609-654-6266
Fax: 609-654-4309
E-Mail: custserv@infotoday.com
URL: <http://www.infotoday.com>

InfoSynthesis, Inc.
195 E. 5th Street, Suite 807
St. Paul, MN 55101
Toll Free: 800-784-7036
URL: <http://www.usscplus.com/index.htm>

Knowledge Express Data Systems
3000 Valley Forge Circle
STE 3800
King of Prussia, PA 19406
Toll Free: 800-529-5337
URL: <http://www.teonline.com/teopro/pr32846.html>

Leadership Directories, Inc.
104 5th Avenue
New York, NY 10011
Phone: 212-627-4140
Fax: 212-645-0931
E-Mail: info@leadershipdirectories.com
URL: <http://www.leadershipdirectories.com>

LEXIS-NEXIS
9443 Springboro Pike
P.O. Box 933
Dayton, OH 45401-0933
Phone: 937-865-6800
Toll Free: 800-227-4908
Fax: 937-865-6909
URL: <http://www.lexis-nexis.com>

Maps a la carte, Inc.
205 Indian Hill Road
Groton, MA 01450
Phone: 978-448-2321
Fax: 978-448-3861
E-Mail: comments@topozone.com
URL: <www.topozone.com>

MARCIVE, Inc.
P.O. Box 4750
San Antonio, Texas
78265-7508
Phone: 210-646-6161
Toll Free: 800-531-7678
Fax: 210-646-0167
E-Mail: info@marcive.com
URL: <http://www.marcive.com/web1.htm>

MicroPatent
250 Dodge Avenue
East Haven, CT 06512-3358
Phone: 203-466-5055
Toll Free: 800-648-6787
Fax: 203-466-5054
E-Mail: info@micropat.com
URL: <http://www.micropat.com/0/index9809.html>

National Information Services Corporation
NISC USA
Wyman Towers
3100 St. Paul Street
Baltimore, Maryland 21218
Phone: 410-243-0797
Fax: 410-243-0982

E-Mail: sales@nisc.com
URL: <http://www.nisc.com>

National Learning Corporation
212 Michael Drive
Syosset, NY 11791
Phone: 516-921-888
Toll Free: 800-645-6337
Fax: 516-921-8743
URL: <http://www.passbooks.com/index.html>

National Library of Medicine
8600 Rockville Pike
Bethesda, MD 20894
Phone: 301-496-6531
Toll Free: 800-638-8484
E-mail: custserv@nlm.nih.gov
Service Desk Phone Number: 888-FINDNLM (888-346-3656)
Information: URL: <http://www.nlm.nih.gov/databases/>

NERAC, Inc.
One Technology Drive
Tolland, CT
Phone: 860-872-7000
Fax: 860-875-1749
URL: <http://www.nerac.com>

Oceana Publications, Inc.
75 Main Street
Dobbs Ferry, NY 10522
Phone: 914-693-8100
Fax: 914-693-0402
E-Mail: info@oceanalaw.com
URL: <http://www.oceanalaw.com>

OCLC (FirstSearch)
6565 Frantz Road
Dublin, OH 43017
Phone: 614-764-6000
Toll Free: 800-848-5878
Toll Free: 800-848-8286 (in Ohio)
Fax: 614-764-6096
E-Mail: job@oclc.org
URL: <http://www.oclc.org>

Omnigraphics, Inc.
615 Griswold Street
Detroit, MI 48226
Toll Free: 800-234-1340
Fax: 800-875-1340
URL: <http://www.omnigraphics.com>

Oryx Press
P.O. Box 33889
Phoenix, AZ 85067-33889
Toll Free: 800-279-6799
Fax: 800-279-4663
E-Mail: info@oryxpress.com
URL: <http://www.oryxpress.com>

Ovid Technologies, Inc.
333 Seventh Avenue
New York, NY 10001
Phone: 212-563-3006
Toll Free: 800-950-2035
Fax: 212-563-3784
E-Mail: sales@ovid.com
URL: <http://www.ovid.com>

Primary Source Media (Research Publications)
12 Lunar Drive
Woodbridge, CT 06525
Phone: 203-397-2600
Toll Free: 800-444-0799
Fax: 203-397-3893
E-Mail: sales@psmedia.com
URL: <http://www.galegroup.com/psm/>

Research Institute of America (RIA)
90 Fifth Avenue
New York, NY 10011
Phone: 212-645-4800
Toll Free: 800-742-3348; 800-431-9025
Fax: 212-337-4280
URL: <http://www.riatax.com>

Research Publications. See Primary Source Media.

Questel-Orbit
8000 Westpark Drive
McLean, VA 22102
Phone: 703-442-0900
Toll Free: 800-456-7248
Fax: 703-893-4632
URL: <http://www.questel.orbit.com>

Scholarly Resources
104 Greenhill Avenue
Wilmington, DE 19805
Phone: 302-654-7713
Toll Free: 888-772-7817
Fax: 302-654-3871
E-Mail: sales@scholarly.com
URL: <http://www.scholarly.com>

SilverPlatter Information, Inc.
100 River Ridge Drive
Norwood, MA 02062-0543
Phone: 781-769-2599
Toll Free: 800-343-0064
Fax: 781-769-8763
E-Mail: us_customerrelations@silverplatter.com;
info@silverplatter.com
URL: <http://www.silverplatter.com>

STN International
FIZ Karlsruhe
P.O. Box 2465
D-76012 Karlsruhe, Germany
Phone: 07247 808555
Fax: 07247 808131
E-Mail: helpdesk@fix-karlsruhe.de
U.S. Branch Office:
c/o Chemical Abstracts Service
2540 Olentangy River Road
P.O. Box 3012
Columbus, OH 43210-0012
Phone: 614-447-3600
STN Help Desk Toll Free: 800-848-6533
Fax: 614-447-3713
URL: <http://www.cas.org/stn.html>

Thomson & Thomson
500 Victory Road
North Quincy, MA 02171-3145
Phone: 617-479-1600
Toll Free: 800-692-8833
Fax: 617-786-8273
URL: <http://www.thomson-thomson.com>

The Trademark Register
2100 National Press Building
Washington, DC 20045
Phone: 202-347-2138
URL: <http://www.trademarkregister.com>

University Publications of America. See Congressional Information Service.

WeatherDisc Associates, Inc.
4584 N.E. 89th
Seattle, WA 98115
Phone: 206-524-4314
Fax: 206-433-1162
E-Mail: cliff@atmos.washington.edu

West Group
620 Opperman Drive
St. Paul, MN 55164-0526
Phone: 612-687-7000
Toll Free: 800-328-9352
Fax: 612-687-7302
URL: <http://www.westgroup.com>

Index

by Christine Karpeles

The abbreviation "fig" denotes a figure or illustration.

Jean Sears is currently the head of the Government Documents Department at Miami University Libraries in Oxford, Ohio. She has worked in the government information field for more than 25 years, and previously she was the president of the Ohio Government Documents Round Table as well as a recipient of their Clyde award for outstanding achievement or service in the field of government information. Ms. Sears holds a master of science degree in librarianship from Western Michigan University.

Marilyn K. Moody has just left her position as director of the Science and Engineering Library at the University at Buffalo (SUNY) and is now the Associate University Librarian for Information and Research Services at the University of California, Santa Barbara. Ms. Moody has written numerous articles for a variety of library and information science journals and is the editor of *Internet Reference Services Quarterly*. She also serves as a visiting associate professor for the LEEP distance learning program at the University of Illinois Graduate School of Library and Information Science, teaching the government publications course. A popular speaker, Ms. Moody has given many workshops and presentations on electronic government information, using the Internet and the Web, and the digital library. In addition, she is an active member of several national, state, and regional professional organizations. Ms. Moody holds a masters degree in library science from the University of Illinois.